Frequently Asked Questions

Ten Best Tips

Page

193 To prevent Security Center alerts from popping up (without disabling Security Center's monitoring of your firewall, automatic updates, and antivirus status), in Security Center click Change The Way Security Center Alerts Me.

241 While the Welcome screen is displayed, you can open the Log On To Windows dialog box by pressing Ctrl+Alt+Delete two times. This allows you to log on using an account that isn't shown on theWelcome screen (Administrator, for example).

248 Pressing the Windows logo key+L is a terrific shortcut for switching users or locking your computer. If your keyboard doesn't have a Windows logo key or you prefer using a mouse, you can create a program shortcut that provides single-click access to the same feature.

516 Anything stored in %UserProfile%\Favorites appears on your Favorites menu or Favorites bar. Most people use this folder exclusively for Internet shortcuts, but you can put shortcuts to files and folders there as well.

651 As a quicker way to display or hide a toolbar, right-click any toolbar. This action displays the View, Toolbars submenu.

880 It's difficult to work with the tiny thumbnail images in the Scanner And Camera Wizard. You'll generally find it most efficient to copy all images to your hard disk, where you can cull the shots you don't want to keep and then work with the rest.

960 Run the Windows XP Network Setup Wizard on every system that's connected to your network. Doing so is the only reliable way to ensure that your network has the proper baseline configuration. Afterwards, you can manually adjust settings and enable or disable features as required.

1020 The My Network Places folder can hold shortcuts to folders and files you use often. To create such a place, type the complete path (in the form \\computername\sharename\folder) on the wizard's third page. Or drag the folder or file from a Windows Explorer window to the My Network Places window.

1134 You can back up settings (including your password) for each e-mail account in Outlook Express. Choose Tools, Accounts, select the account name, and then click Export. To re-establish the account, import the saved .iaf file.

1257 The Windows XP Backup Utility does not support backing up directly to CD-R or CD-RW devices. However, if you plan your backups carefully you can accomplish the same goal in a two-step process. Back up to a file first, and then copy that backup file to a CD-R or CD-RW.

Microsoft

Microsoft® Windows® XP
Inside Out Deluxe,
Second Edition

Ed Bott, Carl Siechert, and Craig Stinson

PUBLISHED BY
Microsoft Press
A Division of Microsoft Corporation
One Microsoft Way
Redmond, Washington 98052-6399

Copyright © 2005 by Ed Bott, Carl Siechert, and Craig Stinson

All rights reserved. No part of the contents of this book may be reproduced or transmitted in any form or by any means without the written permission of the publisher.

Library of Congress Control Number 2004112805

Printed and bound in the United States of America.

2 3 4 5 6 7 8 9   QWT   9 8 7 6 5 4

Distributed in Canada by H.B. Fenn and Company Ltd.

A CIP catalogue record for this book is available from the British Library.

Microsoft Press books are available through booksellers and distributors worldwide. For further information about international editions, contact your local Microsoft Corporation office or contact Microsoft Press International directly at fax (425) 936-7329. Visit our Web site at www.microsoft.com/learning/. Send comments to *nsideout@microsoft.com*.

Microsoft, Active Desktop, Active Directory, ActiveX, Authenticode, ClearType, DirectX, Encarta, FrontPage, Hexic, HighMAT, Hotmail, IntelliMirror, JScript, Microsoft Press, Mozaki, MSDN, MS-DOS, MSN, NetMeeting, OneNote, Outlook, Picture It!, PowerPoint, SharePoint, Visual Basic, Win32, Windows, Windows Media, Windows NT, and Windows Server are either registered trademarks or trademarks of Microsoft Corporation in the United States and/or other countries.

The example companies, organizations, products, domain names, e-mail addresses, logos, people, places, and events depicted herein are fictitious. No association with any real company, organization, product, domain name, e-mail address, logo, person, place, or event is intended or should be inferred.

Acquisitions Editor: Alex Blanton
Project Editors: Kristine Haugseth and Laura Sackerman
Technical Editor: Mitch Tulloch
Copy Editor: Kate House
Editing and Production: nSight, Inc.

Body Part No. X10-87047

*This book is dedicated to the person with whom
I share my life, that special woman whose
name begins with J.*

—Ed Bott, for Judy

—Carl Siechert, for Jan

—Craig Stinson, for Jean

Contents At A Glance

v

Contents At A Glance

Table of Contents

Part 1
Setup and Startup

Chapter 1
What's New in Windows XP   3

Chapter 2
Installing and Configuring Windows XP   15

What do you think of this book?
We want to hear from you!

Microsoft is interested in hearing your feedback about this publication so we can
continually improve our books and learning resources for you. To participate in a brief
online survey, please visit: *www.microsoft.com/learning/booksurvey/*

Part 2
Keeping Your System Secure

Chapter 9

Securing Files and Folders   273

Chapter 10

Securing Your Internet Connection   305

Chapter 13
Auditing Security   385

Part 3
Customizing Windows

Chapter 14
Tuning Up System Performance   403

Chapter 15
Tweaking the Windows XP Interface   441

Chapter 16
Advanced Internet Explorer Options   503

Chapter 17
Managing User Profiles 545

Chapter 18
Configuring Shutdown and Power
Management Options 565

Chapter 19
Automating Windows XP   591

Part 4
Storage and File Management

Chapter 20
Windows Explorer for Experts   647

Chapter 21
Managing and Finding Files   695

Chapter 22

Managing Disks and Drives   **741**

Chapter 23
Working with Offline Files and Folders   **783**

Part 5
Mastering Digital Media

Chapter 24
Using and Customizing Windows Media Player   **801**

Chapter 25
Managing a Digital Music Collection   833

Part 6
Networking

Chapter 31
Remote Access Options   1041

Chapter 32
Hosting a Web or FTP Site 1073

Chapter 33
Working with Windows Domains 1105

Part 8
System Maintenance and Recovery

Chapter 37
Performing Routine Maintenance   1237

Chapter 38
Monitoring System Activities with Event Viewer   1265

Chapter 41
Editing the Registry   1317

Part 9
Appendixes

Appendix A
Windows Versions at a Glance: Professional, Home Edition, and More   1339

Appendix B
Working with the Command Prompt   1343

Appendix C
Using and Customizing Microsoft Management Console

1365

Appendix D
Managing Services

1379

What do you think of this book?
We want to hear from you!

Microsoft is interested in hearing your feedback about this publication so we can continually improve our books and learning resources for you. To participate in a brief online survey, please visit: *www.microsoft.com/learning/booksurvey/*

Acknowledgments

Many skilled hands contributed to this book. We would like to express our admiration and gratitude to our partners and collaborators at Microsoft Press: Josh Barnhill, product manager; Alex Blanton, Program Manager; Kristine Haugseth, Laura Sackerman, and Sandra Haynes, Project Editors. Our thanks go as well to Bill Teel for supervising the art production and to Debbie Swanson and Robert Lyon for managing the CD.

We also received abundant editorial and production support from Mitch Tulloch, technical editor, and a team of professionals at nSight, Inc.: Kaesmene Harrison Banks, Carmen Corral-Reid, Katie O'Connell, Mary-Beth McDaniel, Peter Amirault, Angela Montoya, Kate House, and Brenda Silva. To all, our heartfelt thanks.

Ed Bott, Carl Siechert, Craig Stinson

We'd Like to Hear from You!

Our goal at Microsoft Press is to create books that help you find the information you need to get the most out of your software.

The Inside Out series was created with you in mind. As part of an effort to ensure that we're creating the best, most useful books we can, we talked to our customers and asked them to tell us what they need from a Microsoft Press series. Help us continue to help you. Let us know what you like about this book and what we can do to make it better. When you write, please include the title and author of this book in your e-mail, as well as your name and contact information. We look forward to hearing from you.

How to Reach Us

E-mail:	nsideout@microsoft.com
Mail:	Inside Out Series Editor
	Microsoft Press
	One Microsoft Way
	Redmond, WA 98052

Note: Unfortunately, we can't provide support for any software problems you might experience. Please go to http://support.microsoft.com *for help with any software issues.*

About the CD

The companion CD that ships with this book contains many tools and resources to help you get the most out of your *Microsoft Windows XP Inside Out Deluxe*, Second Edition book.

What's on the Deluxe Edition CD

Your Inside Out companion CD for the Deluxe Edition includes the following:

- **Microsoft Windows XP Inside Out Deluxe, Second Edition eBook.** This contains the electronic version of the book.
- **Reference eBooks.** In this section you'll find the following eBooks in PDF format: Microsoft Computer Dictionary, Fifth Edition; Microsoft Encyclopedia of Networking, Second Edition; and Microsoft Encyclopedia of Security.
- **Insider Extras.** This section includes sample batch and script files referenced in the book.
- **Windows XP Downloads.** In this section, you'll find a listing of Windows XP downloadable resources, including information about security.
- **Windows XP Information.** This section provides a listing of links that you can consult for additional information about using Windows XP.
- **Expert Zone Columns.** This section provides a downloadable compilation of Web articles written by Windows XP expert Ed Bott.
- **Winodws XP Tips Sites.** In this section, you'll find links to third party sites maintained by Ed Bott and other Windows MVPs: Bob Cerelli, Chris Pirillo, Doug Knox, Jerry Honeycutt, Jim Boyce, Kelly Theriot, and John "PapaJohn" Beuchler.

The companion CD provides detailed information about the files on this CD, and links to Microsoft and third-party sites on the Internet.

> **Note** Please note that the third-party software and links to third-party sites are not under the control of Microsoft Corporation and Microsoft is therefore not responsible for their content, nor should their inclusion on this CD be construed as an endorsement of the product or the site. Please check third-party Web sites for the latest version of their software.

Software provided on this CD is in English language only and may be incompatible with non-English language operating systems and software.

Using the CD

To use this companion CD, insert it into your CD-ROM drive; a license agreement should be presented. If AutoRun is not enabled on your computer, run StartCD.exe in the root of the CD to display the license agreement.

> **Caution** The electronic version of the book and some of the other documentation included on this CD is provided in Portable Document Format (PDF). To view these files, you will need Adobe Acrobat or Adobe Reader. For more information about these products or to download Adobe Reader, visit the Adobe Web site at *http://www.adobe.com*.

System Requirements

Following are the minimum system requirements necessary to run the CD:

- Microsoft Windows XP with Service Pack 2 or later
- 266-MHz or higher Pentium-compatible CPU
- 64 megabytes (MB) RAM
- 8x CD-ROM drive or faster
- 80 MB of free hard disk space (to install eBook files)
- Microsoft Windows-compatible sound card and speakers
- Microsoft Internet Explorer 5.01 or later
- Microsoft Mouse or compatible pointing device

> **Note** System requirements might be higher for the add-ins available on the CD. Individual add-in system requirements are specified on the CD. An Internet connection is necessary to access some of the hyperlinks. Connect time charges might apply.

Support Information

Every effort has been made to ensure that the accuracy of the book and the contents of this companion CD. For feedback on the book content or this companion CD, please contact us by using any of the addresses listing in the "We'd Like to Hear From You" section.

Microsoft Press provides corrections for books through the World Wide Web at *http://www.microsoft/learning/support/*. To connect directly to the Microsoft Press Knowledge Base and enter a query regarding a question or issue that you may have, go to *http://www.microsoft.com/learning/support/search.asp*.

For support information regarding Windows XP, you can connect to Microsoft Technical Support on the Web at *http://support.microsoft.com/windowsxp*.

Conventions and Features Used in This Book

This book uses special text and design conventions to make it easier for you to find the information you need.

Text Conventions

Convention	Meaning
Abbreviated menu commands	For your convenience, this book uses abbreviated menu commands. For example, "Choose Tools, Track Changes, Highlight Changes" means that you should click the Tools menu, point to Track Changes, and select the Highlight Changes command.
Boldface type	**Boldface** type is used to indicate text that you enter or type.
Initial Capital Letters	The first letters of the names of menus, dialog boxes, dialog box elements, and commands are capitalized. Example: the Save As dialog box.
Italicized type	*Italicized* type is used to indicate new terms.
Plus sign (+) in text	Keyboard shortcuts are indicated by a plus sign (+) separating two key names. For example, Ctrl+Alt+Delete means that you press the Ctrl, Alt, and Delete keys at the same time.

Design Conventions

 This icon identifies a new or significantly updated feature in this version of the software.

 Inside Out

These are the book's signature tips. In these tips, you'll get the straight scoop on what's going on with the software—inside information on why a feature works the way it does. You'll also find handy workarounds to different software problems.

Tip   Tips provide helpful hints, timesaving tricks, or alternative procedures related to the task being discussed.

Troubleshooting

Look for these sidebars to find solutions to common problems you might encounter. Troubleshooting sidebars appear next to related information in the chapters. You can also use the Troubleshooting Topics index at the back of the book to look up problems by topic.

Cross-references point you to other locations in the book that offer additional information on the topic being discussed.

 This icon indicates information or text found on the companion CD.

Caution   Cautions identify potential problems that you should look out for when you're completing a task or problems that you must address before you can complete a task.

Note   Notes offer additional information related to the task being discussed.

Sidebar

The sidebars sprinkled throughout these chapters provide ancillary information on the topic being discussed. Go to sidebars to learn more about the technology or a feature.

Part 1

Setup and Startup

Chapter 1

What's New in Windows XP

As we write this second edition of *Microsoft Windows XP Inside Out*, Windows XP is about to celebrate its third birthday. With more than 210 million copies sold so far, Windows XP is arguably the most successful computer operating system ever developed. Part of the reason for that success is that Windows XP represents a vast improvement over the Windows family that began with Windows 95, reached its peak with Windows 98, and ended quietly with Windows Millennium Edition (Windows Me).

For a computer operating system, three years is practically an eternity—and sure enough, Windows XP has changed dramatically since its initial release. Two major service packs have rolled up hundreds of bug fixes, security patches, and performance improvements, and a handful of optional updates have added features aimed primarily at connoisseurs of digital music and video. The resulting operating system, although not perfect, is significantly more secure, reliable, and media-savvy than its three-year-old predecessor.

At Home with Windows XP

This book describes two different versions of Windows XP: Windows XP Professional and Windows XP Home Edition. The two versions are largely identical; Windows XP Professional includes everything in Windows XP Home Edition, plus some additional features targeted toward corporate network users and power users. (The other members of the Windows XP family—Media Center Edition, Tablet PC Edition, and 64-Bit Edition—are built on Windows XP Professional and include extra features designed for use with specific hardware devices.) Near the beginning of each chapter in this book, you'll find a sidebar like this one that points out any version differences in the topics covered by the chapter. The differences are also identified in the chapter's text, but the sidebar gives you a quick rundown of any significant limitations you can expect if you use Home Edition.

At a quick glance, you might not notice the difference between today's Windows XP and the one that debuted in 2001. But look more closely and you'll see a long list of changes, inside and out:

- Hundreds of bug fixes and updated drivers have made the core of the operating system more reliable.
- A slew of security enhancements, including the much improved and renamed Windows Firewall (previously known as Internet Connection Firewall), block hostile software like the Blaster worm and make it more difficult for viruses and other malicious programs to spread.

3

- Microsoft Internet Explorer sports new features that protect your privacy and security by blocking pop-up windows and spyware-infested drive-by downloads.

- Two major updates to Windows Media Player have transformed its user interface and simplified the process of managing a library of digital music and video and burning CDs.

- Setting up a network in your home or small business is simpler than before. This is especially true in the case of wireless networks, thanks to a wizard (new in Service Pack 2) that walks you through the process of connecting to a wireless access point using the most advanced security settings available.

- Windows Update is now configured by default to download and install patches automatically.

- New Tablet PC and Media Center editions of Windows XP take advantage of specialized hardware to provide new features.

And that list only scratches the surface.

In preparing this revised edition, we've taken a fresh look at every component in Windows XP. Our coverage assumes that you've installed the most recent updates, notably Windows XP Service Pack 2 and Windows Media Player 10.

Reality Check

As we noted in the first edition of this book, power users of Windows XP are an obsessive bunch. (We can say that, because we include ourselves in that category.) We're constantly on the lookout for ways to make Windows run faster, work smarter, and perform new tricks. We spend hours scouring books, magazine articles, and the Web to find new tips and techniques to shave a second or two off the time we spend on a task.

Over the past three-plus years, the Windows XP community has amassed an enormous distributed library of advice, insights, explanations, registry hacks, add-ons, elegant workarounds, and undocumented secrets to help master this operating system. Some of these tips and tricks are pure gold, some are just common sense, and a few are downright wrong. For better or worse, the World Wide Web acts like an echo chamber that indiscriminately amplifies this conventional wisdom—and when a piece of misinformation is repeated often enough, it takes on a life of its own.

For this second edition of *Windows XP Inside Out*, we've gone out of our way to track down common myths, misunderstandings, misconceptions, and bogus tips you're likely to encounter on the Internet, especially those related to hot-button topics like security and performance. We've collected our findings under the Reality Check heading in sidebars scattered throughout this book. There we provide our own carefully researched explanation of the underlying facts.

Two particular myths jumped out at us when we searched sites where experts congregate to talk about Windows XP in broad terms.

Myth #1: Windows XP is not that different from earlier versions   This argument crops up most often among folks who have lots of experience with Windows 2000 and Windows NT. As far as they're concerned, Windows XP is just Windows 2000 with a goofy user interface and a few extra bells and whistles. That's an easy misconception to come away with, given that many of the most important features in Windows XP were introduced nearly a decade ago in Windows NT—the NTFS file system, for instance, and a well-designed kernel that keeps the operating system from crashing when an application hangs.

But to focus solely on the Windows XP interface is to miss all the other changes under the hood. Some are purely technical, such as the changes in file permissions that are applied when you use a command-line utility to convert a FAT32 disk to the NTFS format. Other innovations are more substantial. All of the following features, for instance, are exclusive to Windows XP:

- Simple File Sharing is a completely new security model that controls access to shared resources on networks.
- Fast User Switching allows two or more people to use the same computer without requiring one of them to log off.
- Out of the box, Windows XP supports wireless networking—a technology that requires third-party software and considerable tweaking in Windows 2000.
- You can use the Remote Desktop feature (available in Professional edition only) to log on to your computer from across a network or around the world.
- The System Restore and Driver Rollback features let you quickly and easily recover from configuration mistakes that would have required advanced troubleshooting expertise in Windows 2000.

And the list goes on. If you're curious about what else is new in Windows XP—especially after Service Pack 2—take a look at any chapter of this book. We predict you'll find some surprises.

Myth #2: Windows XP is inherently insecure   There's a germ of truth in this observation. From the beginning, Windows XP users have had to deal with a seemingly endless parade of viruses and worms—including the fast-spreading Blaster worm that crippled networks around the world in the summer of 2003. Ironically, though, if you enabled the built-in firewall in Windows XP and installed Critical Updates promptly, you were probably better protected from Blaster than your next-door neighbor running Windows 98 or Windows 2000. Still, the default settings in the original release of Windows XP made it too easy to avoid doing the right thing. The security enhancements in Service Pack 2, which we discuss later in this chapter and at great length in other parts of this book, go a long way toward fixing that problem.

We've learned a lot in the last three years, through a lot of hands-on experimentation and—we freely admit—by paying close attention to the incredible wealth of information our friends and colleagues have shared with us. Our mission in this book is to help you take full advantage of the rich new features in Windows XP while working around its occasional quirks, rough edges, and annoyances. And although the book is published by Microsoft Press, we've taken advantage of our editorial freedom to tell you when we've found a better way than the Windows way.

Windows XP at a Glance

Windows XP brings together two product families that were previously separate and decidedly unequal. From Windows 2000, it inherits a reliable, generally crash-proof foundation. It adds a host of user-friendly features and system utilities that were previously available only in Windows 98 or Windows Me. For good measure, it tosses in some interface enhancements and new capabilities that were previously available only as third-party add-ins. And with the improvements introduced in Service Pack 2, it provides significant new security features.

Most importantly, Windows XP comes in an ever-increasing assortment of distinctly different versions:

- **Windows XP Home Edition**   This budget-priced version is typically bundled with consumer PCs sold for use in homes and very small businesses. It's intended for non-technical users who don't need to connect to corporate networks and don't want to fuss with complicated system and security options. It's compatible with any desktop or notebook PC that has a single CPU and a single video display.

- **Windows XP Professional**   This version includes everything in Home Edition, plus all the networking and security components required to join a Windows domain run by Windows 2000 Server or Windows Server 2003. If your system configuration includes certain types of high-performance hardware, such as a dual-processor motherboard, you'll need Windows XP Professional to fully utilize it.

- **Windows XP Tablet PC Edition 2005**   This recent addition to the Windows XP family includes all of the features and capabilities of Windows XP Professional and is sold only with notebook computers that are equipped with custom screens that can recognize input from a digital pen. Significant upgrades to the original Tablet PC operating system are included in Service Pack 2. We cover the unique features of this operating system in Chapter 6, "Using Windows XP Tablet PC Edition 2005."

- **Windows XP Media Center Edition 2004**   This is another variant of Windows XP Professional sold only with specially equipped hardware. As the name suggests, this edition beefs up the digital media capabilities of Windows XP, with full support for live and recorded TV, movies, and music. PCs running Media Center Edition are as likely to be found in the living room as in the office.

- **Windows XP 64-Bit Edition**   If you own a PC equipped with a 64-bit processor such as Intel's Itanium, this variation of Windows XP Professional allows you to exploit some of its technical features. As we write this, 64-bit computers are a high-priced novelty. A new generation of 64-bit processors, accompanied by an update to this edition of Windows XP, should make the platform much more popular within a few years.

Before you read any farther, check to see which version of Windows XP is installed on your PC. Open Control Panel's System option and look on the General tab. Figure 1-1 shows what you should expect to see if you're running the initial release of Windows XP Professional. If you've installed a service pack, you'll see its details here, too. (You can read more about the

What's New in Windows XP

differences between Windows XP Home Edition and Professional in Appendix A, "Windows Versions at a Glance: Professional, Home Edition, and More.")

Figure 1-1. The System Properties dialog box supplies detailed information about your Windows version and your hardware configuration.

Tip   Get fast access to system settings

You don't have to pass through Control Panel to get to the System Properties dialog box. Hold down the Windows logo key and press Break to open this handy dialog box immediately. No Windows logo key? Create a shortcut to Sysdm.cpl (you'll find it in the %SystemRoot%\System32 folder) and pin it anywhere on the Programs menu. Then open the shortcut's properties dialog box and assign it an easy-to-remember keyboard shortcut such as Ctrl+Alt+Shift+S. Another alternative: Simply right-click My Computer (on the desktop, on the Start menu, or in a Windows Explorer window) and choose Properties.

The following section offers an extremely compressed overview of what makes Windows XP tick.

If you're upgrading from Windows 2000, the architectural changes in Windows XP are subtle and in some instances practically invisible. But if you're moving up from Windows 95/98 or Windows Me, you'll have to deal with new system utilities, a new file system option (NTFS), and a new, somewhat confusing file-sharing infrastructure. The payoff for this added complexity is a significant increase in security and a dramatic decrease in system crashes, hangs, lockups, and mysterious error messages.

Password-protected logins and the ability to set permissions on files and folders make it possible for you to share a PC with others without allowing them to install unwelcome software (including viruses) or delete important files. A friendly Welcome screen and easy-to-use administrative tools make it especially easy to set up a shared PC at home or in a small office, with each user having a customized desktop and Start menu, plus secure access to protected files.

Windows XP offers the most sweeping overhaul of the Windows interface since the introduction of Windows 95. If you choose this new Windows XP interface, you'll notice brighter colors, 3-D windows and buttons with rounded edges and sleek shadows, and richer looking icons. The flash and sizzle, though, aren't as important as the hundreds of changes that grew out of testing in Microsoft's usability laboratory—like the Welcome screen, which simplifies the logon process; a redesigned Start menu that uses two columns instead of one to offer quicker access to common locations and frequently used programs; and a much more comprehensive Help and Support system.

Unlike its predecessors, Windows XP also offers an assortment of wizards and programs to streamline the experience of working with digital photos, music, and video.

In short, Windows XP is a massive collection of code that tries to be all things to all people, from performance-obsessed gamers to buttoned-down corporate executives and spreadsheet jockeys. For the most part, it succeeds. In this book, we cover a broad range of tasks that a well-rounded Windows XP user might tackle at home or at work.

What's New? What's Changed?

For the sake of this book, we assume that you have at least some hands-on experience with Windows XP and several years' worth of experience with other Windows versions. In this section, we provide a brief overview of the most important changes that Microsoft has made to Windows XP in the past three years. With a few exceptions, these changes have been contained in two comprehensive service packs.

In the fall of 2002, about a year after the release of Windows XP, Microsoft released Service Pack 1 (more commonly called SP1) for Windows XP. This package incorporated program updates, bug fixes, security patches, and drivers for more devices than were included with the original release of Windows XP. SP1 also included support for a whole new class of devices that use USB 2, the latest version of Universal Serial Bus technology.

The outwardly visible changes in SP1 were few and generally subtle. The most obvious change was the addition of a Set Program Access And Defaults option in Add Or Remove Programs on the Start menu. This option, shown in Figure 1-2, makes it easy to access your favorite Web browser, e-mail program, media player, and other components while hiding the others. Before the release of SP1, Microsoft components often opened by default even after you installed components from another company. For details about Set Program Access And Defaults, see "Selecting a Web Browser and Other Middleware Components," page 64.

What's New in Windows XP

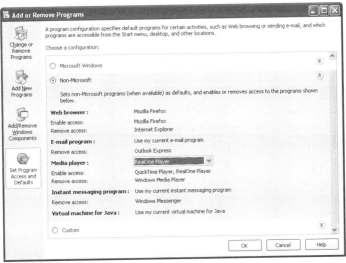

Figure 1-2. With this option in Add Or Remove Programs, you can specify default programs, whether they're from Microsoft or another company.

SP1 also introduced some important changes in Windows Product Activation (WPA). WPA was implemented with Windows XP to combat software piracy—the use of unlicensed versions of Windows. With SP1, Microsoft introduced a change intended to thwart the misuse of specific volume license keys, which can be used an unlimited number of times (unlike the single-use keys that accompany retail copies of Windows XP). These pirated keys have been widely distributed in the warez (illicit software) community. Users who have installed Windows XP using these keys will not be able to install service packs or hotfixes from Microsoft.

The other change to WPA removes an obstacle that sometimes impeded legitimate Windows users. In the original version of WPA, if you change a number of hardware components beyond a certain threshold, Windows requires you to activate your copy of Windows (via an Internet connection or by telephone) before it allows you to log on. (This is done because Windows presumes that a computer with that many different components must be a different machine.) This immediate lockout can be a great inconvenience if it happens to occur while you're unable to activate (for example, on an airplane with no phone or Internet access) or if you're repeatedly swapping hardware in and out to troubleshoot a hardware problem. With SP1, you now have a three-day grace period for so-called "out-of-tolerance" situations. You can continue to work with the unactivated copy of Windows during this interval; by the end of the grace period, you need to contact Microsoft to complete the activation.

For more information about WPA, see "Activating Windows XP," page 32.

In February 2003, five months after the release of SP1, Microsoft re-released the service pack. Service Pack 1a is identical to Windows XP SP1, except that the Microsoft virtual machine (VM) is not installed.

In the summer of 2004, after a lengthy period of testing and development, Microsoft released Service Pack 2 (SP2). This new release incorporated all the changes from SP1, along with new bug fixes and still more drivers for new hardware devices. Unlike its predecessor, however, SP2 includes a slew of new features, some of which dramatically change the way Windows XP works. The stated goal of SP2 is to make Windows XP more secure. The following is a list of some of the most important changes in SP2:

- **Security Center**   This new utility, shown in Figure 1-3, provides a monitoring and control point for three essential security components. If one of these components is disabled or configured incorrectly, a warning icon appears in the notification area.

- **Windows Firewall**   The original release of Windows XP included rudimentary intruder-blocking capabilities in its Internet Connection Firewall. SP2 introduced a significant upgrade and a new name: Windows Firewall. Figure 1-4 shows the basic on/off controls; other tabs allow you to specify which programs the firewall should leave alone. The Windows Firewall is enabled by default on all connections, including local networks, dial-up Internet, and virtual private network (VPN) connections.

Figure 1-3.   Security Center monitors the built-in Windows Firewall and Automatic Updates; it also ensures that antivirus programs (not included with Windows XP) are up to date.

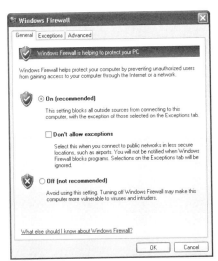

Figure 1-4. The new Windows Firewall, included with SP2, allows you to lock out all external connections—this option is useful when making a wireless connection in a public place.

- **Automatic Updates**   This capability, shown in Figure 1-5, was introduced in the original release of Windows XP and significantly overhauled in SP1. In SP2, the default settings automatically download and install updates without requiring your intervention.

- **Internet Explorer enhancements**   Some of the most insidious security breaches occur on the Web, where unscrupulous page designers try to entice an unsophisticated user into installing a hostile ActiveX control or program. New security features in Internet Explorer block unwanted pop-up windows, prevent downloads of potentially dangerous programs, and give you greater control over browser add-ons, as shown in Figure 1-6.

- **Wireless Networking**   Secure high-speed networks based on wireless technology were an expensive novelty when Windows XP was introduced. Today, wireless networks are inexpensive and extraordinarily popular. Service Pack 2 adds a new Wireless Network Setup Wizard to Windows XP and makes it much easier to secure that network from intruders. Figure 1-7 shows the revamped dialog box that you can use to connect to a wireless network.

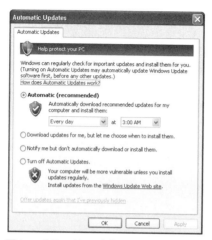

Figure 1-5. New default settings make it less likely that users will skip a Critical Update and leave their PC vulnerable to security breaches.

Figure 1-6. This dialog box, new in SP2, lets you disable suspicious or unwanted browser add-ons.

Chapter 1

What's New in Windows XP

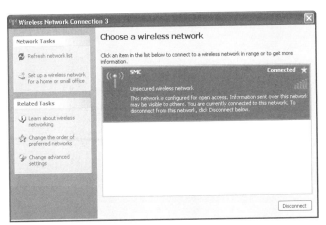

Figure 1-7. Newly designed dialog boxes make it easier to see at a glance whether an available wireless network is secure.

> **Note** New computers should have SP2 pre-installed. If your computer does not yet have SP2, you can order the CD directly from Microsoft or find it at a nearby computer retailer (Microsoft has pledged to make SP2 widely available). If you have a fast enough Internet connection, you can download and install SP2 using Windows Update. (For information about Windows Update, see "Keeping Your System Secure with Windows Update," page 210.) How can you tell whether you already have SP2? Right-click My Computer and choose Properties to open the System Properties dialog box; the General tab shows "Service Pack 2" under the System heading if SP2 has been installed. All of the changes included with Service Pack 1 are incorporated into SP2, so don't worry about having to install the older service pack first—just get SP2.

● **Windows Media Player 10**   Service Pack 2 includes Windows Media Player 9 Series, which was a significant upgrade to the player included with the original release of Windows XP. After SP2 was completed, Microsoft released an even more sweeping upgrade to its all-in-one music and video jukebox. Figure 1-8 shows the newest player at work; if you're still using the older player, you'll want to upgrade, as we explain in Chapter 24, "Using and Customizing Windows Media Player."

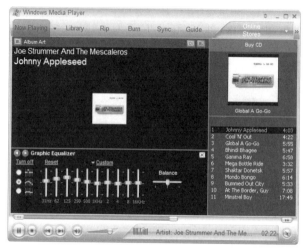

Figure 1-8. The latest version of Windows Media Player simplifies the process of creating and managing a digital music library.

Chapter 2

Installing and Configuring Windows XP

Some Windows users never have to deal with the Windows Setup program. If you buy a new computer with Microsoft Windows XP pre-installed, you may be able to use it forever without having to do anything more than minor maintenance.

For upgraders, hobbyists, and inveterate tinkerers, however, the Windows XP Setup program is inescapable. Knowing how to upgrade properly or perform a clean install can spell the difference between a smooth-running system and a box of troubles. And if you're responsible for multiple Windows installations, you'll want to delve into the Deployment Tools package (which resides on the Windows XP CD) for time-saving strategies.

In this chapter, we'll explain the subtleties and intricacies of the Windows Setup program, explore the workings of the Files And Settings Transfer Wizard, and show you how to set up a computer with multiple versions of Windows.

At Home with Windows XP

Windows XP Home Edition is indistinguishable from the Professional edition when it comes to the core tasks of installing the operating system, updating system files, transferring files and settings between computers, and configuring startup options. Some of the advanced setup options described in this chapter, including the use of answer files and disk imaging, are most commonly used in corporate settings, where Windows XP Professional is a better choice than Home Edition.

Avoiding Compatibility Problems

Many programs originally written for Windows 95, Windows 98, or Windows Me won't run properly under Windows XP. Likewise, some hardware devices use drivers that aren't compatible with Windows XP. The worst possible time to find out about either type of compatibility problem is right after you complete the setup process, when you try to use a favorite program or device.

To spare yourself unnecessary headaches, run the Windows XP Upgrade Advisor before installing Windows XP on a system on which a previous version of Windows is already installed. You can start this abbreviated version of Setup directly from the menu that appears when you insert the Windows XP CD—choose Check System Compatibility, and then click Check My System Automatically. If the CD's opening menu doesn't appear, type **d:\i386\winnt32-checkupgradeonly** (replacing *d* with the correct drive letter, of course) at any command prompt.

When you start the Windows Setup program on a system running Windows 98 or Windows Me, it asks you to enter the product ID, checks for dynamic updates, and then runs a slightly different version of the Upgrade Advisor, giving you the option to check hardware only or to check all installed programs as well. The full option produces the same report you'd see if you had run this utility on its own. If you discover a serious incompatibility, you can (and should) cancel Setup; if the Upgrade Report lists only minor problems, you can continue with confidence.

> **Tip** Use dynamic updates
>
> When you upgrade over an existing Windows version, Setup offers to check for dynamic updates. If you have an active Internet connection, be sure to take advantage of this option. Dynamic updates can include service packs, updated drivers for hardware detected on your system, and upgrade packs for programs you're currently running. Rolling these updates into Windows Setup saves you time and hassle and ensures that you don't have to install a bunch of updates immediately after you boot Windows XP for the first time.

The upgrade report lists problems that you might encounter during the upgrade process, including hardware and software incompatibilities. For some programs, you might be instructed to download upgrade packs. When upgrading over Windows 98 or Windows Me, you might need to uninstall a program before setting up Windows XP, and then reinstall the program after Setup is complete.

Figure 2-1 shows a typical Upgrade Advisor report. Scroll through the entire list to identify any urgent warnings or compatibility issues that require your immediate attention.

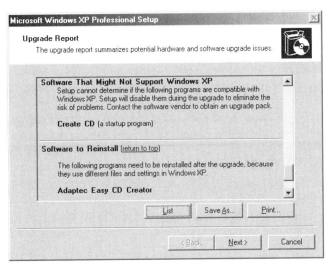

Figure 2-1. Read this upgrade report carefully before continuing with Setup. In some cases, you might need to uninstall programs or find new drivers before going any further.

For the most part, you can safely follow these general guidelines: Business and consumer applications that are compatible with Windows 2000 should work with Windows XP. Applications that were written for Windows 98 or Windows Me are more likely to cause problems, especially if they use virtual device drivers (VxDs). In addition, some programs install differently on Windows 98 and Windows Me than on Windows 2000 and Windows XP—they use different program files or write values to different registry locations, for example. The Upgrade Advisor should flag any such programs, and if they're available, Windows will automatically download upgrade packs as part of the dynamic update process.

When upgrading, be especially vigilant with utility software that works at the system level. If you use a disk partitioning tool, antivirus program, personal firewall software, or other system utility that was originally written for a previous Windows version, it's prudent to assume that it won't work properly with Windows XP. Always look for upgraded versions that are certified to be compatible with Windows XP before continuing with Setup.

Tip Check Windows Catalog to find compatible programs and devices
The Upgrade Advisor is thorough, but it's not exhaustive. If you've installed a program or hardware device that is absolutely essential to your daily productivity, don't assume that it passes muster just because the Upgrade Advisor doesn't flag it as a problem device. The Windows Catalog (*http://www.microsoft.com/windows/catalog*) is regularly updated, and it includes links to additional information and updated drivers.

Preparing to Install Windows XP

Before you install Windows XP, run through this simple checklist:

Confirm that your hardware satisfies the system requirements   Microsoft's official spec sheet says the bare minimum configuration includes a 233 MHz processor from the Intel Pentium/Celeron family or the AMD K6/Athlon/Duron family (or compatible); 64 MB of RAM; 1.5 GB of available disk space; and a video adapter capable of Super VGA (800 × 600) resolution. The recommended configuration is at least a 300 MHz CPU with 128 MB of RAM. You'll also need a mouse or other pointing device, a keyboard, and a CD-ROM or DVD drive.

> **Tip**   Don't skimp on RAM
>
> Defining an acceptable level of performance is strictly a matter of personal preference. The speed of the CPU is probably the least critical element of a Windows XP system. A fast hard disk and gobs of memory will do much more to keep a system with multiple applications and multiple users running smoothly. If you plan to use memory-intensive programs such as Microsoft Outlook, Adobe Photoshop, or Macromedia's Shockwave, don't settle for less than 512 MB of RAM; 1 GB is even better. And if you plan to take advantage of Fast User Switching to allow multiple users to log on simultaneously, you'll need still more RAM— figure on 64 MB for each additional user.

Gather network details   If you need to supply a static IP address and subnet mask, collect this information and have it at hand. Likewise, be sure you know the name of your workgroup or domain. If you plan to set up your network along with the rest of Windows, be sure you're physically connected to the network or that your wireless hardware is working properly.

> For more information about networking your computers, see Chapter 28, "Setting Up a Small Network."

Check hardware and software compatibility   If you need any updated drivers or upgrade packs, download them before you run Setup, and burn them to CD or copy them to floppy disks so that they'll be available when you need them.

Back up your data files and system settings   If you're planning an upgrade, don't underestimate Murphy's Law. Use a reliable backup program or the Files And Settings Transfer Wizard (described in "Moving Windows Settings and Files," page 45) to make a safe copy of important data.

Disable antivirus software and other system utilities   The Upgrade Report should identify utilities that might interfere with Setup. To be on the safe side, disable system utilities before getting started.

Installing and Configuring Windows XP

Setting Up Windows XP

When setting up either edition of Windows XP, you need to first choose one of three installation strategies, each with its own set of pros and cons:

- **Clean install** As the name implies, this installation option sets up a fresh new copy of Windows XP, completely replacing any previous version of Windows on the partition where it's set up and erasing all other files on that partition. Although you can start a clean install by running Setup from an earlier version of Windows, it is much simpler to do so by booting directly from the CD. In either case, you can use an existing partition or define and format partitions during setup.

- **Upgrade over an existing Windows version** You can upgrade to Windows XP Home Edition or Professional from Windows 98, Windows 98 Second Edition, or Windows Me. You can also upgrade to Windows XP Professional from Windows NT Workstation 4 (Service Pack 6) or Windows 2000 Professional (with or without service packs). If you're currently running Windows 3.1 or Windows 95, you cannot upgrade to any version of Windows XP and must perform a clean install. In all upgrade scenarios, Setup preserves most user settings and installed programs and attempts to upgrade device drivers to Windows XP–compatible versions.

- **Side-by-side (multiboot) installation** Use this option (a variation of the clean install process) when you want to preserve an existing copy of Windows. When Setup is finished, you'll be able to choose your OS from a boot menu. You must install the new version on a separate partition; installing multiple Windows versions on a single partition is a recipe for disaster.

Choosing between a clean install and an upgrade is not a cut-and-dried decision. Even on systems that meet the requirements for upgrading, a clean install offers the assurance that you're wiping out all traces of any previous Windows problems caused by installing and uninstalling programs, downloading Web-based components, and over-tweaking the computer's settings. Starting with a clean registry and a solid base of Windows system files should give your computer an opportunity to deliver full performance, unburdened by the past.

On the other hand, an upgrade is sometimes the only way to guarantee that a specific program or driver will work properly. We've seen software and hardware drivers that work well under Windows 2000 but refuse to install properly after a clean Windows XP setup; in many cases, these programs and drivers will continue to work if you upgrade to Windows XP. If you're experiencing this problem, the best choice may be a hybrid of the two approaches. Start with a clean install of Windows 2000 and add any required programs and drivers. After verifying that everything works properly, upgrade to Windows XP.

Chapter 2

Troubleshooting

During setup, some peripherals don't work properly.

Check your system BIOS. An outdated BIOS can cause problems with disk partitioning, power management, peripheral configuration, and other crucial low-level functions. To find out whether an update is available, check with the manufacturer of your computer or its motherboard. Identifying the BIOS and tracking down the appropriate source for updates isn't always easy; you'll find detailed information at the indispensable (and thoroughly independent) Wim's BIOS (*http://www.wimsbios.com*).

After verifying that you're running the most recent BIOS version, use the BIOS setup program to select the "non–Plug and Play operating system" option. This advice may seem counterintuitive—after all, Windows XP is indeed a Plug and Play operating system. However, this setting was intended for use with earlier Windows versions, and if it's set incorrectly it can prevent the Windows XP boot loader from accessing devices at startup.

Most Windows Setup options are fairly straightforward. A clean setup consists of the following four distinct steps:

- **File copy**   This step copies the Windows Setup files to a folder on the partition where they can run when you restart the system. If you boot from the CD, Setup skips this step and loads the files directly from the CD.

- **Text mode setup**   On a clean install, this step is where you select (and if necessary, create and format) the partition you want to use for the Windows XP system files.

- **GUI mode setup**   This is the graphical portion of Windows Setup. In a clean interactive installation, this is where you select regional settings (language and time zone, for instance) and enter details such as the product key, computer name, and administrator password.

- **Windows Welcome**   This is the final portion of Setup, where you have the option to create user accounts and activate Windows. System manufacturers sometimes modify these options to add their own logos, custom registration screens, and additional options or features. (In previous versions, this stage was also known as Out Of Box Experience, or OOBE. The OOBE label refers to your experience when you take a new computer out of the box and set it up for the first time.)

Note   All the files used for this portion of Setup are included in the Oobe folder in the System32 folder. If you like the mood music that runs during this part of Setup, for instance, you can add it to your list of favorite Media Clips. Open the %SystemRoot%\System32\Oobe\Images folder, right-click Title.wma, and choose Add To Playlist.

Installing and Configuring Windows XP

Performing a Clean Install

The simplest setup scenario of all is installing Windows XP in a newly created partition on a system that does not currently have any version of Windows installed (or, as an alternative, to wipe out a partition containing an existing version of Windows and completely replace it with a clean install of Windows XP). The safest way to embark on a clean install is to boot from the Windows XP CD. Insert the Windows CD and restart your computer. Watch for a boot prompt; typically, you need to press a key to boot from the CD. After the setup process begins, you can follow the instructions as outlined in this section.

> **Note**   You can perform a clean install using a Windows XP upgrade CD. The upgrade CD requires proof that you own an earlier version of Windows—but that earlier version does not need to be installed on the computer's hard drive. Instead, boot from the Windows XP CD and proceed as described in this section. During the setup process, Windows asks you to insert the CD from your old version of Windows to confirm your upgrade eligibility.

> **Note**   For a bootable CD to work properly, you must set the boot order in the BIOS so that the CD drive appears ahead of the hard disk drive and any other bootable media; we recommend setting the CD drive as the first boot device, followed by the hard disk, floppy disk, and any other bootable devices, in whichever order you prefer. The boot options available for every computer are different, as is the technique for accessing the BIOS setup program. During boot, watch for a message that tells you which key to press for setup. If you're lucky, the BIOS setup program on your computer includes a Boot tab where you can specify the order of boot devices; if this option isn't immediately apparent, look for a page called Advanced CMOS Settings or something similar.

Most computers that meet the minimum requirements for Windows XP include the capability to boot from a CD-ROM drive. In some relatively uncommon configurations, however, this option isn't available. This problem is most likely to affect you if your CD-ROM is connected to a SCSI adapter that doesn't allow booting from a CD, or if you're trying to install Windows XP on a notebook computer that doesn't include an integrated CD drive. Try one of these alternatives to work around the problem:

- Download the Windows XP setup disk file and use it to create a set of bootable floppy disks. The resulting setup disk set boots the computer, loads the necessary drivers to access the CD-ROM drive, and then begins the setup process. To get the setup disk file, go to the Microsoft Download Center (*http://www.microsoft.com/downloads*) and search for "windows xp setup disk." Be sure you select the file for the version of Windows XP you plan to install; the Windows XP Professional file won't work properly with a Windows XP Home Edition CD and vice versa. Similarly, match the service pack level of the setup disk file to the one on your Windows CD, if it has one.

● Start your computer from a Windows 98/Me emergency boot disk. This floppy disk includes generic CD drivers that allow you to access most IDE and SCSI drives. From the MS-DOS prompt, run the SmartDrive disk-caching utility (Smartdrv.exe), and then start Windows Setup using the Winnt.exe command. (Because this program is running from MS-DOS, you can't use the 32-bit Setup program, Winnt32.exe.)

Tip **Don't skip SmartDrive**

If you have to copy files from a CD to your hard disk using MS-DOS, the SmartDrive utility is essential. Without this helper, copying the Setup files can take hours; with SmartDrive installed, the process practically flies by. Look for the Smartdrv.exe file on the MS-DOS startup disk. If it's not there, you can copy it to your boot floppy from the \Windows \Command folder of any version of Windows 95/98/Me.

● If you can access the Windows XP CD from your previous Windows version and you have a FAT32 partition that is separate from the one on which you plan to install Windows XP, copy the i386 folder from the CD to that partition. (If you have only a single partition available, you'll be unable to perform a clean install using this technique, because you won't be able to wipe out the current system partition without also erasing your Setup files. Likewise, if the second partition is formatted using NTFS, you will not be able to access it from a Windows 98/Me boot floppy.) Then restart the computer using the Windows 98/Me emergency boot disk and run Setup from a command prompt, again using the Winnt command.

Note Where does Setup install Windows XP system files? The exact name of the folder varies. On a clean install, Setup creates a top-level folder called Windows on the drive you designate and then copies system files there. On an upgrade, Setup uses the current path for %WinDir%—for Windows 98 or Windows Me, that's typically C:\Windows; for Windows NT 4 and Windows 2000, the drive letter may vary, but the name of the system folder is usually \Winnt. When performing a clean install, you can specify a different folder name, but your safest choice is to use the default name.

Whether you started from a previous Windows version or booted from a CD, your next stop (after Setup restarts, of course) will be a series of text-mode Setup screens. If your system currently contains a working version of Windows XP, you'll see a screen that offers to repair the installation for you. Press Esc to bypass this screen and reach a disk setup screen similar to the one shown in Figure 2-2.

Installing and Configuring Windows XP

Troubleshooting

Your system crashes after text-mode setup is complete.

The most common cause of a Stop error (also known as the Blue Screen of Death, or BSOD) during Setup is a missing or incompatible driver for a disk subsystem. If your computer includes a high-performance IDE controller (typically identified in the BIOS as ATA-66, ATA-100, or SATA) or an SCSI boot device, Windows XP might not include a compatible driver for that controller.

The best solution to this dilemma is to download a driver that is compatible with Windows XP (in most cases, a driver designed for Windows 2000 will work just as well). Copy the driver files to a floppy disk, and restart your system. When text-mode setup begins, look for a prompt along the bottom of the screen that asks you whether you have a storage device that uses a custom driver. Press F6 at this point; when Setup finishes loading its files, it will prompt you to supply the floppy disk containing the custom driver.

If you can't find a compatible driver for your high-speed IDE controller, you can usually continue with Setup by shutting down your system and switching the drive cables to the standard IDE controller (you may need to adjust BIOS options as well). Disk performance will suffer somewhat, but you'll be able to complete setup using the built-in IDE drivers. You can supply the correct drivers (and switch the controller cables) later.

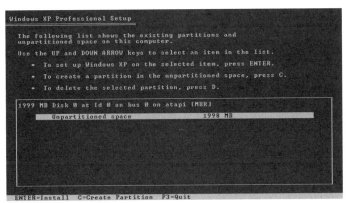

Figure 2-2. This disk management screen is visible only if you boot from the Windows XP CD or choose the option to specify the installation partition.

From this screen, you can do any of the following tasks:

Select an existing partition on which to install Windows XP   Use this option if you already created and formatted an empty partition in preparation for setting up Windows, or if you plan to install Windows XP on a preexisting partition that currently contains data or programs but no operating system. Do not choose this option if a previous version of Windows is already installed on the selected partition. The result in that case might be to leave behind unwanted system files and leftovers from previously installed programs, defeating the purpose of doing a clean install.

Create a new partition from unpartitioned space   Use this option to set up one or more partitions on a new drive or on an existing drive after deleting partitions. By default, Setup offers to use all unpartitioned space on the current disk. You can specify a smaller partition size if you want to subdivide the disk into multiple drives.

Delete an existing partition   Choose this option if you want to do a clean install on a drive that currently contains an earlier version of Windows. Because this operation deletes data irretrievably, you must respond to at least two "Are you sure?" confirmation requests. After deleting the partition, you can create a new one and select it as the destination for your Windows XP installation.

Upgrading a Previous Windows Version

To upgrade to Windows XP, start your current version of Windows, insert the Windows XP CD, and choose Install Windows XP from the Welcome To Microsoft Windows XP menu. Do not boot from the CD and try to perform an upgrade; that won't work. (If you prefer working at a command prompt in Windows, skip the CD menu and type *d*:\i386\Winnt32.exe, substituting the correct letter of your CD-ROM drive for *d*.) On the first page of the Windows Setup Wizard, select Upgrade (Recommended) and click Next.

If you choose to upgrade, the Windows Setup program asks you to enter a few pieces of information, including the product key; the remainder of the process continues completely unattended. Setup replaces your existing Windows files, but it preserves user settings, such as desktop appearance, color schemes, network connections, and so on. It also retains the programs you have installed and all their settings. (As noted earlier in this chapter, the Upgrade Advisor report identifies any programs that are incompatible with Windows XP.) After several reboots that typically require no attention from you, the upgrade installation completes, and you're ready to pick up where you left off—with Windows XP as your new operating system.

After the upgrade is complete, run through the following checklist to confirm that the process went smoothly and to clean up any loose ends:

Reset passwords for migrated user accounts   When upgrading over an installation of Windows 98 or Windows Me, Setup adds an account for each user that had a profile in the previous operating system, but discards the passwords for each such account. As administrator, you can manually add each user's password.

Run the Network Setup Wizard   The upgrade should preserve your network and Internet settings. The Network Setup Wizard helps set up file sharing and configures Windows Firewall, among other tasks.

Check that all essential programs and devices work properly   Don't assume that the Upgrade Advisor was 100 percent accurate. Be sure to test each of your programs and devices to make sure they're operating as you expect. If you encounter serious problems, you can try to fix them or uninstall Windows XP and restore your previous operating system.

Consider upgrading your system drive to NTFS   On an upgrade from Windows 98 or Windows Me, the Setup program does not automatically convert drives to NTFS but leaves them in FAT32 format. If you're satisfied that your system is working properly, you can significantly tighten security by using the Convert utility to change the format to NTFS.

> For more details about converting drives to NTFS, see "NTFS or FAT32: Which Disk Format Should You Choose?" page 746.

Save your Administrator password   On an upgrade to Windows XP Professional, you're required to set a password for the built-in Administrator account (in Home Edition, this password is intentionally left blank). Write this password down and squirrel it away in a safe place. (And, no, a sticky note on the side of your monitor is not a safe place!)

Troubleshooting

You encounter problems installing Windows.

Check for the existence of a log file named Setuperr.log in the %SystemRoot% folder (normally C:\Windows). It should list any errors and warnings that occurred during setup, and can help you pinpoint exactly where the process went awry. If Setuperr.log doesn't provide enough information, try running Winnt32.exe with the /Debug switch. For more information about using this switch, see "Controlling Setup with Switches," page 30.

Windows XP Setup also creates several other log files that can be useful in tracking down installation problems. The most interesting of these is %SystemRoot%\Setupact.log, which contains a list of actions (such as file copies and registry changes) in the order they occurred during the graphical part of setup. Other log files include %SystemRoot%\Comsetup.log (installation information about Optional Component Manager and COM+ components), %SystemRoot%\Setupapi.log (information recorded each time an .inf file executes), %SystemRoot%\Debug\Netsetup.log (information about network setup, including workgroup and domain membership), %SystemRoot%\Security\Logs\Scesetup.log (information about actions taken by the application of the configured security template), and %SystemRoot%\Repair\Setup.log (information used by Recovery Console during repair operations).

Microsoft Windows XP Inside Out Deluxe, Second Edition

Installing Windows XP on a Computer with Other Operating Systems

If your computer already has a 32-bit version of Windows installed *and* you have at least two disk partitions defined, you can install a clean copy of Windows XP without disturbing your existing Windows installation. At boot time, you choose your Windows version from a startup menu. Although this is typically called a dual-boot system, it's more accurate to call it a multiboot configuration, because you can install multiple copies of Windows NT, Windows 2000, and Windows XP.

Having the capability to choose your operating system at startup is handy if you have a program or device that simply won't work under Windows XP. When you need to use the legacy program or device, you can boot into your other Windows version without too much fuss. This capability is also useful for software developers, who need to be able to test how their programs work under different operating systems.

For experienced Windows users, installing a second copy of Windows XP in its own partition can also be helpful as a way to experiment with a program or device driver that is not certified to be compatible with Windows XP without possibly compromising a working system. After you finish setting up the second, clean version of Windows XP, you'll see an additional entry on the startup menu that corresponds to your new installation. (The newly installed version is the default menu choice; it runs automatically if 30 seconds pass and you don't make a choice.) Experiment with the program or driver and see how well it works. If, after testing thoroughly, you're satisfied that the program is safe to use, you can add it to the Windows XP installation you use every day. If it causes problems, you can remove the program or driver.

> **Tip**   Use third-party utilities to manage partitions
>
> Although you can install multiple copies of Windows NT, Windows 2000, and Windows XP, you can have only one copy of Windows 95, Windows 98, or Windows Me on a multiboot system that is managed by the Windows XP boot manager. If you want to be able to choose from two or more Windows versions from the Windows 95/98/Me product line in addition to Windows XP, you need to use a third-party boot manager program. Symantec's highly regarded Norton PartitionMagic (*http://www.symantec.com/partitionmagic*) includes a capable utility called BootMagic. (Be sure to check compatibility carefully; PartitionMagic version 6 and earlier will not work properly with Windows XP.) Another esteemed boot manager is included in BootIt Next Generation, a partition and multiboot manager from Terabyte Unlimited (*http://www.bootitng.com*).

To add Windows XP to a system where an existing version of Windows is already installed, first make sure that you have an available partition (or unformatted disk space) separate from the partition that contains the system files for your current Windows version.

Installing and Configuring Windows XP

Inside Out

Install a second copy of Windows in a single partition

You might want to install multiple copies of Windows (say, for example, a copy of Windows XP Professional and a copy of Windows XP Home Edition) in a single partition, perhaps because it simplifies partition management or sharing programs. Some well-known computer advice Web sites explain how to do this and, in fact, the installations should actually proceed without a hitch. But take our advice: Don't do it! It's a sure recipe for disaster. These installations will have a hybrid registry (the user portion of the registry will be shared between Windows versions, but the machine portion will be separate for each Windows version) and numerous other conflicts that are bound to cause problems. For more information, see "Avoiding Dual-Boot Disasters," page 29.

There is one (and only one) circumstance in which it is desirable to install a fresh copy of Windows XP on a partition that already contains Windows system files. This option is relevant if you have only a single disk partition available and you're unable to start your existing installation of Windows XP even after using all the repair techniques described in Chapter 39, "Recovering After a Computer Crash." In that case, you might choose to boot from your Windows XP CD and perform a clean install in a new folder on the same partition. After setup is complete, you should be able to access your data files through the new Windows XP installation. Use this option as a last resort, and then only to recover data so that you can restore it after fixing the underlying problem, wiping the hard drive clean, and reinstalling Windows XP.

The target partition can be a separate partition on the same physical disk, or it can be on a different hard disk. If your system contains a single disk with a single partition used as drive C, you cannot safely create a multiboot system unless you add a new disk or use third-party software such as PartitionMagic to shrink the existing partition and create a new partition from the free space. The new partition does not need to be empty; however, it should not contain system files for another Windows installation.

Follow these steps to set up Windows XP on a multiboot system:

1. After starting your current Windows version, insert the Windows XP CD.

2. From the Welcome To Microsoft Windows XP menu, choose Install Windows XP.

   If the Welcome menu doesn't appear, CD AutoPlay is probably disabled on your computer. In that case, open the Run dialog box and type *d*:\i386 \Winnt32.exe (substitute the correct letter of your CD-ROM drive for *d*).

3. From the first Windows Setup dialog box, select New Installation (Advanced) from the Installation Type list. Click Next to continue.

4 When prompted, accept the End User License Agreement (EULA) and enter the 25-character product key.

5 In the Setup Options dialog box, click the Advanced Options button.

6 In the Advanced Options dialog box, select I Want To Choose The Install Drive Letter And Partition During Setup, as shown on the next page.

Installing and Configuring Windows XP

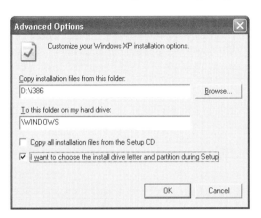

> **Caution**   This option is crucial to a successful multiboot installation! If you get distracted and forget to select this option, the Setup program will automatically upgrade your existing Windows installation and you will lose your current operating system.

7   Click through the remaining steps of the wizard and allow the computer to restart. At that point, you will start in text-mode setup, where you can specify the disk and partition on which you want to install Windows XP.

The Setup program automatically handles details of adding the newly installed operating system to the startup menu.

Avoiding Dual-Boot Disasters

We can't say it strongly enough: Do not install two or more versions of Windows on a single partition! Doing so can cause serious problems with applications, many of which reside in the \Program Files folder on the boot partition (the partition where the operating system is installed).

Many programs use different versions of executable files and dynamic link libraries for Windows 95/98/Me and Windows NT/2000/XP. If you try to share such a program between two Windows versions, it won't work properly in at least one Windows version. In addition, you may experience these problems:

- Program preferences, options, and settings you've chosen in one operating system don't show up when you use the other operating system because each stores its own registry entries.

- If you uninstall an application, its entries still show up on the Start menu, on the Add/Remove Programs list, and throughout the registry of the other operating system—yet the program files are gone.

Chapter 2

You might encounter still other problems with multiple operating systems on a single partition. And if you call Microsoft Product Support Services for help with such problems, you'll be told—politely, to be sure—that you need to reformat your drive and start over. Microsoft does not support such installations. That alone should be a clear indication that it's not a good idea!

Although we recommend that you use separate partitions for each operating system, there's no reason you can't share data on a common drive that's available to all operating systems. In fact, you might want to change the target folder location of your My Documents folder in each operating system so that it points to the same folder.

Removing an Operating System from a Dual-Boot System

Some people set up Windows XP as a dual-boot configuration while they evaluate or migrate to the new operating system. But once the migration is done, you'll want to uninstall the earlier operating system to recover its disk space and to speed up booting. No problem.

The easiest way to remove any operating system from a dual-boot system is to delete its entry from Boot.ini. (For information about this file, see "Configuring Startup Options," page 72.) Then boot into the remaining operating system and delete the files related to the operating system you want to remove. Or, for a more aggressive approach, you can format the partition of the operating system you removed from Boot.ini.

Controlling Setup with Switches

When using the Winnt32.exe command to start the Windows Setup program, you can modify the program's behavior with a number of command-line switches. Table 2-1 lists the most useful of these switches.

Table 2-1. Command-Line Setup Switches for Winnt32.exe

Switch	What It Does
/checkupgradeonly	Runs the Upgrade Advisor without installing Windows XP.
/cmd:*command_line*	Specifies a command to be carried out after the graphical portion of Setup has completed; often used to install applications as part of the Windows XP Setup.
/cmdcons	Adds the Recovery Console to the Windows XP startup menu (see "Adding the Recovery Console," page 76).
/copydir:*folder_name*	Creates a subfolder within the Windows XP folder and copies the contents of the specified folder there; useful if you need to make drivers available for later installation.
/copysource:*folder_name*	Creates a temporary subfolder within the Windows XP folder; this subfolder is deleted when Setup finishes.

Chapter 2

Table 2-1. **Command-Line Setup Switches for Winnt32.exe**

Switch	What It Does
/debug*level*	Creates a log file of setup errors, %SystemRoot%\Setuperr.log. Replace *level* with one of the following numbers: 0 records only severe errors 1 records errors 2 records warnings (this is the default debug level) 3 records information 4 records detailed information for debugging Each level includes all information from levels with lower numbers.
/makelocalsource	Instructs Setup to copy installation source files to your local hard disk; use this option if the CD will be unavailable during installation.
/noreboot	Eliminates forced reboot after file-copying phase of Setup; useful if you need to execute another command before restarting.
/s:*sourcepath*	Specifies source location of Windows XP Setup files, typically on a server; repeat this switch up to eight times to specify multiple servers.
/syspart:*drive_letter*	Allows you to copy Setup files to a hard disk, mark the disk as active, move it to another machine, and restart to continue Setup on the new computer; must be used with /tempdrive and can be run only on Windows NT/2000/XP machines.
/tempdrive:*drive_letter*	Used in conjunction with /syspart to specify the primary partition to be used for storing Windows XP Setup files and installing a new copy of Windows XP; an upgrade installation will be placed on the partition from which Winnt32.exe is run.
/udf:*ID[,UDB_file]*	Identifies a Uniqueness Database (UDB) file that modifies an answer file (see "Using Answer Files for Automated Installation," page 36).
/unattend[*seconds*][:*answer_file*]	Used in conjunction with an unattended Setup, as described in the next section; optional [*seconds*] parameter is only required on Windows NT 4 upgrades, and the file name can be omitted if the default name Unattend.txt is used.

Chapter 2

Activating Windows XP

Windows XP includes an antipiracy feature called Windows Product Activation (WPA). As in previous Windows versions, you must enter a 25-character product key during the setup process. However, WPA adds a new requirement: After Setup completes, you must activate your installation within 30 days, either by connecting to a Microsoft activation server over the Internet, or by making a toll-free call to an interactive telephone activation system.

WPA is a mechanism designed to enforce license restrictions by preventing the most common form of software piracy: casual copying. Typically, a Microsoft Windows XP license entitles you to install the operating system software on a single computer. If you use the same CD and product key to install Windows XP on a different system, you'll be unable to activate the software automatically. Here's what you need to know about WPA:

- **Under most circumstances, activation is automatic and instantaneous** If you purchase a shrink-wrapped copy of Windows XP and install it on a new computer, you can activate over the Internet, and the process should take no more than a few seconds. If you need to use the phone, the process takes longer, because you have to enter a 50-digit identification key (either by using the phone's dial pad or by speaking to a customer service representative) and then input the 42-digit confirmation ID supplied in response, as shown in Figure 2-3.

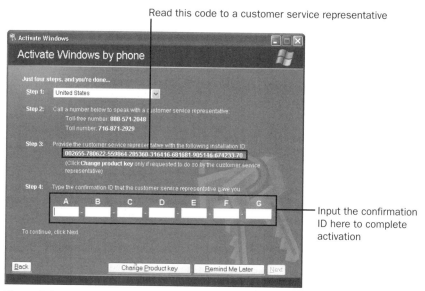

Read this code to a customer service representative

Input the confirmation ID here to complete activation

Figure 2-3. Activating a copy of Windows over the phone is considerably more complex than doing it over the Internet.

Installing and Configuring Windows XP

> **Tip** Don't rush to activate
>
> When you install a retail copy of Windows XP, you're prompted during the final stage of Setup to activate the product. We recommend that you choose not to activate it immediately. Instead, give yourself at least a week to verify that Windows XP works properly on your hardware and that you won't be required to replace any hardware or the entire computer. After you're confident that Windows XP is completely compatible with your hardware, you can safely activate. Use the persistent reminder balloons in the notification area, or click the Start button and choose the Activate Windows shortcut at the top of the All Programs menu.

- **Within 30 days of installing Windows XP, you must activate the software**   If you choose the phone option, you'll see a list of toll-free numbers.

- **Activation is not registration**   The activation process is completely anonymous and does not require that you divulge any personal information. If you choose to register your copy of Windows XP, this is a completely separate (and optional) task.

- **You're allowed to reinstall Windows an unlimited number of times on the same hardware**   During the activation process, Windows XP transmits an encrypted file that serves as a "fingerprint" of key components in your system. If you reinstall Windows XP on the same hardware, the activation server checks the new fingerprint against the one stored in its database. If they match, activation is automatic.

- **Multiple hardware upgrades may require you to reactivate Windows**   The activation software is designed to prevent attempts to "clone" an activated copy of Windows and install it on another computer. If you replace or upgrade four or more components from a list of 10 components on your computer in a period of 120 days or less, the activation mechanism may mistakenly assume that you've installed the operating system on a new computer. In that case, you'll be required to call the WPA clearinghouse and get a new activation code. The list of components included in the hardware "fingerprint" includes your display adapter, primary hard disk, volume serial number, SCSI adapter, IDE disk controller, CD-ROM drive, network adapter (based on its MAC address), CPU type, CPU serial number, and the amount of installed RAM. It does not include Zip drives, digital cameras, or similar peripheral devices. If the computer is marked as dockable, however (as most notebook computers are), the requirements are relaxed significantly, and you can safely upgrade seven of the components on the list (including the network adapter) or nine components (if the network adapter remains unchanged) before being forced to activate Windows again.

- **Copies of Windows XP sold with new computers may be exempt from WPA**   If you purchase a new computer on which Windows XP is pre-installed, the activation process may have been completed before you took delivery. In addition, copies of Windows sold this way are frequently tied via software to the BIOS of that computer (this method of installation is called System Locked Pre-Installation, or SLP). You may reinstall that copy of Windows XP an unlimited number of times on the computer it came with, regardless of how many upgrades you make, as long as you don't change the

Microsoft Windows XP Inside Out Deluxe, Second Edition

BIOS. In fact, you can replace the motherboard on a system activated with SLP as long as the new part is from the same manufacturer and uses the same BIOS identifier. However, you may be prohibited by the license agreement from transferring that copy of Windows to another computer.

● **Many corporations are also exempt from WPA requirements** Businesses that purchase as few as five copies of qualified Microsoft software, including Windows XP, through a Microsoft Volume Licensing (VL) program receive VL media and product keys that do not require activation. Under the terms of a volume license agreement, each computer with a copy of Windows XP must have a valid license.

For more details on volume licensing programs for Windows and other Microsoft software, check the Microsoft Volume Licensing home page at *http://www.microsoft.com/licensing*. For an exhaustive technical discussion of Product Activation, read the white paper at *http://www.microsoft.com/technet/prodtechnol/winxppro/evaluate/xpactiv.mspx*.

Inside Out

Back up Wpa.dbl to avoid activation when reinstalling

Want to prevent at least some activation headaches? Make a backup copy of Wpa.dbl, a tiny file stored in the %SystemRoot%\System32 folder. This file contains the hardware "fingerprint" information used to determine whether activation is required. If you need to reinstall Windows XP on a system that has already been activated, you can restore this file and bypass the need for activation—if your hardware hasn't changed appreciably since the original activation. Windows also creates a backup copy of this file, called Wpa.bak, at startup. This backup copy can be a lifesaver if you encounter problems after a hardware upgrade. If Windows refuses to run because your new hardware has triggered the activation code, you may be able to recover using this workaround: Restore your old hardware, start your computer in Networked Safe Mode, and rename Wpa.bak to Wpa.dbl. If all goes as it should, you'll be reactivated and able to continue working.

Tip Recover your product key

After you install Windows, the product key gets squirreled away, usually never to be seen again. But you might need to retrieve the product key at some point. For example, in our office we have many Windows XP CDs and many accompanying product keys—and our sloppy recordkeeping doesn't always make it easy to figure out which product key was used on a particular system. If we need to reinstall Windows (or if we retire a computer and want to install its copy of Windows on a new computer), we find out which product key we need by using a freeware application called Keyfinder (*http://www.magicaljellybean.com/keyfinder.shtml*). This application displays the product keys that were used to install Windows and Microsoft Office on a computer.

Installing and Configuring Windows XP

Automated Setup Options

If you plan to install Windows XP on one or two computers, running the Setup program from the CD is your best choice. But if you're planning to upgrade an entire office full of computers, you can save a substantial amount of time by automating the installation. The two most popular options are:

- **Unattended setup**   This option uses a batch file and a script (called an answer file) to bypass the Setup program's prompts and fill in answers automatically. You can choose from five unattended modes.
- **Disk imaging (cloning)**   In this option, you set up Windows on a sample computer and then run the System Preparation utility (Sysprep.exe), which removes the unique security identifier (SID). You can then use a disk cloning program such as Symantec Ghost (*http://www.symantec.com/ghost*) or Drive Image (*http://www.symantec.com/driveimage*) to copy the entire partition to a new computer; when it starts up, it runs a Mini-Setup program that completes in 5–10 minutes instead of the hour or more that full Setup requires.

> **Note**   Large organizations with existing networks built around Windows 2000 Server or Windows Server 2003 can deploy Windows XP on hundreds or thousands of machines with relative ease using Remote Installation Services (RIS) and Microsoft Systems Management Server (SMS). These options require substantial up-front preparation by information technology specialists, but the payoff can be dramatic. You can find more information about RIS at the Windows Server 2003 Web site (*http://www.microsoft.com/windowsserver2003*). SMS allows an administrator to manage and monitor installations from a central location. For information about SMS, visit *http://www.microsoft.com/smserver*.

Installing the Deployment Tools

The Windows XP Professional and Home Edition CDs include a selection of utilities and Help files that make it possible to use the automated installation processes described in this section. The Microsoft Windows Corporate Deployment Tools are located in a compressed Cabinet file (a compressed archive that is similar to a .zip file but uses the .cab extension). Before you can use these utilities, you have to copy them to your hard disk.

From Windows Explorer, open the \Support\Tools folder on the Windows XP CD, and double-click Deploy.cab. Select all files in this compressed folder, and copy them to a folder on your hard disk.

> **Tip**   **Keep support files together**
> If you've already installed the Support Tools, why not keep the Deployment Tools in the same location? Create a new subfolder called Deploy in the %ProgramFiles%\Support Tools folder and use it to store the deployment utilities.

The following files are included in Deploy.cab:

- **Setupmgr.exe**   This executable file opens the Microsoft Setup Manager Wizard, which is used for creating answer files. It includes a help file (Setupmgr.chm), which is accessible only from within the Setup Manager Wizard.

- **Sysprep.exe**   This executable file runs the System Preparation Tool, which is used for creating and deploying disk images.

> **Caution**   Do not run Sysprep.exe on any system unless you intend to make an image of that system. Sysprep is a powerful tool that removes unique security identifiers from a Windows computer. If you run it by mistake on a working system, you will wipe out the security settings on that computer and may suffer unintended consequences, such as losing the ability to access files in your user profile.

- **Setupcl.exe**   This small program is used by Sysprep.exe to create unique security identifiers (SIDs).

- **Deploy.chm**   This file is the Microsoft Windows Corporate Deployment Tools User's Guide, in Compiled HTML Help format; it provides detailed instructions and technical information about the deployment process. Double-click to browse its contents.

- **Ref.chm**   This file contains compiled HTML Help that provides reference information about the utilities and support files used in the deployment process. Double-click to browse its contents.

In addition, three specialized utilities that are intended primarily for use by computer manufacturers are included within the Deploy.cab collection on the Windows XP CD:

- **Cvtarea.exe**   Used in conjunction with Convert.exe (the utility that converts a drive to NTFS format) to create an unfragmented placeholder file for NTFS system files. The file is overwritten by the Master File Table during the conversion to NTFS.

- **Oformat.com**   An enhanced version of the Windows 98 Format.exe program (an MS-DOS application) that creates a FAT32 volume with clusters that are aligned optimally for conversion to NTFS format.

- **Factory.exe**   Helper program used with Sysprep.exe to make changes to a standard configuration before delivering it to end users.

For more information about these files, read the descriptions in the Deployment Tools User's Guide (Deploy.chm).

Using Answer Files for Automated Installation

The most tedious part of performing a clean Windows XP installation is waiting. At several points during the installation process, the Setup program stops and waits for you to fill in essential information—your name, the computer's name, network settings, and so on. Instead of waiting around for those dialog boxes to appear, you can create an *answer file*—a text file that automatically fills in the blanks for you and allows Setup to continue

Installing and Configuring Windows XP

unattended. An answer file can also contain answers to a number of questions that aren't posed by the interactive Setup program, which means that you actually have much greater control over installations. You can use an answer file whether you install from the Windows XP CD or from a shared network folder.

Inside Out

Automate installation of your other programs

The automated setup solutions we discuss in this chapter were designed for offices, but they may be ideal even if you only have one or two computers. If you're a dyed-in-the-wool hardware tinkerer and you regularly strip your system to bare metal and rebuild it with new components, use an answer file to take the tedium out of rerunning Setup each time. If you store your favorite customizations in .reg files or save them using the Files And Settings Transfer Wizard, you can be up and running in no time.

Of course, there's much more to setting up a system than installing Windows. First, of course, you'll want to install the latest service pack if it's not included in your Windows installation files. (Most copies of Windows XP sold in 2003 and later have Service Pack 1a. Beginning in late 2004, most copies integrate Service Pack 2.) In all likelihood, additional hotfixes need to be installed as well. The "Microsoft Windows XP Hotfix Installation and Deployment Guide," available online at *http://www.microsoft.com/windowsxp/pro/ downloads/servicepacks/sp1/hfdeploy.asp*, provides a (somewhat convoluted) description of how to include hotfixes when you install Windows XP from a network drive.

A better solution is to create a bootable Windows XP installation CD slipstreamed with the current service pack (that is, the service pack files are integrated so that they install as part of the original setup). To do that, in addition to a Windows XP CD and the service pack full installation file, you'll need a program for burning bootable CDs. (The CD-burning capability built into Windows XP can't make a bootable CD.) Among the most popular are Ahead Software's Nero (*http://www.nero.com*) and Roxio's Easy Media Creator (*http:// www.roxio.com*). You'll find instructions for creating such a CD at the Elder Geek on Windows XP site (*http://www.theeldergeek.com/slipstreamed_xpsp1_cd.htm*) and the Infini-Source site (*http://www.windows-help.net/windowsxp/winxp-sp1-bootcd.html*). (These well-written instructions explain how to slipstream Service Pack 1, but presumably comparable instructions are available for Service Pack 2 by the time you read this.) You can use a slip-streamed installation CD just the way you'd use an ordinary Windows XP CD: You can install directly from it or use an answer file.

But why stop with just an updated version of Windows? Once you have a slipstreamed installation CD, you can also install your applications as part of your automated installation process. A terrific site, *http://unattended.msfn.org*, explains how to do just that, and includes specific instructions and files for a number of popular applications.

If you decide to include service packs, hotfixes, and applications in your unattended setup, you'll still need to use an answer file, as described in the following sections.

Chapter 2

Creating an Answer File

To create an answer file, open the Windows Setup Manager Wizard (Setupmgr.exe) and follow its prompts. Most of the wizard's dialog boxes are self-explanatory, with fill-in-the-blank forms that match up neatly with questions that are familiar to anyone who has interactively run Setup from the Windows XP CD. If this is the first time you're using the wizard, you'll probably want to create a new answer file and designate it for a Windows unattended installation. If you already have an answer file and you need to change one or more details in that file (such as the product key or computer name), choose the Modify An Existing Answer File option.

> **Note** The Windows Setup Manager Wizard on the Windows XP CD runs on Windows XP Professional or Home Edition and on Windows 2000. It will not run on any earlier version of Windows.

The following list describes some of the more interesting options:

- **User Interaction Level** This page, shown in Figure 2-4, lets you choose one of five options that control how much the user sees during installation (for example, you can hide Windows Setup pages for which you've provided the answers) and whether you want the user to be able to override the answers you provide in the answer file. If you choose anything other than the Fully Automated option, you can leave selected answers blank; this technique is useful when you want the user to provide specific information (such as a user name) during Setup.

- **Distribution Folder** If you plan to install from a CD, you can ignore this option. However, if you want to install from a network share, you can specify it here; this option gives you the flexibility to add other files as well, such as drivers not found on the Windows XP CD.

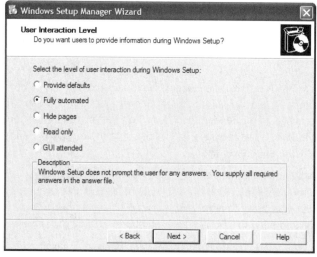

Figure 2-4. Check the Description panel at the bottom of this dialog box to see how each script-based option works.

● **Computer Names** This page, shown in Figure 2-5, allows you to enter the name of each computer individually, or you can import a text file that contains the names. You can specify more than one computer name here if you want to use this answer file to automate installation of Windows XP on multiple computers. If you're willing to accept computer names that follow no pattern, you can allow Setup to create each computer's name on the fly by appending seemingly random letters and numbers to the first few letters of your organization's name.

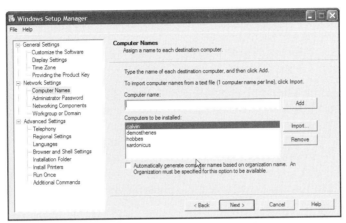

Figure 2-5. If you need to set up multiple computers, specify a group of names in this dialog box and then use the same answer file for each installation.

> **Tip   Create custom names**
> If you enter multiple computer names in the Setup Manager Wizard, you need to customize the batch file used to start the Setup program. Add the /udf switch after either Winnt32.exe or Winnt.exe, and copy the .udf file (which is automatically created by Setup Manager) to the same location as the answer file.

After you finish filling in the blanks in the Setup Manager Wizard, it creates an answer file and stores it using the name and location you specify. Saving the answer file to a floppy disk makes it especially easy to use if you plan to install from a CD.

> **Tip   Use descriptive names**
> The Setup Manager Wizard uses Unattend.txt as its default file name, but you can choose a different name if you prefer. Descriptive names can be helpful if you create multiple answer files to handle different hardware configurations—you might choose Notebook.txt as the name of the answer file to use for portable configurations, for instance.

Customizing an Answer File

The easiest way to customize an answer file—if you simply need to modify some settings you made with Setup Manager—is to restart Setup Manager. On the wizard's second page, select Modify An Existing Answer File and specify the file name.

But there's much more you can do with an answer file; the Setup Manager Wizard guides you through only the most commonly used settings. If you want to get more creative with your automated installations, open Ref.chm, the online reference guide that is included as part of the Deployment Tools collection. This Compiled HTML Help file provides a complete refer-ence to all the answer file parameters in the Unattend.txt section. The information is well organized and clearly presented, although its sheer bulk can be overwhelming. You might consider some of these additions or modifications:

- Consider adding Win9xUpgrade=Yes to the [Unattended] section if you're upgrading computers that are currently running Windows 98 or Windows Me. Without these keys (which Setup Manager does not add), Setup installs Windows XP on the same partition as the existing operating system, but in a separate folder. This produces an improperly configured dual-boot system that's practically guaranteed to cause prob-lems later. Use the [Components] section to specify which accessory programs are installed. You can use this option to prevent distractions like the Pinball game from being installed, for example.

- Use the [Win9xUpg] section to control how user accounts and passwords on Windows 95/98/Me computers are migrated to Windows 2000.

- Edit the [SystemRestore] section to configure System Restore options, including the percentage of disk space potentially used for saved configuration information.

- Use the [Fax] section to configure the fax service.

Answer files are plain ASCII text files that follow a consistent organization and syntax. The file consists of section headers—a section header is a word enclosed in square brackets on a line by itself—followed by keys and values. Each key begins on a new line, and it's usually fol-lowed by an equal sign and a value for the key. If a value contains any spaces, it must be enclosed in quotation marks. You can include comments in an answer file by putting a semi-colon at the beginning of each comment line. The Windows XP Preinstallation Reference includes three sample Unattend.txt files that you can examine in more detail.

> **Note**   In previous versions of the Setup Manager Wizard, passwords were stored in the answer file as ordinary text. In the Windows XP version of this utility, your passwords are considerably more secure. When you enter the Administrator password for the target com-puter, be sure to select the Encrypt Administrator Password In Answer File check box. This option eliminates the chance that a snoop can peek into the answer file and steal the pass-word for the Administrator account.

Installing and Configuring Windows XP

Using an Answer File During Setup

To use an answer file, include the /Unattend switch (along with the file specification for the answer file) on the command line for Winnt32.exe, the Windows XP Setup program. For example, if you're installing from the Windows XP Professional CD and you want to use an answer file named Unattend.txt that's stored on a floppy disk, enter this command line:

```
d:\i386\winnt32 /unattend:a:\unattend.txt
```

> **Tip** Combine a CD and a floppy for a clean install
>
> Of course, you can also use an answer file to automate the installation on a new computer—and you don't have to enter any command lines at all. If your computer can boot from the Windows XP Professional or Home Edition CD, save the answer file on a floppy disk and name it Winnt.sif. Insert the CD and the floppy disk and turn on the computer. Setup runs from the CD and uses Winnt.sif as its answer file.

If you used the Setup Manager Wizard to create the answer file, the process of using the resulting Unattend.txt file is even simpler. Setup Manager creates a batch file using the same file name (but with a .bat extension) and location that you specified for the answer file. Simply navigate to the folder where you saved the answer file (usually the distribution folder, if you set one up, or a floppy disk) and open the batch file. If you copy the batch file, the answer file, or both from the location where Setup Manager originally stored them, you might need to edit the batch file to update the path information.

Troubleshooting

Unattended Setup stops unexpectedly.

Even simple errors in answer files can cause Setup to stop before it ever gets started—and you won't get any hints about where the problem lies. If you receive a message saying that your Setup script file is "inaccessible or invalid," check each line to see that it follows the proper format. Be sure that all values with spaces are enclosed in quotation marks, and be especially vigilant for stray commas.

Using Disk Imaging

Windows XP, like its predecessor Windows 2000, includes Sysprep, a program that allows you to install a system, complete with Windows applications, and then duplicate it to other systems. After the system has been duplicated, the end user starts up the new system and runs either the Windows Welcome portion of Windows Setup (if you choose the Disk Duplication option) or an abbreviated "Mini-Setup" routine that requires only about five minutes to run (if you choose the Automating Mini-Setup option). Because Sysprep duplicates an entire hard disk partition, you can use it to copy complete systems that include additional customizations and installed applications.

> **Note** Why is Sysprep necessary? Unlike Windows 98 and Windows Me, each computer running any member of the Windows NT family (including Windows XP and Windows 2000) must have a unique security identifier, or SID. If two computers on a network have identical SIDs, the result is chaos. Because the Setup program automatically creates a unique SID for each Windows installation, cloning a running Windows XP system won't work—the clone would have the same SID as the original computer. Sysprep solves this problem by removing the SID on the master system, before you create the clone. When you transfer the image to the new system and start it up for the first time, Sysprep generates a unique SID.

Chapter 2

Using Automated Installations: The Simplest Way

If you have a small office—a few dozen computers or less—you don't need to pass an MCSE (Microsoft Certified Systems Engineer) exam to become a Setup whiz. Instead, you can follow this simple, straightforward method for automating your installations:

1 Install Windows XP on one computer.

2 Install the Deployment Tools on the same computer.

3 Use the Windows Setup Manager Wizard to create an answer file. If you already have a network setup, use Setup Manager to create a distribution folder. Otherwise, tell Setup Manager that you'll install from the CD.

4 Using the information in Ref.chm, edit the answer file you created to include any additional customizations you want.

5 If the computers you're targeting for installation don't have a working network connection, copy the answer file, the batch file, and the .udf file (if any) created by Setup Manager to a floppy disk.

6 At each computer, connect to the distribution folder (if you already have a working network) and run the batch file, or run it from the floppy disk. (If you specified more than one computer name in the answer file, you'll need to append the specific computer name to the command line when you run the batch file.)

The process of creating an answer file should take a few minutes—an hour if you decide to customize it extensively. You can easily save 30 minutes or more on each unattended installation, compared to the time it would take to sit in front of the computer and respond to its prompts. That's a healthy return on your investment of time.

Installing and Configuring Windows XP

Sysprep might not be right for you. Although this utility makes it easy to duplicate fully configured systems, it has the following restrictions and limitations:

- Most importantly, the master and target computers must have identical hard drive controllers, identical hardware abstraction layers (HALs), and identical BIOS versions. Although other components—such as modems, sound cards, network cards, and so on—need not be identical, this limitation effectively restricts the use of Sysprep to fleets of identical computers. If you have a varied collection of computers of different ages and manufacturers, chances are good that Sysprep won't work for all of them.

- You'll need third-party software (or a hardware device) for disk duplication. Sysprep merely prepares the image for copying and then runs a version of Setup after the image has been copied to a new computer. But to actually make the copy, you'll need a program such as Symantec Ghost or Drive Image (both from Symantec) or a disk-duplicating device.

- The hard disk on the target computer must be at least as big as the one on the master computer.

- The master computer on which you prepare the Sysprep partition must be a clean install with no user accounts or profiles and no encrypted data. The user will be able to set up accounts when he or she turns on the computer and completes the setup process.

If these restrictions aren't a problem for you, you can follow these steps to use Sysprep:

1 Install Windows XP on a master computer. (Because you might go through this process several times before you get everything set up just the way you want, you should create an answer file and use it for setting up the master computer. See the preceding section, "Using Answer Files for Automated Installation," page 36.)

> **Note** Do not join a domain during this initial setup, even if you intend to do so later; running Sysprep removes the SID that allows the computer to connect to the domain. Set up the master computer in a workgroup. When Windows Welcome or the Mini-Setup program runs on each target computer, you can choose to join a domain.

2 Log on to the computer using the Administrator account.

3 Customize the computer as desired, and install applications that you want to be included on all target computers.

4 Create a folder named \Sysprep on the system partition. Extract Sysprep.exe and Setupcl.exe from the Deploy.cab file in the \Support\Tools folder on the Windows XP CD and copy them to this folder.

5 Run Sysprep.exe. In a few moments, the system will shut down by itself (if it's ACPI-compliant) or display a message stating that it's safe to turn off the computer.

6 Duplicate the hard disk. Depending on the duplication method, you might need to remove the hard disk from the system or you might need to boot from a floppy disk that starts the third-party disk-duplication software.

When you start a computer that contains a duplicated disk (or, for that matter, when you turn on the master computer, if it still contains the master disk), Sysprep automatically:

1 Detects Plug and Play devices.
2 Runs the Windows Welcome portion of Windows Setup, which lets you set up user accounts and activate Windows.
3 Deletes the \Sysprep folder and its contents.
4 Reboots the computer.

This entire process takes only a few minutes, much less time than Setup normally requires.

If you chose the Automating Mini-Setup option, the process takes slightly longer but is still quite speedy. You can automate Mini-Setup by creating an answer file to provide some (or all) of the requested information. Use the Setup Manager Wizard to create the answer file, being sure to select Sysprep Install on the Product To Install page. The file uses the same format, sections, keys, and values as an ordinary answer file. Settings that are unnecessary or inappropriate in the disk-imaging process are ignored. You must name the answer file Sysprep.inf, and you must place it in the \Sysprep folder before you run Sysprep.exe. Table 2-2 shows the information that Mini-Setup requests, along with the answer file sections and keys that you can use to automate the process.

Table 2-2. Answer File Keys for Automating Mini-Setup

Mini-Setup Requests This Information	Use These Keys to Automatically Answer
Your agreement to the terms of the End User License Agreement (EULA)	[Unattended] OemSkipEula
Regional settings	[GuiUnattended] OemSkipRegional (provide settings in the [RegionalSettings] section)
Name and organization	[UserData] FullName, OrgName
Product key	[UserData] ProductID
Computer name	[UserData] ComputerName
Administrator password	[GuiUnattended] AdminPassword
Modem dialing information	[TapiLocation] AreaCode, CountryCode, Dialing, LongDistanceAccess
Date, time, and time zone	[GuiUnattended] TimeZone
Network identification	[Identification] DomainAdmin, DomainAdminPassword, JoinDomain, JoinWorkgroup

Installing and Configuring Windows XP

Troubleshooting

Computer repeatedly reboots after entering computer name.

One of the advantages of Sysprep is that you can customize the system in many ways before you clone the drive. Many administrators use this capability to configure services appropriately. Disabling the Telephony service is usually good advice, but don't do that if you're going to run Sysprep. If you disable the Telephony service and then run Sysprep, a bug in Windows can cause recurring reboots. In that case, you need to disable the service *after* you run Mini-Setup.

Moving Windows Settings and Files

If you upgrade an existing computer to Windows XP, all of your data and most of your programs should survive Setup intact. But what do you do if Windows XP is already installed on a new computer, or if you've decided to do a clean install on your existing system? In previous versions, you would have had to use third-party utilities or go through a tedious backup and restore process. With Windows XP, you can use a utility called the Files And Settings Transfer Wizard to handle most of the grunt work.

Inside Out

Install Windows updates before you move files and settings

Although you might be tempted to use the Files And Settings Transfer Wizard immediately after installing Windows XP, we suggest you curb your enthusiasm. Run Windows Update first, and install all necessary updates. The version of the Files And Settings Transfer Wizard included in the original Windows XP release had a handful of bugs; these bugs were fixed with Service Pack 1. After you've made sure the new computer is up to date, fire up the wizard and transfer your files and settings.

With the help of this wizard, you can migrate settings and files from your old computer to the new one. Although the wizard has its limitations, it's highly flexible and offers an impressive number of customization options. You can save settings from any 32-bit version of Windows (including Windows 95) and restore saved files and settings on Windows XP Home Edition or Professional, using either of these options:

- **Make a direct connection**   You can connect two computers over a local area network or using a serial cable and transfer settings directly from the old computer to the new one. A Fast Ethernet connection is by far your best choice, especially if you want to transfer a large number of data files. Direct cable connections are significantly slower.

- **Save your settings to a file**   If a direct connection isn't practical or possible (if you're planning to wipe out an existing partition so that you can do a clean install on the same computer, for example), you can save the wizard's output to a compressed file and then restore it after you finish Setup. Save the file to removable media such as a floppy disk, flash disk, Zip disk, or CD-RW, or to a network folder.

Tip   **Migrate multiple users**

If your old computer is set up with multiple user profiles, you must run the Files And Settings Transfer Wizard separately for each user when saving and restoring files. If the original system is running Windows NT/2000/XP, start by migrating all settings and files for a user with an account in the Administrators group. This ensures that file associations and other common settings are captured. Then, for each succeeding user, customize the migration settings so that you collect only personal data and settings. Be sure to restore the files and settings in the same order. Log on as the first user and restore the first, complete set. Then log on using a different user account and migrate that user's files and settings, repeating this process until all files and settings are restored.

By default, the Files And Settings Transfer Wizard migrates the following items:

- **User-specific settings**   This category includes visual settings, such as your current theme, wallpaper, and screen saver; folder and taskbar options; accessibility options; phone, modem, and dial-up networking connections; and network printers and drives (as defined in the My Network Places folder).

- **Internet settings**   The wizard copies the contents of your Favorites folder and cookies to the new computer. It does not, however, retain user names, passwords, and other details saved by Microsoft Internet Explorer's AutoComplete feature.

- **E-mail**   The wizard collects mail account settings, messages, and address books from Microsoft Outlook Express and Microsoft Outlook. It does not keep track of individual identities in Outlook Express; all mail for all identities is merged during the transfer.

- **Application settings**   Registry settings and preference files for a long list of programs are copied automatically. Naturally, this list is heavy on Microsoft programs—Office 97/2000/XP, Works 2001, and Money 2001, among many others. But the list also includes more than 30 third-party programs, including Netscape Communicator, AOL Instant Messenger, ICQ, Eudora, Adobe Photoshop, Acrobat Reader, Lotus SmartSuite, Quicken, WordPerfect Office 2000, WinZip, WinAmp, and RealPlayer. The wizard does not migrate program files; instead, it copies the settings and preference files to the correct location on the new computer and uses them when you install the program.

> **Tip**   **See the full list of migrated programs**
>
> Is your favorite program on the list of programs whose settings are migrated by the Files And Settings Transfer Wizard? You can view the full list by opening a text file called Migapp.inf, which is stored in the Valueadd\Msft\Usmt folder on the Windows XP CD. (After installation, this and other setting files are available in %SystemRoot%\System32\Usmt.) Entries here define the registry settings and user files that are migrated for each program. You'll notice that some of the applications listed in Migapp.inf do not appear to be the latest versions. Microsoft has had several updates to Money, for example, since Money 2001, the version identified in Migapp.inf. In many cases, the registry settings for newer versions are the same as for older ones, however. So if your version is later than one listed in the .inf file, the wizard is likely to perform the transfer successfully anyway.

● **Files and folders**   For folders that are typically used for data files—My Documents, My Pictures, and Shared Documents, for instance—all files are migrated automatically, regardless of extension. In all other locations, the wizard uses a long list of extensions to identify which data files should be transferred. You can add or remove extensions from this list and specify additional folders that you want the wizard to copy to the new computer.

Pay careful attention to the wizard's options when moving data. The transfer method and options you choose can have a profound effect on how long the process takes and how successful you are. The following sections contain detailed instructions and tips on how to migrate files and settings safely and successfully.

Transferring Files and Settings Between Computers

If you're replacing your old computer with a new one running Windows XP, your best bet is to connect the two computers over a local area network and use the Files And Settings Transfer Wizard. This technique is not only the fastest way to get your new computer up and running, it's also the best way to avoid losing data. Because your existing data files remain intact on the old computer, you can recover easily if the wizard inadvertently leaves behind a crucial data file.

To get started, install Windows XP on the new computer and ensure that the old and new computers can successfully connect over your network. Then follow these steps to run the Files And Settings Transfer Wizard:

1.   On the new computer, click the Start button and then choose All Programs, Accessories, System Tools, Files And Settings Transfer Wizard. (To skip the cascading menus, you can also type **migwiz** at any command prompt, including the Run dialog box.) Click Next at the opening page.

2.   When prompted, choose the New Computer option and click Next.

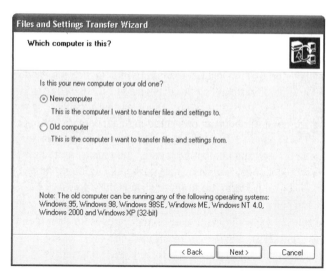

3 In the following dialog box, choose the I Will Use The Wizard From The Windows XP CD option and click Next.

4 At the old computer, insert the Windows XP CD into the CD-ROM drive. From the Welcome To Microsoft Windows XP menu, choose Perform Additional Tasks and then click Transfer Files And Settings. Click Next.

5 Choose the Old Computer option and click Next. If your old computer is not running Windows XP, the Old Computer option is automatically selected and this page does not appear. Proceed to step 6.

6 In the Select A Transfer Method dialog box, choose the Home Or Small Office Network option and click Next. (If this option is not available, verify that your network connection is working properly and start over with the new computer.)

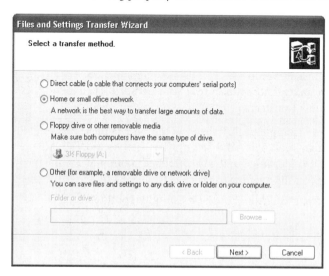

Installing and Configuring Windows XP

You can now complete the wizard using the procedures described in "Choosing Files and Settings to Transfer," page 50.

Tip   Avoid the direct cable option

The Direct Cable option in the Select A Transfer Method page of the Files And Settings Transfer Wizard sounds promising. Trust us, it's not. To connect two computers using this technique, you must use a null modem cable—a specially wired serial cable popularized by the venerable LapLink program. Serial connections are painfully slow; even at their theoretical top speed of 115,200 bits per second, they're only marginally faster than a decent dial-up Internet connection. If all you're transferring is settings, you'll find it easier to use ordinary floppy disks. If you have several hundred megabytes of data, beg, borrow, or buy an external USB hard drive (or even a Zip drive) and use it instead.

Saving Files and Settings to a Folder or Drive

If it's impossible or impractical to connect the old and new computers directly, use the Files And Settings Transfer Wizard to store your saved settings in one or more files. Follow these steps to do so:

1   At the old computer, insert the Windows XP CD into the CD-ROM drive. From the Welcome To Microsoft Windows XP menu, choose Perform Additional Tasks and then click Transfer Files And Settings. Click Next.

2   When prompted, choose the Old Computer option and click Next. If your old computer is not running Windows XP, this option is automatically selected and this page does not appear. Proceed to step 3.

3   In the Select A Transfer Method dialog box, choose either of the following options:

   ■ **Floppy Drive Or Other Removable Media**   The drive list shows all removable drives that are identified by letter, including standard 3.5-inch (1.44 MB) floppy drives, Zip drives (100 MB and 250 MB capacity), USB flash drives, Compact Flash and other memory card readers, and CD-RW drives, if you have packet-writing software such as Adaptec's DirectCD installed. If you choose a floppy drive from this list, the What Do You Want To Transfer page of the wizard defaults to the Settings Only option, eliminates the option to transfer e-mail messages and settings, and warns you that transferring files may require a large number of floppy disks.

   ■ **Other (For Example, A Removable Drive Or Network Drive)**   Choose this option if you want to save files and settings to a folder on a local or network drive. When you select this option, the What Do You Want To Transfer page of the wizard defaults to the Both Files And Settings option.

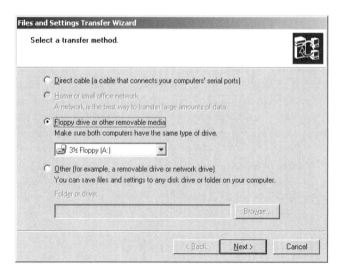

You can now complete the wizard using the procedures in the following section.

Note When you choose the Other option, the Files And Settings Transfer Wizard creates a folder called Usmt2.unc in the location you specify. It then stores the files and settings to be migrated in one or more files, using the names Img00001, Img00002, and so on. The maximum size of each such file is 2 GB.

Choosing Files and Settings to Transfer

When you reach the point in the Files And Settings Transfer Wizard where you actually begin saving data, you can choose Settings Only, Files Only, or Files And Settings from the What Do You Want To Transfer? page of the wizard. It's also possible to customize the options you choose here. Pay very close attention to these options, because they might not behave as you expect.

Settings Only

Generally speaking, you should choose the Settings Only option when you want to minimize the amount of data you need to move from the old computer to the new one. Unfortunately, the Settings Only option can drag along a startling amount of data if you don't understand the inner workings of the Files And Settings Transfer Wizard. The wizard behaves differently, depending on which transfer method you've chosen. For instance, if you choose a 3.5-inch floppy drive as the destination on a system running Windows 98, the list on the right side of the page should resemble the example in Figure 2-6.

Installing and Configuring Windows XP

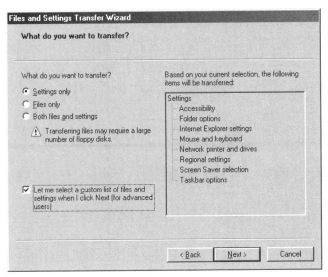

Figure 2-6. If you specify that you want to save settings to a floppy drive, the Files And Settings Transfer Wizard offers this minimal list.

That selection doesn't take up much room at all—in this example, the total amount of data to be transferred fits easily on two floppy disks, as the message that appears informs us.

But when you change the destination to a folder on a local hard drive, the list of items under the Settings heading changes, as you can see in Figure 2-7. The new list includes 11 new entries, including settings for such items as Microsoft Office, Outlook Express, RealJukebox 2, and Windows Media Player. (The list of settings is dynamically created, so the entries for Office and RealPlayer/RealJukebox appear only if those programs are installed on the computer where you're running the Files And Settings Transfer Wizard.)

Although the Settings Only option is still selected, just as before, the list of settings is greatly expanded, and this time it includes some data files. The resulting data file in this example adds up to a whopping 131 MB—most of it consisting of e-mail messages from Outlook Express and the Personal Store file from Outlook 2002.

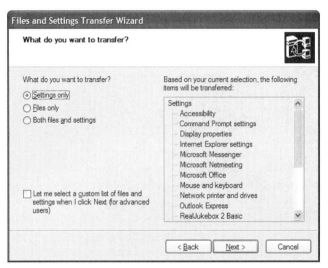

Figure 2-7. When you choose to save settings on a local or network drive, the Settings Only list gets considerably longer.

Tip **Calculate how much space you need**

If you choose Other on the Select A Transfer Method page and then specify a location other than a removable drive, the Files And Settings Transfer Wizard starts saving files without giving you the slightest indication of how much space you'll need. The only way to get a reliable indication of how much disk space you'll gobble up is through a two-step process. Specify a floppy drive as your destination, even if you intend to save your files and settings to a local or network drive instead. After the wizard completes its preliminary calculations, it displays a message that tells you how much space you're about to use. If the result is what you expected, cancel the wizard and start over, this time specifying the location where you really want to save your files and settings.

If you're unsatisfied with either of these options—for instance, if you don't want to transfer your e-mail messages to the new computer—you must choose the option to customize your files and settings, as described in "Customizing the List of Saved Files and Settings" on page 54.

Files Only

When you use the Files And Settings Transfer Wizard to move files from one computer to another, the wizard actually performs two distinct operations, although this division is not immediately apparent. The list of items to be transferred consists of two groups, as the example in Figure 2-8 shows:

● **Specific Folders** By default, this category identifies commonly used storage locations and migrates *all* files it finds in those locations, regardless of their extension.

Installing and Configuring Windows XP

● **File Types**   Scroll through this category and you'll see that it consists of a long list of file extensions—more than 160 in all. Using this option, the wizard searches every folder on every local drive for files with those extensions. You cannot exclude any drive or folder from this search.

The Specific Folders category works exactly as expected. The wizard grabs all files in your My Documents and My Pictures folder, for example, and restores them to the same location on the new computer. The wizard uses class identifiers (CLSIDs) to identify the proper location of these folders, so your files should end up in the correct location even if you've installed Windows XP on a different drive or changed the location of the My Documents folder on either the old or new computer.

The File Types category, however, can have unexpected (and unwelcome) results. The list of file extensions includes a long list of media file types, including music files in the MP3 and Windows Media Audio formats. If you have a large collection of songs you've copied from CDs or downloaded from the Internet and those files are stored on a separate drive, the Files And Settings Transfer Wizard will dutifully try to gather them up and move them to your new computer. If your collection is measured in multiple gigabytes, the process will seem to take forever, and if you're storing the saved settings to a local drive, you'll probably run out of disk space during the process.

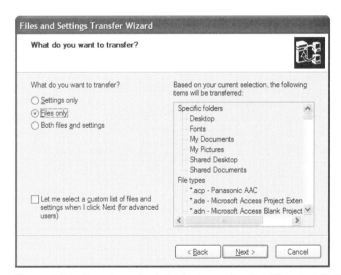

Figure 2-8.   Be extremely vigilant when using the Files And Settings Transfer Wizard to move files, or you could end up moving several gigabytes of data.

The only solution is to use the option to create a custom list of your files and settings, as described later in this section.

Both Files And Settings

No surprises here: This option combines the default settings from the Settings Only and Files Only options.

Customizing the List of Saved Files and Settings

You can safely get away with using the default settings for the Files And Settings Transfer Wizard if you satisfy the following conditions:

- Your old and new computers are networked and you plan to transfer files and settings over that network connection.
- You have at least as much total disk space on the new computer as on the old one.

If the partitioning scheme on the new computer is different from that on the old one, however, or if your data files are meticulously organized in folders other than My Documents, you should consider customizing the way the Files And Settings Transfer Wizard works. When you reach the What Do You Want To Transfer? page on the old computer, select the options shown in Figure 2-9. Choose Both Files And Settings, and then select the Let Me Select A Custom List of Files check box.

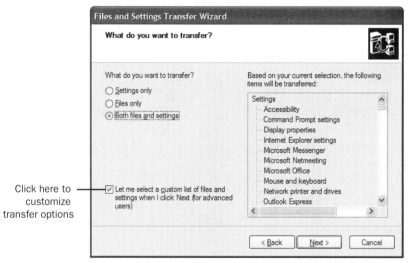

Click here to customize transfer options

Figure 2-9. Select this check box to tell the wizard you want to choose which files and settings are transferred.

Chapter 2

Installing and Configuring Windows XP

After choosing this option, click Next to display the Select Custom Files And Settings page. On this page, you can add or remove settings, files, file types, and folders to customize the way the Files And Settings Transfer Wizard works. Figure 2-10 shows this page after customizing some settings.

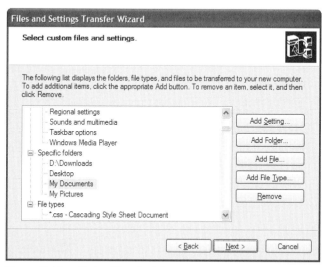

Figure 2-10. If the Files And Settings Transfer Wizard is too aggressive, rein it in by removing some options from this list.

You can customize the Files And Settings Transfer Wizard using these five buttons:

- **Add Setting** This option shows items you've removed from the Settings list. It's also useful if the wizard is displaying a shortened list of settings because you've chosen to save settings to a floppy disk. You cannot create custom settings here.

- **Add Folder** Use this option if you store data in a location other than the default system folders and you want the wizard to migrate all files and subfolders from that folder, regardless of their extension. In Figure 2-10, for example, we've added the Downloads folder from drive D. You can add an unlimited number of folders to this list.

- **Add File** Choose this option if you want to be certain that you migrate a specific file from a specific location without also transferring other files in that folder. You can add an unlimited number of files to this list.

- **Add File Type** If you use an application that produces data files with an extension that is not on the list of file types migrated by the Files And Settings Transfer Wizard, choose that file type here. Note that you can hold down the Ctrl key to select multiple file types.

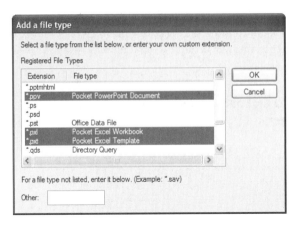

- **Remove**   Select any setting, folder, file, or file type, and click this button to remove it from the list.

Inside Out

Clear all file types with a single keystroke

In the Files And Settings Transfer Wizard, the Specific Folders and File Types settings are combined in the Files Only option. If you want to transfer only files from locations that you define, you have to clear the entire File Types list, one entry at a time; the interface doesn't allow you to eliminate the entire group, as you might expect. Fortunately, there's an easy (if less than intuitive) shortcut. Click to select the first item under the File Types heading. Hold down the Alt key and then press and hold the R key. This deletes the selected item and immediately starts removing the remaining items as well, a process that takes only a few seconds.

Here are some pointers to help you use the Files And Settings Transfer Wizard more effectively:

Check the list of file types carefully   The default list of file types includes a huge number of file types that most people never use. In addition, it includes some file types that you might prefer not to migrate, such as music or video files. By trimming this list so that it includes only the file types you want to collect, you can speed up the collection process and keep the size of the transferred files manageable.

Always prefer folders over file types   If you're highly organized and you know that all your MP3 and WMA files are in a specific location, add that folder to the Specific Folders list and remove those entries from the File Types list. This also helps ensure that all your files go to the location you prefer on the new computer instead of being automatically moved into the My Music folder.

Know where applications store their data and preferences   Many small Windows utilities keep settings and preferences in specific files in specific locations. If you use any such utilities, use the Add File button to specify that you want those files transferred.

Use custom settings to back up parts of your system   If you use custom settings in the Files And Settings Transfer Wizard, you can save specific groups of settings and files. By removing all options from the wizard and then adding back only those you want to keep, you can save a specific group of settings in a single file on a floppy or network drive.

Restoring Files and Settings on Your New Computer

If you use a network or cable connection to transfer files between two computers with the Files And Settings Transfer Wizard, you control both ends of the process. After you establish a connection and finish collecting files from the old computer, the new computer will generate a random password as a security measure. You'll be prompted to enter that password on the old computer. (This is an essential security precaution to prevent an intruder from using the Files And Settings Transfer Wizard to steal information over a network.) The transfer proceeds automatically after you supply the correct password.

If you've saved the files and settings to a floppy disk or a local or network drive, follow these steps to continue the transfer process:

1   Run the Files And Settings Transfer Wizard on the new computer and then choose New Computer from the Which Computer Is This page. Click Next.

2   When prompted on the next page, choose I Don't Need The Wizard Disk, as shown here. Click Next.

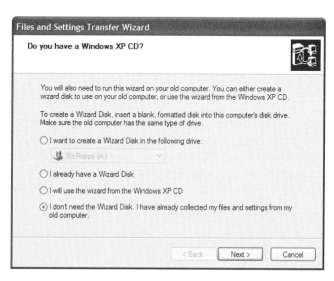

3 On the next page, specify the location where the files and settings are stored. Choose a floppy drive or other removable media from the removable media list, or choose Other and click the Browse button to locate the local or network drive on which the saved files reside.

4 Click Next to begin the transfer.

Accessibility Options

As in previous versions, Windows XP includes three accessibility options designed to make the operating system more usable for persons with vision, hearing, or mobility impairments. These tools are available for use during setup—when using Windows Setup, click the Accessibility Options button; from a command prompt, add the /a switch to the Winnt.exe command. These options can also be adjusted after setup on a per-user basis. You can use any of the following tools alone or in combination:

- **Magnifier** This tool enlarges part of the screen, making it easier for persons with vision impairments to see objects and read text.

- **Narrator** This tool converts on-screen text to speech and sends it to your computer's speakers. This option allows people who are blind or have severe vision impairments to use Windows.

Tip Let the Magnifier window float

The Magnifier tool can be useful for anyone whose vision is less than perfect. You don't have to use it all the time to benefit from it. Normally, the Magnifier window sits in a fixed location at the top of the screen and tracks the movement of the mouse pointer. That default location is extremely wide and short; in this configuration, you can adjust its height, but only by reducing the size of the window you're actually working in. You may find it easier to work with the viewing window by undocking it and adjusting its dimensions. Point to the Magnifier pane, click, and drag to the location where you want it to appear. Drag the window borders to change the height or width of the Magnifier pane.

- **On-Screen Keyboard** This tool provides an alternate means for Windows users with impaired mobility to enter text using a pointing device. Options on the Keyboard menu let you change keyboard layouts; options on the Settings menu let you control how the on-screen keyboard works—you can choose whether to select a letter by clicking, for example, or by allowing the pointer to pause over a key for a specific amount of time.

All three accessibility tools are available to any user, at any time, by clicking Start and choosing All Programs, Accessories, Accessibility. The Accessibility Wizard, also found on this menu, walks you through the process of adjusting Windows Display settings and configuring accessibility options.

Troubleshooting

After experimenting with the Accessibility Wizard, your visual settings are changed unexpectedly.

During its Q&A process, this wizard makes changes to the size of objects such as fonts and icons used in the Windows interface. Even if you back out of the wizard and tell it not to apply any changes, you may find that your taskbar and tray icons have been changed. To restore your preferred settings, open Control Panel's Display option and click the Themes tab. If you previously saved your settings, choose the saved theme here; otherwise, choose one of the default Windows Themes.

If you want accessibility options to be available at all times, even before logging on to the computer, you need to enable the Utility Manager. This option (shown below) allows you to quickly start or stop an accessibility option. Although the Utility Manager is available from the Accessibility group on the Accessories menu, you can access it more quickly by using its built-in keyboard shortcut: Windows logo key + U. This shortcut is the only way to display the Utility Manager before logging on.

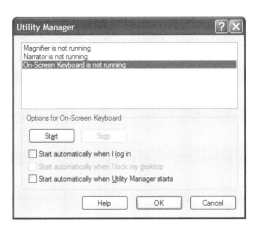

Adding and Removing Windows Components

In previous Windows versions, you could select a Custom Setup option, which allowed you to pick and choose from a lengthy menu of available components during the initial Windows installation. In Windows XP, no such option is available. When you run the Setup program from a CD, you get the standard complement of Windows components, including multimedia tools, games, wallpaper, and other frills you might prefer to do without. In addition, some optional components (mostly advanced services) are left out. In this section, we'll show you how to tweak a Windows installation so that you end up with the pieces you want and no more.

After you complete the Setup process, open Add Or Remove Programs from Control Panel and then click Add/Remove Windows Components. This opens the Windows Components Wizard, shown in Figure 2-11.

By selecting or clearing boxes shown here, you can add or remove any of a small list of optional Windows components. In some cases, a component includes subcomponents that can be individually installed or removed; click the component name (instead of the check box) and click the Details button to see a list of available subcomponents. If you're setting up an office computer, for instance, you can navigate to Accessories And Utilities and uninstall the entire Games group, or, on the next sublevel, individually remove Solitaire, Freecell, and other time-wasters.

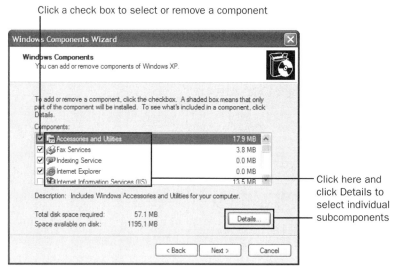

Figure 2-11. This dialog box lets you install or remove a limited number of Windows options.

Table 2-3 lists the optional components available in a default installation of Windows XP.

Table 2-3. Optional Windows Components

Component	Installed by Default?	Comments
Accessories And Utilities	Yes	Click the Details button to remove some or all accessories (including desktop wallpaper and document templates) and games.
Fax Services	No	The best way to add fax capabilities to Windows XP is to open the Printers And Faxes folder and click the Set Up Faxing link under Printer Tasks.
Indexing Service	Yes	To enable, disable, or configure this service, use the Search pane in Windows Explorer. Clear this box only if you want to completely remove the service. (For more details, see "Using Indexing Service and Query Language," page 724.)
Internet Explorer	Yes	Clear this box to remove the Internet Explorer icon from the Desktop and Start Menu. This option does not remove any Internet Explorer components.
Internet Information Services (Professional Only)	No	Select this box to add a personal Web server to Windows XP. Click the Details button to select individual subcomponents. (For more details, see Chapter 32, "Hosting a Web or FTP Site.")
Management And Monitoring Tools	No	This option adds two Simple Network Management Protocol (SNMP) agents designed for use with centralized administration tools.
Message Queuing (Professional Only)	No	This option adds software that allows applications to communicate with other applications over a corporate network.

Chapter 2

Table 2-3. **Optional Windows Components**

Component	Installed by Default?	Comments
MSN Explorer	Yes	Microsoft's all-in-one Web package integrates a browser with e-mail and messaging capabilities. If you're comfortable with Internet Explorer (or another browser) and a full-strength e-mail program, you can remove this option and reclaim 20 MB of disk space.
Networking Services	No	Click the Details button to see the options listed here. Most Windows users don't need the RIP Listener or Simple TCP/IP Services. The Internet Gateway Device Discovery And Control Client option, installed by default, enables the detection of and interaction with Internet gateway devices, such as routers and computers running Internet Connection Sharing. The UPnP User Interface option enables communication with other types of Universal Plug And Play (UPnP) devices. For information on these options, see "Advanced Networking Components," page 994, and Microsoft Knowledge Base articles 821371, 323713, and 821980.
Other Network File And Print Services	No	Install this option to add Print Services for UNIX, which allows UNIX-based network clients to connect to Windows printers.
Outlook Express	Yes	Clear this box to remove access to Outlook Express from the Start menu. This option does not uninstall Outlook Express.
Update Root Certificates	Yes	Automatically downloads the most current security certificates for secure e-mail, Web browsing, and software delivery.

Table 2-3. **Optional Windows Components**

Component	Installed by Default?	Comments
Windows Media Player	Yes	Clear this box to remove access to Windows Media Player from the Start menu. This option does not uninstall Windows Media Player.
Windows Messenger	Yes	Clear this box to remove access to Windows Messenger from the Start menu. This option does not uninstall Windows Messenger.

> **Tip**   Keep users out of the Windows Components Wizard
>
> If you want to prevent access to the Windows Components section of Add Or Remove Programs, you can do so by setting a group policy. In Group Policy (Gpedit.msc), open User Configuration\Administrative Templates\Control Panel\Add Or Remove Programs. Double-click the Hide Add/Remove Windows Components Page policy and select Enable to prevent users from making changes to your installed components.

A handful of additional Windows components that are part of a full Windows XP Professional installation can actually be removed as well, although they're initially hidden from the list in the Windows Components Wizard. To unhide these components so that you can remove them or at least see if you want to remove them, you need to edit the Setup Information file that contains details about each component. To add Pinball to the list of optional components, for instance, follow these steps:

1   Open Windows Explorer, navigate to the %SystemRoot%\Inf folder (a hidden folder), and then select the Sysoc.inf file. (Before making any changes, make a backup copy.)

2   In Notepad or a similar text editor, open Sysoc.inf.

3   Each hidden component has its own line in this file, with the word *hide* near the end of the line. For the Pinball program, this line reads as follows:

```
Pinball=ocgen.dll,OcEntry,pinball.inf,HIDE,7
```

Edit the line to read:

```
Pinball=ocgen.dll,OcEntry,pinball.inf,,7
```

4   Save Sysoc.inf and reopen the Windows Components Wizard, where you'll see the newly available component.

Chapter 2

63

> **Caution** By removing the word *hide* from entries in Sysoc.inf, you can add them to the list of Windows components that can be removed. If you're not 100 percent certain of the consequences, don't do it! Removing Windows Messenger, for instance, makes it more difficult to connect with another Windows XP user via the Remote Assistance feature. And in some cases, restoring an option to the list of components that can be removed has no practical effect. Even after addingTerminal Server to the list, for example, you cannot select or remove it. The check box simply doesn't respond to clicks.

Selecting a Web Browser and Other Middleware Components

 When you install Windows XP Service Pack 1 or later, a new option appears in the Add Or Remove Programs dialog box. This option, imposed as a condition of settlement of the antitrust suit brought by the United States Department of Justice against Microsoft, gives Windows users the option to remove access to a number of Microsoft programs that were previously tightly integrated into Windows. This list of "middleware" components includes the following:

- **Web Browser**   The Microsoft default program is Internet Explorer.
- **E-mail Program**   Unless you specify otherwise, Windows uses Outlook Express for this function.
- **Media Player**   In Windows XP, Windows Media Player is the default utility for playing sounds, videos, and media files.
- **Instant Messaging Program**   Windows Messenger is integrated into a number of places in Windows XP, including Internet Explorer and Outlook Express.
- **Virtual Machine for Java**   In the past, Microsoft included its own Java VM. Although it's no longer available from Microsoft, you can continue to use it if it's installed on your computer.

Installing and Configuring Windows XP

What's the Story with Java Virtual Machines?

A virtual machine for Java (also known as a Java run-time environment, or JRE) allows Java applets to run on Windows-based computers. Java applets are used on many Web sites, among other places. The original version of Windows XP (as well as all earlier versions of Windows going back to Windows 95) included the Microsoft Java Virtual Machine (MSJVM). Because of a longstanding legal dispute between Microsoft and Sun Microsystems, the developer of Java, the MSJVM was removed from Windows XP Service Pack 1a and later. Although installing the service pack as an upgrade doesn't remove an existing MSJVM installation, performing a clean install from a Windows XP Service Pack 1a or Service Pack 2 integrated CD results in a system without a Java virtual machine. You can download a Java VM from Sun; visit *http://www.java.com*.

Microsoft and Sun settled their differences in April 2004, and the upshot is this: The MSJVM is no longer being enhanced, but Microsoft will continue to address MSJVM security issues through the end of 2007. After that time, although the MSJVM will continue to function, Microsoft does not plan to support it in any way. Therefore, you should plan to switch to another Java VM.

You don't need to remove the MSJVM in order to use the Sun Java VM. However, there's no reason to keep it around, either. To remove the MSJVM, search microsoft.com for the MSJVM Removal Tool. If it's not available (it's not at this writing), you can use the following manual procedure.

1 At a command prompt, enter this case-sensitive command:

RunDll32 advpack.dll,LaunchINFSection java.inf,UnInstall

2 Click Yes to confirm your intention, and then reboot the computer when prompted.

3 Delete the following files:

%SystemRoot%\Inf\Java.pnf

%SystemRoot%\System32\Jview.exe

%SystemRoot%\System32\Wjview.exe

4 Delete the %SystemRoot%\Java folder.

5 Using a registry editor, delete the following registry keys:

HKLM\Software\Microsoft\Java VM

HKLM\Software\Microsoft\Internet Explorer\

AdvancedOptions\JAVA_VM

For more information about MSJVM and making the transition to Sun Java VM, visit *http://www.microsoft.com/java*.

Chapter 2

Clicking the Set Program Access And Defaults icon on the left reveals the options shown in Figure 2-12. With the help of options in this dialog box, you can change the default program used for any of the five tasks listed here. You can also remove easy access to any or all of the Microsoft programs used to perform these tasks.

If you installed a retail copy of Windows XP and then added Service Pack 1 or Service Pack 2, the first option, Microsoft Windows, is selected. This option maintains the status quo, with all five categories being assigned to their default Microsoft programs.

Choosing the Non-Microsoft option removes access to all five Microsoft programs listed above. If you previously had icons for Internet Explorer, Outlook Express, and other programs on the Start menu, the Quick Launch bar, or the desktop, they are removed. If you have not installed alternative programs for e-mail and Web access, the E-mail and Internet choices at the top of the Start menu change to generic icons, and clicking either one opens the Internet Options dialog box.

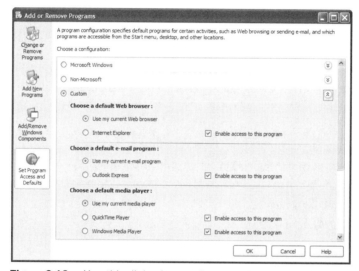

Figure 2-12. Use this dialog box to change default programs used with Windows and to hide access to Microsoft programs and utilities.

Finally, you can banish some Microsoft programs while keeping others available. After installing the alternate software (the Mozilla Web browser, for instance, or RealPlayer), open the Set Program Access And Defaults dialog box and choose the Custom option. For each category, you can choose whether to use the currently installed program or the Microsoft default. In addition, you can choose to hide access to one or more of the programs while allowing access to others.

> **Note** Because this non-Microsoft option is relatively new, not all alternative programs work with it yet. If your favorite non-Microsoft Web browser or media player doesn't respond when you select these options, check with the developer and see if a new version is in the works.

Chapter 2

Installing and Configuring Windows XP

 Inside Out

Access default programs even after you've hidden them

When you choose the drastic Non-Microsoft option, the code that runs Internet Explorer, Outlook Express, and other utilities is still available on your computer. If you don't install an alternative Web browser, Internet Explorer will still start up when you double-click an Internet shortcut or type a Web address in the Run box. Likewise, you can launch any program by typing the name of its executable file in the Run box: **iexplore** for Internet Explorer, **msimn** for Outlook Express, **wmplayer** for Windows Media Player, and **msmsgs** for Windows Messenger.

Configuring System Restore Options

When a rogue program or buggy driver causes your computer to crash, the System Restore feature can be a lifesaver. (For details on how you can use System Restore, see "Undoing Configuration Mistakes with System Restore," page 1288.) However, if you accept its default settings this feature will gobble up a hefty chunk of disk space and can have unexpected (and unpleasant) side effects, including the deletion of recently downloaded files with no warning. Before you need to use System Restore, familiarize yourself with its workings and learn how to customize it so that it doesn't take you by surprise. You can take charge of System Restore in several ways.

To access the full set of System Restore options, open System in Control Panel and click the System Restore tab, shown in Figure 2-13.

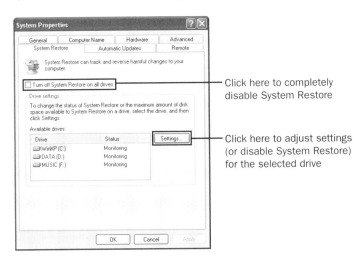

Click here to completely disable System Restore

Click here to adjust settings (or disable System Restore) for the selected drive

Figure 2-13. By default, System Restore monitors changes to every drive on your system and sets aside up to 12 percent of each drive for storing its data.

Using this dialog box, you can adjust any of the following settings:

- **Drive space used** By default, System Restore is configured to allow its files to occupy up to 12 percent of available disk space on every drive. On a 30-GB drive, that adds up to an excessive 3.6 GB of storage space. To rein in space usage for a specific drive, click the Settings button to the right of that drive and move the slider control to the left, as shown in Figure 2-14.

- **Drives to be monitored** By design, System Restore keeps tabs on every drive on your system. If you've set aside one or more drives exclusively for data, you can safely turn off System Restore monitoring on those drives. This action has the effect of reclaiming the space used for restore points; it also prevents System Restore from inadvertently wiping out files on those drives. To exclude a drive from monitoring, open the System Properties dialog box and click the System Restore tab. Select the drive to exclude, click the Settings button, and select Turn Off System Restore On This Drive. Note that this option is not available on the drive that contains your system files.

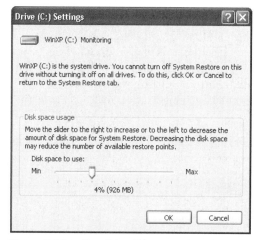

Figure 2-14. Use this slider to reduce the appetite of System Restore. The setting shown here is one-third the normal 12 percent allotment, but should be sufficient for most uses.

> **Note** The default location for System Restore data is d:\System Volume Information, where d is the letter of each drive. Each restore point is stored in its own subfolder, under the name _restore*GUID*, where *GUID* is a unique 32-character alphanumeric identifier. This location cannot be changed. On an NTFS drive, these files are not accessible to users, even those in the Administrators group; the default NTFS permissions grant access only to the System account.

Chapter 2

Installing and Configuring Windows XP

> **Caution** System Restore is a powerful tool, and you shouldn't disable it without a good reason. If you're extremely low on disk space and a hard disk upgrade is impractical or impossible (as on some notebook computers), you might choose to do so. Otherwise, let it run.

Inside Out

Specify the files and folders to be monitored

By default, System Restore maintains a strict hands-off policy on all files stored in your My Documents folder and its subfolders, in the %SystemRoot%\Downloaded Program Files folder, and a number of other folders used by Windows. (A complete list of excluded folders is in the hidden %SystemRoot%\System32\Restore\Filelist.xml file.) Every other folder on your system is fair game, however, and the results can be disconcerting. After you use System Restore to roll back your system to a previous configuration, you may discover that the utility wiped out executable files, scripts, dynamic link libraries (DLLs), TrueType fonts, VBScript (.vbs) files, and files using other monitored formats that were stored outside of your My Documents folder and that had been downloaded after the date of the restore point you selected. If you routinely download programs or create PDF files in a non-protected location, you may want to specifically declare that location to be exempt from System Restore monitoring. To do so, you must add a value to the registry. Follow these steps:

1 Open Registry Editor (Regedit.exe) and select the following key:

HKLM\System\CurrentControlSet\Control\BackupRestore\FilesNotToBackup

2 Choose Edit, New, Multi-String Value.

3 Give the new value a name that describes the location you're about to specify—My Downloads, for instance.

4 Double-click the newly created value. Enter the full path of the folder you want to protect from monitoring and then click OK.

Note that the change you just made will not go into effect until after you set your next restore point manually or Windows creates a system checkpoint. Therefore, it's good practice to set a fresh restore point after making changes.

Tip   Customize System Restore intervals

System Restore settings and preferences are stored in the registry, in the key HKLM\SOFTWARE\Microsoft\WindowsNT\CurrentVersion\SystemRestore. Most of the values found here can be adjusted safely and easily using the System Restore tab of the System Properties dialog box. However, some settings can only be adjusted by editing the values stored in this registry key.

Normally, System Restore automatically creates restore points every 24 hours. To adjust this interval, change the value RPGlobalInterval from its default setting of 86,400 seconds (24 hours). Cut this figure in half, to 43,200, if you want to save restore points twice a day; triple it, to 259,200, if you want restore points created every three days.

By default, System Restore deletes restore points after 90 days. To adjust this interval, change the value RPLifeInterval from its default setting of 7,776,000 seconds (90 days). A value of 2,592,000 seconds (30 days) should be sufficient

If you ever receive a "low disk space" warning for any drive, check your System Restore settings immediately. The utility will shut down on its own if free disk space drops below 200 MB on any single partition. When this happens, you receive no warning. The only indication appears when you open the System Restore properties dialog box, where each drive letter's status is listed as Suspended.

Windows might not turn System Restore back on automatically. To do so manually, try the following workaround:

1   From Control Panel, open the System tool and click the System Restore tab.

2   Select the Turn Off System Restore On All Drives option and click Apply. This completely shuts down System Restore.

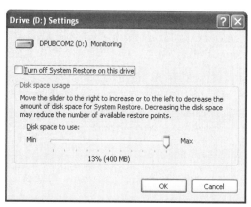

3   Clear the Turn Off System Restore On All Drives option and click Apply. The Status column for each drive changes to Monitoring, an indication that System Restore is working again.

4 From the Available Drives list, select the entry for any drive that you want to exclude from System Restore protection and click the Settings button.

5 Select the Turn Off System Restore On This Drive option, and click OK. Repeat for other drives you want to exclude from System Restore.

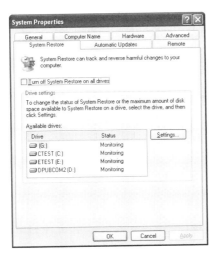

6 Click OK to close the System Restore dialog box.

If the drive that produced the "low disk space" warning is normally full (as might be the case on a drive used to store a large archive of media files that never change), be sure to exclude that drive so that it doesn't continually disable System Restore.

Configuring Startup Options

For most users, most of the time, starting up Windows is a simple process: Turn on the computer, wait for the Welcome screen to appear, click your logon name, and away you go.

> For more details about customizing the Windows logon process, see "Controlling How Users Log On," page 239.

On multiboot configurations, the process gets slightly more complicated, thanks to a startup menu that allows you to choose from different operating systems.

Customizing Multiboot Menus

If more than one operating system is installed on your computer, a boot menu appears each time you start the machine. This boot menu lets you choose which operating system you want to run. (For information about setting up multiple operating systems, see "Installing Windows XP on a Computer with Other Operating Systems," page 26.) By default, the boot menu stays on screen for 30 seconds; an on-screen timer lets you know how much time you have left. If you don't choose an option before the timer runs out, the default operating system (usually the most recent installation of Windows XP) starts up. While the boot menu is visible, you can press the Up or Down Arrow key to highlight a different operating system, which also stops the timer's countdown. Press Enter to start the selected operating system.

At any time, you can change the menu's display time and specify which operating system starts by default. To adjust boot menu settings, follow these steps:

1 Open System in Control Panel and click the Advanced tab. (Alternatively, click the Start button, right-click My Computer, and choose Properties.)

2 In the Startup And Recovery section, click Settings to display the dialog box shown in Figure 2-15.

3 In the Default Operating System list, select the operating system that you want to be initially highlighted on the boot menu and started by default.

4 To adjust the length of time (in seconds) that the boot menu is displayed, change the number to the right of Time To Display List Of Operating Systems. Choose any number between 1 and 99. To set the boot menu so that the default operating system starts automatically, clear the check box at the left, or enter 0.

Choices you make in this dialog box actually write changes to the Boot.ini file, which is stored in the root of the system drive. You can also click the Edit button to open the file in Notepad and edit it directly.

> **Note** You can't rename the operating systems in the Default Operating System list from this dialog box; to do that, you must edit Boot.ini, as described in the following section, "Modifying Boot.ini."

Chapter 2

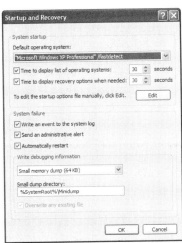

Figure 2-15. Control the boot menu by setting options in the System Startup section of this dialog box.

Overview of the Startup Process

When you turn on your computer, it goes through an elaborate startup process. The process begins when your computer performs its power-on self test (POST), which is followed by the POST for each adapter card that has a BIOS, such as SCSI adapters and video cards. The system BIOS then reads the master boot record (MBR)—the first sector on the first hard disk—and transfers control to the code in the MBR, which is created by Windows XP Setup. This is where Windows takes over the startup process. Here's what happens next:

1. The MBR reads the boot sector—the first sector of the active partition—which contains code that starts Ntldr, the bootstrap loader for Windows XP. The initial role of Ntldr is to switch the system to protected mode with paging enabled (to allow full memory addressing), start the file system, read the Boot.ini file, and display the boot menu.

   Note that Ntldr must be located in the root folder of the active partition, along with Ntdetect.com, Boot.ini, Bootsect.dos (if you're going to dual boot), and Ntbootdd.sys (if you're using certain SCSI adapters for the drive with the boot partition). For more information about sectors, partitions, and drives, see Chapter 22, "Managing Disks and Drives."

2. If you select Windows XP from the boot menu, Ntldr runs Ntdetect.com to gather information about the currently installed hardware. Ntldr then uses the Advanced RISC Computing (ARC) path specified in Boot.ini to find the boot partition—the one where Windows XP is installed—and loads the two files that constitute the Windows XP core: Ntoskrnl.exe and Hal.dll. Both files must be located in the %SystemRoot%\System32 folder.

3 Ntldr continues by reading the files that make up the registry, selecting a hardware profile and control set, and loading device drivers.

4 At this point, Ntoskrnl.exe takes over and starts Winlogon.exe, which in turn starts Lsass.exe (Local Security Administration), the program that displays the Welcome screen (or the Windows logon dialog box) and allows you to log on with your user name and password.

Understanding the boot process can help you to pinpoint problems that occur during startup. For more information, see "Using Advanced Startup Options," page 1285.

Modifying Boot.ini

To adjust some startup options, you might need to open Boot.ini and edit it manually. Because this file is set with the hidden and system attributes, it doesn't ordinarily appear in Windows Explorer; to edit it, use either of these techniques:

- Open the Run dialog box and type **c:\boot.ini**. (This assumes that drive C contains your startup files.)
- Open System in Control Panel, click the Advanced tab, click the Settings button under Startup And Recovery, and click the Edit button in the System Startup section.

ARC Paths in Boot.ini

In the [operating systems] section of the Boot.ini file, you'll find a somewhat cryptic line for each installed copy of Windows XP, Windows 2000, or Windows NT. This line uses Advanced RISC Computing (ARC) paths to specify the location of the boot partition. On a system that uses standard IDE drives, the ARC path in Boot.ini looks like this:

multi(0)disk(0)rdisk(0)partition(2)\WINDOWS

The first parameter identifies the disk controller. In the multi( ) form, it should always be 0.

The disk parameter is not used in the multi( ) form and should always be 0.

The rdisk parameter in the multi() form specifies the ordinal number on the controller (starting with 0) of the disk that contains the boot partition. Thus, if multiple hard disks are installed, the first disk is 0, the second is 1, and so on.

The partition parameter identifies the partition number of the boot partition. Partitions on a disk are numbered starting with 1.

The last part of the ARC path (usually \WINDOWS or \WINNT) identifies the path to the folder where that version of Windows is installed.

Two additional ARC structures identify disks using scsi( ) and signature( ) as the beginning of the ARC path, as described in Knowledge Base articles 227704 and 102873. It's rare that you'd ever need (or want) to edit any of the ARC paths in Boot.ini. (The most likely reason is if you've used a third-party utility like PartitionMagic to add or remove partitions on your boot or system drive.) In fact, if you don't have a deep understanding of disk structures, you can render your system unable to start by editing these settings incorrectly. But if you need to revive a system that's lost its Boot.ini and other key startup files, you might need this information.

In either case, the Boot.ini file opens in Notepad. A typical Boot.ini file might look like this:

```
[boot loader]
timeout=30
default=multi(0)disk(0)rdisk(0)partition(2)\WINDOWS
[operating systems]
multi(0)disk(0)rdisk(0)partition(2)\WINDOWS="Microsoft Windows XP
  Professional" /fastdetect
C:\="Microsoft Windows Millennium Edition"
```

With two exceptions, the [boot loader] section contains items that are more easily changed through the Startup And Recovery dialog box, as explained in the previous section. One exception is if you want the boot menu to be displayed until you press Enter, regardless of how much time elapses. To configure your boot menu to work that way, set the timeout value to –1. (You can't set that value in the Startup And Recovery dialog box.)

The other exception that requires you to edit Boot.ini is when you want to change the descriptions or optional parameters in the [operating systems] section. Each line represents a boot menu item and includes the ARC path of the operating system's boot partition (see "ARC Paths in Boot.ini"), the text that appears on the boot menu (enclosed in quotation marks), and optional parameters. You can adjust each item as follows:

- Change the text description for each operating system—particularly if multiple copies of the same operating system are installed on your computer. If you've installed a second, clean copy of Windows XP to test a few new programs, for instance, you might want to change its description to "Windows XP Pro–Clean Install."

- Append a parameter to the Windows 2000 or Windows XP line (following /Fastdetect, a parameter that disables serial mouse detection). Most parameters are for development and debugging purposes only. *Microsoft Windows XP Professional Resource Kit,*

Second Edition (Microsoft Press, 2003) contains a more complete list. Here are two parameters you might want to try:

- /Noguiboot eliminates the Windows splash screen during startup. Instead you get to continue staring at the horizontal bar at the bottom of the screen.

- /Sos displays the name of each driver as it loads and provides additional text descriptions of what's occurring during startup. It also shows the Windows XP build number, service pack level, number of processors, and amount of installed memory, providing a quick confirmation that Windows is installed correctly and that it's properly recognizing your computer's configuration.

- Remove an item from the menu. Doing so won't free the space used by the operating system whose line you remove; it simply removes the item from the menu. However, you can subsequently remove that operating system's files after you boot into one of the remaining operating systems in the list.

Caution Don't remove the line that matches the default setting in the [boot loader] section.

Adding the Recovery Console

The Recovery Console is a no-frills command-line environment that you can use to recover from serious startup problems. With the Recovery Console, you can log in as a member of the Administrators group and access files and folders on your hard drives, format drives, start and stop services, replace corrupt files, and so on.

Note For details about how to use the Recovery Console in case of disaster, see "Making Repairs from the Recovery Console," page 1295.

Although you can run the Recovery Console by booting directly from the Windows XP CD, it's much more convenient to set it up as a startup option on your boot menu. Do it now, before you need it, by following these steps:

1 Insert the Windows XP CD into your drive.

2 At a command prompt, type *d*:\i386\winnt32.exe /cmdcons (replacing *d* with the letter of your CD drive).

A Windows Setup message appears, describing the Recovery Console option.

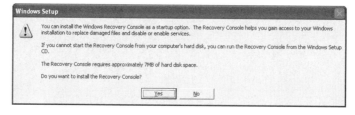

3 Click Yes to install the console.

The next time you start your computer, you'll see a "Microsoft Windows Recovery Console" entry on the boot menu.

Troubleshooting

You can't install the Recovery Console

Once Windows XP Service Pack 2 has been applied to a computer, you can't use a CD with the original version of Windows XP or with Windows XP SP1 (or SP1a) to install the Recovery Console as described in the preceding steps. In other words, if you upgrade an original or SP1 machine to SP2, you can't install Recovery Console using your Windows CD. If you try, you'll be presented with an error message and no way to continue. Fortunately, there are workarounds:

- If one is available to you, use a Windows XP CD that has SP2 integrated. Retail and OEM copies sold after mid-2004 include SP2. This is the safest and easiest workaround.
- Use Add/Remove Programs to uninstall Service Pack 2. Follow the preceding steps to install the Recovery Console from your Windows XP CD. Then reinstall Service Pack 2, which will update your Recovery Console installation as well as your Windows XP installation.
- Boot from your Windows XP CD and run the Recovery Console as described in "Making Repairs from the Recovery Console," page 1295.

Chapter 2

If you decide for whatever reason that you no longer want the Recovery Console on the boot menu, follow these steps to remove it:

1 Edit the Boot.ini file to remove the Recovery Console entry (as described in "Modifying Boot.ini," page 74.) The entry should look like this:

```
C:\cmdcons\bootsect.dat="Microsoft Windows Recovery Console" /cmdcons
```

2 Open Windows Explorer, browse to the root directory of the drive specified in the Boot.ini entry for Recovery Console, and then delete the Cmdcons folder. (Because this is a hidden system folder, you might need to adjust folder options to make it visible, as described in "Hidden Files and Folders," page 672.)

3 In the root directory, delete the file Cmldr.

Removing the Recovery Console will recover about 7 MB of disk space.

Help and Support Options

Did you give up on the Windows Help system years ago? Most experienced Windows users quickly learned to skip right past the Help files in Microsoft Windows 95 and 98, which are aimed at novices and are hampered by a Help engine that's extremely awkward to navigate. The reservoir of Help content in Microsoft Windows Me and Microsoft Windows 2000 is much deeper, and the HTML-based interfaces are slicker and easier to use. However, in both of those Windows versions, the online Help file is still essentially a user manual that's been carved into small pieces and grows increasingly outdated with each Windows update.

Not so in Microsoft Windows XP. The Help And Support Center in both the Home and Professional editions includes a tremendous collection of resources for Windows users at every level of experience.

At Home with Windows XP

For the most part, the Help And Support Center in Windows XP Home Edition looks and works just like the one in Windows XP Professional. Topics that relate only to Professional, of course, are omitted, as are links to tools that are available only in Professional. If you are a frequent user of the Command Prompt window, you'll be disappointed to discover that although both editions support most of the same commands, Home Edition does not include Help for the commands.

Two Help And Support Center features are not available in Home Edition.

- The ability to install and use Help files from different versions of Windows.
- The ability for an expert to initiate a Remote Assistance session instead of depending on the novice to get things going.

Besides the traditional tutorials and reference material, you'll find the following extras integrated into the Windows XP Help And Support Center.

- Links to system tools and utilities, including Disk Defragmenter, System Configuration Utility (Msconfig), Network Diagnostics, and Windows Update, all of which run within the Help And Support Center window.

- Syntax and usage information for 175 command-line options, organized alphabetically (Windows XP Professional only).

- Dozens of troubleshooting tools, covering a huge assortment of common and not-so-common problems.

- Links that collect up-to-date information about your system and its current configuration, with details about all installed hardware, software, and services. Such information can help you or a support technician diagnose a problem.

- Easy access to error logs, status of services, and other advanced system information.

- Access to Group Policy settings (Windows XP Professional only).

- Links to external information sources, including the Microsoft Knowledge Base and an assortment of Windows-focused newsgroups.

- Access to Remote Assistance, which allows a Windows XP user to ask a friend for help; the more experienced user can connect directly to the machine experiencing the problem via the Internet or a local area network and make needed repairs or configuration changes directly.

Using the Help And Support Center

When you open the Help And Support Center, your first stop is always the home page. Figure 3-1 shows the options available from this page.

The left-hand column lists common Help topics. (This list replaces the Help Contents page found in previous Windows versions.) The links in the two groups on the right, each identified by a green arrow, lead to tools and support resources. The Did you know? list in the lower right contains headlines provided by Microsoft support. This area can be customized by third parties as well; if your copy of Windows was included with a new PC, the system manufacturer might have customized the Help And Support Center by providing links to its support site here.

The toolbar at the top of the Help And Support Center window provides basic browser-style navigation tools. Back and Forward buttons let you move through recently viewed topics. Although the toolbar icons closely resemble those used in Microsoft Internet

Explorer, note that the Home, Favorites, and History buttons take you to the respective pages within the Help And Support Center only.

Help and Support Options

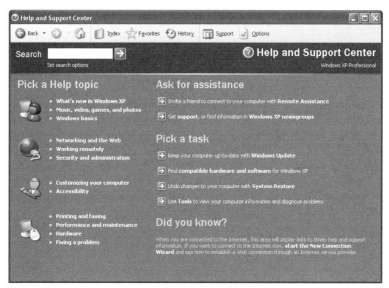

Figure 3-1. The Help And Support Center home page includes links to basic information, troubleshooting tools, and external support resources.

Troubleshooting

There's no Help And Support command on the Start menu.

Ordinarily, you open the Help And Support Center by choosing Start, Help And Support. If the command doesn't appear on your Start menu, you can always open the Help And Support Center by choosing Start, Run, and typing **helpctr**. If you want to restore the command to your Start menu, right-click the Start button and choose Properties. On the Start Menu tab of the Taskbar And Start Menu Properties dialog box, click Customize. In the Customize Start Menu dialog box, click Advanced, and then, in the Start Menu Items list, select Help And Support.

If the Help And Support check box is selected but you still have no Help And Support command on the Start menu, then the command has been disabled by policy. Choose Start, Run, and type **gpedit.msc** to open Group Policy. In the console tree, select User Configuration\Administrative Templates\Start Menu And Taskbar. Then, in the details pane, double-click Remove Help Menu From Start Menu and select Not Configured or Disabled. (Either choice restores the command to the Start menu.) For more information about Group Policy, see Appendix F, "Group Policy." Note that the Group Policy console is not available in Windows XP Home Edition.

Tip Save time by playing Favorites

The Windows XP Professional Help file is truly massive, consisting of nearly 10,000 individual topics drawn from more than 200 Compiled Help (.chm) files. When you uncover a particularly useful topic that you know you'll want to refer to later, click the Add To Favorites button just above the topic window and spare yourself the hassle of searching for it again. By default, each entry in the Help And Support Center Favorites list uses the title of the topic as its name. Use the Rename button at the bottom of the Favorites list to give a list item a name that's more meaningful to you. (This is especially important with Glossary entries, which are all initially named *Glossary* in the Favorites list.) Items in the Favorites list appear in the order in which you add them; unfortunately, there's no way to reorder these items.

Caution Avoid adding items to the Favorites list when you have multiple instances of the Help And Support Center open. Changes you make in one window may not be reflected in other windows, and the list of Favorites visible in the last window you close will be saved, possibly wiping out any entries you saved in other windows.

 # Troubleshooting

Help has stopped working.

The Help And Support Center uses two related modules: the Microsoft Help Center Service (Helpsvc.exe) and the Help And Support Center executable (Helpctr.exe). Under some circumstances, clicking the Help And Support Center icon might not produce a result. If you look in the Windows Task Manager, you'll see that both modules are running; you might also see multiple instances of Helpctr.exe, which could be causing your Help access problem. To solve this problem, follow these steps:

1 Press Ctrl+Shift+Esc to open Windows Task Manager.

2 Click the Processes tab and then click the Image Name heading to sort the list in alphabetical order.

3 Highlight each instance of Helpctr.exe in the list and click End Process. Repeat until all instances are gone from the list and then close Task Manager.

4 Open Control Panel's Services option (in the Administrative Tools group, under Performance And Maintenance Options).

5 Select Help And Support from the list of services, right-click, and then choose Restart.

After completing this procedure, you should be able to restart the Help And Support Center.

Searching for Help Topics

Got a friend who needs a refresher on a basic Windows feature or task? Sometimes a well-written, step-by-step tutorial from the Help files is just the thing you need to help someone who's struggling with Windows XP. Sending them detailed instructions saves you time and increases the chance that they'll get the results they need.

To find tutorials and instructions, you could navigate through the categories, scanning each list until you find the topic you're looking for. But there's a faster way: Choose a general category from the Help And Support Center home page and then use the Search box to locate the exact topic you need.

Follow these steps to search for specific topics:

1. Click a category in the Pick A Help Topic list on the home page to display its list of topics.
2. Enter a word or phrase in the Search box. Look just below the Search box and you'll see an option (already selected) that restricts your search to the category you chose on the home page.
3. Click the green arrow to the right of the Search box to perform the search.
4. Click a topic title from the list on the left to display its contents in the pane on the right.

> **Tip** **Keep drilling to maximize Search efficiency**
> You can customize search options to display a much longer list of topics than the default number of 15. (For more information, see "Customizing the Help And Support Center," page 87.) Providing yourself with a long list of topics from which to choose is the best way to ensure that your search covers enough ground, but it can also produce information overload. If your initial search returns too many hits and quickly scrolling through the list doesn't turn up the topic you want, enter additional search terms and select the Search Within Previous Results option to narrow the topics list. It might take several such searches to find exactly the right topic, but this search technique is extremely effective.

Search results are broken down into the following three groups:

- **Suggested Topics**   This group is based on a comparison between the search terms you entered and keywords defined in the Help files. Because the search is performed against a relatively small index file, this list appears almost immediately; however, the quality of the results depends on the keywords assigned by the Help file authors.
- **Full-Text Search Matches**   This group displays topics where the content of the Help information matches the word or phrase you entered. Although these files are also indexed, the search universe is much larger, and it typically takes longer to display the results.
- **Microsoft Knowledge Base**   This group displays the results of a search of Microsoft's extensive collection of documentation for bug fixes and technical explanations that aren't available in the local Help files. The list of found articles matches the search terms and uses settings defined in the Options dialog box.

Chapter 3

Figure 3-2 shows the results of one such search. Note that the search terms entered are highlighted in each topic.

By default, Windows highlights each occurrence of your search terms.

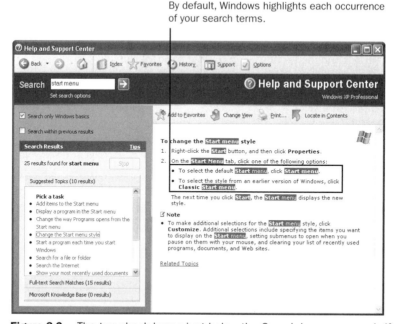

Figure 3-2. The two check boxes just below the Search box appear only if you choose a category in the Pick A Help Topic list on the home page before starting your search.

To launch a search that uses the entire Help file, enter the text in the Search box on the home page. Search terms are not case sensitive, and if you enter two or more words, the Search algorithm looks for topics containing that exact combination before looking for topics that contain the individual words. To set Search options so that results display only topics containing a specific phrase, enclose that phrase in quotation marks. Search ignores a long list of common insignificant words, such as *a, for, from,* and *like.*

You can use the AND, OR, NOT, and NEAR operators to tell the Help And Support Center how you want it to handle multiple search terms. If you're experienced with Boolean syntax, you can use this type of search string to fine-tune the list of results. For instance, searching for **Internet NOT sharing** finds topics related to Internet Explorer and the basics of connecting to the Internet, while filtering out topics that cover Internet Connection Sharing. These operators work inconsistently in some cases, so be prepared to experiment a bit. If you search for **Start NOT menu,** for instance, you'll turn up some topics containing the phrase *Start menu,* which should be rejected by this syntax.

Chapter 3

Help and Support Options

> **Tip** Take the fast lane to the Knowledge Base
>
> With the help of TweakUI, one of the Microsoft PowerToys for Windows XP that you can down-load for free from *http://www.microsoft.com/windowsxp/pro/downloads/powertoys.asp*, you can create a search alias that will accelerate your access to specific entries in the Knowl-edge Base. Once you've set up this search alias, you can jump straight to a particular Knowledge Base article using Internet Explorer. Click in the Address bar and type **mskb** followed by a space and the article ID number. For example, you could go directly to article 823390 ("How to get help with MSN") by typing **mskb 823390**.
>
> To set up the search alias, expand Internet Explorer in TweakUI's main menu, select Search, and click Create. In the Prefix box of the Search Prefix dialog box, type **mskb**. In the URL box, type **http://support.microsoft.com/?kbid=%s**. Then click OK.

Using the Help Index

If you're not sure of the exact term you're looking for, Search can be frustrating. In such a case, you might have better results scrolling through the Help Index, which lists the keyword entries for each topic. To switch to this view, click the Index button. Figure 3-3 shows what you'll see next.

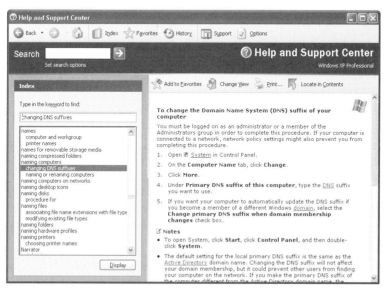

Figure 3-3. Use the Index to scroll through a lengthy list of topics, organized alphabetically by keyword.

The text box in the Index list resembles the Search box, but it behaves quite differently. As you enter text in this box, the Index selection jumps to the first topic that matches the characters you entered. The comparison is based on the beginning of the entry; if you type **networking**, for instance, the Index selection will jump to the group of topics that begin with that keyword, skipping over the Home Networking entry.

Chapter 3

Save Help Topics as Shortcuts

Because the Internet Explorer engine is at the heart of the Help And Support Center, each topic has its own URL. If you know how to manipulate these URLs, you can save a specific Help topic as an external shortcut. Using that shortcut, you can jump directly to the specific topic without having to go through the Help And Support Center first. Unfortunately, Windows XP does not let you create a shortcut to a Help topic directly. To create a shortcut, follow the process outlined below:

1 Open the topic for which you want to create a shortcut, right-click anywhere on the page (except on a link), and choose Properties.

2 Select the entire URL from the Address field (be sure to scroll down to select the full address).

3 Press Ctrl+C to copy the URL to the Clipboard.

4 Right-click the desktop (or in a folder where you want to save the shortcut) and choose New, Shortcut.

5 In the Create Shortcut dialog box, type **%systemroot%\pchealth\helpctr\ binaries\helpctr /url** followed by a space, and then paste the copied URL.

6 Click Next, give the shortcut a name, and click Finish.

Shortcuts you create in this fashion work with URLs in two common Help formats.

● The Help Center Pluggable protocol (with the prefix *hcp://*) is less common and is typically used for Help topics that link to external applications and locations, such as Remote Assistance or Windows newsgroups.

● HTML Help protocol (with the prefix *ms-its://*) is used for access to information in Compiled Help (.chm) files. If you just want quick access and don't mind opening this type of URL in the Windows 2000–style HTML Help viewer, you can use the Hh.exe Help engine. Open the Create Shortcut wizard (right-click the desktop, and then choose New, Shortcut) and type **hh** followed by a space and the Help topic's URL. The resulting shortcut opens the selected topic in a window that lists only topics from the same Help file.

For more information about HTML Help URLs, see Knowledge Base article 235226, "INFO: HTML Help URL Protocols."

> **Tip** If you want a quick overview of every wizard in Windows XP, open the Help And Support Center, click Index, and then jump to the group of topics under the keyword *wizards*. You'll find documentation on two dozen Windows XP wizards listed here, with step-by-step instructions for a wide range of common tasks.

Customizing the Help And Support Center

You can customize the look and feel of the Windows XP Help And Support Center window, and you can also adjust search options. To work with these settings, click the Options button on the Help And Support Center toolbar.

Clicking the Change Help And Support Center Options link in the left pane displays the dialog box shown in Figure 3-4.

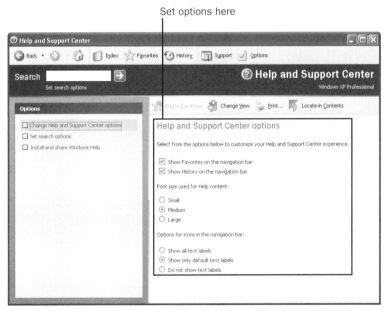

Figure 3-4. Use these options to adjust the appearance of the Help And Support Center window.

To squeeze the maximum amount of information into each Help topic window, set the font size to Small. (If your vision is less than perfect, however, the Small font size might be too small to be comfortably readable.) To reduce the amount of space used by the navigation toolbar and the options buttons at the top of the topic window, choose the Do Not Show Text Labels option. Although you can hide the Favorites and History buttons, it is not possible to hide the navigation toolbar itself.

Tip   In Windows Me and Windows 2000, the only way to change the font size used in Help windows is to globally change the fonts used throughout Internet Explorer. The Windows XP design decouples these two settings so that you can separately control font settings for the Help And Support Center and full browser windows.

To change default search settings for the Help And Support Center, click the Set Search Options link and work with the dialog box shown in Figure 3-5.

Chapter 3

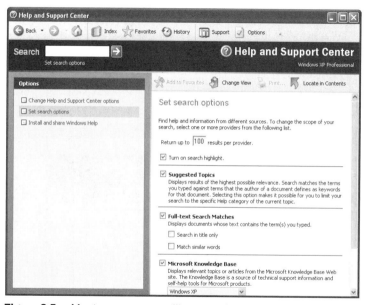

Figure 3-5.   Most power users will want to increase the number of entries returned by a search from the default 15; a value of 100 should be plenty.

The following Search options are adjustable:

Return Up To nnn Results Per Provider   The default value of 15 is too small for any wide-ranging search. Although you can enter any number up to 999, a value in the 50–100 range should be adequate.

Turn On Search Highlight   When this option is selected, Windows highlights each occurrence of your search term in topics that appear as a result of a search. Figure 3-2 shows an example.

> **Tip** **Turn off the search highlight**
> The search highlight can be helpful in drawing your focus to the section of a topic in which you're most interested. Unfortunately, it can be a distraction as well. If the highlight is too much for you, click the Set Search Options link right below the Search box. Clear the Turn On Search Highlight check box, and then click the Back button in the navigation bar to return to your now pristine topic.

Suggested Topics   When this option is selected (the default setting), Windows uses the index of keywords for every search. Note that clearing this check box removes the capability to restrict a search to a specific topic.

Full-Text Search Matches   This option is also selected by default, although the two options beneath it are not. Use the Search In Title Only option to ignore the body text of Help topics; in general this option has little to recommend it. Choose Match Similar Words if you want to extend searches to alternate forms of a word—for instance, if you enter **network**, the search results will also include topics that contain the word *networking*.

Microsoft Knowledge Base   These options are similar to those on Microsoft's Knowledge Base Web page. If you prefer the Help And Support Center interface, you can use the Select A Product Or Topic list to conduct searches for information about related products (such as Microsoft Outlook Express and Internet Explorer) or technology areas (such as keyboards and device drivers). To maximize your chances of getting answers, select All Windows Products from this list.

Sharing Help Files

In Windows XP Professional only, a third link in the Help And Support Center Options pane offers you the choice to Install And Share Windows Help. This option enables you to install Help content from a CD or a shared folder, for a related Windows product, such as Windows XP Home Edition. The option is most useful if you're responsible for multiple computers running different versions of Windows XP or Windows Server 2003. This capability is of obvious benefit to Help Desk professionals, but it can also be useful on a home network that includes a mix of PCs running Windows XP Professional and Home Edition. By switching to the Home Edition Help content, you can look up answers to troubleshooting questions without having to exit Windows XP Professional and without the risk of being confused by the differences between the two editions.

> **Tip**   Don't overestimate the capabilities of the Share Windows Help feature. Only systems running Windows XP and Windows Server 2003 can share Help files. A Windows XP machine cannot install Help files for earlier Windows versions, such as Windows Me or Windows 2000, nor can earlier Windows versions install Help files from Windows XP.

Chapter 3

To set up the capability to access Help files from Windows XP Home Edition on a system running Windows XP Professional, first make sure that you have the Windows XP Home Edition CD in the CD-ROM drive, and then follow these steps:

1 From a PC running Windows XP Professional, open the Help And Support Center and then click Options.

2 Choose Install And Share Windows Help from the Options pane on the left.

3 In the Share Windows Help pane on the right, click Install Help Content From A CD Or Disk Image.

4 Click Browse, select the \I386 folder on the Windows XP Home Edition CD, and then click Find.

5 Select Windows XP Home Edition from the list of available Help versions and then click Install. Windows XP copies a number of files from the CD to your hard disk. When the process is complete, the Status column reads Already Installed.

After you've successfully added the extra Help files to your system, you can return to the Help And Support Center at any time to switch between Help versions. Choose Install And Share Windows Help again, and then select the Switch From One Operating System's Help Content To Another option. The Switch Help Version dialog box shows a list of available Help files. Click Switch to load the Home Edition Help files. Once you've found the answers you were looking for, repeat this process and switch back to the Professional Help files.

Chapter 3

Help and Support Options

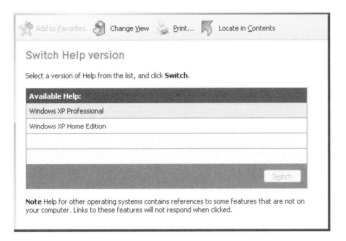

If your local area network includes several Windows XP Professional machines, you can set up shared Help files on each one without having to shuffle CDs between multiple machines. After installing the Help files for Windows XP Home Edition or Windows .NET Server, choose the Install And Share Windows Help option again and then select the Share Your Help Content With Others On Your Network option to make the newly shared files available over the network.

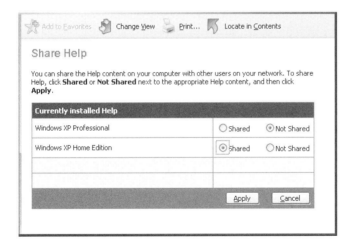

From another networked machine running Windows XP Professional (or Windows Server 2003), select the Install Help Content From Another Windows Computer option. Enter the name of the machine containing the shared Help files, click Find, select the Help version that you want to install, and then click Install to load those files. This procedure has the same result as if you had installed the Help files from the CD—the full Help database is copied to the second PC.

The final menu choice in the Install And Share Windows Help pane allows you to remove installed Help files belonging to another Windows version. Use this option if you no longer need the extra Help files and you want to reclaim the disk space they're gobbling up.

Connecting to Another PC with Remote Assistance

If you've ever tried to help a novice user troubleshoot a Windows problem over the phone, you know how frustrating the entire process can be. It's usually difficult for an inexperienced user to accurately communicate detailed configuration information, especially if the problem involves technically challenging areas, such as hardware drivers or network protocols. Because you're not looking over the user's shoulder, you can't see error messages or informational dialog boxes, so you have to rely on the user to read this crucial information back to you. Even when you successfully pin down the problem and find a solution, you have to walk the user through a potentially daunting repair process. And if the registry needs editing—well, good luck.

With Windows XP, on the other hand, you can eliminate most of those headaches using a cool support tool called Remote Assistance. This feature, available in both Windows XP Professional and Home Edition, lets you open a direct connection between two machines over the Internet or over a local area network. Even if you're hundreds or thousands of miles away, you can watch as the user demonstrates the problem and take control of the screen to make repairs quickly and accurately. You can investigate Control Panel settings, run diagnostic tools, install updates, and even edit the registry of the problem-plagued PC. Repairs that might have taken hours the old-fashioned way can be accomplished in a few minutes using this tool.

> **Note** Behind the scenes, Remote Assistance uses Windows XP Terminal Services to share a desktop and other resources between two PCs. Although this is the same underlying code used in the Remote Desktop feature, Remote Assistance is fundamentally different in two ways. First, in a Remote Assistance session, both users must be present at their respective PCs and must agree to establish the connection. Second, you can use Remote Assistance to connect to a PC running Windows XP Home Edition, whereas incoming Remote Desktop connections can only be enabled on Windows XP Professional.

Remote Assistance is designed for informal, peer-to-peer use by Windows users without an extensive technical background. Although the user interface hides most of its complexities, a basic understanding of how Remote Assistance connections work can help you make reliable connections without compromising the security of either computer.

How Remote Assistance Works

The two parties in a Remote Assistance session are called the *novice* and the *expert*. To use Remote Assistance, both parties must be using Windows XP, both must have active Internet

Help and Support Options

connections or be on the same local area network, and neither can be blocked by firewalls. Creating a complete Remote Assistance session is a three-step process:

1 The novice sends a Remote Assistance invitation, typically using Windows Messenger or e-mail.

2 The expert accepts the invitation, opening a terminal window that displays the desktop of the novice's machine.

3 The expert views the desktop in a read-only window and exchanges messages with the novice using text or voice chat. Before the expert can work with objects on the remote PC, the novice must enable the Allow Expert Interaction option.

At the heart of each Remote Assistance connection is a small text file called an *RA ticket*. (More formally, its type is Microsoft Remote Assistance Incident and its extension is .msrcincident.) This file uses XML fields to define the parameters of a Remote Assistance connection. When you use Windows Messenger to manage the connection, the RA ticket is never visible. When a novice sends a Remote Assistance request via e-mail, however, the RA ticket rides along as an attachment to the message. The expert has to double-click this file to launch the Remote Assistance session.

Remote Assistance works by creating a direct connection between two computers using the TCP/IP protocol. For this connection to be successful, both computers involved must be able to communicate using their respective IP addresses.

Troubleshooting

Double-clicking an RA ticket results in an error message.

If you're experiencing problems with a Remote Assistance connection and you're using an RA ticket (not Windows Messenger), make sure the ticket file is pointing to the correct IP address. If you received the invitation via e-mail, save the rcBuddy.MsRcIncident file and open it using Notepad or another text editor.

Look at the RCTICKET field, which follows this format:

```
RCTICKET="65538,1,ip_address:3389;machine_name:3389,encrypted_connection_info
```

Check the ip address value to be certain it points to the current IP address of the novice's machine and, if necessary, edit it. But don't tamper with the encrypted connection_info data.

A Remote Assistance connection is relatively easy when both parties have public IP addresses provided by an Internet service provider. In that scenario, the computers connect directly, sending and receiving data on TCP port 3389. Routers along the Internet connection between the two computers are able to recognize the addresses of the two computers and send the respective packets to their correct destinations. Internet Connection Firewall in Windows XP automatically opens this port when you request a Remote Assistance connection.

Chapter 3

Remote Assistance connections are also straightforward and typically trouble-free on a private network, such as a workgroup in a home or small office. In that case, each machine can communicate directly with the other without having to pass through any routers.

> **Tip** Use a VPN if possible
>
> On a corporate network, the preferred way to work around firewalls is to establish a virtual private network (VPN) connection. This allows all traffic to pass through the firewall and eliminates the need to create possible security holes by opening specific ports. For more information, see "Connecting to a Virtual Private Network," page 1070.

What happens if one or both sides of the connection are using private IP addresses assigned through Network Address Translation (NAT)? That's when Remote Assistance gets complicated. Because these addresses are reserved for exclusive use on private networks, they cannot be routed over the Internet. Instead, a software or hardware-based NAT device handles the grunt work of passing data between the single public IP address it uses to communicate with the Internet and the private IP addresses on the local network. How it performs that job determines whether the Remote Assistance connection will succeed or fail. The exact outcome depends on how the computer acquired the private IP address:

Internet Connection Sharing   When you use Internet Connection Sharing (ICS) from Windows XP or Windows Me, the ICS server hands out private IP addresses to all other computers on the network. The ICS server listens for Remote Assistance traffic on TCP port 5001 and forwards it to port 3389, allowing the connection to succeed on its end, regardless of whether the computer in question is playing the role of novice or expert. If computers on both ends of the connection are using any combination of public IP addresses and private addresses supplied by ICS, the Remote Assistance session should work perfectly.

> **Note**   If your network includes an ICS server running Windows 98 Second Edition or Windows 2000, Remote Assistance will not work properly.

UPnP-compatible hardware router or residential gateway   If the source of a private IP address is a hardware router or residential gateway, the connection will be successful if the router supports the Universal Plug and Play (UPnP) standard. Most routers manufactured in 2001 or earlier do not support UPnP, although a firmware upgrade may add this capability.

Non-UPnP-compatible hardware router or residential gateway   If both computers are behind NAT devices that are not UPnP compatible, it is not possible to complete a Remote Assistance connection. If only one computer is using a private IP address whose source is a hardware router or residential gateway that is not UPnP compatible, making a successful connection is often possible, although it requires jumping through some hoops. In this configuration, your best bet is to use Windows Messenger to create the Remote Assistance connection. The novice initiates the connection to the expert on a random port; the expert then uses this port to initiate a connection back to the novice.

The trickiest connection of all involves a novice who is behind a non-UPnP NAT device, such as a router or residential gateway on a cable or DSL connection, and who is unable or unwilling to use Windows Messenger. In that case, you may be able to make a Remote Assistance connection work by editing the RA ticket file. Find the address of the NAT device (the public IP address it uses to connect to the Internet) and the private address of the novice's computer; then follow these steps:

1   On the NAT device attached to the novice's network, open port 3389. Traffic on this port must be able to reach the novice machine before it can complete the Remote Assistance connection. In the popular Linksys router product family, for example, you accomplish this goal by using the Forwarding option in the router's Control Panel.

2   Open the Help And Support Center and create a Remote Assistance invitation, saving it as a file on your desktop or in another convenient location. This ticket file includes a pointer to your private IP address; if the novice sends this ticket to an expert who is not on the same private network as you, it will fail because the novice computer will not be able to find a route to the expert's IP address.

3   Open Notepad or another text editor and edit the RCTICKET field, adding the external IP address of the NAT device before the internal IP address. For instance, if your NAT device uses an external IP address of 24.100.255.255 and your private IP address is 192.168.1.105 and your machine name is Groucho, this field should read as follows (the added information is shown in bold):

```
RCTICKET="65538,1,24.100.255.255:3389;192.168.1.105:3389;groucho:3389,
encrypted connection info
```

4   Send the RA ticket file to the expert. When he or she double-clicks this file, the information you added will allow the file to work its way over the Internet to your NAT device and then into your computer on port 3389.

Tip   **Watch for disconnected dial-up connections**
Dynamic IP addresses assigned by a dial-up Internet service provider pose special problems. When you create an invitation and send it via e-mail, Remote Assistance embeds the current IP address in that invitation. If you lose the dial-up connection and have to reconnect, the ISP will almost certainly assign a new IP address, rendering the invitation unusable. At that point, you have two options: Cancel the invitation and issue a new one, or use a text editor to change the existing invitation so that it points to the newly assigned IP address. To discover the new IP address, open a Command Prompt window and type **ipconfig**.

Chapter 3

Sending a Remote Assistance Invitation

By default, Windows XP requires that a user request assistance before a Remote Assistance connection is made. From the Help And Support Center home page, click Invite A Friend To Connect To Your Computer With Remote Assistance. (You can also reach this page from the Remote Assistance shortcut on the All Programs menu.) Choose Invite Someone To Help You. The Remote Assistance pane, shown in Figure 3-6, provides three methods to send an invitation for assistance:

Windows Messenger If you're currently signed on to Windows Messenger, a list of available contacts appears in the Remote Assistance pane. Choose a name and click Invite This Person. Because each user is authenticated through a .NET Passport, there's no need to provide a separate password for this request. The expert sees the request directly in the Messenger window and can click a link to launch the connection.

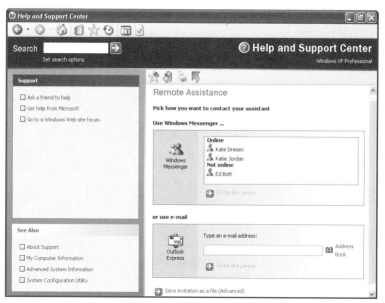

Figure 3-6. Choose any of these three methods to send a Remote Assistance invitation.

E-Mail To send an invitation via e-mail, enter an e-mail address or click the Address Book icon to select a name from the Windows Address Book; then click Invite This Person. You can enter the text you want to appear in the body of the message, as shown on the next page, and then click Continue to set an expiration time and password. Click Send Invitation when you've filled in all the details.

Save Invitation as a File (Advanced)   This option is for use when another connection type is impossible or impractical. As with the e-mail option, you can define an expiration time and password. After saving the file locally, you're responsible for transferring it to the remote assistant, typically by attaching it to an e-mail message or saving it on a floppy disk or a shared network location.

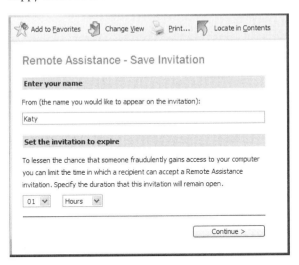

Chapter 3

Initiating a Remote Assistance Session as the Expert

A weakness of Remote Assistance is that it ordinarily depends on the novice—someone who is having trouble using his or her computer—to initiate a Remote Assistance session by sending an invitation. Depending on how the novice and expert computers are connected and the novice's general computer aptitude, this hurdle might prevent the novice from ever getting the needed help.

Inside Out

If Messenger is impractical, pick up the phone.

If you need to send a Remote Assistance invitation (or help someone else send an invitation to you), Windows Messenger is by far the quickest and easiest option. You get immediate confirmation that the invitation has been received and accepted, and the Messenger window handles the connection details without requiring any file attachments. Skip the extra steps in the Help And Support Center and send the invitation directly from Messenger by choosing Tools, Ask For Remote Assistance. The next best option? Pick up the phone. Advise the expert to be on the lookout for an e-mail request, negotiate a mutually agreeable time, provide the expert with the Remote Assistance password, and give a general description of the problem. After making contact via telephone, send the Remote Assistance request via e-mail.

An expert running Windows XP Professional (but not Windows XP Home Edition) can initiate a session with another Windows XP Professional user on the same local area network. To do this, the expert must first configure the novice's computer to accept unsolicited Remote Assistance requests, as follows:

1. At a command prompt on the novice's computer, type **gpedit.msc** to open Group Policy. (Alternatively, from the expert's computer, open the novice computer's Group Policy remotely. For details, see "Starting Group Policy for a Remote Computer," page 1415.)

2. In Group Policy, open Computer Configuration\Administrative Templates\System\Remote Assistance, and then double-click Offer Remote Assistance.

3. On the Setting tab, select Enabled.

4. Specify whether you want helpers to be able to remotely control the computer or simply view it remotely.

5. Click Show to display the list of permitted helpers. In the Show Contents dialog box, shown in Figure 3-7, click Add to add a user account or security group to the list. In the Add Item dialog box, type the name of the account or group. Then click OK to close each dialog box.

Chapter 3

> **Note** Add a familiar user account to the novice machine
>
> If the computers about to establish a Remote Assistance connection are not joined to a domain, you must enter the name of a user account that exists on both the novice's machine and the expert's machine. This account's password must be the same on both computers. For this reason, you'll probably find it most convenient to add a user account to the novice machine, using the name that the expert uses to log on to his or her machine. For details, see "Creating a New User Account," page 234.

6 Turn off Simple File Sharing.

In Control Panel, open Folder Options (in the Appearance And Themes category). On the View tab, clear the Use Simple File Sharing (Recommended) check box.

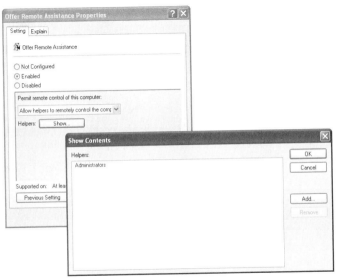

Figure 3-7. Specify the names of users and groups who are allowed to initiate a Remote Assistance session with this computer.

> **Caution** Disabling Simple File Sharing has effects that reach far beyond Remote Assistance. For information about the differences between Simple File Sharing and classic sharing, see "Simple File Sharing vs. Advanced Permissions," page 275.

Troubleshooting

An error appears when the expert tries to connect.

If you, as expert, offer Remote Assistance as described in the preceding procedure, you might receive an "Access to the requested resource has been disabled by your administrator" error message after you click Connect. This message appears when the novice's computer has not been configured to accept unsolicited Remote Assistance requests. You must use Group Policy on the novice's computer to enable the Offer Remote Assistance setting (as described earlier in this chapter).

If the message reads "Permission denied," be sure that Help And Support Center on the expert's computer is running in the context of a user account that matches one on the novice's computer (that is, it has the same user name and password on both machines). In addition, be sure that Simple File Sharing is disabled on the novice's computer.

Once the novice's computer is set up in this way, an expert can initiate an unsolicited Remote Assistance session by following these steps:

1. On the Help And Support Center home page, click Use Tools To View Your Computer Information And Diagnose Problems (under Pick A Task in the right column).

2. In the Tools pane on the left side, click Offer Remote Assistance.

3. Type the name or IP address of the novice's computer, and click Connect.

Note The expert must be logged on using an account that has the same user name and password as a "permitted helpers" account on the novice's computer. Alternatively, the expert can use the Runas command to open the Help And Support Center. For example, if both computers have an account named Smartypants, a user on the expert machine could open the Help And Support Center by entering the following command in a Command Prompt window:

```
runas /user:smartypants "%systemroot%\pchealth\helpctr\binaries\helpctr"
```

4. If Windows prompts you to do so, select the name of a user on the novice's computer.

5. Click Start Remote Assistance.

A dialog box appears on the novice's screen; if the novice accepts your invitation, the Remote Assistance session begins.

Chapter 3

Working in a Remote Assistance Session

After the expert launches the connection request and the novice grants permission, a two-pane Remote Assistance window opens on the expert's machine. The left pane is used for text chat; the pane on the right displays the novice's desktop, as shown in Figure 3-8.

As the expert, you'll use the toolbar at the top of the Remote Assistance window, shown here, to take control of the remote desktop, send a file, or disconnect when the session is complete. (The novice has similar options available on a toolbar whose format is slightly different.)

For obvious security reasons, clicking the Take Control button sends a request to the novice, who has to grant permission before you can actually begin working with the remote desktop. At any time, the novice can cut off your ability to control the session by tapping the Esc key; or you can click the Release Control button on the Remote Assistance toolbar.

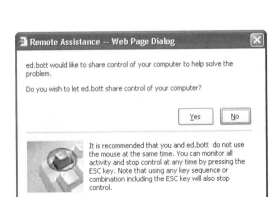

Regardless of your expert credentials, your actions in a Remote Assistance session are governed by the privileges assigned to the novice user's account. When connecting to a machine belonging to a user with a limited account, for instance, you might be unable to edit the registry or make necessary configuration changes unless you can supply an administrator's password (using the Run As dialog box).

Ed and Katy can discuss the problem in this chat pane

Ed can work on Katy's screen in this window

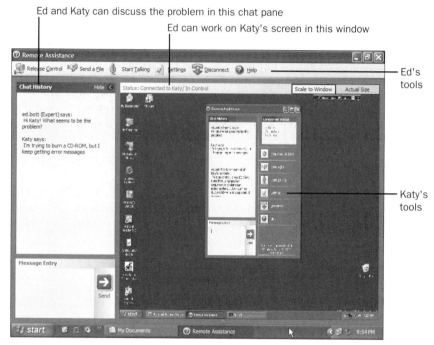

Ed's tools

Katy's tools

Figure 3-8. Use the two tabs in the top right corner of this window to switch between zoomed and actual views of the remote desktop.

For more details about running an application or utility with another user's account privileges, see "Running a Program as Another User," page 127.

Maintaining Security

Remote Assistance is a powerful tool. In the wrong hands, it's also potentially dangerous, because it allows a remote user to install software and tamper with a system configuration. In a worst-case scenario, someone could trick an unsuspecting novice into allowing access to his or her machine, and then plant a Trojan application or gain access to sensitive files.

Tip   Use Group Policy to control Remote Assistance

With Group Policy (Gpedit.msc), you can disable or restrict the ability of users on a computer to request Remote Assistance. In Group Policy, open the Computer Configuration\Administrative Templates\System\Remote Assistance folder, and double-click Solicited Remote Assistance. To prevent users from sending invitations, select Disabled. To restrict users, select Enabled, and then set the options that determine whether experts can control or view the computer and the maximum allowable ticket time. Settings you configure here override any settings you make in the System Properties dialog box.

Chapter 3

Four essential security precautions can slam the door on Remote Assistance–generated security breaches.

- Set a short expiration time on Remote Assistance invitations sent via e-mail. An expiration time of one hour should be sufficient for most requests. (Note that the invitation must be *accepted* within the specified time; you don't need to specify the length of the Remote Assistance session.) An expired RA ticket file is worthless to a potential hacker.

- Assign a strong password to Remote Assistance invitations. Because e-mail is fundamentally insecure, never send a Remote Assistance invitation without password-protecting it first. This option is selected by default when you create an invitation. Communicate the password by telephone or in a separate e-mail message; don't include it with the RA ticket.

- Manually expire invitations when they're no longer needed. To do so, open the Remote Assistance page in the Help And Support Center and then click the View Invitation Status link. The resulting window shows all recently issued invitations and allows you to resend, delete, or change the expiration date of an invitation.

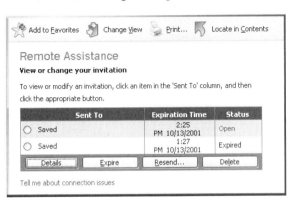

Chapter 3

- Disable Remote Assistance on any machine where the possible benefits of a Remote Assistance session are outweighed by potential security risks. To completely disable Remote Assistance on a given machine, open System in Control Panel, click the Remote tab, and then clear the Allow Remote Assistance Invitations To Be Sent From This Computer check box. If that step seems too drastic, you can limit Remote Assistance capabilities so that an expert cannot take control of the remote machine. On the Remote tab, click Advanced and then clear the Allow This Computer To Be Controlled Remotely check box.

Inside Out

Extend your welcome with a long-lasting invitation

In some cases, you may want to create a long-term Remote Assistance invitation. If you're the expert for a friend or family member, for instance, there's no need to create a new invitation each time the novice gets stuck. Instead, have that person create an invitation and save it as a file. From the novice's machine, open the Help And Support Center, select the Save Invitation As A File option, and specify the maximum expiration time of 99 days. Send the invitation to your own system, store it in a convenient place there, and use it each time you get a call for help. Note that this option will not work if the novice has a dial-up Internet account whose IP address changes with each new connection; it's most effective when the novice has a cable modem or other always-on connection with a fixed IP address.

Improving Remote Assistance Performance

You might shudder at the thought of accessing another desktop over a dial-up connection. Surprisingly, the performance can be quite usable. You wouldn't want to use this sort of connection for everyday work, but for troubleshooting, it's good enough.

You can maximize Remote Assistance performance over a dial-up link by observing these precautions.

- Try to connect at 56 Kbps, if possible.
- Reduce the visual complexity of the novice machine as much as possible. Reduce the display resolution to 800 × 600 and use only as many colors as is absolutely necessary. (Remote Assistance automatically disables wallpaper and other nonessential graphics.)
- Turn off desktop animations and other sophisticated visual effects, and avoid opening windows that contain complex graphics unless absolutely necessary.
- Close any unnecessary applications on the novice machine.
- Don't let the novice move the mouse on the novice machine, if possible, when you are in control of the screen.

Chapter 3

Other Support Resources

Official Help resources are the first line of support, but they're not the only source of answers. Windows-related newsgroups can be a gold mine of information and are particularly useful when your problem involves an unusual error message or a specific combination of hardware. If you can find a post from another user who has experienced the same problem, you might also find a solution, or at least get clues that will point you in the right direction.

To search newsgroups from the Help And Support Center, start at the home page, and click the Get Support, Or Find Information In Windows XP Newsgroups link; then click Go To A Windows Web Site Forum, and click Go To Windows Newsgroups. This opens a browser window with a Web-based interface to Windows XP–related newsgroups.

Note If you want to maintain an archive of newsgroup posts, skip this Web view and use Outlook Express, as described in "Saving Messages Before They're Deleted from the Server," page 1172.

Contacting Microsoft Support

The Help And Support Center includes a variety of tools you can use to initiate support requests directly with Microsoft. From the home page, click the Get Support link, and then click Get Help From Microsoft. If you have an active Internet connection, you can submit a support request directly to Microsoft.

Before initiating a support request, be sure to check your support eligibility. You may be eligible for free support, or you may be required to pay a per-incident fee. The details vary depending on how and when you purchased your copy of Windows.

If you're eligible for support but do not currently have access to an Internet connection, you can save configuration information to a file and submit it later, when you're connected to the Internet again. To do this, follow these steps:

1 Open the Help And Support Center and click Get Support, Or Find Information In Windows XP Newsgroups.

2 Click the Get Help From Microsoft link.

3 Sign in using your .NET Passport and supply any required personal information.

4 At the Microsoft Online Assisted Support page, click the View Other Support Options link.

Chapter 3

5 Click Save Information About This Computer To Submit To Microsoft Online Assisted Support.

6 Specify a location for the file and save the resulting file. Later, when you connect to the Internet, you can transmit the file to a support engineer.

As Figure 3-9 shows, this procedure is almost completely automatic.

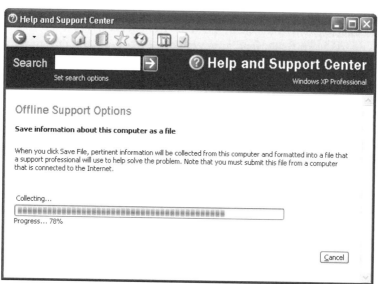

Figure 3-9. When you submit an online support request, Windows gathers all necessary files and submits them automatically.

Chapter 4

Installing, Uninstalling, and Managing Programs

Compared to most earlier versions of Microsoft Windows, the process of adding a new program is simpler and safer in Windows XP. For anyone upgrading from Windows 2000, the changes are mostly in the area of compatibility: Many programs that refuse to run properly under Windows 2000 (especially games) do better under Windows XP. On the other hand, programs that depend on virtual device drivers (VxDs) simply won't run under Windows XP (or Windows 2000, for that matter).

If you're accustomed to Windows 95, Windows 98, or Windows Me, you'll notice two dramatic improvements in the way the operating system manages installed programs. First, Windows XP file protection prevents a rogue program from compromising your operating system by installing outdated or incorrect versions of crucial system files. Second, a greatly improved Add Or Remove Programs dialog box in Control Panel makes it easier to manage installed programs.

How User Rights Affect Program Setup Options

When you attempt to install a program under Windows XP, your setup options depend on the permissions available to you through the account you used to log on. If you're running under an administrator account, you can install any program without restrictions (barring compatibility problems, of course). You can also choose to remove, modify, or repair that program at any time.

At Home with Windows XP

The program management actions described in this chapter work exactly the same way whether you use Windows XP Professional or Windows XP Home Edition. The only part of this chapter that does not apply to Home Edition users are references to the Power Users group, a security group with privileges between those granted to computer administrators and those granted to limited users. The Power Users group is not available in Home Edition.

For instructions on how to manage users and groups, including a computer administrator account, see "Working with User Accounts," page 232.

If you log on with a limited user account, however, you will be blocked from installing any program that can be run by other users—in other words, most programs. You can start the setup program, but it will typically stop before successfully completing. Setup problems can be especially vexing with older applications that aren't certified for use with Windows 2000/XP. With most certified programs, the error message will be easy to understand, like this message that appears when a limited user tries to install a new copy of Microsoft Office XP.

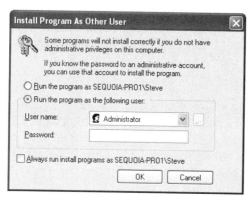

Tip   Use the Run As option to install from your everyday limited account
When Windows blocks installation with the dialog box shown above, you can complete the installation by selecting the name of an administrator account and providing its password; the setup program then runs in the context of that user. This option is often more convenient than logging off and logging back on, particularly if you use a limited account as your everyday account.

Legacy applications that assume the user is running Windows 95/98 behave unpredictably when confronted with the more stringent security model of Windows XP. In these cases, the error message that appears when a limited user is blocked from setting up a program can be bafflingly irrelevant, as demonstrated here.

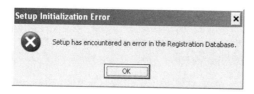

Chapter 4

Troubleshooting

You're having trouble installing a program for a user with a limited account.

Unfortunately, many applications that were originally designed for Windows 95/98 and Windows Me stumble when they encounter the multiuser environment of Windows 2000 and Windows XP. Sooner or later (probably sooner), you'll run into problems setting up a third-party program for a user with a limited account. Even after you successfully install the software, you might discover that the program refuses to run. Here's where to look for possible solutions:

- **Is an upgrade available?**　A later version of the program might work properly under Windows XP.

- **Is there a published workaround?**　Contact the support department of the software developer and search public newsgroups. An experienced support professional or another user of the product might be able to suggest a way to bypass the problem. If the company has its own support database, don't restrict your search to Windows XP–related issues; a workaround for Windows 2000 is likely to succeed under Windows XP as well.

- **Can you adjust permissions in the registry?**　The program might be encountering a problem because it requires that the current user be allowed to modify keys or values in a protected part of the registry. If you can determine which keys are causing the problem, you might be able to log on using an administrator's account, adjust permissions using Registry Editor, and solve the problem.

- **Does temporarily "promoting" the user help?**　Try changing the user's account type from Limited to Computer Administrator, and then run the setup routine for the program. After setup completes successfully and you confirm that the program will run, see if any user data files are being stored in a system location. If so, move those files to the user's profile and change the account back to Limited. This technique might help get past a glitch caused strictly by a simple design flaw in the setup program. (For example, some setup programs are designed to prevent installation by any user who is not a member of the Administrators group—even if the account has all of the requisite privileges.)

In some cases, you might discover that the best solution to the problem is to sidestep it completely. Find a Windows XP–compatible program that accomplishes the same goal as the one that's giving you problems. If you can't find a suitable replacement, allow the user to run the program with an administrator's account as described in the final section of this chapter.

The setup program might squawk when it tries to copy files to protected folders, where limited users lack appropriate permissions, or it might complain that it couldn't create a specific registry key or value. The only programs that can successfully be installed under a limited user account are those that copy files only to the user's profile, modify registry settings only

Chapter 4

in the HKEY_CURRENT_USER hive, and install shortcuts only for the currently logged-on user. If the setup program tries to step outside these bounds, it fails.

On a system that has been upgraded from Windows 2000, some accounts might belong to the Power Users group. This type of user account should be able to install most applications, but any setup program that replaces operating system files or installs a service will fail; the system blocks access to these crucial parts of the file system and registry by all users except administrators. Nevertheless, security purists recommend that you log on for everyday computing tasks using an account in the Power Users group and use a computer administrator account only when the task requires it.

The Power Users group is on the list of default groups in Windows XP Professional, but it's not available when you create or change an account using Control Panel's User Accounts dialog box. To work with this group, use the Local Users And Groups snap-in from the Computer Management console.

Caution   Don't be lulled into a false sense of security by the fact that you're logged on using an account in the Power Users group instead of an administrator's account. Running under a limited account provides excellent protection, but is too restrictive for most experienced Windows users to tolerate. The modest restrictions on Power Users still leave your system open to tremendous damage. Power Users can inadvertently install a virus or Trojan horse program, for instance, or trigger the "blue screen of death" by replacing signed drivers with newer, untested versions (buggy video or disk drivers are especially troublesome). They can also create problems by editing keys and values in the HKLM\Software registry hive.

Installing Programs

As in previous versions of Windows, you can manage the installation of programs through Add Or Remove Programs, which you reach through Control Panel. The Add Or Remove Programs dialog box used in Windows XP is similar to the one introduced in Windows 2000 and dramatically different from its bare-bones predecessor in Windows 95/98 and Windows Me. As Figure 4-1 shows, the list of currently installed programs provides detailed information about each program, including the amount of disk space the program occupies, how often it's been used, and the date the program was last started. You'll also find buttons to uninstall or modify the program.

Indiscriminately installing software is rarely a good idea. A poorly written program can create system instabilities, cause conflicts with other programs, and impede system performance by using excessive amounts of RAM or CPU time. Before installing a new program, ask the following questions:

- **Is it compatible with Windows XP?**   Look for a definitive statement of compatibility on the software package or on the software developer's Web site. Also, check Microsoft's database of compatible applications, Windows Catalog (*http://www.microsoft.com/windows/catalog*). You'll find a link to Windows Catalog near the top of the Start, All Programs menu. For more information about compatibility issues, see "Forcing Older Programs to Run Properly," page 121.

- **Are any patches available?** Checking for updates before installing a new program can spare you painful installation headaches.

- **Are there known problems with the program?** A quick search through public news-groups via Google's online Usenet archive (*http://groups.google.com*) might turn up valuable setup hints or convince you not to even try to install a particular program.

- **Can it be uninstalled easily?** If the program's setup routine was written with a recent version of InstallShield, Wise Install, or Microsoft's Windows Installer, it will almost certainly include tools that allow you to remove it completely. The older the program, the more likely its uninstall procedure is incomplete.

Figure 4-1. Select each item in the list of currently installed programs for detailed information; note the link to additional support information.

Tip Set a restore point first

Even if you're absolutely convinced that a new program is well tested and completely safe, it's *always* a good idea to manually create a System Restore checkpoint first. Give the restore point a descriptive name that clearly identifies it. If you run into unforeseen problems, uninstall the program and then use System Restore to remove any leftover program files and registry entries. For more details, see "Undoing Configuration Mistakes with System Restore," page 1288.

Looking for Support Shortcuts

Thoughtful software developers embed links to support resources and tools directly in the program's listing in the Add Or Remove Programs dialog box. If you've installed Office 2003, for example, the support link leads to the dialog box shown here. Programs that use Windows Installer (including all recent versions of Office) might also include a Repair button like the one shown here, which can be used to quickly fix problems caused by missing or damaged program files.

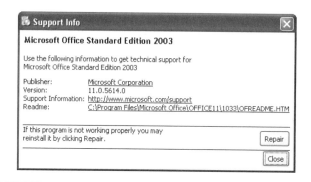

Installing 32-Bit Windows Programs

Virtually all modern 32-bit Windows programs start the setup process through a file called Setup.exe. Windows can track down the proper setup file automatically when you use the Add New Programs tab on the Add Or Remove Programs dialog box, shown in Figure 4-2. Click the CD Or Floppy button to search removable media. Use the Browse button in the resulting dialog box to search in other locations (including your default downloads folder or a shared network folder).

On corporate networks, the Add New Programs tab also lists applications that a network administrator has made available to authorized users and groups over a network built around Windows 2000 or Windows 2003 servers. Using Windows Installer, administrators can configure a program so that it installs automatically when the user needs it. A program installed this way will appear in either of these two configurations:

- When an application has been *assigned* to a user, shortcuts to the program appear on the user's Start menu or desktop, and relevant file types are preassociated with the application. As soon as the user chooses the menu item, activates the shortcut, or opens an associated document, the application is installed. An application assigned to a specific user is available to that user wherever he or she logs on. An application can also be assigned to a computer, in which case the application is automatically installed when the computer starts up. (If someone uninstalls the assigned application, it is automatically reinstalled at the next logon.)

● An application that is *published* to a user is installed only when the user chooses that option from the list of available programs at the bottom of the Add New Programs window.

Figure 4-2. Click the CD Or Floppy button to quickly locate setup files. The network programs section at the bottom of the window appears only if you're part of a domain, and programs appear in this section only when configured by a network administrator.

To learn more about the second option on the Add New Programs tab—Add Programs From Microsoft— see "Keeping Your System Secure with Windows Update," page 210, for information about using Windows Update to automatically install new features or drivers.

Tip Turn off Start menu notifications

After you install a program, Windows announces additions to the Start menu with a pop-up balloon and highlights the changes on the menu itself. Some folks like the extra guidance, but if you find it distracting and condescending, turn off this notification. Right-click the Start button and choose Properties. On the Start Menu tab, click Customize, and then click the Advanced tab. Clear the Highlight Newly Installed Programs check box.

Inside Out

Setup programs and security warnings

Sometimes when you run a program, a security warning like the one shown below appears.

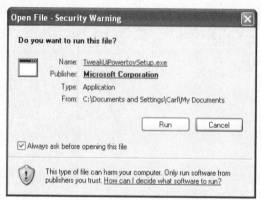

This type of message often appears with setup programs, but it can appear when you launch *any* type of executable program. You might wonder why you get the warning with some programs, but not others. Here's what's going on:

When you download a file using Internet Explorer and you save it to an NTFS volume, Internet Explorer creates an alternate data stream that is stored with the file (more about data streams in a moment). This data stream identifies the file as one that was downloaded from the Internet. Because many viruses, worms, and other nasties arrive in program files downloaded from the Internet, beginning with Service Pack 2 Windows displays the extra warning message that also includes information about the program's publisher and digital signature. (Of course, before you download a program using Internet Explorer, you must successfully run Internet Explorer's gauntlet; by default, it blocks program downloads and displays a message in the Information Bar. For more information, see "Protecting Your System from Unsafe and Unwanted Software," page 315.)

If the security warning appears when you run a setup program that you're going to run only once, it's not too intrusive. But if it appears on a program that you run more often, you'll want to get rid of the warning once you're sure that the program is safe. You can do that by clearing the Always Ask Before Opening This File check box, of course. But you can also disable the warning by right-clicking the program's icon in Windows Explorer and choosing Properties; then click the Unblock button. Either action removes the alternate data stream from the file.

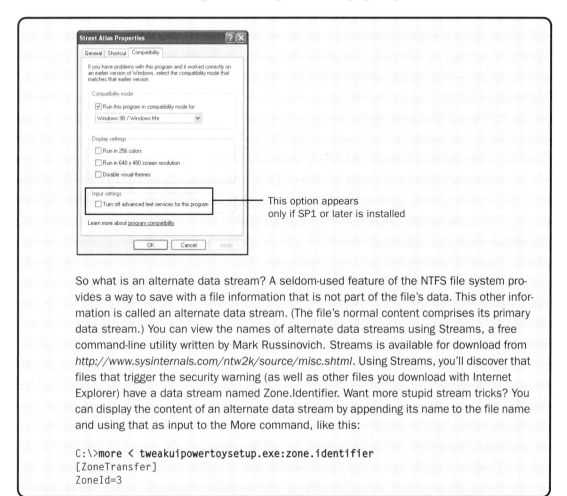

This option appears
only if SP1 or later is installed

So what is an alternate data stream? A seldom-used feature of the NTFS file system provides a way to save with a file information that is not part of the file's data. This other information is called an alternate data stream. (The file's normal content comprises its primary data stream.) You can view the names of alternate data streams using Streams, a free command-line utility written by Mark Russinovich. Streams is available for download from *http://www.sysinternals.com/ntw2k/source/misc.shtml*. Using Streams, you'll discover that files that trigger the security warning (as well as other files you download with Internet Explorer) have a data stream named Zone.Identifier. Want more stupid stream tricks? You can display the content of an alternate data stream by appending its name to the file name and using that as input to the More command, like this:

```
C:\>more < tweakuipowertoysetup.exe:zone.identifier
[ZoneTransfer]
ZoneId=3
```

Chapter 4

Installing and Running 16-Bit Windows Programs

Windows XP does an impressive job of running programs that were written years ago for Windows 3.x. To run these older 16-bit programs under a 32-bit operating system, Windows XP launches a subsystem—a *virtual machine*—that mimics "386 enhanced mode" in the older Windows 3.x environment.

Although Windows XP allows you to run these 16-bit programs, you'll encounter a few glitches:

- Most 16-bit programs do not support long file names. (Windows XP maintains the links between short and long file names, however, so that a long file name is preserved and saved after a file is modified using a 16-bit application.)

- In general, 16-bit applications do not run as fast as comparable 32-bit applications. The 16-bit programs are restricted to using a single thread, even on a multithreaded operating system such as Windows XP. And calls made by a 16-bit application must be translated for the 32-bit operating system. This translation process, called *thunking*, adds to execution time.

- Some 16-bit applications require 16-bit device drivers, which are not supported in Windows XP. Applications that directly access hardware must supply a Windows XP virtual device driver and a Windows XP 32-bit device driver, or they won't run.

- Dynamic link libraries (DLLs) written for 16-bit applications cannot be used by 32-bit applications, and vice versa. Because the setup program for most applications installs all of the DLLs needed by the application, you won't be aware of this distinction most of the time. But if, for example, you have a macro written for Microsoft Word 6 (a 16-bit application) that accesses one or more DLLs, it won't work with Word 2002 (a 32-bit application).

Many 16-bit programs use the Windows 3.*x*–vintage Win.ini and System.ini files to store program-specific configuration information (some programs use private .ini files as well). Windows XP retains bare-bones copies of Win.ini and System.ini in the %SystemRoot% folder. If you encounter problems with a 16-bit application, you might find clues in these two files.

> **Tip** **Learn how to spot a 16-bit application**
>
> Because most Windows 3.*x*–based programs run properly under Windows XP, it's sometimes difficult to tell 16-bit and 32-bit applications apart. Here are two methods for determining whether an application is 16-bit or 32-bit: Right-click the program's executable file and then choose Properties. If you see a Version tab, it's a 32-bit program. Or, if the program is running, press Ctrl+Alt+Delete to open Windows Task Manager. On the Processes tab, look in the Image Name column for the name of the program's executable file. If any 16-bit programs are running, you'll find an entry for Ntvdm.exe, the virtual DOS machine. Just above it in the list, you'll see indented entries for Wowexec.exe (the Windows on Windows subsystem) and the executable name of each 16-bit program running in that virtual machine.

By default, Windows XP treats each running 16-bit application as a thread within a single virtual machine. If you're running multiple 16-bit applications, they share a common memory space, and a crash in one Windows 3.*x*–based application will typically bring down all the others—causing you to lose any unsaved information in all 16-bit applications. If you regularly run multiple 16-bit applications and one of them hangs or crashes frequently, you should run it in a separate memory space. To do so, follow these steps:

1 Create a shortcut to the program. Right-click the shortcut icon, and then choose Properties.

2 On the Shortcut tab, click the Advanced button.

Installing, Uninstalling, and Managing Programs

3 Select the Run In Separate Memory Space check box. (See Figure 4-3.)

4 Click OK, and then close all open dialog boxes to apply the change.

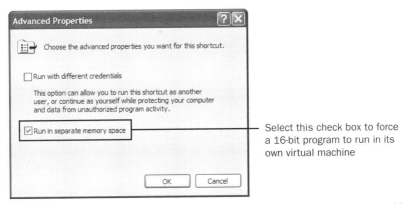

Select this check box to force
a 16-bit program to run in its
own virtual machine

Figure 4-3. A program running in separate memory space won't cause problems for other 16-bit programs running at the same time.

Before deciding to run multiple 16-bit applications on separate virtual machines, you should weigh the tradeoffs. The downside is that this approach uses extra memory. (Windows Task Manager can help you measure the exact differences in RAM consumption for each scenario as explained in "Monitoring Memory Usage," page 409.) However, there are several benefits, including preemptive multitasking, better responsiveness, and the ability to run multiple instances of applications that normally do not allow you to do so. In general, this option is best reserved for mission-critical legacy applications.

Note Command.com, the MS-DOS command processor, is a 16-bit application included with Windows XP. If you type **command** in the Run box, Windows starts a new MS-DOS virtual machine. Don't confuse this option with Cmd.exe, the 32-bit Windows XP Command Prompt program. For most command-line tasks, Cmd is preferred; reserve Command.com for those rare occasions when you want to run a 16-bit MS-DOS program.

Installing and Configuring MS-DOS Programs

By definition, all programs originally written for MS-DOS are 16-bit programs. As such, they run on a virtual machine alongside their 16-bit counterparts developed for Windows 3.*x*.

To control the behavior of MS-DOS-based programs, you use a properties dialog box whose design hasn't changed much since Windows 95. Custom property settings for each program are stored in a shortcut file called a *program information file* (PIF).

Chapter 4

Tip Set global PIF options

Is the default MS-DOS environment not quite right? You can adjust the default settings that apply to all MS-DOS programs by editing the settings stored in %SystemRoot%_default.pif. When you double-click the icon for an MS-DOS-based program and Windows can't find a matching PIF, it uses the settings recorded here. Likewise, when you create a new PIF, it starts with these default settings. If you want an MS-DOS batch file to run each time any MS-DOS program starts up, save the file as %SystemRoot%_default.bat.

You can create multiple shortcuts (PIFs) for a single MS-DOS program, each with its own custom settings, such as a default data file or working directory. When you right-click the icon for an MS-DOS executable file and make any changes to its properties, Windows saves your changes in the same folder, creating or updating a file with the same name as the executable file and the extension .pif. You can change the name of the shortcut file or move it to another folder.

The PIF format is binary and can't be edited except through the properties dialog box. Right-click the icon for the MS-DOS program's executable file to display this dialog box, which adds four tabs containing options that are exclusively available to MS-DOS programs. Using the Misc tab, shown in Figure 4-4, for instance, you can disable Windows shortcut keys that conflict with shortcuts in the MS-DOS program. Options on other tabs allow you to adjust the amount of memory allocated to a program, specify the program's initial display mode (full-screen or windowed), and change the icon associated with the program, among other things.

Figure 4-4. The Font, Memory, Screen, and Misc tabs in this dialog box control settings that are exclusive to MS-DOS programs.

Chapter 4

> **Note** For a concise explanation of each option in the properties dialog box for an MS-DOS program, right-click the option and then use the context-sensitive What's This? command. Alternatively, click the title bar's question mark icon and then click the option that needs explanation.

You can run any character-based program written for MS-DOS in full-screen mode or in a window. (Graphics-based programs run only in full-screen mode.) If you run a program in full-screen mode, it looks exactly like it does when you run it under MS-DOS. If you run it in a window, it has a title bar, a Control menu, and other familiar window management features.

> **Tip** **Switch to full screen and back again**
> To switch an MS-DOS program window between full-screen and windowed views, use the keyboard shortcut Alt+Enter. If the Alt+Enter shortcut is disabled (because it's used by the MS-DOS program for another purpose) and the program is currently in full-screen view, press Alt+Tab or Ctrl+Esc to switch to another program, or tap the Windows logo key to display the Start menu. Then right-click the taskbar button for the program you switched from. Choose Properties from the shortcut menu, click the Options tab in the properties dialog box, and then select the Window option button.

Running some MS-DOS programs properly might require that you change the system configuration used by the MS-DOS virtual machine. Two files, Autoexec.nt and Config.nt, serve this function in Windows XP. These two files serve a purpose similar to that of Autoexec.bat and Config.sys in MS-DOS and Windows 95/98, with several important differences:

- Autoexec.nt and Config.nt are located by default in the %SystemRoot%\System32 folder. (The corresponding files on an MS-DOS or Windows 95/98 machine are in the root folder of drive C.)
- In Windows XP (as in Windows 2000), you can create custom versions of Autoexec.nt and Config.nt for specific applications. To associate your custom configuration files with a specific application, copy the default files to a separate location and edit them as needed. Next, open the properties dialog box for the MS-DOS program, click the Advanced button on the Program tab, and then enter the correct locations as shown below. (Note that this dialog box includes a Compatible Timer Hardware Emulation check box. This option imposes a performance penalty, so you should select it only if your application won't run with the box cleared.)

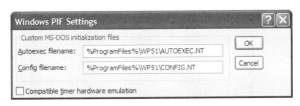

Chapter 4

- Commands you enter in these two files affect only the MS-DOS subsystem. Many commands, such as Buffers and Break, are ignored, although they can be entered for compatibility purposes when an MS-DOS program insists that they be present. Windows XP includes its own versions of Himem.sys, Ansi.sys, Country.sys, and Setver.exe. Avoid using the following unsupported and unnecessary Windows 95/98 drivers in Config.nt: Emm386.exe, Smartdrv.sys, Ramdrive.sys, and Dblspace.sys/Drvspace.sys. Windows XP ignores all entries in Autoexec.nt except those defined by Set or Path commands, which it adds to the startup environment for that MS-DOS virtual machine.

Making a Program Available to All Users

Most of the time, when you install a Windows program from an administrator's account, its shortcuts are placed in %AllUsersProfile%\Start Menu\Programs, so that any user who wants to run that program can do so. Exceptionally well-written programs ask you whether you want to install the program for all users or only for the currently logged-on user. (This option is especially appropriate when you're installing a utility program that you don't want other users to be able to run.)

What should you do when setup installs a program only for the currently logged-on user? If you want other users to have access to the program, you have two choices:

- Log on using each user account and rerun the setup program. This option gives you the flexibility to make a program available to selected users, but it has one significant drawback: You have to remember to run that setup program again every time you create a new user account.

- For simple programs that don't require per-user settings to be added to the registry before running, you might be able to simply add a shortcut to %AllUsersProfile%\Start Menu\Programs. To ensure that a program is available to all current and future users, move the program's shortcut from your personal profile to the All Users folder. To move the program's shortcut, follow these steps:

    1 Click the Start button, right-click the shortcut or group you want to move, and then choose Cut from the shortcut menu.

    2 Right-click the Start menu and then choose Explore All Users.

    3 Select the Programs folder, right-click, and then choose Paste.

Use the same basic procedure, only in reverse, if you want to move a program shortcut or group from the All Users folder to your personal profile so that it is no longer available to other users. They will still be able to launch the program from the Run box or from an Explorer window, but you will have removed the most visible means of access to the program.

Forcing Older Programs to Run Properly

Windows XP goes to heroic lengths to run many 32-bit Windows applications that refused to run under Windows 2000. The list of compatible software includes thousands of productivity titles and games. Unfortunately, not all programs that ran correctly under previous Windows versions will run under Windows XP, and some can cause serious problems. When you attempt to install a program that is known to have compatibility problems, Windows XP should display a message like the one shown here. Don't take this message lightly! If a patch is available, download and install it immediately. If no patch is available, do not install the program.

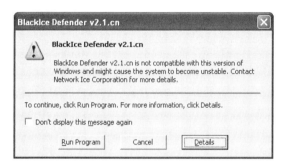

If you run across a program that worked flawlessly under a previous Windows version but refuses to install or run under Windows XP, you might be able to run the program by adjusting its compatibility options. (This functionality was available in Windows 2000 via a Resource Kit utility called Apcompat.exe.) You can reset compatibility options with the Program Compatibility Wizard or use the properties dialog box for a program shortcut. Both options have the same effect—they try to fool the underlying program into believing that it's running on an earlier version of Windows. This strategy is especially effective at getting around a setup program that stops when it finds a Windows version number it doesn't understand.

> **Note** Tinkering with compatibility options is a risky strategy, especially when the program in question is a low-level utility such as an antivirus program or disk partitioning tool that was not specifically designed for Windows XP. Even a seemingly innocuous CD-burning program can become a major troublemaker if it tries to install an incompatible device driver. When in doubt, your best bet is to do more research before trying to tweak compatibility options.

To use the Program Compatibility Wizard, open the All Programs menu and then click Accessories. Click the program shortcut to launch the wizard and follow its step-by-step instructions. This is the only way to adjust compatibility settings on programs that are on removable media (including CDs) or on shared network drives.

If you've successfully set up a program but it refuses to run, the easiest and fastest way to set compatibility options is to work directly with a program shortcut. Right-click the shortcut icon and choose Properties, and then click the Compatibility tab, as shown in Figure 4-5.

Chapter 4

Select the Run This Program In Compatibility Mode For check box, and choose one of the four available operating systems: Windows 95, Windows 98/Windows Me, Windows NT 4.0 (Service Pack 5), or Windows 2000. Use the Display Settings options to deal with programs that experience video problems when run at higher resolutions and color depths. The Input Settings option (which appears only if you've installed Service Pack 1 or later for Windows XP) disables "advanced text services," which include handwriting recognition and speech recognition. Because advanced text services reduce performance, you should disable them for your older programs that can't use these cutting-edge input methods.

> For additional tools and documentation about working with existing applications and ensuring that applications you develop are compatible with Windows XP, visit the Windows Application Compatibility page at *http://www.microsoft.com/windows/appcompatibility/*.

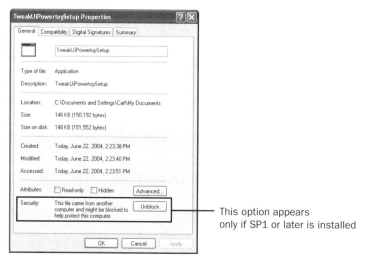

This option appears only if SP1 or later is installed

Figure 4-5. Use these compatibility options to fool an older Windows program into running on Windows XP.

Managing Installed Programs

In its default view, the Add Or Remove Programs dialog box lists installed programs in alphabetical order by program name. If you're ready to do some spring cleaning, use the drop-down Sort By list in the upper right corner to sort by the date last used. Programs you haven't used recently are possible candidates for removal. If your goal is to free up disk space, sort by size; the biggest disk hogs appear at the top of the resulting list.

For programs that include multiple setup options, use the Add Or Remove Programs dialog box to rerun setup and remove installed components or add options that you previously bypassed. Programs that use Windows Installer as their setup engine typically offer a Change button for this purpose. Installer-based applications (including major Microsoft Internet

Explorer upgrades) may also offer a Repair option, typically buried under a support link. In theory, Windows Installer should be able to detect problems caused by a damaged or deleted DLL and repair the component automatically when you run the application—prompting you for installation media if necessary. Use the Repair button to completely refresh the set of installed program files and accompanying registry keys and values.

Inside Out

Correct the usage data

When you select an item in the list of currently installed programs, Windows displays the program's size, its frequency of use, and the date it was last used—at least it's supposed to. That information is often incomplete and inaccurate, however.

The size is provided by the program's installer; Windows makes no attempt to verify its accuracy. Some installers, particularly older ones, don't provide size information, so this section is blank.

Frequency of use is shown as one of three values: Rarely (for items that have been used fewer than three times in the last 30 days), Occasionally (items that have been used from three to ten times in the last 30 days), or Frequently (items that have been used more than ten times). Unfortunately, Windows does a poor job of tracking usage, and these values are wrong as often as not. Similarly, the date last used is not always recorded correctly.

What can you do to get more accurate information? It sometimes (but not always) helps to remove the registry keys that Add Or Remove Programs reads when you open it. If the keys don't exist, it rebuilds them from a variety of other nooks and crannies in the registry. Here's how you force Windows to rebuild these keys:

1   Use a registry editor to back up the HKLM\SOFTWARE\Microsoft\Windows\
    CurrentVersion\App Management\ARPCache key, including all its subkeys.

2   Delete HKLM\SOFTWARE\Microsoft\Windows\CurrentVersion\App Management\
    ARPCache.

3   Open Add Or Remove Programs. (This will take a bit longer than usual, since it needs
    to first rebuild the ARPCache key.)

If you're not satisfied with the result, return to your registry editor, delete the new version of ARPCache, and then restore the backup you created at the beginning of this excursion to the inner workings of Add Or Remove Programs.

Service Pack 2 adds a tiny, but welcome, improvement to the Add Or Remove Programs dialog box shown in Figure 4-1 on page 111. The Show Updates check box toggles the appearance of service packs, hotfixes, and other items installed by Windows Update in the list of

Chapter 4

installed programs. These updates appear as subentries indented below the program they update. Over a period of time, Windows Updates adds dozens of items to the list, and these rarely removed items add lots of clutter, sometimes making it more difficult to find a program that you want to update or remove.

Uninstalling Programs

To remove an installed Windows program, open the Add Or Remove Programs dialog box from Control Panel, select the program's entry in the list on the Change Or Remove Programs page, and click the Remove or Change/Remove button.

> **Caution**   Click the Remove button at your own risk. Although most installer programs are courteous enough to ask your permission before launching the uninstaller program, some programs simply remove themselves, immediately and without any further prompting.

Here are some basic facts you should know about uninstalling programs:

- Windows XP warns you if you attempt to remove a program while other users are logged on. For safety's sake, you should always completely log off any other user accounts before attempting to remove a program.

- Most uninstall programs leave at least a few traces of the program behind, either inadvertently or by design. For instance, programs that create data files typically do not remove custom user settings and data files as part of the uninstall process.

- You can remove programs from the Add Or Remove Programs dialog box only if they were originally installed with a Windows–compatible setup program. Some programs (typically utilities) work by copying their files to a folder. In this case, you uninstall the program by manually removing its files and any shortcuts.

- In some cases, a poorly written uninstall routine may leave a phantom entry behind in the list of installed programs, even after it has successfully removed all traces of the program itself. To remove an item from the list in this case, remove entries manually, using Registry Editor. Detailed instructions are available in Knowledge Base article 314481, "How to Manually Remove Programs from the Add or Remove Programs Tool."

Managing Program Shortcuts

During setup, most Windows-compatible programs typically create one or more shortcuts on the Start menu (and occasionally on the desktop and Quick Launch toolbar as well). By tweaking shortcuts, you can control exactly how and when programs start up. Here are some useful improvements you can make to a generic program shortcut:

- **Specify startup options**   Create multiple versions of a program shortcut for special purposes. Many programs allow command-line arguments (the name of a file or

Chapter 4

startup folder, for instance) or startup switches that control default settings. With Microsoft Word, for instance, you can use the /T switch followed by a template name (don't add a space) to create a new document using that template. Open the shortcut's properties dialog box, and enter the arguments or switches immediately after the command name in the Target box, as shown in Figure 4-6. (Note that in this example we've also adjusted the Start In location and added a shortcut key.)

Figure 4-6. Tweak the properties of program shortcuts to set command-line arguments, assign shortcut keys, and add ScreenTips.

- **Assign a shortcut key**   Click in the Shortcut Key field and press a key combination that you want to use for launching or switching to this program. The shortcut key you assign must consist of one character key (a letter, number, or symbol) plus at least two of the following three keys: Ctrl, Alt, and Shift. (If you press a character key only, Windows automatically adds Ctrl+Alt.) Shortcut keys work only when assigned to a program shortcut on the Start menu, the All Programs menu, or the desktop. The shortcut key you define will not work if it conflicts with a combination used in the program whose window currently has the focus.

Tip   Put the Windows logo key to work

Most keyboards sold with Windows PCs include a Windows logo key that's hard-wired to several useful system functions. (For a complete list of Windows logo key shortcuts, search the Help And Support Center for "Natural Keyboard Shortcuts.") Windows doesn't allow you to use the Windows logo key as part of user-defined shortcuts, but a utility called WinKey adds this capability. Download it from Copernic Technologies at *http://www.copernic.com/winkey*.

- **Add a ScreenTip**   The text in the shortcut's Comments field appears in the ScreenTip when you hover the mouse pointer over the shortcut. You can add comments to your custom shortcuts to explain their purpose. Likewise, if you would like to remove the comment text of an existing shortcut, delete it here.

Chapter 4

For tips on how to customize the Start menu and Quick Launch bar, see "Making It Easy to Start Your Favorite Programs," page 443.

Deleting Obsolete Program Shortcuts

 Just as your Internet Explorer Favorites menu invariably ends up with a collection of dead links, your Start menu, desktop, and other folders will accumulate dead program shortcuts and other links. This can occur, for example, when you uninstall a program but not all of the program's shortcuts get deleted. When you click one of these dead links—that is, a shortcut whose target no longer exists in its original location—Windows offers to search for the target file. The search usually comes up empty.

Windows doesn't provide an easy way to find and remove dead links. However, the Windows XP Resource Kit Tools include a utility called Link Check Wizard (Chklnks.exe). This useful application scans your system's hard drives for shortcut files, checks each one to see if the target file still exists, and lists the dead links, which you can selectively remove. You can install the Link Check Wizard as part of the Resource Kit Tools included on this book's companion CD.

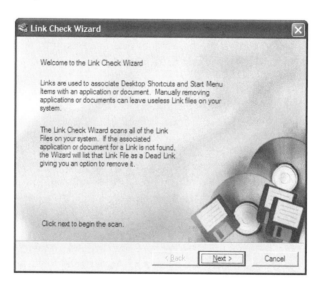

Here's a hidden feature of Link Check Wizard: In the list of dead links that it generates, right-clicking a link name displays information about the link, including its location and the (former) location of the target file.

Running a Program as Another User

In some situations, you might not be able to run a program using the account under which you're currently logged on. This is most likely if you're logged on using an account in the Users group (that is, as a limited user) or the Power Users group and the program you want to use requires administrative privileges. You have three options:

- If Fast User Switching is enabled on your computer, click the Start button, choose Log Off, and then click the Switch User button. Log on using an administrative account and run the program. If the program will take some time to complete, you can allow it to remain running in the background while you switch back to your regular user account. Fast User Switching is not available on a Windows XP Professional machine that is joined to a domain. For more information, see "Configuring Fast User Switching," page 246.

- For immediate access to a program without leaving your currently logged-on account, use the Run As option. The Run As menu choice is available when you right-click any shortcut or program icon. On some special-purpose shortcuts—most notably short-cuts placed on the All Programs menu by Microsoft Office—you have to hold down the Shift key as you right-click to display the Run As option. Select the option shown here, The Following User, and enter the user name and password of an account that has the desired permissions.

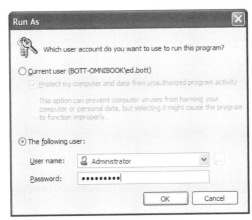

Tip   Choose an account each time

You can configure any program shortcut so that Windows prompts you for logon credentials every time you double-click that shortcut. This is an ideal solution for the Computer Management option in the Administrative Tools folder, for instance. To specify this option, right-click the shortcut icon and choose Properties. On the Shortcut tab, click the Advanced button and select the Run With Different Credentials check box.

● Use the Runas command from a command window, from the Run dialog box, or in the Target field of a shortcut's properties dialog box to specify that you want a program to start with a specific user account. For instance, you can create a shortcut that opens a Command Prompt window using another user's permissions by typing the following syntax in the Target field of the shortcut's properties dialog box (substituting the actual user name, of course):

```
runas /user:username cmd
```

After you issue the command or activate the shortcut, you'll be prompted to enter the password for the specified user account. For security reasons, you cannot save the password with the shortcut. Note that the Runas command does not work with Microsoft Management Console (MMC) shortcuts; if you're logged in as a limited user and you want to start the Computer Management console using an administrator's account, right-click and use the Run As command on the shortcut menu.

The Run As menu choice works with most third-party programs and many Windows utilities and Control Panel options. (Hold down the Shift key when right-clicking a Control Panel icon to use this option.) A handful of applications that are started indirectly by Windows XP cannot be started with the Run As menu choice. You'll strike out if you try to use Run As with Windows Explorer, for instance. The option is also unavailable for desktop items created by the system and for objects in the Network Connections folder. Interestingly, a full menu of options is available when you press Shift and right-click any icon in the Printers And Faxes folder, and then choose Run As. Use this option if you're running under an ordinary user account and need to delete or pause items in the print queue that were created by another user.

Inside Out

Use Run As to run programs more safely

In Windows XP, you can prevent a program from taking advantage of administrative permissions by using an option in the Run As dialog box. Right-click the program shortcut and choose Run As from the shortcut menu. In the Run As dialog box, select Current User, and then select the Protect My Computer And Data From Unauthorized Program Activity check box. This option runs the program using the credentials of the current user (and, therefore, that user's privileges), with one significant restriction: It prevents the program from making any changes to the registry. This option is especially effective when you're trying out a new program that is untrusted; by selecting this check box, you can safely run the program and see if it generates any error messages or displays any unusual behavior.

Chapter 5

Setting Up and Troubleshooting Hardware

It's probably only a slight exaggeration to say that no two computers are alike. Motherboards, disks and controllers, video and network adapters, and peripherals of all shapes and sizes combine to create a nearly infinite number of possible computer configurations.

Although Microsoft Windows XP doesn't work with every computer peripheral ever made, the list of compatible devices is extensive and impressive. For supported hardware upgrades, Windows detects the device automatically and installs the correct driver software so that you can use the device and its full array of features.

If Windows has a problem with a device, you have your choice of troubleshooting tools. Although the basic Device Manager interface closely resembles its predecessors, the Windows XP version of this essential utility is more versatile.

A Crash Course in Device Drivers

Before Windows can work with any piece of hardware, it requires a compatible, properly con-figured device driver. *Drivers* are compact control programs that hook directly into Windows and handle the essential tasks of communicating your instructions to a hardware device and then relaying data back to you. After you set up a hardware device, its driver loads automati-cally and runs as part of the operating system, without requiring any further intervention on your part.

At Home with Windows XP

You'll encounter no differences in working with hardware devices when you switch between computers running Windows XP Home Edition and Windows XP Professional. The proce-dures for installing devices, working with device drivers, and troubleshooting hardware prob-lems are the same in both versions of Windows. However, Windows XP Professional does include a command-line utility called Driverquery that is not available in Home Edition.

Windows XP includes an enormous library of drivers—for printers, keyboards, scanners, mice and related pointing devices, digital cameras, and other devices—in the %SystemRoot%\Driver Cache\i386 folder. All drivers stored here are certified to be fully compatible with Windows XP and digitally signed by Microsoft. When you install a new Plug and Play–compatible device, Windows checks this location first. If it finds a suitable driver, installation proceeds automatically. (The original release of Windows XP stored this cache of signed, certified drivers in a single compressed file called Driver.cab. A supplement to this driver collection is included with each service pack; Service Pack 1, for instance, includes a file called Sp1.cab, which contains updated versions of some of the drivers that were in the original Driver.cab file as well as new signed drivers that became available after the initial release of Windows XP. In addition, Microsoft regularly makes new, certified drivers available through Windows Update.)

To be properly installed in Windows XP, a hardware driver must have a Setup Information file (with the extension .inf). This is a text file that contains detailed information about the device to be installed, including the names of its driver files, the locations where they are to be installed, any required registry settings, and version information. All devices with drivers found in Driver.cab include corresponding Setup Information files, located in the %SystemRoot%\Inf folder. When you install a new driver, it might also add a Setup Information file to this folder.

The basic structure of a Setup Information file is similar to an old-fashioned Windows 3.*x*–style .ini file. Each piece of setup information appears on its own line under a bracketed section heading, as in the following example (taken from a much larger .inf file for Kodak's DC-200 and DC-210 digital cameras):

```
;
; DC240 and compatible USB camera
;
[DC240]
Include=sti.inf
Needs=STI.USBSection
CopyFiles=DC240.Files,Kodak.Color
AddReg=DC240.AddReg
DeviceData=DC240.DeviceData
SubClass=StillImage
DeviceType=2
Capabilities=0x35
UninstallSection=
Events=DC240.Events
ICMProfiles=kodak_dc.icm
[DC240.Services]
Include=sti.inf
Needs=STI.USBSection.Services
[DC240.DeviceData]
Server=local
UI DLL=sti.dll
UI Class ID={4DB1AD10-3391-11D2-9A33-00C04FA36145}
```

Chapter 5

Although the Setup Information file is a crucial part of the driver installation process, you don't work with it directly. Instead, this file supplies instructions that the operating system uses during Plug and Play detection, or when you use the Add Hardware Wizard or a Setup program to install a device.

> **Note** The syntax of Setup Information files is complex, and the intricacies of .inf files can trip up even experienced software developers. If you find that a driver setup routine isn't working properly, you might be tempted to try editing the Setup Information file to work around the hang-up. Trust us: That approach is almost certain to fail. In fact, by tinkering with .inf files, you run the risk of corrupting registry settings and crashing your system.

Are Signed Drivers Safer?

Windows XP includes a mechanism for attaching a digital signature to a driver file. A digitally signed driver is relatively easy to spot, because it's consistently marked by the logo shown here.

In its default settings, Windows XP warns you if you're attempting to install a driver that isn't digitally signed. During the driver setup process, you'll see a strongly worded message like the one shown in Figure 5-1.

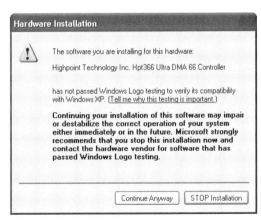

Figure 5-1. Take this warning seriously. Unsigned, incompatible drivers can cause performance and stability problems.

In general, you should prefer signed drivers for two reasons:

- The digital signature confirms that the driver has undergone extensive compatibility testing in Microsoft's Windows Hardware Quality Labs (WHQL). It represents a strong assurance that the driver follows installation guidelines and that you can count on it not to cause your system to crash or become unstable.

● The signature means that the driver hasn't been tampered with by other installation programs or by a virus or Trojan horse program.

Don't underestimate the negative consequences that can result from installing an unsigned driver that turns out to be faulty. Because hardware drivers access low-level functions in the operating system, a badly written driver is much more likely to cause blue-screen errors than a buggy program. Even a seemingly innocuous driver can result in sudden crashes that result in loss of data and prevent you from restarting your computer.

Sometimes you will have to make the difficult decision of whether to install an unsigned driver or give up the use of a piece of hardware. If the hardware device is essential and replacing it would be prohibitively expensive, you might decide that the risk is worth it. In other cases, the choice is more difficult, as in the case when you have to choose between a signed driver that offers a minimal set of features and an unsigned alternative driver that allows you to take advantage of special features that are specific to your hardware.

Tip   **Give unsigned drivers a workout**

If you decide to take a chance on an unsigned driver, your best strategy is to back up your data first, install the new driver, and then thoroughly test it right away, without introducing any additional software or drivers. (Windows automatically sets a System Restore point when you install an unsigned driver.) Run every application that's installed on your computer. Try to run a few CPU-intensive and disk-intensive tasks at the same time. Open and save files, especially big, complex ones. Try running disk utilities such as Chkdsk and Defrag. If the new driver is going to cause problems with the hardware and software you currently use, you want to find out immediately after installing it so you can roll back to your previous configuration with as little hassle as possible.

As noted earlier, Windows XP normally warns you if you're about to install an unsigned driver. If you're an experienced Windows user and you're confident of your ability to identify and select compatible drivers, you can change the default settings to eliminate this warning completely. You can also change system settings to prevent users from installing any unsigned drivers, a strategy that might be appropriate on a shared machine where you're concerned that kids or coworkers will undermine system stability by trying to install an incompatible device. To adjust driver-signing policies, follow these steps:

1   From Control Panel, open System and click the Hardware tab.

2   Click the Driver Signing button.

3   In the Driver Signing Options dialog box, shown in Figure 5-2, choose the action you want Windows to take whenever a user is about to install an unsigned driver.

■   **Ignore**   This option allows the user to install any unsigned driver without having to click through a warning message.

- ■ **Warn** This is the Windows XP default. Users can choose to override the warning and install an unsigned driver.
- ■ **Block** When this option is selected, Windows will not allow any unsigned drivers to be installed.

4 To apply the selected action only to the current user, clear the Make This Action The System Default check box. To apply the selected action to all users, select this check box. (This option is available only if you're logged on as an administrator.)

5 Click OK to apply the changes.

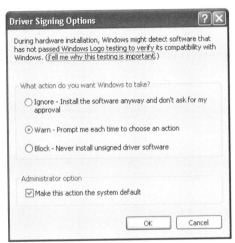

Figure 5-2. Take your choice: You can tighten or loosen driver security with this dialog box.

In the case of specific drivers that are known to cause serious problems, a Windows XP feature called Windows Driver Protection will refuse to install that driver regardless of the policy you've set. When you run the Add Hardware Wizard and point to a driver that is in the database of blocked drivers, you see a dialog box like the one shown in Figure 5-3.

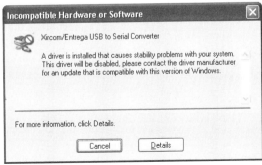

Figure 5-3. Windows Driver Protection blocks installation of drivers that are known to cause serious stability problems.

Inside Out

Establish a driver policy

The Make This Action The System Default option is equivalent to using Local Security Policy to set driver-signing policies. (Local Security Policy is a Microsoft Management Console [MMC] snap-in that's available only in Windows XP Professional.) Security policies provide an effective way to prevent users from making unwanted changes to the driver-signing policy you establish; one specific setting you choose in Local Security Policy determines which Driver Signing Options dialog box options are available to nonadministrative users. After you, as an administrator, set the system default action for handling unsigned drivers (using the Driver Signing Options dialog box or Local Security Policy), only options that are at least as strict appear in the Driver Signing Options dialog box when displayed by a nonadministrative user. (All three options are always available to administrators, although an administrator must select Make This Action The System Default to select an option less strict than the current default.)

If you'd prefer to implement this setting as a part of Local Security Policy (there's no advantage to doing so, unless you have other policies to set), follow these steps: In Control Panel, choose Administrative Tools (in the Performance And Maintenance category), Local Security Policy. In the Local Security Settings console, open Security Settings\ Local Policies\Security Options. Double-click Devices: Unsigned Driver Installation Behavior. Select one of the three options, which, despite the different wording, correspond to the options in the Driver Signing Options dialog box: Silently Succeed (Ignore), Warn But Allow Installation (Warn), or Do Not Allow Installation (Block).

Windows provides multiple warnings and notifications when it takes the drastic step of blocking a driver. The Add Hardware Wizard concludes with a Cannot Install This Hardware message, which includes the text "This driver has been blocked from loading." The pop-up message in the notification area also displays a failure message, as shown here. However, failed driver installations are not recorded in Event Viewer.

Will Drivers Written for Other Windows Versions Work with Windows XP?

If a signed, Windows XP–compatible driver is not available for a given device, you might be able to use a driver originally written for a previous version of Windows.

For the best chance of success, find a driver written for Microsoft Windows 2000. Many (but certainly not all) Windows 2000 drivers work properly in Windows XP.

Some Windows Driver Model (WDM) drivers that were originally written for Microsoft Windows Me might also work in Windows XP, but only if the accompanying Setup Information (.inf) file includes specific instructions for Windows 2000/XP.

Drivers originally written for Microsoft Windows 95/98 or Microsoft Windows NT 4 or earlier are unlikely to work properly with Windows XP, because the architectural differences between those operating systems and Windows XP are just too great.

> **Tip** **Dig deep for drivers**
> It's not always clear from the labeling on the outside of a floppy disk or CD that the drivers it contains are for multiple Windows versions. Sometimes the structure of the disk itself can offer important clues. Look for a Win2000 or W2K subdirectory, for example, and point the Add Hardware Wizard to that location when prompted. If a suitable .inf file is available, you may be able to complete the installation.

Setting Up a New Device

Since its introduction in Windows 95, Plug and Play technology has evolved tremendously. Early incarnations of this technology were notoriously unreliable, leading some users to dismiss the feature as "plug and pray." In recent years, however, hardware and software standards have converged to make most device configuration tasks completely automatic. With true Plug and Play devices, Windows XP handles virtually all of the work of configuring computer hardware and attached devices. For Plug and Play to work properly, all the pieces of a computer system must be capable of working together to perform hardware configuration tasks, specifically:

- The system BIOS must be capable of responding to Plug and Play and power management events. By definition, any system with an ACPI BIOS includes this capability. Non-ACPI computers with a Plug and Play BIOS are capable of performing a subset of Plug and Play functions but will not be as capable as ACPI computers.

- The operating system must be capable of responding to Plug and Play events. Windows XP fully supports the Plug and Play standard.

- The device must be capable of identifying itself, listing its required resources (including drivers), and allowing software to configure it. The Microsoft "Designed for Windows" logo identifies hardware that meets all these requirements.

- The device driver must be capable of interacting with the operating system and responding to device notification and power management events. A Plug and Play driver can load automatically when Windows detects that a device has been plugged in, and it can suspend and resume properly along with the system.

> **Tip**   **Run setup software first**
>
> In many cases, new hardware devices include a setup CD that contains driver files and utility software. The best time to run this CD is *before* plugging in the device. If the drivers are signed, the setup program copies the driver files and Setup Information (.inf) file to your hard disk so that installation can proceed automatically when you plug in the device.

In Windows XP, Plug and Play support is optimized for USB, IEEE 1394 (FireWire), PCM-CIA (PC Card), and PCI devices. By definition, any USB or PCMCIA device is a Plug and Play device, as are virtually all PCI devices. Devices that connect to a parallel or serial port may or may not be fully Plug and Play compatible, and legacy devices that use the ISA bus are by definition not capable of being managed by Plug and Play. If your computer includes one or more USB 2 ports, you must have the proper drivers installed before USB 2 devices will be detected correctly. This support was not available in the original release of Windows XP but was added in Service Pack 1.

Managing the Plug and Play Process

When you install a Plug and Play device for the first time, Windows reads the Plug and Play identification tag in the hardware's BIOS or firmware. It then compares that ID tag with a master list of corresponding tags drawn from all the Setup Information files in the hidden %SystemRoot%\Inf folder. If it finds a signed driver with a matching tag, it installs the correct driver file (or files) and makes other necessary system modifications with no intervention required from you. Unlike previous Windows versions, which display the progress of Plug and Play operations in dialog boxes, Windows XP provides more subtle indications in the form of pop-up messages in the notification area. You might see a series of these notifications, culminating with the final message shown here.

When Windows detects a Plug and Play device (after you've plugged it into a USB port, for instance) but cannot locate a suitable signed device driver, it starts the Found New Hardware Wizard.

> **Note**   Any user can install a new device if a signed driver for that device is included in the Windows Driver Cache. To install any other driver, however (signed or unsigned), you must be logged on as a member of the local Administrators group to install hardware drivers. If you're logged on using an account without administrative permissions, you'll be prompted to supply an administrator's user name and password during hardware setup.

Chapter 5

The basic workings of the Found New Hardware Wizard should be familiar to anyone who's ever installed a device in any version of Windows. As Figure 5-4 shows, the wizard's opening screen offers two choices.

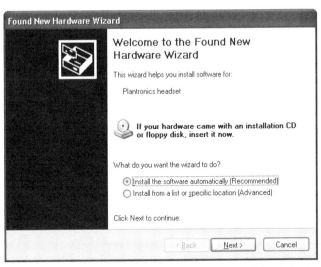

Figure 5-4. Select the second option instead of the default choice if you intend to use a downloaded hardware driver rather than a CD or floppy disk.

The exact procedure to follow next varies, depending on where the driver you plan to install is located:

- **The new device came with an installation CD or floppy disk containing Windows XP–compatible drivers** Choose the first option, Install The Software Automatically (Recommended), and then click Next. This option searches all removable drives and looks for suitable Setup Information files. If only one compatible driver is available, the wizard installs it automatically; if the wizard finds more than one compatible driver, it presents a list of drivers that match the Plug and Play ID tag of the new device and allows you to choose.

- **You've downloaded a Windows XP–compatible driver to a local or network drive** Choose the second option, Install From A List Or Specific Location (Advanced). After you click Next, you see the dialog box shown in Figure 5-5.

Chapter 5

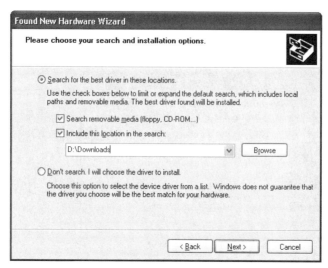

Figure 5-5. If you've downloaded a new driver, use this dialog box to specify its location.

Follow these steps to point the wizard to the correct driver files:

1 Choose the first option, Search For The Best Driver In These Locations.

2 Select the Include This Location In The Search option.

3 Enter the full path of the folder that contains the downloaded driver and Setup Information file, or click Browse to point to this location.

4 Click Next to search the specified location. Follow the prompts to complete the installation.

● **You want to choose a specific driver for the new hardware** Use this option to select a specific driver from several choices that might be compatible with the new device. For instance, you might want to bypass a signed driver included with Windows XP and instead use the manufacturer's unsigned driver, so that you can enable specific features of the new device.

To install an unsigned driver in place of a signed driver, follow these steps:

1 From the Found New Hardware Wizard, choose the second option, Install From A List Or Specific Location (Advanced). Click Next.

2 Select the Don't Search. I Will Choose The Driver To Install option, and click Next. The wizard displays a list of compatible drivers like the one shown on the next page.

Chapter 5

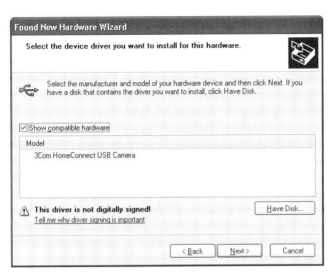

3 To expand the list so that all drivers in the selected device class are available, clear the Show Compatible Hardware check box.

4 Choose a device from the list, and click Next to complete the installation.

Configuring Non–Plug and Play Devices

As you might suspect, Windows will not automatically set up a non–Plug and Play device. However, the Windows XP Driver Cache contains hundreds of drivers for such devices, most of them relatively old but still worthwhile. Also, many non–Plug and Play devices have Windows 2000 drivers that are compatible with Windows XP and can be downloaded. If you own such a device, use the Add Hardware Wizard to complete the hardware setup process. After downloading compatible hardware drivers (or verifying that Windows XP includes built-in drivers for the device in question), follow these steps:

1 If the device includes a CD or a downloadable Setup program, run it now. This option places the driver files on your hard disk and simplifies later installation steps.

2 Connect the new hardware to your computer. In the case of an internal device such as an add-in card, turn off the computer, add the device, and then restart.

> **Note** Although you can try to run the Add Hardware Wizard without first installing a device, you're wasting your time. The wizard will shut down without completing its assigned task if you try to take this shortcut.

Chapter 5

3   Open Control Panel, open System, and then click Add Hardware Wizard on the Hardware tab.

4   Click Next to skip past the Welcome screen and begin searching for the installed device.

If the wizard finds the new device, you can select it to install the correct driver and finish the wizard. In most cases, the wizard won't find the new device and will instead prompt you to search for the device.

5   Click Yes when asked whether you've already installed the new device, and click Next to continue. The wizard displays a list of devices currently installed on the computer, similar to the one shown here.

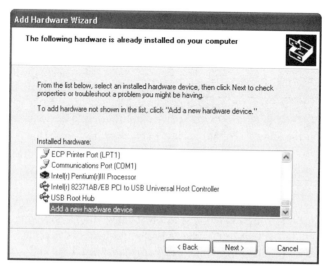

6   If the device you're trying to install is included in this list, select it. Otherwise, scroll to the bottom of the list and select Add A New Hardware Device. Click Next to continue.

7   On the next wizard screen, choose how you want to select the device to be installed.

  ■   For printers, network cards, modems, and other devices that can be detected mechanically, choose Search For And Install The Hardware Automatically (Recommended). After you click Next, the wizard quickly runs a detection module that searches for anything on its list of non–Plug and Play devices. If it finds the new device, it installs the driver automatically, and your work is finished. If the wizard doesn't find any new hardware, you'll be prompted to click Next and look manually; in this case, proceed to step 8.

  ■   If you'd prefer to skip the detection process, choose Install The Hardware That I Manually Select From A List (Advanced) and click Next.

8   From the Common Hardware Types list, select a hardware category (or the inclusive Show All Devices category) and click Next.

Chapter 5

9 From the master list of available drivers, which will look similar to the one shown in Figure 5-6, select the device manufacturer and the correct model. Click Next to continue. Follow the prompts to complete the wizard.

On the final page, the wizard reports on the result of the installation. If you encounter any problems, follow the troubleshooting links listed there.

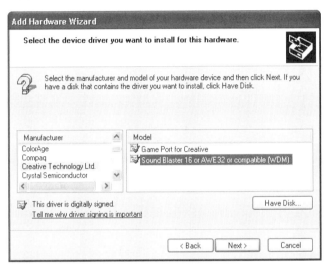

Figure 5-6. This master list shows all available device drivers, broken down by category and by manufacturer.

Finding Information About an Installed Driver

Knowing what hardware drivers are installed on your computer can make a huge difference when it comes to troubleshooting problems or configuring advanced features for a device. In every case, your starting point is Device Manager, a graphical utility that provides detailed information about all installed hardware, along with controls that you can use to configure devices, assign resources, and set advanced options. To open Device Manager, use any of the following techniques:

- From any command prompt, type **devmgmt.msc**.
- Right-click the My Computer icon on the Start menu or the desktop, choose Manage, and then select Device Manager from the left pane of the Computer Management console, under System Tools.
- From Control Panel, double-click the System icon and click the Device Manager button on the Hardware tab.

Chapter 5

141

As Figure 5-7 shows, Device Manager is organized as a hierarchical list that inventories every piece of hardware within or connected to your computer. The default view shows devices by type.

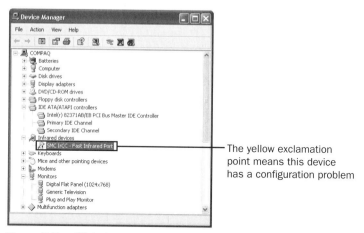

The yellow exclamation point means this device has a configuration problem

Figure 5-7.   Click the plus sign to the left of each category in Device Manager to see individual devices within that category.

Tip   Change the Device Manager view

You can change the default view of Device Manager to organize entries in the list by resource or by connection. Use Device Manager's View menu to switch between any of the four built-in views. Resource views are especially useful when you're trying to track down problems caused by IRQ conflicts. Choosing either the Resources By Type view or the Resources By Connection view shows a list of all devices in which you can see how DMA, IO addresses, and IRQs are assigned. Another option on the View menu lets you show hidden devices.

Viewing Device and Driver Details

To view information about a specific device, double-click its entry in Device Manager's list of installed devices. Each device has its own multitabbed properties dialog box. At a minimum, each device includes two tabs, General and Driver. The General tab lists basic facts about the device, including the device name, the name of its manufacturer, and its current status, as shown in Figure 5-8.

Chapter 5

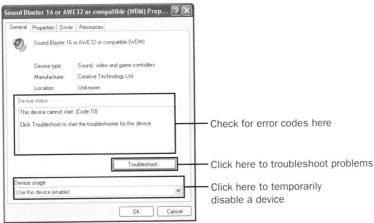

Check for error codes here

Click here to troubleshoot problems

Click here to temporarily disable a device

Figure 5-8. The General tab supplies basic information about a device and whether it is currently functioning properly.

The Driver tab, shown in Figure 5-9, lists version information about the currently installed driver for the selected device. Although the information shown here is sparse, it covers the essentials. You can tell at a glance who supplied the driver and whether it's digitally signed; you can also determine the date and version number of the driver, which is important when deciding whether you should download and install an available update.

Figure 5-9. The Driver tab, which is available for every installed device, offers valuable information and tools for managing installed drivers.

To view additional information about an installed driver, click the Driver Details button. As you can see from Figure 5-10, the Driver File Details dialog box provides far more comprehensive information, including the names and locations of all associated files. Selecting any file name from this list displays details for that file in the lower portion of the dialog box.

Chapter 5

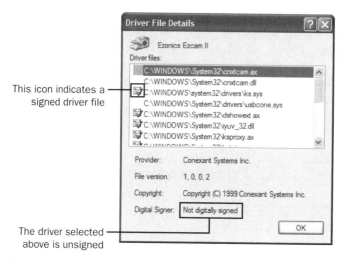

This icon indicates a
signed driver file

The driver selected
above is unsigned

Figure 5-10. This detailed view of an installed driver provides important information about each file the device uses. In this example, a number of files are not digitally signed.

In addition to this basic information, the properties dialog box for a given device can include any number of custom tabs. The Lucent Win Modem shown in Figure 5-11 is an extreme example, with a total of seven tabs, including the basic information on the General and Driver tabs. (Settings for modems are also available from the Phone And Modem Options dialog box in Control Panel.)

Figure 5-11. Any device that requires system resources includes the Resources tab in its Device Manager entry.

Inside Out

Take inventory of installed drivers

If you're running Windows XP Professional and want a more compact record of installed drivers in a format that you can review later, use the Driverquery command. Entering this command with no switches produces a simple list of installed devices and drivers. You can modify the output of the command with a variety of switches, and you can redirect the output of the command to a file so that you can load it in another program. For instance, you can use the /V switch to produce a detailed (verbose) listing, and add the /Fo switch with the Csv parameter to generate the output in a format suitable for use in Microsoft Excel:

```
driverquery /v /fo csv > drvlist.csv
```

Open Drvlist.csv in Excel to see a neatly formatted and highly detailed list of all your hardware. (For a full list of the switches available for the Driverquery command, add the /? switch or search for Driverquery in the Help And Support Center.)

By design, the information displayed in Device Manager is dynamic. When you add, remove, or reconfigure a device, the information stored here changes as well. To save a printed record of the settings for one or more devices, open Device Manager and choose Action, Print. For the most complete record of device settings and installed drivers, select the All Devices And System Summary option in the Print dialog box. But make sure you're prepared for the output, which can easily run to more than 20 pages!

Inside Out

Back Up Drivers

A nifty shareware program offers another solution to managing installed device drivers. Instead of simply displaying or printing all the pertinent information about drivers, HunterSoft My Drivers collects all of the files that comprise your device drivers and stores them so that they can be reinstalled easily. It backs up all your device drivers— whether they came from the original Windows installation, from the CD that came with the device, or from a downloaded file—into a single location for easy retrieval. My Drivers is available from a variety of shareware sites or directly from the developer, Huntersoft, at *http://www.zhangduo.com*.

Chapter 5

Troubleshooting Hidden and Unknown Devices

By default, Device Manager displays information about all currently installed and connected Plug and Play devices. To view devices that use non-Plug and Play drivers, as well as previously installed devices that are not currently connected, you need to tweak Device Manager slightly.

- To view non–Plug and Play devices, open Device Manager and choose View, Show Hidden Devices. In the default Devices By Type view, the formerly hidden devices appear under the Non–Plug And Play Drivers branch.

- To view devices that were once installed but are no longer attached to the computer, open a Command Prompt window and enter the command **set DEVMGR_SHOW_ NONPRESENT_DEVICES=1**. Then, from the same command prompt, type **devmgmt.msc** to open Device Manager. Choose View, Show Hidden Devices. The new instance of Device Manager now shows "ghosted" entries for devices that were once present. This technique is especially useful for fixing problems caused by leftover drivers after replacing a network card or video card—just delete the ghosted device.

- To see advanced details about a device, open a Command Prompt window and type the command **set DEVMGR_SHOW_DETAILS=1**. Then, from the same command prompt, type **devmgmt.msc** to open Device Manager. This environment variable adds a Details tab to every entry in the Device Manager list. The value shown under Device Instance Id is especially useful for tracking down devices that are detected incorrectly. The full details for a device ID shown here can be found in the registry, under HKLM\System\CurrentControlSet\Enum. Although we don't recommend idly deleting the found key, this information might provide enough information to figure out why a device isn't being identified properly.

Setting the DEVMGR environment variables described in this section affects only the instance of Device Manager launched from that Command Prompt window. If you want the changes to be persistent, open Control Panel, open System, click Environment Variables on the Advanced tab, and define new variables for either or both settings. If you add these variables to the User Variables section, the settings apply only to the current user; if you edit the System Variables section, the extra information is visible in Device Manager for all users of the current computer.

Adjusting Advanced Settings

Some devices include specialized tabs in the properties dialog box available from Device Manager. Controls on these additional tabs allow you to change advanced settings and properties for devices. For instance:

- Network cards and modems typically include a Power Management tab that allows you to control whether the device can force the computer to wake up from Standby mode. This option is useful if you have fax capabilities enabled for a modem, or if you use the Remote Desktop feature over the Internet on a machine that isn't always running at full power. On portable computers, you can also use this option to allow Windows to turn off a device to save power.

● The Volumes tab for a disk drive contains no information when you first display the properties dialog box for that device. Click the Populate button to read the volume information for the selected disk; you can then choose any of the listed volumes, as shown in Figure 5-12, and click the Properties button to check the disk for errors, run the Defrag utility, or perform other maintenance tasks. Although you can perform these same tasks by right-clicking a drive icon in the My Computer window, this option may be useful in situations where you have multiple hard disks installed and you suspect that one of those disks is having mechanical problems. Using this option allows you to quickly see which physical disk a given volume is stored on.

Figure 5-12. After you click the Populate button, the Volumes tab lists volumes on the selected drive and gives you full access to troubleshooting and maintenance tools.

● DVD drives offer an option to change the DVD region, which controls what disks can be played on that drive, as shown here.

Caution The DVD Region setting actually increments a counter on the physical drive itself, and that counter can be changed only a limited number of times. Be extremely careful with this setting, or you might end up losing the capability to play any regionally encoded DVDs in your collection.

● When working with network cards, you can often choose from a plethora of settings on an Advanced tab, as shown in this example. Randomly tinkering with these settings is almost always counterproductive; however, you may be able to solve specific performance or connectivity problems by adjusting settings as directed by the device manufacturer or a Microsoft Knowledge Base article.

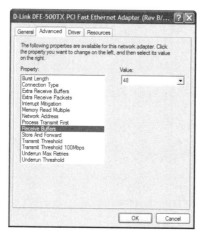

● Self-powered USB hubs (hubs that are connected to an AC power source) include a Power tab like the one shown here. Use the information on the Power tab to calculate the amount of power required by devices that draw power from the hub. If the total power requirement is more than the hub can supply, you might need a new hub.

Chapter 5

Setting Up and Troubleshooting Hardware

> **Tip   View devices over the network**
>
> You can use Device Manager to inspect settings on a remote computer. This option can be useful when troubleshooting from a distance. To view devices on another computer, open the Computer Management console (Compmgmt.msc), select the Computer Management icon at the top of the left pane, and choose Action, Connect To Another Computer. This feature allows you to view information but not change device settings. If you need to change device settings over a network, use Remote Assistance (described in "Connecting to Another PC with Remote Assistance," page 92) or a Remote Desktop connection (described in "Using Remote Desktop Connection," page 1051).

Viewing and Changing Resource Assignments

If you've worked with MS-DOS and early versions of Windows, you've probably struggled with device conflicts, most often when two or more pieces of hardware lay claim to the same IRQ. On modern computers with an ACPI BIOS and Windows XP, those sorts of conflicts are mercifully rare. In the original design of the IBM Personal Computer, IRQs were in short supply, with a total of 15 available, many of those reserved by system devices, such as communications ports, keyboards, and disk controllers. With older Windows versions, problems could occur when adding a new device such as a sound card or network adapter. If the new device was hardwired to a specific IRQ that was already in use, or if there were no free IRQs, the device simply would not work.

On computers running Windows 2000 and Windows XP with a mix of PCI add-in cards, the operating system takes advantage of the ACPI features on the motherboard to share scarce IRQs among multiple devices. In Device Manager, you can check resource allocations at a glance by choosing Resources By Type or Resources By Connection from the View menu. In the example shown here, IRQ 9 is being managed by the Microsoft ACPI-compliant system (an ISA device) and is shared successfully by two PCI devices; a pair of video cards are peacefully coexisting on IRQ 11.

Chapter 5

Under most circumstances, you cannot use Device Manager to change resource settings for a specific PCI or USB device. Resources are allocated automatically by the operating system at startup, and the controls to change resource settings are unavailable. Resource conflicts are most common with legacy devices, such as ISA-based sound cards that are not fully compatible with Plug and Play. Figure 5-13 shows the resource settings for a Plug and Play device that is in conflict with a legacy device. In this example, you might be able to adjust resource settings manually from the Resources tab: Clear the Use Automatic Settings check box and cycle through different settings to see if any of the alternate configurations resolve the conflict.

Figure 5-13. The message at the bottom of this dialog box identifies a resource conflict. To resolve the problem, adjust settings for the non–Plug and Play device.

If you suspect that a hardware problem is caused by a resource conflict, you can access an overview of resource usage by opening the System Information utility (Msinfo32.exe), which is found on the All Programs menu under Accessories, SystemTools. Open Hardware Resources in the console pane and pay special attention to the Conflicts/Sharing entry, shown in Figure 5-14, and the Forced Hardware item. Don't be alarmed if you see a number of devices sharing a single IRQ; that's perfectly normal.

For more information about the System Information utility, see "Digging Deeper with Dedicated System Information Tools," page 1408.

For legacy devices whose resources can't be assigned by Windows, you'll need to adjust jumpers on the card or device, or use a software-based setup/configuration utility to change resource settings for that device.

Setting Up and Troubleshooting Hardware

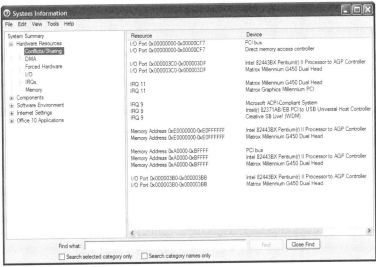

Figure 5-14. All the devices shown in this example are sharing resources properly. If two unrelated devices try to share a resource other than an IRQ, you may need to adjust device settings manually.

Troubleshooting

Resource conflicts prevent a device from working.

If two devices are in conflict for a system resource, try any of these strategies to resolve the problem:

1 With PCI devices, try swapping cards, two at a time, between PCI slots. On some motherboards, IRQs and other resources are assigned on a per-slot basis, and moving a card can free up the proper resources. Check the motherboard documentation to see which IRQs are assigned to each slot and experiment until you find an arrangement that works.

2 If the conflict is caused by a legacy (ISA) device, replace it with a Plug and Play–compatible PCI device.

3 Use jumpers or a software utility to change settings on a legacy device so that it reserves a different set of resources. You will need documentation from the manufacturer to accomplish this goal.

If you have problems with PCI devices, the device itself might not be to blame. When drivers and ACPI BIOS code interact improperly, conflicts can result. Check for an updated hardware driver (especially if the current driver is unsigned), and look for a BIOS update as well.

Chapter 5

Managing Installed Drivers

If you're having a hardware problem that you suspect is caused by a device driver, your first stop should be Device Manager. Open the properties dialog box for the device, and use the following buttons on the Driver tab to perform maintenance tasks:

- **Update Driver** This choice starts the Hardware Update Wizard.
- **Roll Back Driver** This option uninstalls a recently updated driver and "rolls back" your system configuration to the previously installed driver. Unlike System Restore, this option affects only the selected device. If you have never updated the selected driver, Windows offers to run a troubleshooter when you click this button.
- **Uninstall** This button completely removes driver files and registry settings for the selected device. This option is available from Safe Mode if you need to remove a driver that is causing blue-screen (Stop) errors. You can also use this capability to remove a driver that you suspect was incorrectly installed and then reinstall the original driver or install an updated driver.

> **Tip** Double-check System Restore settings
>
> When you install a new, unsigned hardware driver, Windows XP automatically attempts to create a new System Restore checkpoint. That doesn't mean it will be successful, especially if a problem with your System Restore settings has caused this utility to suspend operations temporarily. To make certain that you can roll back your changes if necessary, set a new System Restore checkpoint manually before making any kind of hardware configuration change. (For more details, see "Undoing Configuration Mistakes with System Restore," page 1288.)

Updating a Device Driver

Microsoft and third-party device manufacturers frequently issue upgrades to device drivers. In some cases, the updates enable new features; in other cases, the newer version swats a bug that might or might not affect you. If you've downloaded a new driver for a device that's currently installed on your computer, use the Upgrade Hardware Wizard to install it properly.

If the new driver includes a setup program, run it first, so that the proper files are copied to your system. Then start the wizard from Device Manager by double-clicking the entry for the device you want to upgrade and clicking Update Driver on the Driver tab. This wizard uses the same procedures as the Add Hardware Wizard. Follow the procedures outlined in "Setting Up a New Device," page 135, to point the wizard to the correct location for the driver and complete the update.

Chapter 5

> **Tip** Check driver versions
>
> How do you know whether a downloaded version is newer than the currently installed driver on your system? A good Readme file should provide this information and is the preferred option for determining version information. In the absence of documentation, file dates offer some clues, but they are not always reliable. A better indicator is to inspect the properties of the driver files themselves. After unzipping the downloaded driver files to a folder on a local or network drive, right-click any file with a .dll or .sys extension and choose Properties. On the Version tab, you should be able to find details about the specific driver version, which you can compare to the driver details shown in Device Manager.

Rolling Back to a Previous Driver Version

Unfortunately, updated drivers can sometimes cause new problems that are worse than the woes they were intended to fix. This is especially true if you're experimenting with unsigned drivers or beta versions of new drivers. If your troubleshooting leads you to suspect that a newly installed driver is the cause of recent crashes or system instability, consider removing that driver and rolling your system configuration back to the previously installed driver.

In earlier Windows versions, this process was cumbersome and tricky. In Windows XP, it's as easy as clicking a button. Open Device Manager and double-click the entry for the device you want to roll back. Then go to the Driver tab and click Roll Back Driver. The procedure that follows is straightforward and self-explanatory.

Uninstalling a Driver

There are at least three circumstances under which you might want to completely remove a device driver from your system:

- You're no longer using the device, and you want to prevent the previously installed drivers from loading or using any resources.
- You've determined that the drivers available for the device are not stable enough to use on your system.
- The currently installed driver is not working correctly, and you want to reinstall it from scratch.

To remove a driver permanently, open Device Manager and double-click the entry for the device in question. On the Driver tab, click Uninstall. Click OK when prompted to confirm that you want to remove the driver, and Windows removes files and registry settings completely.

Chapter 5

Inside Out

Manage Plug and Play drivers

Removing and reinstalling the driver for a Plug and Play device requires a little extra effort. Because these drivers are loaded and unloaded dynamically, you can remove the driver only if the device in question is plugged in. Use the Uninstall button to remove the driver before unplugging the device. To reinstall the device driver without unplugging, open Device Manager and choose Action, Scan For Hardware Changes.

Troubleshooting

Your computer experiences sporadic blue screens, lockups, or other strange behavior.

When your computer acts unpredictably, chances are good that a buggy device driver is at fault.

If you're experiencing unexplained computer problems, a powerful troubleshooting tool called Driver Verifier (Verifier.exe) is a terrific way to identify flawed device drivers. Instead of your computer locking up at a most inopportune time with a misleading Blue Screen of Death (BSOD), Driver Verifier stops your computer predictably at startup with a BSOD that accurately explains the true problem. Although this doesn't sound like a huge improvement (your system still won't work, after all), Driver Verifier performs a critical troubleshooting step: identifying the problem. You can then correct the problem by removing or replacing the offending driver. (If you're satisfied that the driver really is okay despite Driver Verifier's warning, you can turn off Driver Verifier for all drivers or for a specific driver. Any driver that Driver Verifier chokes on should be regarded with suspicion, but some legitimate drivers bend the rules without causing problems.)

Driver Verifier works at startup to thoroughly exercise each driver. It performs many of the same tests that are run by WHQL as part of the certification and signing process, such as checking for the way the driver accesses memory.

Beware: If Driver Verifier finds a nonconforming driver—even one that doesn't seem to be causing any problems—it will prevent your system from starting. Use Driver Verifier only if you're having problems. In other words, if it ain't broke …

To enable Driver Verifier, open a command prompt, type **verifier**, and press Enter. In the Driver Verifier Manager dialog box, shown below, select Create Standard Settings. In the next dialog box, select the type of drivers you want to verify; unsigned drivers are a likely cause of problems. Complete the wizard and restart your computer.

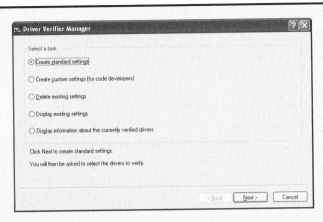

If your computer stops with a blue screen when you next log on, you've identified a problem driver. The error message includes the name of the offending driver and an error code. For information about the error codes, see Microsoft Knowledge Base article Q315252, "A Partial List of Driver Error Codes That the Driver Verifier Tool Uses to Report Problems." To resolve the problem, boot into Safe Mode (press F8 during startup) and disable or uninstall the problem driver. You'll then want to check with the device vendor to get a working driver that you can install.

To disable Driver Verifier so that it no longer performs verification checks at startup, run Driver Verifier Manager again and select Delete Existing Settings in the initial dialog box. Alternatively, at a command prompt, type **verifier /reset**. (If you haven't yet solved the driver problem, of course, you'll be stopped at a BSOD, unable to disable Driver Verifier. In that case, boot into Safe Mode and then disable Driver Verifier.)

You can configure Driver Verifier so that it checks only certain drivers. To do that, open Driver Verifier Manager, select Create Standard Settings, click Next, and select the last option, Select Driver Names From A List. This option lets you exempt a particular driver from Driver Verifier's scrutiny—such as one that Driver Verifier flags but you are certain is not the cause of your problem.

You can read more about Driver Verifier online at the MSDN site, *http://msdn.microsoft.com* (search for **driver verifier verifier.exe**).

Chapter 5

Enabling and Disabling Specific Devices

Installing and uninstalling device drivers can be a hassle. If all you want to do is enable or disable a specific device, you can do so from Device Manager. Open the properties dialog box for the selected device, click the General tab, and toggle the Device Usage setting between Use This Device (Enable) and Do Not Use This Device (Disable). The drivers for a disabled device remain available, but Windows does not load them.

You might choose to disable the driver for a device if you use it infrequently and want to avoid having it use resources or cause stability problems at other times. Enable the device when you want to use it, and keep it disabled the rest of the time. For the most part, however, the capability to enable and disable devices is used in conjunction with hardware profiles.

This capability is most common with notebook computers attached to docking stations, where your video settings, storage devices, and other hardware options vary depending on whether the notebook is in the docking station or not. However, you can also use profiles to set up specialized configurations on a desktop computer. For instance, on a graphics workstation with multiple imaging devices, you might want to avoid conflicts by choosing different combinations of enabled devices for different user profiles. If you use multiple network devices to manage connections to different networks, you might want to use hardware profiles for this task as well.

By default, Windows creates a single user profile, Profile 1, when you first install Windows. If you have a notebook computer with a Plug and Play–compatible docking station, Windows automatically creates Docked and Undocked configurations for you and loads the proper configuration when you connect or disconnect from the docking station. To work with hardware profiles, open Control Panel, open System, click the Hardware tab, and then click Hardware Profiles. Figure 5-15 shows the available options.

The best way to create a new profile is to copy an existing profile and then enable or disable devices as needed. Follow these steps to create a second profile on a system that currently has only one:

1. Open Control Panel, double-click System, and click Hardware Profiles on the Hardware tab.

2. In the Hardware Profiles dialog box, select Profile 1 and click Copy.

3. In the Copy Profile dialog box, enter a descriptive name for the new profile or accept the default, Profile 2. Click OK.

4. In the Hardware Profiles section, specify which profile you want Windows to use at startup.

   - To always choose from a menu of available profiles, choose Wait Until I Select A Hardware Profile.

■ To set a default profile, use the up and down arrows to arrange the Available Hardware Profiles list so that your preferred profile is at the top. Then choose Select The First Profile Listed If I Don't Select A Profile In *nn* Seconds and specify a default waiting period (in seconds).

5 Restart your computer and choose the profile you want to modify. Open Device Manager and adjust the Device Usage settings for each device you want to enable or disable, as follows.

■ Choose Use This Device (Enable) for any device you want to make available for that profile.

■ Choose Do Not Use This Device In The Current Hardware Profile (Disable) for any device that should remain disabled in the current profile.

■ Choose Do Not Use This Device In Any Hardware Profiles (Disable) to disable a device regardless of which profile is selected.

6 After configuring all devices in the current profile, close Device Manager.

7 To adjust other profiles, log on using the selected profile and repeat step 5.

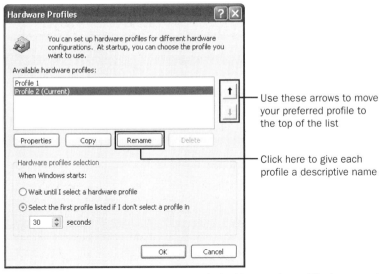

Figure 5-15. On Plug and Play notebook docking stations, Windows creates profiles automatically. To create a new profile, click Copy.

Decoding Hardware Errors

When Windows encounters a problem with a device or its driver, it changes the icon in Device Manager and displays an error code on the General tab of the device's properties dialog box. Each code is identified by a number and a brief text description. Table 5-1 contains a partial list of error codes and suggested actions you should take to try to resolve them.

Table 5-1. Common Device Manager Error Codes

Error Code	Error Message	What To Do About It
1	This device is not configured correctly. (Code 1)	After downloading a compatible driver for the device, click the Update Driver button and follow the wizard's prompts to install the new driver.
3	The driver for this device might be corrupted, or your system may be running low on memory or other resources. (Code 3)	Check available memory and, if necessary, close some programs to free up RAM. If you have sufficient memory, try uninstalling and reinstalling the driver.
10	This device cannot start. (Code 10)	Device failed to start. Click the Update Driver button to install updated drivers if available. The Troubleshoot button may provide useful information as well.
12	This device cannot find enough free resources that it can use. If you want to use this device, you will need to disable one of the other devices on this system. (Code 12)	The device has been assigned one or more I/O ports, IRQs, or DMA channels used by another device. This error message can also appear if the BIOS is configured incorrectly (for example, if a USB controller doesn't get an IRQ from the BIOS). Check BIOS settings. Use the Resources tab to identify the conflicting device.
14	This device cannot work properly until you restart your computer. (Code 14)	The driver has probably been installed correctly, but will not be started until you reboot the system.
16	Windows cannot identify all the resources this device uses. (Code 16)	A legacy device is improperly configured. Use the Resources tab to fill in the missing details.
18	Reinstall the drivers for this device. (Code 18)	Click the Update Driver button to start the Update Hardware Wizard and reinstall the driver.

Chapter 5

Table 5-1. **Common Device Manager Error Codes**

Error Code	Error Message	What To Do About It
19	Your registry might be corrupted. (Code 19)	Incorrect or conflicting information is entered in the registry settings for this device. Try using the Troubleshooting Wizard to identify the specific problem. If that is unsuccessful, uninstall and then reinstall the driver. Try using System Restore to roll back the configuration to a point where the device worked properly.
21	Windows is removing this device. (Code 21)	The system will remove the device. Wait a few seconds, and then refresh the Device Manager view. If the device continues to display, restart the computer.
22	This device is disabled. (Code 22)	The device has been disabled using Device Manager. To enable it, click the Enable Device button.
24	This device is not present, is not working properly, or does not have all its drivers installed. (Code 24)	This is a catch-all error that can be caused by bad hardware or corrupt or incompatible drivers. This message also appears after you use the Remove Device option. Use the Troubleshooting Wizard to identify the specific problem.
28	The drivers for this device are not installed. (Code 28)	After downloading a compatible driver for the device, click the Update Driver button and follow the wizard's prompts to install the new driver.
29	This device is disabled because the firmware of the device did not give it the required resources. (Code 29)	This is most commonly seen with SCSI adapters, third-party disk controllers, and other devices that supply their own BIOS. Check the documentation for the device to learn how to re-enable it.
31	This device is not working properly because Windows cannot load the drivers required for this device. (Code 31)	Windows was unable to load the driver, probably because it is not compatible with Windows XP. After downloading a compatible driver for the device, click the Update Driver button and follow the wizard's prompts to install the new driver.

Chapter 5

Table 5-1. Common Device Manager Error Codes

Error Code	Error Message	What To Do About It
32	A driver service for this device was not required, and has been disabled. (Code 32)	The driver has been disabled. The start type for this service is set to Disabled in the registry. If the driver really is required, change the start type in the BIOS, using the BIOS setup utility as defined in the documentation for the device. If the device previously worked properly, use System Restore to return to a working configuration.
33	Windows cannot determine which resources are required for this device. (Code 33)	This error typically indicates a misconfigured legacy device or a hardware failure. See the documentation for the device for more information.
34	Windows cannot determine the settings for this device. Consult the documentation that came with this device and use the Resource tab to set the configuration. (Code 34)	This legacy device requires a forced configuration. Change the hardware settings (using jumpers or a software utility), and then use Device Manager's Resources tab to set the forced configuration.
35	Your computer's system BIOS does not include enough information to properly configure and use this device. To use this device, contact your computer manufacturer to obtain a firmware or BIOS update. (Code 35)	This error is specific to multiprocessor systems. Check with the system manufacturer for a BIOS upgrade.
36	This device is requesting a PCI interrupt but is configured for an ISA interrupt (or vice versa). Please use the computer's system setup program to reconfigure the interrupt for this device. (Code 36)	IRQ translation failed. This error usually occurs on Advanced Power Management (APM) machines. Check BIOS settings to see if certain IRQs have been reserved incorrectly. Upgrade to an ACPI BIOS if possible.

Table 5-1. Common Device Manager Error Codes

Error Code	Error Message	What To Do About It
37	Windows cannot initialize the device driver for this hardware. (Code 37)	After downloading a compatible driver for the device, click the Update Driver button and follow the wizard's prompts to install the new driver.
38	Windows cannot load the device driver for this hardware because a previous instance of the device driver is still in memory. (Code 38)	Restart the computer.
39	Windows cannot load the device driver for this hardware. The driver may be corrupted. (Code 39)	The driver is missing or corrupted, or is in conflict with another driver. Look for an updated driver or reinstall the current driver. If the device worked previously, use System Restore to roll back to a working configuration.
40	Windows cannot access this hardware because its service key information in the registry is missing or recorded incorrectly. (Code 40)	Information in the registry's service key for the driver is invalid. Reinstall the driver.
41	Windows successfully loaded the device driver for this hardware but cannot find the hardware device. (Code 41)	Windows loaded the driver but cannot find the device. This error occurs with legacy devices because Plug and Play cannot detect them. Use Device Manager to uninstall the driver and then use the Add Hardware Wizard to reinstall it.
42	Windows cannot load the device driver for this hardware because there is a duplicate device already running in the system. (Code 42)	Restart the computer.
43	Windows has stopped this device because it has reported problems. (Code 43)	A driver has reported a device failure. Uninstall and reinstall the device. If that doesn't work, contact the device manufacturer.

Chapter 5

161

Table 5-1. **Common Device Manager Error Codes**

Error Code	Error Message	What To Do About It
44	An application or service has shut down this hardware device. (Code 44)	The device has been halted by an application or service. Restart the computer.
47	Windows cannot use this hardware device because it has been prepared for "safe removal," but it has not been removed from the computer. (Code 47)	The device has been prepared for ejection from a PCMCIA slot, a USB port, or a docking station. Unplug the device and plug it in again, or restart the computer.
48	The software for this device has been blocked from starting because it is known to have problems with Windows. Contact the hardware vendor for a new driver. (Code 48)	Contact the hardware vendor for a compatible driver.

Using Windows XP Tablet PC Edition 2005

The Tablet PC is a new type of PC that combines the basic features of a notebook computer with the capability to enter and edit data using a pen and a specially digitized screen. The result literally turns the PC on its end, with a default portrait orientation that resembles a sheet of letter-sized paper. When you use a Tablet PC, you don't need a keyboard and mouse to input text and to use the operating system. For basic Web browsing, you can use the pen as a mouse, moving the scroll bars and clicking hyperlinks by dragging and tapping the pen's tip. You can carry your Tablet PC to a meeting and enter your handwritten notes directly on the screen, using an accessory application called Windows Journal or a much more powerful program called Microsoft OneNote 2003 (a member of the Microsoft Office system). You can add handwritten annotations to Microsoft Word documents and Microsoft Excel spreadsheets and share the marked-up files with people who don't have a Tablet PC. You can send handwritten notes to other people via e-mail or Windows Messenger, or you can convert your handwritten notes to text and then insert the information into other documents.

At Home with Windows XP

Windows XP Tablet PC Edition is a superset of Windows XP Professional. If your notebook computer has Windows XP Home Edition, then it's not a Tablet PC, and the information in this chapter does not apply.

Although individual computer manufacturers customize their Tablet PC designs with unique hardware features and software utilities, a handful of characteristics define the genre:

- The *digitizer* resembles a standard notebook screen, with the crucial distinction that it can accept input from a stylus.
- The *tablet pen* (better known as the *stylus*) resembles a ballpoint pen with a soft plastic tip and a button on the side, just above the tip. You can use the pen as a pointing device; in programs that explicitly support Tablet PC features, you can also write or draw

directly on the screen, as you would on a sheet of paper. Because the Tablet PC uses an *active* digitizer, you must use a pen that is specifically designed for use with your computer. (The digitizer doesn't respond if you try to use an ordinary ballpoint pen or a fingernail; in fact, you may end up damaging the screen.)

● *Tablet buttons* allow access to some common functions when a keyboard is unavailable. Typically, these buttons are built into the computer's case, in the area alongside the display. Default buttons include Up, Down, and Enter, as well as a Security button that has the same effect as pressing Ctrl+Alt+Delete on a conventional keyboard.

The final ingredient, of course, is software—specifically, Microsoft Windows XPTablet PC Edition, which includes all the features of Windows XP Professional and adds a combination of drivers, utilities, and user-interface enhancements that allow you to use the stylus as an extremely versatile input device.

> **Note** Tablet PC hardware typically uses one of two configurations. *Slate* designs do not include a built-in keyboard (although they can accept an external keyboard or mouse) and are intended for use primarily with a pen. *Convertible* designs resemble a conventional notebook, with a keyboard and pointing device; by rotating the screen on a hinge and folding it over the keyboard, you can switch the PC into a position that allows you to work with the pen in a more natural fashion. From a software point of view, there is no fundamental difference between the two designs.

The most radical difference in Windows XP Tablet PC Edition is support for a new type of data called *ink*. Although it superficially resembles a simple bitmap, ink-based data contains a wealth of information in addition to the simple shape. When you scribble a handwritten note or sketch a figure in a program that supports the ink data type, Windows records the direction, pressure, speed, and location of the tablet pen as it moves and stores the resulting marks as a compressed graphic. If you enlarge a piece of data that was stored as ink, Windows uses this stored data to ensure that it keeps its proper shape. By recognizing the combinations of strokes that represent handwritten letters, the operating system can convert even bad handwriting into text, with surprising accuracy. You don't have to convert ink into text to get the benefits of handwriting recognition, either. The handwriting recognizer in Windows XP Tablet PC Edition automatically converts handwriting to text and stores the resulting text along with the ink, allowing you to locate words and phrases in a data file composed exclusively of handwritten notes if you so desire.

> **Note** Although you need a stylus to create ink on a Tablet PC, anyone who uses Windows XP can view ink-based data. In addition, some users running Windows XP Home Edition or Professional can also create ink using a mouse. Certain ink-aware programs—including Adobe Reader 6 and Microsoft Office 2003—install a Tablet PC component called Wisptis.exe (the acronym combines two names from the Tablet PC development toolkit, Windows Ink Services Platform and Tablet Input Subsystem). Because this code is installed on all Windows platforms, not just Tablet PCs, you can create ink using those programs on any Windows XP computer.

You can enter text directly into any Windows program using the Tablet PC Input Panel. Use the Input Panel's on-screen keyboard to enter characters and other symbols by tapping them, or enter text as handwriting in the Input Panel's writing pad and let the recognizer convert it to text. Programs that recognize ink as data allow some advanced features as well. If you use Office XP or Office 2003, for instance, you can annotate a Word document or an Excel worksheet with digital ink and then send it by e-mail to a colleague or coworker.

Windows XP Service Pack 2 (SP2) includes a sweeping set of revisions to Tablet PC features, including performance enhancements, a radically redesigned Tablet PC Input Panel, and a new name: Windows XP Tablet PC Edition 2005. In this chapter, we assume that you have purchased a new Tablet PC with SP2 preinstalled or have upgraded an older release of Windows XP Tablet PC Edition to SP2.

Setting Up Your Tablet PC

During the initial setup of a new Tablet PC, you should follow the hardware manufacturer's instructions to make sure that all of the PC's components are working properly. To adjust hardware settings after you've used your Tablet PC for a while, open Control Panel and double-click Tablet And Pen Settings.

Adjusting for Left-Handed Use

Are you left-handed? If so, you're probably accustomed to a world where everything seems to have been designed backwards. In the case of a Tablet PC, the operating system assumes you'll hold the tablet in your left hand and manipulate the pen with your right hand. Open Control Panel, double-click Tablet And Pen Settings, and then click the Settings tab. Adjust the Handedness option so that Windows can more accurately recognize your "backwards" handwriting; next, change the Menu Location setting so that menus and ScreenTips fly out to the right, where they aren't covered by your hand.

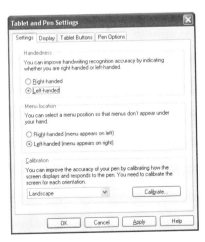

Chapter 6

Calibrating the Screen

Accurately mapping the relationship between pen and screen is essential to using a Tablet PC effectively. The precision with which you can control the pointer's location with the pen depends in part on how you hold the pen and your posture in relation to your tablet. If the digitizer is off by even a few pixels, tapping the screen to click a button or select a menu option won't produce the expected result. Calibration has to be performed separately for both Landscape and Portrait orientations. Open Control Panel, Tablet And Pen Settings. On the Settings tab, tap Calibrate to display a series of four on-screen targets; tap the center of each target in turn, and then switch orientation and repeat the process.

Tip Test your calibration changes

When you calibrate the screen, try to orient the tablet surface and your head so that they are in the same position they will be in when you use the computer. After calibrating your tablet, use it for a while to see how well the pen directs the pointer. Let some time pass before calibrating again. If the pointer doesn't follow the pen well over the entire screen, hold the pen more upright. If the pointer and pen track well together over most of the screen but not in a specific area, try calibrating the tablet again.

Changing Orientation

Tablet PCs are designed so that you can change the screen orientation from landscape to portrait (and back to landscape) without rebooting. This versatility is especially important in convertible Tablet PCs, where you might work in landscape orientation for part of your day, using the keyboard and built-in pointing device to create and edit a spreadsheet, and then switch into portrait mode to take handwritten notes at a meeting. Most convertible PCs change screen orientation automatically when you pivot the screen on its hinge; to change orientation manually, open Control Panel, double-tap Tablet And Pen Settings, and tap the Display tab. Make a selection from the drop-down Orientation list and tap OK.

This change in orientation happens almost instantaneously.

If opening this dialog box seems like a cumbersome way to change orientation, you're right. Simplify the process by defining a predetermined sequence of orientations, which you can then cycle through using a shortcut menu. On the Display tab of the Tablet And Pen Settings dialog box, tap Change and enter up to four orientations in the numbered boxes. Windows switches to the next item in this sequence each time you choose the Change Screen Orientation choice on the Tablet PC menu in the notification area.

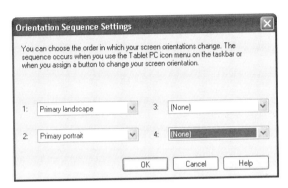

Note The Primary Portrait and Primary Landscape orientations are generally appropriate for right-handed Tablet PC users. The Secondary Portrait and Secondary Landscape options invert these two display orientations. Normally, you use a convertible Tablet PC's keyboard in Primary Landscape mode; changing to Primary Portrait orientation rotates the screen so that the taskbar and start button appear along what had been the left edge of the display. You might prefer the Secondary Portrait display if your power cord attaches at an angle that is inconvenient for working in the Primary Portrait orientation, or if the tablet buttons are in an inconvenient location. On a convertible design, it's hard to imagine a scenario in which the Secondary Landscape orientation—where the screen is essentially upside-down— would be useful. On a slate-style Tablet PC, however, this orientation could be practical.

The options at the bottom of the Display tab also allow you to adjust the brightness of the screen. You can choose separate brightness levels that kick in depending on whether the Tablet PC is plugged in or operating on batteries.

Redefining Tablet PC Buttons

Each Tablet PC design is different, but most include a number of buttons that you can customize to perform any of a long list of actions, including standard keyboard commands (Down Arrow, Up Arrow, and Enter, for example) or running an application. These buttons are typically found around the display, in easy reach of your hands when using the computer as a tablet. To customize them, open the Tablet And Pen Settings dialog box from Control Panel and tap the Tablet Buttons tab. Figure 6-1 shows the available settings for a Toshiba Tablet PC with three customizable buttons.

Chapter 6

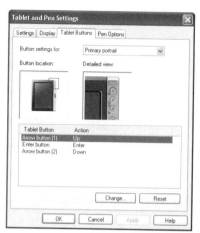

Figure 6-1. Tablet buttons give you access to your most needed keyboard commands.

Inside Out

Use a custom button to manage power

One member of Microsoft's Tablet PC design team offers a clever power-saving tip that uses customized hardware buttons: Redefine one of those buttons so that it blanks the screen when pressed. When you're using a battery-powered Tablet PC in a meeting or at home on the couch, push the "blank screen" button whenever you're not actually using the Tablet PC—when you pause to take a phone call, for instance, or leave to fix a snack. Because the display uses a fairly large percentage of the PC's power, the savings can add up. A tap of the pen on the screen turns the display back on. If your Tablet PC doesn't have a specific menu option that performs this function, use the Launch Application option and define its target as **%windir%\system32\scrnsave.scr** (the Blank screen saver).

By default, the tablet buttons perform the same actions for all screen orientations; however, you can assign different actions to the buttons for different orientations. Using the buttons for actions associated with the keyboard is most helpful when you're using the tablet with the pen only. When browsing the Web, for instance, you might find it helpful to redefine the Up Arrow and Down Arrow buttons so that they emulate the Mouse Wheel Up and Mouse Wheel Down actions instead. Having quick access to these actions is not nearly as helpful on a convertible Tablet PC when the full keyboard is available. For that configuration, consider defining the tablet buttons to launch applications you use frequently.

Configuring the Pen

The Pen Options tab in the Tablet and Pen Settings dialog box includes settings for how the pen performs actions you are used to carrying out with the mouse. Table 6-1 lists the four pen actions and the settings you can change.

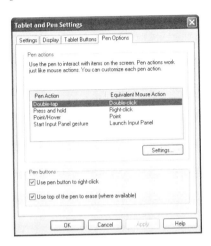

Table 6-1. Settings for Pen Actions

Pen Action (Mouse Equivalent)	Settings
Double-tap (double-click)	The maximum pause that can occur between two taps and still have the tablet recognize the action as a double-tap
	The distance that can separate two taps and still have them be recognized as a double-tap
Press and hold (right-click)	The amount of time you need to press and hold the pen against the screen to emulate a right-click
	The amount of time that passes while you press and hold the pen before you have to select a right-click action
Point/hover (point)	The amount of space you can move the pen and still have the pen's hovering be recognized as pointing to an object or an area on the screen
Start Input Panel gesture	The extent of the side-to-side movement you need to make with the pen to open Input Panel

> **Tip**   Some pens with buttons have a combination button that acts as a right-click if pushed one way and an eraser if pressed differently. The Pen Options tab includes a setting for whether to use the top of the pen as an eraser. You can select this setting independently of the setting to use the pen button to right-click.

Using the Pen

The pen is the device you use to write notes, enter text and other information, and interact with the user interface on a Tablet PC. In Windows Journal or in OneNote 2003, or when you're using the writing pad or character pad in the Input Panel, you write with the tablet pen just as you would with any writing instrument. When the on-screen keyboard is active in the Input Panel, tap the characters and symbols with the pen to enter text and numbers. You can use the pen to activate regular keyboard shortcuts as well.

You can use the pen in four basic ways:

- **Use your pen as a mouse**   The pen can be used like a mouse at any time in any application in which you would use a regular mouse. The pen can provide both left and right mouse button actions as well as other familiar mouse operations. Table 6-2 lists pen actions that correspond to familiar mouse movements.

- **Use your pen as a text input device**   By entering handwritten text or tapping the on-screen keyboard in the Input Panel, the pen can be used in lieu of a regular keyboard to input text in any application.

- **Create a bitmap image**   Some applications, especially drawing programs, accept pen input and convert it to bitmap images. The images can be inserted into documents or attached to e-mail messages.

- **Create a document using rich ink**   Applications that fully support ink as a data type are still relatively rare, but you can perform some remarkable feats with those that do exist. Using Word 2003, for instance, you can insert handwritten comments and annotations or enter text into a frame within a document. In the latter case, you can select a block of handwriting stored as ink, right-click, choose Copy To Text from the shortcut menu, and use the converted text elsewhere. OneNote 2003 goes even farther, building an index of your handwritten notes and allowing you to search through an entire collection for a word or phrase.

Table 6-2. Comparison of Mouse and Pen Actions

Mouse Action	Pen Equivalent
Point	Hold the pen's point over the screen without touching it
Single-click	Tap the item with the tip of the pen and then lift it
Double-click	Point to the item and then tap twice
Right-click	Press and hold until the pointer changes to a mouse icon, or press the side button on the pen and tap the item

As on a desktop computer or a conventional laptop, shortcut menus save time and effort on a Tablet PC. You can use the pen as you would use a mouse to right-click. To open a shortcut menu with the pen, press the pen tip against the screen until the mouse icon appears, and then lift the pen off the screen. Point at the command you want, and then tap it.

Some pen designs incorporate a button that serves the same function as the right button on a conventional mouse; these designs make it even easier to open shortcut menus. To right-click with a pen button, hold down the pen button before you make contact with the screen, tap the item you want to right-click, and then lift the pen off the screen before releasing the pen button.

Entering Text with the Input Panel

When you use a Tablet PC without a keyboard, how do you enter text into dialog boxes, Web forms, your browser's address bar, or a document created using a Windows program that doesn't support ink as a data type? Try the Tablet PC Input Panel. The Input Panel is a relatively small box that pops up on demand and allows you to enter handwritten characters that are converted on the fly and inserted as if you had typed them; you can also tap on a virtual keyboard to enter text directly without tussling with handwriting recognition.

Note The on-screen keyboard appears on the Welcome screen, allowing you to log on to your account by entering your password. The ink-to-text conversion option isn't available here for practical reasons: The handwriting recognition module normally tries to match your input to words in its dictionary; it's easily flummoxed by a secure password that consists of random mixed-case letters and numbers that can't be found in any dictionary. The on-screen keyboard is also a security feature: You don't want a casual bystander or a deliberate snoop to watch the Input Panel show you each character of your password as you enter it.

In Windows XP Tablet PC Edition 2005, the Input Panel is dramatically improved compared to its predecessor. In addition, the Write Anywhere feature, which allowed you to scribble text in an oversized box on the screen, is gone for good. If you were frustrated by the process of entering text on a Tablet PC before Service Pack 2, you'll find the new Input Panel more flexible, more accurate, and much easier to use.

Note We don't cover using the Input Panel for speech recognition in this book. For information about requirements for speech recognition, see the Speech Tutorial in the Windows XP Tablet PC Edition Help And Support Center.

Chapter 6

To open the Input Panel, use one of the following three techniques:

- Tap the Input Panel icon in the taskbar, just to the right of the Start button. This opens the Input Panel in docked mode, at the top or bottom of the screen (by default, it appears along the bottom, just above the taskbar).

Note Although the Input Panel button looks like it's part of the Quick Launch toolbar, it's actually a custom toolbar that appears automatically on any Tablet PC. It can't be hidden or moved, and you can't add icons to it.

- Use the Input Panel gesture. To make this gesture, hold your pen just over the screen and quickly move it in a side-to-side slashing motion three or four times. When you use this technique, the Input Panel is docked, not floating.
- Tap to position the insertion point in a dialog box, a form, a document, or any place where you would normally use the keyboard to enter text. Allow the pen point to hover over the insertion point for a second until the Input Panel icon appears just below the insertion point. Tap the icon to open a floating Input Panel.

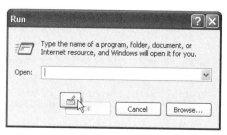

Of these three options, the floating Input Panel is by far the most useful. It appears exactly where it's needed, so you can see where you're inserting the text as you write it. If you're entering more than a few characters, the floating Input Panel expands to offer extra lines on demand. You might prefer the docked Input Panel when you expect to enter a few characters at a time in several locations within a document you're editing.

To switch between floating and docked modes, tap the Tools And Options button at the right of the Input Panel, just below the Close button. The menu that appears allows you to dock the panel at the top or bottom of the screen or allow it to float.

The three icons on the left side of the Input Panel let you switch between its three distinct personalities:

- The Writing Pad offers a blank surface for entering freeform text. As you enter text, your ink remains in the entry window, with the recognized text appearing below the line. When you're finished with text input, tap the Insert button to enter the text at the insertion point.

Tools And Options
button

- The Character Pad provides individual slots for entering each letter or number. By default, the Input Panel converts each character you input to text immediately. Also by default, the text does not appear at the insertion point until you tap Insert. This method is useful when entering text that does not correspond to words in a dictionary, such as proper names, serial numbers, or passwords. By recognizing each character, you avoid the possibility that Windows will transform your input into something other than what you typed.

- The On Screen Keyboard mimics a conventional keyboard. Tap in the document to position the insertion point, and then use the pen to tap the characters, numbers, and symbols you want to enter. Tap Shift to enter an uppercase letter or other symbol, and tap the arrow keys to move the insertion point. Any character you type is entered immediately.

When you're entering handwritten text, a small selection of useful buttons called *quick keys* appear at the right of the Input Panel. Tap the appropriate button to add a space or press Enter, for instance, or to delete or backspace over text. Tap Num to open a numeric keypad (especially useful when working with spreadsheets) and Sym to display a selection of common symbols that are difficult to enter as ink. (Similarly, if you tap in Internet Explorer's Address bar, you'll see the selection of shortcuts shown here, which make it easier to navigate on the Web.)

Fine-Tuning Handwriting Recognition

By default, the Input Panel shows you how your handwriting has been recognized before inserting the resulting text in the document. When you're using the Writing Pad and you notice a recognition error, tap the word that was recognized incorrectly to display a dialog box that contains alternate word choices and a series of boxes where you can edit each character individually. Figure 6-2 shows the editing window in action.

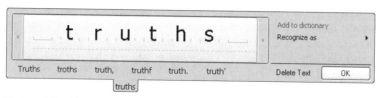

Figure 6-2.   Tap a word from the list at the bottom of the Writing Pad editing window, or tap beneath any character to adjust only that character.

If the Input Panel recognized your word incorrectly and none of the options along the bottom of the editing box is correct, tap beneath any letter to edit that character directly. Menu choices beneath each character allow you to delete a letter, add or remove spaces, or change case. You can also write a new letter over any character in this window. This same interface is available in the Character Pad, which doesn't allow you to select alternate words.

Note   Don't be distracted if the Writing Pad seems to recognize a letter incorrectly as you write it. Some of the handwriting recognition "smarts" are based on letter combinations and dictionary entries. The Input Panel may guess wrong initially, but by the time you get to the end of the word, you may find that it's been recognized correctly after all.

To erase handwritten text, learn the scratch-out gesture. In the Writing Pad and Character Pad, you can use this short, quick, repeated left-to-right motion to erase ink (this gesture also works in Windows Journal, but not in OneNote 2003 or Word 2003). Make sure that your pen stays on the screen as you make the gesture, directly on the text you want to erase, and keep the lines horizontal; if you're unsuccessful, you may need to draw more or longer lines.

Customizing the Input Panel

Depending on your work style, you may want to modify the behavior of the Input Panel to suit the way you work. Click the Tools And Options button at the right of the Input Panel and click Options to change any of the following settings. You can hide the Input Panel icon that appears in text as you type, move the Insert button to the left side of the dialog box, and change the thickness of the default ink, among other actions.

One particularly useful option lets you eliminate the need to tap the Insert button to enter text. In the Options dialog box, this setting is independent for the Character Pad and the Writing Pad.

On the Character Pad tab, select Automatically Recognize Writing As Text After a Pause, and then adjust this value using the slider. This setting controls how long it takes for recognized characters to appear in the text entry area. Choose one of the three options in the Action That Inserts Text box to control when and how your text is inserted. You can change this setting from the default, which requires you to tap the Insert button, to specify that you want text entered when you enter text after a space or start a new line.

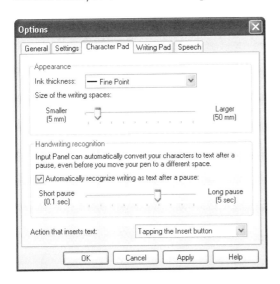

On the Writing Pad, the options to automatically insert text are based on how long you pause after a burst of writing. On the Writing Pad tab in the Options dialog box, select Automatically Insert Text After A Pause and adjust the interval to as long as 10 seconds. The second option, Automatically Insert Individual Characters After A Pause, controls the behavior of the editing panel that appears when you tap a recognized word.

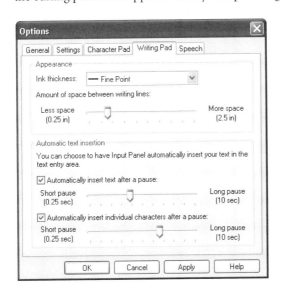

Using Windows Journal

Windows XP Tablet PC Edition includes Windows Journal, an accessory application that works like an electronic version of a legal pad with an endless supply of paper. Using Journal, you can take your tablet to a meeting and enter electronic ink notes directly on "pages," without having to use the Input Panel. (For some tasks, such as entering or removing line breaks, you may need to use the On Screen Keyboard.) The operating system stores and indexes your handwritten notes, which you can then retrieve and update or edit. You can also search through a series of notes using the words and phrases you've written as the criteria.

> **Note** Windows Journal is a useful program that shows off the capabilities of the Tablet PC well. However, it pales in comparison to Microsoft OneNote 2003, a member of the Microsoft Office system that starts with the same basic metaphor of an infinitely expandable loose-leaf notebook but does much, much more. OneNote works on desktop PCs as well, but it's especially useful on a Tablet PC. For details on OneNote as well as a free downloadable trial version, visit *http://www.microsoft.com/onenote*.

To start Windows Journal, tap its shortcut on the All Programs menu. To begin a note, write a name for the note in the Note Title box at the top of the page. (This title will be used as the default file name for the note when you save it.) You can then write on the screen with the tablet pen as if you were using pencil and paper.

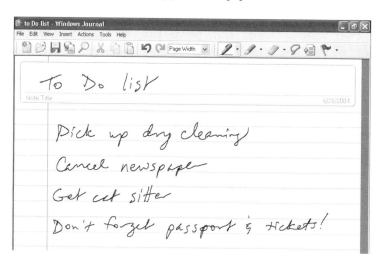

You can select all or a portion of a note and convert the handwriting to text. You can also draw by hand in Journal, include graphics files in the notes you create, print notes, and create notes that occupy multiple pages. In this section, we give an overview of Windows Journal, rather than a comprehensive guide on its functions and features.

Writing in Journal

When you write notes in Journal, you can choose different degrees of fineness for the pen's point or use the pen as a highlighter to emphasize a portion of a note. When necessary, you can use your pen as an eraser by tapping the Eraser button on the Journal toolbar. The Pen And Highlighter Settings dialog box, shown here, supplies options for which pen point to use and other preferences. You can change the width of the pen's point, the color of the digital ink, and the tip style. You can make similar selections for using the pen as a highlighter on the Highlighter Settings tab.

To add or remove space between the information you have written in a note, use the Insert/Remove Space command. Position the dotted line and pointer where you want to adjust the white space, place the tip of your pen on the screen, and then drag.

> **Tip** Space is inserted or removed in one-line increments by default. You can gain finer control by clearing the option Insert Space In Full Line Increments on the View tab of the Options dialog box in Journal.

Converting Notes to Text

You can copy and paste handwritten notes into another note. Use the Selection tool on the Journal toolbar to select the portion of the note you want to reuse.

Windows Journal can also convert your handwritten notes to text. You can correct the words or phrases that Journal doesn't recognize correctly and then store the text with the note or use it in a different application.

To convert your notes to text, select the handwriting you want to convert, and then choose Convert Handwriting To Text from the Action menu. Journal displays the Text Correction dialog box, shown on the next page.

Chapter 6

177

The text that Journal did not recognize is highlighted, and the corresponding ink from the note is displayed for comparison. Correct the text by tapping an incorrect word and choosing the correct word from the list of alternatives provided on the right. You can also tap a word or phrase you need to correct and then tap the Input Panel icon that appears near it. The Input Panel shows a list of alternatives and gives you a familiar writing surface to make a correction that isn't on the list.

The words displayed as alternatives in the Text Correction dialog box in Journal are drawn from the same source as those you see when correcting in the Input Panel. The list of alternatives on the right of the Text Correction dialog box is a little longer and offers a wider range of words. Both features use the same dictionary, so any changes you make to the custom dictionary in Journal will appear in the Input Panel, and vice-versa.

How Handwriting Is Recognized in Journal

Every time you put ink on a page, Journal assesses the strokes to see whether they might form a word. If Journal recognizes the strokes as a word, the strokes are grouped and the handwriting recognizer records its guess for the word as well as several alternatives. The list of possible words is stored as part of the Journal note. The recognition process takes place in the background so that it doesn't interfere with your work. If you choose to convert your handwriting to text, the recognition is already complete.

This method of writing and handwriting recognition differs from that which users of Pocket PC or Palm devices are used to. With those devices, you enter one character at a time or draw letters following a prescribed path. If you prefer one of these methods over the Journal method, stick with Writing Pad, where you can display a character recognizer that lets you enter text in a manner similar to these popular mobile devices.

While the Text Correction dialog box is open, you can rearrange text by dragging and dropping (watch as the ink in the Journal note is highlighted when you select the recognized text). Use the On Screen Keyboard to add or remove line breaks. By default, the correction tool enters a line break wherever a new line appeared in the Journal note. You can remove these line breaks by tapping the Options button and clearing the option to preserve line breaks.

When you tap OK in the Text Correction dialog box, a Journal message asks whether you want to copy the converted text to the Clipboard, preserving your original ink, or replace the ink in the note with a text box containing the text.

> **Note**   You can also use the Copy As Text command on the Edit menu to convert a handwritten note to text and place the text on the Clipboard. The Copy As Text command displays the Text Correction dialog box prior to copying the text.

Journal Page Setup Options

The Page Setup dialog box in Journal provides the means to change the line style of the Journal page. Formats range from wide- or narrow-ruled lines to variations of a quadrille grid (commonly used in engineering drawings) to custom formats you set up yourself. You can also change the color of the writing pad and choose illustrated backgrounds.

Saving and Finding Notes

Each note you write in Windows Journal is stored by default in the My Notes folder as a Windows Journal Note file type, with a .jnt extension. Journal uses its recognized version of what you write in the Note Title box as the default file name. You can change the file name by replacing the text in the Save As dialog box or by opening the file in Windows Explorer and using standard Windows file-management techniques. In either case, you might want to use the On Screen keyboard in the Input Panel to enter a name.

To see a list of notes you've written recently, tap View Recent Notes on the Journal toolbar. You can then open a note based on its inked title or its file name; the list of available Journal notes includes both columns.

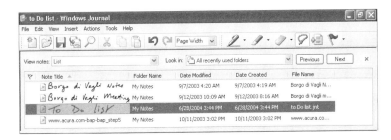

When you need to find a note you've saved, tap File, Search to display Journal's search pane, shown here.

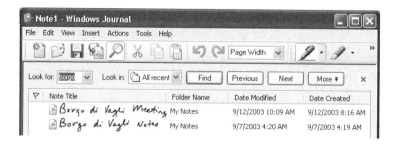

In the Look For box, pick a word or phrase you've used to search with in the past, or use the Input Panel to write or tap in the term you want to search by. Select the location to search in the Look In box. The search pane displays a list of the notes in which Journal has found the word or phrase you searched for.

As mentioned earlier, Journal performs background recognition of your handwriting and stores the list of probable words and alternatives. This word list is used for both converting your ink to text and for finding words in your notes. When you search your notes, Journal shows items in which the search text matched the words it recognized as well as the main alternatives. By finding alternatives, a search is more likely to find the text you're looking for, but you will also see several near misses.

Note If you use the search tool on the Start menu to search for text within documents, it will find matches in handwritten words, text boxes, and imported document text in Journal notes. Search only finds the handwriting recognizer's most likely word, however, and not any of the alternates.

Text boxes and text in imported documents can be included in a search of notes, but the results depend on how the text was inserted in the note. Text boxes created from converted handwriting retain their alternative word lists, and these are included in the search. If a text box contains text copied from another program, no alternative list exists and only exact matches are found. Likewise, imported text is included in most searches but only returns exact matches. If you don't want alternative words or the imported text included in your search, tap the More button in the search pane, and clear the options for close matches or document image text.

Sharing Journal Notes

If you need to share a note with another Tablet PC user, you can send the note as an e-mail attachment in the note format. The recipient can open the note in Windows Journal to read and edit it. If the recipient doesn't have a Tablet PC, they can download the Windows Journal Viewer (details and download links included with Knowledge Base article 816091, "Overview of Windows Journal Viewer 1.5 and Windows Multilingual User Interface Update," at *http://support.microsoft.com/?kbid=816091*). You can also save notes in MHTML format (the Web archive format used in Internet Explorer) or as TIFF files (viewable in any graphics program or in Internet Explorer) and forward those as attachments to colleagues, friends, and family.

Microsoft Office and the Tablet PC

Microsoft Office XP and Office 2003 support Tablet PC features in two ways: You can import an image of an Office document into Journal and add annotations to it, or you can add ink directly into an Office document. To add pen support to Office XP, you first need to download and install the free Office XP Pack for Tablet PC (available by searching at *http://www.microsoft.com/downloads*). Office 2003, by contrast, has ink support fully integrated. Using Office 2003 with your Tablet PC, you can:

- Create and send handwritten e-mail messages (recipients see them as ink or graphics).
- Take notes and underline key points on slides while delivering a PowerPoint presentation.
- Add ink annotations and ink comments to Word documents and Excel spreadsheets.
- Create documents and presentations using handwriting.

Annotations in a Word document, for example, appear in a layer that floats above the text layer on the page. Annotations in Word are readable even on a computer that's not a Tablet PC, as shown in Figure 6-3.

Chapter 6

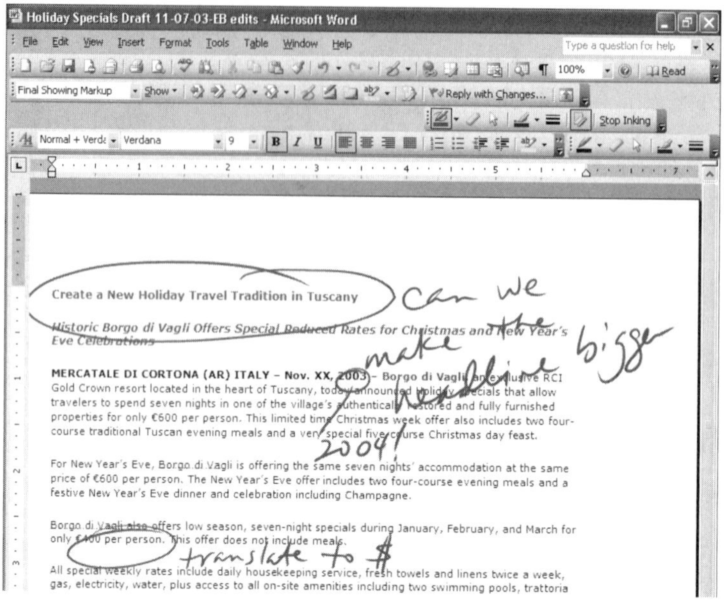

Figure 6-3. You can view ink annotations and comments in Word on any computer, not just a Tablet PC.

For more information about using Office 2003 with a Tablet PC, search the Office 2003 Help system for *Tablet PC.*

Part 2

Keeping Your System Secure

Security Essentials

In the early days of personal computing, security—if it was considered at all—was a mere afterthought. But as personal computers have become more powerful, more complex, and more connected, they've also become more vulnerable. Because of its ubiquity, computers running Microsoft Windows make an especially juicy target for those who would like to steal your valuable personal data, appropriate your computing resources and bandwidth, or simply create havoc. Security can no longer be an afterthought, but it needn't be an all-consuming passion either.

In this chapter, we examine in detail each of three essential security steps—using a firewall, getting updates, and using antivirus software. Beyond these basic steps, there's much more you can do, and toward the end of the chapter and throughout this book we look into some more advanced methods for ensuring that your computer is protected from the bad guys.

At Home with Windows XP

Security essentials are equally important whether you use Windows XP Professional or Home Edition. Fortunately, all the security features described in this chapter work the same in both versions. This chapter does explain how to configure Windows Firewall using Group Policy, a feature that's not available in Home Edition. However, you can make the same settings using other methods we describe.

Windows Security Issues

Some pundits have identified "Windows security" as an oxymoron on a par with "jumbo shrimp" and "work party." Indeed, a historical account of security vulnerabilities in Windows (and attacks that exploit those vulnerabilities) is lengthy. A seemingly endless barrage of viruses and worms that can infect Windows-based computers—Sobig, Blaster, MyDoom, Netsky,

Bagle, and Bugbear were among the most prevalent in 2003 and 2004—took advantage of security holes in Windows to spread their evil. (It should be noted that Microsoft produced patches for most of these holes before they were exploited. Computers with up-to-date patches are immune from most of these viruses.) Each version of Windows has been more secure than the one that preceded it, but Service Pack 2 (SP2) for Windows XP encompasses numerous features that make it far more secure than earlier versions.

SP2 is essentially a brand new version of Windows XP. Due primarily to security enhancements, many of the core binaries have been recompiled, which is why Service Pack 2 is significantly bigger than Service Pack 1. Windows XP SP2 is the second operating system product that Microsoft has developed using a new security methodology that's part of the widely discussed Trustworthy Computing initiative. (The first was Windows Server 2003.) And the results show.

But all software has bugs, and none is completely secure. Achieving security is an ongoing process.

> **Note** If your copy of Windows doesn't include Service Pack 2 and you haven't done so already, install Service Pack 2 on your Windows XP computers. This essential upgrade includes a number of security enhancements, along with a slew of minor improvements. (How do you know if it's installed? Right-click My Computer and choose Properties. On the General tab, under System, the words "Service Pack 2" should appear.) If you don't have Service Pack 2 on CD—Microsoft makes these CDs very easy to get—you can use Windows Update to install Service Pack 2. But be prepared for a long update session, particularly if you have a dial-up connection.

Security Threats

When people talk about security threats these days, they're generally referring to viruses, worms, and Trojan horse programs. Understanding how these programs work is essential to keeping them out of your computer and network. Let's start with some definitions:

- A *virus* is a piece of code that replicates by attaching itself to another object. A virus doesn't have to be a self-contained program; in fact, many outbreaks of seemingly new viruses actually involve rewritten and repackaged versions of older virus code. When a virus infects a computer running Windows, it can attack the registry, replace system files, and take over e-mail programs in its attempt to replicate itself. The virus payload is the destructive portion of the code. Depending on the malicious intent and skill of the virus writer, the virus can destroy or corrupt data files, wipe out installed programs, or damage the operating system itself.

- *Worms* are independent programs that replicate by copying themselves from one computer to another, usually over a network or through e-mail attachments. Many modern worms also contain virus code that can damage data or consume so many system resources that they render the operating system unusable.

● A *Trojan horse program* (also known as a "back door" program) acts as a stealth server that allows intruders to take control of a remote computer without the owner's knowledge. Like the Greek myth after which they're named, Trojan horse programs typically masquerade as benign programs and rely on gullible users to install them. Computers that have been taken over by a Trojan horse program are sometimes referred to as zombies. Armies of these zombies can be used to launch crippling attacks against Web sites.

Computer viruses date back to the 1980s, when they were most commonly transmitted through infected floppy disks. In recent years, though, virus outbreaks have become faster and more destructive, thanks to the ubiquitous nature of the Windows platform and popular e-mail programs such as Microsoft Outlook and Outlook Express, coupled with the soaring popularity of the Internet. Virus writers have become more sophisticated, too, adding smart setup routines, sophisticated encryption, downloadable plug-ins, and automatic Web-based updates to their dangerous wares. Polymorphic viruses can mutate as they infect new host files, making discovery and disinfection difficult because no two instances of the virus "look" the same to virus scanners. A new class of so-called stealth viruses can disguise themselves so that installed antivirus software can't detect them. If you know where to look in the virus underground, you can find point-and-click virus-authoring software, which lets even a non-programmer build a fully functional, destructive virus.

Many viruses and worms spread by attaching themselves to e-mail messages and then transmitting themselves to every address they can find on the victim's computer. Some bury the virus code in an executable file that masquerades as something innocuous, such as an animated greeting card. When the victim opens the attachment, the animated file plays in its own window, disguising the virus activity.

Other viruses hidden in e-mail attachments try to cloak their true identity by appending an additional file name extension to the infected attachment. This strategy relies on the intended victim using the default settings of Windows Explorer, which hide extensions for known file types. With file name extensions turned off, the attachment might appear to be an innocuous Microsoft Word document, for example, and an unwary recipient would be more likely to open it.

Although most viruses and worms arrive as e-mail attachments, email isn't the only method of transmission. Malicious code can also be transmitted to unprotected machines via network shares, through ActiveX controls and scripts, and by HTML-based e-mail messages or Web pages. The infamous Code Red and Nimda worms represent particularly virulent examples of "blended threats" that replicate using multiple vectors.

The Biggest Security Threat

Among some critics, Windows has had a long-held reputation as a security disaster waiting to happen. The reputation—at least with earlier versions of Windows—was not altogether undeserved, but Windows itself is not the cause of many security problems today. A far greater threat comes from "social engineering," modern implementations of scams by what used to be called "con (confidence) men."

Pernicious schemes abound, all of them intended to extract some valuable information from you or to provide access to your computer. Phishing is an online scam that uses the logo and other graphics from legitimate firms (usually banks, credit card companies, and the like) in an e-mail message or Web site facsimile. Although many of these scams are written by crooks who lack language skills, some are very well executed and quite convincing. The intent is to fool you into providing your account number, password, PIN, or other information that the perpetrators can use to clean out your account.

To avoid being hooked by a phishing scam, be suspicious! Most legitimate companies don't ask for sensitive personal information by e-mail. Don't click links in suspicious messages. (If you hover the mouse pointer over a link, you'll often find that the destination site is different from the link's text.) Instead, if you want to visit the site of the apparent sender, type the URL of the company's home page into your browser's address bar and log in to your account in the usual way.

Viruses and worms often pull another trick to win your confidence. In the e-mail messages they scatter about, they often spoof the return address to make it appear that the message came from someone other than the actual sender. And because the apparent sender's name and address is often extracted from the same computer where the virus found your e-mail address, there's some chance that you know the person. "Oh, a message from my old pal," you say. "Let's open it up and see what he has to say…"

Regardless of whether you think you know the sender, the rule nowadays for e-mail attachments is simple: Don't open them unless they're from someone you trust and you're confident that the trusted person sent the file intentionally. If you have any doubt, contact the sender and ask.

Using a firewall, current updates, and antivirus software to batten down the hatches effectively stops most external attacks. The only way for Trojan horse programs, spyware, adware, and other unwanted programs to infect your computer then, is for the perpetrator to convince you to take some action to install these nefarious programs. Be skeptical, and don't let yourself get sucked in.

Basic Prevention

The threats are numerous and the consequences of an attack on your computer's security can be severe. But the good news is that it's relatively simple to protect a standalone computer or computers in a small network from most threats. In a broad educational effort called "Protect Your PC," Microsoft points out three essential steps to safeguard your computer. The logo shown in Figure 7-1 and its variants appear throughout the Microsoft Web site, in advertisements, promotional brochures, and other materials to encourage computer users to visit *http://www.microsoft.com/protect* and learn more about these three steps:

1   Use an Internet firewall.

2   Get computer updates.

3   Use up-to-date antivirus software.

Figure 7-1.   Microsoft's ubiquitous 1, 2, 3 educational campaign extols the importance and simplicity of taking basic steps to protect your PC.

What's New in Service Pack 2

Although Service Pack 2 introduces an assortment of new features and updates ranging from support for Bluetooth devices to a new Show Updates check box in Add Or Remove Programs, its primary focus is on making your computer experience more secure. Some of the security enhancements apply to areas that are covered elsewhere in this book, such as the features to enhance browser security (see Chapter 10, "Securing Your Internet Connection") and the network security changes (see Chapter 28, "Setting Up a Small Network"). But many of the most visible and most important improvements have been made to components relating to the basic prevention tasks outlined in the preceding section, including:

● **Security Center**   This new Control Panel application monitors the status of your firewall program, computer updates, and antivirus program; alerts you to possible problems; and provides access to the tools and information you need to fix problems. For details, see "Monitoring Windows XP Security," page 190.

● **Windows Firewall**   This replacement for Internet Connection Firewall, which was included in the original version of Windows XP, is eminently more configurable than its predecessor. It protects all network connections—LAN (wired and wireless), dial-up, and virtual private network (VPN)—and it is enabled for all connections by default from the moment you install SP2. In addition, it protects your computer during startup. For details, see "Blocking Intruders with Windows Firewall," page 194.

189

- **Windows Update** Automatic Updates, a Control Panel application that manages the download and installation of updates from Microsoft, was overhauled in Service Pack 1; in Service Pack 2, it's revamped again. Likewise, the Windows Update Web site has undergone a facelift to make it easier to use. More importantly, Windows Update, the service that provides security patches, updates, and hardware drivers for Windows and its components, will soon be a part of Microsoft Update, which provides security patches and updates for other Microsoft applications, such as Microsoft Office. When this is fully implemented for all Microsoft applications, Automatic Updates can ensure that high priority updates for all your Microsoft programs are installed promptly.

In addition, SP2 includes numerous security-related enhancements under the hood. For example:

- The Alerter and Messenger services are disabled by default. These services, which date back to the first version of Windows NT, provide a crude form of instant messaging between computers. But in recent years, spammers discovered they could send annoying unsolicited messages over the Internet to computers running the Messenger service.

- Data execution prevention (DEP) is implemented as a way to shut down security exploits that manage to insert and execute code in unexpected memory locations. (This is how many buffer overrun attacks work.) It does this by marking all memory locations used by a process as nonexecutable except those locations explicitly identified as having executable code. If a malicious program attempts to run in a memory location marked as nonexecutable, Windows closes the program.

  In addition to the software support implemented by Service Pack 2, DEP requires a compatible processor. Intel Itanium processors and Advanced Micro Devices (AMD) processors in the Opteron and Athlon 64 families support DEP. Both companies, along with Transmeta, have announced that other processors released in 2004 or later will also support DEP (sometimes referred to as NX, for *no execute*). To determine if your computer's processor is compatible with DEP, in Control Panel open System, click the Advanced tab, click Settings in the Performance box, and click the Data Execution Prevention tab. If your processor does not support DEP, a message at the bottom of the dialog box lets you know.

 # Monitoring Windows XP Security

Your first encounter with the security features included with Service Pack 2 is likely to be a pop-up message from the new Windows Security Center. If you've just installed the latest version of Windows XP (or just upgraded an older version to SP2), you might see a message like the one shown in Figure 7-2 competing for your attention with the invitations to take a tour of Windows, activate Windows, and get a .NET Passport. This is an indication that Security Center is on the job, monitoring your computer's essential security settings.

Figure 7-2. Warning messages pop up above the Windows Security Alerts icon in the notification area at logon if your computer's security settings need attention.

Clicking the notification area balloon or the icon from which it emanates opens Windows Security Center, a control panel for monitoring and managing the three security essentials: firewall, updates, and antivirus. You can also open Security Center via its icon in Control Panel or by typing **wscui.cpl** at a command prompt. Figure 7-3 shows the various elements in Security Center.

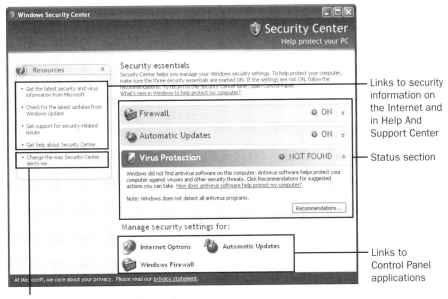

Link to Security Center alert settings

Figure 7-3. Security Center collects security-related information and settings in a single window.

The status section provides at-a-glance information about your security settings. For each item, if everything is okay, you'll see a blue bar with the word *ON*. Clicking the blue bar expands it to display descriptive information. Items that need your attention have an orange or red bar, and status is indicated by phrases such as *Off, Check Settings, Out of Date, Not Found*, or *Not Monitored*. Below the bar appears explanatory text and buttons that let you correct the problem (or configure Security Center so that it won't bother you).

> **Note** If your computer is joined to a domain, Security Center is turned off by default. Although you can still summon it from Control Panel in this situation, the status section is absent. No icon appears in the notification area, and Security Center does not monitor your computer's security status. The only function of Security Center while it's turned off is to provide an attractive container for links to security-related Control Panel applications and online security information. To fully enable Security Center on a domain-based computer, you must make a Group Policy setting. For details, see "Security Center," page 1110.

Security Center is designed to work with third-party firewall programs as well as with Windows Firewall, but many such programs written before the release of SP2 in mid-2004 are not properly recognized by Security Center. It checks for the presence of other software firewalls using Windows Management Instrumentation (WMI), but some firewalls don't respond in an expected way. If you've turned off Windows Firewall in favor of an unrecognized third-party firewall, Security Center suggests with a red bar that your computer has no firewall protection. Click the Recommendations button to display the dialog box shown in Figure 7-4. If you don't want to use Windows Firewall and you don't want to be bothered with alerts from Security Center, select the check box near the bottom of the dialog box: I Have A Firewall Solution That I'll Monitor Myself. You won't receive any further alerts, and thereafter Security Center passively indicates the status as Not Monitored. If you decide you'd rather use Windows Firewall, in the same dialog box you can click Enable Now to turn on Windows Firewall for each of your network connections, without so much as a visit to Windows Firewall or Network Connections.

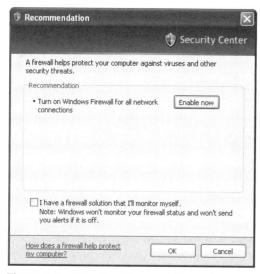

Figure 7-4.   Selecting the check box tells Security Center to stop monitoring firewall status and to stop sending alerts about its status.

Note Security Center does not detect any type of hardware firewall device. If your network has one, you can select the check box in the Recommendation dialog box to avoid the warnings—or you can enable Windows Firewall. Although it's not a good idea to run more than one software firewall on a computer, there's usually no reason not to run a software firewall as an extra layer of protection behind your hardware firewall.

Similarly, Security Center is designed to work with third-party antivirus programs. Using WMI queries, it checks for the presence of antivirus software, and also checks to see if the software (including its virus definitions) is up to date and whether real-time scanning is enabled. Unfortunately, many antivirus programs that predate SP2 go unrecognized. To avoid incessant warnings from Security Center, use a workaround similar to the one for unrecognized firewalls: Click Recommendations in the related red warning bar and then select I Have An Antivirus Program That I'll Monitor Myself.

Tip Disable Security Center alerts
Selecting the I Have… check box in either of the Recommendation dialog boxes, as described in the preceding paragraphs, causes Security Center to stop monitoring a particular security component and, therefore, to stop displaying security alert messages like the one shown in Figure 7-2. However, you might want to disable the alerts but *not* disable Security Center monitoring. This ensures that alerts don't pop up at inopportune times, such as during a presentation. To disable alerts, in Security Center click Change The Way Security Center Alerts Me, the last link in the Resources pane on the left side. In the dialog box that appears, shown below, you can selectively disable Security Center alerts by clearing one or more check boxes.

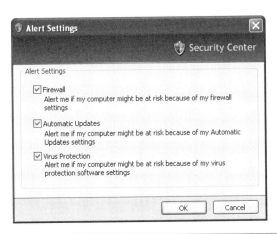

Naturally, you can use the links at the bottom of the Security Center window to open Control Panel applications in which you can refine your security settings. As shown in Figure 7-3, by default Security Center includes icons for Internet Options, Automatic Updates, and Windows Firewall. At the time of this book's publication, we're not aware of any third-party firewall or antivirus programs that add their own icons to the mix. But Security Center is designed to easily accommodate them, so that with a complement of properly designed programs, it serves as the heart of your basic security operations.

Blocking Intruders with Windows Firewall

Your first line of defense in securing your computer is to protect it from attacks by outsiders. Once your computer is connected to the Internet, it becomes just another node on a huge global network. A *firewall* provides a barrier between your computer and the network to which it's connected by preventing the entry of unwanted traffic while allowing transparent passage to authorized connections.

Using a firewall is simple, essential, and often overlooked. You'll want to be sure that all network connections are protected by a firewall. You might be comforted by the knowledge that your portable computer is protected by a corporate firewall when you're at work and that you use a firewalled broadband connection at home. But what about the dial-up connection you use when you travel? Viruses like Sasser and its ilk find unprotected dial-up connections to be an easy mark. In fact, although dial-up users are less vulnerable to certain types of attacks just because of their relatively short connection time, they are particularly vulnerable to Internet worms like Sasser because many Internet service providers (ISPs) don't offer effective firewall protection for this type of connection.

And it makes sense to run a firewall on your computer (sometimes called a *personal firewall*) even when you're behind a corporate firewall. Other people on your network might not be as vigilant as you are about defending against viruses, so if someone brings in a Sasser-infected portable computer and connects it to the network, you're toast—unless your network connection has its own firewall protection.

> **Caution**   This bears repeating. In today's environment, you should run firewall software on each networked computer; don't rely on corporate gateway firewalls and gateway antivirus solutions to protect your computer from another infected computer inside the perimeter. It was this kind of vulnerability that led to the Blaster worm's quick and wide proliferation throughout supposedly protected networks in 2003. Administrators who fret about installing, maintaining, and restricting usage of yet another application on every desktop throughout an enterprise can take solace in the fact that Windows Firewall can be centrally managed through Group Policy.

Windows XP includes a firewall now called, cleverly enough, Windows Firewall. Part of Service Pack 2 for Windows XP, Windows Firewall replaces the Internet Connection Firewall (ICF) that was included in earlier versions of Windows XP. Like ICF, Windows Firewall is a stateful filtering firewall that drops all inbound traffic except traffic sent in response to a request sent by your computer and unsolicited traffic that has been explicitly allowed by creating an exception. You notice nothing if an inbound packet is dropped, but you can (at your option) create a plain-text log of all such events.

Stateful Filtering Explained

Most firewalls work, at least in part, by *packet filtering*—that is, they block or allow transmissions depending on the content of each packet that reaches the firewall. A packet filter examines several attributes of each packet and can either route it (that is, forward it to the intended destination computer) or block it, based on any of these attributes:

- **Source address** The IP address of the computer that generated the packet.
- **Destination address** The IP address of the packet's intended target computer.
- **Network protocol** The type of traffic, such as Internet Protocol (IP).
- **Transport protocol** The higher level protocol, such as Transmission Control Protocol (TCP) or User Datagram Protocol (UDP).
- **Source and destination ports** The number that communicating computers use to identify a communications channel.

Packet filtering alone is an inadequate solution; incoming traffic that meets all the packet filter criteria could still be something you didn't ask for or want. *Stateful packet filtering* goes a step further by restricting incoming traffic to responses to requests from your computer. Here's an example of how stateful filtering works to allow "good" incoming traffic:

1. You enter a URL in your browser's address bar.
2. The browser sends one or more packets of data, addressed to the Web server. The destination port is 80, the standard port for HTTP Web servers; the source port is between 1024 and 65535 (Windows arbitrarily selects an available port number in that range when establishing the connection.)
3. The firewall saves information about the connection in its state table, which it will use to validate returning inbound traffic.
4. The Web server sends a reply (the contents of the Web page you requested) addressed to your computer's IP address and source port.
5. The firewall receives the incoming traffic and compares its source and destination addresses and ports with the information in its state table. If the information matches, the firewall permits the reply to pass through to the browser. If the data doesn't match in all respects, the firewall silently discards the packet.
6. Your browser displays the received information.

But Windows Firewall differs from ICF in much more than name. Among the important improvements that are added with SP2 for Windows XP:

- **Windows Firewall protects internal and external connections.** As suggested by the name, Internet Connection Firewall was intended to protect your computer's Internet connection, but it wasn't easy to properly configure it for connections to your local area network. Recognizing the fact that many security threats can come from your own network, the more appropriately named Windows Firewall now plays nicely with LAN connections.

- **Windows Firewall is enabled by default for all connections.** By default, Windows Firewall is enabled for all network connections on a computer with SP2 installed. This includes wired LAN connections, wireless connections, dial-up connections, and VPN connections. Any new connections you create have Windows Firewall enabled by default.

- **Global configuration options apply to all connections.** With ICF, you had to make firewall settings (such as exceptions to allow incoming traffic) separately for each connection. With Windows Firewall, you can make settings globally. Windows Firewall also lets you make settings for individual connections; any per-connection settings override the global settings.

- **You're protected during startup.** If Windows Firewall is enabled, Windows provides stateful filtering while it is connecting to your network. During startup, Windows Firewall provides basic protection for network startup tasks such as obtaining an IP address from a DHCP server and Group Policy updates from a domain controller. Full protection according to your Windows Firewall configuration then becomes effective when the Windows Firewall service starts. With ICF, you had no firewall protection until the service started, which left a brief interval in which the computer could be attacked.

- **You can specify a scope for each exception.** When you set up an exception in ICF (that is, you specify a port through which unsolicited inbound traffic is allowed), the incoming traffic could originate from any IP address. Windows Firewall lets you restrict the scope for exceptions by limiting it to traffic from an IP address that is part of your local subnet or from a list of IP addresses that you specify.

- **You can create exceptions for programs.** With Windows Firewall, you can create an exception by specifying the name of the program or service for which you want to allow unsolicited incoming traffic. This way, you don't need to know which port(s) and protocol(s) are used by a program in order to create an exception; Windows Firewall figures it out for you.

- **Windows Firewall supports two profiles on domain-based computers.** The domain profile is used when the computer is connected to the domain and the standard profile is used when the computer is not connected or connected to a different network. Each profile has a separate list of exceptions and settings. Windows Firewall switches profiles automatically when you connect or disconnect the computer from the domain network.

- **Internet Protocol version 6 (IPv6) is supported.** IPv6, sometimes called "the next generation Internet," is a protocol that will someday supplant the current Internet Protocol, which is more accurately called IPv4. When that day arrives, Windows Firewall is ready. For more information about IPv6, visit *http://www.ipv6.org.*

- **Configuration can be done with command lines or using Group Policy.** The user interface for configuring Windows Firewall is convenient for ad hoc management of the firewall on a single computer. But if you perform certain tasks repeatedly, or if you have to configure multiple computers, it's much easier to set up a batch program or script that contains the commands needed to perform the task. Likewise, Group Policy (particularly in a domain environment) eases the burden of repetitive tasks. In addition, you can configure the operational mode and exceptions list for Windows Firewall during unattended setup.

Enabling or Disabling Windows Firewall

You manage Windows Firewall through its Control Panel application, which is new with Service Pack 2. (In previous versions of Windows XP, ICF was managed through a tab in the properties dialog box for each network connection.) You can, of course, open Windows Firewall directly from Control Panel. Category View users will find its icon in Network And Internet Connections as well as in Security Center. Other ways to open Windows Firewall include:

- In Security Center, click the Windows Firewall link.
- In the Network Connections folder, click Change Windows Firewall Settings (in the task pane under Network Tasks).
- In the properties dialog box for a network connection, click the Advanced tab and then click Settings in the Windows Firewall box.
- At a command prompt, type **firewall.cpl.**

> **Note** Security Center and Network Connections make ideal launch pads for Windows Firewall because both show at a glance whether Windows Firewall is enabled. Security Center, of course, dedicates the top part of its status section to firewall status. In Network Connections, each connection for which Windows Firewall is enabled has a small padlock in its icon.

Regardless of how you open Windows Firewall, you'll see a dialog box like the one shown in Figure 7-5. To enable Windows Firewall for all network connections, select On. To disable Windows Firewall, of course, select Off. In general, the only reason to turn off Windows Firewall is if you have installed a third-party firewall that you plan to use instead of Windows Firewall.

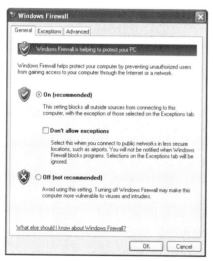

Figure 7-5. The General tab of the Windows Firewall dialog box houses the main on/off switch for Windows Firewall.

Preventing All Incoming Traffic

The Don't Allow Exceptions check box on the General tab provides additional safety. When it's selected, Windows Firewall rejects *all* unsolicited incoming traffic—even traffic that would ordinarily be permitted by an exception. (For information about exceptions, see "Allowing Connections Through the Firewall," on the next page.) Invoke this mode when extra security against outside attack is needed. For example, you might disable exceptions when you're using a public wireless hotspot or when you know that your computer is actively under attack by others.

> **Note** Selecting Don't Allow Exceptions does not disconnect your computer from the Internet. Windows Firewall does not block outbound traffic, so even in "no exceptions" mode, you can still use your browser to connect to the Internet. Similarly, other outbound connections—whether they're legitimate services or some sort of spyware—continue unabated.

Disabling Windows Firewall for Individual Connections

Windows Firewall ordinarily monitors all network connections for unwanted traffic. In some situations, you might want to disable its protection for one or more connections while leaving it on for others. (For example, you might have a print server on your internal LAN connection that refuses to work with Windows Firewall—but you still want to protect your external dial-up connection.) That's easily done, as follows:

1 In Windows Firewall, click the Advanced tab.

2 Clear the check box of each connection for which you want to disable Windows Firewall.

Allowing Connections Through the Firewall

In some situations, you want to allow other computers to initiate a connection to your computer. For example, your computer might be set up as a Web server that you want to make available to Internet users. A more likely scenario is that you want to share some of your computer's folders with other users on your network. Or perhaps you use an instant messaging program that requires inbound connections so others can contact you. In each of these cases, you set up an *exception* in Windows Firewall. An exception pokes a small hole in the firewall and allows a certain type of traffic to pass through the firewall.

Working with Exceptions

You manage exceptions that apply to all connections on the Exceptions tab, shown in Figure 7-6. The list of programs and services that initially appears on the Exceptions tab depends on which services and programs are installed on your computer; you can add others, as described in the following sections. To allow an exception for a program or service that's already been defined, simply select its check box.

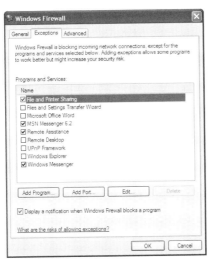

Figure 7-6. The list of programs and services on your computer might not include all those shown here, and it might include others.

Each exception increases your security risk to some degree, so you should clear the check box for all exceptions you don't need. If you're confident you won't ever need a particular exception, you can select it and then click Delete. (A handful of predefined exceptions don't allow deletion, but as long as their check boxes are not selected, there's no danger.)

Creating an Exception for a Program

When you run a program that needs to allow an inbound connection, you can create an exception in any of three ways:

● You can click Unblock when Windows Firewall blocks a program and asks if you want to keep blocking.

● You can set up a program exception on the Exceptions tab in Windows Firewall.

● You can open a port on the Exceptions tab in Windows Firewall. (For details, see "Opening a Port," on page 202.)

Note A *port* is a somewhat arbitrary number that two computers use to identify a particular communications channel. In order for two computers to connect to each other using TCP/IP, both have to agree on which port number (from 1 to 65535) each computer will use.

Creating an exception for a program using either of the first two methods is usually the easier and more secure approach. You don't need to know which port (or ports) the program uses. And Windows Firewall allows the exception only while the program is running, whereas an exception created for a port you open is allowed whenever Windows itself is running, regardless of whether the affected program is actually running.

When a program attempts to open a listening port and you haven't allowed an exception for it, Windows Firewall displays a Windows Security Alert dialog box similar to this:

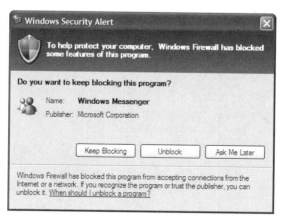

Clearly, you have three options. But exactly what each of those options does is not clear!

● If you click Keep Blocking, Windows Firewall does not create an exception. This means that your program is unable to accept incoming connections, so it might not work properly.

● If you click Unblock, Windows Firewall creates an exception for the program and enables the exception. The program's listening port is then open for incoming connections.

● If you click Ask Me Later, Windows Firewall creates an exception for the program—but it does not enable the exception. The program does not accept incoming connections unless you explicitly allow them.

If you choose Unblock or Ask Me Later, you can see the newly defined exception with a visit to the Exceptions tab in Windows Firewall. (See Figure 7-6.) You can learn more about the exception by selecting it and clicking Edit.

From the Exceptions tab, you can set up a program exception without waiting for the Windows Security Alert dialog box to appear. Follow these steps:

1   Click Add Program. The Add A Program dialog box appears.

2   In the Add A Program dialog box, select the program for which you want to allow incoming connections. Or click Browse and navigate to the program's executable file if it isn't shown in the Programs list.

3   Click Change Scope to display the dialog box shown in Figure 7-7.

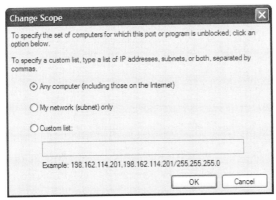

Figure 7-7.   The scope options are the same for creating a program exception or opening a port.

4 Select the range of computers from which you want to allow incoming connections.

- Any Computer means just that—any computer on your network or on the Internet. (Other defenses, such as NTFS permissions or some form of password authentication, might keep out unwanted users, but Windows Firewall will not.)

- My Network (Subnet) Only allows inbound connections only from computers in the same subnet as yours. (For information about subnets, see "Diagnosing IP Address Problems," page 984.)

- Custom List lets you specify one or more computers by their IP address. These can be computers on your local area network or computers with public IP addresses on the Internet.

> **Tip** If you don't want to be bothered with the Windows Security Alert dialog box, clear the Display A Notification When Windows Firewall Blocks A Program check box on the Exceptions tab.

Opening a Port

Another way to create an exception for an incoming connection is to open a port. If the instructions for a program or service you want to use indicate that it needs to use a particular port, use the following procedure to open the specified port.

1 In Windows Firewall, click the Exceptions tab.

2 Click Add Port. The Add A Port dialog box appears.

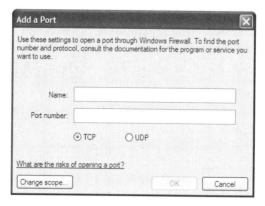

3 In the Add A Port dialog box, make the following entries:

- In the Name box, type a descriptive name for the program or service.

- In the Port Number box, type the port number needed by the program or service.

- Select either TCP or UDP to match the protocol needed by the program or service.

4 Click Change Scope.

5   In the Change Scope dialog box (see Figure 7-7 and step 4 in the previous section), select the range of computers from which you want to allow incoming connections.

Creating Exceptions for a Server

If you run Web, FTP, or mail server software on your computer, or if you want to enable out-side connections to a similar service, you need to create a firewall exception for the server. Similarly, if the server runs on another computer on your network but the network connection through which outside computers will connect to the server is on your computer, you need to create a firewall exception. Windows Firewall has exceptions defined (but not enabled) for many common server types, and you can define others.

> **Note**   An exception you define on the Exceptions tab, as described in the preceding sections, applies to all network connections. Exceptions you create for a server, as described in this section, apply to a single connection.

To enable a service, follow these steps:

1   In Windows Firewall, click the Advanced tab.

2   Select the network connection for which you want to allow an exception for incoming connections.

3   In the Network Connection Settings box, click Settings. The Advanced Settings dialog box appears.

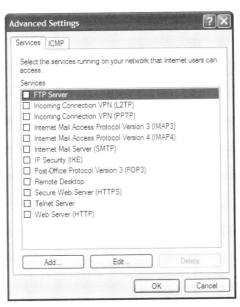

4 To use one of the predefined services, select its check box.

5 If the service is running on another computer on your network, click Edit. In the Service Settings dialog box that appears, specify the IP address of the computer hosting the service.

6 To add a service that isn't on the list of predefined services, click Add. In the Service Settings dialog box, enter the following information:

- A descriptive name for the service
- The name or IP address of the computer hosting the service
- The port number that external computers will use to access the service
- The port number that the service is listening to on your network
- The protocol (TCP or UDP)

Troubleshooting

Windows Firewall doesn't work, or it prevents connections between computers.

Windows Firewall is an essential component of Windows security—but because its very purpose is to isolate computers from one another, it's one that can cause problems when you try to communicate between computers. A document that you can download from the Microsoft Web site, "Troubleshooting Windows Firewall in Microsoft Windows XP Service Pack 2," describes solutions to a number of common problems. To get the latest version of the document, go to *http://www.microsoft.com/downloads* and search for "troubleshooting windows firewall."

Enabling Ping and Other Diagnostic Commands

The TCP and UDP protocols are used to transmit data. But Internet communication also relies on Internet Control Message Protocol (ICMP) to communicate status, control, and error information between computers. In addition, widely used troubleshooting tools such as Ping and Tracert use ICMP to establish network connectivity. Because ICMP carries no data, it can't be used to break into your machine and steal information. But hackers do use ICMP messages for scanning networks, redirecting traffic, and carrying out Denial of Service (DoS) attacks.

By default, Windows Firewall blocks most types of outgoing and incoming ICMP messages. With options accessed from the Advanced tab in Windows Firewall, you can allow certain types of ICMP packets. There's seldom a reason to enable any of these options except for troubleshooting purposes, and they can expose your computer to certain security risks.

To specify ICMP settings for all connections, on the Advanced tab, click Settings in the ICMP box. A dialog box like the one shown in Figure 7-8 appears.

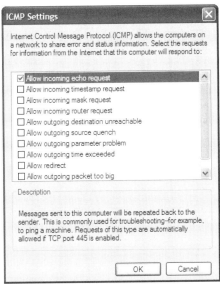

Figure 7-8. As you select each item, the description box at the bottom of the dialog box explains how the item is used.

To specify ICMP settings for an individual connection, on the Advanced tab, select the network connection. Click Settings in the Network Connection Settings box, and then click the ICMP tab. The same list of ICMP options appears. (Actually, you might notice one difference: If the connection you selected does not support IPv6—and most do not at this time—

the list doesn't include Allow Outgoing Packet Too Big, which is an IPv6-only option.) Any settings you make in this dialog box override the global settings you make in the dialog box shown in Figure 7-8.

> For more details about Ping, Tracert, and other essential utilities, see "Network Troubleshooting Tools," page 991.

Logging Firewall Activity

When Windows Firewall blocks traffic, it doesn't display an (annoying) on-screen alert as some third-party personal firewalls do. However, you can configure Windows Firewall to store a record of its activity in a log file. To enable logging, follow these steps:

1 In Windows Firewall, click the Advanced tab.

2 In the Security Logging box, click Settings. The Log Settings dialog box appears.

3 Select the check boxes for the kinds of events you want to log—dropped packets, successful connections, or both.

> **Tip** Log dropped packets only
>
> You'll get the most useful security information by logging only dropped packets, so that Windows Firewall records each connection that was blocked. Logging successful connections tends to create a large file with information that you probably don't need. A log of dropped packets, however, can lead you to IP addresses that are probing your computer and that you might want to act against.

4 Specify a file name for the log if you don't want to use the default (%SystemRoot%\Pfirewall.log).

5 To keep a log from getting too large, specify a maximum file size.

6 Click OK.

To read your log, open it in Notepad or another text editor. Figure 7-9 shows a sample of a Windows Firewall log.

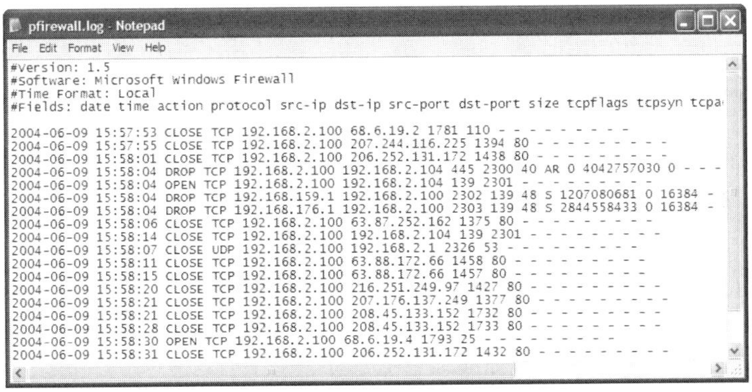

Figure 7-9. A firewall log captures a lot more information than you ever thought you'd need.

The log uses the W3C Extended Log format, a standard logging format that allows you to analyze data using third-party utilities. To understand what the columns mean, look at the column headers in line 4 (they don't align over the data below, but they're in the correct order). The most significant columns are the first eight, listed in Table 7-1.

Table 7-1. The First Eight Columns of a Windows Firewall Log

Item	Description
Date	Year-Month-Date of occurrence
Time	Hour:Minute:Second of occurrence
Action	Operation logged by the firewall; possible values are OPEN, CLOSE, DROP, and INFO-EVENTS-LOST
Protocol	Protocol used for the communication; possible values are TCP, UDP, and ICMP
Source IP	IP address of the computer that initiated the communication
Destination IP	IP address of your computer
Source Port	The port number of the sending computer
Destination Port	Port that the sending computer tried to access on your computer

Inside Out

Use Microsoft Excel to view firewall logs

Do you have Microsoft Office installed on your computer? If so, skip Notepad and use Microsoft Excel to analyze Windows Firewall log files. After converting the space-delimited text file to Excel columns, you can sort, filter, and search the output. Try using Excel's Auto-Filter capability to pick out specific IP addresses or ports from the log; this technique can help zero in on attackers quickly.

Controlling Windows Firewall with Group Policy

If you have Windows XP Professional, Group Policy provides another way to control Windows Firewall. And like the Netsh command (described in the following section), it allows you to do some things you can't do with the Control Panel application alone. To examine the available settings, at a command prompt type **gpedit.msc** to open Group Policy. Navigate to Computer Configuration\Administrative Templates\Network\Network Connections\Windows Firewall, which contains two folders, Domain Profile and Standard Profile.

Why two profiles? You might want different settings depending on whether your computer is connected to a corporate network or not. For example, with a portable computer you might want the firewall locked up tight while you're not traveling or working at home, but have exceptions for certain programs when you're using the corporate network. Windows Firewall uses the settings specified in the Domain Profile folder whenever your computer is joined to a domain; it uses the settings in the Standard Profile folder at all other times. The available settings, which you can examine by clicking either folder, are the same in each folder. Select a policy to display information about how it works; double-click it to make settings.

Note For more information about Group Policy, see Appendix F, "Group Policy." For information about domains, see Chapter 33, "Working with Windows Domains."

Using the Netsh Command to Manage Windows Firewall

If you need to make firewall settings repeatedly—on a single computer as conditions change or, perhaps, on a fleet of computers—you'll find working with the Windows Firewall Control Panel application to be a bit cumbersome. Fortunately, Service Pack 2 introduces another improvement over ICF: command-line control. The Netsh Firewall command provides an alternative way to view or modify all manner of settings—more, in fact, than you can set using the Control Panel application. For example, you can enable Windows Firewall with this command:

```
netsh firewall set opmode enable
```

This command enables logging of dropped packets in a file named C:\Fw.log:

```
netsh firewall set logging c:\fw.log 4096 enable
```

With dozens of keywords and options, the Netsh Firewall command is quite complex. The best way to learn about its various possibilities is through online help. Start in the Help And Support Center. A search for "netsh firewall" returns a suggested topic page titled "Configuring Windows Firewall from the command line," which provides a good overview. For more details, use the help available from the command line. You'll need to do it in several steps, appending another keyword each time. Start by entering **netsh firewall ?** at a command prompt. This returns a list of each of the keywords that you can put after *firewall*—Add, Delete, Dump, Help, Reset, and Set—along with a brief description of each. Next you might type **netsh firewall set ?** to learn about each of the Set options. Then you'd type **netsh firewall set opmode ?**—and so on, until you reach a screen that shows the command syntax and explains all the parameters for the command you've entered.

> **Note** You can make settings for the Domain Profile or the Standard Profile using Netsh Firewall, just as you can with Group Policy. In commands where it's relevant, you use the Profile parameter, which you can set to Domain, Standard, or All. (If you don't specify a profile, your settings apply to the current profile, which depends on whether your computer is joined to a domain.)

 The ability to control the firewall with command lines (and with scripts) makes it possible to create little programs to perform oft-needed tasks easily. This book's companion CD contains a program called Firewall Quick Switch.vbs that enables or disables Windows Firewall more easily than going through the Control Panel application. For more information about this program, see "Enabling or Disabling Windows Firewall," page 638.

Alternatives to Windows Firewall

The firewall software supplied with Windows XP provides good protection against intrusion. Many third-party software firewalls have features not included in Windows Firewall. One feature that differentiates some firewalls is the ability to monitor outbound communication. (Windows Firewall is concerned only with blocking unwanted inbound traffic.) Some viruses and Trojan horses do their mischief by lodging themselves on your system, reading your address books, and then using your computer to launch DoS attacks and export copies of themselves via your Internet connection—in essence, making your computer the creator of mischief on others' computers.

However, there's disagreement among security experts about whether outbound filtering truly enhances security. After all, you won't have a need for outbound filtering until an attacker is able to place a program on your computer (for example, as an e-mail attachment or by offering an attractive-sounding program on a Web site) and then persuade you to run the program.

A good independent source of information about firewalls is the ICSA Labs Web site (*http://www.icsalabs.com/html/communities/firewalls/*), where you'll find information about firewalls and how they work, criteria for an effective firewall, and a buyer's guide that is updated annually. After checking a product to confirm its ability to be installed by a nonexpert user, support Microsoft networking capabilities while providing protection, support concurrent dial-up and LAN connectivity, maintain consistent protection across multiple successive dial-up connections, block common external network attacks, restrict outgoing network communication, and log events in a consistent and useful manner, ICSA Labs certifies a program that meets its criteria.

Keeping Your System Secure with Windows Update

Over time, Microsoft publishes changes to Windows. Some changes are minor additions to the Windows feature set. Other changes are designated as critical updates; these patches (also known as *hotfixes*) repair bugs that can hamper your system's performance, compromise its security, or cause system crashes. Periodically, Microsoft gathers these patches into collections called *rollups* and makes them available for download. And less frequently, Microsoft releases a *service pack*, a thoroughly tested collection of updates and bug fixes. Applying a service pack to your computer is functionally equivalent to (but much simpler than) individually installing all the fixes it contains.

> **Note** With earlier versions of Windows, you must reinstall a service pack whenever you add or remove Windows components or make certain hardware changes. With Windows XP, that's no longer the case. However, you do need to reinstall a service pack if you do any of the following after its installation:
>
> ● Reinstall Windows XP (even if you do an in-place upgrade installation).
>
> ● Repair your Windows installation using Windows Setup (see "Repairing and Reinstalling Windows," page 1301, for details).
>
> ● Use System Restore to revert to a restore point created before you installed the service pack
>
> ● Upgrade from Windows XP Home Edition to Windows XP Professional.

Using Windows Update Manually

The most reliable way to install updates to your computer is with the help of Windows Update. This online service provides one-stop access to the entire collection of updates for Windows and the various programs included with it. The list of available updates includes service packs, updated device drivers, and security updates. To run Windows Update, use any of the following techniques:

● In the Help And Support Center, under Pick A Task, click Keep Your Computer Up-To-Date With Windows Update.

- Open the Start menu and choose All Programs, Windows Update.
- At a command prompt, type **wupdmgr**.
- In Internet Explorer, open the Tools menu and choose Windows Update.
- In Internet Explorer, browse to *http://windowsupdate.microsoft.com*.

The first method displays Windows Update within the Help And Support Center window, as shown in Figure 7-10. If you use any of the other methods, Windows Update appears in an Internet Explorer window.

Tip   Hide updates that you don't ever want to install

The Optional Software Updates category include a slew of updates that you probably have no need for, including patches designed to provide compatibility with hardware you don't own, updates to components you don't use, and regional updates that don't apply to you. If you skip an update, though, it's waiting for you the next time you check Windows Update, unless you customize the display to hide unwanted items. To do so, in the list of updates presented by Custom Install, select Hide This Update for each item you want to eliminate. (The option is unavailable for high priority updates.)

If you later change your mind—or if you just want to see a list of the updates you've chosen to hide—click Restore Hidden Updates (under Other Options in the left navigation pane of Windows Update).

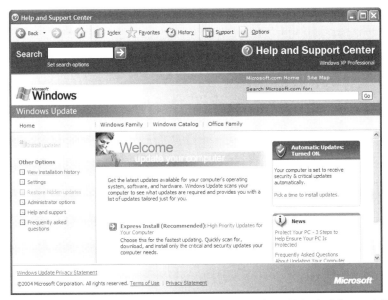

Figure 7-10.   Windows Update can run as part of the Help And Support Center, as shown here, or in an ordinary Internet Explorer window.

> **Note** The first time you use Windows Update, you might need to install its ActiveX control. You can tell if you need to do this if the Information Bar in Internet Explorer drops down with a warning: "To help protect your security, Internet Explorer stopped this site from installing an ActiveX control on your computer." Click the Information Bar and choose Install ActiveX Control. A security warning box then pops up to inform you that Microsoft Corporation is the publisher of the Windows Update control. Click Install.

To begin the update process, click either Express Install or Custom Install.

- Express Install queries the Windows Update server only for critical updates, security updates, service packs, and update rollups—known collectively as *high priority updates*. After a moment's time, Windows displays a list of these updates, along with their number, total size, and estimated download time. You can click any of the listed updates to view more information, but the most expedient action is to simply click the Install button. These high priority updates should be installed as soon as they become available.

- Custom Install (see Figure 7-11) provides access to miscellaneous noncritical software and hardware enhancements and updates in addition to the high priority updates sought by Express Install. Click each of the three links on the left side—Review High Priority Updates, Select Optional Software Updates, and Select Optional Hardware Updates—to view information about available updates in those categories. Read the description for each item, and then select the check box for each update that you want to install. (Because you'll almost certainly want to install all high priority updates, they're selected by default.) After you finish selecting items, click Go To Install Updates for a final review, and then click Install.

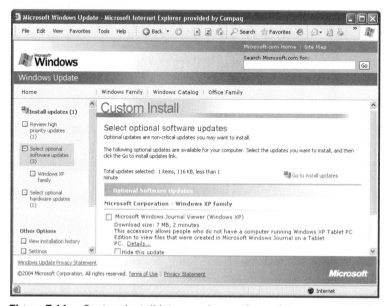

Figure 7-11. Custom Install lets you choose the updates you want to install.

Automating Your Updates

Windows updates are not distributed on a regular basis. Instead, they're published when the need arises, such as when a patch is developed for a newly discovered security vulnerability. In Windows XP, you can eliminate the necessity to check for updates manually by using a feature called Automatic Updates. With this feature enabled, you can instruct Windows to periodically check for high priority updates. Using the preferences you define, Automatic Updates checks for new high priority updates, downloads them in the background, using a small segment of your available Internet connection bandwidth, and—with your permission—installs them automatically.

> **Note** Automatic Updates retrieves only high priority updates. To view, download, and install other Windows updates and newly released drivers, you need to visit the Windows Update site.

Each Windows XP Service Pack has included a major overhaul of the Automatic Updates feature, and Service Pack 2 is no exception. In the original release of Windows XP, you could choose to be alerted when new updates were available, and Windows would download them for you to install, but the operating system wouldn't actually perform the updates. With SP2 installed, the Automatic Updates dialog box includes new options, including the ability to install high priority updates on a specified schedule.

After you first install Windows XP, the operating system is persistent about reminding you to set up the Automatic Updates feature. You can adjust the related options at any time by opening Automatic Updates, which you can do in any of the following ways:

- Open Security Center and click Automatic Updates. (For more information about Security Center, see "Monitoring Windows XP Security," page 190.)
- Open System in Control Panel (in the Performance And Maintenance group) and click the Automatic Updates tab.
- Open Automatic Updates in Control Panel (if you use Classic view).
- Enter **wuaucpl.cpl** at a command prompt or open a shortcut to this command.

To enable Automatic Updates, select one of the first three options available to you, as shown in Figure 7-12:

- **Automatically Download Recommended Updates For My Computer And Install Them** Choose this option if you want the Automatic Updates process to live up to its name completely. In this "set it and forget it" configuration, Windows Update checks for high priority updates on the schedule you specify (by default at 3:00 A.M. every day, although you can change the schedule to weekly and change the time as well), downloads each one as soon as it appears, and installs the update for you. Beware, however: If an update requires restarting your computer, Windows will do so with no regard to whether any applications are open. This option is most appropriate if you leave your computer turned on.

213

- **Download Updates For Me, But Let Me Choose When To Install Them**   This option is most appropriate for users with high-speed, always-on Internet connections—cable modems and DSL, for instance. An icon in the notification area alerts you when a download has arrived. You can accept or reject any download.

- **Notify Me But Don't Automatically Download Or Install Them**   If you don't want to tie up your dial-up Internet connection downloading updates, choose this option. An icon in the notification area alerts you when a download is available; you decide whether and when to download and install it.

Figure 7-12.   To choose how Windows checks for updates, select one of the first three options.

Selecting Turn Off Automatic Updates disables Automatic Updates. Doing so is appropriate if you want to manage updates from a network location instead of having each computer download and install updates individually. (For details, see the following section.)

To install an update that you previously rejected, open Automatic Updates; then click the Offer Updates Again That I've Previously Hidden link. (This link will be unavailable until at least one update has been declined.)

Downloading Update Files for Multiple Computers

Some of the available updates are quite large, often exceeding 5 MB of data. Also, sometimes the file size shown in Windows Update is misleading; it indicates only the size of the installer for the update, not the update itself, which might be considerably larger. Particularly if you have a slow Internet connection, you'll want to minimize the bandwidth consumed by downloads from Windows Update.

Although it's not very well advertised (compared to the myriad ways to start Windows Update, only a portion of which are enumerated earlier in this chapter), Microsoft maintains Web sites where you can download standalone installable versions of the security patches and other updates for Windows. After downloading these patches and updates, you can burn them to CD or make them available on a network server for installation on multiple computers. A site called Windows Update Catalog offers updates for Windows XP, Windows 2000, and Windows Server 2003.

The easiest way to access Windows Update Catalog is to open Windows Update, click Administrator Options (in the left pane), and then click Windows Update Catalog. Alternatively, you can use this link: *http://go.microsoft.com/fwlink/?LinkId=8973.*

If there is a computer running Windows Server 2003 on your network, a better option is available to you. Windows Update Services (which replaces Software Update Services) is a free add-on that helps to automate updates of Windows, Microsoft Office, and other Microsoft products throughout your organization. For more information about Windows Update Services, visit *http://www.microsoft.com/windowsserversystem/wus.*

Troubleshooting

Windows Update doesn't work.

When you start Windows Update, it might display a "software update incomplete" message. (This message appears before you have an opportunity to scan or select updates to install.)

Windows Update requires the use of an ActiveX control, which is installed automatically with Service Pack 2. If you have not yet installed Service Pack 2, this control should be downloaded and installed the first time you access the Windows Update site. To successfully install the ActiveX control, you must:

● Be logged on as a member of the Administrators group.

● Enable (with prompting) the download and running of signed ActiveX controls. (Use settings on the Security tab of the Internet Options dialog box; for more information, see "Controlling ActiveX Downloads," page 319.)

● Click Install in the Security Warning dialog box that asks whether you want to install the Windows Update control.

Once the ActiveX control is installed, an explanatory message appears if a nonadministrative user tries to run Windows Update.

Disabling Windows Update

Windows Update gives any Windows user with administrative rights the ability to locate, download, and install security fixes, drivers, and other updates. That's fine on a personal computer, but in a business setting you might decide that you prefer to give a single network administrator the right to install updates rather than relying on individual users to keep their systems up to date. If the computers in question are running Windows XP Professional, you can set a policy that prevents individual users (even administrators) from using the Internet version of Windows Update. (Group Policy is not available in Windows XP Home Edition.) With this configuration, you can (and should) download and save individual updates and install them manually on each computer.

The following procedure disables manual access to Windows Update on a local computer running Windows XP Professional, shuts down Automatic Updates, and removes all links to the Windows Update site:

1 At a command prompt, type **gpedit.msc** to open the Group Policy console.

2 In the console tree, open User Configuration\Administrative Templates\Windows Components\Windows Update.

3 Double-click Remove Access To Use All Windows Update Features.

4 Select Enabled. This option eliminates all manual access to Windows Update for all local users. (Select Disabled to restore access to Windows Update.)

5 In the console tree, open Computer Configuration\Administrative Templates\ Windows Components\Windows Update.

6 Double-click Configure Automatic Updates.

7 Select Disabled. This option completely removes the Automatic Updates tab from the System option in Control Panel.

> **Tip** The policies in Computer Configuration\Administrative Templates\Windows Components\Windows Update let you configure Automatic Updates in a number of other ways that are not available in the Automatic Updates control panel; you might want to peruse the other options before you close Group Policy.

Several other Windows features also trigger Windows Update. Specifically, the operating system may access Windows Update on its own in any of the following three circumstances:

- When you install a Plug and Play device that does not have a signed driver already installed

- When you click the Update Driver button from the properties dialog box for an installed device

- When you run the Add Printer wizard

If you decide that you want to lock these back doors to Windows Update with a policy, follow these steps:

1 At a command prompt, type **gpedit.msc** to open the Group Policy console.

2 In the console tree, open User Configuration\Administrative Templates\System.

3 Double-click Configure Driver Search Locations.

4 Select Enabled and then choose the Don't Search Windows Update option.

For more information about Group Policy, see Appendix F, "Group Policy."

Blocking Viruses and Worms with an Antivirus Program

The third step in Microsoft's basic PC protection strategy—use up-to-date antivirus software—is one that requires third-party software. Windows XP does not include any antivirus software. Partisans on one side say that it's Microsoft's absolute duty to include a complete security solution, including antivirus software, as part of the operating system. On the other side, people concerned about Microsoft's industry dominance fear that bundling antivirus in the operating system will destroy competition. While Microsoft waits for the dust to settle, viruses continue to sprout like tornados, occasionally touching down and cutting a swath of damage. (Trivia note: At one time, Microsoft did include an antivirus program with its operating system. That operating system was MS-DOS 6.2.)

Finding an Antivirus Program

Plenty of good antivirus programs are available. You can start your search at the Microsoft Antivirus Partners page, *http://www.microsoft.com/security/partners/antivirus.asp*, which provides brief summaries and links to about two dozen publishers of antivirus software. (If you're averse to typing, you'll find a link to this site in Windows Security Center. In the Virus Protection bar of the status section, click Recommendations. Then, in the Recommendation box, click How?.) CERT Coordination Center also maintains a list of antivirus vendors on its Computer Virus Resources page at *http://www.cert.org/other_sources/viruses.html*.

Both of these resources provide lists of products but little or no independent evaluation. Besides the usual review sites managed by computer magazines, you should look to ICSA Labs, which tests antivirus programs and certifies those that meet its criteria for effectiveness. You can find lists of certified programs at *http://www.icsalabs.com/html/communities/antivirus/certifiedproducts.shtml.*

Using an Antivirus Program

Installing an antivirus program is a good first step. But you're not done yet! The initial setup enables the antivirus scanning engine—the code that checks files for possible viruses. The most important part of the package is the database of virus definitions (sometimes called the *signature file*). After installing an antivirus package on a new computer, update it to the latest definitions immediately. Then configure the program to enable these features:

- Install updates to program files and virus definitions at least weekly.
- Scan each file that you access in any way. This feature is typically called "real-time scanning" (or something similar) to differentiate it from scheduled scans, which periodically scan the files stored on your computer to find infected files.
- Scan e-mail attachments and block access to infected files.

Tip   Disable System Restore if you have a virus

If your computer is infected with a virus, your antivirus program should detect the problem and, more importantly, help you eradicate the problem. However, virus-infected files might remain in your System Restore cache. Therefore, to completely remove a virus, turn off System Restore, which removes all saved restore points. Finish cleaning up your system, and then turn System Restore on again. For more information, see Knowledge Base article 831829, "How antivirus software and System Restore work together."

Learning More About Viruses and Virus Protection

The Internet is a rich source of complete and accurate information about viruses, worms, and other hostile software. Unfortunately, a random search of the Internet for information about "computer viruses" also turns up a long list of links to sites that are incomplete, out-of-date, or run by scam artists. We strongly recommend that you start your search for definitive information with the vendor that supplies your antivirus software, because that company is most likely to have information and step-by-step instructions that are directly applicable to your system configuration. Virtually every major company that produces antivirus software offers a searchable Web-based list of viruses. In addition, we suggest bookmarking the CERT Coordination Center site, which offers up-to-date, unbiased information about currently active viruses (*http://www.cert.org/nav/index_red.html*).

The CERT Coordination Center Computer Virus Resources page at *http://www.cert.org/ other_sources/viruses.html* provides lots of general information about viruses—how they've evolved, how they work, how you can protect against them, and how you can recover from an infection. For more information from a company that's not trying to sell you an antivirus program, check out "The Antivirus Defense-in-Depth Guide," which was produced by members of the Microsoft Solutions for Security group. You can download this white paper from Microsoft by visiting *http://go.microsoft.com/fwlink/?linkid=28734*.

Advanced Security Tools and Techniques

Is that all there is to securing your computer? Unfortunately, no. While the three steps outlined in Microsoft's strategy and described in this chapter go a long way toward ensuring that your computer remains safe, there's much more you can do. Many Web sites and many books are devoted solely to the topic of computer security. (In fact, we wrote one: *Microsoft Windows Security Inside Out for Windows XP and Windows 2000*, Microsoft Press, 2003.)

In the remaining sections of this chapter we touch on some of the additional steps you might want to look into and list sources for more information.

Identifying Vulnerabilities with Microsoft Baseline Security Analyzer

Windows Security Center monitors and reports the status of the most basic security components. Microsoft also makes available a tool that performs a more comprehensive test for security vulnerabilities, Microsoft Baseline Security Analyzer (MBSA). (Download Microsoft Baseline Security Analyzer from *http://www.microsoft.com/technet/security/tools/mbsahome.mspx*.)

Using this application, you can test a dozen or more different aspects of your system, including your settings in Internet Explorer and Microsoft Outlook Express, your password-strength policy, your Microsoft Office macro security settings, the security settings for your operating system services, and whether you've installed all necessary service packs and hotfixes. As Figure 7-13 shows, you can use MBSA to scan a group of computers on a network, using domain names or IP addresses to define which computers to check.

Microsoft Baseline Security Analyzer maintains a log of its findings, and you can compare these logs over time to monitor your progress on the security front. But for a better way to collect, monitor, and compare MBSA output for multiple systems, you might want to take advantage of the scripting capabilities built into the most recent versions of MBSA. For information about MBSA scripting, including sample scripts that you can use on your own network, visit *http://www.microsoft.com/technet/security/tools/mbsascript.mspx*.

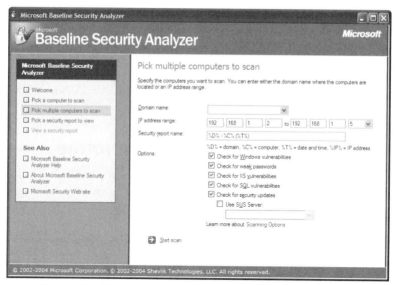

Figure 7-13. Use Microsoft Baseline Security Analyzer to check security settings for one computer or a range of computers on your network.

Keeping Up with Security News

It's an unfortunate fact of life: Security has become an unwanted but essential part of the computing experience. Therefore, you might want to schedule periodic visits to security-related Web sites and subscribe to security-related newsletters or RSS (Really Simple Syndication) feeds. Some resources you might want to check out include:

- Microsoft's security home page at *http://www.microsoft.com/security* offers links to information about the latest security updates (which you already have installed if you use Automatic Updates), current security threats, security training sessions, guidance centers, and other information.

- Microsoft TechNet Security (*http://www.microsoft.com/technet/security*) provides more technical details, aimed primarily at information technology professionals. You can view the latest issue of the Microsoft Security Newsletter at *http://www.microsoft.com/technet/security/secnews/newsletter.htm*; to subscribe, visit *http://www.microsoft.com/technet/security/secnews/default.mspx*

- You can sign up for e-mail alerts of new Microsoft security bulletins at *http://www.microsoft.com/security/bulletins/alerts.mspx*.

- If you'd rather learn about Microsoft security bulletins via RSS, point your aggregator to *http://www.microsoft.com/technet/security/bulletin/secrss.aspx*.

- You can also find valuable technical information on current security threats at *http://www.cert.org*, a site maintained by the CERT Coordination Center, a federally funded research institute operated by Carnegie Mellon University.

Chapter 8

Managing User Accounts, Passwords, and Logons

At Home with Windows XP

With respect to features described in this chapter, the most significant differences between Windows XP Professional and Windows XP Home Edition are the following:

- In Windows XP Home Edition, Simple File Sharing is the only available file-sharing mode. Simple File Sharing provides Home Edition users with an easier-to-understand user interface, but it reduces the granularity with which you can assign permissions to shared resources. For an overview of the differences between Simple File Sharing and the alternative sharing mode available to Professional users, see "Simple File Sharing vs. Windows 2000–Style Sharing," page 230. For more details about these differences, see "Simple File Sharing vs. Advanced Permissions," page 275.

- In Windows XP Home Edition, you can't log on to the Administrator account except in Safe Mode. For information about the Administrator account, see "What Happened to the Administrator Account?" page 249.

Certain procedures described in this chapter are available only in Windows XP Professional, because they involve the use of MMC snap-ins that are not included in Windows XP Home Edition. Wherever possible, we describe workarounds that are available to Home Edition users. For example, the Local Users And Groups snap-in (lusrmgr.msc) is not included in Windows XP Home Edition. The Net User and Net Localgroup commands are available in both versions of Windows XP, however, and you can do the same things (and more) with these command-line utilities that you can do with Local Users And Groups.

Using security concepts that are central to the industrial-strength security in Microsoft Windows NT and Windows 2000, Windows XP allows you to restrict access to your computer so that only people you authorize can use the computer or view its files. This is a sharp departure from Windows 95/98/Me, in which bypassing security was as simple as pressing Esc when Windows asked you for a password. With Windows XP, you can

- Require each user to identify himself or herself when logging on
- Control access to files and other resources that you own
- Audit system events, such as logons and the use of files and other resources

For information about auditing, see Chapter 13, "Auditing Security."

Of course, if your computer is in a secure location where only people you trust have physical access to it, you might not have such concerns. Because the designers of Windows XP were able to provide for the needs of those who want convenience as well as those who need security, Windows XP works for you, too. You'll still probably want to create a user account for each person who uses the computer, because associated with each account is a user profile that stores all manner of information unique to that user: favorite Web sites, desktop background, document folders, and so on. With features such as the Welcome screen and Fast User Switching, described in this chapter, you can log on or switch between user accounts with only a few clicks.

Introducing Windows XP Security

The Windows XP approach to security is discretionary: Each securable system resource—each file or printer, for example—has an owner, who has discretion over who can and cannot access the resource. Usually, a resource is owned by the user who created it. If you create a file, for example, you are the file's owner under ordinary circumstances. (Computer administrators, however, can take ownership of resources they didn't create.)

Note To exercise full discretionary control over individual files, you must store those files on an NTFS volume. Windows XP supports the FAT and FAT32 file systems used by MS-DOS and Windows 95, Windows 98, and Windows Me for the sake of compatibility. However, the FAT and FAT32 systems were not designed with security in mind. To enjoy the full benefits of Windows XP security, you must use NTFS. For more information, see "NTFS or FAT32: Which Disk Format Should You Choose?" on page 746.

To determine which users have access to a resource, Windows assigns a *security ID* (SID) to each user account. Your SID (a gigantic number guaranteed to be unique) follows you around wherever you go in Windows. When you log on, the operating system first validates your user name and password. Then it creates a *security access token*. You can think of this as the electronic equivalent of an ID badge. It includes your user name and SID, plus information about any security groups to which your account belongs. (Security groups are described later in this chapter.) Any program you start gets a copy of your security access token.

Whenever you attempt to walk through a controlled "door" in Windows (for example, when you connect to a shared printer) or any time a program attempts to do so on your behalf, the operating system examines your security access token and decides whether to let you pass. If access is permitted, you notice nothing. If access is denied, you see an unavailable menu or dialog box control or, in some cases, you get to hear a beep and read a refusal message.

In determining whom to pass and whom to block, Windows consults the resource's *access control list* (ACL). This is simply a list of SIDs and the access privileges associated with each one. Every resource subject to access control has an ACL.

Permissions and Rights

Windows distinguishes two types of access privileges: permissions and rights. A *permission* is the ability to access a particular object in some defined manner—for example, to write to an NTFS file or to modify a printer queue. A *right* is the ability to perform a particular system-wide action, such as logging on or resetting the clock.

The owner of a resource (or an administrator) assigns permissions to the resource via its properties dialog box. For example, if you are the printer owner or have administrative privileges, you can restrict someone from using a particular printer by visiting the properties dialog box for that printer. Administrators set rights via the Local Security Policy console in the Administrative Tools folder. If you have an administrative account and you're using Windows XP Professional, you can use Local Security Policy to grant someone the right to load a device driver.

> **Note** In this book, as in many of the Windows XP messages and dialog boxes, *privileges* serves as an informal term encompassing both permissions and rights.

In Depth: Security Identifiers

Windows XP security relies on the use of a security identifier (SID) to identify a user. When you create a user account, Windows assigns a unique SID to that account. The SID remains uniquely associated with that user account until the account is deleted, whereupon the SID is never used again—for that user or any other user. Even if you re-create an account with identical information, a new SID is created.

A SID is a variable-length value that contains a revision level, a 48-bit Identifier Authority value, and a number of 32-bit subauthority values. The SID takes the form S-1-*x*-*y1*-*y2*-.... S-1 identifies it as a revision 1 SID; *x* is the value for the IdentifierAuthority; and *y1*, *y2*, and so on are values for subauthorities.

You'll sometimes see a SID in a security dialog box (for example, on the Security tab of a file's properties dialog box while Simple File Sharing is not enabled) before Windows has had time to look up the user account name. If a SID on a Security tab doesn't change to a name, it's because it's a SID for an account that has been deleted; you can safely delete it from the permissions list because it'll never be used again. You'll also spot SIDs in the hidden protected operating system folder \Recycler (each SID you see in this folder represents the Recycle Bin for a particular user), in the registry (the HKEY_USERS hive contains a key, identified by *SID*, for each user account on the computer), and deep in the %UserProfile%\Application Data\Microsoft folder structure, among other places.

Not all SIDs are unique (although the SID assigned to your user account is always unique). A number of commonly used SIDs are constant among all Windows XP installations. For example, S-1-5-18 is the SID for the built-in System account, a hidden member of the Administrators group that is used by the operating system and by services that log on using the System account. You can find a complete list of such SIDs, called *well-known SIDs*, on the Microsoft TechNet Web site at *http://www.microsoft.com/TechNet/prodtechnol/winxppro/reskit/prnc_sid_cids.asp*.

User Accounts

The backbone of Windows XP security is the ability to uniquely identify each user. During setup—or at any later time—a computer administrator creates a user account for each user. The *user account* is identified by a user name and (optionally) a password, which the user provides when logging on to the system. Windows then controls, monitors, and restricts access to system resources based on the permissions and rights associated with each user account by the resource owners and the system administrator.

In addition to such "normal" user accounts, Windows provides two special accounts that have predefined sets of permissions and rights: the Administrator account and the Guest account.

- **Administrator account** Every computer running Windows XP has a special account named Administrator. This account has full rights over the entire computer. It can create other user accounts and is generally responsible for managing the computer. Many system features and rights are off limits to accounts other than Administrator (or another account that belongs to the Administrators group).

- **Guest account** The Guest account resides at the other end of the privilege spectrum. It is designed to allow an infrequent or temporary user such as a visitor to log on to the system without providing a password and use the system in a restricted manner. (By default, the Guest account is disabled on a clean install of Windows XP; no one can use an account that's disabled.) The Guest account is also used to access shared network resources on your computer when Simple File Sharing is enabled.

For information about using the Administrator account, see "What Happened to the Administrator Account?" on page 249. For information about using the Guest account, see "Setting Up a Secure Guest Account," page 272.

Local Accounts and Groups vs. Domain Accounts and Groups

Windows stores information about user accounts and security groups in a security database. Where the security database resides depends on whether your computer is part of a workgroup or a domain.

A *workgroup* setup (or a standalone computer) uses only local user accounts and local groups—the type described in this chapter. The security database on each computer stores the local user accounts and local groups that are specific to that computer. Local user accounts allow users to log on only to the computer where you create the local account. Likewise, a local account allows users to access resources only on that same computer. (This doesn't mean that you can't share your resources with other network users, even if you're not part of a domain. For details, see Chapter 30, "Managing Shared Folders and Printers.") With such a setup, you avoid the initial expense of purchasing and configuring Microsoft Windows Server 2003—but because you must manage user accounts on each individual computer, this process becomes unwieldy with more than five or ten computers.

Chapter 8

The alternative is to set up the network as a domain. A Windows *domain* is a network that has at least one machine running Windows Server 2003, Windows 2000 Server, or Windows NT Server as a domain controller. A *domain controller* is a computer that maintains the security database, including user accounts and groups, for the domain. With a *domain user account*, you can log on to any computer in the domain (subject to your privileges set at the domain level and on individual computers), and you can gain access to permitted resources anywhere on the network.

In general, if your computer is part of a Windows domain, you shouldn't need to concern yourself with local user accounts. Instead, all user accounts should be managed at the domain controller. But you might want to add certain domain user accounts or groups to your local groups. By default, the Domain Admins group is a member of the local Administrators group, and Domain Users is a member of the local Users group; members of those domain groups thereby assume the rights and permissions afforded to the local groups to which they belong.

Domain-based accounts and groups are also known as *global accounts* and *global groups*.

For more information about working with domains, see Chapter 33, "Working with Windows Domains."

Account Types

Account type is a simplified way—new in Windows XP—of describing membership in a security group, a collection of user accounts. Groups allow a system administrator to create classes of users who share common privileges. For example, if everyone in the accounting department needs access to the Payables folder, the administrator can create a group called Accounting and grant the entire group access to that folder. If the administrator then adds all user accounts belonging to employees in the accounting department to the Accounting group, these users will automatically have access to the Payables folder. A user account can belong to one group, more than one group, or no group at all.

Groups are a valuable administrative tool. They simplify the job of ensuring that all members with common access needs have an identical set of privileges. Although you can grant privileges to each user account individually, doing so is tedious and prone to errors—and usually considered poor practice. You're better off assigning permissions and rights to groups and then adding user accounts to the group with the appropriate privileges.

Permissions and rights for group members are cumulative. That means that if a user account belongs to more than one group, the user enjoys all of the privileges accorded to all groups of which the user account is a member.

Windows XP classifies each user account as one of four account types:

- **Computer administrator**   Members of the Administrators group are classified as computer administrator accounts. The Administrators group, which by default includes the Administrator account and all accounts you create during Windows XP setup, has more control over the system than any other group. Computer administrators can:
    - Create, change, and delete user accounts and groups
    - Install programs
    - Share folders
    - Set permissions
    - Access all files
    - Take ownership of files
    - Grant rights to other user accounts and to themselves
    - Install or remove hardware devices
    - Log on in Safe Mode

- **Limited**   Members of the Users group are classified as limited accounts. By default, limited accounts can:
    - Change the password, picture, and associated .NET Passport for their own user account
    - Use programs that have been installed on the computer
    - View permissions (if Simple File Sharing is disabled)
    - Create, change, and delete files in their document folders
    - View files in shared document folders

- **Guest**   Members of the Guests group are shown as guest accounts. Guest accounts have privileges similar to limited accounts. A user logged on with the Guest account (but not any other account that is a member of the Guests group) cannot create a password for the account.

- **Unknown**   The account type for a user account that is not a member of the Administrators, Users, or Guests group is shown as Unknown. Because accounts you create with User Accounts in Control Panel are automatically assigned to the Administrators group or the Users group, you'll see the Unknown account type only if you upgraded your computer from an earlier version of Windows (for example, new users in Windows 2000 are assigned by default to the Power Users group) or if you use the Local Users And Groups console or the Net Localgroup command to manage group membership. (The Local Users And Groups console is not available in Windows XP Home Edition.)

Chapter 8

There's nothing wrong with accounts of this type, and if you need to use other security groups to classify the accounts on your computer, you should do so. In User Accounts, all the usual account-management tasks are available for accounts of Unknown type, but if you want to view or change group membership, you'll need to use Local Users And Groups or the Net Localgroup command.

Tip Reserve administrator accounts for special occasions

A limited account is the best and safest type for everyday use. Limited accounts and their limited privileges provide fewer opportunities for malicious hackers to cause problems; a limited account also prevents some self-inflicted damage, such as accidentally deleting shared files. Unfortunately, some programs don't work properly when accessed by a limited account. Try making your own account a limited account (or, if you use Windows XP Professional, a member of the Power Users group) and see whether you can perform all of your normal computing activities. When you need to run a program that doesn't work with limited accounts or you need to make administrative changes, use a separate administrator account that you set up for the purpose. (Log on using your administrator account or use the Run As command. For details about Run As, see "Running a Program as Another User," page 127.) If this becomes too cumbersome, change your everyday account back to an administrator account.

For information about the User Accounts option in Control Panel, see "Working with User Accounts," page 232. For information about the Local Users And Groups and Net Localgroup management tools, see "Advanced Account Setup Options," page 252.

A clean installation of Windows XP Professional creates the following groups—each with predefined rights and permissions—in addition to the Administrators, Users, and Guests groups:

- **Backup Operators** Members of the Backup Operators group have the right to back up and restore folders and files—even ones that they don't otherwise have permission to access. Backup operators also have access to the Backup Utility program.

- **HelpServicesGroup** This group is used by Microsoft and computer manufacturers for Remote Assistance, enabling technical support personnel to connect to the computer (only with your permission, of course!).

For information about Remote Assistance, see "Connecting to Another PC with Remote Assistance," page 92.

- **Network Configuration Operators** Members of this group have administrative privileges in areas that relate to setting up and configuring networking components.

- **Power Users** The Power Users group is intended for those who need many, but not all, of the privileges of the Administrators group. Power Users can't take ownership of files, back up or restore files, load or unload device drivers, or manage the security and auditing logs. Unlike ordinary users, however, Power Users can share folders; create, manage, delete, and share local printers; and create local users and groups.

- **Remote Desktop Users**   Users in this group can connect to the computer via the Remote Desktop feature, if it is enabled.

> For information about Remote Desktop, see Chapter 31, "Remote Access Options."

- **Replicator**   Members of the Replicator group can manage the replication of files on the domain, workstation, or server. (File replication, a feature of Windows NT Server and its successors, is beyond the scope of this book.)

Except for HelpServicesGroup, these additional groups are not included on a computer running Windows XP Home Edition. Applications that you install might create additional security groups.

> **Note**   A computer that is a member of a domain offers two standard account types, and they're slightly different from the ones that appear on a workgroup computer. A *standard user* is a member of the Power Users group, and a *restricted user* is a member of the Users group.

User Profiles

Windows limits access to information through the use of user profiles. A *user profile* contains all the desktop settings for a user's work environment. But it's much more than that. In addition to storing the user's personal registry settings for everything from desktop background to the author initials used in Microsoft Word, the profile contains a number of files that are specific to a user, such as cookies the user receives while using Microsoft Internet Explorer, documents in the My Documents folder and its subfolders, and shortcuts to network places.

By default, each user who logs on to a computer has a local user profile, which is created when the user logs on for the first time. Local user profiles are stored in %SystemDrive%\ Documents And Settings. Each user's profile is stored in a subfolder, with the user name as the folder name. The full path of one of the profiles on a computer in our office is C:\ Documents And Settings\Cheryl, for example. (The entire path for the current user's profile is stored in another commonly used environment variable, %UserProfile%.)

In general, each user account has full access to its own user profile and can create, change, and delete files within the profile as well as make settings that are stored in the profile. Non-administrative accounts have only limited access to profiles belonging to other users; by default, these users can view files but not make any changes to another user's profile.

> For more information about the content of user profiles and managing them, see Chapter 17, "Managing User Profiles."

Simple File Sharing vs. Windows 2000–Style Sharing

A primary feature of Windows XP is the ability to securely allow or deny access to files, printers, and other resources. Yet maximum flexibility—the ability to specify permissions at a granular level (for example, separate permissions for reading a folder directory, reading a file, changing a file, adding a new file, deleting a file, and so on) for individual users or groups—requires an option-filled user interface that many users find daunting.

Windows XP addresses this potential confusion by introducing Simple File Sharing, a stripped-down interface that makes it easy to set up common security arrangements. Simple File Sharing differs from classic (Windows 2000–style) file sharing in the following ways:

- The Sharing tab in a folder's properties dialog box provides fewer, simpler options, as shown in Figure 8-1. This simplified Sharing tab controls share permissions *and* NTFS file permissions. (Many Windows NT and Windows 2000 users were confused by this subtle, yet important, distinction; placing all the controls on this tab makes it clear what you need to do to share with other local users and network users.)

- The properties dialog box for a folder, file, or printer does not have a Security tab. As Figure 8-2 shows, the Security tab is revealed when Simple File Sharing is disabled.

- Permissions are set only at the folder level; you can't apply permissions to individual files (except with the arcane Cacls and Xcacls command-line utilities).

- Your options for sharing folders and the files they contain are few: You can share with all other local users, you can share with network users, and you can prevent other users from viewing one or more of your private folders.

- Network users who connect to your computer are authenticated using your computer's Guest account. This means that network users who access a shared folder on your computer have only those privileges and permissions that are specifically granted to the Guest account.

For information about setting permissions, see Chapter 9, "Securing Files and Folders." For information about sharing with other users on your network, see Chapter 30, "Managing Shared Folders and Printers."

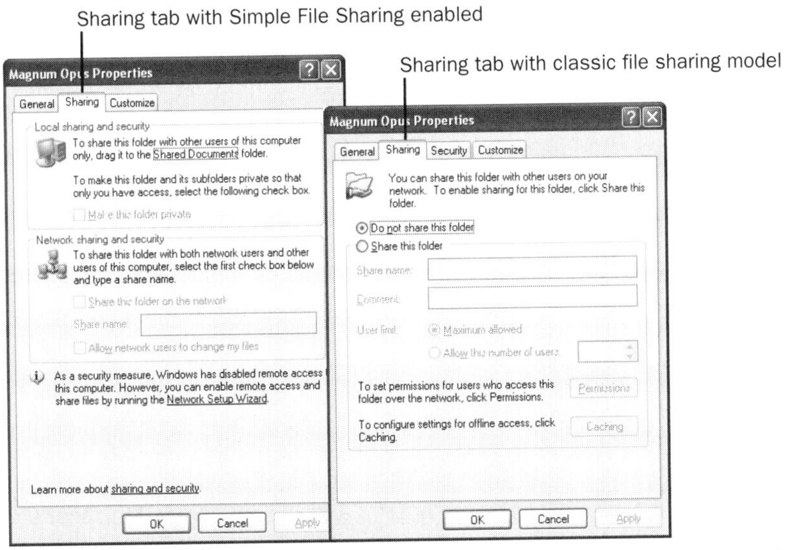

Sharing tab with Simple File Sharing enabled

Sharing tab with classic file sharing model

Figure 8-1. Simple File Sharing consolidates a small number of sharing and security options on a single tab.

Figure 8-2. With classic sharing, the Security tab for a file (as shown here) or a folder lets you specify various permissions for individual users and groups.

Chapter 8

If you use Windows XP Home Edition, you don't have a choice: Simple File Sharing is your only option.

If you use Windows XP Professional, you can choose to use Simple File Sharing or the classic sharing and security interface. To switch between them, open Folder Options (in Control Panel's Appearance And Themes category), click the View tab, and select or clear the last item in the Advanced Settings box, Use Simple File Sharing (Recommended). Simple File Sharing is enabled by default on computers that are not members of a domain.

Inside Out

Switch sharing methods quickly

Even power users sometimes appreciate the cleaner, simpler approach provided by Simple File Sharing. It's one of those settings that you might like to be able to switch to and from quickly and easily—using Simple File Sharing most of the time and disabling it when you need to set special permissions for a particular object. Making the change through the user interface requires, at a minimum, six clicks. To switch back and forth rapidly, you might want to create a script that changes the ForceGuest value of the HKLM\System\CurrentControlSet\Control\Lsa registry key. Setting ForceGuest to 0 disables Simple File Sharing; setting it to 1 enables the feature. You can find such a script, called ToggleSharingOptions.vbs, on the companion CD. (For a details about ToggleSharingOptions.vbs, see "Controlling Access with NTFS Permissions," page 282.) After you have a registry-toggling switch, you might want to assign a shortcut key to it or place a shortcut in an easily accessible location. (For general information about scripts, see "Automating Tasks with Windows Script Host," page 623. You'll find a sample script that toggles registry settings in the sidebar titled "Batch Programs vs. Scripts: Which Should You Use?" on page 624.)

Working with User Accounts

When you install Windows XP, its setup program encourages you to create at least one user account in addition to the Administrator and Guest accounts that Windows Setup creates. (If you don't create an account during setup, Windows creates a computer administrator account named Owner. Unless your name is Owner, you'll probably want to rename this account, as described later in this chapter.) If you upgrade to Windows XP and you had local accounts set up in your previous operating system (that is, you were using Windows NT or Windows 2000, or you had enabled user profiles in Windows 95/98/Me), Windows Setup migrates those accounts to your Windows XP installation. Accounts that you migrate from Windows NT/2000 maintain their group memberships and passwords. Accounts you create during setup, as well as accounts you migrate from Windows 95/98/Me, are members of the Administrators group and have no password.

Note An administrator account with a blank password creates a security risk! (Note that when you upgrade from Windows 95/98/Me, Windows XP retains the user accounts you had set up in your previous operating system, but it removes the password associated with those accounts.) Although new security features in Windows XP prevent *network* logon by an account with a blank password, someone with physical access to your computer can log on without providing a password. And because they have administrative privileges, they have full access to your computer. In other words, until you assign a password to each account that Windows Setup creates in Windows XP, anyone can log on and can view or modify your files and settings.

Through User Accounts in Control Panel, Windows XP provides a simple post-setup method for creating new accounts, making routine changes to existing accounts, and deleting accounts. If your computer is not a member of a domain, when you launch User Accounts in Control Panel you'll see a window similar to the one shown in Figure 8-3.

If your computer is a member of a domain, the version of User Accounts that appears looks nothing like the one shown in Figure 8-3. Rather, it's similar to Users And Passwords in Windows 2000. For more information, see "Advanced Account Setup Options," page 252.

Note To create accounts or make changes to other accounts, you must be logged on as an administrator. Users without administrative privileges can use User Accounts only to create, change, or remove their own password; change their picture; or link their account to a .NET Passport.

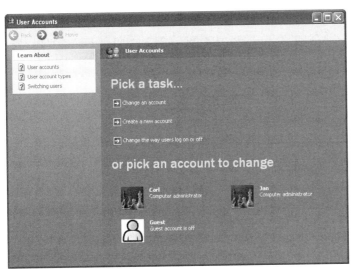

Figure 8-3. User Accounts on a workgroup computer has a clean, simple interface.

Creating a New User Account

User Accounts offers a convenient Create A New Account link on its home page and it lets you create a new account with a minimum of fuss. You need to supply only a name for the account and decide whether you want the account to be a computer administrator account or a limited account.

> **Note**   The name you provide when you create a new account with Windows is used for both the user name and the full name. The *user name* is the primary name used internally by Windows. You use it when you log on without the benefit of the Welcome screen and when you specify the account name in various commands and dialog boxes for setting permissions. The *full name* is the name that appears on the Welcome screen, at the top of the Start menu, and in User Accounts. You can change either name at any time after the account is created.

If you want to specify any other information about the account—including setting a password—you must make changes after you create the account, as described in the following section. Alternatively, you can use the Local Users And Groups snap-in or the Net User /Add command, both of which allow you to create an account and make several other settings simultaneously. For more information, see "Advanced Account Setup Options," page 252.

> **Tip**   Don't use spaces in the user name
>
> User Accounts allows you to include spaces in the user name when you create an account. Don't do it. Spaces in user names cause complications with some applications and when you use command-line tools for managing user accounts. If you want a space to appear on the Welcome screen and on the Start menu (for example, if you want to display your full name, including first and last name), create your account name without a space. (For example, use just your first name or, if that's the same as another account name, use your first name and last initial without a space.) After you create the account, you can change the full name without changing the user name, as described in the following section.

Changing Account Settings

Making routine changes is easy with User Accounts. Don't bother clicking the Change An Account link, which leads to a window that shows all the accounts that you can change. Instead, at the bottom of the User Accounts home page, simply click the name of the account you want to change. You'll see a window similar to the one shown in Figure 8-4.

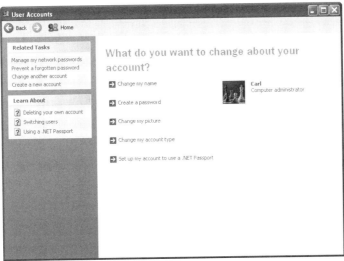

Figure 8-4. User Accounts provides easy access to commonly changed account information.

> **Note** If you open Control Panel, User Accounts while logged on as a limited user, you bypass the first User Accounts window—the one shown in Figure 8-3—which shows all the user accounts and lets an administrator perform certain other tasks. Instead, you go directly to a pared-down version of the account-change window shown in Figure 8-4. In that window, you can create, change, or remove your password; change your picture; or link your account to a .NET Passport. A limited user cannot change the name or account type, nor can a limited user modify other accounts.

In this window, you can make the following account changes to your own account or other accounts on your computer:

- **Name** Although User Accounts doesn't explain the distinction, when you change the name here you're changing the full name (the one that appears on the Welcome screen, on the Start menu, and in User Accounts), not the user name. Changing the name here—after creating a short user name without spaces—allows you to create a friendly name that appears on-screen.

- **Password** You can create a password and store a hint that will provide a reminder for a forgotten password. If the account is already password protected, User Accounts allows you to change the password or remove the password. For more information about passwords, see "Setting Logon Passwords," page 260.

- **Picture** If you don't want a user to be identified as a rubber ducky (or whatever icon Windows selects for the account), you can change the picture associated with the account name at the top of the Start menu and in User Accounts. (The picture doesn't appear if your computer is a member of a domain or if you use the classic Start menu.) As shown in Figure 8-5, clicking the change-picture link shows all the pictures stored in %AllUsersProfile%\Application Data\Microsoft\User Account Pictures\Default Pictures, but you're not limited to those choices (most of which are no more or less appropriate than the rubber ducky icon).

Click to select one of your own pictures

Click to snap a picture with an attached camera

Figure 8-5. Select a picture that reflects your personality.

Click Browse For More Pictures, and you can select any picture in bitmap format (.bmp extension), Graphics Interchange Format (GIF), Joint Photographic Experts Group (JPEG) format, or Portable Network Graphics (PNG) format, such as a picture of yourself or a favorite scene. Windows reduces the picture to fit the picture box and stores the resulting file in %AllUsersProfile%\Application Data\Microsoft\User Account Pictures with the account's user name as the file name.

● **Account type**   With User Accounts, you can change the account type to Computer Administrator (which adds the account to the Administrators group) or Limited (which adds the account to the Users group). If you want to add the account to other groups, you must use Local Users And Groups or the Net Localgroup command. For more information about those alternatives, see "Advanced Account Setup Options," page 252.

Tip Access the account change windows quickly
If you want to change your own picture, you can jump directly to the picture-changing window shown in Figure 8-5 by opening the Start menu and clicking your picture. Then, if you want to change other settings for your account, click the Back button to display the window shown in Figure 8-4. To display the window shown in Figure 8-3 on page 233 (so you can make changes to other accounts), click Home.

For your own account (that is, the one with which you're currently logged on), you can make the following additional changes:

- **.NET Passport**   You can set up your own account to use a .NET Passport or change the Passport currently associated with your account. For more information about .NET Passport settings, see "Setting Up a .NET Passport," page 269.

- **Network passwords**   Under Related Tasks, you'll find the Manage My Network Passwords link, which lets you manage stored user names and passwords that you use to access network resources and Web sites. For more information, see "Gaining Access to Shared Folders on Another Computer," page 1020.

- **Password reset disk**   The Prevent A Forgotten Password link, also under Related Tasks, launches a wizard from which you can create a password reset disk. For more information, see "Recovering from a Lost Password," page 266.

Deleting an Account

You can delete any account except one that is currently logged on. To delete an account, open User Accounts and click the name of the account you want to delete. Then click Delete The Account. User Accounts gives you a choice, shown in Figure 8-6, about what to do with the account's files:

- **Keep Files**   Windows copies certain parts of the user's profile—specifically, files and folders stored on the desktop and in the My Documents folder—to a folder on your desktop, where they become part of your profile and remain under your control. The rest of the user profile, such as e-mail messages and other data stored in the Application Data folder, Internet favorites, and settings stored in the registry, will be deleted after you confirm your intention in the next window that appears.

- **Delete Files**   After you select Delete Files and confirm your intention in the next window, Windows deletes the account, its user profile, and all files associated with the account, including those in its My Documents folder.

Note   User Accounts won't let you delete the last local account on the computer, even if you're logged on as Administrator. This limitation helps to enforce the sound security practice of using an account other than Administrator for your everyday computing.

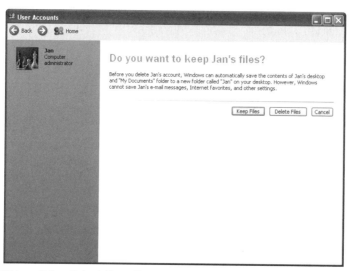

Figure 8-6. Select Keep Files to avoid losing files in the account's My Documents folder.

After you delete an account, of course, that user can no longer log on. Deleting an account also has other effects you should be aware of. You cannot restore access to resources that currently list the user in their access control lists simply by re-creating the account. This includes files to which the user has permission and the user's encrypted files, personal certificates, and stored passwords for Web sites and network resources. That's because those permissions are linked to the user's original SID—not the user name. Even if you create a new account with the same name, password, and so on, it will have a new SID, which will not gain access to anything that was restricted to the original user account.

You might encounter another predicament if you delete an account. If you use a tool other than User Accounts to delete the account, the user's original profile remains in the Documents And Settings folder. If you later create a new account with the same name, Windows creates a new profile folder, but because a folder already exists with that user's name (for example, C:\Documents And Settings\Josie), it appends the computer name to the user name to create a convoluted folder name (for example, C:\Documents And Settings\Josie.SEQUOIA). The extra folder not only consumes disk space, but leads to confusion about which is the correct profile folder. (In general, the one with the longest name is the most recent. But you can be certain only by examining files in the profile folder.) To avoid this problem, use User Accounts to delete accounts because it properly deletes the old profile along with the account.

Inside Out

Delete an unused profile when you delete an account

If you delete an account with a tool other than User Accounts, the account's profile continues to occupy space in the Documents And Settings folder and in the registry. You don't want to delete the files or registry entries directly because a simple mistake could affect other accounts. Instead, right-click My Computer and choose Properties. Click the Advanced tab and then click Settings under User Profiles. Select the account named Account Unknown (the deleted account), and click Delete.

Controlling How Users Log On

If your computer is not part of a domain, Windows XP offers two different methods for users to log on:

- **Welcome screen** The Welcome screen, shown in Figure 8-7, offers an easy way for users to log on. Users simply click their name and, if required, type their password. For more information, see "Using the Welcome Screen," page 241.

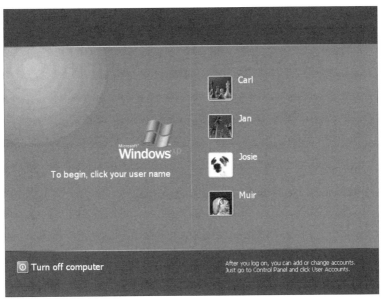

Figure 8-7. The Welcome screen provides the simplest logon system for computers shared by only a handful of users.

> **Note** Don't be misled by the fact that the word *Welcome* appears nowhere on the Welcome screen, yet the classic logon screen shows a Welcome To Windows dialog box. In dialog boxes and in help, references to the Welcome screen refer to the logon screen shown in Figure 8-7.

- **Classic logon**   The alternative to the Welcome screen is the sequence of logon screens used in Windows NT and Windows 2000. When the Welcome screen is disabled (or on a domain-based computer, which doesn't support the Welcome screen), after Windows completes its startup tasks, you'll see one of the following dialog boxes: Welcome To Windows, shown in Figure 8-8, or Log On To Windows, shown in Figure 8-9.

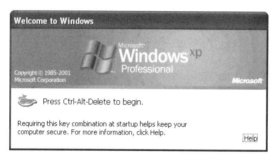

Figure 8-8.   If this dialog box appears, press Ctrl+Alt+Delete to initiate the logon process.

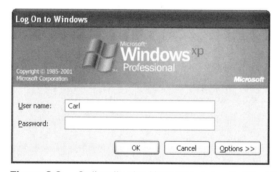

Figure 8-9.   Ordinarily, the User Name box is filled in with the name of the last user who logged on.

Systems set up for the greatest security initially display the Welcome To Windows dialog box that invites you to log on by pressing Ctrl+Alt+Delete. When you do so, the Log On To Windows dialog box appears. Type your name and password to log on.

> **Tip** Hide the name of the last user to log on
>
> Local Security Settings contains a policy that you might want to enable if you don't use the Welcome screen. Ordinarily, the name of the last user who logged on appears in the User Name box of the Log On To Windows dialog box. On a system that's used primarily by a single user, this is a convenient feature that allows the user to log on again without typing his or her name each time. But it's also a bit of a security hole, because anyone can learn a valid user name just by looking at this dialog box. If you're using Windows XP Professional, you can prevent the last-used name from appearing by typing **secpol.msc** at a command prompt to open Local Security Settings. In Local Security Settings, open Local Policies\Security Options. Then enable the policy named Interactive Logon: Do Not Display Last User Name.

> **Tip** Skip the Ctrl+Alt+Del requirement
>
> If you don't want to be bothered by the Welcome To Windows dialog box or pressing Ctrl+Alt+Del to reach the Log On To Windows dialog box, make the following change:
>
> 1 At a command prompt, type **control userpasswords2** and press Enter. (If your computer is joined to a domain, you can simply open User Accounts in Control Panel.)
>
> 2 In the User Accounts dialog box that appears, click the Advanced tab.
>
> 3 Under Secure Logon, clear the Require Users To Press Ctrl+Alt+Delete check box.
>
> Be aware that doing so removes a security feature. Because a component of the Windows XP security system prevents any other application from capturing this particular key combination, pressing Ctrl+Alt+Delete ensures that the next dialog box that appears, Log On To Windows, is displayed by the operating system and not by a rogue application that's trying to capture your password, for example.

Using the Welcome Screen

Except on computers that are part of a domain (a configuration that doesn't support the Welcome screen), Windows XP is configured by default to use the Welcome screen.

> **Tip** Log on using hidden accounts
>
> While the Welcome screen is displayed, you can display the Log On To Windows dialog box shown in Figure 8-9 by pressing Ctrl+Alt+Delete twice. This allows you to log on using an account that isn't shown on the Welcome screen (Administrator, for example). Note, however, that this trick works only when no other users are logged on.

If your system is not using the Welcome screen and you want it to, follow these steps:

1 While logged on as an administrator, open User Accounts in Control Panel.

2   Click the Change The Way Users Log On Or Off link.

If a warning message about offline files appears, simply click Cancel. As the message points out, offline files and Fast User Switching are incompatible, but you don't need to disable offline files to enable only the Welcome screen.

3   Select Use The Welcome Screen, and then click Apply Options.

By default, whenever the screen saver kicks in and you subsequently press a key or move the mouse, you'll find yourself back at the Welcome screen. This provides some protection against someone using your computer when you've stepped away. To resume working, you'll need to click your name and enter your password. If you'd rather return to work without going through these extra steps, do the following:

1   Right-click the desktop, and choose Properties to open the Display Properties dialog box.

2   Click the Screen Saver tab.

3   Clear the check box labeled On Resume, Display Welcome Screen (if Fast User Switching is enabled) or On Resume, Password Protect (if Fast User Switching is disabled).

Your decision to use the Welcome screen has other, perhaps unexpected, effects as well. For example, if you use the Welcome screen, pressing Ctrl+Alt+Delete after you're logged on displays Windows Task Manager, an invaluable little program that lets you end hung applications and shows running tasks and processes, how much memory and processor time each is using, and a concise summary of several performance metrics, among other information. (For more information about Task Manager, see Chapter 14, "Tuning Up System Performance.") If you have disabled the Welcome screen, however, pressing Ctrl+Alt+Delete displays the Windows Security dialog box, shown in Figure 8-10.

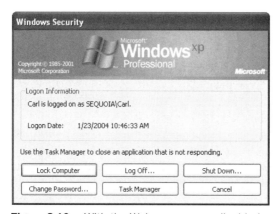

Figure 8-10.   With the Welcome screen disabled, pressing Ctrl+Alt+Del displays this dialog box instead of Task Manager.

Troubleshooting

You can't enable (or disable) the Welcome screen.

If you have problems enabling or disabling the Welcome screen with User Accounts, you can edit the registry or set a policy that implements the logon style you want to use.

In either Windows XP Professional or Windows XP Home Edition, you can enable or disable the Welcome screen with a registry setting. Use Registry Editor to change the LogonType value in the HKLM\Software\Microsoft\Windows NT\CurrentVersion\WinLogon key. Set it to 0 to use the classic logon or 1 to use the Welcome screen.

In Windows XP Professional, you can also enable or disable the Welcome screen with a policy. Follow these steps:

1. At a command prompt, type **gpedit.msc** to open the Group Policy console.
2. Open the Computer Configuration\Administrative Templates\System\Logon folder.
3. Double-click the Always Use Classic Logon policy.
4. Select Enabled to use the classic logon, Disabled to use the Welcome screen, or Not Configured to cede control to the registry setting. (A policy setting overrides the setting you make in User Accounts or in the registry.)

For more information about group policy, see Appendix F, "Group Policy."

Tip Whether you use the Welcome screen or not, you can get to Task Manager with another single keystroke: Ctrl+Shift+Esc.

Inside Out

Create an invisible account

You can prevent an account from appearing on the Welcome screen, thereby creating a "hidden" account. (It's not completely hidden, because the account is visible to administrators in Local Users And Groups, and the account's profile in the Documents And Settings folder is visible to all users.) Use Registry Editor to open HKLM\Software\Microsoft\Windows NT\CurrentVersion\Winlogon\SpecialAccounts\UserList. Create a new DWORD value, setting its name to the user name of the account you want to hide and leaving its value set to 0.

> Be careful with this trick: You won't be able to get to the account with Fast User Switching because the account doesn't appear on the Welcome screen, and pressing Ctrl+Alt+Delete two times at the Welcome screen to display the Log On To Windows dialog box works only when no other users are logged on. Therefore, if you want to use this type of hidden account, you should either disable Fast User Switching (for details, see "Configuring Fast User Switching," page 246) or resign yourself to using the account only when no one else is logged on.

Other minor changes also mimic the behavior of Windows 2000 and Windows XP when your computer is part of a domain. For example, the button at the bottom of the Start menu changes from Turn Off Computer to Shut Down. And the dialog box that appears after you click that button provides a list of shutdown options instead of separate buttons for each option.

 Troubleshooting

The Welcome screen doesn't display any accounts.

You might find yourself staring at a Welcome screen that asks you to click a user name—but there are no user names to click. This can occur if you manage to delete all local user accounts (User Accounts won't let you do this, but other account-management tools aren't as protective) or, in some cases, if you upgrade your computer from an earlier version of Windows.

If you're using Windows XP Professional, press Ctrl+Alt+Delete two times to display the Log On To Windows dialog box. Type **Administrator** in the User Name box, and enter the password you created for the Administrator account during setup. Logged on as Administrator, you can run User Accounts and create one or more new accounts, which will thereafter show up on the Welcome screen.

Windows XP Home Edition users can't log on using the Administrator account, which is prevented by account restrictions from logging on. Instead, you must start Windows XP in Safe Mode by pressing F8 at the beginning of the startup process. After you're up and running in Safe Mode, you can run User Accounts to create one or more new accounts.

Bypassing the Logon Screen

If your computer has only one account (aside from Administrator and Guest), and if that account doesn't have a password, Windows XP automatically logs on as that user during startup. You won't see the Welcome screen or any other logon screens; Windows launches straight to your desktop.

You might want to set up your computer to log on this way even if it has more than one user account. This kind of logon can be convenient in several situations: if you're the primary user of the computer but other people occasionally need to use it; if you occasionally need to log on as a different user to install software or perform other tasks; or if you have set up a password for your account (so that you could use scheduled tasks or connect remotely, operations that are available only to accounts with passwords), but you still want it to log you on automatically at startup.

> **Note** *Automatically logging on* means that the system effectively enters your user name and password when you turn on the power. Anyone who has physical access to your computer can then log on as you and have access to all computer resources (including Web sites for which you've saved passwords) that you normally have.

You can set up your computer to log on automatically by following these steps:

> **Tip** **Bypass automatic logon or prevent others from bypassing**
> If you've configured your system to log on automatically, you can suppress the automatic logon by holding down the left Shift key as the system boots. If you want to prevent users from bypassing the automatic logon (thereby ensuring that your system always starts with a particular account), you can use a registry setting to make the system ignore the Shift key. Use Registry Editor to navigate to HKLM\Software\Microsoft\ WindowsNT\CurrentVersion\Winlogon. If the string value IgnoreShiftOverride doesn't exist, create it. Set this value to 1 to ensure that your system always starts with its auto-logon account.

1   At a command prompt, type **control userpasswords2** and press Enter. Doing so launches the Windows 2000–style User Accounts application.

2   On the Users tab, clear the Users Must Enter A User Name And Password To Use This Computer check box and then click OK. Note that the Users Must Enter A User Name And Password To Use This Computer check box doesn't appear if your computer is a member of a domain. Only computers that aren't part of a network or are part of a workgroup can bypass this dialog box. Domain users must enter a user name and password, even to log on locally.

The Automatically Log On dialog box appears.

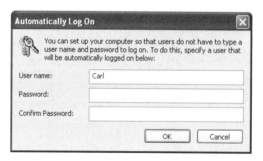

3 Type the user name and password for the account that you want to be logged on to each time you start your computer.

After you make this change, you can use other accounts on the computer by logging off and then logging on to another account or by using Fast User Switching.

Configuring Fast User Switching

Fast User Switching, a feature that made its first appearance in Windows XP, allows multiple users to be logged on to a computer at the same time. As the feature name suggests, you can quickly switch among users. This might be convenient, for example, if one user logs on, opens several documents, and begins downloading a huge file from the Internet. Meanwhile, another user comes along and wants to quickly check e-mail. With Fast User Switching enabled, it's no problem. The second user can log on, log off, and return control to the first user. While the second user is logged on, the first user's applications (such as the download process) continue to run.

To switch to another user account, press the Windows logo key+L. This displays the Welcome screen, from which the second user can click his or her name and enter a password, if required.

> **Tip**   If your keyboard doesn't have a Windows logo key (or you prefer using the mouse), you can get to the Welcome screen by clicking Start, Log Off. In the Log Off Windows dialog box, click Switch User.

Fast User Switching won't work in every situation. To enable the feature you must observe the following requirements:

- The Welcome screen must be enabled.
- The computer must not be joined to a domain.
- Offline files must be disabled.

● Although it's not an absolute requirement, the computer should have more than 64 MB of memory. By default, Fast User Switching is disabled on computers that have only 64 MB. (In any case, to run Windows XP effectively, you should have at least 128 MB.)

To enable Fast User Switching, follow these steps:

1 While logged on as an administrator, open User Accounts in Control Panel.

2 Click the Change The Way Users Log On Or Off link to see the following screen.

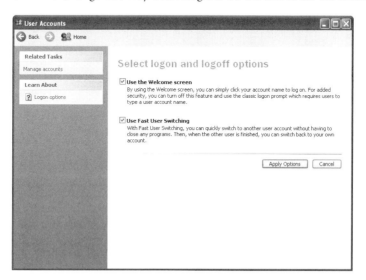

3 Select Use Fast User Switching and, then click Apply Options.

Note If a warning message about offline files appears, open the Folder Options dialog box by clicking OK. You must disable offline files before you can enable Fast User Switching.

Tip Check your e-mail without switching

The logon screen for Fast User Switching shows which users are logged on (a note under each name indicates the number of programs each has running or, for users who are logged on but have no programs running, their logon status). In addition, the logon screen displays the number of unread messages in a user's Inbox below each user name. To use this feature, simply start Microsoft Outlook Express or Windows Messenger and leave it running when you switch users. (If you don't leave the e-mail program running, Windows continues to display the number of unread messages that remained when you last closed it.) And if you don't like this unread messages feature? Microsoft Knowledge Base article 304148, "Overview of the Mail Notification Display on the Windows XP Welcome Screen," at *http://support.microsoft.com/?kbid=304148* explains how to disable it with a registry edit.

Logging Off or Locking Your Computer

When you're finished using your computer, you want to be sure that you don't leave it in a condition in which others can use your credentials to access your files. To do that, you need to log off, switch users, or lock your computer.

- **Log off**   With this option, all your programs close and dial-up connections are ended. To log off, choose Start, Log Off, and click Log Off.

- **Switch users**   With this option, which is available only if Fast User Switching is enabled, your programs continue to run. Your account is still logged on, but (if it's protected by a password) only you can return to your session. To switch users, press the Windows logo key+L or choose Start, Log Off, and then click Switch Users. Either method takes you to the Welcome screen for Fast User Switching.

- **Lock your computer**   With this option, which is available only when Fast User Switching is disabled, your programs continue to run. However, only you or another administrator can unlock the computer. If another administrator unlocks the computer, Windows closes your programs (without saving any open documents) and logs you off. To lock a computer, press the Windows logo key+L or (if the Welcome screen is disabled) press Ctrl+Alt+Delete and click Lock Computer. If you press Ctrl+Alt+Delete when the Welcome screen is enabled, choose Lock Computer from the Windows Task Manager Shut Down menu.

Tip   Create a shortcut for switching users or locking your computer

The Windows logo key+L is a terrific shortcut for switching users or locking your computer. But if your keyboard doesn't have a Windows logo key or you prefer using a mouse, you can create a program shortcut that provides single-click access to the same feature. Follow these steps to create a switch/lock shortcut on your desktop:

1   Right-click the desktop and choose New, Shortcut.

2   On the first page of the Create Shortcut Wizard, type **rundll32.exe user32.dll,LockWorkStation** and click Next.

3   Type a name for the shortcut (**Lock Workstation** would be appropriate), and click Finish.

4   Right-click the new shortcut and choose Properties.

5   On the Shortcut tab, click Change Icon.

6   In the text box, type **shell32.dll** and press Enter.

7   Select an icon that tickles your fancy; you'll find several with lock, key, and user images. Then click OK.

8   In the Shortcut Key box, type the shortcut key you want to use (for example, Ctrl+Alt+L).

To immediately display the logon screen (if Fast User Switching is enabled) or lock your computer (if Fast User Switching is disabled), simply double-click your new shortcut or type the shortcut key you assigned. To make it accessible with a single click, even when your desktop is covered with other windows, move the shortcut to the Quick Launch bar.

In any case, if you want to prevent others from using your account, you must protect your account with a password. When you choose any of these options, Windows hides whatever you were working on. Your computer continues to run (subject to power management settings), and any resources shared by your computer remain available to other users on the network.

What Happened to the Administrator Account?

Ordinarily, the Administrator account is hidden from view. It appears on the Welcome screen only in the following situations:

- No other administrative user accounts exist.
- You start your computer in Safe Mode (by pressing F8 during startup).
- The Administrator account is logged on and you're using Fast User Switching.

Nonetheless, the account does exist, and it takes care of some important functions. First, because it can't be deleted, it provides a safety net in case you somehow manage to delete all other accounts. You can log on as Administrator and then create other accounts. Second, it's the only account that can log on to the Recovery Console, your last-ditch opportunity for repairing a damaged system.

> **Note** By default, the Administrator password in Windows XP Home Edition is blank. This isn't the gaping security hole that you might imagine, however, because in Home Edition the Administrator account is barred from logging on locally or through a network connection. You do, however, need to know that the password is blank if you ever need to run Recovery Console, which requires the Administrator password. If the blank password concerns you, you can change it. For details, see "Securing the Administrator Account."

Logging On as Administrator

If you're using Windows XP Professional, you can log on as Administrator. If the Welcome screen is enabled, press Ctrl+Alt+Delete twice at theWelcome screen to display the Log On To Windows dialog box. (Be sure that no other account is logged on when you do this.) If the Welcome screen is disabled, press Ctrl+Alt+Delete one time as you would to log on with any other account. Type **Administrator** in the User Name box, and enter the password you created for the Administrator account during setup.

> **Note** Except in Safe Mode, Windows XP Home Edition users can't log on using the Administrator account, because it is prevented by account restrictions from logging on. To log on to the Administrator account using Windows XP Home Edition, first make sure that your system is not set up to bypass the logon screen. (See "Bypassing the Logon Screen," page 244.) Then press F8 while booting and choose Safe Mode from the menu that appears.

Making Administrator the Only Administrative Account

If your applications support it, you're better off using a limited account (or a Power Users account) as your everyday logon account and using an administrator account only when you need to perform administrative tasks. You can use any administrator account for those tasks, but if you prefer, you can use the Administrator account. Here's how you can set up your system to easily use Administrator in this way:

1 At a command prompt, type **lusrmgr.msc** to open Local Users And Groups.

2 In the console tree, click Groups.

3 Double-click the Administrators group and remove all accounts except Administrator.

4 Open the Users or Power Users groups, and then click Add to add each of the accounts you removed.

With all administrative accounts except Administrator removed, the Administrator account becomes accessible from the Welcome screen.

> **Note** Use this procedure only with Windows XP Professional. With Windows XP Home Edition, you can't use Local Users And Groups (although you can make the group membership changes with the Net Localgroup command). But more important, the Administrator account is not allowed to log on in Windows XP Home Edition, so even if you get it to appear on the Welcome screen, you won't be able to use it.

Inside Out

Add Administrator to the Welcome screen

If you're using Windows XP Professional, you can add Administrator to the Welcome screen, without eliminating all other administrative accounts, by modifying the registry. Use Registry Editor to navigate to HKLM\Software\Microsoft\WindowsNT\ CurrentVersion\Winlogon\ SpecialAccounts\UserList. In this subkey, create the new DWORD value *Administrator*. Then set this value to 1. To remove Administrator from the Welcome screen, return to the registry and set the Administrator value to 0.

Chapter 8

Securing the Administrator Account

Because an account named Administrator exists on almost every computer running Windows XP, and because this account is all-powerful, malevolent hackers might attempt to break into a computer using the Administrator account. After all, they already know the user name, so they just need to figure out the password. You can make your Administrator account more secure in two ways:

- **Use a secure password** If you're logged on as Administrator, you can use User Accounts to set a password. But if you want to create a randomly generated secure password, open a Command Prompt window and type this command:

  ```
  net user administrator /random
  ```

  Windows displays the new password it creates. Be sure to write it down and store it in a safe place!

- **Change the name of the account** It doesn't need to be cryptic like a password; it just needs to be something other than "Administrator," the name that every hacker already knows and expects to find. To change the name, follow these steps:

  1. At a command prompt, **type secpol.msc** to open Local Security Settings. (Alternatively, you can double-click the Local Security Policy shortcut in Control Panel's Administrative Tools folder.)

  2. Open Local Policies\Security Options.

  3. In the details pane, double-click Accounts: Rename Administrator Account.

  4. Type the new name for the Administrator account.

Note Because the Local Security Settings snap-in isn't available in Windows XP Home Edition, you can't use it to change the name of the Administrator account. However, you can change the user name by launching the Windows 2000–style User Accounts. At a command prompt, type **control userpasswords2**. Then select Administrator and click Properties. Be sure you change the user name, not the full name.

Tip Create a phony Administrator account

After you rename the Administrator account, you can create a new user account named Administrator. Put this account in the Guests security group and give it a strong password. Such an account serves two purposes: It's a decoy that'll keep attackers occupied (and won't give up anything of value if they do manage to crack it), and it helps you to determine whether someone is trying to break into your system. (Check the security log in Event Viewer to see whether someone is attempting to log on as Administrator.)

Advanced Account Setup Options

Windows XP includes no fewer than four different interfaces for managing users and groups:

- **User Accounts**   Located in Control Panel, User Accounts provides the simplest method to perform common tasks. For more information, see "Working with User Accounts," page 232.

- **User Accounts (Windows 2000 style)**   If your computer is joined to a domain, opening User Accounts in Control Panel displays a different version from the version described above, as shown in Figure 8-11. If your computer is not joined to a domain, you can open this version by typing **control userpasswords2** at a command prompt.

  The capabilities of this version of User Accounts are few (you can add or remove local user accounts, set passwords, and place a user account in a single security group), but it has a handful of unique features that you might find compelling. With this version, you can:

  - Change an account's user name
  - Configure automatic logon (for more information, see "Bypassing the Logon Screen," page 244)
  - Eliminate the Ctrl+Alt+Delete requirement if you're not using the Welcome screen

Figure 8-11.   On a domain member computer, User Accounts looks like Users And Passwords in Windows 2000.

Note   If your computer is not a domain member, yet you find yourself using this version of User Accounts frequently, create a shortcut to it. Store the shortcut in Control Panel's Administrative Tools folder.

- **Local Users And Groups**   This Microsoft Management Console (MMC) snap-in provides access to more account management features than User Accounts and is friendlier than command-line utilities. For more information, see "Using the Local Users And Groups Snap-In," page 255.

- **Command-line utilities**   The Net User and Net Localgroup commands, though not particularly intuitive (starting with the name—we're talking about local accounts and groups, not network-based accounts!), provide the most complete and direct access to various account tasks. For more information, see "Using the Net User and Net Localgroup Commands," page 256.

With varying degrees of ease, all of these options allow an administrator to create, modify, and delete local user accounts and security groups. The availability and appearance of each of these options depends on which version of Windows XP you have (the Local Users And Groups console is not available in Windows XP Home Edition) and whether your computer is a member of a domain (Users And Passwords in Control Panel is completely different for domain members). Which interface you choose depends in part on whether you prefer a graphical interface or a command prompt.

But you'll also find that each tool offers capabilities that the others do not. To help you decide which tool to use for a particular task, Table 8-1 shows the common account-management tasks that can be performed with each interface.

Table 8-1. Account-Management Tool Tasks

Task	User Accounts in Control Panel (Workgroup)	User Accounts in Control Panel (Domain)	Local Users And Groups Console	Command-Line Utilities
Local User Accounts				
Create user account	✓	✓	✓	✓
Delete user account	✓	✓	✓	✓
Place account in a group	✓ [1]	✓ [1]	✓	✓
Change user name		✓	✓	
Change full name	✓	✓	✓	✓
Change description		✓	✓	✓
Change picture	✓			

Table 8-1. **Account-Management Tool Tasks**

Task	User Accounts in Control Panel (Workgroup)	User Accounts in Control Panel (Domain)	Local Users And Groups Console	Command-Line Utilities
Set a password	✓	✓[2]	✓	✓
Set a password hint	✓			
Set password restrictions			✓	✓
Set logon hours				✓
Enable or disable account	✓[3]		✓	
Unlock account			✓	✓
Set account expiration date				✓
Specify profile and logon script			✓	✓
Link account to .NET Passport	✓	✓		
Local Security Groups				
Create			✓	✓
Delete			✓	✓
Rename			✓	✓
Set group membership			✓	✓
Add a domain account to a group		✓[1]	✓	✓

[1]With User Accounts, you can add an account to only one group. In the workgroup version of User Accounts, you can add an account only to the Administrators or Users group.

[2]With User Accounts, you can set the password only for a local account other than the one with which you're currently logged on.

[3]With User Accounts, you can enable or disable the Guest account, but not other user accounts.

Chapter 8

Using the Local Users And Groups Snap-In

Local Users And Groups, an MMC snap-in, offers more advanced capabilities than either version of User Accounts. Local Users And Groups is not available in Windows XP Home Edition.

You can start Local Users And Groups, shown in Figure 8-12, in any of the following ways:

- In Computer Management, open System Tools, Local Users And Groups.
- At the command prompt, type **lusrmgr.msc**.
- If your computer is a domain member, in User Accounts click the Advanced tab, and then click the Advanced button.

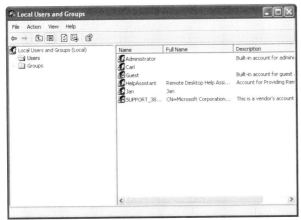

Figure 8-12. Through its austere interface, Local Users And Groups offers more capabilities than User Accounts.

Table 8-2 lists the procedures for performing various tasks with the Local Users And Groups snap-in.

Table 8-2. Local Users And Groups Procedures

Task	Procedure
Local User Accounts	
Create	Right-click Users and choose New User.
Delete	In Users, right-click the account and choose Delete.
Change user name	In Users, right-click the account and choose Rename.
Change full name or description	In Users, double-click the account to display the General tab of the properties dialog box.
Set or change password	In Users, right-click the account and choose Set Password.

Table 8-2. Local Users And Groups Procedures

Task	Procedure
Set password restrictions	In Users, double-click the account to display the General tab of the properties dialog box.
Enable or disable	In Users, double-click the account to display the General tab of the properties dialog box, and then clear or select the Account Is Disabled check box. (When an account is disabled, the user can't log on or access resources on the computer.)
Unlock after too many unsuccessful logon attempts	In Users, double-click the account to display the General tab of the properties dialog box, and then clear the Account Is Locked Out check box.
Set group membership	In Users, double-click the account and then click the Member Of tab.
Specify profile and logon script	In Users, double-click the account and then click the Profile tab. For details, see "Working with User Profiles," page 550.
Local Security Groups	
Create	Right-click Groups and choose New Group.
Delete	In Groups, right-click the group and choose Delete.
Rename	In Groups, right-click the group and choose Rename.
Set group membership	In Groups, double-click the group to display the properties dialog box. You can add local user accounts, domain user accounts, and domain groups to a local group. In the Select Users dialog box that appears when you click Add, use the Locations button to specify the computer name (for local users) or domain name (for domain users and groups).

Using the Net User and Net Localgroup Commands

If you prefer a terse Command Prompt window to a gooey utility, you'll want to use Net.exe for managing local users and groups. To change any local user account or group information, you need to be logged on as a member of the local Administrators group. (Alternatively, you can use Run As to launch the Command Prompt window, or you can precede each command you enter in a Command Prompt window with **runas /user:administrator.**)

In the following sections, we describe only the most common Net commands (and their most common parameters) for managing local users and groups. This isn't an exhaustive reference, however. You can get that information from online help or by typing **net help _command_**, replacing _command_ with the word that follows _Net_ in the examples below. For instance, to get more information about the Net Localgroup command, type **net help localgroup**. This provides more help than typing **net localgroup /?**, which shows only the command syntax.

Net User

The Net User command lets you view, add, modify, or delete user accounts.

Viewing user account information   Typing **net user** with no parameters causes the program to display the name of your computer and a list of local user accounts. If you follow *Net User* with the name of a local user account (for example, **net user jan**), Net User displays all information about the user account, as shown in the sample that follows.

```
C:\>net user

User accounts for \\SEQUOIA

-------------------------------------------------------------------------------
Administrator          Carl                          Guest
HelpAssistant          Jan                           SUPPORT_388945a0
The command completed successfully.


C:\>net user jan
User name                Jan
Full Name                Jan
Comment
User's comment
Country code             000 (System Default)
Account active           Yes
Account expires          Never

Password last set        1/4/2004 12:43 PM
Password expires         Never
Password changeable      1/4/2004 12:43 PM
Password required        Yes
User may change password Yes

Workstations allowed     All
Logon script
User profile
Home directory
Last logon               1/4/2004 11:54 AM

Logon hours allowed      All

Local Group Memberships  *Users
Global Group memberships *None
The command completed successfully.
```

Chapter 8

Adding or modifying a user account   Following Net User *username*, you can append any or all of the parameters shown in Table 8-3. For example, you can add a new account for a user named Josie, create a complex password, and prevent Josie from changing the password with the following command:

```
C:\>net user Josie /add /random /passwordchg:no
Password for Josie is: nkHRE$oU

The command completed successfully.
```

Table 8-3. Useful Parameters for the Net User Command

Parameter	Description
password or * or /Random	Sets the password. If you type an asterisk (*), Net User prompts for the password you want to assign; it does not display the password as you type it. The /Random switch generates a hard-to-crack, eight-character password.
/Add	Creates a new user account. The user name must be 20 characters or fewer and can't contain any of these characters: " / \ [ ] : ; | = , + * ? < >
/Fullname:"*name*"	Specifies the user's full name.
/Comment:"*text*"	Provides a descriptive comment (maximum length of 48 characters).
/Passwordchg:yes or /Passwordchg:no	Specifies whether the user is allowed to change the password.
/Active:no or /Active:yes	Disables or enables the account. (When an account is disabled, the user can't log on or access resources on the computer.)
/Expires:*date* or /Expires:never	Sets the expiration date for an account. For *date*, use the short date format set in Regional Options. The account expires at the beginning of the day on the specified date; from that time on, the user can't log on or access resources on the computer until an administrator sets a new expiration date.
/Passwordreq:yes or /Passwordreq:no	Specifies whether the user account is required to have a nonblank password.
/Times:*times* or /Times:all	Sets the times when an account is allowed to log on. For *times*, enter the days of the week you want to allow logon. Use a hyphen to specify a range of days or use a comma to list separate days. Following each day entry, specify the allowable logon times. For example, type **M-F,8am-6pm; Sa,9am-1pm** to restrict logon times to normal working hours. Use All to allow logon at any time; a blank value prevents the user from ever logging on.

Chapter 8

> **Note** The last three switches in Table 8-3 (/Expires, /Passwordreq, and /Times) allow you to make settings that you can't make (or even view) using Local Users And Groups. These switches provide some powerful options that are otherwise available only with Windows 2000 Server or Windows Server 2003.

Deleting a user account To remove a user account from the local security database, simply use the /Delete switch with the Net User command, like this:

```
C:\>net user josie /delete
The command completed successfully.
```

Net Localgroup

The Net Localgroup command lets you view, add, modify, or delete local security groups.

Viewing group information Type **net localgroup** with no parameters to display the name of your computer and a list of local groups. If you follow Net Localgroup with the name of a group (for example, **net localgroup "power users"**), Net Localgroup lists the members of the group.

Adding or deleting a group Following Net Localgroup *groupname*, append /Add to create a new group or append /Delete to remove an existing group. When you add a group or view its information, you can optionally add a descriptive comment (maximum length of 48 characters) by appending the /Comment:"*text*" switch.

Adding or deleting group members You can add local user accounts, domain user accounts, and global groups to a local group (though you can't add other local groups). To do so, enter the names of the users or groups you want to add after the group name (separate multiple names with a space) and include the /Add switch. For example, to add Jan and Josie to the Power Users group, use this command:

```
C:\>net localgroup "power users" jan josie /add
The command completed successfully.
```

To delete one or more group members, use the same syntax, replacing the /Add switch with /Delete.

Working with Domain Accounts

By appending the /Domain switch to any of the Net User or Net Localgroup commands described in this chapter, you can view, add, modify, or delete domain user accounts and global groups—as long as you log on as a member of the Domain Admins group. You don't need to specify the domain name; the Net User and Net Localgroup commands always work with the primary domain controller of your computer's primary domain.

Setting Logon Passwords

By default, Windows XP is somewhat insecure. User accounts that you create during setup (as well as user accounts that are migrated from Windows 95/98/Me during an upgrade) have administrative privileges and no password. Because the Welcome screen shows every defined user account, if you don't set passwords, anyone who has physical access to your computer can log on as an administrator by simply clicking a name on the Welcome screen. Requiring a password for each account (particularly administrator accounts) goes a long way toward securing your computer.

Chapter 8

> **Note**   You needn't worry about someone logging on to your computer remotely (over the network, the Internet, or with Remote Desktop Connection, for example) if your account doesn't have a password. New security features in Windows XP prevent remote logon by any account with a blank password. When you don't have a password in Windows XP, the risk comes only from people who have physical access to your computer.
>
> This feature is enforced by a policy, which is enabled by default. If you have Windows XP Professional, you can confirm that the policy is enabled, as follows. At a command prompt, type **secpol.msc** to open Local Security Settings. Open Local Policies\Security Options and be sure that the Accounts: Limit Local Account Use Of Blank Passwords To Console Logon Only policy is enabled. (If you use Windows XP Home Edition, you needn't worry; the policy can't be disabled.)

 Troubleshooting

Windows requires a logon password but you don't have one.

Ordinarily, a user who has no logon password assigned can log on simply by clicking her or his name on the Welcome screen. But in some cases, clicking the name displays a request for a password, and nothing you type (even just pressing Enter) satisfies the request.

This sometimes occurs when auditing is enabled. You can solve the problem by disabling auditing (for details, see "Enabling Auditing," page 387), but a much better solution is to assign a logon password—even a short one—to the user.

Creating a Secure Password

A password is of little value if it's easily guessed by an intruder. Obviously, you shouldn't use your name or something equally transparent. However, even a random word provides little security against a determined intruder—some hackers use tools that try every word in the dictionary. By observing the following guidelines, you can create a password that's difficult to crack:

- Use at least eight characters.
- Use a mixture of uppercase letters, lowercase letters, numbers, and punctuation (for example, OneWorld7).
- Avoid including your name or user name in the password.
- Use random sequences instead of words, or intersperse numbers and punctuation within words (for example, oNe6Wo7RlD).
- Consider using the initials of a phrase that you can easily remember. For example, you could remember the password WdYw2gT? as "Where do you want to go today?"

Inside Out

Use a long password to foil common cracking tools

You'll get even better security if your password is at least 15 characters long. (In Windows XP and Windows 2000, passwords can be up to 127 characters long; in Microsoft Windows NT, the limit is 14 characters.) Longer passwords become exponentially more difficult to crack, but they have another seldom-documented benefit. When you set a password for a user account, Windows XP creates and stores two different hashes for the password: a Windows NT hash (NT hash) and a LAN Manager hash (LM hash). The LM hash is a holdover from early network operating systems and is easily cracked. But if you define a password of 15 or more characters the LM hash can't be cracked because LM hashes are formed using only the first 14 characters. If you don't want to use passwords longer than 14 characters, you can instead disable LM hashing entirely; for details, see Knowledge Base article 299656 "How to prevent Windows from storing a LAN manager hash of your password in Active Directory and local SAM databases" (*http://support.microsoft.com/?kbid=299656*). Whether you use long passwords or disable LM hashes, any password cracking program that relies on the common technique of LM hash extraction will not work.

Not everyone agrees that your password must be an unpronounceable collection of apparently random letters, numbers, and symbols. Some experts argue that such cryptic passwords are less secure than those made up of several words interspersed with numbers and symbols, because you're almost certainly going to write down a cryptic password (and then that piece of paper becomes a possible security risk). You can find an interesting discussion of password security in "Ten Windows Password Myths," an article written for SecurityFocus by Mark Burnett (*http://online.securityfocus.com/infocus/1554/*).

Tip Use spaces
You can use any character in a Windows logon password, including spaces. With one or more spaces in a password, it's easier to come up with a long yet memorable password; you might even incorporate several words separated by spaces and other symbols. Don't use a space as the first or last character of your password, however; some applications trim spaces from these positions.

Troubleshooting

You can't log on.

Even when you're *certain* you know the password, you might have trouble logging on. First, be aware that passwords are case sensitive: You must type capital letters and lowercase letters exactly as you did when you created the password. If you still can't get on, be sure the Caps Lock key is not on.

Setting a Password

The simplest way to set a password for yourself or for another user (if you're logged on as an administrator) is with User Accounts in Control Panel. Click the name of the user for which you want to set a password and then click Create A Password. A window like the one shown in Figure 8-13 appears.

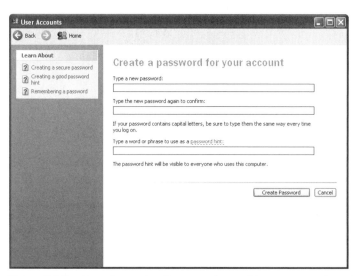

Figure 8-13. User Accounts allows you to provide a password reminder hint that becomes available on the Welcome screen.

You can set a password with the other account management tools, but User Accounts is the only tool that lets you specify a password hint. The password hint is available by clicking the question mark icon that appears after you click your name on the Welcome screen. Be sure your hint is only a subtle reminder—not the password itself—because any user can click your name and then view the hint.

Caution You can safely set the initial password for another user as described here, or you can use any of the other account management tools to set the password. But do not remove or change a user's password using any of these methods unless the user has forgotten the password and has absolutely no other way to access the account. (For more information, see "Recovering from a Lost Password," page 266.) If you change or remove another user's password, that user loses all personal certificates and stored passwords for Web sites and network resources. Without the personal certificates, the user loses access to all of his or her encrypted files (for information about encrypted files, see Chapter 11, "Encrypting Confidential Information") and all e-mail messages encrypted with the user's private key. Windows deletes the certificates and passwords to prevent the administrator who makes a password change from gaining access to them—but this security comes at a cost!

Troubleshooting

You can't access encrypted files because an administrator changed your password.

When an administrator removes or changes the password for your local account, you no longer have access to your encrypted files and e-mail messages. That's because your master key, which is needed to unlock your personal encryption certificate (which, in turn, is needed to unlock your encrypted files), is encrypted with a hash of your password. When the password changes, the master key is no longer accessible. To regain access to the master key (and, by extension, your encrypted files and e-mail messages), change your password back to your old password. Alternatively, use your Password Reset Disk to change your password.

When you change your own password (through User Accounts or with your Password Reset Disk), Windows uses your old password to decrypt the master key and then re-encrypts it with the new password, so your encrypted files and e-mail messages remain accessible.

Tightening Password Security

Even if you convince everyone who uses your computer to use passwords, you can be sure that they won't always follow the secure practices of choosing a difficult-to-crack password and changing it periodically. If security is a serious concern in your organization, you can take the following measures to help ensure that users don't make it easy for hackers to guess their passwords:

- You can use the Net User command to generate a complex password for each user. In a Command Prompt window, type **net user *username* /random**.

Tip **Generate stronger random passwords**

The Net User command conveniently generates an eight-character password and assigns it to a user account. A number of online services and stand-alone programs are available for randomly generating strong passwords of any length you specify. Check out some of these programs at the following Web sites:

- WinGuides.com Password Generator (*http://www.winguides.com/security/ password.php*)

- The JavaScript Source Password Generator (*http://javascript.internet.com/ passwords/password-generator.html*)

- Segobit Advanced Password Generator (*http://www.segobit.com/apg.htm*)

- Hirtle Random Password Generator-Pro (*http://www.hirtlesoftware.com*)

- InfoTech Professional Random Password Generator (*http://www.mark.vcn.com/ password*)

A Web search for "password generator" turns up many more.

- If you have Windows XP Professional, you can set password policies that place restrictions on the types of passwords users can provide and how often users can (or must) change them.

The easiest way to set password policies is with the Local Security Settings console, shown in Figure 8-14. To open Local Security Settings, in Control Panel open Administrative Tools, Local Security Policy. (If you use Category view, AdministrativeTools is under Performance And Maintenance.) Alternatively, type **secpol.msc** at a command prompt.

To see the policies that set password behavior for all accounts, open Account Policies\ Password Policy. Table 8-4 describes each of these policies.

 You'll find a lot more information about these and other account policies in "Threats and Countermeasures: Security Settings in Windows Server 2003 and Windows XP," a white paper from Microsoft that is included on this book's companion CD.

As an alternative to the Local Security Settings console, you can set a number of these policies using the Net Accounts command. In Table 8-4, the appropriate switch to set a policy is shown next to the policy name as it appears in Local Security Settings. For example, to set the maximum password age to 21 days, type **net accounts /maxpwage:21** at a command prompt.

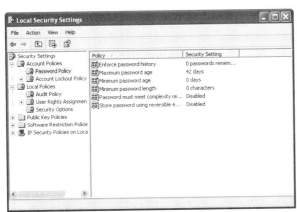

Figure 8-14. With Local Security Settings, you can set password requirements for all local user accounts.

Table 8-4. Account Policies

Policy	Net Accounts Switch	Description
Enforce password history	/Uniquepw:*number*	Specifying a number greater than 0 (the maximum is 24) causes Windows to remember that number of previous passwords and forces users to pick a password different from any of the remembered ones.
Maximum password age	/Maxpwage:*days*	Specifying a number greater than 0 (the maximum is 999) dictates how long a password remains valid before it expires. (To override this setting for certain user accounts, open an account's properties dialog box in Local Users And Groups and select the Password Never Expires check box.) Selecting 0 means the password never expire. (With the Net Accounts command, use the /Maxpwage:unlimited switch if you don't want a password to ever expire; 0 is not an acceptable value.)
Minimum password age	/Minpwage:*days*	Specifying a number greater than 0 (the maximum is 999) lets you set the amount of time a password must be used before a user is allowed to change it. Selecting 0 means that a user can change the password as often as he or she likes.

Table 8-4. Account Policies

Policy	Net Accounts Switch	Description
Minimum password length	/Minpwlen:*length*	Specifying a number greater than 0 (the maximum is 14) forces a password to be longer than a certain number of characters. Specifying 0 permits a user to have no password at all. *Note: Changes to the minimum password length setting do not apply to current passwords.*
Password must meet complexity requirements	N/A	Enabling this policy requires that a new password be at least six characters long; that the password contain a mix of uppercase letters, lowercase letters, numbers, and punctuation (at least one character from three of these four classes); and that the password does not contain the user name or any part of the full name. *Note: Enabling password complexity does not affect current passwords.*
Store password using reversible encryption for all users in the domain	N/A	Enabling this policy effectively stores a password as clear text instead of encrypting it, which is much more secure. The only situation in which you should even consider enabling this policy is when you have a particular application that needs access to the user password for authentication.

> **Note** If you set a maximum password age so that a password expires automatically, Windows reminds the user to change the password at each logon, beginning 14 days before the password expires. If you want to change the reminder period, in Local Security Settings, open Local Policies\Security Options. Double-click the Interactive Logon: Prompt User To Change Password Before Expiration policy, and set the number of days before the expiration date that you'd like the warning to begin appearing.

Recovering from a Lost Password

It's bound to happen: Someday when you try to log on to your computer and are faced with the password prompt, you will draw a blank. Windows XP offers two tools that help you to deal with this dilemma:

- **Password hint** Your hint (if you've created one) is available by clicking the question mark icon that appears after you click your name on the Welcome screen. (It's not available if you don't use the Welcome screen.) For more information, see "Setting a Password," page 262.

● **Password Reset Disk**   The Password Reset Disk allows you (or anyone with your Password Reset Disk) to change your password—without needing to know your old password. As standard practice, each user should create a Password Reset Disk and keep it in a secure location. Then, if a user forgets the password, he or she can reset it using the Password Reset Disk.

> **Note**   You can make a Password Reset Disk only for your local user account. If your computer is joined to a domain, you can't create a Password Reset Disk as a back door to your domain logon password. However, in a domain environment, a domain administrator can safely change your password and you'll still have access to your encrypted files.

Inside Out

Create a password reset disk without a floppy

Many modern computers don't have a floppy disk drive. On such computers, the Forgotten Password Wizard nonetheless suggests using a floppy disk and, in most cases, offers no other option. Even if your computer includes a drive that can write to CDs or DVDs, the wizard won't let you use it to create a password reset disk. What to do?

You could, of course, buy a floppy disk drive; internal and external models are available. Unless you have other uses for it, however, it's silly to invest in technology that's rapidly becoming obsolete. Instead, use the wizard with one of these devices:

● USB flash drive

● USB external hard drive

● Card reader for flash memory

● Digital camera (this doesn't work with all cameras)

Whenever you attach one of these devices (with the exception of some cameras), the wizard page that normally tells you to insert a floppy disk sprouts a list of usable drives (still including the nonexistent floppy disk drive). The same list of acceptable drives appears when you invoke the Password Reset Wizard from the Welcome screen while the removable drive is attached.

Both solutions require a little forethought on your part. You must create the hint when you set your password, and you must create the Password Reset Disk before you actually need it.

To create a Password Reset Disk, you'll need to know your current password and you'll need to have a floppy disk available. Follow these steps:

1   Log on using the account for which you want to create a Password Reset Disk.

2 In Control Panel, click User Accounts.

3 If you're logged on as an administrator, click your account name.

4 Click Prevent A Forgotten Password (in the task pane under Related Tasks) to launch
the Forgotten Password Wizard.

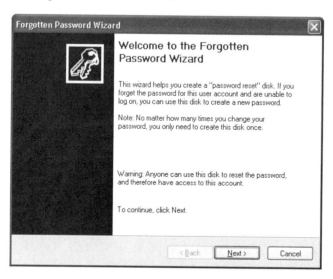

5 Follow the wizard's instructions.

You can have only one Password Reset Disk for each user account. If you make a new one, the
old one is no longer usable.

⚙ Troubleshooting

The Forgotten Password Wizard writes to the wrong drive.

The Forgotten Password Wizard—which, after all, doesn't even know whether your computer really has a floppy disk drive—sometimes saves its information to the wrong drive.
For example, on one floppyless system we tested, the wizard wrote to the root of drive C
instead of to the removable flash drive. Luckily, because the wizard creates only a single
file, the solution is easy. Simply move the Userkey.psw file to the appropriate media (which
doesn't need to be a bootable disk).

Setting Up a .NET Passport

Your user account can be linked to a .NET Passport—a service that provides single sign-on access to a number of Web sites and a secure way to make online payments. With Passport, you provide your user name and password one time and gain access to your Hotmail account, Windows Messenger, and a large number of Web sites. Your Passport profile can also contain (at your control, of course) your credit card numbers so that you can easily make online payments. This service is much easier than the systems used by early e-commerce sites, where you needed a different user name and password for each site you visited. If you used credit cards for online payments and your credit card number changed, you had to update your information at each site.

You'll need to use a Passport if you plan to use Windows Messenger to communicate with other Internet users or use the built-in Web publishing and photo-print ordering features of Windows XP. Microsoft and other businesses that use the .NET Passport technology offer many more services as well.

To create a Passport (if you don't already have one) and link it to your user account so that you're automatically logged on to Passport when you log on to your computer, follow these steps:

1   Open User Accounts in Control Panel.

2   If you're logged on as an administrator, click your user name.

3   Click Set Up My Account To Use A .NET Passport, which launches the .NET Passport Wizard.

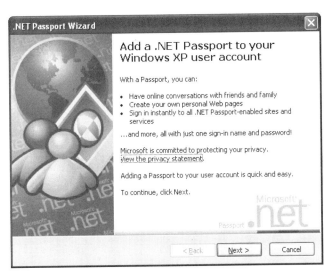

4   Follow the wizard's instructions. You can link your Passport to one of your existing e-mail addresses or you can obtain a new, free e-mail account; the wizard leads you either way.

Banishing .NET Passport Reminders

After installing Windows XP, you'll repeatedly see a reminder encouraging you to set up a .NET Passport. You can disable these reminders—and you don't have to set up a .NET Passport to do so. Here's how:

1   In Registry Editor, navigate to HKCU\Software\Microsoft\MessengerService.

2   If the PassportBalloon registry value doesn't already exist, create a new binary value with that name.

3   Double-click the PassportBalloon value and set it to 0A 00 00 00.

4   Click OK and then close Registry Editor.

Note   Even if your computer is a domain member, you might want to create a Password Reset Disk for a local user account on your computer. To do that, log on as the local user. Press Ctrl+Alt+Delete to open the Windows Security dialog box. Click Change Password, and then click Backup to launch the Forgotten Password Wizard.

When you've forgotten your password but valiantly try to remember, one of two things happens if you don't provide the correct password:

● If you have created a Password Reset Disk, Windows displays a message that includes either a Use Your Password Reset Disk link (if your computer is configured to use the Welcome screen) or a Reset button (if you're not using the Welcome screen).

Click the link or the button to launch the Password Reset Wizard. You'll need your Password Reset Disk, of course. The Password Reset Wizard asks you to create a new password and hint. Log on with your new password, and then return your Password Reset Disk to its safe storage place. You do not need to make a new Password Reset Disk.

● If you have not created a Password Reset Disk, Windows displays a message that tells you, in effect, to type your password correctly.

In this situation, if you can't remember the password and the hint doesn't jog your memory, you're out of luck. An administrator can log on and change or remove your password for you, but you'll lose access to your encrypted files and e-mail messages.

Setting Up Windows XP on a Shared Computer

Whether you're setting up a computer for your family to use at home or to be used in a business, it's prudent to set it up securely. Doing so helps to protect each user's data from inadvertent deletions and changes as well as malicious damage and theft. When you set up your computer, consider these suggestions:

Chapter 8

- **Control who can log on.** Create accounts only for users who need to log on locally (that is, at your computer as opposed to over a network). Delete or disable other accounts (except the built-in accounts created by Windows).

- **Change all user accounts except one to limited accounts.** You'll need one administrative account for installing programs, creating and managing accounts, and so on. All other accounts—including your own everyday account—can run with limited privileges.

> **Note** You'll find that certain programs—particularly programs written for earlier versions of Windows—won't run for users with limited accounts. If that's the case, try adding the users who need the affected programs to the Power Users group. (If your computer is not joined to a domain, you'll need to use Local Users And Groups or the Net Localgroup command to add users to this group. For details, see "Advanced Account Setup Options," page 252.) You can also coax some such programs into working by setting the compatibility mode to an earlier Windows version. (See "Forcing Older Programs to Run Properly," page 121.) If the programs still won't run, change the affected users to administrators.

- **Be sure that all accounts are password protected.** This is especially important for administrator accounts and for other accounts whose profiles contain important or sensitive documents. You might not want to set a password on your toddler's account, but all other accounts should be protected from the possibility that the tyke will accidentally click the wrong name on the Welcome screen.

- **Restrict logon times.** You might want to limit the computing hours for some users. You can limit logon times with the Net User *username* /Times command. (For details, see "Using the Net User and Net Localgroup Commands," page 256.) And if you use Windows XP Professional, you can forcibly log off users if they are still logged on at the end of their allowable logon time. To do that, at a command prompt, type **secpol.msc** to open Local Security Settings. Open Local Policies\Security Options and enable the policy named Network Security: Force Logoff When Logon Hours Expire.

- **Restrict access to certain files.** You'll want to be sure that some files are available to all users, whereas other files are available only to the person who created them. You can implement such protections with all versions of Windows XP. If you have Windows XP Professional, you can further refine your file protection scheme by selectively applying permissions to varying combinations of files, folders, and users. For details, see Chapter 9, "Securing Files and Folders."

- **Restrict the amount of disk space available to each user.** If you have Windows XP Professional, you can set disk quotas for each user, thereby preventing your teenager from filling the whole hard drive with downloaded music files or a coworker from gobbling up disk space with scanned photographs, for example. For details, see "Setting Quotas for Disk Space Use," page 774.

Chapter 8

● **Turn on the Guest account only when necessary.**   You might occasionally have a visitor who needs to use your computer. Rather than logging on with your own account and exposing all your own files and settings to the visitor, turn on the Guest account in such situations. To do that, log on as an administrator. In Control Panel, open User Accounts, click Guest, and then click Turn On The Guest Account. To disable the account, return to the same window and click Turn Off The Guest Account.

> **Note**   You'll find a lot more detailed information about securely setting up a computer for shared use in our earlier book, *Microsoft Windows Security Inside Out for Windows XP and Windows 2000* (Microsoft Press, 2003).

Setting Up a Secure Guest Account

By default, the Guest account has access to your computer's programs, to files in the Shared Documents folder, and to files in the Guest profile. But no password is required to use the account, so you'll want to be sure that the Guest account doesn't expose items that a casual user shouldn't see or modify. In fact, the default settings place pretty tight restrictions on the Guest account, but you should ensure that these rather obscure settings are still in place:

● **Prevent network logon by the Guest account.**   This prevents a user at another computer from using the Guest account to log on over the network. In Local Security Settings (Secpol.msc), open Local Policies, User Rights Assignment. Be sure that Guest is listed in the Deny Access To This Computer From The Network policy.

Do not include Guest in this policy if you use Simple File Sharing and you are sharing your computer's folders or printers. Simple File Sharing requires the use of the Guest account for network access.

● **Prevent a Guest user from shutting down the computer.**   In Local Security Settings, open Local Policies, User Rights Assignment. Be sure that Guest is not listed in the Shut Down The System policy. (Even with this policy in place, anyone—including guests—can shut down the computer from the Welcome screen. You can set a policy that allows only a logged-on user to shut down the computer. To do that, open Local Policies, Security Options, and disable the Shutdown: Allow System To Be Shut Down Without Having To Log On policy.)

● **Prevent a Guest user from viewing event logs**   In Registry Editor, open HKLM\System\CurrentControlSet\Services\Eventlog. Visit each of the three subkeys—Application, Security, and System—and be sure that each contains a DWORD value named RestrictGuestAccess set to 1.

Chapter 9

Securing Files and Folders

When two or more people use the same computer, how do you keep each user from snooping in files and folders that should be private? How do you allow easy access to files that should be shared? And how do you keep untrained users from accidentally wiping out important files? Out of the box, anyone with a user account on a Microsoft Windows XP computer has virtually unlimited access to files and folders. In either edition of Windows XP, you can lock up your personal files and folders by selecting a single check box, even if you know nothing about security. And with Windows XP Professional and some advanced access control options, you can exercise precise control over who is able to access any file or folder on any drive.

At Home with Windows XP

Because Simple File Sharing is the only file-sharing mode available in Windows XP Home Edition, users of Home Edition will be concerned mostly with the first third of this chapter. The material beginning on page 282 ("Controlling Access with NTFS Permissions") addresses the more granular permission settings available to users of Windows XP Professional.

It is possible, but not easy, to apply NTFS file system permissions to NTFS-formatted disks on Home Edition systems. To do this, you need to start Windows XP in Safe Mode or use the terse syntax of the Cacls command. If you're an administrator who manages file-sharing on Home Edition systems and requires the full set of security features available via NTFS, this entire chapter will be relevant to you. In particular, be sure to read the description of the Safe Mode "back door" in the tip on page 275, and the section on Cacls ("Setting Permissions from a Command Prompt," page 298).

If the bulk of your previous computing experience is with Microsoft Windows 95, Microsoft Windows 98, or Microsoft Windows Me, the entire notion of file and folder security is probably an alien concept. Those consumer-based operating systems offer only the most rudimentary security. On the other hand, if you're a seasoned Microsoft Windows NT or Microsoft Windows 2000 user, you probably already understand the basics of access control; your challenge with Windows XP will be understanding its new and radically different Simple File Sharing interface.

This chapter focuses exclusively on sharing and securing files among users who log on to the same computer. If you're interested in learning how to share files and folders over a network, see "Sharing a Folder over a Network," page 1001.

How Setup Decisions Dictate Your Security Options

Three factors dictate how much control you have over access to shared files and folders on a computer running Windows XP:

- **Disk format** Access controls, which determine whether a given user can open a folder, read a file, create new files, and perform other file operations, are available only on NTFS-formatted drives. On drives formatted with FAT32, most local security options are unavailable. Any user can access any file without restriction.

> For more details about the differences between NTFS and FAT32, see "NTFS or FAT32: Which Disk Format Should You Choose?" page 746.

- **Windows XP edition** By default, Windows XP Home Edition and Windows XP Professional share a simplified security interface that allows you to set a limited number of access controls based on built-in group memberships. If you use Windows XP Professional, you can configure your system to use more complex security options that closely resemble those found in Windows 2000. We discuss the differences between these options later in this section.

- **User account settings** During setup, Windows XP creates a group of shared folders specifically designed to hold files for all users of that computer. (If your computer is joined to a Windows domain, these shared locations are unavailable.) Each user with an account on the machine can designate certain folders as private.

> For more details about differences in security options and the Windows interface when running under a domain, see "Domains vs. Workgroups," page 1106.

NTFS vs. FAT32

When it comes to security, the single most important factor is the file system you've chosen for the drive containing the Windows system files and user profiles. If the drive is formatted using the FAT32 file system, none of the options discussed in this section apply to you. The only way to enable file system permissions is to convert the drive to NTFS format.

> For instructions on how to convert a FAT32 partition to NTFS, see "Converting a FAT32 Disk to NTFS," page 748.

> **Tip** **Access NTFS permissions from Home Edition**
> Throughout this book, we note that users of Windows XP Home Edition are locked out of the full range of file security options. However, there is one noteworthy exception: When you restart Home Edition in Safe Mode (as described in "Using Safe Mode," page 1286), you'll find the full Windows 2000–style access control editor. This back door is designed for recovery of protected files after a system crash, but a determined Home Edition user can take advantage of it to set permissions on files and folders. Our take? If you understand NTFS permissions and need to use them, get Windows XP Professional.

Simple File Sharing vs. Advanced Permissions

In a clean installation or an upgrade over Windows 98/Me, Windows XP assigns default security settings that work like on/off switches. This Simple File Sharing interface initially makes all the files in your user profile (including your My Documents folder, desktop, Start menu, and Favorites) visible to anyone who has an administrator's account on your computer (users with limited accounts are restricted from viewing files in other profiles). As Figure 9-1 shows, opening the My Computer window displays a separate icon for the folder that holds each user's personal documents, along with an icon for a Shared Documents folder. (See the following section for a full discussion of how the Shared Documents folder works.)

This low-security configuration is similar to the standard setup on a machine running Windows 95/98/Me. In an environment where all users trust each other completely, it makes collaborating easy. If you and a coworker share a computer, you can each keep your personal files organized in your My Documents folder for convenience; if you need to look at a file that your coworker created, you open his or her My Documents folder. Likewise, at home, you and your spouse can browse each other's files.

But some environments demand less trust and more protection. On a home computer, for example, parents might want to keep financial data and other private files out of the reach of children—not just to ensure privacy, but also to protect the files from accidental changes or deletion. By selecting a check box on the Sharing tab of a folder's Properties dialog box, you can designate as private all or part of your user profile. After you've selected that option, your files are visible only when you log on using your account.

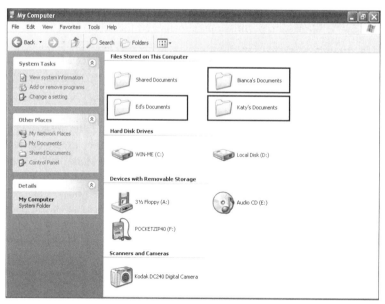

Figure 9-1. By default, the My Computer window shows an icon for every user's My Documents folder.

It's certainly easy to make a folder private—all you do is right-click a folder, choose Sharing And Security, and select the Make This Folder Private check box—but this Simple File Sharing option suffers from some significant limitations:

- The Make This Folder Private option is available only within your user profile. If you use a program that stores its user data in any other location, you cannot protect that folder from unauthorized access. Likewise, if you've created a second partition on which you store digital images, media files, or other space-gobbling data, you have no way to protect those files from unauthorized access or accidental deletion.

- Protection applies to all files and subfolders within a folder for which you select this option. You cannot protect an individual file, nor can you single out files or subfolders within a protected folder and make them available to others.

- The private setting is an all-or-nothing proposition. When you select the Make This Folder Private check box, Windows sets permissions on that folder so that you and only you can access files stored in that location. Clear the check box, and any user who logs on to the computer can view the files stored in the folder.

- When Simple File Sharing is enabled and you move or copy files or folders between a private folder and a shared location, the moved or copied objects always take on the security attributes of the destination folder. This behavior changes if you disable Simple File Sharing. See "Troubleshooting Permission Problems," page 301, for more details.

Caution   The Make This Folder Private option is ineffective unless you've configured your account with a password. If you neglect this step, any other user can go to the Welcome screen, click your logon name, and gain complete access to your files. If you try to make a folder private on an account that has no password, a dialog box reminds you of this basic fact and offers to help you set a password.

How Simple File Sharing Works

There's nothing magical about Simple File Sharing. This user interface hides the full set of NTFS permissions and applies a strictly defined set of permissions to selected objects. Behind the scenes, here is what's happening:

- **Default permissions**   When you create a new user account and log on for the first time, Windows XP creates an empty set of user profile folders and assigns Full Control permissions to the new user. In addition, Windows assigns Full Control permissions to the built-in Administrators group and the System account. Windows designates the logged-on user as the Creator Owner of these folders; the owner has full rights to work with the files and folders and to change the access controls on these files. (For more details on what ownership means, see "Taking Ownership of Files and Folders," page 300.)

- **Private folders**   Selecting the Make This Folder Private option removes the Administrators group from the list of permitted users, leaving only the user's account and the built-in System account on the Permissions list. (A member of the Administrators group can regain access only by taking ownership of the folder, a drastic action that is recorded in the computer's event logs and is immediately obvious to the previous owner.)

- **Shared folders**   As the name implies, the Shared Documents folder and its subfolders are available for use by anyone with an account on the computer. Members of the Administrators group have Full Control permissions over this folder and all its subfolders. Members of the built-in Power Users group (available only in Windows XP Professional) have all rights except the ability to change permissions or take ownership of files in this folder. Finally, those with limited accounts (members of the built-in Users group) can read and open files in the Shared Documents folder but cannot create new files, modify existing files, or copy or move files to this location.

If you want to break through any of these limitations, you can disable the Simple File Sharing interface and use the full complement of Windows 2000–style file permissions. As noted previously, these options are available only if you're running Windows XP Professional, and only on NTFS-formatted drives. To make the switch, open any Windows Explorer window (the My Documents or My Computer window will do) and choose Tools, Folder Options. Click the View tab, scroll to the bottom of the list, and then clear the Use Simple File Sharing (Recommended) check box.

Chapter 9

> **Note** You must be a member of the Administrators group to change file sharing options.

After you make this change, you'll notice a new Security tab in the properties dialog box for any folder stored on an NTFS drive. Figure 9-2, for example, shows the Security settings for a subfolder in the user Ed's My Documents folder. The Allow check boxes are unavailable because these settings are inherited from a higher-level folder. For details about inheritance, see "Applying Advanced Security Settings," page 285.

When you turn off Simple File Sharing, you plunge into a confusing and potentially dangerous set of options. Even expert Windows users struggle with the proper use of NTFS permissions, and if you make a mistake you can make folders and files inaccessible to yourself and other authorized users. Before you decide to forego the Simple File Sharing interface, make sure that you completely understand the consequences. Read the rest of this chapter carefully, and if you share files and folders over a network, read Chapter 30, "Managing Shared Folders and Printers," as well, because these settings also have a profound impact on network security.

Figure 9-2. When you disable Simple File Sharing, you expose the full range of NTFS permissions for files and folders.

Default Locations for Shared Files

As noted in the previous section, Windows XP sets aside a group of folders for users to share documents with one another. By default, these folders are located in the All Users profile (on a default setup, the path is C:\Documents And Settings\All Users). File and folder permissions are set so that administrators have full access to these folders.

Note If your computer belongs to a Windows domain, the shared folder shortcuts referred to in this section aren't available at all. In workgroup setups and on standalone computers, the exact location of each shared folder is defined in the registry using values under the following key: HKLM\SOFTWARE\Microsoft\Windows\CurrentVersion\Explorer\Shell Folders.

Sorting out the exact location and behavior of shared folders can be confusing. When you open a shared folder in a Windows Explorer window, the folder name that appears in the Address bar doesn't always match the label that appears under the folder icon and in the title bar of the open window. The registry values that define shared folders use completely different names as well. In addition, some shared folders are hidden and at least one doesn't work as you might expect. Confused? The following list is not exhaustive, but it should help you make sense of the most frequently used shared folders:

- **Shared Documents** To access this folder, open the My Computer window. The Shared Documents shortcut actually points to the Documents folder in the All Users profile. Its location is stored in the registry using the value Common Documents.

- **Shared Pictures** You'll find this subfolder in the Shared Documents folder. Its actual name, confusingly, is My Pictures. Its location is stored in the registry using the value CommonPictures.

Shared Pictures

- **Shared Music** This subfolder is also found in the Shared Documents folder. The actual name of this folder is My Music, and its location is stored in the registry using the value CommonMusic.

Shared Music

- **Shared Video** This folder appears in the Shared Documents folder if Windows Movie Maker is installed. The folder's actual name is My Videos, and its location is stored in the registry using the value CommonVideo.

- **Desktop** Any files you copy or move to the Desktop folder in the All Users profile show up on the desktop of all users on the system. Users with limited accounts can view and open these files but cannot rename or delete them. This location is stored in the registry as Common Desktop.

Chapter 9

- **Start Menu**   As is the case with the Desktop folder, shortcuts or files you add to this common location appear on the Start menu for all users and can be changed only by members of the Administrators or Power Users group. This location is stored in the registry as Common Start Menu.

- **Favorites**   You might expect this folder to behave like the Desktop and Start Menu folders, merging its contents with the user's personal Favorites collection. Unfortunately, it doesn't. In fact, this folder does nothing at all.

Tip   Get to shared folders faster

Instead of typing the full path to the All Users profile every time you want to work with files and shortcuts stored there, get in the habit of using shortcuts based on the system variable %AllUsersProfile%. That variable works in all shortcuts and is especially useful on systems on which you have multiple versions of Windows XP installed. By using this system variable, you don't have to remember whether the current system is using the copy of Windows on drive C or drive D. If you're logged on as an administrator, you can also right-click the Start button and choose Open All Users or Explore All Users to get to the shared Start Menu folder.

Keeping Your Own Files Private

If you create a new account during setup, or if the Windows Setup program automatically creates your user account when you upgrade from Windows 98 or Windows Me, your account starts out with no password. As the final step when you add a password to your own account from User Accounts in Control Panel, Windows displays the dialog box shown in Figure 9-3, which offers to help you make your files and folders private. (This option appears only when Simple File Sharing is in effect and does not appear with limited accounts or accounts whose user profiles are stored on a FAT32 drive.)

Figure 9-3.   If you choose this option, Windows resets the permissions on your user profile so that only you can view or open your files and folders.

Using this option to make your files private is convenient, but it's not the only way to exercise your right to privacy. Regardless of which choice you make when presented with this dialog box, you can change your mind later. You can add or remove protection from your entire profile, or apply the Make This Folder Private option to selected subfolders in your profile, as discussed in the previous section.

To protect your entire profile, follow these steps:

1 In the Run box or at any command prompt, type **%systemdrive%\documents and settings**.

2 Right-click the icon labeled with your user name, and choose Sharing And Security.

3 Under Local Sharing And Security, select the Make This Folder Private check box, as shown in Figure 9-4.

Figure 9-4. Select the Make This Folder Private check box to prevent other users from accessing files in your user profile.

4 Click OK to close the dialog box and apply your changes.

Other users who log on to the same computer and open the My Computer window can no longer see the folder icon that represents your My Documents folder if you've made your user profile private. Users who try to access your profile by opening the Documents And Settings folder will receive an "access denied" error message when they double-click the folder that contains your profile. The result is the same if another user tries to open a subfolder that you've made private.

Chapter 9

281

Troubleshooting

The Make This Folder Private option can't be selected.

The Sharing And Security command is available when you right-click any folder icon. Under some circumstances, however, the Make This Folder Private option appears dimmed and you are unable to select this check box (or clear it, if it's already checked). If you encounter this problem, run through the following checklist:

- **Is the drive formatted using NTFS?** The Make This Folder Private option will always be unavailable on FAT32 partitions.

- **Is the folder in your profile?** You cannot use the Make This Folder Private option on any other folder, including those in another user's profile.

- **Is a parent folder already set as private?** If you're trying to protect a subfolder in your user profile and the dimmed box is checked, you almost certainly have already used the Make This Folder Private option on a parent folder or on the entire profile. Work your way up the folder tree until you find the folder where you set this option.

You can apply protection to selected subfolders within your user profile. For instance, you might want other users to be able to work with some files in your My Documents folder while keeping other files protected. To set up this sort of partial protection, create a subfolder and give it a descriptive name like *Private*. Then move the files and folders you want to protect into that subfolder, and select the Make This Folder Private option for that folder only.

To remove protection from a folder, clear the Make This Folder Private check box. You might have to log off and log back on again before other accounts recognize the change in permissions.

Controlling Access with NTFS Permissions

If you're frustrated by the limitations of Simple File Sharing, you do have an alternative—that is, if you're running Windows XP Professional and if the drive that contains the files you want to protect is formatted with the NTFS file system. (On a machine running Windows XP Home Edition, the only way to adjust permissions on individual files or folders is by restarting in Safe Mode or using the Cacls utility from a command prompt, an option we describe in "Setting Permissions from a Command Prompt," page 298.) By disabling Simple File Sharing and using the full range of NTFS access controls, you can accomplish any or all of the following goals:

- **Control access to any file or folder on any NTFS-formatted drive.** This is a dramatic improvement over Simple File Sharing, which allows you to protect files in your user profile only.

- **Allow different types of access for different users or groups of users.** For instance, you might allow your teenagers read-only access to your collection of digital music

Chapter 9

files, so that they can play them but not erase them to make room for their own down-loaded tunes. You and your spouse, on the other hand, get full rights to add or delete any files. This is a significant change from the all-or-nothing access controls available via Simple File Sharing.

● **Fine-tune permissions on specific files or folders.** In a folder that contains the templates you use to create new documents or Web pages, you might want to restrict users to read-only access, while blocking their ability to overwrite or delete files. Anyone can open a new file based on an existing template, but you can be certain that the revised file won't inadvertently replace one of your carefully crafted templates.

Inside Out

Setting Permissions in Windows XP Home Edition

An undocumented loophole in Windows XP Home Edition makes it possible (although not easy) to set individual file and folder permissions by starting in Safe Mode. On a home computer where the drive containing the Documents And Settings folder is formatted with NTFS, for instance, you might have three accounts, all in the Administrators group: Mom, Dad, and Katy. Mom and Dad each need to be able to do online banking with Quicken or Microsoft Money, but daughter Katy isn't allowed near those files. If Mom stores the data file in her private My Documents folder, both Katy and Dad are locked out. If she stores the data file in the Shared Documents folder, Katy can access it. The solution? Mom needs to take the following steps:

1 Create the data file in her (Mom's) My Documents folder.

2 Copy the data file to the Shared Documents folder. (Leave the existing file in the My Documents folder as a backup in case of problems.)

3 Restart the computer in Safe Mode (see "Using Safe Mode," page 1286, for instructions), and log on from the Welcome screen.

4 Open Windows Explorer, and navigate to the Shared Documents folder.

5 Right-click the file whose permissions are to be adjusted, and choose Properties from the shortcut menu. Click the Security tab and remove all accounts except Mom, Dad, and System, each of which should have Full Control. (You may need to change inheritance settings, as described in "Applying Permissions to Subfolders Through Inheritance," page 292.)

6 Restart the computer, log on using each account, and try to access the file. If the permissions work as expected, delete the backup copy.

You can use this same technique to restrict access to any folder stored on an NTFS-formatted volume.

Caution Setting NTFS permissions without understanding the full consequences can lead to unexpected and unwelcome results, including a complete loss of access to files and folders. Working with the built-in permission sets—Full Control, Modify, and so on—is the safest strategy. If you plan to tinker with special permissions, set up a folder and fill it with test files so that you can experiment safely. When you're certain you've worked out the correct mix of permissions, apply them to the folders containing your real working files and delete the test folder.

The best way to begin working with permissions is to start by using the Make This Folder Private option on any folders you want to protect in your user profile. This sets a baseline of default permissions that guarantee you'll have exclusive access to those files. After completing that process, you're ready to turn off the Simple File Sharing interface and reveal the more complex Security tab, with its full array of NTFS permissions. To do so, from any Windows Explorer window, click Tools, Folder Options. On the View tab, clear the Use Simple File Sharing (Recommended) check box.

As a general practice, you should be consistent in your use of either the Simple File Sharing interface or full NTFS permissions. Switching back and forth indiscriminately can wreak havoc with network shares, as we point out in Chapter 30, "Managing Shared Folders and Printers." If you normally use Simple File Sharing, but occasionally need to work with the full set of permissions, you can bypass the dialog boxes with this simple script, which toggles between the two modes. Open Notepad or any plain text editor and enter the following text:

```
' ToggleSharingOptions.vbs
' Toggles between Simple Sharing and full NTFS permissions
Option Explicit
Dim strOldForceGuestValue, WshShell

On Error Resume Next

Set WshShell = WScript.CreateObject("WScript.Shell")
strOldForceGuestValue = _
  WshShell.RegRead("HKLM\SYSTEM\CurrentControlSet\Control\Lsa\forceguest")

If strOldForceGuestValue = "1" Then
  WshShell.RegWrite _
    "HKLM\SYSTEM\CurrentControlSet\Control\Lsa\forceguest", 0, "REG_DWORD"
  WScript.Echo "Full permissions are now available"
Else
  WshShell.RegWrite _
    "HKLM\SYSTEM\CurrentControlSet\Control\Lsa\forceguest", 1, "REG_DWORD"
  WScript.Echo "Simple sharing is now on"
End If
```

Alternatively you can copy the ToggleSharingOptions.vbs file from the companion CD included with this book.

Save the file in the Windows folder or in the All Users\Desktop folder asToggleSharing Options.vbs. Create a shortcut to the script and add it to the All Programs menu; for even faster access, assign a keyboard shortcut to the script.

Applying Advanced Security Settings

To view and edit NTFS permissions for a file or folder, right-click its icon, choose Properties, and then click the Security tab. This dialog box lists all the groups and users with permissions set for the selected object. As the example in Figure 9-5 shows, you can assign different permissions to each user—in this case, Katy can read and play (Execute) files in the Music Downloads folder but is forbidden to change existing files (Modify) or create new ones (Write).

In Windows XP, the owner of a file or folder (typically the person who creates the file) has the right to allow or deny access to that resource. In addition, members of the Administrators group and other authorized users can grant or deny permissions. You can add individual users to the list of users and allow or deny specific types of file and folder actions. You can also assign permissions to built-in groups (Administrators, for instance) or create your own groups and assign permissions that way. As we'll explain later in this section, some permissions don't need to be explicitly defined but instead are inherited based on permissions from a parent folder. All permissions are stored in the file system as part of the access control list (ACL).

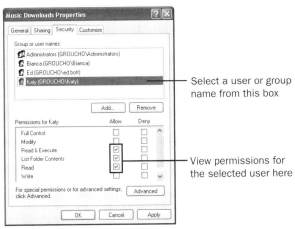

Select a user or group name from this box

View permissions for the selected user here

Figure 9-5. View and edit permissions for the selected user in the list at the bottom of this dialog box; each user or group can have a different set of permissions.

Chapter 9

For more details about creating and managing user accounts and groups, see "Working with User Accounts," page 232.

If the user or group whose permissions you want to edit is already listed at the top of the Security tab, you can select check boxes in the Allow column to add permissions, or clear boxes to remove permissions. Select check boxes in the Deny column only if you want to explicitly forbid certain users from exercising a specific permission. Deny access control entries take precedence over any other permission settings that apply to an account, such as those granted through membership in a group. If you want to completely lock out a specific user or group from access to a selected file or folder, select the Deny check box on the Full Control line.

Tip   Be careful with the Deny box

On the average home or small business computer, resist the temptation to select any of the check boxes in the Deny column on the Security tab. This option is typically used on large, complex networks where many groups of users are defined (individual departments, for example) and administrators want to exercise tight control over sensitive files in specific locations. Unraveling the interactions between Allow and Deny permissions can be a daunting task. On a machine with a handful of users, it's almost always simpler to define permissions by selecting and clearing check boxes in the Allow column.

In most cases, you can safely assign permissions by selecting a user or group name and then selecting one or more of the predefined groups of permissions listed at the bottom of the Security tab. Table 9-1 describes the basic function of each of these entries.

Table 9-1. How Permissions Control File and Folder Access

Permission	How It Controls Access to Files and Folders
Full Control	Gives the designated user or group full control over the selected file or folder, as the name implies. Selecting this box selects all check boxes below it as well. Users with Full Control can list contents of a folder, read and open files, create new files, delete files and subfolders, change permissions on files and subfolders, and take ownership of files.
Modify	Allows the user to read, change, create, and delete files, but not to change permissions or take ownership of files. Selecting this check box selects all the options listed below it.
Read & Execute	Allows the user to view files and execute programs. Selecting this check box selects the List Folder Contents and Read boxes as well.
List Folder Contents (folders only)	Provides the same individual permissions as Read & Execute and is available only on the Security tab for a folder. The only difference between the two permissions is in the way they are inherited.

Table 9-1. How Permissions Control File and Folder Access

Permission	How It Controls Access to Files and Folders
Read	Allows the user to list the contents of a folder, view file attributes, read permissions, and synchronize files. This is the most basic permission of all.
Write	Allows the user to create files, write data, read attributes and permissions, and synchronize files.
Special Permissions	If this permission is selected, the assigned permissions don't match any of the built-in templates shown here. Click the Advanced button to see details.

Note When the Read & Execute permission is applied to a folder, this permission is inherited by all files and subfolders within the folder. The List Folder Contents permission, on the other hand, though functionally identical, is inherited by subfolders but not by files within the folder or subfolders. For details about inherited permissions, see "Applying Permissions to Subfolders Through Inheritance," page 292.

To set permissions for a group or user who isn't listed in the Group Or User Names box, follow these steps:

1 Open the properties dialog box for the file or folder, and click the Security tab.

2 Click Add.

3 Type the name in the Select User Or Group dialog box shown here; when entering multiple names, separate them with semicolons. (Note that you must type the user name, which may be different from the full name that appears on theWelcome screen.)

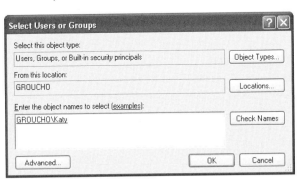

4 Click Check Names to confirm that you entered the names correctly.

5 Click OK to return to the Security tab and set permissions for the newly added user(s).

Chapter 9

Inside Out

Entering Group and User Names

On a standalone computer or on a computer that is part of a workgroup and is not joined to a Windows domain, the list of available group and user names is drawn only from the account database on the local computer—that is, the computer at which you're logged on. If your machine is a domain member, you can click the Locations button and choose whether you want to specify permissions based on users of the local computer or those in the domain's directory. If you're entering names of users on a Windows domain, enter a portion of the name and then click the Check Names button.

Unfortunately, you can't use the same shortcut to select users and groups defined in the local computer's account database; instead, you have to enter the user's name in full, and if you're off by even a single letter you'll get an error message. (Windows will, however, fill in the computer or domain name for you automatically.) To see a list of available local users and groups, click the Advanced button, and then click Find Now. The resulting list includes all user accounts, groups, and special accounts on the local computer.

When adding or removing permissions, follow these basic principles:

- **Start from the top and work down.** By default, permissions you set on a folder apply to all files and subfolders within that folder. (For more details, see "Applying Permissions to Subfolders Through Inheritance," page 292.) Managing file access is much easier when you have a consistent set of permissions for all files in a location, with exceptions only where needed.

- **Organize shared data files in common locations.** If shared data is scattered over multiple drives and folders, it's too easy to inadvertently let permissions get out of sync. Try to consolidate shared data files into a single group of folders. When data is all in one place, you'll find it easier to manage permissions and make proper backups.

- **Use groups whenever possible.** This is especially important in a small business setting. Take advantage of the built-in Administrators, Power Users, and Users groups for basic permissions. If you need to define custom permissions so that several users can access files stored in multiple folders, use group-based permissions to simplify the process. Create a new local group and add the users who need access to the files in question. (For details, see "Using the Local Users and Groups Snap-In," page 255.) Open the properties dialog box for the first folder, click the Security tab, add the newly created group, and grant the appropriate permissions to that group. Repeat this process for each additional folder. Later, when one member of the group leaves and another one joins, you can change the group membership and automatically update the permissions for all folders without having to go through each folder's properties dialog box again.

> For more information about how to create and manage local groups, see "Working with User Accounts," page 232.

- **Steer clear of special permissions.** Unless you're a wizard at understanding the interplay of NTFS permissions, resist the temptation to tweak special permissions for individual files or folders. The built-in security settings (Full Control, Modify, Read & Execute) cover most needs adequately.

- **Grant only the level of access that users require.** If a specific user needs to read files stored in a certain location, but does not need to create new files or edit existing ones, grant that user only the Read permission. This precaution is especially important to prevent novices and untrained users from wiping out important data files accidentally.

 Troubleshooting

You can't change file or folder permissions.

If you're unable to set custom permissions, look for the symptom in this list and try the following problem-solving techniques:

- **The Security tab is not visible** Do you see only a Sharing tab? If so, choose Tools, Folder Options, and clear the Use Simple File Sharing (Recommended) check box. If, after making this change, you still see only a Sharing tab, check the properties for the drive; the most likely explanation is that the drive is formatted using the FAT32 file system. The Security tab is visible only on NTFS drives.

- **You've made changes, but the check marks disappear** This may not be a problem at all. If you set permissions and apply them to anything other than the default location—This Folder, Subfolder, And Files—Windows adds a check mark in the Special Permissions box (when viewing permissions for a folder, you have to scroll to the bottom of the Permissions list to see this box). You can view the applied permissions by clicking Advanced, selecting the user or group, and clicking Edit.

- **Permission settings are unavailable** Check your user account rights. You must be logged on as a member of the Administrators group or be the owner of an object to set its permissions. These settings will also be unavailable if the selected object is inheriting its permissions from a parent folder. To set custom permissions on such an object, you have to remove the inheritance, as described later in this chapter, in "Applying Permissions to Subfolders Through Inheritance," page 292.

Working with Built-in Users and Groups

In addition to the standard local groups (Administrators and Users, for instance), Windows XP includes a number of special identities. These users and groups, which are built into the system and can't be deleted, are used to apply special permissions to system resources (including files and folders); in many cases, these identities are placeholders that apply to user accounts based on the way a given account uses the system.

> **Note** Special identities are often referred to as *well-known security identifiers* (*SIDs*).

The most common special identity you're likely to encounter in everyday use is the Everyone group, which includes all users who log onto the system. On a drive that's been newly converted to NTFS, the Everyone group is assigned the Full Control permission. As you would expect, this has the effect of allowing anyone who logs on to the computer to do anything with files and folders on that drive, unless further restrictions are placed on subfolders and files.

Understanding these built-in accounts and groups is crucial to using advanced NTFS permissions effectively. Table 9-2 lists the most common special identities.

Table 9-2. Special Identities Available in Windows XP

Special Identity	Description
Everyone	Includes every user who accesses the computer, including Guests. This group does not include Anonymous logons.
Creator Owner	Identifies the user who created the selected file or folder or who has taken ownership of it since it was created.
Authenticated User	Includes any user who logs on with a user name and password. Unlike the Everyone identity, this group does not include users who log on as Guest, even if the Guest account has been assigned a password.
Interactive	Includes any user that logs on locally or through a Remote Desktop connection.
Anonymous Logon	Identifies network logons for which credentials are not provided, such as connections to a Web server. Anonymous and Interactive logons are mutually exclusive.
Dialup	Includes any user who accesses the computer over a dial-up connection.
Network	Includes any user that logs on over the network. Does not include Interactive logons that use Remote Desktop over a network.

Some of these special identities are esoteric, and the average user will never need to apply them. But others can be extremely powerful additions to your security toolkit. For instance, you can use the following combinations of permissions to tighten security on your computer:

- For shared data folders, assign the Read & Execute permission and the Write permission to the Users group, and the Full Control permission to the Creator Owner special identity. In this configuration, every user who creates a file or folder becomes that object's owner and has the ability to read, modify, and delete it. Other users can read and modify documents created by other users but can't accidentally delete them.

- If you have a second drive in your system and you want to prevent all access to files on that drive by anyone using the Guest account, change the default permissions on the root of the drive. Add the Authenticated Users group and give it Full Control, and then remove the default Everyone group.

Caution One of the most common mistakes made by users who are inexperienced with NTFS permissions is removing the Everyone group from the root of a drive—or worse, selecting the Deny box next to Full Control for this group. If you try to take either of these drastic measures in Windows XP Professional, the system displays a dialog box warning you that you're about to deny all access to all files on the drive to all users—which is almost certainly not the intended result! Remember, more restrictive permissions always override more lenient permissions. As a rule of thumb, the best strategy for the permissions on the top-level folder for any drive is to make sure that all users who will access files on that drive have the proper level of access. After you've organized data on that drive, tighten up permissions on each subfolder so that it's accessible by the correct users and groups.

Windows XP includes three special identities that are reserved for software and system processes and are never used by human users. The Batch identity provides permissions for any batch process (such as a job launched via Task Scheduler) that needs to access a resource on the computer. The Service identity is used by system services and is controlled by the operating system. (For more information about services, see Appendix D, "Managing Services.") The System identity allows the operating system itself to access protected resources. As a general rule, permissions for these three groups are set by the operating system and should never be adjusted by users.

Caution Tampering with the default permissions on the drive that contains Windows system files is a bad idea. As part of the setup process, Windows XP applies specific permissions to the root of the system drive; to the Windows, System32, and Documents And Settings folders; and to specific subfolders within each of these locations. Changing the default permissions will not improve security and will almost certainly cause some users or programs to have problems. If you've made a mess of permissions in a system folder and you need to know how to put things right again, search the Microsoft Knowledge Base for a Windows XP–specific update to article 244600, "Default NTFS Permissions in Windows 2000."

Chapter 9

Applying Permissions to Subfolders Through Inheritance

Files and subfolders can inherit permissions from a parent folder. By default, any new permissions you assign to a folder are passed on to subfolders as well. Thus, when you create a new subfolder in your My Documents folder, it inherits the permissions you've set for your profile. If you made your user profile private, the new subfolder and any files you create or store within it will be private as well.

You can prevent permissions from being inherited by changing the inheritance options for a folder. You can specify that subfolders or files (or both) no longer inherit permissions that have been assigned to the parent folder containing them. Instead, only permissions you explicitly apply to files and subfolders will apply.

To see the inheritance options for a selected folder, right-click the folder icon, choose Properties, and then click the Security tab. Click Advanced to display the Advanced Security Settings dialog box. The Inherited From column in the Permission Entries list shows the parent folder from which a given set of permissions is inherited. In the example shown in Figure 9-6, the Everyone group inherits Full Control permissions from the ACL on the root folder of drive E, whereas the other permissions, designated as <not inherited>, have been applied directly to this folder.

In this example, the inherited permissions are getting in the way of the tight security we want to apply to this folder. To remove the inherited permissions, clear the Inherit From Parent The Permission Entries That Apply To Child Objects check box. You see the following dialog box, which warns you to specify how you want to reset the permissions on the selected folder.

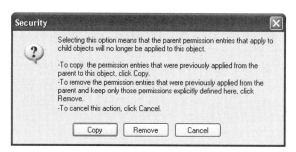

Choose one of the following three options:

- **Copy**   This option copies the permissions from the parent folder to the current file or folder and then breaks the inheritance link to the parent folder. After choosing this option, you can adjust the permissions to suit your security needs.

- **Remove**   This option removes any permissions that were inherited, keeping only those permissions that you've explicitly assigned to the file or folder.

- **Cancel**   This option closes the warning dialog box and leaves the inheritance options intact.

Chapter 9

When you remove inherited permissions from a folder, it becomes a new top-level folder. By default, any permissions you assign to this folder ripple down the hierarchy of subfolders and to files within those subfolders as well.

For an excellent illustration of how these settings all work together, look at the permissions on your user profile after you choose the Simple File Sharing option to make the folder private. Using Simple File Sharing, click the Make This Folder Private option, and then turn off Simple File Sharing. When you click the Advanced button on the Security tab of the "private" folder, you'll see that the Inherit From Parent The Permission Entries That Apply To Child Objects check box has been cleared and that the permissions on the folder now include only the System account and your user account, both with Full Control permissions. The net effect is to block out every user except you.

These permissions are applied directly to the current folder

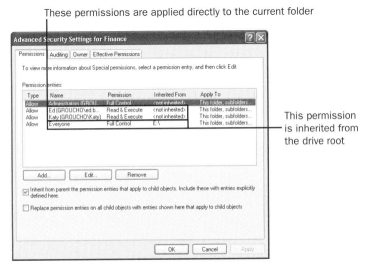

This permission is inherited from the drive root

Figure 9-6. The list of permissions shown here helps you identify which permissions are inherited from parent folders.

In some cases, you may want to apply two or more sets of permissions to the same folder for the same group, with each set of permissions having different inheritance settings. For instance, say that you and several coworkers on a shared computer are working on a top-secret project. You've set up a shared folder called Project X Files for use by everyone who has an account on your computer. In the main folder, you've stored a handful of document templates that you want members of the team to use when creating new documents; you've also set up subfolders to hold files that are currently being worked on.

In this scenario, you might want the Everyone group to have Read & Execute access to files within a top-level folder, and Full Control over subfolders. Using this arrangement of permissions, you can allow users to open templates stored in the top-level folder, while

Chapter 9

293

protecting those templates from accidental changes or deletions. By using a different set of permissions on subfolders, you can allow users to create new files and modify previously saved documents. To apply permissions with this level of fine-grain control, follow these steps:

1. Open the properties dialog box for the top-level folder you want to adjust (Project X Files, in this example), and click the Security tab. Then Click Add.

2. In the Select Users Or Groups dialog box, enter **Administrators** and click OK.

3. Choose Administrators from the Group Or User Names List at the top of the properties dialog box, and then select the Allow box to the right of the Full Control entry in the Permissions list. Click Add again.

4. This time, enter **Everyone** in the Select Users Or Groups dialog box and click OK.

5. Choose Everyone from the Group Or User Names List, and then select the Allow box to the right of the Read & Execute entry in the Permissions list.

6. Click the Advanced button to open the Advanced Security Settings dialog box.

7. If necessary, clear the Inherit From Parent The Permission Entries That Apply To Child Objects check box (and then select Copy when the security warning appears).

8. Select the entry for Everyone, and click the Edit button to open the Permission Entry dialog box (shown here). Open the Apply Onto list, choose This Folder And Files, and click OK.

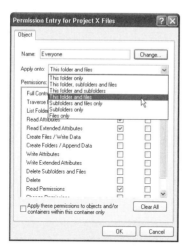

9. From the Advanced Security Settings dialog box, click Add.

10. In the Select User Or Group dialog box, enter **Everyone** and click OK.

11. In the Permission Entry dialog box, check the Full Control box, choose Subfolders Only from the Apply Onto list, and then click OK.

The resulting set of permissions should look like the one shown in Figure 9-7. With these settings, you and other members of the Administrators group can add and change files in the main folder; you can also add subfolders. All other users can view and open files in the main folder but can't create new files, change existing files, or delete files or subfolders. They can, however, save files in the subfolders you create.

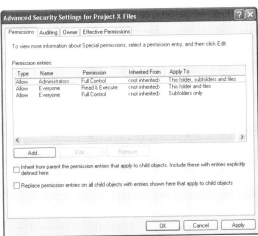

Figure 9-7. By applying different sets of permissions to files and subfolders, you can fine-tune permissions for a group of folders all at once.

What's the advantage of using inherited permissions in this fashion? Each time you create a subfolder, Windows automatically applies the proper permissions to it, using the inheritance settings you defined. Without these settings, you would be forced to define permissions from scratch for each new subfolder. That's a lot of needless work, with the potential for errors and inconsistencies. More important, if you decide to change the permissions later—for instance, changing the Full Control permission for subfolders from the Everyone group to a more limited group of users—you can make a single change and have the changes apply to all the child folders automatically.

Testing the Effect of Permissions

Because file and folder permissions can come from a variety of settings, it's sometimes difficult to figure out exactly what each user can and can't do with a given file or folder. As a general rule, you can figure out *effective permissions* by combining all the NTFS permissions assigned to an individual user account and to all of the groups to which that user belongs. Thus, if a user has Read & Execute permission for a folder set through her user account and is also a member of a group that has been assigned Write permissions for that folder, she has both Read and Write permissions for the folder.

Chapter 9

On a scale of complexity, calculating effective permissions is more difficult than programming a VCR and only slightly less taxing than quantum physics. Fortunately, Windows XP Professional includes a new tool that does the calculations for you. To see what the effect of all NTFS permissions will be on a given user or group, follow these steps:

1   Right-click the file or folder in question, and then choose Properties.

2   On the Security tab, click Advanced and then click the Effective Permissions tab.

3   Click Select to open the Select User Or Group dialog box.

4   Enter the name of the user or group for which you want to check effective permissions, and then click OK.

> **Note**   Anyone who's ever struggled to figure out Windows 2000 permissions will really appreciate the Effective Permissions dialog box in Windows XP. It's a wonderful addition, and if you're going to use NTFS permissions you should learn its ins and outs. Unfortunately, it also includes one potentially confusing interface element. The Group Or User Name box looks like a place to enter text directly, but it doesn't work that way in practice. You have to display the Select User Or Group dialog box to enter a name.

The resulting dialog box shows the effective permissions that apply to the user or group you selected. These permissions are presented using the complete list of available permissions from the Advanced Security Settings dialog box, which are far more detailed than those shown on the Security tab. This level of detail can be difficult to decipher, but it's crucial in identifying subtle changes that can compromise security. In the example in Figure 9-8, for instance, the user named Ed has permissions that are equivalent to Read & Execute; in addition, he can change permissions on the selected object.

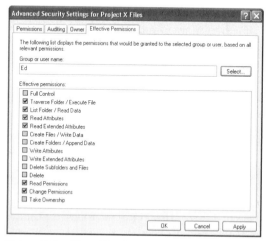

Figure 9-8.   Use this dialog box to see how permissions through user accounts and groups combine for a given user. Check marks indicate which permissions are assigned.

The effective permissions calculation looks up all local and domain groups to which a user or group belongs and takes those permissions into account in its summary. A check mark identifies permissions that have been assigned. The resulting display is a snapshot of permissions based on other settings. You can't change any permissions from this dialog box.

> **Note**　The effective permissions calculation does not include the Anonymous Logon or Authenticated Users group, nor does it include settings granted because a user is the Creator Owner of an object. In addition, the calculation does not consider whether you're logging on interactively or over a network. If you've customized any of these permissions, you'll need to account for the differences.

Using Special Permissions

Don't be misled by the long list of so-called special permissions that you see when you click Advanced on the Security tab, select a user or group name, and then click Edit. Whenever you use NTFS permissions, whether it's through the Simple File Sharing model or the more full-featured Security dialog box, your actions result in changes to this list. Using the built-in permission options—Full Control, Modify, and so on—actually sets predetermined groups of permissions here. Figure 9-9, for instance, shows the results when you select the Allow box next to the Read & Execute entry—Windows actually sets five individual permissions in response to the single click.

Figure 9-9.　In general, you don't need to adjust these so-called special permissions. Using the check boxes on the Security dialog box makes the adjustments for you.

When dealing with unusual access control situations, the best solution is usually to start by applying the predefined basic permission that comes closest to the desired result. Then add or remove special permissions as needed. Table 9-3 lists the full set of special permissions that are applied when you set each of the predefined permission options.

Table 9-3. Special Permissions Applied by Basic Permissions

Basic Permission	Special Permissions
Read	List Folder / Read Data Read Attributes Read Extended Attributes Read Permissions
Read & Execute List Folder Contents	All Read special permissions listed above Traverse Folder / Execute File
Write	Create Files / Write Data Create Folders / Append Data Write Attributes Write Extended Attributes
Modify	All Read & Execute permissions listed above All Write special permissions listed above Delete
Full Control	All special permissions listed above Delete Subfolders And Files Change Permissions Take Ownership

Setting Permissions from a Command Prompt

Cacls.exe, a command-line utility available in both Windows XP Professional and Home Edition, provides another way to view and edit permissions. With Cacls (short for *Control ACLs*), you can view existing permissions by typing **cacls** *filename* at a command prompt, replacing *filename* with the name of the file or folder you're interested in (wildcards are acceptable as well). The resulting list of permissions is terse, to say the least. Next to each user account name, Cacls displays a single letter for any of three standard permission settings: F for Full Control, C for Change, and R for Read. Any other combination of settings from the Security tab or the Advanced Security Settings dialog box generates output only a programmer could love.

Cacls is useful for quickly finding the permissions for an object—particularly if you're already working in a command prompt window. As an administrator, especially when working with Windows XP Home Edition, it's an indispensable part of your toolkit.

> **Tip** Get a more powerful permission tool
> If you like Cacls, you'll love Xcacls. As the name suggests, it's an extended version of the basic utility included with Windows 2000 and Windows XP. This utility is included in the Support Tools collection found on the Windows XP CD in \Support\Tools\Support.cab.

You can also set permissions with Cacls. In fact, in Windows XP Home Edition, using this utility is the only way to adjust individual permissions without restarting in Safe Mode. Use the switches listed in Table 9-4 to modify the effects of Cacls.

Table 9-4. Command-Line Switches for Cacls.exe

Switch	What It Does
/T	Changes permissions of specified files in the current directory and all subdirectories
/E	Edits access control list instead of replacing it
/C	Continues on "access denied" errors
/G user:perm	Grants specified user access rights; if used without /E, completely replaces existing permissions
/R user	Revokes specified user's access rights (must be used with /E)
/P user:perm	Replaces specified user's access rights
/D user	Denies access to specified user

In conjunction with the /G and /P switches, use one of the following four letters where indicated by the *perm* placeholder:

- F (for *full control*) is equivalent to selecting the Allow box next to the Full Control entry on the Security tab.
- C (for *change*) is equivalent to selecting the Allow box for next to the Modify entry.
- R (for *read*) is equivalent to selecting the Allow box for Read & Execute entry.
- W (for *write*) is equivalent to selecting the Allow box for Write entry.

Note that wildcards can be used to specify more than one file in a command and that you can specify more than one user in a command. For instance, if you've created a subfolder called Archives in the Shared Documents folder and you want Carl to have Full Control permissions and Craig to have Read permissions in that folder, open a command prompt window, navigate to the Shared Documents folder, and type the following command:

```
cacls archives /g carl:f craig:r
```

If you then decide that you want to revoke Craig's access rights and give Read permissions to the Administrators group, type this command:

```
cacls archives /e /r craig /g administrators:r
```

Chapter 9

Caution Just because you *can* set permissions with Cacls doesn't mean that you should. It's easy to make a mistake that causes you to lose existing permissions on a file. If you're using Windows XP Professional, there's no reason to use Cacls to set permissions. If you're using Windows XP Home Edition, try the Cacls command on a test folder first and make sure that your settings have the desired effect before you use this command on your actual working files.

Taking Ownership of Files and Folders

When you create a file or folder on an NTFS drive, Windows XP designates your user account as the owner of that object. That status gives you the right to allow or deny permission for other users and groups to access the file or folder. As owner, you can lock out every other user, including all members of the Administrators group.

So what happens if you turn over responsibility for a document (or an entire folder full of documents) to another user? As the owner, you can allow the other user to take ownership of the object. In addition, any member of the Administrators group can take ownership of any file or folder, although he or she cannot transfer ownership to other users.

Turning over the ownership of a file or folder makes sense when you want someone else to be responsible for setting permissions for that object. To ensure a smooth transition of power, use either of the following techniques.

If you're a member of the Administrators group, follow these steps:

1 Right-click the file or folder icon, and choose Properties.

2 On the Security tab, click Advanced to open the Advanced Security Settings dialog box for the file or folder.

3 Click the Owner tab. As the example in Figure 9-10 shows, this dialog box identifies the current owner and allows you to transfer ownership to the Administrators group or to your account.

4 Select either name from the Change OwnerTo list, and click OK.

If you're not an administrator, you must first be granted the right to take ownership of a file or folder explicitly. To do this, ask the current owner or any member of the Administrators group to add your account to the ACL for the file or folder and give you the Take Ownership permission. This permission can be found at the bottom of the list of special permissions available by clicking Edit in the Advanced Security Settings dialog box. Ultimately, the ability for an administrator to take ownership of files and folders means that you can't count on absolute privacy for any files stored on an NTFS drive. No matter how securely you lock them up, an administrator can break through the lock by taking ownership of the files. This is a brute force solution, however, and it's not something that can be easily hidden. If you're concerned about security and you want to monitor changes in ownership of file-system objects, configure your system so that Take Ownership events in a particular location are audited. You'll find step-by-step instructions on how to do this in "Seeing Who Has Tried to Access Your Files and Folders," page 391.

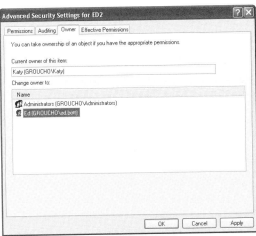

Figure 9-10. Only members of the Administrators group have the right to take ownership of files and folders.

Troubleshooting Permissions Problems

NTFS permissions are straightforward and uncomplicated when the Simple File Sharing interface is enabled. In this configuration, users do not have the ability to manipulate file and folder access controls directly. You can select one or more folders within your user profile and make those locations private, but no other security settings are available for customization. With Simple File Sharing enabled, when you move or copy files or folders from a folder you've made private into any other location on an NTFS volume, the moved or copied objects take on the security attributes of the destination folder—in most cases, that means they're freely available to all other users. When you drag a file out of your private My Documents folder and drop it into the Shared Documents folder, for instance, that file is accessible by all other users of the local computer. Conversely, when you move a file from the Shared Documents folder into your private My Documents folder, it becomes a private file accessible only to you.

But if you disable Simple File Sharing and work directly with NTFS permissions, ordinary file management tasks can have unintended and confusing consequences. In fact, even when a user has been granted Full Control permissions for a given folder, he or she may

Chapter 9

encounter an "access denied" error message when trying to open, rename, delete, or copy a file or folder.

To understand why this problem occurs, you need to understand what happens when you move or copy files or folders from one location to another. During the move, the permissions for the files or folders may change. With Simple File Sharing disabled, Windows XP follows a strict set of rules when applying permissions during a move or copy operation. Note the different results that apply depending on whether you're moving or copying the object and whether the destination is on the same drive or on a different drive:

- **When you copy a file or folder to an NTFS drive...** The newly created folder or file takes on the permissions of the destination folder, and the original object retains its permissions. This is true regardless of whether the destination is on the same NTFS drive as the original file or on a separate NTFS drive. You become the Creator Owner of the new file or folder, which means you can change its permissions.

- **When you move a file or folder within a single NTFS drive...** The moved folder or file retains its original permissions and you become the Creator Owner.

- **When you move a file or folder from one NTFS drive to another...** The moved folder or file picks up the permissions of the destination folder and you become the Creator Owner.

- **When you copy or move a file or folder from a FAT32 drive to an NTFS drive...** The newly created folder or file picks up the permissions of the destination folder and you become the Creator Owner.

- **When you copy or move a file or folder from an NTFS drive to a FAT32 drive...** The moved or copied folder or file in the new destination loses all permission settings, because the FAT32 file system is incapable of storing these details.

When Simple File Sharing is disabled, you may discover, after dragging a file from your My Documents folder into the Shared Documents folder, that other users are unable to access that file. This result will occur if the following conditions apply:

- The drive that contains the Documents And Settings folder is formatted using the NTFS file system.

- You've made your entire user profile private (as you were prompted to do when you added a password to your account).

- You've created a group of files (or a subfolder) in your My Documents, My Music, or My Pictures folder, and you want to share those files with other users by dragging them to the Shared Documents folder.

Chapter 9

Because both locations are on the same NTFS-formatted drive, dragging any file or folder from your user profile to the Shared Documents folder moves the selected object without making any changes to its access control list. As a result, other users can see the icon for the file or folder but are greeted with an "access denied" error message when they double-click it. Frustrating, isn't it? The solution to this dilemma is simple. If you've disabled Simple File Sharing, never *move* a file from your personal profile to a shared location. Instead, get in the habit of *copying* the file. The new copy inherits the permissions from the destination folder (Shared Documents), and is therefore available to every user. After copying the file or folder, you can safely delete the original from your private folder.

Another common cause of permission problems has an equally simple solution. After you add a user account to a group that has been assigned permissions for a file or folder, the user must log off and log back on to have access to the files.

Tip   **Don't overlook inherited permissions**
When trying to sort out why a user is having problems accessing a given file or folder, look first in the Advanced Security Settings dialog box. Pay particular attention to the Inherited From column in the Permission Entries list. The data here will often show you the exact source of an unexpected permission problem.

Chapter 9

Chapter 10

Securing Your Internet Connection

Your connection to the Internet lets you download music files, load your favorite Web sites in a browser window, and receive e-mail from just about anywhere. Unfortunately, that connection can also carry dangerous data, such as viruses and spyware. Some rogue programs arrive as e-mail attachments; others are disguised as seemingly innocuous downloads. A malicious intruder who convinces you to install an unsafe program or figures out how to exploit an unpatched security hole can connect to your computer and poke around in your personal files, or install a program that allows him to literally take over your computer.

To put it in the simplest possible terms: When your computer is connected to the Internet, you're at risk. That fact is undeniable, but it needn't be alarming. You can manage the risk if you understand its nature and take some relatively simple and straightforward precautions.

In the original release of Microsoft Windows XP, Internet Explorer offered only a modest degree of protection against the possibility of downloading and installing unsafe or unwanted programs—including spyware and viruses. It took exceptional care, constant vigilance, and advanced skills to avoid infection. Service Pack 2 significantly enhances the ability of Windows XP to prevent hostile code from being installed in the first place, without requiring intervention on your part, and it provides new tools that allow you to disable, remove, and otherwise manage browser add-ons.

At Home with Windows XP

All of the tools, techniques, and protective measures we discuss in this chapter are available in both Microsoft Windows XP Home Edition and Windows XP Professional.

Internet Explorer also allows you to categorize Web sites according to the degree of trust you accord them. Based on a site's reputation or your own direct knowledge of it, you can apply stricter or more lenient security standards. Thus, you can deal with the Web in much the same way you deal with the world at large—giving reputable Web sites and other trusted contacts the benefit of the doubt and exercising greater caution with unknown or suspicious parties.

In Chapter 7, "Security Essentials," we introduced the basic components that make up the Windows XP security infrastructure. In this chapter, we provide additional details about how to protect your Internet connection, with a special emphasis on security features in Internet Explorer and Microsoft Outlook Express. And because they're closely related to issues of security, we also discuss some measures you can take to enhance your privacy online.

 # What's New in Service Pack 2

Some of the most important features in Windows XP Service Pack 2 (SP2) are specifically designed to increase your security as you move around on the Internet. This partial list includes some of the new features, as well as some existing features that have been improved:

- **Restrictions on automatic downloads in Internet Explorer**   You now have to specifically approve any software download, and Web page designers can no longer repeatedly prompt you to download a file or install a program.

- **Improved handling of downloaded files, including e-mail attachments**   If you're familiar with earlier versions of Windows, you'll note a cleaner download dialog box, with a new file handler icon and explanatory text along the bottom of the box. In addition, behind the scenes, Windows now checks for publisher information in all executable files.

- **An effective pop-up blocker**   This option eliminates a major annoyance and lessens the likelihood that an unsophisticated user will be tricked into clicking an unsafe link. (We discuss this feature in more detail in "Blocking Pop-Ups," page 522.)

- **Tighter ActiveX security**   ActiveX controls are executable programs that enable or enhance features in other programs; they're most commonly used to add capabilities to Internet Explorer. Unfortunately, ActiveX controls can also deliver spyware, adware, or other hostile code. With SP2, you decide when to install an ActiveX control; Web pages are no longer allowed to display an Authenticode dialog box that forces you to reject an ActiveX control. In addition, unsigned ActiveX controls are blocked from installation unless an administrator specifically changes default system security settings.

- **An interface to control browser add-ons**   The open architecture of Internet Explorer makes it easy to add toolbars, search panes, and utility programs that expand the capabilities of the browser. Used properly, this feature can make Web browsing more productive. However, poorly written add-ons can cause frequent browser crashes, and some add-ons contain code that produces undesired effects, such as spawning pop-up windows or redirecting the browser to unwanted sites. In SP2, you can see which add-ons are installed and disable or remove those you don't want as well as those that have been shown to cause crashes.

● **New advanced security settings** SP2 improves several important security options that were formerly almost invisible or buried several layers deep in dialog boxes. The most important of these settings tighten the existing Security Zone features and add new choices on the Advanced tab of the Internet Options dialog box.

Another Internet Explorer-specific SP2 feature is the Information Bar. As Figure 10-1 shows, this thin band appears above the contents of the current Web page, just below any visible toolbars. On the left side of the status bar on the bottom of the page, the Windows security icon indicates that Windows took a security precaution on your behalf.

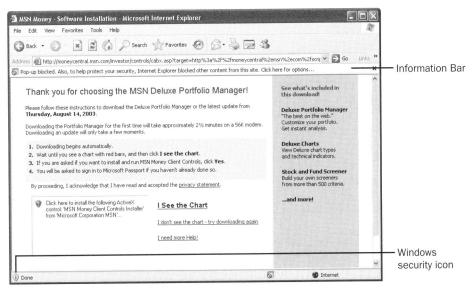

Figure 10-1. When Internet Explorer blocks multiple events—in this case, a pop-up window and an attempted ActiveX installation—you'll need to click the Information Bar to see details.

The Information Bar appears in response to events that previously might have triggered an intrusive warning dialog box, such as a blocked pop-up window or an attempt to download a program or install an ActiveX control. If you want to act on this relatively subtle notification, you need to click or right-click the Information Bar (both actions produce the same result) and choose the appropriate action from the context menu.

> **Tip** Use the keyboard to get to the Information Bar
>
> As with virtually every part of the Windows interface, you can navigate to the Information Bar without using a mouse. Press Tab to move the focus around the Web page and the browser window (press Shift+Tab to move it in the opposite direction). The Information Bar is after the last browser toolbar in the Tab sequence. When the Information Bar changes color to indicate that it has been selected, press Shift+F10—a standard keyboard shortcut—to display the menu.

Should You Switch Browsers?

Although Internet Explorer is the default browser in Windows XP, it isn't your only option. In this chapter, we focus on Internet Explorer because it's widely used, but we've logged many hours with alternative browsers as well. Some security experts recommend avoiding Internet Explorer when possible and using Mozilla, Firefox, or Opera instead. They argue that Internet Explorer's history of security problems and the fact that it is the target of relentless attacks makes it too dangerous to use. We think the sweeping security enhancements in Service Pack 2 resolve many of the serious issues that plagued earlier versions, but we also have no quarrel with anyone who prefers to use a different browser. Just be aware that as long as you use Windows XP, you can't escape Internet Explorer. Some sites don't work properly with non-Microsoft browsers, and some operating system features (including Windows Update) rely on Internet Explorer components to perform basic functions. Even if you rarely use Internet Explorer, it's important that you install all security patches when they're available.

The Information Bar is subtle—perhaps a little too subtle, which is why Windows also plays a sound when an event triggers the Information Bar. If you're annoyed by the sound, you can shut it off or change to a sound file that is more esthetically pleasing:

1 Open Control Panel and double-click Sounds And Audio Devices (under Sounds, Speech, And Audio Devices if your Control Panel is arranged by category).

2 On the Sounds tab, scroll to the Windows Explorer section of the Program Events list and select Information Bar.

3 To change the notification sound, choose an alternate sound from the Sounds list, or click Browse to select a custom WAV file. Select (None) from the top of the Sounds list to turn off the sound.

4 Click OK to save your changes.

Settings for the Information Bar are enabled on the basis of security zones. If you want to disable the Information Bar for a particular type of behavior, you can do so on a zone-by-zone basis. When you disable an SP2 security feature in this fashion, Internet Explorer uses the less restrictive behavior of SP1 and earlier versions of Windows XP. (For more details, see "Defining Security Zones for Web Sites," page 328.)

Setting Up Your Internet Connection

Before you can secure your Internet connection, you have to make sure it's set up properly. If you follow our advice and run the Network Setup Wizard (for more details, read "Using the Network Setup Wizard," page 958), Windows will do most of the work for you. It doesn't matter whether you're connected via a cable modem or a dial-up connection—the wizard sets you up so that you can reliably connect to your Internet service provider; it then turns on Windows Firewall so that you're protected from external threats.

With a few exceptions, most desktop computers in home and small offices will have a single Internet connection. Who would want to set up a second Internet connection? You might, if you fall into one of the following categories:

- You need a secondary dial-up account on a desktop computer that's normally connected via broadband. If your cable or DSL service occasionally fails and you require nonstop access for your business, it's comforting to know that you can get connected—albeit slowly.

- You travel frequently with a notebook computer and you need a way to connect to the Internet from a hotel phone.

- You travel frequently with a notebook computer and you need a second dial-up account for use in areas where your main dial-up account doesn't have a local access number. (This situation is especially common for anyone who travels globally.)

- Your office requires that you make a dial-up or virtual private network (VPN) connection to log on to the network. (For more details on setting up a VPN, see "Connecting to a Virtual Private Network," page 1070.)

- Your notebook computer has an Ethernet jack or a wireless adapter. You use the wired connection in your office; you use the wireless adapter in coffee shops, airports, and other locations that offer "hot spot" connections.

These days, you're most likely to use a broadband connection for your primary Internet access. But as the above list makes clear, the most common type of secondary network connection is a dial-up connection. If you upgrade to Windows XP, your previous connection settings should transfer to the new operating system without any problems. If

Chapter 10

you're setting up a dial-up connection from scratch, Windows XP includes a wizard that automates the process.

> **Note** When you create a dial-up connection, its settings are stored in the Network Connections folder, available via Control Panel.

To set up a new dial-up connection in Windows XP, start by gathering all the necessary account information from your Internet service provider, including access numbers, logon names, passwords, and any other configuration details, such as the names of e-mail servers. Then follow these steps:

1 From Control Panel, open the Network Connections folder (in the Network And Internet Connections category) and click the Create A New Connection link in the Network Tasks pane. Alternatively, choose File, New Connection. Click Next to skip the Welcome screen of the New Connection Wizard.

2 On the wizard's Network Connection Type page, select Connect To The Internet and then click Next to open the Getting Ready page.

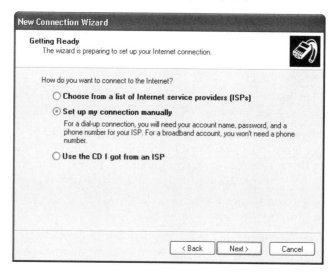

3 Choose Set Up My Connection Manually and then click Next. The Internet Connection page displays.

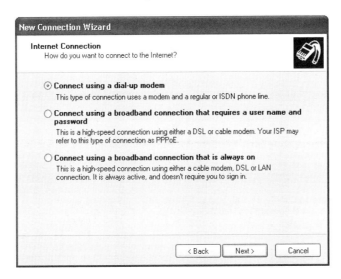

4   Select Connect Using A Dial-Up Modem and then click Next. The Connection Name page appears.

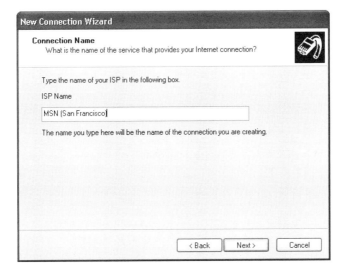

5   Enter a descriptive name for the new connection in the ISP Name box. This is the label that will appear beneath the connection icon in the Network Connections folder. Click Next to continue.

Chapter 10

> **Tip** **Describe your dial-up connection**
>
> Adding extra detail to the connection name can make dial-up connections easier to use later. On portable computers, it helps to include the location along with the name of the ISP—for example, MSN Seattle or Earthlink Dallas. If you set up multiple connection icons, one for your usual dial-up number and others for numbers you use when traveling, label each one clearly—MSN (Home) or MSN (Dallas), for instance.

6 On the Phone Number To Dial page, enter the exact number you need to dial to connect to the ISP, including any necessary prefixes or area codes. Click Next to open the Internet Account Information page.

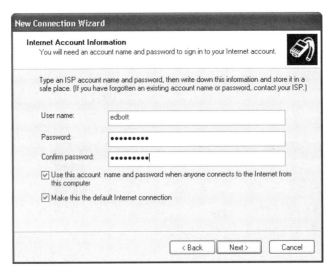

7 Fill in the User Name and Password boxes and retype your password in the Confirm Password field. In addition, clear either or both of the following options, if necessary (both are enabled by default):

- ■ **Use This Account Name And Password When Anyone Connects To The Internet From This Computer**   Select this option if you want to enable automatic dialing from all user accounts. Clear this check box if you want to allow this connection to be used only when you've logged on to your Windows XP account.

- ■ **Make This The Default Internet Connection**   Leave this option selected if this connection is your primary means of access to the Internet. Clear this check box if this is a backup connection.

Click Next to continue.

8 On the final page of the wizard, review your settings and click Finish to create the connection.

Tip **Get quicker access to connections**

If you use a dial-up connection regularly, you'll quickly lose patience with the rigmarole of locating the Network Connections dialog box every time you want to go online. Make your life a little easier by using shortcuts on the desktop and the Start menu, which will put your connection no more than two clicks away at any time. When you set up a new connection, a new dial-up connection icon is added to your Network Connections folder. Windows also adds a cascading Connect To menu to the Start menu, listing your available dial-up options. If this menu isn't visible, you can add it easily by following these steps:

1 Right-click Start and choose Properties to open the Taskbar And Start Menu Properties dialog box.

2 On the Start Menu tab, click Customize.

3 If you're using the Windows XP Start Menu, click the Advanced tab and scroll through the Start Menu Items list until you locate the Network Connections category. Select Display As Connect To Menu and then select OK. If you're using the Classic Start Menu option, click the Expand Network Connections option and click OK.

After you finish with the wizard, you can work with your connection by opening the Network Connections folder. To dial the connection manually, double-click the connection icon and click the Dial button.

Chapter 10

To create a "hands-free" connection that dials automatically without requiring your intervention, make sure you've saved all necessary logon information, including your user name and password, with the connection. Then follow these steps:

1   In the Network Connections folder, right-click the connection icon and choose Set As Default Connection. (If the Cancel As Default Connection option is available, you can skip this step.)

2   From Control Panel, open Internet Options and select the Connections tab.

3   Select the dial-up connection from the list and then choose Always Dial My Default Connection. Click OK to close this dialog box.

4   Open Internet Explorer and browse to any page. When you see the Dial-Up Connection dialog box, shown here, select the Connect Automatically check box and click Connect.

Protecting Your System from Unsafe and Unwanted Software

Based on one recent survey of crashes submitted via the Online Crash Analysis tool in Windows XP, Microsoft concluded that roughly half of reported failures in the Windows operating system are directly traceable to what it calls "deceptive software." That is a remarkable statistic, especially when you realize that this type of rogue program barely existed when Windows XP was first being developed. As we explain in this section, spyware, adware, and other similarly unsavory types of software represent a major security risk.

How does deceptive software end up on a computer? The simplest route is the most direct: You click a link on a Web page or in an e-mail message that leads directly to an executable file. For example, an advertisement (often written as an ActiveX control) may make extravagant claims about a free program. When an unsophisticated computer user clicks the ad, the program offers to install itself via an Authenticode dialog box, which can easily be mistaken for an official Windows stamp of approval.

In some cases, the setup routine for one program surreptitiously installs additional programs in the background. This is particularly true of software designed for use with underground file-sharing networks. When we installed one widely used song-swapping program, for instance, we found that it installed four well-hidden add-ins along with the main application, resulting in an increase in pop-up advertisements and changes to the way the browser handled search requests and mistyped URLs. The most vicious types of deceptive software typically attempt to exploit security holes to install themselves automatically, without your approval or even your knowledge.

It should come as no surprise that the makers of this sort of software employ all sorts of tricks to mislead, deceive, and cajole you into installing their wares, by extolling the program's benefits and glossing over or omitting any mention of its undesirable behavior. For someone with a basic understanding of computer security issues, the principal security concern when browsing is to ensure (insofar as it is possible) that anything you download is safe and that any potentially undesirable behavior is fully disclosed. If you share a computer or network with unsophisticated computer users who cannot reasonably be expected to consistently reject unsafe software, your goal should be to prevent them from having to make potentially confusing choices in the first place.

Chapter 10

Spyware? Adware? What's the Difference?

Unfortunately, you'll find little consistency in the use of terms and descriptions when you read articles about unsafe or unwanted software. Some sources use the word *spyware* as a broad brush that covers even the most innocuous browser add-ons. In this book, we use the term *deceptive software* to refer to a wide continuum of programs, scripts, and browser add-ons that are typically installed without full disclosure of exactly how they work. Programs in this category interfere with legitimate requests to retrieve information from some Web sites and, in extreme cases, interfere with the operation of the computer itself. Some developers go out of their way to hide the fact that their program is installed at all and make the process of removing it as difficult as possible.

Depending on how a particular program or add-on works, you may hear it referred to by a number of specialized terms:

- *Spyware* is the term used to describe programs that gather information about you and your browsing activities without your knowledge and informed consent. These programs can store that information and use it to modify your computer's behavior, or they can send the data to the software developer or to a third party.

- *Adware* refers to a class of programs that display advertisements—usually in pop-up windows, on the desktop, or in the browser window. These programs often contain spyware-like features in that they monitor your movements around the Web so that they can provide ads that are ostensibly related to your interests.

- *Home-page hijackers* are scripts or programs that modify your browser settings to change your default home page. This type of exploit often affects search settings as well. Some especially egregious offenders modify the registry or place files on the affected computer that block the user's ability to change these settings. The new home page is often disguised to look like a Web portal or a legitimate search page, although a minority of programs in this category send the victim to X-rated sites.

In all three categories, the motive for infecting your computer is usually economic, with the owner receiving cash for referrals to Web pages that originate from the stealthily installed program. Other examples of deceptive software—less common but more dangerous—include *dialers*, which configure a computer to make unsolicited (and usually expensive) dial-up connections, and *Trojan horses*, which allow an intruder to take over a compromised computer and use it to attack other computers or forward spam.

Downloading Executable Files

In the original release of Windows XP, as in previous versions of Windows, a single dialog box typically stood between your computer and a piece of hostile code. In Windows XP with Service Pack 2 installed, you have several more layers of protection. When you click a link that points directly to an executable program file, Windows displays a Security Warning dialog box like the one shown in Figure 10-2.

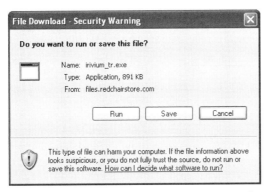

Figure 10-2. You must approve two separate Security Warnings to download and install a program in Internet Explorer.

If you click Save, you can download the file to your hard disk. After the download is complete, you can run the program by clicking Run in the Download Complete dialog box or double-clicking the program's icon in the location where you saved it. In either case, you see a second Security Warning dialog box. The color of the Windows security icon in the lower left corner of the dialog box indicates whether the program is digitally signed: A red icon indicates an unsigned program and a yellow icon identifies a signed program. (A blue icon appears for downloads that are not executable, such as Microsoft Word documents.) If you're certain that the program is safe, click Run.

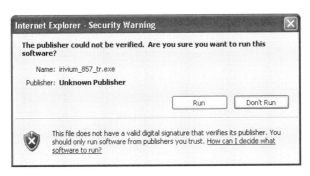

Chapter 10

> **Tip** **How do you know that a program is safe?**
>
> When an executable file isn't digitally signed, it's impossible to make a definitive determination of whether it's safe. In those circumstances, you can't be too cautious. In our experience, you can tip the odds in your favor by using common sense. Make sure the download is from a verifiable source. Use your favorite search engine to look for complaints about the program or its publisher—be sure to search the Web and Usenet newsgroups via Google Groups (*http://groups.google.com*)—and don't install anything until you're comfortable that you can resolve any reported problems if they crop up on your PC. Be sure to scan any downloaded files for viruses and spyware before installing. Finally, set a System Restore point before installing any software, so that you can undo the configuration changes if you're unhappy with the installation.

 ## Dealing with Automatic Downloads

Some Web pages are designed to initiate downloads automatically when you navigate to the page in your browser. In some cases, the page designer's intent is to be helpful by supplying download or installation instructions on the page and only asking the user to approve the download. However, this tactic can be abused by unscrupulous Web site owners who display a download dialog box and use the text on the underlying page to convince the user that a potentially harmful program is actually benign. If the user tries to cancel the dialog box, it may pop back up repeatedly—a "social engineering" trick designed to confuse the visitor into clicking OK to get rid of the annoying prompts.

Automatic downloads are blocked by new security features in SP2. When you encounter a page in the Internet zone that tries to "force" a download that the user has not initiated by clicking on a page element, the following message appears in the Information Bar: "To help protect your security, Internet Explorer blocked this site from downloading files to your computer. Click here for options…."

> **Note** This prompt may appear even when you click a page element, if that click runs a script that opens another page that is coded to prompt for a download. Automatic downloads are not blocked from Web sites that are in the Trusted Sites zone.

If you didn't intend to download a file, you can safely ignore the prompt, and it won't be repeated—SP2 limits download prompts to once per page access. If you want to download the file, click or right-click the Information Bar and choose Download File. This action eliminates the block; you can then proceed with the download as described in the previous section.

Troubleshooting

An automatic download fails.

You visit a Web page that attempts to automatically download a file, but after you click the Information Bar the download doesn't begin. What happened? The most likely explanation is that the Web designer has used a script on the page that causes the browser to automatically begin the download and then jump to a new page; because the entire script runs without checking whether the first part was blocked for security reasons, the download doesn't have a chance to begin. Click your browser's Back button to reenter the original page and attempt to begin the download again. If the automatic download still doesn't start, look for a direct link to the download; most page designers provide this alternative for visitors who have scripting disabled. If that fails, and you are certain the site is trustworthy, consider adding the site to the Trusted Sites zone and then reload the page—just be sure to remove the site from the Trusted Sites zone after the download is complete.

Note that if you download a data file (an MP3 file or a Word document, for example), a program (a shareware product, for example), or a helper application (an accessory, such as Adobe Reader, that assists Internet Explorer in rendering a particular kind of content), you are given the choice between saving the item to disk and installing or running it. To be safe, you should always save and scan, rather than installing or running directly.

Controlling ActiveX Downloads

ActiveX controls are small programs that enhance the functionality of a Web site, using a technology developed by Microsoft. They're used for such things as enabling the capability for you to play games with other Internet users, displaying stock tickers, and displaying animation. Windows Update uses an ActiveX control to compare installed patches and updates on your system with those available on Microsoft's servers. ActiveX controls, like executables that you run from the Start menu or a command line, essentially have full access to your computer's resources, although they are subject to some security restrictions.

> **Note** You cannot download an ActiveX control, scan it for viruses, and install it separately. ActiveX controls must be installed on the fly. Although the inability to scan for viruses in advance may sound like a security risk, you're protected from known viruses if you've configured your antivirus software to perform real-time scanning for hostile code. If the ActiveX control contains the signature of a known virus or worm, the antivirus software will intercept it and refuse to allow the installation to proceed. As with any program you download and install, of course, you need to exercise caution and ensure that the download is safe before allowing it on your computer.

Chapter 10

319

Before Windows XP SP2, a Web page could offer to install an ActiveX control by displaying a so-called "Authenticode" dialog box. This text-heavy security warning, shown in Figure 10-3, was difficult to read and understand, and it was easy for software developers to fill in the fields for the name of the software with a lengthy description practically guaranteed to fool an unsophisticated user.

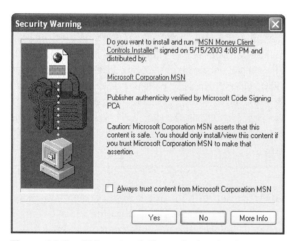

Figure 10-3. This potentially confusing (and potentially harmful) dialog box has been completely redesigned in Windows XP Service Pack 2.

As a result, Microsoft completely reworked the ActiveX download interface in SP2. When code on a Web page tries to install an ActiveX control on a computer running Windows XP with SP2, you see one of two warning messages in the Information Bar:

● If the control is unsigned, the message reads "To help protect your security, Internet Explorer stopped this site from installing an ActiveX control on your computer. Click here for options…." If you decide to overrule this decision by clicking the Information Bar and then choosing Install ActiveX Control from the menu, you see a dialog box with a red Windows security icon and the stern message shown here. Click OK to return to the page. The ActiveX control is not installed.

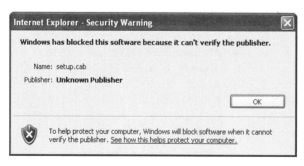

Chapter 10

● If the control is digitally signed, the message reads "This site might require the following ActiveX control: '*control_name*' from '*publisher_name*'. Click here to install...." In this case, you can allow the download to continue by clicking or right-clicking the Information Bar and then choosing Install ActiveX Control from the menu. The Security Warning dialog box displays a yellow icon, along with the name of the program and its publisher. Click More Options to see the full dialog box, as shown here. If you're certain the program is safe, click Install to continue; click Don't Install if you're not confident of the program's safety.

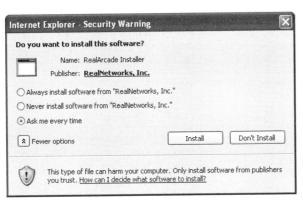

In the Security Warning dialog box for a signed control, note that the publisher's name is a hyperlink. Click this link to see the Digital Signature Details dialog box, which provides information about the certificate used to sign the program. Do not let your guard down! The existence of a digital signature does not guarantee that a program is safe to install or use; but by carefully examining these details (and, if necessary, doing additional research), you can learn more about the developer of the software, which you can then use to make an informed decision about whether to install the program.

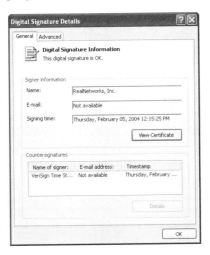

Some businesses refuse to allow the use of any ActiveX control that is not approved by an administrator. Others disallow all ActiveX controls. If you need to tighten the security settings imposed on ActiveX controls in the Internet zone, choose Internet Options from the Tools menu in Internet Explorer. On the Security tab, click Internet, and then click Custom Level. In the ActiveX Controls And Plug-ins section, adjust any of the options shown in Table 10-1.

Table 10-1. ActiveX Security Settings

Setting	Description
Automatic prompting for ActiveX controls	Disable (default) displays the Information Bar before allowing downloads; choose Enable to display a dialog box for all ActiveX controls.
Binary and script behaviors	Enable (default) allows scripts and programs to use an ActiveX control; choose Disable or Administrator Approved to tighten security.
Download signed ActiveX controls	Prompt (default) requires that you confirm before install-ing a signed control; choose Disable to prevent installa-tion. (Note: We strongly caution against choosing Enable, which weakens security to an unacceptable level.)
Download unsigned ActiveX controls	Disable (default) blocks installation of any unsigned con-trol; choose Prompt if you need to install a custom con-trol that is unsigned but trustworthy. (Note: Again, we strongly caution against choosing Enable, which weakens security to an unacceptable level.)
Initialize and script ActiveX controls not marked as safe	Disable (default) blocks any attempt to use an ActiveX control that is not specifically approved for use with scripts; choose Prompt to allow this type of activity on a case-by-case basis. (Note: As noted for the previous two settings, we strongly caution against choosing Enable, which weakens security to an unacceptable level.)
Run ActiveX controls and plug-ins	Enable (default) allows ActiveX controls to function, sub-ject to other security settings; choose Prompt to approve each control as it's used, Disable to block use of all ActiveX controls, or Administrator Approved to allow only those that have been flagged as acceptable by an Administrator.
Script ActiveX controls marked safe for scripting	Enable (default) allows Web pages to use script with cer-tain ActiveX controls; choose Prompt to approve each control as it's used, or Disable to block all scripting of ActiveX controls.

If you tighten any of these security settings and then visit a page that uses an ActiveX control, you may see one of the following messages in the Information Bar:

- "Your security settings do not allow Web sites to use ActiveX controls installed on your computer. This page may not display correctly. Click here for options…."
- "Internet Explorer has blocked this site from using an ActiveX control in an unsafe manner. As a result this page may not display correctly."

To work around either of these errors, you need to change the appropriate security setting for the Internet zone or add the site you're visiting to the Trusted Sites zone. For more information, see "Defining Security Zones for Web Sites," page 328.

Controlling Scripts

Scripts are small snippets of code, written in a scripting language such as JavaScript or VBScript, that run on the client computer (that is, *your* computer, not the Web provider's) to enhance the functionality of a Web page. (A scripting language is a simple programming language designed to perform limited tasks.) These should be distinguished from Active Server Pages (Web pages with the extension .asp), which employ a server-side scripting technology and don't, by themselves, represent a security hazard.

Scripts are generally harmless and are widely used in modern Web design. However, a would-be attacker can construct a hostile script to take advantage of security holes on a computer running Windows XP; when embedded in Web pages or in HTML-formatted e-mail messages, that script can wreak havoc on an unpatched computer. Security experts sometimes advise users to disable active scripting as a security measure. If you decide to take this extreme step, be prepared for some of your favorite Web sites to stop working properly. (For instance, you can't search for articles in the Microsoft Knowledge Base when scripting is disabled.) To work around this limitation, you'll have to add sites—manually, one at a time—to the Trusted Sites zone.

With those caveats having been said, if you're still determined to disable scripting, follow these steps:

1. Choose Internet Options from the Tools menu.
2. On the Security tab, click the Internet icon and then click Custom Level.
3. In the Settings list, locate Active Scripting (under the Scripting heading) and click Disable.
4. Click OK to save your settings, and then click OK to close the Internet Options dialog box.

If this option is too extreme but you're still concerned about security risks from scripts, consider choosing Prompt instead of Disable in the Settings list. For sites in the Internet zone

Chapter 10

that use scripting, you'll be forced to endure a blizzard of prompts such as this one, but as long as your mouse finger holds up you'll be able to successfully navigate through even the most script-heavy page.

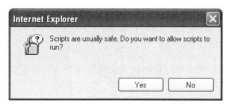

To Trust or Not to Trust?

Microsoft offers a digital signing technology, called Authenticode, that can be used to guarantee that an executable item comes from the publisher it says it comes from and that it has not been changed, deliberately or otherwise, since it left the publisher's hands. The digital signature verifies each bit of the signed file by comparing it to a hash value; if even a single bit of the file has changed, the comparison fails and the signature is invalid. With Service Pack 2 installed, Windows XP blocks installation of any code that has an invalid signature—by definition, this indicates that the program file is corrupt (possibly because it was damaged during downloading) or that it has been tampered with.

A digital signature doesn't promise that the signed item is healthy and benevolent. It confirms only that the bits you're about to download are the authentic work of a particular party and haven't been tampered with on their way to you. However, it is prudent to regard an unsigned item, or an item without a valid signature, as a potential threat.

Assuming the signature is valid, you can use the information contained within that signature to make an additional determination—do you trust the person or organization that attached the signature to the file? If the publisher is reputable and the Security Warning message reports that the item has been digitally signed, you must decide how much confidence you have in the publisher.

In earlier versions of Windows XP, the dialog box used with signed downloads included a check box that allowed you to specify that you always trusted the publisher using that certificate. By selecting this check box, you could automatically install future downloads from your favorite publishers without having to see the Security Warning dialog box every time.

Windows XP SP2 adds the counterpart to that feature—a check box that lets you identify a publisher as untrusted. If you determine that a particular company's widely distributed ActiveX controls and programs don't belong on your computer, you can designate that publisher as untrusted, and no user of your computer will be able to install software that uses that publisher's digital certificate.

Normally, you make choices about whether or not to install a signed item on an individual basis. But you may choose to trust a particular publisher and allow their software to be installed automatically without any prompting. Or you may decide that the publisher of a particular program is not trustworthy and you do not want any products from that publisher to be installed on your computer, under any circumstances.

To block programs from a given publisher, follow these steps:

1. Visit a Web page that attempts to install an ActiveX control.
2. Click the Information Bar and choose Install ActiveX Control. The Authenticode dialog box opens.
3. Choose the Never Install Software From Publisher option.
4. Click Don't Install.

After you make this choice, Internet Explorer will notify you any time you visit a site that tries to install or use software from the untrusted publisher. A Manage Add-Ons icon will appear in the status bar, at the right side of the bottom of the browser window. Also, a balloon tip will alert you that an add-on or program has been disabled or blocked.

To remove a publisher from the Untrusted Publishers list, choose Internet Options from the Tools menu in Internet Explorer. On the Content tab, click Publishers. Click the Untrusted Publishers tab, select the publisher name, and click Remove.

> **Caution** Do not remove the two Microsoft Corporation entries from the Untrusted Publishers list. As the text in the Friendly Name column explains, these two entries represent certificates that were issued several years ago to an untrusted source and were signed with Microsoft's master certificate. The revocation means that a ne'er-do-well can't exploit these phony certificates to install a virus or Trojan horse program that appears to have been published by Microsoft.

Managing ActiveX and Java Controls

If you'd like to take inventory of all the ActiveX controls and Java applets that you've downloaded and installed on your computer, follow these steps:

1. In Internet Explorer, choose Tools, Internet Options.
2. Click the General tab and then click Settings.
3. In the Settings dialog box, click View Objects.

Chapter 10

As Figure 10-4 shows, these steps take you to the Downloaded Program Files folder (%SystemRoot%\Downloaded Program Files), where you can see a listing of installed ActiveX controls and Java applets, and view the properties of each item. (Scripts are embedded in Web pages, not downloaded as separate files, so they don't appear in the Downloaded Program Files folder.)

> **Note**   This listing is by no means complete. Windows includes an enormous collection of ActiveX controls that it uses for various functions, and programs like Microsoft Office also install ActiveX controls that don't appear in the Downloaded Program Files folder. As the name suggests, this listing shows only ActiveX controls that you've downloaded and installed using your Web browser.

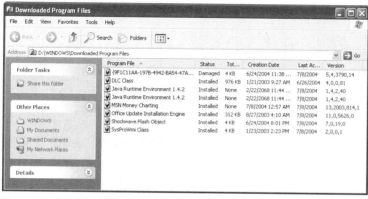

Figure 10-4.   The Downloaded Program Files folder lists installed ActiveX controls and Java applets and identifies damaged programs.

The most useful columns in this display are Status and Version. If a downloaded item stops working properly, that fact will be reported in the Status column. The Version column, meanwhile, can help you determine whether you need to update a control or utility. If you suspect that a newer version of an item is available for download, right-click its entry in the Program File column and choose Update from the shortcut menu. Internet Explorer will go to the site from which you downloaded the control or applet, check for an update, and download it if one is available.

Note that you can't tell from the icon associated with an item whether that item is an ActiveX control or a Java applet. The only way to know which species an item belongs to is by right-clicking it and choosing Properties from the shortcut menu. (Look at the Type field on the General tab.) The properties dialog box, shown in Figure 10-5, includes information about the item's dependencies (other files that must be present for the item to work properly), as well as the URL from which you downloaded the item.

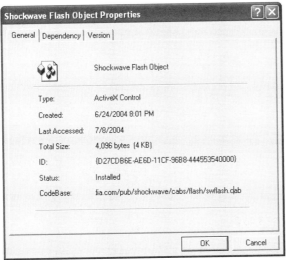

Figure 10-5. A downloaded program's properties dialog box tells you whether it's an ActiveX control or a Java applet, in addition to other details about the item.

Managing Browser Add-ons

Internet Explorer is extraordinarily customizable. Developers and their add-ons can extend its capabilities in highly visible ways, by adding new toolbars, Explorer bars, menus, and buttons. A programmer can also hook into the browser's core features to extend its search capabilities, manage the process of filling in forms, and save bookmarks—these are just a few of the tricks that popular add-ons can perform. These add-ons take the form of browser extensions, browser helper objects (BHOs), toolbars, Java applets, and ActiveX controls, to name just a few of the options available.

Unfortunately, add-ons have a dark side as well. A poorly written add-on can interfere with the smooth operation of Internet Explorer, resulting in mysterious crashes and other glitches; a malicious add-on can cause unnecessary pop-up windows, slow system performance, and reveal details about you and your browsing habits to an untrusted third party. Beginning with Service Pack 2, Windows XP offers a Manage Add-Ons dialog box that shows you all currently installed add-ons and allows you to disable those that are suspicious or known to cause problems.

To open this dialog box, choose Manage Add-Ons from the Tools menu. Figure 10-6 shows this dialog box on a computer with a relatively small number of installed add-ons.

Chapter 10

327

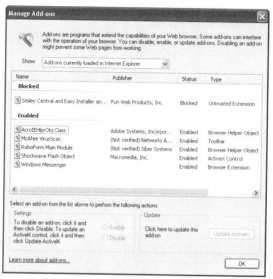

Figure 10-6. This dialog box shows add-ons currently in use by Internet Explorer as well as those you've blocked.

The Manage Add-ons dialog box displays a fair amount of detail about each add-on, including its publisher (if known), type, and the specific file with which it is associated. Use this list to enable or disable add-ons—click an entry in the list and choose Enable or Disable under Settings below. In the case of installed ActiveX controls, you can click the Update ActiveX button to check for a newer version than the one currently installed.

The drop-down Show list at the top of the dialog box allows you to toggle between a full list of all available add-ons and a shorter list of only those that are currently in use.

Unfortunately, the Manage Add-ons dialog box does not include a mechanism for removing add-ons. If you want to permanently remove one of the items on this list, you need to find the program that originally installed it and then remove that program. If you can't identify which program is responsible for a specific add-on, use your favorite search engine to look for clues, using the name of the add-on and the file with which it's associated as search terms. Be aware also that the Manage Add-ons dialog box may not detect all add-ons, especially hostile programs that were deliberately designed to thwart easy removal.

Defining Security Zones for Web Sites

Internet Explorer's security zones are key elements to browsing the Web and using the Internet without fear. By default, all Web sites you visit are assigned to the Internet zone, and Internet Explorer severely restricts the action of sites in the Internet zone. If you're concerned about security, you can lock down security zones even more tightly if you like.

By default, Internet Explorer allows you to work with four security zones:

- The Internet zone includes all sites that are not included in any other category.
- The Local Intranet zone is for sites on your local network, typically behind a firewall. These sites are highly trusted.
- The Trusted Sites zone (empty on a clean installation of Windows) allows you to specify sites where you allow certain actions—such as running ActiveX controls or scripts—that you might not permit on other sites in which you have a lower degree of trust.
- The Restricted Sites zone (also empty on a clean installation) allows you to specify sites where you want to specifically disallow actions that might otherwise be permitted. This zone is the default for HTML-formatted e-mail you read using Outlook or Outlook Express.

> **Note**   A fifth zone, called Local Machine (often referred to alternatively as My Computer), is not normally configurable and its settings are not displayed on the Security tab of the Internet Options dialog box.

When you open a Web page using Internet Explorer, Windows applies restrictions on what that page can do, based on the security zone for that page. Initially, any sites you connect to internally (that is, your own company's sites, which you access by means of an intranet connection) are automatically assigned to the Local Intranet zone, and the Local Intranet zone is accorded a "medium-low" level of security settings. All the rest of the Internet is lumped into the Internet zone, which is given a "medium" level of security settings. As you roam the Internet, if you come upon a site that you trust implicitly, you can move that site into the Trusted Sites zone. Internet Explorer, by default, applies a "low" level of security settings to the Trusted Sites zone. When you discover a site that warrants a high degree of wariness, you can move that site into the Restricted Sites zone. The security settings that apply there, by default, are described as "high."

Before Service Pack 2 (SP2), content opened from a local file system was considered secure and was assigned to the Local Machine zone. Although this decision was logical, it also allowed security holes that outside attackers exploited successfully. By convincing Internet Explorer that a Web page or a chunk of hostile code was running in the Local Machine zone, an attacker could read files and install programs, actions that aren't permitted in the Internet zone. SP2 introduces a new set of restrictions called Local Machine Zone Lockdown that block scripts, objects (such as ActiveX controls), and actions that are potentially dangerous in the Local Machine zone. HTML files that use the *res:* prefix, such as Help files, are allowed to run from local storage.

Chapter 10

When you encounter a page that is attempting to run prohibited content, such as a script from the local zone, you'll see this error message in the Information Bar: "This page has been restricted from running active content that might be able to access your computer. If you trust this page, click here to allow it to access your computer." If you do trust the page, click the Information Bar and use the shortcut menu to remove the lockdown restrictions.

Adding Sites to a Zone

To change the zone in which a site resides, or to reconfigure the security settings associated with a zone, you use the Security tab of the Internet Options dialog box (choose Tools, Internet Options, and then click the Security tab), which is shown in Figure 10-7. As the figure shows, Internet Explorer uses a different icon to depict each zone.

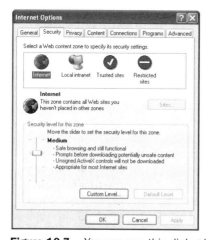

Figure 10-7. You can use this dialog box to add sites to particular zones or modify the security settings associated with a zone.

Whenever you visit a site, the icon and name of the site's zone appear at the right side of the status bar, like this.

To add a site to your Trusted Sites or Restricted Sites zone, follow these steps:

1 On the Security tab of the Internet Options dialog box (shown in Figure 10-7), select Trusted Sites or Restricted Sites.

2 Click Sites. You'll see the following dialog box (or one similar if you selected Restricted Sites).

3   Type the URL for the site (or copy and paste from the Address bar) and then click Add.

When you're adding sites to the Trusted Sites zone, the default settings require that Internet Explorer verify that the site's server is secure (in other words, that it begins with *https:*) before establishing a connection. To add a non-SSL site to the list, clear the check box at the bottom of the Trusted Sites dialog box. (After adding the site, you can select the check box again.) When you add a domain (such as *http://www.edbott.com*) to either of these zones, all URLs located within that domain are assigned to the zone you selected.

Note   Note that the URLs *http://edbott.com* and *http://www.edbott.com* are not considered to be the same domain; if you want to add all possible pages for a domain to a security zone, you must consider all possibilities. To add all possible pages on a particular domain, enter only the domain name (*edbott.com*) and leave off the prefix.

By default, Internet Explorer populates the Local Intranet zone with the following:

- All intranet sites that you haven't moved into either the Trusted Sites zone or the Restricted Sites zone
- All sites that bypass your proxy server, if one exists on your network
- All network servers accessed via UNC paths (*server_name*)

Chapter 10

To remove one or more of those categories (so that the affected category joins the Internet zone), select Local Intranet in the Internet Options dialog box and then click Sites. You'll see the following dialog box. Clear the appropriate check boxes.

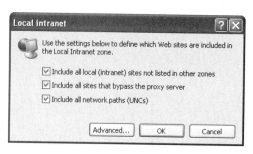

If you want to add a site to the Local Intranet zone, click the Advanced button. Then type the site's URL and click Add.

Changing a Zone's Security Settings

Any site placed in a security zone receives the same privileges and restrictions as all other sites in that zone. You can change the overall security settings associated with the zone, however, and thereby change the security settings for all of its member sites. To change the security settings associated with a zone, follow these steps:

1 Choose Tools, Internet Options, and then click the Security tab (shown earlier in Figure 10-7).

2 Click the icon for the zone you want to adjust.

3 In the Security Level For This Zone section of the dialog box, click the Default Level button to reveal a slider control (if the slider isn't already visible).

4 Move the slider up to apply more stringent security measures, or down to be more lenient. As you move the slider from level to level, the description to the right of the slider summarizes the current level's settings.

To fine-tune the settings for a zone, or to read all of the particulars about the current level of settings, click Custom Level. In the Security Settings dialog box that appears, shown in Figure 10-8, you can use the option buttons to adjust individual settings.

If you've customized a security zone and you're unhappy with the settings, click the Reset button in the Security Settings dialog box to restore the default security level.

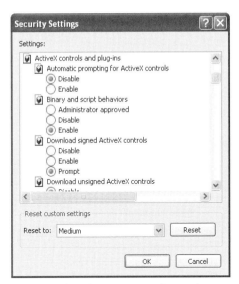

Figure 10-8. For most security settings, you can choose between Disable, Enable, and Prompt.

Blocking Objectionable Content

The Internet undoubtedly has something to offend every taste and moral standard. Although objectionable content is not a security issue in the sense that it threatens the well-being of your hardware and data, some users might consider it a threat to other aspects of their well-being, so we'll briefly discuss the most important features of Internet Explorer's Content Advisor. When Content Advisor is enabled, if a user tries to go to a Web page that is beyond the limits you set, Internet Explorer won't show the page. Instead it displays a warning message. Users who know the supervisor password (you supply this password when you first enable Content Advisor) can bypass the warning and view the page.

By default, Internet Explorer includes a single set of ratings, the Recreational Software Advisory Council's (RSAC) Internet rating system (known as RSACi). This system divides potentially objectionable content into four categories: language, nudity, sex, and violence. Each category has five levels, numbered 0 through 4. A higher number indicates more explicit or intense content. The RSAC no longer exists, and the RSACi system is being supplanted by the Internet Content Rating Association (ICRA) system, which has a much larger number of categories, each of which you can choose to allow or not allow. If you intend to use Content Advisor, we recommend that you install the ICRA system in addition to the default RSACi. (For details about the two systems, see the ICRA Web site at *http://www.icra.org.*)

Chapter 10

To install the ICRA rating system and set up Content Advisor, follow these steps:

1   Download the Icra.rat file (the extension is short for "ratings") from *http://www.icra.org/icra.rat* and save it to the %SystemRoot%\System32 folder.

2   Open Internet Explorer, choose Tools, Internet Options, and then click the Content tab.

3   Click Enable under Content Advisor. (If you've already enabled Content Advisor, click Settings instead.) The Content Advisor dialog box appears.

4   On the General tab, click the Rating Systems button to display a list of available rating systems and categories.

> **Tip**   You can also install other rating systems, although RSACi and ICRA ratings are currently applied to more Web sites than any other system. To learn about other systems, click the Find Rating Systems button on the General tab.

5   Click Add, select the Icra.rat file you downloaded in Step 1, and then click OK in the Rating Systems dialog box.

6   Click the Ratings tab, select a category, and then drag the slider to set the limits you want. As you move the slider, a description of the current setting appears below the slider. Repeat this step for each category.

7   Click Apply or OK. If you haven't already set up a supervisor password, supply and confirm your supervisor password in the Create Supervisor Password dialog box that appears.

The supervisor password is the master key that lets you change the Content Advisor settings or bypass the Content Advisor protections. Write this password down in a safe place so that if you forget it, you won't be blocked from modifying or disabling Internet Explorer's content restrictions.

Tip **Disable a forgotten password**

If you forget your password, don't panic. Open Registry Editor and navigate to HKLM\
Software\Microsoft\Windows\CurrentVersion\Policies\Ratings. Then delete this key's Key
value. Restart the computer, return to the Internet Options dialog box, and click the Disable
button on the Content tab. If you're concerned that your kids might be savvy enough to
make this registry fix themselves, use registry permissions to control access to that key
(using the Permissions control on the Edit menu). (Exercise caution when editing the registry. For information about using Registry Editor, see Chapter 41, "Editing the Registry.")

Blocking Unrated Sites

Not all Internet content is rated. By default, Content Advisor blocks pages that don't have a
rating, simply because it has no way of knowing what types of content are on such pages. Just
as when you attempt to view a site with unacceptable ratings, when you attempt to view an
unrated site, you'll see a dialog box similar to the one shown in Figure 10-9.

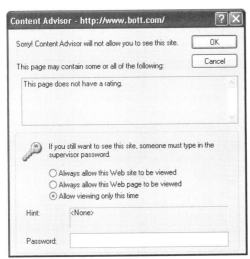

Figure 10-9. Content Advisor blocks pages with ratings beyond the limits you set and pages
that aren't rated.

If you don't want this type of protection, you can change the default behavior. Open Internet Options, click the Content tab, and then click Settings. In the Content Advisor dialog
box, click the General tab, shown in Figure 10-10, and select Users Can See Sites That Have
No Rating.

Figure 10-10. The General tab lets you block unrated sites, bypass blocking, and change the supervisor password.

Because so many sites are unrated—including both "good" sites and "bad" ones—Content Advisor lets you create your own ratings for particular sites. To set up a list of sites that you want to allow or disallow, regardless of their claimed content rating, click the Approved Sites tab in the Content Advisor dialog box. Type each site's URL and then click Always or Never.

Turning Off Blocking

If you change your mind about blocking offensive material, simply display the Internet Options dialog box, click the Content tab, click the Disable button, and then enter your supervisor password. Blocking will remain turned off until and unless you return and click the Enable button (which alternates with the Disable button).

Using E-Mail Safely

The biggest hazard associated with e-mail is the potential for messages to harbor hostile code. As we note in "Blocking Viruses and Worms with an Antivirus Program," page 217, e-mail is the most common (although by no means the only) transmission vector for viruses, worms, and Trojan horse programs. Hostile software can be attached to messages in executable format, requiring the recipient to click on the program to run it. Executable files can be hidden within compressed (.zip) files, which have a greater chance of slipping through filters but require an extra step on the user's part before they can infect a PC. Rogue content can also be included in an e-mail message's HTML code, where it can take advantage of security flaws to execute automatically, with or without requiring any action by the message recipient. (As we explain throughout this chapter, however, staying safe does not require that you forgo attachments or HTML. You just need to take some simple measures to protect yourself.)

Chapter 10

The other security risk associated with e-mail is the ease with which your inbox can become a dumping ground for all manner of unwanted communication. At its best, spam is a nuisance that significantly degrades the value of e-mail. If you share your computer with other people, or if your PC is connected to a home or business network spam can become a considerably greater hazard. The content of spam messages—pornographic images, for instance—can pose a problem if your kids are the recipients. Unsolicited e-mail messages may also contain links to Web sites that can use scripts or social engineering to lure an unsuspecting user into installing a dangerous program.

(You can use identities in Microsoft Outlook Express to segregate your mail from that of other people who use your computer, including your children. For more information, see "Managing Identities," page 1143.)

Guarding Against Hazardous E-Mail Attachments

The cardinal rules for dealing with potentially hazardous e-mail attachments are as follows:

- Don't open any attachment that's potentially executable. Save it instead, and scan it with your virus checker before running it.

- Don't open attachments from unknown parties. Save and scan them. If you can't verify that an attachment is harmless, hit the Delete key.

- If you receive an unexpected attachment from someone you know, be suspicious. Many viruses do their dirty work by harvesting addresses from the victim's computer or by forging the return address. When in doubt, ask the supposed sender if the attachment is legitimate.

It's not always easy to tell whether an attachment contains executable code. (Data files in applications that support programming languages such as Visual Basic for Applications, for example, can include potentially harmful macros, so even a Word document can—at least in theory—be dangerous.) If you're in any doubt, save and scan.

The best way to protect yourself against dangerous attachments is to use an e-mail program that can prevent you from opening (or even saving) a potentially executable attachment. Microsoft Outlook 2003, Outlook 2002 (and Outlook 2000 with E-Mail Security Update), and Outlook Express 6 offer slightly different implementations of this behavior. Outlook Express 6, which is included with Windows XP, is set by default to prevent you from saving or opening any attachment that could possibly be a virus. If a message arrives containing such an attachment, Outlook Express notifies you that it has blocked access to the attachment. When you are so notified, you can either ignore the attachment or temporarily remove the default protection, save the attachment to disk, scan it, and then reinstate the default protection. (To remove the default virus protection, choose Tools, Options, click the Security tab, and then clear Do Not Allow Attachments To Be Saved Or Opened That Could Potentially Be A Virus. To reinstate the protection, select this check box.)

> For more information about the security features in Outlook Express, including its ability to warn you if a virus appears to be sending mail from your system, see "Blocking Dangerous Attachments," page 1166.

If your e-mail program does not offer the ability to block access to potentially infected attachments, you will need to be vigilant yourself. Get into the save-and-scan habit and you can be reasonably sure you won't become a victim of an attachment-borne virus.

> **Caution**   Many experienced Windows users believe they can hold viruses and worms at bay merely by practicing safe computing. They're wrong, as victims of Klez and other auto-executing viruses will ruefully attest. These bits of hostile code are written to exploit security holes in Windows, and they can execute on an unpatched system, infecting the user's computer and spewing out infected e-mails, if the victim simply opens or previews the message. Any sensible e-mail security strategy must include software that blocks known viruses as well as a routine that ensures that all critical updates and patches are installed as soon as they're available.

Guarding Against Rogue HTML Content

If you can receive HTML-formatted mail, you can enjoy all of the graphics, sound, and formatting that HTML brings to Web content. Along with those benefits, however, comes the possibility that an e-mail sender might intentionally or unintentionally embed destructive code within the message, such as a hostile snippet of script, a link to a dangerous ActiveX control or Java applet, or a deliberately malformed URL designed to exploit a security flaw in Windows. If you use Outlook Express or Outlook, you can take advantage of Internet Explorer's security zones to protect yourself. If you use a different e-mail program, check to see whether it includes a comparable security mechanism. If you receive your e-mail exclusively through Internet Explorer (for example, if you're a Hotmail user, and you don't prefer to receive your mail in Outlook Express or another client program), you're already enjoying the protection afforded by the browser.

Outlook Express and Outlook are both set by default to use the security settings assigned to the Restricted Sites security zone. If you have not altered these settings, this means that all active controls will be disabled. If you find this stricture too confining, you can switch Outlook Express or Outlook to the Internet zone (which is, by default, much more permissive with regard to active content), or you can modify the settings associated with the Restricted Sites zone. For information about security zones, see "Defining Security Zones for Web Sites," page 328.

Defending Yourself Against Spam

In its simplest definition, spam is unsolicited commercial e-mail. In practice, it's a nuisance that clutters up your inbox with junk mail—much of it clearly illegal and often offensive. If you're unlucky enough to get on one of the many lists that spammers use to blast out their junk e-mail, your inbox can become so clogged with garbage that your real messages are lost in the muck.

Unfortunately, there's no foolproof way to ward off spam. The best approach uses a combination of filtering at the server (to prevent obvious spam from ever reaching your inbox) and by your e-mail program to separate known "good" e-mail from messages that are likely to be spam.

Caution The worst thing you can do is reply to the spam sender. Most spam includes phony return addresses anyway, so the effort is pointless. For those messages that actually do go back to a legitimate address, you simply confirm that your address is valid, and you encourage the spammer to promote your address to his "preferred" list of confirmed addresses. The likely result? More unwanted messages.

Unsolicited advertising messages usually include instructions telling you how to get yourself removed from the sender's address list. Unfortunately, however, spam purveyors are not known for their ethical standards. In many cases, the spammer is sending his or her message to thousands of e-mail addresses without actually knowing which addresses are currently valid. If you respond—even to request removal—you might simply be confirming that the message has reached a live body, thereby inviting a renewed flood of spam.

If you use Outlook Express, you can apply the Block Sender command to ward off messages from a particular mailer. This tactic is usually ineffective, however, because the majority of spammers use fake e-mail addresses, and even those mass marketers who use a legitimate return address frequently change domain names to bypass filters. Rules that filter out messages containing particular words or phrases are similarly ineffective, as spammers use creative misspellings to bypass those rules. If spam is a serious problem, consider switching to an e-mail provider that has more aggressive and effective blocking solutions at the server, and consider installing anti-spam software on the client side that captures those messages that make it through the filters. Outlook 2003 has excellent spam-blocking tools built-in; Outlook Express does not.

Chapter 10

In *Microsoft Windows Security Inside Out* (Microsoft Press, 2003), we cover basic and advanced spam-fighting techniques in detail. The following suggestions are summarized from the discussion in Chapter 11 of that book, "Blocking Spam."

- **Guard your e-mail address as if it were gold**   Never post it in a public place, such as a Web-based discussion board. Don't use it to sign up for online contests (which are often fakes, used by spammers to harvest e-mail addresses). And don't give it to strangers until you're certain that they can be trusted. Instead, set up a "throwaway" e-mail account at a free service like Hotmail and use it for any correspondence outside of your trusted circle of family and friends. If the free account is taken over by spam, shut it down and start a new one.

- **Use server-based spam-blocking solutions, when they're available**   An increasing number of ISPs filter out spam, but most do so only if you request it. Both Hotmail and MSN offer junk mail-filtering features that can be set to different levels, including one that blocks all messages unless they come from contacts in your address book. Check with your e-mail provider and find out if this service is available.

- **Learn to use e-mail filters effectively**   Virtually all e-mail programs allow you to set up rules to process incoming messages. The best strategy for using these filters is to define rules that identify the messages you want to receive. The first few rules in the list should allow messages from people who are in your address book and from mailing lists that you subscribe to. Use additional rules to block messages from known spammers and those containing terms associated with spam. Finally, set up a rule for everything that isn't handled by one of these rules, moving any such messages to a Possible Spam folder. Go through this folder every couple days, picking out the occasional legitimate message and deleting the rest.

Protecting Your Privacy

Cookies constitute the most serious potential threat to your privacy online, because these small text files can provide unknown parties with personally identifiable information—your e-mail address, for example—as well as information about your habits and predilections. Handling cookies, like handling active Web content, requires a serious evaluation of tradeoffs—in this case, the convenience afforded by being recognizable to your regular Web haunts versus the vulnerability that comes from being (in some respects) watched.

Internet Explorer offers an elaborate set of features for filtering cookies based on various parameters. For more details on how these features work, see "Managing Cookies," page 525.

Guarding Passwords and Other Sensitive Data

Windows XP provides a secure system for storing sensitive data associated with your use of the Web, such as saved user names, passwords, and Web form data you "remember" using the AutoComplete feature in Internet Explorer. The Protected Storage service, which runs as part of the Local Security Administration subsystem (Lsass.exe) manages this data store and decrypts the data only when it can verify that the request is accompanied by the correct logon credentials.

Inside Out

Manage AutoComplete data

Windows XP doesn't include any tools for exploring and managing saved AutoComplete data. For that task, you need to use third-party utilities. *PC Magazine*'s AutoWhat? 2 utility, for instance, scans the AutoComplete list and displays the names of fields for which data is stored. You can add or remove values associated with each form field, and if you remove all the stored data for a field, Windows removes the field name from the AutoComplete list. You can learn more about AutoWhat? 2 at *http://www.pcmag.com/article2/ 0,1759,4681,00.asp*.

A much more powerful tool, Protected Storage Explorer, allows you to view all sorts of saved data from the Protected Storage service, including passwords for e-mail accounts in Outlook and Outlook Express, saved forms data, saved user names and passwords on Web pages, and cached logon credentials for Web sites that require authentication. However, you cannot change or delete individual entries. This utility was developed by James and Jeremy Pullicino and is available at *http://www.codeproject.com/tools/PSExplorer.asp*.

For all-purpose management of forms, passwords, and Web logons, we highly recommend AI RoboForm. This program integrates tightly with Internet Explorer and other browsers, saving passwords, form data, credit card details, and other commonly used information and providing automatic logons when you access pages that require a password. You can encrypt your saved data with a strong password, back up your data to a USB key or network location, and easily move your settings from one PC to another. For details, visit *http:// www.roboform.com*.

The ability to see saved passwords can be a tremendous convenience if you once saved a Web site password but have since forgotten it. Using a tool like Protected Storage Explorer lets you see the saved password in plain text and write it down. Does the fact that you can view saved passwords and other data constitute a security risk? It can, if your computer is in a location that isn't physically secure. If you leave your computer unattended without logging off or locking the screen, an unscrupulous intruder can sit down and use one of these tools to inspect all of your saved passwords. The moral of the story? If you want your secrets to be safe, lock your computer!

Chapter 10

Some earlier versions of Windows stored passwords in a weakly encrypted text file with the extension .pwl. In Windows XP, this data is stored in a secure portion of the registry. The saved data is encrypted using your logon credentials, and for security reasons you cannot view the hashed data directly. Instead, Windows allows programs to query the store for specific data. If you've saved your password for an Outlook Express account, for instance, it's stored here.

The AutoComplete feature in Internet Explorer allows you to save form data and user name/password combinations associated with Web pages. As you begin entering data in a field on a Web form, AutoComplete consults its list of previous entries and proposes possible matches—thereby reducing the amount of typing you have to do. Likewise, when Internet Explorer detects matching user name and password fields on a Web page, it saves the data as a matched pair. Each chunk of data gets its own 15-digit encrypted pointer, saved as a DWORD value in HKCU\Software\Microsoft\Internet Explorer\Intellliforms\SPW. The Protected Storage service uses this index to query the encrypted data store and return the saved data when a program asks for it.

When it comes to entering passwords, AutoComplete can be both a help and a hazard. If you're prone to forgetting your passwords, AutoComplete can do your remembering for you and save you time and frustration. On the other hand, AutoComplete can also make it easier for someone else to log onto one of your private accounts.

If you'd rather do without AutoComplete for user names and passwords, follow these steps:

1   Choose Tools, Internet Options.

2   Click the Content tab.

3   Click AutoComplete.

The AutoComplete Settings dialog box appears.

4 Clear User Names And Passwords On Forms.

5 To erase Internet Explorer's memory of user names and passwords that you've already recorded, click Clear Passwords.

Note The Protected Storage service is used only for Internet Explorer's AutoComplete details. Windows XP uses a different mechanism to store other secrets, including private keys and certificates.

If you like using AutoComplete for user names and passwords but want to forgo it for particularly sensitive accounts, click Clear Passwords (to get back to an initial state, before Internet Explorer began remembering any of your passwords), and then make sure that Prompt Me To Save Passwords is selected. As you use your various accounts, you will be prompted each time you enter a password that Internet Explorer can (optionally) remember. Let it record passwords for the accounts you're not concerned about and decline its offer to remember the ones that are more critical.

You can delete individual saved entries from the AutoComplete list. To do so for a single value, go to the Web page associated with the saved data. Click in the box that contains the form field or logon name and press the Down Arrow key to select the stored item (you may need to press this key repeatedly if you have a number of items stored for that field). When you've selected the data you want to get rid of, press the Delete key. If you select a logon name that is associated with a password, Windows displays a dialog box asking if you want to also delete the stored password.

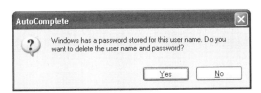

Clearing Your History

Internet Explorer keeps track of Web sites you've recently visited and presents links to those sites in the History bar. This feature, which is convenient for retracing your steps, also makes it easy for others with access to your computer to know where you've been. If you would rather delete this information, follow these steps:

1 Choose Tools, Internet Options.

2 Click the General tab.

3 Click Clear History.

By default, Internet Explorer maintains 20 days' worth of history. You can modify that number upward or downward using the Days To Keep Pages In History box on the General tab in the Internet Options dialog box. To minimize the amount of history that Internet Explorer records, set this value to 0.

Note Internet Explorer always records the sites you visited today and lets you return to those sites via the History bar, even if you set the Days To Keep Pages In History value to 0. If you set this value to 1, Internet Explorer keeps today's sites and yesterday's sites.

Finding Additional Security Resources

Microsoft maintains a security Web site (*http://www.microsoft.com/security*) that publicizes current virus threats, any newly discovered security vulnerabilities (and their remedies), and other important matters relating to your security online. It's a good idea to visit this security site from time to time. If you want more technical details, add the Microsoft TechNet Security site (*http://www.microsoft.com/technet/security*) to your Favorites list and visit it regularly as well. To receive timely notice of security bulletins from Microsoft via e-mail, subscribe to the Microsoft Security Notification Service. You can do so by visiting the Microsoft Profile Center at *http://register.microsoft.com/regsys/pic.asp*, or by sending a blank e-mail message to *securbas@microsoft.com*.

You can also find valuable technical information on current security threats at *http://www.cert.org*, a site maintained by the CERT Coordination Center, a federally funded research institute operated by Carnegie Mellon University. The United States Computer Emergency Readiness Team provides security bulletins for computer users at all technical levels via its Web site, *http://www.us-cert.gov*.

Chapter 10

Encrypting Confidential Information

Organizations of all sizes—and even home computer users—are likely to have sensitive data that must never be available to others. Financial data—your accounting data, personal finance data files, and so on—certainly falls into this category. But your computer might also be the repository for marketing plans, trade secrets, medical history, diaries, phone books, and similar information. Two popular trends in computing, interconnected computers (on a local area network or on the Internet) and portable computers, put this data at risk. If someone can obtain a file by downloading it from your computer or by borrowing (or stealing) your portable computer, they will know your secrets.

Microsoft Windows XP provides a way to prevent the loss of confidential data. The Encrypting File System (EFS) encodes your files so that even if someone is able to obtain the files, they won't be able to read them. The files are readable only when you log on to the computer using your user account (which, presumably, you have protected with a strong password). In fact, even someone else logging on to your computer won't have access to your encrypted files, a feature that provides protection on systems that are shared by more than one user.

At Home with Windows XP

To take advantage of the Encrypting File System (EFS), you must be using Windows XP Professional. EFS is not available on computers running Windows XP Home Edition.

Beware the Dangers of EFS!

EFS provides secure encryption of your most important information. The encryption is so secure that if you lose the key to decrypt your data, the information is effectively lost. By default, Windows XP provides no "back door" if your private key is lost.

You can innocently lose your key in a number of ways. Among the worst:

- Working with the Certificates dialog box or the Certificates console (Certmgr.msc), you can inadvertently delete the encryption certificate, which contains the key.

- You might have your data stored in encrypted folders on a second volume (drive D, for example). You notice that your computer is running sluggishly and its hard drive is overflowing with junk files—so you decide to reinstall Windows from scratch. Not worrying about your files on another partition, you format drive C and reinstall Windows. Although it's not apparent, reinstalling Windows creates new security identifiers (SIDs) for each user, even if you do everything exactly the same way each time you run Setup. As a result, each user's encryption certificates are also different from the ones they replaced, and they can't be used to access the encrypted data stored on drive D. Even the Administrator account—which also has a new SID—can't decrypt the files from a different Windows installation.

Fortunately, with a little care, these drastic scenarios can be prevented. To learn about EFS and then begin safely using it for your important files, we recommend that you follow this approach:

1. Create an empty folder and encrypt it. (For details, see "Encrypting Folders and Files" on the next page.)

2. Create a nonessential file in the encrypted folder (or copy a file to the folder), and verify that you can use it as you would any ordinary file.

3. If your computer is not part of a domain, create a *data recovery agent*, a second user account that can be used to decrypt files should your personal encryption certificate become lost or corrupt. (For details, see "Creating a Data Recovery Agent," page 356.)

4. Back up your file recovery certificate and your personal encryption certificate. (For details, see "Backing Up Your Certificates," page 360.)

   Note that you won't have a certificate to back up until after you have encrypted at least one folder or file. A new Windows installation doesn't have encryption certificates; one is created the first time a user encrypts a folder or file.

You are now ready to begin using EFS for your important confidential files. Remember: If you encrypt files on a computer that is not joined to a domain, be sure to set up a data recovery agent. Back up both your personal certificate and the data recovery agent's file recovery certificate. Review the best practices listed at the end of this chapter to ensure that you don't leave any loopholes in your security.

Encryption is the process of encoding sensitive data using a key algorithm. Without the correct key, the data can't be decrypted. Windows XP uses encryption for several purposes:

- Encrypting files on an NTFS volume (a disk partition formatted with the NTFS file system) (see "Encrypting Folders and Files" below)
- Encrypting data sent between a Web browser and a server using Secure Sockets Layer (SSL) (see "Enabling a Secure (Encrypted) Connection," page 1096)
- Encrypting data sent between computers using a virtual private network (VPN) (see "Allowing Remote Access via a Virtual Private Network," page 1065)
- Encrypting or signing e-mail messages

Encrypting Folders and Files

The Encrypting File System (EFS) allows you to encrypt files on a local NTFS volume so that only you can use them. This offers an additional level of protection beyond that provided by NTFS permissions, which you can use to restrict access to your files by others who log on to your computer. NTFS permissions are vulnerable in a couple of ways. First, all users with administrative privileges can grant themselves (or others) permission to access your files. What's worse, anyone who gains physical access to your computer can boot from a floppy disk (or from another operating system, if your computer is set up for dual booting) and use a utility such as NTFSDOS (available at *http://www.sysinternals.com*) to read the files on your hard drive—without having to provide a user name or password. Portable computers, which are more easily stolen, are especially vulnerable to this type of information loss.

> **Note** On most computers, you can use BIOS settings as another protection against this type of loss. Set your BIOS so that a password is required to start the computer or to enter the BIOS setup program, and set the boot options so that the computer can't be booted from a floppy disk. Unfortunately, this type of protection can also be circumvented. For example, removing the hard drive and installing it in another computer makes its files available to someone with the proper tools.

EFS provides a secure way to store your sensitive data. Windows creates a randomly generated file encryption key (FEK) and then transparently encrypts the data, using this FEK, as it is being written to disk. Windows then encrypts the FEK using your public key. (Windows creates a personal encryption certificate with a public/private key pair for you the first time you use EFS.) The FEK, and therefore the data it encrypts, can be decrypted only with your certificate and its associated private key, which are available only when you log on with your user name and password. (Designated data recovery agents can also decrypt your data.) Other users who attempt to use your encrypted files receive an "access denied" message. Even administrators and others who have permission to take ownership of files are unable to open your encrypted files.

Chapter 11

For information about data recovery agents, see "Recovering Encrypted Files and Folders," page 364.

You can encrypt individual files, folders, or entire drives. We recommend that you encrypt folders or drives instead of individual files. When you encrypt a folder or drive, the existing files it contains are encrypted, and new files that you create in that folder or drive are also encrypted automatically. This includes temporary files that your applications create in the folder or drive. (For example, Microsoft Word creates a copy of a document when you open it for editing. If the document's folder isn't encrypted, the temporary copy isn't encrypted—giving prying eyes a potential opportunity to view your data.) For this reason, you should consider encrypting your %Temp% and %Tmp% folders, which many applications use to store temporary copies of documents that are open for editing, in addition to the folders where your sensitive documents are stored.

Securing the Paging File

If you're truly concerned about the possibility of your computer falling into the wrong hands, you should be sure that you don't leave any tracks in the paging file. By default, when you shut down your system, the paging file remains intact. People who have access to your computer can conceivably look through the unencrypted paging file to find information they shouldn't have.

You can foil such snooping by changing a registry entry. Use a registry editor to navigate to the HKLM\System\CurrentControlSet\Control\Session Manager\Memory Management key, and set the value of ClearPageFileAtShutdown to 1. After you do that, Windows fills the paging file with zeros whenever you shut down. Keep in mind that this could slow down your system—don't make this change unless your security needs demand it.

Caution   Before you encrypt anything important, you should back up your file recovery certificate and your personal encryption certificate (with their associated private keys), as well as the data recovery agent certificate, to a floppy disk. Store the disk in a secure location. If you ever lose the certificate stored on your hard disk (because of a disk failure, for example), you can restore the backup copy and regain access to your files. If you lose all copies of your certificate (and no data recovery agent certificates exist), you won't be able to use your encrypted files. No back door exists, nor is there any practical way to hack these files. (If there were, it wouldn't be very good encryption.) For details, see "Backing Up Your Certificates," page 360.

To encrypt a folder, follow these steps:

1 Right-click the folder, choose Properties, click the General tab, and then click Advanced, as shown below. (If the properties dialog box doesn't have an Advanced button, the folder is not on an NTFS-formatted volume and you can't use EFS.)

> **Tip** **Move folders to an NTFS volume for encryption**
>
> Your important files are likely to be in your My Documents folder; other at-risk files might be in a Temp folder. Ordinarily, these folders are on your boot partition. If the boot partition is not an NTFS volume, you can't encrypt those folders. If it's not feasible to convert your boot partition to NTFS (if you need FAT format for dual-boot capabilities, for example), there is a solution if your computer has more than one volume: Format another volume as NTFS and move your important folders there. Because My Documents and Temp are special folders, simply moving them with Windows Explorer won't do the job, however. (In fact, doing so will cause severe problems; don't even try.) You can safely move these folders using other methods, however. For details, see "Moving Folders from the Standard Profile Locations," page 555.

2 Select Encrypt Contents To Secure Data. (Note that you can't encrypt compressed files. If the files are already compressed, Windows clears the Compressed attribute. Because encryption and compression are mutually exclusive, this section of the dialog box really should contain option buttons rather than check boxes—with the addition of a "Neither" option button.)

3   Click OK twice. If the folder contains any files or subfolders, Windows then displays a confirmation message.

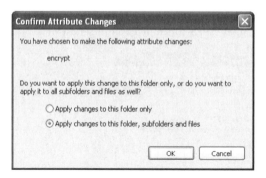

Note   If you select Apply Changes To This Folder Only, Windows doesn't encrypt any of the files currently in the folder. Any new files that you create in the folder, however, including files that you copy or move to the folder, will be encrypted.

Inside Out

Add encryption commands to file and folder context menus

If you frequently encrypt and decrypt files and folders (for most users, it's a one-time "set it and forget it" operation), you'll find that it's rather tedious to right-click, choose Properties, click Advanced, select or clear a check box, and click OK twice every time you want to change encryption status. If you're comfortable using a command-line interface, you can use the Cipher command to perform these tasks. (For details, see "Using the Cipher Command," page 355.) But if you'd prefer to work with Windows Explorer, you can use an easier method: Add encryption commands to the shortcut menu that appears when you right-click a folder or file.

To add encryption commands, follow these steps:

1   Use Registry Editor to open the HKLM\Software\Microsoft\Windows\ CurrentVersion\Explorer\Advanced key.

2   Open the Edit menu, and choose New, DWORD Value.

3   Name the new value **EncryptionContextMenu**.

4   Double-click the EncryptionContextMenu value, and set its data to **1**.

This change takes effect the next time you start Windows Explorer. When you right-click a folder or file that's not encrypted, the shortcut menu includes an Encrypt command; a Decrypt command appears if the target is already encrypted.

To encrypt one or more files, follow the same procedure as for folders. You'll see a different confirmation message (shown in Figure 11-1) to remind you that the file's folder is not encrypted and to give you an opportunity to encrypt it. You generally don't want to encrypt individual files, because the information you intend to protect can too easily become decrypted without your knowledge. For example, with some applications, when you open a document for editing, the application creates a copy of the original document. When you save the document after editing, the application saves the copy—which is not encrypted—and deletes the original, encrypted document. Static files that you use for reference only— but never for editing—can safely be encrypted without encrypting the parent folder. Even in that situation, however, you'll probably find it simpler to encrypt the whole folder.

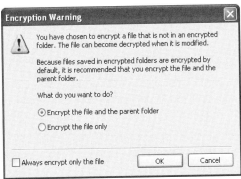

Figure 11-1. In this dialog box, a message advises you to encrypt folders rather than individual files.

Note You can't encrypt any files that have the system attribute, nor any files located in %SystemRoot% or its subfolders. (Those files are usually system files, and the system might be rendered unusable if some of its essential files were encrypted.) Also, you can't encrypt any files or folders in a roaming profile.

If you see a message box like the one shown here when you try to encrypt a file or folder, EFS has been disabled on your computer. Although the box's four buttons might lead you to believe that you have a choice in the matter, you don't. Regardless of which button you click, Windows refuses to encrypt your files—just as if you clicked Cancel. To solve this problem, you need to enable EFS. For details, see "Disabling or Reenabling EFS," page 365.

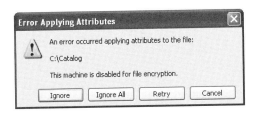

Other than the fact that their names in Windows Explorer are green (instead of the black text used for ordinary uncompressed files), you'll notice no significant difference in working with encrypted folders or files while you're logged on using the same account as when you encrypted them. But encrypted files do act differently in several subtle ways. Table 11-1 describes the important differences.

Table 11-1. Behavior of Encrypted Files

When You Do This	This Happens
Log on using a different account	• If you try to open an encrypted file, you get an "access denied" message.
	• If you try to decrypt an encrypted file by clearing the encryption attribute, you get an "access denied" message.
	• If you have Modify or Full Control permission, you can delete or rename an encrypted file.
Copy or move an unencrypted file to an encrypted folder	• The copy in the encrypted folder becomes encrypted.
Copy an encrypted file	• If you copy an encrypted file to an NTFS volume on your computer or another computer running Windows XP or Windows 2000, it remains encrypted. (If EFS is disabled on the target computer, Windows warns that the copied file will lose its encryption.)
	• If you copy to a FAT volume (including floppy disks) or to an NTFS volume on a computer that is running Windows NT, the file becomes decrypted.
Move an encrypted file	• If you move the file to another folder on the same volume, it remains encrypted.
	• Moving the file to another volume is essentially a "copy and then delete" process; moving your own encrypted files is handled as in copy operations, described above.
	• If you move someone else's encrypted file to a FAT volume, you get an "access denied" message.
Rename an encrypted file	• The file is renamed and it remains encrypted.
Delete an encrypted file	• If you delete to the Recycle Bin, the restorable file remains encrypted.

Table 11-1. **Behavior of Encrypted Files**

When You Do This	This Happens
Back up an encrypted file using Backup	● You've picked the best way to back up encrypted files or move them between systems! The files in the backup media remain encrypted, whether they're on disk or tape. (Because most removable media can't be formatted as NTFS, an ordinary copy becomes decrypted.)
Use encrypted files on a different computer	● Your personal encryption certificate and its private key must be available on the computer. You can copy the keys manually. For details, see "Backing Up Your Certificates," page 360.
	● If you use roaming profiles, your encryption keys are automatically available on all computers you log on to with your user account. For more information, see "Using Roaming User Profiles," page 559.

Caution Other users with permission to delete a file (that is, users with Modify or Full Control permission) can't use your encrypted files—but they can make them difficult for you to use. Any such user can rename your files, which can make them difficult to find, and delete your files. (Even if the user merely deletes them to the Recycle Bin and doesn't remove them altogether, the deleted files are unavailable to you because you don't have access to any other user's Recycle Bin.) Therefore, if you're concerned about protecting your files from other authorized users as well as from a thief who steals your computer, you should modify the NTFS permissions to prevent any type of modification by other users. For more information, see "Applying Advanced Security Settings," page 285.

Decrypting Folders and Files

Like the encryption process, decryption is done transparently. That is, you simply work with your encrypted files exactly the same way you work with unencrypted files. When Windows detects that a file you're accessing is encrypted, it finds your certificate and uses its private key to decrypt the data as it is read from the disk.

To permanently decrypt a folder or file, simply clear the Encrypt Contents To Secure Data check box in the Advanced Attributes dialog box. If you decrypt a folder, Windows asks whether you want to decrypt only the folder or the folder and its contents. If you choose the latter option, Windows prohibits you from decrypting any files for which you don't hold a valid encryption certificate. If you change the attribute for a file that you encrypted, Windows decrypts it without further ado. If you attempt to decrypt a file that someone else encrypted, you get an "access denied" message.

Chapter 11

Inside Out

Identify encrypted files in Windows Explorer

Unless you use a command-line utility like Cipher.exe, it's difficult to see at a glance which files are encrypted and which are not. Right-clicking each file and then choosing Properties, General, Advanced (followed by Cancel, Cancel) is tedious. Fortunately, there's an easier way. In Windows Explorer, use Details view. Choose View, Choose Details, and then select Attributes. Encrypted files show a letter *E* in the Attributes column. You can also set an option so that the names of encrypted files appear in a different color from other file names. In Folder Options, click the View tab, and select Show Encrypted Or Compressed NTFS Files In Color.

Allowing Others to Use Your Encrypted Files

After you have encrypted a file, you can allow others to access the file transparently, just as you can. This capability, which is new in Windows XP, lets you secure a file with EFS, yet make it available to other users you designate. The other users you select may be users with whom you share your computer, or they can access the file over the network. To enable another user to use one of your encrypted files, follow these steps:

1   Right-click an encrypted file and choose Properties. On the General tab, click Advanced.

2   In the Advanced Attributes dialog box, click Details.

Note   The Details button is unavailable when you initially encrypt a file. You must encrypt the file and then return to the Advanced Attributes dialog box to use Details. Note also that the Details button is available only when you select a single file; if you select a folder or multiple files, the button is unavailable.

3   In the Encryption Details dialog box, click Add. The Select User dialog box appears, as shown in Figure 11-2.

4   Select the name of the user to whom you want to give access, and then click OK.

Note   Only users who have an EFS certificate on your computer appear in the Select User dialog box. The easiest way for a user who shares your computer to create a certificate (and therefore appear in this list) is for that user to log on and encrypt a file. Network users should export their own certificates (for details, see "Backing Up a Personal Encryption Certificate," page 362); you can then import the certificate to your computer.

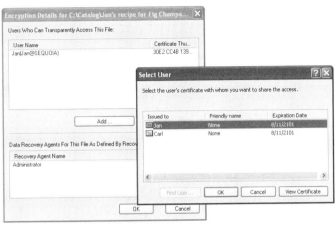

Figure 11-2. You can provide access to any account that has an EFS certificate on your computer.

Using the Cipher Command

If you prefer to use the command line, a non-GUI alternative to the Advanced Attributes dialog box is available for encrypting and decrypting folders and files. Like the Windows Explorer methods described earlier in this chapter, Cipher.exe allows you to encrypt or decrypt folders or individual files. If you specify a folder, you can choose whether to include existing files and subfolders.

To display the encryption state of the current folder and its files, type **cipher** with no parameters.

To encrypt or decrypt a folder or file, include the path and the appropriate switches. Use the /E switch to encrypt the folders or files you specify or the /D switch to decrypt. For example, to encrypt the My Documents folder, including its files and subfolders, type **cipher /e /a / s:"%userprofile%\my documents"** at a command prompt.

You can use wildcards in the file specification. You can also specify multiple folders and files in a single instance of the command; simply separate each name with a space. Table 11-2 shows the most commonly used switches for Cipher; for a complete list, type **cipher /?** at a command prompt.

Chapter 11

Table 11-2. Command-Line Switches for Cipher.exe

Switch	Description
/E	Encrypts the specified folders.
/D	Decrypts the specified folders.
/S:folder	Performs the operation on folder and its subfolders (but not files).
/A	Performs the operation on specified files and files in specified folders.
/K	Creates a new file encryption key for the user running Cipher. If this option is used, all other switches are ignored.
/R	Generates a data recovery agent key and certificate. The key and certificate are placed in a .pfx file, and the certificate alone is placed in a .cer file.
/U	Updates the user's file encryption key or data recovery agent key on every encrypted file on local drives.
/U /N	Lists every encrypted file on local drives without changing anything.

Strengthening EFS Protection

EFS provides extremely strong protection against attackers. Multiple levels of encryption make the system all but impossible to crack. You can strengthen security even more by using Triple Data Encryption Standard (3DES) to encrypt and decrypt files instead of the default algorithm, expanded Data Encryption Standard (DESX). However, although 3DES is more secure, it is also slower because it processes each block of each file three times.

To enable 3DES protection, follow these steps:

1. In the Run dialog box, type **secpol.msc** to open Local Security Settings.
2. Select Security Settings\Local Policies\Security Options.
3. In the details pane, double-click System Cryptography: Use FIPS Compliant Algorithms For Encryption, Hashing, And Signing.
4. Select Enabled and click OK.

Creating a Data Recovery Agent

A *data recovery agent* is another user account, usually Administrator, that can be used to access your encrypted files. This allows you to recover encrypted files if something happens to your private key.

Windows XP does not create a default data recovery agent on standalone computers. If you are a member of a domain, the domain administrator is the default data recovery agent.

> **Note** A data recovery agent can recover only files that are encrypted *after* the recovery certificate is created and the data recovery agent is designated, as described in the following sections. The agent won't have access to preexisting encrypted files. That's because when a file is encrypted, EFS uses the public key of the account that's encrypting the file and of each designated data recovery agent. Therefore, only the data recovery agents whose certificates are installed at the time a file is encrypted can decrypt the file.

To create a data recovery agent, you must create a file recovery certificate and then designate a user to be the data recovery agent.

Generating a File Recovery Certificate

To generate a file recovery certificate, follow these steps:

1. Log on as Administrator.
2. At a command prompt, type **cipher /r:***filename*, where *filename* is the name you want to assign to the stored certificate file. Do not include a file name extension.
3. When prompted, type a password that will be used to protect the files you create.

This generates both a .pfx file and a .cer file with the file name you specify.

> **Note** These certificate files allow anyone to become a data recovery agent. Be sure to copy them to a disk and put it in a secure, safe place. Then erase these files from your hard drive.

Inside Out

Poor man's data recovery: use a Password Reset Disk

The reason Windows XP does not have a default data recovery agent for stand-alone computers is to provide enhanced security. In Windows 2000, a thief who's able to crack the Administrator account (the default data recovery agent) has access to all the encrypted files on a stolen computer. With Windows XP, the only way a thief can get to your encrypted data is by knowing your user name and password.

This extra security comes with some risk: If you forget your password, you're locked out of your own files, and you have no practical way to access them. For that reason, we suggest creating a data recovery agent as one solution. However, another solution that's easier and perhaps more secure is to create a Password Reset Disk. For details, see "Recovering from a Lost Password," page 266.

Chapter 11

Designating Data Recovery Agents

You can designate any user as a data recovery agent. We recommend that you use the Administrator account.

> **Caution** Do not designate the account you use to create encrypted files as a data recovery agent. Doing so provides little or no protection. If the user profile is damaged or deleted, you will lose all the keys that allow decryption of your files.

Follow these steps to designate a data recovery agent:

1 Log on to the account that you want to designate as a data recovery agent.

2 In Certificates (Certmgr.msc), select Certificates–Current User\Personal.

3 Choose Action, All Tasks, Import to launch the Certificate Import Wizard, and then click Next. The File To Import page appears.

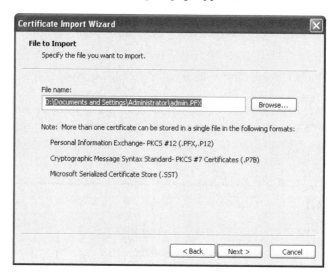

4 Enter the path and file name of the encryption certificate (a .pfx file) you exported and click Next. (If you click Browse, you must select Personal Information Exchange in the Files Of Type box to see .pfx files.)

5 Enter the password for this certificate, and then select Mark This Key As Exportable. Click Next.

6 Select Automatically Select The Certificate Store Based On The Type Of Certificate, and then click Next. Click Finish.

7 In Local Security Settings (Secpol.msc), click Security Settings, Public Key Policies, Encrypting File System.

8 Choose Action, Add Data Recovery Agent. Click Next.

9   On the Select Recovery Agents page, click Browse Folders and then navigate to the folder that contains the .cer file that you created. (The Browse Directory button searches Active Directory, a feature of domains based on the Windows 2000 Server and Windows Server 2003 families.) Select the file and click Open.

The Select Recovery Agents page now shows the new agent as USER_UNKNOWN. This is normal, because the name is not stored in the file.

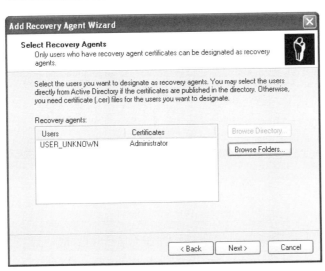

10 Click Next and then click Finish.

The current user is now the data recovery agent for all encrypted files on this system.

Removing the Private Key

To prevent someone from simply logging on as Administrator and viewing another user's encrypted files, you can export and remove the data recovery agent's private key. Keep the key in a secure location—without it you can't use the file recovery certificate.

To remove the data recovery agent's private key, follow these steps:

1   Log on to the account you designated as a data recovery agent.

2   In Certificates (Certmgr.msc), select Certificates–Current User\Personal\Certificates.

3   Right-click the File Recovery certificate (identified in the Intended Purposes column), and then choose All Tasks, Export to launch the Certificate Export Wizard. Click Next.

4   Select Yes, Export The Private Key, and then click Next.

5   Select both Enable Strong Protection and Delete The Private Key If The Export Is Successful, and then click Next.

Chapter 11

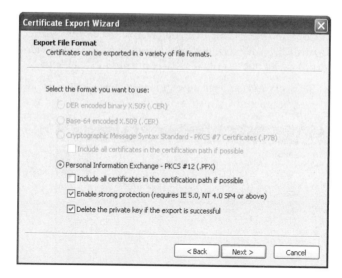

6   Enter a password twice, and then click Next.

7   Specify the path and file name for the exported file.

8   Click Next and then click Finish.

As with the file recovery certificates, you should copy the file to a removable disk, store it in a secure location, and remove the file from your hard disk.

The data recovery agent's public key is now used to encrypt a copy of the FEK with each encrypted file, but because the private key is not available, the data recovery agent can't view the files. To reestablish the data recovery agent's access to encrypted files, import the private key you just exported, using the same procedure as for importing a personal certificate.

For details, see "Importing a Personal Encryption Certificate," page 363.

Backing Up Your Certificates

When you use encryption for the first time (and you don't already have a certificate that's valid for EFS), Windows creates a self-signed certificate for EFS. (*Self-signed* means that the certificate is not granted by a trusted certification authority that can confirm your identity. Such verification is unnecessary for this purpose; in this case, the signature merely confirms that the certificate was created while your account was logged on.) This certificate becomes your personal encryption certificate, and it contains the public/private key pair used for encrypting and decrypting files while you're logged on.

Each user who encrypts files on a system has a personal encryption certificate. In addition, Windows can create a certificate for the designated data recovery agent. This certificate, whose purpose is File Recovery, is not the same as the user's personal encryption certificate, whose purpose is shown as Encrypting File System.

All users should have a backup of their personal encryption certificate. More importantly, the system administrator should have a backup of the file recovery certificate and the data recovery agent's private key. Without one or the other of the certificates, encrypted files are unusable.

Backing Up a File Recovery Certificate

The file recovery certificate provides an administrative alternative for decrypting files if a user's personal encryption certificate is unavailable for any reason. Having a backup of this certificate is essential if you plan to use EFS.

To back up the file recovery certificate, follow these steps:

1 Log on as a member of the Administrators group.

2 In Local Security Settings (Secpol.msc), go to Security Settings\Public Key Policies\ Encrypting File System.

> **Tip** If you have an aversion to command prompts, you can open Local Security Settings by opening Control Panel, Performance And Maintenance, Administrative Tools, Local Security Policy.

3 Right-click the certificate issued to Administrator (or another account) for the purpose of File Recovery, choose All Tasks, Export to launch the Certificate Export Wizard, and then click Next. The Export File Format page opens.

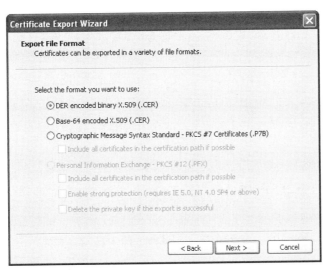

4 Select DER Encoded Binary X.509 (.CER), and then click Next.

5 Specify the path and file name for the exported file.

6 Click Next and then click Finish.

Chapter 11

Backing Up a Personal Encryption Certificate

To back up a personal encryption certificate, follow these steps:

1 Log on as the user whose certificate you want to back up.

2 On the Content tab of the Internet Options dialog box (in Internet Explorer, choose Tools, Internet Options), click Certificates to open the Certificates dialog box.

> **Note** If you prefer, you can use the Certificates snap-in for Microsoft Management Console for this procedure. We chose to open the Certificates dialog box via Internet Options because this route is available and easily understandable to all users; no special privileges are required.

3 On the Personal tab, select the certificate that shows Encrypting File System in the Certificate Intended Purposes box at the bottom of the dialog box.

> **Note** Windows creates this certificate the first time you encrypt a folder or file. Unless you have encrypted something—or you created an encryption certificate in some other way—the certificate won't exist.

4 Click Export to launch the Certificate Export Wizard, and then click Next.

5 Select Yes, Export The Private Key, and then click Next twice.

6 Specify a password for the .pfx file; it doesn't need to be the same as your logon password. Click Next.

7 Specify the path and file name for the exported file.

8 Click Next and then click Finish.

Chapter 11

As you'll see in the next section, the import process makes it very easy to install your personal encryption certificate on another computer—and thereby provide access to your encrypted files. For that reason, be careful to observe these guidelines:

- When you export your certificate, be sure to protect it with a password that can't be guessed easily. Unlike with logon attempts, no policies exist to prevent further attempts after a certain number of incorrect guesses. (On the other hand, be sure to use a password that *you* can remember when the need arises!)

- Be sure to keep your certificate files—whether they're on a floppy disk, a hard disk, or some other medium—in a secure place.

Importing a Personal Encryption Certificate

You will need to import your personal certificate—one that you exported to disk using the procedure in the preceding section—in either of the following situations:

- You want to use your encrypted files on a different computer.

- Your original personal certificate is accidentally lost or becomes corrupt.

To import a personal encryption certificate, follow these steps:

1. Open Control Panel, Network And Internet Connections, Internet Options. On the Content tab of the Internet Properties dialog box, click Certificates to open the Certificates dialog box.

2. Click Import to launch the Certificate Import Wizard, and then click Next.

3. Enter the path and file name of the encryption certificate (a .pfx file) you exported, and then click Next. (If you click Browse, you need to select Personal Information Exchange in the Files Of Type box to see .pfx files.)

4. Enter the password, select other options if so desired, and then click Next.

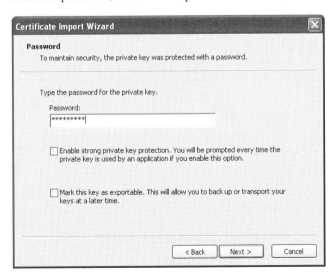

5 Select Place All Certificates In The Following Store, click Browse, and then select Personal. Click OK, Next, and then Finish.

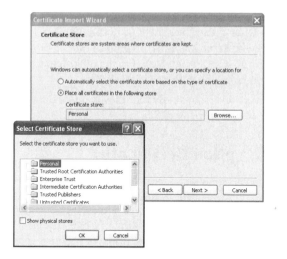

Creating a New Personal Encryption Certificate

If you lose your personal encryption certificate, you can create a new one using Cipher.exe, the command-line encryption utility. At a command prompt, simply type **cipher /k** to create a new personal encryption certificate for the user running Cipher. (By using the Runas command to launch Cipher, you can create certificates for other users.) Of course, you can't use the new certificate to decrypt files that were encrypted using the public key from your old certificate.

Recovering Encrypted Files and Folders

The security policy for a computer or a domain can include a data recovery policy. This policy designates one or more users as data recovery agents; these users can decrypt encrypted files even if the personal encryption certificate that was used to encrypt the file is no longer available. This makes it possible to recover encrypted files after an employee leaves a company, for example.

If your computer is not part of a domain, there is no default data recovery agent and you should create one, as described earlier in this chapter. In a Windows 2000 Server or Windows Server 2003 domain environment, the default data recovery agent is the Administrator account for the domain.

If your computer is a member of a domain, the domain administrator can designate additional users as data recovery agents. Using the domain's Enterprise Certificate Authority, the domain administrator creates data recovery agent certificates for these users and adds them to Public Key Policies\Encrypted Data Recovery Agents in Local Security Settings or, more likely, in the domain security policy.

Whether your computer is a domain member or in a workgroup, best practices suggest not storing the private key associated with the data recovery agent's file recovery certificate on the computer. (If it's stored on the computer, the user designated as the data recovery agent has access to all users' encrypted files, a situation that removes the privacy protection that EFS is designed to provide.) To restore the data recovery agent's file recovery certificate when it's needed, take the following steps:

1 Log on as Administrator.

2 Use the Certificates dialog box to import the file recovery certificate. Use the same procedure as for importing a personal encryption certificate. For details, see "Importing a Personal Encryption Certificate," page 363.

> **Note** If you don't have a domain with an Enterprise Certificate Authority and you want to use an account other than Administrator as the data recovery agent, log on as that user, and then restore the Administrator's file recovery certificate to the personal store. Thereafter, any time you log on with that user account, you can work with any encrypted files on the system.

If you're in a situation where you need to recover encrypted files, you need to know which user accounts are authorized to decrypt the files. For a single file, you can view its Encryption Details dialog box, as shown in Figure 11-2 on page 355. (Right-click the file and choose Properties. On the General tab, click Advanced, Details.) To learn about multiple files, you're better off with the command-line utility Efsinfo.exe, which shows who encrypted each file and who has permission to decrypt it, including any data recovery agents. Efsinfo.exe is on the Windows XP CD-ROM in \Support\Tools\Support.cab; it's not installed by default. In addition to the help generated by typing **efsinfo /?** at a command prompt and the help available in the Help And Support Center, Microsoft Knowledge Base article 243026 has more information about Efsinfo.

Also, a utility called EFSDump, from the good people at Sysinternals, is available at *http://www.sysinternals.com/ntw2k/source/misc.shtml*. Like Efsinfo.exe, EFSDump shows who encrypted a file and who has access to it.

Disabling or Reenabling EFS

If you want to prevent users from encrypting files on a particular machine, you can disable EFS. If your computer is part of a domain, domain-level policies determine whether EFS can be used on a workstation. For standalone computers and computers that are part of a workgroup, the following sections explain how to control the availability of EFS.

> **Caution** Disabling EFS not only prevents users from encrypting any additional folders or files, it also prevents access to existing encrypted files.

Disabling and Reenabling EFS for All Folders and Files

To disable EFS on a computer that is not part of a domain, follow these steps:

1 At a command prompt, type **regedit** to open Registry Editor.

2 Open the HKLM\Software\Microsoft\Windows NT\CurrentVersion\EFS key.

3 Choose Edit, New, DWORD Value.

4 Type **EfsConfiguration** as the name for the new value.

5 Double-click the new value and change its value data to 1.

6 Restart the computer.

To reenable EFS, return to the same value and change it to 0.

> **Note** Intrepid tweakers might come upon a check box called Allow Users To Encrypt Files Using Encrypting File System (EFS) and assume that clearing it disables EFS. Unfortunately, it has no effect in a workgroup environment. If you want to check it out for yourself, open Local Security Settings (Secpol.msc), select Public Key Policies, right-click Encrypting File System, and choose Properties.

Disabling EFS for Individual Folders or Files

You might want to prevent the encryption of files in a certain folder to ensure that they remain available to everyone who has access to the folder. To disable encryption within a folder, use Notepad (or another text editor) to create a file that contains the following lines:

```
[Encryption]
Disable=1
```

Save the file as Desktop.ini in the folder in which you want to prevent encryption. Any encrypted files already in the folder remain encrypted, but users who attempt to encrypt any other files will be stopped with this message: "The directory has been disabled for encryption."

Disabling encryption in this fashion doesn't disable encryption altogether, even within the folder you've set up. If you copy or move encrypted files into the folder, they remain encrypted. And if you create a subfolder within the folder, you can encrypt the subfolder and any files it contains.

It's possible, but generally not practical, to prevent certain files from being encrypted. You can do this in any of the following ways, each of which has a drawback:

● Store the file in %SystemRoot% or one of its subfolders—folders in which encryption is never allowed. (Drawbacks: Windows makes it difficult to browse to these folders, and storing the file here might not mesh with your system of file organization.)

- Use the Attrib command to set the file's System attribute. (Drawback: By default, Windows Explorer does not display system files, so they're difficult to find.)
- Remove Write permissions from the file for users you want to prevent from encrypting. (Drawback: Removing Write permissions also prevents users from editing the file.)

Best Practices for Safe Encryption

If you don't implement EFS correctly, you can undermine your security efforts. For example, your editing program may leave unencrypted temporary files on your drive. Or worse, you can render your encrypted files unusable. To avoid these pitfalls, follow these suggestions:

- Encrypt the My Documents folder and any other local folder you use for storing documents. This ensures that files created by Microsoft Office are encrypted.
- Encrypt the %Temp% and %Tmp% folders. This ensures that any temporary files are encrypted.
- Always encrypt folders, not files. When a folder is encrypted, all files created in that folder are encrypted. Many editing programs save a new copy of the document you are editing. This copy will be encrypted if you encrypt the folder, but it will be plain text if you encrypt only the original file.
- Export and protect the private keys for recovery accounts, and then remove them from the computer. This prevents someone from accessing your files using the data recovery agent account.
- Export the personal encryption certificate for each account.
- Don't destroy file recovery certificates when you change data recovery agent policies. Keep them until you are sure all files that are protected by them have been updated.
- When printing, avoid using spool files, or encrypt the folder in which they are created.
- Secure your paging file so that it is overwritten when Windows shuts down. (See the sidebar "Securing the Paging File," page 348.)

Chapter 12

Securing Your Computer with Templates

Microsoft Windows XP is rife with security options—various settings you can implement to ensure that the bad guys are locked out of your computer and that people to whom you want to grant access can use your computer and its resources. You can specify user rights, which determine the accounts that are permitted to perform certain tasks. You can configure numerous settings that determine how your computer operates. You can apply permissions to every file, printer, and other resource, specifying exactly what type of access is granted to each user. And on and on. We describe in detail these security options—and many others— in *Microsoft Windows Security Inside Out for Windows XP and Windows 2000* (Microsoft Press, 2003).

Fortunately, the default settings in Windows are appropriate in most cases, and you don't need to spend an inordinate amount of time reviewing and setting security options. In certain situations, you might need to grant an additional user right to a particular user account or user group—a task we explain in this chapter. Once you know how, it's quite easy. But what if you need to apply uniform, non-default security settings to all the computers on your network? Although making settings on one computer is not particularly difficult, it's not a job you want to repeat any more than necessary. Security templates provide a solution.

At Home with Windows XP

If you use Windows XP Home Edition, you might as well skip right past this chapter; the settings described here rely on Microsoft Management Console (MMC) snap-ins that are included only with Windows XP Professional. (Don't worry about your computer's security, however. Windows XP Home Edition enjoys the same security protection as Professional; the difference is that in Home Edition you can't change the settings.)

The final topic of this chapter is Security Configuration And Analysis, a Microsoft Management Console (MMC) snap-in that allows you to compare your current security settings with those of a security template and apply the template settings if you choose.

Setting User Rights

A *user right* is authorization to perform an operation that affects an entire computer. (A *permission*, by contrast, is authorization to perform an operation on a specific object—such as a file or a printer—on a computer.) For each user right, you can specify which user accounts and groups have the user right. To review or set user rights, use the Group Policy console. (At a command prompt, type **gpedit.msc** to open Group Policy.) Navigate to Computer Configuration\Windows Settings\Security Settings\Local Policies\User Rights Assignment. Then double-click a user right to view or change the list of authorized users and groups, as shown in Figure 12-1.

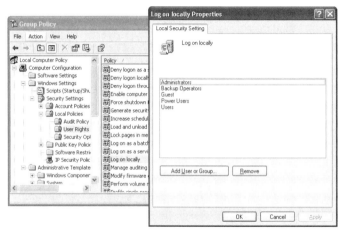

Figure 12-1. To review or change the local setting for a user right, double-click the user right in User Rights Assignment.

For more information about Group Policy, see Appendix F, "Group Policy."

> **Tip** **Use the Local Security Settings console**
> The Local Security Settings console displays a subset of the Group Policy console's content, thereby providing a shorter path to User Rights Assignment. Local Security Settings is useful when you're not setting other policies, such as the ones in the Administrative Templates folders. To open Local Security Settings, double-click Local Security Policy in Control Panel's Administrative Tools folder, or type **secpol.msc** at a command prompt.

Ten of the user rights—Access This Computer From The Network, Allow Logon Through Terminal Services, Log On As A Batch Job, Log On As A Service, Log On Locally, and their corresponding "Deny" user rights—are known more precisely as *logon rights*. They control how users are allowed to access the computer—whether from the keyboard ("locally") or through a network connection, or whether as a service or as a batch facility (such as Task Scheduler). You can use these logon rights (in particular, Log On Locally and Deny Logon Locally) to control who can log on to your computer. By default, Log On Locally is granted to the local Guest account and members of the Administrators, Backup Operators, Power Users, and Users groups. If you want to prevent certain users from logging on at the keyboard (but still allow them to connect via the network, for example), create a group, add the unwelcome user accounts to it, and then assign the Deny Logon Locally user right to the new group. Like deny permissions, deny logon rights take precedence over allow logon rights, so if a user is a member of both a group that is allowed to log on (such as Power Users) and a group that is not (such as the one described in the previous sentence), the user will not be allowed to log on. (Such users are rebuffed with an error message after they type their user name and password in the Log On To Windows dialog box.)

For a description of each user right, see *Microsoft Windows XP Professional Resource Kit* (Microsoft Press, 2003). Another useful reference is "Threats and Countermeasures: Security Settings in Windows Server 2003 and Windows XP," a white paper from Microsoft that includes a description of each user right along with a discussion of security vulnerabilities exposed by each user right granted and effective countermeasures. "Threats and Countermeasures" is included on this book's companion CD. Table 12-1 lists the default rights assigned to the built-in user groups.

Chapter 12

Table 12-1. Default User Rights of Built-In User Groups in Windows XP Professional

Group	Default Rights
Administrators	• Access this computer from the network
	• Adjust memory quotas for a process
	• Allow logon through Terminal Services
	• Back up files and directories
	• Bypass traverse checking
	• Change the system time
	• Create a page file
	• Create global objects*
	• Debug programs
	• Force shutdown from a remote system
	• Impersonate a client after authentication*
	• Increase scheduling priority
	• Load and unload device drivers
	• Log on locally
	• Manage auditing and security log
	• Modify firmware environment values
	• Perform volume maintenance tasks
	• Profile single process
	• Profile system performance
	• Remove computer from docking station
	• Restore files and directories
	• Shut down the system
	• Take ownership of files or other objects
Backup Operators	• Access this computer from the network
	• Back up files and directories
	• Bypass traverse checking
	• Log on locally
	• Restore files and directories
	• Shut down the system
Everyone	• Access this computer from the network
	• Bypass traverse checking

Table 12-1. Default User Rights of Built-In User Groups in Windows XP Professional

Group	Default Rights
Guest (account)	• Deny logon locally • Deny access to this computer from the network† • Log on locally
Power Users	• Access this computer from the network • Bypass traverse checking • Change the system time • Log on locally • Profile single process • Remove computer from docking station • Shut down the system
Remote Desktop Users	• Allow logon through Terminal Services
Users	• Access this computer from the network • Bypass traverse checking • Log on locally • Remove computer from docking station • Shut down the system
Not assigned to any group	• Act as part of the operating system • Add workstations to domain • Create a token object • Create permanent shared objects • Deny logon as a batch job • Deny logon as a service • Deny logon through Terminal Services • Enable computer and user accounts to be trusted for delegation • Generate security audits • Lock pages in memory • Log on as a batch job • Log on as a service • Replace a process-level token • Synchronize directory service data

* This user right is available only with Service Pack 2 or later.

† The Guest account is removed from the list of accounts with the Deny Access To This Computer From The Network right when you enable network file sharing.

Using Security Templates

If you decide to change some of the default settings for user rights or other security options, you can make the changes in Group Policy or in Local Security Settings, as described in the preceding section. If you want to apply the same changes to a number of computers in your network, however, making the settings can be tedious. In this common situation, you're better off using *security templates*, files that contain preconfigured security settings for various purposes. You can also use security templates to restore your security settings to a known condition if experimentation with various settings has compromised your secure system. A security template can contain the following types of settings:

- Account Policies, including Password Policy and Account Lockout Policy settings (For details about these settings, see "Tightening Password Security," page 263.)
- Local Policies, including Audit Policy, User Rights Assignment, and Security Options settings (See "Enabling Auditing," page 387, and "Setting User Rights," page 370.)
- Event Log (See "Working with Log Files," page 1272.)
- Restricted Groups (See "Controlling Security Group Membership," page 378.)
- System Services, which determines the startup type for each service (See "Using the Services Snap-In," page 1379.)
- Registry, which sets permissions on registry keys (See "Changing Registry Key Permissions," page 1333.)
- File System, which sets permissions on folders and files (See "Controlling Access with NTFS Permissions," page 282.)

 Inside Out

Propagating Group Policy settings

Security templates do not include settings for policies in Group Policy's Administrative Templates folders. Therefore, you can't use security templates to apply those settings to other computers. (The ability to centrally manage and apply Group Policy settings is one of the strengths of domain-based networks that use Microsoft Windows 2000 Server or Windows Server 2003.)

However, you can propagate your policy settings to other computers relatively easily: After you make the necessary changes on one computer, simply copy the Registry.pol files to each computer on which you want to apply the policies. For the settings in Computer Configuration\Administrative Templates, copy %SystemRoot%\System32\GroupPolicy\Machine\Registry.pol to the same folder on the target machine. For the User Configuration\Administrative Templates settings, copy the Registry.pol file stored in %SystemRoot%\System32\GroupPolicy\User.

Security templates are saved as ordinary text files with a .inf file name extension. By default, they're stored in %SystemRoot%\Security\Templates. Although you could edit these plain-text (but rather cryptic) files in Notepad or another text editor, you don't need to. The Security Templates snap-in for MMC provides a much better and easier means to view, modify, create, and delete security templates.

Each security template that comes with Windows is configured for specific purposes. You can use these templates as is, modify them, or create new ones from scratch. Table 12-2 describes the templates included with Windows XP Professional.

Table 12-2. Security Templates Included with Windows

Template Name	Description
Compatws	This template removes all users from the Power Users group and relaxes the default permissions for members of the Users group. This setting allows members of the Users group to run certain applications that aren't properly designed for Windows security, without granting them the additional administrative privileges (such as the ability to create user accounts) granted to Power Users.
Hisecdc and Hisecws	These templates are intended for configuring a highly secure domain. They include all the settings in the Securedc and Securews templates, plus additional settings that require more secure authentication, restrict security group membership, and require data signing and encryption in most network communications. Hisecdc is intended for domain controllers; Hisecws is for workstations.
Rootsec	This template applies permissions to the root folder of the system drive, using the Windows XP default permissions. If you inadvertently change those permissions, this template provides a quick and easy way to restore them. The permissions propagate to all child objects that inherit permissions from the parent, but they aren't applied to child objects for which explicit permissions have been set.
Securedc and Securews	These templates configure strong password, lockout, and audit settings; require the use of strong authentication protocols; restrict anonymous users; and configure Server Message Block (SMB) packet signing. They're intended for creating secure domains. Use Securedc on domain controllers and Securews on workstations.
Setup Security	This template contains the default security settings that were applied when Windows XP was installed on your computer. As such, it makes a good disaster recovery template, allowing you to easily revert to the original Windows configuration.

Chapter 12

> **Note** Except for Setup Security.inf, none of the furnished templates includes a complete set of security settings. Instead, they're designed to modify only a specific subset while leaving other settings unchanged.

Inside Out

Restoring default security settings

You can restore default NTFS permissions and other security settings with a hidden template. Windows XP includes a template called Defltwk.inf that includes all the default security settings (including NTFS permissions, user rights assignments, policies, registry permissions, and so on) as originally configured by Microsoft for a clean installation of Windows on a new machine. (For a number of reasons, some of these settings might be different from the settings in Setup Security.inf.) Unlike the other predefined templates, Defltwk.inf is stored in %SystemRoot%\Inf, a hidden folder. Because of its storage location, it doesn't appear by default in the Security Templates snap-in, where it would be more likely to get changed inadvertently. Instead, Defltwk.inf is intended to be used only with the Security Configuration And Analysis snap-in or Secedit.exe, the tools for analyzing current settings and applying settings. Read more about Defltwk.inf in Knowledge Base article 266118, "How to Restore the Default NTFS Permissions for Windows 2000." (The article refers only to Windows 2000, but Defltwk.inf is also included with Windows XP.)

Using the Security Templates Snap-In

Security Templates is an MMC snap-in that allows you to view, create, and edit security templates. No console furnished with Windows XP includes the Security Templates snap-in; you'll have to create your own, as follows:

1 At a command prompt, type **mmc**.

2 Open the File menu and choose Add/Remove Snap-In.

3 On the Standalone tab in the Add/Remove Snap-In dialog box, click Add.

4 Select Security Templates, and then click Add.

5 Click Close, and then click OK.

By default, the Security Templates snap-in displays the templates stored in %SystemRoot%\ Security\Templates, as shown in Figure 12-2. To view templates stored in another folder, including those stored on a network drive, right-click Security Templates in the console tree, and choose New Template Search Path.

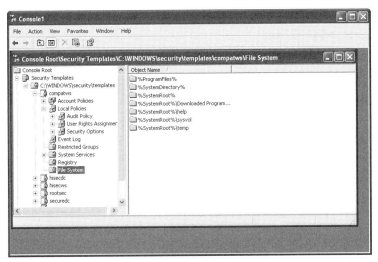

Figure 12-2. The Security Templates snap-in lets you set permissions on folders and files and make other security settings.

To create a new template, in the console tree, right-click the folder where you want to store the template, and choose New Template. Enter a name and, optionally, a description of the template.

You can view the description for a template in two ways:

- In the console tree, select the folder that contains the templates. The description of each template appears next to its name in the details pane.
- Right-click a template name (in the console tree or the details pane), and choose Set Description.

If you want to modify the settings in an existing template and also want to keep the original template unchanged, right-click the template name and choose Save As. After you specify a name for your copy of the template, it appears in the console tree. Note that none of the changes you make to a template are saved to disk unless you select the template and choose Action, Save or right-click a template name and choose Save. (The Save command on the File menu saves the console layout and settings—not the template settings.) If you have unsaved templates when you close the MMC console, Windows asks which of these templates you want to save. Select the ones you want to save, and then click Yes.

Note The Security Templates snap-in is a tool only for viewing, creating, and modifying templates. Changes you make in the snap-in are saved in template files, but this snap-in does not apply template security settings to a computer. To apply the settings in a template, use the procedures described in "Applying Template Settings," page 381.

Chapter 12

Reviewing Account Policies, Local Policies, Event Log, and System Services Settings

You can easily review account policies, local policies, the event log, and system services settings. In the Security Templates snap-in, expand the folders in the console tree until the policy in which you're interested is displayed in the details pane. Then double-click the policy name to open the properties dialog box; Figure 12-3 shows an example. If you want the policy to be controlled by the security template, select Define This Policy Setting In The Template, and then specify the setting you want. Your choices for policy setting depend on the specific policy. (For example, some policies require you to select among two or more options, whereas others provide a text box or spin box with which you can specify a numeric value.)

Figure 12-3. The properties dialog box for each policy has options comparable to those in the Local Security Settings console.

Controlling Security Group Membership

With restricted groups policies, you can control membership in security groups. When you apply a security template with restricted groups policies, any user accounts that are currently members of a group whose membership is restricted are removed from that group. For example, if you create a restricted group policy for Administrators that includes only Ed and Carl in that group, applying the template adds Ed and Carl to the group (if they're not already members) and removes all other accounts. Restricting group membership in this way is a one-shot deal; administrators can subsequently add or remove members from the group.

To add a group to the list of restricted groups, right-click Restricted Groups and choose Add Group. In the Add Group dialog box, type the name of the security group you want to add, or click Browse to display a list of all security groups. In the Select Groups dialog box, click Advanced, and then click Find Now to display the list.

To control the membership of a restricted group, double-click the group name to display the properties dialog box for the group, as shown in Figure 12-4. Next to the Members Of This Group box, click Add. In the Add Member dialog box, type a user name, or click Browse to display a list of user names. You can separate multiple names with semicolons, or you can simply repeat the process to add other names.

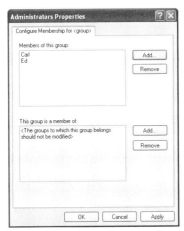

Figure 12-4. After applying the template, only user accounts listed in the top box remain in the group; if no names appear, the group is empty.

Configuring Permissions on Folders, Files, and the Registry

The File System and Registry sections of a security template let you apply permissions to folders, files, and registry keys, overriding any permissions currently protecting the items you specify. Just as with Windows Explorer and Registry Editor, you can specify a discretionary access control list (DACL), which grants (or denies) access permissions to users and groups. You can also specify a system access control list (SACL), which specifies the security events to be recorded in the Security log.

For information about permissions on folders and files, see "Controlling Access with NTFS Permissions," page 282. For information about applying permissions within Registry Editor, see "Changing Registry Key Permissions," page 1333. For information about setting SACLs, see "Seeing Who Has Tried to Access Your Files and Folders," page 391.

If the folder or file on which you want to configure ACLs does not appear in the details pane when you select File System, right-click File System (or right-click an empty area of the details pane), and choose Add File. The Add File command opens the Add A File Or Folder dialog box, which lets you browse all folders and files in My Computer. The steps for adding a registry key are similar: Right-click Registry and choose Add Key. In the Select Registry Key dialog box, you can expand the registry hierarchy and select the key you want to configure.

Chapter 12

379

When the folder, file, or registry key of interest appears in the details pane, simply double-click it to configure it. A dialog box similar to the one shown in Figure 12-5 appears. To set ACLs, select the first option, and then specify how you want to set permissions on child objects (subfolders and files within the specified folder, or subkeys within the specified registry key). The options to propagate inheritable permissions and replace existing permissions correspond to the similarly worded options in the Advanced Security Settings dialog box, which opens when you click Advanced on the Security tab in Windows Explorer or Registry Editor.

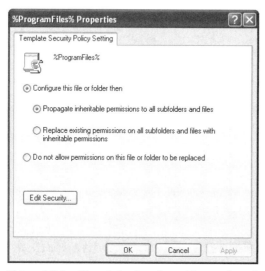

Figure 12-5. The dialog box for setting registry key permissions is nearly identical to this one. Minor wording variations refer to keys instead of files and folders.

Select Do Not Allow Permissions On This File Or Folder To Be Replaced if you want to ensure that permissions on the folder, file, or key are *not* changed when a security template is applied. Why not just omit this object name from the Registry or File System folder in the template? This option prevents changes that might be inflicted through inheritance by settings on a parent object.

Finally, of course, you need to specify the permissions for the object. Click Edit Security, and you'll see a dialog box that includes a Security tab just like the one in Windows Explorer or Registry Editor. This dialog box shows the object's current security settings.

Applying Template Settings

After you've configured a template to include the settings you want, you can apply the settings to your local computer. You do this with Security Configuration And Analysis, an MMC snap-in that manages a database of security settings from one or more templates. You can also use this snap-in to compare your current settings to those in the templates database.

> **Tip** Before you apply your template settings, you might want to analyze your configuration to see what differences exist between your current settings and the settings in your security template. For details, see "Analyzing System Security," in this chapter.

To use Security Configuration And Analysis, you must add it to an MMC console. Use the same procedure as described for the Security Templates snap-in; for details, see "Using the Security Templates Snap-In," page 376. Initially, the Security Configuration And Analysis snap-in looks like no other, displaying only an empty console tree and, in the details pane, sparse instructions for tasks whose purpose isn't clear.

> **Tip** To house all your security management tools in one place, create a console that includes the Group Policy, Security Templates, and Security Configuration And Analysis snap-ins. Save the console in your Administrative Tools folder.

Go ahead and follow these instructions:

1. Right-click Security Configuration And Analysis and choose Open Database.
2. In the Open Database dialog box, type a name for a new database, and then click Open. (If you want to use a database that you've created previously, select it instead.)
3. In the Import Template dialog box, select a security template, and then click Open.
4. If you want to import another security template into the database, right-click Security Configuration And Analysis, and choose Import Template.

Now you're ready to actually apply your settings. Right-click Security Configuration And Analysis, and choose Configure Computer Now. In the Configure System dialog box, type the path and name for a log file if you don't want to accept the default file. Click OK. (Why it's called an *error* log file is another mystery of Security Configuration And Analysis; it's a log of all configuration actions, not only errors.) Windows applies your settings, and you're once again left at the same cryptic console display. To see what has occurred, right-click Security Configuration And Analysis and choose View Log File; the log file appears in the details pane.

Inside Out

Applying template settings from a command line or batch program

You might find it more convenient to apply template settings with Secedit.exe, a command-line utility. This utility can make applying settings on multiple computers easier. You could, for example, store the security database (.sdb) file on a shared network drive, along with a one-line batch program that applies the settings. A command-line utility also makes it easy to set up security configuration as a scheduled task.

Before you use Secedit, you must create a security database file with Security Configuration And Analysis, as described in the numbered steps in the preceding section. Then, to apply your settings, use the command **secedit /configure /db *databasefile***, where *databasefile* is the path and name (including the extension) of the database file. You can omit the path if the database is in the current directory. For example, if you leave the security database file in the default location, you'd enter the following:

```
secedit /configure /db
"%userprofile%\my documents\security\database\mysettings.sdb"
```

With additional command-line parameters, you can instruct Secedit to apply only certain types of settings specified in the database, control the location and display of the log file, and set other options. In addition, you can use Secedit to compare your computer settings with security database settings, extract a security template file from a security database, and more. For details, type **secedit /?** at a command prompt.

Analyzing System Security

The Security Configuration And Analysis snap-in has that name for a reason: In addition to applying template settings (configuration), it compares a computer's current security settings with those in a security database file (analysis). This comparison provides an easy way to comprehensively review security settings. You can see which settings have been changed, how your computer compares with one of the highly secure template configurations, and so on.

To perform an analysis, open Security Configuration And Analysis in MMC, and then create or open a security database. (See the preceding section, "Applying Template Settings," for details.) Right-click Security Configuration And Analysis, and choose Analyze Computer Now. In the Perform Analysis dialog box, modify the log file name if you want, and then click OK. After the analysis is complete, the console tree sprouts new branches, identical to those in a template in the Security Templates snap-in. For each policy in the Account Policies, Local Policies, and Event Log folders, the details pane shows the database setting and the current computer setting. A symbol in a policy's icon indicates at a glance the results of the analysis of that policy:

	A circled green check mark indicates that the two settings match.
	An *X* in a red circle identifies policies in which the database setting differs from the computer setting.
	A circled exclamation point or question mark indicates that the computer setting was not analyzed; this typically occurs in policies that are relevant only on a domain controller.

Double-click a policy to see its properties dialog box, as shown in Figure 12-6. The dialog box displays the current settings for the computer and in the database. If you want to change the setting in the database, select Define This Policy In The Database, make your setting, and click OK.

Differences between the database settings and computer settings in the Restricted Groups, System Services, Registry, and File System folders are indicated with icons similar to those just shown. Instead of displaying the settings in the details pane, however, Security Configuration And Analysis displays the word *Investigate* alongside items with differences. Double-click any such items in the Restricted Groups or System Services folder to display a properties dialog box, similar to the dialog box shown in Figure 12-6, that shows both settings and allows you to modify the database setting.

Security Configuration And Analysis has another quirk as well. Double-clicking an item in the Registry or File System folder doesn't open the properties dialog box unless the item is at the bottom of the hierarchy. To view the properties dialog box for a folder or a key that has child objects, right-click it and choose Properties.

Chapter 12

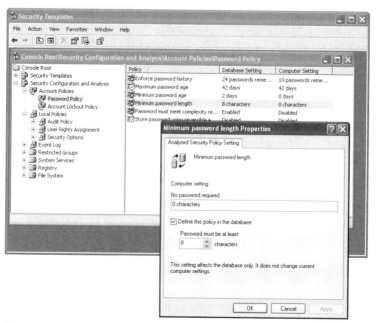

Figure 12-6. The properties dialog box for a policy shows computer's current setting and the value in the security database. You can change the database value if you want to.

Auditing Security

As a secure operating system, Microsoft Windows XP is designed to prevent unauthorized access to a computer's files, folders, and printers. But if a user inadvertently makes improper settings or if an intruder is especially determined, someone might gain access to resources that should be off limits. Monitoring, or *auditing*, system usage can be a helpful tool in the administration of system security. For example, repeated attempts to log on with the wrong password might be an indication that unauthorized users are trying to gain access to your system. Repeated failure to access a folder might indicate that software has been incorrectly installed or that security for the folder is set up incorrectly.

Windows XP provides the ability to audit security events by recording attempts to access system resources. In this chapter, we describe the various auditing tools that you, as a system administrator or resource owner, can use. We examine their purpose and use and explain what information they can supply when used properly.

About Auditing

When a user attempts to access a system resource, Windows checks the resource's access control list (ACL) to determine whether the user should be allowed access. This is the essence of Windows XP security.

At Home with Windows XP

In Windows XP Home Edition, account logon, account management, logon, policy change, and system events are audited for both successful incidents and failed attempts. You cannot enable auditing for directory service access, object access, privilege use, or process tracking events, or disable the categories that are already enabled, without additional tools.

> **Note** Even if your computer is configured to use Simple File Sharing (the default configuration in standalone and workgroup environments), Windows still uses ACLs. With Simple File Sharing, the standard user interface provides fewer options for viewing and editing ACLs, but the lists—and the protection they provide—are still in place. For more information about the Simple File Sharing model, see "Simple File Sharing vs. Windows 2000–Style Sharing," page 230.

If auditing is enabled, you can also request that Windows audit access to a given resource. (For more information, see "Enabling Auditing," page 387.) Windows will then record in a log file any attempts to access that resource. You might direct Windows to record all failed print jobs on a given printer, for example, or to record all failed file-read requests for a certain folder.

Windows records this information in the Security log (Secevent.evt), one of the three system-wide logs that Windows manages. The other two are the System log (Sysevent.evt), which records events generated by components of the operating system—such as display or network drivers—and the Application log (Appevent.evt), which records events generated by applications. For example, Backup Utility generates events when you erase a tape or restore files, and records the events in the Application log.

> **Note** For information about the System and Application logs, see Chapter 38, "Monitoring System Activities with Event Viewer."

Avoid auditing if you don't need it. Security audits, like IRS audits, can be time-consuming. (OK, security audits aren't *that* bad.) When you enable auditing, the system must write an event record to the Security log for each audit check the system performs. Because this can severely degrade system performance, you should audit only the events that are important to you.

Ensuring That You Don't Miss Any Security Events

By default, when the Security log becomes full, Windows erases the oldest entries when it needs to make a new entry—just as it does with the System log and the Application log. But if security is critical to your operation, you can make a registry setting that ensures that events can be deleted only by a member of the Administrators group. (Even without this registry setting, only administrators—and others with the Manage Auditing And Security Log right—can view the Security log or clear its contents. To prevent people from covering their tracks, no one can delete individual entries; authorized individuals must delete all or none.)

This solution is rather drastic and should therefore be used only when it's essential that every security event be preserved. With this registry entry, the system halts when the Security log becomes full, preventing all further use—and possibly losing data if document files happen to be open when this occurs. If you want to enable this level of security, here's how it's done:

1 In Event Viewer, right-click Security and choose Properties. (Type **eventvwr.msc** at a command prompt to launch Event Viewer.)

2 On the General tab, select either Overwrite Events Older Than or, for maximum security, Do Not Overwrite Events (Clear Log Manually).

3 Use Registry Editor to change or create a DWORD value named CrashOnAuditFail in HKLM\System\CurrentControlSet\Control\Lsa. Set its value to 1. (Alternatively, in Windows XP Professional, you can use Group Policy to make this registry change. Go to Computer Configuration\Windows Settings\Security Settings\Local Policies\ Security Options and enable the Audit: Shut Down System Immediately If Unable To Log Security Audits policy.)

4 Restart the computer.

After you've followed these steps, the computer will halt when the Security log is full. At that point, you need to restart the computer and log on as a member of the Administrators group; no other accounts are allowed to log on. Your first action after logging on should be to review, export if desired, and clear the Security log. You then need to reset the value of the registry entry to 1. (The operating system automatically sets it to 2, which is the mechanism that prevents other users from logging on.) To restore the computer to normal operation (that is, it continues to run even if the Security log is full), set the value to 0.

Naturally, if you employ this trick, you should take steps to avoid having the security log fill up and lock the machine at inopportune moments. Review and then clear the log periodically. (Export the log contents first if you want to preserve them.) You might also want to increase the size of the log. For more information, see "Working with Log Files," page 1272.

Enabling Auditing

No events are written to the Security log until you enable auditing, which you do via Local Security Settings. (In Windows XP Home Edition, security auditing is enabled for certain events. Because Home Edition doesn't include Local Security Settings, you cannot change which events are audited unless you use a tool like Auditpol.exe—included in the Windows 2000 Resource Kit—or a comparable third-party tool.) Even if you set up auditing for files, folders, or printers, as explained later in this chapter, those events aren't recorded unless you also enable auditing in Local Security Settings.

> **Note** To enable auditing, you must be logged on with an account that has the Manage Auditing And Security Log privilege. By default, only members of the Administrators group have this privilege. For information about privileges, see "Setting User Rights," page 370.

> **Note** Like most other settings in Local Security Settings, the audit policy settings can be overridden by domain-level policy settings. If your computer is part of a Windows 2000 Server or Windows Server 2003 domain, you should use domain-level Group Policy to make audit policy settings instead of using Local Security Settings.

To enable auditing, follow these steps:

1 In Control Panel, open Administrative Tools, Local Security Policy. (If you use Category view, you'll find Administrative Tools under Performance And Maintenance.) Alternatively, you can type **secpol.msc** at a command prompt.

2 Expand Local Policies and then click Audit Policy to display the list shown in Figure 13-1.

3 Double-click each policy for which you want to enable auditing, and then select Success, Failure, or both.

Figure 13-1 shows the types of activities you can audit. Some, such as account management and policy change, can provide an audit trail for administrative changes. Others, such as logon events and object access, can help you discover how to better secure your system. Still others, including system events and process tracking, can assist you in locating problems with your system. Table 13-1 provides more details.

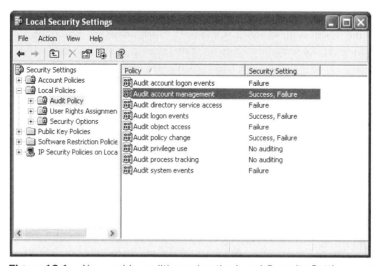

Figure 13-1. You enable auditing using the Local Security Settings console.

Table 13-1. **Events That Can Be Audited**

Audit Policy	Description
Audit account logon events	Account logon events occur when a user logs on or logs off another computer that uses this computer to validate the account. This happens only on a server running Windows 2000 or Windows Server 2003, and is therefore not applicable on a computer running Windows XP.
Audit account management	Account management events occur when a user account or group is created, changed, or deleted; when a user account is renamed, enabled, or disabled; or when a password is set or changed.
Audit directory service access	Directory service access events occur when a user accesses an Active Directory object that has its own system ACL. (This is the same as object access except that it applies only to Active Directory objects in a Windows domain.)
Audit logon events	Logon events occur when a user logs on or logs off a workstation or connects via a network.
Audit object access	Object access events occur when a user accesses a file, folder, printer, registry key, or other object that is set for auditing.
Audit policy change	Policy change events occur when a change is made to user rights assignment policies, audit policies, or trust policies.
Audit privilege use	Privilege use events occur when a user exercises a user right (other than logon, logoff, and network access rights, which trigger other types of events).
Audit process tracking	Process tracking includes arcane events such as program activation, handle duplication, indirect object access, and process exit. This policy is generally not useful for everyday security concerns.
Audit system events	System events occur when a user restarts or shuts down the computer or when an event occurs that affects system security or the Security log.

Troubleshooting

Windows requires a logon password but you don't have one.

Ordinarily, a user who does not have an assigned logon password can log on simply by clicking his or her name on the Welcome screen. In some cases, clicking the name displays a request for a password, and nothing you type (even just pressing Enter) satisfies the request.

New security features in Windows XP prevent users who don't have a password from logging on in certain situations. (This is done to prevent someone who knows your account name from logging on via a network or the Internet, for example—but it can affect local logons as well.) One of those situations can occur when auditing is enabled.

You can solve the problem by disabling auditing (and setting the CrashOnAuditFail value to 0 if you have changed it), but a much better solution is to assign a logon password—even a short one—to each user. To do that, visit User Accounts in Control Panel.

Viewing Security Events

Before we examine how to audit events, let's first take a look at Event Viewer—the Microsoft Management Console snap-in that allows you to examine the events that have been recorded. Event Viewer is in Computer Management, under System Tools. For the uncluttered view, go instead to Control Panel, Administrative Tools, Event Viewer, or simply type **eventvwr.msc** at a command prompt. You can use Event Viewer to examine any of the three logs: System, Security, or Application. If you select the Security log, you'll see a window similar to the one shown in Figure 13-2.

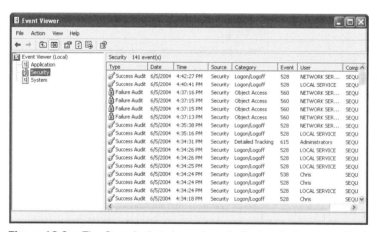

Figure 13-2. The Security log shown here indicates that an unauthorized user has apparently been attempting to use an object. These unsuccessful access events, identified with a lock icon, happened within a few seconds of each other.

Note   For more information about Event Viewer, see Chapter 38, "Monitoring System Activities with Event Viewer."

> **Note** You must be logged on as a member of the Administrators group to view the Security log. (A system administrator can grant Security log access to other groups and user accounts by assigning the Manage Auditing And Security Log right. For details, see "Setting User Rights," page 370.)

If you want more information about an event in the Security log, double-click the event, or select it and then choose Action, Properties. The Event Properties dialog box appears, similar to the one shown in Figure 13-3.

Figure 13-3. This Event Properties dialog box indicates that Barbara has tried to open the file 37-01.bmp without permission.

By carefully examining all unsuccessful logon events, you might be able to find a pattern in attempts to gain access to the system. You can then take measures to tighten security, such as warning users to change their passwords and monitoring the Security log more closely for specific events.

Seeing Who Has Tried to Access Your Files and Folders

If you are logged on as a member of the Administrators group (or if the Manage Auditing And Security Log right has been assigned to your logon account), you can set up auditing of certain files or folders on your system. Windows XP can audit a variety of events and can audit different events for different users.

> **Note**   The files and folders that you want to audit must reside on an NTFS volume; FAT volumes do not support auditing.

Avoid auditing too many successful events. Although auditing is a useful technique for monitoring access to your system, you should be careful when auditing busy folders or files—and be particularly careful about auditing successful accesses. Each time a user successfully completes an operation on the file or folder, Windows XP writes one or more records to the Security log to reflect the access. This slows down your system and adds many events of little value to the log, thereby making it more difficult to find real security breaches. On the other hand, selectively auditing successful file access can be beneficial in some situations. For example, you might want to log all access to a payroll database file, which would allow you to track down who did what (and when) as well as find out if someone without the proper authority accessed the file.

Use the Security tab in the properties dialog box for a file or folder to display its audit settings. You can specify the users and groups whose access to the selected file or folder you want to audit. For each user and group, you can specify which types of access should generate entries in the Security log. You can specify different auditing events for each user and group.

> **Note**   The settings you make on the Auditing tab of the Access Control Settings dialog box (as described in the following procedure) are effective only if you also enable auditing. If you haven't done so already, visit Local Security Settings to enable auditing. Be sure to set Audit Object Access events to audit success and failure. (See "Enabling Auditing," page 387.)

To set up auditing for files and folders, follow these steps:

1   If your computer is not a member of a domain, in Windows Explorer, choose Tools, Folder Options. Click the View tab and then clear the Use Simple File Sharing (Recommended) check box. Click OK.

    Disabling Simple File Sharing allows the Security tab to appear when you look at an object's properties.

> **Note**   After you make the audit settings you want for various files and folders (as described in the following steps), you can restore Simple File Sharing by returning to Folder Options and selecting the same check box. Thereafter the Security tab isn't visible in the properties dialog box for files and folders, but the audit settings you made remain in effect.

2   Right-click a file or folder in Windows Explorer and choose Properties.
3   Click the Security tab.

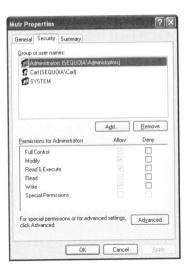

> **Note**   If the selected file or folder is not stored on an NTFS volume, the Security tab doesn't appear, because auditing and other security features are implemented only for NTFS volumes.

4   Click Advanced. The Advanced Security Settings dialog box appears.

5   Click the Auditing tab. For each object, you can specify different audit settings for different users.

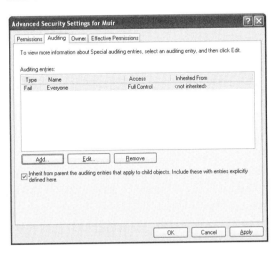

6   Click Add to add a new user or group, or select an existing user or group and then click Edit to change its audit settings.

7   If you click Add, the Select User Or Group dialog box appears. In this example, the Everyone group is being selected. Click OK.

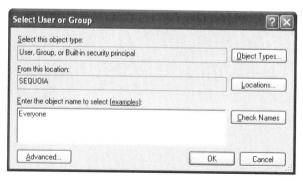

8   Whether editing an existing entry or adding a new one, in the Auditing Entry dialog box, select the types of access you want to audit for the selected user or group (in this case, Everyone).

The different types of access you can audit for success or failure are the same types of access for which you can set permissions.

9   If you're making audit settings for a folder, select the scope of objects you want audited from the Apply Onto list.

If you select an event's Successful check box, Windows generates a Security log record (containing, among other information, the time and date) each time the specified user or group successfully attempts the event for the specified file or folder. Similarly, if you select an event's Failed check box, Windows generates a Security log record each time the specified user or group unsuccessfully attempts the event for the specified file or folder.

> **Tip** Change audit settings for more than one file or folder at once
>
> You can change audit settings for multiple files or folders simultaneously. If you select more than one file or folder in Windows Explorer and then click the Security tab in the properties dialog box, the changes you make affect all the selected files or folders. If the existing security settings are not the same for all the items in your selection, a message appears, asking whether you want to reset the audit settings for the entire selection.

Seeing Who Has Tried to Use Your Printers

Windows XP can audit several printer events as well as audit different printer events for different users. If you have a color printer that uses expensive ink cartridges, for example, you might want to know who's causing it to run dry so frequently. You can manage all the printer security features through the Printers And Faxes folder.

> **Note** You must be logged on as a member of the Administrators group (or your logon account must have the Manage Auditing And Security Log right) to set up auditing of printers.

To set up printer security auditing, follow these steps:

1 Use Local Security Settings to enable auditing. Be sure to set Audit Object Access events to audit success and failure. (For details, see "Enabling Auditing," page 387.)

2 If your computer is not a member of a domain, in Windows Explorer, choose Tools, Folder Options. Click the View tab and then clear the Use Simple File Sharing (Recommended) check box.

   Disabling Simple File Sharing causes the Security tab to appear when you look at a printer's properties dialog box. (Yes, the Simple *File* Sharing setting also applies to printers.)

> **Note** After you make the audit settings you want for your printers (as described in the following steps), you can restore Simple File Sharing by returning to Folder Options and selecting the same check box. Thereafter the Security tab isn't visible in the properties dialog box for printers, but the audit settings you made remain in effect.

3 From the Start menu, choose Printers And Faxes.

4 Right-click the icon for the printer you want to audit and choose Properties.

5 Click the Security tab.

6 Click Advanced. The Advanced Security Settings dialog box appears.

7 Click the Auditing tab.

The Auditing tab for a printer object is nearly identical to the one for a file object, as shown.

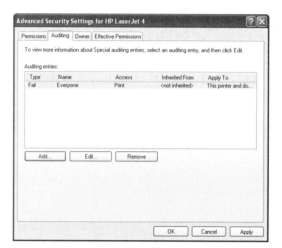

8 Click Add to add a new user or group, or click Edit to change audit settings for an existing user or group. If you click Add, specify the new user or group in the Select User Or Group dialog box that appears and then click OK.

9 In the Auditing Entry dialog box (similar to the one shown here), select the types of access you want to audit.

For a printer, often the most useful information comes from auditing failures rather than successes. Logging printer successes generates a large number of relatively useless log entries.

You might want to do this for only a short time to identify users who should not have access to a printer. Printer failures, on the other hand, create few entries and can be used to quickly identify people who attempt to access a printer for which they do not have permission.

When Windows logs a printer event, such as successful printing or a deletion from the print queue, the event record is written to the System log. In contrast, security events, such as attempts to access a printer for which an account does not have permission, result in an event record being written to the Security log.

> **Tip**   **Monitor possible printer malfunctions and errors from the print queue**
> It is often useful to monitor unsuccessful print jobs and deletions from the print queue, because these events might indicate a problem with the printer or difficulty using the printer. These are printer operation events, however, not security events. On the Advanced tab of the Print Server Properties dialog box, select Log Spooler Information Events. (To display the Print Server Properties dialog box, in the Printers And Faxes folder, choose File, Server Properties.) For more information, see "Setting Server Properties," page 1033.

Seeing Who Has Shut Down Your Computer—And Why

Windows XP includes a feature that requires anyone who shuts down the computer to specify a reason for the shutdown and, optionally, to include a textual description of the reason. While not a security auditing feature like the other features described in this chapter, this capability, called Shutdown Event Tracker, can be useful in monitoring what's going on with your computer. (In fact, Shutdown Event Tracker is not intended as a security tool at all; rather, its purpose is to collect information for analysis and problem solving.) For example, information collected by Shutdown Event Tracker can help you to keep track of problematical programs and offer revealing insights into user behavior.

> **Note**   If you just want to know who shuts down your computer, configure the Audit Logon Events policy, as described earlier in this chapter. Use Shutdown Event Tracker only if you want to know *why* your computer gets shut down.

The other auditing tools described in this chapter monitor surreptitiously, and they record their findings in the Security log. Shutdown Event Tracker, on the other hand, is an in-your-face impediment that records data in the System log, another of the three logs that appear in Event Viewer. When Shutdown Event Tracker is enabled, choosing the Shut Down command on the Start menu displays a dialog box that's much larger than the normal Shut Down Windows dialog box, as shown in Figure 13-4.

Figure 13-4. Shutdown Event Tracker forces you to specify the reason you are shutting down the computer.

The OK button is unavailable—and therefore you can't complete the shutdown—until you select a reason in the Options box or type in the Comment box. The Options box offers the following choices for planned shutdowns:

- Other (Planned)
- Hardware: Maintenance (Planned)
- Hardware: Installation (Planned)
- Operating System: Upgrade (Planned)
- Operating System: Reconfiguration (Planned)
- Application: Maintenance (Planned)

By clearing the Planned check box, the following options become available for unplanned shutdowns:

- Other (Unplanned)
- Hardware: Maintenance (Unplanned)
- Hardware: Installation (Unplanned)
- Operating System: Upgrade (Unplanned)
- Operating System: Reconfiguration (Unplanned)
- Application: Maintenance (Unplanned)
- Application: Unresponsive
- Application: Unstable

Regardless of your selection, you can add a descriptive comment. A comment is required if you select Other in the Options box.

Note Shutdown Event Tracker is effective only if your computer is configured to use the classic logon—not the Welcome screen. (For information about classic logon vs. Welcome screen, see "Controlling How Users Log On," page 239.)

You'll find a record for each shutdown in the System log. To find them quickly, filter for USER32 as the Event Source and 1074 as the Event ID. (For more information, see "Filtering the Log Display," page 1272.)

To enable Shutdown Event Tracker, follow these steps:

1   Use a registry editor to open the HKLM\Software\Microsoft\Windows\CurrentVersion\Reliability key.

2   If one doesn't exist already, create a DWORD value named ShutdownReasonUI.

3   Set the ShutdownReasonUI value to 1. (Setting it to 0 restores the default behavior.)

Part 3

Customizing Windows

Tuning Up System Performance

Every Windows user has experienced sudden, unexplained slowdowns in system performance. Routine actions that normally take a few microseconds suddenly cause your computer to stop responding. Your hard disk chatters incessantly. You're forced to wait when switching between programs. Surprisingly, you don't need an engineering degree, an oscilloscope, or expensive third-party software to track down the cause of these performance problems and solve them.

With one quick keyboard combination, you can open the Windows Task Manager, which helps you monitor essential hardware resources, including your central processing unit (CPU), memory, and network adapter. You can quickly spot programs that are using excessive amounts of system resources and just as quickly determine whether a sudden slowdown is caused by too little memory. Sometimes the reason a system turns sluggish is because too many programs or services are running in the background. We'll show you how to trim the fat using some well-hidden Windows utilities.

To monitor performance over time, you can use the Performance Console, a sophisticated and extraordinarily customizable tool that gives you a more detailed look at your computer's overall performance. In this chapter, we'll provide detailed instructions to help you master this expert tool as well.

At Home with Windows XP

All of the tools for monitoring and adjusting system performance described in this chapter are available in both editions of Microsoft Windows XP. The System Configuration utility (Msconfig.exe) is also available in both editions. The Group Policy console (Gpedit.msc), which can be used to enable or disable particular startup applications, is not included with Windows XP Home Edition, however.

Reality Check

Among diehard tweakers, the urge to squeeze out every last bit of performance from a computer is irresistible. As a result, even a casual Web search turns up dozens of tips intended to help you improve performance in Windows XP. Many of these tips repeat information that we cover in this chapter, including the truism that the best way to tune up Windows is to throw hardware at it. Nothing speeds up a sluggish system like a healthy dose of extra RAM.

Unfortunately, many of the Windows-tuning tips we uncovered in our Web searches are of dubious value, and a few can actually hurt performance when indiscriminately applied. Some of these spurious tips are derived from techniques that worked with older Windows versions but are irrelevant with Windows XP; others are based on seemingly logical but erroneous extrapolations of how would-be experts think Windows XP works.

In this section, we debunk the most popular pieces of misinformation we've found. We also explain how to tell the difference between legitimate tuning techniques and those that have a negligible or even negative effect on performance.

Swap File Confusion

By far, the most common instances of performance-related misinformation revolve around the subject of page files, also known as *swap files*, *paging files*, or *virtual memory*. Virtual memory uses disk space to simulate physical RAM, allowing a Windows user to work beyond the limits of installed RAM. (We discuss this topic at length in the section "Monitoring Memory Usage," later in this chapter.) The following are some widely published myths about the proper configuration of virtual memory in Windows XP:

- **If your computer has a large amount of memory installed (1 GB or more), you should eliminate your swap file completely.** Although you can configure Windows so that it does not set aside any virtual memory, no reputable source has ever published benchmarks establishing any performance gains from doing so, and Windows XP simply wasn't designed to run without a swap file. If the goal is to conserve disk space, a more sensible strategy is to configure Windows to create a page file with a relatively small minimum size and monitor its usage over time to see how much virtual memory the operating system actually uses in daily operation.

- **Creating a swap file of a fixed size improves performance.** The logic behind this tip dates back to the earliest days of Windows. On 1990s-vintage hardware, dynamically resizing the swap file caused noticeable delays in system response and also resulted in excessive fragmentation. The memory management subsystems in Windows XP have been tuned to minimize the likelihood of performance problems.

- **Making a handful of registry tweaks can make virtual memory work more efficiently.** The values in question are found under HKLM\System\CurrentControlSet\Control\Session Manager\Memory Management. Manually adjusting the LargeSystem Cache value isn't necessary; you can tweak this setting using the System option in Control Panel, as we explain later in this chapter. Changing the DisablePagingExecutive setting from its default of 0 to 1 prevents Windows from paging user-mode and kernel-mode drivers and kernel-mode system code to disk. If you have a very large amount of memory (1 GB or more), modifying this setting may indeed provide some gains in performance.

For an excellent discussion of these issues, see the article by Microsoft MVP Alex Nichol, "Virtual Memory in Windows XP," at *http://www.aumha.org/win5/a/xpvm.htm*.

Prefetch Pros and Cons

Another widely circulated tip of dubious value recommends that Windows XP users clean out the Prefetch folder and consider disabling the Prefetch function. Some sites even provide links to utilities that automate these functions. We discuss the Prefetch feature in the section "Advanced System Tweaks," at the end of this chapter. To summarize briefly: Prefetch performs a valuable function by monitoring Windows as it starts up and similarly observing programs as they load. The Prefetch folder contains a record of all the files loaded and, more importantly, the order in which to load page faults (the 4-KB segments of data and code that make up each of those files). Windows XP uses this information to speed up the boot process and to load programs more efficiently on subsequent occasions. The Windows Disk Defragmenter also uses these layouts to optimize the arrangement of program files on the disk.

Clearing out the Prefetch folder forces Windows to run programs the inefficient way, but only once, since it rebuilds the layout file the next time you run that program. Disabling the Prefetch function eliminates Windows' ability to optimize program loading. In either case, it's hard to find a logical reason why the tweak should result in a performance improvement. In fact, when we used a stopwatch to measure Windows boot times with and without Prefetch enabled, the results were indisputable: Having the Prefetch layout handy routinely improved startup times by nearly 40 percent.

Is it necessary to clear out the Prefetch cache occasionally to eliminate obsolete files and to minimize wasted disk space, as some Web sites claim? Hardly. A typical Prefetch folder uses 3–6 MB of disk space, and Windows flushes entries that are older than a few weeks. Our take? The developers responsible for the memory management subsystem of Windows XP did a remarkable job when they devised this feature. Don't turn it off.

Shutting Down Services

Our Web searches turned up several sites focusing on Windows XP services. One sensible piece of advice is to minimize the use of unnecessary background applications and system services. A few sites take this advice to an extreme, however, urging Windows users to shut down virtually all system services, including System Restore and Automatic Updates. We don't agree that the average Windows user should perform this sort of radical surgery on Windows. In less-than-expert hands, the Services console is a minefield; some Windows services can be safely disabled, but indiscriminately shutting down services is a prescription for trouble. That advice is doubly true for features designed to protect system reliability and security. In Appendix D, "Managing Services," we list all standard services and provide our recommended startup settings.

In fact, one element is consistently missing from virtually every collection of performance-related tips: a systematic effort to measure and document the effect of each such adjustment. In our experience, most performance problems in Windows XP are caused by resource bottlenecks: a shortage of RAM, a CPU that can't keep up with demanding tasks, or a hard disk that hasn't been defragmented. After you've dealt with those big issues, you might be interested in playing around with registry hacks and system settings that promise to squeeze a few percentage points of extra speed from your system. If so, we have one piece of advice: Keep a stopwatch handy, so you can see for yourself whether the end result is what you really intended.

Detecting Common Performance Bottlenecks

Most performance problems can be traced to a handful of common bottlenecks that boil down to the same basic problem: trying to do too much work with too few resources. Fortunately, Windows XP includes a wonderful utility that makes it easy to spot problems and in some cases fix them immediately. Veterans of Windows 2000 and Windows NT know the Windows Task Manager well; if you're accustomed to the bare-bones Task Manager from Windows 95, Windows 98, or Windows Me, you'll be impressed with the greatly expanded capabilities in the Windows XP version.

Note One performance problem that affects Windows 95/98/Me users is not found in any of the editions of Windows XP. After upgrading, you no longer need to worry about system resource limitations caused by the infamous 64-KB User and GDI heaps in those Windows versions. Windows XP is immune from the crashes and forced reboots that result when individual programs drain system resources. With enough memory, you'll find that you can run multiple applications safely and reliably, without holding your breath in fear that opening one more window will cause the system to lock up.

The Windows Task Manager provides a continuously updated display of exactly what's going on with your system's key internal resources. You can see at a glance which applications and processes are running, along with information about how much memory and what percentage of the CPU each process is using. (We discuss these essential capabilities later in this chapter, in "Managing Programs and Processes," page 418.) You can keep tabs on your network connection to determine whether your network adapter is a bottleneck. And if you're willing to customize the Task Manager, you can dig into a wealth of esoteric performance indicators as well, some of which can be extremely useful in helping you find and fix performance problems.

Tip **Match programs with processes**

Process is the technical term for any program code that runs in its own address space. In Windows Task Manager, the Processes list includes applications that you start from the All Programs menu, as well as subsystems and services that are managed by the operating system. To match a running program with the specific process it's using, right-click the program name on the Applications tab of Windows Task Manager and then choose Go To Process.

If you're using the Welcome screen to log on to Windows, you can open the Windows Task Manager at any time by pressing Ctrl+Alt+Delete. If you're not using the Welcome screen or if you're joined to a Windows domain, press Ctrl+Alt+Delete and then click the Task Manager button in the Windows Security dialog box. And regardless of your system configuration, you can always go directly to Task Manager by pressing Ctrl+Shift+Esc.

As Figure 14-1 shows, Windows Task Manager is a multitabbed dialog box. The Applications, Processes, and Performance tabs are visible on all Windows XP systems. The Networking tab is visible only if the computer is configured with a network adapter, and the Users tab is shown only if Fast User Switching is enabled. A status bar at the bottom of the window, visible on all tabs, displays the number of processes that are currently running, the percentage of your CPU's processing capacity that's currently in use, and some information about your system's current memory usage.

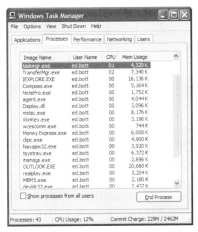

Figure 14-1. Each entry on the Processes tab of Windows Task Manager provides useful details about memory and CPU usage for that process.

Troubleshooting

Windows Task Manager is missing its menus.

If Windows Task Manager mysteriously appears without its title bar, menu bar, tabs, and status bar, don't be alarmed. You inadvertently double-clicked in the Task Manager window and switched to this stripped-down interface. It's not a bug; it's a feature, designed to give you a clearer, less cluttered picture of system information. To toggle between this resizable window and the normal view, double-click anywhere except within the list box that displays the names of programs and processes.

The Performance tab, shown in Figure 14-2, provides four graphs and some tabular data. The CPU Usage and PF Usage graphs display the percentage of your CPU's processing capacity and the amount of virtual memory (page file) capacity that your system has reserved for future use as of the most recent update of Windows Task Manager. The CPU Usage History and Page File Usage History line graphs show the same performance measures over time. (For more details about page file usage, see "Making the Most of Virtual Memory," page 415.)

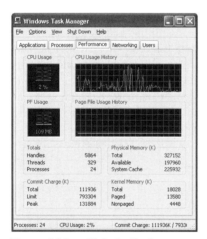

Figure 14-2. Click the Performance tab to get a big-picture view of CPU, memory, and page file usage.

How much history the two history graphs record depends on Windows Task Manager's current update speed and the width of its window. Each vertical gridline in these graphs represents six update intervals. If you widen the window, you see more history. By default, Windows Task Manager updates its data once every two seconds. To increase the frequency to twice per second, in Task Manager, click View, choose Update Speed, and then change the frequency from Normal to High. To reduce the update frequency to once every four seconds, choose the Low setting from the Update Speed menu. If you want to study the graph of the most recent history, you can stop all updates by clicking View and choosing Update Speed,

Paused. At any frequency, you can force an immediate update by pressing F5 (the system-wide shortcut for the Refresh command) or choosing Refresh Now from the View menu.

On the vertical axis, all four graphs are scaled from 0 to 100 percent. Increasing the height of the window expands the axis without changing its end points, making the graphs easier to read.

> **Tip**   **Get a close-up of CPU usage**
>
> Double-clicking anywhere within the Performance tab—on the graphs themselves or the surrounding matter—removes everything but the CPU Usage and CPU Usage History graphs, allowing you to see more detail without expanding the window. With the window thus altered, you can resize the display and keep it on top as you work. To toggle to the Processes or Applications tab, press Ctrl+Tab. To return Windows Task Manager to its normal display, double-click again.

The remainder of the Performance tab provides some "snapshot" statistics about the current state of your computer's memory; these are discussed in the following section.

> **Caution**   The numbers you see throughout Windows Task Manager can provide useful general information about your system, but they can also mislead you. In some cases, the numbers are technically accurate, but don't actually provide meaningful information that you can use to solve performance problems. For instance, despite its name, the Page File Usage History graph actually indicates when space in the page file was committed or reserved, not when Windows began swapping data between physical memory and your hard disk. If you're planning to make changes on the basis of numbers you see here, be sure to test the effect of those changes carefully to ensure that the results are as you expect.

Monitoring Memory Usage

The most common reason a Windows system slows down is that you've filled every bit of physical memory. When this happens, Windows begins a process called *paging*—that is, moving blocks of program code and data files (each block is called a *page*) out of memory and onto disk. A modest amount of paging is perfectly normal, but excessive paging can take a terrible toll on overall system performance. This type of performance problem is especially noticeable when trying to switch between several memory-intensive programs on a computer that doesn't have enough RAM to keep up. The result is nearly nonstop "thrashing" as the disk tries in vain to shuffle data to and from the much faster memory chips.

For a quick snapshot of current memory usage, open Windows Task Manager and examine the bottom of any tab. The statistic at the far right, Commit Charge, lists two numbers, presented as a fraction. The first number (the numerator) represents your current *total commit charge*—the total amount of physical and virtual memory in use by all running processes. (*Virtual memory* is memory backed by your page file.) The second number (the denominator) represents your total available memory, physical and virtual. By itself, this number will

Chapter 14

only tell you whether you're about to completely run out of memory—in other words, when commit charge is nearly equal to available memory.

To uncover more details about your current memory usage, click the Performance tab and look at the series of tables in the bottom half of the dialog box. Beware: The numbers and labels here can be absolutely baffling and can steer even an expert Windows user into the wrong conclusions. Table 14-1 explains how you can use this data to answer common questions about memory usage.

Table 14-1. Decoding Task Manager Performance Data

Value	What It Means
Totals	
Handles	Unique identifiers that allow a program to access system resources such as files, registry keys, fonts, and bitmaps. In theory, this value can be used to identify programs that fail to restore memory properly after being shut down. In practice, this information is mostly useful to developers who are using specialized debugging tools to troubleshoot memory leaks in applications.
Threads	Objects within processes that run program instructions. Multithreaded programs can perform multiple operations simultaneously. As with handles, this value is generally most useful to a software developer while testing an application for memory leaks.
Processes	Total number of processes (programs, subsystems, and services) running for all users of the local computer. (This number is also displayed in the lower left corner of the Task Manager window.)
Commit Charge (K)	
Total	Total amount of physical and virtual memory currently in use by the operating system and all programs, measured in kilobytes. (This value is also displayed in the lower right corner of the Task Manager window.) Commit charge increases as you open additional programs and data files and should decrease when you close programs and files.
Limit	Total amount of physical and virtual memory available for use by the operating system and all programs, measured in kilobytes. (This value is also displayed in the lower right corner of the Task Manager window.) To raise this limit, add more RAM or increase the size of the page file, or both.

Table 14-1. Decoding Task Manager Performance Data

Value	What It Means
Peak	Highest amount of memory that has been in use during the current session, measured in kilobytes. If this value regularly approaches or equals the Limit value, your system might need more memory.
Physical Memory (K)	
Total	Total amount of physical RAM installed in the computer, measured in kilobytes. Divide by 1024 to convert to megabytes.
Available	Total amount of physical RAM, measured in kilobytes, that Windows will make available to programs before swapping data to virtual memory. Windows will always try to reserve some physical RAM for additional applications, even when the total commit charge exceeds the total amount of physical RAM installed.
System Cache	Total amount of physical RAM, measured in kilobytes, used to store recently accessed programs and data. Windows will try to use as much physical RAM as possible for this function, but will release RAM from the file system cache when needed for programs and operating system functions.
Kernel Memory (K)	
Total	Total amount of RAM, measured in kilobytes, used by core components of the operating system, including device drivers.
Paged	The total amount of memory, measured in kilobytes, used by Windows core components and mapped to pages in virtual memory.
Nonpaged	Amount of operating system and driver code, measured in kilobytes, that must be run in physical memory and cannot be paged to virtual memory.

If your system starts to slow down and you suspect that memory is the issue, a quick scan of the Performance tab can provide important clues. If Total Commit Charge is higher than Total Physical Memory, for instance, Windows must swap pages between fast RAM chips and the much slower virtual memory in the page file, causing the system to slow down. Figure 14-3 shows a computer that barely meets Microsoft's minimum RAM requirements; its performance is under severe stress as the numbers here clearly illustrate.

Chapter 14

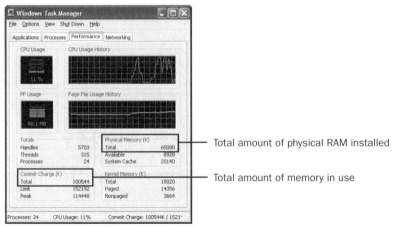

Total amount of physical RAM installed

Total amount of memory in use

Figure 14-3. When Total Commit Charge is higher than Total Physical Memory, the result is excessive paging—and reduced performance.

In this example, the Total Commit Charge is 100,544 KB (roughly 98 MB), well over the computer's physical RAM of 65,080 KB (64 MB). In this configuration, a significant percentage of the programs and data currently used by the system are running from slow, disk-based virtual memory, and excessive paging will occur each time the user switches between running programs or attempts to load a new data file.

Now look at Figure 14-4, which depicts a system that is loaded with 1 GB of physical RAM— roughly eight times the minimum amount of memory that Microsoft recommends for satisfactory use of Windows XP.

Despite running 35 separate processes, including a number of demanding Microsoft Office applications, this computer is currently using less than a quarter of its Total Physical Memory for programs and data, as evidenced by the Total Commit Charge of 238,952 KB. The excess RAM is not going to waste, however, because Windows has devoted a huge portion of it to caching previously loaded programs and data files. The result is a tremendous boost in apparent speed in everyday use. Each time you start a program or load a file, Windows first checks to see whether that file is already stored in the cache; if the file is there, it loads in a fraction of the time it would take to access the file from the hard disk. An operation that might take eight to ten seconds when running from the hard disk can complete in two to three seconds if the necessary files are already in the cache.

Even if you're not experiencing noticeable performance slowdowns, it's a good idea to check memory usage occasionally. Pay special attention to the Commit Charge Peak setting, which tells you the maximum amount of memory you've used during the current Windows session. If this number is consistently higher than the amount of physical RAM installed on your machine, your system cache is being starved of the physical memory it needs to run properly.

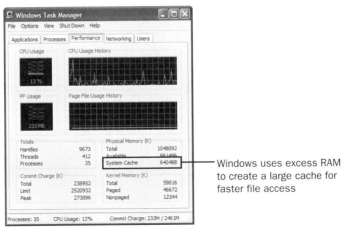

Windows uses excess RAM to create a large cache for faster file access

Figure 14-4. Because this computer has far more physical RAM than it typically uses, Windows is able to allocate a huge amount of memory to the system cache.

Inside Out

Add RAM for better performance

If you use applications that routinely load and reload extremely large data files, such as video editing programs, computer-aided drafting (CAD) tools, or database management software, you stand to get an especially large boost from the Windows file cache. For systems running this type of software, there's no such thing as too much RAM. The improvement in performance from a simple RAM upgrade can be breathtaking, especially on a computer whose CPU and hard disk are relatively slow.

Not surprisingly, the best cure for memory-related performance problems is usually to add more RAM. You can also delay the onset of paging by shutting down unneeded programs and services to free up memory. To identify the specific programs that are gobbling memory, open Windows Task Manager, click the Processes tab, and click the Mem Usage column heading twice to sort the list in descending order, so that processes using the most RAM appear at the top of the list, as shown in Figure 14-5.

This view of running programs and processes is especially useful when you're about to start a memory-intensive program on a system that is nearly out of physical RAM. By shutting down applications that are presently using more than their fair share of RAM, you can often reclaim enough memory to avoid the slowdown caused by excessive paging.

Chapter 14

Figure 14-5. Click any heading to sort by that column. In this example, clicking the Mem Usage heading twice lets you see which applications are memory hogs.

Avoiding CPU Overload

For most home and business computing tasks, the CPU chip is rarely a source of anything more than momentary slowdowns. A sudden burst of CPU activity might cause your computer to temporarily slow to a crawl, but it should normally snap back to life in a few seconds. The two most common CPU-related problems occur when a program consistently asks for more than your computer can deliver.

- **CPU-intensive software** Programs designed for transforming and editing digital media often make inordinate demands on the CPU. Programming tools, CAD software, and even some games can have the same effect, which is especially noticeable when you try to run other tasks in the background. With these types of programs, a faster CPU can make a noticeable difference.

- **Poorly written programs** In some cases, a program grabs onto the CPU with the tenacity of a puppy protecting its favorite chew toy and won't let go. As a result, the program uses a high percentage of the processor even when it's apparently doing nothing. If you spot a program that hogs the CPU in this fashion, contact the software developer to see if an updated version is available.

To see how much processor time each process is consuming at any given moment, open Windows Task Manager and click the Processes tab. Find the name of the program or service in the Image Name column and observe the value in the CPU column. (Select the row to highlight its values; doing so also makes it easier to keep track of a process when the list is sorted by CPU usage.) This value should change dynamically as a program works its way through tasks. Compressing a file using the popular WinZip program, for instance, might use a high percentage of your CPU's available cycles, but this should settle down to zero after the program has completed its work. This value is expressed as a percentage, where the total of all running processes always adds up to 100.

> **Note**   If the CPU column has to add up to 100, what happens when your system is doing little or nothing? Windows XP uses a "placeholder" process called System Idle Process that indicates when the CPU is not being fully utilized by existing processes. If this value isn't visible, select the Show Processes From All Users check box in the bottom left corner of the Processes tab.

If you display the Processes tab and sort the resulting list in descending order using the CPU column, you can quickly see how much of your CPU's processing power an individual task requires. Armed with this information, you can determine whether and when to multitask, and when you should allow a program to run on its own. Using Windows Media Player to copy a track from a CD to disk, for instance, can practically take over some CPUs, using 90 percent or more of available CPU cycles. If that's the case on your system, you'll get best results by avoiding any other background activity while the track is being copied.

> **Tip**   **Keep an eye on your CPU**
>
> It's difficult to know when your CPU is under stress until you discover it the hard way—by watching an application struggle to get started. Here's a trick that can give you a quick graphic display of current CPU usage.
>
> Open Windows Task Manager. From the Options menu, choose Hide When Minimized. Now minimize the Task Manager and watch as it takes an unobtrusive place in the notification area at the right of the taskbar (sometimes referred to as the system tray). This icon serves as a bar-style CPU graph, glowing bright green to indicate when the CPU is in use. To see the exact percentage of CPU usage at any given moment, let the mouse pointer rest over the Task Manager icon briefly until a ScreenTip appears. To restore the Task Manager, double-click the tray icon or press Ctrl+Alt+Delete.

Making the Most of Virtual Memory

As noted earlier, Windows does not live on RAM chips alone. In addition to using physical RAM to store programs and working data, Windows creates a hidden file on your primary hard disk and uses that file to swap pages of data out of physical memory when necessary. This page file is also sometimes referred to as a *swap file* or *paging file*. (In fact, different dialog boxes throughout Windows XP use different terms to refer to this file.) In the interest of convenience and consistency, we use the term *page file* throughout this book.

In a default Windows XP installation, Windows creates the page file in the root folder on the same drive that holds the Windows system files. The size of the page file is determined by the amount of RAM in your system: By default, the minimum size is 1.5 times the amount of physical RAM on your system, and the maximum size is three times the amount of physical RAM (twice the minimum). You can see the page file in a Windows Explorer window if you configure Windows to show hidden and system files; look for Pagefile.sys in the root of your system drive.

An option in the System Control Panel lets you see your current page file settings and adjust them as needed. You can change the size of the page file, move it to another drive, or split it over several physical drives to improve performance.

To view and change page file settings, follow these steps:

1 Log on using an account in the Administrators group and open System in Control Panel.

2 On the Advanced tab, click Settings in the Performance section.

3 In the Performance Options dialog box, click the Advanced tab.

4 Click Change to display the Virtual Memory dialog box, shown in Figure 14-6.

Figure 14-6.   If you're careful, tweaking the size of the page file can improve system performance.

5 Look in the Total Paging File Size For All Drives box to see the current settings for the page file.

6 Choose any drive in the list at the top of the dialog box to adjust the settings for that drive. The following options are available:

   ■ **Custom Size**   Enter a value in the Initial Size (MB) box to specify the starting size (in megabytes) for the Pagefile.sys on the selected drive. In the Maximum

Size (MB) box, enter a value (also in megabytes) that is at least as large as the initial size but is smaller than 4096 MB (4 GB).

- **System Managed Size** Select this option to instruct Windows XP to dynamically manage the size of the page file for the selected drive. This is the preferred option if you intend to override the default Windows settings.

- **No Paging File** Choose this option for any drive for which you don't want to create a page file. Make sure that a page file exists on at least one drive.

7 After making changes for an individual drive, click Set to record your changes.

8 Repeat steps 6 and 7 for other drives, as needed. Click OK to close the dialog box when you're finished.

How big should your page file be? A large page file is appropriate for systems with relatively low RAM configurations—on a system with 128 MB of RAM, for instance, a page file of 192 MB to 384 MB makes perfect sense. With higher RAM counts, overly large page files simply waste disk space. If you have 512 MB or more of RAM, your Total Commit Charge never approaches the total physical memory installed on your computer, and you're short of free disk space, you might want to set your page file to a fixed size, where the initial and maximum sizes are identical and are equal to the total amount of installed RAM. Be aware, however, that this option can result in out-of-memory error messages if your computing requirements change over time.

Based on experiences with previous versions, some Windows users advocate creating a fixed-size page file, where the initial size and maximum size are identical. In theory, this strategy should improve performance by preventing Windows from storing the page file in fragments on a single physical disk. In practice, however, the design of the page file is such that it tends to use large blocks of disk space; as a result the impact of fragmentation on the page file is minimal. You might notice a very small performance hit when Windows increases the size of the page file, but that's a one-time operation and won't affect everyday performance.

> **Tip** Play it safe with your page file
>
> On systems with 512 MB or more of physical memory, the large initial size of the page file can consume excessive amounts of disk space. On a system with 1 GB of RAM, for instance, the starting page file size is 1.5 GB, and under normal circumstances it's likely that this file will never be used. The best strategy for page-file management in this configuration is to set Initial Size (MB) to be relatively small—say, 512 MB—while setting a large Maximum Size (MB) so that Windows can increase the page file size if necessary. These settings keep disk space use in check but prevent the possibility of out-of-memory errors. If disk space is really tight, set the initial page file size to its minimum of 2 MB and set the maximum size to a value that is at least as large as the amount of installed memory. Use your computer normally for a few weeks and allow Windows to create a page file of the proper size. Use Task Manager to monitor the size of the page file and make certain that it's below the maximum size you specified.

Do you have two or more physical disks installed in your computer? Moving the page file to a fast drive that doesn't contain your Windows system files is a good idea. Using multiple page files split over two or more physical disks is an even better idea, because your disk controller can process multiple requests to read or write data concurrently. Don't make the mistake of creating two or more page files using multiple drive letters on a single physical disk, however. If you have a single hard disk that contains C, D, and E drives and you split the page file over two or more of these partitions, you might actually make your computer run more slowly than before. In that configuration, the magnetic heads on the physical disk have to do more work, loading pages from different portions of the same disk sequentially, rather than loading data from a single contiguous region of the hard disk.

If you decrease the size of either the minimum or maximum page file settings, or if you create a new page file on a drive, you must restart your computer to make the change effective. Increasing the size of a page file typically does not require that you restart your computer.

Caution   If you have plenty of physical memory installed in your computer, you might be tempted to completely disable your page file. Don't do it! By design, Windows XP requires a page file for a number of core functions, and several third-party programs will generate out-of-memory errors if you try to get rid of all virtual memory. Remember, Windows doesn't actually use the page file until it's needed, so you won't gain any performance advantage by tweaking your system in this fashion.

Windows XP is capable of dynamically increasing the size of your page file if needed. This option works only if you have selected the System Managed Size option or if you have specified a maximum size that is larger than the current size of the page file in the Performance Options dialog box.

For more details about improving performance of hard disks, see "Defragmenting Disks for Better Performance," page 1241.

Managing Programs and Processes

In Windows Task Manager, the Applications tab lists all running programs that have corresponding taskbar buttons. The entries you see here are approximately the same as the ones presented by the Windows Alt+Tab task switcher. As Figure 14-7 illustrates, each entry in the Task column consists of descriptive text and not a program name, as is found on the Processes tab. This text is identical to the text displayed in the program's title bar.

In its default Details view, the Applications tab includes a Status column. Most of the time, the entries in this list will read *Running*. If an application hangs or freezes for any reason, you see the words *Not Responding* in this column instead. In that case, you can attempt to shut down the misbehaving program by selecting its entry and clicking End Task. Don't be too quick on the trigger, however: Not Responding doesn't necessarily mean that an application

Tuning Up System Performance

is irredeemably lost. If the program in question is using every bit of resources to handle a difficult task, it might simply be too busy to communicate with Windows Task Manager. Before you decide to end the program, give it a chance to finish whatever it's doing. How long should you wait? That depends on the task. If the operation involves a large data file (performing a global search and replace in a large Microsoft Access database, for instance), it's appropriate to wait several minutes, especially if you can hear the hard disk chattering or see the disk activity light flickering. But if the task in question normally completes in a few seconds, you needn't wait more than a minute.

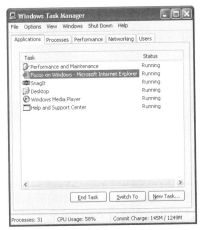

Figure 14-7. The Applications tab lists all running programs with a corresponding taskbar button; it doesn't include hidden programs and system processes.

Tip Be smart about shutdowns

When you shut down an application by clicking the End Task button on the Applications tab, the effect is the same as if you had chosen to shut down the program using its menus or by right-clicking its taskbar button and choosing Close. If the program can respond to the shutdown request, it should prompt you for confirmation or give you a chance to save open files, if necessary. By contrast, the End Process button on the Processes tab zaps a process immediately and irrevocably, closing any open files without giving you a chance to save them. Whenever possible, you should try the End Task option first and reserve the drastic End Process option for situations in which you have no alternative.

As noted earlier, the items listed on the Applications tab represent only a portion of the total number of programs and services running on a Windows computer at any given time. To see the entire list of running processes and gain access to a broader selection of tools for managing them, click the Processes tab.

In its default view, the Processes tab lists programs and services that are directly accessible to the user. Note in the example shown here that 30 processes are currently running (as evidenced by the value in the lower right corner of the dialog box). So why does the list display only a dozen entries?

The short list shows only processes that can be directly controlled by the user. If you select the Show Processes From All Users check box, the list expands to include all currently running processes. In this case shown below, the list of all users includes the built-in System, Network Service, and Local Service accounts. On a system where Fast User Switching is enabled, you may see processes "owned" by other logged-on users; in addition, on a computer running a server application such as Internet Information Services, you may see listings for accounts created and managed by the server, such as IWAM_*computername*.

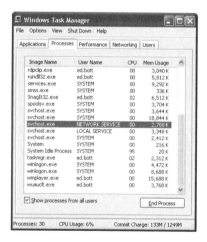

For each process, Windows Task Manager includes the following information by default: Image Name (the name of the process), User Name (which user started the process), CPU (the percentage of the CPU's capacity that the process is currently using), and Mem Usage (the amount of memory the process requires to perform its regular functions, sometimes referred to as its *working set*).

Inside Out

Interpret memory usage correctly

If you add up the figures in the Mem Usage column, you'll notice that the total does not correspond to any figure on the Performance tab. That's perfectly normal. In the curious language of software developers, the number to the right of each entry in the Processes list represents the sum of the memory pages in its current working set. Those pages might not have been used in days or weeks, but Windows doesn't remove them until it needs the pages for something else. In addition, some chunks of code are shareable. Two or more programs in the list might be using the same code, stored in the same physical location in memory; however, each entry in the Processes list will count that amount of memory separately. Use the numbers in the Mem Usage column as a general guideline, but don't assume that they're completely accurate.

Processes are sorted initially by the order in which they were started, with the most recent entries at the top. You can sort by any column by clicking the column heading (click a second time to reverse the sort order). As noted earlier, this is a good way to identify processes that are using more than their fair share of memory or CPU time.

With a modest amount of work, you can customize the Processes tab so that it shows far more information about each running process than the lean default view. To change the columns displayed on this tab, choose View, Select Columns, and then add or remove entries from the dialog box shown here.

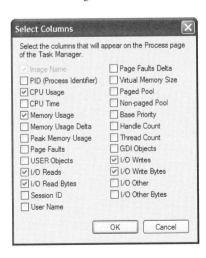

Most of these columns correspond to entries available in the Performance console (described later in this chapter, in "Advanced System Performance Measurement," page 431). After selecting the columns you want to see, click OK. You can then rearrange the display by dragging column headings to the left or right and dragging the border of any column heading to change its width. If necessary, resize the Task Manager window to see more data. Figure 14-8, for instance, shows the addition of four columns that measure disk reads and writes on a per-program basis. If your hard disk starts thrashing for no apparent reason, switching to a view like this one can help you quickly determine which program is responsible.

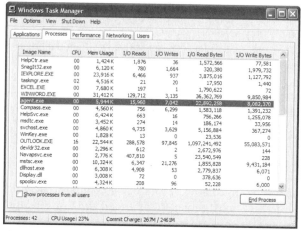

Figure 14-8. Customize the display of data on the Processes tab to identify other performance bottlenecks, such as disk input/output.

Giving Programs an Extra Dose of CPU

For each running process, Windows assigns a *base priority*—a ranking that determines how that process shares CPU cycles with other processes. By default, the base priority for most processes is Normal. A handful of essential system services run with a base priority of High, including Task Manager (Taskmgr.exe), the Windows Logon process (Winlogon.exe), and the Client/Server Runtime Subsystem (Csrss.exe). The High setting helps ensure that these processes take priority even when another program is hogging the CPU.

You can add the Base Priority column to the display of data on the Processes tab of Windows Task Manager. You can also change the base priority of any process by selecting the name of the process in the Processes tab, right-clicking, and choosing Set Priority. The six available settings appear on a submenu, as shown on the next page.

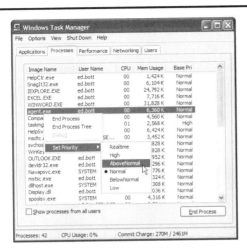

Because the base priority for any process is set by its program code, any changes you make using Windows Task Manager remain in effect for the current session only. If you always want to run an application at a priority level other than its default, you can create a shortcut that uses the Start command to start the application. Type **start /?** in a command prompt window to display the arguments that let you run a program at a priority level other than its default.

Like so many performance-related tweaks, this one should be used sparingly, and only when you're absolutely certain of the consequences. For the most part, we suggest that you avoid tinkering with this feature, because its headache-generating capability far outweighs its potential to solve problems. Consider using this option to assign a lower-than-normal priority to a CPU-hogging task that otherwise interrupts other essential activities, for example, but be certain to test the consequences carefully before employing this technique on a regular basis. Be extremely cautious when using the Realtime priority, which can allow a process to lock up a system so tightly that not even Task Manager can break in; the result can be data loss. This option is not recommended for normal use; in theory, it might be useful on a dedicated machine that runs only a single, critical CPU-intensive task.

On a dual-CPU system running Windows XP Professional, you have one additional option: You can assign a process that is normally shared by both processors to a single processor by right-clicking its entry in the Processes list and choosing Set Affinity from the shortcut menu. This command does not appear on the shortcut menu on single-processor systems. This option too should be used sparingly, and only when a particular task uses all available CPU cycles from both processors and interferes with performance of other programs.

Chapter 14

Configuring Programs That Run Automatically

Chapter 14

An extremely common performance problem occurs when Windows automatically loads an excessive number of programs at startup. The result, especially on systems with minimal memory, is unpleasant: Startup takes unnecessarily long, applications that you never use steal memory from programs you use frequently, and the page file gets more of a workout than it should. Some programs, such as antivirus utilities, need to start up automatically. But in most cases you're better served by running programs when you need them and closing them when they're not needed.

Overcrowded startups are most common on computer systems sold in retail outlets, where Windows XP is preinstalled, along with a heaping helping of applications. In some cases, the bundled programs are welcome; but a free software program is no bargain if it takes up memory and you never use it. After purchasing a new PC, it's always a good idea to look through the list of bundled software so that you can keep the programs you plan to use and discard the ones you don't want or need. In previous versions, you could spot the symptoms of an overstuffed system by looking at the long line of icons in the notification area at the right of the taskbar. Because Windows XP tidies these icons regularly, you might not realize that you have a problem on your system.

> For more details about customizing the taskbar and notification area, see "Removing Unneeded Icons from the Notification Area," page 494.

Tracking down programs that start automatically isn't as easy as it sounds. A program can be configured to run at startup by any of the following methods:

- **Startup folder (User)**   The %UserProfile%\Start Menu\Programs\Startup folder contains shortcuts that run when a specific user account logs on.

- **Startup folder (Common)**   Shortcuts in the %AllUsersProfile%\Start Menu\Programs\Startup folder run automatically whenever any user logs on.

- **Run key (Machine)**   Programs listed in the registry's HKLM\Software\ Microsoft\ Windows\CurrentVersion\Run key are available to all users.

- **Run key (User)**   Programs listed in the HKCU\Software\Microsoft\Windows\ CurrentVersion\Run registry key run when the current user logs on. A similar subkey, HKCU\Software\Microsoft\Windows NT\CurrentVersion\Windows\Run, may also be used.

- **Load value**   Programs listed in the Load value of the registry key HKCU\Software\ Microsoft\Windows NT\CurrentVersion\Windows run when any user logs on.

- **Scheduled Tasks folders**   You can use Scheduled Tasks to specify per-user tasks that run at startup. In addition, an administrator can set up startup tasks for your user account; by default such tasks are listed only in the administrator's Scheduled Tasks

Tuning Up System Performance

folder, not your own. Other users can also schedule tasks that run when you log on; these tasks run as background processes only.

● **Win.ini**   Programs written for 16-bit Windows versions may add commands to the Load= and Run= lines in the [Windows] section of this startup file located in %SystemRoot%, a legacy of the Windows 3.1 era.

● **RunOnce and RunOnceEx keys**   This group of registry keys identifies programs that run once and only once at startup. These keys may be assigned to a specific user account or to the machine.

  ▪ HKLM\Software\Microsoft\Windows\CurrentVersion\RunOnce

  ▪ HKLM\Software\Microsoft\Windows\CurrentVersion\RunOnceEx

  ▪ HKCU\Software\Microsoft\Windows\CurrentVersion\RunOnce

  ▪ HKCU\Software\Microsoft\Windows\CurrentVersion\RunOnceEx

● **RunServices and RunServicesOnce keys**   As the names suggest, these rarely used keys can control automatic startup of services. They may be assigned to a specific user account or to a computer.

● **Winlogon key**   The Winlogon key controls actions that occur when you log on to a computer running Windows XP. Most of these actions are under the control of the operating system, but you can also add custom actions here; if you set up automatic logon using the Windows XP version of Tweak UI, for instance, your saved settings are stored here. The HKLM\SOFTWARE\Microsoft\Windows NT\CurrentVersion\ Winlogon\Userinit and HKLM\SOFTWARE\Microsoft\Windows NT\CurrentVersion\ Winlogon\Shell subkeys can automatically launch programs.

● **Group Policy**   The Group Policy console includes two policies called Run These Programs At User Logon that specify a list of programs to be run whenever any user logs on. (For more information, see "Using Policies to Control Startup Applications," page 428.)

● **Policies\Explorer\Run keys**   Using policies to specify startup programs, as described in the previous paragraph, creates corresponding values in either of two registry keys: HKLM\Software\Microsoft\Windows\CurrentVersion\Policies\Explorer\Run or HKCU\Software\Microsoft\Windows\CurrentVersion\Policies\Explorer\Run. It is possible for a legitimate program or rogue process to create or modify these registry values directly—that is, without using the Group Policy object. Note that disabling the Run These Programs At User Logon policies in Group Policy Editor does not prevent Windows from launching the items listed in the Policies\Explorer\Run registry keys.

● **BootExecute value**   By default, the multi-string BootExecute value of the registry key HKLM\System\CurrentControlSet\Control\Session Manager is set to *autocheck autochk *. This value causes Windows, at startup, to check the file-system integrity of your hard disks if your system has been shut down abnormally. It is possible for other programs or processes to add themselves to this registry value. (Note: Microsoft warns

Chapter 14

against deleting the default BootExecute value. For information about what to do if your system hangs while Autocheck is running, see Microsoft Knowledge Base article 151376, "How to Disable Autochk If It Stops Responding During Reboot.")

- **Shell service objects** Windows loads a number of helper dynamic-link libraries (DLLs) to add capabilities to the Windows shell. The list of authorized objects includes a DLL to create the CD Burning folder, for instance, as well as another that permits Internet Explorer to check Web sites for updates. Writers of viruses and Trojan horse programs have also discovered the HKLM\SOFTWARE\Microsoft\Windows\CurrentVersion\ShellServiceObjectDelayLoad key, however, and some have used this location to surreptitiously start up unauthorized software.

- **Logon scripts** Logon scripts, which run automatically at startup, can open other programs. Logon scripts are specified in Group Policy in Computer Configuration\Windows Settings\Scripts and User Configuration\Windows Settings\Scripts (Logon/Logoff).

Windows XP includes a System Configuration Utility, Msconfig.exe, which allows you to see most of the programs that run at startup. Although it resembles the Windows 98/Me utility of the same name, it adds important features not found in those operating systems. For anyone upgrading to Windows XP from Windows 2000, this utility is a completely new addition. To start the System Configuration Utility, type **msconfig** in the Run dialog box and press Enter.

> **Note** Neither the System Configuration Utility nor either of the third-party startup managers recommended later in this section recognizes startup applications specified via the Group Policy console. (See "Using Policies to Control Startup Applications," page 428.)

Figure 14-9 shows the System Configuration Utility's Startup tab, which lists each startup item, the name and full path of the command used to start that item, and the location of the startup entry.

The Startup tab of the System Configuration Utility is intended for use as a troubleshooting tool (it's not intended to be a full-time startup manager). By clicking Disable All, you can clear every check box in the list, preventing Windows from starting any programs automatically at startup; then, through an iterative process of restoring one or two programs at a time to the list, you can restart programs and see which one is causing a particular problem.

To test whether it's safe to remove a single program from the list of those that start automatically with Windows, clear the check box to the left of the program's name on the System Configuration Utility's Startup tab and restart. After verifying that your system works properly without that program starting automatically, you can safely remove it, following these guidelines:

- **Look first for an option in the program itself** Most programs that start automatically allow you to change this behavior by clearing a check box in an Options or Preferences dialog box. It might take some digging around, but this is always the preferred option.

- **Remove the program shortcut from the Startup folder** Be sure to look in the Startup folder for your profile and the corresponding folder in the All Users profile. This option won't work if the auto-start option is set in the registry. You can move the shortcut to another location if you think you might want to restore it later.

- **As a last resort, edit the registry manually** This technique is messy, risky, and not always successful; some particularly persistent programs will restore the startup values in the registry the next time you run the program.

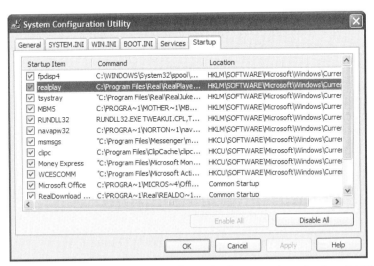

Figure 14-9. To stop a program from starting up automatically, clear the check box next to its entry.

Tip Get help managing the startup process

Although the System Configuration Utility is a priceless troubleshooting tool, it lacks a few features. For instance, although you can disable a shortcut or registry entry using the System Configuration Utility, this utility won't allow you to permanently remove entries from your startup configuration or to choose from a menu of startup configurations each time you begin working with Windows. Fortunately, a quick search on the Web can help you find several useful free or low-cost alternatives. Our favorite is Startup Control Panel, written by Mike Lin and available at *http://www.mlin.net/StartupCPL.shtml*. An alternative program that we recommended in previous editions of this book is Startup Cop, written by Neil J. Rubenking for PC Magazine. That program is no longer available; its replacement, Startup Cop Pro, is available only with a paid subscription to the PCMag.com Utility Library at *http://www.pcmag.com/utilities*.

If you would prefer to use an automated tool to uncover all automatically starting programs, try AutoRuns, a freeware utility created by the good folks at Sysinternals and available at *http://www.sysinternals.com/ntw2k/source/misc.shtml#autoruns*. For a meticulously organized, searchable list that explains the source and purpose of many common startup programs, visit Paul Collins' Start-Up Applications page at *http://www.sysinfo.org/startupinfo.php*.

No matter how you choose to control programs that auto-start, resist the temptation to use the System Configuration Utility as a permanent startup manager. Doing so impairs its ability to work effectively as a troubleshooting tool; if you experience a startup problem, you'll have to keep careful records to determine which programs have been disabled for troubleshooting purposes and which should be permanently shut down. In addition, some particularly persistent programs actually restore their auto-start entries to the Registry when you restart, overriding your startup choices. Finally, using the System Configuration Utility slows down startup times by causing the dialog box shown here to appear each time you start your computer; after you click OK, the System Configuration Utility opens with the Selective Startup option selected.

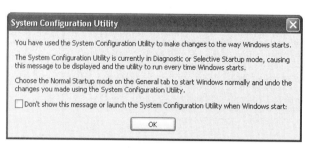

If you used the System Configuration Utility for troubleshooting and you've successfully resolved the issue you were testing, choose the Normal Startup option on the General tab and click OK to close the utility. The next time you start your computer, it will run through its complete startup routine and all the options you cleared will be enabled again.

If you insist on using the System Configuration Utility as a startup manager—something we strongly advise against—disable the warning dialog box to avoid accidentally restoring the full startup configuration. After restarting your computer, select the Don't Show This Message Or Launch The System Configuration Utility When Windows Starts check box and then click OK. The startup options you disabled using the System Configuration Utility remain disabled until you restore them. If you open the System Configuration Utility without making changes, you must click Cancel to close it, or it will prompt you to restart your computer.

Using Policies to Control Startup Applications

The Group Policy console (Gpedit.msc) includes three policies that affect startup applications (and documents):

- Run These Programs At User Logon
- Do Not Process The Run Once List
- Do Not Process The Legacy Run List

Tuning Up System Performance

Each of the above policies appears in two places in Group Policy:

- Computer Configuration\Administrative Templates\System\Logon
- User Configuration\Administrative Templates\System\Logon

Changes at either node affect all users of the current computer. If startup programs are specified for the Run These Programs At User Logon policy in both nodes, all such programs are run at startup—the Computer Configuration programs first, followed by the User Configuration programs. If policy settings at the two nodes conflict, the Computer Configuration settings take priority. To view or modify any of these policy settings, log on as a member of the Administrators group and run Gpedit.msc. Note that the Group Policy console is not available in Windows XP Home Edition.

For more information about Group Policy, see Appendix F, "Group Policy."

Run These Programs At User Logon

This policy lets you specify a list of startup applications. To implement the policy, in the details pane of the Group Policy console, double-click Run These Programs At User Logon Then select Enabled, click Show, and click Add. In the Add Item dialog box, type the name of an executable, or a document associated with an executable. If necessary, specify the complete path of the item, so that Windows can find it at startup. (If you're not sure whether the full path is necessary, try using the Start menu's Run command to run the item. If the Run command requires the path, Group Policy requires it as well.)

Do Not Process The Run Once List

Enabling this policy prevents Windows from processing the contents of HKLM\SOFTWARE\Microsoft\Windows\CurrentVersion\RunOnce. Windows includes the policy as a security measure. If you're concerned that a virus or Trojan horse might use the RunOnce key to launch some malicious code on your system, enable the policy. Be aware, though, that many legitimate programs rely on this key to complete their setup routines.

Do Not Process The Legacy Run List

What Group Policy calls the "legacy run list" is the list of programs launched at startup via the registry keys HKLM\SOFTWARE\Microsoft\Windows\CurrentVersion\Run and HKCU\SOFTWARE\Microsoft\Windows\CurrentVersion\Run. Like the policy described in the previous paragraph, this one appears to be included as a security measure. If you're concerned about the possibility that a rogue application might infiltrate your system via one of these registry keys, enable the policy. Be aware, though, that many legitimate programs—virus checkers, for example—rely on one of these registry keys for startup launch. If you

Chapter 14

decide to enable the policy, you will need to find another way to launch such programs. Startup Control Panel, described earlier in this section (see the Tip "Get Help Managing the Startup Process," page 427) provides an easy way to move startup programs from registry keys to your Startup folder. Simply right-click an item in Startup Control Panel, choose Send To, and then choose either Startup (Common) or Startup (User).

Controlling Services at Startup

Services are software components that perform specific system functions, typically working closely with key operating system code and hardware. On a typical system running Windows XP Home Edition or Professional, 50 services, some consisting of multiple processes and others grouped under a single process, may be running at any given time. Services perform tasks as diverse as managing Plug and Play activities, monitoring hard disks, overseeing security accounts, and synchronizing the system clock with Internet-based time servers.

For more details about Windows XP services, see Appendix D, "Managing Services."

Some services are essential to the operation of Windows; others are optional and can safely be disabled to free up memory and other resources. The best way to manage services is via the Services console (Services.msc), which is also included as part of the Services and Applications node in the Computer Management console. The Services tab of the System Configuration Utility, shown in Figure 14-10, allows you to temporarily disable one or more services so that you can test how your system runs without that service.

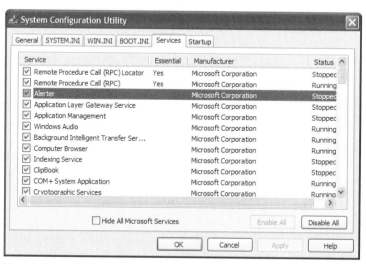

Figure 14-10.   As with the Startup tab, you can clear check boxes here to stop specific services from loading when Windows starts.

The four columns on the Services tab list the name of the service, whether the service is essential to the operation of Windows, the manufacturer of the service, and the current status (Running, Stopped, or Paused) of the service.

This tool is most appropriately used very sparingly. In particular, although the Services tab includes a Disable All button, this option is not recommended for anything except the most drastic troubleshooting.

Tip Look for third-party services

The Hide All Microsoft Services check box at the bottom of the Services tab serves an important function by highlighting added services (such as third-party disk defragmenters and antivirus programs) that are not part of the Windows operating system. If you're experiencing performance or stability problems, choose this option to see the short list of third-party services. By temporarily disabling one or more of these services (preferably through the Services console), you might be able to identify the cause of a problem quickly.

Advanced System Performance Measurement

As noted earlier, the Windows Task Manager provides a quick snapshot of system performance. A more robust system tool, the Performance console, allows you to monitor a much longer list of performance metrics than is available in Windows Task Manager. You can also log performance data to disk files or export it to programs like Microsoft Excel for detailed analysis, set "alerts" that cause Windows XP to take specified actions when performance thresholds are crossed, and monitor remote systems as well as your local machine.

Note The Performance console is a snap-in to Microsoft Management Console (MMC). For more information about MMC-based utilities, see Appendix C, "Using and Customizing Microsoft Management Console."

To begin using the Performance console, open the Administrative Tools option in Control Panel and then double-click the Performance icon. (Or, if you're comfortable at the command line, type **perfmon.msc** to open the console directly.)

The Performance console, shown in Figure 14-11, has two components: System Monitor and Performance Logs And Alerts. The latter is subdivided into Counter Logs, Trace Logs, and Alerts. System Monitor provides graphical displays and textual information about your system's current state and recent history. Performance Logs And Alerts lets you track your system over longer periods of time, recording data in disk files for subsequent analysis. You can use the Alerts section of Performance Logs And Alerts to indicate actions that your computer should take if performance measures meet specified thresholds. In this chapter, we focus exclusively on using the System Monitor component. For details on how to create and reuse system logs and set up alerts, see *Microsoft Windows XP Professional Resource Kit* (Microsoft Press, 2003).

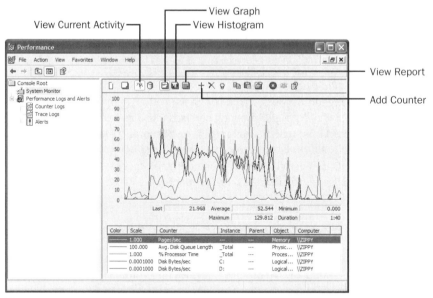

Figure 14-11. The System Monitor component of the Performance console can provide graphical information about your system's current and recent status.

The Performance console can track everything from relatively mundane but core activities, such as processor time and disk access, to exotic and highly technical measurements, such as the number of nonpaging read bytes per second handled by the network redirector. Whatever you decide to track, you add it to the Performance console in the form of an *object* and a *counter*:

- **Object** This is any portion of a computer's resources that can be assigned characteristics and manipulated as a single identifiable element. Typical objects on most computers include the processor, memory, page file, and physical and logical disks. The complete list of objects varies from one system to another, depending on what hardware is installed, what network protocols are used, and so on.

- **Counter** This tracks various types of information about the objects to which they are assigned. The available counters vary from object to object. For the Processor object, for example, the available counters include % Interrupt Time, % Processor Time, Interrupts/sec, and several others.

Some counters report instantaneous values. Others report the average of the current value and the value at the previous sampling interval. Still others report the difference between the current value and the previous value. If you're uncertain about what a particular counter represents, click Explain in the Add Counters dialog box, as explained in "Adding Counters."

Some objects can appear more than once in the Performance console; each such counter is considered a separate *instance*, allowing you to measure and compare the same type of performance using different software processes or hardware devices. The Process object has an instance for each process that's running. The PhysicalDisk object has an instance for each physical disk installed in the computer, and so on. Objects that have multiple instances typically include an instance that supplies information about the total of all the individual instances. So, for example, you could create multiple instances of the IO Data Bytes/sec counter, which measures all data that a process reads and writes from all sources (disk, network, and devices). In this example, the counter that tracks total IO Data for all running processes would give you an accurate measurement of overall system performance; by adding counters for each running process, you could see if a particular process is responsible for more than its fair share of this total.

Monitoring Current and Recent Information with System Monitor

In its Chart view, System Monitor shows the current state of one or more counters, along with a certain amount of very recent history. (At the default sampling interval of one second, the duration of a System Monitor chart is 1 minute and 40 seconds.) Alternative views show the current state of counters as a histogram or a textual report. To switch between Chart, Histogram, and Report views, use the View Graph, View Histogram, and View Report buttons on the toolbar (see Figure 14-11). Alternatively, right-click anywhere on the chart, choose Properties from the shortcut menu, and then select the view you want on the General tab of the System Monitor Properties dialog box.

Adding Counters

In any view, System Monitor's details pane is initially blank, waiting for you to select one or more of its myriad available performance measures. (A red vertical bar appears at the left side of the chart. If you do not see this bar, click the View Current Activity button on System Monitor's toolbar.) To make your selection, click the Add button on the toolbar or right-click the chart and choose Add Counters from the shortcut menu. The Add Counters dialog box, shown in Figure 14-12, appears.

To monitor your own computer, choose Use Local Computer Counters. To monitor a remote computer, choose Select Counters From Computer and then select the name of the computer you want to watch.

To specify what you want to monitor, begin by selecting an object from the Performance Object list. The remaining two lists in the dialog box then show the counters and instances available for the selected object. You can select counters and instances singly, or you can make multiple selections. (Hold down the Shift key to select adjacent items or the Ctrl key to select

433

items that are not adjacent.) You can also use the All Counters and All Instances option buttons to select all the items in a list.

If you're not sure what a particular counter counts (more than a remote possibility, given the number of available counters), select it in the counters list and then click Explain. A paragraph of descriptive prose will descend from the bottom of the dialog box.

After you've selected a combination of object, counter, and instance, you can click Add to add the combination to your chart, histogram, or report. Once you've finished adding counters, click Close to return to the Performance console. You can add as many counters as you like to your chart, histogram, or report. Note, however, that a chart with many counters can be difficult to read. If you need to track a large number of performance measures at one time, consider using multiple instances of the Performance console and putting some of the counters on the second or subsequent instance.

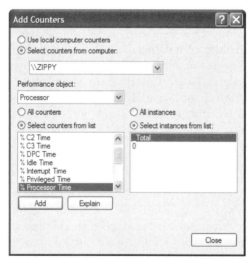

Figure 14-12. To tell System Monitor what you want to monitor, select an object, a counter, and an instance from the lists in this dialog box.

Changing the Chart's Display Characteristics

System Monitor's Chart and Histogram views plot all counters against a single vertical axis scaled, by default, from 0 to 100. A default scaling factor is applied to each counter so that counters with large values (such as PhysicalDisk(_Total)\Disk Read Bytes/sec, which measures the number of bytes per second read from all physical disks and might reach the high hundreds of thousands or more) can coexist meaningfully in a chart with low-value counters (such as PhysicalDisk(_Total)\Disk Reads/sec, which measures the number of read operations per second).

It's quite possible that, in order to make a chart intelligible, you will need to adjust its scale or the scaling factor for one or more counters (or both the scale and one or more scaling factors). In particular, you will need to make some kind of adjustment if System Monitor represents one or more of your counters as a horizontal line along the top edge of the chart. That's System Monitor's way of saying that your data, given its current scaling factor, exceeds the highest value of the vertical axis. The following five options represent adjustments that can make the visual display of performance data more useful:

Changing the Vertical Axis Scale

To change the scale, right-click the chart or histogram and choose Properties from the shortcut menu. On the Graph tab of the System Monitor Properties dialog box, type values in the Maximum and Minimum text boxes. Note that because all of System Monitor's many counters return positive values exclusively, you cannot set the minimum scale point to less than 0. On this tab, you can also add horizontal or vertical gridlines, supply a descriptive label for the vertical axis, and give the chart a title. These options are especially useful if you create special-purpose Performance consoles designed to focus on specific performance characteristics of a system.

Changing a Counter's Scaling Factor

To change the scaling factor for a counter, go to the Data tab of the System Monitor Properties dialog box, select the counter, and then adjust the value of the Scale field. The default scaling factor is called Default, which tells you nothing about the value that System Monitor has chosen to use. To see what the default value actually is, check the Scale column in the chart's legend. For help in deciding what scaling factor might be appropriate, check the Minimum and Maximum values in the Value bar—the numeric fields that appear directly below the chart, above the legend.

Note, however, that theValue bar displays information only about the counter that's currently selected in the legend. Therefore, when adjusting the scaling factor for a particular counter, it's a good idea to select it in the legend *before* you open the System Monitor Properties dialog box, shown here.

Changing Colors, Fonts, and Titles

Other options on the various tabs of the System Monitor Properties dialog box let you change colors and fonts for your chart or histogram, as well as for chart elements. You can also use Width, Color, and Style lists on the Data tab to modify the appearance of selected counters. Be aware, though, that the Style options are available only for the default line width. If you choose a nondefault width, you get the default (solid) line style.

Emphasizing a Particular Line

With several counters displayed on the same chart, it can sometimes be hard to tell which is which. If you double-click a line on the chart, System Monitor highlights the associated counter in the legend. But when lines are close together, it can be difficult to be sure that you've double-clicked the right one. The Highlight button (the light bulb) on the toolbar can help. When you click the Highlight tool (or use its keyboard shortcut, Ctrl+H), System Monitor displays the current chart line in a bold width and contrasting color. With highlighting on, you can move up and down through the legend and see at a glance which chart line belongs to which legend entry.

Changing the Sampling Interval

As noted earlier, System Monitor samples counters at one-second intervals by default and adjusts its display to show 100 sampling intervals. You can alter the sampling interval by going to the General tab of the System Monitor Properties dialog box. Integers from

1 to 3888000 (one second to 45 days) are accepted. To set up a console that shows page-file usage over a two-hour period, for instance, enter 72.

To freeze the current chart (stop sampling), clear the Sample Automatically Every check box on the General tab of the System Monitor Properties dialog box. Alternatively, click the Freeze Display button (the red "X") on the toolbar, or use its keyboard shortcut, Ctrl+F.

Saving and Reusing System Monitor Settings

To copy the current chart's properties to the Clipboard, press Ctrl+C, or click the Copy Properties button on System Monitor's toolbar. To paste properties from the Clipboard, press Ctrl+V, or use the Paste Counter List button. By using the Clipboard in this fashion, you can replicate a chart in a separate instance of System Monitor. Alternatively, you can use the Clipboard to restore the current state of a chart after making changes to it—provided, of course, that you haven't cleared the Clipboard in the meantime. Note that the Paste Counter List tool pastes all properties stored on the Clipboard, not just the counter list.

Advanced System Tweaks

A handful of advanced features in Windows XP allow you to tune performance settings to match your computing needs. In some cases, these options happen automatically, and knowing how to tune them can be useful.

Troubleshooting

Multiple instances of Svchost.exe appear in Task Manager.

This is perfectly normal. Service Host (Svchost.exe) is a core piece of Windows XP code that collects a number of lower-level system-critical services and runs them in a common environment. By gathering multiple functions together, this arrangement reduces boot time and system overhead and eliminates the need to run dozens of separate low-level services. Because different groups of services have different requirements in terms of system access and security, Windows XP creates a number of different groups. To see a list of which services are associated with each Svchost instance, open a Command Prompt window and type **tasklist /svc /fi "imagename eq svchost.exe"**.

Several interesting ways to adjust performance characteristics appear when you open System in Control Panel, click the Advanced tab, click Settings in the Performance section, and then click the Advanced tab. In the resulting Performance Options dialog box, shown in Figure 14-13, the two top options let you tune CPU and memory usage.

In the Processor Scheduling section, Programs is selected by default. If you multitask heavily and you're willing to sacrifice some zip in foreground program execution in exchange for faster background processing, select the Background Services option.

In the Memory Usage section, you can also shift the default settings, which are optimized for running programs. Choosing the System Cache option reserves a much larger percentage of available physical memory for use in the cache. This option is most useful if you use extremely data-intensive applications, such as video editing programs or large databases.

Note The System Cache option changes the setting of the LargeSystemCache value in HKLM\CurrentControlSet\Control\SessionManager\Memory Management from 0 (the default) to 1. Based on experience with Windows 2000, a number of Web sites recommend manually editing the registry to make this change; in Windows XP, however, using Control Panel is a safer option. You must restart your system to make this change effective.

To improve the speed of starting applications, Windows XP continually monitors files that are used when the computer starts and when you start applications. It then creates an index (in the %SystemRoot%\Prefetch folder) that lists segments of frequently used programs and the order they're loaded in. This prefetching process improves performance by allowing the operating system to quickly grab program files.

Figure 14-13. By default, the first two options here are optimized to help you run programs most effectively.

The prefetching code is even more effective when used in conjunction with the built-in Disk Defragmenter utility, Defrag.exe. Every three days, during idle times, this utility rearranges program code, moving it to the outside of the disk to make it more efficient when loading. To force Windows to perform this optimization without having to run a full defragmentation, use the Defrag.exe command with the –b switch; for instance, type **defrag c: -b**.

This command forces the command-line version of Defrag.exe to run, optimizing boot files and applications while leaving the rest of the drive undisturbed.

Chapter 14

Tweaking the Windows XP Interface

In the development of Microsoft Windows XP, the *user interface*—everything that connects you, the user, to the computer—underwent its first major overhaul since the introduction of Windows 95. The basic elements remain in place, and most of the tips and techniques you used in earlier versions of Windows work equally well in the bold new interface of Windows XP. But you'll also discover much that is new.

As in previous versions of Windows, the default configuration provided by the Setup program provides a decent color arrangement, a serviceable screen resolution, appropriately sized buttons and icons, and so on. But because one size does not fit all, Windows XP gives you many ways to tailor the appearance and behavior of your Start menu, desktop, taskbar, and other elements. In this chapter, we explore these choices and offer suggestions on how to set up your system so that it works best for *you*.

At Home with Windows XP

When it comes to customization of the user interface, Windows XP Professional and Windows XP Home Edition are essentially alike: what you can do in one, you can do in the other as well. A couple of tweaks involving the My Recent Documents menu (the Start menu section that provides shortcuts to your 15 most recently opened documents) require the use of the Group Policy snap-in (Gpedit.msc), which is not available in Windows XP Home Edition. You can work around that small limitation easily enough, however, by downloading the free Tweak UI utility from *http://www.microsoft.com/windowsxp/pro/downloads/ powertoys.asp*. A description of Tweak UI appears at the end of this chapter.

User profiles allow two or more users of a machine to establish individual settings that will be remembered and restored each time they log on. That means you're free to paint your workspace purple without offending someone else who also needs to use the same machine. Nearly all the customizing steps described in this chapter are profile-specific, which means that they affect only the current user account.

> **Note** The default interface described in this chapter is the one you see if you install a retail version of Windows XP. If Windows came preinstalled on your computer, the computer manufacturer might have provided a desktop and Start menu that's different from what you see here. The procedures for changing those defaults, however, should be the same on any computer.

A Road Map to the Windows XP User Interface

Figure 15-1 shows some of the elements of a typical Windows XP desktop. The first thing you'll notice, if you're familiar with earlier versions of Windows, is the distinct lack of clutter.

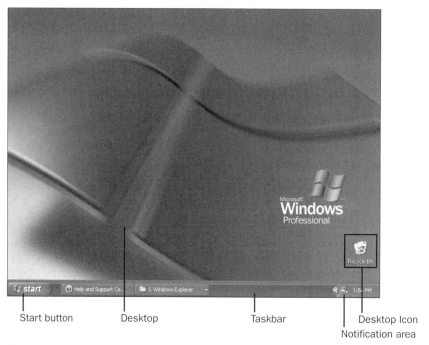

Start button   Desktop   Taskbar   Desktop Icon

Notification area

Figure 15-1. A default Windows XP desktop includes these elements.

- A default configuration of Windows XP has only one desktop icon, Recycle Bin, but you can add as many as you like. If you upgraded from an earlier version of Windows, your old desktop icons are still in place.

- The notification area (some people call it the system tray) displays only the icons you choose. Windows hides the icons you seldom use (but that some programs insist on putting there), displaying only the ones that you're actively using. The others are available with a single click.

- The taskbar doesn't squeeze in a button for every open window. Instead, when enough windows are open to fill the taskbar, Windows combines buttons from the same application (such as multiple Microsoft Word documents) into a single button that you can expand with a quick click.

- By default, the taskbar doesn't include the Quick Launch toolbar or any other toolbar.

Making It Easy to Start Your Favorite Programs

The purpose of an operating system is not to impress you with its snazzy looks or nifty animated menus and sounds. Although these adornments might enhance your experience, the real purpose is to run the programs you need for work or play. Windows offers a number of different methods for starting a program:

- Click the program's shortcut on the Start menu. This is, by far, the most common method and usually the easiest. (The following sections are devoted to tuning up the Start menu to work the way you work.)

- Click the program's icon on the Quick Launch toolbar or another toolbar. Toolbars are extremely handy, yet little understood. (For details, see "Using the Quick Launch Bar and Other Desktop Toolbars," page 456.)

- Double-click the program's icon on the desktop or in another folder.

- Type the name of the program's executable file in any of these locations:
  - The Run dialog box (click Start, Run or press the Windows logo key+R)
  - The Address toolbar (include the file's path)
  - The Address bar in Windows Explorer (include the file's path)

- Press the shortcut key assigned to the program shortcut.

> **Tip** Open a file to start a program
> You can also start a program by using any of the techniques listed here to open one of the program's documents. Instead of clicking the program's icon or typing its name, click a document icon or type the document's name to open the specified document in its associated program.

Setting the Appearance of the Start Menu

It all begins (and ends, as some wags are fond of pointing out) with the Start menu, which provides access to nearly everything you need to do in Windows. This invaluable command post appears at a single click or keystroke. (On newer keyboards, press the Windows logo key;

on any keyboard, press Ctrl+Esc.) Windows XP offers two different versions of the Start menu, as shown in Figures 15-2 and 15-3.

As these figures demonstrate, the layout of the new default Start menu is completely different from the more compact one that appeared in earlier versions of Windows (now called the classic Start menu). The default Start menu makes it easy to access items (such as My Computer) that were on the desktop in earlier versions. (Although the desktop seems like a convenient place to store such icons, they're usually covered by windows when you need them.) The default menu offers prominent shortcuts to your Web browser and e-mail program, along with shortcuts to your most-used programs.

To switch between the two Start menu options, right-click the Start button and choose Properties. The Taskbar And Start Menu Properties dialog box appears, as shown in Figure 15-4. Select either Start Menu or Classic Start Menu.

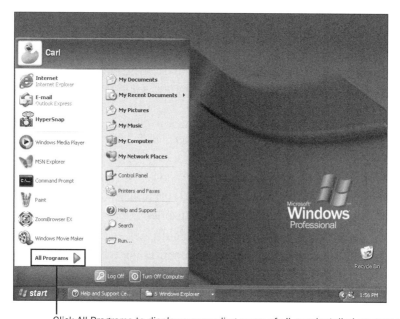

Click All Programs to display a cascading menu of all your installed programs

Figure 15-2. The default Start menu places frequently used programs on the left side and frequently used folders on the right side.

Tweaking the Windows XP Interface

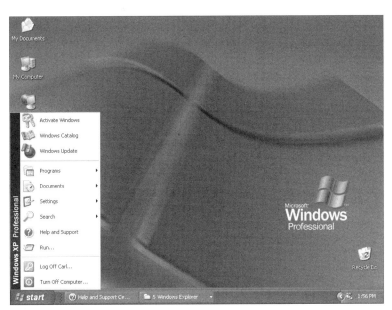

Figure 15-3. The classic Start menu is the same as the Start menu in earlier versions of Windows.

Figure 15-4. You can also reach the Taskbar And Start Menu Properties dialog box via Control Panel. (If you use Category view, you'll find Taskbar And Start Menu under Appearance And Themes.)

Chapter 15

> **Note** By default, when you switch to the classic Start menu, icons for My Documents, My Computer, My Network Places, and Internet Explorer appear on the desktop. And when you switch back, these icons disappear. Whichever menu you select, however, you can override this default and choose which icons you want on your desktop. For details, see "Controlling Desktop Icons," page 468. Tweak UI also provides check box control over the standard desktop icons. For more information, see "Customizing Windows XP with Tweak UI," page 501.

While you're in the Taskbar And Start Menu Properties dialog box, you might want to make one other appearance-related change that allows more items to fit on the menu:

- If you choose the default Start menu, click Customize and then, on the General tab of the Customize Start Menu dialog box, select Small Icons.

- If you choose Classic Start Menu, click Customize and then, in the Customize Classic Start Menu dialog box, select Show Small Icons In Start Menu (near the bottom of the Advanced Start Menu Options list).

With either menu version, choosing small icons changes only the appearance of the main Start menu. Cascading submenus always use small icons, and there's no option to display them with large icons.

This glimpse beyond the Customize button shows lots of other Start menu customization options, which is the topic of the following section.

> **Tip** Change your name and icon
> One advantage of the default Start menu over the classic Start menu is that the top of the menu shows at a glance who is currently logged on. You can change your user profile name and the icon that appears alongside it. (The same name and icon appear on the Welcome screen.) To change the name or icon, visit User Accounts in Control Panel. For more information, see "Changing Account Settings," page 234.

Controlling the Content of the Start Menu

Regardless of which Start menu you choose, much of the menu is customizable. You can add, delete, move, copy, sort, and rename most menu items. You can turn some into cascading menus, which allow you to navigate to a particular item of interest without even clicking; all you need to do is point at an item to open its submenu.

The default Start menu, shown in Figure 15-5, shows programs on its left side. Closer inspection shows that the left side is further divided into three areas:

- **Pinned items list** Items at the top of the menu always appear on the menu. You decide which programs you want here, and in which order.

- **Most frequently used programs list** Windows monitors which programs you use most often and adds them to this list automatically. Each program that is added knocks off a less-used program. Programs are listed in the order of their usage, with the most frequently accessed items at the top. You can control the number of items that appear here and you can remove items from this list, but you can't add items or change their order.

- **All Programs button**   This is the entry point to a traditional menu of all installed programs. The content that appears here is the same content you see when you click Programs on the classic Start menu, plus any items that appear at the top of the classic Start menu (above Programs). You're free to rearrange these links in whatever way works best for you.

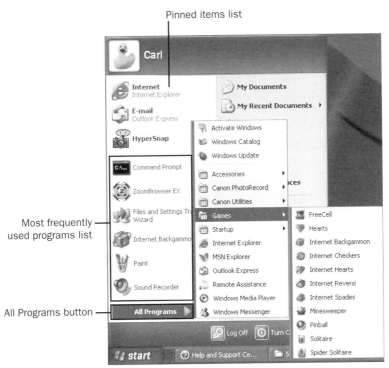

Figure 15-5. The menu that appears when you click All Programs includes items from the top of the classic Start menu as well as the classic menu's Programs menu.

> **Note** Items on the pinned items list and most frequently used programs list do not appear anywhere on the classic Start menu. A close replacement for the pinned items list, however, is the top of the Start menu, above the Programs folder. You can add any items you like to this part of the classic Start menu.

Adding an Item to the Menu

To add a program to the pinned items list, right-click it and choose Pin To Start Menu. You can right-click a program wherever it appears—on the Start menu, in Windows Explorer, or on the desktop. Alternatively, you can drag a program icon (or a document icon) to the Start button.

To add a program or document to any part of the All Programs menu, drag it there. If you have a shortcut on your desktop, for example, that you would also like to appear somewhere on the Start menu, simply click it, hold down the mouse button, and move your mouse pointer to the Start button. When the Start menu opens, after a moment's delay, you can drag the desktop shortcut to a location within the All Programs menu. As you move the mouse, a dark line shows where the new item will appear when you release the button.

> **Note** If you drag a shortcut to the Start button and release the mouse button before the Start menu opens, the new item will appear in the pinned items list. If you're using the classic Start menu, items you drop on the Start button appear at the top of the menu.

You can use the same technique to drag items from Windows Explorer windows to the Start menu. Windows leaves the dragged item in its original location and plants a copy on the Start menu. If the dragged item isn't a shortcut to begin with, Windows creates a shortcut to it on the Start menu. Thus, for example, you can drag a folder to the Start menu without changing the folder structure of your drive in any way; on the menu, Windows simply creates a pointer (a shortcut) to the folder.

> **Caution** Windows creates a shortcut only if you drag a file or folder to the pinned items list or the All Programs menu (or to the top of the Start menu or Programs menu if you're using the classic Start menu). Dragging a file or folder to one of the document links, such as My Documents or My Pictures, causes Windows to *move* the item to that folder instead of creating a shortcut. Just as you can when dragging items in Windows Explorer, you can determine what Windows will do by noticing the icon as you drag it: If it's going to create a shortcut, the mouse pointer includes a small boxed arrow.

> **Tip Remove the orange highlight from new program shortcuts**
> When you install a new program, by default, Windows highlights in orange the additions to your Start menu for a few days. This makes it easier to find the new items and makes you aware of added items that you might have otherwise overlooked. Some users find the highlights distracting, however. If you want to remove the highlights, open the Taskbar And Start Menu Properties dialog box. On the Start Menu tab, click Customize. Click the Advanced tab and clear the Highlight Newly Installed Programs check box.

If you're not sure how to get to a Windows Explorer window that displays the item you want on the Start menu, you can use the Search command to locate it—and then drag the item from the Search Results window to the menu. For example, suppose you want to put Notepad at the top of your Start menu, but you're not quite sure where Notepad lives. Open the Start menu and click Search. Tell Search to find Notepad, and when Notepad.exe appears in the Search Results pane, simply drag it to the Start button.

Controlling the Pinned Internet and E-Mail Items

By default, the Start menu includes two links in the pinned items list: one for your Web browser and one for your e-mail program. If you don't use these links, you can remove them in the same way that you remove other links: Right-click and choose Remove From This List.

To change the program that is started by each of these items or to restore either one if you removed it in error, follow these steps:

1 Right-click the Start button and choose Properties to open the Taskbar And Start Menu Properties dialog box.

2 On the Start Menu tab, click Customize to open the Customize Start Menu dialog box.

3 Under Show On Start Menu, select the check box for each item that you want to appear. Then select which of your installed Web browsers and e-mail programs you want the pinned item to start.

Deleting an Item from the Menu

To remove a program or document from the Start menu, follow these steps:

1 Click the Start button and then release the mouse button.

2 Right-click the item you want to delete.

3 For an item on the pinned items list or most frequently used programs list, choose Remove From This List from the shortcut menu. For an item in the All Programs menu, choose Delete from the shortcut menu and then click Yes in the Confirm File Delete or Confirm Shortcut Delete dialog box.

The shortcut menu that appears when you right-click a pinned item also includes an Unpin From Start Menu command. Choosing this command deletes the program from the pinned items list, but if it happens to be one of your most frequently used programs, it instantly reappears on the most frequently used programs list. To ensure that the program doesn't appear on either list, choose Remove From This List.

> **Note** Deleting a shortcut from the Start menu does not uninstall the program; it deletes only the shortcut to the program.

Moving or Copying a Menu Item

To move an item from one part of the Start menu to another, simply grab and drag it. Click the Start button, release the mouse button, move the mouse pointer to the item you want to move, and then click again and hold down the mouse button. Now move the mouse in the direction of the item's new destination. As you do, Windows draws a thick line to show where the item will land if you release the mouse button.

To copy an item to a new location, follow the same steps as for moving, but hold down the Ctrl key while you drag. A plus sign (+) next to the mouse pointer confirms that you're copying, not moving. Release the mouse button first, and then release the Ctrl key.

Troubleshooting

You can't drag items on the Start menu.

You might find that you can't drag items to, from, or within the Start menu; when you drag items over the Start menu, an "unavailable" symbol appears instead of a black line that indicates the destination. In this case, you need to enable the Start menu's drag-and-drop capability. To do that, right-click the Start button, choose Properties, and click Customize. If you're using the default Start menu, click the Advanced tab and then, in the Start Menu Items box, select Enable Dragging And Dropping. If you're using the classic Start menu, in the Advanced Start Menu Options box in the Customize Classic Start Menu dialog box, select Enable Dragging And Dropping.

Tweaking the Windows XP Interface

Dragging items from the left side of the default Start menu to the All Programs menu always copies the item; you don't need to hold down the Ctrl key. The same is true for items you drag from the All Programs menu to the pinned items list.

The drag-and-drop techniques that let you rearrange menu items also work for moving and copying items to off-menu locations. Thus, for example, if your menu gets crowded, you can move some items from the menu to your desktop, to a toolbar, or to a folder. In all cases, Windows creates a shortcut in the new location.

Sorting Menu Items

Windows lets you move or copy menu items to any location on the All Programs submenu, as described in the previous section. Although this allows you to place them in any order that suits you, you might prefer to revert to a more orderly approach. You can ask Windows to re-sort a single submenu in its default order: folders in alphabetical order, followed by menu items in alphabetical order.

Inside Out

Sort Your Menus Automatically

Even if you never change the Start menu order manually, your menu can soon become jumbled because new programs you install ordinarily place their shortcuts at the bottom of the menu. If you prefer to have your menus always sorted alphabetically, you can use a registry trick to force alphabetical sorts: Remove permissions to the registry key that controls menu order.

1 Open Registry Editor and select HKCU\Software\Microsoft\Windows\CurrentVersion\ Explorer\MenuOrder.

2 On the Edit menu, choose Permissions.

3 In the Permissions For MenuOrder dialog box, click Advanced.

4 In the Advanced Security Settings For MenuOrder dialog box, clear the Inherit From Parent check box.

5 In the Security dialog box that appears, click Copy.

6 Click OK to return to the Permissions For MenuOrder dialog box, and then clear the Full Control access control entry for your own account and for any security groups that you're a member of, leaving the Read access control entry in place.

Without Full Control permissions, Windows is prevented from rearranging menu items. Your programs remain in alphabetical order, even when new items are installed. The downside to this change is that you can no longer make your own ad hoc rearrangements, and any such arrangements you made previously are lost. To revert to default behavior, reinstate Full Control permissions, then log off and log on again.

Chapter 15

To sort a single submenu, follow these steps:

1 Click the Start button and then release the mouse button.

2 Move the mouse pointer to the submenu you want to sort.

3 Right-click an item on the submenu and choose Sort By Name from the shortcut menu.

If you use the classic Start menu, you can sort all submenus within the Programs submenu at once, as follows:

1 Right-click the Start button and choose Properties.

2 In the Taskbar And Start Menu Properties dialog box, on the Start Menu tab, click Customize.

3 In the Customize Classic Start Menu dialog box shown here, click Sort.

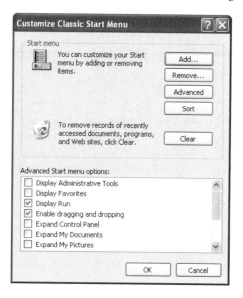

Note Windows maintains the sort order for the default Start menu and the classic Start menu separately. Therefore, changes you make to one Start menu—whether you change the order by dragging or sort the items with a sort command—do not appear if you switch to the other menu style. The sort orders for both menus are stored in the HKCU\Software\Microsoft\Windows\CurrentVersion\Explorer\MenuOrder registry key. The classic menu order is stored in the Start Menu subkey, and default menu order is stored in the Start Menu2 subkey.

Renaming a Menu Item

In earlier versions of Windows, it wasn't easy to rename an item on the Start menu. In Windows XP it is, thanks to an additional shortcut menu command. To rename a menu item, follow these steps:

1 Click the Start button and then release the mouse button.

2 Right-click the menu item you want to rename and choose Rename.

3 Edit the name (or type a new one) and then click OK.

Troubleshooting

No shortcut menu appears when you right-click.

When you right-click an item on the Start menu, a shortcut menu should appear. If instead the menu flashes and no shortcut menu appears, the Enable Dragging And Dropping check box has been cleared. Although it's not apparent from the name, this option enables shortcut menus as well as drag-and-drop capability. To enable the option, right-click the Start button, choose Properties, and then click Customize on the Start Menu tab of the Taskbar And Start Menu Properties dialog box. If you're using the default Start menu, click the Advanced tab and then, in the Start Menu Items box, select Enable Dragging And Dropping. If you're using the classic Start menu, the option appears in the Advanced Start Menu Options box in the Customize Classic Start Menu dialog box.

Managing the Most Frequently Used Programs List

The list of most frequently used programs —the items that appear on the default Start menu between the pinned items list and the All Programs link—is controlled by Windows. It keeps track of your program usage so that the programs you use most appear here automatically. The most frequently used programs list does not appear anywhere on the classic Start menu.

The most frequently used programs list includes only shortcuts to .exe files; other executable files you open do not appear, regardless of how often you run them. In addition, the following items are excluded by default (for more information, see Knowledge Base article 282066, "Frequently Used Programs Not Automatically Added to the Start Menu"):

- Programs listed in the AddRemoveApps value of the registry key HKLM\Software\ Microsoft\Windows\CurrentVersion\Explorer\FileAssociation. By default, the following items are excluded: Setup.exe, Install.exe, Isuninst.exe, Unwise.exe, Unwise32.exe, St5unst.exe, Rundll32.exe, Msoobe.exe, and Lnkstub.exe. By modifying this registry value, you can tailor this exclusion list to suit your needs.

- Programs whose HKCR\Applications*Appname* registry key include the string value NoStartPage. For example, the registry key HKCU\Applications\Explorer.exe includes the string value NoStartPage, so shortcuts to Explorer.exe never appear on the most frequently used programs list. By default, the items excluded are Explorer.exe,

Icwconn1.exe, Inoculan.exe, Mobsync.exe, Navwnt.exe, Realmon.exe, and Sndvol32.exe. You can add an item to this exclusion list by finding its HKCU\ Applications*Appname* key and adding the string value NoStartPage.

● Items whose shortcut names include any of the following text: Documentation, Help, Install, More Info, Readme, Read Me, Read First, Setup, Support, What's New, Remove. This list of exclusion strings is specified in the AddRemoveNames value of HKLM\ Software\Microsoft\Windows\CurrentVersion\Explorer\FileAssocation.

To specify the number of programs that appear on the most frequently used programs list, right-click the Start button, choose Properties, and click Customize on the Start menu tab of the Taskbar And Start Menu Properties dialog box. On the General tab of the Customize Start Menu dialog box, enter the value you want in the Number Of Programs On Start Menu box. You can specify any number from 0 (if you hate the feature) through 30 (if you have a gigantic screen, high resolution, and lots of different programs).

Using Windows Explorer to Modify the All Programs Menu

The All Programs submenu of the Start menu is merely a collection of shortcuts stored on your computer. Therefore, you can use Windows Explorer to add, delete, move, and copy items in the All Programs menu instead of using the procedures described in the preceding sections. (You can't use Windows Explorer to establish the sort order, however. That information is stored in the registry, plus the sort order is best modified by working directly within the Start menu.)

The All Programs submenu contains the links stored in two different folders (along with all their subfolders, which create the cascading menu structure): %UserProfile%\Start Menu and %AllUsersProfile%\Start Menu. The items in your own user profile appear only when you're logged on, whereas those in the All Users profile appear no matter who is logged on. Items from the two folders are merged into a seamless list.

Store the items that you want to appear at the top of the All Programs menu in the Start Menu folders. (If you use the classic Start menu, items in the Start Menu folders appear at the top of the Start menu, above the Programs menu.) Store the shortcuts and folders that you want to appear in the lower part of the All Programs menu in the Start Menu\Programs folders. (In the classic Start menu, these items appear on the Programs menu.)

To work with these items in Windows Explorer, you can use the usual techniques to navigate to the folders. But an easier way is to right-click the Start button and choose Open (to open %UserProfile%\Start Menu) or Open All Users (to open %AllUsersProfile%\Start Menu). If you prefer to display the Folders bar in Windows Explorer, choose the Explore or Explore All Users command instead.

The Clear List button gives you an opportunity to wipe the slate clean. After you click it, Windows begins monitoring your program usage anew, adding a program to the list each time you start one.

Unlike the folders and items in the All Programs menu, the most frequently used programs list is buried deep in the registry, and there's no practical way to edit it directly. Instead, let Windows add programs as it sees fit, use the Remove From This List command and the Clear List button to remove items, and use Pin To Start Menu to be sure that your favorite programs remain within easy reach.

Using Personalized Menus

With personalized menus, a feature that's available only when you use the classic Start menu, Windows displays the menu items you use most frequently and hides the others. This reduces clutter and leads to shorter menus, which are easier to scan and use. A double arrow at the bottom of a submenu indicates the presence of seldom-used items. To display these items, click the double arrow. Or if you simply wait a few seconds, Windows senses your momentary confusion and expands the menus, as shown in Figure 15-6. The newly visible items appear on a light-colored background so that they're easier to spot.

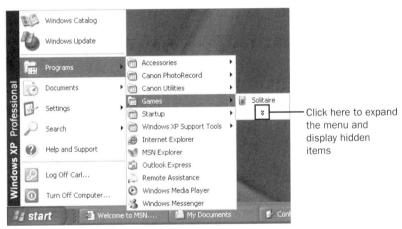

Figure 15-6. Personalized menus hide seldom-used menu items.

Some users love personalized menus; others loathe this feature. Fortunately, Windows gives you a choice. To enable or disable personalized menus, follow these steps:

1. Right-click the Start button and choose Properties.
2. On the Start Menu tab, click Customize.
3. In the Advanced Start Menu Options list in the Customize Classic Start Menu dialog box, select or clear the Use Personalized Menus check box.

> **Note** The personalized menu setting in the Customize Classic Start Menu dialog box affects only the Start menu. To enable or disable personalized menus in other programs that use them, such as Microsoft Internet Explorer or Microsoft Office, set the option within that program.

> **Tip** Scroll your Programs menu if it gets too long
>
> Windows has another trick for dealing with an overgrown Programs menu. If your Programs menu is too tall for your screen, Windows normally displays it in multiple columns, which can quickly outgrow the screen's width. For a cleaner alternative, select Scroll Programs in the Advanced Start Menu Options list in the Customize Classic Start Menu dialog box. This option appends an arrow at the top or bottom of a menu if it won't fit vertically; point to the arrow to scroll the menu in that direction.
>
> This same option is available to users of the default Start menu. Right-click the Start button, choose Properties, and click Customize. In the Customize Start Menu dialog box, click the Advanced tab and then select Scroll Programs in the Start Menu Items box.

Using Policies to Restrict Start Menu Contents

If your responsibilities include setting up Windows XP systems for relatively inexperienced users, you might want to take a look at the policy options for controlling Start Menu contents that are available via the User Configuration\Administrative Templates\Start Menu And Taskbar node of the Group Policy console (Gpedit.msc). You can use these policies to remove potential hazards, such as the Run command, or potential distractions, such as My Pictures and My Music. Note that the Group Policy snap-in is not available in Windows XP Home Edition. For more information, see Appendix F, "Group Policy."

Using the Quick Launch Bar and Other Desktop Toolbars

A *toolbar* is a collection of icons that simplify commonplace tasks. Windows includes a toolbar called Quick Launch that docks on your taskbar and populates itself with three icons: Internet Explorer, Show Desktop, and Windows Media Player. With the toolbar in place, a single click of an icon initiates an action. The Show Desktop icon displays the desktop, in the process minimizing whatever windows might be open; clicking Show Desktop again restores all windows to their previous size and position. The other two icons simply start their corresponding programs.

In addition to the Quick Launch toolbar, the following toolbars can be displayed on the taskbar or elsewhere on your desktop:

- **Address** The Address toolbar provides a place where you can enter an Internet address or the name and path of a program, document, or folder. When you press Enter or click the Go button, Windows takes you to the Internet address, starts the program, opens the document, or displays the folder in a Windows Explorer window. The Address toolbar is functionally equivalent to the Start menu's Run command or the Address bar in Windows Explorer or Internet Explorer.

- **Links**   The Links toolbar provides a set of shortcuts to selected Internet sites. It is equivalent to the Links toolbar in Internet Explorer or Windows Explorer.

- **Desktop**   The Desktop toolbar provides copies of all the icons currently displayed on your desktop. You might find this toolbar handy if you're using an HTML page as background for your desktop and your normal desktop icons get in the way.

- **Language Bar**   If you have installed an application that supports Advanced Text Services (such as Office), Windows, by default, displays the Language Bar. In addition to simplifying work in multiple languages, the Language Bar provides access to speech recognition, handwriting recognition, and text-to-speech features.

Additional application-specific toolbars might also be available on your system. Windows Media Player, for example, can minimize itself into a taskbar-docked toolbar, allowing easy access to player controls. (For information about installing and "Using the Mini Player Toolbar," page 820.)

To give you an idea of the flexibility of toolbars, Figure 15-7 shows an unrealistically cluttered collection of them. It's unlikely that anyone would want all these toolbars displayed at once—at least in the fashion shown here—but you might want to use one or more on your desktop.

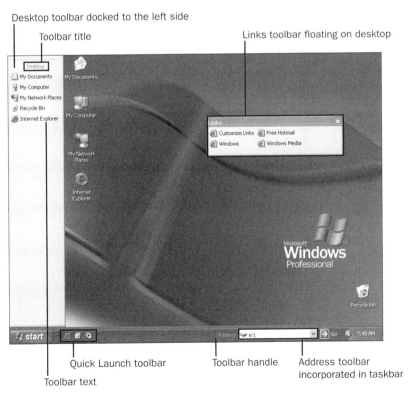

Desktop toolbar docked to the left side

Toolbar title

Links toolbar floating on desktop

Quick Launch toolbar

Toolbar handle

Address toolbar incorporated in taskbar

Toolbar text

Figure 15-7.   You can customize these four standard toolbars and create your own new toolbars.

Chapter 15

You can customize any of the supplied toolbars except for Address. So, for example, you can add icons for your own programs or shortcuts to the Quick Launch toolbar, remove links from the Links toolbar that you don't find useful (or add links to your own favorite sites), and so on. You can also create entirely new toolbars, as discussed in a section below.

Desktop toolbars initially appear on the taskbar, but you can *float* them on the desktop or *dock* them against any side of the desktop. Thus, for example, you can have your taskbar docked against the bottom edge of the desktop and line the other three edges with toolbars. Tips on positioning toolbars are discussed in a section below.

Installing and Removing Toolbars

To install a new toolbar or remove one you're currently using, right-click any unoccupied part of the taskbar or any existing toolbar. Choose Toolbars from the shortcut menu that appears, and then choose from the ensuing submenu. A check mark beside a toolbar's name means that it is already displayed on the taskbar. Clicking a checked toolbar name removes that toolbar from the taskbar.

To remove a toolbar that is not on the taskbar—or to add another toolbar to it—right-click an unoccupied part of the toolbar, choose Toolbars, and then choose from the submenu. You can also click the Close button on a floating toolbar to remove it from the desktop.

Troubleshooting

The Show Desktop tool is missing.

The Show Desktop tool is not an ordinary program shortcut. If it is deleted, the procedure for recreating it is not obvious. Follow these steps:

1   Open Notepad and type the following text:

```
[Shell]
Command=2
IconFile=explorer.exe,3
[Taskbar]
Command=ToggleDesktop
```

2   Save the new file as Show Desktop.scf.

3   Drag the file's icon to the Quick Launch bar or another location where you want the shortcut to appear.

Chapter 15

Troubleshooting

The Language Bar always appears at startup.

From one startup to the next, Windows retains all settings on the Toolbars submenu except for the Language Bar command. If you never want to see the Links toolbar, for example, you can right-click your taskbar, choose Toolbars, and clear the check mark next to the Links command, and that toolbar will not return unbidden. To remove the Language Bar permanently, however, you need to follow a different procedure. Open Regional And Language Options in Control Panel, click the Languages tab, click the Details button, click the Language Bar button, and then clear Show The Language Bar On The Desktop. With Language Bar thus removed, you can still call it back by right-clicking the taskbar and choosing Toolbars, Language Bar.

Sizing and Positioning Toolbars

Before you can move or resize toolbars that are on the taskbar, the taskbar must be unlocked. To do that, right-click an unoccupied area of the taskbar and, if a check mark appears next to the Lock The Taskbar command, click the command to clear the check mark. Alternatively, open the Taskbar And Start Menu Properties dialog box and, on the Taskbar tab, clear the Lock The Taskbar check box.

Note Even when the taskbar is locked, you can add or remove toolbars and icons and you can make other changes in toolbar appearance. Locking only prevents you from moving or resizing toolbars or the taskbar itself. Locking the taskbar does not affect toolbars that are not on the taskbar.

When the taskbar is not locked, a dotted vertical bar appears at the left edge of every toolbar positioned on the taskbar. (If the taskbar is displayed vertically against the left or right edge of the desktop, the bar is horizontal and appears at the top of the toolbar.) This is the toolbar's *handle* (shown in Figure 15-7). To move a toolbar out onto the desktop, position the mouse pointer on the handle. When the pointer changes shape, drag the toolbar. (If the toolbar title is displayed, you can grab it instead.) To dock a toolbar against a different edge of the desktop, drag it all the way to that edge. When you release the mouse button, the toolbar will dock.

Note You can dock toolbars only against the edges of the whole desktop. If your desktop spans two or more monitors, you can't dock a toolbar against a screen edge that's adjacent to the edge of another screen.

Chapter 15

On the desktop, a toolbar takes the form of a simple window, with a title bar and a Close button. You can move a desktop toolbar around by dragging its title bar or close it by clicking the Close button. To reposition a toolbar on the taskbar, simply drag its title bar to the taskbar. To change the size of a desktop toolbar, simply drag one of its borders.

You can also use the handle to change a toolbar's size or position on the taskbar. Assuming your taskbar is horizontal, dragging the handle to the right decreases the width of the toolbar and makes more room for the toolbar on the left. Dragging to the left has the opposite effect.

Any toolbar that's docked to the edge of the desktop can be set to auto-hide. To do that, right-click the toolbar's title bar or any unoccupied space and choose Auto-Hide. With that setting in place, the toolbar retreats into the side of the desktop, leaving only a thin line as a reminder of its presence. When you want to use the toolbar, simply move the mouse pointer to the edge of the desktop, and the toolbar springs into view.

Customizing Toolbars

To remove a tool from a toolbar, right-click it and choose Delete from the shortcut menu. To add to a toolbar a tool that starts a program or opens a document, drag the item's icon from the desktop or a Windows Explorer window and deposit it wherever you want it to appear on the toolbar. To change the properties for a particular tool, right-click and choose Properties; you'll see the familiar Properties dialog box for a shortcut file.

Troubleshooting

You can't modify a toolbar icon.

When you modify certain toolbar icons, you might get a message that your changes can't be saved and that access is denied. This can occur if a Quick Launch icon has its read-only attribute set. The solution, which you're not likely to intuit from the error message, is quite simple: Right-click the icon, choose Properties, click the General tab, and clear the Read-Only check box.

Toolbars can be displayed with or without their titles, and their tools can be displayed with either large or small icons, and with or without identifying text. To avail yourself of any of these customizing options, right-click the toolbar you want to modify (not on a tool, however). Choose View followed by Show Title to suppress or display the toolbar title; choose Large Icons or Small Icons to change the icon size; choose Show Text to suppress or display tool text.

Note that if you don't display tool text, you can still see the name of any tool simply by moving your mouse pointer over it and pausing for a moment.

Tweaking the Windows XP Interface

Inside Out

Create a cascading menu of your folders and files

When set up in a certain way, the Desktop toolbar can provide a cascading menu of all the folders and files on your system. Follow these steps to set up this handy feature:

1. Display the Desktop toolbar somewhere on the taskbar, and be sure its toolbar title is displayed.

2. Reduce the Desktop toolbar's size by dragging its handle (and the handles of surrounding toolbars, if necessary) until it displays only the toolbar title ("Desktop") and a double arrow.

Now when you click the toolbar's double arrow, a menu of desktop items appears. Desktop items that contain other folders and files (such as My Computer, My Documents, and My Network Places) cascade to show their contents when you point at them.

Creating a New Toolbar

Any folder on your system can become a toolbar. This includes Windows system folders such as Printers And Faxes or Control Panel. To create a new toolbar, right-click an existing toolbar or a spot on the taskbar, choose Toolbars, and then choose New Toolbar. In the next dialog box, navigate to a folder and click OK.

The folder's name becomes the name of the new toolbar, and each item within the folder becomes a tool.

Tip Create a toolbar by dragging a folder

You can quickly and easily make a toolbar of any folder by dragging the folder to the edge of the desktop and releasing it. Doing so docks the new toolbar to the edge where you dropped it. You can still change the size of the icons and whether the toolbar title or button text appears, and you can still move the toolbar to another location.

Most toolbars are representations of folders that exist somewhere on your system. To see a toolbar's underlying folder in a Windows Explorer window, right-click the toolbar and choose Open Folder. If you prefer to make your additions, deletions, and other changes in Windows Explorer instead of working directly on the toolbar, you can do so. Table 15-1 shows the file locations for the three standard toolbars.

Table 15-1. Folder Locations of Standard Toolbars

Toolbar	Location
Quick Launch	%AppData%\Microsoft\Internet Explorer\Quick Launch
Links	%UserProfile%\Favorites\Links
Desktop	%UserProfile%\Desktop and %AllUsersProfile%\Desktop

Chapter 15

Making It Easy to Open Your Favorite Documents

When Microsoft introduced the My Documents folder in Windows 98, many longtime computer users with roots in MS-DOS and the earliest versions of Windows objected vociferously. Aside from the name, which some found cloying, they didn't want to be told where to store their documents. (By the way, you can change the name of My Documents in the same way that you change the name of any other folder: Right-click and choose Rename.) But the implementation of My Documents has been greatly improved in subsequent versions of Windows, and it provides the easiest and best place to organize and store your documents. Its advantages include the following:

- Windows provides easy access to the My Documents folder (and its subfolders) through the Start menu, the task pane in Windows Explorer, common File Open and File Save dialog boxes, and other places.

- Using My Documents makes it easy to share the documents you want to share and keep private the ones you don't want to share (particularly if you use Windows XP Home Edition, in which it's difficult to modify the default share permissions and NTFS permissions).

- Keeping your documents in My Documents and its subfolders makes it much easier to back up your documents or move them to another computer en masse. Gathering your documents from their far-flung locations all over your drive is an essential first step in developing a practical backup strategy.

Of course, you're still free to store your documents where you want, but there's really no reason *not* to use My Documents. Clicking a link to My Documents—and you'll see lots of them in Windows XP—leads you directly to your document storage location, where you can open your document of choice with a simple double-click.

For information about moving the My Documents folder, see "Moving Folders from the Standard Profile Locations," page 555.

To access documents that you share with others, either in the Shared Documents folder or in a folder on a network drive, simply create a shortcut to the shared folder in your My Documents folder. That way My Documents becomes the single access point for all your documents—private, shared locally, and shared on the network.

Tip Archive your old documents in a different folder

To keep the My Documents folder from becoming unwieldy—both in the number of folders and files you need to wade through to find the one you want and in the amount of data you must back up—use it only for documents that you're actively working with. Every month or so, move the documents you no longer use to a folder (not in My Documents) named Archives (or something equally descriptive). This speeds up your backup routine considerably: Your My Documents folder, which you should back up frequently, remains relatively small, and you only need to back up the Archives folder when you add files to it.

Many programs, by default, store the documents they create in a folder other than My Documents. If the program allows it, override those defaults! For example, unless you use roaming user profiles, move your Outlook Express message store to My Documents. (In Outlook Express, click Tools, Options, Maintenance, Store Folder, Change.)

Working with Recently Opened Documents

The Start menu contains an item called My Recent Documents (on the classic Start menu, its name is simply Documents) that contains shortcuts to 15 of your most recently used documents. To open one of these documents, simply click its name.

 Troubleshooting

Recent documents don't appear on the Start menu or on the File menu in Microsoft Office applications.

Ordinarily, documents you open are added to the My Recent Documents list on the Start menu. In addition, documents you have recently opened in Office applications (such as Microsoft Word and Microsoft Excel) appear at the bottom of the application's File menu, for easy reuse. However, you might find that documents you open are not added to either location. Furthermore, the Options dialog box settings that control this feature in Office applications is unavailable. This problem occurs when a policy prevents the creation of shortcuts to recently opened documents. The policy can be set through Group Policy (Gpedit.msc), but most people make the setting (inadvertently) through Tweak UI, a popular utility available from Microsoft. You can solve the problem—and resume adding recently opened documents to the menus—in either of two ways:

- **Use Tweak UI**   Open Tweak UI and click Explorer. In the Settings box, select Allow Recent Documents On Start Menu and Maintain Document History. For more information about Tweak UI, see "Customizing Windows XP with Tweak UI," page 501.

- **Use Group Policy**   At a command prompt, type **gpedit.msc** to open Group Policy. Navigate to User Configuration\AdministrativeTemplates\Start Menu And Taskbar. In the details pane, double-click Do Not Keep History Of Recently Opened Documents. Select Disabled and then click OK. (Group Policy is not available in Windows XP Home Edition.)

If you intentionally set the policy to prevent the appearance of recent documents on the Start menu, but you want recent documents listed on your applications' File menus, make the policy change explained above. Then remove the Recent Documents menu from the Start menu. For details, see "Removing the My Recent Documents Menu" on page 465.

Note By default, My Recent Documents doesn't appear on the Start menu in Windows XP Home Edition. To display it, right-click the Start button, choose Properties, and click Customize. On the Advanced tab of the Customize Start Menu dialog box, select List My Most Recently Opened Documents.

Removing Items from the My Recent Documents Menu

You can prune individual items from the My Recent Documents menu in the same way that you remove items from other parts of the Start menu: Right-click an item and choose Delete from the shortcut menu. Notice when you remove an item in this way, however, that My Recent Documents still contains 15 items! That's because the My Recent Documents menu reflects the contents of a hidden folder called Recent, which is stored as part of your user profile. Windows keeps shortcuts to all recently used documents in the %UserProfile%\Recent folder but displays only the most recent 15 on the My Recent Documents menu.

To clear the whole menu, including the backup supply of shortcuts, follow these steps:

1 Right-click the Start button, choose Properties, and click Customize.
2 If you're using the default Start menu, click the Advanced tab and click Clear List. If you're using the classic Start menu, click the Clear button.

Note that you can't add items to the My Recent Documents menu by making direct additions to the Recent folder. For the purposes of building this menu, Windows simply ignores anything in the Recent folder that it didn't put there itself. When you use the Clear List command, however, *everything* in the Recent folder is deleted, no matter how it got there.

If you have privacy concerns about the recently opened documents list—specifically, the ability of others to snoop in your Recent folder after you log off to see what you've been up to—you'll want to enable a policy that clears the list automatically each time you log off. Follow these steps:

1 At a command prompt, type **gpedit.msc** to open Group Policy.
2 Open User Configuration\Administrative Templates\Start Menu And Taskbar.
3 Double-click the Clear History Of Recently Opened Documents On Exit policy.
4 On the Setting tab, select Enabled.

Note Changes you make with Group Policy affect all users on your computer. Group Policy is not available in Windows XP Home Edition. However, you can also use Tweak UI, in either Windows XP Professional or Windows XP Home Edition, to clear your document history on exit. (Click Explorer, then select Clear Document History On Exit). Note that this Tweak UI setting affects the current user only. For more information about Tweak UI, see "Customizing Windows XP with Tweak UI," page 501.

Removing the My Recent Documents Menu

If you find that you have no use for the My Recent Documents menu, you can remove it from the Start menu. The method you use depends on which Start menu you use, and whether you're working with Windows XP Professional or Windows XP Home Edition.

- To remove My Recent Documents from the default Start menu, in either edition of Windows XP, right-click the Start button, choose Properties, and click Customize. On the Advanced tab of the Customize Start Menu dialog box, clear the List My Most Recently Opened Documents check box. This change affects only the default Start menu.

- In Windows XP Professional, you can remove the My Recent Documents menu from the classic Start menu by using Group Policy. At a command prompt, type **gpedit.msc** to start Group Policy. Open User Configuration\Administrative Templates\Start Menu And Taskbar. Double-click Remove Documents Menu From Start Menu and select Enabled. (This change affects the default Start menu as well as the classic Start menu.)

- To remove the My Recent Documents menu from the classic Start menu in Windows XP Home Edition, you need Tweak UI. In Tweak UI, click Explorer, and then clear Allow Recent Documents On Start Menu. If necessary to make the change take effect, either log off and log back on or switch to the default Start menu and then back to the classic Start menu. For more information about Tweak UI, see "Customizing Windows XP with Tweak UI," page 501.

> **Note** Removing My Recent Documents from the Start menu does not remove existing shortcuts from the Recent folder, nor does it prevent the creation of new shortcuts. Therefore, if you reenable the list's appearance on the Start menu, the list will be up to date. Also note that disabling the My Recent Documents menu via Tweak UI removes the Recent Documents section from the Advanced tab of the Customize Start Menu dialog box. To reinstate My Recent Documents after you have taken this step, you must first return to Tweak UI and select the Allow Recent Documents On Start Menu check box. Then go back to the Advanced tab of the Customize Start Menu dialog box and select List My Most Recently Opened Documents.

Customizing the Start Menu with Shortcuts to Other Folders

In addition to shortcuts to programs and recently opened documents, both versions of the Start menu provide links to a handful of other common folders and destinations. But the links that appear by default are only a compact subset of the available links.

You can add other links and delete those you don't want. In addition, you can set up certain Start menu items as cascading menus. Instead of opening Control Panel in its own window and then double-clicking one of its icons, for example, you can configure it as a cascading menu, with its utilities available as a submenu of the Start menu, as shown in Figure 15-8.

Chapter 15

Figure 15-8. Control Panel is one of several items that can be set up as a cascading menu.

The following items can be included or excluded as top-level items on the default Start menu, at your option:

- Links to folders and files
  - Favorites
  - My Computer
  - My Documents
  - My Music
  - My Network Places
  - My Pictures
- Settings and configuration items
  - Administrative Tools
  - Control Panel
  - Network Connections
  - Printers And Faxes
  - Set Program Access And Defaults
- Links to other tasks
  - Help And Support
  - Run
  - Search

To select the items you want to appear and, in some cases, specify whether you want a link or a cascading menu, right-click the Start button and choose Properties to open Taskbar And Start Menu Properties. Click Customize and then click the Advanced tab. Make your selections in the Start Menu Items box, shown in Figure 15-9.

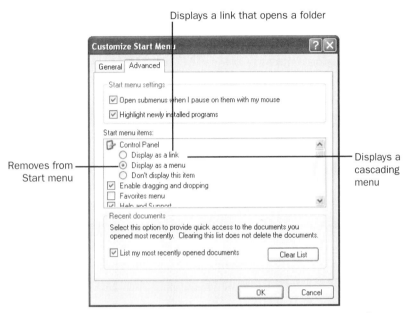

Figure 15-9. You can make your Start menu as comprehensive or as Spartan as you like.

If you use the classic Start menu, your choices are similar, yet fewer. The Customize Classic Start Menu dialog box (right-click the Start button, choose Properties, and click Customize) lets you choose three optional items:

- Administrative Tools
- Favorites
- Run

In addition, the Customize Classic Start Menu dialog box includes several "expand" check boxes, which display the following items as cascading menus:

- Control Panel (on the Settings menu)
- My Documents (on the Documents menu)
- My Pictures (on the Documents menu)
- Network Connections (on the Settings menu)
- Printers And Faxes (on the Settings menu)

Managing Desktop Clutter

Usability studies at Microsoft show that desktop clutter—accumulated icons from various program installations, stored documents, and Windows itself—stifles productivity. The designers of Windows XP have taken to heart those study results and produced a desktop that, by default, contains only a single desktop icon (Recycle Bin). Key system icons are now located where they're more accessible, on the Start menu. The Desktop Cleanup Wizard automates the process of relocating other seldom-used desktop icons. But in the words of a Windows XP product manager, "The desktop is yours to abuse as you see fit." Windows XP makes it easier to restore system icons to the desktop should you decide that location works best for you.

With a desktop that's no longer littered with icons, you might want to choose a more interesting background or put some useful Web content on your desktop. The following sections describe these desktop-management options in detail.

Controlling Desktop Icons

The desktop icons that appear by default depend upon your choice of Start menu. With the default menu, you get only a Recycle Bin icon. Switching to the classic menu adds icons for My Documents, My Computer, My Network Places, and Internet Explorer. (If you upgraded from an earlier version of Windows or migrated from another computer using the File And Settings Transfer Wizard, your desktop might have additional icons.)

To control which of these system icons appear on your desktop, follow these steps:

1 Right-click an unoccupied area of the desktop and choose Properties. Alternatively, open Display (in the Appearance And Themes category) in Control Panel. Either action opens the Display Properties dialog box.

2 In Display Properties, click the Desktop tab and then click Customize Desktop.

3 In the Desktop Icons section of the General tab, select the items you want to appear.

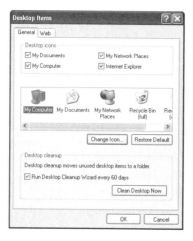

While you've got the Desktop Items dialog box open, you might want to examine its other features:

● If you're really into customization, you can change the icon used for any of the system folders displayed in the center of the dialog box. If you upgraded from Windows 98, you'll find an interesting collection of icons in your %ProgramFiles%\Plus!\Themes folder. A clean installation of Windows XP doesn't have too many interesting alternatives (you might, however, want to check the hodgepodge of icons in %SystemRoot%\System32\Shell32.dll), but the capability exists nonetheless.

Note If you're interested in creating your own icons for the desktop or for use elsewhere in Windows, you'll find an excellent description of the process in the MSDN Library at *http://msdn.microsoft.com/library/en-us/dnwxp/html/winxpicons.asp*.

● A more interesting option is the Desktop Cleanup Wizard. This wizard, which you invoke by clicking Clean Desktop Now, displays a list of all the shortcuts on your desktop, along with the date each shortcut was last used, as shown in Figure 15-10. You select the items you no longer need to have on your desktop, and the wizard moves the selected items to a desktop folder it creates named Unused Desktop Shortcuts. Your seldom-used shortcuts are still available; you just need to dig into the folder to use them instead of searching for them on the desktop. (You should delete shortcuts you'll never need again. That's a task you'll need to do manually; Windows doesn't presume to know which ones can be safely deleted altogether.)

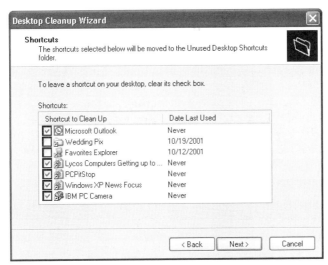

Figure 15-10. The wizard selects shortcuts that haven't been used in a long time (or ever), but you can override its choices on this page.

Inside Out

Create a *really* clean desktop

If you want the ultimate clean desktop, you have the following options:

- You can toggle the display of all desktop icons in one fell swoop by right-clicking the desktop and choosing Arrange Icons By, Show Desktop Icons.

- In Windows XP Professional, you can remove the Recycle Bin icon—but you must use a policy to do so. At a command prompt, type **gpedit.msc** to open Group Policy. Open User Configuration\Administrative Templates\Desktop. Double-click the Remove Recycle Bin Icon From Desktop policy and select Enabled. Your deleted files continue to collect in the Recycle Bin (depending on your Recycle Bin settings, of course), but its icon is no longer available on the desktop or in Windows Explorer. (Note that, like all local group policies, settings you make here affect all users of your computer.) In the Desktop policy folder, you'll notice policies that remove other desktop items. Policy settings override any settings a user makes in the Desktop Items dialog box. For more information about policies, see Appendix F, "Group Policy."

- In either edition of Windows XP, you can use Tweak UI to enable or disable the display of icons for Internet Explorer, My Computer, My Documents, My Network Places, and Recycle Bin. Click Desktop, and then select or clear check boxes as desired. For more information about Tweak UI, see "Customizing Windows XP with Tweak UI," page 15xx.

After you've populated your desktop with icons, you might want to control the arrangement of those icons. Right-clicking the desktop and choosing Arrange Icons By produces a submenu with a number of useful commands. The Name, Size, Type, Modified, Auto Arrange, and Align To Grid commands work just as they do in Windows Explorer to sort and lay out your icons. (For details, see "Sorting and Grouping Icons," page 665.) Show Desktop Icons hides or displays all desktop icons. The last two commands on the menu—Lock Web Items On The Desktop and Run Desktop Cleanup Wizard—provide handy shortcuts to options in the Desktop Items dialog box. Lock Web Items On The Desktop prevents you (or others) from moving Web content that you've displayed on your desktop (see "Displaying Web Content on Your Desktop," page 476). Run Desktop Cleanup Wizard invokes the wizard that was described earlier in this chapter (see "Managing Desktop Clutter," page 468).

As an ordinary folder, the desktop can store much more than system icons and program shortcuts. If you're not careful, it can become a repository for all manner of documents, downloaded files, shortcuts, and so on. Although it's nice to have some of these items in this convenient location, you'll probably want to avoid the clutter created by injudicious use of the desktop as a storage depot. Instead, use My Documents and its subfolders, which provide a good way to organize your documents and, in fact, are just as accessible.

Inside Out

Tidy up on a schedule

The Desktop Items dialog box includes a check box that allows you to schedule the Desktop Cleanup Wizard every 60 days. (The wizard itself doesn't run automatically. Instead, at the designated time, a reminder appears if your desktop has any unused shortcuts. Clicking the reminder starts the wizard.) Selecting the check box is the easiest way to ensure that you run the wizard periodically. But you're not stuck with a 60-day recurrence. To have the wizard reminder appear more or less frequently, open Registry Editor and navigate to HKCU\Software\Microsoft\Windows\CurrentVersion\Explorer\Desktop\CleanupWiz. Double-click the Days Between Clean Up value, select the Decimal option, and enter the desired number of days between reminders. (If the value doesn't exist, create a new DWORD value named Days Between Clean Up.)

Troubleshooting

When you delete a desktop item, it also disappears from other users' desktops.

The items that appear on your desktop (aside from the My Documents, My Computer, My Network Places, and Internet Explorer icons) come from two sources: %UserProfile%\Desktop (your own profile) and %AllUsersProfile%\Desktop (the All Users profile). Items in the latter folder appear on the desktop of everyone who uses your computer. Ordinarily, items that you place on your desktop are stored as part of your profile. But the setup routines for some programs add a shortcut to the All Users desktop so that everyone can access the program. When you delete a desktop item, if it's stored in the All Users profile, your deletion affects everyone's desktop—not just your own. Windows gives no indication that your change might affect others, nor is there any visual clue to an item's actual location. Before you delete an item from your desktop—whether manually or with the Desktop Cleanup Wizard—you might want to confirm its location. Right-click its icon and choose Properties. On the General tab, see whether the Location field shows All Users or your own user name.

To recover shared items that you've already deleted, move them from your Unused Desktop Shortcuts folder to %AllUsersProfile%\Desktop (if you used the Desktop Cleanup Wizard to remove them) or restore them from your Recycle Bin (if you deleted them manually). To remove a shortcut from your desktop but keep it on others, you'll need to copy it to the Desktop folder in each user's profile and then delete it from the All Users profile.

Making Desktop Icons Easier to See

If your vision is impaired or if you use a high display resolution on a small monitor, you might find it difficult to see desktop icons or the label that appears below each one.

To change the size of the icons, right-click the desktop, choose Properties, click the Appearance tab, and click Effects. In the Effects dialog box, select Use Large Icons. For more precise control of icon size, on the Appearance tab of the Display Properties dialog box, click Advanced. In the Advanced Appearance dialog box, shown in Figure 15-11, select Icon in the Item list. Then adjust the size of the icon (in pixels) and the text below the icon. If you make significant changes to the default settings, you might also need to adjust the space between icons so they don't overlap. In the Item list, select Icon Spacing (Horizontal) and change the size; repeat with Icon Spacing (Vertical).

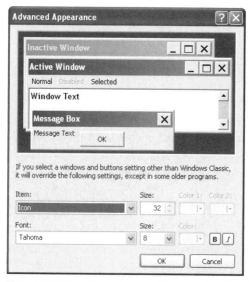

Figure 15-11. If your icon settings go too far afield, you can return to the default settings shown here.

Note Whether you use the Effects dialog box or the Advanced Appearance dialog box to modify the icon size, your change affects Icons view in Windows Explorer as well as desktop icons.

Tweaking the Windows XP Interface

Your difficulty in reading icon labels might also be resolved by disabling a particular visual effect instead of modifying icon size. To find out, follow these steps:

1   Right-click My Computer and choose Properties. (Alternatively, open System in Control Panel's Performance And Maintenance category.)

2   In the System Properties dialog box, click the Advanced tab and then, under Performance, click Settings. This opens the Performance Options dialog box.

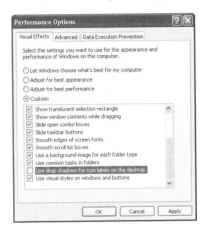

3   On the Visual Effects tab, clear the Use Drop Shadows For Icon Labels On The Desktop check box.

With this option disabled, icon labels appear on a solid rectangular background, which provides better contrast (and gives your computer a tiny performance boost).

Changing the Background

You can perk up any desktop with a background image. You can use a small image repeated (*tiled*) to fill the desktop, a centered image, or an image stretched to cover the entire desktop. Your background can be supplied by a graphics file in any of several common formats: bitmap (.bmp or .dib extension), Graphics Interchange Format (.gif), Joint Photographic Experts Group (.jpg or .jpeg), or Portable Network Graphics (.png). Alternatively, you can drape your desktop with a Hypertext Markup Language (HTML) file stored on your computer or on a network drive, complete with live links. (HTML is the programming language used to encode Web pages.)

To select a background, right-click the desktop, choose Properties from the shortcut menu, and click the Desktop tab. This takes you to the dialog box shown in Figure 15-12.

Figure 15-12. Using the Desktop tab in the Display Properties dialog box, you can set a picture or an HTML page as your desktop background.

Select an image file from the Background list, or click the Browse button to find an HTML file or an image that's not in the list. (The list initially includes image files from your My Pictures folder, %SystemRoot%, and %SystemRoot%\Web\Wallpaper.) If you don't want a background image, select (None), which appears at the top of the list.

After choosing an image file, you can choose either Center, Tile, or Stretch from the Position list. If you choose Center, the color indicated in the Color box surrounds the image if it's not big enough to fill the screen. If you choose Tile, your image is repeated as often as needed to fill the screen. If you choose Stretch, Windows resizes your image to fit the screen (possibly distorting it beyond recognition in the process).

Inside Out

Cover multiple monitors with multiple images

If more than one monitor is connected to your computer, you might want to have a different background image appear on each monitor. You can't do that with an ordinary desktop background—the type you select on the Desktop tab. If you use the Desktop tab to make your selection, Windows repeats the one image on each monitor. However, you can achieve the desired effect by placing an image as a Web item on each monitor. Then click each Web item's maximize button, or open its Control menu and choose Cover The Desktop. (This command, in fact, causes the image to cover the current monitor, not the entire desktop.) For information about Web items, see "Displaying Web Content on Your Desktop," page 476.

Tweaking the Windows XP Interface

> **Note** If you choose an HTML file as your background, it covers the entire desktop except for the space occupied by the taskbar and any other desktop toolbars. Any desktop icons you have displayed overlay the HTML document. An HTML document you display this way won't have any scroll bars. Therefore, an HTML file used as your desktop background should be designed so that the entire page fits on your screen so that its text and images don't interfere with your desktop icons. If you want an HTML document on your desktop but you don't want these constraints, use the procedures in the following section, "Displaying Web Content on Your Desktop."

Inside Out

Display the Windows version number on the desktop

You might find it useful to have a visual indication of which version of Windows you're currently running, particularly if you administer several computers or if you boot among several operating systems on your own computer. A minor change to the registry displays this information in the lower right corner of your desktop. To enable this feature, use Registry Editor to navigate to the HKCU\Control Panel\Desktop key. Open the PaintDesktopVersion value and set it to 1. To remove the text, change the value back to 0. You'll need to log off and back on for the change to take effect. (If you don't see the version number when PaintDesktopVersion is set to 1, right-click the desktop, choose Properties, click the Desktop tab, and click Customize Desktop. On the Web tab of the Desktop Items dialog box, clear Lock Desktop Items.)

Note that if you're using an evaluation version of Windows, this version information is always displayed on the desktop—regardless of the setting of this registry value—as a reminder that the version will expire after a period of time.

An alternative method for applying an image to the background exists for pictures stored on your computer and for pictures on Web pages.

- **Pictures stored on your computer** Any image stored in a picture folder can be applied to the background by selecting it and then clicking Set As Desktop Background in the Picture Tasks section of the Windows Explorer task pane. Alternatively, right-click the image and choose Set As Desktop Background. (A picture folder is one to which the Pictures or Photo Albums template has been applied using the Customize tab in the folder's Properties dialog box.)

- **Pictures on Web pages** If you see an image on a Web page that you'd like to use as your desktop background, right-click the image and choose Set As Background.

Inside Out

Use a patterned background

Earlier versions of Windows offered a different type of background: patterns. A *pattern* is a small bitmapped image that is repeated over the entire screen. It's only two colors, but it lets you dress up the display for a minimum amount of memory. Support for patterns is now gone from the Display Properties dialog box, but you can implement them through the registry by following these steps:

1 Start Registry Editor and open HKCU\Control Panel\Patterns.

2 Find the value for the pattern you want, double-click the value, and copy its data.

3 Open HKCU\Control Panel\Desktop and create a new string value named Pattern.

4 Double-click the Pattern value and paste the value data you copied in step 2.

5 On the Desktop tab of the Display Properties dialog box, select (None) as the background.

6 Log off and log back on.

Displaying Web Content on Your Desktop

You can choose to display Web content on your desktop. Web content—sometimes called Active Desktop items—can include items such as stock or news tickers that can be updated from the Internet automatically at scheduled times. Your desktop can also contain an HTML document, complete with links to other HTML documents.

Figure 15-13 shows a desktop with two Web items—a stock market ticker and a satellite-tracking graphic. These items are updated periodically from the Internet.

Tip   Add Web images to your desktop quickly
If you want to add an image (such as a webcam image) from a Web page to your desktop, the easiest way to do so is to right-click the image and choose Set As Desktop Item.

You can turn any Web page or link into desktop Web content directly from Internet Explorer. To use the current page, right-drag the icon from the Address bar to the desktop, and then choose Create Active Desktop Items Here from the shortcut menu that automatically appears. To use the target of a link, right-drag the link from your browser window to the desktop.

Tweaking the Windows XP Interface

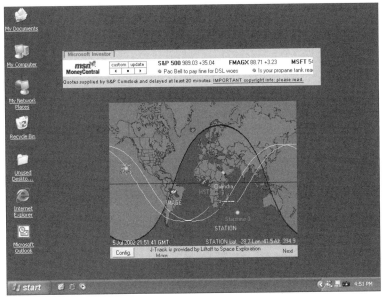

Figure 15-13. This stock market ticker and satellite-tracking graphic provide updated information.

To add Web content to your desktop, follow these steps:

1. Right-click the desktop, choose Properties, click the Desktop tab, and click Customize Desktop.

2. In the Desktop Items dialog box, click the Web tab and then click New. The New Desktop Item dialog box appears.

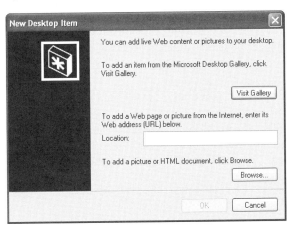

From this dialog box, you have three choices:

- If you know the Uniform Resource Locator (*URL*—an item's address on the Internet or your intranet) of the item you want to add, type it in the Location box and click OK.

- If you want to display a local file (such as a picture or an HTML document) or the target of an Internet shortcut, click Browse and navigate to the item you want.

- Click Visit Gallery to display the Desktop Gallery Web site. (When you go to this page, you might see a security warning window asking whether you want to download a Microsoft ActiveX control. Go ahead and click Yes if you see this message.) The Visit Gallery link takes you to a Microsoft Web site that provides a few free items of content designed expressly for display on your desktop. However, as of this writing, the site had not been updated for more than two years. You can find more recent offerings (mostly inexpensive, some free) by using a Web search engine to look for "Active Desktop."

3   After you click OK in the New Desktop Item dialog box or add an item from the Desktop Gallery, you might be asked to confirm that you want to add the item to your desktop. After you confirm, you'll see a dialog box that looks something like this.

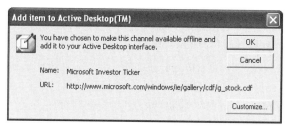

To add the item to your desktop and accept the vendor's default update schedule, simply click OK. If you want to set up your own schedule, click Customize. This starts the Offline Favorite Wizard, which lets you specify the schedule for updating the content.

> **Tip**   Display folder contents on your desktop
>
> Displaying a folder as a desktop item provides convenient access to a folder's contents because it's always on the desktop. You can choose any view available in Windows Explorer, and the desktop item displays any folder customization you've created. To add a folder to your desktop, type the complete path of the folder you want to display in the Location text box in the New Desktop Item dialog box. (This is one place where you can't use environment variables like %UserProfile%.)

After your Web content is displayed on your desktop, you can interact with it exactly as you would if you were working within a Web browser. When you click a link, Windows activates your browser, connects to the Internet if you're not already online, and then performs the action stipulated by that link.

Moving and Sizing Web Content

Web items displayed on your desktop are windows, albeit unconventional ones. You can move them around, change their sizes, lock them in place, and close them. You can't minimize them, however.

To move one of these windows, follow these steps:

1 Make sure the window isn't locked in place. Right-click the desktop and choose Arrange Icons By. If a check mark appears by Lock Web Items On Desktop, choose the command to clear the check mark.

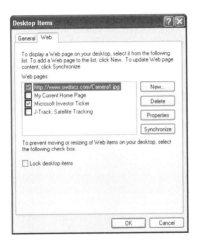

2 Move your mouse pointer somewhere near the window's top edge and pause there. After a moment, a border pops up from the top edge.

3 Drag this border to move the window.

To change a window's size, point to one of the window's borders. When your mouse pointer changes to a two-headed arrow, drag.

The icons in the top border are similar in operation to the icons in an ordinary window's title bar.

▼	Displays the Control menu
☐	Expands window to cover the entire desktop (or the current screen if you're using multiple monitors)
◱	Expands window to cover the entire desktop except for a resizable area on the left side, where desktop icons appear
▣	Restores window to normal size
✕	Closes window

Updating Web Content

Web content on your desktop doesn't update continuously; it updates only at scheduled intervals and when you request an update. To update all items immediately, open Display Properties (right-click anywhere on the desktop and choose Properties on the shortcut menu), select the Desktop tab, click Customize Desktop, and then click Synchronize. Alternatively, open the Start menu and choose All Programs, Accessories, Synchronize; in the Items To Synchronize dialog box, select one or more items and click Synchronize. To update a single item, point to the top edge of the item, click the down arrow that appears in the upper left corner to open the Control menu, and choose Synchronize.

To change an item's update schedule, visit its properties dialog box. Here are some ways to get there:

- Point to the top edge of the item, click the down arrow that appears in the upper left corner to open the Control menu, and choose Properties. (This method is available only when the Lock Desktop Items check box isn't selected.)
- Right-click the desktop, choose Properties, and click Desktop, Customize Desktop, Web. In the Desktop Items dialog box that appears, select the item whose schedule you want to change and click the Properties button.
- On the Start menu, point to All Programs, Accessories, and then choose Synchronize. Select the item whose schedule you want to change and click the Properties button.

> **Tip** To see when an item was last updated, choose Synchronize from the Accessories folder of the Start menu. In the Last Updated column, you'll find the date and time of the most recent update for each item.

Removing Web Content from Your Desktop

What do you do when you're tired of looking at that news ticker, weather map, or other desktop item? You can suppress its display by simply closing it, which you can do in any of the following ways:

- Point to the top edge of the Web item and then click the Close button (the X icon that appears in the upper right corner). (This method is available only when the Lock Desktop Items check box isn't selected.)

- Point to the top edge of the item and then choose Close from the Control menu that appears when you click the down arrow in the upper left corner of the border. (This method is available only when the Lock Desktop Items check box isn't selected.)

- In the Desktop Items dialog box, click the Web tab and then clear the check box next to the window name. (Select the check box to reopen the window.)

Windows continues to update a Web item even if it's not being displayed. To prevent further updates, open the Desktop Items dialog box. Select the item, click Properties, and then clear the Make This Page Available Offline check box on the Web Document tab.

If you want to permanently delete an item, click the Web tab in the Desktop Items dialog box. Select the item you want to delete and then click Delete.

Changing Colors, Fonts, and Visual Effects

One of the most talked-about features in Windows XP is its bright (some say cartoonish) new look. The new visual style—which includes rounded corners on windows and buttons, new desktop icons, bright colors, and more legible fonts—is one part of a theme that was dubbed *Luna* during its development. A desktop *theme* is a predefined set of colors, fonts, sounds, and other elements. Themes are not new to Windows, of course; they've been around since Microsoft Plus! was released for Windows 95. But Windows XP implements themes through a new visual styles engine that allows much greater customization. Instead of merely changing the color of a title bar, theme developers can change its texture, pattern, and shape!

Out of the box, Windows XP includes two distinct visual styles:

- **Windows XP style**   This is the new style that you see in illustrations throughout this book.

- **Windows classic style**   This style, marked by rigidly rectangular windows and solid colors, is the style that appears in Windows 95/98/Me and Windows NT/2000.

> **Note**   Certain windows—notably command prompt windows and windows for some earlier programs—don't conform to the new Windows XP style. Instead, they have square borders, along with title bar buttons, scroll bars, and other elements that follow the Windows classic style. That's because they run outside the control of the Themes service. It's perfectly normal—and unchangeable.

Chapter 15

Inside Out

Determine your personal preferences

Throughout this chapter, we explain lots of options, but offer few specific recommendations. That's because every user's needs and tastes are different. The authors of this book each have different desktop layouts, and we change them occasionally as requirements or whims move us. In case you're wondering how we set up our own systems, here's the desktop of one of our computers.

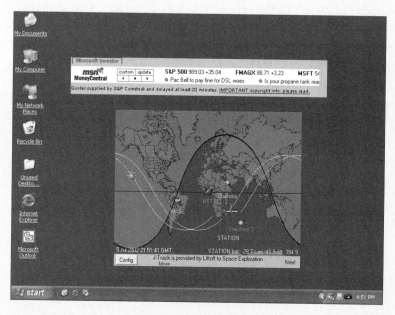

- After having the taskbar on the right side for many months, we've moved it back to the bottom of the screen, and it's two buttons high. This allows room for plenty of taskbar buttons—this computer typically has 10–15 open windows—and it makes room for eight Quick Launch buttons. The extra height also makes room for the complete date and time to appear in the notification area.

- The Quick Launch bar is on the taskbar, and it's sized to just accommodate buttons for eight frequently used tasks. Though some users prefer shortcut keys or a carefully arranged Start menu—and many dislike the clutter imposed by the Quick Launch bar—it works well for us.

- The Desktop toolbar appears as just a title at the right end of the taskbar. Because My Computer and My Documents icons folders are at the top of the Desktop namespace (even when their icons are not displayed on the desktop), clicking the double-arrow yields a cascading menu of all documents and other files on the system.

- The Address toolbar—which we use often—is docked to the top of the screen. It's rolled down in the preceding illustration, but it's set to auto-hide.

- The desktop is littered with icons. (We've been meaning to clean it up, honest.)

- We've customized the notification area to always show the new-mail icon and a few others that we use regularly. The rest are hidden—some permanently, others when inactive.

- We use the new-style Start menu (not shown in the illustration), but have removed several items (My Pictures, My Music, and so on) that we don't use and added a few others (such as Favorites).

To meet the publishing requirements of this book, we reduced the resolution to 800 x 600 for this illustration. Ordinarily, we run at 1152 x 864. At that resolution, the toolbar, taskbar, icons, and even the webcam picture of Yellowstone's Old Faithful occupy much less relative space than this illustration suggests. Nonetheless, the screen is quite cluttered.

Note that most of these settings on this heavily used system are wildly different from the austere default Windows settings. (They're probably also wildly different from what you would choose!) Don't be afraid to experiment.

To select a theme based on one of these visual styles, open Display Properties, shown in Figure 15-14. You can get there by right-clicking the desktop and choosing Properties, or by choosing Display in Control Panel's Appearance And Themes category. Make your selection in the Theme list.

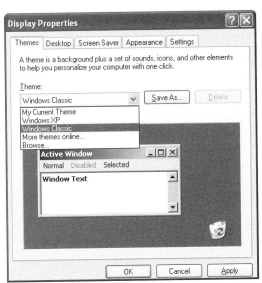

Figure 15-14. The bulk of the Themes tab is devoted to showing a preview of the selected theme.

Chapter 15

> **Tip** Use ClearType for sharper text
>
> ClearType can sharpen text for easier reading. It's intended for use on LCD monitors, but it improves text appearance on some CRT displays too. Try it; if you don't like it, switch back. To enable ClearType, open Display Properties and click Appearance, Effects. Then select Use The Following Method To Smooth Edges Of Screen Fonts and click ClearType in the list below. You can also try the Standard setting, designed for CRT users. For information about how ClearType works, visit Microsoft's ClearType site, at *http://www.microsoft.com/typography/ClearTypeInfo.mspx*. Microsoft also offers a valuable ClearType "tuner" that lets you optimize the way ClearType works on your system. You'll find the tuner at *http://www.microsoft.com/typography/cleartype/tuner/1.htm*. Additional information about ClearType is available in the Knowledge Base; see article 306527, "How to Use ClearType to Enhance Screen Fonts in Windows XP."

Both styles permit considerable customization. You can create your own theme by making changes to the items listed in Table 15-2. When you have everything set the way you like, return to the Themes tab in Display Properties and click Save As. Themes you save in My Documents or in %SystemRoot%\Resources\Themes appear on the Theme list.

Table 15-2. Theme Components You Can Change

Component	How to Change
Background	In Display Properties, click the Desktop tab and specify Background, Position, and Color.
Colors	In Display Properties, click the Appearance tab and select a Color Scheme. If none of the predefined schemes pleases your eye, click Advanced, where you can select your own color for each item. Note that the list of color schemes changes depending on your choice of Windows And Buttons style. Note also that many choices you make in the Advanced Appearance dialog box (such as the color of the active title bar) have no effect on ordinary windows if you choose the Windows XP visual style.
Fonts	In Display Properties, click the Appearance tab and select a Font Size. If you want to use a different font or size, click Advanced, where you can select your own font for each item that displays text.
Icons for My Computer, My Documents, My Network Places, and Recycle Bin	In Display Properties, click Desktop, Customize Desktop and select images for the desktop icons. Note that a theme doesn't record your choices of which icons appear on the desktop; it includes only your choice of icon for each item.

Chapter 15

Tweaking the Windows XP Interface

Table 15-2. Theme Components You Can Change

Component	How to Change
Mouse pointers	In Mouse Properties (open Mouse in Control Panel's Printers And Other Hardware category), click the Pointers tab and select individual pointers or a preset scheme.
Screen saver	In Display Properties, click the Screen Saver tab and select a screen saver.
Sounds	In Sounds And Audio Devices Properties (in Control Panel's Sounds, Speech, And Audio Devices category), click the Sounds tab and then select sounds for various events.
Visual style	In Display Properties, click the Appearance tab and select a Windows And Buttons style.

> **Tip** If you come up with a combination of sights and sounds that you particularly like, be sure to save it. If you don't, your changes are discarded when you select another theme.

Modifying the Predefined Color Schemes

To modify one of the supplied color schemes (a group of settings that also includes fonts and sizes of certain interface elements), open Display Properties and click the Appearance tab, shown in Figure 15-15. In the Windows And Buttons list, select a visual style and then select a scheme in the Color Scheme list.

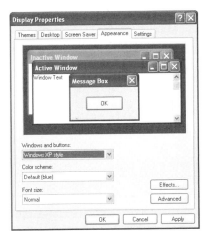

Figure 15-15. The available color schemes depend on the visual style you choose in the Windows And Buttons list.

Click Advanced to display the Advanced Appearance dialog box, shown in Figure 15-11, page 472. In the sample window, click the screen element you want to change. Then use the lists and buttons at the bottom of the dialog box to make your color, font, and size selections. For title bars, you can specify two colors; Windows creates a gradation from Color 1 (at the left end of the title bar) to Color 2 (at the right end). The Item list includes some items that don't appear in the sample window, so you might want to review it in its entirety before you move on.

The Color button for each item opens a selection of 20 standard colors. If you don't see the one you're looking for, click the Other button. Windows then displays a Color dialog box, as shown in Figure 15-16. Should you fail to find exactly the color you want in the Basic Colors palette, you can define your own custom colors. Change the color that appears in the Color|Solid box, either by adjusting the positions of the hue/saturation crosshair and the luminosity arrow or by specifying numeric values. When you have found the color you want, click Add To Custom Colors. If you want to replace an existing custom color, select it before you specify your new color.

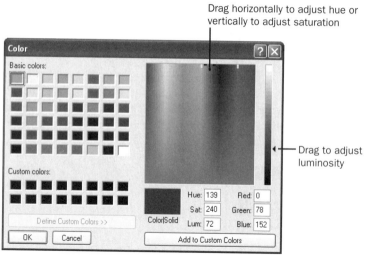

Figure 15-16. If you know a color's RGB specification, you can enter the values directly in the Red, Green, and Blue boxes.

Note If you select Windows XP Style in the Windows And Buttons box on the Appearance tab, some settings you make in the Advanced Appearance dialog box will have no effect on most windows. Though it's bound to cause some confusion, this is intentional. By design, the Windows XP visual style settings override some of these settings. How do you know which settings and which windows are overridden? Experiment. If you manage to make your screen illegible, you can always return to one of the original themes or color schemes.

Troubleshooting

Windows and buttons have square corners, even with the Windows XP theme selected.

If your display looks more like that of an earlier version of Windows—for example, the windows and buttons don't have round corners, the Close button doesn't stand out from other title bar buttons, and the Start button doesn't stand out on the taskbar—the first thing to check is that Windows XP Style is selected in the Windows And Buttons box on the Appearance tab of Display Properties. But what if the Windows XP Style choice isn't available? Visual styles are implemented by the Themes service. If the service isn't running, Windows reverts to the classic Windows styles, which don't rely on the Themes service.

To restore the Windows XP styles, open the Services console (at a command prompt, type **services.msc**), select Themes in the right pane, and then click the Start link on the Extended tab or the Start Service button on the toolbar.

If that doesn't fix the problem, right-click My Computer and choose Properties to open System Properties. Click the Advanced tab and then click Settings under Performance. On the Visual Effects tab, select Use Visual Styles On Windows And Buttons (the last item in the Custom box).

Installing Additional Themes

If you examine the Theme list on the Themes tab of Display Properties, you'll find the item More Themes Online near the bottom of the list. This is a link that takes you to *http://www.microsoft.com/windows/plus,* a site where you can read about, sample, and buy Microsoft Plus! for Windows XP, which includes four additional themes: Aquarium, da Vinci, Nature, and Space—along with various other attractions. The four Plus! themes, like their predecessors in earlier Plus! editions, supply thematically related wallpaper, animated pointers, sound schemes, and screen savers.

Figure 15-17 provides a look at the wallpaper, color scheme, and Normal Select pointer (note the space-shuttle image resting on the OK button) for the Space theme. Unfortunately, a silent, motionless, black-and-white screen shot can't begin to convey the full effect of this theme or any of the others that come with Plus! The stunning three-dimensional graphics of the Plus! screen savers, in particular, have to be seen to be appreciated. The package includes eight such screen savers, four of which are not attached to themes. You can, of course, apply any of the screen savers without opting for any of the related thematic material.

As additional inducement for you to buy, Plus! provides three games and assorted other media-oriented goodies: a voice interface for Windows Media Player, a CD label creator, a tool for creating custom playlists in Windows Media Player, and a utility for converting MP3 files to WMA. Plus! runs in both editions of Windows XP. Minimum requirements are a 500 MHz processor (750 MHz recommended), 64 MB of memory (128 MB recommended), and 300 MB of hard disk space. To install the screen savers and games, you need a 3-D graphics accelerator card with at least 16 MB of memory.

Figure 15-17. Microsoft's Plus! package comes with four additional themes: Space (shown here), Nature, da Vinci, and Aquarium.

Going Retro: Reverting to Windows 2000 (or Earlier)

You might decide that the new look of Windows is not for you. Because old habits die hard, you might find it easier (as might other users in your organization) to stay with the familiar interface of earlier Windows versions. To do that, you really need to change only two settings:

1. In Display Properties, click the Themes tab and select Windows Classic in the Theme list. (Optionally, you can select your favorite color scheme on the Appearance tab.)

2. In Taskbar And Start Menu Properties, click the Start Menu tab and select Classic Start Menu. (If you want to go all the way, click the Taskbar tab and clear Group Similar Taskbar Buttons and Hide Inactive Icons.)

Chapter 15

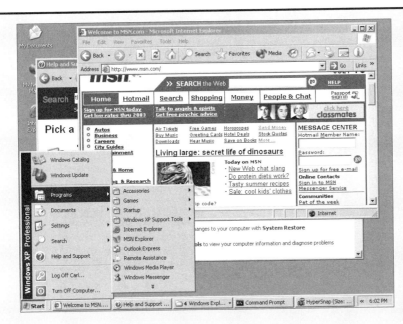

Before you do this, however, try the new interface for a while. You might find the improvements helpful. If you are really sure you want to re-create the look and feel of earlier versions of Windows, you should probably also take the following steps:

1. Open User Accounts in Control Panel, click Change The Way Users Log On Or Off, and clear Use The Welcome Screen.

2. Right-click My Computer and choose Properties. In the Performance section of the Advanced tab of the System Properties dialog box, click Settings. Then select Adjust For Best Performance.

3. Run Services.msc, double-click Themes, change Startup Type to Manual, and click Stop.

If your goal is to re-create the Windows 2000 ambience, you won't need to have the Themes service running. Stopping the service will make some additional memory available to your system.

Skinning Windows XP

Prior to the initial release of Windows XP, rumors were flying that Microsoft was going to make the newest version of the operating system completely "skinnable"—that is, that users would be able to overhaul the appearance and behavior of windows, menus, and controls in ways that go well beyond switching wallpaper and color schemes. In the end, however, in the interest of maintaining consistency and relative simplicity, Microsoft chose not to integrate skinning features into Windows XP, but instead to provide "hooks" for skinning products from third parties.

The most widely used of these products is WindowBlinds, from Stardock. WindowBlinds is one component of a suite of customizing products called Object Desktop. If your taste for novelty goes way beyond what you can do with the native Windows XP interface, you'll want to investigate WindowBlinds and Object Desktop at *http://www.stardock.com*. With a complete set of skinning tools, you'll be able to do such things as reposition buttons and controls, add rollup buttons to windows (buttons that shrink windows into their title bars instead of collapsing them onto the taskbar), add background images to the Start menu—and much, much more.

Stardock also maintains a Web site (*http://www.wincustomize.com*) where users can upload their latest creations and download those of fellow skinners. Figure 15-18 shows a sample skin downloaded from WinCustomize.com.

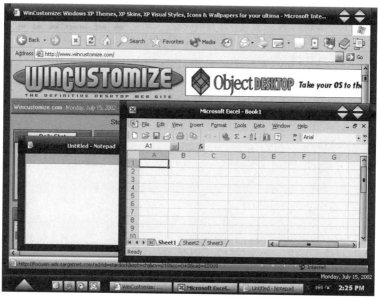

Figure 15-18. This WindowBlinds skin, downloaded from *www.wincustomize.com*, features bright blue pinstriped window borders, rollup buttons, and a black-and-white gradient-filled Start menu button that doesn't say "Start."

Customizing Visual Effects for Better Performance

Before you leave the topic of colors, fonts, and visual effects, you might want to consider what impact these snazzy visual effects have on performance. With a late-model, high-powered computer, you're not likely to notice any slowdown. But if you're using a computer that's more than a few years old, you can probably improve its performance by eliminating some visual effects. It's nice that menus fade in and fade out, that windows perceptibly shrink to the taskbar when minimized, and so on. But it is just eye candy, after all, and it's not worth slowing your computing experience for.

Chapter 15

You'll find a collection of performance-related settings for visual effects by following these steps:

1. Right-click My Computer (on the Start menu, the desktop, or in a Windows Explorer window) and choose Properties to open the System Properties dialog box. Alternatively, open System in Control Panel (in the Performance And Maintenance category).

2. Click the Advanced tab and then click Settings under Performance. The Performance Options dialog box appears.

3. Make your selections in the dialog box. If you choose Adjust For Best Appearance, Windows selects all the option boxes. If you choose Adjust For Best Performance, all the option boxes are cleared. If you choose Let Windows Choose What's Best For My Computer, Windows leaves all options selected if your computer is reasonably quick. To make your own selection of options, choose Customize and then select and clear option boxes to suit your tastes.

Customizing the Taskbar

The taskbar houses the Start button, the notification area, and a button for each running program. You can use these task buttons to switch from one running program to another. You can also click a task button to minimize an open window or to reopen a minimized window. Your taskbar might also hold one or more toolbars—collections of icons that let you start programs quickly. For information about using toolbars on the taskbar, see "Using the Quick Launch Bar and Other Desktop Toolbars," page 456.

Changing the Taskbar's Size and Appearance

The default location of the taskbar is along the bottom edge of the desktop. Before you can move or resize the taskbar, it must be unlocked. Right-click an unoccupied area of the taskbar and, if a check mark appears next to the Lock The Taskbar command, choose the command to clear the check mark. You can move the taskbar to any other edge of the desktop if you want to try something a little different. Click an unoccupied area of the taskbar and drag toward another edge of the desktop. By default, the taskbar shows one row of buttons (or one column, if your taskbar is docked against the left or right edge of the desktop). If you keep toolbars on the taskbar, you might find it convenient to expand the taskbar to two or even three rows. Simply position the mouse along the inner border of the taskbar (the edge closest to the center of the screen). When the mouse pointer becomes a two-headed arrow, drag toward the center of the screen to expand the taskbar.

Making More Room on the Taskbar

In previous versions of Windows, active users who like to keep many windows open simultaneously had to figure out which tiny taskbar button represented which window. As new windows opened, each taskbar button was reduced to fit, leaving no room for the taskbar title.

Windows XP offers a better way: taskbar grouping. With this feature, when the taskbar fills up, Windows consolidates taskbar buttons from a single application (for example, several Internet Explorer windows) under one taskbar button. A number on the button indicates how many application instances it contains. Clicking the button displays a list of windows, as shown in Figure 15-19. As you might expect, right-clicking an item in the list displays the same shortcut menu that you'd see if the window had its own button; with this menu, you can move, resize, or close the window.

Figure 15-19. Click one of the taskbar button's list items to select its window.

In addition to reducing taskbar clutter, taskbar grouping offers some other benefits that aren't immediately apparent. The menu that appears when you right-click the group button provides several useful commands. With a single click, you can:

- Display all windows in the group (choose Cascade, Tile Horizontally, or Tile Vertically), without affecting any other open windows.
- Minimize all windows in the group.
- Close all windows in the group.

Tweaking the Windows XP Interface

To enable taskbar grouping, open the Taskbar And Start Menu Properties dialog box, as shown in Figure 15-20. You can find it in Control Panel (in the Appearance And Themes category) or, more simply, by right-clicking an unoccupied area of the taskbar and choosing Properties. Select Group Similar Taskbar Buttons.

Figure 15-20. Reduce clutter and gain window-management features by enabling taskbar grouping.

Inside Out

Customize taskbar grouping

By default, taskbar grouping comes into play only when the taskbar fills up. Even if you have multiple windows from the same application open, if there's room for a separate button for each window, that's what you get.

You might prefer to have all similar windows grouped together all the time. To do that, you'll need to edit the registry. Use Registry Editor to open HKCU\Software\Microsoft\Windows\ CurrentVersion\Explorer\Advanced. Create a new DWORD value named TaskbarGroupSize.

This setting controls how many windows are allowed before Windows starts grouping them under a single taskbar button. A setting of 2 groups related windows as soon as you open a second window, even if there's plenty of room on the taskbar; 3 enables grouping as soon as you have three or more similar windows; and so on. If you prefer to prevent taskbar grouping unless your taskbar gets *really* crowded, use a higher setting (say, 5). You must log off and then back on before this setting takes effect.

You can also increase button space by removing the clock from the taskbar. If you don't need Windows to display the time of day, you can probably squeeze at least one more button onto the bar by removing the clock. In the Taskbar And Start Menu Properties dialog box, clear Show The Clock.

Getting the Taskbar Out of Your Way

By default, the taskbar remains visible even when you're working in a maximized program. If that's inconvenient for any reason, you can tell it to get out of the way. The Taskbar And Start Menu Properties dialog box, shown in Figure 15-20, offers two options to control this behavior.

- **Keep The Taskbar On Top Of Other Windows**   Clearing this check box means that you'll be able to see the taskbar at all times *except* when a window is maximized or placed over the taskbar.

- **Auto-Hide The Taskbar**   With this option selected, the taskbar retreats into the edge of the desktop. To display the taskbar, move the mouse pointer to the edge of the desktop where the taskbar is "hidden."

Note   Regardless of how you set options in the Taskbar And Start Menu Properties dialog box, you can make the taskbar visible at any time by pressing the Windows logo key or Ctrl+Esc.

Note   Locking the taskbar (an option in the Taskbar And Start Menu Properties dialog box and on the shortcut menu that appears when you right-click the taskbar) does not prevent you from using either of the preceding options. Locking merely prevents you from inadvertently moving or resizing the taskbar or any toolbars in the taskbar.

Removing Unneeded Icons from the Notification Area

The notification area (formerly known as the system tray or the status area) can become crowded with tiny icons—many of which don't "notify" you of anything. A variety of programs use the notification area to provide program-starting icons. But many of those programs seldom need to be started; they continue to do their job without any intervention from you. Windows XP adds a new feature that hides icons you don't use. Like the programs on the left side of the Start menu, the notification area adapts to the way you work. And also like the Start menu, you can specify your own preferences that override the adaptive behavior of Windows XP.

Chapter 15

With this icon-hiding feature enabled, only active icons and icons you specify appear in the notification area. Others are only a click away: Click the arrow at the left end of the notification area to display the hidden icons, as shown in Figure 15-21.

Click to display hidden icons

Figure 15-21. Clicking the arrow expands the notification area to reveal all icons.

To enable this feature, select Hide Inactive Icons in the Taskbar And Start Menu Properties dialog box (to get to this dialog box, right-click the Start button and choose Properties). To specify which icons should be hidden, click Customize to display the dialog box shown in Figure 15-22. For each icon—including icons that have been displayed in the past as well as ones that are currently in the notification area—you can choose whether to hide or show.

Figure 15-22. You determine which icons you want to be visible and which ones you want to be accessible only when you expand the notification area.

Streamlining Control Panel

Earlier versions of Windows had a single Control Panel—a collection of icons that led to assorted configuration tools and settings. As computers became more complex, the number of icons in Control Panel increased, giving pause to users plunging into Control Panel for the first time. Windows XP addresses this confusion by dividing Control Panel icons into categories, and putting a friendly face on the new Control Panel, shown in Figure 15-23.

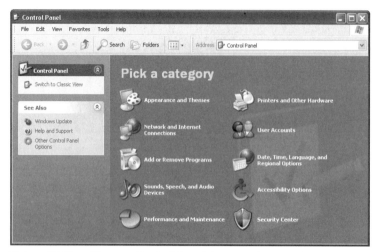

Figure 15-23. The new Control Panel is pretty but requires an extra step to reach your destination.

Experienced users are likely to find the new Control Panel more of a hindrance than an aid, but fortunately, it's easy to revert to the single-level Control Panel of old, shown in Figure 15-24.

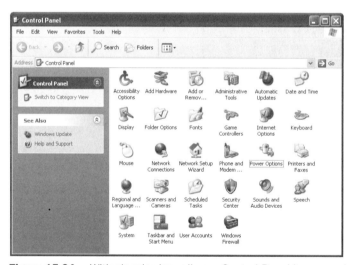

Figure 15-24. With classic view, all your Control Panel icons are in one place.

Resetting Control Panel will probably be one of the first changes you'll make on a new computer.

Inside Out

Customize Control Panel categories

Some programs and devices install their own Control Panel applications. These applications should go into the proper category if you use Category view, but applications not written to Windows XP specifications might not. If you want to change the category in which a Control Panel application appears, you can do so with a registry edit.

The HKLM\Software\Microsoft\Windows\CurrentVersion\Control Panel\Extended Properties\ {305CA226-D286-468e-B848-2B2E8E697B74} 2 key contains the category information. Each DWORD value, which uses the full path to a .cpl (Control Panel) file as its name, should have one of the following settings.

Category	Value Data
Accessibility Options	0x00000007
Add or Remove Programs	0x00000008
Appearance and Themes	0x00000001
Date, Time, Language, and Regional Options	0x00000006
Network and Internet Connections	0x00000003
Other Control Panel Options	0x00000000
Performance and Maintenance	0x00000005
Printers and Other Hardware	0x00000002
Security Center	0x00000010
Sounds, Speech, and Audio Devices	0x00000004
User Accounts	0x00000009
No category	0xFFFFFFFF

Although Control Panel provides a suitable means of access to settings you make only occasionally, you might prefer a more direct way to open certain configuration tools. Table 15-3 shows the command line you can use to reach each of the standard Control Panel applications. In many cases, you can use a command line to go directly to a particular tab of interest, saving another click. You can use these command lines at a command prompt, of course, but for frequently used items they'll be of more use encapsulated in a shortcut or used in a batch program or script. You can create a shortcut for any Control Panel item by right-clicking it in Control Panel and choosing Create Shortcut from the shortcut menu. The resulting shortcut, however, provides no access to the command string that invokes the Control Panel item. To incorporate command strings for Control Panel items in a batch program or script, use the command strings listed in Table 15-3.

> **Tip**   Run a DLL as an alternative to Control.exe
>
> As an alternative to using Control.exe to start Control Panel items—the method used in most Table 15-3 entries—you can run a dynamic-link library (DLL) as an application. In each instance, replace **control** with **rundll32.exe shell32.dll,Control_RunDLL**. (Note that the second parameter—Control_RunDLL—is case sensitive.) This method works better in some programming languages.

Table 15-3. **Commands to Open Control Panel Items**

Control Panel Option	Command
Accessibility Options	**control access.cpl,,x** where *x* is replaced by one of these values: 
Add Hardware	**control hdwwiz.cpl**
Add or Remove Programs	Change or Remove Programs **control appwiz.cpl** Add New Programs **control appwiz.cpl,,1** Add/Remove Windows Components **control appwiz.cpl,,2** Set Program Access and Defaults **control appwiz.cpl,,3**
Administrative Tools	**control admintools**
Automatic Updates	**control wuaucpl.cpl**
Date and Time	**control timedate.cpl,,x** where *x* is replaced by one of these values:

Chapter 15

Table 15-3. Commands to Open Control Panel Items

Control Panel Option	Command
Display	**control desk.cpl,,*x*** where *x* is replaced by one of these values:

Folder Options	**control folders**
Fonts	**control fonts**
Game Controllers	**control joy.cpl**
Internet Options	**control inetcpl.cpl,,*x*** where *x* is replaced by one of these values:

Keyboard	**control main.cpl,@1,*x*** where *x* is replaced by one of these values:

Mouse	**control main.cpl,,*x*** where *x* is replaced by one of these values:

Network Connections	**control netconnections**
Network Setup Wizard	**control netsetup.cpl**

Chapter 15

499

Table 15-3. Commands to Open Control Panel Items

Control Panel Option	Command
Phone and Modem Options	**control telephon.cpl,,x** where x is replaced by one of these values:

```
Phone and Modem Options          [?][X]
  Dialing Rules | Modems | Advanced
        |          |        |
        0          1        2
```

Power Options	**control powercfg.cpl**
Printers and Faxes	**control printers**
Regional and Language Options	**control intl.cpl,,x** where x is replaced by one of these values:

```
Regional and Language Options          [?][X]
  Regional Options | Languages | Advanced
        |              |           |
        1              2           3
```

Scanners and Cameras	**control scannercamera**
Scheduled Tasks	**control schedtasks**
Security Center	**control wscui.cpl**
Sounds and Audio Devices	**control mmsys.cpl,,x** where x is replaced by one of these values:

```
Sounds and Audio Devices Properties          [?][X]
  Volume | Sounds | Audio | Voice | Hardware
    |        |        |       |        |
    0        1        2       3        4
```

Speech	**control speech**
System	**control sysdm.cpl,,x** where x is replaced by one of these values:

```
System Properties                                   [?][X]
      System Restore   | Automatic Updates  |   Remote
  General | Computer Name | Hardware | Advanced
    |    |      |        |      |        |
    0    4      1        5      2        6      3
```

Taskbar and Start Menu	**rundll32.exe shell32.dll,Options_RunDLL 1**

Tweaking the Windows XP Interface

Table 15-3. Commands to Open Control Panel Items

Control Panel Option	Command
User Accounts	Workgroup version (not available in domain environment)
	control userpasswords
	Windows 2000/domain version
	control userpasswords2
Windows Firewall	**control firewall.cpl**
Wireless Link	control irprops.cpl,,*x* where *x* is replaced by one of these values:

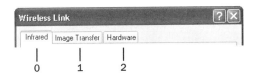

Customizing Windows XP with Tweak UI

Tweak UI, shown in Figure 15-25, is one of a set of PowerToys created by Microsoft to enhance the functionality of Windows XP. You can download any or all of the PowerToys, free of charge, from the Microsoft Web site at *http://www.microsoft.com/windowsxp/pro/ downloads/powertoys.asp*.

As its name suggests, Tweak UI provides all sorts of ways to tweak the Windows user interface. You can use Tweak UI, for example, to change the appearance of shortcut icons, prevent particular applications from appearing on the most frequently used programs section of the Start menu, add folders of your choice to the Places bar that appears along the left side of the common File, Open and File, Save dialog boxes—and much, much more.

Some of Tweak UI's options (such as the one that lets you change the threshold at which Windows groups similar items on the taskbar) are alternatives for procedures described elsewhere in this chapter. A few provide functionality that would otherwise be inaccessible to users of Windows XP Home Edition. Many others are simple menu-pick avenues to customizations that would otherwise require you to edit the registry.

If you have used the version of Tweak UI that was available at the time when Windows XP first shipped, be aware that Microsoft has withdrawn that version and replaced it with another. If you plan to download the newest version, you must uninstall the old one first. You'll find that, in the latest incarnation, each of the PowerToys can be downloaded and installed (as well as uninstalled) individually.

Chapter 15

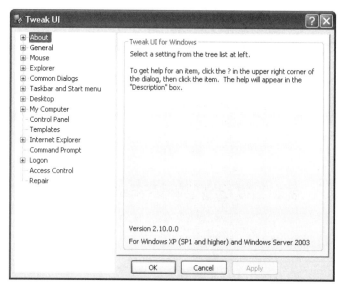

Figure 15-25. Tweak UI, a free but unsupported utility from Microsoft, gives you many additional ways to customize the appearance and behavior of Windows XP.

Because Microsoft does not officially support Tweak UI, you won't be able to call Product Support Services if you run into difficulty with it or any of the other PowerToys. It's not likely that you will need support, however. We consider the PowerToys safe, reliable, and extremely useful.

Chapter 16

Advanced Internet Explorer Options

Microsoft Windows XP comes with Microsoft Internet Explorer 6 as its default tool for accessing Web pages from the Internet or a local intranet. Reflecting the range of expertise of Windows users, Internet Explorer can be used with little or no modification by novices, yet also has extensive possibilities for tailoring by expert users. In this chapter, we discuss many of these advanced configuration features.

Choosing a Default Web Browser and Java Virtual Machine

If you prefer another browser to Internet Explorer, you can (if you want) remove Internet Explorer's icons and Start menu shortcuts. To do this, choose Add Or Remove Programs in Control Panel. Click Add/Remove Windows Components. Then, when the Windows Components Wizard appears, clear the check box next to Internet Explorer, and click Next. Internet Explorer is then removed from your desktop, Start menu, and Quick Launch toolbar.

After you install another browser, you can specify it as the top choice on the Start menu's pinned items list. For details, see the sidebar "Controlling the Pinned Internet and E-Mail Items," page 449.

At Home with Windows XP

With the exception of a few customizations involving Group Policy (which is unavailable in Windows XP Home Edition), everything in this chapter applies equally to both versions of Windows XP.

If you have installed Service Pack 1 or Service Pack 2 for Windows XP, you have another, more comprehensive tool for easing access to one browser and hiding access to others that have been installed. Use the Set Program Access And Defaults option within Add Or Remove Programs (you'll also find a shortcut on the Start menu) to specify which browser you want to appear on your Start menu, desktop, and elsewhere. This tool also changes the browser that's associated with HTML files (and other files normally viewed in a browser) to the one you choose. For more information about Set Program Access And Defaults, see "Selecting a Web Browser and Other Middleware Components," page 64.

Set Program Access And Defaults also lets you select which virtual machine (VM) you want to use for running Java applications. For information about Java virtual machines, see "What's the Story with Java Virtual Machines?" page 65.

Customizing the Internet Explorer User Interface

Like Windows Explorer, Internet Explorer offers three optional toolbars and lets you customize each in various ways. You can add buttons to or remove them from the Standard Buttons toolbar, add links to or remove them from the Links toolbar, remove the Go button from the Address toolbar, and rearrange all of these elements to suit your tastes and optimize the space at the top of your screen. After you have positioned your toolbars (and the menu bar) to your liking, you can take advantage of the program's toolbar-locking feature to prevent anyone (yourself included, of course) from accidentally upsetting your carefully wrought layout.

Repositioning Toolbars

Figure 16-1 shows the Internet Explorer menu bar and three toolbars in one of their many possible arrangements. At the left edge of each of the four elements are dotted handles. To change the position of any element, drag its handle. Note that you can move the menu bar this way, as well as the toolbars. If you don't see any handles, your toolbars are locked. To unlock them, choose View, Toolbars, and then choose Lock The Toolbars to toggle the lock off.

To display a toolbar that isn't currently displayed, choose View, Toolbars, and then select the name of the toolbar. Choose the same command again to hide the toolbar. Note that the menu bar is not optional: You can move it, but you can't hide it altogether.

Figure 16-1. You can rearrange toolbars by dragging their handles.

If you really want to conserve space at the top of your screen, you can put the most essential interface elements—the menu bar, the Address bar, and the Standard Buttons toolbar—all on one line. Remove the Go button from the Address bar (pressing Enter after typing a URL in the Address bar is equivalent to clicking Go) by right-clicking it and choosing Go Button from the shortcut menu. Then reduce the Address bar to a reasonable width. If the menu bar and Standard Buttons toolbar don't fit entirely, Internet Explorer truncates them on the right and displays chevrons to indicate that it has done so. Clicking a chevron displays a small palette containing the remaining items (as shown in Figure 16-2, a picture of the screen at 800 × 600 resolution).

Figure 16-2.   Click a chevron to show toolbar or menu bar elements that aren't otherwise visible.

Tip   Press F11 for full-screen display

Actually, you can hide the menu bar—by pressing F11. This action puts Internet Explorer into a full-screen mode, in which only the Standard Buttons toolbar is visible (even if you've hidden it in Internet Explorer's normal display mode). While in full-screen mode, you can dock additional toolbars, as well as the menu bar, so that they abut the Standard Buttons toolbar, but everything you choose to display is squeezed into a single row at the top of the screen. In full-screen mode, Internet Explorer is maximized, even if it was previously not maximized, and the Windows taskbar is covered. In other words, you get every available square millimeter of screen space for interacting with the Web pages you visit. You can still display the taskbar by hovering your mouse at the bottom of the screen (if that's where you've chosen to put it), and you can return Internet Explorer to its normal display style by pressing F11 a second time.

Chapter 16

Tailoring the Standard Buttons Toolbar

To edit the content of the Standard Buttons toolbar, choose View, Toolbars, Customize (or right-click the toolbar and choose Customize from the shortcut menu). To add a button to the toolbar, drag it from the Available Toolbar Buttons window of the Customize Toolbar dialog box, shown in Figure 16-3, to the location of your choice in the Current Toolbar Buttons window. To remove an item, select it in the right window and click Remove. To change the order in which toolbar buttons appear, drag them upward or downward within the Current Toolbar Buttons window. If you use a truncated toolbar like the one shown in Figure 16-2, you will probably want to make sure that the buttons you use most often are in the part of the toolbar that's always visible.

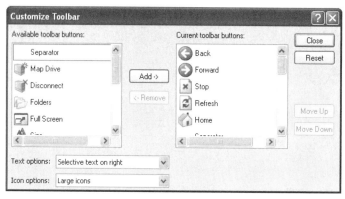

Figure 16-3. The Customize Toolbar dialog box lets you populate the Standard Buttons toolbar with only those tools that you find most useful.

Note that the Standard Buttons toolbar is designed to be extensible. That is, other applications can add their own tools to it. In Figure 16-2, for example, some of the buttons on the toolbar's expanded palette were added by Microsoft Encarta. You can add and remove such application-specific buttons via the Customize Toolbar dialog box, exactly as you would add or remove an Internet Explorer button.

Tip Start Internet Explorer without a home page

If you use a dial-up connection, you might find it annoying to have to wait for the home page to appear each time you start Internet Explorer. To start the browser more quickly, have it open without a home page—by choosing Tools, Internet Options; clicking the General tab; and then clicking Use Blank. As an alternative to using a blank home page, you can launch Internet Explorer from a shortcut with the following command string: **iexplore –nohome**. However, when you start this way, some of the browser's menu commands are unavailable until you actually load a page.

Inside Out

Control toolbar customization with Group Policy

On systems running Windows XP Professional, you can use Group Policy to configure the content of the Standard Buttons toolbar. By doing so, you can prevent nonadministrative users (and administrators who don't know about Group Policy) from making changes to your custom arrangement. Type **gpedit.msc** at a command prompt to launch Group Policy. Then open User Configuration\Administrative Templates\Windows Components\Internet Explorer\Toolbars.

In the details pane, double-click Configure Toolbar Buttons. Select Enabled, select the buttons you want to include, and then click OK.

To make this policy effective, you must also enable another policy in the same folder: Disable Customizing Browser Toolbar Buttons. If you don't do that, Internet Explorer reverts to its previous toolbar settings immediately after opening the next time. In addition, of course, enabling this policy prevents users from making changes to the toolbar arrangement.

While you're here, you might want to consider the Toolbars folder's final policy, Disable Customizing Browser Toolbars. Enabling this policy prevents users (including yourself) from selecting or repositioning toolbars as described in the preceding section. (Unfortunately, Group Policy enforces this restriction in a ham-handed way. Instead of removing the dotted handles, as when the toolbars are locked, the dotted handles remain and the mouse pointer changes to suggest that moving is possible. However, dragging the handles actually does nothing.)

For more information about Group Policy, see Appendix F, "Group Policy."

Chapter 16

Customizing the Links Toolbar

The Links toolbar is designed to hold shortcuts to your most favorite favorites—the Web sites you use every day. Windows initially populates it with links to various Microsoft sites, which perhaps you don't need. You can replace those. To remove an item from the Links toolbar, right-click it and choose Delete from the shortcut menu.

The simplest way to add a shortcut to a favorite Web site is as follows:

1. Display the Web site.
2. Drag the Internet Explorer icon at the left edge of the Address bar and drop it on the Links toolbar.
3. Right-click the new Links item, choose Rename from the shortcut menu, and then type a short name.

The last step is optional, of course, but toolbar real estate is scarce, and you don't want to fill the space with a verbose shortcut name.

Troubleshooting

Internet Explorer displays third-party toolbars incorrectly.

Third-party toolbars are available from a number of search vendors (Google, for example), antivirus vendors, and other sources. Some users have reported that Internet Explorer occasionally gets its wires crossed about which toolbars to display—showing, for example, the antivirus toolbar when the search toolbar is selected, or vice versa. If you experience this sort of problem, try choosing Tools, Internet Options; clicking the Advanced tab; and then clearing the Enable Third-Party Browser Extensions (Requires Restart) check box. After doing this, close all Internet Explorer windows, restart Internet Explorer, select the same check box, close again, and restart once more. That should unravel the mixup.

You can use the same check box to get rid of all your third-party toolbars (that is, remove them from the View, Toolbars submenu) should you ever tire of them completely. To get rid of a specific third-party toolbar, see if an uninstall routine is provided in the Add Or Remove Programs section of Control Panel. Alternatively, you can disable specific third-party toolbars without removing them from your system using Internet Explorer's Tools, Manage Add-ons command. For information about Manage Add-ons, see "Managing Browser Add-ons," page 327.

Inside Out

Bury the Links folder—or create a more useful links toolbar

As constituted in a fresh installation of Internet Explorer, the Links toolbar probably serves its vendor's interests more than your own. Because it promotes particular Web sites that Microsoft (or another entity that has created a customized version of Internet Explorer for you) would like you to visit, some people find this toolbar downright annoying. You can suppress its display, of course, by deselecting the Links item on the View, Toolbars submenu. But the folder from which its contents are derived—%UserProfile%\Favorites\Links—is unaffected by this action. Moreover, if you delete this folder from your hard disk and subsequently choose View, Toolbars, Links, Internet Explorer not only displays an empty Links toolbar, it also re-creates an empty Links folder to accommodate the empty toolbar. You can get rid of this hardy creature (the folder, not the menu command) permanently by running Registry Editor, navigating to HKCU\Software\Microsoft\Internet Explorer\Toolbar, double-clicking the LinksFolderName value, and deleting the text *Links* in the Edit String dialog box. After taking this step, if you erase the %UserProfile%\Favorites\Links folder, Internet Explorer will not re-create it, even if you opt to redisplay the Links toolbar.

What Internet Explorer *will* do if you redisplay the Links toolbar after making the registry edit just described is interesting and potentially useful: It will turn your entire Favorites folder into a toolbar, displaying as much of it as it can squeeze onto a single line (with whatever toolbars may be occupying that line). If you click the chevron at the right side of this customized Links toolbar, any favorites that don't fit on the toolbar become available via a drop-down menu. This form of favorites access can be particularly handy if you like to work in full-screen mode and don't choose to display the menu bar. As the illustration below shows, you can get to a favorite site by navigating a cascading submenu, and the menu retires gracefully from the scene when you aren't using it.

Configuring Internet Explorer to Work with Other Programs

Internet Explorer maintains connections with six programs related to your use of the Internet:

- An HTML editor
- An e-mail client
- A newsgroup reader
- An Internet conferencing program
- A calendar program
- A contact manager

When you click a particular kind of link on a Web page—a *mailto* link, for example—Internet Explorer opens the appropriate program. To configure these support programs, choose Tools, Internet Options, and then click the Programs tab, shown in Figure 16-4. Select your programs from the categorized lists. (Note that the choices available in these lists depend on the software installed on your system and might not match the ones shown in the figure.)

Chapter 16

Figure 16-4.   You can configure support programs on the Programs tab of the Internet Options dialog box.

Using (or Refusing) AutoComplete

Internet Explorer's AutoComplete features can help reduce keystrokes (and keystroke errors) by remembering URLs you type, data you enter into Web forms, logon names, and passwords. Not everyone welcomes this kind of assistance, though. Depending on your tastes, you might want to use all, none, or only some of the browser's AutoComplete services.

> **Note**   An interesting article about AutoComplete, written from the developer's perspective, may be found at *http://msdn.microsoft.com/library/default.asp?url=/workshop/author/forms/autocomplete_ovr.asp.*

The dialog box shown in Figure 16-5 (which you can display by choosing Tools, Internet Options; clicking the Content tab; and then clicking the AutoComplete button) provides control over all but one of the AutoComplete options. (The other option, called Inline AutoComplete, appears in a different dialog box. For more information, see "Using Inline AutoComplete," page 513.) Here you can select any or all of the following check boxes:

- Web Addresses—to enable auto-completion of data typed in the Address bar
- Forms—to enable auto-completion of data that you provide to Web pages themselves, such as the names and shipping addresses that you supply on e-commerce sites
- User Names And Passwords On Forms—to have Internet Explorer remember logon credentials for various sites that you visit

Caution If you select User Names And Passwords On Forms, Internet Explorer always prompts before collecting a new password. The password itself appears on screen as a string of asterisks and is encrypted (via the Protected Storage service) for storage on your disk. A person reading over your shoulder or prowling your hard disk will therefore not be able to pick up your password when AutoComplete supplies it. Nevertheless, someone making unauthorized use of your Windows XP user account could interact with Web sites for which you have AutoComplete user name and password data, effectively impersonating you. Unless you are sure that no one else will ever use your account, you might want to decline the browser's offer to remember logon credentials.

For more about security considerations relating to AutoComplete, see "Guarding Passwords and Other Sensitive Data," page 340.

Figure 16-5. You can turn various AutoComplete options on or off individually.

Caution With AutoComplete for User Names And Passwords turned on, Internet Explorer prompts before saving a new logon name and password. If you decline the offer for the site in question, it won't prompt again for that site. The only way to get another chance to save your credentials will be to clear all passwords and start again.

If you want Internet Explorer to remember logon credentials for new sites that you visit, be sure to select Prompt Me To Save Passwords, as well as User Names And Passwords On Forms. If you clear this suboption, the AutoComplete feature will retain entries that it already has recorded but will not record any new ones.

Troubleshooting

AutoComplete does not save any user names or passwords.

If you have selected the User Names And Passwords On Forms option in the AutoComplete Settings dialog box, but Internet Explorer does not preserve logon credentials for any site, it's possible that you have inadvertently turned off the Protected Storage service, upon which AutoComplete depends. To see if this is the case, choose Start, Run, type **services.msc**, and scroll down to the Protected Storage item. If the Status column does not say *Started*, right-click Protected Storage and choose Start from the shortcut menu. Then close the Services console and restart Internet Explorer.

According to Knowledge Base article 306895 (*http://support.microsoft.com/?kbid=306895*), AutoComplete can also fail to record logon credentials if RSABase.dll is incorrectly registered. For details about correcting this problem, see this article. The article also describes a more drastic procedure that might correct the problem in the event that the Protected Storage service is running and you've tried re-registering RSABase.dll.

Clearing the AutoComplete History

If Internet Explorer's memory bank of AutoComplete entries starts to feel like a nuisance or a security hazard, you can induce immediate amnesia by clicking Clear Forms or Clear Passwords in the AutoComplete Settings dialog box. Each of these buttons deletes a particular category of entries. As the text below the buttons indicates, to clear Web address entries, you have to go elsewhere—to the General tab of the Internet Options dialog box. Clicking Clear History there covers your tracks on the History Explorer bar in addition to clearing Auto-Complete entries.

Tip Delete AutoComplete items selectively

If you make occasional typing errors, the AutoComplete feature has a tendency to collect useless, misspelled entries right along with helpful ones. This accumulation of missteps leads some users to turn the whole feature off in frustration. There's a simpler solution: To get rid of a mistyped AutoComplete entry, press Down Arrow as many times as necessary until the unwanted item is selected, and then press the Delete key.

Tip Save keystrokes by pressing Ctrl+Enter

With or without AutoComplete, you can reduce labor in the Address Bar with a handy keyboard shortcut. Pressing Ctrl+Enter prepends http://www. and appends .com to whatever you've already typed.

Using Inline AutoComplete

The AutoComplete entries collected by the options shown in Figure 16-5 appear in drop-down lists as you type. To use an entry, you select it with your mouse or with cursor keys. Inline AutoComplete works differently. With this feature turned on, Internet Explorer attempts to read your mind as you type in the Address Bar. Type **www.m**, for example, and Inline AutoComplete might propose *www.microsoft.com*, as the following illustration shows:

In this illustration, the drop-down list of AutoComplete entries includes two lengthy URLs beginning with *www.microsoft.com/downloads/details.aspx*. If you wanted to return to the Microsoft downloads site without entering either of these entire URLs, the drop-down entries would not be helpful. But with Inline AutoComplete, you could press the End key after typing **www.m**, then type the letter **d**. Inline AutoComplete would fill out the word *downloads*, and you'd be good to go.

To turn on Inline AutoComplete, choose Tools, Internet Options, and then click the Advanced tab. In the Browsing section of the Settings list, select Use Inline AutoComplete.

Managing Your Favorites

Internet Explorer maintains a repository of shortcuts to your favorite Web sites in the folder %UserProfile%\Favorites. Any time you discover a site that you know you'll want to return to, you can add a shortcut to that site to the Favorites folder. To return to a favorite site, just select it from the Favorites menu, from the Favorites Explorer bar, or from the Favorites submenu of your Start menu (if you set your Start menu to display Favorites).

You can display the Favorites Explorer bar in any of the following ways:

- Choose View, Explorer Bar, Favorites.
- Press Ctrl+I.
- Click the Favorites button on the Standard Buttons toolbar.

If the Favorites submenu does not appear on your Start menu, you can put it there as follows:

1 Right-click the Start button.
2 Choose Properties from the shortcut menu.
3 In the Taskbar And Start Menu Properties dialog box, click the Start Menu tab.
4 Click Customize next to the Start menu style you're using.

Chapter 16

5 If you're using the new Windows XP Start menu, click the Advanced tab and select Favorites under Start Menu Items. If you're using the classic Start menu, click Display Favorites in the Advanced Start Menu Options list.

Tip Use the full Favorites menu

By default, Internet Explorer hides items on your Favorites menu that you haven't used for a while. Since many users, over time, build long Favorites lists that require scrolling, having the menu "personalized" in this manner can be a help. It minimizes clutter and lets you move quickly to the items you need regularly. (You can always click the small arrow at the bottom of the menu to reveal the temporarily hidden items.) On the other hand, some users are averse to having *anything* hidden and find the personalized menu system a major annoyance. If you're in this group, choose Tools, Internet Options; click the Advanced tab; and then clear Enable Personalized Favorites Menu.

Adding an Item to Your Favorites List

Internet Explorer makes it easy to add the currently displayed Web page to your Favorites. Any of the following methods will work:

- Press Ctrl+D.
- Display the Favorites bar; then drag the Internet Explorer icon at the left side of the Address bar and drop it into the Favorites bar.
- Choose Favorites, Add To Favorites.
- Click the Add button at the top of the Favorites bar.
- Right-click anywhere within the current page (but not on a link) and choose Add To Favorites from the shortcut menu.

Using the Ctrl+D Keyboard Shortcut

Pressing Ctrl+D while on a Web site adds the current page to the top level of your Favorites folder. Because most users quickly accumulate so many favorites that they need to use subfolders to organize them (each folder representing a category of favorites), you can think of this option as a fast but temporary method for adding a favorite. After you've created a few favorites in this manner, you'll probably want to use the Organize Favorites command to put these quickly created items into subfolders.

Tip Use your wheel mouse to change text size

Internet Explorer's View, Text Size command lets you increase or decrease the size of text on a Web page—an invaluable aid if you're trying to read a page full of print in high resolution. If you have a wheel mouse, you can take advantage of a handy mouse shortcut for this command: Hold down Ctrl while you roll the wheel forward to decrease text size or backward to increase it. Be sure to note that changing the text size on screen also affects the size of text when you print.

Ctrl+D also uses the full name of the current Web page as the favorite name. Because Web pages often have verbose names (*Welcome to the Microsoft Corporate Web Site*, for example, instead of just *Microsoft*), you'll probably want to rename the resulting favorites before consigning them to appropriate subfolders.

Dragging the Current Page to the Favorites Bar

To add the current page to your Favorites bar, you can drag the icon at the left edge of the Address bar and drop it anywhere within the Favorites bar. If you want the item to go inside an existing subfolder that isn't open, pause your mouse pointer over the folder icon. After a half second or so, the folder will open, and you can position the item appropriately within the subfolder.

After you have added a favorite in this manner, you can edit its name by right-clicking it and choosing Rename from the shortcut menu.

Tip Type a top-level favorite into the Address Bar
If a favorite is stored in the top level of your Favorites folder (not in a subfolder of Favorites), you can type its name directly in the Address Bar. For example, if you have *www.microsoft.com* assigned to a top-level favorite named MS, you can simply type **ms** and press Enter. Internet Explorer will execute the favorite shortcut, exactly as it would if you had selected it with the mouse. (If you type the name of a Favorites subfolder, the folder appears in Windows Explorer.)

Using the Add To Favorites Command

If you choose Favorites, Add To Favorites, or if you click the Add button at the top of the Favorites bar, the Add Favorite dialog box, shown here, appears. (If you don't see the lower portion of the dialog box, which shows your Favorites folder tree, click the Create In button.)

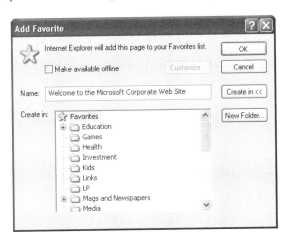

To finish creating the new favorite, follow these steps:

1 Edit the favorite name in the Name text box (keeping in mind that short names are easier to find on your Favorites bar or Favorites menu).

2 Select the name of the folder in which the favorite should reside. (Select a parent folder and click New Folder if the folder you want doesn't exist yet.)

3 Click OK.

Tip Add folders and files to your Favorites list

Anything stored in %UserProfile%\Favorites appears on your Favorites menu or Favorites bar. Most people use this folder exclusively for Internet shortcuts, but you can put shortcuts to files and folders there as well. Putting a shortcut to a folder or document you're currently working on makes that document easier to reach while you're working in Internet Explorer.

Editing Favorites

Favorite Web sites are recorded as Internet shortcuts in your %UserProfile%\Favorites folder. You can edit these shortcuts the same way you would edit any other kind of shortcut. Right-click the item you want to edit (on the Favorites menu, on the Favorites bar, or in the Favorites folder) and choose Properties from the shortcut menu. Figure 16-6 shows the properties dialog box for a favorite Web site.

You might want to edit a favorite item for the following reasons:

- To change the name of the favorite
- To change its URL
- To change its icon
- To assign it a keyboard shortcut
- To make it available offline or change its offline-update parameters

To change the name that appears in your Favorites menu, click the General tab and edit the text in the box at the top of the dialog box. To change the URL, edit the URL box on the Web Document tab. To select a different icon for this shortcut, click Change Icon on the Web Document tab.

Figure 16-6. You can edit a favorite in various ways, including adding a keyboard shortcut to activate it.

Tip Open Internet shortcuts in new windows

To ensure that Internet Explorer always opens a Web shortcut in a new window, rather than replacing the material you're currently looking at, choose Tools, Internet Options, and then click the Advanced tab. In the Browsing section of the Settings list, clear the Reuse Windows For Launching Shortcuts option.

Assigning a Keyboard Shortcut

Favorites, which are Internet shortcuts, can have keyboard shortcuts, just like file and folder shortcuts. For more information about assigning keyboard shortcuts to shortcuts, see "Creating and Customizing Document Shortcuts," page 701.

Making a Favorite Available Offline

If you select Make This Page Available Offline on the Web Document tab of a favorite's properties dialog box, Internet Explorer downloads a copy of the page to your Temporary Internet Files folder (%UserProfile%\Temporary Internet Files) and updates that page at periodic intervals (every day at a particular time, for example). You can then read the page without having to reconnect to the Internet. You might find it convenient to make favorite pages available offline, particularly if you use a dial-up connection. Then let Internet Explorer connect and download those pages for you at night so that you can read them at the start of your next workday.

You can also use the offline availability feature as a way of checking for changes in a favorite's content. Each time it downloads the favorite page, Internet Explorer can check the current content against the previous download and notify you via e-mail if there are differences.

When you select Make This Page Available Offline, Internet Explorer adds a Schedule tab and a Download tab to the properties dialog box. Use the Schedule tab to specify the schedule that you want Internet Explorer to follow for updating the Temporary Internet Files copy of your page. (You can also indicate that you want to update only on demand.) Use the Download tab, shown in Figure 16-7, to specify additional download parameters.

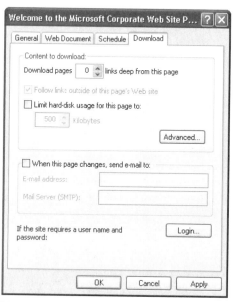

Figure 16-7. You can use the Download tab to specify a maximum size for the offline copy of your favorite—among other parameters.

Tip Turn off the flash and noise

If you're annoyed by blinking banner ads or Web pages that insist on serenading, you can hit the mute button in either of two ways. To silence the current page, simply press Esc (but wait until the content has finished loading before pressing Esc; otherwise, you might not get the whole page). To squelch the animations or sound permanently, choose Tools, Internet Options, and click the Advanced tab. In the Multimedia section, clear Play Animation In Web Pages or Play Sound In Web Pages.

If you need only the favorite page itself and none of the pages to which it is linked, leave the Download Pages value at 0. Otherwise, specify the depth to which you want Internet Explorer to go. Keep in mind that the size of your download increases dramatically as you increase this depth value; to prevent things from getting totally out of hand, you can select Limit Hard-Disk Usage For This Page To and specify a maximum file size.

To have Internet Explorer send you e-mail notification of changes in your favorite's content, select When This Page Changes, Send E-Mail To, and then supply your e-mail address and the address of your e-mail system's SMTP (outgoing mail) server. (If you're not sure what that address is, look for it in the account properties dialog box in your e-mail client program, or consult your network administrator.)

Organizing Favorites

Internet Explorer provides a small dialog box, shown in Figure 16-8, that you can use to add subfolders to your Favorites tree, move items between folders, rename folders and shortcuts, and delete favorites or folders. You can open this dialog box by choosing Favorites, Organize Favorites, or by clicking the Organize button at the top of the Favorites bar.

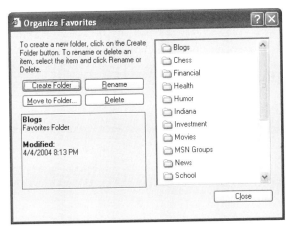

Figure 16-8. If you find this small Organize Favorites dialog box confining, you can reorganize your favorites in Windows Explorer instead.

An easier way to organize your favorites is to use Windows Explorer. In recognition of that fact, Internet Explorer provides an easy way to get to the %UserProfile%\Favorites folder: Hold down the Shift key while you open the Favorites menu and choose Organize Favorites. Figure 16-9 shows the result.

> **Tip**   You can also get to the Favorites folder by choosing Run on the Start menu and typing **favorites**. You don't have to include %UserProfile%.

Figure 16-9. Pressing the Shift key while choosing Favorites, Organize Favorites takes you straight to the Favorites folder in Windows Explorer.

Importing, Exporting, and Sharing Your Favorites

Got a batch of favorites you want to share? Internet Explorer's File, Import And Export command lets you save any branch of your favorites folder tree (or the entire tree) as an HTML file (named Bookmark.htm, by default), suitable for e-mailing to a friend, for maintaining as a backup of your Favorites folder, and for use as an alternative route to your favorite Web sites. As Figure 16-10 shows, folders in your Favorites tree become headings in the Bookmarks file, and each favorite becomes a link.

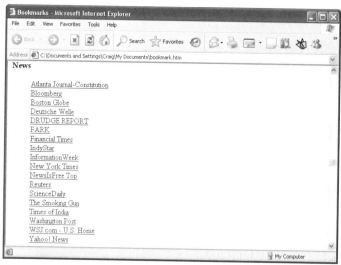

Figure 16-10. Internet Explorer can export your favorites tree (or any branch of it) to an HTML file in which each Favorites subfolder becomes an outline heading and each exported favorite becomes a link.

> **Tip** **Print your favorites**
>
> To create a printed record of your favorites and the URLs to which they're linked, follow these steps:
>
> 1 Export your favorites.
>
> 2 Open the exported HTML file in Internet Explorer.
>
> 3 Choose File, Print. On the Options tab of the Print dialog box, select Print Table Of Links.
>
> Unless you have lots of time and paper, you'll want to avoid selecting the Print All Linked Documents option, which will proceed to open all your favorites and print their contents.

To export favorites, choose File, Import And Export. The Import/Export Wizard appears and guides you through the rest of the process.

You can use the same command and the same wizard to merge a set of links in an HTML file into your own Favorites tree. The wizard will prompt for a file name and for the branch of your current Favorites tree to which you want to import the new links.

Using Third-Party Favorites (Bookmark) Managers

A number of free or inexpensive third-party products are available to help you manage your favorites and expand on features in Internet Explorer. Among the features offered by these advanced bookmark managers are the following:

- The ability to annotate favorites
- Advanced sorting capabilities
- The ability to search bookmarks for particular characteristics
- The ability to check your favorites list periodically and flag those with unreachable URLs

If you have a particularly large stash of favorites and you have difficulty keeping tabs on them all using Internet Explorer's native feature set, you might want to check out some of these third-party products. Use Internet Explorer's searching features to look for "bookmark managers." For more information about searching the Internet, see "Searching the Internet," page 534.

Another way to manage favorites is to use services available at various Web sites. The advantage of storing your favorites list on the Web is that you can access it, use it, add to it, and so on, from any computer, anywhere. The principal disadvantage is speed. (Another disadvantage, given the volatility of the dot-com world, is the possibility that the site that stores your favorites today might be gone tomorrow. Be sure you keep a local backup.) Connecting to the site that stores your bookmarks in addition to connecting to the sites to which your bookmarks take you inevitably adds overhead to the surfing experience.

Chapter 16

Blocking Pop-Ups

Beginning with the version shipped with Windows XP Service Pack 2, Internet Explorer includes a tool that can eliminate most pop-up windows. With this feature turned on, you'll be spared the annoyance of advertising that appears unbidden in windows lying either over or under the Web sites you visit. Pop-up Blocker is turned on by default. To determine or change its status, choose Tools, Pop-up Blocker. If the feature is on, the Pop-up Blocker submenu displays a command to turn it off—and vice versa.

In its default configuration, Pop-up Blocker suppresses most new windows that are spawned directly by Web sites you visit. (Pop-up Blocker calls these "automatic pop-ups.") If you initiate an action that opens a new window (by clicking a link), Pop-up Blocker assumes you want the new window to open and does not interfere. You can configure the feature to be more or less permissive than it is by default. (See "Setting the Filter Level" below.)

Pop-up Blocker, by default, operates only on sites in the Internet and Restricted Sites security zones. It does not suppress the display of new windows generated by sites in the Local Intranet and Trusted Sites zones. This default arrangement is also customizable. (See "Allowing Pop-up Blocker to Work in the Local Intranet or Trusted Sites Zone," page 525.)

Pop-up Blocker maintains an exception list of sites that you want it to ignore. If you regularly visit a site that generates new windows and Pop-up Blocker is getting in your way, you can easily add that site to the exception list. (See "Allowing Pop-ups from Specific Sites," page 524.)

> **Tip** Bypass Pop-up Blocker temporarily
>
> You might occasionally find it convenient to allow a pop-up window from a particular site, without changing the pop-up blocker so that it always permits pop-ups from that site. To squelch the pop-up blocker temporarily, hold down the Ctrl key while clicking the link that spawns the pop-up. You can also give a temporary pass to a particular site by clicking the Information Bar that appears at the top of the Internet Explorer window when a pop-up is suppressed. The first item on the menu that appears, Temporarily Allow Pop-ups, displays the window that was just suppressed.

Setting the Filter Level

Pop-up Blocker offers three standard levels of vigilance, called Low, Medium, and High. The default is Medium. The characteristics of these levels are as follows:

- **High** Pop-up Blocker tries to suppress all new windows, including those that result from your own actions. ActiveX controls may not work in this setting.

- **Medium**   Pop-up Blocker allows new windows that result from links that you click. New windows that would otherwise appear as a result of data submitted on forms might be suppressed. If you discover this to be the case for a particular site, consider adding that site to the exception list. If it happens on several sites and that creates a problem, set the registry value UseTimerMethod to 1 (see "Creating a Custom Filter Level," next).

- **Low**   Pop-up Blocker tries to permit all new windows except those that arise automatically when you visit a Web site. Pop-up Blocker also turns a blind eye to all new windows arising on secure (HTTPS) sites.

To change from one standard filter level to another, choose Tools, Pop-up Blocker, Pop-up Blocker Settings. (Alternatively, choose Tools, Internet Options, click the Privacy tab, and then click Settings.) In the Pop-up Blocker Settings dialog box, shown in Figure 16-11, open the Filter Level drop-down list and select one of the three settings.

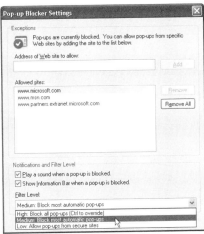

Figure 16-11.   You can use the Pop-up Blocker Settings dialog box to configure the Filter level, modify the list of exempted Web sites, and adjust notification options.

Creating a Custom Filter Level

Pop-up Blocker's filtering behavior is determined by four DWORD values of the registry key HKCU\Software\Microsoft\Internet Explorer\New Windows. Those values, each of which can be set to 0 (no) or 1 (yes), are as follows:

- **BlockUserInit**   This determines whether Pop-up Blocker suppresses windows arising from clicks on links within a Web site. In the High level, BlockUserInit is 1; in the other two levels, it is 0.

- **UseTimerMethod**   Some pop-up windows appear not as a result of clicked links but of data submitted on Web forms. With UseTimerMethod set to 1, such pop-ups are permitted; otherwise, they are suppressed. UseTimerMethod is set to 0 in the High and Medium levels.

- **UseHooks**   This value, if set to 1, enables Internet Explorer to display an ActiveX control that is instantiated by a Web site you visit. If UseHooks is set to 0, most ActiveX controls are suppressed as pop-ups. UseHooks is 0 only in the High level.

- **AllowHTTPS**   This value, if set to 1, causes Pop-up Blocker to snooze when you visit a secure site. AllowHTTPS is 1 only in the Low level.

The four registry values and their standard settings are summarized in Table 16-1.

Table 16-1. Registry Keys That Control Pop-up Blocker Filtering Behavior

Registry Value	Standard Filter Level Setting		
	High	Medium	Low
BlockUserInit	1	0	0
UseTimerMethod	0	0	1
UseHooks	0	1	1
AllowHTTPS	0	0	1

You can create a custom filter level by using a registry editor to change one or more of these values. If the four values do not conform to one of the three standard constellations shown in Table 16-1, the Filter Level drop-down list in the Pop-up Blocker Settings dialog box displays Custom.

Allowing Pop-Ups from Specific Sites

Because some Web sites might not function properly if they aren't allowed to generate pop-ups, and because you might actually welcome pop-up advertising from particular sites, Internet Explorer's Pop-Up Blocker can maintain an exception list of exempted URLs. These URLs are user-specific and are maintained as values in the registry key HKCU\Software\Microsoft\Internet Explorer\New Windows\Allow.

If Pop-up Blocker suppresses a pop-up from a site that you want to be on the exception list, click the Information Bar at the top of the screen, and choose Allow Pop-ups From This Site. If you know in advance that you want to exempt a site, choose Tools, Pop-up Blocker, Pop-up Blocker Settings. (Alternatively, you can choose Tools, Internet Options; click the Privacy tab; and then click the Settings button in the Pop-up Blocker section of the dialog box.) In the Pop-up Blocker Settings dialog box, shown in Figure 16-11, enter the address of the Web site you want to exempt, and then click Add.

Configuring Notification Options

When Pop-up Blocker prevents a window from appearing, you are informed, by default, in the following ways:

● An Information Bar appears.

    Pop-up blocked. To see this pop-up or additional options click here…   **✕**

● An icon appears in the status bar.

● A sound is played.

To suppress either the Information Bar or the notification sound, choose Tools, Pop-up Blocker, Pop-up Blocker Settings. Then clear one or both of the check boxes in the Notifications and Filter Level section of the Pop-up Blocker Settings dialog box.

> **Tip** **Change the blocked pop-up sound**
> If you don't fancy the sound that Internet Explorer uses to announce a blocked pop-up, you can assign a different sound via the Sound And Audio Devices Properties section of Control Panel. You'll find the event you need to configure—Blocked Pop-up Window—under the Windows Explorer heading. (Internet Explorer doesn't have its own heading in this dialog box.)

Allowing Pop-up Blocker to Work in the Local Intranet or Trusted Sites Zone

Pop-up Blocker normally naps whenever you visit sites in the Local Intranet and Trusted Sites security zones, on the assumption that you've given your blessing to anything that goes on at such sites. If you want to apply the blocker to either or both of these security zones, follow these steps:

1. Choose Tools, Internet Options, and click the Security tab.

2. Select the zone you want to adjust, and click Custom Level.

3. In the Miscellaneous section of the Settings list (it's near the bottom of the list), under the heading Use Pop-up Blocker, select Enable.

Managing Cookies

A *cookie* is a small text file that enables a Web site to personalize its offerings in some way. The Web site downloads the cookie to your hard disk (Internet Explorer stores it in the folder %UserProfile%\Cookies), and then reads the cookie from your hard disk on your subsequent visits to the site. Cookies can be used for a variety of purposes, such as recording logon information, shopping preferences, pages that you have visited, searches that you have performed, and so on. In general, cookies provide benefits to users as well as to Web content providers. They make the Web sites you visit more responsive to your needs and preferences.

Nevertheless, because cookies can provide Web sites with personal information about you (your e-mail address or telephone number, for example), and because some sites might not use this information in ways that you would regard as beneficial, cookies are a mixed blessing. A cookie can only provide a Web site with information that you supply while visiting the site (a cookie can't scurry around your hard disk, reading your address book and financial records, for example), and this information can be read only by the site that created the cookie. Nevertheless, because it's not always obvious who's sending you a cookie and what purposes that cookie will serve, many users are understandably wary about allowing cookies on their systems.

In versions earlier than Internet Explorer 6, your cookie management options were limited to allowing all cookies, blocking all cookies, or being prompted every time a site wanted to read or write a cookie. In practice, the second and third of these options created so much inconvenience that most users gave up and accepted all cookies. (Some sites will not even allow you to log on if you block all cookies, and if you request a confirmation prompt for every cookie transaction, you spend most of your time responding to confirmation prompts.)

Internet Explorer 6 (and subsequent versions) supports the Platform for Privacy Preferences (P3P) standard. This enables Internet Explorer to filter cookie transactions (that is, block cookies or admit them) on the basis of the cookie's content and purposes, in accordance with your stated privacy preferences. (For information about P3P, visit the World Wide Web Consortium site at *http://www.w3.org/P3P*.)

Sites that support P3P supply information about their use of cookies in the form of a *compact privacy statement*—special HTML tags embedded in the site's HTTP header that indicate what kind of cookies are used and for what purposes. When you access a site, Internet Explorer compares the site's compact privacy statement with your expressed privacy preferences, and then accepts, blocks, or *restricts* the cookies. (To restrict a cookie means to allow it for the current session only, deleting it from your hard disk when you leave the Web site.) Thanks to Internet Explorer's P3P support, you can now choose to block certain kinds of cookies, while allowing the rest. (You can also still choose to be prompted each time a site wants to use a cookie.)

To express your preferences regarding cookies, choose Tools, Internet Options, and then click the Privacy tab. On the Privacy tab of the Internet Options dialog box, shown in Figure 16-12, use the slider to choose one of the following settings:

- Block All Cookies
- High

Chapter 16

- Medium High
- Medium
- Low
- Accept All Cookies

The default setting is Medium. Table 16-2 summarizes these options on the next page.

> **Note** If you don't see a slider on your Privacy tab, you are currently using "advanced" or imported privacy settings. You can clear those settings and make the slider appear by clicking Default.

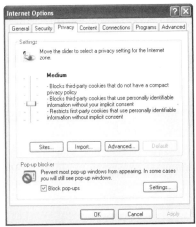

Figure 16-12. Use the slider in this dialog box to select a policy for accepting, rejecting, and restricting cookies based on their source and purpose.

> **Note** Your privacy setting applies only to sites in the Internet zone. By default, all cookies are accepted in the Trusted Sites and Local Intranet zones. (You can override these defaults by importing custom privacy settings. Doing so requires knowledge of XML programming; for details, see the overview "How to Create a Customized Privacy Import File" at *http://msdn.microsoft.com/workshop/security/privacy/overview/privacyimportxml.asp*) Cookies from sites in the Restricted Sites zone are always rejected, and you can't override that default. For more information about Internet Explorer's security zones, see "Defining Security Zones for Web Sites," page 328.

Table 16-2. **Effects of Privacy Settings on New and Existing Cookies**

Privacy Setting	Effects
Block All Cookies	• Blocks all new cookies • Prevents Web sites from reading existing cookies • Ignores per-site settings
High	• Blocks cookies from sites that do not have a compact privacy statement • Blocks cookies that use personally identifiable information without your explicit consent • Allows Web sites to read existing cookies • Can be overridden by per-site settings
Medium High	• Blocks cookies from third-party sites that do not have a compact privacy statement • Blocks third-party cookies that use personally identifiable information without your explicit consent • Blocks first-party cookies that use personally identifiable information without your implicit consent • Allows Web sites to read existing cookies • Can be overridden by per-site settings
Medium (default)	• Blocks third-party cookies that do not have a compact privacy statement • Blocks third-party cookies that use personally identifiable information without your implicit consent • Accepts first-party cookies that use personally identifiable information without your implicit consent, but deletes those cookies when you close Internet Explorer • Allows Web sites to read existing cookies • Can be overridden by per-site settings

Chapter 16

Table 16-2. Effects of Privacy Settings on New and Existing Cookies

Privacy Setting	Effects
Low	• Blocks third-party cookies from sites that do not have a compact privacy statement
	• Accepts cookies from third-party sites that use personally identifiable information without your explicit consent, but deletes those cookies when you close Internet Explorer
	• Accepts all first-party cookies
	• Allows Web sites to read existing cookies
	• Can be overridden by per-site settings
Accept All Cookies	• Accepts all new cookies
	• Allows Web sites to read existing cookies
	• Ignores per-site settings

To make an informed choice, you need to understand the following terms:

- **Compact privacy statement** Information in a Web site's HTTP header that indicates the source, purpose, and lifetime of cookies used by that site. (Some cookies, called *session cookies*, are designed to be deleted when you leave a site. Other cookies have a fixed expiration date—usually sometime in the next decade or beyond.)

- **Personally identifiable information** Information that a site could use to contact you, such as your name, e-mail address, or home or work address; also, the credentials (name and password) you use to log on to a site.

- **Explicit consent** Giving explicit consent, also known as *opting in*, means that you have taken some kind of affirmative step to allow a site to use personally identifiable information.

- **Implicit consent** To consent implicitly means not to have *opted out*—that is, not to have taken an affirmative step to deny a Web site permission to use personally identifiable information.

- **First-party cookie** A cookie used by the site that you are currently viewing. First-party cookies are generally used to personalize your experience with a Web site.

- **Third-party cookie** A cookie used by a site other than the one you're currently viewing—such as an advertiser on the site you're currently viewing.

Chapter 16

> **Note** Some Web sites will not function at all if you block their cookies. If you find that a particular site you trust does not let you on with your current privacy setting, you can make an exception for that site, and change your setting in Internet Explorer to accept all of that site's cookies, regardless of your current privacy setting. (For details, see "Overriding Your Privacy Setting for Particular Web Sites," page 531.)
>
> You can find a detailed discussion of cookies and other privacy issues in *Microsoft Windows Security Inside Out for Windows XP and Windows 2000* (Microsoft Press, 2002).

Viewing a Site's Privacy Report

When Internet Explorer blocks or restricts a cookie, it displays this icon on your status bar. (Choose View, Status Bar, if your status bar is not visible.)

To find out what cookie was blocked and why, double-click this icon. You will see the site's Privacy Report dialog box, which will indicate which cookies were blocked or restricted. To learn more about why a cookie was blocked or restricted, double-click it in the Privacy Report dialog box.

To read the privacy report for any site, and to find out whether or not Internet Explorer has blocked or restricted cookies from that site, choose View, Privacy Report. Figure 16-13 shows part of the Privacy Report dialog box for the Microsoft Encarta Web site (*http://encarta.msn.com*). Note that three cookies have been served (two from Microsoft's Passport service, a third from Encarta) and that all three have been accepted—that is, they have met the privacy specifications for this user. If a cookie had been rejected, the word *Blocked* would have appeared in the Cookies column. You can limit the dialog box to show only the names of sites with blocked cookies by selecting Restricted Web Sites from the Show list.

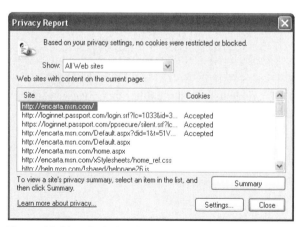

Figure 16-13. A site's privacy report provides information about all parties contributing content to that site. Double-click a site URL to read its privacy policy (if any).

Double-clicking the entry for the first accepted cookie in this example reveals the privacy statement for Microsoft Corporation, shown in Figure 16-14.

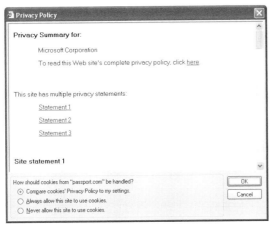

Figure 16-14. This Privacy Policy dialog box shows the privacy policy for an accepted cookie.

Overriding Your Privacy Setting for Particular Web Sites

If, after reading a site's privacy statement (or discovering that it doesn't have one that conforms to the P3P standard), you decide that you want to block or accept all cookies from that site, regardless of the privacy setting that you have chosen in the Internet Options dialog box, select either Always Allow This Site To Use Cookies or Never Allow This Site To Use Cookies in the site's Privacy Policy dialog box.

You can also specify per-site privacy settings by clicking Sites on the Privacy tab of the Internet Options dialog box. The Per Site Privacy Actions dialog box appears, as shown in Figure 16-15. To allow or block all cookies from a site, enter the site's address and then click Allow or Block. As you add settings for individual sites, the sites will be listed in the Managed Web Sites portion of the dialog box.

Chapter 16

531

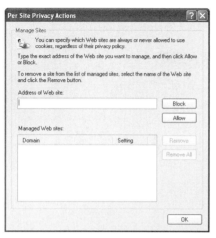

Figure 16-15. The Per Site Privacy Actions dialog box lists all sites that you designate to be exceptions to your privacy policy.

Dispensing with Automatic Cookie Handling

If you want, you can tell Internet Explorer to forget about privacy settings assigned on a site-basis and institute uniform policies for all first-party and all third-party cookies regardless of their sites of origin. For example, you can tell Internet Explorer to accept all first-party cookies and to issue a prompt for all third-party cookies (allowing you to block or accept third-party cookies on a case-by-case basis). To override automatic cookie handling, click Advanced on the Privacy tab of the Internet Options dialog box. The Advanced Privacy Settings dialog box appears, as shown in Figure 16-16.

This dialog box also includes a check box that tells Internet Explorer to accept all session cookies, which are cookies that a Web site will delete at the end of your current session. Session cookies are usually benign (they're used for such things as keeping track of what's in your shopping cart), so if you are planning to override automatic cookie handling, this is normally a safe option to select.

Asking Internet Explorer to prompt you for all third-party cookies is an excellent way to learn which of the sites you visit regularly rely on third-party cookies. After a few days' experience with this setting, you can return to automatic cookie handling and tell Internet Explorer to always block cookies from any particularly troublesome third parties that you notice.

Advanced Internet Explorer Options

Figure 16-16. Clicking Advanced on the Privacy tab of the Internet Options dialog box lets you institute uniform policies for all first-party and third-party cookies.

> **Note** Per-site settings trump advanced settings. If you decide to block either first-party or third-party cookies (or both) through the Advanced Privacy Settings dialog box, be sure to remove any per-site settings that allow cookies. Otherwise, the sites to which you gave carte blanche earlier will continue to drop cookies on your plate. To do this, click Edit on the Privacy tab of the Internet Options dialog box. Select specific sites, and click Remove, or simply click Remove All.
>
> Advanced settings don't affect cookies already stored on your computer. Be sure to delete existing cookies for sites that you want to block (or be prompted for). Otherwise, those sites will continue to read your current cookie data. (You might want to back up those cookies before deleting them—just in case you find that a site doesn't work without its cookies.)

Backing Up Your Cookies

Because cookies—particularly the ones you intentionally allow your system to accept—are more likely to be beneficial than harmful, it's smart to back them up from time to time. Internet Explorer's Import/Export Wizard lets you do just that. Choose File, Import And Export, and then follow the wizard's steps to export your cookies. The wizard creates a single text file, stored by default in My Documents.

The command to export cookies was included in Internet Explorer to provide users with a way to transfer their cookies to the format used by Netscape browsers. But it works just as well as a backup tool. If you ever need to restore your cookies, choose File, Import And Export again, and point the wizard to the file you exported earlier.

Searching the Internet

Internet Explorer 6 provides the following ways to search for sites, businesses, and people on the Internet:

- Search Companion
- Classic Internet Search
- Address bar

Search Companion and Classic Internet Search provide alternative search behaviors on the Search Explorer bar. That is, you can configure Internet Explorer to use one or the other when you display the Search bar. Searching in the Address bar bypasses the Search bar. Whenever you type anything in the Address bar, Internet Explorer attempts to parse your typing into a URL (an Internet address). If it cannot do so, it hands your entry off to a search provider.

Using Search Companion

To summon Search Companion, display the Search bar, using any of the following methods:

- Click Search on the Standard Buttons toolbar.
- Choose View, Explorer Bar, Search.
- Press Ctrl+E.

Search Companion appears in the Search Explorer bar, the pane on the left side of Internet Explorer, as shown in Figure 16-17. If instead you see Classic Internet Search (shown in Figure 16-19 on page 537), you can switch to Search Companion as follows:

1 Click the Customize button on the Search bar.
2 Select Use Search Companion.
3 Click OK.
4 Close all Internet Explorer windows and restart Internet Explorer.

Tip **Set Internet Explorer to use a favorite search provider**

Both Search Companion and Classic Internet Search are set up (initially, at least) to let you use a variety of search providers. If the current default provider doesn't satisfy a search need, you can move on to another one. However, if you have a favorite search service that you plan to use exclusively, this default user interface will get in your way. To set up Internet Explorer to use a single search provider in the Search bar, see "Using a Single Search Provider," page 538. Alternatively, you can simply bookmark that provider's Web site and select it from your Favorites menu, the Favorites bar, or the Links toolbar. You might even consider making that search provider's site your home page in Internet Explorer. (To do that, display the provider's site. Then choose Tools, Internet Options, click the General tab, and click Use Current.)

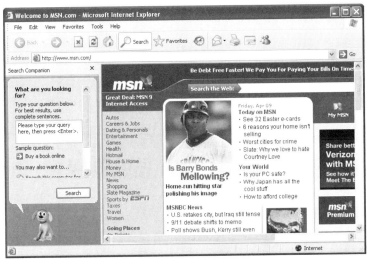

Figure 16-17. Search Companion in Internet Explorer looks, feels, and sounds like Search Companion in Windows Explorer.

As it does in Windows Explorer (see "Locating Files with Search Companion," page 718), Search Companion in Internet Explorer comes with animated characters to personalize your search experience, including Rover and Merlin. If you prefer, you can turn off the companions by clicking the Change Preferences link on the opening pane of Search Companion, and then clicking Without An Animated Screen Character.

Search Companion invites you to express your wishes in plain English sentences. This too is optional, of course. Whether you phrase your query like Tarzan or Henry James, Search Companion takes the significant words in your search string (ignoring conjunctions, articles, and prepositions) and passes them to the default search engine (which you can change, as you'll see in a moment).

Search Companion also presents a sample search question, drawn at random from a store of such questions. (You might see anything here from *Find comics* to *How bad is the traffic in Phoenix?* to *Read reviews of lawn tractors.*) For amusement, you can click the sample question and see what emerges in the other pane.

In most cases, after responding to your search question (by displaying the results in the right pane), Search Companion will propose some follow-up questions. Sometimes those questions will seem related to your initial query, and sometimes not. Occasionally you'll be given an opportunity to exercise your credit card (for example, *Buy a Movie*).

Forwarding Your Query to Other Search Engines

Often, the most useful item in Search Companion's follow-up menu is Automatically Send Your Search To Other Search Engines (it's near the bottom of the follow-up menu; you might need to scroll to get to it). Clicking this link opens the menu shown in Figure 16-18, which

Chapter 16

you can use to try your query with another search provider. (If you don't see the one you want, click Send Search To More Search Engines.)

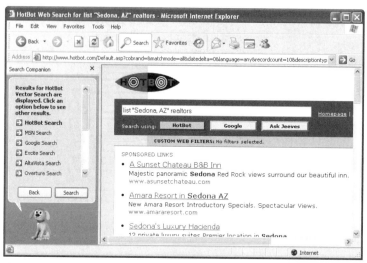

Figure 16-18. Search Companion can pass your query to other search engines, in addition to its default engine.

Changing the Default Search Engine

Search Companion's factory-default search provider is MSN. You can make a different engine the default as follows:

1 Open Search Companion and click the Change Preferences link.

2 Click Change Internet Search Behavior to see the search engines displayed here.

3 Make a selection and click OK.

Chapter 16

Using Classic Internet Search

To use Classic Internet Search, first display the Search bar. Classic Internet Search appears in the Search bar with the title *Search* and a small toolbar that includes New, Next, and Customize buttons, as shown in Figure 16-19. If instead you see Search Companion (the Search bar's title will display *Search Companion*), you can switch to Classic Internet Search as follows:

1. Click the Change Preferences link at the bottom of the Search bar.
2. Click Change Internet Search Behavior.
3. Click With Classic Internet Search.
4. Click OK.
5. Close all Internet Explorer windows and then restart Internet Explorer.

Classic Internet Search operates in either of two modes. If you use the Search Assistant (shown in Figure 16-19), you start by selecting one of seven search categories (if you don't see all seven, click the More link). After you've made this initial selection, the rest of the Search bar presents edit boxes appropriate for your selection.

If you prefer, you can dispense with Search Assistant and deploy a single search provider for all your queries in Classic Internet Search (see "Using a Single Search Provider," page 538).

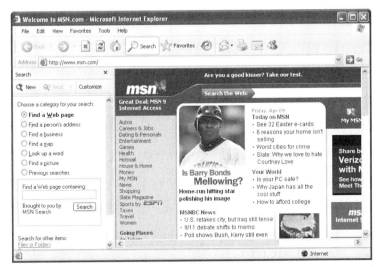

Figure 16-19. Classic Internet Search's Search Assistant lets you choose from broad categories—such as Web page, address, and business.

Search Assistant begins by using the default search provider for the category you've chosen. (You can modify this default.) After it has completed a search using the default provider, you can click the Next button at the top of the Search bar to repeat the search with another provider. (To use a particular provider, click the arrow beside the Next button and then choose from the list.)

Chapter 16

Changing Search Assistant's Default Providers

To change the default provider for each search category (as well as the order in which the Search Assistant cycles through available search providers when you click Next), follow these steps:

1 Click Customize.

2 In the Customize Search Settings dialog box, shown here, be sure that Use Search Assistant is Selected.

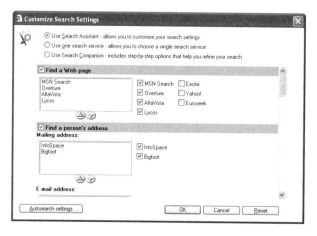

3 In each search category (you will have to scroll the dialog box to see all the categories), select the names of the providers you want to include.

4 To change the order in which Search Assistant consults a provider, select that provider and then click the up or down arrow. For example, to make Overture the default provider for Web page searches (assuming that Search Assistant is currently set as shown above), select Overture in the Find A Web Page list window and click the up arrow.

5 Clear the check boxes for any search categories that you don't want Search Assistant to include. For example, if you don't think you'll ever need to search for pictures on the Internet, scroll down to Find A Picture and clear its check box.

Using a Single Search Provider

To use a favorite search provider exclusively in the Search bar, follow these steps:

1 Click the Customize button on the Search bar.

2 In the Customize Search Settings dialog box, select Use One Search Service For All Searches.

3 Select a provider and click OK.

Searching from the Address Bar

Often the simplest way to search is to type a search string directly in the Address bar. For example, if you start typing something that Internet Explorer doesn't recognize as a URL, like this,

Internet Explorer passes what you have typed to the current default Autosearch provider, like this.

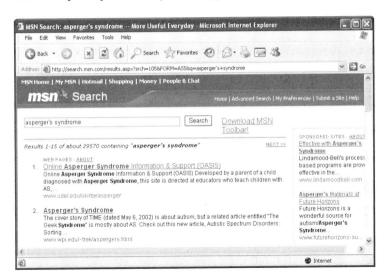

You can change the default Autosearch provider as follows:

1 Display the Search Explorer bar, using Classic Internet Search.

2 Click Customize.

3 In the Customize Search Settings dialog box, click Autosearch Settings.

Chapter 16

539

4 In the Customize Autosearch Settings dialog box, shown here, select a search provider.

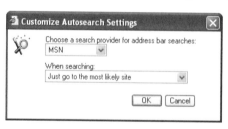

5 To change the behavior of the search provider (for example, to switch from showing a list of search hits to going straight to the most likely hit), choose an option from the When Searching list. The options available vary by provider.

Inside Out

Create search shortcuts with Tweak UI

Tweak UI, one of the PowerToys that you can download from Microsoft's Web site at *http://www.microsoft.com/windowsxp/pro/downloads/powertoys.asp*, enables you to create your own custom Address bar searches. In Tweak UI, expand Internet Explorer and select Search. Then click Create to define a search. For example, to provide fast access to Google, in the Prefix box, type **g**. (You can use any string you like as an identifier; to be useful, it should be short and meaningful.) In the URL box, type **http://www.google.com/search?q=%s**. Then, if you want to search Google for information about the Pacific Crest Trail, for example, in Internet Explorer's Address bar, type **g pacific crest trail**. Internet Explorer replaces the %s parameter with the text you type after the prefix. In this example, Internet Explorer converts your entry to *http://www.google.com/search?q=pacific+crest+trail*.

You can create your own Address bar searches for all manner of Web sites that offer some sort of search capability, including sites with weather conditions, stock quotes, comparison shopping information, recipes, and more. The trick is to perform a search on the site in which you're interested. Copy the resulting URL to the URL box in Tweak UI, but replace the search terms you use with **%s**. Here are some other ideas for custom Address bar searches you can create with Tweak UI:

- To display a Microsoft Knowledge Base article for which you know the article ID, use prefix **kb** and URL **http://support.microsoft.com/default.aspx?scid=kb;en-us;%s**. For example, type **kb 300698** to view the article with that ID.

- To automatically jump to the first result returned by Google, use prefix **gl** and URL **http://www.google.com/search?q=%s&btnl=I'm+Feeling+Lucky**. (Note that the letter following "&btn" is a capital *l*.)

Chapter 16

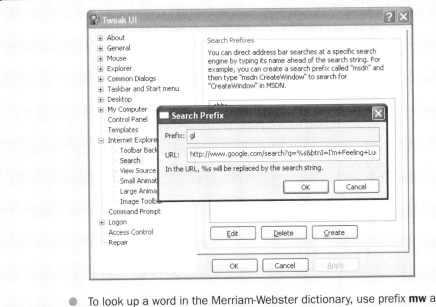

- To look up a word in the Merriam-Webster dictionary, use prefix **mw** and URL **http:// www.m-w.com/cgi-bin/dictionary?%s**.

- To find the meaning of an acronym or abbreviation, use prefix **abbr** and URL **http:// www.acronymfinder.com/af-query.asp?String=exact&Acronym=%s&Find=Find**.

By default, Internet Explorer replaces each space in your search phrase with a plus sign. If the target site uses other characters in place of spaces (many use %20, for example), you can specify the correct characters by making a change in the registry. Using Registry Editor, open HKCU\Software\Microsoft\Internet Explorer\SearchUrl, and then open the subkey for the prefix you saved in Tweak UI. You can then change the data for the "space" value and for any other character that needs to be replaced.

Managing the Web Cache

When you browse sites on the Internet, Internet Explorer stores copies of everything you download (including HTML pages and graphics) in a Temporary Internet Files folder. This cache of recently visited sites enables Internet Explorer to redisplay pages more quickly—particularly pages (such as the MSN home page) that are made up of many separate files, pages that use a lot of unchanging graphics, and so on. When you revisit a Web page, Internet Explorer checks to see if you have a version of the page's files in your cache. If you do, the program loads what it can from the cache instead of downloading material again from the Internet.

Changing the Size of the Cache

Temporary Internet files are stored by default in various subfolders of the hidden system folder %UserProfile%\Local Settings\Temporary Internet Files. If you're curious about the contents of the cache, you can take a look at it as follows:

1 Choose Tools, Internet Options, and click the General tab.

2 Click Settings.

3 In the Settings dialog box, shown in Figure 16-20, click View Files.

By default, Internet Explorer reserves a maximum of about three percent of the space on your system disk for the Web cache. On today's gigantic disks, that's probably way more than you need. You can free up some disk space without suffering any loss of browsing functionality by reducing the cache size. To do this, display the Settings dialog box and drag the slider to the left (or enter a smaller number in the edit box).

Figure 16-20. The Settings dialog box lets you control how Internet Explorer uses its Web cache.

Moving the Cache

If you want to move the cache—to a different disk, for example—you can do that from the Settings dialog box as well. Click Move Folder. In the Browse For Folder dialog box, select the new folder and click OK.

Controlling How Internet Explorer Uses the Cache

The Settings dialog box gives you four options that control how Internet Explorer exploits its Web cache. Each option strikes a different balance between the desire for quick display and the need for current information. As you consider these options, remember that the cache is

Chapter 16

particularly critical to performance on systems that use a dial-up connection to the Internet. If you're working with a broadband connection, the benefit you receive by having Internet Explorer reload pages from the cache is considerably less significant.

The options are as follows:

- **Every Visit To The Page**   This option causes Internet Explorer to check the Web for newer versions of cached pages every time you visit those pages. If the temporary files are still current, Internet Explorer displays them. Otherwise, it downloads new pages and displays them. This option ensures that the information you see is always current, but it can slow your browsing.

- **Every Time You Start Internet Explorer**   This option causes Internet Explorer to check for newer versions once per Internet Explorer session. A check is made the first time you visit a page after you open Internet Explorer, but not again until you close and reopen the browser. If, however, you have Internet Explorer open over the course of several days and you revisit a page that you visited on a previous day, Internet Explorer does check the files again.

- **Automatically**   This option, the default, is the same as the Every Time You Start Internet Explorer option, except that Internet Explorer tabulates how often pages are actually updated. If a page is not updated frequently, Internet Explorer reduces the frequency with which it checks that page.

- **Never**   With this option, Internet Explorer never checks for newer files and always displays what is in the cache.

Troubleshooting

Internet Explorer can only save images as bitmaps.

If you right-click an image in Internet Explorer and choose Save Picture As, you should be given the option to save the image either in bitmap format (.bmp) or in the format with which the image was posted to the Web (typically .jpeg or .gif). If you find you can only save images as bitmaps, try clearing the cache (click Delete Files on the General tab of the Internet Options dialog box). Usually, that will solve the problem. If it does not, it's possible that you have a damaged file (an ActiveX control or Java object, for example) in your Downloaded Program Files folder. On the General tab of the Internet Options dialog box, click Settings. Then, in the Settings dialog box, click View Objects. Display the Downloaded Program Files folder in Details view. Look for any files marked Damaged or Unknown in the Status column. If you find such a file, right-click it and choose Remove. Close the Internet Options dialog box and again try to save an image in its native format. For more information, see article 810978, "Internet Explorer Saves Images As Bitmaps (.bmp Files)," in the Microsoft Knowledge Base at *http://support.microsoft.com/?kbid=810978*.

Chapter 16

> **Tip** Ensure that the Web page is up-to-date
>
> If Internet Explorer appears to be reading from the cache when it should be downloading afresh (for example, if you find yourself looking at yesterday's headlines on a newspaper site), hold down the Shift key while you click Refresh (or press Shift+F5).

Emptying the Cache Automatically

Some users who are particularly concerned with privacy like to cover their tracks by having Internet Explorer purge the Web cache whenever they quit the browser. To do this, follow these steps:

1. Choose Tools, Internet Options.
2. Click the Advanced tab.
3. In the Security section of the Settings list, select Empty Temporary Internet Files Folder When Browser Is Closed.

Using Internet Explorer as an FTP Client

You can use Internet Explorer to access File Transfer Protocol (FTP) sites as well as Web sites. By default, Internet Explorer displays FTP sites in "folder view"—making them look and function almost exactly like local or network folders.

To view an FTP site that allows anonymous access, simply type the URL in the Address bar—of either Internet Explorer or Windows Explorer. To connect to an FTP server that requires you to provide your user name and password, you can include your logon information in the Address bar, like this:

```
ftp://name:password@ftp.microsoft.com
```

Alternatively, after you arrive at the site, you can choose File, Login As and provide your credentials. Regardless of who you log on as—even if you use anonymous logon—you can tell who you're logged on as by looking at the status bar (choose View, Status Bar if it isn't visible).

Internet Explorer's FTP support excludes the following functionality:

- Connecting to the Internet using a CERN proxy server or Web proxy server
- Connecting to a Virtual Address Extension (VAX) or Virtual Memory System (VMS) FTP server
- Using Internet Explorer from within a separate program or service
- Copying files from one server to another

If you prefer a non-folder approach to FTP browsing, choose Tools, Internet Options, and then click the Advanced tab. In the Browsing section, clear Enable Folder View For FTP Sites.

Chapter 17

Managing User Profiles

As you've undoubtedly discovered, Microsoft Windows XP offers users all manner of customization possibilities. Using various settings in Control Panel and elsewhere, users can control the appearance of their desktop, taskbar, Start menu, folder windows, and other items; specify sounds that play when certain events occur; add or remove programs; and so on. This is terrific for a single computer operated by a single user who wants to master his or her working environment.

But if, as an administrator, you have to keep more than one computer humming along and keep more than one user productive, you might want to perform some of this customization for the user. With tools provided by Windows XP, you can configure settings for users who lack the knowledge, experience, or time to do it themselves. Just as importantly, you can impose restrictions that prevent inexperienced or devious users from damaging their setup.

In this chapter we describe user profiles, a feature of Windows XP that controls each user's computing environment. Administrators can work with profiles in various ways to customize a system for one or more users.

At Home with Windows XP

Because Windows XP Home Edition does not include a practical way to work with NTFS permissions or a GUI method for assigning a profile to a user account, it's impractical—although not altogether impossible—to set up and work with roaming user profiles in Home Edition. This feature, which is best suited to a domain environment, is rarely used in workgroup environments. The same limitations also prevent all but the most masochistic Home Edition users from using mandatory user profiles.

And because Windows XP Home Edition does not support Group Policy, you can't use scripts specified in Group Policy that run at logon, logoff, startup, and shutdown. You can, however, specify the *location* of a script to run at logon by using the Net User command-line utility.

All the other features of user profiles described in this chapter apply to both versions of Windows XP.

Introducing User Profiles

A *user profile* contains all the settings and files for a user's work environment. This includes the user's personal registry settings for mouse pointers, view settings used in Microsoft Word, files that are specific to the user (such as cookies the user receives while using Microsoft Internet Explorer), documents in the My Documents folder and its subfolders, and shortcuts to network places.

Location and Content of User Profiles

By default, each user who logs on to a computer has a local user profile, which is created when the user logs on for the first time. Local user profiles are stored in %SystemDrive%\Documents And Settings. Each user's profile is stored in a subfolder where the user name is the folder name (for example, C:\Documents And Settings\Jan). The entire path for the current user's profile is stored in another commonly used environment variable, %UserProfile%.

> **Note** If you upgraded from Windows NT 4 (instead of performing a clean installation of Windows XP or upgrading from another version of Windows), user profiles are stored in %SystemRoot%\Profiles.

Within a user's profile folder, you'll find a hierarchy of folders, as shown in Figure 17-1. The root of the profile (that is, the subfolder of Documents And Settings where the user name is the folder name) contains Ntuser.dat, which is the user portion of the registry (in other words, the HKCU hive). In addition, a computer that's a member of a Windows NT Server domain might have an Ntuser.pol file, a file that has system policy settings. (System policy is the Windows NT predecessor to Group Policy, which was introduced with Windows 2000.)

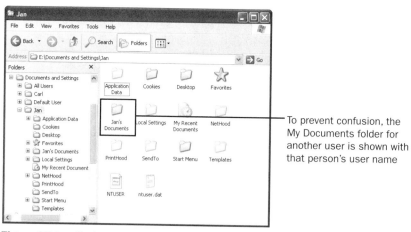

To prevent confusion, the My Documents folder for another user is shown with that person's user name

Figure 17-1. Each user profile contains a number of folders, including several hidden ones.

The profile includes the following folders:

- **Application Data** This hidden folder contains application-specific data, such as a custom dictionary for word processing programs, junk sender lists for an e-mail program, a CD database for a program that plays music CDs, and so on. Application vendors decide what information to put in this folder.

- **Cookies** This folder contains Internet Explorer cookies.

- **Desktop** This folder contains all items stored on the user's desktop, including files and shortcuts.

- **Favorites** This folder contains Internet Explorer favorites.

- **Local Settings** This hidden folder contains settings and files that don't roam with the profile, either because they're machine specific or because they're so large that it's not worthwhile to include them in a roaming user profile, which must be copied from and to a network server at each logon and logoff. (Roaming user profiles are discussed in the next section.) For example, the staging area for burning CDs—which is machine specific *and* potentially large—is stored in a subfolder of Local Settings. The Local Settings folder contains four subfolders:

    - **Application Data** This hidden folder contains machine-specific application data.

    - **History** This folder contains the user's Internet Explorer browsing history.

    - **Temp** This folder contains temporary files created by applications.

    - **Temporary Internet Files** This folder contains the offline cache for Internet Explorer.

- **My Documents** This folder is the default target for the My Documents shortcut that appears on the Start menu, in the Windows Explorer task pane (under Other Places), and elsewhere. My Documents is the default location for storing user documents in most applications. When you view the profile folders for another user, the user's name replaces *My*, although the actual folder name for all users is My Documents.

- **NetHood** This hidden folder contains the shortcuts that appear in My Network Places.

- **PrintHood** This seldom-used hidden folder can contain shortcuts to items in the Printers And Faxes folder.

- **Recent** This hidden folder contains shortcuts to recently used documents; the most recent of these can appear on the Start menu. Although it appears in Windows Explorer as My Recent Documents, the actual folder name is Recent.

- **SendTo** This hidden folder contains shortcuts to the folders and applications that appear on the Send To submenu. Send To is a command that appears on the File menu in Windows Explorer when you select a file or folder; it also appears on the shortcut menu when you right-click a file or folder.

- **Start Menu** This folder contains the items (such as shortcuts to applications and documents) that appear on the Start menu's All Programs submenu.

● **Templates**   This hidden folder contains shortcuts to document templates. These templates are typically used by the New command in Windows Explorer (on the File menu and the shortcut menu) and are referenced by the FileName value in the HKCR*class*\\ShellNew key, where *class* refers to the extension and file type.

> **Note**   Group Policy settings always take precedence over user-configured settings in user profiles. This allows administrators to foil users who have the knowledge and permissions to make changes directly in their own user profile. For more information, see Appendix F, "Group Policy."

Types of Profiles

Windows XP Professional supports three types of profiles:

● **Local user profiles**   A local user profile is stored in the %SystemDrive%\\Documents And Settings (or %SystemRoot%\\Profiles) folder on the local hard disk. Windows creates a local user profile the first time a user logs on to the computer. If the user makes changes to the profile, the changes affect only the computer on which the changes are made.

● **Roaming user profiles**   A roaming user profile is stored on a network server, which makes it available when a user logs on to any computer on the network. Windows creates a local copy of the user profile the first time a user logs on to a computer. If the user makes changes to the profile, Windows merges the changes into the server copy when the user logs off; therefore, the revised profile is available the next time the user logs on to any computer. Roaming profiles are easily managed by and are ideally suited to Windows Server 2003 and Windows 2000 Server. With some extra effort, however, you can achieve some of the benefits of a roaming user profile even without a server edition of Windows. For details about this workaround, see "Using Roaming User Profiles," page 559.

● **Mandatory user profiles**   A mandatory user profile is one that can be changed only by an administrator. Like a roaming user profile, a mandatory profile is stored on a network server, and Windows creates a local copy when a user who has been assigned a mandatory profile logs on for the first time. Unlike a roaming user profile, a mandatory profile is not updated when the user logs off. This makes mandatory profiles useful not only for individual users whom you want to severely restrict, but also for multiple users (for example, all users in a certain job classification) to whom you want to apply consistent job-specific settings. Multiple users can share a mandatory user profile without affecting others. Users who have been assigned a mandatory profile can make profile changes while they're logged on (unless prevented by policy settings), but the network copy remains unchanged. Although a copy of the profile—changes and

Chapter 17

all—remains on the computer after a user logs off, at the next logon Windows recopies the original profile from the network share. For information about assigning a mandatory user profile, see "Using Mandatory User Profiles," page 563.

> **Note** Windows XP Home Edition uses local user profiles. As stated earlier in the At Home sidebar, it's possible, but not practical, to implement roaming or mandatory profiles in Home Edition.

Common Profiles

In the profiles folder (%SystemDrive%\Documents And Settings or %SystemRoot%\Profiles), you'll find two profiles that aren't associated with a particular user account: All Users and Default User. (The Default User folder is hidden.)

- **All Users**   The content of the All Users folder appears for all users who log on to a workstation, in addition to the content of each user's own profile folder. For example, items in the All Users\Desktop folder appear on the desktop along with items that the current user has saved on the desktop. Similarly, the Start menu shows the combined contents of the All Users\Start Menu folder and the current user's Start Menu folder. The All Users\Documents folder (which appears as Shared Documents in Windows Explorer) contains documents that are available to all users. The exception is the All Users\Favorites folder, which appears to serve no purpose whatsoever.

  By default, only members of the Administrators group and the Power Users group can add items to the Desktop and Start Menu folders in the All Users profile. All users can add items to the Shared Documents folder.

> **Tip**   **View the Start Menu folder**
> Windows offers a simple way to get directly to either branch of the Start menu hierarchy. Right-click the Start button and choose Open or Explore if you want to look at the Start Menu folder within the current user profile; choose Open All Users or Explore All Users to view the All Users\Start Menu folder in Windows Explorer.

- **Default User**   When a user logs on to a computer for the first time (and his or her account is not set up to use a roaming profile or mandatory profile), Windows creates a new local profile by copying the content of the Default User folder to a new folder and giving it the user's name. Therefore, you can configure the Default User profile the way you want new users' initial view of Windows to appear. With the default security settings, only members of the Administrators group can make changes to the Default User profile.

Chapter 17

Setting Up a Default Profile

You can populate the Default User profile with files that you want each new user to have available. In particular, you might want to supply a set of Internet links, a few desktop short-cuts, and perhaps some documents. You can easily do this by copying the appropriate shortcuts and files to the Favorites, Desktop, and My Documents folders. (Because the Default User folder is hidden, you'll first need to display hidden folders by opening Folder Options and selecting Show Hidden Files And Folders on the View tab.)

Be sure that you *copy* files to the Default User profile so that they inherit the appropriate permissions from the destination folder. If you *move* files to the folder, they retain their existing permissions, which will likely prevent them from being copied to the new user's pro-file when it is created.

Like the other user profiles, the Default User profile contains Ntuser.dat, which is the user-specific portion of the registry. The registry-controlled settings in the Default User profile become the initial settings for a new user who signs on. Therefore, you can make settings therein that become the default settings for new accounts. The trouble with this is that it's not as easy to make registry settings in the Default User profile as it is to copy files to it, as described in the preceding paragraphs. You can make the settings in either of two ways:

- If you know precisely what needs to be changed in the registry to implement a certain setting or feature, you can modify the Default User profile in Registry Editor. In Reg-istry Editor, make changes to the HKU\.DEFAULT branch of the registry. From that key, navigate to the same subkey that you would use within HKCU to make a change to your own profile.

- You can create a new account, log on using that account, and make all the settings you want. Configure the desktop, menus, mouse, and other options as you want new users to see them. Then log off and log on using your administrative account. Copy the profile for the user account you created to the Default User folder. Be sure you copy as described in "Copying a User Profile," on page 552; do not use Windows Explorer to copy the profile information.

Working with User Profiles

Armed with the knowledge of where profiles reside and what they contain, you might be tempted to manipulate them directly from Windows Explorer or a command prompt. Although you can safely add, modify, or remove items in a profile, such as the Start menu and desktop items, you should not move, copy, or delete entire profiles in this manner. Instead, you should use the User Profiles dialog box, shown in Figure 17-2. To get there, right-click My Computer and choose Properties (or choose System in Control Panel). On the Advanced tab, click Settings under User Profiles.

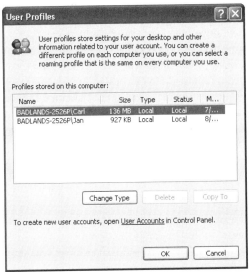

Figure 17-2. Use the User Profiles dialog box to copy or delete a user profile.

Note Users who are not members of the Administrators group can't see other user profiles in the User Profiles dialog box, nor can they delete, copy, or change their own profile.

Removing a User Profile

The User Profiles dialog box indicates the disk space occupied by a profile. Because each user's documents are stored in their profile, this space can be significant. To recover the space occupied by unused profiles, you can remove the profile in either of two ways (shown in order of desirability):

● Open User Accounts in Control Panel and delete the user account associated with the profile. For details, see "Deleting an Account," page 237. This method deletes the user account as well as the profile, and also offers a way to save the profile's documents.

● From the User Profiles dialog box, simply select a profile and click Delete. You cannot delete a profile that is currently logged on. Deleting profiles in this manner (instead of using Windows Explorer, for example) ensures that the appropriate profile also gets removed from the registry. (Each user profile occupies a subkey of HKLM\Software\ Microsoft\Windows NT\CurrentVersion\ProfileList.)

 One of the Resource Kit tools included on the companion CD, Delprof.exe (User Profile Deletion Utility), provides a third way to remove unwanted profiles. With a single command, it can delete all profiles, including cached roaming profiles, or all profiles that haven't been used in a specified amount of time.

Chapter 17

551

Note If you use roaming user profiles, Windows ordinarily saves the copy of the profile that has been copied to the local hard drive. Windows uses this local copy if the network copy happens to be unavailable the next time the user logs on. If you have a computer that's available to many users, this occasional convenience can cost a lot of disk space. You can force Windows to automatically delete the local copy of a roaming profile when a user logs off. To do that, open Group Policy (Gpedit.msc), go to Computer Configuration\Administrative Templates\System\User Profiles, and enable the policy named Delete Cached Copies Of Roaming Profiles. Other policies in the same folder also affect how roaming profiles are applied. For more information, see Appendix F, "Group Policy."

Copying a User Profile

Copying a user profile (by selecting a profile in the User Profiles dialog box and clicking Copy To) doesn't add the profile to the registry; that happens the first time a user who has been assigned the profile you copy logs on. But copying from the User Profiles dialog box instead of using Windows Explorer has an important advantage: Windows assigns the proper permissions to the copy. That is, it gives Full Control permission to the user or group you specify and removes permissions for other nonadministrative users. Such permissions are necessary to allow a user access to his or her own profile—but no one else's.

Note You cannot copy a profile that is currently logged on, including your own. If you want to copy your own profile, you'll need to log on using a different account.

Inside Out

Automatically back up your profile

Because so much of your important data is stored in your profile, you might want to store two copies of the profile on different drives. By using some techniques that are intended for managing roaming profiles, you can create automatic local backups. (This procedure works only if you have Windows XP Professional.) Here's how:

1 Copy the profile you want to use to another drive. You'll need to log on using a different administrator account because you can't copy the profile you're currently using. In the User Profiles dialog box, select the profile and click Copy To. In the Copy To dialog box, specify a folder on a different drive. You don't need to change the permitted users.

2 Open Local Users And Groups (Lusrmgr.msc), open Users, and double-click your user name. On the Profile tab, specify the path to the profile copy in the Profile Path box.

Now when you log on, Windows copies the profile you created on the other drive to the Documents And Settings folder. This copy becomes your working copy, and any changes you make to settings or files are recorded there. When you log off, the profile in Documents And Settings is then copied back to the other drive. Easy backup!

 Troubleshooting

An error prevents you from logging on.

If you get a profile-related error when you try to log on or if you notice such an error in the Application event log, it could be caused by one or more of the following conditions:

- Your account doesn't have sufficient access permissions. Your account must have (at least) Read access to the %UserProfile% folder, whether it's a local profile or a roaming or mandatory profile stored on another computer.

- Your account doesn't have sufficient access permissions to the profiles folder—the folder that contains the individual profiles (%SystemDrive%\Documents And Settings on most computers). The Everyone account should have Full Control access to the folder. In addition, if it's a shared folder on a network drive, the Everyone account should have Full Control access to the share.

- Your system is low on hard disk space.

- The profile has been corrupted. In most cases, the only solution to this situation is to delete the profile. Before you take that drastic step, try using System Restore to revert to a working profile. Be aware, however, that this will roll back *all* profiles to the time of the restore point.

Assigning a Profile

If you want to assign a profile to a user account, you use Microsoft Management Console with the Local Users And Groups snap-in. You can find this snap-in under System Tools in Computer Management, or you can open it in its own window by typing **lusrmgr.msc** at a command prompt. In the Users folder, double-click the name of the user you want to assign the profile to and click the Profile tab, shown in Figure 17-3.

On the Profile tab, you can specify the following:

- **The location of the user profile**   (Note that you need to do this only if you want to use a profile that's not stored in the default location, such as a roaming user profile or a mandatory user profile.) For more information, see "Using Roaming User Profiles," page 559.

- **The location and file name of a logon script**   A *logon script* is a program that runs each time the user logs on. For more information, see "Using Scripts That Run at Logon, Logoff, Startup, and Shutdown," page 556. (With the Net User command, you can specify the script location with the /Scriptpath switch.)

● **The path to the user's home folder**   The *home folder* is a folder in which a user can store his or her files and programs. Although most programs use My Documents as the default folder for File Open and File Save, some older programs use the home folder. The home folder is also the initial current folder for Command Prompt sessions. The home folder can be a local folder or on a shared network drive, and multiple users can share a common home folder. To specify a local home folder, enter a path specification in the Local Path text box. To use a folder on a network server as a home folder, choose Connect and select a drive letter (Windows maps the folder to this letter at each logon) and specify the full network path to the folder. (With the Net User command, you can specify the script location with the /Homedir switch.) If you don't specify a home folder, Windows uses %UserProfile% as the home folder.

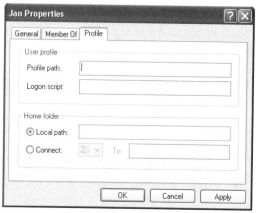

Figure 17-3.   Use the Profile tab to specify a user profile, a logon script, and a home folder.

> **Note**   Local Users And Groups is not available in Windows XP Home Edition. You can achieve the same result, however, by using the /Profilepath switch with the Net User command. For details, type **net help user** at a command prompt.

Troubleshooting

Your files are missing, or you have two profiles.

A common problem with profiles is that, for one reason or another, you end up with more than one profile for a user account. The symptoms are deceiving: All of a sudden, your documents are missing, programs are missing from the Start menu, or your settings have changed. This usually occurs when you join a domain and then log on using the same user name as you used before joining the domain. In this case, you have (perhaps unwittingly) created two user accounts: a local account and a domain account. And each account is associated with its own profile.

If you haven't yet used your new profile to store any documents or make any settings and you are able to determine which account is associated with each profile, you can remedy this situation simply by assigning the correct profile to your account.

A better solution is to use the File And Settings Transfer Wizard. Log on with the account you no longer plan to use and save your files and settings. Then log on with the other account and import your information. For more information about using the File And Settings Transfer Wizard, see "Moving Windows Settings and Files," page 45.

In some cases—particularly if you just want to retrieve your documents—it's easier to use Windows Explorer to move the documents from one profile to another. (The profile folders in Documents And Settings each begin with your user name, but at least one of them will have the computer or domain name appended to make it unique.)

Whichever way you move your information, you can then remove the profile you no longer need. (Ordinarily, that would be the profile associated with the local account, assuming you normally log on with your domain account.)

Moving Folders from the Standard Profile Locations

You can easily change the location of the My Documents folder and its subfolders, My Music and My Pictures. You might want to do this if the drive where your profile is stored becomes full, for example. As an alternative to using a different location on your computer, you might consider moving these document folders to a shared folder elsewhere on the network. Storing such data on a network server apart from the user profile offers two important benefits:

- Storing user data in a central location can make backup easier.
- Separating user data from the user profile speeds up the logon and logoff process for users with roaming profiles. (If a user's documents are stored within the profile, they are copied from the network server to the local computer at each logon, and then copied back at each logoff. By storing them apart from the profile, each file is fetched only as it's needed.)

To move My Documents, follow these steps:

1 Right-click My Documents and choose Properties. On the Target tab, click Move.

2 Select the path of the folder where you want to keep My Documents, either on your own computer or in a shared network folder. Here the Data folder is selected on a network server.

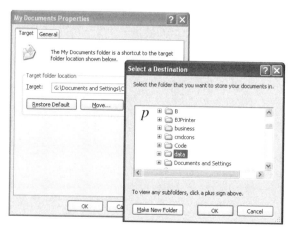

3   Click OK on each screen. Click Yes if you want to move the existing documents to the new target location.

> **Note**   It's possible—but not at all advisable—to move the entire Documents And Settings folder. For details, see Microsoft Knowledge Base article 236621, "Cannot Move or Rename the Documents and Settings Folder."

To move My Music or My Pictures, simply use Windows Explorer to move the folder to the desired location. Windows XP automatically updates all references to the folder, including those on the Start menu.

Unless you use roaming user profiles to move them en masse, moving other profile folders isn't practical if your computer isn't joined to a domain. In a domain-based network, Group Policy settings allow an administrator to use folder redirection to store the data files from a user's profile on a network server. The Folder Redirection extension in Group Policy for domain-based accounts allows administrators to easily change the actual location of the Application Data, Desktop, My Documents, and Start Menu components of the user profiles—and users won't even notice the difference.

Using Scripts That Run at Logon, Logoff, Startup, and Shutdown

With user profiles or Group Policy, you can implement scripts that run automatically. Any executable file—that is, a batch program (.bat or .cmd extension), a Windows Script Host (WSH) script (.vbs, .js, or .wsf extension), or a program (.exe or .com extension)—can be used as a logon script. For information about batch programs and WSH scripts, see Chapter 19, "Automating Windows XP."

Logon scripts are commonly used to map network drives to a drive letter, to start certain programs, and to perform other similar tasks that should happen at each logon. As with most tasks in Windows, you can use other methods to perform each of these—but a logon script offers a convenient, flexible method.

Note that using system environment variables such as %UserName% makes it easy to use the same script for different users. Windows substitutes the correct user name when it runs the script.

To use a logon script for a local user account, specify the script's path and file name in the Logon Script box on the Profile tab of the user's properties dialog box (shown earlier in Figure 17-3 on page 554).

Windows XP Professional (but not Home Edition) also offers support for four other types of scripts:

- Group Policy logon scripts, which run whenever a user logs on
- Group Policy logoff scripts, which run whenever a user logs off
- Group Policy startup scripts, which run whenever the computer starts up
- Group Policy shutdown scripts, which run whenever the computer shuts down

Like ordinary logon scripts, you can use any executable file type for any of these scripts. Though you're free to store scripts anywhere you like, each type of script has a default location.

Logon script	%SystemRoot%\System32\GroupPolicy\User\Scripts\Logon
Logoff script	%SystemRoot%\System32\GroupPolicy\User\Scripts\Logoff
Startup script	%SystemRoot%\System32\GroupPolicy\Machine\Scripts\Startup
Shutdown script	%SystemRoot%\System32\GroupPolicy\Machine\Scripts\Shutdown

Note that the %SystemRoot%\System32\GroupPolicy folder is hidden.

To implement any of these scripts, start Group Policy (Gpedit.msc) and go to Computer Configuration\Windows Settings\Scripts (for startup and shutdown scripts) or User Configuration\Windows Settings\Scripts (for logon and logoff scripts).

Chapter 17

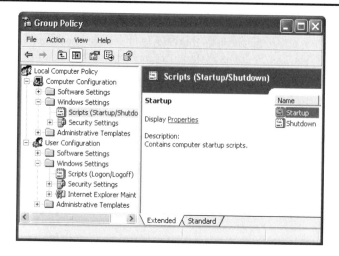

When you double-click an entry in one of these folders, you'll notice some additional improvements over legacy logon scripts:

- You can specify more than one script for each of these events, and you can specify the order in which they run.

- You can specify command-line parameters for each script.

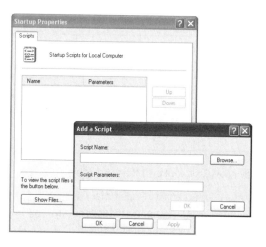

Group Policy also offers a number of policy settings that affect how scripts run—synchronously or asynchronously, hidden or visible. (In this case, *synchronously* means, in effect, that nothing else runs until the script finishes running.) You'll find these settings, along with more complete explanations of their effects, in Computer Configuration\Administrative Templates\System\Scripts and in User Configuration\Administrative Templates\System\Scripts. Some policy settings appear in both places; if the settings are configured differently, the one in Computer Configuration takes precedence.

Using Roaming User Profiles

A roaming user profile allows a user to log on to any workstation and see his or her familiar settings on the desktop, the Start menu, and so on. Roaming user profiles work by storing the user profile in a shared network folder. When the user logs on, the profile information is copied from the shared network folder to the local hard disk. When the user logs off, the profile information—which might have changed during the computing session—is then copied back to the shared folder.

If you use more than one computer, you might find roaming user profiles useful. For example, if you have a small business with a front office and a back office, you might find yourself spending equal time in each location. Although it's relatively easy to set up your data files in a shared network location for easy access, you'll probably find that your productivity suffers because little changes in settings—your personal spell-checking dictionary in Word, for example, or your list of favorite Web sites—are different in the two locations. Using roaming user profiles solves this problem.

Ordinarily, roaming user profiles are a feature of domain-based networks (that is, a network that uses a member of the Windows Server 2003, Windows 2000 Server, or Windows NT Server family as a domain controller). With a bit of extra work, however, you can enjoy some of the same benefits in a workgroup environment. In a domain environment, user accounts and computer accounts are centrally managed at the domain level, so you need to make settings only one time and in only one place. Accessing a profile for the first time from a new computer happens automatically. By contrast, with a workgroup, you must explicitly create similar user accounts on each computer where you want to log on before you're allowed to log on.

To make this work in a workgroup environment, each user whom you want to set up with a roaming profile must have an account on each computer where that user will log on, plus an account on the computer that contains the shared profiles folder. The user account on each computer must have the same user name and password.

> **Caution**   Our own experimentation showed that configuring roaming profiles and mandatory profiles in a Windows XP–only workgroup environment is difficult, at best. Because of the way settings are applied (particularly settings related to the theme engine and Start menu), not all settings roam properly, and operation is somewhat unpredictable if you don't configure everything correctly. If having these features perform perfectly is important to you and your business, you should seriously consider upgrading to Windows Server 2003, which makes user configuration much easier and more reliable.

Setting Up the Shared Folder for Roaming Profiles

Because you'll need to view and modify permissions, the computer where you're planning to store roaming profiles must be running Windows XP Professional and Simple File Sharing must be disabled.

To set up the shared folder, follow these steps:

1 Log on as a member of the computer's Administrators group.

2 Using Windows Explorer, create a folder called Profiles.

3 In Windows Explorer, right-click the new Profiles folder and choose Sharing And Security.

4 On the Sharing tab of the Profiles Properties dialog box that appears, select Share This Folder. The default sharing permissions, which provide Full Control share access to Everyone, are appropriate.

5 Click the Security tab (if you created the folder on an NTFS volume), and ensure that Everyone has Full Control permission.

Setting Up User Accounts

To set up the user accounts for your workgroup, follow these steps:

1 On each computer (including the "server" that you set up in the preceding procedure), log on as a member of the Administrators group.

2 Right-click My Computer and choose Manage.

3 In Computer Management, go to System Tools\Local Users And Groups\Users.

4 If the user account you want doesn't already exist, choose Action, New User, and create a user account. Be sure to use the same user name and password on each computer. Clear the User Must Change Password At Next Logon check box before you click Create.

5 In the right pane of the Computer Management window, double-click the name of the user to display the properties dialog box.

6 Click the Profile tab. In the Profile Path box, type the network path to the shared profiles folder, as shown in Figure 17-4.

Figure 17-4. The %UserName% environment variable is expanded to the user name when you move to another field or click OK.

The advantage of using the %UserName% environment variable is merely convenience: You can use the same string for every user, without having to pause to figure out the correct name of the profile folder.

Note A *client* computer—not the one where the profile is stored—can run Windows XP Home Edition. Although Home Edition does not include the Local Users And Groups snap-in, you can use other tools to achieve the same results. If necessary, create a new user account and assign a password with User Accounts in Control Panel. To assign a profile path, use the Net User command. For example, to make the same assignment shown in Figure 17-4 for a user named Josie, at a command prompt, type **net user josie/profilepath:\\badlands\profiles\josie**.

Troubleshooting

Windows doesn't use the shared profile.

If you forget to set up a user account on the computer with the shared profiles folder, Windows displays a warning when the user attempts to log on. If a local copy of the user profile already exists, Windows uses that copy; if not, Windows creates a temporary profile (based on the Default User profile) in a folder called Temp, which is not saved when the user logs off. To solve the problem, simply create a user account on the "server"; be sure you use the same user name and password as on the client computer.

Creating the Profile

To create a profile to be used as a roaming user profile and copy it to the shared profiles folder, follow these steps:

1. Create a profile by logging on (ideally with a temporary user account you create for the purpose) and making the settings you want.

2. Log off and then log back on as a member of the Administrators group.

Note If you are copying a profile from a computer other than the one that contains the shared profiles folder, the account you log on with must have the same name and password as an account that has administrative privileges on the target computer.

3. Right-click My Computer and choose Properties. In the System Properties dialog box, click the Advanced tab and then click Settings under User Profiles.

4. Select the profile you created and click Copy To.

5. In the Copy Profile To box, type the full path of the destination profile folder. For example, if you want to create a profile for a user named Josie in the Profiles share on the computer named Badlands, type \\badlands\profiles\josie. Be sure the destination folder you specify doesn't exist; if it does, Windows deletes its contents before copying the profile.

Chapter 17

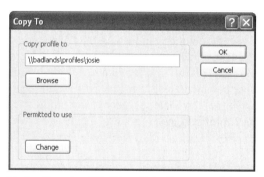

6   Under Permitted To Use, click Change and then type the name of the user who will use the profile.

When you click OK in the Copy To dialog box, Windows copies the user profile to the specified folder and sets permissions on the destination folder and its contents. Windows gives Full Control permission to the Administrators group, the user or group you entered in the Permitted To Use box, and the System account. This prevents nonadministrative users from accessing a profile other than their own.

If you copied the profile from one computer to a shared folder on another computer, the permissions that Windows creates are not exactly right, and you must take one more step to correct them. On the computer with the shared profiles folder, right-click the new profile folder, choose Properties, and click Security. If one of the names shows the security identifier of an unknown user, as shown in Figure 17-5, you must add the correct user account (Josie, in this case) and give it Full Control permission. You can remove the unknown user, although it's not necessary to do so. (The unknown account is actually the correct user name, but it's the account from the source computer, not the account on the local computer. This is one of the hazards and annoyances of relying on separate security databases—as the workgroup model does—rather than using the centralized security database used by domains. For more information, see "Local Accounts and Groups vs. Domain Accounts and Groups," page 225.)

Figure 17-5.   If the permissions for the profile folder don't include the local user account, the user won't be able to log on.

Chapter 17

Using Mandatory User Profiles

A mandatory user profile works much like a roaming user profile: When a user logs on, the profile is copied from a network location to a local folder, thereby providing familiar settings. The difference is that a mandatory profile isn't updated with user changes when the user logs off.

To assign a mandatory user profile to one or more users, follow the same procedures as described for using roaming user profiles. Then, on the computer where the shared profile is stored, make the following changes:

1 Change the folder permissions to remove Full Control, Modify, and Write permissions for the user account (or accounts) that will use the profile—leaving the account with only Read & Execute, List Folder Contents, and Read permissions.

2 Change the name of the hidden Ntuser.dat file (in the profile's top-level folder) to Ntuser.man. (Be sure you change Ntuser.dat, not Ntuser.dat.log, which ordinarily has a hidden extension.) The .man extension identifies a mandatory profile.

Troubleshooting

Certain files are unavailable to the roaming profile.

You might encounter problems if certain user profile settings rely on files that are stored on the local hard drive. For example, you might set the desktop background to a file stored on drive C. When you log on at another computer, the background doesn't appear (unless the same file happens to be in the same location on the other computer). You can alleviate such problems by redirecting My Documents to a shared network folder and then using it to store documents and other files that you want to access from different computers.

Chapter 17

Configuring Shutdown and Power Management Options

In the past, power management has been the concern primarily of laptop-toting road warriors and others who use battery-powered portable computers. Those computers' short battery life—as little as one hour between charges—demanded that users monitor battery charge levels closely and do everything possible to minimize battery consumption. Systems were designed to turn off certain components when not in use and to switch the whole system to a low-power state after a period of inactivity.

Recent years have seen tremendous advances in battery technology. In addition, current models of devices such as displays and hard drives draw less power than their predecessors. This combination of technology advances has led to greatly increased battery life for portable computers—suggesting that power management is no longer an important topic. In fact, it has become even more important.

At Home with Windows XP

Microsoft Windows XP Professional and Windows XP Home Edition are both adept at managing power. All descriptions and procedures in this chapter apply equally to both editions of the operating system.

The dawn of the new millennium brought rolling blackouts to California and soaring electricity prices for nearly everyone. Now proper power management is as important for desktop computer users as it is for battery-powered computer users. Although the advances in hardware technology have achieved considerable power savings, operating system power management features still provide a significant boost in battery life for portable computers.

Power management and shutdown features provide three primary benefits to users of all computers:

- Minimized power consumption, which lowers power costs for desktop users and increases battery life for portable users
- "Instant-on" capability
- An orderly shutdown in case of power outage

How Does Your Computer Manage Power?

Windows XP—along with an OnNow-capable computer and suitable applications— manages a computer's power in such a way that power usage (and noise) is minimized, but the computer and its peripherals are instantly available when needed. Based on settings you make, Windows XP switches the computer and its peripherals to a low-power state when they're not in use. An OnNow-capable system can be wakened by events received from an application, a modem, a network connection, or other devices. This capability allows scenarios such as these:

- You have a computer set up as a host for Internet Connection Sharing and a shared printer. It can be in a quiet, low-power sleep state until another computer on your network needs an Internet connection or a printer, whereupon the computer becomes instantly available.
- You have a computer set up as a telephone answering device. It wakes from a low-power state whenever the phone rings.
- You have security devices, such as break-in detectors or a camera. During suspected security breaches, these devices wake a computer from a low-power state so it will automatically send e-mail or pager alerts.
- You have maintenance and other tasks scheduled to run when a computer's not being used. Tasks in the Scheduled Tasks folder can be configured to wake the computer at the appointed time and perform the task.

Some of these capabilities are dependent upon your computer being compliant with the Advanced Configuration and Power Interface (ACPI) specification.

For information about ACPI, see "ACPI vs. APM," page 584.

What Is OnNow?

OnNow is a Microsoft initiative to advance PC hardware so that it supports instant-on capability, yet appears to be off (that is, it's quiet and uses little or no power) when it's not in use. This has ramifications beyond eliminating the need to go get a cup of coffee to occupy the time after you switch on your computer: It allows devices and applications to wake the computer from a low-power state and immediately get to work. Microsoft set the following design goals for a typical consumer PC running Windows XP:

- Boot from power off to a usable state in 30 seconds.
- Resume from hibernation in 20 seconds.
- Resume from standby in five seconds.

Although these goals are met only by compliant hardware, meeting them relies on several under-the-hood improvements in Windows XP. For example, changes were made in the boot loader that greatly reduce the time spent seeking data on hard disks. The boot process was also optimized to perform certain steps concurrently and to avoid or postpone the loading of processes and services that aren't needed at boot time.

Configuring Your Computer's BIOS

For Windows XP power management features to work properly, you should disable all power management features in your computer's BIOS. Run its setup program (usually accessed by pressing Delete or F1 during the computer's power-on self test; watch the screen for a message explaining how to enter setup), and browse the menus for all settings related to power management. With ACPI, power management should be under the exclusive control of the operating system. When the operating system and the BIOS contend for control, problems often result.

Conserving Power on All Computers—Even Desktops!

There used to be an ongoing debate: Should you turn your computer off when you're not using it or leave it on all the time? Proponents of leaving a computer on claimed that turning the power on and off—causing motors to start and stop and other components to heat up and cool down—would shorten its life. This assertion was never widely accepted and, in fact, others argued that leaving a computer on all the time would wear out bearings and other moving parts more quickly. So the issue of whether your computer will last longer if it's turned off or left on when not in use has never been satisfactorily resolved. (Besides, no matter which routine wears out your computer faster, the machine is likely to become obsolete long before it wears out.) Regardless, it makes sense to turn off your computer (or switch to a low-power state) simply for the energy savings.

Chapter 18

> **Note** Screen savers—programs that display varying patterns on your computer's screen while you're not using it—can be fun, but they don't save energy. In fact, by keeping the monitor on and by using CPU cycles, they actually consume more energy than if you didn't use a screen saver at all.

How much power does a desktop computer consume? Unlike many appliances, you won't find a sticker that specifies power consumption on the back of a computer. And specifications for most computers don't indicate power consumption because so many variables exist. Each expansion card or other device you install in the computer consumes power; more power is consumed when the computer is in use than when it's inactive; power management features control power consumption; and so on.

You can use an ammeter to get an idea of how much power your computer uses. Or you can visit the Web site of American Power Conversion Corporation (APC), a company that makes uninterruptible power supplies (UPSs) and surge protectors. The APC site provides a page that calculates the power needs of your computer, at *http://www.apcc.com/template/size/apc*.

How much money can you save by effectively using power management? Suppose your computer uses 300 watts and you use it eight hours a day. Without power management (in other words, if you leave the computer on at full power), during the other 16 hours of the day, the computer consumes 4.8 kilowatt-hours (KWH). Assuming power in your area costs, say, 15 cents per KWH, by putting your system in a low-power state during your non-working hours, you could save on the order of 72 cents per day. And if you pay the bill for several computers, the potential savings are significant.

Of course, you can realize these savings with any computer and with any operating system by simply remembering to turn the system off when you're not using it. Windows XP and an OnNow-capable computer, however, switch to low-power (or no-power) states automatically after a period of inactivity. Besides turning off your computer at night, using ACPI can reduce power consumption while you're away at lunch or working away from your computer. Also, using Windows power management enables the computer to return to a working state much more quickly than rebooting.

 Inside Out

Take a Direct Route to Power Options

Navigating through menus to get to the section of Control Panel that provides power-management options can be tedious. Here's a fast way to get there: Right-click the desktop and choose Properties. In the Display Properties dialog box, click the Screen Saver tab and click Power.

And for command prompt aficionados, here's an even quicker method: At a command prompt, type **powercfg.cpl**.

Configuring Shutdown and Power Management Options

> If you find that you need to visit Power Options Properties often, you can include its icon in the notification area so that it's only a click away. To do that, select Always Show Icon On The Taskbar on the Advanced tab of the Power Options Properties dialog box.

To configure any of the Windows XP power management features, open Power Options in Control Panel. (If you use Category view in Control Panel, you'll find Power Options under Performance And Maintenance.) Figure 18-1 shows the Power Schemes tab of the Power Options dialog box.

Figure 18-1. The appearance of your Power Options Properties dialog box depends on your system—whether it's ACPI-compliant, whether it has a battery, whether it has power backup in the form of a UPS, and so on.

Using Standby to Reduce Power Use

Standby uses only enough power to preserve the contents of memory—typically only a few watts. Its advantages over hibernation are that it doesn't require free disk space and it allows nearly instant system reactivation. Use standby when you're planning to not use your computer for a few minutes or a few hours; use hibernation for longer periods of disuse.

On systems that support standby, you can configure the system to switch to standby automatically after a period of inactivity or you can switch to standby manually.

To enable automatic switching, follow these steps:

1 In the Power Options Properties dialog box, click the Power Schemes tab.

2 Specify a time in the System Standby box and click OK or Apply.

Power States: Standby vs. Hibernation

Although your computer appears to be either on or off, the ACPI specification actually defines six different power states, which are described in the following table.

State	Description
S0 Working	The computer is on. The CPU is fully up and running. Under the direction of the operating system or device settings, other devices may be running in a low-power state.
S1 Standby	The computer appears to be off. (Some systems have a blinking light to indicate they're in a sleep state.) The display and drives are powered off, but power remains for the CPU, memory, and fans.
S2 Standby	The computer appears to be off. Same as S1 Standby, but the CPU and cache are powered off.
S3 Standby	The computer appears to be off. Minimal power is provided to refresh RAM; all other devices are powered off.
S4 Hibernate	The computer appears to be off. The system is completely powered off, but the contents of RAM have been saved to disk.
S5 Off	The computer is off. The system is completely powered off and nothing has been saved.

Not all computers support all six power-saving states and, in fact, Windows XP presents only four choices to users (S1, S2, and S3 are all variants of the condition called *standby*): working, standby, hibernation, and off.

What's the difference between standby and hibernation? In a nutshell, standby simply shifts to a low-power state by shutting down hard drives, fans, the CPU, and other power-hungry components—but it continues to draw some power to retain the contents of memory and to be ready to spring back to life quickly. Hibernation saves the contents of memory to the hard disk and then shuts off all power. The following table shows the features that differentiate standby and hibernation.

Advantage	Standby	Hibernation
Uses no power		✓
Powers down more quickly	✓	
Returns to work state more quickly	✓	
Doesn't require disk space	✓	
Preserves data even if power goes off		✓

Inside Out

Prevent Loss of Work with a UPS

If the power goes out while your computer is on standby, you lose whatever is in memory. If you have any unsaved documents, for example, they're gone. With a UPS, however, you can prevent data loss during blackouts. Although the blackout might last longer than the battery run time provided by the UPS, you can prevent loss, even if your computer happens to be on standby and you're away when the power goes out. To do so, make the following settings in Power Options:

● Enable hibernation. (On the Hibernate tab, select Enable Hibernate Support.)

● Specify a time—less than the battery run time—for the computer to switch to hibernation. (On the Power Schemes tab, set a time for System Hibernates under Running On Batteries.)

Thereafter, your computer switches to standby after the specified amount of time has elapsed without any input from the keyboard, mouse, or other devices.

To configure other standby options, follow these steps:

1 In the Power Options Properties dialog box (shown in Figure 18-2), click the Advanced tab.

Figure 18-2. Use the Advanced tab in the Power Options dialog box to specify button actions.

2 If you're concerned about somebody else waking your computer from standby, select Prompt For Password When Computer Resumes From Standby. This option has no effect if your account doesn't need a password to log on to Windows.

3 For each button under Power Buttons, choose Standby—or another action if you prefer. (Despite its possible appearance in the dialog box, not all computers have a sleep button.)

> **Tip** If you configure your power button to do something other than shut down (its traditional function), you can still force the computer to power off completely. Simply press and hold the power button for several seconds.

Troubleshooting

Your computer won't enter standby or hibernation.

Power management features—especially standby and hibernation—rely on device drivers that support power management in addition to compatible hardware. In particular, incompatible video drivers can prevent these features from working. The built-in VGA driver, for example, is a bare-bones driver that doesn't support power management. If standby and hibernate don't work, try installing an updated driver for your display adapter.

To switch to standby manually, use either of these methods:

● Press the button on your computer or keyboard (for example, the power button or sleep button) that you've configured to switch to standby.

● On the Start menu, choose Turn Off Computer. In the window that appears (Figure 18-3), click Stand By.

Figure 18-3. A fourth option—Hibernate—is hidden. Hold down the Shift key to see it.

If your computer is a member of a domain, the procedure is slightly different: On the Start menu, choose Shut Down. A dialog box like the one shown in Figure 18-4 appears. Select Stand By in the list and then click OK.

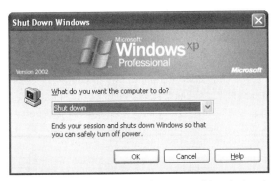

Figure 18-4. Domain members see this window instead of the one shown in Figure 18-3.

Shutting Down Your Computer

Despite the quick-resume advantages provided by standby and hibernation, you'll still want to shut down your computer completely on occasion. You can do this in either of two ways:

- On the Start menu, choose Turn Off Computer, Turn Off. (If your computer is part of a domain, click Start, Shut Down, select Shut Down, and then click OK.)
- Press the computer's power button. (If you've configured the power button to switch to standby or hibernation, press and hold the button for several seconds to perform a complete shutdown.)

In Windows XP, these two methods perform a controlled shutdown in exactly the same way: The operating system notifies applications that it's going to shut down (giving them an opportunity to save unsaved work), waits for responses, and then shuts down. This is a departure from Microsoft Windows 2000, in which pressing the power button performs a "critical action" shutdown. In this type of shutdown, Windows notifies applications and devices about the impending shutdown—but doesn't wait for a response. Some people discovered this difference in Windows 2000 and used the power switch to shut down more quickly. What they didn't realize is that they risked losing unsaved data with this method; Windows XP now eliminates that confusing distinction.

Troubleshooting

A hung application prevents shutdown.

If you need to shut down in a hurry—or if a frozen application prevents you from shutting down in the normal ways—you can use the following procedure. Be aware, however, that you won't get an opportunity to save open documents. Windows shuts down immediately— no "Windows is shutting down" or other messages. To perform an emergency shutdown, press Ctrl+Alt+Delete to display Task Manager. Open the Shut Down menu and hold down the Ctrl key as you click Turn Off. Poof!

Chapter 18

If your computer is part of a domain, the procedure is similar. Press Ctrl+Alt+Delete and then hold down Ctrl when you click Shut Down. In this situation, you'll get a warning message pointing out—quite correctly—that this should be used only as a last resort.

As an alternative to the instant shutdown procedure just described, you can use the End Task and End Process buttons in Windows Task Manager to terminate a task or process that appears to be unwilling to go quietly (or quickly). And as an alternative to terminating processes and tasks via Windows Task Manager, you can use the command-line programs Tskill or Taskkill. Tskill is available in both Windows XP Home Edition and Windows XP Professional. Taskkill, which offers some options not available in Tskill, is available in Windows XP Professional only. For details about the syntax of these commands, open a Command Prompt window and type the command name followed by /?.

Hibernating for Maximum Power Savings

Hibernation is a way of shutting down your computer without shutting down the operating system. Hibernation is an option on many systems, even if they're neither Advanced Power Management (APM) nor ACPI-compliant. When you hibernate, Windows XP copies everything in memory to disk and then powers down all components of your computer. When you emerge from hibernation (by pressing your computer's power button), the memory image that was copied to disk is restored, and you're ready to go back to work.

Hibernation saves time because it relieves Windows of all the housekeeping chores it would normally perform during shutdown and restart. Instead of having to close files on shutdown, redetect hardware, reconstitute the hardware-specific sections of your registry, reload drivers, and restart programs, the operating system simply saves and restores the state of your computer.

Caution   *Never* boot into another operating system while your computer is hibernating. That is, if your computer is set up so that it can boot into an operating system other than Windows XP, do not hibernate Windows XP and then boot into another operating system. Doing so can corrupt or destroy your stored data. When Windows hibernates, it stores the contents of RAM—which usually includes part of the hard disk's master file table (MFT). If you boot to another file system, make some changes to the data on disk, and then resume from hibernation, Windows restores the MFT from the stored hibernation file—which likely means your changes will be overwritten.

Tip   If you want to boot to another operating system, be sure you shut down or restart your computer rather than hibernating.

Inside Out

Don't Try to Relocate the Hibernation File

When you hibernate, Windows XP stores the contents of memory on your computer's boot partition in a file named Hiberfil.sys. As long as hibernation is enabled, you can't delete it, rename it, or move it to another disk or partition. That's because of its integral role in the boot process. When you turn on the power, Ntldr (the bootstrap loader program for Windows XP) looks for the existence of Hiberfil.sys on the boot partition. At that point in the boot process, no other programs or drivers are running and the registry isn't accessible—so it's not possible to specify another location. If the file exists, Ntldr then checks to see whether a flag is set to indicate that the computer is in hibernation. If so, its contents are restored to memory. (If the file doesn't exist or the hibernation flag isn't set, Ntldr then proceeds to run the normal boot sequence.)

If you need the space occupied by Hiberfil.sys, you must disable hibernation by clearing the check box on the Hibernate tab in the Power Options dialog box.

Because hibernation puts your work into nonvolatile storage, it's a safer way to reduce power during periods of inactivity than standby. If you experience a power failure while your computer is hibernating, you won't lose anything because your computer's memory has been copied to disk. On the other hand, hibernation requires an amount of free disk space equivalent to the amount of your computer's random access memory. If you have a 128-MB system, for example, you need 128 MB of free disk space to hibernate. Moreover, it takes longer to emerge from hibernation than to come off standby, because the operating system has to restore data from disk.

To configure your system for hibernation, in the Power Options Properties dialog box, click the Hibernate tab and select Enable Hibernation.

You can configure other hibernation options to:

- Set an inactivity time limit to automatically switch to hibernation (Power Schemes tab).
- Assign a button on the computer to switch the computer to hibernation (Advanced tab).
- Require a password to resume from hibernation (Advanced tab; although the check box mentions only standby, it affects emergence from hibernation also).

Chapter 18

Inside Out

Beware of the Expiring Password

If you use password security on your computer—and, unless it's in a locked closet that's not connected to a network or the Internet, you probably should—you might also use policies that cause passwords to expire periodically. If your password happens to expire while your computer is in hibernation (and you've enabled the password prompt on resume option), you've got a problem: Windows won't let you resume from hibernation. Therefore, you can't set a new password. Granted, it's an unusual set of circumstances, but we know from personal experience that it's possible. There is a workaround: Using Safe Mode (after pressing the power button, press F8 and choose Safe Mode), log on as Administrator. As Administrator, you can change the password for the hibernated account and then reboot.

To hibernate manually, use either of these methods:

● Press the button on your computer or keyboard (for example, the power button or sleep button) that you've configured to hibernate.

● On the Start menu, choose Turn Off Computer. In the window that appears (see Figure 18-3 on page 572)—here's the tricky part—hold down the Shift key. The Stand By button changes to Hibernate; click it before releasing Shift and the computer will hibernate rather than enter standby mode. (If your computer doesn't support standby, then the button always appears as Hibernate, and you won't need to press the Shift key.)

Troubleshooting

Your system reboots or shuts down instead of hibernating.

A faulty device driver is probably causing a blue-screen error during the hibernation process. To see whether that's the case, open the System Properties dialog box (press Windows+Break or, in Control Panel, open Performance And Maintenance, System) and click the Advanced tab. Under Startup And Recovery, click Settings. In the Startup And Recovery dialog box, select the Write An Event To The System Log check box and clear Automatically Restart. Close the dialog boxes and try to hibernate. Now, if a blue-screen error occurs, it remains on-screen and you can use it to help pinpoint which driver is causing the problem.

If you have an APM system that shuts down instead of hibernating, try the following. Open Device Manager (Devmgmt.msc) and choose View, Show Hidden Devices. Open NT Apm/ Legacy Support and be sure that the NT Apm/Legacy Interface Node device is enabled.

Configuring Shutdown and Power Management Options

Waking Up Your Computer

You can bring your computer back from standby or hibernation simply by pressing the power button. In a few seconds, you'll be back to where you were when the computer powered down—or at a dialog box asking for your password before allowing access. But you can also configure various devices and applications to wake the computer. For example, if the keyboard device is configured to wake the computer, pressing any key powers up the computer.

Troubleshooting

Your system won't emerge from standby.

First check with your system vendor to be sure you have the latest BIOS. If a new BIOS doesn't enable your system to emerge from standby, the problem is likely to be with a device driver. Try removing or disabling all your peripheral devices. If you can then emerge from standby properly, add devices one at a time and test whether your system emerges from standby after each addition. When you find the device that causes the problem, check with its vendor to see whether an updated driver is available.

In some cases, a problematic device driver prevents a particular device from waking. For example, your computer resumes from standby, but the mouse doesn't work. You can sometimes fix this problem by disabling the option that allows the problem device to wake the computer. If the mouse doesn't work, for example, go to the properties dialog box for the mouse as described next and clear the check boxes on the Power Management tab.

To enable a hardware device—such as the keyboard, mouse, modem, network card, and so on—to wake the computer, follow these steps:

1. In Device Manager (type **devmgmt.msc** at a command prompt), double-click the name of the device for which you want to enable power management.

2. In the device's properties dialog box, click the Power Management tab, shown in Figure 18-5. (If the dialog box has no Power Management tab, the device can't be used to wake the computer.)

3. Select the appropriate check boxes for your situation.

Chapter 18

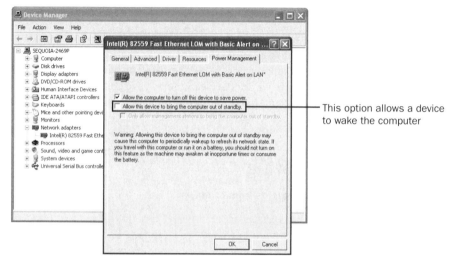

This option allows a device to wake the computer

Figure 18-5. On the Power Management tab, you direct your computer to wake from a low-power state when it receives a signal from a device.

OnNow-aware applications can also be configured to wake the computer. For example, items in the Scheduled Tasks folder can be configured to run at predetermined times, even if the computer is on standby.

Inside Out

Dealing with Unwelcome Awakenings

Does your computer wake up in the middle of the night, even when no one touches it? Some broadband Internet providers periodically probe your computer to see whether it's still connected. If your network interface card is configured to wake the computer, one of these probes will do it. If you don't want to disable the wake-on-LAN feature, you can ensure that probes from your Internet connection don't rouse your computer by turning off the computer's power completely before you and your computer retire: Shut down Windows and flip off the switch on your power strip or UPS. (Be sure, however, that your computer is not on standby when you do this.)

Follow these steps to enable power management for a scheduled task:

1 Open the Scheduled Tasks folder (choose Start, All Programs, Accessories, System Tools, Scheduled Tasks).

2 Create a new task or select an existing one.

3 Double-click the task to open its properties dialog box and click the Settings tab.

4 Select the appropriate check boxes under Power Management, shown in Figure 18-6.

Figure 18-6. You can configure tasks to wake the computer if it's sleeping or prevent them from running if the computer isn't running on AC power.

 Troubleshooting

Your APM machine has problems emerging from standby.

If your computer uses APM for power management and sometimes fails to come out of standby, check the time-out settings in your BIOS setup program. If these thresholds are lower than the ones set in the Power Options Properties dialog box, you might sometimes be unable to emerge from standby. To resolve the problem, set the BIOS time-out settings to their maximum values.

Using Power Schemes

A *power scheme* is a named combination of power-reduction settings. Windows XP provides a number of predefined schemes, which appear on the Power Schemes tab in Power Options. (See Figure 18-1 on page 569.) You can alter the supplied schemes or add your own.

To modify an existing power scheme, simply select it in the Power Schemes list, adjust the settings below, and then click OK. To create a new scheme, edit an existing one. Then click Save As and supply a new name.

Conserving Power on Portable Computers

All of the power-management features that reduce power consumption on desktop computers work equally well on portable computers. In addition, several other features benefit users of late-model, battery-powered portable computers:

- When the computer's lid is closed, the display is switched off.
- When a portable computer is running on battery power, the display is dimmed; it automatically returns to full brightness when the computer is plugged in.
- Some portable computers can be configured so that when they're running on battery power, the processor runs at a lower speed, which consumes less power. (To configure this option, visit the Advanced tab in the Power Options Properties dialog box.)
- A portable computer can be configured so that when it's running on battery power and it enters a low-battery or critical-battery condition, it automatically raises an alarm, switches to a low-power state, or runs a program. This feature is especially useful when your computer is on standby and you're not around—it can automatically hibernate to preserve your data when the batteries run down. (To configure this option, visit the Alarms tab in the Power Options Properties dialog box, shown below.)

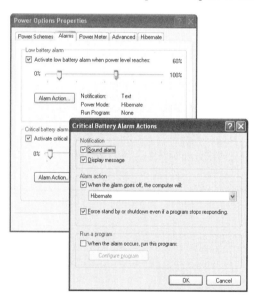

Displaying a Power Status Indicator

As in many corners of the Windows XP user interface, the Advanced tab of the Power Options Properties dialog box presents nothing the least bit advanced. It's simply a catch-all location for miscellaneous user-interface elements.

One of those elements in the Power Options Properties dialog box is an option to display a power status icon in your taskbar's notification area. Should you accept, a battery icon appears while you're running on batteries, and a power-cord icon appears when you're not. When your battery power falls below about 50 percent, the battery icon changes to a "half-full" appearance.

Double-clicking the icon provides more detailed information about your battery's condition. Right-clicking the icon generates a shortcut menu, from which you can return to the Power Options Properties dialog box.

Protecting Your Data During a Power Outage

You've been working on an important document—your doctoral thesis, a new musical composition, a financial projection—for several hours. Suddenly the screen goes blank and the room becomes dark. Amazingly, it's *then* that the proverbial light bulb blinks on above your head: "I should have saved that document!" If the power goes off, the computer's memory—including any changes to unsaved files—is erased.

The first way to protect your data is to back it up frequently:

- Use your program's autosave feature, if there is one. For example, you can configure Microsoft Word to save AutoRecover information every few minutes. (On the Tools menu, choose Options and then click the Save tab.) The next time you start Word (after the power comes back on), it opens your document with the last-saved AutoRecover information.

- Get in the habit of saving frequently. In most programs, Ctrl+S is the keyboard shortcut for saving the current document. Press Ctrl+S every few minutes, whenever you get up from your desk, or even each time you pause to think about what to type next. This action should become so instinctive that you do it automatically.

- Establish—and follow—a regular backup routine. Should the lights go dim and your files somehow become scrambled, you'll at least be able to restore the document as it existed at the time of your most recent backup. It beats starting over. For more information, see "Smart Backup Strategies," page 1254.

Of course, these precautions defend against disasters other than power outages. For real protection against data loss in the event of a power outage, you need a UPS—an uninterruptible power supply. A UPS is essentially a battery backup system. When the lights go off, the battery kicks in to provide power. Most UPSs also provide some form of power conditioning, which reduces or eliminates surges, spikes, and brownouts (low voltage). Any of these conditions can damage electronic equipment as well as your data.

Configuring a UPS

The easiest type of UPS to configure is the kind that connects to your computer's USB port. If you have this type of UPS, plug it into one of the USB ports on your computer—not to a USB hub. When you do that, it installs its driver and modifies the Power Options Properties dialog box appropriately: It adds an Alarms tab and a Power Meter tab, as shown in Figure 18-7. It also adds to the Power Schemes tab settings for shutdown times while running on batteries. (Don't be concerned that the UPS tab has disappeared; it's only necessary for UPSs that connect to a standard serial port.)

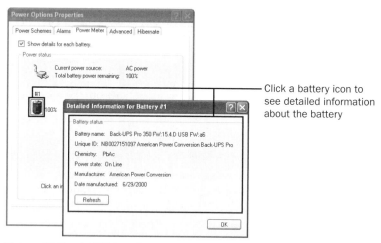

Click a battery icon to see detailed information about the battery

Figure 18-7. A USB-interface UPS typically adds a Power Meter tab, with which you can monitor your battery's charge.

> **Tip** Save open documents before you leave your computer
>
> Even if you have a UPS, you should save your open documents and close your applications before you leave your computer. Most UPSs designed for personal computers keep the computer running for only a few minutes before it's forced to shut down—and any documents left open at that time are lost just as if you had no UPS protection at all. By saving open documents before you leave your computer, you avoid data loss in the case of a blackout that lasts longer than your batteries.
>
> Of course, the one time you neglect to follow that advice will be right before the power goes out. Windows XP offers a better solution: Configure your computer to hibernate when the UPS battery reaches a critically low level. To do that, in Power Options, click Configure on the UPS tab or click the Alarms tab. (Where you find the setting depends on which UPS model you have.)

If your computer uses a serial-interface UPS, a UPS tab appears in your Power Options Properties dialog box, as shown in Figure 18-8. You should visit this corner of the power-management UI to make sure that your UPS is properly identified and configured. If the UPS tab doesn't already identify the manufacturer and model of your UPS, click Select. In the ensuing dialog box, you can specify a manufacturer and model as well as the port to which the UPS is connected.

Figure 18-8. Use the UPS tab to configure and monitor a serial-interface UPS.

To configure the actions taken by your UPS and by Windows XP should your normal power become unavailable, click the Configure button. In the UPS Configuration dialog box, shown in Figure 18-9, you can specify such things as a program that should run either when the UPS battery is close to exhaustion or when your system has been running on UPS battery power for a specified period of time.

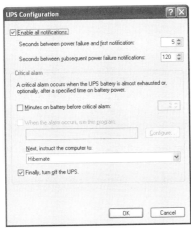

Figure 18-9. In the UPS Configuration dialog box, you can tell Windows XP what you want it to do when the power is out and the UPS battery is approaching exhaustion.

Chapter 18

ACPI vs. APM

Windows XP provides three levels of power-management support:

- On computers that are fully compliant with the ACPI specification—a requirement of OnNow-capable computers—the operating system maintains efficient and reliable control of the power supplied to your monitor, disk drives, peripherals, and motherboard components, reducing power to those components appropriately when your computer is inactive.

- On many systems that are not ACPI-compliant but that use an APM 1.2 BIOS, Windows can provide a serviceable, if somewhat less versatile, form of power management.

- On some earlier systems that do not have an APM 1.2 BIOS, the operating system can still conserve power by having the operating system shut down the monitor and disk drives during periods of inactivity. If you have a pre-APM BIOS, you might also be able to manually put your system into hibernation when you don't plan to use it again for a while.

The advantage of ACPI over APM is that ACPI puts power management completely in the control of the operating system. Because ACPI is an operating-system specification, Windows XP can provide a consistent approach to power management across all ACPI-compliant systems, thereby ensuring reliability while reducing training costs and user perplexity. With applications that are designed for ACPI, an ACPI-compliant system can also track the status of running or scheduled programs and coordinate power transitions with applications as well as hardware.

APM, on the other hand, is a BIOS specification. To manage power on a system that incorporates an APM BIOS but is not fully compliant with ACPI, Windows must work cooperatively with the BIOS. Because differences exist between the various APM BIOSs that are in use, APM-enabled systems differ considerably in their power-management behavior. Therefore it's impossible to say with certainty what power-management features will be available on your own APM system, exactly how those features will be implemented, and whether all your power-management features will work with 100 percent reliability.

In addition to reliability and consistency, other advantages of ACPI include the following:

- **Control of USB and FireWire devices**   ACPI systems can track the status of devices connected to your computer via USB or IEEE 1394 (FireWire). Because APM cannot monitor such devices, an APM system might attempt to go into standby or hibernation when a peripheral is active.

- **Support for wake-on-LAN and wake-on-ring**   An ACPI system can be configured to emerge from standby or hibernation when data arrives over the local area network or modem. Windows cannot take advantage of wake-on-LAN or wake-on-ring with systems that use APM.

Chapter 18

- **User definition of the power and reset buttons** On an ACPI system, you can configure the power and reset buttons to do what you want them to do. You can set the power button so that it puts the system into standby or hibernation, for example, rather than turning the computer off—thereby making it less likely that you'll inadvertently cut the power to your system. (For more details on power button configuration, see "Using Standby to Reduce Power Use," page 569.)

- **Better battery management** Under ACPI, Windows can provide separate meters for each battery on the system. Under APM, Windows represents multiple batteries as though they were a single composite battery.

- **Dynamic configuration of PC cards** On ACPI systems, you can insert and remove PC (PCMCIA) cards, and the operating system responds appropriately without requiring you to reboot.

- **Multiprocessor support** APM power management is not available on multiprocessor systems.

Determining Whether Your System Is ACPI-Compliant

During setup, Windows XP decides whether your computer is ACPI-compliant. If it is (according to the Setup program's judgment), Setup installs an ACPI hardware abstraction layer (HAL). Otherwise, Setup installs a standard APM (non-ACPI) HAL. The decision algorithm is as follows:

1. Setup looks to see whether your BIOS is on a list of BIOSs known to be incompatible with ACPI. (This list is in the [NWACL] section of a file named Txtsetup.sif, which is located in the \i386 folder of the Windows XP CD-ROM.) If your BIOS is on the list, you get the non-ACPI HAL.

2. If your BIOS isn't on the known-to-be-incompatible list, Setup checks the BIOS date. If it's later than January 1, 1999, you get the ACPI HAL.

3. If the BIOS date is prior to January 1, 1999, Setup checks a known-to-be-good BIOS list (located in the [GoodACPIBios] section of Txtsetup.sif). If your BIOS is listed, you get the ACPI HAL. If it's not, Setup installs the non-ACPI HAL.

How do you know whether Setup deemed your computer to be ACPI-compliant? You can use Device Manager to determine whether your computer is using ACPI for power management, by following these steps:

1. Open Device Manager. (At a command prompt, type **devmgmt.msc**.)

    You can also reach Device Manager from the System Properties dialog box. Press the Windows+Break, click the Hardware tab, and then click Device Manager.

Chapter 18

585

2 Open the System Devices entry.

If your system is ACPI-compliant (and the Windows XP Setup program has installed an ACPI HAL), you'll find an item called *Microsoft ACPI-Compliant System*.

Tip You can also check for ACPI compliance in the Power Options Properties dialog box. If it includes an APM tab, your system is not ACPI-compliant. (The absence of an APM tab, however, does not necessarily mean that your system *is* ACPI-compliant.)

Upgrading to ACPI Support

In some cases, a BIOS update can make a standard PC ACPI-compliant. If your computer is shown in Device Manager as a Standard PC and you want to upgrade to ACPI support, your first step is to check with your computer vendor to get the latest BIOS. In most cases, updating the BIOS doesn't require swapping out the BIOS chip (as it did on early PCs); rather, you copy a vendor-provided program to a floppy disk and boot the computer from the floppy disk. The program writes new data to the BIOS.

If you use a BIOS update to upgrade a system from APM to ACPI support, you must reinstall Windows XP after performing the upgrade. That's because ACPI support is dependent on an ACPI HAL, which you can get only by reinstalling Windows. You can perform an upgrade installation. (In other words, you don't need to perform a clean install.) This is a relatively painless operation that retains your existing settings, programs, and files.

Caution Do not use the Hardware Update Wizard or any other driver update procedure to change from Standard PC to an ACPI HAL (or the reverse). There's a good chance that your computer won't boot after making such a change. Even if it does boot, other severe problems could occur later. That's because changing the HAL is much more complex than simply changing a driver; all hardware must be redetected, support for Plug and Play and other hardware must be changed, and the part of the registry that stores information about installed hardware must be modified. The only supported way to make these changes is by rerunning Setup, as described above.

If you've already made this mistake, there's hope. Boot from your Windows XP CD and let Setup find the existing Windows installation. It should ask if you want to repair it. Answer in the affirmative, and Setup will reinstall the correct HAL while leaving all your other files and settings in place.

During setup, you can force Windows to install the standard PC HAL or an ACPI HAL rather than relying on the Setup program's judgment about your computer's level of ACPI support. There's seldom reason to do so—although symptoms of noncompliance might not be immediately apparent, Setup is usually right about which computers properly adhere to the ACPI specification—but you might need to do this if you encounter power-related problems with one HAL or the other. To specify which HAL to install, follow these steps:

1. Boot from the Windows XP CD to initiate setup.

2. At the point in text-mode setup where a message at the bottom of the screen reads "Press F6 if you need to install a third party SCSI or RAID driver," press F5. (That's right: press F5 at the F6 prompt.)

3. Use the Up Arrow key and Down Arrow key to scroll through the list of computer types. Highlight the one you want and then press Enter.

Enabling APM Power Management

If your system is not ACPI compliant and an APM tab appears in the Power Options Properties dialog box, you can use APM for power management. On some systems, the Windows XP Setup program enables APM power management automatically. These are systems with BIOSs known to cooperate effectively with Windows XP. On other systems, Windows provides support for APM power management, but you have to enable it yourself. You do that by going to the APM tab in Power Options and selecting the Enable Advanced Power Management Support check box. You do not have to restart your system after enabling APM power management. If you subsequently disable APM, however, you do need to restart.

 Troubleshooting

Windows won't allow you to enable APM.

If you can't enable APM, installing the NT Apm/Legacy Interface Node device might solve the problem. To do that, run the Add Hardware Wizard. In the wizard's list of installed hardware, select Add A New Hardware Device. Select manual installation and then, in the list of common hardware types, select NT Apm/Legacy Interface Node. For more information about the Add Hardware Wizard, see Chapter 5, "Setting Up and Troubleshooting Hardware."

APM is designed to monitor hardware interrupts and I/O port data traffic at the BIOS level to determine whether your system is active or inactive. The BIOS measures periods of inactivity against thresholds that you set via your system's BIOS Setup program. If the BIOS timer arrives at a preset threshold, the BIOS sends a message to Windows requesting some form of power transition (standby, for example). Windows verifies that your computer is ready for the requested power reduction and then tells the BIOS to go ahead with the requested transition. On a portable computer, the BIOS might also monitor battery

Chapter 18

status and send Windows a power-reduction request when battery strength falls below a specified threshold.

Troubleshooting

The Power Options Properties dialog box doesn't have an APM tab.

If you think Windows should provide APM support for your computer, but there's no APM tab in Power Options, the first thing to investigate is your computer's BIOS setup program. If APM is disabled in the BIOS when Windows is installed, the Windows XP Setup program does not install APM support. If APM is disabled in your system's BIOS, try reenabling it and reinstalling Windows XP.

If you still don't have APM support after taking these measures, your BIOS might be one that Windows XP regards as troublesome and declines to support. You can confirm this by running the program Apmstat.exe, which is one of the support tools included on your Windows XP CD-ROM. To install the support tools, navigate to the \Support\Tools folder on the CD, and then run Setup.

It's best to run Apmstat with the *verbose* switch in a Command Prompt window, like this:

```
apmstat -v
```

If the news from Apmstat is disagreeable, your next step is to contact your hardware vendor and see whether a BIOS upgrade is available. Microsoft strongly recommends that you do not try to circumvent its decision not to support your current BIOS.

Unfortunately, Windows cannot discriminate between the various possible reasons for an APM power-transition request. It cannot tell, for example, whether the BIOS is asking for power reduction because the system is idle, because battery power is low, or because the user has pressed the computer's sleep button.

Inside Out

Set the BIOS Inactivity Threshold High

Because Windows tries to honor the BIOS request under all circumstances, the system might attempt to go into standby or hibernation at a time when the computer is not actually idle. To avoid such problems, if you're using an APM system, set the BIOS inactivity thresholds to their highest possible values or disable these thresholds altogether. (On some systems, APM will not work if you disable the BIOS power-reduction thresholds.) With BIOS thresholds disabled or set to high values, you can rely on activity timers provided by Windows for power management. (For information about adjusting BIOS power-management settings, consult the documentation that came with your computer.)

Administering Power Options from the Command Prompt

Beginning with Service Pack 1 both Windows XP Professional and Windows XP Home Edition include Powercfg.exe, a command-utility that provides access to all the functionality of the Power Options section of Control Panel. With Powercfg.exe, you can do such things as query a system's power-management features, activate a particular power scheme, set battery alarms, and enable or disable wake-up capability for particular devices. You can also its import and export commands to copy power settings from one system to another.

For a complete description of the syntax of this powerful tool, open a Command Prompt window and type **powercfg /?**.

Chapter 18

Automating Windows XP

If you use your computer very much—and if you're reading this book you probably do—you probably find yourself repeatedly performing the same steps to accomplish the same ordinary tasks. Such a task might be a routine maintenance activity, such as backing up your data or cleaning detritus from your hard disk, or it might be a job that requires many steps. Computers excel at repetitive actions, and Microsoft Windows XP provides several ways to automate such tasks:

- **Task Scheduler** This service launches programs on a regular schedule or upon certain events, such as logging on to your computer.
- **Batch programs** These programs, a throwback to the earliest days of MS-DOS, still provide an easy, reliable way to run a sequence of programs and commands. Most programs can be started from a command prompt, which means they can be started from a batch program.
- **Windows Script Host** This feature allows you to run scripts written in VBScript, JScript, and other languages. Although learning how to use Windows Script Host is more difficult than learning how to create batch programs, scripts can interact with the operating system and with other programs in much more powerful ways.

In some cases, you'll find it useful to combine these techniques. For example, suppose your computer has two hard disks and you want to defragment them weekly. You can set up a scheduled task to run the Defrag command, but it can defragment only a single drive. Rather than setting up a separate task for each hard disk—and having to manage multiple schedules—create a batch program that includes a command to defragment each hard disk, and then create a scheduled task to run the batch program once a week.

At Home with Windows XP

All of the ways to automate Windows XP described in this chapter can be used in both editions of the operating system. To curtail the capabilities of the Task Scheduler by means of policies, however, you need to use Windows XP Professional.

For more information about defragmenting, see "Defragmenting Disks for Better Performance," page 1241.

Scheduling Tasks to Run Automatically

Windows XP includes a flexible, easy-to-use scheduling tool that allows you to automate chores that need to be performed at regular intervals. You can view, create, modify, and delete scheduled tasks with a visit to the Scheduled Tasks folder: In Control Panel, choose Performance And Maintenance, Scheduled Tasks.

Tip   Find the Scheduled Tasks tool

If you prefer navigating the Start menu—or if you want to find a shortcut to the Scheduled Tasks folder that you can put in a more convenient location—choose Start, All Programs, Accessories, System Tools, Scheduled Tasks. Alternatively, in Windows Explorer you can navigate to %SystemRoot%\Tasks.

Running a Program at a Scheduled Time

Task Scheduler, the name of the service that runs scheduled tasks, can be used to launch any program, script, or document on a schedule you specify. To create a scheduled task, open Add Scheduled Task in the Scheduled Tasks folder. The Scheduled Task Wizard that appears when you choose Add Scheduled Task is mostly, but not entirely, self-explanatory. Here are some aspects of the wizard that might not be apparent at first glance:

- You can schedule any application, script, batch program, shortcut, or linked document— anything that you can execute on a command line. You can also specify command-line arguments, but doing so requires a visit to the task's properties dialog box after you have created the task.

- If you schedule a task to run When My Computer Starts, that task will run as a noninteractive process when the computer starts and will continue to run, regardless of who is logged on, until the system is shut down or you terminate the task. (Because you are the task's owner, only you or a member of the Administrators group can terminate it. To terminate a noninteractive process, right-click its name in the Scheduled Tasks folder, and choose End Task. Alternatively, press Ctrl+Shift+Esc to open Windows Task Manager, click the Processes tab, select the process, and then click End Process.)

- If you schedule a task to run When I Log On, the task actually runs when *anyone* logs on. If you log on, the task runs interactively (provided, of course, that it was designed to run that way). If someone else logs on, the task runs as a noninteractive process.

> **Note** Logon tasks do not run when you use Fast User Switching to switch to another person's profile—even if the new user has not already logged on. Logon tasks that are not already running run only when someone logs on while all users are logged off.

● The screen shown in Figure 19-1 prompts you for a user account name and a password. If you're logged on as a member of the Administrators group, you can specify a user account and password other than your own here, thereby creating an interactive task for another user. Even if you're merely scheduling a task for your own account, however, you must supply your account name and password (the latter twice) in this dialog box—despite the fact that you've already given your password at logon.

If you don't provide a password, an error message appears after you finish creating the task, warning that the task won't run because "access is denied." You can resolve the problem by opening the properties dialog box for the task and, on the Task tab, click Set Password. Note, however, that if you subsequently change your password (a sound security practice), you'll need to revisit each task and reset the password in each one. With Service Pack 2 for Windows installed, an alternative solution exists. On the Task tab of the task's properties dialog box, select Run Only If Logged On. With this check box selected, the task runs at the appointed time if you are logged on; you don't need to enter your password separately for each task. Run Only If Logged On enables the task even if you change your password or lock your computer. (Your account must have the requisite privileges to run the task, of course. For example, if the task requires administrative permissions, you must be logged on with an account that is a member of the Administrators group.)

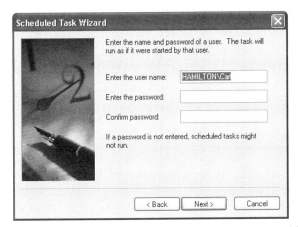

Figure 19-1. If you're an administrator, you can use this screen to schedule interactive tasks for other accounts.

● If you schedule a recurring task or one that will run at some distant point in the future, be aware that the password you specify must be valid at the time the task runs. If you change your password periodically, or if you set up a task for a user account that changes its password periodically, you might need to reenter the password down the line. You can do that by right-clicking the task in the Scheduled Tasks folder and choosing Properties from the shortcut menu.

● Unless the Remove Advanced Menu policy has been enabled (see "Restricting the Task Scheduler with Policies," page 599), the wizard's last page includes a check box that asks whether you want to open "advanced properties" for the new task when you click Finish. What appears if you select this check box is actually the normal properties dialog box for the task. To set true advanced properties, click the Schedule tab, and then click Advanced. In the Advanced Schedule Options dialog box, you can do such things as set repeat parameters and an end date for your new task. You can always come back to these options later by right-clicking the task in the Scheduled Tasks folder and choosing Properties from the shortcut menu. (For more information about advanced scheduling options, see "Advanced Scheduling Options" on page 596.)

Inside Out

Work around the quirks of logon tasks

If you set up a logon task for your own use, expecting it to run interactively, and someone else logs on before you, that task will run noninteractively when you log on. Windows XP leaves the task running when the other user logs off (because you own it) and does not start a second, interactive instance when you log on. The quickest way to get your task running the way you intended is to open Scheduled Tasks, right-click the task and choose End Task, and then right-click it again and choose Run.

Inside Out

Create scheduled tasks with drag and drop

You can create a scheduled task by simply dragging an executable (program or document) from Windows Explorer or the desktop to %SystemRoot%\Tasks. Windows XP sets up a .job (scheduled task) file for the object you drop and gives it a default schedule—every day at 9 A.M. Note, however, that this new scheduled task will not run until you authenticate it with a user name and password. To do that, right-click the new .job file in the Tasks folder and choose Properties from the shortcut menu. On the Task tab of the properties dialog box, fill out the Run As box, click Set Password, and supply the appropriate password. (Alternatively, select Run Only If Logged On if you don't want to enter your password and you plan to be logged on when the task is scheduled to run.) You can also delete existing .job files by dragging them from the Tasks folder to the desktop.

Troubleshooting

Your logon task appears not to run.

When someone other than the owner of a logon task logs on, the task runs as a noninter-active task, which means it displays no obvious indication that it's running. (This makes logon tasks ideal for certain background tasks, such as checking for viruses or monitoring computer usage remotely.) If you want a particular interactive program to start whenever you log on—say, for example, you would like a to-do list to open in Notepad—place a short-cut to the program in the Startup group instead of using a logon task.

Inside Out

Run scheduled tasks without a password

A security feature in Windows XP prevents accounts with no password (that is, a blank password) from logging on except at the Welcome screen. (This prevents easy access to the user's profile from a nefarious Internet hacker, for example.) Because Task Scheduler uses Run As capability to launch tasks, you must use an account that has a password to run scheduled tasks.

If your computer is in a location where you can safely use it without password-protecting your account, there is a simple workaround: Create a separate user account for running scheduled tasks and assign a password to that account.

Alternatively, you can disable the feature that limits the capabilities of accounts without a password. *Be aware that doing so makes it easier for a hacker to gain access to your computer from elsewhere on the network or on the Internet; we don't recommend this approach in most situations.* To disable the blank-password protection, open Local Security Settings (Secpol.msc) and navigate to Local Policies\Security Options. Double-click the Accounts: Limit Local Account Use Of Blank Passwords To Console Logon Only policy, select Disabled, and click OK. (To restore the protection, select Enabled.) If you are a Home Edition user, you must edit the registry directly to make this change: Use Registry Editor to open the HKLM\System\CurrentControlSet\Control\Lsa key. Change the set-ting of the limitblankpassworduse value to 0. (To restore the protection, set it to 1.)

Monitoring Scheduled Tasks

You can get useful information about the status of a scheduled task by displaying the Sched-uled Tasks folder in Details view. Among other things, you can learn when the task last ran (or was scheduled to run), when it's scheduled to run again, and who created the task.

A Note About Security

The behavior of the Windows XP Scheduled Tasks facility points to a fact that you should always keep in mind when working on a network or sharing your own machine with other user accounts: It's possible for someone else to start a process that runs invisibly while you're logged on to your own account. Even though a process started by someone else is limited by the privileges available to that other user, it's possible for such a process to monitor your activities. If you work with data that you don't want others to see, keep that data on an NTFS volume and use NTFS file security to restrict others' access.

Tasks can be designated as hidden, and by default hidden tasks don't appear in the Scheduled Tasks folder. To make them appear, choose Advanced, View Hidden Tasks. (You can't create a hidden task using the Scheduled Task Wizard or by editing an existing task. Hidden tasks can be created only by applications that are programmed to invoke this feature, which was introduced with Service Pack 2 for Windows XP.)

If a task fails to run, Details view tells you so but doesn't tell you why. To get diagnostic information, choose View Log from the Scheduled Tasks folder's Advanced menu. The log (%SystemRoot%\Schedlgu.txt) appears as a plain-text file in Notepad.

Tasks that fail to run because the computer is off at the appointed hour, or because the computer is on battery power and you've stipulated that the task shouldn't run in that condition, are recorded as missed tasks. You can be notified about missed tasks by choosing Notify Me Of Missed Tasks from the Scheduled Tasks folder's Advanced menu. If you miss a task because your computer is off, a message to that effect appears at your next logon.

 Inside Out

Find the latest log entry

Task Scheduler doesn't add new events to the end of the log file. Rather, it creates a sort of circular log file: When it records a new entry after reaching the log's size limit, it replaces the oldest entry still in the log. To find the most recent entry, use Notepad's Find command to search for *****. The newest entry precedes a line that reads "[***** Most recent entry is above this line *****]."

Advanced Scheduling Options

Visiting the properties dialog box for a task gives you the opportunity to modify the task's schedule, change the password or user name associated with the task, add command-line arguments for the task, or even change the application that is scheduled to run. The properties dialog box also provides some useful advanced scheduling options.

Caution Don't disable the Task Scheduler service by stopping it in the Services snap-in or with the Stop Using Task Scheduler command on the Advanced menu. Although they don't appear as scheduled tasks, several behind-the-scenes optimizations rely on the Task Scheduler service. In particular, optimizations that improve disk layout (by moving files around on disk for the best performance), boot time, and application opening time run as scheduled tasks.

Tip Use a batch program to schedule sequential tasks

When you have a group of tasks you want to perform periodically, you can create a scheduled task for each one and modify its properties to suit your needs. Doing so, however, makes it difficult to ensure that the tasks run in a certain order or that one task doesn't start until a prerequisite task is complete. For example, you might want to remove unneeded files from your hard drives, defragment each one, and then back them up. The most reliable method in such a case is to combine the command line for each task in a batch program and then create a scheduled task that runs the batch program. This has one other advantage: If you need to change scheduled task properties—say, to modify the schedule or enter your new logon password—you need to apply that change to only one task.

If you don't know if the command line performs a particular task (the command line for the Windows Backup Utility is particularly hairy), first set up the task in the normal way. That is, use the Scheduled Task Wizard or, in Backup Utility, use the Backup Or Restore Wizard. Then open the properties dialog box for each task you created to extract its command line to put into your batch program. For information about creating a batch program, see "Automating Command Sequences with Batch Programs," page 606.

The Show Multiple Schedules check box, on the Schedule tab, lets you assign more than one schedule to the same task. You could, for example, arrange to have your task run every Friday at 5 P.M. and also at 5 P.M. on the 30th day of every month. When you select this check box, a New button appears. Click New to enter a second or subsequent schedule.

Figure 19-2 on the next page shows the dialog box that is displayed when you click Advanced on the Schedule tab. Here you can specify an end date for a recurrent task or specify a repeat interval for a recurrent task. If you select RepeatTask, you can use the Time or Duration option to tell the system when to quit repeating. To repeat every two hours until 11 P.M., for example, you could select Repeat Task, set the Every fields to 2 and Hours, select Time, and specify 11 P.M. To run at 30-minute intervals for four hours, you could set the Every fields to 30 and Minutes, select Duration, and then specify 4 hours and 0 minutes.

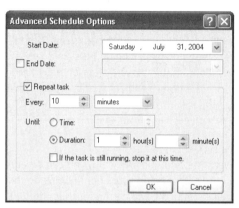

Figure 19-2. Click Advanced on the Schedule tab to produce the Advanced Schedule Options dialog box, where you can set end dates and recurrence parameters.

On the Settings tab, shown in Figure 19-3, you can provide a termination order for a task that has run too long, stipulate that a task not run if the computer is in use at the scheduled time (or stop running if someone begins using the computer), and tell the system not to run a task if the computer is running on battery power. On ACPI-compliant computers, the Power Management section of this dialog box includes a Wake The Computer To Run This Task check box. Selecting this check box ensures that your task will run at the scheduled time, even if the computer is in standby at the time. (For information about ACPI, see "ACPI vs. APM," page 584.)

On the Settings tab, you can also select a check box that will remove the task object from the Scheduled Tasks folder if, on the current schedule, it's never going to run again.

Figure 19-3. The Settings tab of a task's properties dialog box provides power-management control and other useful options.

> **Note** A computer is considered to be "idle" when there's no keyboard or mouse activity.

Restricting the Task Scheduler with Policies

The Task Scheduler node in the Group Policy console (Gpedit.msc) includes seven policies that you can use to curtail features relating to scheduled tasks. These policies are listed in Table 19-1. (The Group Policy console is available in Windows XP Professional only.)

Table 19-1. Task Scheduler Policies

Policy	Effect When Enabled
Hide Advanced Properties Checkbox in Add Scheduled Task Wizard	Simplifies the Scheduled Task Wizard by eliminating the option to set advanced scheduling properties.
Hide Property Pages	Prevents users from viewing and changing the properties of new and existing tasks, including their schedules, Run As accounts, and passwords.
Prevent Task Run Or End	Prevents users from running or stopping a task manually.
Prohibit Drag-and-Drop	Prevents users from creating a task by dragging an executable to the Tasks folder.
Prohibit New Task Creation	Eliminates the Add Scheduled Task item from the Tasks folder. Administrators can still use the Schtasks command to create new tasks.
Prohibit Task Deletion	Prevents users from deleting tasks from the Tasks folder. Administrators can still use the Schtasks command to delete tasks.
Prohibit Browse	Eliminates the Browse button from the Scheduled Task Wizard and from the Task tab of a task's properties dialog box.

Note the following:

- All of the policies affect task scheduling via the Scheduled Tasks folder only. None of them restrict users' ability to use the Schtasks command (described in the next section).

- Hide Property Pages prevents users from changing the characteristics of tasks once they have been scheduled. Unless you also enable Prohibit New Task Creation, users can still set task properties while creating new tasks.

- The purpose of Hide Advanced Properties Checkbox in Add Scheduled Task Wizard is to simplify the Scheduled Task Wizard. Users can still set a task's advanced properties by returning to the properties dialog box after the task has been created.

If you choose to enable any of these policies, be aware that your settings apply to all users of the current computer, regardless of whether you work within Computer Configuration\ Administrative Templates\Windows Components\Task Scheduler or User Configuration\ Administrative Templates\Windows Components\Task Scheduler. (If you make different changes to both Group Policy nodes, the Computer Configuration changes take priority.) For more information about policies and the Group Policy console, see Appendix F, "Group Policy."

Scheduling Tasks with the Schtasks Command

The Scheduled Tasks facility provides a friendly and versatile method of creating and managing scheduled tasks. In some instances, however, you might find it easier to manage scheduled tasks from a command prompt. For those occasions, Windows XP provides the Schtasks command, a replacement for the venerable At command that was included with previous versions of the Windows NT platform.

> **Note** You can continue to enter At commands at the command prompt or in batch programs; tasks that you set up this way appear in the Scheduled Tasks folder, identified as At*n*, where *n* is a task ID supplied by the system. If you edit an At task in Scheduled Tasks, however, the task is upgraded to a "normal" scheduled task. At that point, you can no longer delete the task at a command prompt, and you must supply user credentials (account name and password) before the task can run.

With Schtasks, you can create, modify, delete, end, view, and run scheduled tasks, on your own computer or on another computer on your network. The Schtasks command is a boon not only for Windows XP users who prefer working at an MS-DOS-style prompt, but more importantly, for you to manage scheduled tasks from batch files.

> **Note** The Schtasks command is available only to computer administrators. Others who attempt to use it are rebuffed with the message "ERROR: Access is denied."

Schtasks is a rather complex command with lots of command-line switches and other parameters (its description in the Help And Support Center runs to 16 densely packed pages of text), but it has only six main variants:

- **Schtasks /Create** This variant, which you use to create a new scheduled task, is the most complex because of all the scheduling flexibility. You can, for example, set up a schedule at an interval expressed in minutes, hours, days, weeks, or months—in addition to the event-based schedules, such as on startup, on logon, and when the system is idle.

- **Schtasks /Change** This variant allows you to modify an existing task. You can change the program that the task runs, the user account under which the task runs, or the password for the user account.

- **Schtasks /Delete** This variant deletes an existing scheduled task or, optionally, all scheduled tasks on a computer.
- **Schtasks /End** This variant stops a program that was started by a scheduled task.
- **Schtasks /Query** This variant displays all scheduled tasks on a computer, including those that were created by other users.
- **Schtasks /Run** This variant immediately starts a scheduled task, ignoring the schedule that was created for the task.

You can get more information about each of these variants of Schtasks by viewing the descriptions in the Help And Support Center or by appending /? to one of these commands at a command prompt. For example, for detailed information about Schtasks /Run, at a command prompt type:

```
schtasks /run /?
```

A few examples should give you an idea of the power of the Schtasks command. Suppose, for example, you want to take a break every four hours at 20 minutes past the hour to play a bit of Solitaire. The following command sets up a task that launches Solitaire on that schedule:

```
schtasks /create /tn "Solitaire break" /tr sol.exe /sc hourly /mo 4 /st 00:20:00
```

In this example, the /Tn switch specifies the name of the task, /Tr specifies the name of the executable program (if the program is not stored in the %SystemRoot%\System32 folder, you must specify the complete path to the program), /Sc specifies the schedule type, /Mo specifies the interval, and /St specifies the starting time.

When you create a task as shown in this example, you'll see that Schtasks prompts you for the password for your account. You can bypass this prompt by appending /**rp** *password* to the command, where *password* is your logon password.

The following example creates a scheduled task that runs a script on the last Friday of each calendar quarter. (This isn't a script that's included with Windows; it's a made-up name intended to spark ideas on your part!)

```
schtasks /create /tn "Quarterly wrap-up" /tr c:\apps\qtrwrap.vbs
  /sc monthly /mo last /d fri /m mar,jun,sep,dec
```

By default, tasks scheduled via the Schtasks command run under the user account that's currently logged on. To make them run under a different user account, use the /Ru switch followed by the user account name you want to use; you'll also need to know the logon password for that account. To use the built-in System account, append /**ru** "**System**" to the command. No password is required for the System account, but because only administrators can use Schtasks, this doesn't present a security problem.

Because the System account cannot log on interactively, you can't see or interact with programs run by the System account.

Chapter 19

If you're familiar with the At command from Windows NT and Windows 2000, you'll see that Schtasks offers several improvements:

- You specify tasks using a friendly name rather than a serial ID number.
- You have many more options in setting up schedules, including specifying the last (or first, second, and so on) day of a month, specific times of day, and various other intervals.
- You can view, modify, run, or end an existing scheduled task.

Downloading Web Pages at a Scheduled Time

Most of the time, you'll use Microsoft Internet Explorer or another browser while you're connected to the Internet. If you prefer, you can have Internet Explorer visit your favorite Web sites at night (for example) and then deliver the goods for you to read offline the following morning.

To schedule a page for automatic download, it must be in your list of Favorites. Pages included on the Favorites menu have a Make Available Offline option; enabling this option (and specifying a schedule) causes Internet Explorer to fetch pages at the appointed time.

> **Note** Making a page available offline—with or without specifying a schedule—makes it possible for you to view the page even when your computer isn't connected to the Internet.

 Inside Out

Get Web page updates with RSS

A technology called RSS (Really Simple Syndication) provides a better alternative than offline Web pages for downloading updates to Web pages. With RSS, an update appears on your computer only when a page has changed. (This is a huge timesaver, as you don't need to periodically visit a site and then try to determine if it has any new content.) RSS requires the use of an RSS aggregator, a program that reads the RSS feed for the sites in which you're interested. It also requires that the site provides an RSS feed, an XML rendition of the site's most recent changes. The RSS phenomenon is growing by leaps and bounds, but at the time of this book's publication in 2004, RSS feeds could be found primarily on news and technology sites. For sites without an RSS feed, offline Web pages still provide a useful way to keep up.

Adding a Page to Your Offline Web Pages List

You can add a page to your offline Web pages list (that is, make it available offline) when you create the favorite or at any time later on.

Follow these steps to add a page to your Favorites folder, make it available offline, and specify a download schedule:

1 Display the page, and then choose Favorites, Add To Favorites.

2 In the Add Favorite dialog box, select Make Available Offline.

3 Click the Customize button to start the Offline Favorite Wizard.

With this wizard, you can specify the following:

- Whether Internet Explorer should also download pages that are linked from the page you're saving as a favorite

- When Internet Explorer should download the pages

If you choose to use an existing named schedule, Windows doesn't show you exactly what that schedule is. The best course of action is to select an existing schedule and proceed blindly ahead. After you've saved the favorite, open its properties dialog box (right-click its entry in the Favorites menu and choose Properties), click the Schedule tab, and then make any necessary adjustments.

- Whether the page requires a user name and password for access

4 Change the name and location of the favorite if you like, and then click OK.

To set up a download schedule for an existing favorite, follow these steps:

1 Open the existing favorite page's properties dialog box. (Right-click its entry on the Favorites menu or on the Favorites bar and then choose Properties from the shortcut menu.)

Don't bother using the shortcut menu's Make Available Offline command. It launches the Offline Favorite Wizard—forcing you to step through several pages even if you don't want to change any default settings—and it doesn't offer many of the options that are available in the properties dialog box.

2 On the Web Document tab of the page's properties dialog box, select Make This Page Available Offline.

3 Click the Schedule and Download tabs, and make settings as described in the following section.

For more information about adding favorites and organizing the list, see "Managing Your Favorites," page 513.

Changing Offline Web Page Settings

The properties dialog box for an offline Web page is the place where you can set up a synchronization schedule, determine exactly what is downloaded, and set up e-mail notification of changes. Do one of the following to view the properties dialog box:

- Right-click the page's entry on the Favorites menu or on the Favorites bar, and then choose Properties from the shortcut menu.

- Choose Organize Favorites from the Favorites menu, right-click the page, and then click Properties.

Setting up a synchronization schedule By default, Internet Explorer synchronizes your locally stored copy of an offline Web page with the original version only when you choose Synchronize from the Tools menu. Using the Schedule tab in the properties dialog box, you can set up a schedule for synchronizations. At the appointed times, Internet Explorer connects to the Internet (if you're not already connected) and updates the offline page by downloading the current version of the online page.

Take these steps to set up a synchronization schedule:

1 On the Schedule tab of the page's properties dialog box, select Use The Following Schedule(s).

2 If the schedule you want to use isn't in the list, click Add. The New Schedule dialog box appears.

3 Specify the number of days between updates and the time you want the updates to occur, and give the schedule a name. Select the check box if you want to connect to the Internet at the appointed time. (If you don't select the box and you're not already connected to the Internet, the connection dialog box waits for your go-ahead.) Then click OK.

4 Select the check box next to each named schedule you want to use for this page.

> **Tip** Create complex schedules
>
> The New Schedule dialog box allows you to set up schedules that update, at most, once per day. To update more frequently, you can create several schedules. But there's a better way: Set up a daily schedule, and then, on the Schedule tab, select the schedule and click Edit. In the schedule's properties dialog box that appears, click the Schedule tab. Here you can schedule updates at any of several intervals, upon certain events, or on certain days of the week or month; you can even create multiple schedules. And by clicking the Advanced button, you can schedule updates as often as every minute and set an ending time for scheduled updates. For more information about advanced scheduling options, see "Advanced Scheduling Options," page 596.

> **Tip** **Prevent synchronization while traveling**
>
> Futile attempts by Internet Explorer to make a dial-up connection while you're away from
> a phone line can be annoying. To prevent such interruptions, on the Schedule tab of the
> properties dialog box for the offline page, select the synchronization schedule and click
> Edit. Then, on the Settings tab, select Don't Start The Task If The Computer Is Running
> On Batteries.

Setting up download and e-mail notification options   Visit the Download tab in the
properties dialog box (shown in Figure 19-4) in the following circumstances:

● You want to change the level to which Internet Explorer downloads linked pages.

The default is zero, which means you download only the offline page—but not any
pages that are reached by links on the original page. You can specify up to three levels,
but be aware that the amount of material that Internet Explorer will have to download
increases exponentially as you select deeper levels of links.

If you choose to include linked pages, you can limit the download to include only links
to other pages at the same site (this prevents downloading pages linked to banner ads,
for example) or only links to HTML pages. (Click Advanced to set the latter option.)

Figure 19-4.   The Download tab allows you to determine what is downloaded automatically. Clicking Advanced displays the Advanced Download Options dialog box.

- You want to change the kinds of items that Internet Explorer downloads—for example, exclude images or add sound and video. (Click the Advanced button to set these options.)

- You want to impose a maximum download size for the page.

- You want to receive e-mail notification when the page changes. (Enter your e-mail address and the name of your mail server; this feature works only with SMTP-based (Simple Mail Transfer Protocol) mail systems, which excludes many Internet mail accounts.)

- The page requires a user name and password for access. (Click the Login button to enter this information.)

Automating Command Sequences with Batch Programs

A *batch program* (also commonly called a *batch file*) is a text file that contains a sequence of commands to be executed. You define the sequence of commands, name the sequence, and then execute the commands by entering the name at a command prompt. Any action you can take by typing a command at a command prompt can be encapsulated in a batch program.

When you type the name of your batch program at the command prompt, the command interpreter opens the file and starts reading the statements. It reads the first line, executes the command, and then goes on to the next line. On the surface, this seems to operate just as if you were typing each line yourself at the command prompt. In fact, however, it can be much more complicated because you can use parameters with batch programs to vary their behavior just as you can with other types of programs. Batch programs can also respond to values returned by programs and to the values of environment variables.

Recording Keyboard and Mouse Actions as Macros

As an alternative to learning a programming language (such as the batch language or a script language you can use with Windows Script Host), your needs might be met by a simple macro recorder—a program that records keystrokes and mouse actions and then plays them back upon demand. A number of macro recorder programs are available at little or no cost on the Internet. You might want to try the following:

- Aldo's Macro Recorder (*http://www.aldostools.com/macro.html*)

- EZ Macros (*http://www.americansys.com/ezmacros.htm*)

- Macro Magic (*http://www.iolo.com/mm/*)

A search for "macro" or "macro recorder" on any search engine or shareware download site is likely to turn up dozens of programs in this category.

Inside Out

Understand how duplicate file names are handled

In Windows XP, you can name your batch programs with the .bat or .cmd file name extension. The Windows XP command interpreter, Cmd.exe, attempts to execute commands from any file with either of these extensions. When you type the name of a batch program at a command prompt, Cmd.exe looks first for a file with a .bat extension. If you have two batch programs in the same folder with the same base name but different extensions, the .bat file will be executed—not the .cmd file. You can override this behavior by including the extension when you type the file name.

The rules for capitalization in batch programs are the same as at the command prompt—there are none. Commands and labels are not case sensitive, and you can mix capital and lowercase letters at will. (With certain commands, however, switches and parameters are case sensitive.) In the examples in this book, we show commands in lowercase because that's the easiest to type (although we capitalize command names in explanatory text). On the other hand, we use uppercase for labels so that they stand out clearly. We use mixed case for messages that appear on the screen and for names used when creating folders or files, because the capitalization is retained when the text is transferred to screen or disk.

Note Several examples in this chapter include commands that won't fit on a single line on the printed page of this book. The second and subsequent lines of such commands are indented. You, however, should type these commands on a single line.

Using Batch Commands

Batch commands are the commands that generally make sense only when used within a batch program. With a few exceptions, Windows XP has the same batch program commands as MS-DOS. We start by summarizing all the batch commands, in Table 19-2, and then look at some Windows XP batch programs. We explain some of the commands, but for most of them, this table—along with the command reference in Windows XP—should suffice. (For details about the online command reference, see "Getting More Information About Command-Line Tools," page 609.)

Table 19-2. Batch Commands

Command	Purpose
@	Prevents the line from being displayed on the screen when used as the first character in a line.
Echo [Off | On]	Turns screen echoing off or on.
Echo *msg*	Displays *msg* on the screen.

Table 19-2. **Batch Commands**

Command	Purpose
Echo.	Displays a blank line on the screen.
Rem *msg*	Identifies *msg* as a comment.
If [Not] Errorlevel *num cmd*	Executes *cmd* if the error level value returned from the previous command is greater than or equal to *num*. (*Not* reverses the logic.)
If [Not] Exist *file cmd*	Executes *cmd* if *file* exists. (*Not* reverses the logic.)
If [Not] *txt1* == *txt2 cmd*	Executes *cmd* if *txt1* is the same as *txt2*, including case. (*Not* reverses the logic.)
Goto *label*	Transfers control to the line marked by *label*.
: *label*	Names the line to be reached by a Goto command.
For %%*var* In (*set*) Do [*cmd*] %%*var*	Loops through the items in *set*, executing *cmd* for each loop and replacing any instances of *var* with the matching item from *set*, which can be a list separated by spaces or can contain the wildcard characters * and ?.
Shift	Shifts command-line parameters one place so that %2 becomes %1, %3 becomes %2, and so on.
Call *batfile args*	Executes *batfile* with *args* and then returns to the calling batch program.
Setlocal	Makes current environment variables local to this batch program; any changes to variables are known only in this batch program until Endlocal is executed.
Endlocal	Makes environment variables known to the system; any changes made after Endlocal remain in effect when the batch program terminates.
Pushd *path*	Saves the current folder on a stack and changes to *path*.
Popd	Changes to the last folder saved by Pushd and removes it from the stack.
Pause	Suspends processing until a key is pressed.
Title	Sets the title of the Command Prompt window.

> **Tip** Find batch programming resources online
>
> The command-line help in Windows provides good reference material about each command, but it is short on practical information about how to string together a series of commands to make a useful batch program. A Finnish professor, Timo Salmi, has put together an excellent assortment of links to more information about batch programming, and has also compiled a collection of useful batch tricks. You'll find this information at *http://www.uwasa.fi/~ts/http/http2.html#batch*.

Getting More Information About Command-Line Tools

Windows XP Professional includes information about command-line tools in its graphical Help And Support Center, but it's hard to find. (The help is also available in Windows XP Home Edition, but it's even harder to find because there's no direct link to it.) In either version, however, you can get a complete list of supported commands by typing **help** at a command prompt. For help on a particular command, type **help** followed by the name of the command (for example, **help xcopy**) or type the name of the command followed by /? (for example, **xcopy /?**).

If you prefer the graphical help, which provides more information, you can get to it via this path in Windows XP Professional:

1. Click Start, Help And Support.
2. On the Help And Support Center home page, under Pick A Task, click Use Tools To View Your Computer Information And Diagnose Problems.
3. Under Tools in the contents pane, click Command-Line Reference A-Z.

If you use the graphical help frequently, you'll want to add this page to your Help And Support favorites list. (Click Add To Favorites.) But you can also get to detailed graphical help quickly from a command prompt—the place where you're most likely to be when you need the information. This is the only way for Windows XP Home Edition users to open graphical help about command-line tools. You can get directly to this help page by typing this unwieldy command at a prompt:

```
%systemroot%\pchealth\helpctr\binaries\helpctr
  /url ms-its:%systemroot%\Help\ntcmds.chm::/ntcmds.htm
```

You can go directly to the help for a particular command by replacing the last occurrence of "ntcmds" with the name of the command you're interested in. Typing this cryptic string, of course, is no easier than navigating through the pages of the Help And Support Center. But with a couple of tricks, you can eliminate all of the messy typing and make it much easier to get right to the help you want.

First, use Doskey—a program that creates command-line macros—to encapsulate the preceding command in a macro named *h*. To create the macro, at a command prompt type:

```
doskey h=%systemroot%\pchealth\helpctr\binaries\helpctr
  /url ms-its:%systemroot%\Help\ntcmds.chm::/$1.htm
```

With this macro—which includes $1 as a replaceable parameter—you type **h** followed by a space and the name of the command about which you want information. For example, to get information about Doskey, you'd type **h doskey**. To display the index page that lists all of the commands, type **h ntcmds**.

A Doskey macro that you enter at a command prompt works only within that session. Your macro won't work in other command prompt windows you open, and it's gone altogether

609

when you close the window in which you created it. You can save your macros to a file and load them with a short command each time you open a command prompt window, but there's a better way.

Employ the second trick, which uses the registry's AutoRun value to cause the macro to be automatically created in *every* command prompt session you open. Follow these steps:

1 Open Registry Editor. (For information about Registry Editor, see Chapter 41, "Editing the Registry.")

2 Navigate to HKLM\Software\Microsoft\Command Processor. (This key affects all users who log on to your computer. If you want the help macro to be available only for your user account, go to HKCU\Software\Microsoft\Command Processor instead.)

3 Double-click the AutoRun value (if it doesn't exist, create a string value called AutoRun) and type the following command (the same one described above) in the Value Data box:

```
doskey h=%systemroot%\pchealth\helpctr\binaries\helpctr
  /url ms-its:%systemroot%\Help\ntcmds.chm::/$1.htm
```

4 Click OK and close Registry Editor.

 If you don't want to get your hands dirty by delving into the registry, the companion CD contains a script called Command-line help.vbs that makes this registry change for you.

 Inside Out

Use other command-line tools for batch programs

 The Windows Resource Kit Tools include a number of command-line tools that are especially useful in batch programs. This book's companion CD contains a subset of the Windows Resource Kit Tools, including the following tools of particular simplicity and utility:

- Ifmember.exe checks to see whether the current user is a member of a specified security group. You can use this information to take different actions depending on group membership.

- Logtime.exe creates a log file with a date and time stamp that indicates when it ran. When included in a batch program, it provides a record of when the batch program ran; if you run it before and after a particular set of commands, you can calculate how long it took to run the commands.

- Now.exe displays the current date and time along with an optional message that you specify. You can use this tool to track the progress of a batch program.

- Sleep.exe causes a batch program to stop running for a specified amount of time.

For more information about using these tools, install the Windows Resource Kit Tools. Doing so installs a help file that explains each tool in detail.

Inside Out

Avoid echoing comments

Using the Rem command is the documented way to put comments in your batch programs, but it is intrusive—the command looks like part of the comment. Furthermore, if you leave echoing on while debugging a batch program, all of your comments are echoed, making it harder to read commands. A better way to add comments to code is to use two colons:

```
:: This line is for humans; computers ignore it
```

This kind of comment is never echoed. Be sure to use two colons; using only one creates a label that might conflict with a legitimate label. Although this commenting style is handy, we use the conventional Rem statement in this book's examples to avoid confusing readers who miss this sidebar.

Creating a Simple Batch Program

The most important step in writing a batch program (or any other kind of computer program) is to state the problem correctly. In this example, the problem is to connect to a dial-up connection by repeatedly dialing different connections until a successful connection is made. If a connection fails (because the line is busy or you enter the wrong password, for example), the program should try another dial-up connection.

This batch program relies on Rasdial.exe, the command-line version of the dialing component used by dial-up connections. The program uses dial-up connections that you have previously created in the Network Connections folder.

To create a batch program, use a plain-text editor, such as Notepad. (When you save the file, be sure to give it the .bat or .cmd file name extension.) The following listing shows Dial.bat:

```
@echo off
rem Connects to a Dial-up Connection
title Dialing Connections

:START
echo Connecting to MSN
rasdial msn pct_hiker *
if not errorlevel 1 goto end

echo Connecting to Earthlink
rasdial earthlink swdocs *
if not errorlevel 1 goto end

echo Connecting to local ISP
rasdial "pasadena isp" swdocs *
if errorlevel 1 goto start

:END
title Command Prompt
```

You'll find Dial.bat—along with several other example batch programs—on the companion CD.

You execute a batch program by typing its name at the command prompt, like this:

```
C:\>dial
```

By default, batch programs display each line on the screen before attempting to execute it. Because this is seldom desirable, most batch programs start with the same line that ours starts with:

```
@echo off
```

The at sign (@) tells the program not to display the Echo Off command. The Echo Off command tells the program not to display any more lines for the rest of the batch program.

The line that follows the descriptive Rem statement

```
title Dialing Connections
```

sets the title of the Command Prompt window to Dialing Connections, as shown in Figure 19-5. This title helps orient users to the task at hand.

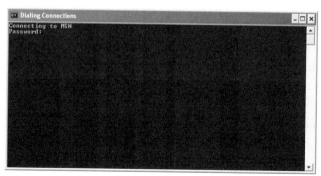

Figure 19-5. The Title command sets the title of the Command Prompt window.

Between the Start and End labels are three sets of dialing commands—one for each Internet service provider (ISP) for which we've created a dial-up connection. As we've used it here, the parameters following Rasdial are the connection name (the name that appears in the Network Connections folder) and the user name. The asterisk causes Rasdial to prompt for your password; you can put the password in your batch program (in plain text) if you're sure that it won't be compromised.

Like many programs, when Rasdial exits, it sets an error level, which is simply a numeric result code. The If statement in Dial.bat tests the error level for values of 1 *or greater*. An error level of 0 indicates a successful connection. (Rasdial uses many other values to indicate various error conditions. For a list of error codes, type **hh netcfg.chm** to open Network Connections help; on the Contents tab, open Troubleshooting and select Error Messages.)

Each of the If commands includes a Goto command that directs processing to the correct part of the batch program. When a Goto is executed, the command interpreter jumps to the line with the matching label and starts executing the lines it finds following the label. (A *label* is a line starting with a colon.) Following the first two connection attempts, if the error level value is *not* greater than or equal to 1, the command processor transfers control to the End label; otherwise, it drops down to the next statement. In the final If statement, the program jumps back up to the Start label if the error level is greater than or equal to 1.

The Goto End statement prevents the subsequent commands from being executed by directing processing to the End label. Without these statements, Rasdial would dial the second and third connections, even if the first one was successful.

The single statement that follows the End label simply resets the window title.

Better Options for Testing Error Level Values

If you want your batch program to take different actions based on different error level values, you can use successive If statements to test for each value. With MS-DOS and earlier versions of Windows, it was necessary to test error level values in decreasing order, because the condition is true if the error level value is equal to or greater than the value you specify. But if you're writing a batch program for use only on computers running Windows 2000 or Windows XP, you can use comparison operators to more easily act on different error level values. To do that, you must use the %ErrorLevel% environment variable, which expands into the current error level value. For example, you might use a statement like the following to jump to a certain section of the program if Rasdial sets the error level to 676—the result code that indicates the line is busy:

```
if %errorlevel% equ 676 goto busy
```

The available comparison operators are Equ (equal to), Neq (not equal to), Lss (less than), Leq (less than or equal to), Gtr (greater than), and Geq (greater than or equal to). You can use comparison operators only if command extensions are enabled. For information about command extensions, see "Using Command Extensions," page 1348.

Using Advanced Techniques

This section offers a few example batch programs that illustrate some additional programming techniques.

 You can find these batch programs—Rsbackup.bat, CleanRecent.bat, and Alphabetize.bat—on the companion CD.

Backing Up the Removable Storage Database

This batch program creates a backup copy of the Removable Storage database. It illustrates some commonly used techniques, including stopping and starting services and using environment variables. The following program is called Rsbackup.bat:

```
@echo off
rem Backs up the Removable Storage database
title Removable Storage Backup
echo Removable Storage database backup in process...

echo Stopping the Removable Storage service
net stop "removable storage" > nul

echo Copying the Removable Storage database
xcopy /y %systemroot%\system32\ntmsdata %systemroot%\system32\ntmsdata
  \backup\ > nul

echo Starting the Removable Storage service
net start "removable storage" > nul

echo.
echo Removable Storage database was backed up to
echo %SystemRoot%\System32\NtmsData\Backup\
title Command Prompt
```

The first command to examine is Net Stop:

```
net stop "removable storage" > nul
```

The Net command is frequently included in batch programs because it can be used to control so many functions in Windows. In this case, we are stopping the Removable Storage service to ensure that it doesn't have the database files open when we try to copy them. To stop or start a service, you can use the service's "friendly name" (that is, the name that appears in the Services snap-in), as we've done here, or you can use the actual service name if you know it. (In the case of Removable Storage, the service name is Ntmssvc.) Throughout the program, Echo statements keep the user informed of the progress. Therefore, we use > Nul to redirect the output of the Net statement to the Nul device—colloquially known as the "bit bucket"—because its output is redundant.

The Xcopy command then makes a copy of the files:

```
xcopy /y %systemroot%\system32\ntmsdata systemroot%\system32\ntmsdata\
  backup\ > nul
```

On most computers, the Removable Storage database files are stored in C:\Windows\System32\Ntmsdata. However, if you installed Windows in a different folder, the files will be in a different location. In this Xcopy statement, %SystemRoot% is an environment variable that specifies where Windows is installed on the local computer. By using environment variables, we can ensure that our batch programs work on any computer that is running Windows XP.

Table 19-3 lists some useful environment variables. You can see the current environment variables for your computer by typing **set** at the command prompt. To use an environment variable in a batch program or at the command prompt, precede and follow its name with a percent sign (%). When the batch program executes, the value of the environment variable replaces its name in the batch program. (For more information, see "Using Environment Variables," page 1357.)

Table 19-3. Useful Environment Variables

Environment Variable	Value
AppData	Location of the Application Data folder for the current user (for example, C:\Documents And Settings\CarlS\ Application Data).
CommonProgramFiles	Location of the Common Files folder (typically C:\Program Files\Common Files).
ComSpec	Executable file for the command processor (typically C:\Windows\System32\Cmd.exe).
HomeDrive	Drive letter that's mapped to the home folder for a user profile. By default, it's the same as the letter of the system volume (typically C).
HomePath	Folder for a user profile on the home drive (for example, \Documents And Settings\CarlS). Together, HomeDrive and HomePath specify the default folder for a user profile.
OS	Operating system on the user's workstation (Windows_NT on a system running Windows XP, Windows 2000, or Windows NT).
Path	Application search path. When you type the name of an executable at a command prompt, Windows looks in each folder in the search path if the executable file is not in the current folder.
ProgramFiles	Location of the Program Files folder (typically C:\Program Files).
SystemDrive	Drive on which the system folder resides (typically C).
SystemRoot	System folder; the folder that contains the Windows XP operating system files (typically C:\Windows).
Temp	Folder for storing temporary files (for example, C:\ Docume~1\CarlS\Locals~1\Temp—the short path name for C:\Documents And Settings\CarlS\Local Settings\Temp).
UserDomain	Domain the user is logged into (for example, SWDOCS) or, if the computer is not logged into a domain, the name of the computer (for example, SEQUOIA).
UserName	User's logon name (for example, CarlS).

Table 19-3. Useful Environment Variables

Environment Variable	Value
UserProfile	Location of the current user's profile (for example, C:\ Documents And Settings\CarlS).
Windir	Same as SystemRoot; included for compatibility with earlier versions of Windows.

When the database files have been copied, another Net command restarts the Removable Storage service:

```
net start "removable storage" > nul
```

Cleaning Out the Recent Documents List

The batch program that follows, called CleanRecent.bat, removes some of the files from the recently used documents list that you see if you select My Recent Documents from the Start menu. Removing document types that you don't want on this list allows room for more of the documents that you do want to see.

```
@echo off
rem Cleans unwanted file types from the Recent folder
title Clean Recent
echo Cleaning Recent folder...
for %%t in (wav log ini) do del "%userprofile%\recent\*.%%t.lnk"
echo.
echo Done cleaning Recent folder.
title Command Prompt
```

> **Note** CleanRecent.bat is effective only if you have cleared the option to hide file name extensions on the View tab in Folder Options before you opened the documents that appear on the Recent menu. If extensions don't appear on the Recent menu, this program can't identify the files to be deleted.

This batch program uses the For...In...Do command to repeatedly execute the Del command. The document type file name extensions that you want to remove from the list are enclosed in the parentheses. The For command executes the Del command once for each entry in this list. The variable %%T contains the current extension and is substituted in the Del command. This is effectively the same as typing three Del commands.

Note that the file names have an .lnk extension added. This is because the Recent folder contains shortcuts (which have the extension .lnk) rather than containing the actual recently used files.

Alphabetizing Your Favorites Menu and Your Start Menu

This batch program is somewhat more complex than the ones we have looked at so far. It uses more advanced techniques to control program flow.

Alphabetize.bat alphabetizes your Favorites menu and the Programs branch of your Start menu. (You can have it act on your Favorites menu, your Start menu, or both.) The menus become unsorted as you add new items—which are appended to the bottom of the menu—or manually reorder them by dragging menu items. Windows XP does include a Sort By Name command on the shortcut menu that appears if you right-click one of these menus. But Alphabetize.bat offers something more: If you decide you like the previous order better, Alphabetize.bat can restore the previous order—giving it an "undo" capability. Furthermore, Alphabetize.bat reorders the entire menu, including its submenus, whereas the Sort By Name command doesn't sort the contents of submenus.

> **Note** Alphabetize.bat works only with the classic Start menu, not the default Start menu.

The order information for the Start and Favorites menus is kept in the registry. To alphabetize, this batch program exports the current settings to a file and then simply deletes the appropriate keys from the registry. Without an order specified in the registry, Windows alphabetizes the lists. As you add or move menu items, Windows re-creates the order information in the registry.

In the Alphabetize.bat listing that follows, we've included line numbers for reference. Note that you can't use line numbers in an actual batch program.

```
 1 @echo off
 2 rem Alphabetizes Favorites and/or Start menu
 3 setlocal
 4 if not exist "%appdata%\inside out\" md "%appdata%\Inside Out\"
 5
 6 if "%1" == "" goto usage
 7 if "%1" == "/?" goto usage
 8 if /i %1 == help goto usage
 9 set type=%1
10 set action=%2
11 if "%2" == "" set action=sort
12
13 set startmenu=false
14 set favorites=false
15 goto %type%
16 :STARTMENU
17 set startmenu=true
18 goto %action%
19 :FAVORITES
20 set favorites=true
21 goto %action%
22 :BOTH
23 set startmenu=true
24 set favorites=true
25 goto %action%
26
27 :SORT
28 :SORTFAVORITES
29 if not %favorites% == true goto sortstartmenu
```

```
30 reg export "HKCU\Software\Microsoft\Windows\CurrentVersion\Explorer\
   MenuOrder\Favorites" "%AppData%\Inside Out\Favorites.reg" > nul
31 reg delete "HKCU\Software\Microsoft\Windows\CurrentVersion\Explorer\
   MenuOrder\Favorites" /f > nul
32 if %errorlevel% equ 0 echo Favorites alphabetized.
33
34 :SORTSTARTMENU
35 if not %startmenu% == true goto :eof
36 reg export "HKCU\Software\Microsoft\Windows\CurrentVersion\Explorer\
   MenuOrder\Start Menu" "%AppData%\Inside Out\Start Menu.reg" > nul
37 reg delete "HKCU\Software\Microsoft\Windows\CurrentVersion\Explorer\
   MenuOrder\Start Menu" /f > nul
38 if %errorlevel% equ 0 echo Start Menu alphabetized.
39 goto :eof
40
41 :UNDO
42 :UNDOFAVORITES
43 if not %favorites% == true goto undostartmenu
44 if not exist "%appdata%\inside out\favorites.reg" goto noundofile
45 reg import "%appdata%\inside out\favorites.reg" > nul
46 echo Favorites order restored.
47
48 :UNDOSTARTMENU
49 if not %startmenu% == true goto :eof
50 if not exist "%appdata%\inside out\start menu.reg" goto noundofile
51 reg import "%appdata%\inside out\start menu.reg" > nul
52 echo Start menu order restored.
53 goto :eof
54
55 :NOUNDOFILE
56 echo No file exists to restore.
57 goto :eof
58
59 :USAGE
60 echo.
61 echo Usage:
62 echo Alphabetize StartMenu^|Favorites^|Both [Undo]
63 echo.
64 echo Example:
65 echo Alphabetize Favorites
66 echo.
67 echo Add Undo to restore previous settings.
```

Lines 1 through 3 take care of some basic setup functions. They identify what this batch program does and turn echoing off. The Setlocal command specifies that environment variables created or changed by this batch program should be "local" to this batch program and should not affect other programs.

Line 4 creates a folder under the Application Data folder called Inside Out. Because the Md (make directory) command displays an error if the folder already exists, we use If Not Exist so that the Md command is executed only if the folder does not exist.

The second section of the batch program, lines 6 through 11, checks for command-line parameters. The %1 that appears in several of these lines represents the first argument on the command line, %2 represents the second, and so on up to %9. If you type the command **alphabetize a**, for example, the command interpreter sees this as the first line in this section of the batch program:

```
if "a" == "" goto usage
```

Using Local Environment Variables

In many cases, a batch program needs to change a standard environment variable, such as Path. But changing this critical variable without restoring it when you are finished could cause problems for other programs. If you're writing the batch program for your own use, it's not difficult to restore modified variables, although it gets tiresome after awhile. But if you're writing a batch program to be run by others, you probably won't even know what settings to restore.

Windows XP addresses this problem with the Setlocal and Endlocal commands. Setlocal makes any further settings or changes to environment variables local to the current batch program. Endlocal returns handling of environment variables back to normal mode—any further changes remain after the batch program terminates.

You might want to use a batch program to modify environment variables for either of two reasons. First, this might be the primary purpose of the batch program, as it is in the following short batch program (call it Addpath.bat), which adds a folder to the end of the search path:

```
@echo off
set path=%path%;%1
```

But more often, you will use environment variables to save values or change program behavior within the batch program. The simple rule is to use Setlocal at the start of the batch program and Endlocal at the end. Even if your batch program sets only a temporary environment variable, you want to be sure that the variable is cleared on termination. For example:

```
setlocal
rem Set new path
set path=d:\bin
rem Do something with the new path
.
.
endlocal
rem Path goes back to its original value after EndLocal
```

The test for equality would not be True, so the Goto statement would not be executed. But if you type **alphabetize** (without any arguments), the command interpreter would see

```
if "" == "" goto usage
```

and the Goto statement would be executed. Notice in Alphabetize.bat that %1 is surrounded by quotation marks. This isn't a requirement. We could just as easily have written %1$==$. All we're doing is making sure that the command interpreter always sees something on both sides of the equal signs. Without a character there, it sees the line as

```
if == goto usage
```

The result would be a syntax error, causing the batch program to terminate. The quotation marks are a readable way to be sure neither side is ever empty.

The first line of this section (line 6), therefore, is for the case when no command-line parameters are used, and it sends the command processor to the Usage label (line 59), where the program displays instructions for using Alphabetize.

Lines 7 and 8 do the same thing: They answer calls for help. Because the comparison in an If statement requires an exact match, in line 8 we used the /I switch, which causes the If statement to ignore case. This switch is available only if command extensions are enabled. The /I switch overcomes a major limitation of earlier versions of MS-DOS and Windows, in which you'd need to set up several If statements to test for capitalization variants of the word *help*. For example, you might test for *help*, *HELP*, and *Help*—and you still wouldn't catch every possible form.

If the command line includes parameters that are not requests for help, lines 9 through 11 come into play. The Set commands assign the command-line parameters to environment variables that we can use later in the batch program. If the second command-line parameter is blank ("%2" == ""), the action is assumed to be Sort and is set to that value.

In lines 13 through 25, we set a group of environment variables that are used to tell the remainder of the batch program what to do.

Replaceable Parameters

Besides %1 through %9, you should be aware of two other useful replaceable parameters: %* and %0.

%* represents *all* the command-line arguments. One useful place for this parameter is in a For...In...Do statement. For example, you could enhance CleanRecent.bat (the batch program described in the preceding section) by changing its For statement to read

```
for %%t in (%*) do del "%userprofile%"\recent\*.%%t.lnk
```

You would then type the extensions you want to delete (separated by spaces) on the command line. You could type any number of extensions.

%0 represents the command name (in other words, the name of the batch program).

Lines 13 and 14 set the environment variables StartMenu and Favorites to their default value of False. The Goto %Type% command (line 15) sends processing to the label that matches the

Type variable set earlier. Because labels are not case sensitive, it doesn't matter whether the user types **both**, **Both**, or some other variant. The rest of this section sets the StartMenu and Favorites variables to True if they are to be processed. They remain set to False if they are not to be processed. The Goto %Action% commands (lines 18, 21, and 25) send processing to the proper section of the batch program—to the Sort label (line 27) or the Undo label (line 41).

Now we are ready to start the actual work. Lines 27 through 39 sort the menus, and lines 41 through 57 restore the old menu arrangements.

The Sort section starts by checking that the value of the variable Favorites is True, in line 29. If it is not, the processing of Favorites is skipped. Next, the Reg Export command (line 30) creates a file that contains the current Favorites order. The environment variable AppData is used to locate the Inside Out folder that was created at the beginning of the batch program. After the backup file is made, the Reg Delete command (line 31) removes all the Favorites order information from the registry. Without this information in the registry, the menu reverts to its default alphabetical order. The /F switch does this without confirmation, and > Nul eliminates the completion message.

Using Pushd and Popd to Change to a Different Folder

A common sequence of events in a batch program is to move to a specific folder, do some work there, and then return to the original folder. The problem is that your batch program can be run from any folder. If you don't know where you are, you can't go back. Pushd and Popd to the rescue.

The Pushd command saves the current folder and changes to a new one. The Popd command restores the original. Normally, you need these commands only in batch programs, but an example from the command prompt shows how they work:

```
C:\bat>pushd \data
C:\data>pushd sales
C:\data\sales>popd
C:\data>popd
C:\bat>
```

You can probably figure out intuitively what's going on here, but if you're not a programmer, you might wonder what "push" and "pop" in the command names mean. *Push* means to put something onto a *stack*, in this case a stack of folder names. *Pop* means to take the top item—the only one you can get at—off the stack.

In the example, we first push the Bat folder onto the stack. If we popped now, we would return to the Bat folder. Instead we push another folder, Data. We have to pop it off the stack before we can get to the Bat folder. Of course, in a batch program we would be doing some work in each folder before we pushed another one or popped to restore the old one.

Reg sets the error level value to 0 upon successful completion or to 1 if an error occurs. The If statement in line 32 echoes a message of success if the error level is 0. This form of the If statement works only with Windows 2000 and Windows XP; if you want to create a program for use on computers running earlier versions of Windows, you could instead use the more traditional form:

```
if not errorlevel 1 echo Favorites alphabetized.
```

The SortStartMenu section (lines 34 through 39) performs the same process on the Start menu. Lines 35 and 39 demonstrate another feature introduced in Windows 2000: the Goto :EOF command. This special label, which must include the colon, causes the command processor to jump to the end of the batch program—in other words, to end execution. With MS-DOS and earlier versions of Windows, you must create a label at the end of the file and use it as the target of the Goto command to achieve the same result.

The Undo section of the batch program, lines 41 through 57, restores the original menu order. Again, the first check is to be sure that the Favorites are supposed to be processed (line 43). Then the If Not Exist command in line 44 checks to be sure that a backup file exists. If the file doesn't exist, the NoUndoFile section (lines 55 through 57) displays a message to that effect.

The Reg Import command (line 45) does the actual work. It imports the contents of the backup file to the registry, restoring the previous order.

The UndoStartMenu section (lines 48 through 53) performs the same process on the Start menu.

It's a good idea to make batch programs self-documenting. The Usage section, lines 59 through 67, does just that. This section consists of a series of Echo commands that display the correct usage of this batch program. Note the use of the Echo command followed by a dot, which displays a blank line for improved legibility. (If you use *Echo* alone, it reports the state of the echoing function—on or off.)

The interesting thing about line 62 is the use of the escape symbol (^) to indicate that the pipe symbol (|) should be treated as a character and not interpreted as a pipe symbol. Without the escape symbol, the command interpreter would try to pipe the Echo command and the first few words to whatever follows the pipe symbol, which would cause a syntax error. You must use the escape symbol any time you want to echo a pipe symbol (|), a greater than sign (>), a less than sign (<), an ampersand (&), or a caret (^).

Although this batch program illustrates some advanced techniques of batch processing, it also demonstrates some limitations. If you misspell the first parameter, which should be Favorites, StartMenu, or Both, the batch program will fail. For example, if you type **alphabetize favorits**, the batch program displays this message:

```
The system cannot find the batch label specified - favorits
```

There is no way to trap for this error or to change the message to something more meaningful.

Likewise, if you happen to type one of the options for the first parameter as the second parameter, the batch program goes into an endless loop. For example, if you type **alphabetize favorites both**, the batch program appears to hang. It is actually very busy jumping back and forth between various labels, but the only way to stop it is to press Ctrl+Break.

These limitations are typical of complex batch programs. Batch programs provide a quick way to do simple tasks, but other tools (such as Windows Script Host) are better for more complex tasks.

A final word about debugging batch programs: You usually have to do some experimenting to get your batch programs to work exactly the way you want. You can write the batch program in one Command Prompt window and test it in another. To see exactly what the command interpreter sees, change the first line to

```
rem @echo off
```

This "comments out" the Echo Off command so that each line echoes to the screen with parameters and environment variables filled in before it is executed. In our sample file, you would probably also want to temporarily remove the redirection to Nul from each command so that you could see all the output.

Automating Tasks with Windows Script Host

Microsoft Windows Script Host (WSH) provides a way to perform more sophisticated tasks than the simple jobs that batch programs are able to handle. You can control virtually any component of Microsoft Windows and of many Windows-based programs with Windows Script Host scripts.

To run a script, you can type a script name at a command prompt or simply double-click the script's icon in Windows Explorer. Windows Script Host has two nearly equivalent programs—Wscript.exe and Cscript.exe—that, with the help of a language interpreter dynamic-link library such as Vbscript.dll, execute scripts written in VBScript or other scripting languages.

With WSH, the files can be written in several different languages, including VBScript (a scripting language similar to Microsoft Visual Basic) and JScript (a form of JavaScript). Windows Script Host is, in fact, just what its name says: a host for script languages. VBScript and JScript interpreters come with Windows XP; interpreters for Perl, KiXtart (Kix), Python, Rexx, and other languages are available elsewhere.

Because WSH scripts can access ActiveX controls, they provide great flexibility. Several objects are provided with Windows Script Host that allow you basic control of Windows and your computer. By using ActiveX, you can control many of the programs on your computer. For example, you can create a WSH script to display a chart in Microsoft Excel.

As an introduction, here's the WSH "Hello World" script. It's as short as it can get in any programming language:

```
WScript.Echo "Hello World"
```

Using a plain-text editor such as Notepad, put this line in a file with a .vbs file name extension (Hello.vbs, for example), and you have a working WSH script. Simply double-click the file's icon in Windows Explorer to run your script.

Batch Programs vs. Scripts: Which Should You Use?

This chapter describes two rather different methods for automating repetitive tasks: batch programs and scripts. The method you should use depends in part on your comfort level. For tasks that can be performed by either method, choose the one that's easiest for you. Batch programs are generally easier to write and debug, particularly if you're already familiar with the batch command language used in MS-DOS and earlier versions of Windows. You'll find, however, that many tasks can't be performed by batch programs. And even those that can are often done better with a script, which provides better program logic, user feedback, and error handling. To give you an idea of how batch programs and scripts compare for a simple procedure, examine the examples below and on the next page.

As you can see, it's sometimes possible to use nearly identical program logic in both languages. These programs examine the registry to see whether hidden files (those with the hidden attribute set) are displayed in Windows Explorer. If not, the programs modify the registry so that hidden files, super-hidden files (those with the system and hidden attributes set), and all file name extensions are displayed. If hidden files are already displayed, the programs modify the registry so that these items are not displayed. Of course, you can make these display changes with a trip to the Folder Options dialog box instead of modifying the registry directly. But that's rather tedious, and you may want to switch between these settings frequently—the perfect application for a batch program or a script.

Here's the batch program, called ToggleHiddenExplorerStuff.bat:

```
:: Script to toggle Windows Explorer display of hidden files,
:: super-hidden files, and file name extensions

@echo off
setlocal

set key = HKCU\Software\Microsoft\Windows\CurrentVersion\Explorer\Advanced
set hiddenvalue=Hidden
set superhiddenvalue=ShowSuperHidden
set fileextvalue=HideFileExt

reg query %key% /v %hiddenvalue% | find "0x2" > NUL
if errorlevel 1 goto Hide

:Show
reg add %key% /v %hiddenvalue% /t REG_DWORD /d 1 /f > NUL
reg add %key% /v %superhiddenvalue% /t REG_DWORD /d 1 /f > NUL
reg add %key% /v %fileextvalue% /t REG_DWORD /d 0 /f > NUL
```

```
echo.
echo Windows Explorer will show hidden files and file name extensions.
echo You might need to change to another folder or press F5 to refresh
echo the view for the change to take effect.
goto :eof

:Hide
reg add %key% /v %hiddenvalue% /t REG_DWORD /d 2 /f > NUL
reg add %key% /v %superhiddenvalue% /t REG_DWORD /d 0 /f > NUL
reg add %key% /v %fileextvalue% /t REG_DWORD /d 1 /f > NUL
echo.
echo Windows Explorer will not show hidden files and file name extensions.
echo (These are the default settings.) You might need to change to another
echo folder or press F5 to refresh the view for the change to take effect.
```

Here's the equivalent script version, ToggleHiddenExplorerStuff.vbs, written in VBScript:

```
' Script to toggle Windows Explorer display of hidden files,
' super-hidden files, and file name extensions

Option Explicit
Dim dblHiddenData, strHiddenKey, strSuperHiddenKey, strFileExtKey
Dim strKey, WshShell
On Error Resume Next

strKey = "HKCU\Software\Microsoft\Windows\CurrentVersion\Explorer\Advanced"
strHiddenKey = strKey & "\Hidden"
strSuperHiddenKey = strKey & "\ShowSuperHidden"
strFileExtKey = strKey & "\HideFileExt"

Set WshShell = WScript.CreateObject("WScript.Shell")
dblHiddenData = WshShell.RegRead(strHiddenKey)

If dblHiddenData = 2 Then
    WshShell.RegWrite strHiddenKey, 1, "REG_DWORD"
    WshShell.RegWrite strSuperHiddenKey, 1, "REG_DWORD"
    WshShell.RegWrite strFileExtKey, 0, "REG_DWORD"
    WScript.Echo "Windows Explorer will show hidden files and file " & _
        "name extensions. You might need to change to another folder " & _
        "or press F5 to refresh the view for the change to take effect."

Else
    WshShell.RegWrite strHiddenKey, 2, "REG_DWORD"
    WshShell.RegWrite strSuperHiddenKey, 0, "REG_DWORD"
    WshShell.RegWrite strFileExtKey, 1, "REG_DWORD"
    WScript.Echo "Windows Explorer will not show hidden files or file " & _
        "name extensions. (These are the default settings.) You might " & _
        "need to change to another folder or press F5 to refresh the " & _
        "view for the change to take effect."
End If
```

ON THE CD Both programs are included on the companion CD.

Finding Scripting Resources

You won't learn how to write a script in this chapter. You must know a scripting language, or else use the resources described in the following paragraphs to learn one. (If you know Visual Basic, you already know a scripting language.) Our intent here is to show you some of what you can do with Windows Script Host and help you find the widely scattered information you need to use it effectively.

Wscript vs. Cscript

Windows XP includes two programs that run WSH scripts. Cscript.exe is the command-line version, and Wscript.exe is the GUI version. Although this sounds like a big distinction, for most scripts the differences are pretty small. Try running Hello.vbs—a one-line program described on page 623—with each program to see the difference. At the command prompt, type these two lines:

```
cscript hello.vbs
wscript hello.vbs
```

Figure 19-6 shows the results. Cscript displays the words "Hello World" in a Command Prompt window. Wscript displays a small dialog box with the message "Hello World" and an OK button. With Cscript, you use command-line parameters to change the properties of a script file. Wscript, in contrast, provides a dialog box to set the properties. Type **wscript** at a command prompt to display the properties dialog box.

Output from Cscript.exe

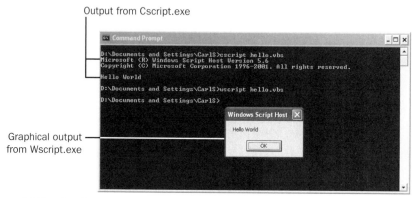

Graphical output
from Wscript.exe

Figure 19-6. Cscript.exe, the console version, displays its result in a Command Prompt window, whereas Wscript.exe generates a dialog box.

Note that Cscript and Wscript command-line options use two slashes. This differentiates them from command-line options for the script being executed, which use a single slash. To see all the command-line options, type **cscript //?** (or **wscript //?**) at a command prompt.

Scripts and Security

Much has been made about the security risks posed by Windows Script Host. The power and flexibility afforded by WSH can be used by forces of evil just as easily as they can be used to make your life simpler. Indeed, the infamous I Love You and Anna Kournikova e-mail worms were powered by VBScript attachments. Luckily, you can make some simple changes that reduce the chance that you'll accidentally run a nefarious script.

As a first line of defense, be sure that the file name extension is always displayed for script files. (This would have tipped off many people who opened an e-mail attachment named Anna Kournikova.jpg.vbs. Because the extension is not displayed by default, many hopeful fans expected to see a picture of the tennis star.) Second, change the default action for scripts from Open to Edit. This causes the files to open harmlessly in Notepad if you double-click a file. To make these changes, follow these steps:

1 In Windows Explorer, choose Tools, Folder Options.

2 Click the File Types tab.

3 Select the JS (JScript Script File) file type and then click Advanced.

4 Select the Always Show Extension check box.

5 In the Actions list, select Edit and click Set Default. Then click OK.

6 Repeat steps 3 through 5 for JSE (JScript Encoded Script File), VBE (VBScript Encoded Script File), VBS (VBScript Script File), and WSF (Windows Script File) file types.

7 Click Close when you've secured all of the script file types.

Changing the default action to Edit makes it more difficult to run scripts that show up as e-mail attachments, which is one of the most likely places to find a malevolent script. However, it also makes it more difficult to execute legitimate scripts from trusted sources: You must save the attachment and then, in Windows Explorer, right-click it and choose Open. You can use this same technique (right-click and choose Open) to run any script stored on your computer, but if you want to avoid that inconvenience for a script that you *know* to be harmless, simply create a shortcut to the script. (Be sure the Target text in the shortcut's properties dialog box begins with *wscript.exe* or *cscript.exe*; if you include only the script name, this trick won't work.) Double-clicking the shortcut runs the script without further ado.

One of the biggest hurdles to learning to use WSH is finding the information you need. The scripting language, whether it is VBScript or JScript, is separate from the objects you use in your scripts, and each piece has separate documentation. You must find the reference guide for both the scripting language you choose and the objects you use. Throughout this chapter, we tell you where to find the relevant documentation, most of which is available on Microsoft's Web site. The Microsoft TechNet Script Center (*http://www.microsoft.com/ technet/scriptcenter/default.mspx*) focuses exclusively on WSH scripting (primarily using VBScript) and has loads of sample scripts you can learn from (and use), along with tools and other useful information. You'll also find the Microsoft Windows 2000 Scripting Guide here;

although it's been around awhile, it's still one of the best resources available for learning how to use scripts to manage your computer. However, at the time of this book's publication, it doesn't have much in the way of language reference documentation. For that information, you're better off at the Windows Script section of the Microsoft Developer Network (MSDN) Library (*http://msdn.microsoft.com/scripting*). Browsing this site can be confusing, however. The site describes the use of the scripting languages and their associated objects, but it also provides information for software developers who want to add scripting capabilities to their programs—which is another topic altogether.

> **Tip**   For a wealth of third-party information about scripting and batch programming, visit Rob van der Woude's Scripting Pages Web site, at *www.robvanderwoude.com*. Replete with instruction, examples, and links to Microsoft and other third-party information sources, van der Woude's site covers Kix, Perl, and Rexx, as well as batch files and WSH.

Choosing a Scripting Language

Windows Script Host doesn't care whether you use VBScript, JScript, or some other scripting language. All the objects are available to any language, and in most situations, you can choose to use the language with which you are most comfortable. In this book, we use VBScript. You can actually mix languages in the same program.

VBScript is a major subset of Visual Basic. If you know Visual Basic, there is little that you can't do in VBScript. One of the biggest differences is that VBScript has only Variant variables. You simply use Dim and the variable name; you can't add a variable type because they are all the same. You can find documentation of VBScript at *http://msdn.microsoft.com/ library/en-us/script56/html/vtoriVBScript.asp*.

Here is a short script, called Folders.vbs, that shows some of the elements of a script written in VBScript:

```
Option Explicit

Dim objWSShell
Dim strMsg
Dim intCtr

Set objWSShell = WScript.CreateObject("WScript.Shell")
WScript.Echo "Your desktop is " & objWSShell.SpecialFolders("Desktop") _
    & vbNewLine

strMsg = "All your special folders are:" & vbNewLine
For intCtr = 0 To objWSShell.SpecialFolders.Count - 1
    strMsg = strMsg & objWSShell.SpecialFolders.Item(intCtr) & vbNewLine
Next
WScript.Echo strMsg
```

You can find Folders.vbs—and all the other example scripts from this chapter—on the companion CD.

The script starts with an Option Explicit statement, which tells the VBScript interpreter to require you to use a Dim statement for every variable in the script. This helps to prevent errors from misspelled variable names and is accepted as good programming practice.

The Set statement creates a WScript Shell object, which is used to access the special folders. One of the properties of the Shell object is the SpecialFolders object. The SpecialFolders object lets you retrieve the path and file name of any of the special folders on your system. For example, this script retrieves the path specification of the Desktop folder, as shown in Figure 19-7 below.

Figure 19-7.   Folders.vbs initially displays the location of your Desktop folder.

The next section of the script, the For…Next loop, displays the folder paths of all the special folders. This section demonstrates a technique that makes scripts work well with both Wscript and Cscript. Instead of putting a WScript.Echo statement inside the loop, we add each result to the strMsg string and then display this string after the loop is finished. When run with Cscript, the results are the same. However, when run with Wscript, accumulating the results into a string and using one WScript.Echo statement means that one dialog box is displayed for the entire loop (as shown in Figure 19-8), rather than one dialog box for each special folder.

Figure 19-8.   The For…Next loop builds a string that is displayed in a single dialog box.

Using the Script File Format

For WSH scripts, you can use VBScript in files with the .vbs extension and JScript in files with the .js extension. Windows Script Host adds another level of tags that provide more flexibility and power. In fact, WSH files, which use the .wsf extension, are actually Extensible Markup Language (XML) files that use tags, as shown in the following example (Hello.wsf):

```
<?XML version="1.0"?>
<package>
<job id="job1">
<?job debug="true"?>
<script language="VBScript" src="MyScript.vbs"/>

<script language="VBScript">
<![CDATA[
    WScript.Echo "Hello World"
]]>
</script>
</job>
</package>
```

Table 19-4 describes the function of each of these tags, plus a few others.

Table 19-4. Useful XML Tags in WSH Files

Tag	Description
<?XML version="1.0"?>	Marks your code as compliant with XML 1.0. This tag is optional now but might be required by future XML tools.
<package> </package>	Encloses multiple jobs in a single file. The <package> tag is optional if you have only one pair of <job> tags.
<job id="job1"> </job>	Identifies jobs in a file. When you have multiple jobs in a file, you can run any one with this syntax: Cscript //Job:MyFirstJob MyScripts.wsf
<?job debug="true"?>	Allows use of the script debugger. You can add error="true" to this tag to allow error messages for syntax or run-time errors.
<script language="VBScript" src="MyScript.vbs"/>	Includes, or merges, another file into the current one when the script runs. This tag allows you to easily reuse code.
<script language="VBScript"> </script>	Encloses a script. In a single job, you might have several scripts—even in different scripting languages.
<![CDATA[ ]]>	Indicates that the parser should treat your code as character data and not interpret the characters in it. Use this tag if you use the XML tag.

Table 19-4. **Useful XML Tags in WSH Files**

Tag	Description
<object>	Defines objects that can be referenced by the script.
<reference>	Provides a reference to an external type library, allowing you to use defined constants from that type library.
<resource>	Isolates text or numeric data that should not be hard-coded in a script.

Debugging Scripts

To debug scripts, you first need to install Microsoft Script Debugger. You can download it from *http://msdn.microsoft.com/downloads/list/webdev.asp*.

Also, if you want to debug a .wsf file, you must add the line <**?job debug="true"?**> to your script file. (It goes right below the <job> tag.) Without this line, the debugger will not open.

> **Note** After you have installed the debugger, the messages you see when you encounter a script error while you browse the Internet are different. At the bottom, the message asks, "Do you want to debug the current page?" If you click Yes, the debugger appears with the page loaded. Because you are probably looking at someone else's site, however, you probably want to click No.

You can find the documentation for Script Debugger at *http://msdn.microsoft.com/scripting/debugger*. Keep in mind that you can use this same debugger to debug both client and server scripts for Web pages; most of the documentation is focused on those activities. (In fact, Windows Script Host might not be mentioned in the debugger documentation at all.)

You start the debugger using command-line switches with the Cscript or Wscript commands. The //X switch starts the debugger, loads the script into the debugger, and stops at the first line of the script. The //D switch starts the debugger only when an error is encountered. It also loads the program in the debugger and stops at the line where it encountered the error.

Here's an example of debugging a very simple script, which we call Debug.vbs:

```
main()

Function main()
x = 99
WScript.echo "Hello once"
WScript.echox "Error 1 here"
WScript.echo "Hello twice"
End Function
```

After creating this script, at the command prompt type

```
wscript //d debug.vbs
```

The words "Hello once" should appear in a small dialog box. When you click OK, Script Debugger appears, with the error highlighted, as shown in Figure 19-9.

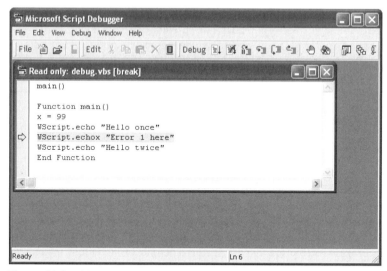

Figure 19-9. When you run a script with the //D switch and an error occurs, Script Debugger appears and highlights the error.

The debugger helps you find your error, but you can't fix errors here. As you notice at the top of the document window, the file is identified as read-only. You can open another instance of the file in the debugger and edit that file. The debugger provides an editor that is on a par with Notepad.

Using Other Debugger Windows

At this point, the debugger can provide some additional information, but you are effectively done running the script. Three additional windows, all available both from the View menu and from the right side of the toolbar, allow you to see more information about your script:

- **Running Documents**   This window shows you scripts that are currently running. Besides Windows Script Host, you are likely to see Microsoft Internet Explorer here. If you right-click a script in this window, one command appears on the menu: Break At Next Statement. This command provides a way to "invite" a script into the debugger.

● **Call Stack** This window displays the call history to the current point in the current script. This can help you figure out just how you got where you are.

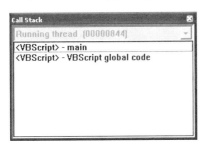

● **Command** This window allows you to view and manipulate variables in your script. In the following example, the first line "printed" the value of *x*. (A question mark is shorthand for the Visual Basic Print command.) Then the value of *x* was changed to 100 and displayed again.

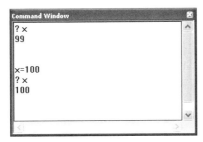

When you work in the Command window, you must use the same language as the currently running script. If you are running a VBScript file, for example, type a question mark followed by a space and the variable name to display a variable's value. If you are running a JScript file, simply enter the name of the variable. You can also view and change an object's properties in the Command window.

Stepping Through Scripts

When you start the debugger using the //X command-line switch, the debugger opens with the first line of the script highlighted. You can move through the script and see how the program flow works. All the debugging information is available so that you can check the value of variables and object properties and see how they are changed by the operation of the script.

The Debug toolbar—one of three toolbars in Script Debugger—contains the tools you need to step through a script. Table 19-5 describes the buttons on the Debug toolbar.

The debugging process is to step through the script, line by line, until you find an error. When you determine that a specific part of the script works, you can set a breakpoint at the beginning of the untested part and then click Run to get to that point quickly.

Table 19-5. **Script Debugger's Debug Toolbar**

Button	Name	Description
	Run	Executes the script until it hits a breakpoint, an error, or comes to the end of the script
	Stop Debugging	Runs the script outside the debugger
	Break At Next Statement	Activates an open server script in the debugger; not useful for WSH files
	Step Into	Advances the script by one statement; steps into functions and subroutines
	Step Over	Advances the script by one statement; executes but does not display functions and subroutines
	Step Out	Advances the script until it exits the current function or subroutine
	Toggle Breakpoint	Inserts or removes a breakpoint at the line containing the insertion point
	Clear All Breakpoints	Clears all breakpoints
	Running Documents	Displays the Running Documents window
	Call Stack	Displays the Call Stack window
	Command Window	Displays the Command window

When you believe that your functions and subroutines are working correctly, you can speed up debugging by clicking Step Over to execute them as one step, instead of using the Step Into button.

Introducing Objects

You can't do much with WSH without using objects. An *object* is a variable comprising both routines and data that is treated as a discrete entity. Some objects are built into the scripting language; others are provided by the operating system. One of the previous script examples used the WScript.Shell object to gain access to the Windows shell. Table 19-6 describes the objects that are built into VBScript. They are documented, along with the VBScript language, at *http://msdn.microsoft.com/library/en-us/script56/html/vtoriVBScript.asp*.

Table 19-6. VBScript Objects

Object	Description
Class object	Provides access to the events of a created class
Debug object	Sends output to a script debugger
Dictionary object	Stores data in key/item pairs
Drive object	Provides access to the properties of a disk drive or network share
Drives collection	Collection of all available Drive objects
Err object	Provides information about run-time errors
File object	Provides access to all of the properties of a file
Files collection	Collection of all File objects within a folder
FileSystemObject object	Provides access to your computer's file system
Folder object	Provides access to all of the properties of a folder
Folders collection	Collection of all Folder objects contained within a Folder object
Match object	Provides access to the read-only properties of a regular expression match
Matches collection	Collection of regular expression Match objects
RegExp object	Provides simple regular expression support
SubMatches collection	Collection of regular expression submatch strings
TextStream object	Facilitates sequential access to a file

Windows Script Host provides the objects described in Table 19-7. They are documented, along with Windows Script Host, at *http://msdn.microsoft.com/scripting* (click Windows Script Host Documentation).

Table 19-7. Windows Script Host Objects

Object	Description
Scripting.Signer object	Provides a way to sign a script with a digital signature and verify the signature
WScript object	Exposes properties that specify the path of the running scripting host (Wscript.exe or Cscript.exe), its arguments, and the working mode (interactive or batch); also provides methods to create and read objects
WshArguments object	Returns a pointer to the collection of command-line parameters
WshController object	Provides access to a method for creating a script to run on a remote computer
WshEnvironment object	Retrieves system environment variables
WshNamed object	Provides access to the named command-line parameters in the WshArguments object
WshNetwork object	Maps the network, making it easy to connect and disconnect remote drives and printers
WshRemote object	Provides access to the remote script process
WshRemoteError object	Exposes error information that results when a remote script ends in error
WshScriptExec object	Provides information about a script run with the Exec method
WshShell object	Starts new processes, creates shortcuts, and provides the Environment collection to handle environment variables such as SystemRoot, Path, and Prompt
WshShortcut object	Creates an object reference to a shortcut
WshSpecialFolders object	Accesses the Windows shell folders such as the Desktop folder, the Start Menu folder, and the My Documents folder
WshUnnamed object	Provides access to the unnamed command-line parameters in the WshArguments object
WshUrlShortcut object	Creates an object reference to a URL shortcut

Using the FileSystemObject

One of the objects you will probably use often is FileSystemObject. This object gives you access to the files and folders on your computer. The following example, called FileProp.vbs, shows how to use this object; Figure 19-10 on the next page shows the result.

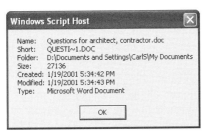

Figure 19-10. The FileProp.vbs script quickly displays some file properties that aren't easily viewed in Windows Explorer.

```
' Displays properties of file on command line

Option Explicit
Dim strArg, objFileSys, objFile, strMsg

If WScript.Arguments.Count < 1 Then
    WScript.Echo "Usage: FileProp <filename>" & vbNewLine & _
"Or drag and drop a file on this file."
    WScript.Quit (1)
End If

Set objFileSys = CreateObject("Scripting.FileSystemObject")

strArg = objFileSys.GetAbsolutePathName(WScript.Arguments(0))

Set objFile = objFileSys.GetFile(strArg)
strMsg = "Name: " & vbTab & objFile.Name & vbNewLine
strMsg = strMsg & "Short: " & vbTab
strMsg = strMsg & objFile.ShortName & vbNewLine
strMsg = strMsg & "Folder: " & vbTab
strMsg = strMsg & objFile.ParentFolder & vbNewLine
strMsg = strMsg & "Size: " & vbTab
strMsg = strMsg & objFile.Size & vbNewLine
strMsg = strMsg & "Created: " & vbTab
strMsg = strMsg & objFile.DateCreated & vbNewLine
strMsg = strMsg & "Modified:" & vbTab
strMsg = strMsg & objFile.DateLastModified & vbNewLine
strMsg = strMsg & "Type: " & vbTab
strMsg = strMsg & objFile.Type & vbNewLine
WScript.Echo strMsg
Set objFile = Nothing
Set objFileSys = Nothing
```

This script first checks to see whether the command line contains any parameters. If none are found, it displays a usage message and quits. The script works with drag and drop because Windows adds the name of dropped files to the command line. If you drop more than one file on this script, it displays information about the first one only.

After the error checking is out of the way, the script creates a FileSystemObject object and then uses that object to get the full path name of the file. Using the full path name, it gets a File object.

The script then builds a string by concatenating various properties of the File object. When the entire string is built, the script displays it with the Echo method of the WScript object. You can also use the MsgBox function to display strings. This function allows you to specify which buttons appear, to change the title from Windows Script Host to a message you specify, and to respond to the button a user clicks. Whereas the WScript.Echo method works differently in Cscript and Wscript, the MsgBox function works the same way in both: It always displays a dialog box. To see the difference, try replacing the WScript.Echo line in the previous script with the following line:

```
MsgBox strMsg, vbOKOnly, "File Properties"
```

Finally, the script releases the File object and the FileSystemObject object by setting the variables to the built-in value Nothing, which releases the resources used by the objects. It's not important to do this in a small script such as this one because it happens anyway when the script ends, but in more involved scripts, releasing the objects when you've finished with them can reduce the resources your script requires.

Example Scripts

In this section, we present two sample scripts that demonstrate some of the techniques you can use with Windows Script Host.

Enabling or Disabling Windows Firewall

You might have an occasional need to disable Windows Firewall for a few moments to bypass its protections. This script provides an easy way to disable or enable the firewall. You could take the traditional path—click Start, open Control Panel, open Security Center, open Windows Firewall, and then try to remember why you wanted to change the setting in the first place—or you could simply double-click the desktop shortcut for a script like the one that follows.

```
'****************************************************************************
'*
'* File:        Firewall Quick Switch.vbs
'*
'* Function:    Displays the status of Windows Firewall and allows you
'*              to enable or disable the firewall.
'*
'*
'* Usage:       Click Yes to enable, No to disable, or Cancel to do
'*              nothing.
'*
'*
'****************************************************************************

Option Explicit

Dim objFirewall
Dim objPolicy
Dim strPrompt
Dim strTitle
```

```
Set objFirewall = CreateObject("HNetCfg.FwMgr")
Set objPolicy = objFirewall.LocalPolicy.CurrentProfile

'Check firewall status and build strings for message box.
If objPolicy.FirewallEnabled Then
    strPrompt = "Windows Firewall is enabled." & VbNewLine
    If objPolicy.ExceptionsNotAllowed Then
        strPrompt = strPrompt & "No exceptions are allowed." & vbNewLine
    Else
        strPrompt = strPrompt & "Specified exceptions are allowed." & _
            vbNewLine
    End If
Else
    strPrompt = "Windows Firewall is disabled" & VbNewLine
End If
strPrompt = strPrompt & VbNewLine
strPrompt = strPrompt & "Do you want to enable Windows Firewall?"
strTitle = "Windows Firewall"

' Display the message box and act on resulting button click
Select Case MsgBox(strPrompt, vbYesNoCancel, strTitle)
    Case VbYes        'Enable firewall
        objPolicy.FirewallEnabled = vbTrue
    Case VbNo         'Disable firewall
        objPolicy.FirewallEnabled = vbFalse
    Case VbCancel     'Do nothing
End Select
```

This script checks the current settings of Windows Firewall: whether it's currently enabled and, if so, whether the program and service exceptions you've specified are allowed to pass through the firewall. It displays this information in a dialog box and asks whether you want to enable the firewall, as shown in Figure 19-11.

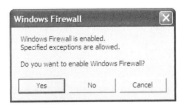

Figure 19-11. The top of this dialog box displays the current firewall status.

For consistency, the question posed by the script is always "Do you want to enable Windows Firewall?"—even if the firewall is already enabled. This way, clicking Yes always enables the firewall and clicking No always disables the firewall.

This script is pretty basic; you might want to modify it to control more firewall settings (such as controlling whether exceptions are allowed) or to handle command-line arguments (so that you can enable or disable without displaying the dialog box).

For more information about Windows Firewall, see "Blocking Intruders with Windows Firewall," page 194.

Controlling Your Computer and Other Computers

A popular use for scripts is to control your computer—that is, make various settings, adjustments, and tweaks—or to control another computer on your network. Creating a script to control a frequently changed setting often provides a quicker, easier way to perform the task than doing it manually, which can entail traversing through several cascading menus, dialog boxes, and tabs. Many tweaks require a time-consuming visit to the registry, where an inadvertent mistake made in the haste of a quick setting change can wreak havoc.

Enabling or disabling Windows Firewall, as shown in the previous example program, is one of hundreds of tasks that can be made easier with a script. Ready-made scripts to control all manner of settings are readily available on the Web; two of our favorite sites for scripts to manage Windows XP are Bill James' VBScript Tools page at *http://www.billsway.com/ vbspage* and Kelly Theriot's site at *http://www.kellys-korner-xp.com*.

But the mother lode of scripts and, better yet, scripting tools, is at the Microsoft TechNet Script Center (*http://www.microsoft.com/technet/scriptcenter/default.mspx*). Here you'll find a treasure trove of scripts for managing all facets of a local or remote computer, organized by function. Two tools that rely on Windows Management Instrumentation (WMI) to report on and control computers are available at the Script Center and deserve special mention.

- Scriptomatic generates scripts that display (but do not alter) various computer settings.

- Tweakomatic, shown below, goes much further. It generates scripts for many more settings, creates scripts that make settings as well as display them, and makes it easier to create scripts that manage another computer on your network.

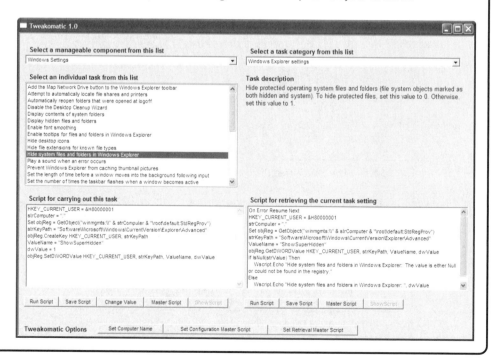

Both of these tools are written by The Scripting Guys, and they're worth checking out just for the entertainment value provided by the documentation. These tools generate scripts that are ready to use, which makes the tools useful for scripting novices. But they also provide a great assist to scripting pros, not only because they relieve some of the typing drudgery, but because they expose objects and properties that are not readily discovered otherwise.

Note, however, that you can't use a script to control another computer that's running Windows XP with Service Pack 2 installed with default settings. That's because Windows Firewall on the remote computer blocks execution of WMI scripts. To make these scripts work, you need to go to each remote computer and open the appropriate ports in the firewall, which you can do with the following script:

```
Set objFirewall = CreateObject("HNetCfg.FwMgr")
Set objPolicy = objFirewall.LocalPolicy.CurrentProfile

Set objAdminSettings = objPolicy.RemoteAdminSettings
objAdminSettings.Enabled = vbTrue
```

Keeping a Journal

The following script, named Journal.vbs, helps you keep an ad hoc journal by opening a text file and adding a time stamp, as shown in Figure 19-12. For consistency with other scripts in this chapter, we've included comments, used standard naming conventions, included error-checking routines, and otherwise dressed up Journal.vbs. But at its heart, this script demonstrates how you can use scripting to perform simple automation tasks merely by having a script launch a program or play back keystrokes.

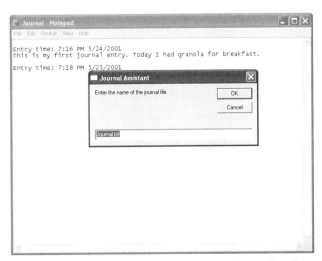

Figure 19-12. Journal.vbs opens a file in Notepad and then types the time and date at the end of the file.

```
'*****************************************************************************
'*
'* File: Journal.vbs
'*
'* Function: Opens a text file and adds a time stamp.
'*
'* Usage: Uses a command-line argument for the file name to open.
'* If there is no command-line argument, prompts for it.
'*
'*****************************************************************************

Option Explicit

Dim shell
Dim strFileName
Dim strPrompt
Dim strTitle
Dim strDefault

' Check for a command-line argument.
If WScript.Arguments.Count Then
    ' Use the command-line argument for the file name.
    strFileName = WScript.Arguments(0)
Else
    ' No command-line argument. Ask for a file name.
    strPrompt = "Enter the name of the journal file."
    strTitle = "Journal Assistant"
    strDefault = "Journal.txt" ' propose a name
    strFileName = InputBox(strPrompt, strTitle, strDefault)
    ' If the user clicks Cancel or enters nothing, exit.
    If strFileName = "" Then
        WScript.Quit
    End If
End If

' Start Notepad with the specified file.
Set shell = CreateObject("WScript.Shell")
shell.Run("Notepad " & strFileName)
shell.AppActivate "Notepad"
WScript.Sleep 100 ' allow time for Notepad to get going

' Move to the end of the file and add the time stamp.
shell.SendKeys "^{END}{ENTER}{ENTER}" ' move to end of file
shell.SendKeys "Entry time: " ' add a text string
shell.SendKeys "{F5}{ENTER}" ' add the time stamp
```

There are four ways to specify the text file you want to use as a journal:

- Enter the file name at the prompt that the script presents.
- Start the script from a command prompt and include the file name on the command line.
- Use a shortcut to the script that includes the file name in the shortcut's Target box.
- Drag the file from Windows Explorer and drop it on the script or a shortcut to the script. (If you drop a file onto a shortcut to which you have added a file name, the dropped file overrides the file in the shortcut and the dropped file is opened.)

When the script starts, it checks to see whether there is a command-line argument. If so, it is used as a file name. If not, the script uses the InputBox function to request a file name.

After the script has a file name, it opens Notepad and displays that file. Then it uses the Send-Keys method to manipulate Notepad.

SendKeys does as its name implies: It sends keystrokes to a program. In the SendKeys syntax, most keys are represented by their normal characters. Keys that don't produce characters, such as Enter or Backspace, are represented by special character codes, as listed in Table 19-8. Keys you use in combination with other characters (Shift, for example) are also represented by codes.

Table 19-8. Codes for SendKeys Method

Key	Code
Backspace	{BACKSPACE}, {BS}, or {BKSP}
Break	{BREAK}
Caps Lock	{CAPSLOCK}
Delete	{DELETE} or {DEL}
Down Arrow	{DOWN}
End	{END}
Enter	{ENTER} or ~
Esc	{ESCAPE} or {ESC}
Help	{HELP}
Home	{HOME}
Insert	{INSERT} or {INS}
Left Arrow	{LEFT}
Num Lock	{NUMLOCK}

Table 19-8. Codes for SendKeys Method

Key	Code
Page Down	{PGDN}
Page Up	{PGUP}
Print Screen	{PRTSC}
Right Arrow	{RIGHT}
Scroll Lock	{SCROLLLOCK}
Tab	{TAB}
Up Arrow	{UP}
Function keys F1 through F16	{F1} through {F16}
Shift	+
Ctrl	^
Alt	%

Part 4

Storage and File Management

Windows Explorer for Experts

Getting Windows Explorer and the other components of the Microsoft Windows XP user interface to look and work in a manner that's congenial and congruent with your level of expertise is critical to your satisfaction with Windows XP. Fortunately, Microsoft made Windows Explorer highly customizable. You don't need to use it the way it came out of the box (although you certainly may). To help you tailor the interface to suit your working style, this chapter presents a brief expert's tour of Windows Explorer.

At Home with Windows XP

Windows Explorer works essentially the same way in both versions of Windows XP. The Folder Options dialog box, which is described in this chapter, contains one option that's not available in Windows XP Home Edition—the option to disable Simple File Sharing. To customize the places bar in common dialog boxes using Group Policy, you need Windows XP Professional. Home Edition users can perform this customization with Tweak UI, however.

Choosing Between Common Tasks and Classic Folders

One of the first customization decisions you'll probably want to make while working with Windows Explorer in Windows XP is whether or not to retain the pane of links to common tasks that Windows Explorer can display along the left side of your folder windows, as shown in Figure 20-1. These links can be useful. You can use them to copy and move files, attach files to e-mail messages, display pictures as slide shows, play music, and so on; you can also use links in the Other Places section of the pane to move quickly to other folders. But this "task pane" does consume screen space, so there might be times when you'd rather not see it. Unfortunately, your decision about whether to use or lose the task pane is global—that is, you can't have it displayed in some folders and not displayed in others. Fortunately, you can switch between one mode and the other quickly and easily.

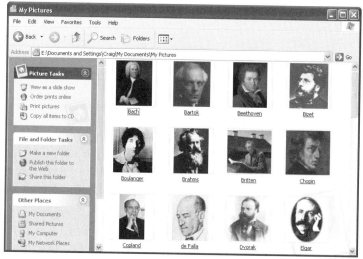

Figure 20-1. You can display links relevant to current folder content in order to perform common tasks quickly and easily.

The task pane is displayed by default. To turn it off, follow these steps:

1. In Windows Explorer, choose Tools, Folder Options.
2. On the General tab of the Folder Options dialog box, shown in Figure 20-2, select Use Windows Classic Folders.

> **Note** Another way to get to the Folder Options dialog box is via Control Panel. Open Control Panel, choose Appearance And Themes (if you're using Category View), and then click Folder Options. A better alternative for frequent Folder Options users: Create a shortcut (on your desktop or in another convenient location) using the command **control folders**.

Chapter 20

> **Tip** If you use it often, put it on the toolbar
>
> If you make frequent trips to the Folder Options dialog box, you can save time by putting a Folder Options button on the Windows Explorer Standard Buttons toolbar. For details, see "Customizing the Toolbars," page 650.

Figure 20-2. Select Use Windows Classic Folders to remove the task pane from all windows.

Toggling Between Folder Views

Unlike the Explorer bars that can also take up residence along the left edge of your Windows Explorer windows, the task pane does not come with a Close button. If you want to see it some of the time but not all the time, you have to toggle it in and out of view by returning to the Folder Options dialog box. That's not too onerous if you put the Folder Options command on your toolbar, but it's still less convenient than you might like.

Here's an alternative approach: Toggle the task pane by clicking the Folders button on the Standard Buttons toolbar. Clicking the Folders button replaces the task pane with the Folders bar, which shows an outline of your computer's storage resources. A second click removes the Folders bar and replaces it with the task pane. (For more information about the Folders bar, see "Using the Folders Bar," page 656.) With the Folders bar displayed, you still don't have the maximum space available for files, but the left side of your screen is given over to something just as useful as the task pane. And you can switch between the task pane and Folders bar with a single click.

Using the Details Section of the Task Pane

The lowest section of the task pane is like a miniature Properties dialog box—it provides useful information about the currently selected item or items. For example, with the first item in the folder shown in Figure 20-1 selected, the Details pane looks like this.

If all the items in the folder displayed in Figure 20-1 were selected, the details section would look like this.

In 800 × 600 resolution, you might not see the Details section without scrolling the task pane. If you find it more useful than one or more of the sections that appear above it, you can bring it into view by collapsing the sections you don't need to see. Click the double-arrow in the upper right corner of a section to collapse it. (Click again to expand it.)

Customizing the Toolbars

Windows Explorer offers three toolbars: Standard Buttons, Address bar, and Links. You can display these toolbars in any combination. To display or hide a toolbar, choose View, Toolbars, and then select the toolbar you want (or don't want) from the submenu.

The Radio toolbar that was available in earlier versions of Windows has been replaced by the Media Explorer bar. For information about the Media Explorer bar, see "Using Explorer Bars," page 653.

> **Tip** For a quicker way to display or hide a toolbar, right-click any toolbar. This action displays the View, Toolbars submenu.

You can change the size or position of any toolbar by dragging the handle that appears at the left edge of the toolbar, shown here.

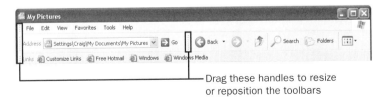

Drag these handles to resize or reposition the toolbars

To put a toolbar on a new line, drag it downward by its handle. If two toolbars appear on the same line and you want to reverse their order, drag one of them down, and then drag it up on the other side of the second toolbar.

> **Note** If you can't move or resize the toolbars, they are probably locked. Open the View menu, select Toolbars, and click Lock The Toolbars to unlock them.

Note that the menu bar can also be repositioned. If you want to see it below the toolbars, simply drag it downward. To eliminate the menu bar altogether (and completely fill the screen with Windows Explorer), press F11. Press F11 again to return Windows Explorer to its previous appearance.

> **Tip** Lock the toolbars
>
> After you have arranged the toolbars to your satisfaction, you can lock them so that you don't inadvertently change their current sizes and positions. Choose View, Toolbars, Lock The Toolbars. The handles at the left edges of the toolbars become solid when locked. To unlock the toolbars so that you can move them around, choose View, Toolbars, Lock The Toolbars again.

If a toolbar is too wide to be displayed entirely in its current position (and given the current window size), Windows Explorer displays a chevron at the right edge. Click the chevron to display the toolbar items that don't fit.

Chapter 20

In addition to repositioning and resizing the toolbars, you can customize the content of the Standard Buttons toolbar. You can specify which buttons to include, what order they should appear in, how big the icons should be, and whether and how to display text labels for the icons.

> **Tip   Go button, be gone!**
> The Go button at the right side of the Address Bar toolbar is a bit of a redundancy. If you select an address from the Address bar list, Windows Explorer takes you to that address directly. If you type an address in the Address bar, Windows Explorer takes you to that address as soon as you press Enter. The only time you would need the Go button would be if you typed an address and, for some reason, didn't care to press the Enter key. Clicking Go would then accomplish the same feat as pressing Enter. To remove the Go button and make more room for other items, right-click the Go button and select Go Button from the shortcut menu.

To customize the Standard Buttons toolbar, follow these steps:

1   Choose View, Toolbars, Customize. The following dialog box appears.

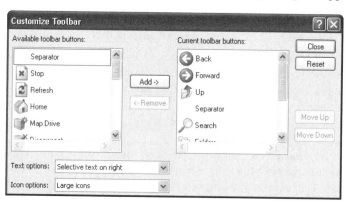

2   To add a button, select it in the left box and click Add. To remove a button, select it in the right box and click Remove.

3   To change the position of a button, select it in the right box and click Move Up or Move Down. Alternatively, you can drag a button to its desired position.

4   To change the position of or eliminate descriptive text, choose from the Text Options list.

5   To change the size of toolbar icons, choose from the Icon Options list.

Displaying the Status Bar

Unlike earlier versions, the Windows XP version of Windows Explorer does not display the status bar by default. To make the status bar visible, choose View, Status Bar. The status bar, shown here, provides useful information, such as the number of objects selected (or the total number of objects in the displayed folder) and their total size.

Using Explorer Bars

The View, Explorer Bar command opens a menu on which you can choose from five Explorer bars: Search, Favorites, Media, History, and Folders. You might have additional Explorer bars, courtesy of applications that you have installed. If so, these additional Explorer bars will also be available via the View, Explorer Bar command.

The Explorer bar you select appears along the left edge of the Windows Explorer window, replacing the task pane if you have chosen to display task panes. Figure 20-3 shows a Windows Explorer view of My Computer with the History bar in place.

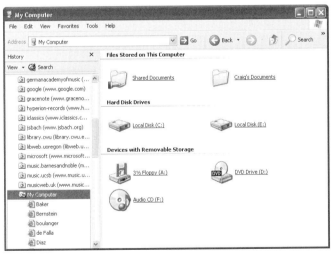

Figure 20-3.   The History bar is most commonly used in Microsoft Internet Explorer but can be useful in Windows Explorer as well.

Chapter 20

You can use the same Explorer bars in both Internet Explorer and Windows Explorer. Some of the Explorer bars (History, for example) are more commonly used in the Internet context. But all have some utility in Windows Explorer as well. The following sections offer brief descriptions of the Explorer bars and the use to which they can be put in Windows Explorer.

Using the Search Bar

Choosing the Search Explorer bar displays the Search Assistant, which helps you search for files and folders. This action is equivalent to choosing Search from the Start menu, except that the Search Assistant is set by default to look in the current folder. When you search using the Explorer bar, the results of your search appear in the main part of the Windows Explorer window. To return to the normal folder display, click Back on the Standard Buttons toolbar.

The Search bar can be opened by either of two keyboard shortcuts: F3 and Ctrl+E. It can also be opened and closed by clicking the Search button that appears by default in the Standard Buttons toolbar. For more information about searching for files, see "Locating Files with Search Companion," page 718.

Using the Favorites Bar

The Favorites Explorer bar displays the contents of your Favorites folder, located at %UserProfile%\Favorites. The contents of this folder also determine what appears in Windows Explorer's Favorites menu.

Most users store links to commonly visited Internet sites in their Favorites folder, but you can put any kind of shortcut (or folder or file) there. For example, if there's a folder or document you need frequently for a project you're working on, you can create a shortcut to it, store the shortcut in your Favorites folder, and then use the Favorites Explorer bar as a way to move to the folder or open the file.

The simplest way to add a folder to your Favorites bar (and Favorites menu) is as follows:

1   Display the folder you want to add in Windows Explorer.

2   Display the Favorites Explorer bar.

3   Click the Add button at the top of the Favorites bar. The following dialog box appears.

4   Click Create In to expand the dialog box if you want to place the new favorite in an existing Favorites subfolder or to place it in a new folder (click the New Folder button in the expanded dialog box to do that). Otherwise, click OK.

To add a file to the Favorites bar, hold down the Alt key while dragging the file to the Favorites bar. The new item is placed at the bottom of your Favorites bar. If you're going to be using it frequently, you might want to drag it toward the top of the list.

The keyboard shortcut for the Favorites bar is Ctrl+I. Unlike the Search and Folders bars, the Favorites bar has no buttons on the Standard Buttons toolbar by default, but you can add one by customizing the toolbar.

Using the Media Bar

The Media Explorer bar has followed a tortured evolutionary path. It replaced the Radio toolbar that was available in earlier versions of Windows, but beginning with Windows XP Service Pack 2, the Media Explorer bar has become extinct. If you have not yet installed SP2, the Media bar enables you to find and play media files in Windows (or Internet) Explorer. Links on the Media bar take you to various places within WindowsMedia.com. For more information about WindowsMedia.com, see Chapter 24, "Using and Customizing Windows Media Player."

Using the History Bar

The History Explorer bar shows you what Web sites you've visited and what document files (local and networked) you've opened recently. Like the Favorites bar, it's used mostly in the Internet Explorer context. But the History bar can also help you find your way back to a recently used document; it's particularly useful if the document you want is no longer available via the Start menu's My Recent Documents folder. It's also a help if you want to return to a recently visited Web site and you don't want to open Internet Explorer to do it. When you open a Web site in Windows Explorer, Windows Explorer effectively becomes Internet Explorer.

> **Tip**   To see the names of recently opened local documents in the History bar, open the folder named My Computer. To see the names of networked documents, open the name of the remote computer.

You can sort the History bar in any of the following ways:

- **By Date**   In chronological order by date
- **By Site**   In alphabetical order by site name
- **By Most Visited**   In order of most visited (most visited sites at the top, least visited at the bottom)
- **By Order Visited Today**   In order of sites most visited today

To select a sorting order, click the View button at the top of the History bar.

You can also filter the History bar to show only items that meet a search criterion. This can be quite useful. If you've visited hundreds of Web sites in the last two weeks but you only want to know about the ones containing the text *Windows XP*, you can use the History bar's Search tool. Click the Search button at the top of the History bar, enter your search string, and then click Search Now, as shown here.

To return to the full history, click View and then select a sort order.

The History bar's handy keyboard shortcut is Ctrl+H, and you can add a History button to your Standard Buttons toolbar.

Using the Folders Bar

The Folders bar is probably the most useful Explorer bar from a file management perspective. The Folders bar displays all your storage resources, both local and remote, in a hierarchical tree. You can use the tree as a navigational tool (hop straight to a distant folder by expanding and selecting that branch of the tree) and as a copy or move target (drag an item from a folder window and drop it on the appropriate entry in the Folders bar).

> **Tip** Hold down the right mouse button while you drag
>
> Windows has logical and consistent defaults for whether it copies or moves when you drag an item onto the Folders bar. In most cases, it moves when the source and destination are on the same disk, and it copies if the source and destination are on different disks. But it's easy to forget and move when you mean to copy—or vice versa. To avoid mishap, form the habit of right-dragging. When you drop the item on its target, you can choose the action you want from the shortcut menu that appears.

Chapter 20

The Folders bar is so useful that the shortcut menu for every folder includes a command that opens the selected folder in Windows Explorer with the Folders bar displayed. Right-click any folder or shortcut to a folder and choose Explorer (instead of Open), and Windows Explorer displays the selected folder as well as the Folders bar.

Navigating the Folders Bar in Simple Folder View

In Windows XP, unlike earlier versions of Windows, if you click a folder name in the Folders bar, Windows Explorer displays the folder's contents and expands the folder branch you clicked. Click another folder name, and Windows Explorer closes the branch where you were, opening the one you just clicked in its place. If you want to expand a branch without closing a previous one, click the item's plus-sign icon, not its name.

This new navigational mode is a big help when you're working with folders that have a lot of subfolders. In previous versions of Windows, it was easy to get lost in the details (the sub-folders) and lose track of the larger structure (the top-level set of folders). If you prefer the previous navigational mode, however, you can restore it by following these steps:

1 Choose Tools, Folder Options.

2 Click the View tab.

3 In the Advanced Settings list, clear Display Simple Folder View In Explorer's Folders List.

Choosing View Options

Windows Explorer provides six distinct ways of viewing items in a folder:

- Details
- List
- Thumbnails
- Tiles
- Icons
- Filmstrip

You can choose these options either from the View menu or by clicking the Views button on the Standard Buttons toolbar.

> **Note** Filmstrip view is available only in *picture folders*—that is, folders that use either the Pictures or Photo Album template. (For more information about folder templates, see "Choosing a Folder Template," page 667.) Filmstrip view also requires that you choose Show Common Tasks In Folders, on the General tab of the Folder Options dialog box. You don't have to display the task pane; you can display an Explorer bar instead.

Chapter 20

If you've used earlier versions of Windows, you're probably familiar with Details and List views, and perhaps also with Thumbnails view. (Details view presents a columnar display of file names and attributes. List view offers a compact display, consisting only of small icons and file names. In Thumbnails view, Windows Explorer displays previews of file contents, if it can; you see miniature images of graphics and HTML files, for example.) Windows veterans will also notice that the Small Icons view of yore is no more.

The new Tiles view generates larger and more colorful icons than the previous Large Icons view. In Tiles view, Windows Explorer also displays a generous three lines of text to describe each file. This allows it to give you more information about each file than you would see in Icons view, which simply shows icons and file names. The information that appears in Tiles view depends on the file type. With Windows Media Audio (WMA) files, for example, Windows Explorer displays performer names as well as file names.

In Filmstrip view, shown in Figure 20-4, the currently selected picture (or the first picture, if none is selected) appears in a larger size in the center of the window (with the help of the Windows Picture And Fax Viewer accessory). Below the selected image, Windows Explorer displays four buttons. The first two buttons let you change which picture is displayed in the larger frame by clicking backward and forward through the folder. The other two buttons allow you to rotate the current picture clockwise or counterclockwise. If you rotate a picture, the Windows Picture And Fax Viewer saves the rotated image under the current file name, overwriting the image that was saved under that name before. To keep the original and create a rotated copy, use the task pane to copy the original first.

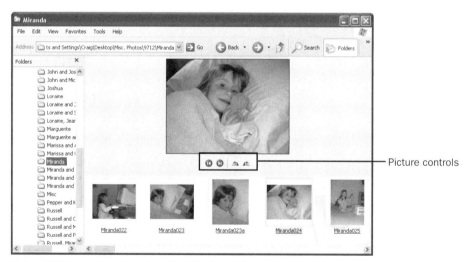

Figure 20-4. In Filmstrip view, the Windows Picture And Fax Viewer accessory shows a larger version of the selected file. You can also turn your folder into a slide show.

As Figure 20-4 shows, you don't have to have the task pane visible to use Filmstrip view. But if you do display the task pane, you can use its first Picture Tasks link to generate a slide show from all the pictures in your folder by clicking View As A Slide Show (see Figure 20-1).

Making All Folders Use the Same View

If you want all your folders to use the same view—Details or Tiles, for example—set up one folder the way you want it. Then do the following:

1. Choose Tools, Folder Options.
2. Click the View tab.
3. Click Apply To All Folders.

After you have made all your folders look more or less the same, you can still apply distinct views to individual folders. For example, you might want to have 90 percent of your folders use Details view but still display your picture folders in Thumbnails or Filmstrip view. No problem: Use the Apply To All Folders command to make all the folders use Details view. Then go to your pictures folders and override the default by applying Thumbnails or Filmstrip view.

To return all of your folders to their default views, go back to the Folder Options dialog box, click the View tab, and then click Reset All Folders.

Inside Out

Adjust the customization limit

If you've been using one of the original editions of Windows XP, or Windows XP with Service Pack 1 (SP1), it's possible that you've experienced problems with the retention of folder display customizations in Windows Explorer. Versions of Windows XP prior to Service Pack 2 (SP2), by default, remembered a paltry maximum of 400 display customizations. If you customized the display settings for a 401st folder, Windows "forgot" the settings you had applied to your first folder, and so on. Increasing the default beyond 400 required a registry edit.

The good news is that SP2 has bumped the customization maximum from 400 up to 5000. That's probably enough. But you can increase it further if you still find yourself losing folder settings. To do so, follow these steps:

1. Open Registry Editor (choose Start, Run, and type regedit).
2. Navigate to HKCU\Software\Microsoft\Windows\ShellNoRoam.
3. In Registry Editor's right pane, double-click the value BagMRU Size.
4. In the Edit DWord Value dialog box, enter a new customization maximum.

The Edit DWord Value dialog box uses hexadecimal notation by default. If you're more comfortable with decimal notation, click the Decimal button, and then specify your new maximum.

If you're using a version of Windows prior to SP2, you might not find a BagMRU Size value in the HKCU\Software\Microsoft\Windows\ShellNoRoam registry key. You can still adjust the customization maximum—by adding this value yourself. After navigating to HCKU\Software\Microsoft\Windows\ShellNoRoam, choose Edit, New, DWord Value. Name the new value BagMRU Size, double-click the new value, and enter an appropriate value (something larger than the default 400!). Better still: consider SP1's recurrent bouts of customization amnesia one more reason to download and install SP2.

Note that version 2.10.0.0 of the excellent Tweak UI utility—the latest version available at the time this book was in production—includes an Explorer\Customizations command that purports to adjust the customization limit without requiring you to open a registry editor. This command appears, however, to update the wrong registry value—Bag MRU Size, instead of BagMRU Size.

Note also that adjusting the BagMRU Size value—either directly through a registry editor or indirectly by means of another program—is an undocumented procedure, unsupported by Microsoft.

Changing Views in Common Dialog Boxes

You can change from one view to another inside the common dialog boxes used by many Windows applications—the Open and Save dialog boxes, for example. To select a different view in one of these dialog boxes, click the arrow on the dialog box's Views button and then choose a view from the menu that appears.

The common dialog boxes open in List view by default in all but certain system folders. Unfortunately, you can't make a view change for a particular folder persistent. You can switch from List to Details when you open a file, for example, but the next time you open a file, you'll be back in List view again. (This generalization does not apply to Microsoft Office applications, which don't use the common dialog boxes. Your choice of views in Office Open and Save dialog boxes is persistent.)

The places bar that appears along the left edge of the common dialog boxes provides a one-click shortcut to five storage locations. By default, the five locations in the places bar are My Recent Documents, Desktop, My Documents, My Computer, and My Network Places. Using either of two tools—Group Policy and Tweak UI—you can replace these standard locations with ones that are more useful to you.

Troubleshooting

Files and folders are sorted incorrectly in the common dialog boxes.

The standard Open and Save dialog boxes used by Notepad, Paint, WordPad, and many other applications normally display folder contents in ascending order by name, with sub-folders appearing before files. It's possible to make a persistent change in this sort order, however. If you right-click within a common dialog box, choose Arrange Icons By, modify the current sort order, and then dismiss the dialog box while holding down the Ctrl key, Windows records the new sort order in the registry (in the ShellState value of the key HKCU\Software\Microsoft\Windows\CurrentVersion\Explorer) and maintains that order the next time you open a common dialog box. It doesn't matter whether you exit by cancel-ing (clicking the big X or the Cancel button) or by following through with the dialog box's nor-mal action (clicking Save or Open). As long as you are pressing Ctrl at the time, the system remembers how the folder contents are currently sorted.

This feature (let's be generous and call it that, since it can work to your advantage if you don't prefer the conventional sort order) might drive you crazy if you use it accidentally. For-tunately, it's easy to restore the original sort order. Right-click again, choose Arrange Icons By, choose Name, and hold down Ctrl while clicking Cancel.

Note the following: The sort order recorded in the registry applies to the current user only, is preserved in all common dialog boxes (again, this excludes Microsoft Office applications, which use their own enhanced versions of the common dialogs), and—alas—has nothing to do with the current view. If there's a way to make your preferred view—Thumbnails, Tiles, Icons, List, or Details—persist in the common dialog boxes, we haven't found it yet.

Customizing the Common Dialog Boxes with Group Policy

To customize the places bar using Group Policy, you need Windows XP Professional, and you must be logged on as an administrator. With those prerequisites in place, follow these steps:

1. At a command prompt, type **gpedit.msc** to open Group Policy.

2. In the tree pane, select User Configuration\Administrative Templates\ Windows Components\Windows Explorer\Common Open File Dialog.

3. In the Details pane, double-click Items Displayed In Places Bar.

4. Select Enabled, and then make entries in each of the five item boxes. You can enter any of the following:

   - The path to a local folder or mapped network folder (for example, **c:\work**)
   - The UNC path to a shared network folder (for example, **\\sequoia\projectx**)

661

- **CommonDocuments**, which displays Shared Documents (%AllUsersProfile%\
  Documents)
- **CommonMusic**, which displays Shared Music (%AllUsersProfile%\
  Documents\My Music)
- **CommonPictures**, which displays Shared Pictures (%AllUsersProfile%\
  Documents\My Pictures)
- **Desktop**, which displays the desktop (%UserProfile%\Desktop)
- **MyComputer**, which displays My Computer
- **MyDocuments**, which displays My Documents (%UserProfile%\
  My Documents)
- **MyFavorites**, which displays Favorites (%UserProfile%\Favorites)
- **MyMusic**, which displays My Music (%UserProfile%\My Documents\
  My Music)
- **MyNetworkPlaces**, which displays My Network Places (%UserProfile%\
  Nethood)
- **MyPictures**, which displays My Pictures (%UserProfile%\My Documents\
  My Pictures)
- **Printers**, which displays Printers And Faxes
- **ProgramFiles**, which displays program files (%ProgramFiles%; by default,
  C:\Program Files)
- **Recent**, which displays My Recent Documents (%UserProfile%\Recent)

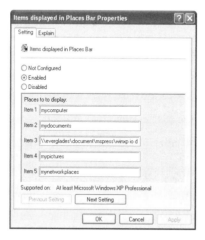

If you use Group Policy to configure the places bar, you should make entries in all five text boxes. If you don't, Windows inserts for each missing item a placeholder icon that doesn't work properly. Also, note that to specify subfolders of the folders listed above, you need to include the full path. For example, %UserProfile\My Documents\TaxDocs works, but MyDocuments\TaxDocs.does not.

> **Tip** Put links to shared network folders on the places bar only if your computer and the computer with the shared folder are always connected to the network. If either computer is disconnected when you choose File Open or File Save, you'll have to endure a lengthy wait while Windows tries to find the folder.

If you prefer to get rid of the places bar altogether, you can do that with Group Policy also. Open Group Policy as described in steps 1 and 2 of the preceding procedure, double-click Hide The Common Dialog Places Bar, and select Enabled.

Customizing the Common Dialog Boxes with Tweak UI

Tweak UI for Windows XP, a program you can download from *http://www.microsoft.com/windowsxp/pro/downloads/powertoys.asp*, also lets you customize the Open and Save dialog boxes.

Tweak UI for Windows XP is an application created by Microsoft for expert tweakers, but it is not a program formally supported by Microsoft. If you're comfortable with that arrangement, you'll find a lot to like in Tweak UI. You can use it to customize all kinds of details of the Windows user interface that are otherwise inaccessible to end users. When it comes to customizing the places bar, Tweak UI offers a couple of advantages over Group Policy:

- It works in Windows XP Home Edition as well as Professional.
- Its <none> option allows you to have fewer than five icons on the places bar.

To configure the places bar with Tweak UI, start Tweak UI (if you use the default setup, you'll find an icon for it in the Start, All Programs, Powertoys For Windows XP folder) and select Common Dialogs\Places Bar in the left pane. As shown in Figure 20-5, you can use any of the valid entries permitted by Group Policy (listed in the preceding section) or you can select from a short list of common places.

Chapter 20

Figure 20-5. Microsoft's Tweak UI program lets you modify the places bar in the common Open and Save dialog boxes.

Customizing Details View

In Details view, Windows Explorer presents a table of properties for each folder and file. The properties that appear by default in this table depend on the kind of files the folder contains. With picture folders, for example, Details view includes columns that report the dimensions of each picture and the date the picture was taken. In music folders, the default columns include Artist, Album Title, Duration, and so on.

You can customize the columns that appear in any folder's Details view by choosing View, Choose Details. As Figure 20-6 shows, the list of available properties is extensive.

With the Choose Details dialog box, you can also rearrange the order in which columns appear, and change the width of any column. You'll probably find it easier to make these kinds of changes directly, however—by adjusting columns with your mouse in Windows Explorer. Drag a heading to the left or right to reposition it. Drag the right edge of a column heading to change that column's width.

> **Tip** You can also choose which columns to display in Details view by right-clicking any column heading.

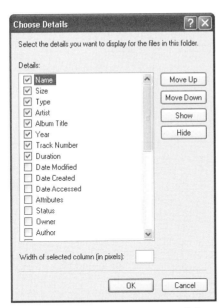

Figure 20-6. You can show any of these properties in a folder's Details view.

Sorting and Grouping Icons

In Details view, you can sort the contents of a folder by clicking a column heading. For example, to display a folder's contents by file size (smallest to largest), click the Size heading. Click the column heading again to reverse the sort order.

In other views, you can sort the contents by choosing View, Arrange Icons By, and then selecting a sort key from the submenu. The available sort keys depend on the folder type. As Figure 20-7 shows, with a music folder you can sort by Artist, Album Title, Year, Track Number, and Duration, as well as by Name, Size, and Type.

Figure 20-7 also illustrates a nifty feature of Windows Explorer in Windows XP. In all views except List and Filmstrip, you can use the Show In Groups command (on the Arrange Icons By submenu) to organize your folders by some category of your choosing—size, date, name, or type, for example. When you have a lot of items in a folder, displaying the contents in groups can help you locate the one you need. The Show In Groups command can also make it more pleasant to look at a small folder that contains significantly different kinds of items—such as My Computer, as shown in Figure 20-8.

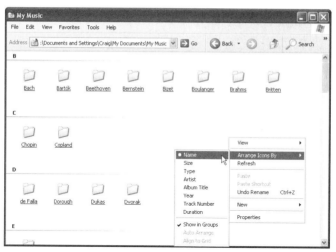

Figure 20-7. The Show In Groups command makes it easier to find files and folders.

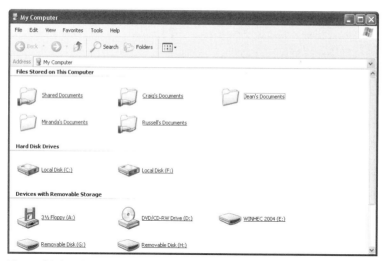

Figure 20-8. Grouping items by type makes for a more pleasant display, even in a folder with relatively few items.

> **Note** **Remove the Files Stored On This Computer group**
> Some users prefer not to take up space in My Computer with the Files Stored On This Computer group (as shown in Figure 20-8). You can eliminate that group from My Computer as follows:
>
> **1** Open Registry Editor.
>
> **2** Navigate to HKLM\Software\Microsoft\Windows\CurrentVersion\Explorer\ My Computer\NameSpace\Delegate Folders.
>
> **3** Below this key, you'll see a subkey called {59031a47-3f72-44a7-89c5-5595fe6b30ee}. Delete this subkey and close Registry Editor.

Choosing a Folder Template

Windows XP does not include the Customize This Folder Wizard, which lets you assign pictures and HTML templates as backgrounds to folders in earlier versions of Windows Explorer. Instead of taking you to the wizard, the View, Customize This Folder command now puts you on the Customize tab of the folder's Properties dialog box, as shown in Figure 20-9, where you can choose one of the folder templates that Windows supplies, assign a picture to a folder (the picture will appear on the folder's icon in Thumbnails view) or change a folder's icon altogether.

Figure 20-9. On the Customize tab of a folder's Properties dialog box, you can choose a template, assign a picture, and change the folder icon.

The seven supplied templates are as follows:

- Documents (for any file type)
- Pictures (best for many files)
- Photo Album (best for fewer files)
- Music (best for audio files and playlists)
- Music Artist (best for works by one artist)
- Music Album (best for tracks from one album)
- Videos

Most of the time, you'll find that Windows applies an appropriate template without any help from you. If you use Microsoft Windows Media Player to copy tracks from an audio CD to your hard disk, for example, Windows Media Player (by default) creates an artist folder, stores an album folder within that artist folder, and stores the individual audio tracks in that album folder. The Music Artist template is applied to the artists folder, and the Music Album template is applied to the album folder—as you would expect. If Windows finds ordinary documents in a folder (that is, not media files), it assigns it the Documents template, and so on.

To choose a template other than the one Windows assigns by default, follow these steps:

1 Right-click a blank space in the folder.
2 Choose Customize This Folder.
3 In the Use This Folder Type As A Template list, choose a template.

Your choice of template (or, more typically, the choice that Windows makes) affects the following:

- The tasks that appear at the top of the task pane
- The default view (Filmstrip for a Photo Album template, for example)
- Whether Windows should display four pictures or only one on the folder icon in Thumbnails view
- The background image for the folder

Note The Customize This Folder command is not available for certain system folders, such as My Documents, My Music, Shared Music, and Shared Pictures.

Putting Pictures on Folder Icons

Folder icons that appear in a folder displayed in Thumbnails view can be decorated with pictures. Windows XP uses this feature to "preview" the contents of picture, video, music album, and music artist folders. When you copy audio tracks to your hard disk with Windows Media Player, Windows adorns the artist folder with album art from the albums contained within that folder. When Windows discerns that a folder contains pictures, it plants up to four of those pictures on the folder icon, as shown in Figure 20-10. When it detects videos, it displays the first frame of up to four videos.

Figure 20-10.   Windows displays up to four pictures on folder icons for folders containing image files.

Windows fancies up your folder icons for media folders automatically. All you need to do to take advantage of this feature is make sure the parent folder (the one with the adorned folder icons) is displayed in Thumbnails view.

You can also put your own pictures on folder icons, and they don't have to be pictures contained within the folder in question. To dress up an icon yourself, return to the Customize tab of the folder's Properties dialog box (shown in Figure 20-9 on page 667), click Choose Picture, and specify. If you change your mind and want to remove the picture, click Restore Default.

> **Tip**   An alternative way to assign a picture to a folder icon is to store a copy of the picture in the folder and name it *Folder*.

Choosing Advanced Folder Options

The View tab of the Folder Options dialog box, shown in Figure 20-11, offers a potpourri of advanced options that govern various aspects of Windows Explorer's behavior. Some of these are self-explanatory and relatively inconsequential. Others are less obvious and can have a significant impact on how you work in Windows XP. The following sections provide brief descriptions of these options.

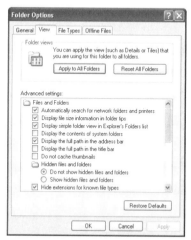

Figure 20-11. The Advanced Settings list includes obvious and obscure miscellany.

Automatically Search for Network Folders and Printers

By default, Windows scans your network periodically for newly shared printers and folders, adding those that it finds to My Network Places and your Printers And Faxes folder. You might want to clear this check box if you're disconnected from the network most of your day. Otherwise, leave it selected; it's a convenience you might as well enjoy.

Display File Size Information in Folder Tips

If you pause your mouse pointer over a folder icon, Windows Explorer normally displays a "folder tip" that describes the contents of the folder and tells you how much space the folder's contents consume.

Chapter 20

If you'd rather skip the file size information and see only a description of the folder contents, clear Display File Size Information In Folder Tips. If you'd rather see no folder tips at all, clear Show Pop-Up Description For Folder And Desktop Items. Clearing the latter check box also suppresses the file size information, regardless of how the former check box is configured.

Display Simple Folder View in Explorer's Folders List

This check box enables the simple-folder navigational method described earlier in this chapter (see "Navigating the Folders Bar in Simple Folder View," page 657).

Display the Contents of System Folders

One of the ways that Windows XP tries to protect you from damaging your operating system is by discouraging you from even opening folders containing system files—such as %ProgramFiles%, %SystemRoot%, and %SystemRoot%\System32. If the Display The Contents Of System Folders check box is clear (its default state), Windows displays this message when you try to display a system folder.

If you're an experienced Windows user, you might object to being shut out of the system folders. You can display system files by selecting Display The Contents Of System Folders. You can also enable the display of system folders selectively. If you leave the Display The Contents Of System Folders check box clear, you'll see the warning screen the first time you visit a system folder. Click Show The Contents Of This Folder, and the folder's contents will be visible thereafter, regardless of how the check box is set. Note that this is a per-user setting; other user accounts will still find the system folders blocked—unless they too click the link that lets them in.

Display the Full Path in the Address Bar and Title Bar

By default, Windows Explorer displays the full path of the current folder in the Address bar but only the folder name in the Windows Explorer title bar. You can shuffle these options any way you like by manipulating two Advanced Settings options. If you like to display the Address bar alongside the Standard Buttons toolbar, you might find that you seldom have room for the full path in the Address bar. The title bar for the Windows Explorer window, on the other hand, typically has room for long paths. So, it's possible you'll want to reverse the defaults. On the other hand, if you use the Folders bar, you might find that you don't need the full path specification in either location.

Experiment to see what works best for you. Be aware that if you display the full path on the title bar, Windows also displays it in your taskbar buttons. These typically do not have room for full paths; when necessary, Windows simply truncates text in the taskbar buttons, though if you pause the pointer over the button the full path and name will appear.

Do Not Cache Thumbnails

Windows normally caches the images that appear in Thumbnails view in a hidden file named Thumbs.db so that it can redisplay the images more quickly each time you reopen a folder in Thumbnails view. Selecting the Do Not Cache Thumbnails check box can free up a bit of disk space, but it might cause delays when you open folders.

> **Note** Changing this setting does not delete any existing instances of Thumbs.db; it merely prevents the creation of new cache files.

Hidden Files and Folders

By default, Windows Explorer hides files and folders that have either the hidden attribute or the system attribute set. The operating system keeps these items out of sight, on the assumption that what you can't see you can't delete, rename, or corrupt.

To make hidden files and folders visible, select Show Hidden Files And Folders. (If you don't see this option, double-click Hidden Files And Folders.) To make visible files and folders with both the system and the hidden attributes set (the so-called "super-hidden" items), clear Hide Protected Operating System Files (Recommended).

> **Note**   In earlier versions of Windows, if hidden files were not displayed in Windows Explorer, they were also invisible to the Search command. In Windows XP, you can search for hidden items, regardless of your settings in the Folder Options dialog box. For more information, see "Locating Files with Search Companion," page 718.

Hide Extensions for Known File Types

Windows Explorer normally displays file name extensions only for file types unknown to the registry, leaving you to discern the type of most files by their icons, screen tips, the tags that appear below file names in Tiles view, or the Type column in Details view. This behavior results in cleaner, leaner displays in Windows Explorer as well as in the dialog boxes that you use to open and save files. The disadvantage of hiding extensions is that it makes it harder for you to change a file's extension. For example, suppose you want to change the name of the file *Notes.txt* to *Notes.doc*—so that it will open automatically in WordPad (or Microsoft Word) instead of Notepad. If the extension is hidden, you will see the entry *Notes* in Windows Explorer. If you simply add *.doc* to the end of this entry, you will see *Notes.doc* in Windows Explorer. But the new name of the file will be *Notes.doc.txt*, and the file will still be associated with Notepad. To change the extension, you must first make the extension visible.

> **Tip**   Use Open With to see a file's extension
>
> If you just want to know what a file's extension is, and Windows Explorer is hiding extensions for known file types, right-click the file name and choose Open With. (If Open With presents a submenu, select Choose Program on the submenu.) Near the top of the Open With dialog box, you'll find the full name of the file, extension included.

 The companion CD included with this book includes a batch file and a VBScript file, both of which toggle all of Windows Explorer's "hide" settings on or off. Run ToggleHiddenExplorerStuff.bat or ToggleHiddenExplorerStuff.vbs once to make hidden and super-hidden files visible and to show extensions; run it a second time to return these settings to their defaults.

> **Tip**   Show extensions for particular files only
>
> To see the extensions for a particular known file type, while hiding all the others, use the File Types tab in the Folder Options dialog box. Select the file type whose extension you want to see, click Advanced, and then select the Always Show Extension check box.

673

Hide Protected Operating System Files (Recommended)

If this option is selected (as it is by default), Windows Explorer hides files that have both the system attribute and the hidden attribute set.

Launch Folder Windows in a Separate Process

Windows Explorer normally uses the same memory space for all open folder windows. If you select the Launch Folder Window In A Separate Process check box, the memory used by each window will be segregated. (The name of the option is misleading; you'll still have only one Explorer.exe process running, but that process will use separate memory spaces for each window.) If Windows Explorer is prone to crashing on your system, you might want to try selecting this check box. Otherwise, there's no good reason to do so, and you'll conserve memory by leaving it clear.

Managing Pairs of Web Pages and Folders

If you save a Web page using Internet Explorer's Web Page, Complete option (choose Web Page, Complete (*.htm, *.html) in the Save As Type list), Internet Explorer saves the Web page's text in one file and puts all the associated graphics and other supporting documents in a folder with the same name. For example, if you save the Microsoft home page (*http://www.microsoft.com/homepage/ms.htm*) under its default name, Microsoft Corporation, you will get a file named Microsoft Corporation.htm and a folder called Microsoft Corporation_files. The folder contains the various image, style sheet, and script files that support the HTML file.

By default, Windows Explorer links such file-and-folder pairs. The file and folder are shown as separate items, but actions taken upon one are applied to both. Delete or move either the file or the folder, for example, and Windows Explorer moves or deletes both items. This behavior makes it less likely that you'll "break" a saved Web page by separating its component parts.

Keeping the file and folder linked is generally a good idea. But you can sever the link for a particular file-folder pair by renaming either the file or the folder and answering a confirmation prompt. You can also prevent Windows Explorer from linking the file and folder in the first place by choosing Show Both Parts And Manage Them Individually in the Advanced Settings list. (If you don't see these options, double-click Managing Pairs Of Web Pages And Folders.) For more information about how file-and-folder linkage works, see the Inside Out sidebar on the next page.

Chapter 20

Inside Out

More about file and folder linkage

By default, Windows Explorer does its best to keep HTML documents connected with associated image files, style sheets, and scripts. If a file with the extension .htm or .html resides in the same folder as a similarly named subfolder, then any of the following commands, when applied to either the file or the folder, are always applied to both: Copy, Cut, Paste, Move, Delete, and Send To. Attempting to rename either the file or the folder results in a warning message. Thus, for example, if a folder contains an HTML file called MyPage.htm and a subfolder called MyPage_files, Windows Explorer will treat those items as an unbreakable unit to the extent that it can.

If for some reason you want to defeat this behavior, you can do so by choosing Tools, Folder Options in Windows Explorer. On the View tab of the Folder Options dialog box, under Managing Pairs Of Web Pages And Folders, select Show Both Parts And Manage Them Individually. Note that this section of the Folder Options dialog box offers two alternatives: Show And Manage The Pair As A Single File, and Show Both Parts But Manage As A Single File. The difference between the two? Nothing. The first of these alternatives should hide the supporting folder, but it does not. Perhaps a future version of Windows will eliminate this bug.

Be aware that the file-and-folder-linkage option concerns Windows Explorer, not Internet Explorer. That is, the setting in effect is applied to all similarly named pairs, regardless of how the option was set when the pairs were created.

Also note the following: The _files designation, which Internet Explorer appends to supporting-file folders, is case-sensitive. Change _files to _Files, and the folder will no longer be linked to the HTML document. To accommodate languages other than English, however, a variety of other suffixes can be used to link folders with HTML documents. Thus, for example, the folder MyPage-Dateien (the German equivalent of MyPage_files) will be linked with MyPage.htm. For a list of these alternative suffixes, see Microsoft Knowledge Base article 252721 (*http://support.microsoft.com/?kbid=252721*).

Remember Each Folder's View Settings

By default, Windows Explorer remembers the view settings you assign to a folder—that is, the next time you open a folder, it looks the same way it did the last time you were there. Not everyone prefers this behavior. If you like to maintain a consistent look in all your folders (for information about how to do this, see "Making All Folders Use the Same View," page 659), and change the view only occasionally for some special situations, you might rather have Windows restore your default view when you close a folder. If that's the case, clear Remember Each Folder's View Settings.

Restore Previous Folder Windows at Logon

When you logged on to previous versions of Windows, Windows Explorer reopened any folders that were open when you logged off. Because many users found the convenience of reopening folders more than outweighed by the extra time required to complete the logon, Windows XP has made this behavior optional—and has disabled it by default. To have your previously opened windows reopened at logon, select Restore Previous Folder Windows At Logon.

Show Control Panel in My Computer

Earlier versions of Windows included the Control Panel folder in My Computer. Windows XP, by default, eschews the folder-style presentation of Control Panel options in favor of a Control Panel menu, but lets you switch back to the "classic view" Control Panel if you prefer the old way. With either the new style or the old, however, you have the option of including Control Panel in the My Computer folder. To put it there, select Show Control Panel In My Computer.

Note that Control Panel appears in the Folders bar under My Computer, regardless of how this option is set, as shown in Figure 20-12.

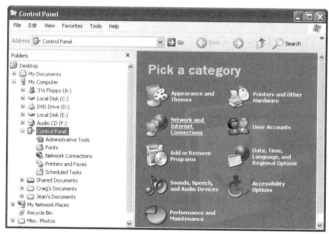

Figure 20-12. Regardless of whether Control Panel appears in your My Computer folder, it appears under My Computer in the Folders bar.

Show Encrypted or Compressed NTFS Files in Color

By default, the names of encrypted NTFS files and folders are displayed in green; the names of compressed files and folders appear in blue. If you like black better, clear the Show Encrypted Or Compressed NTFS Files In Color check box. (For information about using encryption, see Chapter 11, "Encrypting Confidential Information." For information about using NTFS compression, see "Implementing NTFS Compression," page 705.)

Show Pop-Up Descriptions for Folder and Desktop Items

This option enables pop-up descriptions when you select folders or desktop items. If you don't need the information, or if the pop-up information becomes distracting or gets in your way, clear this check box to disable it.

Use Simple File Sharing (Recommended)

The last check box in the Advanced Settings list enables or disables Simple File Sharing. For additional information about Simple File Sharing, see "Simple File Sharing vs. Windows 2000–Style Sharing," page 230.

Because you can't disable Simple File Sharing in Windows XP Home Edition, this option appears only in Windows XP Professional.

Using Cascading Folder Menus

Most users know that you can put a shortcut to any folder on your Start menu (or desktop) and then use the shortcut as a simple way of opening that folder in Windows Explorer. Less obvious is the fact that you can put a whole branch of your file system on the Start menu, and then use cascading submenus to get to any point within the branch. Figure 20-13 shows an example in which a remote folder has been added to the local Start menu. When you add a system of subfolders to the menu this way, you can open any subfolder by navigating to it in the menu, right-clicking it, and then choosing either Open or Explore from the shortcut menu. (Choose Explore to open the folder with the Folders bar.)

To add a branch of your folder structure to the Start menu, follow these steps:

1   In Windows Explorer, open the parent of the folder that you want to be the root of the cascading system.

2   Drag the icon for the root folder to the Start button, and hold it there while the Start menu opens.

- If you're using the Windows XP–style Start menu, drag the folder to All Programs, and wait while the All Programs menu opens. Drag the folder to the place where you want it, and then release the mouse button.

- If you're using the classic Start menu, drag the folder to the top portion of the menu, position it where you want it, and then release the mouse button.

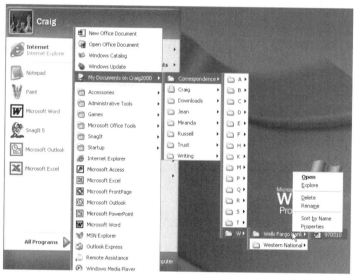

Figure 20-13.   Adding a branch of your file system to your Start menu lets you navigate quickly to distant folders.

Windows creates a shortcut to your folder in the place where you release the mouse button. Note that if you're using the Windows XP–style Start menu, you *can* create that shortcut at the top of the left portion of the menu, but if you put it there, the shortcut opens the root folder only. If you want to be able to cascade the subfolder structure, you need to position the root folder within All Programs.

Working with File Types and File Associations

The File Types tab of the Folder Options dialog box (choose Tools, Folder Options, File Types) displays a list of your registered document file types. A few entries from this long list are visible in Figure 20-14.

By selecting file types from the Registered File Types list, you can perform a number of tasks:

- Change the default action for a file type.
- Change the application associated with a file type.

- Change a file type's icon.
- Specify whether a file type's extension should be displayed in Windows Explorer.
- Specify whether a file type should be opened immediately after being downloaded.
- Add, edit, and delete commands on a file type's shortcut menu.

Figure 20-14.   On the File Types tab you can change such things as the default actions for document types.

Changing the Default Action for a File Type

A file type's default action is the one that occurs when you double-click it (or single-click it if you've set up Windows Explorer for single-click starting). If you right-click a file in Windows Explorer, the default action is shown in boldface on the shortcut menu. Most commonly, the default action for a document is to open it for editing or display it in its parent application—the application with which it is associated. There are exceptions, however. The default action for a .reg file, for example, is to merge the file's data with the registry. To edit the .reg file, you need to choose a nondefault command (Edit) from the shortcut menu. Alternatively, you can change the default action to Edit.

To change a file type's default action, follow these steps:

1   In the Registered File Types list on the File Types tab, select the file whose default action you want to change.

2   Click Advanced.

3   In the list of available actions, select the action you want to be the default.

4   Click Set Default.

This figure shows the result of setting .reg files to be edited by default.

Changing the Application Associated with a File Type

Perhaps the simplest way to change the application associated with a file type is to right-click it in Windows Explorer and choose Open With from the shortcut menu. In the Open With dialog box, select the application you want to associate with the file type, and then select Always Use The Selected Program To Open This Kind Of File.

Alternatively, you can accomplish this change in the Registered File Types list. Select the file you want to change, click the Change button, and then select the program you want associated with the file type, as shown on the next page.

> **Tip** Use a third-party tool to minimize file association hassles
>
> It's a common occurrence: You decide to test out a trial version of some new product, and after installing it, you discover that the trial version has "hijacked" a number of file types for its own use. Restoring these file types' prior associations is a major hassle. Associate This, a utility available at *http://www.spearit.com/about_AssociateThis.html*, can help you avoid this kind of problem. Associate This notifies you whenever a program changes a file-type association and lets you undo the change. Alternatively, you can set it to block association changes for all or particular extensions.

Chapter 20

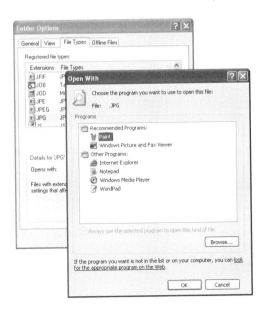

Changing a File Type's Icon

To change the icon used for a file type, follow these steps:

1 Select the file type in the Registered File Types list on the File Types tab.

2 Click Advanced.

3 Click Change Icon.

4 Choose a new icon from the Change Icon dialog box.

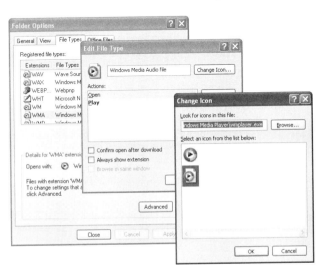

Chapter 20

If you don't find an icon to your liking in the Change Icon dialog box, click Browse and navigate to another program that might offer something you prefer. Icons are commonly stored within .exe, .dll, and .ico files.

Making the Extension of a Particular File Type Visible

If you have set Windows Explorer to hide extensions for known file types (that is, if you have left its default behavior in place), you can still display extensions for particular kinds of files. In the Registered File Types list, select the file type whose extension you want to see. Then click Advanced and select Always Show Extension.

Specifying Download Behavior

To specify that files of a particular type should always be opened as soon as you have finished downloading them, select the file type in the Registered File Types list. Click Advanced and then clear Confirm Open After Download.

> **Note** Indiscriminately opening certain types of files you download could be disastrous to the health of your computer if those files contain viruses or worms. Files with extensions that indicate they are executable files are the ones you need to watch most carefully, such as .bat, .vbs, .exe, or .com.

Customizing a File Type's Shortcut Menu

The menu that appears when you right-click a file in Windows Explorer is derived from various registry keys and from the file %SystemRoot%\System32\Shell32.dll. You can add, edit, or prune this shortcut menu by editing the registry directly, but with registered file types, you can often get the job done by working with the Registered File Types list in the Folder Options dialog box in Windows Explorer—and save yourself a trip to the registry. Nevertheless, some customizations do require direct registry edit. For a list of those tasks and the steps to complete them, see "Customizing Shortcut Menus by Editing the Registry," page 684.

Adding a Shortcut Menu Command

To add a new command to a shortcut menu, select the file type in the Registered File Types list, click Advanced, and then click New. On the Action line of the New Action dialog box, type the command as you want it to appear on the shortcut menu. On the Application Used To Perform Action line, type the command string you want to use.

Chapter 20

For example, .log files are associated with Notepad, by default. Suppose you would like to open them occasionally in WordPad instead. You can use Open With to open the files in WordPad, of course, but let's assume that you'd like to streamline the process by having an Open With WordPad command on the shortcut menu. Here's how to do it:

1 In the Extensions column of the Registered File Types list, select LOG.

2 Click Advanced.

3 In the Edit File Type dialog box, click New.

4 Enter information in the New Action dialog box as shown here.

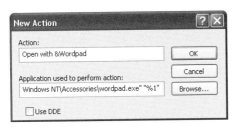

The ampersand before *WordPad* in the Action text box is optional; it makes the letter *W* a shortcut key for the new command. The *%1* at the end of the command string is a place-holder for the name of the file that you right-click. Enclosing *%1* in quote marks ensures that WordPad will be able to handle long file names and paths that include space characters.

Note the following:

● Don't use environment variables, such as %SystemRoot%, in your command strings. If you need to include variables, see "Customizing Shortcut Menus by Editing with the Registry," page 684.

● To create a command without a placeholder, you need to modify the registry directly. You can create a shortcut menu command that simply runs a program, such as Tweak UI or Registry Editor, but you can't do it through the Folder Options dialog box, because Windows Explorer will append *%1* to your command string if you don't put the placeholder in yourself.

● When you work with the shortcut menu for a particular file extension in the Folder Options dialog box, you're actually modifying the shortcut menu for a class of files that might well encompass several different extensions. Depending on how your system is set up, for example, changes to .log files might also affect files with the extensions .dic, .exc, .scp, .txt, and .wtx.

Chapter 20

683

Changing a Shortcut Menu Command

To edit an existing shortcut menu command, follow these steps:

1 Select the file type in the Registered File Types list.

2 Click Advanced.

3 In the Actions list of the Edit File Type dialog box, select the command you want to edit.

4 Click Edit.

5 Make your changes on the Action line, and then click OK.

> **Note** With certain file types (such as Folder), you might find that the Edit and Remove buttons are unavailable in the Edit File Type dialog box. In such cases, modifying or removing commands from the shortcut menu requires a direct registry edit. For more information, see "Customizing Shortcut Menus by Editing the Registry," page 684.

Removing a Shortcut Menu Command

You can usually remove a command from a file type's shortcut menu by choosing Tools, Folder Options in Windows Explorer, selecting the file type on the File Types tab of the Folder Options dialog box, clicking Advanced, selecting the verb you want to remove in the Actions list of the Edit File Type dialog box, and then clicking Remove. If the Remove button is unavailable, you'll need to modify the registry directly. See "Editing the Registry to Remove a Shortcut Menu Command," in the section that follows.

Customizing Shortcut Menus by Editing the Registry

By working directly in the registry, instead of using the Folder Options dialog box, you can do the following:

- Make per-user shortcut-menu modifications (changes made through the Folder Options dialog box are per-computer).

- Add commands to the extended shortcut menu (the menu that appears when you hold down Shift while right-clicking an object).

- Specify command strings that include environment variables, such as %ProgramFiles%.

- Add commands to the shortcut menus of all members of a "perceived" file type (a super category, such as Image, that encompasses files with a variety of extensions, such as .bmp, .gif, .ico, .jpe, .jpeg, .jpg, .png, and .tiff).

- Customize the shortcut menus of unregistered file types.

- Create shortcut menu commands that apply to all file types.

- Customize the shortcut menus of system objects, such as My Computer or Recycle Bin.

- Remove or edit a shortcut menu command when the Remove and Edit buttons are unavailable in the Folder Options dialog box.

Of course, if you simply prefer working in the registry to working through dialog boxes, you can create ordinary shortcut menu customizations for registered file types this way as well.

How Shortcut Menu Information Is Recorded in the Registry

Shortcut menu customizations can be recorded in either of two main branches of the registry. Per-computer commands appear under HKCR, and per-user commands appear under HKCU\Software\Classes. (HKCR is actually a link to HKLM\Software\Classes, so this division is as you would expect; settings applying to all users of a computer are recorded in HKey_Local_Machine, while settings applying to the current user appear in HKey_Current_User.) Menu customizations that you create through the Folders Options dialog box are per computer and are therefore recorded in HKCR. Per-user class registrations were not supported prior to Windows 2000 and are still relatively uncommon.

If you run Registry Editor and examine HKCR, you will find, at or near the top of this root key, a long list of subkeys for all the various file extensions known to your system. The default value of each of these extension subkeys identifies the extension's ProgID. Farther down in HKCR, you will find a subkey matching this ProgID value. So, for example, the default value of HKCR\.log, on most systems, is *txtfile*. Farther down in HKCR is the key HKCR\txtfile, the various subkeys of which record information—including shortcut menu data—that pertains to .log files and all other file extensions (such as .txt) whose ProgID is *txtfile*.

Figure 20-15 illustrates these relationships. The upper part of the figure shows HKCR\.log, whose default value is *txtfile*. The lower part of the figure shows HKCR\txtfile, whose Shell subkey records shortcut menu commands for files of this class.

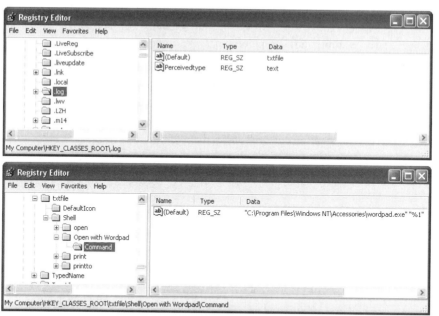

Figure 20-15. Because .log files belong to the class txtfile, shortcut menu commands for .log files appear under the Shell subkey of HKCR\txtfile.

Creating a Per-Computer Shortcut Menu Command

To create a per-computer shortcut menu command, follow these steps:

1 At a command prompt, type **regedit** to run Registry Editor.

2 In HKCR, locate the extension key for the file type whose menu you want to customize. Note the default value of this key.

3 Also in HKCR, locate the key that matches the default value you found in step 2.

4 If this key does not already have a Shell subkey, create it. (Choose Edit, New, Key, and name the key *Shell.*)

5 Create a subkey of Shell, and give it the text of your new command, as you want it to appear on the shortcut menu.When you create a shortcut menu command through the conventional user interface (the Folder Options dialog box), Windows applies your menu text to the default value of the new verb subkey. This step is not essential, however. If you omit it, Windows uses the name of the subkey as the menu command.

6 Create another subkey within the one you just created, and name this subkey *Command.*

7   As the default value of Command, enter the command string that your command
    should execute. Do not use environment variables in this command string. Enclose
    the command string in quote marks. To supply the name of the file or folder that you
    right-click as an argument for the command, follow the command string with the
    placeholder *%1*. Enclose the *%1* separately in quote marks.

Creating a Per-User Shortcut Menu Command

Shortcut menu commands typically apply to all users at a given computer. At times, though,
you might want to create menu structures that are specific for your user profile. That way,
you don't cause any distress or confusion for other users of your machine. More important,
perhaps, a per-user structure stays with you if you use a roaming profile and log on at a different computer in your domain.

Creating a per-user command is similar to creating a per-computer command (see the preceding procedure), except that you do your work in HKCU\Software\Classes instead of
HKCR. Also, because per-user file type registrations are relatively rare, you might need to
create the entire structure of keys and subkeys for your file type, rather than just the Shell
and command subkeys. Start by examining HKCR to see what that structure should look
like in HKCU.

For example, suppose you want to create a per-user command for the .bmp shortcut menu.
Looking in HKCR, you see that the default value of HKCU\.bmp is *Paint.Picture*.

Moving over to HKCU\Software\Classes, you find that neither HKCU\Software\Classes\.bmp
nor HKCU\Software\Classes\Paint.Picture yet exists. So you create those keys. Then you finish
the task by creating the appropriate keys and values within HKCU\Software\Classes\Paint.
Picture (again, see the preceding procedure for details on how to do this).

Adding a Command to an Extended Shortcut Menu

The extended shortcut menu is the menu that appears when you hold down Shift while right-
clicking an object. This secondary shortcut menu is a good place to put commands that you
don't need to use very often. By adding one new value to the registry, you can turn an ordinary shortcut menu command into an extended shortcut menu command.

To create an extended shortcut menu command, follow the steps described earlier (see
"Creating a Per-Computer Shortcut Menu Command," page 686, or "Creating a Per-User
Shortcut-Menu Command," page 687). After step 5, in Registry Editor's left pane, select
the key that names your command. Then choose Edit, New, String Value. In the right pane,
double-click the new string value and name it *Extended*. Then proceed with the remaining
steps as described earlier (create a Command subkey, and so on). Figure 20-16 illustrates
an extended shortcut menu command.

Chapter 20

687

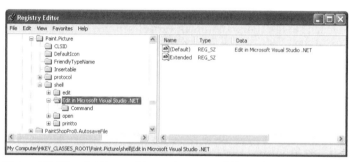

Figure 20-16. Adding a string value named Extended relegates a command to the extended shortcut menu, the menu that appears when you hold down Shift while right-clicking.

Including Environment Variables in Command Strings

If, for some reason, you need to include an environment variable—such as %Systemroot% or %ProgramFiles%—in a shortcut menu command string, you need to make the data type for the default value of your Command key REG_EXPAND_SZ, instead of REG_SZ. Unfortunately, Registry Editor always makes the data type for the default value of a new key REG_SZ, and there's no way to change this type in Registry Editor. Fortunately, you can accomplish the task with the command-line registry editor, Reg.exe.

For example, the following string, entered at a command line, creates the registry key HKCR\FileType\Shell\Verb\Command and gives the default value of that key the data type REG_EXPAND_SZ:

```
Reg add hkcr\filetype\shell\verb\command /ve /t reg_expand_sz
```

Note that if you use the command-line registry editor to supply the data for your Command key's default value, you should use pairs of percent signs, not single percent signs, to mark your environment variables, like this: %%SystemRoot%%. If you use single percent signs, the command interpreter (Cmd.exe) will expand your variables before passing them to the command-line registry editor.

For information about using the command-line registry editor, see "Editing the Registry from the Command Line," page 1335.

Chapter 20

Customizing the Shortcut Menu for All Files of a "Perceived" File Type

Perceived file types are categories of files that encompass other categories. Windows XP supports six perceived types: audio, compressed, image, system, text, and video. On your system, the audio perceived type probably includes files with the extensions .aif, .aifc, .aiff, .au, .cda, .m3u, .mid, .midi, .mp3, .rmi, .snd, .wav, .wax, and .wma, perhaps among others. The text perceived type probably includes .asm, .asmx, .aspx, .c, .css, and so on, in addition to such common types as .txt and .log.

You can add a shortcut menu command for an entire perceived type by working with the registry key HKCR\SystemFileAssociations. To put a command on the shortcut menu for the image perceived type, for example, navigate in Registry Editor to HKCR\SystemFileAssociations\image. Add a Shell subkey if necessary, a subkey under shell for your new verb, and a subkey called Command under the new verb's key. See "Creating a Per-Computer Shortcut Menu Command," page 686, for details about these steps.

Customizing the Shortcut Menu of Unregistered File Types

The registry key HKCR\Unknown tells Windows what to do with files whose extensions are otherwise unregistered. To modify the shortcut menu for such files, add the usual subkeys and values to HKCR\Unknown, following steps described earlier in this section (see "Creating a Per-Computer Shortcut Menu Command," page 686).

Customizing the Shortcut Menu of All File Types

The registry key HKCR* provides data relevant to all file types. You can work with this key in the same manner as with file-specific keys. See Creating a Per-Computer Shortcut Menu Command," page 686, for details.

Customizing the Shortcut Menus of System Objects

System objects, such as My Computer, Recycle Bin, and My Network Places, have shortcut menus, too. Adding commands to the menus of these objects that execute frequently used programs can be a convenient way to reduce desktop and Start menu clutter. You might, for example, want to add Tweak UI or Registry Editor to the shortcut menu (or extended shortcut menu) for My Computer.

To work with system-object shortcut menus, modify the registry key HKCR\CLSID*guid*, where *guid* is the globally unique identifier (GUID) for the object you're interested in. Table 20-1 lists the GUIDs for some items that might be useful to customize.

Table 20-1. GUIDs for customization-worthy system objects

Object	GUID
My Computer	{20D04FE0-3AEA-1069-A2D8-08002B30309D}
My Documents	{450D8FBA-AD25-11D0-98A8-0800361B1103}
My Network Places	{208D2C60-3AEA-1069-A2D7-08002B30309D}
Recycle Bin	{645FF040-5081-101B-9F08-00AA002F954E}

Editing the Registry to Remove a Shortcut Menu Command

In many cases, you can get rid of an unwanted shortcut menu command via the conventional user interface—that is, without editing the registry directly. Choose Tools, Folder Options in Windows Explorer, click the File Types tab, select the file type whose menu you want to prune, click Advanced, select the command you want to eliminate, and click Remove. If you don't find the item you're looking for, however, or if the Remove button is unavailable in the Edit File Type dialog box, you will need to perform surgery in Registry Editor.

Before operating, you might want to consider setting a restore point, so that if you inadvertently remove the wrong organ, you can return your registry to its current state. Once you've done that, run Registry Editor and search for the command text as it appears on your shortcut menus. If the item you want to remove is a per-computer command (it most likely is), you can limit your search to the HKCR root key. If by chance it's a per-user command, start your search instead at HKCU\Software\Classes.

Registry Editor should find an instance of your search string within a subkey structure that looks like this:

```
HKCR\filetype\shell\verb
```

or

```
HKCU\Software\Classes\filetype\shell\verb
```

where *filetype* is a category of files and *verb* is the menu item you've searched for. Select that item in the left pane, press Delete, and check to see if you've removed the item you wanted to remove. If you haven't, run System Restore and try again.

Be aware that some shortcut menu commands are attached to multiple classes of files. If you search HKCR for *&Edit* with Microsoft FrontPage, for example, you're likely to find that shortcut menu command in a number of different registry keys. To remove all traces of a shortcut menu command, you might need to perform multiple surgeries.

Inside Out

Printing folder contents

Windows Explorer does not include a command for printing folder contents. But, of course, the venerable MS-DOS method—generating a directory list with the **Dir** command and redirecting output to the printer—still works. Article 272623 in the Microsoft Knowledge Base (*http://support.microsoft.com/?kbid=272623*) explains how to create a batch file to accomplish this chore and attach the batch file to the shortcut menu for the File Folder file type. Because there are several free Windows utilities that can print folder listings more stylishly than an MS-DOS batch file can (see, for example, *http://www.karenware.com/powertools/ptdirprn.asp*, *http://www.aborange.com/products/dirprinter.php*, and *http://www.widgetech.com/freeware/printdir3_1.shtml*), we don't favor the Knowledge Base article's approach.

If you decide to follow its instructions, however, be sure to make one change. The article instructs you to attach the batch file to the File Folder type. Doing so will run you headlong into an acknowledged bug, as a result of which the default action for folders will change from *open* or *explore* (or whatever else you might have chosen) to *find*. In short, every time you double-click a folder in Windows Explorer, you'll get the Search Assistant.

A separate Knowledge Base article, 321186, (*http://support.microsoft.com/?kbid=321186*) tells you how to restore your previous default. But you can avoid all this hassle by following article 272623's instructions and modifying the shortcut menu for the Folder file type, instead of the File Folder file type.

Using Windows Explorer's Command-Line Syntax

Cascading folder menus, as described earlier in this chapter, are one way to open Windows Explorer with a particular folder displayed. But they might not be the ideal way. Compare the two views of the System32 folder shown in Figure 20-17. The one on the left was generated by a Start menu item; the one on the right was produced by means of Windows Explorer's command-line syntax.

The difference between the two is all in the Folders bar. The command-line string in this case puts the selected folder (System32) at the top of the folder hierarchy, eliminating all folders at higher levels and letting you focus your attention on System32.

This is one example of the usefulness of the Windows Explorer command-line syntax. You can probably find others in your own work. You can use Windows Explorer command strings in shortcuts, with the Start menu's Run command, at the command prompt, or in batch programs or scripts. The syntax is as follows:

```
explorer [/n | /e][,/root,object][[,/select],subobject]
```

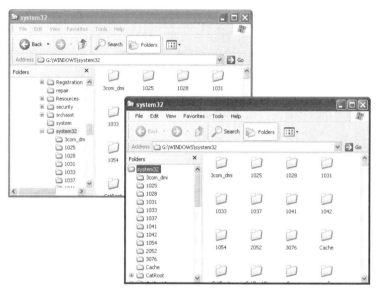

Figure 20-17. The view on the right, produced by a command string, restricts the Folders bar to a particular branch of the file structure.

The switches, all of which are optional, have the following effects:

Switch	Effect
/n	Opens without displaying the Folders bar.
/e	Opens with the Folders bar displayed.
/root,*object*	Restricts Windows Explorer to *object* and all folders contained within object.
/select,*subobject*	Gives the initial focus to the parent folder of *subobject* and selects *subobject*. If */Select* is omitted, *subobject* specifies the folder that gets the initial focus.

Let's look at some examples. To begin,

```
explorer /e,/root,%systemroot%\system32
```

opens Windows Explorer and displays the Folders bar, restricting the namespace to %SystemRoot%\System32 and its subfolders. (This is the syntax used to generate the window on the right side of Figure 20-17.)

To open %SystemRoot%\Cursors in Windows Explorer, with the Folders bar displayed and the file Appstart.ini selected, you must include the file name and extension in the command string, as follows:

```
explorer /e, /select,%systemroot%\cursors\appstart.ani
```

Typing the following opens %SystemRoot% without the Folders bar:

```
explorer %systemroot%
```

The folder is loaded as the subobject focus, not as the root folder—which means that you can navigate upward from %SystemRoot% in the folder hierarchy.

The string

```
explorer /n
```

opens the drive on which Windows XP is installed without displaying the Folders bar, whereas

```
explorer /e,.
```

opens %UserProfile% and displays the Folders bar.

Using GUIDs to Open Shell Folders in Windows Explorer

A GUID is a string of 32 hexadecimal digits enclosed within braces, with hyphens separating the digits into groups of eight, four, four, four, and twelve—like this:

```
{nnnnnnnn-nnnn-nnnn-nnnn-nnnnnnnnnnnn}
```

Windows XP uses GUIDs to identify all kinds of objects, including certain system folders. You can open the following GUIDs in Windows Explorer.

{208D2C60-3AEA-1069-A2D7-08002B30309D}	My Network Places
{20D04FE0-3AEA-1069-A2D8-08002B30309D}	My Computer
{2227A280-3AEA-1069-A2DE-08002B30309D}	Printers And Faxes
{645FF040-5081-101B-9F08-00AA002F954E}	Recycle Bin
{7007ACC7-3202-11D1-AAD2-00805FC1270E}	Network Connections
{D6277990-4C6A-11CF-8D87-00AA0060F5BF}	Scheduled Tasks

Tip **Open Windows Explorer on My Computer**

If you're one of the many Windows XP users who long for the days when Windows Explorer opened by default on My Computer, instead of My Documents, pine no more. Create a shortcut with either of the following command strings:

```
explorer.exe /e, ::{20D04FE0-3AEA-1069-A2D8-08002B30309D}
```

or

```
explorer.exe::{20D04FE0-3AEA-1069-A2D8-08002B30309D}
```

The first of these opens Windows Explorer with the Folders bar in place.

You might find it convenient to incorporate command strings that use GUIDs in shortcuts for opening Windows Explorer, or in batch programs or scripts. When you construct the command string, put a space after the word *explorer* and then two colons. Follow the colons immediately with the GUID, like this:

```
explorer ::{208D2C60-3AEA-1069-A2D7-08002B30309D}
```

If you use one or more of the optional switches (for example, /root,), follow the last character in the string with a space, then two colons, then the GUID, like this:

```
explorer /root, ::{208D2C60-3AEA-1069-A2D7-08002B30309D}
```

If you don't like typing GUIDs, you can copy them from the registry. In Registry Editor, navigate to HKCR\CLSID. Then use Edit, Find to locate search for the folder you want to open—My Network Places, for example. Registry Editor should find a key that has the GUID you want. (Compare it with the preceding table in this book to make sure you have the right one.) Select it and choose Edit, Copy Key Name. You'll be copying the full key path, of course, including My Computer\HKEY_CLASSES_ROOT\CLSID\. But you can edit out the parts you don't need when you paste this text into your command string. If you type the GUID yourself, you can use either capital or lowercase letters. The strings *3AEA* and *3aea* are equivalent, for example.

Chapter 21

Managing and Finding Files

Not long ago, when hard disk capacity was still measured in megabytes, the most serious file management problem facing the typical computer user was how to keep from running out of disk space. Now that disks offering tens and even hundreds of gigabytes are commonplace (and operating systems consume nearly a gigabyte), different issues have come to the fore. Although it might still be true that there's no such thing as a large enough hard disk, for most users, running out of space is a significantly smaller concern than it once was. What matters now is learning how to use storage resources effectively and knowing how to find crucial documents saved in these vast warehouses.

This chapter presents strategies for managing files effectively, discusses some of the file management tools provided by Microsoft Windows XP, and describes the operating system's powerful indexing and search facility. Windows XP Indexing Service comes with an elaborate query language that allows you to locate documents quickly based on their content or other properties. You don't have to master every detail of this language to make good use of the service, but the more you know about it the less likely it is that you'll ever lose an important document.

At Home with Windows XP

All the features described in this chapter work identically in Windows XP Professional and Windows XP Home Edition.

Seven Principles of Effective File Management

It's fashionable to present principles in multiples of seven. So here are our picks for seven principles of effective file management:

Use My Documents   For all the reasons outlined in Chapter 15 (see "Making It Easy to Open Your Favorite Documents," page 462), it's smart to take advantage of My Documents. Most of your applications will expect to save and retrieve documents from this folder anyway, so it's best to build your document storage structure (that is, your folders and subfolders) within the framework of My Documents. If you don't like where Windows XP has set up My Documents (the default location is %UserProfile%\My Documents, which is a subfolder on the drive where Windows is installed), you can move it (see "Moving Folders from the Standard Profile Locations," page 555).

Another virtue of My Documents is that it enforces a prudent separation of documents and executables. Storing documents where programs are stored risks accidental deletion when programs are uninstalled or upgraded. My Documents also discourages you from using your desktop as a document repository. You should use your Windows desktop the way you use your regular desktop—as a temporary surface. It's fine to store something there momentarily (an item downloaded from the Internet, for example, to be read or installed and then deleted or relocated). But if you pile up your everyday work there, you'll not only create visual clutter, you'll also deprive yourself of the organizational services (Details view and the Folders bar, for example) available in ordinary Windows Explorer folders.

Adopt consistent methods for file and folder naming   Both Windows XP Search Companion and Indexing Service can help you find anything. But you can save yourself a lot of trouble by working out a naming scheme for the kinds of documents you create most often and then sticking to that scheme.

Keep file names short   The long file names that Windows began allowing years ago brought welcome relief from the eight-character constraints of MS-DOS and early Windows days. But that doesn't mean you should use descriptive sentences in place of easy-to-recognize names. Long names produce cluttered or truncated displays. Brevity promotes clarity.

Let your folders do some of the naming. Rather than create a file called *Great American Novel Chapter One Fumbling First Effort.doc*, why not build a folder structure like this?

A structure like this can alleviate the temptation to use verbose file names.

Chapter 21

Segregate current and completed work   One way to simplify your storage system is to remove completed work, either by archiving it to an offline storage medium (a backup tape or recordable CD, for example) or by moving it to an archival subfolder. It's also an excellent idea to compress archived documents; even a huge hard disk eventually fills to capacity. For information about using file compression, see "Maximizing Storage Space with NTFS Compression and Compressed (Zipped) Folders," page 704.

Store like with like   Restricting folders to a single document type (or predominantly one type) allows you to take advantage of Windows Explorer's new folder templates and makes it easier for you to find documents you need later on. With all of your pictures for a given trip or time period in a single folder (and nothing else), for example, it's easy to use the new Filmstrip view and slide show feature to find the right picture for your newsletter.

Avoid flat folder structures   If you need to put so many subfolders in a folder that you can't see all of them at a glance in the Folders bar, consider creating an alphabetic menu, like the one shown in Figure 21-1.

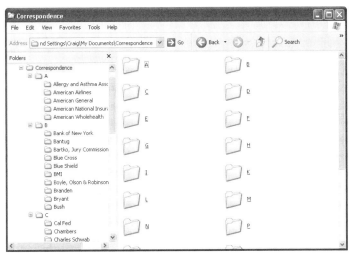

Figure 21-1.   An alphabetic menu can keep your folder structure from becoming too flat.

Use shortcuts and OLE links instead of multiple document copies   If you need to be able to get to the same document from multiple locations, don't create copies of the document. Create shortcuts to it instead. For details, see "Creating and Customizing Document Shortcuts," page 701. Similarly, if you need to reuse boilerplate text in multiple documents, use your application's Paste Link command, instead of its normal Paste command. The resulting object linking and embedding (OLE) link stores a pointer in your document to the boilerplate source. If you change the source, all the documents with links to the source are updated automatically.

Using Tools for File Management

You can move and copy files the same way you move and copy text within a document—by copying or cutting to the Clipboard and then pasting in a new location. But keep in mind that Windows also provides a wealth of tools that make file transfer even simpler, help you track document statistics, enable you to compress and decompress files, and perform other vital document management tasks.

Manipulating Files with the Folders Bar

When you're using Windows Explorer to move or copy files from one folder to another, particularly if the folders are widely separated in your folder hierarchy, the simplest method is often to display the Folders bar and drag the file or files with your mouse. Any folder in the Folders bar can serve as a "drop target." To move an item from Folder A to Folder B, display it in Folder A, display the Folders bar, then drag the item from Folder A and drop it on Folder B in the Folders bar.

Windows Explorer doesn't display the Folders bar by default. You can make it appear by clicking Folders on the Standard Buttons toolbar or by choosing View, Explorer Bar, Folders.

> **Note** The Folders bar is a little easier to work with in Windows XP than it was in earlier versions of Windows. For more information, see "Navigating the Folders Bar in Simple Folder View," page 657.

Inside Out

Use Ctrl+Z to reverse accidental bulk renaming

If you select a group of items in Windows Explorer and then click File, Rename or press F2, it will appear as though you are about to rename only the last item you selected. After you type a new name and press Enter, however, you will find that all items in the selection have acquired the new name—with numbers in parentheses to distinguish one renamed item from another. For example, select three files with dissimilar names, press F2, type **NewName**, and then press Enter. Your three files will be named *NewName*, *NewName (1)*, and *NewName (2)*.

This bulk-renaming behavior is new in Windows XP and might come as a surprise to some users. If you accidentally rename a folder full of files when you mean to rename only one, press Ctrl+Z (or choose Edit, Undo Rename). The last of your files to be renamed (*NewName (2)* in the example just given) will regain its former name. Press Ctrl+Z again and another file will revert. Continue in this manner until all but the intended files have shed their new names.

Inspecting and Setting File Properties

The properties dialog box for a file or folder (or a selection of files or folders) provides a wealth of useful information about the selected item or items. To display this information, right-click the item and choose Properties from the shortcut menu. The kind of information you will see depends on the type of item you have selected. Figure 21-2 shows the General tab of the properties dialog box for the Microsoft Word document used to generate this chapter (while the chapter was still under construction).

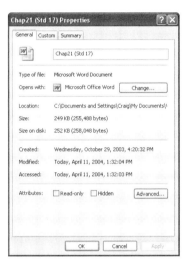

Figure 21-2. The General tab of a document's properties dialog box reports file size, creation date, attributes, and parent application.

As you can see, this part of the properties dialog box provides information about the file's size, location, dates, parent application, and other attributes. There's even a button you can use to change the parent application (Change), should you need to do that. For other and simpler ways to change the association between a document and an application, see "Changing the Application Associated with a File Type," page 680.

Most of the properties shown on the General tab are read-only (that is, they're set by the operating system and can't be changed by you), and you can get most of this information easily enough in Windows Explorer, without displaying the properties dialog box. The Summary and Custom tabs, for documents whose properties dialog box includes these tabs, provide less readily available details and include properties whose value you can set yourself. Figure 21-3 shows the Advanced view of the Summary tab and Figure 21-4 shows the Custom tab for our Word document.

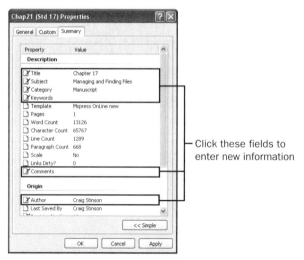

Click these fields to
enter new information

Figure 21-3.   Some of the properties on the Summary tab can be modified at will.

Note   If the Summary tab for a properties dialog box looks significantly different from Figure 21-3 and you see an Advanced button, click Advanced. The Advanced presentation of the Summary tab provides access to more properties than does the Simple presentation.

It might not be obvious from looking at a Summary tab which properties are read-only and which can be set or changed by you. If you're not sure about a property, click on it in the Value column. If the property can be set, an edit box will appear.

As Figure 21-4 shows, the Custom tab lets you create your own properties and set their values. The Name list, shown open in Figure 21-4, enumerates suggested custom properties. But you can type whatever name you want in the Name box. After you provide a value for the item, the Add button becomes available for you to add the property to the file.

Applications that provide user-editable properties, such as Word, provide access to those properties within their own menu systems. In Word, for example, you can choose File, Properties to set the value of properties, such as Title, Subject, and Category, for the current document. But the properties dialog box provides another route to those properties, one that is worth knowing about from a file management perspective.

Tip   Use Indexing Service to locate files by property values
You can use Indexing Service and its query language to look for files on the basis of property values. For example, you can search for all files whose Category property has the value *Manuscript*. For more information, see "Using Indexing Service and Query Language," page 724.

Figure 21-4. You can use the Custom tab to create your own properties and set their values.

Using Details View to See and Compare Properties of Many Files

The most important properties available via the properties dialog box can also be displayed as columns in Windows Explorer's Details view. Details view also lets you sort files on the basis of their property values—from largest to smallest, oldest to newest, and so on.

For more information about customizing Details view, see "Customizing Details View," page 664.

Creating and Customizing Document Shortcuts

Document shortcuts let you open documents from places other than where those documents are stored—from your desktop, for example. (We don't advocate storing documents on the desktop, but using the desktop for shortcuts to documents you're currently involved with is not a bad idea—provided you get rid of the shortcuts when you no longer need them, and provided you don't have security concerns about others who might have access to your computer.)

The simplest way to create a desktop shortcut to a document is as follows:

1. Display the document in Windows Explorer. (Windows Explorer should not be maximized.)

2. Hold down the Alt key and drag the document to your desktop.

3. Rename the shortcut, removing the words *Shortcut to* (an optional step). The small arrow at the lower left of the icon indicates that you're looking at a shortcut.

Chapter 21

701

After you have a shortcut on your desktop, you can assign a keyboard shortcut to it. (As you see, the word *shortcut* can mean many things in Windows.) This keyboard shortcut to your shortcut is a keystroke combination that lets you "run" the shortcut (that is, open the document in its parent application) without first hunting for it on the desktop. To assign a keyboard shortcut, follow these steps:

1 Right-click the shortcut, choose Properties from the shortcut menu, and then click the Shortcut tab.

2 Type a letter or other character in the Shortcut Key box. Windows will prefix your keystroke with Ctrl+Alt+. If you prefer another key combination, you're free to type combinations of Ctrl, Alt, and Shift with your keyboard character.

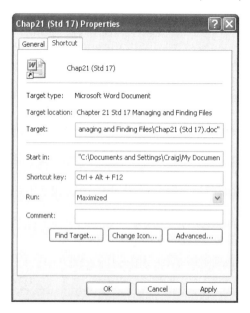

3 While you're in the properties dialog box, you can also use the Run box to tell Windows how you want the document and its parent application to open—minimized, normal, or maximized.

Tip **Test your shortcut's shortcut**

Not all combinations of Ctrl and Alt and a letter or function key can be used in keyboard shortcuts. Those that conflict with existing shortcuts, for example, are disallowed. Rather than try to learn and memorize which ones you can and can't use, just test your shortcut before relying on it. If nothing happens when you type the combination, try another.

Chapter 21

> **Caution** Windows will let you assign keyboard shortcuts to document shortcuts stored in folders other than the desktop. But they won't work.

Protecting Files with the Read-Only Attribute

If you have documents on your hard disk that you keep only for reference—documents that you have no need to change or that must not be changed—it's a good idea to make them read-only. If you edit and then attempt to save a read-only document, your application will present its Save As dialog box, prompting you to supply a new file name and ensuring that the original file remains unmodified.

To give a file read-only status, right-click it and choose Properties from the shortcut menu. On the General tab of the properties dialog box, select Read-Only.

Inside Out

Apply the read-only attribute to folder contents

A folder itself cannot be made read-only. Nevertheless, the properties dialog box for a folder does include a read-only check box. You can use this check box to set or clear the read-only attribute for all *existing* files in the selected folder. This action has no bearing on files that you create subsequently.

In most cases, when you open the properties dialog box for a folder, the Read-Only check box will contain a green square. This indicates either a mixed or undetermined condition. Windows displays this green square because it would take too long to check the state of the read-only attribute for every file in the folder. To apply the read-only attribute to the contents of a folder, click the check box until a check mark appears. To clear the attribute, click the check box until it is empty. When you leave the dialog box, Windows asks whether you want to apply your action to subfolders and files. Be sure you select this option; if you select Apply Changes To This Folder Only, nothing at all happens.

> **Caution** Read-only files can be renamed, moved, deleted—and, of course, read. To keep other users from opening or deleting particular files, use the security features built into Windows XP. (For information about securing files, see Chapter 9, "Securing Files and Folders." For information about encrypting files, see Chapter 11, "Encrypting Confidential Information.") To protect against accidental deletion by yourself, make a backup. (For more information about avoiding accidental erasure of files, see "Using and Configuring the Recycle Bin," page 714.)

Maximizing Storage Space with NTFS Compression and Compressed (Zipped) Folders

Even a huge hard disk eventually fills to capacity. To help you avoid running out of room, Windows XP supports two forms of file compression: NTFS file compression and compressed (zipped) folders. The former, available only on disks formatted with the NTFS file system, is the same compression option offered in Windows 2000. The latter is an implementation of the industry-standard ZIP format (the compression format used by WinZip and other third-party programs). You can use either compression option or both. Here are some essential points to note about NTFS compression and zipped folders:

- NTFS compression achieves only a modest degree of compression but is extremely easy to use. After you have compressed a set of files and folders (or an entire NTFS disk), files look and behave exactly as before, in both Windows Explorer and in the dialog boxes of the applications you use. The only outwardly visible difference is that the names of your files are shown in blue. However, if you look at the properties dialog box for a compressed file, you'll see on the General tab that the Size On Disk value is (usually) considerably smaller than the Size value; with uncompressed files, the Size On Disk value is the same or slightly larger (because of the way disk space is allocated).

- Windows Explorer and your applications decompress NTFS-compressed files when you open them and recompress them when you save. This on-the-fly compression and decompression occurs so quickly that you shouldn't notice any performance effect.

- Files compressed via NTFS compression remain compressed only as long as they stay on NTFS disks. If you move a compressed file to a FAT32 disk or e-mail it, the file on the FAT32 disk or the one attached to your e-mail is expanded to normal size, making it compatible with other machines and other viewers' software.

- NTFS compression is incompatible with NTFS encryption. A file can be compressed or encrypted (or neither), but not both.

- You can get more dramatic compression with zipped folders than with NTFS compression. Moreover, a zipped folder stays compressed, no matter where it is. Thus zipped folders are an ideal way to compress large files for e-mailing or uploading to Internet sites.

- Because zipped folders use an industry-standard compression format, many of your associates will be able to work with your zipped folders, even if they don't use Windows.

- Windows Explorer compresses and decompresses files in zipped folders on the fly. But your applications do not. Therefore, you can open a ZIP-compressed file in its parent application by double-clicking it in Windows Explorer, but you can't open it using an application's Open command.

Because of the differences between the two compression methods, zipped folders are best used for the following purposes:

- For creating compressed archives of files that you no longer need on a regular basis
- For e-mailing large attachments or uploading documents to Internet sites
- For squeezing the maximum amount of free space out of a disk that's getting close to full

NTFS compression, on the other hand, is great for everyday work. You won't get a huge amount of space gain with it, but it's easy to set up and so simple to use that you'll probably forget you're using it.

Implementing NTFS Compression

NTFS compression is implemented by means of a file attribute, much as read-only status is. To compress a file or folder using NTFS compression, follow these steps:

1. Right-click the file or folder (or selection of files or folders) in Windows Explorer and choose Properties from the shortcut menu.
2. On the General tab of the properties dialog box, click Advanced.
3. Select Compress Contents To Save Disk Space and then click OK in both dialog boxes.

If you've selected a folder, you'll see this dialog box.

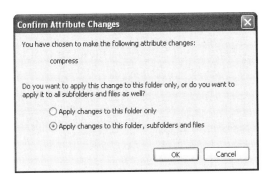

In most cases, you'll want to select the second option. If you apply the compression attribute to the current folder only, files that you subsequently add to the folder will be compressed, but the files that are already there will not be.

You can compress an entire NTFS drive at once. Doing this might tie up your computer for several hours (during which time performance in other programs will be seriously degraded), but you only need to do it once. If you plan to leave the computer unattended while Windows is compressing files, be sure to close all running programs. Windows can't compress files that are open, and if it comes to one that it can't compress, it will idle until you tell it what to do (you can close the file and tell it to try again, or you can tell it to skip the open file and go on). You don't want to come back in the morning and find that the system has been waiting all night for your decision.

Using Zipped Folders

If you have experience with the WinZip program, you're probably familiar with the concept of an archive—a collection of files that are compressed and combined into a single file. In WinZip, you can extract (decompress) files from an archive individually or all at once, and you can add new files to existing archives. The archive itself, in Windows Explorer, might look like this.

Using zipped folders, the same archive looks like this.

Windows Explorer represents the archive as a folder, displaying the folder with a special icon. To see what's in the archive, simply open the folder. To read a file in the archive, double-click it, just as you would double-click a file in a normal Windows Explorer folder. If the file is a document associated with an application, Windows Explorer starts the application, and the application opens a read-only copy of your document. If the item you double-click is executable, it runs—unless it requires additional files that are also compressed. In that situation, you need to *extract* (decompress) all the necessary files first, and then run or install the compressed program (see "Extracting Files and Folders from an Archive," page 711).

Creating a new zipped folder   To create a new archive using zipped folders, follow these steps:

1 In Windows Explorer, display the folder in which you want the new archive to reside.
2 Right-click empty space in the folder.
3 From the shortcut menu, choose New, Compressed (Zipped) Folder.
4 Type a meaningful name for the folder.

Chapter 21

Adding files and folders to a zipped folder   To add files and folders to your archive, simply copy or move them into the zipped folder. If you copy, you then have a compressed version of the copied object inside the zipped folder and the original version outside. If you move, you have only the compressed version—and you free up some space on your disk. Note that Windows Explorer copies by default if you drag files into a compressed folder. If you want to move files or folders, hold down the right mouse button while dragging, then choose Move from the shortcut menu. Or simply cut and paste and items.

Archiving files with the Send To command   You can create an archive and copy one or more files or folders to it in one step by using the Send To command. To compress a single file or folder, follow these steps:

1   Right-click the file or folder.
2   From the shortcut menu, choose Send To, Compressed (Zipped) Folder.

    Windows creates an archive with the same name as the selected object.

To compress a group of files or folders, follow these steps:

1   Select everything you want to compress.
2   Right-click one of the selected objects.
3   From the shortcut menu, choose Send To, Compressed (Zipped) Folder.

The new archive will have the same name as the object you right-clicked. You can then use the Rename command (or press F2) if that's not the name you want to use.

Protecting an archive with a password   The ZIP format supports the use of passwords to prevent unauthorized parties from extracting compressed objects from an archive. If you have used WinZip to assign passwords to archives, Windows XP recognizes and enforces those passwords when you extract objects from the protected archive.

To password-protect a new archive that you create using zipped folders, follow these steps:

1   Select any file in the zipped folder (not the folder itself).
2   Click File, Add A Password, and then complete the Add Password dialog box.

These steps apply the same password to every file in the archive. If the archive includes folders, their contents are password protected as well.

Be aware that new files added to a password-protected zipped folder do not inherit the password. To add password protection to a new file, first remove the current password from all other files in the archive (select any file, choose File, Remove Password, and then complete the Password Needed dialog box). Then add the new file and reinstate your password, using the same procedure you used to create it in the first place.

Chapter 21

707

Using WinZip and Zipped Folders

You can use WinZip *and* zipped folders. If you have WinZip installed on your system, your archives will be displayed either with the WinZip icon or the zipped-folder icon, depending on how you have the association for ZIP files set. If your archives look like folders with zippers, then the default application for ZIP files is Compressed (Zipped) Folder. You can change it to WinZip as follows:

1 In Windows Explorer, click Tools, Folder Options.

2 Click the File Types tab.

3 In the Registered Files Types box, select ZIP. You'll see the following screen.

4 Click Restore. (Alternatively, click Change. Then click WinZip Executable in the Open With dialog box.)

If you have WinZip installed and you leave Compressed (Zipped) Folder as the default application for archives, you will still have access to all the commands that WinZip adds to the shortcut menu for files and folders. And you can still open a zipped folder in WinZip—by right-clicking the folder and choosing Open With, WinZip Executable.

You can disable the zipped folders feature altogether if it interferes with your familiar use of WinZip of a similar program. To do that, at a command prompt type **regsvr32 /u zipfldr.dll**. If you later change your mind and want to reenable Windows XP's built-in support for zipped folders, type **regsvr32 zipfldr.dll** at a command prompt.

Chapter 21

Caution Assigning a password to an archive prevents unauthorized users from extracting (opening) its files. But it does not prevent anyone from opening the zipped folder itself and reading the file names. If the file names reveal confidential information, don't rely on zipped-folder password protection. Password-protecting an archive also does not prevent anyone from deleting objects from the archive. Note, too, that files deleted from a zipped folder do not go to the Recycle Bin, so they are not retrievable.

Inside Out

Be aware that temporary files are not password protected

Windows creates temporary hidden folders during the extraction process. These folders, which contain uncompressed versions of the extracted items, are deleted when you close the zipped folder. If Windows Explorer stops responding for any reason before you have closed an archive, the temporary folders remain on your hard disk, in the parent folder of the zipped folder. Files that were password protected in the archive are not protected in these temporary folders. If Windows Explorer crashes while you work with a zipped folder, be sure to delete the hidden temporary folders.

Working with files and folders in a zipped folder Figure 21-5 shows a zipped folder in Details view, along with the Choose Details dialog box (choose View, Choose Details). In the figure, the task pane has been replaced by the Folders bar.

As you can see, Details view for a zipped folder can offer some useful information about each file. Depending on what you select in the Choose Details box, you can display many properties, including the original and compressed sizes (Size and Packed Size), the compression ratio (Ratio), and whether files have passwords (Has A Password). If you see low numbers in the Ratio column (some file types are much more compressible than others), you might decide that zipping isn't worth the trouble.

Note You can use Search Companion to look for file names within zipped folders. But you can't search for file *content* (specific words or phrases within files) in zipped folders. (For more information about Search Companion, see "Locating Files with Search Companion," page 718.)

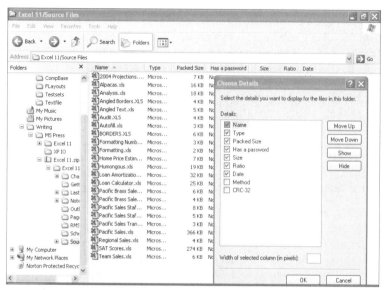

Figure 21-5. Windows Explorer displays an archive's contents as though they resided in a normal folder. The folder itself is a file with the extension .zip.

Inside Out

Be careful where you save a compressed document after editing

When you open a compressed document by double-clicking in Windows Explorer, Windows extracts the document to a temporary hidden folder (a subfolder of %Temp%), then passes a read-only copy of the uncompressed file to its parent application. If you edit the file, you'll need to use Save As, not Save, to preserve your changes. The Save As dialog box might not make it obvious that the proposed folder for your Save As is not the zipped folder from which you opened the original file. Some applications (Microsoft Excel, for example) will actually propose to save the edited version in the temporary folder to which the original file was (temporarily) extracted. If you save your edited file in that location, and you don't happen to have Windows Explorer set to display hidden files and folders, you'll run the risk of being unable to find the file subsequently. To avoid cluttering your disk with hidden temporary files and losing track of files you do want to keep, be sure to save your edits to a working folder.

Although Windows does its best to make them look like ordinary folders in Windows Explorer, your zipped folders are really disguised .zip files, not regular file folders. Therefore, you can't save directly from an application into a zipped folder. If you need to edit a document after opening it from a zipped folder, the best thing to do is extract it to some handy location, such as the desktop. Then, when you have finished, drag the document from its new location back into the zipped folder and confirm the overwrite of your original compressed file.

Extracting Files and Folders from an Archive   To extract a single object or selection of objects from a zipped folder, drag the selection out of the folder—onto your desktop or into another folder. To delete the compressed copy or copies at the same time, right-drag the selection and then choose Move Here from the shortcut menu. To extract all items from a zipped folder, select the folder and click File, Extract All. A wizard will prompt you for a destination folder.

Copying Files to CDs

You don't need special software to write files to a disk in your CD-R or CD-RW drive. The simplest procedure is as follows:

1   Insert a blank CD into the drive (or a CD-RW disk that you're ready to erase and overwrite).

2   Right-click a file or folder, or a selection of files or folders, that you want to copy to a CD.

3   From the shortcut menu, choose Send To, CD Drive.

4   Repeat these steps for all of the items that you want to copy.

5   Open your CD drive in My Computer.

6   Click Write These Files To CD in the task pane, or choose File, Write These Files To CD.

> For information about setting up and configuring a writable or rewritable CD drive, as well as information about using third-party CD burning software, see "Working with Writable and Rewritable CD Drives," page 779.

As an alternative to using the Send To command, you can drag files into the Windows Explorer folder for your CD drive. Or you can use the Copy and Paste commands.

When you copy files and folders into the CD drive's folder, by whatever means, Windows prepares them for transfer to a writable CD. The CD folder becomes, in effect, a staging area for the eventual CD burn. While files are being copied to the staging area, you might see a dialog box like this one.

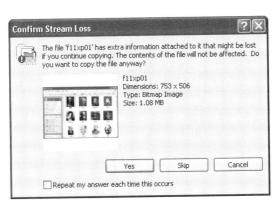

Chapter 21

With some files, Windows Explorer maintains *metadata*—data about the file's data. This information—the dimensions of a graphic image, for example, or the bit rate of an audio file—cannot be copied to the CD. When you see a Confirm Stream Loss dialog box like the one shown on the previous page, your choices are to skip the file or copy it without its metadata. You can also select the check box to keep Windows from displaying similar messages during the current copy process.

After you have moved some files to the CD folder, the folder will look something like Figure 21-6.

Click one of these links to write the CD or to clear files and start over

This banner appears regardless of the view you select

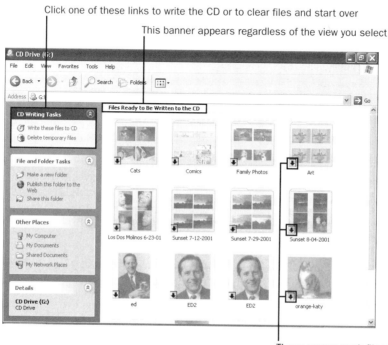

These arrows mark files that are ready to be written to CD

Figure 21-6. Windows adds a downward arrow to the icons for files and folders about to be written to a CD.

Notice that the CD folder does not tell you the total size of the objects in the staging area. (Even if you display the status bar and select everything in the folder, it doesn't provide this information.) To find out whether you're about to try copying more data than will fit on the intended CD, press Ctrl+A, and then right-click an item and choose Properties from the shortcut menu. For your files to fit on a standard CD, this total should be less than 650 MB. With a high-capacity CD, you can go as high as 850 MB.

Inside Out

Make sure that you have plenty of disk space

Burning CDs with Windows XP gobbles up alarming amounts of disk space and demands careful attention if you want to avoid "low disk space" errors. When you drag files or folders into the CD drive window and add them to the Files Ready To Be Written To The CD list, Windows makes a copy of each file in the %UserProfile%\Local Settings\Application Data\Microsoft\CD Burning folder. If you're planning to fill a 700-MB CD with files that are already stored on your computer, that means you'll use up an additional 700 MB of space just making these copies. Then, when you go to write the CD, Windows creates a CD image from the files stored in the CD Burning folder, using an additional chunk of space on a drive or volume you specify in the CD drive properties dialog box. This file, which is hidden, appears in the root of the specified drive under the name CD Burning Stash File. Although Windows cleans up after itself after writing the CD, the net effect causes your system to use temporary space equal to approximately twice the size of the files you plan to copy.

Windows XP writes audio CDs in the Red Book format and data CDs in a combination of the ISO 9660 and Joliet formats. This means that audio CDs can be played in conventional audio CD players and data CDs can be read on systems running other operating systems (Macintosh, for example) and older versions of Windows or MS-DOS.

When you click Write These Files To CD, the CD Writing Wizard appears.

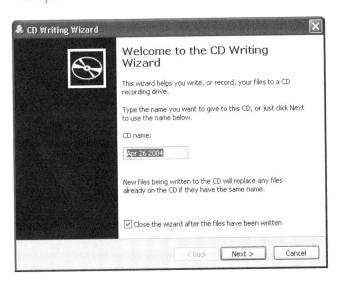

> **Tip** Calculate total data size before you start copying
>
> If you try to copy more data than will fit, the CD Writing Wizard, which manages the burning process, will complain immediately and make you remove some files from the staging folder. In other words, the wizard isn't able to copy as many files as will fit, saving the rest for a second CD. So you might as well save yourself some hassle and figure out in advance whether you've overshot the limit.

On the wizard's first page, you can type a name for the CD. The name you supply—it can be up to 16 characters in length—will help you identify the CD's contents when you open it later in Windows Explorer.

Inside Out

Use a PowerToy to generate CD slide shows

If you save photos or other images to a CD, you can view them as a slide show, just as you can with photos on your hard disk—by clicking View As A Slide Show in the task pane. Users of earlier versions of Windows don't have this snazzy feature, so if you share the CD with them, they'll need an image-viewing application. However, if you install the CD Slide Show Generator, a free PowerToy you can download the Microsoft PowerToys site at *http://www.microsoft.com/windowsxp/pro/downloads/powertoys.asp*, the CD Writing Wizard includes an extra step, which offers to add a picture viewer to the CD. If you choose to include it on the CD, the picture viewer runs automatically when the CD is inserted into a computer running Windows 95 or later.

Using and Configuring the Recycle Bin

The Recycle Bin provides protection against accidental erasure of files. In most cases, when you delete one or more files or folders, the deleted items go to the Recycle Bin, not into the ether. If you change your mind, you can go to the bin and recover the thrown-out items. Eventually, when the bin fills up, Windows begins emptying it, permanently deleting the files that have been there the longest.

The following kinds of deletions do not go to the Recycle Bin:

- Files stored on removable disks
- Files stored on network drives
- Files deleted from compressed (zipped) folders

You can bypass the Recycle Bin yourself, permanently deleting an item, by holding down the Shift key while you press the Delete key. You might want to do this if you need to get rid of some very large files and you're sure you'll never want these files back. Skipping the Recycle Bin in this case will reclaim some disk space.

You can also turn off the Recycle Bin's services permanently. (For more details, see "Disabling the Recycle Bin," on the next page.)

> **Tip** **Search the Recycle Bin**
>
> In earlier versions of Windows, Search Assistant ignored the Recycle Bin. This is no longer the case. To include deleted files in your search, be sure to choose Search Companion's All Files And Folders option. For more information, see "Locating Files with Search Companion," page 718.

Changing the Amount of Space Allocated to the Recycle Bin

Although the Recycle Bin folder (the place where you can see which files have been deleted and from which you can restore deleted files) lists deletions from all local hard drives together, Windows actually maintains separate recycling stores for each drive. By default, when a drive's recycling store reaches 10 percent of the overall capacity of the drive, Windows begins deleting the oldest files from that store permanently. If 10 percent seems like too much (or too little) space to devote to accident prevention, you can specify a different figure, following these steps:

1. Right-click the Recycle Bin icon on the desktop.
2. Choose Properties from the shortcut menu.
3. To specify a new maximum limit that will be applied to all local hard disk drives, make sure that Use One Setting For All Drives is selected on the Global tab, as shown in Figure 21-7. Then move the slider to the left or right.

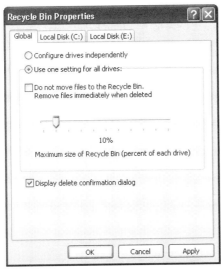

Figure 21-7. Windows normally devotes a maximum of 10 percent of a disk's size to the Recycle Bin.

4 If instead you want to configure your drives' recycling capacities independently, select Configure Drives Independently. Then adjust the slider on each drive's tab.

Disabling the Recycle Bin

If you'd rather do without the Recycle Bin, select Do Not Move Files To The Recycle Bin in the Recycle Bin Properties dialog box. This action is equivalent to setting the maximum capacity to 0 percent, and you can do this for all drives or only particular ones.

Suppressing Confirmation Prompts

Whether the Recycle Bin is enabled or disabled, Windows normally displays a confirmation prompt when you delete something. If that prompt annoys you, go to the Global tab of the Recycle Bin Properties dialog box and clear the Display Delete Confirmation Dialog check box. Unlike the actions just described, disabling the confirmation prompt is something you can only do globally.

To restore an item, select it and then click Restore This Item in the task pane. (If the task pane isn't visible, choose File, Restore.)

Restoring Files and Folders

When you open the Recycle Bin, Windows displays the names of recently deleted items in an ordinary Windows Explorer window, as shown in Figure 21-8. In Details view, you can see when each item was deleted and which folder it was deleted from. You can use the column headings to sort the folder—for example, to display the items that have been in the bin the longest at the top, with more recent arrivals below.

Note that deleted folders are shown only as folders; you don't see the names of items contained within the folder. If you restore a deleted folder, however, Windows re-creates the folder and its contents.

The Restore command puts the item back in the folder from which it was deleted. If that folder doesn't currently exist, Windows asks your permission to re-create it.

If you want, you can restore a file or folder to a different location. Select the item, choose Edit, Move To Folder, and then specify the new location. (Alternatively, you can drag an item out of the Recycle Bin and drop it wherever you want it.)

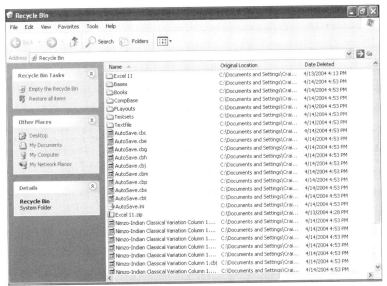

Figure 21-8.   You can get useful information about deleted items by looking at the Recycle Bin's columns in Details view.

Purging the Recycle Bin

A deleted file sitting in your Recycle Bin takes up as much space as it did before it was deleted. If you're deleting files to free up space for new programs and documents, transferring them to the Recycle Bin won't help. You need to remove them permanently. The safest way to do this is to move the items to another storage medium—a different hard disk or a removable disk, for example.

If you're sure you'll never need a particular file again, however, you can delete it in the normal way and then purge it from the Recycle Bin. Display the Recycle Bin, select the item, and then press Delete. (Alternatively, you can simply press Shift+Delete to erase the file without sending it to the Recycle Bin.)

To empty the Recycle Bin entirely, right-click the Recycle Bin icon on your desktop and choose Empty Recycle Bin from the shortcut menu. Or display the Recycle Bin and click Empty The Recycle Bin in the task pane.

Locating Files with Search Companion

The first time you call upon Search Companion—by choosing Start, Search, or by pressing F3 in a Windows Explorer window—you might be greeted by Rover, the search dog. He is friendly—and he's optional. If you'd rather go it alone, without Rover, click Change Preferences. (You might have to scroll the search pane to find this command; it's at the bottom of the menu.) Then click Without An Animated Screen Character.

On the other hand, if you like animated screen characters, you can retain Rover or try one of the several other characters that Windows offers. To review the cast, click Change Preferences, then click With A Different Character. Use the Next and Back buttons to move through the list.

Your decision about whether or not to use an animated character has no bearing on available search options. If you choose Without An Animated Screen Character, the choices in the task pane stay the same as they were before. About the only link you won't find is the Do A Trick link you see when you click on an animated character.

If you're used to searching in earlier versions of Windows, the searching options presented by Windows XP Search Companion will be a bit unfamiliar to you. You can re-create a look that more closely resembles that of Windows 2000 Search Assistant as follows.

1 Click Change Preferences.

2 Click Change Files And Folders Search Behavior.

3 Select the Advanced option and click OK.

In the advanced mode, the user interface is different (and perhaps more congenial, if you're a Windows veteran). But the standard and advanced styles both offer the same choices. Only the presentation is different. (The examples in the remainder of this chapter assume that you chose the standard mode.)

Specifying a Search Type

Search Companion can perform three basic kinds of file searches:

- Digital media
- Documents
- All files and folders

Each of these search types entails a set of defaults about where and how the companion should do its work. You can override some of the defaults. In addition, you can perform any search with or without the help of Indexing Service. We'll look at indexed searches later in this chapter (see "Using Indexing Service and Query Language," page 724).

In addition to these forms of file search, Search Companion offers links that enable you to search for computers on your network, people in your Address Book or Active Directory, or Internet resources. By clicking Computers Or People in Search Companion's first screen, for example, and then clicking A Computer On This Network, you can display the names of all shares on the specified network resource to which your account has access. (Double-click the name of a computer when it appears in the Search Results window to see the names of available shares.)

Searching for Digital Media

To search for digital media, choose Start, Search. Then click Pictures, Music, or Video. The following search pane appears.

You can select any, all, or none of these three check boxes. If you select zero, two, or three check boxes, Search Companion searches all digital media folders before looking at other folders on your hard disk. If you select one, the companion looks first at folders of the selected type. For example, if you select Music, the companion begins by searching music folders.

Other default characteristics of a media search include the following:

- Search Companion examines all document and system folders on all local hard disks, after first looking at folders of the specified media type.
- Search Companion does not look at hidden files and folders.
- Search Companion looks at metadata as well as file names.

The last of these attributes is extremely useful. Although the names of performing artists might not appear in the file names of your music files, for example, you can search for all tracks by a given performer by entering the performer's name in the All Or Part Of The File Name box. You can also enter a genre description in this box or a phrase from a song's lyrics (if lyrics appear in the song's properties dialog box). Figure 21-9 shows the results of a genre search. When searching for photos, you can specify the dimensions of the photo. Type **162 x 200** in the All Or Part Of The File Name box, for example, and the companion will find all pictures measuring 162 pixels by 200 pixels. (Be sure to leave a single space before and after the *x* in the size specification.)

Figure 21-9. Search Companion can locate all music files of a given genre or by a specified performer.

Searching for Documents

To search for documents, choose Search on the Start menu. Then click Documents (Word Processing, Spreadsheet, Etc.). You'll see the following search pane.

The option buttons let you restrict the search to documents last modified within a particular time range. Leave Don't Remember selected to search without regard for modification date. A document search has the following default characteristics:

- Search Companion begins with My Documents and its subfolders and then searches the remainder of your local hard disks.
- Search Companion omits system folders.
- Search Companion omits hidden files.
- Search Companion looks only for files that can be created by end users employing registered applications.

The last point is the crucial difference between a document search and a search for all files. When you search for documents, you get documents only—no folders, no executables, no configuration files, no help files. Use this option to look for your own work, Web pages that you've downloaded, saved e-mail files, and so on. If for some reason the companion fails to turn up a file that you think the Documents option should find, then try searching for all files.

Inside Out

Disregard the duplicates

Search Companion consistently generates duplicate entries for files using its Documents option. Typically a file located in My Documents appears once in the folder My Documents and a second time in the folder %UserProfile%\My Documents. These are, of course, alternative formulations for the same folder, but Search Companion reports its contents twice.

Searching for All Files and Folders

To search for anything and everything, choose Search from the Start menu. Then click All Files And Folders. The following search pane appears.

You can search by file name or by file content—or both. If you specify a file name, Search Companion locates items whose names include your search string. (In other words, there's an implicit asterisk wildcard before and after whatever you type.) If you search for content, you'll find the going slow, unless Indexing Service is turned on and has had time to complete the catalog of your disks. For more information about Indexing Service, see "Using Indexing Service and Query Language," page 724.

If you change any of the settings under the More Advanced Options when performing an all files search, Search Companion retains those settings the next time you perform an all files search. For example, if you always want to search system folders (including Recycle Bin),

Chapter 21

always want to include hidden files and folders, and always want your searches to be case-sensitive, you can set up Search Companion's advanced options the way you want them—and then trust that Search Companion will remember your preferences. Note, however, that this advice applies only to all-files searches. Media and document searches maintain their default settings from search to search. You can override the defaults for any given search (see "Overriding Defaults," on the next page), but your choices will be forgotten the next time you reopen Search Companion.

Searching for Network Files

To search for files located on network shares, open the Look In list in Search Companion's second pane. Click the Browse link at the bottom of the Look In list. Then, in the Browse For Folder dialog box, click My Network Places.

Refining a Search

After Search Companion finishes carrying out a search for you, it asks whether you'd like to "refine" your search. You might expect that a refined search would search the current search results, using more restrictive criteria. In Search Companion, that's not what it means. Search Companion is simply giving you the opportunity to search again. It retains your previous criteria, on the assumption that you will give it additional criteria (telling it to look in more locations, for example), but it doesn't limit the search to the current result set.

Note An all-files search does not look at metadata associated with media files.

Troubleshooting

Windows Search doesn't find a file—even when you know it's there.

When you search based on file content by entering text in the A Word Or Phrase In The File box, the results might be incomplete. That's because, for this type of search, Windows relies on Indexing Service, which catalogs only certain types of files. (For a list of the file types, see "Limitations of Indexing Service," page 725.) In the initial release of Windows XP, even text files with certain common extensions were not cataloged; this problem was resolved with the installation of Service Pack 1 for Windows XP. For more information, including a registry workaround to enable searching of other file types, see Microsoft Knowledge Base article 309173, "Using the 'A Word or Phrase in the File' Search Criterion May Not Work."

Overriding Defaults

After you've made your choice of search type in Search Companion's first pane—media, document, or all files, for example—the second pane appears, in which you specify search criteria. Here you can override the default characteristics associated with your search. (With media and document searches, you might have to click More Advanced Options in this second pane to see the full range of choices available.) The options at your disposal here allow you to do the following:

- Specify file content (a word or phrase contained in the file)
- Specify particular folders or disks to search, excluding others
- Specify a date range (the companion examines the date a file was most recently modified and returns files that fall within your specified range)
- Specify file size parameters
- Include or exclude system folders
- Include or exclude hidden files and folders
- Include or exclude subfolders of the disk or folders you ask to search
- Make the search case sensitive (it is not, by default)
- Search a backup tape

When you choose an all files search, one additional option also appears—the option to specify a file type. You can limit your search to any of the file types registered on your system.

Saving and Reusing Search Criteria

To preserve the criteria that you've used in a search operation for future use, choose File, Save Search. Search Companion creates a Saved Search file (in My Documents by default). To search again with the same criteria, double-click this file, and then click Search.

Using Indexing Service and Query Language

Created for and first delivered with Microsoft Internet Information Services (IIS), Indexing Service is a feature originally designed to facilitate fast and flexible searches for information stored on Web sites. Because its query technology can be applied to ordinary disk storage as well as to Web sites, Indexing Service has become a core component of Windows (beginning with Windows 2000) and is integrated with Search Companion.

Indexing Service extends the power of Search Companion in several ways. First, it can speed up searching dramatically. How much performance gain you'll see depends on many circumstances. But in tests for this book, we often found that some content searches ran on the order of a hundred times faster with Indexing Service than without it.

Chapter 21

Second, Indexing Service's query language lets you find files on the basis of many different properties in addition to the size, date, and file type. With Indexing Service enabled, Search Companion can locate a file on the basis of word count, most recent editor, most recent printing time, and many other attributes.

> For a list of the most useful properties that can be included in Indexing Service queries, see Table 21-1, page 729.

In addition, the query language offers Boolean operators and the ability to find inflected forms of search strings. The Boolean operators allow you to specify more than one criterion in a search (all files written by Bill containing the words *Windows XP*, for example). The ability to find inflected word forms means that, for example, a search for *swim* will also show instances of *swimming*, *swam*, and *swum*.

Security and Indexing Service

Indexing Service obeys the rules of NTFS file security. If a *catalog* (the collection of files used by Indexing Service to record the contents and properties of your files) resides on a local NTFS disk, the access privileges of the user executing a search determine the results of that search. The service will not return the names of files for which the user does not have at least Read access permission. If the catalog is stored on a network drive accessed by means of a Universal Naming Convention (UNC) path, the user might see the names of files for which he or she lacks Read permission but will not be able to open any such files.

By default, Indexing Service creates its catalogs in folders to which only the System account has access. This precaution prevents accidental deletion. More important, it helps maintain security. As long as the default access permissions for the catalog folder are not changed by an administrator, you can be assured that the catalog files themselves are not subject to unauthorized inspection.

Indexing Service never indexes encrypted documents. If a file is encrypted after being indexed, the service removes it from the catalog.

Limitations of Indexing Service

Does using Indexing Service have drawbacks? Not many. But here are some things you should know:

- **Indexing Service requires disk space.**   Because Indexing Service catalogs your disks in the background, during periods when your computer is idle, you don't pay a performance penalty for running the service. You do, however, sacrifice some disk space. Microsoft estimates that the catalog will consume from 15 to 30 percent of the size of the indexed files. Prudence suggests assuming the higher figure is more accurate.

- **Indexing Service catalogs the content of only certain kinds of files.**   By default, Indexing Service catalogs the content of the following document types:
  - HTML files (their text)
  - Text files
  - Documents created by Microsoft Office (version 95 and later)
  - Any other document type for which a suitable filter is installed

  A *filter* tells Indexing Service how to separate meaningful text from file headers, formatting information, and all other nontextual elements. Microsoft provides filters for HTML, text, Office, and mail and news documents. Third parties might provide filters for their own documents. If you use a non-Microsoft office suite, you might want to check with that product's vendor to see whether an Indexing Service filter is available.

  With an optional setting available via Indexing Service MMC console, you can set the service to index files with unknown extensions. (For details, see "Indexing Files with Unknown Extensions," page 735.) If you index files with unknown extensions, the service tries to extract meaningful content from file types other than the ones it catalogs by default.

- **Indexing Service ignores "noise" words.**   The list of words ignored by Indexing Service appears in the file %SystemRoot%\System32\Noise.*xxx*, where *xxx* is a three-letter abbreviation for the language you use. The file is plain text, and you can edit it with Notepad. The noise filter for English, Noise.eng, includes common prepositions and conjunctions, articles, relative pronouns, various forms of the verb *to be* and other common verbs, individual numerals, individual letters, and a handful of other frequently occurring words.

  If you include a noise word in a search string, the service treats that word as a placeholder. For example, in the search string "age before beauty," *before* is a noise word. Indexing Service will treat this string as equivalent to "age after beauty," "age without beauty," and so on.

- **Indexing Service ignores case.**   If Indexing Service is not running, Search Companion can perform case-sensitive content searches. With Indexing Service running, it can't.

- **Indexed searching is not always available, even if you have enabled Indexing Service.**   If the service hasn't finished building its initial catalog, or if it's busy updating the catalog, Search Companion simply dispenses with it, performing an ordinary (unindexed) search.

Activating Indexing Service

The simplest way to start Indexing Service (if it's not already started) is as follows:

1 Choose Search from the Start menu.
2 Click Change Preferences.
3 Click With Indexing Service.

If With Indexing Service doesn't appear on the menu (and Without Indexing Service appears instead), the service is already running. If the menu includes both With Indexing Service and Without Indexing Service, you don't have permission to start (or stop) the service. You need to have an administrator account to configure the service.

Before you can use Indexing Service for queries, the service needs time to generate a catalog. You should let it run overnight before relying on it for queries.

Submitting Index Queries

To use Indexing Service to look for files containing a particular word or phrase, type that word or phrase in the A Word Or Phrase In The File box in Search Companion. (If you're doing a media or document search, you will need to click Use Advanced Search Options to display this box.) To submit a more complex query, enter the query in this same box, but use the syntax of the query language, described in the following sections. Figure 21-10 shows an example of a query that returns all files whose DocAuthor property is Craig.

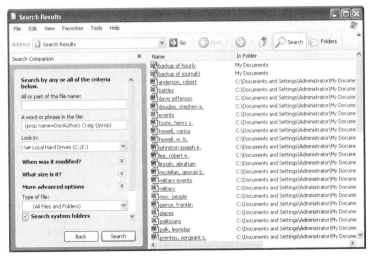

Figure 21-10.   To submit a query, type in the A Word Or Phrase In The File box.

When Search Companion begins searching, it should display the words *Searching by Index*. If it does not, your catalog is not ready for an indexed search. The companion, in that case, will search your files one by one, not its catalog. If the catalog was recently available (that is, if you've already allowed plenty of time for the service to create its initial catalog), then you can assume Indexing Service is merely busy updating the catalog and that it will be available again shortly.

Phrase and Free-Text Query Expressions

Query expressions involving text can take either of two forms, called *phrase* and *free-text*. In a phrase expression, the service looks for exact matches. For example, given the query

```
{phrase} John's debugger eats bugs {/phrase}
```

the service returns only those files that include exactly that four-word string. In a free-text expression, the service treats the text as though each word were separated from the next by a Boolean OR—that is, it returns files that match any of the words. It also looks for inflected forms of verbs. So the query

```
{freetext} John's debugger eats bugs {/freetext}
```

would cause the service to look for files that contain any of the following words: *John's, debugger, eats, bugs, ate, eating, eaten.*

Phrase queries are the default. Therefore, if you simply type some text as your query, without tags such as {freetext} or {phrase}, Search Companion performs a phrase query.

Restrictions on Content Queries

Note the following about query expressions that include text:

- Free-text and phrase expressions cannot be mixed in a single query; that is, you cannot use a Boolean or proximity operator to connect a free-text expression to a phrase expression.
- Enclose your text in quotation marks if it contains any of the following characters: % | ^ # @ $
- Enclose your text in quotation marks if the text you're looking for contains any of the following words: *and, or, not, near, equals, contains.*
- Indexing Service always ignores case.
- You can't use relational operators (>, <, =, and so forth) in content queries.

Working with Properties

Technically, all queries are property queries. When you look for files that contain particular words, you're searching on the basis of the Contents property. Contents is Indexing Service's default property—which is why you can look for a particular word or phrase without having to use a {prop} tag. Table 21-1 lists the most important additional properties that you can use in your queries. Note that not all of these properties are available for every document type.

In addition to the properties listed in Table 21-1, Indexing Service can catalog custom properties associated with a document.

To specify a property in a query, you use the {prop} tag, following this syntax:

```
{prop name=property name} query_expression {/prop}
```

where *property name* is a property like those listed in the left column of Table 21-1, and where *query expression* is the content to be searched for. As an example, to search for documents located in the C:\Press Releases\04 directory, you would type the following:

```
{prop name=directory} C:\Press Releases\04 {/prop}
```

If the query expression (the text between the opening and closing tags) includes wildcard characters, you must also use the {regex} tag. For details, see "Pattern-Matching Queries," page 733.

> **Tip** If the property name includes spaces (this might be the case for a custom property), enclose the property name within quotation marks.

Table 21-1. Useful Document Properties Available for Indexing Service Queries

Property Name	Description
Access	The last time the document was accessed
All	All properties, including Contents; works only for text queries, not numeric queries
AllocSize	The amount of disk space allocated to the document
Created	The time the document was created
Directory	The path to the document, not including the document name
DocAppName	The name of the application that created the document
DocAuthor	The author of the document
DocByteCount	The number of bytes in the document
DocCategory	The document type
DocCharCount	The number of characters in the document
DocComments	Comments about the document
DocCompany	The name of the company for which the document was written
DocCreatedTm	The time the document was created
DocEditTime	The total time spent editing the document
DocHiddenCount	The number of hidden slides in a Microsoft PowerPoint document
DocKeywords	Keywords associated with the document

Table 21-1. **Useful Document Properties Available for Indexing Service Queries**

Property Name	Description
DocLastAuthor	The user who most recently edited the document
DocLastPrintedTm	The time the document was last printed
DocLastSavedTm	The time the document was last saved
DocManager	The name of the manager of the document's author
DocNoteCount	The number of pages with notes in a PowerPoint document
DocPageCount	The number of pages in the document
DocParaCount	The number of paragraphs in the document
DocPartTitles	The names of document parts, such as worksheet names in a Microsoft Excel document or slide titles in a PowerPoint document
DocRevNumber	The current version number of the document
DocSlideCount	The number of slides in a PowerPoint document
DocTemplate	The name of the template used by the document
DocTitle	The title of the document
DocWordCount	The number of words in the document
Filename	The name of the document
Path	The path to the document, including the document name
ShortFileName	The 8.3-format name of the document
Size	The size of the document, in bytes
Write	The date and time the document was last modified

The EQUALS and CONTAINS Operators

In query expressions involving text, use the EQUALS operator when you require an exact match. For example, this query

```
{prop name=docTitle} equals Queen's Gambit Declined {/prop}
```

locates all files whose DocTitle property value is exactly *Queen's Gambit Declined*.

When you care only whether a particular word appears in a property value (no matter what else may be there), use the CONTAINS operator (or no operator; CONTAINS is the default).

For example, to find documents in which the phrase *Queen's Gambit Declined* appears somewhere within any property (including the contents), you could type either of the following:

```
{prop name=all} contains Queen's Gambit Declined {/prop}
{prop name=all} Queen's Gambit Declined {/prop}
```

To find documents in which any of those words (or any of the inflected forms of *declined*) appear, express the text in free-text mode:

```
{prop name=all} contains {freetext} Queen's Gambit Declined {/freetext} {/prop}
{prop name=all} {freetext} Queen's Gambit Declined {/freetext} {/prop}
```

Relational Operators

Indexing Service offers the following relational operators.

Operator	Description
=	Equal to
!=	Not equal to
<	Less than
<=	Less than or equal to
>	Greater than
>=	Greater than or equal to

Date and Time Expressions

Dates and times should be queried in one of the following formats:

```
yyyy/mm/dd hh:mm:ss
yyyy-mm-dd hh:mm:ss
```

The first two year digits are optional. If you omit them, Indexing Service regards all years as falling between 1930 and 2029. You can add an optional three-digit millisecond value to the time value (for example, 2000/04/12 14:54:23.456). All times are recorded in coordinated universal time format (UTC, or Universal Time Coordinate), which is essentially the same as Greenwich mean time.

In conjunction with relational operators, you can express times as offsets relative to the current time, using the following abbreviations.

Abbreviation	Meaning
Y	Year
Q	Quarter (three months)
M	Month
W	Week
D	Day
H	Hour
N	Minute
S	Second

For example, the query

```
{prop name=write} >-1d12h {/prop}
```

returns files last modified within the previous 36 hours.

Boolean Operators

Indexing Service offers the following Boolean operators.

Operator	Short Form	Long Form
AND	&	AND
OR	|	OR
Binary NOT	&!	AND NOT
Unary NOT	!	NOT

The binary NOT operator is used between two properties. For example, in the query

```
{prop name=DocAuthor} Carl {/prop} &! {prop name=DocSubject} Windows {/prop}
```

the binary NOT operator returns documents whose author is Carl and whose subject is not Windows.

The unary NOT operator is used to negate a single query expression. For example, the query

```
{prop name=size} not > 1000
```

returns documents whose size is not greater than 1,000 bytes. The only reason the distinction matters is that the unary NOT is permitted only in queries in which the query expression is a numeric value.

Order of Operator Precedence

The Boolean operators are evaluated in the following order:

1. NOT
2. AND
3. OR

Operators at the same precedence level are evaluated in left-to-right order. You can use parentheses to override the default precedence.

Pattern-Matching Queries

Indexing Service supports three types of pattern-matching queries:

- Queries that use MS-DOS-style wildcard characters (* and ?)
- UNIX-style regular-expression queries
- Queries that look for alternative word forms

Queries That Use MS-DOS-Style Wildcard Characters

Indexing Service recognizes both of the standard MS-DOS wildcard characters, * and ?. The asterisk represents any number of characters, and the question mark represents any single character.

For example, file names with the pattern *.do? can be found with this query:

```
{prop name=filename} {regex} *.do? {/regex} {/prop}
```

Do not omit the {regex} tag. If you do, Indexing Service returns only those files with the characters *do?* before the extension.

Queries That Use UNIX-Style Regular Expressions

Indexing Service supports the UNIX regular-expression syntax. A full treatment of the possibilities this affords is beyond the scope of this chapter. Here, however, is one potentially useful example. The query

```
{prop name=filename} {regex} *.|(do?|,xl?|,mdb|) {/regex} {/prop}
```

returns all files with any of the following extensions: *.do?*, *.xl?*, or *.mdb*.

Queries That Look for Alternative Word Forms

To find words that begin with particular letters, use the asterisk wildcard. For example, the query

```
{prop name=contents} dog* {/prop}
```

returns documents with *dog*, *doghouse*, *doggerel*, *dogmatic*, *doggone*, and so forth.

To find inflected forms of verbs, use the double-asterisk wildcard. For example,

```
{prop name=contents} swim** {/prop}
```

locates files containing *swim*, *swam*, and *swum*—but not *swimmer*.

Administering Indexing Service

The MMC console for administering Indexing Service is Ciadv.msc, shown in Figure 21-11. You can get there by any of the following routes:

- Type **ciadv.msc** at a command prompt.

- Right-click My Computer and choose Manage. In Computer Management, open Services And Applications. Under Services And Applications, select Indexing Service.

- In Search Companion's first pane, choose Change Preferences. In the second pane, choose Without Indexing Service (or With Indexing Service, if the service is currently disabled). In the third pane, choose Change Indexing Service Settings (Advanced).

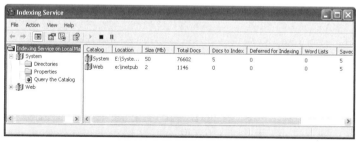

Figure 21-11. You can use this MMC console to administer Indexing Service.

You must be logged on as an administrator to use the Indexing Service console.

If the Indexing Service console does not display the console tree (the left pane), do the following to display it:

1 Choose View, Customize.

2 Select the Console Tree check box and then click OK.

The console tree displays an entry for each catalog created by Indexing Service. By default, that includes a System catalog and, if IIS is installed, a Web catalog. You can also create additional catalogs or delete existing ones in the Indexing Service console.

> For information about creating additional catalogs, see Microsoft Knowledge Base article 308202, "HOW TO: Create and Configure a Catalog for Indexing."

Opening the entry for a catalog reveals the three subentries shown in Figure 21-11: Directories, Properties, and Query The Catalog. Directories shows which folders are indexed by the selected catalog (and lets you make changes to that list). Properties shows which properties are being indexed, and Query The Catalog provides a query form that you can use as an alternative to Search Companion. Queries submitted with this query form generate the same list of files as queries submitted via Search Companion, but the files arrive as hyperlinks rather than as Windows Explorer entries.

When you select a catalog name in the console tree, the details pane of Indexing Service provides status information about the selected catalog.

An Overview of the Indexing Process

Indexing Service creates and maintains its catalogs through the following processes:

Scanning　The service scans the disks and folders to be indexed to determine which files have changed and thus need to be reindexed. A full scan takes place the first time you turn on the service, whenever you add a folder to a catalog, and whenever a serious error occurs. Incremental scans take place whenever the service is restarted (for example, when you restart your computer) and at least once a day.

Creating word lists　A word list is a small temporary index maintained in memory. Documents in a word list are automatically reindexed whenever the service is restarted.

Creating saved indexes　A saved index is a highly compressed temporary disk file optimized for fast response to searches. The service combines word list data into saved indexes whenever a large enough number of word lists have accumulated.

Merging　Merging is the combining of data from multiple word lists and saved indexes into a permanent master index.

Indexing Files with Unknown Extensions

To include files with unknown extensions in all your catalogs, right-click Indexing Service On Local Machine, at the top of the console tree, and choose Properties from the shortcut menu. The dialog box shown in Figure 21-12 appears.

Chapter 21

Figure 21-12. Use this properties dialog box to add unknown file types to your catalog.

On the Generation tab, select the Index Files With Unknown Extensions check box. Indexing Service will then do its best to extract meaningful content from file types for which it lacks a filter. After you've made this change, you must stop and restart Indexing Service for your change to take effect.

To index unknown file types only in a particular catalog, right-click that catalog's name, such as System or Web, in the console tree and then choose Properties. On the Tracking tab, clear the Inherit Above Settings From Service check box. Then go to the Generation tab and select Index Files With Unknown Extensions. (If you don't first clear Inherit Above Settings From Service, the catalog you've selected uses whatever setting you've applied to the service as a whole.) After making this change, stop and restart the catalog to have your change take effect.

Supplying an Alias for a Folder Name

By default, Indexing Service identifies remote folders by their share names and their full UNC paths. The UNC paths appear in the Alias column in the details pane of the Indexing Service console. If this default alias is not to your liking, follow these steps:

1 Right-click Indexing Service On Local Machine.

2 Choose Properties from the shortcut menu.

3 Click the Tracking tab.

Clear the Add Network Share Alias Automatically check box. You can then supply your own alias (if you want) by expanding the catalog entry in the console tree, selecting Directories, double-clicking the directory (folder) name in the details pane, and filling out the ensuing dialog box.

You can also clear the alias default at the catalog level rather than the service level. To do so, right-click the catalog name, choose Properties, go to the Tracking tab, clear the Inherit Above Settings From Service check box, and then clear Add Network Share Alias Automatically.

Stopping, Pausing, and Restarting

To stop the service, right-click Indexing Service On Local Machine and choose Stop from the shortcut menu. To stop the processing of a particular catalog, right-click that catalog's name, choose All Tasks from the shortcut menu, and then choose Stop.

To pause the service or pause the processing of a catalog, follow the same steps, but choose Pause instead of Stop. While the service or a catalog is paused, you can still execute queries, but no further catalog processing occurs. To restart after a pause or a stop, retrace your steps and choose Start.

Changing the Folders Included in a Catalog

To see which folders are included in a catalog, open the catalog's entry in the console tree and select Directories. Figure 21-13 shows a sample of what you might see.

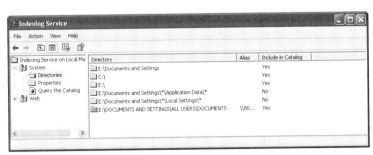

Figure 21-13. The Directories list shows which folders a catalog includes.

Folders with a Yes in the Include In Catalog column are part of that catalog—as are all of their subfolders, with the exception of subfolders explicitly excluded by entries that have a No in the Include In Catalog column.

To add a folder to a catalog, right-click Directories in the console tree, choose New, and then choose Directory. In the ensuing dialog box, supply the path and alias of the folder you want to add. To delete a folder, right-click it in the details pane and choose Delete from

737

Chapter 21

the shortcut menu. To change a folder's status—from included to excluded, or vice versa—double-click the folder in the details pane. In the ensuing dialog box, select Yes or No as appropriate.

Excluding Specific Files on NTFS Disks

To explicitly include or exclude a file on an NTFS-formatted disk from your catalog(s), right-click the file in a Windows Explorer window and choose Properties from the shortcut menu. On the General tab of the properties dialog box, click the Advanced button to display the Advanced Attributes dialog box, shown in Figure 21-14. Clear the For Fast Searching, Allow Indexing Service To Index This File check box to exclude this file from all catalogs.

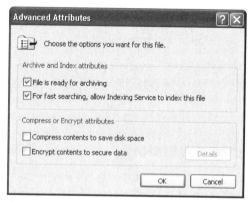

Figure 21-14. You can use this Advanced Attributes dialog box to explicitly exclude a file from your catalog(s).

Manually Rescanning a Folder

You can manually initiate an incremental or full scan of any folder by right-clicking the folder name in the Indexing Service details pane, choosing All Tasks, and then choosing Rescan (Full) or Rescan (Incremental). Microsoft recommends that you do a full rescan if you install a new filter, start or stop the indexing of unknown file types, or edit the noise word file.

Adjusting Indexing Service's Performance Parameters

To adjust Indexing Service's performance parameters, first stop the service. Right-click Indexing Service On Local Machine in the console tree, choose All Tasks, and then choose Tune Performance. These steps take you to the Indexing Service Usage dialog box, shown in Figure 21-15.

Figure 21-15. The Indexing Service Usage dialog box lets you choose a broad performance category.

If none of the first three options listed in this dialog box quite describes your situation, select Customize, and then click the Customize button. The Desired Performance dialog box, shown in Figure 21-16, appears.

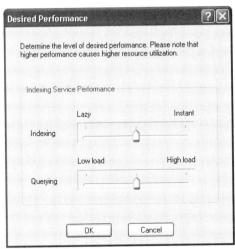

Figure 21-16. The Desired Performance dialog box allows fine-tuning.

The sliders here control the processing priority that Windows gives to the service's catalog building (Indexing) and query processing (Querying). Moving either slider to the right makes the service more responsive while reducing the performance of whatever applications you might be running concurrently with Indexing Service.

Chapter 22

Managing Disks and Drives

When you get right down to it, storage defines what you can and can't do with Microsoft Windows XP. A big hard disk (or two or three) makes it possible for you to download digital media and manage it effectively. By subdividing hard disks intelligently, you can keep data and programs organized, making it easier to find data and back up copies of important files. Windows XP includes built-in support for removable media, too, most notably recordable CD drives, which you can use to create custom music CDs and data backups with relative ease.

At Home with Windows XP

For the most part, disks and drives in all their permutations work the same way in both versions of Windows XP. However, computers running Windows XP Home Edition can't use dynamic disks, one of two types of disk structures. Therefore, Home Edition users can't use simple volumes, striped volumes, or spanned volumes—volume types that are available only on dynamic disks.

We mention in passing one other Professional-only feature in this chapter: file encryption. We describe that feature in depth in Chapter 11, "Encrypting Confidential Information," but Home Edition users can save themselves a trip to that chapter.

Also, this chapter explains how to disable AutoPlay. This procedure is different depending on which version of Windows XP you have (we describe both methods), but the end result is the same.

If you've mastered hard-disk setup utilities from Windows 98 and Windows Me, prepare to unlearn everything you know. Windows XP offers new storage capabilities and a new set of tools. When you set up a new hard disk in Windows XP, you have some important decisions to make: How many partitions will you create? Do you need to combine space from multiple physical disks into a single volume? Which file system will you use to format drives? And how can you configure the built-in CD writing capability of Windows XP so that it works smoothly every time?

Hard Disk Management 101

What appears in My Computer to be a hard disk drive might or might not correlate to a single physical device. A single physical device can be subdivided into partitions, volumes, or logical drives—each appearing in My Computer as a separate drive letter. Conversely, in Windows XP (as in Windows 2000), you can combine storage space from several physical devices so that it appears as a single drive letter.

Let's define the terms used in this chapter:

- A *disk* (or *hard disk*) refers to a physical disk drive installed in your computer. Your computer's first hard disk is identified as Disk 0. If you have additional hard disks installed, they're identified as Disk 1, Disk 2, and so on. As we'll explain in a later section, Windows XP Professional allows you to define a physical disk as a basic disk or dynamic disk, each of which has different tools and capabilities.

- A *basic disk* is a disk that is divided into one or more partitions. A *partition* is a portion of a physical disk that functions as if it were itself a physically separate disk. A *primary partition* is a partition that can be used for starting Windows (and other operating systems). A primary partition cannot be further subdivided. An *extended partition* can be further divided into one or more *logical drives*, each of which can be formatted separately and assigned its own drive letter.

- When a partition or logical drive is formatted for a particular file system (FAT, FAT32, or NTFS) and assigned a drive letter, it's called a *volume*. A volume appears in My Computer as a local disk.

- Whereas basic disks contain only basic volumes (that is, formatted primary partitions or formatted logical drives), *dynamic disks* contain volumes that can be simple, spanned, or striped, with these last two types combining space from multiple dynamic disks. Unlike basic volumes, dynamic volumes can be resized.

Active, System, and Boot Partitions

Three technical terms that can confuse anyone who isn't thoroughly experienced with the ways in which Windows XP works with partitions are *active partition*, *system partition*, and *boot partition*.

The *active partition* on a basic disk is the one from which an x86-based computer boots. On these machines, one primary partition—the one containing the files needed for startup—must be marked active for the computer to start itself and an operating system. The active partition must always be on the first hard disk attached to the system (Disk 0).

If you use Windows XP exclusively, or if you use any combination of Windows XP and Windows 2000, Windows NT, Windows 95/98/Me, or MS-DOS, you do not have to change the active partition. In fact, this option will be unavailable on the Disk Management menu in this type of configuration. If you use another operating system, such as Linux or OS/2, you must mark its system partition as active and reboot in order to use the alternate operating system. If your system contains a drive (including a removable drive) that is capable of starting another operating system, you will see the Active label alongside its status in the Disk Management window.

The *system partition* is the partition that contains the bootstrap files that Windows XP uses to start your system and display the boot menu. On the overwhelming majority of computers, this is the first primary partition on Disk 0, which is identified as drive C. The System label appears in the graphical view in the Disk management window alongside the status indicator for that drive.

The *boot partition* is the partition where the Windows system files are located. On most systems, this is the same as the system partition. On a multiboot system, where drive C contains files from an earlier Windows version and you've installed Windows XP to drive D or drive E, the boot partition is identified as such in the Disk Management window. (And yes, we know that it makes no sense to say that the boot files are on the system partition and the system files are on the boot partition. However, this counterintuitive nomenclature has been a part of the Windows NT family since the earliest days and isn't likely to change any time soon. So make a mental note of these two terms and you won't be confused.)

Chapter 22

Windows XP includes a utility called Disk Management that provides virtually every tool you'll need to manage disks, partitions, volumes, and logical drives. The Disk Management utility is a Microsoft Management Console (MMC) snap-in, and it can be accessed in either of the following ways:

- At any command prompt, type **diskmgmt.msc**.
- Right-click the My Computer icon on the Start menu, choose Manage, and then select Disk Management from the console pane on the left side of the Computer Management window.

As Figure 22-1 shows, Disk Management provides a wealth of information about physical disks and the volumes, partitions, and logical drives in place on those disks. You can use this utility to perform virtually any disk-related task.

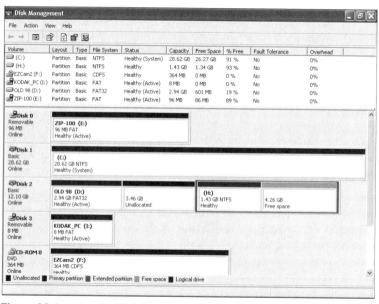

Figure 22-1. Use the Disk Management utility to gather information about and manage hard disks and removable disks.

If you've upgraded to Windows XP from Windows 2000, the Disk Management utility will be refreshingly familiar; the only changes are a few minor improvements to various wizards. If you've recently upgraded from Windows 98 or Windows Me, however, this set of tools will be as welcome as a breath of fresh air. Instead of the ancient and arcane Fdisk and the command-line Format utility, you can use this sleek graphical tool to perform any of the following tasks:

- Check the size, file system, status, and other properties of disks and volumes.
- Create partitions, logical drives, and volumes.
- Format volumes.

- Delete partitions, logical drives, and volumes.
- Assign drive letters to hard disk volumes, removable disk drives, and CD-ROM drives.
- Create mounted drives.
- Convert basic disks to dynamic disks, and vice versa.
- Create spanned volumes and striped volumes, which combine storage space from two or more disks into a single drive letter.
- Extend volumes to increase the size of a drive using free space from the same disk or another disk in the same system.

For the most part, when you make changes to your disk configuration with the Disk Management utility, you don't need to restart your computer. With tasks that are potentially destructive, such as deleting a partition or formatting a drive, you'll still have to click through one or two "Are you sure?" messages. But after you give your assent, Disk Management makes the changes immediately.

Some of these disk management tasks also apply to removable disks (such as Zip disks, USB flash disks, USB hard drives, and CDs). For example, you can use Disk Management to format a Zip disk (although there's no particular reason to, because you can also format from other programs that you're more likely to have open, such as Windows Explorer or a command prompt). More important, you use Disk Management to assign drive letters (or drive paths for mounted drives, if you prefer) to all types of drives—a task you can't perform elsewhere.

> **Note** On workstations that use 64-bit processors such as Intel's Itanium and Windows XP 64-Bit Edition, Disk Management allows you to work with disks that are formatted using the GUID partition table (GPT) instead of the Master Boot Record (MBR). The basic tools for working with GPT disks are the same as those used with MBR disks, but there are some important and subtle technical differences in the newer format. For an excellent overview, search in the Help And Support Center for the "GUID partition table" topic.

In addition, two command-line tools are brand new to Windows XP:

- **Fsutil** This utility (presumably the name means *file system utility*) is designed for support professionals and allows you to find files by security identifier (SID), change the short name of a file, and perform other esoteric tasks.
- **Diskpart** This utility is actually a console application that allows you to manage disks, partitions, and volumes from a command prompt. When you run the Diskpart command, it opens a console window and dumps you at the DISKPART> prompt. If you type **help** and press Enter, you see a screen that lists all available commands, like the one shown here.

> **Caution** These command-line tools are indisputably powerful, but they're not for the faint of heart or for casual experimentation. Both are documented thoroughly in online Help and are intended primarily to be incorporated into scripts rather than for interactive use. The Diskpart command in particular is dense and cryptic, with a complex structure that requires you to list and select objects before you can act on them. Diskpart provides a superset of the commands available through Disk Management. Disk Management offers only those capabilities that are generally safe, whereas Diskpart also provides options that, while necessary in some instances, can destroy your data. Therefore, all but the most expert Windows users should stick with the graphical tool whenever possible. For detailed information about Diskpart, see Knowledge Base article 300415, "A Description of the Diskpart Command-Line Utility."

NTFS or FAT32: Which Disk Format Should You Choose?

The single most important disk decision you have to make on a Windows XP system is which file system to choose for each drive or volume. On a clean install, you face this choice during Windows Setup; on an upgrade from Windows 98 or Windows Me, Setup lets you choose whether to convert the file system used on your existing drive. And you face the issue all over again if you repartition an existing drive or add a second (or third or fourth) drive to an existing system.

File system choices available to you depend on the size of the partition or volume you create. Most of the time, the choice comes down to NTFS or FAT32. On drives that are less than 4 GB in size, the 16-bit version of the FAT file system is also an option.

> **Note** **Avoid FAT**
>
> The 16-bit FAT file format exists in Windows XP for backward compatibility purposes only. Because it was designed in an era when hard disks were dramatically smaller, it's woefully inadequate on modern systems. In the modern era, FAT is appropriate for floppy disks and very small hard-disk partitions only. If you must use a FAT partition for compatibility reasons, try to keep its size under 511 MB.

Which file system should you choose? There's no right or wrong answer. NTFS has significant advantages in reliability, security, and flexibility, but in some system configurations FAT32 is a better choice. Make your decision based on the following factors and how they apply to your needs:

- **Compatibility** Windows 95/98/Me cannot recognize NTFS volumes. On multiboot systems, it's essential that you use FAT32 for any local drives that you want to access when you boot the system using Windows 95, Windows 98, or Windows Me. Note that this restriction does not apply to network access. Assuming you've set up sharing properly, other network users can access your shared folders from computers running any other version of Windows, regardless of the local disk format.

- **Security** On an NTFS volume, you can restrict access to files and folders using permissions, as described in "Controlling Access with NTFS Permissions," page 282. With Windows XP Professional, you can add an extra layer of protection by encrypting files. On a FAT or FAT32 drive, anyone with physical access to your computer can access any files stored on that drive.

- **Reliability** By design, an NTFS volume can recover from disk errors more readily than an otherwise identical FAT/FAT32 drive. NTFS uses log files to keep track of all disk activity. In the event of a system crash, Windows XP can use this journal to repair file system errors automatically when the system is restarted. In addition, NTFS can dynamically remap clusters that contain bad sectors and mark those clusters as bad so that the operating system no longer uses them. FAT and FAT32 drives are more vulnerable to disk errors.

- **Expandability** Using NTFS-formatted volumes, you can expand storage on existing drive letters without having to back up, repartition, reformat, and restore.

- **Efficiency** On partitions greater than 8 GB in size, NTFS volumes manage space more efficiently than FAT32. The maximum partition size for a FAT32 drive created by Windows XP is 32 GB; by contrast, you can create a single NTFS volume of up to 16 terabytes (16,384 GB) using default settings, and by tweaking cluster sizes, you can ratchet the maximum volume size up to 256 terabytes.

Chapter 22

> **Tip** Use Fdisk for extra-large FAT32 drives
>
> Most of the time, the Disk Management utility is the best choice for managing partitions you plan to use with Windows XP. However, under one specific circumstance, you might want to prepare a disk using the tools from Windows 98 or Windows Me instead. Windows XP cannot create or format a FAT32 partition greater than 32 GB in size, but the Fdisk utility from those earlier Windows versions can. Boot from a startup disk prepared by either of those operating systems and use Fdisk to create the partition. After formatting the extra-large FAT32 partition using the Windows 98/Me Format command, restart Windows XP.

To view information about the file system currently used for a given drive or volume, right-click the drive icon in the My Computer window or the volume in the Disk Management window and choose Properties. As Figure 22-2 shows, the file system information appears near the top of the dialog box.

Figure 22-2. This dialog box tells you whether the drive is formatted with NTFS or FAT32.

Converting a FAT32 Disk to NTFS

To convert a FAT or FAT32 disk to NTFS format, use the command-line Convert utility. This utility uses the following syntax:

```
convert d: /fs:ntfs
```

where *d* is the drive letter you want to convert.

The Convert utility can do its work within Windows if the drive to be converted is not in use. However, if you want to convert the system volume or a volume that holds a page file, you might see an error message when you run the Convert utility. In that case, you must schedule the conversion to occur the next time you start Windows. After you restart the computer, you'll see a prompt that warns you that the conversion is about to begin. You have 10 seconds to cancel the conversion. If you allow it to proceed, Windows will run the Check Disk utility and perform the conversion automatically. During this process, your computer will restart twice.

Caution Converting your system drive to NTFS makes it impossible to restore your previous operating system, a fact the Convert utility warns you about in no uncertain terms. If you have set up your system using a multiboot configuration so that you can continue to run Windows 95, Windows 98, or Windows Me, do not convert the system drive to NTFS; doing so will make it impossible to start your previous Windows version.

Inside Out

Align clusters before you convert to NTFS

If you have a drive larger than 512 MB and it was originally formatted as a FAT32 volume using a version of Windows earlier than Windows XP, its 4-KB clusters are probably not aligned on 4-KB boundaries. This situation causes the Convert program to create 512-byte clusters when it converts the drive to NTFS. Because 512-byte clusters generally provide poorer performance than 4-KB clusters, you'll be better off if you realign the partition before you convert, by moving the data area up to a 4-KB boundary. Windows doesn't include a tool for realigning partitions in this manner, but BootIt Next Generation (BootIt NG), a shareware program available at *http://www.bootitng.com*, can perform that task. In BootIt NG, use the Slide button in the Work With Partitions dialog box; be sure to select the Align For NTFS Only check box.

To improve your system's performance, run the Convert command with the /Cvtarea switch. This allows the master file table (MFT), the index of all files and folders on the selected volume, to be created in a single space, rather than being fragmented. Although the Windows XP Disk Defragmenter utility can work with the MFT, it cannot move the first fragment. This limitation practically guarantees that the MFT will be fragmented, unless you follow these steps as part of the NTFS conversion:

1   Use the Windows XP Disk Defragmenter to defragment the drive you plan to convert and consolidate free space on the drive. (For details, see "Defragmenting Disks for Better Performance," page 1241.)

2   Calculate the size of the MFT to be created. The default size of the MFT equals 12.5 percent of the partition size. Thus, on a 10 GB partition, the MFT should be approximately 1.25 GB. If your partition is larger than 40 GB, use 4 GB as the MFT size.

Chapter 22

Note In the next step, you'll create a file with this calculated size. Because the drive hasn't yet been converted to NTFS, you're constrained by the limitations of FAT and FAT32 drives, which can't have a file larger than 4 GB.

3 Use the Fsutil command to create a new contiguous placeholder file equal in size to the MFT you want to create. This file must be created in the root of the drive to be converted. For this example, issue the following command:

```
fsutil file createnew c:\testfile.txt 1250000000
```

You can use any legal file name. For the final parameter, substitute the proper size for the placeholder file, in bytes.

4 Run the Convert command, using the following syntax:

```
convert c: /fs:ntfs /cvtarea:testfile.txt
```

Substitute the correct drive letter as necessary.

5 If necessary, restart your system to complete the conversion.

Inside Out

Converting NTFS permissions on FAT volumes

With Windows 2000, converting a FAT32 system volume to NTFS entails several trade-offs, most notably a reduced level of security, because the Convert utility in Windows 2000 does not adjust default security attributes as the Windows Setup program does. The Windows XP version of the Convert utility (Convert.exe) fixes this deficiency. When you convert a FAT or FAT32 drive under Windows XP, the Convert utility automatically applies the correct default permissions to all system folders. As long as you use the /Cvtarea switch to prevent fragmentation of the MFT, there's no fundamental difference in Windows XP between a converted NTFS volume and one that's created during setup.

Basic and Dynamic Disks

As we mentioned in passing at the beginning of this chapter, Windows XP Professional supports two types of disk structures: basic disks and dynamic disks.

A basic disk is a physical disk that contains primary partitions, extended partitions, and logical drives. This is the same disk structure that has been used by all versions of MS-DOS, Windows 95/98/Me, and Windows NT 4. The partition table—which stores information about the number, type, and placement of partitions on the disk—is located in a 64-byte section of the Master Boot Record (MBR), the first sector on the disk. On a basic disk, you can create a maximum of four partitions, which can include one extended partition. Within an

Chapter 22

extended partition, you can create multiple logical drives, which are the familiar drive structures that appear in Windows Explorer as drive D, drive E, and so on.

A dynamic disk is a physical disk that contains one or more dynamic volumes, which are similar to partitions on a basic disk. Dynamic disks were introduced in Windows 2000 and are incompatible with earlier Microsoft operating systems. A dynamic disk does not have an MBR; instead, it maintains information about the layout of disk volumes in a database stored on the last 1 MB of the disk. When you create partitions using Windows XP (or Windows 2000), the operating system never uses the full space; instead, it reserves 8 MB for the dynamic disk database, so that you can convert a FAT32 disk later. Dynamic disks offer the following advantages:

- You can create an unlimited number of volumes on a disk. In this respect, a dynamic disk is like an extended partition on a basic disk, where you can create an unlimited number of logical drives. However, unlike a logical drive, a simple volume on a dynamic disk can be used as a system partition and can be extended.

- Dynamic disks allow you to combine physical disks in interesting ways. You can extend an existing volume, for instance. If you've created a 30-GB drive D on a dynamic disk for storing your data files and you add a new 60-GB physical disk to your system, you can extend that existing 30-GB volume using all or part of the new disk, effectively creating a 90-GB drive D, without being required to back up or restore data or change drive letters. This sort of disk structure is called a *spanned volume*. You can also create *striped volumes*, in which data is stored in equal-sized 64-KB strips across multiple dynamic volumes on separate physical disks to improve performance. Another advantage: you can make these configuration changes without having to restart your computer.

- Disk configuration information for dynamic disks is stored in a database in a reserved area on the disk itself. If you have multiple dynamic disks on a single system, each one contains a replica of the dynamic disk database for the entire system. This feature makes it somewhat easier to move disks between computers and to recover data from corrupted disks.

The advantages of dynamic disks are especially pronounced in servers for large enterprises, where it's not unusual to see systems configured with five or more physical disks. On desktop systems, however, you must decide whether the possible benefits outweigh the increased complexity and the risk of data loss that can occur if one disk used in a multidisk spanned or striped volume crashes.

> **Note** If you use Windows XP Home Edition, or if you're running Windows XP Professional on a portable computer, the option to convert a basic disk to a dynamic disk is not available.

Chapter 22

Caution If you want to experiment with dynamic disks, do so on a disk that doesn't include important data; don't treat this operation lightly. Although you can convert a dynamic disk back to a basic disk, all data in all volumes on that disk and on any other disks that are part of a spanned or striped volume will be irretrievably lost in the process. If you decide to convert a dynamic disk back to a basic disk, you'll need to have additional space or removable media to back up all your data so that you can restore it to the resulting empty basic disk.

To convert a basic disk to a dynamic disk, follow these steps:

1 Close any programs (other than Disk Management) that are using the disk you're converting. This includes all Windows Explorer windows.

2 In the Disk Management window, right-click the disk you want to convert and choose Convert To Dynamic Disk. (Right-click the disk icon at the left of the graphical view in the bottom of the window.)

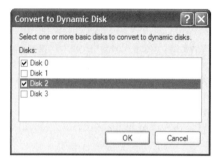

3 If you have more than one disk, select which one(s) you want to upgrade and then click OK.

4 In the Disks To Convert dialog box shown below, click Convert. Click through all warning dialog boxes to complete the conversion.

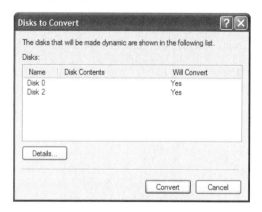

Want to reverse the process and convert a dynamic disk to a basic disk? Unfortunately, this conversion is a destructive process. To convert a dynamic disk to a basic disk, follow these steps:

1 Back up all existing data to another drive or removable media.

2 Delete all volumes on the dynamic disk. (For details, see "Deleting a Partition, Volume, or Logical Drive," page 764.)

3 From the Disk Management window, right-click the disk you want to convert and choose Convert To Basic Disk.

4 After the conversion is complete, restore the backed-up data.

Working with Partitions, Volumes, and Disks

Before you can store data on a physical disk, you have to prepare it for use with Windows. Just as in previous Windows versions, the process of preparing a disk is twofold: First you carve out a space on the disk by creating a partition (or volume, if you're using dynamic disks) and, if necessary, one or more logical drives; then you choose a file system and format the drive. After you assign a drive letter to each newly formatted partition, volume, or logical drive, you're ready to go.

Creating Partitions from Free Disk Space

When you add a new drive to an existing system or delete partitions from an existing drive, you have a wide range of options for using the new disk space. How you choose to divvy up the space is up to you. If you stick with basic disks, your options are similar to those that are familiar from earlier Windows versions. On the other hand, if you're willing to learn the ins and outs of dynamic disks, you can combine disk space in creative ways. In either case, wizards do most of the work.

Creating Partitions on a Basic Disk

To create a new partition on a basic disk, you need free space on your hard disk. (In the default Disk Management view, free space is identified by a black bar with the Unallocated label.) If you add a new hard disk to your system, the entire disk is available for use. You can choose all or part of the available space for use as a primary or an extended partition. If no unallocated space is available, you can make room by deleting an existing partition (and its data).

To create a new partition, follow these steps:

1 In the bottom half of the Disk Management window, right-click an unallocated portion of a disk and choose New Partition from the shortcut menu.

2 Click Next to advance past the Welcome page of the New Partition Wizard.

3 On the Select Partition Type page, select Primary Partition or Extended Partition and click Next.

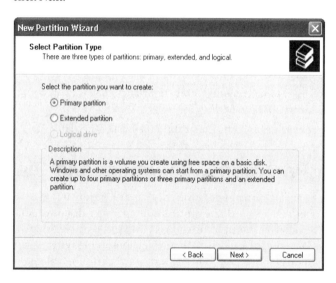

If you create an extended partition, the wizard ends here. Before you can store data on the newly created partition, you must define one or more logical drives within it, as explained in the following section. A primary partition, on the other hand, consists of a single volume, and the remaining steps of the wizard allow you to format that volume. If you select Primary Partition and click Next, the Specify Partition Size page appears, as shown here.

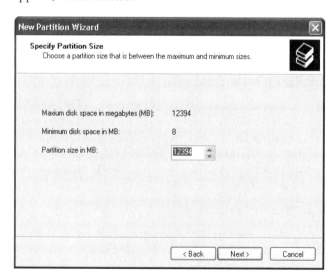

Chapter 22

4   On the Specify Partition Size page, specify how much of the disk's unallocated space you want to use for the new partition. The default value is the entire unallocated space. Click Next to continue. The Assign Drive Letter Or Path page appears.

On the Assign Drive Letter Or Path page, these three options appear:

■   **Assign The Following Drive Letter**   By default, Windows assigns the lowest available drive letter to the partition. The list includes only drive letters that are not currently being used for local disks or for mapped network drives.

■   **Mount In The Following Empty NTFS Folder**   You can create a mounted drive, which appears as a subfolder of another drive. For more information, see "Assigning and Changing Drive Letters or Drive Paths," page 765.

■   **Do Not Assign A Drive Letter Or Drive Path**   Choose this option if you want to create the partition but you do not want to make it available for storage yet. (In that case, before you can use the partition to store and retrieve data, you must return to the Disk Management utility and assign a drive letter or create a mounted drive.)

5   Select one of the above options and click Next to continue. The Format Partition page appears.

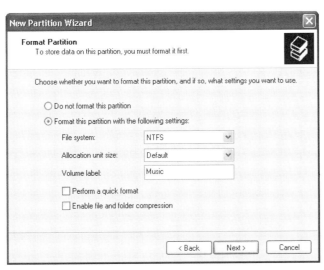

Chapter 22

6   Choose Format This Partition With The Following Settings and then choose from these options:

- **File System**   Choose NTFS or FAT32 from the list. NTFS is selected by default. If the size of the volume is 4 GB (4096 MB) or less, your choices also include FAT. For more information, see "NTFS or FAT32: Which Disk Format Should You Choose?" on page 746.

- **Allocation Unit Size**   The allocation unit size (also known as the cluster size) is the smallest space that can be allocated to a file. The Default option, in which Windows XP selects the appropriate cluster size based on volume size, is the best choice here.

- **Volume Label**   The volume label identifies the drive in the My Computer window. The default label text is New Volume. (You can change this text at any time, as explained in "Assigning or Changing a Volume Label," page 763.)

Select Perform A Quick Format if you want Disk Management to skip the sometimes lengthy disk-checking process. Select Enable File And Folder Compression if you want all data on the new volume to use NTFS compression. (This option is unavailable if you chose the FAT or FAT32 file system.)

7   Click Next, confirm your settings, and click Finish.

Creating a Simple Volume on a Dynamic Disk

On dynamic disks, simple volumes are the equivalent of primary partitions on basic disks. To create a simple volume, log on using an account in the Administrators group and follow these steps:

1   Open the Disk Management window, right-click an unallocated portion of a dynamic disk, and then choose New Volume.

2   In the New Volume Wizard, click Next to move past theWelcome page. The Select Volume Type page appears.

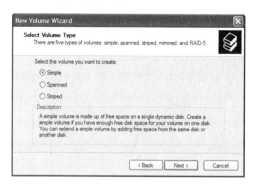

3   On the Select Volume Type page, select Simple. (If you have only one dynamic disk, this is your only choice. If you have multiple dynamic disks and you want to create a spanned or striped volume, see the instructions in the following section.)

> **Note**   Don't be confused by the explanatory text in this dialog box. Although dynamic disks support five different types of volumes, only the three choices shown here are available with Windows XP Professional. The remaining two options—mirrored volumes and RAID-5 volumes—are available only on Windows Server 2003 installations.

4   Click Next. The Select Disks page appears.

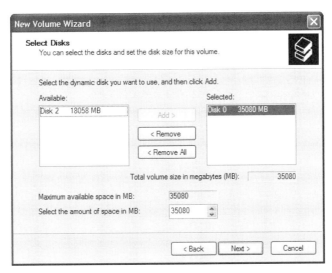

5   On the Select Disks page, select the disk on which you want to create the volume. By default, the disk you right-clicked in step 1 is shown in the Selected box. (To choose a different disk, click Remove, and then select a different available disk and click Add.) By default, the wizard offers to create a new volume using all available unallocated space; if you want to make a smaller volume, change the value in the Select The Amount Of Space In MB box. Click Next to continue.

6   On the remaining wizard pages, specify the drive letter or path and format the disk. These options are identical to those presented in the New Partition Wizard; for details, see "Creating Partitions on a Basic Disk," page 753.

Chapter 22

Combining Volumes from Dynamic Disks

If you have additional unallocated space on a dynamic disk after creating a simple volume—either the same disk or another disk—you can extend an existing volume to increase its size. If you have unallocated space on two or more dynamic disks, you can combine that space to create a volume. These combinations are subject to the following limitations:

- You can extend only simple volumes and spanned volumes on dynamic disks; you can't extend striped volumes or partitions on basic disks.
- You can extend a volume only if it's formatted with NTFS or if it's unformatted; you can't extend FAT or FAT32 volumes.
- You can't extend a system volume or boot volume.

Caution   Weigh the risks carefully before creating a volume that contains space from two or more dynamic disks. If a catastrophic failure occurs on either physical disk, the entire spanned or striped volume and all its data will be lost. Also, you cannot reverse your decision and remove one chunk of space from the extended, spanned, or striped volume. Deleting one part of the volume deletes the entire volume.

Figure 22-3 shows a system that contains four disks, two of which are dynamic disks. In this example, Disk 0 and Disk 2 each contain significant chunks of unallocated space. You could extend the E volume (Music) or the F volume (Backup), or both, using all or part of this unallocated space. You could also create a new spanned or striped volume using the two chunks of unallocated space.

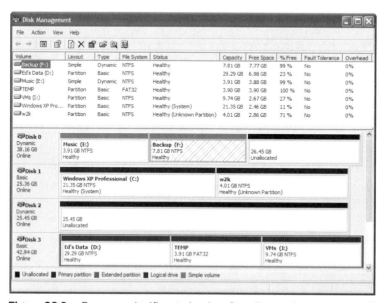

Figure 22-3.   Because significant chunks of unallocated space are available on two dynamic disks, you have a variety of options here.

Figure 22-4 shows the results after extending the two existing simple volumes and creating a new striped volume. First, we extended the E volume (Music), picking up 7.81 GB of space from Disk 2 and turning it into a spanned volume. Next, we created the striped H volume, using all remaining space from Disk 2 plus an equal chunk of space from Disk 0. Finally, we extended the F (Backup) volume, using the remaining 8.81 GB from the end of Disk 0, making it an extended simple volume.

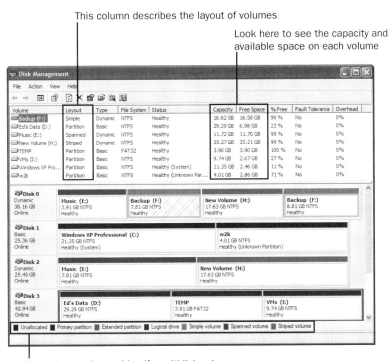

Figure 22-4. Information in the list at the top of this window, combined with color codes and volume labels from the bottom of the window, make it easy to see how storage space is arranged.

Tip Learn to read the numbers

When working with extended, spanned, and striped volumes, the numbers can be confusing. In dialog boxes, values are typically listed in megabytes (MB). In the graphical view at the bottom of the Disk Management window, values are typically listed in gigabytes (GB). Because 1 GB is equal to 1024 MB, the numbers aren't always comparable. For instance, 35080 MB appears in the graphical view as 34.26 GB. As long as you're aware that the value in the graphical view will always appear a bit smaller than the one shown in dialog boxes, you should have no trouble.

To create a spanned or striped volume from unallocated space on two or more dynamic disks, use the New Volume Wizard, as described in the previous section, with the following changes:

● On the Select Volume Type page, select Spanned or Striped.

● On the Select Disks page, use the Add button to select two or more disks and specify the amount of space you want to use from each one. On a spanned volume, the portions of unallocated space on each drive can be of different sizes; in the case of a striped drive (as shown here), the two chunks of disk space must be of equal size—the wizard will adjust the space on both disks if you change the amount at the bottom of the dialog box. In either case, the Select Disks page displays the total volume size you can expect to end up with.

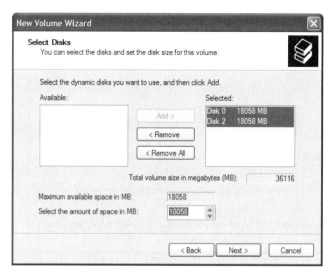

The procedure for extending an existing volume is considerably simpler:

1 In the Disk Management window, right-click the volume you want to extend and choose Extend Volume. This option is available only if unallocated space exists on the same dynamic disk or other dynamic disks in the same system.

2 In the Extend Volume Wizard, click Next to skip past theWelcome page.

3 On the Select Disks page, select which disk (or disks) you want to use by adding them to the Selected list. You can extend a simple volume to use unallocated contiguous space on the same disk, noncontiguous space on the same disk, or space on another dynamic disk (or disks). (In the latter two cases, the volume becomes a spanned volume.) At the bottom of this page, specify how much of the unallocated space you want to use.

4 Click Next and then click Finish.

After a volume is extended, you can extend it again, using additional unallocated space, but you can't reduce its size—except by deleting the entire volume.

Creating Logical Drives

A logical drive is a part of an extended partition that you subdivide and format as a separate volume. A logical drive can have its own drive letter or can be assigned as a mounted volume within an NTFS volume, as described in "Assigning and Changing Drive Letters or Drive Paths," page 765. You use the same wizard to create a logical drive as you do when creating a new partition or volume.

To create a logical drive, open Disk Management and follow these steps:

1 In the graphical view at the bottom of the Disk Management window, right-click the free space within an extended partition and choose New Logical Drive from the shortcut menu.

2 In the New Partition Wizard that appears, click Next to skip past the Welcome page. Click Next to skip the Select Partition Type page as well, where Logical Drive, the only available option, is already selected.

3 On the remaining wizard pages, specify the logical drive's size, drive letter or path, and format, just as you would for a primary partition, as described in "Creating Partitions from Free Disk Space," page 753.

Formatting a Partition, Volume, or Logical Drive

Formatting a partition, logical drive, or volume deletes any existing files and prepares the volume for use. Normally, a wizard handles this task when you create a new partition, logical drive, or volume. You can reformat any drive or volume other than the current system or boot volume at any time. This option is a useful way to start fresh with a partition that you use strictly for temporary files, such as music files that you burn to CD.

To format an existing drive or volume, right-click its icon in the Disk Management utility and choose Format from the shortcut menu. You'll see a dialog box that offers the same choices as those found in the New Partition Wizard and New Volume Wizard, as shown in Figure 22-5.

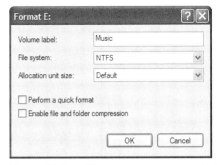

Figure 22-5.   When you format an existing primary partition or logical drive, you can choose the same options as if you were creating it from scratch with the wizard's help.

You can also format any primary partition or logical drive that currently has a drive letter assigned to it from Windows Explorer: Right-click the drive icon and choose Format from the shortcut menu to display the dialog box shown here. Although the layout of this dialog box is different, the options are exactly the same as those found in the Disk Management window.

Finally, if you're a command-prompt fan, you can use the Format command. For volumes and partitions located on hard disks, this option doesn't provide any capabilities that aren't also available from the graphical interface. From a command prompt, use the Format *volume* command. The *volume* parameter specifies the drive letter (which must be followed by a colon), or the mount point or volume name. You can control the Format command using any of the following switches:

/FS:*filesystem*	Specifies the file system to be used—substitute FAT, FAT32, or NTFS for *filesystem*.
/V:*label*	Assigns a volume label using the specified text.
/Q	Performs a quick format.
/C	NTFS only; all files and folders created on the new volume will be compressed by default.
/X	Forces the volume to dismount first if necessary. Caution: Using this switch may cause data loss if applications have open files with unsaved changes.
/A:*size*	Overrides the default allocation unit size. Use the /? switch to see details and restrictions.

Assigning or Changing a Volume Label

In Windows XP, as in previous versions of Windows, you can assign a descriptive text label to any volume. Assigning a label is purely optional, but it's a good practice, especially if you've set up separate partitions to keep your data organized. You can use *Data* as the label for your data drive, *Music* for the drive that holds your collection of digital tunes, and so on. Volume labels appear in the My Computer window alongside the drive letter for a volume, as in the example shown here.

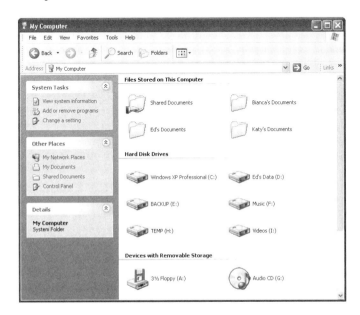

You can enter a volume label when you format a new drive in the final step of the New Partition Wizard or New Volume Wizard, as described in "Creating Partitions from Free Disk Space," page 753. You can change a volume label at any time afterward by right-clicking a volume, choosing Properties, and entering text in the Label box on the General tab. (Or you can edit the volume label directly by clicking the label text in the My Computer window.) Regardless of how you choose to enter the label, you must follow the label rules that are specific to the file system of the underlying drive:

- **FAT/FAT32**   The volume label can be up to 11 characters long and can include spaces. On volumes originally created using MS-DOS or Windows 95/98/Me, the label is displayed in all capital letters. A volume label cannot include the following characters: * ? / \ | . , ; : + = [ ] < > "

- **NTFS**   The volume label can be up to 32 characters long. You can use symbols, punctuation, and special characters, and uppercase and lowercase letters are displayed exactly as you type them.

Deleting a Partition, Volume, or Logical Drive

Deleting a partition, drive, or volume is a radical step, but it's the simplest way to reorganize the layout of partitions on a disk—for instance, if you want to carve a second partition out of a disk that's currently arranged as a single large partition. The only requirement is making certain that all important programs and data have been backed up to another local or network drive, or to an alternative medium such as CD-R/CD-RW.

The most important thing to know about deleting a partition, logical drive, or volume is this: *You will lose all data stored in the partition, drive, or volume when you delete it.* For obvious reasons, you cannot use the Disk Management utility to delete the system volume, the boot volume, or an extended partition that contains logical drives. (You must delete the logical drives first and then delete the partition.)

Caution If you've created any spanned or striped volumes, be especially careful when deleting a volume. Deleting one volume completely wipes out all parts of the spanned or striped volume. All disk regions on all disks that are part of the volume become unallocated space, immediately and irrevocably.

Troubleshooting

When you try to delete a logical drive or volume, you get an error message.

If you checked the drive or volume first and are certain that it is completely empty, try the following techniques:

- Look at the Status line in the Disk Management window. If the word *System* or *Boot* appears in parentheses after the status indicator, you cannot remove the drive or volume from within Windows.

- Is the Windows XP page file configured to use this drive or volume? Follow the procedures outlined in "Making the Most of Virtual Memory," page 415, to view these settings and change them, if needed.

- Did you leave a Windows Explorer window open showing the contents of a folder on this volume or drive? Close all Windows Explorer windows and try again.

- Is an application program using the drive or volume? Check all running programs to see whether one of them is holding a file open on the drive or volume.

If the drive or volume is not configured as the system or boot volume, you should see a dialog box that offers to force the deletion of the selected item. If you're certain that no files you need are currently in use, click Yes to continue.

To delete a logical drive or a volume, first make certain that no other users are currently connected to that drive or volume, either over the network or in another session on the local computer. Then follow these steps:

1 In the Disk Management window, right-click the item you want to delete and choose Explore. Move or back up all files that you want to preserve and then close the Windows Explorer window.

2 Right-click the drive or volume again and choose Delete Logical Drive or Delete Volume.

3 Click Yes in the confirmation dialog box, shown below.

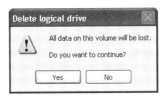

Assigning and Changing Drive Letters or Drive Paths

How does Windows XP assign letters to individual drives? On the degree-of-difficulty scale, the algorithm that Windows XP uses to assign drive letters probably falls mid-way between programming a VCR and Einstein's General Theory of Relativity. It's a complex subject, made more confusing by the fact that the rules for Windows XP are different from those followed by MS-DOS and Windows 95/98/Me. The following list summarizes basic facts you need to know about Windows XP and drive letters:

● On an upgrade installation, Windows XP preserves the drive letters assigned by the previous Windows version. On a clean installation, Windows XP follows the same rules as Windows 2000. (For details, see Knowledge Base article 234048, "How Windows 2000 Assigns, Reserves, and Stores Drive Letters.")

● Assigned drive letters are persistent. Once assigned, drive letters remain the same every time you start Windows XP. This is a big change from the behavior in Windows 95/98/Me, where adding a new CD-ROM drive or hard disk or changing the number and type of partitions on existing drives can cause existing drive letters to change.

● You can assign one (and only one) letter to a primary partition, a logical drive, or a simple volume on a dynamic disk. At any time, you can change any drive letter except those assigned to the system and boot partitions, either for the sake of convenience or because it interferes with the letter mapped to a network drive. You can also remove a drive letter assignment from any volume except the system and boot partitions.

Caution It is possible to change the drive letter assigned to the system and boot partitions in Windows 2000 or Windows XP by editing values in the registry. In general, doing so is not recommended. The only time this option makes sense is when a system configuration unexpectedly causes drive letters to change, so that the letter assigned to the system or boot partition is different from the one that was assigned when Windows XP was installed. This might be the case if you use third-party partitioning tools to alter the layout of partitions on a disk, or if you add or remove a disk controller. If this situation describes your system, read details about this tricky procedure in Knowledge Base article 223188, "How to Restore the System/Boot Drive Letter in Windows."

To change a drive letter assignment, follow these steps:

1 From Disk Management, right-click the volume you want to change (in either the volume list at the top of the window or the graphical view at the bottom), and choose Change Drive Letter And Paths.

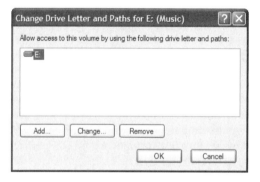

2 To replace an existing drive letter, select it and click Change. To assign a drive letter to a volume that currently has none, click Add.

3 Select an available drive letter from the Assign The Following Drive Letter list and then click OK.

4 Click OK to close the Change Drive Letter And Paths dialog box.

Chapter 22

Inside Out

Swapping drive letters between two volumes

The list of available drive letters in the Add Drive Letter or Path dialog box shows only those that are not currently in use. If you need to swap the drive letters for two volumes, you need to do so in three steps. To swap drive letters G and H, for instance, open Disk Management and follow these steps:

1 Remove the drive letter assigned to drive H, freeing that letter for reassignment.

2 Click drive G and change its assigned drive letter to *H*.

3 Return to the drive formerly designated as H and use the Add button to assign the now available letter G.

Note that the letters *A* and *B* are always reserved for removable drives and cannot be assigned to a volume on a hard disk.

In addition to (or in place of) a drive letter, you can assign one or more *drive paths* to a primary partition, a logical drive, or a simple volume on a dynamic disk. Assigning a drive path creates a *mounted volume*, which appears as a folder within an NTFS-formatted drive that has a letter assigned to it. Besides allowing you to sidestep the limitation of 26 drive letters, mounted volumes offer these two advantages:

- You can extend storage space on an existing drive that's running low on free space. For instance, if your digital music collection has outgrown your drive C, you can create a More Music folder in C:\My Music. Assign a drive path from a new partition to the More Music folder and you've increased the effective storage by the size of the new volume.

- You can make commonly used files available in multiple locations. Say you have an enormous collection of clip art that you store on drive X, and each user has a folder in his or her My Documents folder where they store desktop publishing files. In each of those personal folders, you can create a subfolder called Clipart and assign a drive path to the X partition. That way, the entire clip art collection is always available from any user's desktop publishing folder, without requiring them to manage shortcuts or worry about changing drive letters.

To create a mounted drive, follow these steps:

1 From Disk Management, right-click the volume you want to change (in either the volume list at the top of the window or the graphical view at the bottom), and choose Change Drive Letter And Paths.

2 Click Add to open the Add Drive Letter Or Path dialog box.

Chapter 22

3 Select Mount In This NTFS Folder (this is the only option available if the volume already has an assigned drive letter).

4 Click the Browse button. The Browse For Drive Path dialog box that appears shows only NTFS volumes, and the OK button is enabled only if you select an empty folder. Browse to the location where you want to create the drive path and then select an empty folder, or click New Folder to create one.

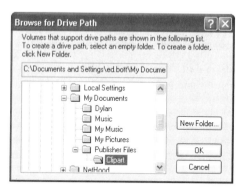

5 Click OK to add the selected location in the Add Drive Letter Or Path dialog box and then click OK to create the drive path.

You can manage files and subfolders in a mounted volume just as if it were a regular folder. If a volume is mounted to a folder located in the root of a drive, it appears in Windows Explorer as a drive icon. However, if the volume is mounted to a subfolder in any other location, the mounted volume appears in Windows Explorer as a folder icon, indistinguishable from a regular file folder. In that case, the only way to tell that this folder is different from other folders is to right-click the folder icon, choose Properties, and then inspect the General tab. As the example shown in Figure 22-6 illustrates, the Type field appears as Mounted Volume, and the Target field identifies the label of the volume that actually contains the files.

If you use the Dir command in a Command Prompt window to display a folder directory, a mounted volume is identified as <JUNCTION> (for *junction point*, another name for mounted volume), whereas ordinary folders are identified as <DIR> (for *directory*, the MS-DOS term for a folder).

> **Caution** When creating mounted volumes, avoid creating loops in the structure of a drive—for example, by creating a drive path from drive X that points to a folder on drive D and then creating a drive path on drive D that points to a folder on drive X. Windows allows you to do this, but it's invariably a bad idea, because an application that opens subfolders (such as a search) can go into an endless loop.

Figure 22-6. The properties dialog box for a mounted drive identifies the volume that actually holds its files.

To see a list of all the mounted drives on your system, open Disk Management and choose View, Drive Paths. A dialog box like the one shown in Figure 22-7 appears. Note that you can remove a drive path from this dialog box; if you do so, the folder remains in the same spot where it was previously located, but it reverts to being a regular, empty folder.

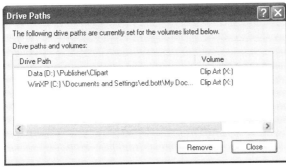

Figure 22-7. This dialog box lists all the mounted drives on a system and shows the volume label, if any, of each mounted drive.

Checking Properties and Status of a Disk or Partition

As with previous Windows versions, you can check the properties of any drive—including its volume label, file system, and the amount of free space available—from the My Computer window. Right-click the drive icon and choose Properties from the shortcut menu. You can see the same details and more by starting from Disk Management. Most of the key information is visible in the volume list, shown by default at the top of the window, with slightly less information available in the graphical view at the bottom of the window. Of particular interest is information about the status of a disk or volume. Figure 22-8 shows where to look for this information.

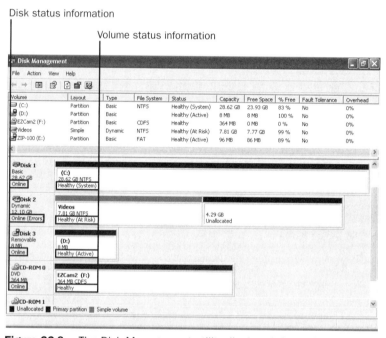

Figure 22-8. The Disk Management utility displays information about the status of each physical disk and volume.

Under normal circumstances, the status information displayed here should report that each disk is online and each volume is healthy. Table 22-1 lists all possible disk status messages you may see on a system running Windows XP Professional or Home Edition, along with suggested actions you should take to resolve possible errors.

Table 22-1. Disk Status

Status	Description	Action Required
Online	The disk is configured correctly and has no known problems.	None.
Online (Errors)	The operating system encountered errors when reading or writing data from a region of the disk. (This status message appears on dynamic disks only.)	Right-click the disk and choose Reactivate Disk to return its status to Online. If errors continue to occur, check for damage to the disk.
Offline	The disk was once available but is not currently accessible. The disk might be physically damaged or it might be disconnected. (This status message appears on dynamic disks only.)	Check the physical connections between the disk and the power supply or disk controller. After repairing connections, right-click the disk and choose Reactivate Disk to return its status to Online. If the damage cannot be repaired, delete all volumes, right-click the disk, and choose Remove Disk.
Foreign	The disk was originally installed on another computer and has not yet been set up for use on your computer. (This status message appears on dynamic disks only.)	Right-click the disk and choose Import Foreign Disks.
Unreadable	All or part of the disk may be physically damaged, or (in the case of a dynamic disk) the dynamic disk database may be corrupted.	Restart the computer. If the problem persists, right-click the disk and choose Rescan Disks. If the status is still unreadable, some data on the disk may be recoverable with third-party utilities.
Missing	The disk is corrupted, disconnected, or not powered on. (This status message appears on dynamic disks only.)	After you reconnect or power on the missing disk, right-click the disk and choose Reactivate Disk to return its status to Online.

Chapter 22

Table 22-1. Disk Status

Status	Description	Action Required
Not Initialized	The disk does not contain a valid signature. It may have been prepared on a system running a non-Microsoft operating system, such as UNIX or Linux, or the drive may be brand new.	If the disk is used by another operating system, do nothing. To prepare a new disk for use with Windows XP, right-click the disk and choose Initialize Disk.
No Media	A disk is not inserted in the drive. (This status message appears only on removable media drives, such as Zip drives and CD-R/CD-RW drives.)	Insert a disk in the drive and choose Action, Rescan Disks.

Table 22-2 describes volume status messages you're likely to see.

> **Tip** Tackle disk problems first
>
> Almost without fail, a disk problem will generate a status indicator for both the disk and any volumes on that disk. For instance, if you see a disk with Online (Errors) in the Status column, you're likely to see Healthy (At Risk) as the volume's status. In this case, your best bet is to try to resolve the disk problem first. If you can successfully do so, the problems with the volume will usually clear up as a matter of course.

Table 22-2. Volume Status

Status	Description	Action Required
Healthy	The volume is properly formatted and has no known problems.	None.
Healthy (At Risk)	Windows encountered errors when reading from or writing to the underlying disk. Such errors are often caused by bad blocks on the disk. After encountering an error anywhere on the disk, Disk Management marks all volumes on that disk as Healthy (At Risk). (This status message appears on dynamic disks only.)	Right-click the disk and choose Reactivate Disk. Persistent errors often indicate a failing disk. Back up all data and run a thorough diagnostic check using the hardware manufacturer's software; if necessary, replace the disk.

Table 22-2. **Volume Status**

Status	Description	Action Required
Healthy (Unknown Partition)	Windows does not recognize the partition; this occurs with some partitions created by another operating system or by a computer manufacturer who uses a partition to store system files. You cannot format or access data on an unknown partition.	If you're certain the partition is unnecessary, use the Disk Management utility to delete it and create a new partition in the free space created.
Initializing	The Disk Management utility cannot determine the disk status because the disk is initializing. (This status message appears on dynamic disks only.)	Wait. The drive status should appear in a few seconds.
Failed	The dynamic disk is damaged or the file system is corrupted.	To repair a failed dynamic volume, check to see whether the disk is online. (If not, right-click the disk and choose Reactivate Disk.) Then right-click the volume and choose Reactivate Volume. If the failed volume is on a basic disk, be sure that the disk is properly connected.
Unknown	The boot sector for the volume is corrupted, and you can no longer access data. This condition may be caused by a virus.	Use an up-to-date virus-scanning program to check for the presence of a boot-sector virus. If no virus is found, boot from the Windows XP CD and use Recovery Console's Fixmbr command to fix the Master Boot Record.

Chapter 22

Troubleshooting

The Check Disk utility runs frequently at startup.

When your system shuts down improperly, Windows runs the Autochk program on all NTFS drives where a disk write was in process at the time of the unexpected shutdown. Problems associated with unexpected shutdowns can be exacerbated if you have write caching enabled on a hard drive connected to a standard IDE controller. Although this option improves performance by delaying the writing of data while you work on other things, it can result in an increased risk of data loss or corruption.

If this is a persistent problem on your system, you should disable write caching on the affected drive. From the graphical display at the bottom of the Disk Management window, right-click the disk's icon and choose Properties. On the Policies tab, clear Enable Write Caching On The Disk. (Note that this option may not be available if your disk is connected to a high-performance ATA-66 or ATA-100 IDE controller.)

After you find the cause of the improper shutdowns and fix the underlying problem, be sure to re-enable write caching.

Setting Quotas for Disk Space Use

Disk quotas allow you to monitor and limit disk-space usage on NTFS-formatted drives and volumes—a handy feature on a multiuser system where a download-happy family member can easily fill up even the most gargantuan physical disk with digital music, videos, and pictures. Using quotas, you can set storage limits for each user and each volume.

 The companion CD includes Diskuse.exe (also known as User Disk Usage Tool). This command-line tool, which is also available as part of the Windows Resource Kit Tools, scans the folder or drive you specify and reports the amount of disk space used by each user. Diskuse can also list all the files owned by the users you specify, and it can list all users whose files occupy more space than an amount you specify. You don't need to set disk quotas to use Diskuse, which is a reporting tool only; it does nothing to actually impose disk space limits.

When you enable disk quotas, Windows tracks volume usage by file ownership. A file counts against a user's quota if the security identifier (SID) of the file's owner is the same as the user's SID. For an in-depth explanation of SIDs and other security issues, see "Introducing Windows XP Security," page 222.

> **Note** Disk quotas rely on the SID, not the user account name. In a workgroup environment—where each user has a separate, identically named user account on each computer—this can cause quotas to be less reliable than in a domain. That's because a user's account on each computer has a different SID. Depending on how a file is created, it might be owned by the user's account on a different computer. If your NTFS volume contains files that are owned by a user account from another computer, you'll see the owner's SID in the Quota Entries window instead of (or in addition to) the user's name.

Enabling Disk Quotas

To enable disk quotas, use the Quota tab in the properties dialog box for a volume. Log on as a member of the Administrators group and then follow these steps:

1. From the My Computer window, right-click any NTFS drive icon and choose Properties (or use the equivalent menu after right-clicking a volume in the Disk Management window).

2. Click the Quota tab and then select the Enable Quota Management check box to enable the other items on the Quota tab.

3. Set the other options on the Quota tab as follows:

   ■ Select Deny Disk Space To Users Exceeding Quota Limit if you want Windows to prevent users from saving files that would exceed their assigned space limit. (They'll see an "insufficient disk space" error message.) If you don't select this check box, Windows doesn't stop users from exceeding their limit—but it allows you to track disk usage by user.

- To specify a default limit for new users (that is, users who don't have an entry in the Quota Entries window, described in the following section), select Limit Disk Space To and set a limit and a warning level. (Exceeding the warning level doesn't trigger a warning to the user, but administrators can use this setting to more easily monitor users who are nearing their limit.) If you don't want to set limits on new users, select Do Not Limit Disk Usage.

- If you want Windows to make an entry in the System log whenever a user exceeds his or her quota limit or warning level, select the appropriate check box.

Managing Disk Quotas

When you enable quotas on a volume that has existing files, Windows calculates the disk space used by each user who has created, copied, or taken ownership of the existing files. The default quota limits and warning levels are then applied to all current users and to any new user who saves a file. To view and modify the quota entries for a given drive, open the properties dialog box for that drive, click the Quota tab, and then click Quota Entries. The Quota Entries window opens, as shown in Figure 22-9.

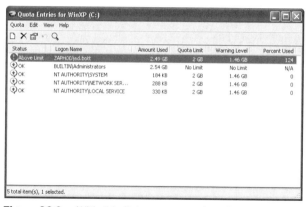

Figure 22-9.   With this list, you can review disk usage and impose limits on a per-user basis.

For each user, Quota Entries displays:

- A status indicator (OK for users who are below their warning level and quota limit, Warning for users who are above their warning level, and Above Limit for users who are above their quota limit)

- The user's logon name

- The amount of disk space occupied by files that the user owns

- The user's quota limit and warning level

- The percentage of the quota limit currently in use

To change a user's limits, double-click his or her entry. A dialog box appears that offers choices for this user similar to the choices offered on the Quota tab for all new users.

> **Note** By default, the Administrators group has no limit—meaning that while you're logged on as a member of the Administrators group, you might be able to create files that exceed the limits of your user account. Although you can set a warning limit for the Administrators group, you cannot set a quota limit.

Setting AutoPlay Options for Removable Drives

On devices that contain removable storage media, Windows is constantly on the lookout for newly inserted media. If you insert a CD or DVD into a drive, or connect a Windows XP–compatible digital camera, or pop a Compact Flash card into an external reader, Windows responds with a dialog box similar to the one shown in Figure 22-10.

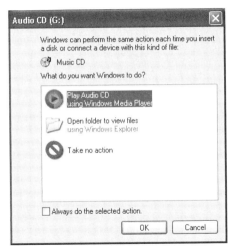

Figure 22-10. When Windows detects that you've inserted a new disk (or other media) into a removable storage device, it asks how you want to handle the content.

The Windows AutoPlay settings allow you to define different default actions for different types of content. For instance, you can specify that you want music CDs to play automatically in Windows Media Player or another application, while disks that contain mixed content should open in a Windows Explorer window so that you can copy them to a local drive.

Inside Out

Disabling AutoPlay

Some people see AutoPlay as a nuisance instead of a convenience. If you're in that camp, you can disable AutoPlay altogether as explained in the following procedures.

If you're running Windows XP Professional, use Group Policy, as follows:

1 At a command prompt, type **gpedit.msc** to open Group Policy.

2 In the console tree, select Computer Configuration\Administrative Templates\ System.

3 In the right pane, double-click Turn Off Autoplay.

4 Select Enabled, and then select CD-ROM Drives or All Drives. The first choice is a bit misleading—selecting CD-ROM Drives disables AutoPlay on DVD drives, removable drives, and network drives, as well as CD-ROM drives. Selecting All Drives indeed disables AutoPlay on all drives, including Compact Flash cards and other non-disk drive types.

5 Click OK and then close Group Policy.

To restore AutoPlay functionality, return to the Turn Off Autoplay policy and set the policy to Not Configured or Disabled.

If you use Windows XP Home Edition, you can't use Group Policy. However, you can edit the registry directly to achieve the same effect. Follow these steps:

1 At a command prompt, type **regedit** to open Registry Editor.

2 Navigate to the HKLM\Software\Microsoft\Windows\CurrentVersion\Policies key.

3 Right-click the Policies key and choose New, Key. Type **Explorer** to replace the default key name, New Key #1.

4 Right-click the new Explorer subkey, and choose New, DWORD Value. Type **NoDriveTypeAutoRun** to replace the default value name, New Value #1.

5 Double-click the new NoDriveTypeAutoRun value, and type **b5** in the Value Data box. (Be sure that Hexadecimal is selected in the Base box.)

6 Click OK, log off, and then log back on.

To restore AutoPlay, return to Registry Editor and delete the NoDriveTypeAutoRun value.

You can adjust the default AutoPlay settings at any time on a per-drive basis. If you decide that you want digital photos on a Compact Flash card to open in a Windows Explorer window instead of in the Scanner And Camera Wizard, that's your right. To adjust AutoPlay settings, open My Computer, right-click the icon for the drive in question, and then choose Properties. On the AutoPlay tab, choose different options for each type of content associated with that drive, as shown here.

Working with Writable and Rewritable CD Drives

Windows XP includes software that allows you to copy files and folders from a Windows Explorer window onto a writable (CD-R) or rewritable (CD-RW) disk in a compatible drive. This software, which is integrated into Windows Explorer, is a light version of Roxio's Easy CD Creator program. If you have a Windows XP–compatible CD recorder, you can copy files and folders from any local folder to a writable or rewritable CD. You can also create audio CDs from Windows Media Player, read from CDs created with packet-writing software such as Roxio's DirectCD, and erase rewritable CDs so that you can reuse them.

Inside Out

Creating music CDs

The built-in CD writing capabilities in Windows XP are useful, but they're not intended for anything but rudimentary use. Using this software, for instance, you can't create CDs using the Universal Disk Format (UDF) file system. (UDF is sometimes called "packet writing.") Without UDF capability, you can't create "disk at once" music CDs, which allow music to flow smoothly from track to track without annoying two-second gaps—a significant flaw for classical and live recordings. If you're serious about creating CDs, you should invest in full-strength CD-recording software, such as Roxio's Easy Media Creator (*http://www.roxio.com*) or Ahead Software's Nero (*http://www.nero.com*). If you do so, be sure to disable Windows XP's built-in recording capabilities, which can conflict with third-party software.

For more details about copying files and folders using a CD burner, see "Copying Files to CDs," page 711.

If you plan to use the built-in CD recording capabilities in Windows XP, check to see that CD recording is enabled on your drive. If you plan to use a third-party program instead, go to the same location to disable recording from Windows Explorer. In either case, you control this option using a check box in the properties dialog box for the CD-RW drive. From the My Computer window, right-click the drive icon and choose Properties. Options on the Recording tab, shown in Figure 22-11, allow you to control how Windows XP works with your CD burner:

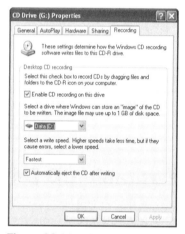

Figure 22-11. Fine-tune CD recording options here.

- Clear the Enable CD Recording On This Drive check box if you want to use a third-party CD recording program. This box should remain selected if you plan to record CDs from within Windows Explorer.

- During the recording process, the CD Writing Wizard creates a CD image that is equal in size to the files you plan to copy. Using the list in the middle of the properties dialog box, you can specify which drive or volume you want to use for these temporary files.

- Normally, Windows configures your CD drive to operate at its fastest speed. If you encounter frequent errors, you might want to reduce the write speed as a troubleshooting step. Choose a speed from the Select A Write Speed list.

- After burning a CD, Windows automatically ejects it from the drive. This action is intended to alert you that the CD is done, so that you can label it or insert another blank CD. Depending on your hardware, this configuration may be less than ideal. If you have a tower computer that sits alongside your chair, for instance, you could inadvertently bump into the CD tray and break it if it pops out when you're not expecting it. To eliminate this possibility, clear the Automatically Eject The CD After Writing check box.

Chapter 22

Troubleshooting

You get frequent errors when writing CDs.

The most common cause of CD writing failures is a buffer underrun—when the flow of data to the CD recorder is interrupted and the laser is unable to continue writing to the disk. When this happens, you end up with a coaster. Fixing persistent buffer underrun problems can be maddening. Here are some places to start:

- **Is your hardware fully compatible and up to date?** Check with the CD-RW drive manufacturer to see whether a firmware update is available.

- **Do you have other CD writing software installed?** If the other software works, disable the Windows XP CD writing capabilities and use the third-party program instead.

- **Are you writing too fast?** Turn down the CD writing speed and see whether that helps.

- **Is your hard disk fragmented? Is it too full? Are you using your fastest hard disk for the location of the CD image?** Clean out unneeded files and defragment all drives on your system. Consider dedicating a separate volume on your fastest physical disk to the temporary files used for CD burning.

- **Are other programs interfering with the CPU?** Shut down screen savers and any background programs that might be getting in the way of the CD writing software.

- **Does the problem happen with one particular brand of blank CDs?** You could have a bad batch. Try a different brand and see whether the problem persists.

In the original release of Windows XP, certain situations resulted in several similar problems:

- The disc is unreadable.

- The disc works in Windows XP, but it's unreadable in Windows 95, Windows 98, or in an MP3 player.

- Some files are lost or missing.

These problems were resolved in Service Pack 1. If you haven't yet installed the latest Windows XP service pack, you can obtain a patch through Windows Update. For more information, see Knowledge Base article 320174, "Compact Disc Recorded in Windows XP Is Missing Files or Folders or Is Unreadable."

Chapter 22

Working with Offline Files and Folders

If you need to take work on the road—even if the road is only your daily commute—you'll appreciate the offline files feature in Microsoft Windows XP Professional. When you make a shared file or folder available for offline use, Windows caches a copy of that file or folder on the hard disk of your local computer. While you're disconnected from the network, you can work with the copy exactly as if it were the original. When you reconnect, Windows synchronizes your cached files with their server counterparts, so that you have up-to-date versions on both your local machine and the server.

Note Throughout this chapter, we use the term *server* to signify the computer on which a shared file or folder resides. That computer might or might not be running one of the server editions of Windows. The features described in this chapter work the same way in a peer-to-peer network setting (such as a typical home or small business network) as in a network that uses one or more domain controllers.

At Home with Windows XP

The offline files and folders feature is available only in Windows XP Professional. If you use Windows XP Home Edition and travel frequently with your notebook computer, you might consider this sufficient reason to upgrade to Professional. Note that only the traveling machine needs the offline files capability. If your portable computer is networked with one or more homebound computers, with each system running Windows XP Home Edition, upgrading the portable computer to Professional will give you the ability to take files on the road and synchronize them on return, even if the other computers continue to run Home Edition.

Even if you don't travel, you might still find the offline files capability of Windows XP to be useful. Offline files can reduce network traffic and ensure continuity on systems that are sometimes disconnected from the network (inadvertently or intentionally). For more information, see "Setting Caching Options on the Server," page 789.

> **Note** Windows XP—both Home Edition and Professional—also allows you to mark favorite Internet sites for offline use. By right-clicking an item in your Microsoft Internet Explorer Favorites folder and choosing Make Available Offline from the shortcut menu, you can *subscribe* to the selected site. Windows then downloads current content to your local hard disk and updates the information periodically, according to the synchronization schedule you specify. For more about this form of offline work, see "Making a Favorite Available Offline," page 517.

Setting Up Your System to Use Offline Files

Before you can cache server-based files and folders on your local system, you have to make sure that the offline files feature is enabled on your local computer. And to enable offline files, you must first *disable* Fast User Switching, if that feature is currently enabled. (With Fast User Switching disabled, you will need to close any running programs before switching user accounts.)

To disable Fast User Switching, open Control Panel, User Accounts, and then click Change The Way Users Log On Or Off. Clear the Use Fast User Switching option. When you no longer need to use offline files, you can return to Control Panel to re-enable Fast User Switching.

To enable offline files, open Control Panel, Folder Options (if you're using Category view in Control Panel, Folder Options is in Appearance And Themes; you can also choose Folder Options from the Tools menu in Windows Explorer). On the Offline Files tab of the Folder Options dialog box, make sure that Enable Offline Files is selected. Figure 23-1 shows this dialog box with default settings.

Figure 23-1. The Offline Files tab of the Folder Options dialog box is where you turn on or off your system's ability to use offline files.

Choosing Setup Options

The most crucial option on the Offline Files tab of the Folder Options dialog box is the first check box—the one that turns the entire feature on or off. The remaining options in this dialog box govern such matters as logoff synchronization, encryption of offline files, and maximum cache size.

The second most crucial option is the third check box—Synchronize All Offline Files Before Logging Off. With this check box selected (its default state), Windows performs what it calls a *full synchronization* whenever you log off your user account. This action ensures that whenever you pack up and go, your cached files match the latest server versions. Be aware, though, that you must actually log off (or shut down) to effect this synchronization. If you simply disconnect from the network, or if you hibernate rather than shutting down (for example, by simply closing the lid of your portable computer, if the computer has been set up to hibernate in this fashion), Windows doesn't have a chance to synchronize your files.

If the option to synchronize at logoff is not selected, you'll get what Windows calls a *partial synchronization*. This means that Windows caches a copy of a server-based file or folder when you mark it Make Available Offline. (For details, see "Making Files and Folders Available Offline" on page 787.) Thus, when you head for the road you'll have *something* to work with—but it might not be the latest version available. So if your purpose in enabling offline files is to take current work with you, select Synchronize All Offline Files Before Logging Off (or get in the habit of manually synchronizing all files before you leave).

Chapter 23

Troubleshooting

Windows can't synchronize certain files when you log off.

Some types of files cannot be synchronized for offline use, including Microsoft Outlook Personal Folders files (.pst), Zip files (.zip), and Microsoft Access files (.mdb). Likewise, if shared files are open (that is, in use by someone else or by another running process) when you synchronize, you'll be unable to synchronize those files. In either case, you'll see the following error message.

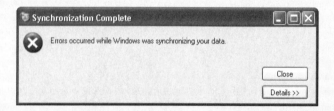

To view the names of the files that Windows was unable to synchronize, click the Details button. If the files are not eligible for synchronization, you can either choose not to synchronize those files, or change the file name extension for each file listed in the Details section to one that is not on the prohibited list. If the synchronization attempt was initiated when you logged off, you'll have no choice but to complete the logoff after dismissing the error message. But if the unsynchronized files are ones you'll need while you're away and they were simply skipped because the files were open, you might want to log back on, arrange to have the files closed (find out who's using them and ask them to desist momentarily), and then log off again.

The option to synchronize all offline files when you log back on (the second check box in Figure 23-1) is cleared by default. Leaving the option in this state gives you the chance to continue working with the offline versions of your files when you return to the office. When you're ready, you can synchronize manually by choosing Tools, Synchronize in Windows Explorer. If this isn't what you want—that is, if you want Windows to synchronize automatically when you reconnect—select the second check box.

For more information about synchronizing manually, see "Synchronizing on Demand, on Idle, or on Schedule," page 793.

If Display A Reminder Every is selected, Windows displays balloon messages in the notification area at periodic intervals when your system is disconnected from the network. You might find this notification useful if you occasionally become disconnected from your network without realizing it. Otherwise, it's likely to be a nuisance—for example, when you are traveling and are well aware that you're offline. Clear the check box if you don't fancy balloons.

When you use offline files, Windows creates a special system folder called Offline Files. You can get to this folder by clicking View Files in the Folder Options dialog box. If you want a desktop shortcut to the folder as well, select Create An Offline Files Shortcut On The Desktop.

If you carry sensitive information on your laptop, you might want to select Encrypt Offline Files To Secure Data. That way, only your own user account will be able to read the cached data. Be aware that many programs (such as Microsoft Word) create temporary files as you work. These files are not encrypted. The program creating the temporary files deletes them in the course of your normal work, but the temporary data remains in an unencrypted form on your hard disk. To maximize security while you work with encrypted offline information, you should also use Windows Explorer to encrypt the folders where temporary files are stored. You can open these folders in Windows Explorer by choosing Start, Run and typing %temp% or %tmp%.

> For more details about encrypting files and folders, see Chapter 11, "Encrypting Confidential Information."

By default, Windows allocates 10 percent of your local hard disk for use in caching offline files. To adjust this setting upward or downward, return to the Offline Files tab of the Folder Options dialog box shown in Figure 23-1 and reposition the slider.

Making Files and Folders Available Offline

After you have set up your computer for offline files, you make individual files and folders available for offline use by right-clicking them in Windows Explorer and choosing Make Available Offline. You select files and folders that reside on the server computer while working from the *client* computer (the one that will go offline), not the server. For example, in Figure 23-2, we've marked the folder \\Vm8200\My Documents\XP IO Second Edition\ Chapter 23 for offline use by navigating to that network folder in My Network Places from the client computer.

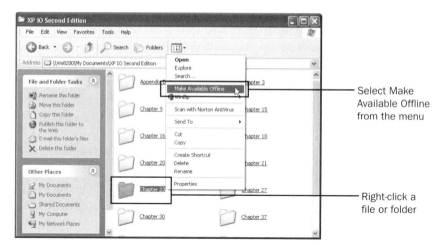

Select Make
Available Offline
from the menu

Right-click a
file or folder

Figure 23-2. To make a file or folder available offline, right-click it from the computer that will go offline, and then select Make Available Offline.

When you mark a folder for offline use, Windows caches all files in the folder. If the folder has subfolders, you'll be asked whether you want to cache those as well. Windows then performs a synchronization on the selected items—that is, it creates copies in the client computer's cache. Icons for cached folders and files thereafter appear in Windows Explorer with a double arrow, as shown here.

Chapter 23

Tip Choose a larger icon size to distinguish shortcuts and cached items

Because Windows uses the lower left corner of folder and file icons for both the single-arrow shortcut symbol and the double arrow cached item symbol, shortcuts and cached items look alike in Windows Explorer's List and Details views. Try Icons or Tiles view if you have trouble telling them apart.

Working Offline

While you're offline, you can work with cached folders and files exactly as if you were online. You can navigate to those items in My Network Places or My Computer, or you can access the files and folders from within your application in the customary ways. In Windows Explorer, you will see the cached folders and their parent folders, but not uncached siblings. For example, in Figure 23-3, the folder Chapter 23 is visible in \\Vm8200\My Documents\XP IO Second Edition, because we marked it for offline use (see Figure 23-2). The sibling folder

Appendix D is also visible, but its icon does not bear the telltale double arrow. That's because one of that folder's subfolders is marked for offline use, but Appendix D itself is not. None of the other siblings of Chapter 23 appears in the XP IO Second Edition folder while the offline computer is disconnected from the network, because none of those folders has been marked for offline use.

 As a reminder of the fact that you're disconnected, Windows displays an "offline" icon in the notification area. You can double-click that icon to read status information.

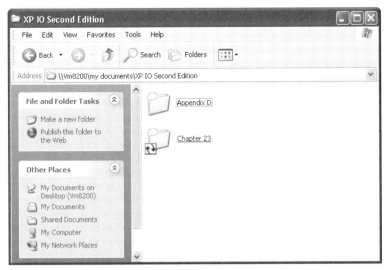

Figure 23-3. When you work offline, Windows Explorer shows only the folders that you've cached, along with their parent folders.

Setting Caching Options on the Server

All discussion of the behavior of offline files and folders so far in this chapter has assumed that the caching property of each network share accessed for offline work is set at its default value. This value, called Manual Caching Of Documents, is one of three possible settings. To adjust the caching property, do the following on the server computer:

1 Type **fsmgmt.msc** at a command prompt. This runs the Shared Folders management console.

2 In the console tree (the left pane), select Shares.

3 In the details pane (the right pane), right-click the share whose property you want to set and then choose Properties.

4 On the General tab of the properties dialog box, click Caching. The Caching Settings dialog box opens, as shown in Figure 23-4.

Note The properties dialog box for a shared folder is not available if you're using Simple File Sharing. To turn Simple File Sharing off, choose Tools, Folder Options in Windows Explorer. On the View tab, clear Use Simple File Sharing (Recommended). After you have changed the server caching options, you can return to Simple File Sharing if you prefer to work in that mode. For more information about Simple File Sharing, see "Simple File Sharing vs. Windows 2000–Style Sharing," page 230.

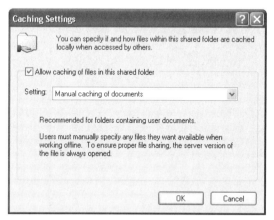

Figure 23-4. You can use this dialog box to control caching behavior for a network share.

The default setting, Manual Caching Of Documents, stipulates that only those files and folders explicitly marked Make Available Offline are cached. When you choose Make Available Offline on the client computer, you are guaranteed that the selected item will be available offline. This is the setting you want to use when you take work out of the office on a portable computer.

The alternative settings for the caching property are Automatic Caching Of Programs And Documents.

Using Automatic Caching Of Documents

When Automatic Caching Of Documents is selected, Windows caches a server-based file or folder automatically as soon as you access it from the client computer. When you open a cached document from a client computer, the cached copy is used, but the original document on the server is also opened to prevent other people from changing the file while you have it open.

Because it doesn't require the separate step of copying a server resource into your cache, automatic caching is more convenient and easier to use than the default manual caching. On the other hand, with automatic caching, Windows doesn't guarantee that your server resources remain in the cache. How long they stay there, in fact, depends on usage. As the amount of disk space you've allocated to the cache is consumed, Windows discards any documents that have not been used recently to make room for newer ones.

Disabling Automatic Caching on Particular Computers

If you use automatic caching as a means of maintaining continuity in an environment where network connections are sometimes broken, you can disable this functionality on particular client computers. You might want to do this, for example, if a particular user needs to know when the network is down. Follow these steps to disable automatic caching on a client:

1 Choose Tools, Options in Windows Explorer.

2 On the Offline Files tab, click Advanced.

3 In the Offline Files–Advanced Settings dialog box, select Never Allow My Computer To Go Offline.

   Alternatively, in this same dialog box, you can disable offline work only when connections to particular servers are broken.

4 Select the option Notify Me And Begin Working Offline, and then add particular servers to the exception list.

5 Add specific servers by clicking Add to open the Add Custom Action dialog box.

6 Type or browse to the name of each computer you do *not* want to cache for offline work and select the option Never Allow My Computer To Go Offline.

Using Automatic Caching Of Programs And Documents

You can use the Automatic Caching Of Programs And Documents setting for folders that contain programs and documents that are read but not changed. Automatic caching of programs can speed up access to programs and documents, because after a file is cached, your system does not have to retrieve it from the server again; only the local copy is opened.

Turning Off Caching for a Specific Share

You can turn the offline files feature off on a per-share basis. To disable caching for a share, clear Allow Caching Of Files In This Shared Folder, in the Caching Settings dialog box (see Figure 23-4).

Chapter 23

How Windows Synchronizes Your Files

When you synchronize your offline files with their server-based copies, Windows XP performs the following operations for each offline file:

- If you have changed the file while offline and the server-based copy has not been changed, Windows updates the server copy with your changes.
- If you have not made changes to your offline copy but the server copy has been changed, Windows updates the copy in your cache.
- If both the server copy and your offline copy have changed, a dialog box appears, as shown in Figure 23-5. You can keep your client version, the server version, or both. (Click the View buttons if you're not sure.)

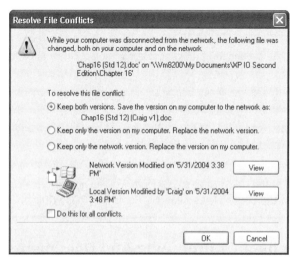

Figure 23-5. When synchronization reveals file conflicts between server and cache, you can keep either version—or both.

- If either the offline copy or the server copy of a file is deleted, the file on the other computer is deleted as well, as long as it wasn't changed while you were offline.
- If the server copy has been deleted and you changed your offline copy, a dialog box appears. You can save your version on the server or delete your offline copy.
- If you delete the offline copy and the server copy has been changed, a dialog box asks whether you want to delete the server copy or use the server copy. If you decide to use the server copy, the server version appears in your offline cache.
- If a new file has been added on the server to a folder that you have marked for offline availability, that new file is copied to your cache.

Synchronizing on Demand, on Idle, or on Schedule

Depending on how you have set up your Offline Files options, Windows may synchronize your work whenever you reconnect your mobile computer to the network. In addition to this default synchronization, you can synchronize on demand. To do this, choose Start, All Programs, Accessories, Synchronize. Or choose Tools, Synchronize in Windows Explorer. The Items To Synchronize dialog box (also known as the Synchronization Manager) appears, as shown in Figure 23-6.

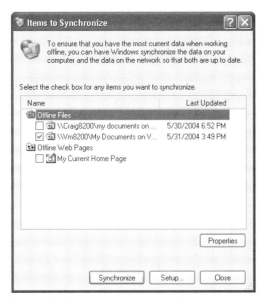

Figure 23-6.   You can use this dialog box to synchronize immediately or set up a synchronization schedule.

To synchronize immediately, select the items you want to synchronize and click Synchronize. For other options, click Setup. The Synchronization Settings dialog box, shown in Figure 23-7, has three tabs. Use the Logon/Logoff tab to fine-tune the way Windows synchronizes at these critical times. Use the other two tabs to set up synchronization when your computer is idle or at other scheduled times.

Chapter 23

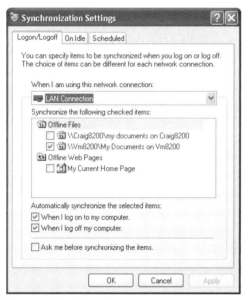

Figure 23-7. The Synchronization Settings dialog box includes a check box that allows you to request a confirmation prompt before synchronization occurs.

> **Tip** By selecting Ask Me Before Synchronizing The Items in the Synchronization Settings dialog box, you can ensure that Windows never synchronizes files without your permission.

Managing the Cache

Windows maintains a system folder that lists all the server-based files you've made available to yourself for offline use. The Offline Files folder, shown in Figure 23-8, also includes information about the synchronization status of each file, the permissions associated with each file, the location of each file's server counterpart, whether the server is currently online or offline, and so on. Files that are stored on servers set for manual caching (see "Setting Caching Options on the Server," page 789) are identified as Always Available Offline. Those that reside on shares set for automatic caching are identified as Temporarily Available Offline. You can launch a cached item (open a document in its parent application, for example) by double-clicking it in the Offline Files folder.

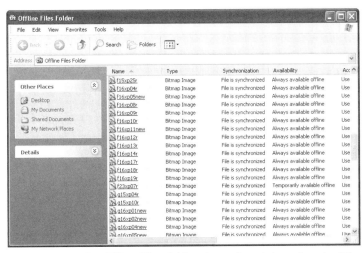

Figure 23-8. The Offline Files folder shows the status of each offline file.

If you opted to create a desktop shortcut for the Offline Files folder when you set up offline files, the easiest way to view the folder is by double-clicking that shortcut. Alternately, you can double-click the Offline Files icon in your notification area and then click View Files. Or you can choose Tools, Folder Options in Windows Explorer, click the Offline Files tab, and then click View Files.

Increasing or Decreasing the Maximum Cache Size

By default, Windows prevents the cache size from exceeding 10 percent of the size of the partition on which Windows is installed. You can increase or decrease that amount by dragging the slider on the Offline Files tab of the Folder Options dialog box (shown in Figure 23-1 on page 785). You cannot move or extend the cache to another partition, however.

Deleting Files from the Cache

When you no longer need offline access to a network resource, return to that resource in My Computer or My Network Places, right-click the item in question, and clear Make Available Offline. If the share involved is set for manual caching (see "Setting Caching Options on the Server," page 789), Windows purges the items from your cache in addition to turning off offline access. If the share is set for automatic caching, items that are currently in the cache remain there. To delete them, choose Tools, Options in Windows Explorer and then click the Offline Files tab. In the Folder Options dialog box (shown in Figure 23-1 on page 785), click Delete Files. Then select the shares whose items you want to delete.

Synchronizing Files with Briefcase

Briefcase provides you with an alternative way to work with files offline and synchronize them with their original counterparts when you reconnect. If you like to transfer work between one computer and another by means of a removable storage medium, such as a diskette or USB flash drive, and you don't have a network connection between the two computers, Briefcase is for you.

To use Briefcase, follow these steps:

1 Put a disk in a removable disk drive of the machine that holds the files you want to use offline and open the removable disk in Windows Explorer.

2 Right-click in the removable disk's folder and choose New, Briefcase.

3 Rename the briefcase (an optional step, but you'll want to do this if you use more than one briefcase at a time).

4 Open the briefcase (it's a folder, almost like any other). Close the dialog box that appears, and then copy files into your new briefcase until the removable disk is somewhat less than full. Don't fill the disk, because you need room for your files to grow as you work with them.

5 Insert the removable disk in your offline computer, and move or copy the briefcase to that computer's hard disk. Move or copy the briefcase *folder*, not the individual files in the briefcase. (This step is optional, but if your transfer medium is a slow performer—a 1.44-MB diskette, for example—you won't want to omit it.)

6 Repeat these steps for as many removable disks as you need, giving each briefcase a unique name.

7 In preparation for synchronizing with your first computer, copy each briefcase on your offline machine to a removable disk. Then transfer the removable disk's contents to your first computer.

8 To synchronize, open a briefcase and then choose Briefcase, Update All. (The Briefcase menu appears on the Windows Explorer menu only when a briefcase folder is displayed.) To synchronize only particular files, select the files you want to synchronize, and then choose Briefcase, Update Selection.

Getting Status Information About Briefcase Files

In Windows Explorer Details view, Briefcase provides useful information about the origin and status of your documents. As Figure 23-9 shows, the Status column shows which files are current and which need updating. The Sync Copy In column tells you where the original version of each file is stored.

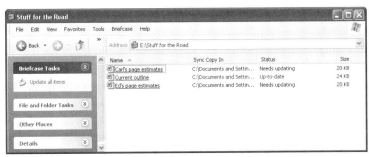

Figure 23-9. Columns in Windows Explorer show which briefcase files need updating and where each file's original version resides.

When your briefcase is online with the computer where it was created, you can also get status information about a particular file by right-clicking it, choosing Properties, and viewing the Update Status tab. Figure 23-10, for example, shows the status for a file that has been changed in the briefcase.

Figure 23-10. The properties dialog box for a briefcase file can tell you which version of the file is more current.

Synchronizing Files

When you're ready to synchronize your briefcase files with their originals, you can either work with one file at a time or update the whole briefcase at once. To update a single file, select it and choose Briefcase, Update Selection. To update the whole briefcase, choose Briefcase, Update All (or click its toolbar equivalent). You'll see an update dialog box similar to the one shown in Figure 23-11.

Figure 23-11. When you choose Update All from the Windows Explorer Briefcase menu, the arrows in this dialog box show you which versions of your files need updating.

The arrows in the center of the dialog box can point in either direction, depending on which versions of your files are changed and which need updating. When you click Update, Windows copies the changed version, no matter where it resides, over the unchanged one. If both files have been modified, the default action is not to update either. If a file was deleted in one location, it will be copied to the other location to replace the deleted file.

If the update action that Briefcase proposes for an item isn't the action you want, right-click its entry in the Update dialog box and then choose the action you prefer.

Separating a Briefcase File from Its Sync Copy

If you move a file from a briefcase to any other folder, the link between that file and its original version is broken. The result is an ordinary copy. You can also sever the link between a file and its sync copy (the copy on the server) without removing it from the briefcase. To do this, select the file and then choose Briefcase, Split From Original. In Briefcase's Status column, the file will then be listed as "orphan."

Mastering Digital Media

Using and Customizing Windows Media Player

Windows Media Player has been a part of Microsoft Windows for more than a decade. In its earliest incarnation, the Media Player program was a bare-bones 16-bit utility that performed only one trick: playing uncompressed (WAV) audio files. Through the years, Microsoft has steadily improved the capabilities of Windows Media Player and tightened its links to Windows. In fact, you practically need a scorecard to keep track of the changes:

- Windows Media Player 8, which was included with the original release of Windows XP in 2001, was widely praised as the most complete and tightly integrated collection of tools for playing and managing digital audio and video that Windows users had ever seen.

- Windows Media Player 9 Series, which was officially released in January 2003 and is included in Service Pack 2, added noteworthy new features to this all-in-one client, without significantly changing the original interface.

- Windows Media Player 10, which was available in a beta version when we wrote this chapter, completely reworked the Player's interface and added a handful of new capabilities. In this chapter, we assume that you have upgraded to Windows Media Player 10.

At Home with Windows XP

Windows Media Player works identically in Windows XP Home Edition and Professional. All the information in this chapter applies equally to both versions. Windows XP Media Center Edition includes a number of additional media-related applications, but its version of Windows Media Player is no different from that found in other editions of Windows XP.

You can use Windows Media Player to play sound and video files stored on a local disk or streamed from Internet sites. It allows you to tune in to radio stations from all parts of the world. You can *rip* tracks from audio CDs (that is, copy them to your hard disk), create custom CDs using a CD-R or CD-RW drive, and download songs to a portable audio player. You can use the Player as a jukebox to listen to all of your favorite songs, in custom sequences that you devise or in random order. If you have a properly configured DVD drive, you can use the Player to screen your favorite movies and concert videos on a desktop or portable PC; with Windows XP Media Center Edition, you can connect your PC to dedicated audio and video components for theater-quality playback.

Windows Media Player is also designed to serve as a gateway to media-related sites on the Internet. If you click Guide in the Features taskbar (the horizontal panel of options at the top of the Player window), the Player becomes a special-purpose Web browser that loads *http://www.windowsmedia.com*, an Internet "magazine" that provides access to all manner of news and entertainment content. You can use links on this site to watch news clips, listen to music, and check out previews of current movies. In Windows Media Player 10, a new Online Stores button allows you to connect to sites that will be happy to sell you various kinds of media items.

The Windows Media Player interface has changed little since the debut of Windows XP. As Figure 24-1 shows, the Player window consists of five main elements when content is playing and Now Playing is selected:

- **Menu bar**   Offers access to Windows Media Player features and options via conventional pull-down menus; the menu bar can be hidden.

- **Features taskbar**   Contains buttons that activate key features and customization options.

- **Playback controls**   Used to manage playback of audio and video files, using VCR-style controls to play, pause, fast-forward, and rewind files; this area also includes a variety of special-purpose buttons that control volume and the appearance of the Player.

- **Quick Access Panel button**   Displays a customizable drop-down list from which you can choose an item to play back; available options include CDs, audio and video clips, playlists, and Media Library categories.

- **Now Playing area**   Center of the Player window; the contents of this area change depending on the current selection in the Features taskbar and any additional customizations you've specified for that type of content. The example shown here includes the Video and Visualizations pane (showing album art), the Enhancements pane (with the graphic equalizer visible), and the Playlist pane.

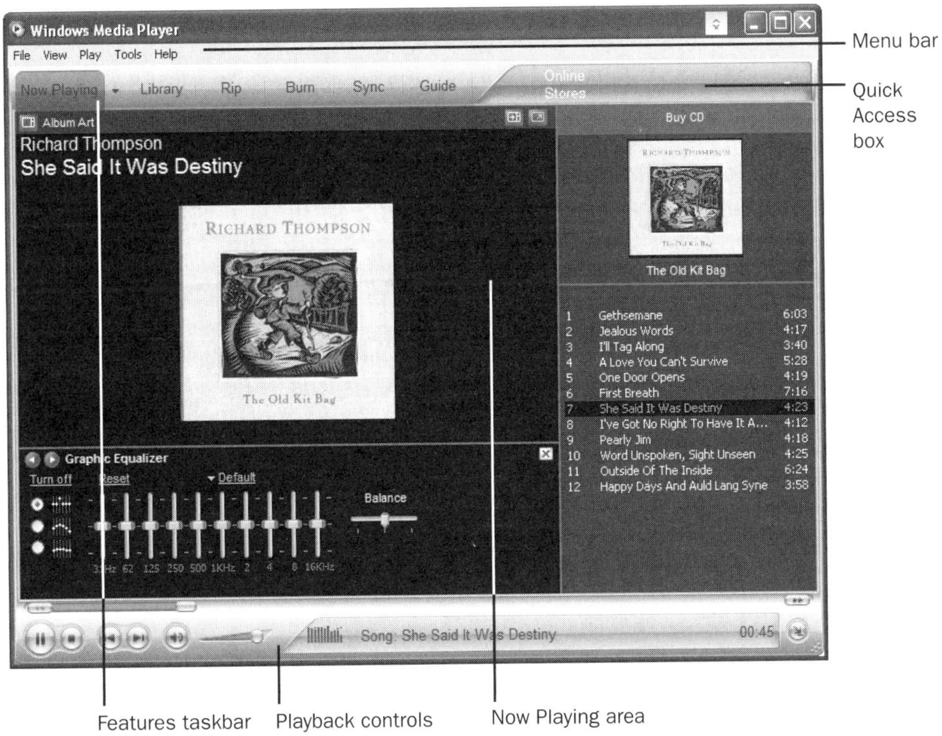

Menu bar

Quick
Access
box

Features taskbar   Playback controls   Now Playing area

Figure 24-1. Five elements of the Windows Media Player interface.

When you click an option other than Now Playing, the Player window allows you to work with your Library of digital media and create playlists for playing back music and video, burning custom CDs, and synchronizing with a portable device. We cover these options in more detail in Chapter 25.

Troubleshooting

Windows Media Player does not connect to Media Guide or to the Windows Media online artist information database.

If you find you never connect to WindowsMedia.com and that Windows Media Player is consistently unable to download track information for your CDs, even when you know you have a functioning Internet connection, you might have inadvertently set the program to stay offline. To see if this is the case, open the File menu. If Work Offline is checked, choose this command to clear the check mark and go back online.

Chapter 24

Windows Media Player 10 offers an extensive array of customization and configuration options. Some of these options simply change the Player's look and feel, but others have a major impact on the quality of your experience. For instance, the file format you choose to use when recording CD audio tracks affects both the quality of the recorded files and the amount of space they take up. In this chapter, we look at how Windows Media Player works and how you can fine-tune it for your own preferences. In Chapter 25, we examine the program's most popular use: creating and managing a digital music collection.

NEW FEATURE! What's New in Windows Media Player

Windows Media Player 9 Series was officially released in January 2003, long after the initial release of Windows XP and several months after Windows XP Service Pack 1 debuted. A beta version of Windows Media Player 10 was publicly released in June 2004; if past experience is any guide, the final release will be available as an optional update.

A default installation of Windows XP Service Pack 1 or earlier includes version 8 of Windows Media Player. Installing Windows XP Service Pack 2 (SP2) updates your system to the final release of Windows Media Player 9 Series. If you choose not to install SP2, you can install the latest code from Windows Update or by starting Windows Media Player and clicking Help, Check for Player Updates.

A full list of the improvements in Windows Media Player since the initial release of Windows XP would run for several pages. In general, the improvements can be grouped into the following broad categories:

- The user interface is cleaner, with usability improvements sprinkled throughout—especially for creating and managing playlists and recording CDs. Enabling mini-player mode allows you to minimize audio playback controls to a compact toolbar that embeds itself in the Windows taskbar.

- Privacy and security options are neatly organized and easy to access, and the default settings greatly improve privacy protection compared to earlier versions.

- Audio and video performance is significantly improved. Surround sound (5.1) audio is fully supported. New Windows Media Audio (WMA) formats allow higher-quality recording, and cross-fading and auto volume leveling eliminate annoying transitions between tracks when playing CDs.

- The Library supplies better tools for organizing music and other media—for instance, you can view your music collection by artist and then by album. You can also assign a rating (1–5 stars) to each track, and see which tunes you've played most often.

- An Advanced Tag Editor gives you more control over the information in music files that identifies artists, song titles, albums, and other attributes. You can automatically update tags and rename files based on downloaded information. The file system is intelligent enough to keep your music library in sync even when you move or rename files.

- You can expand the Player's capabilities with an assortment of plug-ins (such as those found in Microsoft Plus! Digital Media Edition) and premium services.

- Windows Media Player 10 adds support for television broadcasts recorded by Windows XP Media Center Edition.

Controlling File Type Associations

The check boxes shown in Figure 24-2 identify the types of media files that Windows Media Player can render. To get to this list, click Tools, Options, and then click the File Types tab. When you highlight an item in the File Types list, the Description section of the dialog box enumerates the file name extensions that make up the selected file type. Check boxes that are selected in this list denote file types for which Windows Media Player is the default application. (A gray check box indicates a file type for which another program, at one time, has been registered as the default application.) If Windows Media Player is the default application for a file type, double-clicking a file of that type in Windows Explorer (or a shortcut to such a file) launches Windows Media Player, which in turn plays the file.

Figure 24-2. The File Types tab in the Options dialog box lists the kinds of media files that Windows Media Player can render.

As you see, the list of file types is extensive. Not quite everything that moves or plays is there (RealAudio and QuickTime formats are notable absentees), but a great many media formats are represented. Popular audio formats include MP3 and Windows Media Audio, in fixed- and variable-bit-rate encoding. (Windows Media Player 9 Series adds support for Windows Media Audio Lossless format, which compresses audio tracks without any loss of quality.) Supported video formats include Windows Video (AVI and WMV), MPEG movie files, and the Microsoft Recorded TV Show (DVR-MS) format produced on a computer running Windows XP Media Center Edition. Windows Media Player 9 Series also plays streaming audio and video in a variety of formats.

Chapter 24

Windows Media Player does not support the following formats. If you want to share files created in one of these formats, you'll need to use another program for playback, or find a third-party utility to convert the files into a supported format.

- **Advanced Audio Coding (AAC)**   This audio format evolved from the popular MP3 standard and boasts higher quality with significantly smaller file sizes. It is the default format used with Apple Computer's iPod portable music players and the iTunes online music store.

- **Free Lossless Audio Codec (FLAC) and Shorten (SHN)**   Both of these audio formats provide lossless compression. Some portable music players and consumer audio devices support the FLAC format, and the WinAmp music player supports both formats for playback.

- **Ogg Vorbis (OGG)**   This all-purpose compressed media format is suitable for audio, video, and games. It is most widely used for audio tracks and is functionally similar to AAC and WMA in this application. (For more information about this format, visit the Vorbis site at *http://www.vorbis.com.*) Some Web sites offer unsupported releases of the Ogg Vorbis code that reportedly allow clips in this format to play in Windows Media Player 9 Series or later.

- **RealMedia (RM)**   You are most likely to encounter this format, which can be used with audio, video, or both, when playing streaming media from a Web site. Most Web sites that support this format also offer a Windows Media stream as an option. For sites that offer only RealMedia streams, you need to use a player from Real Software (*http://www.real.com.*)

- **QuickTime (MOV)**   Apple Computer controls the rights to this format, which is used to play back video (and, less frequently, audio). To play back files or decode streaming media encoded in this format, you need to download the free QuickTime player from *http://www.apple.com/quicktime.*

Changing the Default Application for Individual File Extensions

The media formats listed in the Options dialog box shown in Figure 24-2 represent types of files; some of these file types use more than one file name extension to identify themselves. The Windows Media (ASF) file type, for example, is associated with eight extensions, including .asf, .asx, and .dvr-ms. If you change Windows Media Player's behavior by selecting or clearing a check box on the File Types tab of the Options dialog box, you are, in most cases, changing the default application for several file name extensions.

To change the default program for a single extension, you might need to use Windows Explorer. Follow these steps:

1   In any Windows Explorer window, locate a file with the extension whose default application you want to modify.

2   Right-click the file and choose Open With.

3   In the Open With dialog box, select the program you want to use as the default for this
    file name extension.

4   Select Always Use The Selected Program To Open This Kind Of File and then click OK.

Changing the AutoPlay Behavior of a CD or DVD Drive

Normally, Windows prompts you to choose an action each time you insert a CD or DVD.
Your options might include displaying the contents of the CD in Windows Explorer, playing
an audio CD or DVD in Windows Media Player or another application, or transferring digital photos to your My Pictures folder. The menu that appears when you insert a CD or DVD
is dynamic, and its choices are determined by the content on the disc and the applications
installed on your computer. When you insert an audio CD, for instance, Windows offers you
the choice of playing the CD with any of your installed media player programs that have registered themselves as being capable of playing music CDs. To change the default program for
a particular type of content and avoid seeing this dialog box in the future, follow these steps:

1   Open My Computer.

2   Right-click the icon for your CD or DVD drive, choose Properties, and then click the
    AutoPlay tab.

3   In the list at the top of the dialog box, shown in Figure 24-3, select a disc type. (In the
    figure, we've selected Music CD. Other options include Pictures, Video Files, Mixed
    Content, and DVD Movie.)

Figure 24-3.   You can specify the action you want Windows to take when you
insert particular kinds of discs into your CD or DVD drive.

4   In the Actions section of the dialog box, select the action that you want Windows to take when you insert a disc of the selected content type. (If you want to preserve your options every time you insert a particular type of disc, select Prompt Me Each Time To Choose An Action.)

5   Click OK.

Managing Multiple Media Players

Because the software market is well supplied with inexpensive (and in some cases free) alternatives to Windows Media Player, it's quite possible that you have other programs that can also play some of the file types mentioned in this chapter. Some are preinstalled on new computers. Others are available for download via the Web. In fact, as we noted in the previous section, you have no choice but to use one of those "other" media players if you want to play back content created in a format that isn't supported by Windows Media Player. If you do use more than one media player, you'll need to specify which kinds of files should open by default with which application. That task is not always as easy as it sounds—left to their default settings, some media players try to attach themselves to as many file types as they can handle, and the most aggressive programs include features that allow them to "reclaim" associations when another player comes along. If you want to split media-playing duties between two programs, with each one assigned to what it does best, you may need to adjust the settings for each one carefully. In particular, you'll need to manually assign each program to the file types you prefer and then ensure that neither program tries to automatically reclaim file types automatically.

If you install another media player after setting up Windows XP, it's possible that the other player will have taken over some of the file types that were originally associated with Windows Media Player. (Similarly, if you installed Windows XP as an upgrade on a computer where you had previously configured another media playing program, Windows Media Player might have assumed control over one or more of that player's assigned file types, as indicated by a gray check box like the one shown in Figure 24-2.) To reinstate Windows Media Player as the default application for one or more formats, choose Tools, Options, click the File Types tab, and reselect the appropriate check boxes. Alternatively, if Windows Media Player is currently the default application for file types that you would rather play back in a different media player, you'll need to take care of the problem by adjusting options in the other player.

Customizing Audio and Video Playback

In general, Windows Media Player produces output that is commensurate with your hardware. The better the sound card, speakers, display adapter, and monitor, the better the performance you can expect. However, you can tweak a variety of settings to improve performance and to change the type of sound and video that Windows Media Player delivers.

Using and Customizing Windows Media Player

Varying Playback Speed

Buried several layers beneath the Player's basic interface is an advanced playback control, introduced in Windows Media Player 9 Series, that allows you to vary the speed of playback. This feature does much more than simply rewind or fast-forward a media clip; it performs time compression and expansion, speeding up or slowing down the pace of playback but maintaining audio and video fidelity—keeping a narrator's voice from sounding like a cartoon character when the video is played at faster than normal speed, for instance. Use this feature to "speed read" an instructional video or documentary, for example, viewing the full program in a fraction of its normal running time while still being able to understand the audio.

To adjust playback speed, click Now Playing in the Features taskbar and then choose View, Enhancements, Play Speed Settings. (If this option doesn't seem to work, choose View, Enhancements, and then click to add a check mark to the left of Show Enhancements.) The main Play Speed Settings control, as shown in Figure 24-4, is a slider that you can drag along a wide range. Drag to the right to speed up playback, to the left to slow things down. (Choosing a negative number causes a video clip to play backwards.) The Slow and Fast presets above the slider work at half-speed and 1.4X normal speed, respectively. Clicking the Previous Frame and Next Frame buttons, just below the slider in the Enhancements pane, pauses playback and steps through a video clip one frame at a time.

Figure 24-4. Click the slider (or use the preset Slow/Normal/Fast options) to change playback speed without distorted audio.

Chapter 24

809

If you're willing to settle for three predefined speeds, use the Fast Play button at the right of the Seek bar. One click increases the speed to 1.4X normal, a second click takes you to 2X, and a third click goes to 5X speed. Click once more to return to normal speed. (Hover the mouse pointer over this button to see ScreenTips that identify what the effect will be.)

Variable-speed playback doesn't work for all types of content; it's unavailable with streaming audio and video clips that are progressively downloaded, for instance. It's effective with Windows Media Video clips and audio files in WMA and MP3 formats. In addition, audio and video fidelity is only maintained at playback rates between 0.5 and 2.0.

Adding Surround Sound Support

With the right hardware, you can adjust your PC's sound from a simple two-speaker stereo setup to full 5.1, 6.1, or 7.1 surround sound. The difference is most noticeable when watching DVDs in a home theater setup or playing games that take advantage of surround sound. Previous versions of Windows Media Player supported analog surround sound, which artificially creates surround effects from conventional stereo tracks. In Windows Media Player 9 Series and later, you can take advantage of digital surround sound, in which each channel contains discrete audio information specifically recorded for that channel. To play back digital surround sound, you need a 5.1-capable sound card, proper drivers for that card, and the proper number of speakers, connected appropriately.

With the proper hardware drivers installed, Windows Media Player automatically recognizes and plays back sounds that are encoded for surround sound. Typically, software utilities included with high-end sound cards allow you to tweak audio performance settings, including adjustments to compensate for less-than-optimum speaker placement. You'll also need to enable advanced speaker configurations in Windows: Open Control Panel and click Sounds and Audio Devices (found in the Sounds, Speech, And Audio Devices category). On the Volume tab, click Advanced and choose the entry in the Speaker Setup list that most closely matches your hardware.

> **Tip** For links to compatibility information, drivers, and a surround-sound test file, see "Are You Ready for 5.1 Audio on Your PC?" at *http://www.microsoft.com/windowsXP/ windowsmediaplayer/51audio.asp.*

Using the Graphic Equalizer and SRS WOW Effects

Windows Media Player includes a 10-band graphic equalizer with numerous preset equalizer settings, shown in Figure 24-5. To adjust the balance of the various frequency bands in your playback, click View, Enhancements, Graphic Equalizer. If the frequency sliders appear dark, click Turn On to enable the equalizer (click Turn Off to disable the equalizer).

Figure 24-5. Windows Media Player's graphic equalizer includes presets for many different kinds of music.

To choose one of the preset equalizer settings, click the Select Preset list, located just above the equalizer controls (in Figure 24-5, Reggae is selected), and make a selection. If none of the preset options quite matches your aural preferences, drag one or more frequency-band sliders upward or downward. When you drag a slider, other sliders might move with it, depending on which of the three options stacked to the left of the sliders is selected. For example, to move one slider without affecting any others, click the top slider option. To change the distribution of sound between your left and right speakers, drag the Balance slider. The Player can "remember" one (and only one) custom Equalizer preset. To save your settings, choose Custom from the bottom of the Preset list and then adjust the frequency-band sliders.

If your sound equipment can take advantage of SRS WOW settings, you can control them in Windows Media Player. To learn more about SRS WOW Effects, which can provide a 3-D sound experience from only two speakers, click the SRS button to open the SRS Labs Web site. To access the effects, choose View, Enhancements, SRS WOW Effects. The Turn On/Turn Off control allows you to toggle the effects. With SRS WOW Effects on, you can select the kind of speakers you're using (normal, large, or headphones), adjust TruBass, and adjust WOW Effect.

Chapter 24

811

Tweaking Video Performance

By default, video clips play back at their original size, and the Player window resizes itself to fit the video clip. You can adjust the default size of the video playback window, change the way the Player window responds to resizing, and adjust the color (hue and saturation), brightness, and contrast of the video image. To access these controls, choose View, Enhancements, Video Settings.

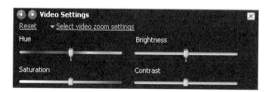

Optimizing Streaming Media Playback

Streaming media servers allow Web users to enjoy lengthy audio or video clips without having to first download a large file. After establishing a connection to the server, Windows Media Player downloads the beginning of the clip and stores it in a *buffer*, which is then used for playback while the Player continues downloading the remainder of the media file. If all goes well, this buffer supplies a steady stream to the Player, masking any momentary glitches in the connection. If the connection should falter long enough that the buffer runs out of content, however, playback stalls as the Player tries to re-establish the connection and fill up the buffer once again.

In general, Windows Media Player does a fine job of automatically sensing the speed of the connection and setting playback parameters for optimal performance. In some cases, you may need to tweak these settings. This is especially true if your connection speed is erratic. If you find that streaming media playback is frequently interrupted, you may want to increase the size of the buffer slightly. To do so, choose Tools, Options. On the Performance tab, click Buffer *nn* Seconds of Content. Try increasing the buffer size in 5-second increments until streaming clips play back reliably.

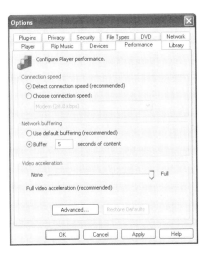

NEW FEATURE! Customizing the Player's Appearance

Even more than most other programs you use, Windows Media Player is a highly customizable application. There's no need to stick with the standard rectangular windows when you're using the Player. In its "full" mode, you can make the window frame and menu bar disappear, giving the program a sleek and curvy appearance, and suppress other elements of the standard user interface as well. If you switch to "skin" mode, you can completely change the Player's appearance by choosing from an assortment of custom visual designs, known as *skins*. Figure 24-6 shows the Player in full mode without frame and menu bar, and Figure 24-7 shows the Player wearing the Windows Classic skin. The same audio track is playing in both guises; all that's changed is the Player's appearance.

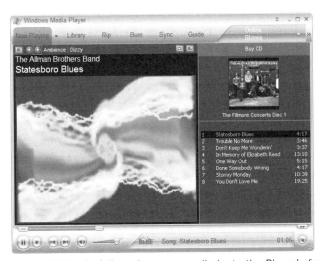

Figure 24-6. In full mode, you can eliminate the Player's frame and menu bar.

Figure 24-7. You can choose from a variety of supplied skins, download others, or even create your own.

Note If you don't see the Player's menu bar because it is hidden as shown in Figure 24-6, press Alt. If Windows Media Player is currently in skin mode, press Ctrl+1 to return it to full mode. Then press Alt if necessary.

Even without using a skin, you can do a great many things to modify the Player's appearance, including several modifications that are new to Windows Media Player 9 Series. You can switch between a normal windowed view with menu bar and the irregularly shaped menu-less form, shown in Figure 24-6 on the previous page. You can display or hide the Features taskbar (the panel along the top of the window). In Now Playing, you can display or hide the current playlist, title, and media information. You can also hide the resize bars, show or hide advanced controls (also known as Enhancements), and switch between a windowed display and a frameless full-screen display. You can change the Player's background color from its default blue to any shade. And you can display one or more of the Player's many visualizations while your music plays. (*Visualizations* are animated designs that Windows Media Player displays while playing music.)

For more information about visualizations, see "Using Visualizations," page 816.

Figure 24-8 shows the controls that allow you to modify the Player's appearance with your mouse while the Player is running in full (not skin) mode.

Show/hide Features taskbar

Enhancements pane

Turn Shuffle on/off

Change Player color

Show/hide menu bar

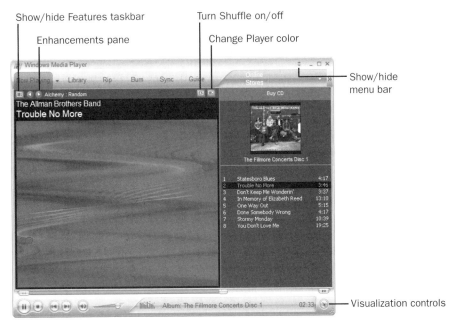

Visualization controls

Figure 24-8. Mouse controls allow you to change the Player's appearance while the program is running in full mode.

Toggling the Menu Bar

The menu bar toggle lets you switch between a normal windowed display and an irregularly shaped display that eliminates the Player's menu bar and title bar. As an alternative to clicking this button, you can click View, Full Mode Options, and then choose Show Menu Bar, Hide Menu Bar, or Auto Hide Menu Bar. (The keyboard shortcuts Ctrl+M and Shift+Ctrl+M also work to show or auto-hide the menu bar, respectively.) If you choose Auto Hide, the menu bar is hidden until you move your mouse into the area where the menu bar would otherwise be, at which point it reappears. If you like the frameless look, you'll probably find this the most convenient way to implement it.

For more information about playback controls, see "Playing Audio CDs," page 822. For more information about playlists, see "Working with Playlists," page 861.

Working with the Enhancements Pane

When you click Now Playing on the Features taskbar, the contents of the main Player window change to show information about the current album, track, or video clip. Choose View, Now Playing Options to see menu choices that allow you to show or hide any of this information. Choose View, Info Center View to specify whether you want to see detailed information about the current album, if available.

Chapter 24

At the bottom of the Now Playing pane, you'll find a subtle improvement introduced in Windows Media Player Series 9: the Enhancements pane. This pane, which is normally hidden, hosts a variety of advanced controls. To make it visible, choose View, Enhancements (or click the Now Playing Options button in the top left corner of the Video and Visualization pane) and select the Show Enhancements option. You can choose one of eight available options by selecting it from the Enhancements menu, or use the Previous Controls and Next Controls arrows in the pane's top left corner to cycle through all eight options in order.

We've already described the Graphic Equalizer and Play Speed Settings controls. The Enhancements menu offers some other useful options as well. For example, the Quiet Mode option lets you reduce the dynamic range of sounds, which can be useful when playing a clip at low volume or listening on headphones. This feature works only with media that was originally encoded with Windows Media Audio Lossless or Windows Media Audio Professional, however. For MPEG-2 movies and compressed audio files in MP3 or WMA format, it has no effect.

Toggling the Playlist Display

A *playlist* in Windows Media Player is a collection of related media items. For example, all the songs on a particular album could make up a playlist. So could all the songs on all albums by a particular performer, or some ad hoc collection of songs that you put together yourself. In Now Playing, the Player normally displays the current playlist, including titles and track times, in a panel at the right side of the Info Center area. The item in the playlist that is currently being played is highlighted in green.

If you would rather not see the playlist, you have two choices. Click the Maximize The Video And Visualization Pane toggle to expand the Info Center area. Or choose View, Now Playing Options and clear the check mark next to Show Playlist; this option leaves album or clip information in place but hides the contents of the current playlist.

Toggling the Taskbar

The Player's Features taskbar appears along the top of the window and offers quick access to common tasks. It's handy for navigation, but it does take up screen space that could be used for visualizations or information about the current album. You can send it away by choosing View, Full Mode Options, Hide Taskbar (if the Features taskbar is hidden, this menu choice changes to Show Taskbar). With the taskbar hidden, you can still navigate via commands on the View, Go To submenu.

Using Visualizations

Visualizations are designs of light and color that change with the frequency and volume of your music, in a style reminiscent of Sixties-era psychedelic light shows. The Player displays visualizations in Now Playing and in many skins. (Not all skins support visualizations, but most do.) Visualizations are grouped into collections with names such as Ambience, Bars

And Waves, and Spikes. To choose one of these visualization collections, click Now Playing and then click the leftmost of the three controls below the Visualizations display. This action opens a menu of collections, as shown in Figure 24-9. After choosing a collection, you can use the other two visualization controls (the left and right arrows) to move between members of the collection. Alternatively, you can pick a visualization by choosing View, Visualizations. Some visualization collections contain a randomization option that rotates among all the collection's visualizations in random order and timing patterns.

Many, but not all, visualizations can be displayed in full-screen mode and are much more effective that way. If the current visualization allows full-screen display, the full-screen toggle appears. Click it or press Alt+Enter, and your entire monitor becomes a light show. Double-click anywhere on the visualization or press Alt+Enter again to return to normal display..

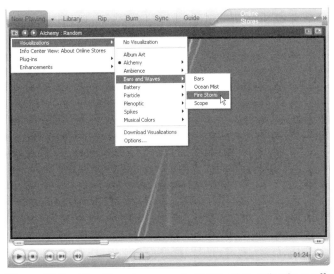

Figure 24-9. The Player's menu of visualization collections offers dozens of choices, as well as the capability to download more.

Troubleshooting

Visualizations do not appear in Now Playing.

If you don't see visualizations in Now Playing, choose View, Visualizations. If No Visualization is selected, choose a different menu option. Also, note that the Player cannot display visualizations during playback of MIDI files, and visualizations might not work for CD tracks when the CD drive is set for analog playback.

Chapter 24

Using Skins

To switch from full mode to skin mode, press Ctrl+2; click View, Skin Mode; or click the Switch To Skin Mode button at the bottom right corner of the full player window. Regardless of which technique you use, the Player applies the current skin. To choose a different skin, start from full mode and click View, Go To, Skin Chooser. Select the skin you want, and then choose Apply Skin. Windows Media Player comes with more than 20 skins, but you're not limited to that set, by any means. Additional skins are available from many sources, and if you have some expertise with XML and JavaScript, you can create your own without great difficulty. For more information about adding skins, see "Adding Skins and Visualizations," on the next page.

> For an excellent tutorial on creating skins, see *Microsoft Windows Media Player for Windows XP Handbook* (Microsoft Press, 2001).

All skins include the most essential controls—for playing, pausing, stopping, skipping to the next track or previous track, adjusting volume, and so on. Beyond these, skin features vary considerably. Some can show the current playlist or the graphic equalizer. Some show the current visualization and let you move to a different one. Some show the name of the current track. You'll need to experiment to see what the different skins can do and where each control is located.

> **Tip** To return from skin mode to full mode, press Ctrl+1.

Most of the Player's menu commands are available in the skin-mode shortcut menu. Right-click anywhere on a skin to display this menu. One item missing from this menu is a command to switch to a different skin. If the Player is displaying its "anchor window" in the lower right corner of your screen, you can click the anchor window and then choose Select A New Skin from *its* shortcut menu. The anchor window looks like this:

It's otherwise not terribly useful, because its commands (and many others) appear on the skin's own shortcut menu. In Windows Media Player 9 Series and later, the anchor window is normally hidden. If it makes an unwanted appearance, you can eliminate it by clicking it and choosing Hide Anchor Window. Alternatively, choose Tools, Options. On the Player tab of the Options dialog box, clear Display Anchor Window When In Skin Mode. Note that closing the anchor window is not the way to hide it—doing that closes the Player and brings your entertainment to a sudden stop.

> **Tip** To make a "skinned" Player window stay on top of all other windows, choose Tools, Options. On the Player tab, select Display On Top When In Skin Mode.

Using and Customizing Windows Media Player

Adding Skins and Visualizations

The simplest way to add more skins to Windows Media Player is to open the Skin Chooser (View, Go To, Skin Chooser) and then click More Skins. This link takes you to a Web page where you can find a long alphabetical list of downloadable skins approved by Microsoft. Downloading is straightforward, and the skins are automatically added to the Player's Skin Chooser list as soon as they're downloaded. Choose a new skin from the list and click Apply Skin to begin using it.

Likewise, the simplest way to get more visualizations is to click Tools, Download, Visualizations. This takes you to Microsoft's official list of supported downloadable visualizations.

For even more skins and visualizations, visit Microsoft's Windows Media Plug-ins site, *http://www.wmplugins.com*. For a lengthy list of links to non-Microsoft sites that offer Windows Media Player add-ins, see the excellent Windows Media Player Mini FAQ at *http://www.nwlink.com/~zachd/pss/pss.html*.

Changing the Player's Color

In a default installation of Windows Media Player 9 Series or later, the background of the full Player window is blue—a dark blue for the area that contains the Show/Hide Menu Bar button, and a smooth, somewhat lighter gradient for the Features taskbar and player controls. To change the background color, choose View, Enhancements, Color Chooser. In the Color Chooser pane, use the Hue slider control to select a color, and use the Saturation slider to adjust the intensity of the selected color. Click Reset to restore the default blue.

Tip   Go gray or black

To make the Player background a neutral gray, slide the Saturation control to the far left. In this setting, Windows Media Player completely ignores the Hue setting and uses a light gray background. The border around video clips is always black. To configure the Playlist region so that it matches this setting, regardless of the chosen background color, select Use Black As Player Background Color in the Color Chooser pane.

Using the Mini Player Toolbar

What do you do if the phone rings while you're playing one of your favorite tunes? In previous versions, the only way to reach the Pause or Mute button was to bring Windows Media Player to the foreground. With Windows Media Player 9 Series and later, you have the option to minimize the player to a tiny toolbar that docks on the Windows taskbar. With the mini Player toolbar enabled, you can control playback and volume without restoring the full Player window. Figure 24-10 identifies each of the toolbar's controls.

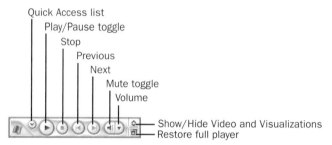

Figure 24-10. The mini Player toolbar offers access to basic playback and volume controls.

To enable the mini Player toolbar, right-click any empty space on the Windows taskbar, click Toolbars, and then click Windows Media Player. With this toolbar selected, the mini Player toolbar will tuck into the right side of the taskbar any time you minimize the Player.

Tip   Shrink the Player

To reduce the Player to its absolute minimum size, point to the sizing handle in the lower right corner and drag up and to the left. When you've dragged as far in each direction as you can go, the only portions of the Player window visible will be the playback controls. If the menu bar is still visible, click the Hide Menu Bar button. In this configuration, you can open the Quick Access panel by right-clicking any playback control; to open any of the (hidden) top-level menus, right-click anywhere in the lower right corner.

Extending the Player's Capabilities

As with most Windows components, Microsoft periodically issues updates that fix bugs or address security issues identified in Windows Media Player. You can check for the availability of an update at any time by choosing Help, Check For Player Updates. If updates or new components are available, a list will be displayed, and you can choose to install or not install any item on the list.

Windows Media Player checks for updates automatically at regular intervals. To customize the interval at which it performs these checks, choose Tools, Options. On the Player tab, select Once A Day, Once A Week, or Once A Month. The default is Once A Week.

Adding and Updating Codecs

A *codec* is a software component used to compress and decompress digital media. Before a sound or video clip can be streamed to your computer from an Internet site or played back from a saved file, your computer must be equipped with a suitable codec. For the most part, you don't have to be concerned about finding and installing codecs for widely supported media types. By default, Windows Media Player is configured to handle this chore automatically. To verify that this option is set, and to change it if necessary, choose Tools, Options. Click the Player tab, and then select the check box labeled Download Codecs Automatically. With this option enabled, providers of streamed media will download needed codecs to you without any necessary action on your part. If the check box is clear, you will be prompted for permission before the Player attempts to download and install a new codec.

You can also download and install third-party codecs that are designed to work with Windows Media Player but not endorsed or supported by Microsoft. You do so at your own risk—a buggy codec can cause the Player to crash, freeze, or suffer reduced performance, even when working with clips in a completely different format than the one supported by the rogue codec. In some cases, especially when playing content that was encoded using an older media-authoring program, you may decide to take the risk and install an untested codec. If you do, be sure to set a restore point using System Restore first. (For more details on how to use System Restore, see "Undoing Configuration Mistakes with System Restore," page 1288.)

Troubleshooting

Visualizations do not appear in Now Playing.

If the Player is unable to play back a particular video clip because a codec is missing, you should see an error message in the following format:

```
Video not available, cannot find 'vids:XXXX' decompressor.
```

where *XXXX* is the official Four-Character Code (FOURCC) that uniquely identifies video stream formats. You can use that code to search for an appropriate codec at Dave Wilson's well-organized site, *http://www.fourcc.org*. If your hunt is successful, follow the developer's instructions to install the codec.

Installing and Configuring Plug-ins

Windows Media Player also supports *plug-ins*—software add-ins that enhance existing features or add new ones. With relative ease, you can find a wide selection of supported plug-ins for Windows Media Player. Microsoft Plus! Digital Media Edition, for instance, includes a slew of plug-ins, including a converter that adds support for Windows Media Audio formats at higher bit rates and a CD label maker. (Details are available at the Microsoft Plus! site at

Chapter 24

http://www.microsoft.com/windows/plus/dme.) Third parties make plug-ins as well, such as the Nero Fast CD-Burning Plug-in, which speeds up CD burning and eliminates the standard two-second gap between tracks on custom audio CDs you burn from Windows Media Player. You can find the Nero add-in and many more at Microsoft's Windows Media Plug-ins site at *http://www.wmplugins.com*.

To work with installed plug-ins, choose Tools, Plug-ins, and select from the menu. To adjust the configuration of a plug-in, choose Tools, Plug-ins, Options. Select a category from the list on the left and then select the plug-in whose settings you want to adjust from the list on the right. Select or clear the check box to enable or open the plug-in; click Properties to change its settings.

Troubleshooting

Plug-ins stop working.

If the Player is closed without being shut down properly, the program assumes that the crash may have been the result of a damaged or faulty plug-in and disables all third-party plug-ins. To re-enable a plug-in, choose Tools, Plug-ins, Options, select the plug-in from the list, and click the check box to its left.

Playing Audio CDs

Playing an audio CD in Windows Media Player is almost as easy as playing it on any conventional CD player: Insert disc, close drive, press Play, enjoy music. The *almost* has to do with your CD (or DVD) drive's AutoPlay settings. As described earlier in this chapter, you can configure the way Windows responds to the insertion of CDs or DVDs containing various kinds of content. If you have set up your system so that the AutoPlay application for music CDs is Windows Media Player, your disc starts playing more or less the moment you insert it (provided it's not busy doing something else).

For more information about setting AutoPlay options, see "Changing the AutoPlay Behavior of a CD or DVD Drive," page 807.

If Windows Media Player is not the AutoPlay application for music CDs, you'll need to start the Player manually after you insert a CD (or switch to it, if it's already running), then click the Play button. The Player will begin playing the first item in the current playlist—which might or might not be your CD. (For more information about playlists, see "Working with Playlists," page 861.) If something other than your CD starts playing, click Stop. Then follow these steps:

1   Click the arrow to the right of Now Playing to open the Quick Access panel.

2   Select your CD (it should be near the top of the list; if you have multiple drives, be sure you select the drive that contains the CD you want to play).

3 Click the Play button; press Ctrl+P; or click Play, Play/Pause.

The Player's playback controls, shown in Figure 24-11, look and function like those on common consumer devices, such as CD players and video cassette recorders.

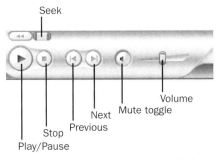

Figure 24-11 labels (Seek, Volume, Mute toggle, Next, Previous, Stop, Play/Pause)

Figure 24-11. The Player uses playback controls like those of other consumer devices.

The Play button becomes a Pause button while the Player is playing. The Mute button is a toggle; click one time for silence, a second time for sound. The Next and Previous buttons move ahead and back one item within the current playlist. You can drag the slider in the Seek control to move to a different place within the item that's currently playing. For example, to start the current track over again, you would drag the Seek slider all the way to the left.

Troubleshooting

Windows Media Player skips when you play a CD.

If you get "skippy" performance, try switching your CD drive to analog playback. Choose Tools, Options, and then click the Devices tab. Select your CD drive and click Properties. In the Playback section of the Properties dialog box, select Analog. If this doesn't solve the problem, select Digital again, and then try selecting Use Error Correction (in the same dialog box).

The Player plays the current playlist in order, once, unless you turn on Shuffle or Repeat (or both):

● If you turn on Shuffle by pressing Ctrl+H or by choosing Play, Shuffle, the Player moves through the playlist in random order.

● If you turn on Repeat by pressing Ctrl+T or by choosing Play, Repeat, the Player plays the current playlist continuously—that is, it repeats the playlist each time it finishes the final track.

Because the Player generates a different random sequence each time you start the program, the shuffle order will be different each time you insert a CD. But if you repeat the CD multiple times in a given listening session, you'll shuffle through the tracks in the same sequence each time. To deliberately change the shuffle order, turn shuffle off and then turn it on again.

While a CD is playing, use the Now Playing window (click Now Playing in the taskbar or choose View, Go To, Now Playing) to enjoy visualizations, see what tracks are coming up in the current playlist, view information about the current album, and more.

If the playlist is not displayed along the right edge of Now Playing, choose View, Now Playing Options, Show Playlist. When the playlist is displayed, you can switch to a different track by double-clicking the track.

 ## Troubleshooting

Your computer slows down while CDs are playing.

Visualizations might have a noticeable impact on system performance on computers with limited resources, especially those with slow CPUs or inadequate video memory. If your other programs slow down while you play CDs, turn off visualizations: Choose View, Visualizations, and then click No Visualization from the top of the list.

Viewing Media Information and Album Art

If you're connected to the Internet, the Player can download information about the CD you're currently playing, including the album cover, track names, a bio of the artist or group, and a review of the album; details about artists and albums are provided by All Media Guide (AMG) (*http://www.allmediaguide.com*). To see what information the Player finds about a particular CD, choose View, Now Playing Options, Show Media Information. Click the links at the top of the Info Center to see information that was automatically detected. (If a visualization is currently playing, you may need to select one of the options on the View, Info Center View menu.) For a more concise view, and to update your Media Library, click the Find Album Info link at the bottom of any page. (To learn more about how Windows Media Player stores this information and how you can work with it, see "Managing Your Media Library," page 850.)

Album art, once retrieved from the Internet, is cached on your computer. Thereafter, even if you're no longer online, you can display the album art in the visualization area of Now Playing. To do this, choose View, Visualizations, Album Art. Figure 24-12 shows Now Playing with album art in the visualization area.

Figure 24-12. The Player can show album art that it retrieved from the Internet in the visualization area, even after you've logged off.

Troubleshooting

The Player doesn't show media information.

If displaying Media Information in the Player doesn't show such information as track titles in the Media Information window or in the playlist, click the Refresh button at the top of the Info Center pane. If that doesn't solve the problem, try ejecting the CD and reloading it. Also, remember that you must be connected to the Internet to retrieve information for a CD.

 # Security and Privacy Issues

Like all Internet-enabled applications, Windows Media Player creates a two-way channel between your computer and an ocean of content. Clicking on a link to a media file can take you to a trusted site or a viper's den. Known security holes in previous versions of Windows Media Player created the potential for an attacker to install a virus or Trojan horse program by exploiting the Player's Web-browsing capabilities. In addition, because the Player is capable of using the Internet to download information about the content you watch or listen to, it raises worrisome privacy issues. Some privacy advocates, for instance, argue that the same connection that downloads information about a music track or DVD is also, at least in theory, capable of sending information about a user's viewing habits to Web sites that have no legitimate need for that information.

Chapter 24

Configuring Security Options

Windows Media Player (9 Series and later) includes several improvements in the underlying architecture of the Player to minimize security risks. In addition, tools that allow you to manage security and privacy options are more accessible than in previous versions.

Most security issues associated with Windows Media Player arise because of its role as a host for Web-based content. Specifically, a hostile URL on a Web page or in an e-mail message can exploit a flaw in Internet Explorer and install hostile code. In addition, malicious scripts can attempt to force the Player into running hostile code, either from a Web-based location or from a local file. The most effective way to guard against this sort of exploit is to ensure that all Windows security patches are installed. In addition, Windows Media Player 9 Series and later provides extra layers of protection that protect against hostile code. To implement these protections, choose Tools, Options, and click the Security tab. Figure 24-13 shows the two adjustments you can make.

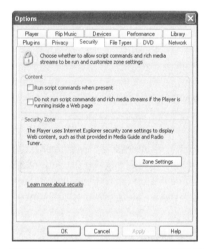

Figure 24-13. These default settings block Windows Media Player from executing scripts, which can contain hostile code.

By default, Windows Media Player 9 Series blocks the execution of all scripts. This feature is designed to prevent a would-be attacker from burrowing into your computer by way of a streaming media file. In one such scenario, an attacker could create a script file using the Advanced Systems Format (.asf), which can contain streaming media (such as an audio or video clip), along with links to URLs and script commands. By enticing you to click one of these links, the attacker might be able to exploit a security hole and load a hostile program. Disabling scripts prevents such an attack from succeeding via Windows Media Player, even if the security hole is unpatched.

This security precaution can, unfortunately, catch innocentWeb-based content in its dragnet. For instance, some sites offer online audio tutorials that are synchronized with a Web-based slide show. As the audio narration plays, the speaker's slides reinforce the underlying messages. If the default security settings are enabled, Windows Media Player 9 Series cannot control Internet Explorer in this fashion. The solution is to open the Options dialog box, click the Security tab, and select the Run Script Commands When Present check box. (Be sure to restore this setting to its more secure level after playing the Web-based presentation.) If an ASF file is embedded in a Web page, the capability to process scripts is enabled. To increase security settings in this scenario, select the second check box, Do Not Run Script Commands And Rich Media Streams If The Player Is Running Inside A Web Page.

Inside Out

Pay attention to the privacy statement

Most people click right past Web-based privacy statements, which typically are written in legalese and obscure more than they inform. The Windows Media Player privacy statement is a noteworthy exception. It's written in plain, nontechnical terms. It's organized in a FAQ format with hyperlinks that let you jump to topics of interest. And it includes step-by-step instructions that explain how to disable features that might affect your privacy, with clear explanations of the consequences of doing so. The information isn't buried, either. When you first run Windows Media Player 9 Series or later, a wizard steps you through setup options; on the Select Your Privacy Options page of that wizard, you'll find a Privacy Statement tab that contains links to the most up-to-date version of this document. If you've already been through this initial setup process, choose Tools, Options. On the Privacy tab, you'll find a Click Here For More Information About Privacy link that leads to the same up-to-date document. (A similar Web page that explains security features is available from a link on the Security tab of the Options dialog box.)

Configuring Privacy Options

As we noted earlier, the connection between Windows Media Player and the Web works both ways. When you connect to a streaming media file or update your digital music collection with information from an online database, you run the risk that someone, somewhere will connect your computer—and by extension, you—with the content you're viewing. If that's an issue that concerns you, one drastic option is to disable the Player's connection to the Internet. Of course, doing so makes it impossible to update music files or acquire licensed content. For a set of less extreme privacy-protecting options, consider the following three potential privacy risks:

- **Cookies**   Because Windows Media Player uses the same underlying components as Internet Explorer, individual sites (including WindowsMedia.com) can, at least in theory, use cookies to track the content played by a particular computer. By using the cookie-management features in Internet Explorer (described in "Managing Cookies," page 525), you can eliminate this possibility. Note that blocking cookies may break some Windows Media Player features, such as the capability to keep track of radio tuner presets.

- **Player ID**   When you connect to a streaming media server, the Player sends a log of the session to the server. This log contains your unique IP address as well as details about your connection. It also includes a unique identifier called a Player ID. By default, this ID is anonymous in Windows Media Player 9 Series and later (a change from the default behavior of the version of Windows Media Player included in the original release of Windows XP). In some rare cases, a site may require that you use a unique Player ID that is capable of identifying your computer. In that case, choose Tools, Options, and select the Send Unique Player ID To Content Providers check box on the Privacy tab.

- **History Tracking**   For each user account, Windows Media Player maintains a history that identifies media files and URLs you play. In addition, it keeps a list of CDs and DVDs you play. Anyone with physical access to your computer can inspect those lists and possibly draw conclusions based on their contents. To eliminate this possibility, you need to adjust several settings on the Privacy tab of the Options dialog box, as shown in Figure 24-14. Clearing the check box at the top, Retrieve Media Information For CDs And DVDs From The Internet, prevents the Player from compiling a list of discs you play. Clearing the Save File And URL History In The Player check box at the bottom disables the history list. Finally, the Clear History and Clear CD/DVD buttons erase the current contents of those lists for the logged-on user.

Figure 24-14.   Adjust options here if you're concerned about threats to your privacy from Windows Media Player.

Watching DVD Movies

DVD playback in Windows Media Player requires a supported DVD drive and a software decoder. If you bought your computer with a DVD drive and Windows XP preinstalled, the computer manufacturer may have included a DVD decoder as part of the software bundled with your new PC, in which case you can safely assume your hardware setup supports playback in Windows Media Player. Most DVD drives sold as retail upgrades also include a software decoder. If you installed Windows XP on an older computer, however, you might need to purchase, download, and install a decoder from the Internet. If this is the case, the first time you insert a DVD disc in your drive, the Player will display an error message with a link to its DVD Troubleshooter. Follow this link and you'll find a list of compatible decoders.

After all the requisite hardware and software is in place, playing a DVD movie in Windows Media Player is as transparently simple as playing an audio CD. If Windows Media Player is the AutoPlay application for DVD movies, it will start automatically and begin playing your movie. If it isn't, start Windows Media Player yourself. Then click Play, DVD Or CD Audio. In the submenu that appears, choose your DVD drive.

While your movie is playing, its chapters appear in the Playlist section of Now Playing. This chapter list provides one means of navigation within the movie—you can jump to a particular chapter by double-clicking it in Now Playing. You can also get to the movie's own menu screen by clicking the Menu button near the lower left corner of Now Playing.

Playback controls appear at the bottom of Now Playing. You can use these to play or pause your movie, to fast-forward or rewind, or to adjust the volume. To jump to the DVD menu (which typically includes options for choosing the language of the soundtrack, adjusting audio settings, and showing subtitles), click the DVD icon at the bottom of the Now Playing screen, just above the playback controls, or choose View, DVD Features. You can also adjust the soundtrack and subtitles from the Play menu, by choosing Audio And Language Tracks or Captions And Subtitles.

To fully appreciate a DVD movie, you probably don't want to see any part of the Player except the portion that shows the movie itself. You can display the movie full screen by choosing View, Full Screen; pressing Alt+Enter; or clicking the View Full Screen button.

In full-screen mode, the Player's playback controls appear temporarily in a bar along the bottom of your screen. Information about the movie you're watching, as well as the chapter list, briefly appear on the right side of the screen (if this list isn't visible, click the Show Playlist button). All of these controls normally fade from view after about three seconds and reappear whenever you move the mouse. To lock them into position, click the pushpin in the bar along the top of the screen. While you're watching the movie on the full screen, you can also right-click at any time to get to the DVD Features menu.

To return to the Player's normal windowed presentation, press Alt+Enter or Esc. Or right-click and choose Exit Full Screen.

Understanding and Protecting Your Digital Rights

Windows Media Player is designed to deal gracefully with media files that are licensed using Microsoft's Windows Media Digital Rights Management (DRM) technology—that is, digital content whose use is governed by a licensing agreement with the content provider. The license associated with a file, which protects the provider against illegal distribution of the media item, specifies how you can use the file and for what period of time. Licensed files are encrypted using digital signatures. The terms of the license are determined by the content vendor; Windows Media Player enforces the terms of that license agreement.

> **Note** Windows Media DRM is one of several licensing schemes available for digital media. If you acquire files from a source that uses an alternative DRM technology, you will be unable to play those clips in Windows Media Player. Check with the supplier of the licensed content to see which media player supports the DRM scheme used in that content.

When you download a media item—a song or a movie clip, for instance—from the Internet, the content provider might provide you with a license. Alternatively, if you play an unlicensed file that requires a license, the Player tries to obtain the license. You might have to register or pay for the license at this time.

> **Tip** If you want to avoid acquiring licensed media, choose Tools, Options. On the Privacy tab in the Options dialog box, clear Acquire Licenses Automatically For Protected Content.

Windows Media DRM licenses may be for an indefinite period of time or may expire after some period of time. In some cases, a license will allow you to play the media item only on the computer on which the item was obtained. In other cases, a license allows you to copy or move the item to other computers (but not necessarily to CDs). If the protected content originated on a CD (that is, if you copied protected content from a CD to your hard disk), you typically are permitted to copy the content onto another CD but not to other computers. Copying to SDMI-compliant portable devices is typically restricted by the same terms that apply to the use of the item on the computer where it was downloaded. (SDMI stands for Secure Digital Music Initiative, a forum that seeks to establish technology specifications for protecting the property rights of digital content providers. For more information, see the forum's Web site at *http://www.sdmi.org.*)

You can read the terms of an item's license by examining the item's properties dialog box. Locate the file in Windows Media Player or in Windows Explorer (usually you'll find it in My Music), right-click it, choose Properties from the shortcut menu, and click the License tab. Figure 24-15 shows the License tab for a downloaded music file. Alternatively, if the file is included in the Player's media library, you can right-click it there, choose Properties, and click the License Information tab. The same information appears in both places.

Figure 24-15. You can read the terms of a media item's license by displaying its properties dialog box, either in Windows Explorer or in the Player's Media Library.

If you have bought licenses that allow you to play the items for an indefinite period of time on your own computer, that doesn't mean you can never move the media items to another computer. You can move them (giving up your privileges on the current computer, of course), but only if you have backed up your licenses. When you move the media to a new computer, you restore the licenses on the new computer.

Note Microsoft allows you to restore your licenses on a maximum of four unique computers. Note that if you reformat your hard disk and reinstall Windows XP, Microsoft considers the new installation to be a new unique computer.

Backing Up Your Licenses

To back up all of your media licenses, follow these steps in Windows Media Player:

1 Choose Tools, License Management.

2 In the License Management dialog box, shown in Figure 24-16, click Browse and then specify a location for your backup. You might want to create at least one backup on a removable medium.

3 Click Back Up Now.

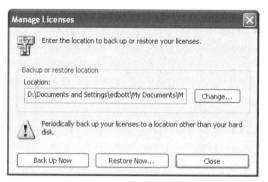

Figure 24-16. If you have digital licenses, back them up! Otherwise you could lose your media collection when you move to a new computer.

Restoring Your Licenses

To restore your licenses, follow these steps:

1. Choose Tools, License Management.

2. In the License Management dialog box, shown in Figure 24-16, click Restore Now. The following appears.

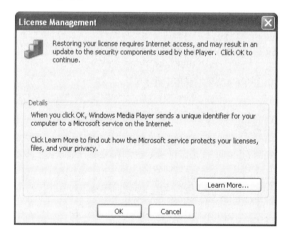

Restoring sends to Microsoft a globally unique identifier (GUID) that enables Microsoft to track how many times you restore your licenses. The company does this to discourage illicit replication of licensed files. (To read more about what information about your computer Windows Media Player might send over the Internet, click Learn More.)

3. Click OK.

Chapter 25

Managing a Digital Music Collection

Windows Media Player works with all sorts of media, but it's especially well-suited for the task of managing digital music files. Using nothing but the Player window, you can download songs from the Internet, copy tracks from CDs, edit song titles and other information stored within files, create custom playlists, copy music to portable devices, and burn custom CDs. (In fact, the same tools you use to manage a music library work with video clips and recorded TV broadcasts as well. We cover those other types of media in this chapter, but our emphasis is on music files.)

In this chapter, we look at how to use Windows Media Player to handle all of these tasks. As in Chapter 24, we assume that you have upgraded to Windows Media Player 10, which represents a major upgrade over previous versions. Our coverage is based on a preview version of Windows Media Player 10; if you're using the final release of this program, or a subsequent upgrade, you may find that some features are different from the descriptions in this chapter, although the basic principles are the same.

At Home with Windows XP

Windows Media Player works identically in Windows XP Home Edition and Professional. All the information in this chapter applies equally to both versions. (Microsoft Windows XP Media Center Edition includes a number of additional media-related applications designed to allow you to record and play back TV programs and to play back a music collection from across the room, using a remote control.) To take full advantage of the capabilities described in this chapter, you may need to upgrade to the most recent version of Windows Media Player.

Configuring Windows Media Player to Copy Music from CDs

Windows Media Player can copy, or *rip*, tracks from audio CDs and store them as files on your hard disk. You can listen to the saved tracks on your PC, burn a collection of tracks to a custom CD, or download tracks to a portable player. Before you start ripping, however, it's smart to answer the following questions:

- Should you use copy protection or not?
- Do you want to use the Windows Media Audio (WMA) or MP3 format?
- At what bit rate should you copy?
- Where should your files be stored, and what naming convention do you want to use?

 Inside Out

Manage the Media Library database

Although the items in your Media Library consist of individual files, the display of information in the player window is drawn from a single indexed database file. In Windows XP, each local user account has a separate Media Library database. For Windows Media Player 9 Series and earlier, the database file is named CurrentDatabase_59R.wmdb, and in Windows Media Player 10 the file name is CurrentDatabase_130.wmdb; in either case, the file is stored in the folder %UserProfile%\Local Settings\Application Data\Microsoft\Media Player. The inner details of this format are not publicly available, and we know of no way to view or edit its data using anything other than Windows Media Player. (When you upgrade to Windows Media Player 10, the old database file remains; you can delete it if you're fussy about small amounts of wasted file space, but it isn't necessary to do so.)

Most information in the library is initially drawn from the WindowsMedia.com database or from metadata (tags) stored in the media files themselves. If you change any of the details displayed in the Media Library window for a given track, that information is saved in your database and is also written as metadata within the underlying files. If the file is in a shared location (on your computer or on a network server), your changes will be reflected in any other user's Media Library the next time they play that track.

Two pieces of information—the rating you assign to individual tracks (on a scale of 1 to 5 stars) and the number of times you've played each track—are stored only in the Media Library database file and not as metadata. If you erase the Library database, this information is irretrievably lost.

Windows Media Player copies each CD track to a separate file and stores it, by default, in the My Music folder of the currently logged-on user (%UserProfile%\My Documents\My Music). The Player downloads information about each track—the name of the artist, album, and song, for instance—from the WindowsMedia.com database and inserts that information into the saved file as metadata. It then uses these details to organize your collection of saved files into a hierarchy, with a folder for each artist and a subfolder for each album by that artist. If you don't have enough room on the disk where the My Music folder resides, you can choose an alternative location before you start copying.

In fact, your digital media collection can be drawn from multiple folders. You might keep your favorite tunes—the ones your spouse and kids don't enjoy all that much—in the My Music folder in your personal profile and store ripped tunes from CDs you all enjoy in the Shared Music folder. Windows Media Player automatically keeps track of where your media files are physically stored and updates your library if you use Windows Explorer to move files after adding them to the Media Library. As a result, you can change your mind about file locations at any time, and you won't have to rebuild your Library if you eventually decide to move it to another drive. You should give some consideration in advance to the naming convention that Windows Media Player will use when you rip files (we cover your file-naming choices in "Deciding How to Name Your Files and Where to Store Them," page 839; however, improvements in Windows Media Player 10 make it relatively easy to update the names of existing files if you decide that a new naming scheme is more appropriate.

Deciding Whether to Use Copy Protection

You can copy CD tracks to your hard disk with or without copy protection. When you rip a track from a CD with copy protection enabled, Windows Media Player records a license for each track that allows you to play the file or burn the track to a custom CD, as long as you do so on the current computer; the license prevents you from playing the track on another computer or copying it to an SDMI-compliant portable device (such as an MP3 player). For the average music lover, these restrictions serve absolutely no purpose and are an unnecessary hassle. Backing up and restoring a library of copy-protected music files is cumbersome, and if you lose the licenses, your collection is worthless. We recommend that you configure Windows Media Player to copy CDs without copy protection.

In previous versions of Windows Media Player, copy protection was enabled by default. Beginning with Windows Media Player 10, this setting is off by default. To verify that you aren't inadvertently recording copy-protected files, choose Tools, Options. On the Rip Music tab, make sure Copy Protect Music is cleared.

Click Apply or OK to save the setting.

Choosing an Audio Format and Bit Rate

For practical purposes, files copied from audio CDs to your hard disk must be compressed; without compression, each CD you copy will consume more than half a gigabyte of disk space. Most algorithms used to compress audio (and video) files are *lossy*, which means that they achieve compression by eliminating data. In the case of audio files, the data that's tossed out during the compression process consists mostly of frequencies that humans don't ordinarily hear. However, the more you compress a file, the more likely you are to degrade its audio quality to the point where you'll notice it.

Deciding on the type and amount of compression involves making a trade-off between disk space and audio quality. The level of compression is determined by the bit rate you select for your copied files. Higher bit rates preserve more of the original sound quality of your audio tracks but result in larger files on your hard disk or portable player. Lower bit rates allow you to pack more music onto portable devices with limited storage, at a cost in fidelity.

To express your preferences, choose Tools, Options, and click the Rip Music tab. Choose one of the three available formats from the drop-down Format list. Windows Media Audio, which uses fixed bit rates, is the default choice. Windows Media Audio (Variable Bit Rate) allows the encoder to vary the compression applied to portions of a file, depending on the amount of information in it. Using variable bit rate (VBR) can result in files of much higher quality compared to files of similar size created using fixed bit rates. Choose Windows Media Audio Lossless if you're archiving your CDs or if you want to make custom CDs that are equal in quality to the music source.

Inside Out

Make a perfect copy of a CD track

If you right-click an audio CD and choose Explore from the shortcut menu, you'll see that each track is listed as a small file with the .cda extension. CDA is not a file format; instead, these pointers serve as shortcuts to the actual files, which are stored in a format that is essentially identical to a WAV file. You can't copy a CD track directly to your hard drive from Windows Explorer, and the default Rip options compress the resulting file so that it loses some quality. Using Windows Media Player 10, your best alternative is to use the Windows Media Audio Lossless format. Specifying this as the format when you rip a CD results in files that are smaller than a WAV file but still quite large. This format is the right choice if you want to create a custom CD without degrading audio quality by using a compressed format.

The process of ripping a track from a CD is not perfect. Tiny errors—a single bit here and a couple of bits there—can creep in when you rip a file. Similar errors can result when you use the "copy CD" option available in most commercial CD-burning software. These errors are mostly imperceptible to the human ear, but if you repeat the rip/mix/burn cycle several times the errors can add up and create a click, pop, or other noticeable glitch during playback. Perfectionists who want to make a perfect copy of a single music track or an entire CD should use Exact Audio Copy, written by Andre Wiethoff and available for download from *http://www.exactaudiocopy.de*; this highly regarded program can reliably extract every bit of digital information from the disc, without allowing any data to be lost.

If you select a format other than Windows Media Audio Lossless, use the Audio Quality slider, shown in Figure 25-1, to select a bit rate. Moving the slider to the left produces smaller files; moving it to the right produces better quality.

Figure 25-1. The description underneath the Audio Quality slider gives a rough approximation of the amount of disk space your compressed WMA files will use.

What Happened to MP3?

Windows Media Player, as shipped with Windows XP, does not allow you to create MP3 files from CD audio tracks. It does, however, play any MP3 files that you might have or obtain, without sacrificing fidelity, and it does support the addition of MP3 encoders from third parties.

The WMA format supported by Windows Media Player achieves audio quality equivalent to that of MP3 at much higher compression. A CD track encoded via WMA generally uses no more than half the disk space of an MP3 file of comparable quality. (In some cases, the size of the WMA file is closer to one third the size of the equivalent MP3.)

If you want to rip files from a CD and save them in MP3 format, you can use one of many third-party programs that excel at this task. We recommend downloading one of these three inexpensive third-party plug-ins that allow you to create MP3 files at bit rates of up to 320 Kbps: MP3 PowerEncoder from Cyberlink Corporation; MP3 XPack from InterVideo, Inc.; or CinePlayer MP3 Creation Pack from Sonic Solutions. Conveniently, a link in Windows Media Player takes you to a Web page with direct links to these and other add-ins: Choose Tools, Options. On the Rip Music tab, click Learn More About MP3 Formats.

The Learn More About MP3 Formats and Compare Windows Media Audio To Other Formats links on the Rip Music tab in the Options dialog box, shown in Figure 25-1, bring you to Microsoft Web sites where you can find additional information about the relative strengths and weaknesses of MP3 and WMA.

Windows Media Player provides the following file copying options. As you can see, the amount of disk space consumed by the tracks on an average CD increases as you increase the bit rate.

Format	Bit Rate (Kbps)	Approximate File Size per CD (MB)
WMA	48	22
WMA	64	28
WMA	96	42
WMA	128	56
WMA	160	69
WMA	192	86
WMA VBR	40–75	18–33
WMA VBR	50–95	22–42
WMA VBR	85–145	37–63
WMA VBR	135–215	59–94
WMA VBR	240–355	105–155
WMA Lossless	470–940	206–411

What bit rate is best for you? It depends on how big your disk is (and how many CDs you intend to copy), how much you care about preserving the full spectrum of sound recorded on your CD, and the quality and capabilities of your playback equipment. WMA Lossless offers the best quality, but at a potentially prohibitive cost in disk usage. The WMA VBR format offers higher quality than fixed bit rates, but some portable devices and external media players designed to connect to home audio systems don't support these formats. If you intend to copy the tracks to a portable music device with limited storage, choosing a lower bit rate means you can pack more songs onto the device; however, as we'll explain later in this chapter, Windows Media Player can perform this conversion on the fly when synchronizing with a portable device, allowing you to keep higher-quality copies on your computer.

For most users and typical computer speakers, 64 kilobits per second is the minimum acceptable choice, allowing for generally acceptable audio quality at little expense of disk space. The default bit rate of 128 kilobits per second produces noticeably better sound and strikes an excellent balance between disk usage and audio quality. If you're a discerning audiophile with high-quality playback equipment, you will almost certainly want to choose an even higher bit rate. To determine your own minimum acceptable audio quality, you'll need to perform comparative tests using your own ears and speakers.

Deciding How to Name Your Files and Where to Store Them

By default, Windows Media Player stores CD tracks in My Music, a subfolder of My Documents. If you decide you want to store your Media Library in a different location, choose Tools, Options. On the Rip Music tab, shown in Figure 25-1, click Change. This capability is especially useful if you share a home computer with other family members and want everyone to have access to the same music library. If your songs are stored in your personal profile and you make your profile private, other users will be unable to access the tunes. In this case, move the files to the Shared Documents\Shared Music folder instead.

If you are online when you copy a CD, Windows Media Player connects to the Windows Media online database and gets whatever information is available about that CD. Typically, that includes the names of songs and performers, album names, information about musical genres, and album art. Windows Media Player uses some of this information to create file names for your copied CD tracks. (All of the information Media Player gets from this online repository of information can be used in one way or another, even if it doesn't become part of your file names. The album art, for example, can appear in the Now Playing window when you play tunes from that album and in Windows Explorer when you use Thumbnails view. For more information about the Windows Media online database and the Media Library, see "Viewing Media Information and Album Art," page 824.)

By default, the file names for your tracks are made up of the track number followed by a space character followed by the song title (which probably includes spaces). Such a file name might look like this: 03 You Still Touch Me.wma

In Windows Explorer's Tiles view, a folder of CD tracks named by this convention might look like the one shown in Figure 25-2. Notice that Windows Explorer displays the artist and album title in gray below the track number and song title. This additional information, which is not part of the file name, is recorded as metadata associated with the media file. These details and others also appear in Media Player's Library, if you add a song to the Library, and in Windows Explorer's Details view. In Windows Explorer you can control the categories of additional information that appear by choosing View, Choose Details and selecting or clearing check boxes in the Choose Details dialog box, shown in Figure 25-3 on the next page.

Figure 25-2. In Tiles view, Windows Explorer displays metadata in gray beneath file names. This information (and more) also appears in Details view.

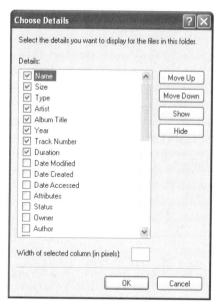

Figure 25-3.   Use the Choose Details dialog box to specify what kind of metadata you want to see in Windows Explorer.

Because Windows Explorer (and the Media Library) can display so much information about a media file by means of its metadata, it's not vital that you include a lot of detail in the actual file name. Using the track number as the beginning of the file name ensures that the tracks on an album always sort correctly within their folder, even when you copy that folder to another drive, device, or media-playing program. However, if you copy a group of songs to a portable player, that device may display and sort by only the file name. Therefore, when you choose a file-naming convention in Windows Media Player, give some thought to how your files will work in your portable device. In that context, if you want to keep all songs from a given artist or album together, the most important information is probably the artist or album name, followed by the track number.

Tip   Avoid generic file names

If Windows Media Player cannot connect to the Internet to identify your CD tracks by accessing the Windows Media online database, it uses generic names such as Unknown Album, Unknown Artist, and Track 1. To keep your files recognizable in Windows Explorer and Windows Media Player's Library, do not accept these generic names. Edit the track information *before* Windows Media Player begins copying tracks and creating disk files. For more information, see "What to Do if Windows Media Doesn't Recognize Your Disc," page 845. If you've already ripped some tracks with these generic names, you can update the album information to add album art, album title, and track details; you can then rename and rearrange the files using the downloaded media information. See "Renaming Ripped Files," page 848, for more details.

In any event, you can tell Media Player how you want your files named as follows:

1. Choose Tools, Options, and click the Rip Music tab.

2. Click File Name to open the File Name Options dialog box.

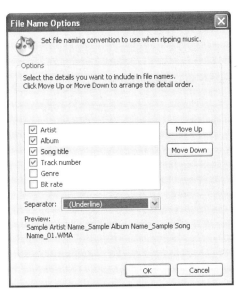

3. Select the check boxes for the information categories that you want to include in your file names, and clear the other check boxes. As you adjust your choices here and in the following two steps, the example in the Preview area of the dialog box shows you the effect on file names.

4. If desired, use the Move Up and Move Down buttons to change the order in which name elements appear.

5. Use the Separator list to change the character that appears between name elements, if you don't want to use spaces. Your alternatives are dashes, dots, underlines, or no separator character at all.

6. Click OK.

Ripping Audio Tracks from CD to Hard Disk

To copy an audio CD to your hard disk, first make sure that you have selected the file format that you want to use and that you have adopted an appropriate naming scheme and location for your copied files. (For details about these configuration decisions, see "Configuring Windows Media Player to Copy Music from CDs," page 834.) Click Rip on Windows Media Player's taskbar and then insert the disc. (If the disc is already in the CD drive, just click Rip.) Windows Media Player might begin playing your CD. That's not a problem; Windows Media Player can play and copy at the same time.

Microsoft Windows XP Inside Out Deluxe, Second Edition

When you're connected to the Internet, Windows Media Player consults its online data sources to determine the name of your disc, as well as the names of the artist(s) and tracks and the genre of music the disc contains. Figure 25-4 shows how Windows Media Player might look after it has successfully found all of this information.

Figure 25-4. If your CD is among the 500,000 or more in the Windows Media database, the album artist and title will appear at the top of the Rip window, and the tracks will be identified by name.

Inside Out

Find a classical music database

The Windows Media online database uses information from a variety of suppliers, including All Media Guide (AMG) and Muze (for UK titles). The total number of albums listed with AMG stands well above 600,000 and is constantly growing. The service is heavily skewed in favor of pop and rock titles and has much less information about classical music CDs. If you want to copy a classical collection to your hard disk, your best bet is to find a third-party CD player that uses an alternative Internet service called CDDB. The CDDB database of classical discs is extensive, and after you have copied your discs via the other product, you can import the resulting files into your Windows Media Player Media Library. For more information, visit *http://www.gracenote.com*.

Managing a Digital Music Collection

By default, Windows Media Player selects the check boxes to the left of all track names when you choose to copy a CD to disk. To copy particular tracks only, clear the check boxes beside tracks that you don't want to copy. To clear or select all the check boxes at once, click the check box in the column heading.

When you copy a CD, the album becomes a playlist in the Media Library. If you'd like to change the order of tracks on the album at this point, before copying, you can drag track names up and down in the Rip window. Or you can do this at any time later on, by selecting the album in your Media Library.

For more information about playlists, see "Working with Playlists," page 861. For more information about Media Library, see "Managing Your Media Library," page 850.

To begin ripping, click Rip Music. If this is the first copy you've made, you might see a message asking you if you're sure the bit rate and format you've chosen are the ones you really want to use. Otherwise, copying begins immediately. Entries in the Rip Status column tell you which tracks are pending, which are being copied, and which have already been ripped to the Library.

You can do other things in Windows Media Player while this is going on—listen to the radio, listen to the CD you're copying, or listen to something else altogether. If you have two CD drives, you can even play one CD while copying another: Open the Quick Access Panel (click the arrow to the right of Now Playing) to choose the disc you want to play after you begin copying the first disc.

Editing Track Information Before You Copy

If the Windows Media online database recognizes your disc but doesn't have all the track names the way you want to see them in your Media Library, click Find Album Info in the Rip window. The downloaded information appears in a pane at the bottom of the window. (You can enlarge this pane by dragging the horizontal split bar that separates it from the original track listing.) To change any part of this information, click the Edit button (just below the album cover). An editing window, similar to the one shown in Figure 25-5 on the next page, will then appear.

Use the boxes at the top of the editing pane to edit the artist name, album name, or genre. Use the boxes below to edit the titles of individual tracks. The names of performers and composers for individual tracks are hidden by default; to show these details and make them available for editing, click the respective column headings.

When you've completed your edits, click Next. The resulting pane displays the results of your editing and gives you a chance to review it for errors. As the text at the top of the pane notes, your edits are sent to WindowsMedia.com, where they may be used to update the database from which the information came. From a personal standpoint, however, the important thing is that editing the album information keeps your own Media Library in good order. Doing so before you begin the copy process ensures that the file names you see later, when you work with your Media Library in Windows Explorer, are correct.

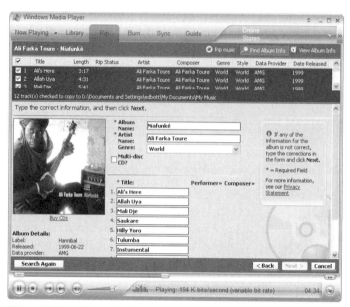

Figure 25-5. If you don't agree with the album and track information returned by the WindowsMedia.com database, edit it here.

Note According to the experts we consulted, the information you submit when you update a Windows Media listing may indeed be used to correct errors or omissions in the online database, although the process can take six weeks or more. In addition, when you submit artist/album/track information for a CD that isn't currently listed in the online database, your input is likely to end up in the database after a similar processing period. If you're an artist or CD producer in the United States, you can submit product information directly to *artist_submissions@allmusic.com*; consumers can send corrections via the form at *http://www.allmusic.com/feedback3.html*.

Tip Pay attention to genre and artist names

The Windows Media online database occasionally abbreviates musical genres in ways that are unnecessary for Windows Media Player. If you're bothered by this—if you'd rather see *Country* than *CTRY*, for example, edit the genre before you copy. It's good to be consistent about genre names, since genres become playlists. You get one playlist for all your Rock tracks, another for all your Jazz tracks, and so on. Artists too become playlists. On albums where different artists perform on different tracks, AMG generally doesn't provide the track-by-track details. If getting the playlists right is important to you, edit before you copy.

What to Do If Windows Media Doesn't Recognize Your Disc

If the Windows Media online database doesn't recognize your disc or if you don't have an Internet connection to retrieve the information, Windows Media Player proposes to use generic information in the Media Library and in the ripped files. If you agree to this, in the Media Library, tracks are named by their order on the disc (Track 1, Track 2, and so on), the Album Artist field is identified as Unknown Artist, and the Album and Genre fields are left blank. Windows Media Player creates a new folder called Unknown Artist (if it doesn't already exist), and then creates a subfolder in that location using the current date and time as part of the folder name—*Unknown Album (12-31-2004 11-53-07 AM)*, for instance. The ripped files are saved in that new folder.

If you accept the generic names, your music will sound fine, but you'll have a hard time finding your way back to it, either in Windows Media Player or in Windows Explorer. In Windows Explorer, your file and folder names will be a jumble of Unknowns.

In previous versions of Windows Media Player, cleaning up this mess was a cumbersome process. In Windows Media Player 10, updating your library and renaming files is considerably simpler (see "Editing Album and Track Info After You Rip," page 847, for details). Of course, if possible, pay attention to the process *before* you rip the tracks from your CD.

If Windows Media Player can't supply the usual information, you can add it manually before you copy, or you can go ahead and worry about track names and metadata later. If you're unable to connect to the Internet to download album information but you're reasonably certain that the CD you're about to copy is in the WindowsMedia.com database, rip away. Windows Media Player will replace the generic information automatically the next time you connect to the Internet. However, if the CD is a custom mix, or if it was created by an obscure artist and isn't in the online database, consider entering the album and track information now, before you start ripping (see the next section for details). This will save you a step or two later. If you're pressed for time, though, don't worry—you can update the information when you're ready.

And what about those not-so-helpful generic file and folder names? You can use one of two techniques we describe later in this chapter to have Windows Media Player rename the ripped files automatically. (See "Renaming Ripped Files," page 848, for details.)

Adding Album and Track Information Before You Rip

Follow these steps to enter album and track information manually before ripping a CD:

1. At the top of the Rip window, click Find Album Info.
2. In the Search For Album Information pane, select Type The Information For A Personally Created (Burned) CD, and click Next.

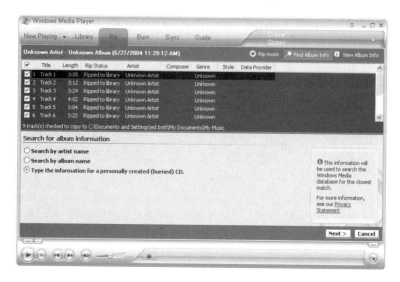

> **Tip**   Double-check the database
>
> If you have access to an Internet connection and you suspect that your CD is actually in the
> database, try searching for it from this screen before you enter information manually.
> Choose Search By Artist Name or Search By Album Name, enter a portion of the artist
> name or album name in the box that appears to the right of your selection, and click Next.
> Follow the prompts to narrow down the Results list to the correct album. If track information
> appears, review the track listings to be sure they're correct. If no track information appears
> or if you notice any errors, click the Edit button, enter the correct track names, and click Fin-
> ish. If you're unable to find a match, select Artist Not Found or Album Not Found, click Next,
> and continue with the steps we list here.

3   Enter information in the fields indicated by red asterisks. At a minimum, you must
enter the Album Name and Artist Name and fill in the Title field for each track. If
you're entering information for a CD that contains tracks by several artists, click the
Performer heading to make this column available for editing. When you finish entering information, the screen should look like the one shown in Figure 25-6. Click Next
to continue.

4   Review the information you have entered. If you see any errors or omissions, click
Back and repeat Step 3. When you're satisfied with the information entered, click
Finish.

5   Click Rip Music to begin copying the tracks to your hard disk.

Managing a Digital Music Collection

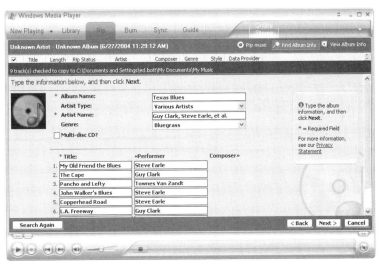

Figure 25-6. The red asterisks indicate fields that are mandatory. We've filled in the Performer column for this collection of tracks by multiple artists.

Windows Media Player will use the information you entered when it creates the file names for your tracks, using the preferences you set in the File Name Options dialog box.

Editing Album and Track Information After You Rip

If you've already created a collection of files using the generic file and folder names, the first thing you should do before editing these details manually is to check the WindowsMedia.com database. If the track information hasn't already been updated for you, right-click the album title (Unknown) in the Media Library and choose Update Album Info. If this isn't successful, you'll need to edit the track information manually.

The form-based editing screen isn't available from the Media Library, unfortunately, but you can accomplish the same task by editing the list directly.

> **Tip** Before you begin the following procedure, decide whether you want the files stored in your My Music folder to be renamed automatically, based on the information you enter. If the answer is yes, choose Options from the Tools menu, click the Library tab, and select Rename Music Files Using Rip Music Settings.

1 Click the Unknown entry in the Library's Contents pane to display the list of tracks.

2 Right-click any heading in the Details pane and choose Album Artist from the list of available columns. You'll need to edit this column, which is normally hidden, to file your tracks correctly.

> **Note**   The Album Artist field is new in Windows Media Player 10. Use it in conjunction with the Artist field when you want to highlight performers on individual tracks. On a compilation CD, for instance, you might enter **Various Artists** in the Album Artist field, and then enter the names of individual performers in the Artist field for each track. On an album that consists of duets with a star artist and various guests, enter the star's name in the Album Artist field. The Album Artist field is used as one of the primary sorting mechanisms in the Library's Contents pane.

3   Click to select any track in the list and then press Ctrl+A to select all available tracks. (If the Unknown category includes more than one album, select just the tracks associated with the album you're editing.)

4   Right-click any track in the list and choose Edit from the shortcut menu. This will put you into an edit mode.

5   Press Tab or Shift+Tab to move from column to column; when the editing box appears in the Album Artist column, enter the name of the artist you want to assign to the album. Because you've selected more than one row, Windows Media Player warns you that the value you enter will appear in that column for all selected rows. Click OK and repeat this procedure to fill in the Album and Genre columns for all tracks.

6   Click the first row in the list to remove the group selection, and then right-click that track name and choose Edit from the shortcut menu.

7   Fill in the track name, and repeat the process as many times as necessary for the rest of the tracks, pressing Up Arrow and Down Arrow to move up or down within the list.

The changes you've made are automatically saved as metadata stored within the files.

Renaming Ripped Files

After you painstakingly edit the album, artist, and track information for tracks you originally ripped using generic names, the Media Library becomes a masterpiece of organization—but the associated file and folder names remain unchanged. The folder that contains the individual tracks, for instance, is still named "Unknown Album (*date and time*)," and it is found inside another folder called "Unknown Artist." The files themselves are similarly generic. (The exact format depends on how you've set your file-naming preferences.)

By adjusting two Library settings, you can tell Windows Media Player to rename ripped files and move them to new folders based on the information in the Media Library. These options are disabled in a default installation. To turn them on, choose Options from the Tools menu, click the Library tab, and select one or both of the following options:

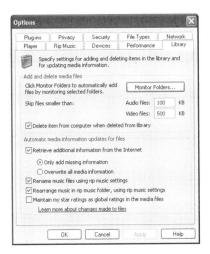

● **Rename Music Files Using Rip Music Settings**   This option renames each individual file, using the current tags and the settings defined in the File Name Options dialog box under Rip Music. It is effective whether you update track information automatically from the WindowsMedia.com database or enter track information manually.

● **Rearrange Music In Rip Music Folder, Using Rip Music Settings**   This option creates new folders and subfolders in the My Music folder, using the artist and album information downloaded from the WindowsMedia.com database, and then moves those files as needed. It does not work when you edit track information manually.

If you select these two checkboxes after you've ripped a CD using generic file and folder names while disconnected from the Internet, each file will be renamed and/or moved as soon as you reconnect—as long as the CD is available in the online database. If you choose the first option after editing track information on a custom CD, you'll need to fool Windows Media Player into making the change by following these steps:

1   Choose Options from the Tools menu, click the Library tab, and ensure that the Delete Item From Computer When Deleted From Library check box is cleared. Click OK to save the change.

2   Right-click the Album in the Contents pane of the Library and choose Delete from the shortcut menu.

3   In the warning dialog box shown on the next page, make sure Delete From Library Only is selected and click OK. The tracks vanish from your Media Library. Don't worry—they'll be right back.

4 Choose Search For Media Files from the Tools menu. (Or press its keyboard shortcut, F3.) Click the Browse button to the right of the Look In box and select the folder that contains the files you want to rename. (It should be in a subfolder beneath the Unknown Artist folder in My Music.)

5 Select New Files And All Existing Files In Library (Slow).

6 Click Search.

After Windows Media Player finishes searching for files in the folder you specified, you should see your tracks in the Media Library again. If you open Windows Explorer, you'll find that the tracks are properly renamed, although the folder retains its generic name. Next, open the My Music folder in Windows Explorer and open the Unknown Artist folder. Rename the Unknown Album subfolder using the correct name of the album. If you already have other albums by this artist, move this subfolder into the folder for the album artist. If this is the first CD you've ripped by the artist, rename the Unknown Artist folder using the artist's name.

Managing Your Media Library

Windows Media Player's Media Library feature displays your collection of media files in a single outlined list, where everything is easy to relocate and replay. Related items in Media Library are automatically gathered into playlists, and you can create additional custom playlists of your favorite tracks.

As Figure 25-7 shows, Media Library uses two panes to display your collection in a view that works much like Windows Explorer. The Contents pane on the left is an outline, and the Details pane at right shows what's included in the current selection in the Contents pane. (If the Playlist pane is visible, it appears to the right of the Details pane.)

Where is all this information stored? As we noted at the beginning of this chapter, the entire Media Library is stored in a single database file. This file, which is not directly editable using any tool except Windows Media Player, contains information about DVDs you've watched and CDs you've played, as well as details about music and video files you've added to your library, whether by recording them from CD or TV, importing previously recorded files, or purchasing tracks from an online service. In addition, the Media Library database contains custom playlists you've created and ratings you've assigned to individual tracks.

Managing a Digital Music Collection

Figure 25-7. Windows Media Player uses a Windows Explorer-style display to organize your media collection.

Inside Out

Clean up the database

Although you can't edit the Media Library database, you can clean it up easily if it becomes corrupted (or if you simply want to get a fresh start). After closing Windows Media Player, open Windows Explorer and browse to the hidden folder %UserProfile%\ Local Settings\Application Data\Microsoft\Media Player. Rename the database file, CurrentDatabase_130.wmdb. Then reopen Windows Media Player and use the Search facility to import music and other media files stored on your computer (see the following section, "Adding Items to Your Media Library," for more details). This step erases the stored details (including customizations) of any CDs and DVDs you've played but have not added to the Library; you'll need to download these details again for each CD in your collection. It also wipes out the star ratings and play counts for any tracks in your library.

Adding Items to Your Media Library

As you have seen, if you copy CDs to your hard disk, those copies automatically become part of your Media Library. Windows Media Player creates entries in the audio section of your library for album titles, artist names, song titles, and musical genres. Adding tracks by copying CDs is, however, only one of several ways to build your library.

Adding Items Automatically

By default, Windows Media Player monitors your My Music and My Videos folders. Any compatible files you add to these locations are automatically added to the Library without any intervention on your part. You can have Media Player check other folders, too—for instance, if you subscribe to an online music service and your purchased tracks are stored in a subfolder that is not in My Music, consider adding that location to the list of monitored folders. Choose Options from the Tools menu, click the Library tab, and then click Monitor Folders. Click Add to browse for folders to make the list longer. Click Remove to clear entries from the list. If you prefer to have complete control over which items get added to your Library, you can disable monitoring by removing all folders from the list.

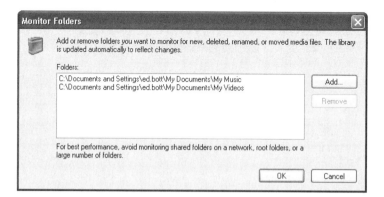

Caution   Heed the warning at the bottom of this dialog box and avoid monitoring shared network folders or the root folder of any drive. We can personally attest that either of these configurations can have adverse effects on the response of Windows Media Player. The dialog box also warns against monitoring "a large number of folders." That's probably good advice, but note that we've had no problems monitoring locations that contain close to 1000 folders; if you have a larger music collection than we do, you may want to consider turning off Monitor Folders and managing your music manually.

Using Search to Add Items

If you already have a collection of songs and other media items in another location on your computer, you can add those files to the Media Library by letting Windows Media Player search your disks for compatible media files. To do this, choose Tools, Search For Media Files, or press F3. Click the Advanced Options button in the Search For Media Files dialog box to reveal the full dialog box, as shown in Figure 25-8.

By default the program searches all local drives, ignoring audio files smaller than 100 KB and video files smaller than 500 KB, and ignoring Windows XP system folders. These defaults filter

Managing a Digital Music Collection

out sounds and videos employed by the operating system (your logon and logoff melodies, for example), while collecting media items that you're likely to want to hear or see again.

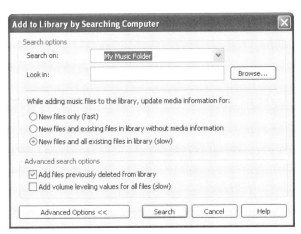

Figure 25-8. Windows Media Player can also populate your Media Library by searching disks for media files.

To limit the search to a particular drive, use the Search On list. To focus on a particular folder and all of its subfolders, click Browse. In the Browse For Folder dialog box that appears, you can specify shared network folders as well as local folders.

Note If you have more than one version of Windows installed on your local hard drive(s), the default search parameters will *not* filter out sounds used by that other operating system. In such a case, if you search all local drives using these defaults, your library will acquire such items as Tada, the Microsoft Sound, and the Windows Logon Sound. No harm is done if these and similar works find their way into your library, but you will probably want to delete them eventually. You should also be wary of running broad search-and-gather operations if you have media-rich applications such as Microsoft Encarta on board. Otherwise your library is likely to collect dozens of inscrutably named audio and video files that might not be terribly useful out of context.

Tip Decide where to store your media files
Are your media files scattered all over your hard disk, in a mishmash of folders? Before importing them into your Media Library, why not reorganize them into a more manageable collection of folders? The best place to store your own collection of music files, of course, is in the My Music folder, which is a part of your personal profile. However, if you have a large collection of specialized media files, such as live music recordings, you might want to keep them in their own folder, separate from the tracks you rip from CDs. For extra-large music collections, consider dedicating a separate volume or even a separate physical drive to music only. (Keeping these files outside of your personal profile also prevents your profile from becoming so large that you can't easily back it up.)

> **Tip** If several users share your computer and you also want to share a music collection, try saving your files in the Shared Music folder; to locate it, open My Computer and then open the Shared Documents folder. You'll have best results if you limit the number of storage locations to no more than a handful of folders.

Adding Items When They Are Played

If you download media from the Internet, you have a choice as to whether to add such items to your Media Library automatically. If you want every item you play to take up residence in the Library, choose Tools, Options, and click the Player tab. Then select Add Music Files To Library When Played. Otherwise, leave this check box clear.

Adding Specific Files or URLs

If you don't add media items automatically the first time you play them, you can drag a media file from Windows Explorer (or your desktop) and drop it onto Media Player's Details pane to bring the item into your library. Or you can choose File, Add To Library. The submenu that appears lets you specify a file, a playlist, URL, or whatever file or playlist is currently playing.

Editing Metadata Tags in the Media Library

Information in the Details pane of Media Library is organized in rows and columns. Much of the information you see in this list is editable—the Track Number, Title, Artist, Album, and Genre, for instance. In fact, you can edit any value that appears in this default list except the data in the Length and File Name columns. Right-click the row where you want to change data and choose Edit from the shortcut menu. While you're editing, you can move from column to column by pressing Tab or Shift+Tab, and move from row to row by pressing Up Arrow or Down Arrow.

If you're going to make the same editing change to an entire column, select all of the rows first (click the first entry and then Shift+click the last entry, or press Ctrl+A to select all items in the currently visible list). Then right-click and choose Edit. Move to the column you want to edit by pressing Tab or Shift+Tab, make the edit in one row, and then press Enter to duplicate the edit to the entire column.

All editable data in the Details pane of Media Library is *metadata* that is stored as tags within your media files. When you edit a track name or change the details of an artist in the Library, Windows Media Player rewrites the information in the underlying file. (To change file names, you need to work in Windows Explorer.) For music files, Windows Media Player can read and write these details by way of *tags* stored directly in the file, using one of the following three formats:

● **ID3v1** This relatively old format is still in wide use for MP3 files. It consists of six fields, each of fixed size, stored in 128 bytes at the end of the file. Windows Media Player can read ID3v1 tags but does not write them.

- **ID3v2** Modern media players that use the MP3 format typically store metadata using these tags, which can contain dozens of fields, each holding an unlimited number of characters. Because these tags are often used to help identify streaming media, they are stored at the beginning of the media file. If you edit the details associated with an MP3 file in Windows Media Player, it writes the data to the file using this type of tag.

- **WMA** These tags are the native format used for Windows Media Audio files. The metadata is stored at the beginning of the file, and the format is functionally equivalent to ID3v2 tags.

When you edit details of a track in your Media Library, Windows Media Player writes the information back to the file containing that track, using either an ID3v2 or WMA tag. This change is permanent. If you use an external tag editor or Windows Explorer to change information stored in a WMA or MP3 file, however, the changes are not reflected in your Library. When you import files into Windows Media Player, the data stored in these tags is used to populate the fields in the Media Library.

Windows Media Player now includes an Advanced Tag Editor (introduced in Windows Media Player 9 Series) that exposes all the tags in your library for editing. You can edit a single file or a group of files, or work through your entire library to add details missing from your collection. To use this tool, click Library, select one or more files in the Details pane, right-click, and choose Advanced Tag Editor. As Figure 25-9 shows, this utility organizes all available tags into a set of five tabs.

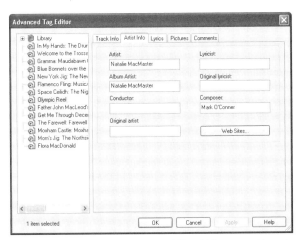

Figure 25-9. Use the Advanced Tag Editor to add and edit details that can't easily be changed in the Library itself, such as Lyricist and Composer.

For music files, the Track Info and Artist Info tabs contain all standard tags. Select a single track, change the value in a field, and then click Apply (to save the changes and continue editing tags) or OK (to save your changes and close Advanced Tag Editor).

> **Caution** Advanced Tag Editor doesn't include an undo feature. If you make a mistake when editing tag information, those changes become part of the underlying files. Before doing any serious tag editing, we strongly recommend that you back up your music collection.

If you select multiple tracks, the interface changes slightly. By default, all fields are unavailable for editing. This is a safety precaution, designed to prevent you from inadvertently renaming a group of tracks with a title you intended to apply to just one. To enable editing for fields that typically are identical for an entire group (such as Genre, Album, or Album Artist), select the check box to the left of the field you want to edit. Make your change and click Apply or OK; the new value you entered replaces the existing contents of that field for all selected tracks.

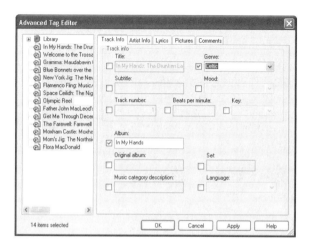

> **Note** Advanced Tag Editor is powerful enough for all but the most obsessive music fans. It's far from perfect, however. For instance, it doesn't allow you to search and replace values in a library (useful when you've misspelled an artist's name). Although you can edit the Track Number field, you can't automatically renumber tracks based on the order in your playlist. You can't manually rename files based on tag information, nor can you extract tag information from the names of downloaded files. And you'll be unable to edit files in formats other than MP3 and WMA, such as OGG or AAC. If you want those features and many more, we recommend an inexpensive third-party utility called eMusicTag Editor, available from AbyssAudio at *http://www.abyssaudio.com*. It uses an easy, Explorer-style interface and supports virtually any type of music file. For serious music collectors, it's a must-have, if only for its undo/redo capability!

You can also edit metadata directly in Windows Explorer. Right-click any MP3 or WMA file and choose Properties, and then click the Summary tab (you may need to click the Advanced button to see this information). Each field shown here is editable. If you select multiple files, you can use this dialog box to edit fields such as the name of the artist or album for all selected tracks. Note that changing metadata stored within each file does not change the information displayed in your Media Library unless you remove the tracks from the Media Library and add them again using the Search tool.

Rating Tracks in Your Music Collection

Every music track in your library has a star rating, assigned on a scale of 1 star (lowest) to 5 stars (highest). By default, all new tracks are Auto Rated at 3 stars. As you play a track, its Auto Rating increases to 4 or 5 stars. (The rating goes up only if you play all the way through a track; if you click the Next button while a track is playing, Windows Media Player assumes you did so because you didn't like the selection.)

If you choose to do so, you can assign ratings to tracks, one at a time or in groups. To adjust a rating, select one or more tracks in the Library's Details pane, choose Rate, and pick a rating from the list. You can also assign a rating by pointing to the Rating column for a track and choosing the correct number of stars. As soon as you assign a rating, Windows Media Player stops using Auto Rating for that track. (To completely remove a rating you've assigned, choose Unrated. In this case, the track will once again have an Auto Rating of 3 stars.)

The Rated Songs category in the Library's Contents pane allows you to sort your Library by user rating (or to see all tracks that you have not yet rated).

Adding Lyrics and Other Details

You can add lyrics to a song's metadata and then display those lyrics in the Now Playing window as you play the song. Start by right-clicking a song's entry in Media Library or in a playlist. Choose Advanced Tag Editor from the shortcut menu and then click the Lyrics tab. Enter or paste the lyrics in the text box provided.

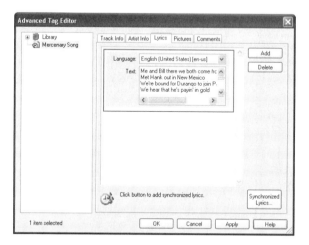

If you want the lyrics to appear karaoke-style, synchronized with music tracks, select the group of lyrics and click the Synchronized Lyrics button. Click Play to hear the song; in the window at the bottom of the dialog box, drag the indicators for each line so that they appear at the appropriate time.

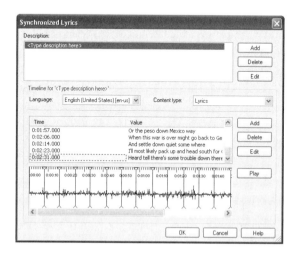

To display the song's lyrics in Now Playing while you play it back, choose View, Now Playing Tools, Lyrics. You can add both static and synchronized lyrics to a file. Static lyrics appear in the Now Playing window in Info Center view when you begin playing the file. Synchronized lyrics take over when you reach the defined markers.

Likewise, use the Pictures tab in Advanced Tag Editor to insert your own pictures into a ripped file. You can add an unlimited number of pictures to a WMA or MP3 file. These can also be viewed in the Now Playing window.

Searching for Items in Your Media Library

As your library grows, you might find it more and more difficult to locate particular items of interest. Windows Media Player's Search command can help.

> **Note** Don't confuse the Search command that searches the items already in your Media Library with the Tools, Search For Media Files command that searches your hard disk(s) for content to add to the library.

To search your library, first click Library in the taskbar (if you're not already there). Enter one or more search terms in the text box at left above the Library. Click the Search button to display the results in the Details pane. A welcome improvement in Windows Media Player 10 allows you to right-click on a track in the results list and choose Jump To Album or Jump To Artist. To see the file in Windows Explorer, choose Open Containing Folder.

Working with Your Media Library in Windows Explorer

Windows Media Player's Media Library and Windows Explorer are tightly integrated, so that you can easily manipulate your Library in either context. If you rename or move a media file in Windows Explorer, Windows Media Player dutifully records the change in the Media Library database; you won't have to rebuild or edit your library in any way. If you delete an item using Windows Explorer, the item will remain in your library. But the first time you try to play it, Windows Media Player will display the deleted track in red and go on to the next track in the playlist. If you right-click the track that now appears in red, and then choose Error Details from the shortcut menu, a dialog box like this one appears.

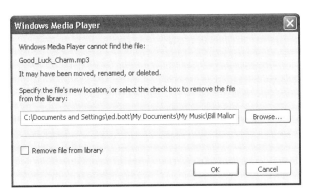

If the item still exists somewhere (other than in your Recycle Bin) and Windows Media Player is mistaken about the deletion, click Browse and help Windows Media Player find it. If you have deleted it and want to remove the listing from your Media Library, select the Remove File From Library check box and then click OK.

When Windows Media Player retrieves information about a ripped CD from the Internet, it downloads JPEG files that show the album cover, storing these files as hidden files in the album folder. In Thumbnails view, Windows Explorer uses the downloaded album art to adorn the folders, as in Figure 25-10; if your music collection includes more than one album by an artist, the folder for that artist displays up to four album images in Thumbnails view.

Figure 25-10. Windows Explorer uses album art in Thumbnails view.

Note To use any album image as folder art, save it in the album folder with the file name Folder.jpg. If you downloaded any album art, it's saved as a hidden file with the same name; saving another file with the same name will replace the current file.

At any level of the folder structure—My Music, an artist folder, or an album folder—Windows Explorer's Contents pane conveniently offers links to relevant tasks. You can play an entire folder (including all of the individual media items in its subfolders) by selecting the folder and clicking Play Selection. Or you can play all media items in My Music by selecting nothing there and clicking Play All. In either case, Windows Explorer passes the list of media items to Windows Media Player, which builds a temporary playlist for the occasion.

If you click Shop For Music Online, Windows Explorer transports you to WindowsMedia.com, where you can do what that link implies. And if you select a folder and click Copy To Audio CD, Windows Explorer passes the selection to Windows Media Player, which builds a playlist and prepares to burn a CD.

For more information about creating custom CDs, see "Burning Custom CDs," page 866.

Deleting Items from Your Media Library

When you delete an item from your Media Library—by right-clicking it in the Details pane and choosing Delete From Library—Windows Media Player removes it from the Library listing immediately. This operation cannot be undone, except to restore the missing information by importing the files again. To remove an item from the library and also delete the file containing that item, choose the other option, Delete From Library And My Computer.

To delete a custom playlist, right-click its name under My Playlists, in the Contents pane. Then choose Delete from the shortcut menu.

Working with Playlists

A *playlist* is a customized list of digital media files that Windows Media Player can play back as a unit, in either linear or random order. If you want to combine tracks from multiple albums or rearrange the order of tracks on a CD, you use a playlist. Windows Media Player 10 supports three distinct uses for playlists: Now Playing lists are for playback, Burn lists for are creating custom CDs, and Sync lists are for synchronizing files with a portable device.

You can build a playlist on the fly for a specific purpose—to play some files or burn a CD, for example. After the task is done, you can clear the list or save it for reuse. Saved lists are stored by default in the My Playlists folder. You can also conduct a search and save its results as an Auto Playlist.

Creating a Custom Playlist

The current playlist appears in the Playlist pane at the right of the Library window. (If the Playlist pane isn't visible in the Library window, click the drop-down arrow to the right of the Add To button, or right-click in any empty space in the Details pane, and then click Show List; this menu choice is a toggle that you can also use to hide the Playlist pane if it's currently showing.) Windows Media Player 10 offers a variety of ways to create a custom playlist:

- Start by entering some text in the Search box and press Enter. Right-click Search Results at the bottom of the Contents pane and choose Add To Now Playing List. (You also have the option to save the results as a named playlist, skipping the Playlist pane.)

- Drag tracks from anywhere in the Library and drop them in the Playlist pane.

- Select one or more tracks and click the Add To button. Normally, this sends the current selection to the Now Playing list; click the drop-down arrow to the right of this button to choose the Burn list or Sync list instead.

- Double-click any album or playlist. The contents of the album or playlist appear in the Now Playing list in the Playlist pane, where you can add or remove tracks or rearrange the order of tracks on the album.

- Select one or more tracks in Windows Explorer, right-click, and use the shortcut menu to add your selection to the Now Playing list, to a Burn or Sync list, or to a saved playlist.

Regardless of which of the above methods you use, your selections appear in the Playlist pane at the right of the Library. The controls just above and below the Playlist pane allow you to work with the current list, as shown in Figure 25-11.

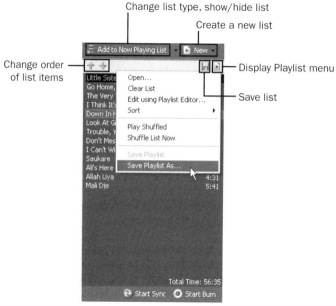

Figure 25-11. To master playlists, learn the function of the controls above the Playlist pane.

Using the controls here, you can change the order of items in a playlist, create a new playlist, save a playlist as a file, clear the current list, or randomly shuffle the list. If you prefer to work in a more formal environment, use the Playlist Editor. Choose File, New Playlist, or click the Playlist button above the Playlist pane and choose Edit Using Playlist Editor from the menu. Click items in the Library pane on the left to add them to the current playlist. In the New Playlist dialog box, use the three buttons below the list to remove or rearrange items on the list. Be sure to save your list after working with it!

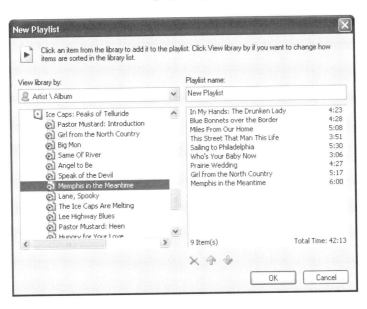

Tip Change the playlist order—permanently

The only way to permanently customize the order of items in a playlist is to save it as a custom playlist. For instance, you might have copied a CD to your disk, in which case the track numbers define the order in which songs on that album are played. Or you might have created an Auto Playlist that finds tracks from your three favorite female vocalists that you've rated with 4 or 5 stars. If you want to play the tracks in a sequence that can't be set by sorting a column in the Details pane, define your preferred custom order by following these steps:

1. Make sure the Now Playing list is empty. If it's not, click the New button above the Playlist pane and choose Now Playing List.

2. Right-click the album, playlist, or artist in the Contents pane and choose Add To Now Playing Playlist.

3. In the Playlist pane, use the Up and Down arrows to arrange the tracks exactly as you like, or drag individual tracks up or down in the list. If you started with an album, the track numbers in the Now Playing list will disappear as soon as you move a single track.

4. Click the Save button (just above the Playlist pane) and give the new playlist a name.

Your custom list will contain the same tracks as the original, but you can now always play back your list in your custom order, and you can rearrange the order whenever you like.

Saving Searches as Auto Playlists

Windows Media Player 10 includes a cool feature that automatically creates playlists for you, based on your preferences. Unlike static playlists, which capture a list of specific tracks in the exact order you specify, Auto Playlists are saved searches that return different results depending on the current contents of your Media Library. Windows Media Player starts you out with a collection of 15 Auto Playlists, as shown in Figure 25-12. These saved searches let you zero in on tracks that you've added recently but not yet rated, for instance, or on low-bit rate files, which you might want to upgrade when you get more storage. You'll find the list of ready-made Auto Playlists at the bottom of the Media Library tree.

Figure 25-12. Auto playlists are essentially saved searches.

With just a little effort, you can also create your own searches and save them as Auto Playlists. The possibilities in Auto Playlists are limited only by your own imagination, and you can even share your saved searches. You'll find the details of each Auto Playlist you create in an XML file stored in the My Playlists subfolder of your My Music folder. Copy that file to the identical location on another computer and the Auto Playlist will be available on that computer as well.

To get started, right-click the Auto Playlists entry in the Contents pane and click New. Enter a name in the box at the top of the New Auto Playlist dialog box and then begin clicking to add criteria to your Search. Start with the green plus sign and use drop-down lists to define criteria. In the example shown in Figure 25-13, we've created an Auto Playlist that includes songs from a trio of talented female artists that are all rated 4 stars or better.

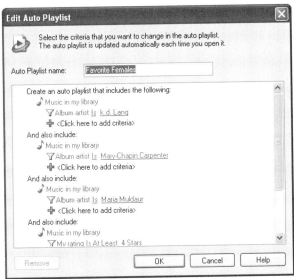

Figure 25-13. Build an Auto Playlist one criterion at a time. Enter each criterion in its own branch and click OK to save. In this example, the contents of the Auto Playlist change when you add tacks by these artists and rate them as 4 stars or higher.

Exporting and Importing Playlists

As noted in the previous section, playlists are saved by default in files within the My Playlists subfolder of My Music. When saving a custom list, you have your choice of several file formats. The default is a file in Windows Media Playlist format, with a .wpl extension. If you suspect you'll play your playlists on a different device or in a program that doesn't support this format, you may need to choose an alternate format, such as an M3U playlist (.m3u). Check the documentation for the other program or device to see what playlist formats it supports.

Windows Media Playlist files use XML tags to specify the file name of each track in the list. Additional information (genre, artist, and so on) are drawn from the Library database using the Globally Unique IDs—the two long alphanumeric strings—that define each track's entry in the WindowsMedia.com database. Note that this playlist format uses relative path references for each track. If you copy the playlist and the files to a CD and play it back on another computer, it should work just fine, even when the current CD drive has been assigned a different letter than on the computer where the playlist was created.

By contrast, older playlist formats such as M3U Playlist (.m3u) use fixed file paths. When you move an M3U playlist to a new computer, Windows Media Player may have trouble locating the files you're trying to play if they're in a different location than they were on the other machine.

Windows Media Player can also import playlists in a wide variety of formats, including formats created by other media programs. Choose File, Add To Library, Add File or Playlist. In the Open dialog box that appears, use the Files Of Type list to specify Media Playlist (*.asx, *.wax, *.m3u, *.wpl, *.wvx, *.wmx) and then choose the playlist file you want to import.

> **Note** All playlist formats are text files. The Windows Media Playlist format uses XML tags to save your selections. You can open any saved playlist in Notepad or another text editor to verify its contents, as shown here.

Burning Custom CDs

If you have a CD burner, Windows Media Player can use it to burn a selection of songs onto a custom CD. You don't need to use Windows Explorer or a third-party CD-burning program to do this (although if you are a demanding CD creator you may choose to use a more powerful program for a variety of reasons).

If the items you want to copy to a CD already exist as an album or a custom playlist, select that item in the Contents pane of your Media Library. Then click Burn in Windows Media Player's taskbar. You'll see a display comparable to the one shown in Figure 25-14.

Your playlist appears in the left pane, with check boxes for each track. Windows Media Player initially selects all check boxes, on the assumption that you want to copy all tracks. The right pane shows the current content of the CD, if any. A list box at the top of the right pane identifies the drive to which Windows Media Player proposes to copy the files. If you have multiple drives and you want to copy to a drive other than the one displayed, choose it from this list. If you have a portable device (other than a CD recorder) installed, that device will also appear in this list.

Note the total time figure at the bottom of the left pane and the available time figure at the bottom of the right pane. If the total time exceeds the available time, some of your tracks will remain unselected. You can accept those deletions or edit the playlist so that the tracks you want to burn will fit on the blank CD.

Figure 25-14. The left pane shows the tracks to be copied and their total playing time; the right pane shows available playing time.

Be aware that if Windows Media Player comes to a track that's too large to fit, it continues to scan the playlist until it finds a track that will fit. That maximizes the amount of music you copy to your CD, but it can interfere with the linear order you might be expecting. If you don't want to copy any more tracks after the first one that doesn't fit, you'll need to clear all of the remaining check boxes. Alternatively, you can clear all check boxes by clearing the single check box that appears at the top of the left pane (next to the word *Title*), and then select tracks until you come to one that won't fit.

Tip   Burn a CD from the Library

You can copy tracks to a CD directly from within the Media Library, by creating a Burn playlist and clicking the Burn button beneath the Playlist pane when you're ready to burn. The information is identical whether you start on the Burn tab or in Media Library, and the resulting CD will be exactly the same regardless of where you start the burning process.

If you change your mind about copying the selected playlist, or if you've accidentally selected the wrong playlist, click Library in the taskbar, then click the New button above the Playlist pane and choose Burn List. The next time you select an album or playlist and click Add To Burn List, your new selection will appear in the Burn list.

If the items you want to copy don't exist as a playlist, go back to the Library and select the track or tracks you want to add to your CD. For each selection, click Add To Burn List. Each selected item is added to the end of the Burn list; you can rearrange the order at any time. To remove an item from the Burn list, right-click the item and choose Remove From List. (If you use the Burn window, you can right-click an item in the Playlist To Copy pane and choose Remove From List.)

By default, Windows Media Player assumes you want to burn an audio disk that can be played back in any home or car CD player. If you would rather burn a data disk consisting of compressed files or a HighMAT CD, click the arrow to the right of the CD icon (at the top of the Playlist pane in the Burn window, at the bottom of the pane in the Library window) and make your selection from the drop-down list.

When you're ready to copy, click the Start Burn button. The CD burning process takes a little while. Windows Media Player first checks each track to make sure that its license (if any) permits copying. Then it converts each file in turn to a temporary .wav audio file. Because .wav files are uncompressed, you might need as much as 1 GB of temporary storage to accommodate this process. By default, Windows Media Player uses the drive on which Windows XP is installed. If you don't have enough room there, choose Tools, Options, and then click the Devices tab. Select your CD burner and then click Properties. On the Recording tab of the properties dialog box, shown in Figure 25-15, select a different disk.

Finally, after each track is checked and converted, Windows Media Player begins copying files to the CD. You can follow the progress of all of these operations by watching the Status column in the Copy To CD Or Device window, or you can return to another part of Windows Media Player and play other media.

By default, Windows Media Player ejects your disc when the copy is complete. If you don't want it to do this, go to the Recording tab of your device's properties dialog box and clear Automatically Eject The CD After Writing.

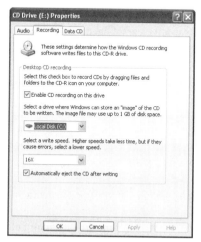

Figure 25-15. The Recording tab of your device's properties dialog box lets you specify the disk used for temporary storage while Windows Media Player burns CDs.

Troubleshooting

Tracks that play continuously in Windows Media Player don't do so on custom CDs.

Windows Media Player puts two-second "spacers" between tracks on CDs that it burns, and you don't have the option of eliminating these spacers. Tracks that are intended to be played continuously thus will be discontinuous when copied to a CD. To eliminate the gaps, use a third-party CD-burning program or install the Nero Fast CD-Burning Plug-in, available from the Windows Media Web site. If you burn CDs with spaces and play them back in Windows Media Player, you can configure the player to use crossfading, which gradually overlaps the end of one track with the beginning of the next on playback. We suggest that you experiment to see if this option is acceptable. Choose Enhancements from the View menu and then click Crossfading And Auto Volume Leveling. In the Enhancements pane, click Turn On Crossfading and specify how much of an overlap you want.

Copying to a Portable Device

Do you own a portable music player? If so, you may be able to synchronize the contents of that device with the digital music collection on your PC. Windows Media Player 10 adds a bevy of new features that let you establish a working relationship between your device and your music collection. After you complete the initial configuration, you can connect the device to your PC (typically via USB cable) and synchronization occurs automatically.

Note Don't let the term "synchronization" fool you. In this case, synchronization is not a two-way street. If you add songs to your portable device, they will not be automatically copied to your computer the next time you synchronize. You'll have to perform that operation yourself.

When you perform a synchronization, Windows Media Player goes through your Library and builds a Sync list. If necessary, it first converts the existing files into a format that is more appropriate for the limited space on a portable device. It then copies the tracks from the PC to the device, erasing any files on the device that are no longer part of the Sync list.

In general, supported devices are those that use a form of flash memory (Compact Flash or Secure Digital cards, for instance) and can also be identified by a drive letter in My Computer. Players that use a hard disk for storage are unlikely to be supported by the Sync feature. No drivers are required to enable sync support—just connect a compatible device to your computer and you'll see a dialog box similar to the one shown in Figure 25-16.

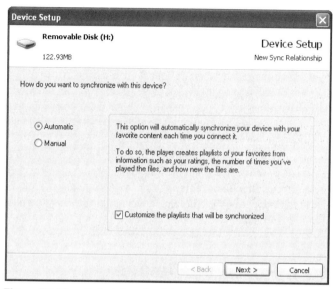

Figure 25-16. Select the check box at the bottom of this dialog box if you want to sync automatically with a custom playlist.

You can set up synchronization partnerships with up to 16 devices on a single computer, each with its own unique settings. To adjust device-specific settings after the initial setup, the device must be connected. Choose Options from the Tools menu, click the Device tab, select the correct drive letter or device from the list, and click Properties. The first thing you should do in the resulting dialog box, shown in Figure 25-17, is to give the device a descriptive name so you don't have to identify it by drive letter.

Figure 25-17. Some synchronization options are unavailable when the hardware doesn't support those features.

In Figure 25-17, note that all of the synchronization options are unavailable. This situation occurs because Windows Media Player correctly detected that this device doesn't support folders and that its entire storage capacity should be used for music and media storage. If you are using a supported device that has a hard disk for storage, these options may be available. You could define a specific amount of storage under Space To Use When Synchronizing; you could use this option to restrict the amount of space used for music storage, for example, to reserve room on the disk for backups of data files that you carry on the road.

If your portable device has limited storage space, you can make the best use of it by adjusting options on the Quality tab of its properties dialog box, shown in Figure 25-18. Under Music Quality Level, select Select Quality Level and then use the slider to choose the bit rate you want to use for all tracks copied to the device (all in WMA format). If you set this option to its lowest level, 64 Kbps, you can significantly increase the number of tracks that fit on your portable music player, albeit at a cost in audio quality.

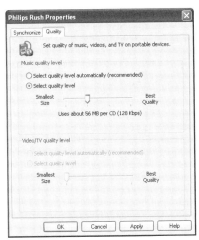

Figure 25-18. To squeeze more tracks onto a portable player (at a cost in audio quality), move the Music Quality Level slider to the left.

Inside Out

Speed up file syncs

Each time you sync with a portable player whose quality settings are lower than those of your music library, Windows Media Player transcodes those tracks—converting them to the lower bit rate in a temporary folder before copying them to the device itself. If you have ample space on your primary hard disk, you can speed up this process by allowing more room for the Transcoded Files Cache and configuring Windows Media Player to perform this operation in the background. To find these options, open the Options dialog box and click Advanced on the Devices tab. Transcoded files are stored in the default location (in your profile). Buttons in this dialog box let you move the cache to another folder or even another drive, and to delete the files for space-saving purposes.

When you connect a device that has a defined relationship with one PC to a different computer, you see a dialog box that allows you to transfer the partnership to the new computer or just synchronize the device one time using the current Library. All other actions are the same after you make this choice.

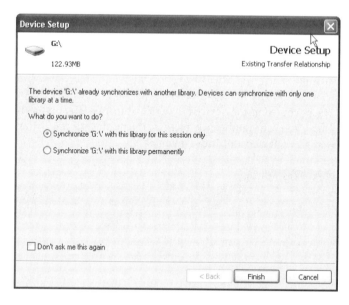

This initial setup process asks you to make two choices when creating a relationship:

- **Manual or automatic synchronization?**   Manual or automatic synchronization? With the Manual option, you connect your device, confirm that the synchronization details are correct, and then click the Sync button. With the Automatic option, synchronization begins as soon as you connect your device, using the current sync settings.

- **Custom playlist or priority syncronization?**   You can designate one or more playlists for Windows Media Player to use when synchronizing, or you can allow the program to use its built-in list or priorities to choose music for you.

If you entrust Windows Media Player with the responsibility to build that list, it uses a set of built-in rules to try to guess which tracks are your favorites. For music, its top priorities are as follows, in order:

- Any playlists you have created
- Music auto-rated at 5 stars
- Music added in the last month
- Music rated at 4 or 5 stars
- Music played in the last month

In addition, if your device supports pictures, TV, and video files, those file types will be added, but their priority is much lower on the list.

To adjust these settings afterwards, click the Display Properties And Settings button on the Sync tab, just above the Sync List pane, or open the Options dialog box, select the connected device, and click Properties. Click Settings in the properties dialog box to display the Synchronization Settings dialog box shown here.

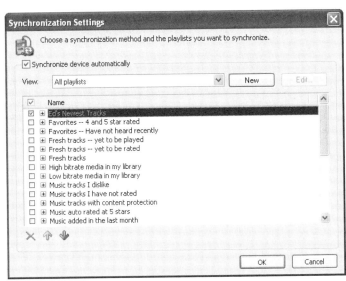

In this example, we've created a custom playlist called Ed's Newest Tracks and defined it as the only playlist to be used when synchronizing. By managing that single playlist, we can control which tracks appear on the device without worrying about the built-in rules or having to assign ratings.

Tip   **What if you don't own a compatible device?**
If your portable player isn't on the list of supported portable players, you'll need to find an alternate strategy for filling it with music. Most devices include some sort of software designed to help with this task. For hard disk-based devices, we recommend an all-purpose utility called FileSync (available from *http://www.fileware.com*). You can specify settings by file or folder, filter out certain types of files (so that album art doesn't waste disk space on your device, for instance), and save settings for reuse. It's useful for many other types of tasks as well.

Chapter 26

Organizing and Editing Images

Microsoft Windows XP does a spectacular job with all sorts of image files, including digital photos and scanned documents. Out of the box, it works with hundreds of imaging devices to help you convert photos and documents from a digital camera or a scanner into a Windows-compatible format, move the resulting files to your computer, and keep those images organized. When working with image files, you'll use the following tools:

- **Scanner And Camera Wizard**   If your imaging device includes a Windows XP–compatible driver, you're home free. This straightforward wizard makes short work of getting images into your computer.

- **Additional wizards**   Built-in wizards and dialog boxes help you shrink the size of files so that you can send them by e-mail, publish images to Web sites, manage the details of printing pictures, and order prints from online suppliers.

- **Windows Explorer enhancements**   Throughout Windows Explorer, you'll find features designed to make working with digital image files easier, most notably a Filmstrip view (new in Windows XP) that combines thumbnails and a preview pane. These enhancements are immediately visible in the My Pictures folder, but you can customize any folder that contains image files to give yourself access to the new image-handling tools.

- **Windows Picture And Fax Viewer**   This tool, also new to Windows XP, offers an easy way to preview (and in some cases, annotate) image files.

At Home with Windows XP

All of the features described in this chapter are available in Windows XP Home Edition as well as Windows XP Professional.

Setting Up a Scanner or Digital Camera

To take advantage of the image-handling features in Windows XP, start with the right hardware. Specifically, you need a digital camera or scanner that supports the Windows Image Acquisition (WIA) standard and connects to your computer via a Universal Serial Bus (USB), SCSI, or IEEE 1394 (FireWire) cable. When you plug in a WIA-compliant device and supply the correct drivers, Windows automatically recognizes it, installs the drivers, and adds an icon for the device in Control Panel's Scanners And Cameras folder. By right-clicking this device icon and opening the properties dialog box, you can configure options that are specific to that device, including color profiles and how to respond when specific actions occur, as shown in Figure 26-1.

Tip   Give new life to an old camera

Do you have an older digital camera that doesn't include WIA drivers? If it still takes perfectly good pictures, don't toss it out. As long as it uses industry-standard memory cards (Compact Flash or SmartMedia for example), you can get an external memory reader that connects via the USB port on your computer. A number of companies, including SanDisk (*http://www.sandisk.com*) and Kingston Technology (*http://www.kingston.com*), make reliable and inexpensive readers that are compatible with Windows XP. Instead of connecting the camera directly to the computer, you transfer the memory card to the reader. Windows recognizes digital memory cards as generic storage devices (look for an icon in the My Computer window) and provides the exact same image-handling features you would get with a WIA-compatible camera. Card readers also help you conserve your camera's battery power, because you don't have to leave the camera turned on while you transfer pictures.

Figure 26-1.   From the Scanners And Cameras folder, you can associate specific actions with events, such as clicking the Scan button on a flatbed scanner.

WIA-aware imaging programs like Microsoft Office XP or Office 2003, Microsoft Picture It! 2000 or later, and Adobe Photoshop can communicate directly with WIA-compatible imaging devices. For Windows programs that are only compatible with devices that use the older TWAIN standard, WIA provides a compatibility layer that allows you to capture and transfer images without having to install extra software. When Windows makes a WIA device available through the TWAIN compatibility layer, its device name includes "WIA-" as a prefix. The TWAIN compatibility layer isn't perfect; for instance, it supports only the BMP (Windows Bitmap) file format and doesn't allow you to use the automatic document feeders found on many high-end flatbed scanners.

With older devices that do not have WIA drivers and communicate with Windows via a serial port, you'll be unable to take advantage of any image-handling features found in Windows XP. These devices typically hook into Windows using proprietary interfaces; any such device won't show up in the Scanners And Cameras folder and won't be available for use with Windows XP wizards.

In some cases, you may have to choose between the software and drivers that came with your device and the WIA-based features in Windows XP. If the manufacturer's software includes device-specific features, such as the ability to program buttons on a scanner or to access configuration options in a camera, it may be your best choice. When you choose this option, you'll lose the ability to work with the device through the Scanner And Camera Wizard, but for some devices the trade-off may be worth it.

> **Tip**   Use System Restore before experimenting
>
> It's impractical to switch between the WIA-based imaging features in Windows XP and those found in a device manufacturer's proprietary software. If your device works when you plug it into a Windows XP system but you want to experiment with the manufacturer's software to decide whether its features are a better fit for you, be sure to set a System Restore checkpoint before installing the software and drivers. If you decide you prefer the WIA-based tools, uninstall the software package and then use System Restore to remove the manufacturer's drivers and restore your system to its previous configuration. For full details, see "Undoing Configuration Mistakes with System Restore," page 1288.

Finally, if the built-in picture-handling capabilities of Windows XP don't do everything you want, you have the option to use a full-featured image-management program instead. One of our favorites is Picasa. It makes short work of transferring pictures from camera to computer, performing simple edits such as red-eye removal, organizing photos into collections, categorizing and tagging images for easy retrieval, and sharing photos online. Picasa is available at *http://www.picasa.com*.

Saving and Editing Images

To transfer images from a digital device to your computer, your simplest option is to use the Scanner And Camera Wizard. Because each class of device is inherently different, the exact choices available to you depend on your starting point.

On systems where multiple WIA-compatible devices are installed, you can begin with the Scanner And Camera Wizard (click the Start button and then choose All Programs, Accessories). You'll see a dialog box like the one in Figure 26-2. Pick a device and click OK to begin working with the wizard.

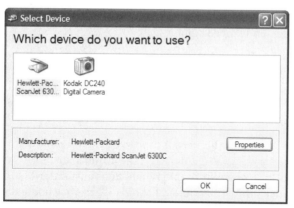

Figure 26-2.   If you have multiple imaging devices, you can select one and adjust its properties if necessary from this dialog box.

Inside Out

Learn the secrets of smarter cropping

When you're scanning photographs on a flatbed scanner, knowing a few simple secrets can save you hours of tedious cropping. For starters, place a sheet of clean white paper behind the image, to serve as a background. When you reach the Choose Scanning Preferences step of the wizard, don't just click Next; if you do that, the wizard will scan the entire image area, and you'll have to manually crop the resulting image file. Instead, *always* click Preview. After the preview scan is complete, the wizard displays the scan and selects the image automatically—a task that's much easier thanks to the plain white background you provided. After you verify that the selection is correct, click Next to complete the scan.

To scan a document or photo, start by double-clicking the device icon in the My Computer window or in Control Panel's Scanners And Cameras folder. (If you're using the Category view of Control Panel, you'll find this option under Printers And Other Hardware.) As Figure 26-3 shows, the controls on the Choose Scanning Preferences wizard page allow you to select the picture type, preview the image, and (if necessary) crop it to suit your needs. With scanners that include a document feeder, you can also choose the paper source and page size.

Choose a preset picture type or...

Click here to specify custom scan settings

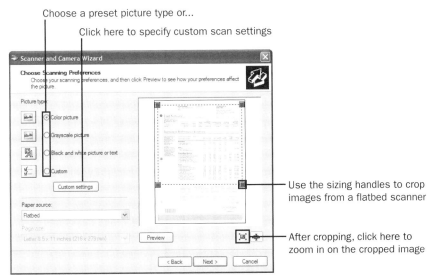

Use the sizing handles to crop images from a flatbed scanner

After cropping, click here to zoom in on the cropped image

Figure 26-3. This dialog box gives you quick access to all scanning controls.

With a digital camera, the wizard behaves a bit differently. As soon as Windows detects that you've connected a camera to the computer, it fires up the Scanner And Camera Wizard, reads the images stored in the camera's memory, and displays thumbnails of the stored images, as shown in Figure 26-4.

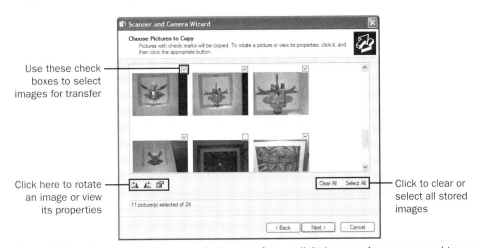

Use these check boxes to select images for transfer

Click here to rotate an image or view its properties

Click to clear or select all stored images

Figure 26-4. Use the wizard to transfer images from a digital camera's memory card to your hard drive.

By default, all the stored images are selected. If you want to copy the entire group to your hard drive, click Next. If you can tell at a glance that some of the images aren't keepers, clear the check mark above those thumbnails before going to the next step. What if you only want to transfer one or two images from a memory card that contains dozens of images? Save yourself some effort: Click Clear All at the lower right and then select only the images you want.

> **Tip** **When in doubt, copy**
>
> It's difficult to work with the tiny thumbnail images in the Scanner And Camera Wizard. You'll generally find it most efficient to copy all images to your hard drive, where you can cull the shots you don't want to keep and then work with the rest. Although the thumbnail viewer in the Scanner And Camera Wizard includes tools for rotating images, this task is also best left for the larger Preview window.

If you're a digital camera fanatic, you can skip the wizard altogether and automatically copy all images to your hard drive every time you connect a WIA-compatible camera. (If you're using a USB-based memory-card reader, this option isn't available.)

Follow these steps to set up this option:

1 With the camera connected and powered on, open the Scanners And Cameras folder in Control Panel.

2 Right-click the camera icon and choose Properties.

3 In the properties dialog box, click the Events tab, and adjust the settings as shown here.

When you select these options, Windows automatically creates a subfolder in the My Pictures folder (using the current date as the folder name), copies all pictures from the camera to that folder, and deletes the images from the camera's memory so that you can start fresh.

In the final step of the Scanner And Camera Wizard, you specify the location where you want the images stored. If you've selected multiple images, you also specify a group name. The wizard tacks on consecutive numbers at the end of the group name for each individual image—Pictures 001, Pictures 002, and so forth.

Tip   Skip the wizard for faster results

If you don't like the wizard's step-by-step approach, you can cut straight to the chase and work directly with images stored on a digital camera. After connecting the device, open the My Computer window and double-click the camera icon to display stored images directly in a Windows Explorer window. Select one or more images, and then use the Copy The Selected Items link in the task pane to copy the images to a folder of your choice. When you use this technique, the image files use the default names supplied by your camera—typically a combination of a prefix and automatic numbering. If necessary, you can change these names afterwards in Windows Explorer.

Finally, you can scan or acquire an image directly from any WIA-compatible application. In Microsoft Paint, for example, choose File, From Scanner Or Camera to open a simplified version of the Scanner And Camera Wizard. Instead of being saved to a file, the resulting image appears in the Paint window, where you can crop or edit it before saving.

Choosing the Right File Format

When you capture an image with a digital camera, the camera settings define the file format used. As a result, when you transfer images, you're not given a choice of formats. But when you scan a document, the final step of the Scanner And Camera Wizard involves the dialog box shown in Figure 26-5. The name and location fields are self-explanatory, but choosing the right file format isn't always so easy.

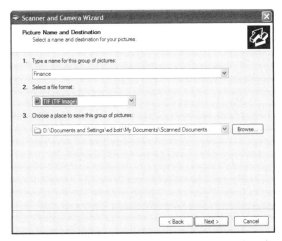

Figure 26-5.   After scanning an image, save it using a descriptive name and one of four default file formats.

Chapter 26

Select a format. The following four formats are the most popular for scanned documents, although your scanner may offer a different set of choices.

- **BMP** saves the file in the Windows Bitmap format. Because this format does not support compression, images tend to be very large. This is rarely the right choice for scanned images unless you intend to open the image in Paint (or another image editing program), make changes to it, and save it in another format immediately.

- **JPG** is the three-letter extension used to identify images that use the Joint Photographic Experts Group (JPEG) format. Because it is highly compressible, this is one of two popular formats used for Web graphics. (The other is Graphics Interchange Format, or GIF.) It's an excellent choice if the scanned image is destined for use on the Web. However, the compression used to create JPEG files results in a permanent loss of detail. If you want to preserve as much detail as possible, choose a different format.

- **TIF** is the three-letter extension for the Tag (or Tagged) Image File Format (TIFF), which is compatible with a large number of software applications. Although TIFF files can be compressed, the compression does not result in a loss of detail; of course, the trade-off is that TIFF files are generally larger than GIF or JPEG files. This is the best choice for graphics that will be used in desktop publishing programs. It's also the default format for faxes received through the Windows XP Fax Service. When scanning multiple pages using an automatic document feeder, choose this format to save the files in multipage TIFF format, in which all pages are merged into a single file.

- **PNG** stands for Portable Network Graphics, a format that is platform independent, highly compressible, and safe for use on Web pages because it's supported by virtually all modern browsers. Although some experts predict it will someday replace GIF, as of this writing it is still not widely used. The PNG filter used in Windows XP tends to produce relatively large images with no loss of detail.

> **Note** Previous versions of Windows included a useful image viewing and editing tool called Kodak Imaging. This tool is no longer available in a clean installation of Windows XP, although it is preserved if you upgrade from Windows 98, Windows Me, or Windows 2000. You'll sorely miss Kodak Imaging if you routinely work with multipage TIFF files, because the Windows XP Picture And Fax Viewer doesn't offer any way to add, delete, or rearrange individual pages in such a file. If you need this capability on a regular basis, you'll need to adopt an appropriate image-editing utility. Microsoft Office XP and Office 2003 include the excellent Microsoft Office Document Imaging utility. If you're not an Office user, consider the feature-rich, easy-to-use IrfanView (*http://www.irfanview.com*).

Need to convert a graphics file after saving it to your hard disk? Open Microsoft Paint (click the Start button, choose All Programs, Accessories, and click Paint). Unlike the noticeably underpowered Paint utility in Windows 95/98/Me, which could only work with BMP files, the Windows XP version is surprisingly robust. It still works with BMPs, of course, but you can also open and save picture files in JPEG, GIF, TIFF, and PNG formats. (You cannot, however, choose custom options such as compression levels for any of these formats.)

Chapter 26

Compressing and Shrinking Image Files

When you initially capture or scan an image, the size of the file can be enormous. That's all well and good if you have a large hard drive and you intend to send the digital photo to a color printer using high-quality paper. The larger size means more detail and thus a better image. But large file size is a serious hindrance if you plan to send an image as an e-mail attachment or upload it to a Web site. In either of those cases, your most important consideration is reducing the image to a size that can be conveniently downloaded without sacrificing quality.

Shrinking Images for E-Mail

If you plan to send digital photos to a friend or relative via e-mail, you'll run into problems if you don't plan carefully. If the recipient has a dial-up Internet connection, for instance, they probably won't appreciate tying up the line for a half-hour as your 6 MB attachment in TIFF or BMP format trickles in. With some Internet service providers (ISPs), attachments over a specified size are summarily rejected or can exhaust the user's quota on the server, causing all incoming messages to be rejected until he or she downloads your attachment.

If you manually attach an image file to a message, Microsoft Outlook Express, Outlook 2000/2002, and other e-mail client programs *will* send the original, uncompressed image. (Outlook 2003 includes an excellent set of tools for reducing oversized digital images in outgoing messages; if you use it as your default e-mail program, you can safely skip this section.) Windows XP can help you shrink the size of the image and convert the file to a compressible format, if you use the right technique. To do so, follow these steps:

1 Open a Windows Explorer window and select one or more picture files.

2 Click the E-Mail This File link in the File And Folder Tasks pane. If you make multiple selections, the wording of this task link changes to apply to the selected items or to all items in a folder. (If this option isn't visible, right-click the selection and choose Send To, Mail Recipient from the shortcut menu.)

3 In the Send Pictures Via E-Mail dialog box, the Make My Pictures Smaller option is selected by default. Click the Show More Options link to display the expanded version of this dialog box, as shown here.

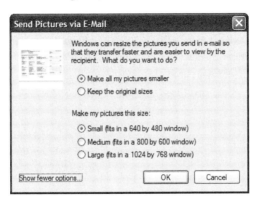

By default, this option converts BMP and TIFF images to JPEG format. (Because GIF and JPEG images are already compressible, using this option leaves those file formats alone.) It then compresses the file substantially and resizes the image so that it fits within a space no larger than 640 × 480 pixels (the exact dimensions of the resized image depend on the proportions of the original picture). If you're willing to accept a larger file size in exchange for more detail, you can select the Medium (800 × 600) or Large (1024 × 768) options instead.

4   Select the Small, Medium, or Large option and click OK. Windows opens your default e-mail program, creates a new message, and attaches the compressed image file(s).

5   Add message text, insert the recipient's address, and click the Send button without worrying that you'll be overloading someone's inbox.

Troubleshooting

The Make My Pictures Smaller option is unavailable.

Under some circumstances, the Make My Pictures Smaller option doesn't appear when you try to send files via e-mail from Windows Explorer. The culprit is a DLL that is no longer registered with the Windows shell. The fix is simple. Click Start, Run. In the Open box, type **regsvr32 shimgvw.dll** and press Enter.

The results of such file compression can be startling. Table 26-1 shows the before and after file sizes of four images. In all cases, the compressed file is less than half the size of the original, and in the case of large TIFF and BMP files, the compression ratio is as much as 99 percent.

Table 26-1. How Compression Affects Graphics File Sizes

Original Picture Specifications	Original Size and Format	Compression	
		Small (640 x 480)	**Large (1024 x 768)**
Scanned text document (B&W, 150 dpi, 8½ x 11 inches)	268 KB JPEG	36 KB JPEG	126 KB JPEG
Scanned magazine page (grayscale, 150 dpi, 8½ x 11 inches)	1.11 MB TIFF	16 KB JPEG (text unreadable)	85 KB JPEG (text readable)
Color photo from digital camera (24-bit color, 192 dpi, 1280 x 960 resolution)	556 KB JPEG	56 KB JPEG	235 KB JPEG
Scanned color photo (24-bit color, 300 dpi, 3 x 5 inches)	6 MB BMP	12 KB JPEG	66 KB JPEG

Caution   Using the technique described in this section to shrink and compress an image file invariably causes a loss of data. When you're sending a snapshot to your parents, the decrease in quality is probably a fair tradeoff for the faster, slimmer e-mail attachment. But if the scanned image contains text, or if the recipient wants to be able to print a high-quality copy, check the compressed image before you click Send. Where quality is crucial, you might have better results using the ZIP format to compress the original file without losing any data. Or look for a third-party image editing program such as IrfanView (*http://www.irfanview.com*) or Paint Shop Pro (*http://www.jasc.com*), which gives you greater control over compression.

Optimizing Image Files for the Web

Overly large image files are just as unwelcome on Web sites as they are in e-mail. Professional Web developers make a science out of "optimizing" graphics files for use on Web pages. Windows XP offers a limited set of tools for compressing image files and transferring them to a select number of Web-based locations that are specifically configured to hook into the wizard's dialog boxes. Currently, this group includes free or paid sites hosted by MSN Groups. If you have a Web site hosted elsewhere, you won't be able to access it through this wizard.

To launch the Web Publishing Wizard, select one or more graphics files (or an entire folder) and click the Publish To The Web link in the task pane. After confirming, and if necessary, changing your file selection and choosing a Web-based destination, you'll end up at the dialog box shown in Figure 26-6. As in the Send Pictures Via E-Mail dialog box, you can choose from three image sizes.

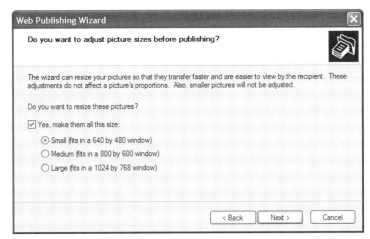

Figure 26-6.   To avoid wasting Web server space and speed up page loading times, choose the Small option when uploading image files.

If you prefer to leave all your files their original size, clear the Yes, Make Them All This Size check box. Otherwise, choose one of the three options, and complete the wizard to compress and upload the files in a single operation.

885

Compressing Image Files

The simplest way to compress a bitmap image to make it more suitable for uploading to the Web is to open it in Paint, and then use Paint's Save As command to convert it to a JPEG file. You can reduce the size of your BMP files by as much as 95 percent using this simple procedure.

Windows XP doesn't include any batch conversion tools, but a couple of easy workarounds let you reduce the size of several image files at once. The first method is to download the Image Resizer PowerToy from *http://www.microsoft.com/windowsxp/pro/downloads/ powertoys.asp*. (Don't be concerned about the "pro" in that URL; the PowerToys work with both Windows XP Professional and Windows XP Home Edition.) Like the other PowerToys available from this site, Image Resizer is offered free but not supported by Microsoft. We can attest to its reliability, though.

Once you have downloaded and installed Image Resizer, a Resize Pictures command appears on the shortcut menu whenever you select one or more image files. Choosing the command produces the following dialog box. (Click Advanced if you don't see the full dialog box.) You can change the size of an entire folderful of images at once with this command.

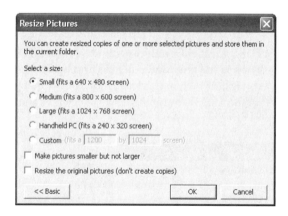

Note that Image Resizer can change the size of your pictures, but not the file format. A BMP file resized this way remains a BMP file and still consumes far more bits than a comparably sized JPEG. If you need to make a significant reduction in the file size of a batch of images— say, if you're getting ready to upload a folder of scanned photos to a personal Web site hosted on a server that isn't compatible with the Web Publishing Wizard—you should use a third-party tool such as IrfanView (*http://www.irfanview.com*). If you insist on using Windows XP, you can take the following indirect route to resize a group of pictures and convert them to a different format (the specifics of the format changes are described earlier in this chapter, in "Shrinking Images for E-Mail"):

1 Open a Windows Explorer window, navigate to the folder that contains the images, and then select one or more files.

2 Click the E-Mail The Selected Items link in the task pane.

Chapter 26

3   In the Send Pictures Via E-Mail dialog box, choose the image size you want (Small, Medium, or Large), and click OK.

4   A new mail message window opens; leave it open. Open a new Windows Explorer window and browse to the folder where you want to save the compressed files. (Don't use the original folder.)

5   Select all the attachment icons from the newly created e-mail message, and then drag them out of the message window and into the folder you just opened.

6   Close the message window. Your files are now ready for uploading.

Creating an HTML Slide Show

Want to turn your pictures into a slide show suitable for uploading to a Web site? The Microsoft PowerToys collection includes a tool that lets you do just that. You can download the HTML Slide Show Wizard from *http://www.microsoft.com/windowsxp/pro/downloads/powertoys.asp*. (Like all other PowerToys, this tool is a free utility created by, but not supported by, Microsoft.)

The HTML Slide Show Wizard starts by walking you through the selection of individual images and folders of images to include in your show. Once you've gathered your pictures, you can put them in the order you want by dragging them into the dialog box shown here.

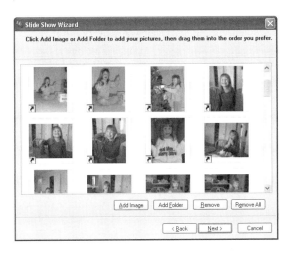

Note   Slide shows created with the HTML Slide Show Wizard can be viewed on your own computer as well as on a Web site. If you show them in Microsoft Internet Explorer, your slides include attractive transition effects. The PowerToys collection also includes a CD Slide Show Generator that lets you add a viewer to custom-burned picture CDs. For information about this PowerToy, see the Inside Out sidebar on page 714.

Chapter 26

The wizard's remaining steps let you name your show, add your own name as the show's author (if you choose), provide a file name and a folder in which to store the show, and choose various options. The most important of these options lets you reduce large images to a size more suitable for Web storage—320 × 240, 640 × 480, or 800 × 600. You can also choose between a simple show and an advanced show. The latter gives your audience a few extra viewing options but requires additional storage. To try out your work locally, simply navigate in Windows Explorer to the folder in which the wizard stored your show, and then double-click the file Default.htm. Figure 26-7 illustrates the wizard's output, as rendered by Internet Explorer in full-screen mode.

Figure 26-7. The HTML Slide Show Wizard generates attractive slide shows suitable for local viewing or uploading to the Internet.

Printing Digital Photos

Digital images are ideal for on-screen viewing, but they're hardly suitable for framing. That's where the Windows XP Photo Printing Wizard comes in. This new addition to Windows allows you to size, crop, and rotate images so that you get the best results on the printed page. This wizard is particularly useful when you want to make best use of expensive photo-quality paper, because it allows you to lay out multiple photos on the page for maximum coverage. Using the wizard also prevents you from inadvertently printing pictures where the subjects are distorted because of a mismatch between the typical 4:3 aspect ratio of many digital cameras and the 3:2 ratio used in standard-size 4 × 6 prints.

The easiest starting point for the Photo Printing Wizard is the Print This Picture link in the Picture Tasks box shown here. (This task box is visible by default in the task pane of the My Pictures folder and any other location you've designated as a place to store pictures or photos.)

If the Picture Tasks pane isn't visible in a Windows Explorer window, you can bring up the wizard easily enough. Select one or more images, right-click, and choose Print from the shortcut menu. (If you want to see the picture in its own window first, right-click and choose Preview to open the file in the Windows Picture And Fax Viewer. From this window, you can launch the Photo Printing Wizard by clicking the Print button.)

The wizard walks you through the following three steps:

1 **Picture Selection**   This window shows the files you selected or, if you didn't make a selection, all image files in the current folder. Use the check boxes above each thumbnail to select or clear an image from the list.

2 **Printing Options**   Choose a printer from the drop-down list, and then click the Printing Preferences button to set printer-specific options. This step is crucial if you intend to use photo paper. Choose color and resolution options here, and specify whether you want to print multiple copies.

3 **Layout Selection**   Here you can specify how you want the photos to be arranged on the page. As Figure 26-8 shows, you can mix and match photographs in each layout.

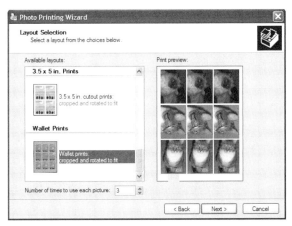

Figure 26-8.   To make most efficient use of expensive photo paper, use the Photo Printing Wizard to lay out images on the page.

You'll need to pay close attention when using the Photo Printing Wizard with images saved using the 4:3 ratio that's standard on most cameras—digital and film. All but one of the nine available layouts crop images during the printing process. Depending on the proportions of the selected images, you could be unpleasantly surprised by the final results. Table 26-2 lists all the available layouts and offers advice for using each one most effectively.

Table 26-2. Photo Printing Wizard Layouts

Layout	How to Use It
Full page prints	The Full Page Fax Print layout is the only layout that doesn't crop any portion of the image. Instead, the image is centered on the page and rotated if necessary, leaving some white space on two sides. The Full Page Photo Print layout crops the image slightly to fill the entire space.
Contact sheet prints	Choose this layout to print out thumbnail images of all selected images (35 per sheet), with the file name printed just below each image. Ideal for creating a printed index to a large library of digital images.
8 x 10 inch prints	Similar to the full page layouts, with slightly more severe cropping. This layout removes about 6 percent (cropped equally from the short edges of the image) of a standard 4:3 photo.
5 x 7 inch prints	A very efficient use of paper, with about 5 percent of the image cropped; the cuts are made equally on the long edges of the image.
4 x 6 inch prints	Cropping removes more than 10 percent of the image, and the effect can be especially severe because the cuts are to the long edges—in other words, an image that is shot in landscape orientation loses equally large slices from the top and bottom. For most efficient use of paper, choose the layout with three photos per 8½ × 11 inch sheet.
3½ x 5 inch prints	This option makes the most efficient use of paper, with less intrusive cropping than the 4 × 6 layout.
Wallet prints	This layout involves virtually no cropping. If you don't need nine copies of a single image, try selecting three images and printing each picture three times.

When using the Photo Printing Wizard, choose layouts carefully and pay close attention to cropping. For casual snapshots, the default cropping might not be noticeable. But for images that are carefully composed, you'll get best results by cropping the image manually in an image-editing program so its proportions match those of the print layout you plan to use.

Organizing Your Digital Picture Collection

Most people throw their digital images into the online equivalent of a shoe box. The Scanner And Camera Wizard can automatically number image files and dump them into folders for you, but that's about the extent of its organizational expertise. If you shoot lots of pictures, learn how to take advantage of information called *metadata* to keep track of extra details.

Image metadata is nonpicture information that's captured and stored within a picture file. Most digital cameras use the Exchangeable Image File (EXIF) format when saving pictures; images may also include metadata that conforms to the International Press Telecommunications Council (IPTC) and Adobe's Extensible Metadata Platform (XMP) standards. (To learn more about the EXIF standard, visit *http://www.exif.org*; for more details about XMP, see *http://www.adobe.com/products/xmp/overview.html*.) EXIF metadata typically includes the date and time the picture was taken, the width and height of the image (in pixels), the resolution (in dpi), and the color depth. Depending on the camera you use, metadata can also include technical information such as the camera model, flash mode, aperture, and exposure time. Some high-end devices even allow you to add audio annotations to images and store them in the same file. A few bits of metadata are available in the ScreenTip that appears when you pause the mouse pointer over an image file, as shown below.

```
Dimensions: 1440 x 2160
Date Picture Taken: 9/19/2003 9:29 AM
Camera Model: KODAK DX3900 ZOOM DIGITAL CAMERA
Type: JPEG Image
Size: 503 KB
```

Windows XP doesn't allow you to edit image metadata. But you can use it in Windows Explorer windows to sort and file images. To see all available metadata for an individual image file, right-click the file icon and then choose Properties. On the Summary tab, click Advanced to display a scrolling list of available metadata properties and values. Image data appears above the Description data, as in the example in Figure 26-9.

Figure 26-9. Image metadata is captured by a camera and stored within each image file.

To really take advantage of metadata, you need to customize the Windows Explorer window so that metadata information is visible. To do so, switch to Details view, right-click any column heading, and then select the names of available fields to make those columns visible. Click More at the bottom of the list to see all possible fields. Here you can select multiple fields and arrange their order in one step.

Figure 26-10 shows the results of customizing Details view for a folder filled with image files. The most noteworthy addition here is the Date Picture Taken column. Click the column heading to sort by this field and gather pictures that were taken around the same time.

You can search for pictures on the basis of their metadata tags. To find all pictures taken with your GR-DVM90 camera, for example, click Pictures, Music, Or Video in the Search Explorer bar, and then select Pictures And Photos. Then click Use Advanced Search Options and enter **GR-DVM90** in the A Word Or Phrase In The File box.

Organizing and Editing Images

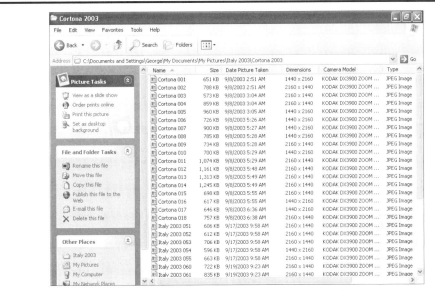

Figure 26-10. Displaying image metadata in a Windows Explorer window makes it a snap to see the date on which a photo was taken.

Tip Avoid wasting paper

Make your choices carefully when choosing a print layout, or you might end up wasting paper accidentally. Pay special attention to the number of photos in your selection and on the layout; if you select three images and then choose the 5 × 7 inch prints layout, which contains slots for two prints, the wizard will put the final image on a page by itself. Rather than waste half a sheet of photo paper, you might want to select a fourth image to fill the remaining space. Or, as an alternative, you could split the job in two. Select two images and print them on a single page; then run the wizard again and print the third image using the same layout, increasing the Number Of Times To Use Each Picture setting to 2.

Caution When you rotate images in Windows XP, your metadata is preserved. However, many image-editing programs (including the Windows XP Image Resizer PowerToy) wipe out all metadata when you make any changes to the image, such as cropping or resizing. To preserve these details, use a third-party tool that can back up metadata before you edit images and restore it to the modified files. The free Exifer for Windows utility (*http://www.friedemann-schmidt.com/software/exifer/*) handles this chore with aplomb and also allows you to add comments and custom fields that can be directly stored as metadata within image files.

Chapter 26

Managing Images in Windows Explorer

In Windows XP, the My Pictures folder is the official storage location for image files of all sorts. When you acquire an image with a WIA-compatible device, it's stored in this folder. When you use Internet Explorer's Image toolbar, you jump straight to this folder. And any modern application that uses image files will use this folder as its default storage location.

> **Tip**   Give My Pictures a new name
>
> Does the My Pictures name set your teeth on edge? Then change it. Windows tracks the actual location of this folder in the registry, using the My Pictures value under the key HKCU\Software\Microsoft\Windows\CurrentVersion\Explorer\Shell Folders. Don't edit this value in the registry, however. To rename this folder, right-click its shortcut on the Start menu or its icon in the My Documents window and choose Rename. You can also move the folder to another location on your hard disk. When you do, Windows records the new name and location, copies all your files, and updates the registry automatically. To specify that you want My Pictures to point to a different location without moving your existing image files, use Tweak UI for Windows XP; click the Special Folders option under the My Computer heading.

Although the My Pictures folder itself has been around for several Windows versions, Windows XP includes the following new file management features that make it easier to work with image files:

- **Thumbnails view**   When you choose this view to display the contents of the My Pictures folder, Windows shows a miniature image of each image file. The icon for each subfolder that contains image files displays thumbnails of the last four images you created or modified in that subfolder.

- **The Picture Tasks box**   This list of links gives you quick access to common tasks you're likely to perform with images. You can order prints online, copy a group of files to a CD, view all the images in the current folder as a full-screen slide show, or launch the Photo Printing Wizard.

- **Filmstrip view**   In the My Pictures folder (and all its subfolders), this new view allows you to quickly preview images, rotate them 90 degrees at a time, and perform common image-related tasks. Figure 26-11 shows this view in action. Note that the "strip" of photos in the bottom of the window scrolls from left to right, whereas the preview pane above it stays in a fixed location.

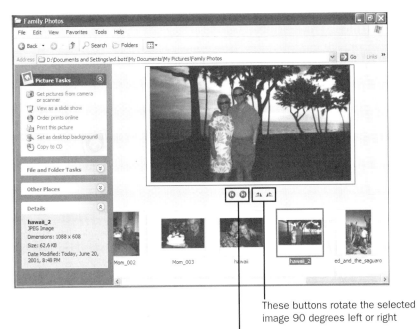

These buttons rotate the selected image 90 degrees left or right

Use these two buttons to quickly preview images

Figure 26-11.   In the new Filmstrip view, you can scroll through thumbnails along the bottom of the folder window and preview selected images.

Tip   Give photos some extra room

Want to clear the title bar, menus, Address bar, and other space-hogging screen elements when working with a folder full of images? Press F11, the Full Screen shortcut key, to banish virtually all the clutter above the preview pane in Filmstrip view. The only thing left will be a scaled-down toolbar. To restore the normal interface elements, press F11 again.

Troubleshooting

Thumbnails or file names don't appear.

In Thumbnails or Filmstrip view, you might encounter some images that simply won't display as a proper thumbnail. A variety of technical problems can cause broken thumbnails, which typically appear as a large red X or a generic image icon. Try one of the following techniques to restore the thumbnail:

- Press F5 to refresh the folder's contents.
- Right-click the image icon and choose Refresh Thumbnail from the shortcut menu.
- Rotate the image 90 degrees clockwise and then rotate it back to its original position. This technique allows Windows to reread the image.
- Open the image file in Paint and save it under another name, using the same format.

If none of these techniques is successful, the file might be in a format that Windows Explorer's thumbnail handler doesn't recognize, even though it can preview the image when selected. If that's the case, try opening the image in Paint and saving it under a new name, using a different file format.

Normally, the name of each image file appears beneath each thumbnail in Thumbnails or Filmstrip view. If these labels disappear unexpectedly, you can make them reappear by switching to any other view (such as List or Details) and then holding down Shift as you choose the Thumbnails or Filmstrip option on the View menu or from the Views button. If you like the cleaner, no-name look, repeat these steps to toggle the display of file names off.

Customizing Folders for Images

When you create a new subfolder in the My Pictures folder, it automatically inherits all of Windows Explorer's image-handling tools. But you can customize other folders to have these tools as well. Say, for instance, that you keep a collection of logos and product pictures in a subfolder on your drive D. Here's how to customize that folder so that it includes Filmstrip view and the Picture Tasks box:

1. Right-click the folder icon and choose Properties.

2. On the Customize tab, choose Pictures from the Use This Folder Type As A Template list.

3. If you want to organize image files in subfolders, select Also Apply This Template To All Subfolders.

4. To define a custom image that will appear on the folder in Thumbnails and Filmstrip views, click the Choose Picture button and select an image file. If you skip this step, Windows Explorer will display the last four images modified. Note that the image you define here will become part of the template for this folder and will appear on every subfolder you create as well.

5 To add a custom icon to identify the folder in all other views, click the Change Icon button and select an icon file. (To see an example, look at the custom My Music and My Pictures icons in the My Documents folder.)

Tip   Make your own icons
Creating custom icons isn't particularly difficult. There are dozens of free and shareware icon editors available, or you can create your own. The rules for an icon are simple: Make it 32 pixels square and save it in BMP format, using the extension .ico.

When you're finished, the dialog box displays the custom image you selected, as in the example shown in Figure 26-12.

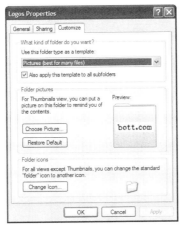

Figure 26-12.   Use these settings to customize any folder on any drive so that it includes image file management tools.

6 Click OK to apply your changes.

Note   When customizing a folder, you can also choose Photo Album from the Use This Folder Type As A Template list. What's the difference? In a Photo Album folder, Filmstrip is the default view; a Pictures folder defaults to Thumbnails view. Otherwise, the two customizations are identical.

Viewing and Annotating Image Files

Unless you install a third-party program to handle image viewing, double-clicking an image file opens the Windows Picture And Fax Viewer. This utility, a Windows XP newcomer, displays images in a resizable preview window that includes a toolbar for common actions. (Even if another program has taken over the default association for a particular image file type, you can still use the built-in Windows tool; in Windows Explorer, right-click one or more files, click the Open With menu, and choose Windows Picture And Fax Viewer.)

If you open an ordinary image file, the toolbar consists of 14 buttons that allow you to resize the image; rotate it 90 degrees in either direction; delete, print, or save the image; and open it for editing.

As Figure 26-13 shows, however, the toolbar is greatly expanded when you open a TIFF image. Nine additional buttons allow you to annotate the image, using text, simple lines and shapes, yellow "sticky notes," and a highlighter tool. Notice, too, the navigation controls in the center of the toolbar, which allow you to move from page to page within a multipage document, such as a fax.

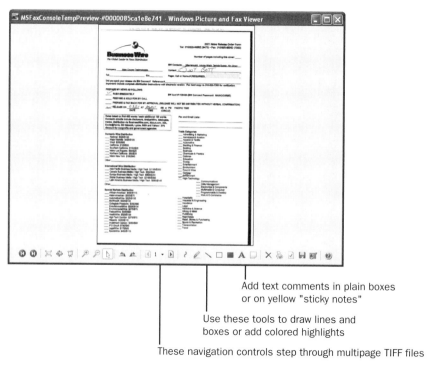

Add text comments in plain boxes or on yellow "sticky notes"

Use these tools to draw lines and boxes or add colored highlights

These navigation controls step through multipage TIFF files

Figure 26-13. Use the tools at the bottom of the Windows Picture And Fax Viewer window to add annotations to a TIFF file.

Chapter 26

Using Windows Movie Maker

If you've owned a video camera for more than a week or two, odds are good that you have a stack of videotapes somewhere in your home or office. Those tapes likely contain nuggets of pure gold—memories of idyllic vacations, perhaps, or recordings of milestone events in your life or the lives of people you love. Unfortunately, those nuggets are probably so deeply embedded in the surrounding gangue that you seldom bother to look for them (let alone look *at* them). It doesn't help that the sequential-access nature of recording tape discourages review, not to mention the fact that much of what most of us put on videotape isn't worth revisiting or inflicting upon others.

But the nuggets are there, so you don't dare discard or reuse those tapes. How to separate the valuable bits from all the rest? Microsoft Windows Movie Maker can help. This program, included with Windows XP, is a highly functional video editing tool, designed to create polished video presentations, complete with animated titles, credits, narration, background music, professional-looking scene transitions, and special effects. But even if you never use any of those fancy features (an unlikely outcome), you'll find that Windows Movie Maker is a terrific tool for memory-mining. With it, you can import your raw video footage, separate it into scenes, assemble the gold into meaningful sequences, and render these distillations into packages that you'll be at ease delivering to friends and family—and watching again yourself.

Windows Movie Maker is a consumer-oriented program, adequate for most personal purposes. But even though it lacks the exotic features of professional video editing programs (such as Adobe Premiere or Pinnacle Liquid Edition Pro), you can use it to create effective business presentations as well—training videos, short movies to post to your company's Web site, product demonstrations, and other similar items.

At Home with Windows XP

Everything described in this chapter applies equally to Windows XP Professional and Windows XP Home Edition.

Whether you use Windows Movie Maker at home or at work, it's an easy place to begin learning the art and craft of video editing. If you become seriously smitten, you can always move on to the hard stuff later.

What You Need to Use Windows Movie Maker

Video editing requires a lot of computing and storage resources. Microsoft's recommended minimum system configuration is a 1.5 GHz microprocessor with 256 MB of RAM. Our experience suggests that you're more likely to capture video footage from your camcorder successfully, without dropped frames, if you double that memory requirement to a half gigabyte.

As for disk space, what you need depends on the image quality you want to achieve and the amount of footage you intend to store. Capturing footage from your digital camcorder using the highest quality, least compressed format, called Digital Video Audio-Video Interleaved (DV-AVI), will consume disk space at the blood-pressure-raising rate of 178 MB per minute, or about 13 GB for a one-hour source tape. You'll want to use this format, if possible, if you intend to copy your finished movies back to videotape, to CDs, or to DVDs. (Windows Movie Maker does not support rendering movies to DVD, but you can use third-party software for this purpose.) If you are planning to prepare videos to watch on a computer, you can choose a more compact format. Capturing digital camcorder footage in the .wmv format at the quality level that Windows Movie Maker recommends for computer playback consumes a mere 14 MB per minute—less than a twelfth of the space used by DV-AVI. If you're planning to publish your work on Web sites, you can choose from a variety of still more compact formats, suitable for downloading at broadband or dial-up speeds. (For details, see "Capturing from Videotape," page 904.)

> **Tip**   Make sure that any partitions on which you plan to capture DV-AVI video are formatted in NTFS. FAT32 partitions have a file-size limit of 4 GB.

> **Tip**   Windows Movie Maker creates large temporary files while it renders projects into movies. As you calculate your disk space needs, it's a good idea to budget 15 GB for this purpose.

However you expect to work, assume that you need a large amount of storage. If you're buying a system expressly for movie making, get the largest disk you can afford (add another disk to your system if that's an option). That will give you the freedom to capture more of your video library and assemble the best parts into satisfactory movies.

If you plan to capture footage from a digital camcorder, you should have an IEEE 1394 (FireWire or iLink) interface and cable. If your computer is of recent vintage and has a built-in 1394 adapter, you're in great shape. If not, you can buy an IEEE 1394 card and plug it into a PCI slot. To capture video from an analog camera or from VHS tape, you'll need an analog capture device.

> **Tip**   If you're contemplating buying a video-capture hardware device—particularly an analog card—you might want to consult Microsoft's Movie Maker newsgroup (microsoft. public.windowsxp.moviemaker) to see what experience others have had with that device.

Introducing Windows Movie Maker

If your Start menu has not been drastically rearranged, you'll find shortcuts for Windows Movie Maker near the bottom of Start, All Programs and Start, All Programs, Accessories, Entertainment. To launch from the Run command, type **moviemk.exe**. Before you get started with the program, take a moment to ensure that you're working with version 2.1 or later (choose Help, About Windows Movie Maker to get your version number). If for some reason you need to download the latest version, you can do so by pointing your browser to *http://www.microsoft.com/windowsxp/downloads/updates/moviemaker2.mspx*.

Figure 27-1 shows the four panes that constitute the Windows Movie Maker window. On the left is a task pane that provides quick access to some of the program's more frequently used commands. You can click the icons next to each heading to hide or reveal subheadings. After your first hour or two with Windows Movie Maker, you'll probably want to be rid of the task pane. By clicking Collections on the toolbar, you can replace it with the more useful Collections tree (shown in Figure 27-2).

> **Note** If you prefer to keep the task list visible in the leftmost pane, you can still navigate your Collections tree by opening the drop-down list in the toolbar.

Task pane   Collections pane

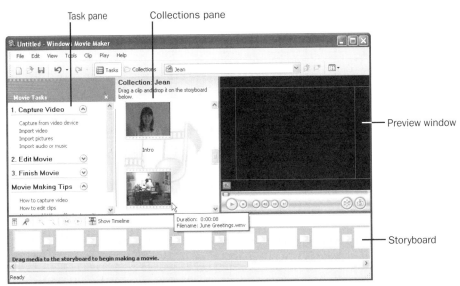

Preview window

Storyboard

Figure 27-1. The Windows Movie Maker screen is divided into four panes.

To the right of the task pane is the Collections pane. In Windows Movie Maker terminology, a *collection* is a virtual folder containing clips, and a *clip* is an element that can be used in a movie—a video scene, a static image, some narration, or some music. (For more about

Chapter 27

901

collections and clips, see "Gathering and Managing Source Materials," page 904.) Because the screen shots for this book use 800 × 600 resolution, the Collections pane in Figure 27-1 is extremely narrow, showing only two clips. You will undoubtedly work at higher resolution, and you'll want to have a large number of clips in view as you assemble your movies.

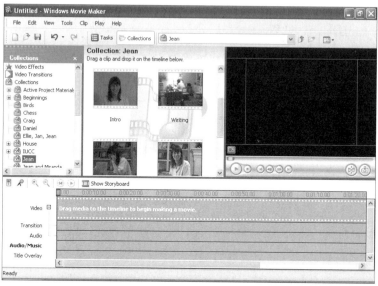

Figure 27-2. The Collections tree enables you to organize your source materials, and the timeline provides an alternative to the storyboard for movie assembly.

Figure 27-1 shows the Collections pane in Thumbnails view. By choosing View, Details (or using the View tool on the toolbar), you can switch to Details view and see such details as the duration and image size of each clip. As the figure shows, however, you can also see some essential information about a clip by reading the ScreenTip that emerges when you point to or hover over the clip with the mouse.

The large dark area to the right of the Collections pane is the Preview pane. This is a miniature media player. You can use it to play the selected clip (whether that clip is video or sound) or to preview your work as you put together a movie.

The process of assembling clips into a movie takes place either in the storyboard, which occupies the fourth pane shown in Figure 27-1, or the timeline, shown in that same bottom-of-the-window pane in Figure 27-2. You can toggle between storyboard and timeline by clicking the Show Timeline or Show Storyboard button (at the top of the pane), by choosing commands on the View menu, or by pressing Ctrl+T.

As you make your movies, you'll probably find yourself switching frequently between the timeline and the storyboard. The storyboard is easier to use for certain tasks, such as adding a visual transition between clips. But using the timeline is the *only* way to accomplish other important tasks, such as adding background music or narration.

Chapter 27

In Figure 27-2, we've toggled the task pane to display the Collections tree and replaced the storyboard with the timeline. The Collections tree shows an outline of your collections folders, somewhat like the Folders bar in Windows Explorer. On your system, the first three entries—Video Effects, Video Transitions, and Collections—will match Figure 27-2. The subentries under the Collections heading, of course, will reflect the folder structure that you establish.

The timeline shown in Figure 27-2 has been expanded to its full five-track glory. You can drag the thick blue pane-divider at the top of the timeline (or storyboard) to make the pane bigger or smaller. By dragging the vertical bars to the left and right of the Collections pane, you can make similar adjustments to the sizes of the other screen elements.

The Process of Making a Movie

Like so many other things you do at your computer, making a movie entails input, processing, and output. With Windows Movie Maker, those steps are as follows:

- Gathering and organizing of source materials (input)
- Sequencing of source materials on the storyboard and timeline, along with the addition of transitions, visual effects, sound, and titles (processing)
- Rendering of the storyboard/timeline sequence into a finished movie (output)

Devoting some thought and energy to the first part of this process—particularly the organization of your raw material—will save you a great deal of time and hassle when you are immersed in the more interesting, creative work. As you work with thumbnails in the Collections pane (or line entries, if you switch to Details view), bear in mind that you are manipulating pointers to data, not the data itself. Similarly, when you create collections folders in which to classify your clips, you are dealing with virtual folders—like the Inbox and Sent Items folders in Microsoft Outlook Express, not the folders on your hard disk. Thus, once you have captured or imported an accumulation of video footage, you can copy your clips (and folders) at will, rename each copy meaningfully, and build a conveniently redundant structure that reflects the multiple contexts in which your clips can be used—all without creating a proliferation of disk-eating data files.

As you assemble materials on the storyboard and timeline, you create a blueprint that Windows Movie Maker will use to render your finished movie. The program calls this blueprint a *project*. You save it—using the File, Save Project command or pressing Ctrl+S—in a file with the extension .mswmm. Unlike your source video files, project files are small. Provided the data objects they reference remain at hand, you can edit and reuse project files indefinitely to make different kinds of movies for different purposes.

When it comes to rendering a finished project, you have five basic choices. You can save the movie to a disk file for viewing in Windows Media Player (or a comparable program), burn it onto a recordable CD, save it as an e-mail attachment, upload it directly to a video hosting provider on the Internet, or (if you have a digital video camera and an IEEE 1394 connection) send it back to videotape. Some of these basic choices have options of their own; for details, see "Rendering Your Project into a Movie," page 928.

Gathering and Managing Source Materials

There are two ways to get video, image, and sound materials into Windows Movie Maker: You can *capture* video, by connecting a video device (such as a camcorder, Web camera, or television tuner), or you can *import* video and other kinds of media from existing files.

Capturing from Videotape

To capture recorded footage from a camcorder or VHS player, start by connecting the camera or player to the appropriate computer interface (your IEEE 1394 port or analog capture card) and turning it on. Set the camera to its playback mode, and in Windows Movie Maker, choose File, Capture Video. (If Plug and Play recognizes your device, you won't have to take this last step; the system will do it for you.) You'll then arrive at the Video Capture Device screen of the Video Capture Wizard, which will look something like this (depending on the video hardware you have installed):

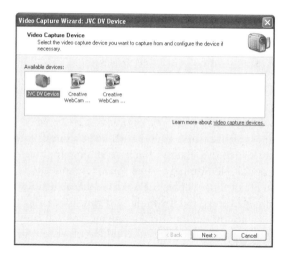

If you're using a digital camera connected to an IEEE 1394 interface, you have nothing more to do on this screen than select your camera in the Available Devices section of the dialog box and click Next. If you're using an analog device, the dialog box includes additional options. You'll need to select your video input source, in the event that your analog capture card has more than one connection line (a composite video connection and an S-video connection, for example). You might also see a Configure button, which lets you specify other settings appropriate for your device. When you're ready to move on, click Next.

The wizard's second screen asks for a file name and disk folder for your captured video. Make these decisions thoughtfully. The clips that will appear in the Collections pane after Windows Movie Maker has captured your footage will be pointers to the file name and folder that you have specified. You can rename those clips to your heart's content, but if you rename or move the disk file, the pointers will become invalid. You can fix the links, but that's a hassle you don't need. It's best to pick a suitably descriptive file name and an appropriate location before you start the capture.

Tip   Avoid "invalid source" hassle

Store your captured video locally. If you put the source files on a network server, Windows Movie Maker will mark clips derived from that source as invalid each time you start the program. You can fix the links (each time) and use the remote source if you need to, but it's a pain. Use local storage if possible.

The wizard's next screen, called Video Setting and shown here, presents the quality/file size tradeoff.

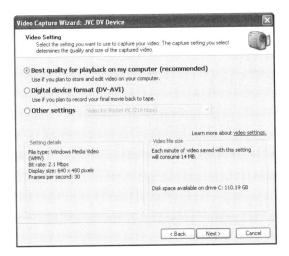

The important thing to keep in mind as you consider the options on this screen is that your capture quality sets an upper limit on the quality of your finished movie. You will confront a similar set of movie-quality/file-size options later on when you render your project, but whatever choices you make then, the rendering process cannot improve on the quality that you capture now. If you know already that you're going to be using this footage only for the purpose of generating movies that will be viewed under constrained circumstances—as e-mail attachments, for example, or for posting to a Web site that viewers might access over dial-up connections—then you might as well opt for modest quality and small file size. To keep your eventual options open, capture at the highest quality that your disk-space budget will allow.

The default option on the Video Settings screen, Best Quality For Playback On My Computer (Recommended) generates a .wmv file of a quality that will play well on standard (that is, not PDA) computer screens. (WMV, which stands for *Windows Media Video*, is Microsoft's standard compressed video format. .wmv files can be viewed in Windows Media Player, versions 7 and later.) The estimated disk size of video captured at this setting is 14 MB per minute.

The second option, Digital Device Format (DV-AVI), is the gold standard for quality. The least compressed format uses disk space at the rate of 178 MB per minute. Use this setting if plan to render your movie back onto digital videotape.

The drop-down list that becomes available if you click the third option, Other Settings, presents all the available choices, including the two just described. Those choices are enumerated in Table 27-1. As you review the options, note that higher bit rates (rates of data transfer) generate smoother playback but can be a prime decision factor for video that will be accessed from an Internet site.

Table 27-1. Video Capture Options

Setting	File Type	Bit Rate	Display Size	Frames per Second	Estimated File Size per Minute
Video for Pocket PC (218 Kbps)	WMV	218.2 K	208×160	20	1 MB
Video for Pocket PC (143 Kbps)	WMV	143 K	208×160	8	1 MB
Video for Pocket PC (Full screen 218 Kbps)	WMV	218 K	320×240	15	1 MB
High-quality video (large)	WMV	Variable	640×480	30	Varies
High-quality video (small)	WMV	Variable	320×240	30	Varies
Video for local playback (2.1 Mbps)	WMV	2.1 M	640×480	30	14 MB
Video for local playback (1.5 Mbps)	WMV	1.5 M	640×480	30	10 MB
Video for LAN (1.0 Mbps)	WMV	1 M	640×480	30	7 MB
Video for LAN (768 Kbps)	WMV	768 K	640×480	30	5 MB
Video for broadband (512 Kbps)	WMV	512 K	320×240	30	3 MB
Video for broadband (340 Kbps)	WMV	340 K	320×240	30	2 MB
Video for broadband (150 Kpbs)	WMV	150 K	320×240	15	1 MB
Video for ISDN (48 Kbps)	WMV	48 K	160×120	15	351 KB

Chapter 27

Table 27-1. **Video Capture Options**

Setting	File Type	Bit Rate	Display Size	Frames per Second	Estimated File Size per Minute
Video for dial-up access (38 Kbps)	WMV	38 K	160×120	15	278 KB
DV-AVI (NTSC)	AVI	25 M	720×480	30	178 MB
High-quality video (NTSC)	WMV	Variable	720×480	30	Varies
Video for Pocket PC 2003 (348 Kbps at 24 fps)	WMV	348 K	320×240	24	2 MB
Video for Pocket PC 2003 (348 Kbps at 30 fps)	WMV	348 K	320×240	30	2 MB
Video for Smartphone 2002 (182 Kbps)	WMV	182 K	160×120	15	1 MB
Video for Smartphone 2003 (182 Kbps)	WMV	182 K	160×120	15	1 MB

If you're capturing from a digital device connected via IEEE 1394, after you make your video settings decision and click Next, you'll see the Capture Method screen:

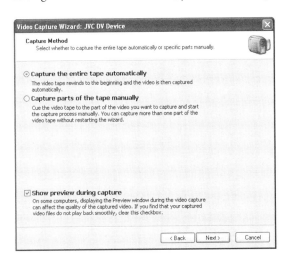

An IEEE 1394 interface can send playback signals to most digital cameras, so if you want to capture the entire tape, simply select the first option, Capture The Entire Tape Automatically. The wizard will rewind your tape (if necessary) and begin the capture process. If you'd rather operate the controls yourself, select the second option. After clicking Next, you will see the Capture Video screen:

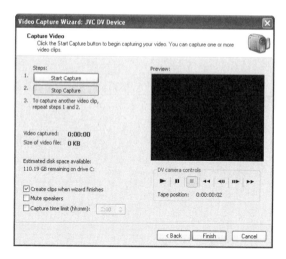

You can use the Preview window and the DV Camera Controls to position your tape appropriately, then use the Start Capture and Stop Capture buttons to begin and end the capture process. Note that you can capture several different sections of a tape this way. Windows Movie Maker will save them all in a single file.

If you're capturing from an analog device, you'll need to operate the camera's playback controls directly. Position your tape slightly ahead of the first frame you want to capture, then click Start Capture and press your camera's Start control. Click Stop Capture and press the camera's Stop control to finish.

The capture process will take as long as the recording that you're capturing. There's no way to speed this along. To reduce the likelihood that your computer might drop frames during the capture, it's best to keep it otherwise idle. If you need to capture an hour's worth of tape, do so at a time when you don't need to be downloading e-mail, crunching numbers, or playing Spider Solitaire.

Previewing During the Capture

One of the last options presented by the Video Capture Wizard before it begins collecting data from your camera, Show Preview During Capture, is selected by default and lets you see and hear the contents of your tape as they're being captured. If you do find that you're losing frames during the capture process, try again with this check box cleared. Unless you're capturing footage from a VHS player that's not also connected to a television, you'll still be able to preview the capture on your camera's playback screen.

Letting Windows Movie Maker Create Clips Automatically

The Capture Video screen includes a handy Create Clips When Wizard Finishes check box. If you leave this selected (its default state), Windows Movie Maker uses its own logic to resolve your captured footage into individual clips (scenes) at the end of the capture process. The program does this by looking for changes in lighting or (on digital tapes) discontinuities in the recorded time stamps. Unless you're capturing only a very small section of tape that records a single continuous scene, you probably want to take advantage of this service. The program's judgment about where to divide your video into clips is by no means infallible (sometimes it seems downright arbitrary), but if you get clips that are too long, you can always split them manually later on. And if the program happens to see a discontinuity where one didn't really exist, you can easily rejoin the resulting clips. (See "Splitting Clips," page 913, and "Joining Clips," page 914.)

Capturing Live Video

Want to perform live for Windows Movie Maker? No problem. Simply set your camcorder to its camera (as opposed to playback) mode and choose File, Capture Video in Windows Movie Maker. You'll see a set of wizard screens similar to the ones shown in the previous section.

If you're capturing from a Webcam or other device that does not normally record sound, you'll have the option of using a microphone plugged into your sound card for audio input. Specify your audio input source on the Video Capture Device screen (typically the choice here will be Microphone, but you might also choose Line In or another setting, depending on your hardware setup). You'll also see a microphone input level meter and an adjustable level setting. You can do a quick sound test here (speak into the microphone and adjust the input level so that the meter stays out of the red zone) before you start capturing.

Importing Media Files into Windows Movie Maker

The File, Import Into Collections command (shortcut: Ctrl+I) lets you turn existing sound, image, and video files into Windows Movie Maker clips. If you want a favorite CD track to serve as background music, for example, use Windows Media Player (or another similar program) to rip the track as a .wma or .mp3 file, then import that file into Windows Movie Maker. Table 27-2 lists the media formats that Windows Movie Maker can import.

Table 27-2. File Formats Supported by Windows Movie Maker

Media Type	Supported Extensions
Audio	.aif, .aifc, .aiff, .asf, .au, .mp2, .mp3, .mpa, .snd, .wav, .wma
Still image	.bmp, .dib, .emf, .gif, .jfif, .jpe, .jpeg, .jpg, .png, .tif, .tiff, .wmf
Video	.asf, .avi, .m1v, .mp2, .mp2v, .mpe, .mpeg, .mpg, .mpv2, .wm, .wmv

> **Tip** You can drag and drop any supported media file into the Collections pane of Windows Movie Maker—an action equivalent to using the File, Import Into Collections command. Copy and paste does not work, however.

You'll notice in Table 27-2 that Windows Movie Maker does not support QuickTime video (files with the extension .mov). If you have QuickTime files that you want to use in your Windows Movie Maker productions, you'll need to convert them to a supported format first. The RAD Video Tools, which you can download from the RAD Game Tools site at *http://www.radgametools.com/bnkdown.htm*, can do this job for you.

> **Tip** Prepare for codecs
>
> If you try to import a video or audio file that uses a codec (a compression/decompression algorithm) that isn't already installed on your system, Windows Movie Maker will not be able to complete the import. To avoid this problem, you can have Windows Movie maker download any codec it needs without intervention from you. To make use of this service, choose Tools, Options, and click the General tab. Then select Download Codecs Automatically.

Working with Clips

Figure 27-3 shows a set of freshly captured video clips. Because the clips came from a digital camera, Windows Movie Maker was able to use each clip's time stamp as a name for that clip. (Analog cameras don't provide this information, so Windows Movie Maker simply uses a sequential naming system.) This information is undoubtedly interesting, but it doesn't tell you anything about the content of the clip. A descriptive name might be more useful, particularly if there are events or actions in the clip that aren't hinted at by the thumbnail.

You can review each clip by selecting it and playing it in the Preview pane, and you can rename any clip by right-clicking it and choosing Rename (or by selecting it and pressing F2). But before you do that, be aware that, although Windows Movie Maker is able to generate a time stamp as a default name for each clip captured from a digital camera, it does not store that time-stamp information as a property of the clip. As Figure 27-4 shows, the properties dialog box for a clip (which you can inspect in the usual way, by right-clicking and choosing Properties) provides data about the clip's duration, time offset within its source file, video and audio parameters (bit rate, frames per second, height, width, and so on), but—aside from that default name—there is no indication of when the clip was shot.

If you switch your Collections pane from Thumbnails view to Details view, you will find a column named Date Taken. Alas, this misnamed column reports the capture date, not the shoot date. Nor will you find the shoot date by inspecting the properties of the clip's source file (the .wmv or .avi file that you captured and stored on your hard disk). Again, the source file's properties will tell you when the video was captured, but not when it was recorded.

Using Windows Movie Maker

Figure 27-3. Freshly captured clips arrive in a folder named to match the name of the source file; the clips themselves are named by their date-and-time stamps, if they originated in a digital camcorder.

Figure 27-4. A clip's properties dialog box provides useful information about the clip's format but no property records when the clip was shot.

To preserve date and time data while assigning descriptive names to your clips, you can create collections folders with date names—July 2004, or Miranda's Twelfth Birthday, for example. This approach runs aground, however, if you want to copy your clips into multiple folders.

Alternatively, you could simply append or prepend descriptions to the default date-time names. The resulting length, however, would make your clip names hard to read when you position them on the timeline or storyboard.

The best method we've found for keeping the date information is to add it as a comment in the Properties dialog box of the source file (see Figure 27-5). Tagging the source file with comments regarding the content and purpose of your captured footage, as well as its date of origin, will help you keep track of the goods.

Figure 27-5. It's a good idea to tag your source files with comments describing the content, purpose, and date of your captured footage.

Previewing Clips

The Preview pane comes with a set of controls that mimic those on your VCR—with a couple of handy additions:

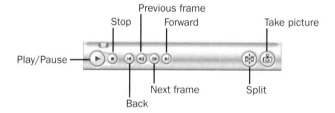

To preview a clip, simply select it and click the Play button. (Alternatively, you can drag a clip and drop it onto the Preview pane.) If you prefer to operate from the keyboard, Table 27-3 lists the available shortcuts.

Table 27-3. Keyboard Shortcuts for Previewing Clips

Action	Command
Play/Pause	Spacebar
Stop	Ctrl+K
Back	Ctrl+Alt+Left Arrow
Previous Frame	Alt+Left Arrow
Next Frame	Alt+Right Arrow
Forward	Ctrl+Alt+Right Arrow
Split	Ctrl+L

Note that the Next Frame and Previous Frame commands advance and rewind the clip by eight one-hundredths of a second, regardless of frames per second at which the footage was captured.

By default, Windows Movie Maker previews clips and projects and also renders finished projects into movies, at the aspect ratio 4 (width) to 3 (height). The Preview pane retains this ratio at two standard sizes—Small (320 × 240) and Large (640 × 480). You can switch between these sizes by right-clicking the pane and choosing Small or Large (the latter is available only when window space permits).

If you prefer the 16:9 aspect ratio used by newer televisions, choose Tools, Options and click the Advanced tab. In the Video Properties section of the dialog box, select 16:9. The Preview pane will adjust its standard sizes to 320 × 180 and 640 × 360. Windows Movie Maker will also render your finished projects at 16:9 while this setting is in effect.

> **Tip** You can also drag the left border of the pane to achieve intermediate sizes (a Screen-Tip reports the current dimensions of the pane as you drag). For a full-screen display, press Alt+Enter while a preview is running. To return to a normal display, click the mouse (or press Alt+Enter again).

Splitting Clips

To divide a clip into two clips, play it in the Preview pane and pause at the desired split point. Then click the Split button or press Ctrl+L. Windows Movie Maker assigns the new clip a sequential name based on the original. You can split both video and audio clips.

Note that you can also *trim* a clip after you have added it to your project. Trimming, which you may do from either the left (beginning) or right (ending) side of a clip, shortens the amount of the clip that is used in your movie without affecting the clip as it is stored in your collections. (See "Trimming Clips," page 919.)

Joining Clips

To rejoin what Windows Movie Maker has put asunder, select the clips you want to reconnect, and then choose Clip, Combine—or press Ctrl+M. You select multiple clips the same way you would select multiple files in Windows Explorer, by holding down the Shift key or by Ctrl-selecting each clip in turn. You can combine as many video clips at once as you please, provided they represent a contiguous block of footage in the source file. The combined clip assumes the name of the first clip in the sequence. Audio clips cannot be joined.

Creating New Clips

If you didn't have Windows Movie Maker create clips for you when you captured your footage, or if you'd just like to let the program have another go at dividing up a long clip, right-click that clip and choose Create Clips. If you're not happy with the result, press Ctrl+Z (or choose Edit, Undo Create Clips).

Taking Still Pictures from Captured Video

Often, as you play through your clips, you'll find moments that would make perfect still pictures. Simply stop the playback when you come to such a point, use the Previous Frame and Next Frame buttons, if necessary, to position the playback exactly where you want it, and then click the Take Picture button (or choose Tools, Take Picture From Preview). Windows Movie Maker captures the image as a JPEG file, with dimensions that match the captured video. If you captured your footage at 640 × 480, for example, you will get a 640 × 480 JPEG file. Windows Movie Maker will create a clip for the image file, and you can use that clip in your movies, if you like. (See "Using Still Images," page 920.)

Working with Collections Folders

When you capture footage from your camera, Windows Movie Maker deposits the clips in a newly created folder whose name matches the name you assigned to your source file. You'll find the name of the folder at the top of the Collections pane, and you'll see an entry for the folder alphabetically positioned in the Collections tree. (If the Collections tree isn't visible, click Collections on the toolbar.)

You don't by any means have to stick with this default scheme. You can create, copy, nest, and delete collections folders to suit your own organizational purposes. The mechanics are simple: To create a new folder at the root level, right-click the entry *Collections* in the collections tree, choose New Folder, and assign a name to the New Folder item that appears. To create a new folder as a subfolder of an existing folder, start by selecting that folder. To move a folder (for example, to make a root-level folder subordinate to something), drag it and drop it. To copy a folder, right-click and choose Copy. If you paste it at the same level of the tree, Windows Movie Maker will give it the original name plus a sequential number.

Chapter 27

Remember that the clip objects you work with in Windows Movie Maker are merely pointers to file data, so you can copy them freely without incurring meaningful storage expense. If you find that it makes sense to file a clip in multiple locations, simply create the appropriate folders and copy the clip. (You can also rename the copies individually.) Figure 27-6 illustrates this useful redundancy. Identical Alice in Wonderland and Fiddler clips appear in two places in the tree—under Miranda\Plays and in a root-level folder called Theater.

Figure 27-6. You can make your Collections tree as redundant as you please, without adding to your storage burden.

To move a clip from one folder to another, drag it from the Collections pane and drop it onto the appropriate entry in the Collections tree. To copy instead of move, hold down Ctrl while you drag.

Backing Up the Collections Database

Windows Movie Maker records the state of your collections—the names of your folders and clips, and the linkages between clips and source files—in a file called Mediatab.dat, hidden and buried deeply within your profile, in %UserProfile%\Local Settings\Application Data\ Microsoft\Movie Maker. This file needs to be included in your regular backup routine. If the file gets erased or damaged, you won't lose your captured video (all of which presumably will still be safely stored in WMV or AVI files elsewhere on your hard disk), but you will have to reimport that footage and rebuild your collections structure.

Should you wish to start afresh, of course, deleting or relocating Mediatab.dat is a simple way to do it. Windows Media Maker will present you with a clean slate and create a new database for you.

> **Tip** **Use AutoRecover**
>
> By default, Windows Movie Maker saves your collections database and current project information (if any) every ten minutes in an AutoRecover file. If the programs stops abnormally, the next time you start you'll have the opportunity to return to the state recorded by the last AutoRecover save. You can change the AutoRecover time interval by choosing Tools, Options, clicking the General tab, and entering a new value in the Save AutoRecover Info Every check box. You can also turn the feature off, although we can't think of a good reason to do that.

Repairing Damaged Links

You can move and rename clips at will, but what happens if you tinker with the names and locations of your source files? If a source file was and remains on an NTFS partition, Windows Movie Maker will *usually* recognize a change in file name and update the links for you. In some cases, though, you might see a display similar to Figure 27-7.

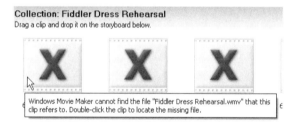

Figure 27-7. If you move a source file, the associated clips might become temporarily unavailable.

Fortunately, the ScreenTip that appears when you point to one of these big red Xs spells out the problem clearly and suggests a remedy. The ScreenTip tells you what file Windows Movie Maker is looking for. If you know what became of it and where it used to live, you can repair the links by restoring the file to its original name and location. In most cases, a simpler fix is to double-click the clip. Windows Movie Maker will ask if you want to browse for the missing file. Answer yes, and—again, assuming NTFS—the program will usually discover the source file's new location without any further intervention from you. If it can't find it, it will ask for your help. If all else fails, of course, you'll have to reimport the clips from their source files.

Assembling Your Project on the Storyboard and Timeline

To create a sequence of video clips that Windows Movie Maker can render into a movie, simply drag those clips from the Collections pane and drop them onto the big rectangles of the storyboard. As Figure 27-8 shows, the storyboard displays a thumbnail of each clip, along with the clip's name. You can add a video transition between two clips by dragging it to the small rectangle between those clips, and you can add a video effect to a clip by dragging it to the star in the lower left corner of the clip's thumbnail. Windows Movie Maker changes the color of the star from gray to blue when an effect is in use. (For more about video transitions and effects, see "Using Video Transitions," page 921, and "Using Video Effects," page 922.)

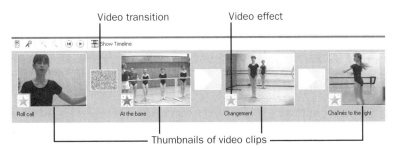

Video transition   Video effect

Thumbnails of video clips

Figure 27-8. The storyboard displays a thumbnail of each video clip in your project. Video transitions appear in the small rectangles, and video effects are marked by a blue star.

While you're putting the project together, you can use the Preview pane at any time to see what you have so far. To play the project starting from a particular clip, select that clip before clicking the Play button.

> **Tip**   To clear everything from your project and start fresh, press Ctrl+Delete, or choose Edit, Clear Storyboard (or Edit, Clear Timeline).

The storyboard is always in insert mode. To place a new clip between two clips that are already on the storyboard, simply drop the newcomer on the second of those clips. Windows Movie Maker inserts your clip and moves everything else to the right. To move a clip, drag it to its new location. Windows Movie Maker inserts at the new location, closing the gap at the old location.

> **Tip**   If you don't like the way a clip on the storyboard is named, delete it (select it and press Delete). Rename it in the Collections pane, then drag it back onto the storyboard. You can't rename objects while they're on the storyboard or timeline.

The storyboard makes it easy to see the beginning content of each clip in your project, but it doesn't, at a glance, show you the relative durations of your clips. If you hover the mouse over a clip, however, Windows Movie Maker reports the clip's duration in a ScreenTip:

Transitions and video effects have names, just as clips do. You can also hover the mouse over a video transition rectangle to see the name of that transition or over a blue star to see what effect you've applied.

To get precise information about when events occur in your movie-in-progress, switch to the timeline. Figure 27-9 shows a timeline view of the project displayed in Figure 27-8.

Click these two buttons to change the scale of the timeline

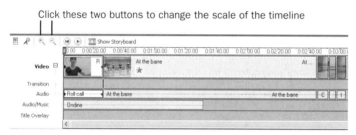

Figure 27-9. The timeline shows when events start and stop. It also displays information about sounds and titles.

Because the space devoted to events on the timeline is proportional to the time they occupy in your movie, some clips appear stretched, while others are scrunched into illegibility. To get a better look at items of short duration, you can expand the scale of the timeline by clicking the Zoom Timeline In button (the plus sign near the upper-left corner of the timeline) or pressing Page Down. Press Page Up or click Zoom Timeline Out to return the timeline to a more compressed scale.

> **Tip** With either the storyboard or the timeline, the quickest way to scroll laterally is by rolling the wheel on your mouse.

As Figure 27-9 shows, the timeline has five separate tracks and conveys some information not shown on the storyboard. (If you don't see the Transition and Audio tracks, click the plus sign to the right of Video. If you still don't see all five tracks, drag the top border of the Timeline pane upward to expand the pane.) These tracks have the following functions:

- **Video** The Video track displays an initial thumbnail for each clip. If you've added a video effect to the clip, a blue star appears.

- **Transition** Video transitions appear on the Transition track. Depending on how you've adjusted the time scale, your transitions might show up as narrow vertical bars.

- **Audio** The Audio track represents the audio captured or imported with your video—the sounds recorded by your camcorder's microphone, for example, or by your computer's microphone if you captured video from a Webcam with a separate microphone. A blue sound graph runs through the middle of the track; the thickest parts of the graph represent the loudest sounds.

- **Audio/Music** If you add narration or background music to your project, those items appear on the Audio/Music track. (For information about managing the sound balance between Audio/Music and Audio, see "Changing the Balance of Sound Between the Audio and Audio/Music Tracks," page 926.) The project shown in Figure 27-9 includes about a minute and a half's worth of background music. Comparing the blue sound graph of the Audio/Music track in this example with that of the Audio track, you can see that the music is relatively quiet and unobtrusive. (For more about managing the interaction of the Audio and Audio/Music elements of your project, see "Working with Sound," page 923.)

- **Title Overlay** Windows Movie Maker includes a titles/credits editor. If you use it to create titles that appear superimposed on the video of your movie, these titles are represented on the Title Overlay track of the timeline. You can also use the editor to generate a title that appears at the beginning of your movie or credits that appear at the end, those items are represented on the Video track of the timeline. (For more about titles, see "Creating Titles and Credits," page 926.)

The first three of these tracks—Video, Transition, and Audio—are bracketed on the timeline, because you can't adjust the positions of items on these tracks independently. If you move two clips joined by a video transition, for example, the transition moves along with the video and audio.

Trimming Clips

One of the handy things you can do on the timeline that you can't do on the storyboard is trim a clip. To lop off the beginning or ending of any clip, audio or video, start by clicking somewhere within the clip. Then move the mouse pointer to the right or left edge of the clip (depending on which side you want to trim). When you see the trim clip (a double-headed red arrow, as shown on the next page) you're ready to trim.

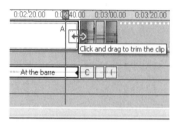

Typically, you'll want to play the clip in the Preview pane before you trim it. When you get to the place where you want to make the cut, pause the player. Use the Previous Frame and Next Frame controls on the Preview pane if necessary to get to the exact frame. The blue bar that runs through the clip marks the place where you paused the player, and you can get a precise trim by dragging the edge of the clip until it aligns with this bar. If you change your mind, or if you trim too much, all you need to do is drag the clip edge back in the other direction again.

Using Still Images

Movies don't always need to move. Sometimes a moment of frozen action is just what's needed.

Still images enable you to create interesting narrated slide shows. They can be handy as stationary backgrounds for overlaid titles. (For more about laying titles over clips, see "Creating Titles and Credits," page 926.) And you can use solid color images (created in Microsoft Paint, perhaps) as static points from which to fade into moving images. Windows Movie Maker makes it easy to fade into a clip from white or black (see "Using Video Effects," page 922), but it doesn't provide a built-in fade-from-purple effect (for example). If that's what you want, you can make a solid purple image in Paint, import it into Windows Movie Maker as a still image clip, add it to your project, then follow it with a fade transition into your next clip.

> **Tip** Check out Plus! Photo Story
>
> Plus! Photo Story, one of several programs included with Microsoft Plus! Digital Media Edition, is expressly designed to create interesting movies from still pictures, complete with narration, background music, and zooming and panning effects. If you need to build a presentation exclusively from stills, you might find Photo Story more versatile and easier to use than Windows Movie Maker. You can also use Photo Story to create a still-based sequence, then import the resulting .wmv file as a Windows Movie Maker clip to be used in your movies. You can read more about Plus! Photo Story and download a trial copy at the Microsoft Plus! site, at *http://www.microsoft.com/windows/plus/dme/photo.asp*.

Still image clips have a default duration of five seconds. You can increase or decrease this duration for a particular clip by dragging its trim handle on the timeline. To change the default duration, choose Tools, Options, click the Advanced tab, and enter a new value in the Picture Duration box. Note that changing the default does not affect pictures you've already added to your project.

Using Video Transitions

If you're tired of using simple cuts between the clips of your movies (that is, abrupt changes from one scene to the next), you can choose from dozens of stylish transitions in Windows Movie Maker's built-in Video Transitions collection. (Most of these are new in version 2, so if you're a veteran of the original Windows Movie Maker, be sure to check them out.) For a sampling of what a transition will look like in your movie, select the transition in the Video Transitions collection and click the Play button in the Preview pane.

> **Tip** **Set your own default images**
>
> Any JPEG images can serve as the pictures that Windows Movie Maker uses to preview transitions. To change from the default images to pictures of your own choosing, navigate to %ProgramFiles%\Movie Maker\Shared. Rename the files Sample1.jpg and Sample2.jpg. Then copy the new images you want to use into this folder and name them Sample1.jpg and Sample2.jpg.

The Microsoft Plus! Digital Media Edition (*http://www.microsoft.com/windows/plus/dme/dmehome.asp*) includes 25 additional video transitions. If the standard library doesn't meet your needs, perhaps these will. Even more transitions are available through third parties (see, for example, Pixélan Software's offerings at *http://www.pixelan.com/mm/intro.htm*).

The easiest way to add a transition to your project is to drag it to the storyboard. Drop the transition in the small rectangle before the clip that you want to transition to. Alternatively, select that clip, select the transition in the Collections pane, and then press Ctrl+D.

Transitions have a default duration of 1.25 seconds. To increase or decrease the time devoted to a particular transition, display the timeline and adjust the time scale (using Page Down and Page Up, or the Zoom Timeline In and Zoom Timeline Out buttons) so that the transition becomes visible as a rectangle on the Transition track. Then click the transition and drag the trim handle to the left or right. To change the default transition time, choose Tools, Options, click the Advanced tab, then adjust the value in the Transition Duration box. Note that changing the default does not affect transitions that you have already added to your project.

To add a Fade transition—in which one video clip simply overlaps another so that the first footage gradually disappears from view while the second emerges—you can work in the manner just described (that is, drag the Fade object from the Video Transitions collection to the storyboard). But as an alternative, click the second clip on the timeline and then drag that clip to the left so that it partially overlaps the preceding clip. As you do this, a bright blue bar tapers to a point at the timeline position where the fade will begin:

Chapter 27

You can see the exact starting time of the fade by reading the ScreenTip. Note that the duration time reported in the ScreenTip is that of the second clip, however, not that of the fade. You can calculate the duration of the fade by noting the timeline position of the playback bar, which marks the start of the second clip. In the example just shown, the playback bar is at 0:00:05.00 and the starting time of the fade is 0:00:03.20, hence the fade will last 1.8 seconds.

If you right-click a clip on the timeline or storyboard, you'll see the shortcut-menu commands Fade In and Fade Out. You can also use these to achieve fade transitions. But these fade options are different in two ways from the fade transition just described. First, they fade in from or out to black, not in from or out to the adjacent clip. Second, they are of shorter duration and their duration can't be changed. Because of these differences, Windows Movie Maker treats them as video *effects*, not video *transitions*. (The Video Effects collection also includes fades into and out of white.) We'll take up the topic of video effects next.

Using Video Effects

With the exception of the four fade effects just mentioned, the video effects available in Windows Movie Maker change the entire appearance of video clips, not just their beginnings or endings. You can use video effects to do such things as brighten or darken a clip, speed playback up or slow it down, invert or flip the action, achieve a grainy or old-movie appearance—and so on. To see what effects are available, select Video Effects, at the top of the Collections tree. To see what a video effect does, select it in the Collections pane and click the Play button in the Preview pane.

You can acquire an additional two dozen video effects by installing Microsoft Plus! Digital Media Edition (*http://www.microsoft.com/windows/plus/dme/dmehome.asp*). Still others are available from third parties.

Video effects, unlike video transitions, can be combined. Thus, for example, you can make your clip both dark *and* grainy by adding both the Brightness, Decrease and Film Grain effects. You can use as many as six effects on the same clip. Using the same effect more than once on the same clip intensifies the effect. For example, using Speed Up, Double twice multiplies the playback speed by four.

Note that some effects cancel one another. The Ease In effect, for example, zooms in on the selected clip (in other words, it crops the clip slowly from the outside toward the center). The speed at which the effect carries out this zoom is timed so that it continues through the duration of the clip. Ease Out does exactly the opposite. With Ease Out, playback of your clip starts zoomed in toward the center, and more and more of the clip is revealed throughout the duration of its playback. Use both these effects together, and the clip simply plays back as though there are no effects in use.

Using Windows Movie Maker

To add an effect to a clip, select the effect you want and drag it to the clip. You can do this with equal facility in both the timeline and the storyboard. Windows Movie Maker darkens the star on the storyboard (in the bottom left-hand corner of the clip) to show that an effect is in place; on the timeline it displays a star that would otherwise not be there.

As an alternative method of adding effects, right-click the clip and choose Video Effects from the shortcut menu. As Figure 27-10 shows, the Add Or Remove Video Effects dialog box that appears lets you add multiple effects at once. It's also a handy way to see what effects are already in place. (Another way to do that is to hover the mouse over the blue square in a clip's storyboard frame.)

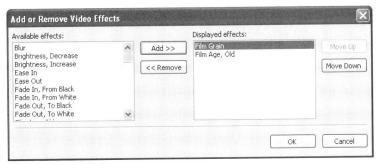

Figure 27-10. Right-clicking a clip and choosing Video Effects lets you add or remove effects—or just see what effects are already in place.

Working with Sound

As we noted earlier, the timeline in Windows Movie Maker reveals two audio tracks. One of these, the Audio track, represents the sound captured on your video source (your camera's microphone, typically, or the microphone at your computer if you captured video from a Webcam). The other, called Audio/Music, lets you add a separate layer of sound—such as background music from a .wma or .mp3 file, sound effects recorded in a .wav file, or a narration that you record to accompany your movie. The Audio track is a component of the Video track, in the sense that its objects cannot be moved or trimmed independently of the video they belong to. Objects on the Audio/Music track, in contrast, are freely movable and may be trimmed at either end.

Tip Use video for audio
By dragging a video clip to the Audio/Music track of the timeline, instead of the Video track, you can use just the sound portion of a video clip. If you happen to have shot some video that includes generically useful sound—lions roaring, cicadas chirping, surf thumping, or whatever—save a copy of that clip in whatever collections folder you use for background sounds, and reapply as needed to the Audio/Music tracks of your movies.

Adding Music or Other Background Sound

To add music to your project, first be sure that you have that music in the form of a Windows Movie Maker clip. If what you want is a CD track, use Windows Media Player to rip the track, then import the resulting .wma file into Windows Movie Maker. (For information about ripping CD tracks, see "Ripping Audio Tracks from CD to Hard Disk," page 841.)

Display the timeline and, if necessary, expand the timeline upward (drag the blue bar at the top of the pane), so that you have a good view of the Audio/Music track. Then drag the clip onto that track. To position an audio/music object *precisely* within a video track, play the video track from the timeline. When you get to the point where you want the sound to be aligned, click the Pause button in the Preview pane. The blue playback pointer in the timeline now provides you with an easy-to-hit target for your sound clip. (Adjust the position of this pointer with the Previous Frame and Next Frame buttons if necessary to get it exactly where you want it.)

Note that unlike video, which can only be appended to the last clip on the Video track or inserted between existing clips, sound clips can be positioned anywhere on the Audio/Music track. Before you drop the clip on the track, as you move the mouse left and right, a bright blue insertion pointer shows where the sound will land if you release the mouse button.

> **Note** If you move the mouse pointer smoothly beneath a set of clips stationed on the Video track, you'll notice that the insertion pointer pauses briefly each time you come to a clip boundary. This behavior is designed to help you align sound clips with video clips.

> **Tip** Clips on the Audio/Music track are not anchored to the video clips with which they're aligned. If the video clips moves (for example, because you insert another video clip or trim a clip), you'll have to realign your sound and video. To avoid frustration, get all your visual blocks in place, and then add sound.

Fading In and Out of Sound Clips

You can add fade-in and fade-out effects to sound clips of any kind. Simply right-click the clip you're interested in and choose Fade In or Fade Out from the shortcut menu.

Adding Narration

If you have a microphone connected to your computer, you can play back all or portions of a project and record a narration to accompany what you see. Follow these steps:

1 Display the timeline and make sure that the Audio/Music track is visible.

 2 Position the playback pointer (the blue bar that runs through all five tracks) where you want to begin your narration. (The Audio/Music track must be vacant at this place; you cannot record a narration over an existing audio/music clip.)

Chapter 27

3   Choose Tools, Narrate Timeline (or click the Narrate Timeline tool on the Timeline toolbar).

4   In the Narrate Timeline window that appears, make sure that the Audio Device and Audio Input Source options are set correctly.

Speak into your microphone at the volume level and distance you're comfortable with; adjust either the Input Level setting, your volume level, or your position relative to the microphone if the meter is going into the red zone or not getting off the floor.

5   If you have other sound clips on the Audio/Music track to the right of your current position, select Limit Narration To Available Free Space on Audio/Music Track. (Otherwise, if your narration goes on too long, subsequent objects will be moved to the right while you speak.)

6   If the video that you're about to narrate has much sound of its own, select Mute Speakers (or turn your speakers off). Otherwise, your microphone will pick up some of that sound along with your voice as you narrate.

7   Click Start Narration. Windows Movie Maker will begin playback of your project at the current playback position, and you can match your words to what you see in the Preview pane. When you've said all you want to say, click Stop Narration.

Windows Movie Maker will prompt you for a file name and location for your newly recorded sound. Then it will import that sound file and create an audio clip for you, deposit that clip in the same folder where the video clip you're narrating resides, and finally place that clip in the desired position on the Audio/Music track. Return the playback pointer to that place and play your project again to make sure everything is the way you want it. Then save your work (or delete the clip from the timeline and try again).

Adjusting Volume Levels

To change the volume level of any sound clip, right-click the clip (on the Audio or Audio/Music track of the timeline) and choose Volume (or simply press Ctrl+U). Then drag the slider left or right in the Audio Clip Volume dialog box. You can also select the Mute Clip check box if what you want is silence. This is a particularly handy option if you're narrating a video clip that includes extraneous unwanted sound.

Changing the Balance of Sound Between the Audio and Audio/Music Tracks

By default, Windows Movie Maker treats the two sound tracks even-handedly. You can adjust the balance, though, so that the background music or narration gets less or more importance than the sound component of your video clips. To alter the balance, choose Tools, Audio Levels or click the Audio Levels tool, at the left edge of the timeline or storyboard toolbar. The Audio Levels dialog box that appears is modeless, which means you can leave it open on screen, begin a playback, and then move the slider to the left or right until you get the balance you're looking for. Note that the Audio Levels setting is global per project. You can't adjust it separately for different parts of a project, but projects can maintain different balance settings.

Trimming and Moving Clips on the Audio/Music Track

You can trim clips on the Audio/Music track from either end, the same way you trim video clips. Click within the clip, move the mouse pointer toward the end you want to trim, and drag the trim handle.

To move a clip on the Audio/Music track, click inside the clip somewhere away from either end. Your mouse pointer will assume the shape of a hand, and the clip will turn solid blue as you drag.

NEW FEATURE! ## Creating Titles and Credits

No movie is complete without titles and credits. Windows Movie Maker includes a rudimentary editor for creating such necessities, complete with a selection of text layout and animation styles. You can use it to create opening titles, closing credits, titles that appear between scenes of your movie, or titles superimposed on still images or video within the movie. In all but the last case, titles join your project on the timeline's Video track, where you can modify their duration by dragging the trim handles. Superimposed titles appear on the Title Overlay track; you can move them to achieve the desired alignment with your video.

To open the title editor, choose Tools, Titles And Credits. The title editor will then ask you to specify where you want your title to appear. After clicking one of the placement options, you'll see the two-box edit screen shown on the next page.

Enter Text for Title
Click 'Done' to add the title to the movie.

Done, add title to movie   Cancel

More options:

Change the title animation

Change the text font and color

(If you've chosen to place your title at the end of the current project, the editor assumes you want to list credits and gives you spaces to enter names and parts.) After you've written your title text, you can click the other two links on this page to customize the font and color, and to choose one of the available animation styles. Figure 27-11 illustrates the Transparent Overlapping Titles animation option for a two-line movie title. (Note that "two-line" means two blocks of text. Whether it gets displayed on two lines or not depends on how much text you supply.)

Figure 27-11.   You can use the title editor to create titles and credits in various styles of animation.

Using AutoMovie to Generate Movies Automatically

The Tools, AutoMovie command, with which Windows Movie Maker concocts a project automatically from the contents of the current Collections folder, might seem more like a gimmick than a useful feature. But if you have a set of clips that tell a coherent story, it's worth letting AutoMovie have a run at your stuff, just to see what it will come up with. Granted, you're not likely to render the result without modification. But perhaps you'll find it a useful starting point that you can edit into something satisfactory. At the very least it will give you ideas.

To use AutoMovie, start by creating a Collections folder with all the video clips that you want your movie to include. (Don't worry about sound at this point.) Then choose Tools, AutoMovie. The following screen will appear:

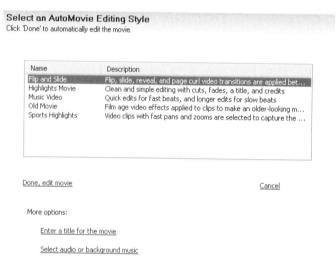

Choose one of the five available movie styles. Click the links at the bottom of the window to specify title text and an audio file for background music (AutoMovie will incorporate the music into your Audio/Music track *without* creating a clip from it—something you can't do on your own!), and then click Done, Edit Movie. Windows Movie Maker will take a few minutes to analyze your audio and video, and then present its work on the timeline and storyboard.

Rendering Your Project into a Movie

With your project fully assembled on the timeline and storyboard, it's time to let Windows Movie Maker make a movie. Choose File, Save Movie File to summon the Save Movie Wizard, shown in Figure 27-12. The wizard's first screen, Movie Location, asks you to choose a destination for your finished movie.

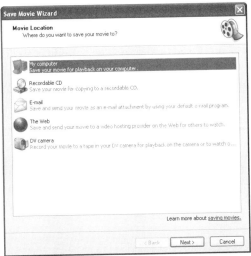

Figure 27-12. You can render your movie to a disk file, a HighMAT-formatted CD, an e-mail attachment, a video hosting provider on the Web, or a FireWire-connected DV camera.

Render in the Correct Format and Aspect Ratio

Before you begin rendering, you might want to confirm that your aspect ratio and video format settings are appropriate. (Choose Tools, Options and click the Advanced tab to see or change your settings.) Windows Movie Maker normally detects the format and aspect ratio of your video footage and sets these parameters accordingly. For the majority of users in the United States, the settings are 4:3 (aspect ratio) and NTSC (video format).

NTSC, which stands for National Television System Committee, is the standard required for broadcast in the United States and hence the standard supported by video devices configured for use in this country. Windows Movie Maker also supports the PAL, or Phase Alternating Line, standard used in some other parts of the world. If you're planning to render your movie back to a digital-video device configured for PAL, you should make sure the video format is set to PAL.

Many recent-vintage camcorders can record in 16:9 widescreen mode as well as the more common 4:3 mode. If your footage was captured at 16:9 and you intend to watch it at that ratio, be sure the aspect ratio setting is 16:9 before you render. You can render 4:3 footage at 16:9 as well, but if you're considering this, be sure to run it through the Preview pane before you render it. Typically, you'll get distortions that you won't be happy with.

Rendering to a Disk File

Your first option is to save the movie on your local (or local network) storage. After you specify a file name and location, you'll be prompted to make a quality decision, similar to the one you might have made when you captured the footage from your camcorder or VCR. If you don't go with the default choice, Best Quality For Playback On My Computer (Recommended), you can click Other Settings and open the drop-down list to see a range of options comparable to the ones listed in Table 27-1 on page 906. (If you don't see the Other Settings option button, click the Show More Choices link.)

If you're having trouble evaluating the size/quality tradeoff, take a look at the option called Best Fit To File Size. As Figure 27-13 shows, with this option, you specify a maximum file size and Windows Movie Maker provides the best quality it can without exceeding your specification. In the Setting Details section of the dialog box, you can see what bit rate and display size the wizard proposes to use.

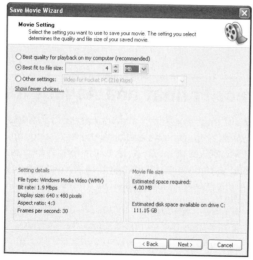

Figure 27-13. The Best Fit To File Size option gives you maximum quality for the file size you specify.

> **Tip** Movie rendering is a processor- and memory-intensive task that will take as long as the movie's play time—and then some. Allow plenty of time.

Rendering to a Recordable CD

Windows Movie Maker supports HighMAT, a recently developed technology that lets you create menu-driven video CDs. (For information about HighMAT, see *http://www.highmat.com* and *http://www.microsoft.com/windows/windowsmedia/consumerelectronics/highmat.aspx.*) With a HighMAT-enabled playback device, your audience will be able to navigate through a disc of your movies, much the way they would navigate scenes on a DVD. Figure 27-14 shows a sample of a HighMAT menu on a CD generated by Windows Movie Maker.

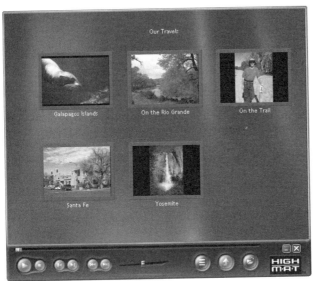

Figure 27-14. You can render a CD full of movies and, on a HighMAT-enabled playback device, navigate them via a thumbnail menu.

With or without HighMAT playback, you can render one or several movies to a recordable CD, using the Save Movie Wizard's second destination option. For each movie, you specify a name and quality setting. When the wizard finishes rendering the first movie, it ejects your disc (in case you want to render the same movie to another disc). To render another movie to the same disc, close the drive, tee up the next project, and return to the wizard. In the lower right corner of the wizard's Movie Setting screen, you'll find an estimate of the file size you're about to create and a report of the available space on your CD.

Rendering to an E-Mail Attachment

The wizard's third destination option lets you save your movie as an e-mail attachment. Because many mail systems impose size limits on message attachments, Windows Movie Maker, by default, will not let you create a movie larger than 1 MB. You can increase that threshold in 1 MB increments to as much as 10 MB; to do this, choose Tools, Options, click the Advanced tab, and adjust the Maximum File Size For Sending A Movie As An Attachment In An E-Mail Message box.

When you choose E-Mail on the Movie Location screen and click Next, Windows Movie Maker immediately begins rendering your project—without asking for any quality decisions on your part. When it finishes rendering, it presents you with a message window in your default e-mail program, with the attachment in place.

Rendering to the Web

If you have an account with a video hosting provider on the Internet, such as Neptune Mediashare (*http://www.neptune.com*), you can use the Save Movie Wizard's fourth destination option to post your movie directly to that Web host. You can use this service as a way of sharing your movies with selected friends and colleagues.

If you don't have such an account, stepping through this option in the Save Movie Wizard (while connected to the Internet) will get you a list of service providers available in your part of the world. (Windows Movie Maker determines where you are by how you've configured Regional And Language Options in Control Panel before downloading service provider information.) You can sign up for an account and post your first movie without leaving the wizard.

When you render to the Web, the wizard presents essentially the same list of quality options that you have for saving locally. But the options that are defined by bandwidth appear at the top of the Movie Setting screen. You should make your choice according to your expectations about how viewers will connect with your Web host.

Rendering to a DV Camera

The Save Movie Wizard's last destination option returns your movie to a DV camera. Your camera must be turned on, set to its playback mode, and connected to an IEEE 1394 port. Put a fresh tape in the camera, click Next, and Windows Movie Maker does the rest.

This option preserves your movie at the maximum possible quality. (Ideally, you want to use this with footage that you've captured at maximum quality, of course.) After you've rendered the movie back to DV tape, you can preserve it, transfer it to another medium, or even recapture it in Windows Movie Maker for further editing as you think of ways to improve it.

Resources for Further Learning

Making a movie is easy. Making a *good* movie is something else. This chapter has carefully steered clear of aesthetic issues. For more on matters of movie-making technique and a wealth of ideas about how to put Windows Movie Maker to work, see *Microsoft Windows Movie Maker 2: Do Amazing Things!*, by John Buechler (Microsoft Press, 2004). Buechler also maintains a valuable Web site at *http://www.eicsoftware.com/PapaJohn/MM2/MM2.html*.

You can also find a wealth of information about Windows Movie Maker on various Microsoft sites. Start with the Windows Movie Maker home page, at *http://www.microsoft.com/windowsxp/using/moviemaker/default.mspx*. Here you can access links to video-oriented newsgroups, troubleshooting, and how-to articles. Microsoft occasionally posts useful and free downloads for Windows Movie Maker as well, so it's a good idea to drop in once in a while and see what's new.

Part 6

Networking

Setting Up a Small Network

Setting up a network on a computer running Microsoft Windows is no longer the complex and sometimes frustrating process it used to be. On a network where every computer is running Microsoft Windows XP, in fact, you may find that your network requires no configuration at all—after you finish setting up Windows, your network is available for immediate access. Even on networks that include a mix of different Windows versions, getting everything connected is usually a straightforward process. (For advice on what to do when the pieces of your network don't fit together so neatly, see Chapter 29, "Tweaking and Troubleshooting a Small Network.")

You can maximize your chances of a trouble-free network setup by selecting the right hardware and configuring it properly. Even if you're a Windows networking wizard yourself, we recommend that you use the Windows XP Network Setup Wizard to automatically set IP addresses, set workgroup names, configure the Windows Firewall, add required registry keys, and adjust system policies. After using the wizard, you can fine-tune network settings to suit your networking needs.

Windows XP Service Pack 2 introduces some significant changes to familiar networking tools and capabilities. Most noteworthy is a complete reworking of the wizard that sets up a wireless network. Security enhancements, including changes to the Windows Firewall, affect other networking features. Throughout this chapter, we assume that you have already installed Service Pack 2.

At Home with Windows XP

This chapter explains how to configure a peer-to-peer network—one that is not part of a domain running Windows Server 2003 or Windows 2000 Server. In this environment, the steps for setting up and configuring a network are the same whether you use Windows XP Professional or Windows XP Home Edition.

In this chapter, we focus exclusively on networks for small workgroups (typically consisting of 10 computers or fewer) that don't include a system running Windows 2000 Server or Windows Server 2003. For details on how to work with domain-based networks, see Chapter 33, "Working with Windows Domains."

Reality Check

The intricacies of networking in Windows XP could fill tens of thousands of pages. So, it should come as no surprise that searching the Internet for tips, tricks, and troubleshooting advice turns up an enormous collection of sites, ranging from simple tutorials to treasure troves of technical information. Even on a small network, tuning and troubleshooting can require delving into the complexities of TCP/IP and other network components. With more complex networks involving multiple operating systems and sophisticated hardware, even certified experts can get lost.

When we trolled the Web for network-related information, we found three topics where the conventional wisdom is likely to confuse or mislead users of Windows XP.

- **Should you use the Network Setup Wizard?** Some popular advice sites strongly recommend not using the wizard. That same sentiment turns up frequently in newsgroup threads devoted to Windows networking. This line of thinking starts with the flawed notion that the Network Setup Wizard somehow forces the user into incorrect default choices. That's simply not true. If you pay attention to each step of the wizard, you'll avoid its two most common pitfalls: renaming your default workgroup to MSHOME and incorrectly bridging multiple connections. Conversely, if you bypass the wizard, you'll need to manually enable the Guest account and adjust local security policies before you can share files. Our advice, for novices and experts alike, is to use the Network Setup Wizard; afterwards, you can tweak any settings that are specific to your network.

- **Is wireless networking unsafe?** In the popular press, discussions of wireless networks often focus on lurid tales of "war driving," in which hackers armed with WiFi-equipped notebooks drive through neighborhoods breaking into unprotected wireless access points. In the technical press, the discussions go further, with information about the weaknesses of Wired Equivalent Privacy (WEP) and advice on how to strengthen your network's security.

  For starters, the threat of drive-by hacking is somewhat overstated. If you live in a densely populated urban area or in an apartment building, you're at a greater risk that a neighbor with a WiFi-ready PC can attach to your wireless network and access shared resources on your computer. If your home is in the suburbs or the country, it's doubtful that anyone will connect to your network by accident, although a determined attacker with a sensitive and directional antenna can sniff out a reliable connection from miles away. At any rate, as we point out in this chapter, you can minimize the risk by not openly advertising your access point and by using the best available security option—WiFi Protected Access (WPA), if it's available, or WEP if it's not.

As for the technical issues of security, virtually all of the detailed information on the Web that was published before mid-2004 has been rendered essentially obsolete by changes in Windows XP Service Pack 2. Unfortunately, the nature of the Web is such that many of those pages will never be updated, and anyone who relies on these instructions will find a solution that is, at best, incomplete. If you're looking for advice on wireless network security in Windows XP, be especially skeptical of anything you read that doesn't explicitly mention the significant changes in SP2.

● **Is TCP/IP inherently insecure?**   The single most controversial network security recommendation we've encountered is the persistent claim that you should avoid using TCP/IP on your local area network. Adherents of this approach argue that you should reserve TCP/IP strictly for your Internet connection and install a second protocol—either NetBEUI or IPX/SPX—for use on your LAN. By unbinding the File and Printer Sharing service from the TCP/IP protocol, they contend, you make it less likely that a hacker can break into your network and access shared files and printers.

Although this argument seems logical, it doesn't stand up to close examination. Specifically:

■ This security routine was originally recommended for Windows 95 and its successors, during the era when most people used dial-up connections and broadband routers were exotic, expensive devices. These days, routers are dirt cheap and offer effective protection from unsolicited outside connections. In addition, Windows XP incorporates security features that block outside access to shared resources by default, and the Network Setup Wizard enables Windows Firewall on network configurations that are potentially unsafe.

■ Windows XP has been in widespread release for more than three years. During that time we have not found a single documented instance where this multiple-protocol configuration would have prevented an attack. The justification is completely theoretical.

■ Unbinding File and Printer Sharing does nothing to protect you from attacks on other ports via your TCP/IP-based connection to the Internet. If you neglect the basics of Internet security—installing Critical Updates and configuring Windows Firewall or a third-party alternative—a would-be attacker can exploit a security hole and install a Trojan horse program that gives him complete control over your PC and your network. So unbinding this service only provides you with the illusion that your network is secure.

■ Adding multiple protocols creates needless complexity and increases the chance that some applications will fail to work properly. It can also slow network communications if the protocols aren't bound in the correct order.

The bottom line? We believe that a Windows XP network works best and is most secure when it uses only TCP/IP, configured with appropriate security precautions. We strongly advise against installing additional protocols unless you specifically need them to communicate with other computers and servers on your network—and even then, these protocols should be used in addition to, not in place of, TCP/IP.

Chapter 28

937

What You Can and Can't Do with a Small Network

With a minimal investment in hardware, you can connect two or more computers and form a simple peer-to-peer network. Because these networks aren't built around a server, they don't allow you to manage users and shared resources centrally; instead, each computer contains its own database of authorized user accounts and shared folders, drives, and printers. Setting up a workgroup-based network offers the following advantages:

- **Shared storage**   By designating certain folders as shared resources, you avoid the need to swap files on floppy disks or to maintain duplicate copies of files; instead, everyone on the network can open a shared report or access a collection of digital photos or music files from a single location.

- **Shared printers**   Sharing a printer allows any authorized network user to print to that device. By setting permissions on shared printers on a home network, you can prevent your kids from wasting expensive paper and ink on a high-quality color photo printer. (This option is available only with Windows XP Professional, and only if Simple File Sharing is disabled.)

- **Shared Internet connection**   Using Internet Connection Sharing (ICS), you can set up Internet access on a single computer and allow every computer on the network to share that connection. This capability is most useful if you have a high-speed Internet connection, such as a cable or DSL modem; however, you can share a dial-up Internet connection and control it from any computer on the network. As we discuss in this chapter, using a hardware router offers significant security and performance advantages over ICS.

For the most part, different versions of Windows can coexist quite peacefully on a network, if you plan carefully. If you intend to use Internet Connection Sharing, you'll have best results if you install Windows XP (Professional or Home Edition) on the computer that has the Internet connection to be shared. You can then use the Windows XP Network Setup Wizard to configure other systems running Windows XP, Windows 2000, Windows Me, or Windows 98.

> **Tip**   Set up a simple server
>
> If your network includes at least one computer running Windows XP Professional, you can use that machine as a workgroup server. Although this configuration doesn't come close to providing the centralized administration and security of a domain-based network, it does allow you to enforce security on a per-user basis. On the Windows XP Professional machine, disable Simple File Sharing and assign permissions to shared folders by selecting users and groups, as explained in "Controlling Access with NTFS Permissions," page 282.

Hardware, Cabling, and Connections

Before you can even think about setting up the networking software in Windows XP, you need to assemble and configure the proper hardware. In addition to two or more computers, you'll need the following components to set up a home or small office network:

- **Network adapters**   Each computer needs an adapter (also called a *network interface card*, or NIC) to communicate with the other computers on the network. Network adapters can be internal (usually installed in a PCI slot) or external (typically connected to a USB port). The overwhelming majority of network adapters conform to the Ethernet standard.

- **A central connection point**   Use a *hub* or *switch* to connect the computers in an Ethernet network. This function is sometimes integrated in a *router* or *residential gateway*, which typically adds network address translation (NAT) capabilities and security features. On wireless networks that use the 802.11b or 802.11g standard, a wireless access point handles these duties. Networks that use the Home Phoneline Networking Alliance (HomePNA) standard do not require a hub.

- **Cables**   On an Ethernet network, you connect each network adapter to the hub using an eight-wire Category 5 patch cable with RJ-45 connectors on each end. HomePNA networks connect to an existing telephone jack with a standard telephone connector (RJ-11). By definition, wireless networks require no cables.

> **Tip**   Connect two computers without a hub
>
> If your home network consists of two computers and you have no plans to expand it, you can save yourself the cost of a hub and use a *crossover cable* instead. A crossover cable is identical to a standard patch cable, except that two wires are reversed, simulating the connection that would take place if the wires were plugged into a hub. Using a crossover cable is an acceptable solution when you want to connect two computers directly to transfer files quickly with a minimum of hassle; using Windows Explorer and a two-computer network is much less hassle than cumbersome solutions that require null-modem cables and extra software. A crossover cable can also serve as a permanent connection between two computers if one computer has an Internet connection and the other doesn't. But as soon as you add a third computer to the network, you'll need additional hardware to serve as a hub.

Although it's not required, most networks also include one additional hardware component: a modem or other device to connect your network to the Internet.

Chapter 28

Ethernet, Wireless, or Phone Line?

When setting up a network, you can choose from three popular technologies, all of which are supported by Windows XP:

- **Ethernet/Fast Ethernet**   This popular networking standard, developed in the mid-1970s, has stood the test of time. The original Ethernet standard (also known as 10Base-T) is capable of transferring data at maximum speeds of 10 megabits per second. The Fast Ethernet standard (also known as 100Base-T) can transfer data at 100 megabits per second. Some network adapters and hubs offer auto-switching (10/100) capabilities, allowing you to mix and match Ethernet and Fast Ethernet components on the same network. (Without this capability, a mixed network will throttle down to the speed of the slowest link.) A relatively new standard called Gigabit Ethernet allows data transfers at 1 gigabit (1,000 megabits) per second. In an office or home that is wired for Ethernet, you can plug your network adapter into a wall jack and install a hub at a central location called a *patch panel*. In a home or office without structured wiring, you'll need to plug directly into a hub.

- **Wireless**   In recent years, wireless networking technology has enjoyed an explosion in popularity, thanks to its convenience and steadily decreasing prices. Although wireless networks were originally developed for use with notebooks, they are increasingly popular with desktop computer users, especially in homes and offices where it is impractical or physically impossible to run network cables. The most popular wireless networks use one of two variants of the IEEE (Institute of Electrical and Electronics Engineers) 802.11 standard, also known as Wi-Fi. Using base stations and network adapters with small antennas, Wi-Fi networks using the 802.11b standard transfer data at a maximum frequency of 11 megabits per second (comparable to Ethernet speeds) using radio frequencies in the 2.4 GHz range. The newer 802.11g standard works at approximately five times the speed (54 megabits per second) using the same 2.4 GHz frequency range. Most 802.11g hardware works with 802.11b networks as well.

  A number of other wireless network standards promulgated by the IEEE's 802.11 Working Group promise benefits such as better security. Be aware that, despite the confusingly similar names, network equipment using one of the wireless standards is generally compatible only with other equipment using the exact same standard. In addition to 802.11b and 802.11g, you might encounter the following:

  - **802.11a**   broadcasts in a different frequency range, 5 GHz, and can reach maximum speeds of 54 Mbps, roughly as fast as 802.11g networks. This standard was quickly overtaken by the 802.11g flavor of Wi-Fi and although it is fully supported by Windows XP, it is, for all practical purposes, obsolete.

▪ **802.1x**   provides a mechanism for authenticating computers that connect to a wireless access point, typically through a Remote Authentication Dial-In User Service (RADIUS) server. This emerging standard is impractical for small networks but is ideal for large organizations that already have one or more authentication servers. (And no, the name is not a typographical error—because this standard applies to conventional wired networks as well as wireless, it contains only a single "1" in its name.)

▪ **802.11i**   incorporates the security components of a wireless connection. Wired Equivalent Privacy (WEP), the authentication system built into the original Wi-Fi standard, turned out to be unacceptably easy to crack. When the 802.11i standard is finalized, it will incorporate a number of encryption techniques, including Temporal Key Integrity Protocol (TKIP) and Advanced Encryption Standard (AES). An interim version of this standard incorporates an improved security infrastructure called Wi-Fi Protected Access (WPA), which is fully supported in Windows XP Service Pack 2.

For the latest technical details, you can read the sometimes dense and dry commentary at the official site of the 802.11 Working Group, *http://www.ieee802.org/11*. For a more readable summary, try the Web site run by the Wi-Fi Alliance at *http://www.wi-fi.org*.

▪ **Phone Line**   Networks that comply with the Home Phoneline Networking Alliance (HomePNA) standard closely resemble Ethernet networks. Early versions of this standard operated at Ethernet speeds of roughly 10 megabits per second; the HomePNA 3 standard claims to work at speeds of up to 128 megabits per second. HomePNA networks don't require a central connection point such as a hub; instead, they employ a daisy-chain topology in which all network adapters communicate directly by plugging into existing telephone jacks and transmitting data on the same wires that carry telephone and fax signals, without interfering with those communications. The availability of cheap wireless network gear has relegated HomePNA technology to a tiny niche; it's most attractive in older homes where adding network cable is impossible and wireless signals are impractical because of distance or building materials. For more information, visit the Home Phoneline Networking Alliance at *http://www.homepna.org*.

Chapter 28

Installing and Configuring Network Adapters

On most systems, you don't need to take any special configuration steps to set up a network adapter. The Plug and Play code in Windows XP handles all the work of loading drivers. If you install an internal adapter and Windows XP includes a signed driver for that adapter, the driver should be installed automatically when Windows detects the adapter (if Windows cannot find a built-in driver, you'll be prompted to supply the location of the driver files). For an external adapter connected to a USB or IEEE 1394 port, the driver loads and unloads dynamically when you attach or remove the adapter.

> For more details about installing hardware, see "Setting Up a New Device," page 135.

As with all hardware devices, you can inspect the properties of a network adapter from the Device Manager window. (See "Finding Information About an Installed Driver," page 141, for details.) Most network adapters include an Advanced tab in the properties dialog box, from which you can configure specialized hardware settings. These settings are invariably hardware-specific, and they can vary dramatically, as the two examples in Figure 28-1 illustrate.

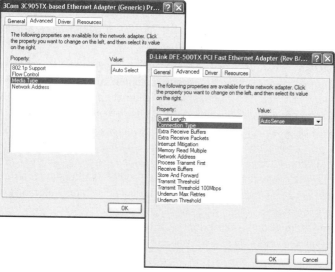

Figure 28-1.   Adjust Advanced properties only for a network card when required for performance or compatibility reasons.

Chapter 28

In general, you should accept the default settings on the Advanced tab of the network adapter's properties dialog box except when you're certain a change is required. In the examples shown in Figure 28-1, for instance, you can see by the selected Property and Value that both adapters are configured to automatically detect (AutoSense) whether the network is operating in 10Base-T or 100Base-T mode. In some cases, this AutoSense or Auto Select capability may cause an adapter to operate at a slower speed than the rest of the network. In that case, you can force it to run at the correct speed by selecting the 100 Mbps speed from the Advanced options list.

> **Tip** **Check compatibility carefully**
>
> In terms of compatibility, networking gear is among the most demanding of all hardware types. As always, your first stop before buying any networking hardware for use with a Windows XP system should be the Find Compatible Hardware And Software For Windows XP option in the Help And Support Center (under Pick A Task in the right pane). Trying to force old, incompatible network hardware to work with Windows XP is asking for trouble. Reliable, compatible, inexpensive network adapters are easy to find. If you're setting up a Windows network, don't settle for anything less.

Making Connections: Cables and Hubs

On a standard Ethernet network, all computers must be connected to a network hub (or a switch, which is physically identical to a hub and performs the same functions with higher levels of speed and efficiency—in this chapter, when we refer to a hub, we mean either a hub or a switch). The hub is usually a small box with a row of jacks that accept RJ-45 connectors. Each jack is called a *port*. Most hubs designed for use on home networks and in small businesses have from four to eight ports. Here are some guidelines to follow when connecting your network to a hub:

- Place the hub in a central location. You must be able to run a cable from the hub to each computer on your network.

- The total length of all cables used on the network should not exceed 100 meters (328.1 feet). For most home networks, this is not an issue.

- It usually doesn't matter which ports you use on the hub, unless one is identified as *uplink*. Uplink ports are used to expand a network's capacity by connecting two hubs or sometimes to connect a hub to a router or broadband modem. On most hubs an uplink port cannot be used to connect to a computer, unless the uplink port has a switch to toggle it into a normal port mode. The uplink port achieves the same purpose as a crossover cable, and a toggle switch simply reverses the crossed-over lines to be able to accept a standard patch cable.

In addition to (or in place of) a hub or switch, your network may use a router or residential gateway. This type of device is specifically designed to connect to an external DSL or cable modem. Most such products designed for use in homes and small offices combine a router and hub; in this type of device, you connect your external DSL or cable modem to the Internet connector (often labeled as wide area network, or WAN) on the router and then connect each computer on the network to a port on the local area network (LAN) side. The simplest type of router is designed with a single Internet or WAN port and a single local port. If you have this type of device, connect the DSL or cable modem to the Internet connector and then connect the local port to your hub.

If you plan to use Internet Connection Sharing and you have an external DSL or cable modem, you'll need to install two network adapters in the computer with the shared Internet connection. The DSL or cable modem connects directly to one network adapter and provides the Internet connection. Connect the second network adapter to the same hub as the other computers in your home network.

If your cable or DSL modem is an internal device, or if you plan to share a conventional dial-up modem rather than a broadband connection, you need to install only one network adapter in the computer that will act as the Internet Connection Sharing host.

Setting Up a Wireless Network

The original release of Windows XP includes a feature called Wireless Auto Configuration, which does most of the work of setting up your wireless network adapter, without requiring a lot of manual tweaking. Wireless Auto Configuration adds the following interface elements to a computer that is equipped with a WiFi adapter:

- A Wireless Networks tab in the Properties dialog box for the wireless adapter.
- Messages in the notification area that indicate the availability of wireless networks and the status of the current connection.
- A Wireless Network Connection dialog box that lists networks available for connection.
- A snap-in for the Services console that allows you to manage the Wireless Zero Configuration service.

Since the original release of Windows XP, Microsoft has issued several updates that provide additional security and wireless configuration features. Windows XP Service Pack 2 (SP2) adds a new Wireless Network Setup Wizard that automatically configures compatible wireless computers, peripherals, and access points and sets security keys using either WEP or WPA. The SP2 version of the Wireless Network Connection dialog box is also different, designed with the goal of making it much easier to create a secure wireless network.

In this section, we assume that you have already connected a wireless access point to your network and followed the manufacturer's instructions to set it up on your network.

Your Wireless Security Options

On a conventional wired network, physical security is a given: If someone plugs a computer into your hub, you'll know about it immediately, and you can trace the physical wire back to the intruder's computer. On wireless networks, however, anyone who comes into range of your wireless access point can tap into your network and intercept signals from it. Finding open access points has become something of a sport; as we noted earlier in this chapter, participants call it *war driving*. Although some war drivers seek open access points just for fun, other users who find their way into your network present several risks:

- **Theft of service**   An intruder might be able to access the Internet using your connection, which could degrade the quality of your Internet service.

- **Denial of service**   An intruder who is unable to connect to your network can still cause some degree of havoc by flooding the network with connection requests. With enough persistence, an attacker could completely deny legitimate users access to the network.

- **Theft or destruction of data**   Outsiders who successfully connect to your network can browse shared folders and printers. Depending on the permissions assigned to these resources, they can change, rename, or delete existing files, or add new ones.

- **Network takeover**   An intruder who manages to log on to the network and exploit an unpatched vulnerability can install a Trojan horse program or tamper with permissions, potentially exposing computers on the LAN to attacks from over the Internet.

To prevent any of these dire possibilities, you can and should configure the best available security for your access point and all wireless devices on your network. Depending on your hardware, you should have a choice of one or both of the following options:

- Wireless Equivalent Privacy (WEP) protects authorized users of a wireless network from eavesdroppers by encrypting the data flow between the networked computer and the access point. Typically, WEP encryption uses a secret key that is either 64 bits or 128 bits in strength. (Confusingly, you may also see references to 40-bit and 104-bit keys, which refer to the unique portion of each WEP key that is separate from the common 24-bit initialization vector.) To enter a WEP key, you supply a string of ASCII or hex characters (5 ASCII or 10 hex characters for a 64-bit key; 13 ASCII or 26 hex characters for a 128-bit key). The key you provide when setting up your wireless adapter must match the key on your access point, and all devices on the network must use the same encryption strength—either 64 or 128 bits. Although WEP offers reasonable security for a home network, it suffers from some known security flaws that make it relatively easy for an attacker to "crack" the key using off-the-shelf hardware. As a result, WEP is inappropriate for use on any network that contains sensitive data.

Chapter 28

● Wi-Fi Protected Access (WPA) is a newer, stronger encryption scheme that was specifically designed to overcome weaknesses of WEP. On a network that uses WPA, clients and access points use a shared network password (called a *pre-shared key*, or *PSK*) that consists of a 256-bit number or a passphrase that is between 8 and 63 bytes long (a longer passphrase produces a stronger key). With a sufficiently strong key based on a truly random sequence, the likelihood of an outside attack is very, very slim. Most network hardware that supports the 802.11g standard also supports WPA. With older hardware, you may be able to add WPA compatibility via a firmware upgrade.

Typically, configuring an access point to support WEP or WPA requires that you use a Web-based configuration utility. Figure 28-2, for instance, shows the configuration settings for an SMC 2804WBR Barricade, which combines a wired router and a wireless access point.

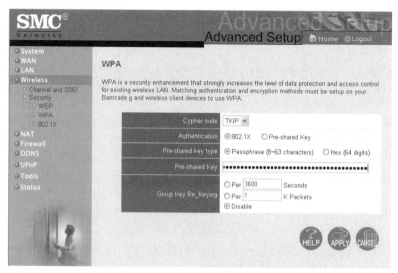

Figure 28-2. Security settings and keys for a wireless access point must match those for your wireless adapter. The Pre-Shared Key setting here works with the WPA-PSK setting in Windows XP.

The alternative to either of these encryption methods is to use no security at all, an option that produces an "open" network. If you own a coffee shop or bookstore and your goal is to provide free Internet access for your customers, this option is acceptable as long as you make sure to protect other computers on your network from unauthorized access. But for most people, the risks of running an open network are unacceptable.

Inside Out

Beef up security at the access point

If your data is sensitive and your network is in an apartment building or an office complex where you can reasonably expect other people to wander into range with wireless adapters, you should take extra security precautions in addition to enabling WPA. Consider any or all of the following measures to protect your wireless access point from intruders:

- Change the network name (SSID) of your access point to one that doesn't match the hardware defaults and doesn't give away any information about you or your business.
- Prevent your access point from broadcasting its SSID; because you know the network name, you can enter it manually, but a would-be intruder will be unable to click to select the network name and will have to guess the name first.
- Consider disabling remote administration of the access point; if you need to change settings, you can do so directly, using a wired connection.
- If you allow remote administration of the access point, set a strong password.
- Upgrade the firmware of your wireless hardware (access point and adapter) to the most recent versions, which may incorporate security fixes.
- If your pool of PCs is small and fixed, use your access point's configuration tools to restrict access to computers using the unique MAC address of each computer's wireless adapter.
- Consider using virtual private networks for wireless connections.

On larger networks with one or more domain servers available, you can set up a Remote Authentication Dial-In User Service (RADIUS) server to allow the most secure option of all, 802.1x authentication. In addition, consider enabling IP Security (IPSec). For more information, see "IP Security and Filtering," in *Microsoft Windows XP Professional Resource Kit Documentation* (Microsoft Press, 2001). In one of our other books, *Microsoft Windows Security Inside Out for Windows XP and Windows 2000* (Microsoft Press, 2002), we provide more information about securing wireless networks and about using IPSec.

Chapter 28

Connecting to a Wireless Network

When you first add a wireless network adapter to a computer and install the appropriate drivers, Windows XP scans for available wireless access points. If it finds at least one, it displays a status message in the notification area. (You must be logged in as an administrator to connect to a wireless network.)

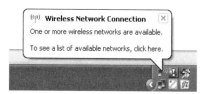

Click the status message to display the Wireless Network Connection dialog box, shown in Figure 28-3. (If the message disappears before you get around to selecting it, right-click the Wireless Network Connection icon in the notification area and choose View Available Networks; or open Network Connections from Control Panel, right-click the icon for your wireless connection, and choose the same option from the shortcut menu.) Click the Connect button to join the network.

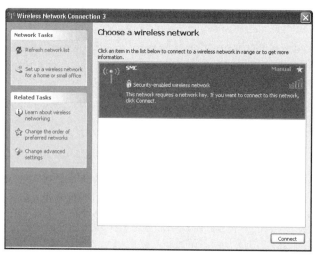

Figure 28-3. Any nearby networks that are broadcasting their network names (SSIDs) are visible here, with secure networks clearly noted.

If the network you select is secure, you'll be prompted to enter your encryption key at this point, as shown in Figure 28-4. After you successfully enter the key, you can begin using the shared Internet connection and any available shared resources on the network.

Chapter 28

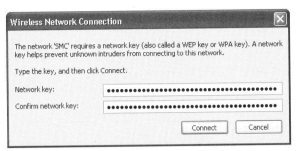

Figure 28-4. When you attempt to connect to a secure wireless network, Windows XP prompts you to enter the appropriate WEP or WPA key.

Troubleshooting

You're unable to connect to your wireless network.

If you're having problems connecting to your wireless network, check the following:

- Does your wireless network adapter support automatic configuration? Check with the hardware manufacturer and, if necessary, update the drivers and firmware for the devices in question.

- Is automatic configuration enabled in Windows? Open the properties dialog box for the wireless network connection; on the Wireless Networks tab, select the Use Windows To Configure My Wireless Network Settings check box. If you are using the manufacturer's software to set up your wireless connection, clear this check box.

- Is the Wireless Zero Configuration service running? Open the Administrative Tools folder in Control Panel and then double-click Services. Check the entry in the Status column for this service. If it doesn't say Started, right-click the entry and choose Start from the shortcut menu.

- Is the access point visible in the Choose a Wireless Network list in the Wireless Network Connection dialog box? If the access point does not broadcast its network name, you need to manually add it to your list of preferred networks, as described in the following section.

Chapter 28

Managing Wireless Network Connections

The first time you connect to a wireless network, Windows XP adds that network to the top of the list of preferred networks. If you take your computer to a different location and connect to a new network, that location is added to the list of preferred networks. Each time you turn on your computer or enable your wireless adapter, Windows XP attempts to make a connection, using the following rules:

- Wireless Auto Configuration tries to connect to each of the preferred networks in the list of available networks (those that have broadcast their SSIDs), in the order that those networks appear.

- If this does not result in a successful connection, Wireless Auto Configuration tries to connect to each preferred network that does not appear in the list of available networks. This strategy should be successful if you are trying to connect to a network that does not broadcast its network name.

- Wireless Auto Configuration next looks in the list of available networks for any ad hoc networks—that is, those that are based on direct connections to another wireless adapter rather than an access point—and attempts to connect to any that are also in the list of preferred networks.

- If all these attempts have failed to make a successful connection, Wireless Auto Configuration looks in the list of preferred networks for the name of any ad hoc network that is not currently available and configures the wireless adapter as the first node in this ad hoc network, making it available for connections by other computers.

Tip Network without an access point

Although the most common way to set up a wireless network is with an access point or residential gateway, you don't need this piece of hardware to set up a wireless network. By using *ad hoc mode* instead of the default *infrastructure mode*, you can connect directly to other computers on the network, as long as each one is equipped with a compatible wireless adapter. If you think of a wireless access point as a server, then a Wi-Fi network running in ad hoc mode is the equivalent of a peer-to-peer network. Wireless access points add the capability to share an Internet connection, assign IP addresses, and enforce security. To switch to ad hoc mode, open the Wireless Network Connection Properties dialog box and then click the Advanced button at the bottom of the Wireless Networks tab. In the Advanced dialog box, select Computer-To-Computer (Ad Hoc) Networks Only. Repeat this process on any other network computers equipped with wireless adapters. Your hardware may require additional configuration before an ad hoc configuration will work properly.

From the above description of the steps that Wireless Auto Configuration takes to make a connection, you can see that the list of preferred networks plays a key role in determining when and how you're connected to a wireless network. As noted earlier, Wireless Auto

Configuration adds a new entry to the preferred list the first time you successfully connect to a network and configures that entry for automatic connections. You can alter the order of networks in the preferred list, add networks manually, remove entries from the list, and configure any entry for Manual rather than Automatic connections. To manage the settings of entries on the list of preferred networks, click Change the Order Of Preferred Networks in the list of tasks along the left side of the View Available Networks dialog box. (Or, alternatively, open the Network Connections folder, right-click the entry for your wireless connection, choose Properties, and then click the Wireless Networks tab.) This action opens the Wireless Network Connection dialog box, where you can manipulate the Preferred Networks list, as shown in Figure 28-5.

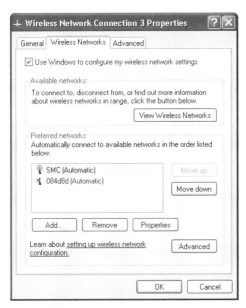

Figure 28-5. The icon to the left of each entry in the Preferred Networks list indicates whether it is currently available.

- To change the order of entries in the Preferred Networks list, select the entry you want to move and then click Move Up or Move Down.

- To delete an entry from the list that you don't plan to use again—for instance, a wireless entry from a network at a hotel you don't plan to return to—select the entry and click Remove.

- To change an entry in the Preferred list from Automatic to Manual, or vice-versa, select the list entry and then click Properties. Click the Connection tab and select or clear the Connect When This Network Is In Range check box.

Chapter 28

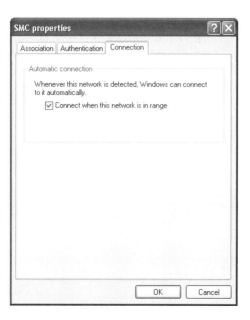

- Click the Advanced button to change the way Wireless Auto Configuration behaves when attempting to connect to new networks. Select the Access Point (Infrastructure) Networks Only check box, for instance, if you want to be certain you never, ever accidentally, connect to another computer with a wireless connection.

The check box at the bottom of the Advanced dialog box, Automatically Connect To Non-Preferred Networks, controls how Wireless Auto Configuration works when it is unable to connect to any network on your preferred list. With this option enabled, Wireless Auto Configuration attempts to connect to any available network, in the order in which they were detected by the wireless adapter. With this option disabled, Windows scans only for entries on your preferred list and notifies you via a status message when a suitable network is available.

After making a successful connection, Wireless Auto Configuration continues to scan for available networks. If a new network becomes available and it is higher on the list than the current connection, Windows drops the existing network and connects to the preferred network.

Configuring a New Wireless Network

Configuring a new network involves specifying four discrete pieces of information. You need to define the network type (infrastructure or ad hoc); specify the network name (SSID); choose authentication and encryption options for security; and enter a security key of the appropriate length and complexity. This last step can be the most tedious, especially if you're using WPA, which requires that you enter a 64-character hexadecimal value for maximum security. In fact, the hassle of creating WEP keys in the original release of Windows XP resulted in this security feature going mostly unused. With its longer keys and more complex architecture, WPA has been even less successful.

Inside Out

Don't type, paste!

Although you can carefully enter a 64-digit WPA key by typing each character, that method is a recipe for frustration, especially if you have more than one or two computers to set up. The new Wireless Network Setup Wizard uses a USB flash drive to enter this information automatically on computers running Windows XP Service Pack 2. If you allow the wizard to generate the encryption key automatically, it saves the key in a text file on the flash drive. To set up a router that doesn't use the flash drive, and for computers running other operating systems, open that text file, copy the key to the Clipboard, and then paste it into the dialog box. This method saves typing and avoids frustrating typos that can cause connections to fail.

The Wireless Network Setup Wizard, a new addition in Windows XP Service Pack 2, tries to take some of the sting out of creating and configuring a secure network. The wizard is built around a new feature called the Smart Network Key architecture, which uses inexpensive USB flash drives to automatically configure routers and workstations on a wireless network. The long-term vision, when all wireless networking hardware supports the Smart Network Key architecture, is to make the process as simple as clicking through a wizard and then using flash drives to transfer the settings throughout all devices on a wireless network.

Even without a full complement of compatible hardware, however, you can use the Wireless Network Setup Wizard to simplify the process of setting up and securing a network.

The wizard runs only on a computer equipped with a wireless adapter and running Windows XP Service Pack 2. To start the wizard, double-click its Control Panel icon or its Start menu shortcut (All Programs, Accessories, Communications), or open the Network Connections folder or the list of available wireless networks and click the Set Up A Wireless Network link under the Network Tasks heading.

1 Click past the Welcome screen. If you have previously configured a network, the next screen lets you choose whether to configure a new device for that existing network or set up a new network. Click Next to continue. If you have not used the wizard before, you'll skip this screen and go straight to the Create A Name For Your Wireless Network screen, as shown in Figure 28-6.

Tip Start from scratch

When the Wireless Network Setup Wizard finishes its work, it writes your network settings to a hidden file named LastFlashConfig.WFC, which it saves in %Appdata%\Microsoft. The data in this file is encrypted as a security measure. If you want to eliminate all traces of a previous configuration and start fresh with your wireless network, delete this file before running the wizard.

Figure 28-6. Be sure the settings you select in the wizard match those defined at the access point.

2 In the Network Name (SSID) box, enter the name of the network as defined at the access point. This is also the place to select the following security options:

- Click Automatically Assign A Network Key to let Windows define a random key at the maximum security level.

- Click Manually Assign A Network Key if your access point and/or other devices are currently configured to use a specific key and you're using the wizard to duplicate that setup.

- By default, the Use WPA Encryption Instead Of WEP box is cleared, meaning your new connection will use WEP security. Select this check box to use WPA instead. Click Next to continue.

> **Note** Why does the Wireless Network Setup Wizard use the relatively insecure WEP as a default setting? For backward compatibility with the large installed base of old equipment, that's why. All wireless hardware supports WEP; only newer equipment supports WPA. If you configure WPA security on a network that uses one or more older devices, you'll be unable to connect those devices to the network. If you know your equipment supports WPA, make sure you change the default to take advantage of the greater security.

3 If you chose the option to manually assign a key, the dialog box shown in Figure 28-7 appears. (The instructions will vary, depending on whether you chose WEP or WPA as your encryption option.) Enter or paste the encryption key and click Next to continue.

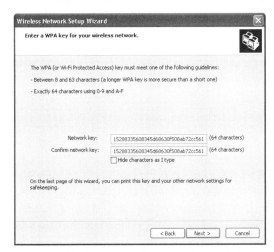

Figure 28-7. Clear the check box beneath these text boxes so that you can proofread as you type a complex key. Leave the box selected if you plan to paste the key from a saved text file.

4   On the How Do You Want To Set Up Your Network page, shown in Figure 28-8, choose the method you want to use when saving your wireless network settings for use on other pieces of your network:

Figure 28-8.   We recommend using a USB flash drive to simplify the process of setting up a wireless network.

- Use A USB Flash Drive copies necessary configuration files to a USB-based portable storage device, along with an AutoRun file and a script that allows the wizard to operate automatically on other computers running Windows XP with Service Pack 2. This is the easier of the two options.

- Choose Set Up A Network Manually if the devices you're configuring do not support USB flash drives.

Tip   Don't be fooled by the Print button

If you choose the Set Up A Network Manually option, the final step of the wizard suggests that you need to print out the resulting settings and retype them at the destination computer. We thought so, too, the first three or four times we used this wizard. But that cumbersome step isn't necessary. Clicking the Print Network Settings button on the final page actually opens Notepad, with the newly created settings file displayed as editable text. For the sake of convenience, you might choose to save that text tile to a common location (a floppy disk or a USB flash drive, for instance) and then open it on the computer where you're performing the next configuration step. This makes it easy to copy and paste the encryption key instead of having to type it from a printed page.

5 Follow the wizard's prompts to complete setup. If you chose to use a flash drive, you'll be instructed to take the drive to your access point and other computers on your network to complete the configuration.

> **Note** As of summer 2004, when we completed this edition of Windows XP Inside Out, no commercially available wireless access points supported the Network Smart Key feature. Based on our experience with this feature, the next generation of access points should be worth waiting for. If you're considering the purchase of a new access point, we recommend that you look for one that supports configuration via Smart Network Key.

To create a new wireless connection from scratch, without using the wizard, or to adjust settings manually for an existing connection, open the properties dialog box for your wireless connection. On the Wireless Networks tab, click Add to create a new network entry; to edit settings, select an entry from the list and click Properties. The Association tab, shown in Figure 28-9, contains the same information entered by the wizard.

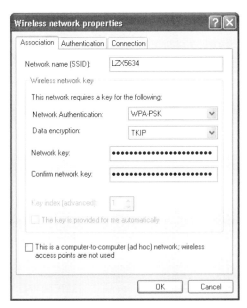

Figure 28-9. Be careful when editing or creating a connection using this dialog box; the security options, in particular, can be confusing.

The Network Name (SSID) text box is self-explanatory, as are the text boxes where you enter and confirm a network key (note, however, that these boxes don't provide any guidance as to the correct length or format of the keys—you're just expected to know those details). The Network Authentication and Data Encryption boxes offer the most potential for confusion.

Under the 802.11 standard, a wireless adapter first has to authenticate to an access point; after this process is successful, the adapter associates with the access point. For Network Authentication, choose Open if you plan to use WEP as your encryption method. The alternative, Shared, is considered insecure. If all of your hardware supports WPA, choose either WPA or WPA-PSK in this box; the exact choice should match the setting on your access point. (A third option, WPA-None, is the correct choice when setting up a secure ad-hoc wireless network.)

In the Data Encryption box, choose WEP if you're using that standard and you chose Open in the previous step. Choose TKIP if you selected any variant of WPA for your Network Authentication method. (AES is an optional, nonstandard encryption algorithm that should be selected only when the manufacturer of your hardware explicitly requires its use.)

Configuring a Default Network Connection

After you've installed your networking hardware (wired or wireless) and configured drivers and other supporting software, Windows creates a local connection that includes the following networking components:

- **Client For Microsoft Networks**   A network client provides access to computers and resources on a network; this client allows you to connect to computers running any 32-bit or 64-bit Windows version.

- **File And Printer Sharing For Microsoft Networks**   This service allows other computers on your Windows-based network to access shared resources on your computer.

- **QoS Packet Scheduler**   This component (installed only on systems running Windows XP Professional) enables Quality Of Service features provided on corporate networks and by Internet service providers. For the most part, these advanced features will not be widely used until Internet Protocol version 6 (IPv6) is also widely used.

- **Internet Protocol (TCP/IP)**   TCP/IP is the default network protocol in Windows XP. It provides easy connectivity across a wide variety of networks, including the Internet. Although TCP/IP has plenty of options you can configure, most users can safely accept the default settings without having to make any configuration changes.

For more details about TCP/IP configuration, see "Setting IP Addresses," page 973, and "Troubleshooting TCP/IP Problems," page 981.

This default collection of clients, services, and protocols is generally all you need to work with a Microsoft network (that is, one where all computers are running 32-bit or 64-bit versions of Windows). For a full discussion of other protocols and networking components, see "Adjusting Network Settings," page 968.

Setting Up a Small Network

To see information about currently defined network connections, open Control Panel, Network Connections. Figure 28-10 shows the information and configuration options available from this window.

Use this list of tasks to work with a network connection

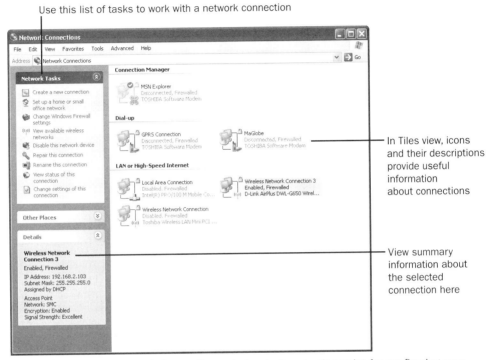

In Tiles view, icons and their descriptions provide useful information about connections

View summary information about the selected connection here

Figure 28-10. The Network Connections window is the starting point for configuring your network.

To see more detailed information about a network connection, double-click its icon in the Network Connections window. Figure 28-11, for instance, shows the status dialog box for a default Local Area Connection.

Tip   Rename your connections
Windows tags your main network connection with the Local Area Connection label. When you add connections, they get equally generic titles, like Local Area Connection 2. You can easily replace these labels with text that's more meaningful to you. For instance, on a computer that's serving as an ICS host, you might give your two network adapters distinctive names like "Comcast Cable Modem" and "Home Network Connection." To edit a connection label, right-click the connection icon and choose Rename from the shortcut menu; then type the descriptive name.

Chapter 28

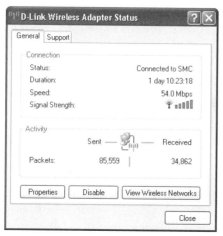

Figure 28-11. The status dialog box provides basic statistics, including uptime, throughput, and the current connection speed.

Using the Network Setup Wizard

After you've successfully installed all the required hardware for your network, run the Network Setup Wizard. Even if your network seems to be working just fine, you should run the Network Setup Wizard anyway. This automated configuration utility sets the proper permissions on shared folders, adds required keys to the registry, configures protocols and binds them to network cards, and enables or disables Windows Firewall. Windows XP Service Pack 2 adds an extra step to the wizard, allowing you to enable or disable file and printer sharing and, if necessary, adjust system policies so that file sharing works properly over the network.

Inside Out

Use the Network Setup Wizard

Are you a Windows expert with a disdain for all wizards? You're not alone. But even if you speak fluent TCP/IP and have multiple certifications in advanced networking, you should make an exception in this case and run the Windows XP Network Setup Wizard on every system that's connected to your network. Doing so is the only reliable way to ensure that your network has the proper baseline configuration. Afterward, you can manually adjust settings and enable or disable features as required.

Chapter 28

If your network includes one computer that you want to use as an Internet Connection Sharing (ICS) host, be sure to configure the Internet connection on that computer first, and then run the Network Setup Wizard on that computer. If all your networked computers have separate Internet connections, or if you use a router or residential gateway to share an Internet connection, you can start with any computer. To start the Network Setup Wizard, open Control Panel, double-click Network Connections, and then click the Set Up A Home Or Small Office Network link under Network Tasks in the left pane. This choice is also available in the My Network Places folder. If you've turned on the Folders bar so that the task pane isn't visible in Windows Explorer, you can access the wizard from the All Programs menu—choose Accessories, Communications, Network Setup Wizard.

To use the Network Setup Wizard, follow these steps:

1. Click Next to skip past the two introductory screens. If the wizard detects that your computer is connected to a router or residential gateway, or if you are running the wizard on other computers after setting up ICS, it offers the choice of using the shared connection or choosing an alternate connection method. Choose the first option: Yes, Use The Existing Shared Connection For This Computer's Internet Access. Click Next and skip to Step 5.

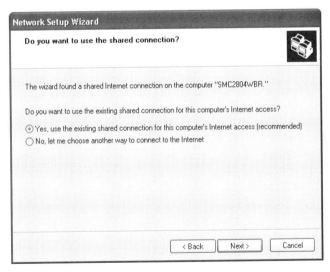

2. If your network doesn't include a router, or if you chose the second option on the previous page, the Select A Connection Method page appears.

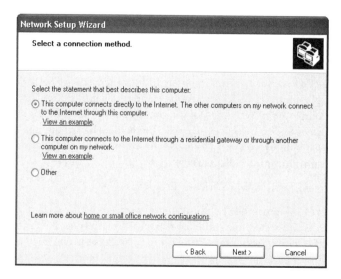

Choose one of these three options:

- **This Computer Connects Directly To The Internet. The Other Computers On My Network Connect To The Internet Through This Computer.** Select this option if you have multiple network connections on the computer and you plan to use one to share Internet access with other computers on the network. Click Next to continue.

- **This Computer Connects To The Internet Through A Residential Gateway Or Through Another Computer On My Network.** If you use a router or residential gateway to manage shared Internet access and it was not detected by Windows XP, select this option and click Next to continue. If you use ICS and you see this screen, stop and check your Internet connection. If ICS is properly set up, the wizard should display a different page, as described at the end of this section.

- **Other.** Select this option if your computer is connected to the Internet directly or through a hub, or if your network does not have Internet access. If you choose this option and click Next, you will see the Other Internet Connection Methods page next.

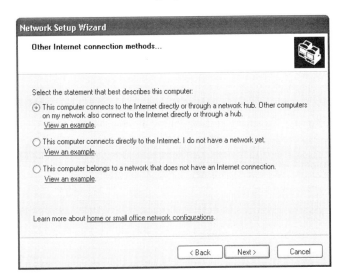

3   If you chose Other on the previous page, choose one of the following options. Otherwise, skip to step 5.

■ **This Computer Connects To The Internet Directly Or Through A Network Hub. Other Computers On My Network Also Connect To The Internet Directly Or Through A Hub.**   If your external DSL or cable modem is connected directly to the hub along with all networked computers, choose this option. Click Next to continue.

Caution   This configuration, in which all computers have individual Internet connections and direct access to other networked computers, potentially exposes your system to serious security risks. On computers running Windows XP Service Pack 1 or earlier, the Network Setup Wizard displays a stern warning about the risks of this configuration immediately after you select it; the resulting configuration turns on the old Internet Connection Firewall and blocks all access to shared resources on the local network. By contrast, with Windows XP Service Pack 2 installed, you'll see a smaller warning dialog box if you choose this configuration and then enable file and printer sharing over your network. If you override this choice and enable file and printer sharing anyway, Windows Firewall allows computers on your local subnet to access shared resources. You should verify that your local subnet doesn't include any untrusted computers, such as those belonging to other customers of your cable company sharing the same IP address range.

Chapter 28

- **This Computer Connects Directly To The Internet. I Do Not Have A Network Yet.** Select this option if you have only one computer and it is directly connected to the Internet. Click Next to continue.

- **This Computer Belongs To A Network That Does Not Have An Internet Connection.** Choose this option if no computer on your network has an Internet connection you want to share. Click Next to continue.

4 If your computer has more than one network connection, one of which is directly connected to the Internet, the Select Your Internet Connection page appears.

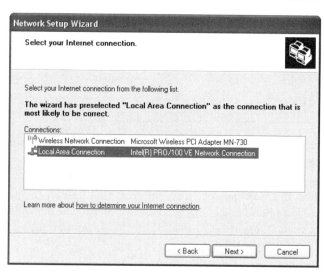

Note In versions of Windows XP before Service Pack 2, the wizard would often inappropriately attempt to bridge multiple network connections, usually causing problems and confusion. The wizard's default behavior now is not to create a bridge. If you're in the small minority of people who need to bridge network connections, you'll need to perform this task manually before or after running the wizard.

5 Confirm that the wizard has selected the correct connection and click Next to continue. The Give This Computer A Description And Name page appears.

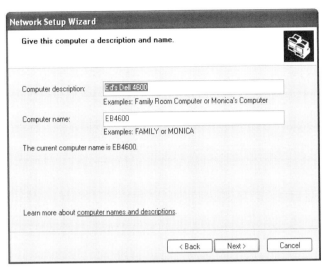

6   Check the name of the computer listed in the Computer Name box. Adjust the name and description if necessary, and click Next to continue.

Caution   Under normal circumstances, you establish the computer name during Setup, and there's rarely a good reason to rename a computer. In fact, doing so can cause problems with some Internet service providers, which insist that your computer have a specific name. It can also cause inconvenience to other users who have created shortcuts to shared resources on your system. One circumstance in which it is desirable to rename a computer is if your preferred logon name is the same as your computer name. Windows XP does not allow you to create a user account whose name is the same as the computer name. In that case, it might be preferable to change the computer name so that you don't have to adopt a different user name.

7   On the Name Your Network page, enter the name of your workgroup. Note that this page is not like the previous page, in which the wizard correctly remembers your computer name. If you don't want to use the default workgroup name of MSHOME, you must manually change it here. (For more details about assigning workgroup names, see "Configuring Workgroup Settings," page 971.) Click Next.

Chapter 28

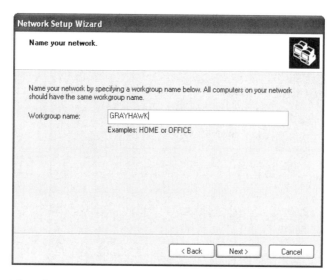

8 The File Or Printer Sharing page, which was introduced as part of Service Pack 2, allows you to enable or disable file and printer sharing. If you enable this option, the wizard creates an exception in Windows Firewall so that traffic from your local network can use TCP ports 139 and 445 and UDP ports 138 and 139. Click Next to move to the Ready To Apply Network Settings page.

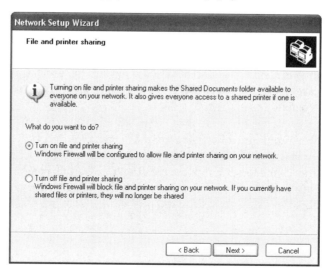

9   Scroll through the summary of changes the wizard is about to make to your network configuration. To make any changes to the settings you chose on the previous pages, use the Back button. If you're satisfied with the results, click Next to apply the changes immediately. The wizard displays an animated graphic while it works.

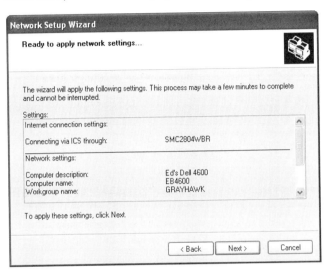

> **Caution**   When you change your network configuration, the Network Setup Wizard temporarily shuts down your Internet connection and breaks off communication with the rest of your network. Do not run the wizard if you're currently in the middle of downloading files from the Internet or if other users are using shared resources on your computer.

10   On the final page of the wizard, you can create a network setup disk for use on systems running previous versions of Windows that are connected to the same network. If your network consists of Windows XP systems only, choose Just Finish The Wizard and click Next to close the wizard.

> **Tip**   Determine which connection is which
>
> If you have two network connections defined, it can be difficult to tell which one is the Internet connection to be shared and which one belongs to your local network. The easiest way to determine which is which is to open the Network Connections window and then temporarily unplug the connection between your external DSL or cable modem and your computer. Within a few seconds, a red X should appear on one of the connections—note the name of that connection and select it when prompted by the Network Setup Wizard. (And don't forget to reconnect that cable before resuming the wizard!)

Chapter 28

967

Adjusting Network Settings

Although the Network Setup Wizard is the preferred way to work with network settings, you may need to adjust settings manually under some circumstances. Windows XP allows you to add, remove, enable, and disable protocols; change network settings; and set IP addresses using options in the Network Connections folder.

Installing and Configuring Protocols

Network *protocols* are the common languages used to transfer data from point to point on a network. A few years ago, it was not uncommon for a computer running Windows to require multiple protocols, and earlier versions of Windows included a plethora of protocols developed for use on different types of networks—most of them completely irrelevant to home and small business users.

Because of the overwhelming popularity of the Internet, however, only one protocol is truly essential anymore. TCP/IP, the default protocol of the Internet, is installed on every computer running Windows XP. For virtually any networking task, TCP/IP is the preferred solution. It works equally well on tiny two-computer networks and massive multinational networks with thousands of workstations. In fact, TCP/IP is so essential to the basic operation of Windows XP that it can't be removed, although it can be disabled.

Two protocols that were once widely used in Windows networks are still available in Windows XP and can be configured for special purposes:

- **IPX/SPX**   This protocol was originally developed for use on networks running Novell NetWare. It's available in Windows XP as an installable option. In the previous edition of this book, we explained how to use IPX/SPX in addition to TCP/IP to work around security issues that result when all network computers share an Internet connection through a hub. Because of the security improvements in Windows XP Service Pack 2, we no longer recommend this configuration. Some older games rely on IPX/SPX.

- **NetBEUI**   This protocol (short for NetBIOS Extended User Interface) is available as an unsupported option in Windows XP. It was originally developed for use on small networks running Windows 3.*x*. Because it works by indiscriminately broadcasting packets over the network, NetBEUI can cause performance problems and should only be used when an existing network configuration requires it.

> **Note**   In most network setups, you don't need to install any additional protocols. For a full discussion of the pros and cons of using alternate protocols as a security measure, see "Reality Check," at the beginning of this chapter.

Chapter 28

In addition, the relatively new Internet Protocol Version 6 (IPv6) is included with Windows XP Service Pack 2. This protocol, listed in network setup dialog boxes as TCP/IP version 6, is still in its infancy but will someday be widely used; it is included here for use in advanced and experimental applications. If you use an application that requires IPv6, the software developer should instruct you to install this protocol.

To install an additional protocol, follow these steps:

1. If you're going to install NetBEUI, insert your Windows XP CD. Use Windows Explorer to copy the following files from the CD's \Valueadd\Msft\Net\Netbeui folder:

   - Copy Nbf.sys to the %SystemRoot%\System32\Drivers folder.
   - Copy Netnbf.inf to the %SystemRoot%\Inf folder. (This is a hidden folder. You can navigate directly to it by typing its name in the Address bar.)

2. From Control Panel, open the Network Connections folder.

3. Select the connection icon you want to edit and then click the Change Settings Of This Connection link under Network Tasks. (If this option isn't visible, right-click the connection icon and choose Properties from the shortcut menu.)

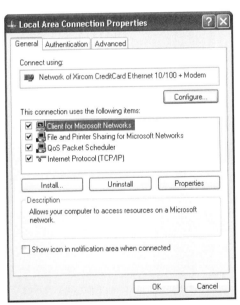

4. From the properties dialog box, click the Install button. The Select Network Component Type dialog box opens.

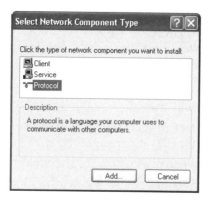

5 Choose Protocol and click Add. The Select Network Protocol dialog box appears.

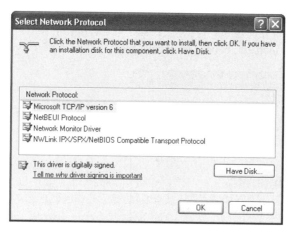

6 Choose the protocol you want to add:

- To install IPX/SPX, select NWLink IPX/SPX/NetBIOS Compatible Transport Protocol and click OK.

- To install NetBEUI, select NetBEUI Protocol and click OK.

- To install IPv6, select Microsoft TCP/IP version 6 and click OK.

You can use the new protocol immediately. In some configurations, you may be required to restart the computer before the new configuration is fully usable.

To temporarily enable or disable the use of a protocol with a specific connection, open the properties dialog box for that connection and select or clear the box to the left of the protocol.

Configuring Workgroup Settings

After your network is properly configured, you should be able to see all other computers on your network by opening My Network Places in Windows Explorer. Click the View Workgroup Computers link under Network Tasks in the left pane of My Network Places to see a list of the computers on your network. (This option is not available if your computer is joined to a Windows domain.)

To communicate properly with one another, all the computers on a peer-to-peer Windows network must be members of the same workgroup. "Joining" a workgroup doesn't require a secret handshake or special security settings. The workgroup name is strictly an organizational tool, which Windows uses to group computers and shared resources on the same network. As the administrator of a workgroup, you might want to change the workgroup name to something that describes your organization or family; if your network is relatively large but does not include a domain server, you may choose to define more than one workgroup.

Inside Out

Arrange protocols in order

For performance or compatibility reasons, networking experts may want to specify the order in which Windows should use different protocols. In Windows XP, this option is still available, although it's well hidden. From the Network Connections folder, choose Advanced Settings from the Advanced menu. The Advanced Settings dialog box, shown below, lets you specify which protocols are available for clients and services on each connection and control the order in which each protocol is used. These settings are strictly for specialized situations. Most networks will do best with the default settings.

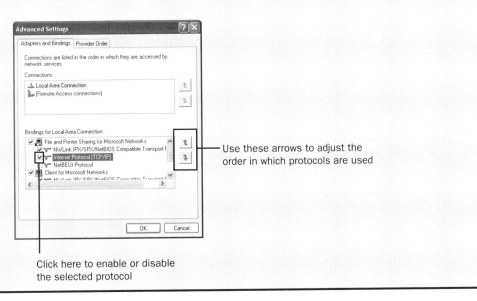

Use these arrows to adjust the order in which protocols are used

Click here to enable or disable the selected protocol

Chapter 28

Caution   Don't let the wizard change your workgroup

Every time you run the Network Setup Wizard, you're required to pass through a page where you enter the name of your workgroup. One usability glitch in this wizard has the potential to temporarily cut off your workgroup if you blast through the wizard without paying enough attention. The wizard automatically defaults to MSHOME as the workgroup name, even if you've specified a different name during Windows Setup, manually, or while running the wizard on previous occasions. Don't just idly click the Next button. Be sure to enter the correct name for your workgroup.

The easiest way to change the workgroup to which your computer belongs is by using the Network Setup Wizard. However, you can also adjust this setting manually, following these steps:

1   Open Control Panel, System, and then click the Computer Name tab.

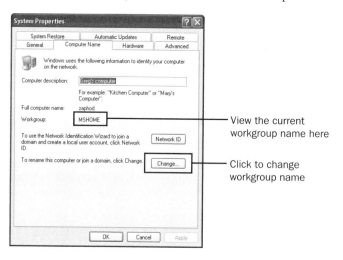

2   Click the Change button. (Don't be confused by the explanatory text for this button, which mentions domains but doesn't use the word *workgroup* at all.) The Computer Name Changes dialog box opens.

3   Select theWorkgroup option and then replace the name of the current workgroup with the name of the workgroup you want to join or create.

4   Click OK to make the change. Two successive message boxes welcome you to the workgroup and remind you that you have to restart your computer to make the change effective.

Note   A workgroup name can legally contain up to 15 characters. It cannot be the same as the name of any computer in the workgroup, and it cannot contain any of the following characters: ; : " < > * + = \ | ? ,

Setting IP Addresses

Networks that use the TCP/IP protocol rely on *IP addresses* to route packets of data from point to point. On a TCP/IP network, every computer has a unique IP address, which consists of four 8-bit numbers (each one represented in decimal format by a number between 0 and 255) separated by periods. In addition to the IP address, each computer's TCP/IP configuration has the following additional settings:

- A *subnet mask*, which tells the network how to distinguish between IP addresses that are part of the same network and those that belong to other networks.

- A *default gateway*, which is a computer that routes packets intended for addresses outside the local network.

- One or more *Domain Name System (DNS) servers*, which are computers that translate domain names (such as *www.microsoft.com*) into IP addresses.

Chapter 28

Windows XP provides several methods for assigning IP addresses to networked computers:

- **Dynamic Host Configuration Protocol (DHCP)**   This is the default configuration for Windows XP Professional and Home Edition. Most Internet service providers (ISPs) start with a pool of IP addresses that are available for use by their customers. ISPs use DHCP servers to assign IP addresses from this pool and to set subnet masks and other configuration details as each customer makes a new connection. When the customer disconnects, the address is held for a period of time and eventually released back to the pool so that it can be reused. Many corporate networks use DHCP as well to avoid the hassle of managing fixed addresses for constantly changing resources; Windows 2000 Server and Windows Server 2003 both include this capability. The Internet Connection Sharing feature in Windows XP includes a full-fledged DHCP server that automatically configures all TCP/IP settings for other computers on the network. Most routers and residential gateways also incorporate DHCP servers that automatically configure computers connected to those devices.

- **Automatic Private IP Addressing (APIPA)**   When no DHCP server is available, Windows automatically assigns an IP address in a specific private IP range. (For an explanation of how private IP addresses work, see the sidebar "Public and Private IP Addresses.") If all computers on a subnet are using APIPA addresses, they can communicate with one another without requiring any additional configuration. APIPA was first introduced in May 1998 with Windows 98 and works the same in all versions of Windows released since that time.

> For detailed technical information about APIPA, including instructions on how to disable it, read Knowledge Base article 220874, "How to Use Automatic TCP/IP Addressing Without a DHCP Server."

- **Static IP Addressing**   By entering an IP address, subnet mask, and other TCP/IP details in a dialog box, you can manually configure a Windows XP workstation so that its address is always the same. This method takes more time and can cause some configuration headaches, but it allows a high degree of control over network addresses.

Static IP addresses are essential if you plan to set up a Web server, a mail server, a virtual private network (VPN) gateway, or any other computer that needs to be accessible from across the Internet. Even inside a local network, behind a router or firewall, static IP addresses can be useful. For instance, you might want to configure the router so that packets entering your network on a specific port get forwarded to a specific computer. If you use DHCP to assign addresses within the local network, you can't predict what the address of that computer will be on any given day. But by assigning that computer a static IP address that is within the range of addresses assigned by the DHCP server, you can ensure that the computer always has the same address and is thus always reachable.

● **Alternate IP Configuration** This feature, new in Windows XP, allows you to specify multiple IP addresses for a single network connection (although only one address can be used at a time). This feature is most useful with portable computers that regularly connect to different networks. You can configure the connection to automatically acquire an IP address from an available DHCP server, and then assign a static backup address for use if the first configuration isn't successful. Note that this configuration affects only IP addresses; it doesn't resolve logon issues caused by mismatched account names or switching between workgroup- and domain-based networks. For a more detailed discussion of these issues, see "Domains vs. Workgroups," page 1106.

To set a static IP address, follow these steps:

1 From Control Panel, open the Network Connections folder and select the connection whose settings you want to change.

2 Use any of the following techniques to open the properties dialog box for the selected connection:

   ■ Select the connection and click the Change Settings Of This Connection link in the Network Tasks pane.

   ■ Right-click the connection icon and choose Properties from the shortcut menu.

   ■ Double-click the connection icon to open the Status dialog box and then click the Properties button on the General tab.

3 From the list of installed network components, select Internet Protocol (TCP/IP) and then click the Properties button.

4 In the Internet Protocol (TCP/IP) Properties dialog box, select Use The Following IP Address and fill in the blanks. You must supply an IP address, a subnet mask, and a default gateway.

5 Select Use The Following DNS Server Addresses and fill in the numeric IP addresses for one or more DNS servers as well. Figure 28-12 shows the dialog box with all fields filled in.

6 Click OK to save your changes. You do not need to reboot after changing your IP configuration.

Chapter 28

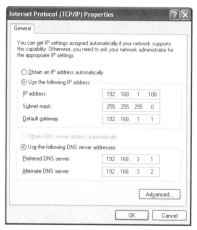

Figure 28-12.   When assigning static IP addresses, you must fill in all fields correctly. Make a mistake and you'll lose your Internet connectivity.

Public and Private IP Addresses

Any computer that is directly connected to the Internet needs a public IP address—one that can be reached by other computers on the Internet, so that information you request (Web pages and e-mail, for instance) can be routed back to your computer properly. When you connect to an Internet service provider, you're assigned a public IP address from a block of addresses registered to that ISP. If you use a dial-up connection, your ISP probably assigns a different IP address to your computer (drawn from its pool of available addresses) each time you connect. If you have a persistent connection to your ISP via a DSL or cable modem, your IP address may be permanent—or semi-permanent, if you turn off your computer when you leave your home or office to travel and your assigned IP address is changed when you reconnect on your return.

On a home or small office network, it's not necessary to have a public IP address for each computer on the network. In fact, configuring a network with all public addresses increases security risks and usually requires an extra fee from your ISP. A safer, less costly solution is to assign a single public IP address to a single computer (or a router or residential gateway). All other computers on the network connect to the Internet through that single address. Each of the computers on the local network has a private IP address that is not directly reachable from the outside world. To communicate with the Internet, the computer or router on the edge of the network uses a technology called network address translation (NAT) to pass packets back and forth between the single public IP address and the multiple private IP addresses on the network.

The Internet Assigned Numbers Authority (IANA) has reserved the following three blocks of the IP address space for use on private networks that are not directly connected to the Internet:

- 10.0.0.0 – 10.255.255.255
- 172.16.0.0 – 172.31.255.255
- 192.168.0.0 – 192.168.255.255

In addition, the Automatic Private IP Addressing feature in all post-1998 Windows versions uses private IP addresses in the range of 169.254.0.0 to 169.254.255.255.

Routers and residential gateways that use NAT almost always assign addresses from these private ranges. Linksys routers, for instance, typically assign addresses starting with 192.168.1.x. The Internet Connection Sharing feature in Windows XP (as in previous versions of Windows) assigns private IP addresses in the 192.168.0.x range. If you're setting up a small business or a home network that will not be connected to the Internet, or that will be connected through a single proxy server, you can freely use these addresses without concern for conflicts. Just make sure that all the addresses on the network are in the same subnet.

To set up an alternate IP configuration, follow these steps:

1. From Control Panel, open the Network Connections folder and select the connection whose settings you want to change.

2. Click the Change Settings Of This Connection link in the Network Tasks pane, or right-click the connection icon and choose Properties from the shortcut menu.

3. From the list of installed network components, select Internet Protocol (TCP/IP) and then click the Properties button.

4. On the General tab of the Internet Protocol (TCP/IP) Properties dialog box, select Obtain An IP Address Automatically.

5. Click the Alternate Configuration tab and then select the User Configured option.

6. Enter the IP address, subnet mask, default gateway, and DNS servers for the alternate connection, as shown on the next page.

Chapter 28

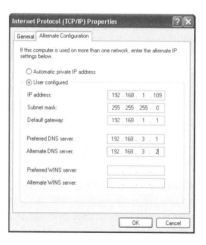

> **Note** You can safely ignore the fields that ask you to enter a preferred and alternate WINS server. WINS stands for Windows Internet Name Service, a name resolution system that maps a computer's NetBIOS name to an IP address. WINS servers are used on large corporate networks to allow domain servers to communicate with computers running older Microsoft operating systems, including Windows NT, Windows 95, Windows 98, and Windows Me. For virtually all home and small business networks, the WINS server details are unnecessary and irrelevant.

7 Click OK to save your changes. You do not need to restart after setting up an alternate configuration.

When you've configured an alternate IP configuration for a network connection, Windows XP looks first for a DHCP server to assign an IP address automatically. If no DHCP server is available, the system falls back to the static IP address defined on the Alternate IP Configuration tab.

Sharing an Internet Connection

To share an Internet connection safely on a small network, you have two options:

● **Install a router or residential gateway** This piece of hardware sits between your network and your Internet connection (usually an external DSL or cable modem, although you can also use a conventional modem in this configuration). To the outside world, the residential gateway appears to be a computer with its own IP address, although it's considerably more secure because it does not have any running programs or disk storage that can be attacked by a would-be intruder. This class of hardware typically uses network address translation (NAT) to assign private IP addresses to computers on your network. Because it's always on, any computer can access the Internet at any time through the gateway device.

> **Tip** **Insist on a UPnP device**
>
> If you're shopping for a router or residential gateway for your network, look carefully. Make sure you get a model that is certified as compatible with Windows XP. In particular, make certain it supports the UPnP standard, which allows Windows XP to configure programs like Windows Messenger and Remote Assistance to work seamlessly with the NAT features of the device.

- **Use Internet Connection Sharing (ICS)**   In this configuration, the computer with the active Internet connection acts as the ICS host computer and shares its Internet connection. All computers on your network route their Internet traffic through the ICS host computer. ICS is most effective with high-speed (cable or DSL) connections, although it works acceptably with dial-up Internet connections. The ICS host computer must have a second network adapter to share a broadband connection; and, of course, the shared connection is only available if the ICS host computer is turned on.

To configure ICS, use the Network Setup Wizard. Run it first on the ICS host, and then on each network computer where you plan to use the shared connection. ICS works as follows:

- The shared connection on the ICS host acquires an IP address from the Internet service provider.
- The wizard enables Windows Firewall on the shared connection.
- The connection to the local network from the ICS host uses the static IP address 192.168.0.1, configured with a subnet mask of 255.255.255.0.
- The Internet Connection Sharing service runs automatically on the ICS host.
- A DHCP allocator on the ICS host automatically assigns IP addresses to other computers on the network. The default range is 192.168.0.2 to 192.168.0.254, with a subnet mask of 255.255.255.0. A DNS proxy on the ICS host eliminates the need to specify DNS servers on other computers on the network.
- Autodial is enabled on the ICS host.

When you use a UPnP-compatible router or a computer running Internet Connection Sharing, Windows XP adds an icon for that device to the Network Connections folder, under the heading Internet Gateway. It also adds a device icon to the My Network Places folder. Double-clicking the connection icon opens a status dialog box such as the one shown on the next page, which displays statistics about the connection and gives you the option to shut down communications in the event of a security threat.

Chapter 28

Troubleshooting

Your shared Internet connection isn't working.

Any of the following circumstances can prevent ICS from working properly:

- **The Internet Connection Sharing service is not running.** From Control Panel, open the Administrative Tools folder, double-click the Services icon, and then check to see that the Status column alongside the Internet Connection Sharing service reads Started. If necessary, right-click the Service entry and choose Start or Restart from the shortcut menu.

- **The wrong network adapter is shared.** Run through the Network Setup Wizard again and confirm that you've selected the correct adapters.

- **The settings on other network computers are incorrect.** Computers running Windows 98, Windows Me, Windows 2000, or Windows XP should be able to connect to the Internet through an ICS host when configured to obtain an IP address automatically and obtain DNS servers automatically. Leave the default gateway field blank when configuring network settings. If necessary, rerun the Network Setup Wizard on the other computers. (Note that this wizard will not run on Windows 95 or Windows 3.1.)

Double-clicking the device icon in My Network Places opens the management interface for that device. If your router uses a Web-based configuration utility, for instance, this icon opens the Web browser and points it to the IP address and port configured for managing the router.

Note that the UPnP User Interface and the Internet Gateway Device Discovery and Control Client must both be installed for this feature to work properly. For a discussion of these networking services, see "Advanced Networking Components," page 994.

Chapter 29

Tweaking and Troubleshooting a Small Network

With Microsoft Windows XP, most simple networks of 10 computers or fewer work just fine. When you encounter network problems, however, the troubleshooting process can be tricky, because it's difficult to determine where the fault lies. In some cases, network problems are directly related to hardware, either on the local computer, elsewhere on your network, or at another stop on the connection between your computer and an Internet destination. But the problem is just as likely to be caused by a faulty configuration on your computer.

In this chapter, we explain how to identify and repair common network configuration problems, including TCP/IP address errors, improper subnet settings, and domain name server (DNS) problems. We also explain how to identify situations where a network is performing at less than its optimum speed, and we show you how to take advantage of a new feature in Windows XP to quickly and easily bridge two networks. Finally, we introduce some advanced networking components that are new to Windows XP.

Troubleshooting TCP/IP Problems

TCP/IP is the default communications protocol of the Internet; in Windows XP it's installed and configured automatically and cannot be removed. Most of the time, your TCP/IP connection should just work, without requiring any manual configuration. When you encounter problems with TCP/IP-based networks, such as an inability to connect with other computers on the same network or difficulty connecting to external Web sites, the problems may be TCP/IP-related. You'll need at least a basic understanding of how this protocol works before you can figure out which tool to use to uncover the root of the problem.

At Home with Windows XP

The techniques described in this chapter work identically in Windows XP Home Edition and Windows XP Professional.

Checking for Connection Problems

Anytime your network refuses to send and receive data properly, your first troubleshooting step should be to check for problems with the physical connection between the local computer and the rest of the network. Assuming your network connection uses the TCP/IP protocol, your most potent weapon is the Ping utility. When you use the Ping command with no parameters, Windows sends four echo datagrams, small Internet Control Message Protocol (ICMP) packets, to the address you specify. If the machine at the other end of the connection replies, you know that the network connection between the two points is alive.

> **Note** Where does the name *Ping* come from? Officially, it's short for Packet INternet Groper. However, it's more likely that this utility, which dates to the earliest versions of UNIX, was originally named after the sound a submarine's sonar system makes when it sends out pulses looking for objects in the sea. The "official" meaning was almost certainly made up after the fact.

To use the Ping command, open Command Prompt window (Cmd.exe) and type the command **ping *target_name*** (where *target_name* is an IP address or the name of another host machine). The return output looks something like this:

```
C:\>ping www.example.com
Pinging VENERA.ISI.EDU [128.9.176.32] with 32 bytes of data:
Reply from 128.9.176.32: bytes=32 time=94ms TTL=242
Reply from 128.9.176.32: bytes=32 time=76ms TTL=242
Request timed out.
Reply from 128.9.176.32: bytes=32 time=81ms TTL=242
Ping statistics for 128.9.176.32:
  Packets: Sent = 4, Received = 3, Lost = 1 (25% loss),
Approximate round trip times in milli-seconds:
  Minimum = 76ms, Maximum = 94ms, Average = 83ms
```

If all the packets you send come back properly in roughly the same time, your TCP/IP connection is fine and you can focus your troubleshooting efforts elsewhere. If some packets time out, the "Request timed out" message appears, as in the example above, indicating that your network connection is working, but that one or more hops between your computer and the target machine are experiencing problems. In that case, repeat the Ping test using the –n switch to send a larger number of packets; **ping –n 30 192.168.1.1**, for example, sends 30 packets to the computer or router at 192.168.1.1.

> **Note** The –n switch is case-sensitive; don't capitalize it.

A high rate of timeouts, also known as *packet loss*, usually means problems elsewhere on the network and not on the local machine. (To see the full assortment of switches available for the Ping command, type **ping** with no target specified.)

If every one of your packets returns with the message "Request timed out," the problem may be the TCP/IP connection on your computer or a glitch with another computer on that network. To narrow down the problem, follow these steps, in order, stopping at any point where you encounter an error:

1. Ping your own machine using either of the following commands:

    ```
    ping 127.0.0.1
    ping localhost
    ```

    This standard IP address corresponds to your computer. If you receive an error, then TCP/IP is not configured properly on your system. For fix-it details, see "Repairing Your TCP/IP Configuration," page 987.

2. Ping your computer's IP address.

3. Ping the IP address of another computer on your network.

4. Ping the IP address of your router or the default gateway on your network.

5. Ping the address of each DNS server on your network. (If you don't know these addresses, see the next section for details on how to discover them.)

6. Ping a known host outside your network. Well-known, high-traffic Web sites are ideal for this step.

7. Use the Pathping command to contact the same host you specified in step 6. This command combines the functionality of the Ping command with the Traceroute utility to identify intermediate destinations on the Internet between your computer and the specified host or server.

Note   **Choose your test site carefully**
In some cases, pinging an external Web site results in a string of "Request timed out" messages, even when you have no trouble reaching those sites. Don't be misled. Some popular sites, including Microsoft's home page, *http://www.microsoft.com*, block all ICMP traffic, including Ping packets, as a routine security measure. Try pinging several sites before concluding that your Internet connection is broken.

If either of the two final steps in this process fails, your problem may be caused by DNS problems, as described later in this chapter. (For details, see "Resolving DNS Issues," page 987.) To eliminate this possibility, ping the numeric IP address of a computer outside your network instead. (Of course, if you're having DNS problems, you may have a hard time finding an IP address to ping!) If you can ping a Web site using its IP address but not by using its name, DNS problems are indicated.

If you suspect that there's a problem on the Internet between your computer and a distant host or server, use the Traceroute utility (Tracert.exe) to pinpoint the problem. Like the Ping command, this utility works from a command line. You specify the target (a host name or IP address) using the syntax **tracert *target_name*** and the utility sends a series of packets out,

Chapter 29

measuring the time it takes to reach each "hop" along the route. Timeouts or unusually slow performance indicate a connectivity problem. If the response time from your network to the first hop is much higher than the other hops, you might have a problem with the connection to your ISP; in that case, a call to your ISP's support line is in order. Problems farther along in the traceroute might indicate congestion or hardware problems in distant parts of the Internet that are out of your ISP's hands and that might disappear when you check another URL that follows a different path through the Internet.

If your testing produces inconsistent results, rule out the possibility that a firewall program or network address translation (NAT) device (such as a router or residential gateway) is to blame. If you're using a third-party firewall program, disable it temporarily. Try bypassing your router and connecting directly to a broadband connection such as a DSL or cable modem. To see whether you're using the Windows Firewall, look in the Network Connections folder for a padlock icon and the word *Firewalled* on the connection icon in question. If you see these indicators, turn off Windows Firewall temporarily, using its Control Panel shortcut.

If the Ping test works with the firewall or NAT device out of the picture, you can rule out network problems and conclude that the firewall software or router is misconfigured. After you complete your testing, be sure to enable the firewall and router again!

Diagnosing IP Address Problems

On most networks, IP addresses are assigned automatically by Dynamic Host Configuration Protocol (DHCP) servers; in some cases, you need to use static IP addresses, which are fixed numeric addresses. Problems with DHCP servers or clients can cause network connections to stop working, as can incorrectly assigned static IP addresses.

Tip   Use these tools instead of Winipcfg

If you've recently switched to Windows XP from Windows 95, Windows 98, or Windows Me, you may be used to using the Winipcfg command to discover details about your IP connection and repair IP-related problems. That command is not available in Windows XP. To perform IP repairs, use the status dialog box from the Network Connections window. For detailed information about IP configuration, use the command-line based Ipconfig utility. Both techniques are described in this section.

To see details of your current IP configuration, follow these steps:

1   Open Control Panel and double-click Network Connections (click Network And Internet Connections if you're using Control Panel's Category view).

2   Double-click the icon for the connection about which you want more information. (Alternatively, you can select the icon and click the View Status Of This Connection link in the Network Tasks pane.)

3   Click the Support tab to see the currently assigned IP address, subnet mask, and default gateway for that connection, as in the example in Figure 29-1.

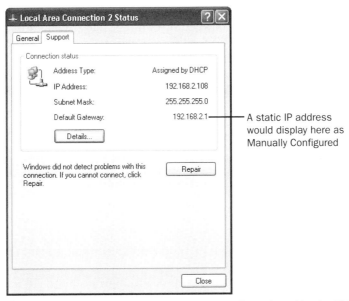

Figure 29-1. This IP address was automatically assigned by the DHCP server in a router.

If those details aren't sufficient—in particular, if you want to see information about DNS servers and when your DHCP address will expire and be renewed—click the Details button. Figure 29-2 shows the results.

Figure 29-2. This dialog box provides extra information about your network connection. Normally, DHCP addresses are renewed automatically at intervals shown here.

Chapter 29

Want still more information? Then fire up a Command Prompt window (Cmd.exe) and use the IP Configuration utility, Ipconfig.exe. Used without any parameters, typing **ipconfig** at a command prompt displays the DNS suffix, IP address, subnet mask, and default gateway of your primary network connection (identified as Local Area Connection in the Network Connections folder, unless you've renamed it). To see exhaustive details about every available network connection, enter **ipconfig /all**.

> **Note** To see a full list of options for the Ipconfig command, use the /? switch.

The actual IP address you see may help you solve connection problems:

- If the address is in the format 169.254.*x.y*, your computer is using Automatic Private IP Addressing (APIPA). This means your computer's DHCP client was unable to reach a DHCP server to be assigned an IP address. Check the connection to your network.

- If the address is in one of the blocks of IP addresses reserved for use on private networks (for details, see "Setting IP Addresses," page 971), make sure that another computer (an Internet Connection Sharing host) or a router or residential gateway is routing your Internet requests to a properly configured public IP address.

- If the address of your computer appears as 0.0.0.0, the network is either disconnected or the static IP address for the connection duplicates an address that already exists on the network.

- Make sure you're using the correct subnet mask for computers on your local network. Compare IP settings on the machine that's having problems with those on other computers on the network. The default gateway and subnet mask should be identical for all network computers. The first one, two, or three sets of numbers in the IP address for each machine should also be identical, depending on the subnet mask. A subnet mask of 255.255.255.0 means the first three IP address numbers of computers on your network must be identical—192.168.0.83 and 192.168.0.223, for instance, can communicate on a network using this subnet mask, but 192.168.1.101 will not be recognized as belonging to the network. Likewise, with a subnet mask of 255.255.0.0, the first two numbers in each address must match—172.16.2.34, 172.16.4.56, and 172.16.83.201 are all valid addresses on a subnet with this mask. In every case, the gateway machine must also be a member of the same subnet. (If you use a router, switch, or residential gateway for Internet access, the local address on that device must be part of the same subnet as the machines on your network.)

> **Note** Are you baffled by subnets and other related technical terms? For an excellent overview of these sometimes confusing topics, read Knowledge Base article 164015, "Understanding TCP/IP Addressing and Subnetting Basics."

Chapter 29

Repairing Your TCP/IP Configuration

If you suspect a problem with your TCP/IP configuration, try any or all of the following repair options:

- **Run the Network Setup Wizard again**   This option is especially useful if you've been tinkering with connection settings, or if you've installed a third-party utility that may have done so. Be sure to choose the correct option for your network configuration and enter the correct workgroup or domain name, as outlined in "Using the Network Setup Wizard," page 958.

- **Use the automated repair option**   Double-click the connection icon in the Network Connections folder and click the Repair button on the Support tab. Selecting this option has the same effect as typing the following commands from a command prompt:

  - **ipconfig /renew**   Automatically renews your IP address from a DHCP server

  - **arp –d**   Flushes the Address Resolution Protocol cache

  - **nbtstat –R**   Reloads the NetBIOS name cache

  - **ipconfig /flushdns**   Clears the DNS cache

  - **ipconfig /registerdns**   Registers the computer's name on the appropriate DNS server

- **Renew your IP address**   If you don't want to perform the full set of repairs, use the **ipconfig /renew** command to renew your IP address from the DHCP server.

- **Restore the base TCP/IP files**   Although you can't uninstall TCP/IP in Windows XP, you can reinstall all its components and reset registry keys to a clean state. To do so, type **netsh int ip reset resetlog.txt**. Note that this step is not as drastic as it sounds and will not tamper with your current network settings.

Resolving DNS Issues

The Domain Name System (DNS) is a crucial part of the Internet. (It's also at the heart of domains based on Windows 2000 Server and Windows Server 2003, a topic we touch on in Chapter 33, "Working with Windows Domains.") DNS servers translate host names (*http://www.microsoft.com*, for instance) into numeric IP addresses, so that packets can be routed properly over the Internet. If you can use the Ping command to reach a numeric address outside your network but are unable to browse Web sites by name, the problem is almost certainly related to your DNS configuration.

Chapter 29

Here are some questions to ask when you suspect DNS problems:

● **Do your TCP/IP settings point to the right DNS servers?**   Inspect the details of your IP configuration and compare the DNS servers listed there with those recommended by your Internet service provider. (You may need to call your ISP to get these details.)

Tip   Translate names to IP addresses and vice versa

The Nslookup command is a buried treasure in Windows XP. Use this command-line utility to quickly convert a fully qualified domain name to its IP address. You can tack on a host name to the end of the command line to identify a single address; type **nslookup ftp.microsoft.com**, for instance, to look up the IP address of Microsoft's FTP server. Or type **nslookup** to switch into interactive mode. From this prompt, you can enter any domain name to find its IP address. If you need more sophisticated lookup tools, you can find them with the help of any search engine. A good starting point is *http://www.dnsstuff.com*, which offers an impressive collection of online tools for looking up domains, IP addresses, and host names. The site also offers form-based utilities that can translate obfuscated URLs and dotted IP addresses, both of which are widely used by spammers to cover their online tracks.

● **Is your ISP experiencing DNS problems?**   A misconfigured DNS server (or one that's offline) can wreak havoc with your attempts to use the Internet. Try pinging each DNS server to see whether it's available. If your ISP has multiple DNS servers and you encounter problems accessing one server, remove that server from your TCP/IP configuration temporarily and use another one instead.

● **Have you installed any "Internet accelerator" utilities?**   Many such programs work by editing the Hosts file on your computer to match IP addresses and host (server) names. When Windows finds a host name in the Hosts file, it uses the IP address listed there and doesn't send the request to a DNS server. If the owner of the server changes its DNS records to point to a new IP address, your Hosts file will lead you to the wrong location.

Inside Out

Match machines and IP addresses quickly

A Hosts file can be useful on a mid-size network where all computers have static IP addresses. By entering computer names and IP addresses in a Hosts file, you eliminate the need to broadcast messages around the network looking for each machine. Instead, Windows finds the machine name and matching IP address in the Hosts file and goes straight to the correct address. To edit the Hosts file, use Notepad or another text editor. Open the Hosts file (it has no extension) in %SystemRoot%\System32\Drivers\Etc. The comments in this file explain its syntax and are very easy to follow.

If you suddenly and mysteriously lose the ability to connect to sites on the Internet, check to see whether you have more than one active network connection. This situation is most common if you've connected to a virtual private network and you also have a broadband Internet connection. In this case, the problem most likely occurs because the VPN connection thinks it is responsible for Internet access too. To fix this problem, follow these steps:

1. Open Control Panel, Network Connections, and click the icon for the active VPN connection.

2. In the Network Tasks pane, click Change Settings Of This Connection to open the properties dialog box for that connection.

3. On the Networking tab, choose Internet Protocol (TCP/IP) and then click the Properties button.

4. In the Internet Protocol (TCP/IP) Properties dialog box, click the Advanced button.

5. In the Advanced TCP/IP Settings dialog box, shown here, clear the Use Default Gateway On Remote Network check box.

6. Click OK and then close all dialog boxes to save your changes.

Temporary DNS problems can also be caused by the DNS cache, which Windows XP maintains for performance reasons. If you suddenly have trouble reaching a specific site on the Internet and you're convinced there's nothing wrong with the site, type this command to clear the DNS cache: **ipconfig /flushdns**.

Chapter 29

989

Fixing Problems with My Network Places

One of the most annoying problems with any network occurs when you open the My Network Places folder and discover that none of the other computers on your network are listed there. When this happens, don't despair. Many times the problem is simply caused by a delay in the Browser service, which is used by all 32-bit Windows versions to maintain a list of computers sharing resources on a workgroup (Windows 2000 and Windows Server 2003 domains use Active Directory instead of the Browser service). If you wait a few minutes, the missing computers will appear.

> **Tip** Allow time for network icons to appear
>
> The rules that govern which computers handle browsing duties on a network are complex and occasionally Byzantine. But as a general rule, on a local network, you shouldn't have to wait longer than 24 minutes, and usually no more than 12 minutes, for the icons for network computers to appear in the My Network Places folder. If your network contains some remote segments, these periods may stretch out to 36 or 48 minutes. If you've waited more than an hour, something is wrong. Want more details about how the Browser service works? Read Knowledge Base article 188001, "Description of the Microsoft Computer Browser Service."

If you can't wait, then use the UNC name or IP address of the other computer and connect directly. If the other computer is named Harpo, for instance, and the Shared Documents folder is shared using its default name, you can connect to it directly by typing **\\harpo\shareddocs** in the Run box.

The opposite problem occurs when you remove one or more computers from your network. When you open the My Network Places folder on one of the remaining computers, you may find one or more shortcuts that point to shared folders that are no longer present. If you find the clutter distracting, you can select the icon for any such shortcut and press Delete. (Note that you may experience a brief delay when attempting to delete shortcuts to unavailable locations.)

You can also prevent Windows XP from automatically adding new icons to the My Network Places folder. Normally, Windows XP searches for shared folders and printers on other networked computers and automatically adds all the shortcuts it finds to My Network Places. To prevent this behavior, open Windows Explorer and chooseTools, Folder Options. On the View tab, clear Automatically Search For Network Folders And Printers.

Even with automatic discovery disabled, Windows XP creates a shortcut in My Network Places when you connect manually to any shared resource. To disable this behavior, open Group Policy (**gpedit.msc**) and navigate to User Configuration\Administrative Templates\Desktop. Open the policy Do Not Add Shares Of Recently Opened Documents To My Network Places and change its setting to Enabled.

Network Troubleshooting Tools

Windows XP contains a huge assortment of utilities you can use to diagnose, monitor, and repair network connections. Most of them are included within Windows itself. A few more are available with the Windows Support Tools collection, which you can install by running the Setup program found in the \Support\Tools folder on the Windows XP CD (Home Edition and Professional). Table 29-1 lists all of the available utilities and summarizes how you can use them.

Table 29-1. Windows XP Network Utilities

Utility Name	What It's Used For
DHCP Server Locator Utility (Dhcploc.exe)	Displays a list of all available DHCP servers on the current subnet, so that you can resolve conflicts caused by the presence of multiple DHCP servers; part of Windows XP Support Tools
Get MAC Address (Getmac.exe)	Discovers the Media Access Control (MAC) address and lists associated network protocols for all network cards in a computer, either locally or across a network
Hostname (Hostname.exe)	Displays the host name of the current computer
IP Configuration Utility (Ipconfig.exe)	Displays all current TCP/IP network configuration values and refreshes DHCP and DNS settings
Name Server Lookup (Nslookup.exe)	Displays information about Domain Name System records for specific IP addresses and/or host names, so that you can troubleshoot DNS problems
Net services commands (Net.exe)	Performs a broad range of network tasks; type **net** with no parameters to see a full list of available command-line options
Netstat (Netstat.exe)	Displays active TCP connections, ports on which the computer is listening, Ethernet statistics, IP routing table, and IPv4/IPv6 statistics
Network Command Shell (Netsh.exe)	Displays or modifies the network configuration of a local or remote computer that is currently running; this command-line scripting utility has a huge number of options, which are fully detailed in Help
Network Connectivity Tester (Netdiag.exe)	Tests the status of your network connection and helps identify and isolate network problems; part of Windows XP Support Tools

Chapter 29

Table 29-1. **Windows XP Network Utilities**

Utility Name	What It's Used For
Network Monitor Capture Utility (Netcap.exe)	"Sniffs" packets on a network (using Network Monitor Driver) and writes the information to a log file so that you can identify suspicious or unauthorized traffic; part of Windows XP Support Tools
NWLink (IPX) Source Routing Application (Ipxroute.exe)	Displays and modifies information about the routing tables used for packets sent by the IPX protocol
PathPing (Pathping.exe)	Combines functions of Traceroute and Ping to identify problems at a router or network link
PPTP Ping utilities (Pptpclnt.exe, Pptpsrv.exe)	Tests the path between virtual private network (VPN) clients and servers to verify that correct ports and protocols are in use; part of Windows XP Support Tools
TCP/IP NetBIOS Information (Nbtstat.exe)	Displays statistics for NetBIOS over TCP/IP (NetBT) protocol, NetBIOS name tables for both the local computer and remote computers, and the NetBIOS name cache
TCP/IP Ping (Ping.exe)	Verifies IP-level connectivity to another Internet address by sending ICMP packets and measuring response time in milliseconds
TCP/IP Route (Route.exe)	Displays and modifies entries in the local IP routing table
TCP/IP Traceroute (Tracert.exe)	Determines the path to an Internet address and lists the time required to reach each hop; useful for troubleshooting connectivity problems on specific network segments

Fine-Tuning Network Performance

Is your network running more slowly than it should? A fast, easy way to measure the performance of all active network connections is to use the Networking tab in Windows Task Manager. To view current networking statistics, open Windows Task Manager by pressing Ctrl+Alt+Delete. (If the Welcome screen is disabled, or if your computer is joined to a domain, click the Task Manager button in the Windows Security dialog box, or use the Ctrl+Shift+Esc shortcut instead.)

For more information about how to use Windows Task Manager, see "Detecting Common Performance Bottlenecks," page 406.

In the example shown here, two network connections are active, so two graphs appear, one for each connection. Note that neither connection is even close to saturating available network bandwidth.

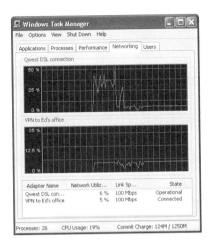

> **Tip** **Rename network connections for clarity**
>
> In the Network Connections folder, Windows automatically creates generic names for every connection—Local Area Connection, for instance. Get in the habit of renaming all connections in this folder with descriptive names. The names you assign will appear in Windows Task Manager graphs, notification area icons, status dialog boxes, and any other place where you can expect to see information about connections. Descriptive names make it much easier to troubleshoot, especially when you have multiple connections active.

On most networks, the speed of the connection to the Internet is the limiting factor for network performance. Plain Ethernet connections, with a theoretical maximum transfer speed of 10 megabits per second, run 3 to 10 times faster than even the fastest cable or DSL connections. You might see excessive network utilization on the local network connection for an Internet Connection Sharing host machine when several other computers on the network are transferring large files such as video clips directly from that machine and not from the network. Wireless connections that are having difficulty reaching a base station may also display performance problems as they automatically throttle down to lower connection speeds. Again, this slowdown will be most obvious when trying to transfer large files between two computers on the network.

Chapter 29

993

Caution In theory, at least, you may be able to improve the performance of a TCP/IP-based network by tweaking specific settings in the registry. The TCP Receive Window (RWIN) and Maximum Transmission Unit (MTU) settings control technical details of how your TCP/IP connection transfers and receives packets. The Internet is awash with sites that claim to offer helpful advice and utilities that you can use to reset these values. Beware! Most of these articles are based on TCP/IP settings from previous Windows versions and do not apply to Windows XP, which does a generally good job of configuring connections properly. In fact, tweaking settings without understanding their consequences is a near-certain route to slower performance, and it may result in connection problems when your tweaked packets hit routers and other connection points on the Internet that can't handle them. If you feel compelled to experiment, set a System Restore checkpoint first, and read the definitive and exhaustive FAQ at the DSL Reports site, *http://www.dslreports.com/faq/tweaks*, before you fire up Registry Editor.

Advanced Networking Components

If you poke around in the Windows Components Wizard (available via Control Panel's Add Or Remove Programs option), you'll find a well-hidden Networking Services category that includes five options. These options are a mixed bag, consisting of two components that are useful to just about anyone with a home network and three that are appropriate only in highly specialized circumstances. The following inventory should help you decide which of these options might be useful on your network:

- **Internet Gateway Device Discovery and Control Client** This component, which is the only one of these five components installed by default in Service Pack 1 and later, allows Windows to detect the presence of Internet connection sharing hardware and software, including routers and computers running Internet Connection Sharing (ICS). For the Internet gateway device to be detected, it must broadcast its presence using Simple Service Discovery Protocol (SSDP).

- **Peer-to-Peer** This option installs specialized services designed for use with applications that use Microsoft's Peer-to-Peer Infrastructure. Despite its confusing name, this option has nothing to do with the conventional definition of a peer-to-peer network, which is a small network without a dedicated server. Rather, it enables a new class of decentralized collaborative applications that share computing resources (such as CPUs and memory), as opposed to merely allowing access to files and printers over a network. With this option installed, Windows Firewall is configured to allow Peer-to-Peer Networking connections.

- **RIP Listener** This option listens for route updates sent by routers that use the Routing Information Protocol version 1 (RIPv1). This service is not used in home or small business networks and would rarely be used in enterprise networks, except on servers.

- **Simple TCP/IP Services** This option installs five protocols—Character Generator, Daytime, Discard, Echo, and Quote of the Day—that are provided for compatibility

Chapter 29

with older UNIX-based networks. They are not needed on home and small business networks.

- **UPnP User Interface**   This option displays icons in My Network Places for UPnP devices, such as routers and network printers, that are detected on the network. Installing this option opens the required Windows Firewall ports for the UPnP service. The information provided by a UPnP device allows the operating system to manage or configure that device. Note that UPnP was formerly known as Universal Plug and Play; the change in name reflects the fact that there is no connection to the Plug and Play capabilities of Windows.

Bridging Two Networks

As we noted in Chapter 28, "Setting Up a Small Network," Windows XP supports a variety of network media types, including Ethernet, Home Phoneline Networking, and wireless connections. In some cases, your home or small business network may consist of two or more different types of physical networks. For instance, you might have two desktop computers (we'll call them A and B) in your upstairs den connected to an Ethernet hub, with Computer A also serving as your Internet Connection Sharing host. In the basement, you have another computer (call it C) that you want to add to the network. Running coaxial cable to that distant location is impractical, and it's too far away for a reliable wireless connection. You do have a phone jack in that location, however, so you've installed a phone-line network adapter and plugged in to that jack. Upstairs, you've installed a phone-line adapter in Computer B.

You now have two networks. Computer A and Computer B can communicate easily, and Computer B and Computer C can do so as well. But Computer A and Computer C have no way to reach each other, which means Computer C is cut off from the Internet as well. How do you bring all three computers into the same network? That's where Windows XP has a big edge over previous Windows versions. Instead of requiring you to install a hardware router and enable IP packet forwarding (a messy and complicated procedure), you can create a network bridge, which brings the two networks together seamlessly and creates a virtual connection between the separate network segments. In this example, you would bridge the two network connections on Computer B. In this configuration, Computer C could communicate directly with Computer A, even sharing its Internet connection.

> **Caution**   In most home and small business setups, a network bridge is unnecessary and you should use Internet Connection Sharing or a router or residential gateway instead. If you plug a wireless access point into a router, for example, instead of hooking it directly to a broadband connection, it will join the other machines on your Ethernet network. Turn off network address translation on the wireless access point, and allow each networked computer equipped with a wireless adapter to receive its IP address directly from the router's DHCP server. This configuration requires that you dive into the access point's setup software and set some advanced options, but the results are worth it from a security and ease-of-administration point of view.

Chapter 29

Although the steps to create a bridge are simple, the concepts behind it are potentially confusing. Here's what you need to know:

- You must be logged on as an Administrator to create a network bridge.
- You can create a bridge using any two Ethernet, IEEE-1394, or Ethernet-compatible wireless adapters. You cannot add a VPN connection, a dial-up Internet connection, or a direct cable connection to a network bridge.
- Any adapter that has Internet Connection Sharing or Windows Firewall enabled cannot be added to the network bridge.
- Although it's technically possible, you should never bridge a connection that has a public Internet address with one that connects to a private network. In that configuration, you should use Internet Connection Sharing instead.
- When you use a network bridge, the machine that has the bridge enabled must be turned on to allow other computers to communicate across the virtual network. If you shut down that computer, you also shut down the bridge.

In versions of Windows XP before Service Pack 2, the Network Setup Wizard attempted to bridge connections automatically when it detected two or more available connections. This capability all too often bridged multiple connections inappropriately; as a result, a change in Service Pack 2 blocks the Network Setup Wizard from bridging connections automatically.

To create a bridge manually, select the first connection, hold down Ctrl, and then select the second connection. Right-click and choose Bridge Connections from the shortcut menu.

After you create the bridge, a new device, Network Bridge, appears in the Network Connections folder, as shown here.

After you create the bridge, the settings for each individual connection are no longer available. To view details of your network configuration, double-click the Network Bridge icon and click the Support tab on the Network Bridge Status dialog box.To change details of the bridged connection, right-click the Network Bridge icon and choose Properties from the shortcut menu. The resulting dialog box, shown in Figure 29-3, lets you adjust configuration details for individual adapters or configure IP settings for the bridged connection.

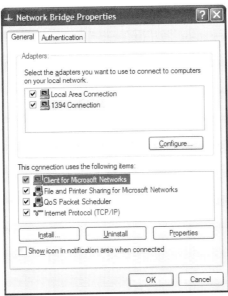

Figure 29-3. To remove adapters from the network bridge, clear the appropriate check boxes in the Adapters section of this dialog box.

You can have only one network bridge on a single computer, although you can, in theory, have as many as 68 network adapters joined in a bridge. To add or remove network adapters from the bridge, right-click the connection icon in the Network Connections window and choose Add To Bridge or Remove From Bridge. If you decide you no longer want to use the network bridge, you can remove it by right-clicking the Network Bridge icon and choosing Delete from the shortcut menu.

Chapter 29

997

Chapter 30

Managing Shared Folders and Printers

By sharing your computer's resources, such as its folders and printers, you let other people on your network use these resources. With Microsoft Windows XP, using network resources and sharing your own resources with other network users is almost as simple and straightforward as using your own computer's resources. Browsing a network folder is just like browsing a folder on your own hard disk. Sending a document to a network printer is just like printing at your own computer.

At Home with Windows XP

Because Windows XP Home Edition supports only Simple File Sharing, some of the material in this chapter will be useful only to users of Windows XP Professional. In particular, Home Edition users might want to skip over the section "Managing Shared Folders" (page 1013), which describes the Shared Folders console—a tool that is of limited utility under Simple File Sharing.

Access to folders shared by other network users is less convenient in Home Edition than in Windows XP Professional, because Home Edition is unable to retain network logon credentials. An effective and not-too-onerous workaround for this limitation is described in the Inside Out sidebar on page 1022.

Windows provides support for networks from a number of vendors and supports the simultaneous use of multiple networking protocols. This means that, assuming your network is set up properly, you should be able to work successfully in a heterogeneous network environment, sharing and accessing resources on computers running Windows XP, Windows 2000, Windows NT, Windows Me, Windows 98, Windows 95, Windows for Workgroups, NetWare, and other operating systems.

Windows XP puts a new wrapper on the sophisticated security settings for resource sharing that have been an integral—and often confusing—part of Windows 2000 and its predecessor, Windows NT. This wrapper, called Simple File Sharing, makes it easy to implement security appropriate for computers shared by multiple users and for many small network workgroups.

This chapter covers the full gamut of sharing options: from the simplicity of Simple File Sharing (select one check box and immediately other network users can view and use files on your computer), to the nitty-gritty details of setting access permissions on a printer, to the arcane command-line tools that let you control shares from a batch program. It's all here.

Introducing Windows XP Sharing and Security Models

Windows XP offers two distinctly different sharing models:

- **Simple File Sharing**   With Simple File Sharing, sharing folders and printers is easy, but your configuration options are limited. For example, sharing a folder in this model requires selecting a single check box, whereupon Windows XP sets appropriate shared resource permissions and NTFS file permissions. But a share created this way is available to all network users; you can't selectively set permissions for different users. With Simple File Sharing, Windows uses the Guest account for all network logons.

- **Classic sharing**   The classic sharing model is similar to the one employed by Windows 2000. When you share a folder, you must set appropriate shared resource permissions and NTFS file permissions to control the folder's use. But you can set varying permissions for individual users or groups (allowing full control to some, read-only access to some, and locking out others altogether, for example). You can also limit the number of simultaneous connections. This additional flexibility comes at the cost of complexity, however. Besides understanding permissions and how to set them, you'll need to set up appropriate user accounts on each computer that allows network access.

Windows XP Home Edition uses Simple File Sharing exclusively. Windows XP Professional can use either Simple File Sharing or classic sharing. To switch between these models, in Control Panel, open Folder Options (in the Appearance And Themes category), click the View tab, and either select or clear the Use Simple File Sharing (Recommended) check box (the last item in the Advanced Settings list).

> **Note**   If your computer is joined to a domain, it always uses the classic sharing model, regardless of your setting in Folder Options.

A Third Model: Share-Level Access in Windows 95/98/Me

If you shared folders or printers in Windows 95/98/Me, you might be familiar with a third sharing model. When not joined to a domain, those operating systems use *share-level access control*. With this type of access control, passwords (one for read-only access and one for full access) are assigned to each shared resource. When a network user tries to use a shared resource, Windows requests a password. Which password the user enters—the full control password, the read-only password, or an incorrect password—determines the user's level of access to the share. Windows makes no attempt to determine who the user is; therefore, anyone on the network who obtains (or guesses) the password has access to the share.

Windows XP, by contrast, always uses *user-level access control*, which means each shared resource allows access only by specified user accounts. To gain access to a shared resource over the network, a user must log on using an account that has access to the share.

You cannot set a password for a particular folder or printer in Windows XP; all access is controlled by permissions granted to specified users.

For more information about the two sharing models in Windows XP, see "Simple File Sharing vs. Windows 2000–Style Sharing," page 230.

Sharing a Folder over a Network

By sharing a folder with other network users, you enable them to access the folder (and the files it contains) directly from their own desktop. Gone are the days of "sneakernet"—copying files to a floppy disk and carrying it over to another computer. To create a shared folder, you must be logged on as a member of the Administrators, Power Users, or Server Operators group. (After a folder has been shared, however, the share is available to network users no matter who is logged on to your computer—or even when nobody is logged on.)

Enabling File Sharing

Sharing is disabled on a clean installation of Windows XP. That's because sharing in a workgroup environment relies on the Guest account, which is disabled by default. The easiest way to configure your computer to share folders, files, and printers is to run the Network Setup Wizard. The Network Setup Wizard also ensures that computers in your network share the same workgroup name; sets up a shared, firewall-protected Internet connection; and attends to other details.

Chapter 30

For information about the Network Setup Wizard, see "Using the Network Setup Wizard," page 958.

If you haven't yet run the Network Setup Wizard, when you right-click a folder that you want to share and choose Sharing And Security, you're likely to see a dialog box similar to the one shown in Figure 30-1. (If the Network Sharing And Security box doesn't look like the one in the figure, sharing is already enabled.)

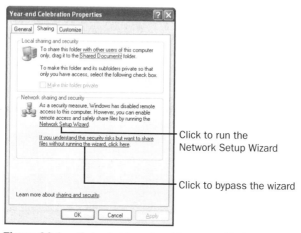

Click to run the
Network Setup Wizard

Click to bypass the wizard

Figure 30-1. If sharing hasn't yet been enabled, you'll see a dialog box like this when you try to share a folder.

You might be curious about the link that offers to bypass the wizard. Clicking it displays a dialog box similar to the one shown in Figure 30-2. Like the one before, this dialog box implores you to use the Network Setup Wizard. But if you've already configured your network so that computers are visible to each other, set up your Internet connection, and so on, you can safely choose the second option, Just Enable File Sharing.

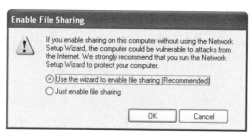

Figure 30-2. This dialog box offers another chance to run the Network Setup Wizard.

Note If the Sharing tab on your computer doesn't resemble the one shown in Figure 30-1 and the properties dialog box also has a Security tab, Simple File Sharing is not enabled on your computer. If your computer is not joined to a domain, you can enable Simple File Sharing simply by visiting the View tab in Folder Options. If you don't plan to use Simple File Sharing, skip ahead to "Restricting Access to Network Shares," page 1007.

Choosing the Just Enable File Sharing option does just two things:

- It enables the Guest account. If you prefer, you can do this manually by typing **net user guest/active:yes** at a command prompt. (Note that enabling the Guest account does not add it to the Welcome screen. To do that, you must open User Accounts in Control Panel and turn on the Guest account. This process enables Guest—if it's not already enabled—*and* removes the Deny Logon Locally user right for the Guest account.)

- It removes the Guest account from the list of accounts with the Deny Access To This Computer From The Network user right. To do this manually, you need to navigate to Local Policies\User Rights Assignment in Local Security Settings (Secpol.msc).

Note There's really no reason to perform these tasks manually. However, the online help doesn't explain what's happening "under the hood," and some users are curious (or concerned) about what changes are being made to their system.

What are the security risks that the dialog boxes shown in Figures 30-1 and 30-2 hint at? If you don't secure your Internet connection, someone on the Internet could gain access to your shared folders, because the Guest account (and the folders it has access to) is available to anybody who finds his or her way into the network. The Network Setup Wizard secures the Internet connection by configuring Internet Connection Sharing and Windows Firewall (if the latter is not already enabled).

Note If you don't plan to use Simple File Sharing and you plan to create accounts on each computer for users who need access to shared network folders, you don't need to enable sharing in the manner described in this section. In fact, by *not* enabling the Guest account, you can create a more secure environment in which only users you designate can access your computer's shared resources. Specifically, if you don't enable sharing as described here, users on other computers must use an account that has the same name and password (the password cannot be blank) as an account on your computer. For more information, see "Restricting Access to Network Shares," page 1007.

Chapter 30

Troubleshooting

A folder's properties dialog box doesn't have a Sharing tab.

If the folder's properties dialog box doesn't have a Sharing tab, be sure your system is set up for sharing. First, check the properties dialog box for the network connection, and be sure that File And Printer Sharing For Microsoft Networks is installed and selected. (For more information, see "Configuring a Default Network Connection," page 958.) Then use the Services tool (right-click My Computer, choose Manage from the shortcut menu, expand Services And Applications, and click Services), and make sure that the Server service is started.

Using the Guest Account for Simple Sharing

The easiest way to set up sharing is with Simple File Sharing enabled. You can share any drive or any folder except Program Files and Windows. (You can share subfolders of these system folders, however.) To share a folder or drive, follow these steps:

1 In Windows Explorer, display the icon for the folder or drive you want to share.

2 Right-click the icon and choose Sharing And Security.

If you're sharing a drive, you'll see a dialog box like the one shown on the next page.

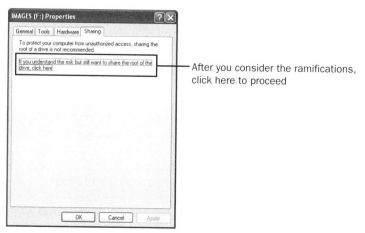

After you consider the ramifications, click here to proceed

Be aware that sharing a drive shares not just its root folder, but all its subfolders as well; everything on the drive is available. And because Simple File Sharing allows any network user to access your shared resources, this opens the full content of your shared drive to anyone on your network. (If the drive is formatted as an NTFS volume, NTFS permissions might be configured to restrict Guest access to some folders, however.) In general, you're better off sharing folders instead of drives; you're exposing fewer of your files to others. However, in certain situations—with a CD-ROM drive or a drive dedicated to music files, for example—you might want to provide such unlimited access. If that's the case, go ahead and click the link in this dialog box.

3 In the Network Sharing And Security box, on the Sharing tab, select Share This Folder On The Network.

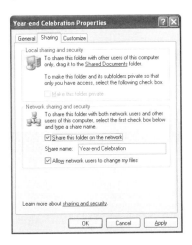

4 Specify a name for the shared resource in the Share Name box. (This is the name that network users see when they browse to your shared folder.) Windows proposes the name of the folder or, for a drive, the volume name and drive letter. Making a change here affects only the name visible on the network; it doesn't change the name of the folder on your computer.

5 If you want to allow network users to create or modify files in your shared folder and its subfolders (subject to the limitation imposed on the Guest account), select Allow Network Users To Change My Files. By default, Windows leaves this check box clear, which means network users can view files and folders in your shared folder but not create or modify them.

When you complete these steps, all network users will be able to find your shared folder in their My Network Places folder (if automatic discovery of network places is disabled, they'll need to browse to the shared folder), view its contents, and—unless you cleared the last check box—change its contents. Regardless of how they're logged onto their own computer, your computer authenticates network users as if they were using the Guest account. Therefore, within the folders you share over the network, network users have the same privileges as those granted to someone logging on locally as Guest.

> **Tip** Hide a shared folder from casual browsers
>
> If you append a dollar sign to the share name (for example, *Elopement$*), the folder is not visible to users who browse the network with My Network Places or Windows Explorer. Users whom you've entrusted with the name of your shared folder can still connect to it by typing its name—including the dollar sign—anywhere network paths are accepted, such as the Address bar, the Add Network Place Wizard, the Map Network Drive dialog box, and so on.
>
> Note, however, that hiding share names that end with a dollar sign is a function of the client computer, not the server. (In this context, *server* means the computer that has the shared folder.) All versions of Windows hide such shares, but if your network includes Apple Macintosh or Linux computers, users on those computers can view the "hidden" shares. Therefore, you can't rely on this method to completely secure your sensitive shared data; you must also set permissions appropriately.

Behind the scenes, here's what Windows does when you share a folder with Simple File Sharing enabled:

- It creates a share and grants shared resource permission to the built-in Everyone group. (The Guest account is a member of the Everyone group.) Depending on the choice you make in the Allow Network Users To Change My Files check box, Windows grants Read permission (if the check box is not selected) or Full Control permission to the Everyone group.

- If the shared folder is on an NTFS-formatted drive, Windows adds an entry for the Everyone group to the folder's access control list (ACL). If Allow Network UsersTo Change My Files is not selected, the ACL allows Read & Execute permission; otherwise, the ACL allows Modify permission. Be aware that, by default, NTFS permissions are inherited by child objects (that is, files and folders in the shared folder, as well as the files and folders they contain).

For information about shared resource permissions vs. NTFS permissions, see "How Shared Resource Permissions and NTFS Permissions Work Together," on page 1008. For information about inheritance, see "Applying Permissions to Subfolders Through Inheritance," page 292.

With Simple File Sharing, sharing is indeed simple and convenient. What Simple File Sharing lacks, however, is the ability to restrict access to certain network users or to impose different restrictions on different users. To do that, you must use classic sharing, as described in the next section.

> **Note** The simple act of enabling sharing makes your computer's Shared Documents folder available on the network, regardless of which other folder you originally intended to share. It appears on other computers as SharedDocs, and all network users can view, modify, and add files in this folder.

Restricting Access to Network Shares

Compared with Simple File Sharing, the classic sharing model provides a quantum leap in control over what you allow other users to do with your resources—and in complexity. Classic sharing allows you to control who can access each resource (instead of allowing access to everyone on the network) and what permissions they have (instead of allowing the same access—modify or read-only—to everyone who connects over the network).

> **Tip** An alternative way to set different permissions for administrators and limited users
> Windows provides another way to set different permissions for different users: the Create Shared Folder Wizard, which you open from the Shared Folders snap-in. For details, see "Creating a New Share Using the Shared Folders Snap-In," page 1015.

To enable classic sharing, in Control Panel, open Folder Options (in the Appearance And Themes category), click the View tab, and clear the Use Simple File Sharing (Recommended) check box.

Classic sharing imposes three fundamental changes in the way you control network access:

- You specify shared resource permissions on a per-user basis. (Simple File Sharing, you'll recall, sets shared resource permissions only for the Everyone group.)
- If the shared folder is on an NTFS volume, you specify ACLs for each object in the share. (Simple File Sharing sets NTFS permissions only for the Everyone group, and hides the ability to view or modify ACLs.)
- Users who connect to your computer over the network are not automatically authenticated as Guest. If a network user's user name and nonblank password matches the user name and password of an account on your computer, Windows authenticates the user as the local account. If the network user's name and password do not match a local account, he or she is authenticated as Guest.

How Shared Resource Permissions and NTFS Permissions Work Together

The implementation of shared resource permissions and NTFS permissions is confusingly similar, but it's important to recognize that these are two separate levels of access control. Only connections that successfully pass through both gates are granted access.

Shared resource permissions control *network* access to a particular resource. Shared resource permissions do not affect users who log on locally. You set shared resource permissions on the Sharing tab of a folder's properties dialog box.

NTFS permissions apply to folders and files on an NTFS-formatted drive. They provide extremely granular control over an object. For each user to whom you want to grant access, you can specify exactly what they're allowed to do: run programs, view folder contents, create new files, change existing files, and so on. You set NTFS permissions on the Security tab of the properties dialog box for a folder or file. For more information, see "Controlling Access with NTFS Permissions," page 282.

It's important to recognize that the two types of permissions are combined in the most restrictive way. If, for example, a user is granted Read permission on the network share, it doesn't matter whether the account has Full Control NTFS permissions on the same folder; the user gets only read access when connecting over the network. In effect, the two sets of permissions act in tandem as "gatekeepers" that winnow out incoming network connections. An account that attempts to connect over the network is examined first by the shared resource permissions gatekeeper. The account is either bounced out on its caboodle or allowed to enter with certain permissions. It's then confronted by the NTFS permissions gatekeeper, which might strip away (but not add to) some or all of the permissions granted at the first doorway.

In determining the effective permission for a particular account, you must also consider the effect of group membership. Permissions are cumulative; an account that is a member of one or more groups is granted all the permissions granted explicitly to the account as well as all permissions granted to each group of which it's a member. The only exception to this rule is Deny permissions, which take precedence over any conflicting Allow permissions. For more information, see "Testing the Effect of Permissions," page 295.

Preparing for Classic Security: Setting Up User Accounts

If the computers in your network are set up as a workgroup (that is, they're not joined to a domain), each computer maintains its own security database of user accounts. By contrast, in a domain environment, information about global user accounts is stored on a domain controller. All computers in the domain refer to the domain controller when they need account information. To secure resources with either type of setup, you create user accounts; you then give those accounts permission to use specific resources. The difference is that in a workgroup, you must create user accounts on each computer instead of doing it once on a server.

On each computer in a workgroup, add a user account for each user who needs access to the computer's shared resources. If you use the same user name and password for each user on every computer on the network, users won't have to log on to each machine individually. Logging on to their local machine allows them to access all the resources for which they have permission.

Follow these steps to add a user account:

1 In Control Panel, open User Accounts.

2 Click Create A New Account.

3 When prompted, enter a user name and then create an account.

4 After the account is created, double-click it and click Create A Password to specify a password for the account.

For each account you create, the user name and password must be identical on all computers.

Note Accounts that you intend to use for network access to shared folders must have a password. Except for the Guest account, Windows security prohibits network access by accounts with a blank password.

For more information about user accounts, see "Working with User Accounts," page 232.

Sharing a Folder Using Classic Security

Provided you are logged on as a member of the Administrators, Power Users, or Server Operators group, you can share folders on your own system with other users on your network.

Tip   Set NTFS permissions first
If you're sharing a folder on an NTFS drive, you should set the NTFS permissions as you want them *before* you share the folder. That way, security restrictions are in place before you make the folder available on the network.

To share a folder or drive, follow these steps:

1 In Windows Explorer, display the icon for the folder or drive you want to share.

2 Right-click the icon and choose Sharing And Security from the shortcut menu.

This takes you to the Sharing tab of the folder's properties dialog box, as shown in Figure 30-3.

Figure 30-3.   To share a folder, choose the Sharing And Security command from the folder's shortcut menu.

3   Select the Share This Folder option.

4   Accept or change the proposed share name.

> **Note**   If the folder is already shared, click New Share and then type the share name. Local drives always have a default administrative share whose share name consists of the drive letter and a dollar sign (for example, *C$*). This share name is not visible to others, and you can't set permissions for the default share—so you'll want to create a new share.

The share name is the name that other users will see in their own My Network Places folders. Windows initially proposes to use the folder's name as its share name. That's usually a good choice, but you're not obligated to accept it. If you already have a shared folder with that name, you'll need to pick a different name.

5   Type a description of the folder's contents into the Comment field.

Other users will see this description when they inspect the folder's properties dialog box in their My Network Places folder (or use Details view).

6   To limit the number of users who can connect to the shared folder concurrently, select Allow This Number Of Users and then specify a number.

If network traffic seriously impacts your system's responsiveness, you might want to take advantage of this option. The default choice, Maximum Allowed, permits up to 10 concurrent users. (If you need to share a folder with more than 10 users at once, you must use a server version of Windows.)

For information about the Caching button in a folder's Properties dialog box, see "Setting Caching Options on the Server," page 789.

Assigning Permissions to a Shared Folder

The default shared resource permission associated with a new share is Full Control to Everyone. That means that anyone on your network can do whatever they want to your files, including delete them. (If the shared folder resides on an NTFS volume, individual folders and files can have their own access restrictions, however.) You can place limits on what particular users or groups of users can do with your shared files by clicking the Permissions button in the dialog box shown in Figure 30-3. Then you'll see the permissions dialog box, shown in Figure 30-4.

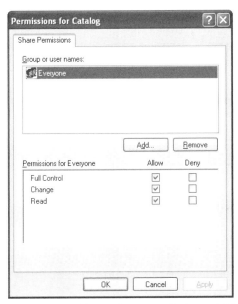

Figure 30-4. To set share permissions, right-click the shared folder in Windows Explorer and choose Sharing And Security. Then click Permissions.

Caution When you share a folder, you also make that folder's subfolders available on the network. If the access permissions you set for the folder aren't appropriate for any of its subfolders, either reconsider your choice of access permissions or restructure your folders to avoid the problem.

Follow these steps to view or set permissions:

1   In the Group Or User Names list, select the name of the user or group you want to manage.

The shared resource permissions for the selected user or group appear below in the permissions list.

2   Select Allow, Deny, or neither for each access control entry:

- ■ **Full Control**   Allows users to create, read, write, rename, and delete files in the folder and its subfolders. In addition, users can change permissions and take ownership of files on NTFS volumes.

- ■ **Change**   Allows users to read, write, rename, and delete files in the folder and its subfolders, but not create new files.

- ■ **Read**   Allows users to read files but not write to them or delete them.

If you select neither Allow nor Deny, it is still possible that the user or group can inherit the permission through membership in another group that has the permission. If the user or group doesn't belong to another such group, the user or group is implicitly denied permission.

Note   To remove a name from the Group Or User Names list, select it and click Remove. To add a name to the list, click Add to open the Select Users Or Groups dialog box, where you can enter the names of the users and groups you want to add. For more information about this dialog box, see "Applying Advanced Security Settings," page 285.

Tip   Disable Guest access to a shared folder

Setting up a share grants permission to the built-in Everyone group by default. The Guest account is included in Everyone. And because Windows authenticates network users who don't have an account on the local computer as Guest, that means that anyone on your network has access to a share. If you want to exclude anyone who does not have a user account on your computer, on the Share Permissions tab, select Everyone and click Remove. Then click Add, type **Authenticated Users**, and click OK. (The built-in Authenticated Users group does not include the Guest account.) Back on the Share Permissions tab, choose Authenticated Users and then select the Allow check box for Full Control. Note that shared resource permissions apply only when the folder (and its files and subfolders) are accessed over a network. They don't protect files or folders when opened locally from the computer on which they reside. If the folder you're sharing is on an NTFS volume, the NTFS permissions protect the files locally, and they also apply to network users.

For information about NTFS permissions, see "Controlling Access with NTFS Permissions," page 282.

Caution Files and folders that are created in a shared folder on an NTFS drive while Simple File Sharing is enabled are owned by the local Guest account. Ownership of files doesn't change when you disable or enable Simple File Sharing. Be aware that, even if you change to classic sharing and impose tighter security on your shared folders, users who log on as Guest (locally or remotely) continue to have full control over files that were created by *any* remote user while Simple File Sharing was enabled (assuming they still have access to the shared folder). To remedy this situation, take ownership of the folder and its contents, and remove Everyone from the ACLs of the folder and its contents.

Managing Shared Folders

Although you can manage your shared folders from Windows Explorer, the Shared Folders snap-in for Microsoft Management Console (MMC) provides a more centralized approach. With this snap-in, you can manage all the shared folders on your computer.

Start the Shared Folders snap-in by opening Computer Management (right-click My Computer and choose Manage) and then navigating to System Tools\Shared Folders. Figure 30-5 shows the Shared Folders snap-in.

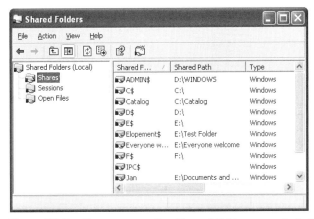

Figure 30-5. You can open the Shared Folders snap-in in its own console window—without all the clutter of Computer Management—by typing **fsmgmt.msc** at a command prompt.

> **Note** To use the Shared Folders snap-in, you must be a member of the Administrators or Power Users group. And to use it for anything other than merely viewing shares, sessions, and open files, you must have Simple File Sharing disabled (which means that Shared Folders is of limited use to users of Windows XP Home Edition).

Viewing and Changing Share Properties

When you open the Shared Folders snap-in, all the shared folders on your computer are visible in the Shares folder. You can modify the properties of any folder by right-clicking it and choosing Properties. The associated properties dialog box appears, as shown in Figure 30-6.

Figure 30-6. Choose Properties in the Shared Folders snap-in to open a dialog box like this.

Note that if you right-click a shared folder in Windows Explorer while Simple File Sharing is disabled, you'll see controls nearly identical to the ones shown in Figure 30-3. The Permissions button shown in Figure 30-3 serves the same purpose as the Share Permissions tab shown in Figure 30-6.

Chapter 30

Understanding Administrative Shares

Some of the shares you see in the Shared Folders list are created by the operating system. Most of these share names end with a dollar sign ($), which makes them "invisible"—they do not appear in the browse list when another Windows user looks at the shares on your computer. They are not inaccessible, however. If Simple File Sharing is disabled on your computer, any user who knows these names can connect to these shares simply by typing the share name rather than selecting it from the browse list. You can't view or set permissions on most of these shares, as you can for shares you create; the operating system restricts access to them to accounts with administrative privileges.

You can stop sharing these administrative shares only temporarily. The share reappears the next time the Server service starts or you restart your computer. Table 30-1 describes the administrative shares that appear on most systems.

Table 30-1. Administrative Shares

Share Name	Description
C$, D$, E$, and so on	Each of these shares allows members of the Administrators and Backup Operators groups to connect to the root folder of a hard drive. You will see one of these (with the appropriate drive letter) for each hard drive on your computer. These shares are often used by backup programs.
ADMIN$	This share is used during remote administration. It maps to the %SystemRoot% folder (C:\Windows on most systems).
IPC$	This share provides the named pipes that programs use to communicate with your computer. It is used during remote administration and when viewing a computer's resources.
PRINT$	This share is used for remote administration of printers.
FAX$	This share appears on fax servers and is used by clients to send faxes and access cover pages stored on the server.

Creating a New Share Using the Shared Folders Snap-In

To share a folder, right-click Shares in the Shared Folders console tree and choose New File Share. The Create Shared Folder Wizard appears. This wizard helps you find the folder you want to share and assists in setting up basic security options, as shown in Figure 30-7. Note that unlike the default share permissions applied when you create a share in Windows Explorer (whether Simple File Sharing is enabled or not), the wizard allows you to easily set different permissions for administrators (members of the Administrators group) and other users (Everyone).

Chapter 30

1015

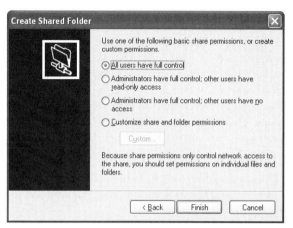

Figure 30-7. The Create Shared Folder Wizard provides an alternative to sharing a folder from Windows Explorer.

Troubleshooting

The New File Share command doesn't appear.

If sharing has not yet been enabled on your computer (by default, sharing is disabled on a new Windows XP installation), the Shared Folders snap-in is of little use. Worse, it doesn't tell you what the problem is or how to solve it. The solution, fortunately, is simple: First, be sure that Simple File Sharing is disabled. (If you disable Simple File Sharing while the Shared Folders snap-in is running, you might need to close and reopen the snap-in before the New File Share command appears.) If that doesn't make the command appear in Shared Folders, then run the Network Setup Wizard or share a folder using Windows Explorer; either action enables sharing. For details, see "Enabling File Sharing," page 1001.

Reality Check

Some users of Windows XP Home Edition have made the discovery that they can get to the Create Shared Folder Wizard by typing **shrpubw** at a command prompt. It might appear that you could use this trick to circumvent the all-or-nothing sharing limitations imposed by Simple File Sharing. Alas, using the wizard to create a share with custom permissions is of no use when Simple File Sharing is enabled—which is all the time in Home Edition. That's because on a machine running Home Edition, all network users are authenticated as Guest. Therefore, it does no good to set up different permissions for different network users because all users are logged on using the Guest account.

Removing a Share Using the Shared Folders Snap-In

Removing a share is as easy as right-clicking the share and choosing Stop Sharing. This is equivalent to visiting the folder's properties dialog box in Windows Explorer and clearing the Share This Folder check box.

Viewing and Disconnecting Sessions

Each user who connects to your computer creates a session. You can use Shared Folders to see who is currently connected to the computer as well as what files they have open. Click Sessions in the console tree to have the current sessions appear in the details pane, as shown in Figure 30-8.

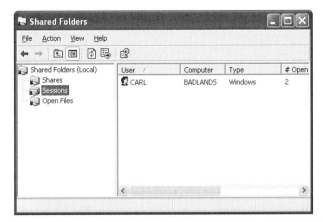

Figure 30-8. The Sessions folder shows all open connections.

> **Tip** **See who is authenticated**
> If you're trying to determine why some users have access to certain folders and others don't, it's helpful to know whether they're being authenticated as themselves or as Guest. That's easy to do with Shared Folders. In the Sessions folder, the rightmost column is titled Guest; its value is either Yes (authenticated as Guest) or No (authenticated as named user).

Besides seeing who is connected, you can also disconnect any or all sessions. Right-click a session and choose Close Session to close a single session. Right-click Sessions in the console tree and choose Disconnect All Sessions to close all the open sessions. Don't do this capriciously; users can lose information if you close a session while they have documents open.

Chapter 30

Viewing and Closing Files

Click Open Files in the Shared Folders console tree to see a list of shared files that are currently open for other users, as shown in Figure 30-9.

You can close an individual file by right-clicking it and choosing Close Open File. You can close all the open files at once by right-clicking Open Files in the console tree and choosing Disconnect All Open Files. If you close a document file before the user has saved new information, you might cause the information to be lost.

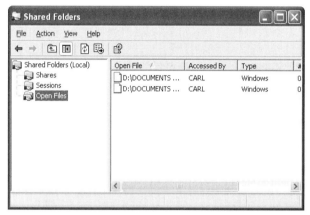

Figure 30-9. The Open Files folder shows all the files that have been opened by current users.

Warning Other Users

Because closing sessions and files can cause a loss of information, you should warn users who have open sessions and files before you close them. The Shared Folders snap-in includes a Send Console Message command for this purpose. The command relies on the Messenger service, however, and because this service has been widely abused by spammers, it is turned off by default in Windows XP Service Pack 2. We recommend alternative methods of notification (instant messaging, e-mail, the telephone, a hearty shout).

If you decide to use console messages, first be sure the Messenger service is turned on at your intended recipients' computers. Then right-click Shared Folders or Shares in the console tree and choose All Tasks, Send Console Message. (This command does not appear when you right-click Sessions or Open Files.)

When the Send Console Message dialog box appears, the names of all the computers with open sessions (which includes all computers with open files) are in the Recipients list. Simply type your warning message and click Send.

Accessing Shared Folders

My Network Places is your gateway to all available network resources, just as My Computer is the gateway to resources stored on your own system. My Network Places replaces the Network Neighborhood folder that appears in earlier versions of Windows—and you'll soon see that more than the name has changed. My Network Places appears in a Windows Explorer window that contains icons for network resources you use. Network places can be shortcuts to network computers, shared folders, Web folders on the Internet or your intranet, or FTP sites.

To open My Network Places (if your Start menu doesn't already include a shortcut to it), open My Computer. Under Other Places, click My Network Places.

You can also use My Network Places to browse your network. Under Network Tasks, click View Workgroup Computers. Doing so displays the computers in your workgroup. Double-clicking a computer displays the shared resources on that computer. While viewing workgroup computers, you can click Microsoft Windows Network (under Other Places) to display a top-level view of your entire corporate network.

Adding a Network Place

By default, Windows periodically searches your network for shared folders and shared printers. Shared resources discovered during this search automatically appear in My Network Places.

Tip   **Disable automatic discovery**

If your network has lots of shared resources that you don't use, you might prefer to disable the automatic discovery feature. To control this feature, follow these steps:

1   In My Network Places (or any Windows Explorer window), open the Tools menu and choose Folder Options.

2   In Folder Options, click the View tab.

3   In the Advanced Settings list, select or clear Automatically Search For Network Folders And Printers.

You can also create your own network places, such as a shortcut to a network resource, a Web site, or an FTP site. To add a network place, open My Network Places and click Add A Network Place (under Network Tasks). The Add Network Place Wizard leads you through the process.

Note   A shortcut to a Web site doesn't open the site in Microsoft Internet Explorer, as a shortcut in your Favorites folder does. Rather, it opens a Windows Explorer view of the folders within a Web site. Therefore, it's most useful as a shortcut to your own Web site or to Web folders on your intranet—where you might use or contribute files—rather than to a public Web site, which might not allow folder views.

Chapter 30

> **Tip**   Go directly to the folder you want
>
> My Network Places can also hold shortcuts to folders and files within a shared folder. To create such a shortcut, type the complete path (in the form *computername**sharename*\\ *folder*) on the Add a Network Place Wizard's third page. Or simply drag the folder or file from a Windows Explorer window to the My Network Places icon or window.

Using Network Places with Applications

The real strength of My Network Places isn't that it allows you to peruse your network, but that it provides fast, easy access to network places that you use day in and day out, without forcing you to traverse a lengthy path to get to each one. After you create a network place, it appears in the Open dialog box or in the Save dialog box that appears in most applications when you choose one of those commands from the File menu. All you need to do is click My Network Places in the places bar on the left side of the dialog box, and shortcuts to all your network places appear, as shown in Figure 30-10.

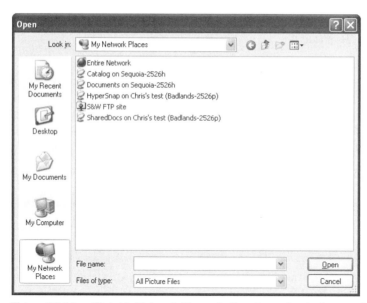

Figure 30-10.   Click My Network Places in the places bar to jump quickly to the network places you use.

Gaining Access to Shared Folders on Another Computer

To open a shared folder on another computer, double-click its icon in My Network Places. (If My Network Places doesn't contain a shortcut to the folder you want, click View Workgroup Computers or Microsoft Windows Network to navigate to it.) If you have the proper permissions, this action displays the folder's content in Windows Explorer. It's not always that easy however. If the user account with which you logged on doesn't have permission to view a network computer or resource you select, a dialog box similar to the one shown in Figure 30-11 appears. To gain access, you must provide the name of an account (and its password, of course) that has permission.

Perhaps the trickiest part of using shared folders is fully understanding what permissions have been applied to a folder and which credentials are in use by each network user. The first rule to recognize is that *all network access is controlled by the computer with the shared resources*; regardless of what operating system runs on the computer attempting to connect to a network share, it must meet the security requirements of the computer where the resource is shared. The following sections explain how to connect to shared folders on various types of servers. (In this context, *server* merely denotes the computer where the folder is shared; it might not be a dedicated server.)

Figure 30-11.   Enter the name and password of a user with an authorized account on the sharing computer or domain.

Windows XP Home Edition or Windows XP Professional with Simple File Sharing Enabled

This is the easiest configuration to use because any network user can easily open any shared folder. For the same reason, of course, it's not appropriate for all networks.

- **Share permissions**   The built-in Everyone group has Full Control or Read access, depending on the Sharing tab setting.
- **NTFS permissions**   Everyone has Modify or Read & Execute access, depending on the Sharing tab setting.
- **How to connect**   All network users are authenticated as Guest, and therefore can open any shared folder simply by double-clicking its shortcut in Windows Explorer.

Chapter 30

Inside Out

Store Your Network Passwords in Windows XP Home Edition

Whether you provide a user name and password when Windows requests them or add them directly to the stored network passwords, if you're using Windows XP Professional, Windows saves the credentials so that you need never enter them again to access the same resource. Unfortunately, the same is not true of Windows XP Home Edition. With a little effort, you can work around this limitation of Home Edition, as follows:

1 Use Notepad or another plain text editor to create a batch program (a plain text file with the file name extension .bat or .cmd).

2 Enter a Net Use command on a separate line in the batch program for each network resource you want to connect to. The command takes the form **net use** *computername**sharename password* **/user:***computername**username*, where *computername* is the name of the sharing computer, *username* is the name of an account on the sharing computer with access rights to the share, and *password* is that account's password.

For example, to make the connection shown in the figure on the facing page, you'd type the following:

```
net use "\\sequoia\budget data" WhI89dd /user:sequoia\carl
```

3 Drag a shortcut for the batch program to the Startup group on your Start menu, or set up a scheduled task so that it runs when you log on.

For more information about batch commands and scheduled tasks, see Chapter 19, "Automating Windows XP." For information about the Net Use command, see "Net Use," page 1037.

Windows XP Professional with Simple File Sharing Disabled or Windows 2000

In a workgroup environment, this configuration is more secure than Simple File Sharing, as it lets the share owner decide who to let in. Computers joined to a domain always have Simple File Sharing disabled, so this information applies to those computers as well.

- Share permissions   By default, Everyone has Full Control. Administrators on the sharing computer can grant or deny permissions to any user or group.

- **NTFS permissions**   By default, a folder inherits the permissions of its parent folder, but administrators on the sharing computer can grant or deny permissions to any user or group.

● **How to connect**   If your local account has the same user name and nonblank password as an account on the sharing computer, you're authenticated using that account and therefore have the access privileges granted to that account. If your local account does not match one on the sharing computer, you're authenticated as Guest and therefore have only the access privileges explicitly granted to Everyone or Guest. (If the Guest account is disabled on the sharing computer, only users with an account matching a local account can connect.)

If you're presented with a dialog box like the one shown in Figure 30-11, enter the user name and password of an account that has been granted the permissions you need. If the account you want to use is a local account on the sharing computer (always the case in a workgroup), enter the user name in the form *computername\username* (for example, **GLACIER\Jan**). To use a domain user account, use the form *domain\username* if your computer is not joined to the domain; if your computer is joined to the domain, you can enter the user name alone.

If you receive an "access denied" error message instead of a user name request, you'll need to add an entry to your stored network passwords. (You can do this only if you're running Windows XP Professional.) In Control Panel, open User Accounts and, if necessary, click your name to make changes for your account. Under Related Tasks, click Manage My Network Passwords, click Add, and then provide the requested information. (If your computer is joined to a domain, the path to Stored User Names And Passwords is slightly different: In User Accounts, click the Advanced tab and then click Manage Passwords.) You might need to log off and log on before you can access the shared folder.

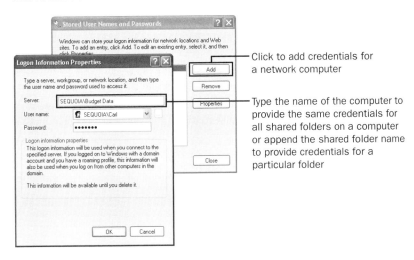

Click to add credentials for a network computer

Type the name of the computer to provide the same credentials for all shared folders on a computer or append the shared folder name to provide credentials for a particular folder

Windows 98 or Windows Me

These versions rely on passwords to protect shared resources; they don't care what user provides the password.

- **Permissions**   When a folder is shared, it can be protected with a password for read-only access, a password for full access, both, or neither.

- **How to connect**   Any network user can open any shared folder simply by double-clicking its icon in Windows Explorer. If the password for your user account matches the password assigned to the folder, the folder opens immediately. If not, Windows asks you to provide the password in a dialog box like the one shown in Figure 30-11 on page 1021. You don't need to provide a user name; that box is disabled.

Working with Mapped Network Folders

Mapping a network folder makes it appear to Windows as though the folder is part of your own computer. Windows assigns the mapped folder a drive letter, making the folder appear like an additional hard drive. You can still access a mapped folder in the conventional manner, by navigating to it through My Network Places. But mapping gives the folder an alias—the assigned drive letter—that provides an alternative means of access.

In general, drive mapping is obsolete, having been supplanted by improvements in and greater reliance on My Network Places. But mapping still offers benefits in some situations:

- **It makes the network folder available to programs that don't use the Windows common dialog boxes.**   With programs that use the common dialog boxes, you can navigate to network folders just as you would with My Network Places. But to read a document from, or save a document to, a network folder using earlier programs, you will probably need to map the folder to a drive letter.

- **It makes the network folder accessible from My Computer.**   Because a mapped folder becomes a virtual drive on your local computer, an icon for the folder appears in the My Computer folder, right alongside your local drives. If you do most of your work with files stored locally but need access to particular network folders, you might find it convenient to map them. That way, you won't have to bother opening My Network Places to find the network folders you need.

Mapping a Network Folder to a Drive Letter

To map a network folder to a drive letter, follow these steps:

1　In Windows Explorer, open the Tools menu and choose Map Network Drive.

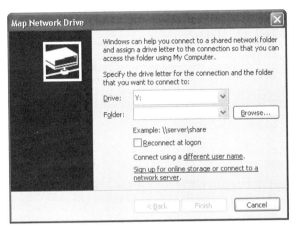

2　Select a drive letter in the Drive box. You can choose any letter that's not already in use.

3　In the Folder box, type the path to the folder you want or, more easily, click Browse and navigate to the folder.

4　Select Reconnect At Logon if you want Windows to connect to this shared folder automatically at the start of each session.

5　If your regular logon account doesn't have permission to connect to the resource, click the Different User Name link, enter a user name and password, and click OK. (This capability is useful if you personally have multiple user accounts. For example, you might have an administrator account that has access to some folders that are not available to your regular logon account.)

6　Click Finish.

Unmapping a Mapped Network Folder

If you change your mind about mapping a network folder, simply right-click the folder's icon in your My Computer folder. Choose Disconnect in the resulting shortcut menu, and the connection will be severed.

Sharing a Printer

If you've figured out how to share a folder over the network, sharing a printer will be easy. You configure all options for a printer—whether you plan to share it or not—using the printer's properties dialog box. To display it, open the Printers And Faxes folder (choose Printers And Faxes in Control Panel or on the Start menu), right-click the printer you're interested in, and choose Properties.

To make a printer available to other network users, simply click the Sharing tab, select Share This Printer, and provide a share name, as shown in Figure 30-12. Windows XP permits spaces and other characters in printer names, but if you're going to share with users of other operating systems, you should observe the following restrictions:

- Use only letters and numbers; don't use spaces, punctuation, or special characters.
- The entire Universal Naming Convention (UNC) name, including the requisite backslashes and your computer name, should be 31 or fewer characters. For example, assume that your computer name is YELLOWSTONE (11 characters). When you add slashes, the length becomes 14 characters, meaning that the share name should be 17 characters or less. This results in a UNC name along the lines of \\YELLOWSTONE\HPLASERJET4000.
- If any MS-DOS users will connect to the printer, the share name must be no longer than eight characters.

Figure 30-12. On the Sharing tab, specify a share name.

Using a Network-Interface Printer

Your print device doesn't necessarily have to be connected directly to the computer that's acting as the print server. That is, it needn't be connected to one of the computer's local ports, such as a parallel port (LPT*x*), a serial port (COM*x*), an infrared (IrDA) port, a universal serial bus (USB) port, or a 1394 port. If your print device has a built-in Ethernet adapter (or if it's connected to a network-interface device such as a Hewlett-Packard JetDirect), all you need to do is set up a standard TCP/IP port—a simple procedure in Windows XP:

1. Be sure that the print device is connected to the network and powered on.
2. Open Printers And Faxes in Control Panel. Under Printer Tasks, click Add A Printer.
3. On the Local Or Network Printer page of the Add Printer Wizard, select the local printer option and clear the automatic detection option.
4. On the Select A Printer Port page, select Create A New Port and then select Standard TCP/IP Port. Click Next to open the Add Standard TCP/IP Printer Port Wizard.
5. On the first page of the Add Standard TCP/IP Printer Port Wizard, click Next.
6. On the Add Port page, type the IP address of the printer. (You can get that by printing a configuration report from the print device or network-interface device. See the device's manual for instructions.) You can accept the Port Name that the wizard proposes or create your own. Click Next.

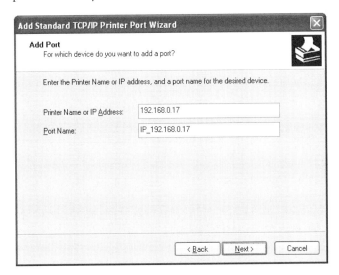

7. The wizard's final page shows your settings and also shows information (such as the adapter type) that confirms successful communication with the print device. Click Finish.

Note If you've already created a printer (if, for example, the print device was initially attached directly to a computer), you can change its port to use a network-interface device. In Printers And Faxes, open the printer's properties dialog box and click the Ports tab. Click Add Port, and in the Printer Ports dialog box that appears, select Standard TCP/IP Port and then click New Port. The Add Standard TCP/IP Printer Port Wizard then opens, and you can proceed with step 5 in the preceding procedure.

Chapter 30

Setting Permissions on Shared Printers

Unlike shared folders, which maintain separate share permissions and NTFS permissions, a single set of permissions controls access to printers, whether by local users or by network users. (Of course, only printers that have been shared are accessible to network users.)

When you set up a printer, initially all users in the Everyone group have Print permission for documents they create, which provides users access to the printer and the ability to manage their own documents in the print queue. By default, members of the Administrators and Power Users groups also have Manage Printers and Manage Documents permission. Table 30-2 shows the basic permissions and associated privileges that Windows XP provides for printers.

Table 30-2. Basic Printer Permissions and Privileges

Permission	Privileges
Print	Print documents
	Control properties of owned documents
	Pause, restart, and remove owned documents
Manage Printers	Share printer
	Change printer properties
	Remove printer
	Change printer permissions
	Pause and restart the printer
Manage Documents	Pause, restart, move, and remove all queued documents

A user account that doesn't have any of these permissions can't connect to the printer, print to it locally, or view its queue.

> **Note**   To set permissions on a printer, you must be using Windows XP Professional, and you must have Simple File Sharing disabled.

If you have Manage Printers permission for a printer, you can change other users' permissions for that printer. To do so, click the Security tab of the printer's properties dialog box and change permissions by clicking Allow or Deny (or neither) as necessary. To add another user or group to the list, click Add. After you type the names of users or groups you want in the Select Users Or Groups dialog box, return to the printer's properties dialog box. Then select each new user or group and assign permissions by clicking Allow, Deny, or neither. (If you select neither, permissions are determined by the user's group membership.)

Setting Hours of Availability and Other Options

The Advanced tab of the printer's properties dialog box, shown in Figure 30-13, includes a number of options that are both intriguing and confusing. Making changes to these options requires Manage Printers permission.

- **Always Available and Available From**   To restrict the availability of the printer to certain times of day, choose Available From and specify the range of times. Print jobs that are sent outside of these hours are held in the queue until the appointed time.

- **Priority**   The Priority setting has a similar purpose: If you create multiple printers for a single print device, documents sent to the printer with the higher Priority setting print ahead of those sent to the other printers. You might want to create a high-priority printer that certain users have permission to use when they need to cut in line to get a document printed quickly. Or you might want to assign Print permission to the high-priority printer to one group of users, and permission to the lower-priority printer to another group of users with different (less urgent) needs.

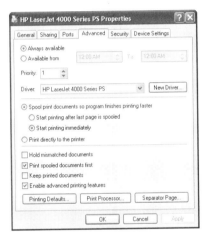

Figure 30-13.   The Advanced tab offers the ability to set the hours of operation for a printer, along with a number of unrelated options.

- **Driver**   This list includes all the printer drivers currently installed on your system; use it to select the correct driver for the print device. If the correct driver isn't in the list, click New Driver to start the Add Printer Driver Wizard.

- **Spool settings**   The four option buttons in the center of the dialog box determine whether a document should be spooled to a hard disk before sending it to the printer. (For information about specifying the location of spool files, see "Setting Server Properties," page 1033.) Spooled documents are then sent to the print device in the background. Ordinarily, you should choose the first and third options, which cause fastest return of control to your application and fastest printing completion. But if you have trouble with complex print jobs being interrupted by pages from another document, choose Start Printing After Last Page Is Spooled.

- **Hold Mismatched Documents**   Selecting this option tells the spooler to check a document's properties against the printer properties and to hold the document in the queue if the properties don't match. For example, a mismatched document can occur when an application specifies a form that's not currently assigned to a printer tray. Correctly matched documents continue to print normally, bypassing any mismatched documents in the queue.

- **Print Spooled Documents First**   Selecting this option directs the spooler to print documents that have completed spooling ahead of documents that are still spooling, even if the latter documents have a higher priority. When this option is cleared, the spooler selects the next document to print based only on its priority. Selecting this option maximizes printer efficiency because the print device doesn't have to wait for an incomplete, high-priority document to finish spooling before it can begin printing a complete, lower priority document.

- **Keep Printed Documents**   When this option is selected, the spooler doesn't delete documents from the queue after they print. You can then reprint a document from the queue rather than from the program that created it, or you can delete the document manually.

- **Enable Advanced Printing Features**   Selecting this option turns on metafile spooling for print jobs from Windows XP and Windows 2000 clients using Windows-based applications. Of more interest to most users, selecting this option enables new options in the common Print dialog box for some printers and some applications, such as Booklet Printing and Pages Per Sheet. The only reason to clear this option is if you have problems printing.

- **Printing Defaults**   Clicking this button displays the printing defaults dialog box—the same one that appears if you right-click a printer and choose Printing Preferences. In this dialog box, you specify default document settings for options such as orientation, two-sided printing, paper tray selection, and so on. Your settings here become the default settings for all users of the printer. (Another reason to create multiple logical printers for a single device: You might want to create printers with different default settings for different types of documents or for users with different needs.)

- **Print Processor**   Clicking this button opens the Print Processor dialog box, a place you'll probably never need to venture. In a nutshell, it displays the available print processors (a *print processor* tells the spooler how to alter a print job depending on the document data type) and the default data type for the selected print processor. *Microsoft Windows XP Professional Resource Kit Second Edition* (Microsoft Press, 2003) provides detailed information about print processors and data types.

- **Separator Page**   Click this button to specify a separator page. For more information on separator pages, see the next section.

Using Separator Pages

A *separator page* prints before each document (much like a fax cover page) and identifies the name of the user who printed the job, the date and time it was sent, and other details. Using separator pages makes finding your document among a stack of others in the printer's output bin easier. In addition, two of the separator pages furnished with Windows XP switch between PostScript and PCL (Printer Control Language, a language used by Hewlett-Packard printers), which is useful for printers that don't automatically switch languages.

Windows XP includes four separator page files, which you can use ready-made or customize. These are the supplied files, which are stored in the %SystemRoot%\System32 folder:

- **Sysprint.sep**   Switches the printer to PostScript and then prints a separator page that includes account name, job number, date, and time.
- **Pcl.sep**   Switches the printer to PCL and then prints a separator page that includes account name, job number, date, and time.
- **Pscript.sep**   Switches the printer to PostScript but does not print a separator page.
- **Sysprtj.sep**   A variant of Sysprint.sep that uses Japanese fonts, if available.

Separator page files are plain-text files with the extension .sep. You can create your own separator pages either by modifying the files supplied with Windows XP or by typing codes into a new plain-text document and saving that document in your %SystemRoot%\System32 folder.

The codes you can use for your separator pages are listed in Table 30-3. Each separator file must start with a single character on a line by itself; that character becomes the *command delimiter*, which identifies commands elsewhere in the file. You can use any character as a command delimiter. In Table 30-3, the @ character is used as the command delimiter. For these commands to work, the first line of your file must contain only a single @ character.

Table 30-3. Separator Page Codes

Code	Description
@N	Prints the user name of the person who submitted the print job.
@I	Prints the job number.
@D	Prints the date, in the date format specified by Regional Options in Control Panel.
@T	Prints the time, in the time format specified by Regional Options in Control Panel.
@L	Prints all characters following @L up to the next @ code or until the page width specified by @W is reached.
@Fpathname	Prints the contents of the file specified by *pathname*.

Chapter 30

Table 30-3. Separator Page Codes

Code	Description
@H*nn*	Sends a printer-specific control code, where *nn* is a hexadecimal value. For example, use @H1B to send an escape code, which has a hexadecimal value of 0x1B (27 decimal).
@W*nnn*	Sets the maximum width of the separator page to the decimal value specified by *nnn*. Any characters beyond this width are truncated. (The default width is 80; the maximum is 256.)
@B@S	Prints in single-width block characters.
@B@M	Prints in double-width block characters.
@U	Turns off block-character printing.
@*n*	Skips *n* lines. (*n* can be 0 through 9.)
@E	Ejects the current page from the printer.

Setting Up a Printer for Non–Windows XP Clients

Your network probably includes computers that are not running Windows XP. By configuring your print server properly, you can make it easy for users of the other systems to use your printers. A Windows XP–based print server includes support for the following types of clients:

- **Windows XP, Windows 2000, Windows NT, and Windows 95/98/Me**   To provide access for these types of clients, click the Sharing tab in the printer's properties dialog box. Click Additional Drivers and then select each of the client types you want to support. When one of these clients connects to the printer for the first time, Windows automatically sets up the printer on the client system.

- **Windows 3.x and MS-DOS**   These clients must install a 16-bit printer driver on their systems and redirect a local port to the network share. For example, you'd configure a printer driver on such a machine to print to LPT1, and then issue this command to the network redirector: **net use lpt1: *server**share*.** (Replace *server* with the computer name of your print server and replace *share* with the share name of the printer.)

- **UNIX**   On the print server, install Print Services For UNIX. (Go to Control Panel, Add/Remove Programs, Add/Remove Windows Components, Other Network File And Print Services, Details, Print Services For UNIX.) You also need to set the TCP/IP Print Server service (the name of Print Services For UNIX as it appears in the Services snap-in) to start automatically. (For information about controlling services, see

Appendix D, "Managing Services.") Set up an LPR port by opening the printer's properties dialog box and clicking Ports, Add Port, LPR Port, New Port. UNIX clients then connect to the printer using the Line Printer Daemon (LPD) service.

● **Internet**   Clients that support Internet Printing Protocol (IPP) can print to a Windows XP print server using HTTP. To provide access for Internet (or intranet) clients, you must install Internet Information Services (IIS). (For details about IIS, see "Setting Up IIS for Internet Printing," page 1101.) To connect to a shared printer using IPP, at the client computer, type **http://*server*/printers/** (replace *server* with the URL or the computer name of the server) in the Address bar of Internet Explorer. Users with the requisite permissions can view the queue, manage the printer, and manage documents. Clicking Connect (under Printer Action in the left frame) automatically installs the printer on the client computer if it's not already installed.

Setting Server Properties

In addition to setting properties for individual printers by using their properties dialog boxes, you can set other properties by visiting the Print Server Properties dialog box. To get there, open the File menu or right-click a blank area of the Printers And Faxes folder and then choose Server Properties.

The first three tabs control the list of items you see in the properties dialog box for a printer:

● The Forms tab controls the list of forms that you can assign to trays using the Device Settings tab in a printer's properties dialog box. You can create new form definitions and delete any that you create, but you can't delete any of the predefined forms.

● The Ports tab offers the same capabilities as the Ports tab in a printer's properties dialog box.

● The Drivers tab offers a list of all the installed printer drivers and provides a centralized location where you can add, remove, or update drivers.

The Advanced tab, shown in Figure 30-14, offers a potpourri of options:

● You can specify the location of spool files. You might want to change to a folder on a different drive if, for example, you frequently run out of space on the current drive when you attempt to print large documents.

● The first three check boxes on the Advanced tab determine which types of events merit entries in the Windows System log, which you can view with the Event Viewer snap-in. For more information, see Chapter 38, "Monitoring System Activities with Event Viewer."

Chapter 30

● The Beep On Errors Of Remote Documents check box causes the print server to notify you audibly of problems with a remote printer.

● The two Show Informational Notifications check boxes control pop-up status messages near the notification area.

● The last two check boxes on the tab control an alternative notification method. Windows XP can cause a message to pop up to let you know when your print job has completed. If you don't select the last check box, the message goes to the first workstation at which the user who printed the job is logged on. If that user account is logged on to more than one workstation, the message might not go to the one that generated the print job. To ensure that it does, select the last check box also, which causes the message to be delivered to the computer that generated the print job.

Windows XP uses the Alerter service on a print server to send notification to users when network printing jobs are complete. By default, the Alerter service does not run automatically in Windows XP. If you plan to use this feature, you'll need to start the Alerter service using the Services snap-in in Computer Management.

To receive such a message, a computer must be running the Messenger service. Users right next to the printer might want to leave this service off (and not be bothered by the pop-up messages), whereas users down the hall can start it so they'll know when print jobs are done.

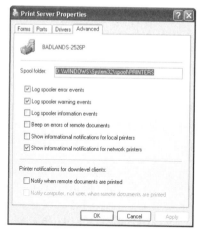

Figure 30-14. Settings you make here affect options available in all printer properties dialog boxes.

Troubleshooting

Your document won't print.

If a document gets stuck in the print queue and you can't delete it, open the Services snap-in in the Computer Management console, and stop the Print Spooler service. Then restart the service.

Inside Out

Set spool folders for individual printers

Your Spool Folder setting on the Advanced tab is stored in the DefaultSpoolDirectory value in the HKLM\Software\Microsoft\Windows NT\CurrentVersion\Print\Printers registry key, and it determines the spool folder for all your local printers. If you want to use a different folder for a particular printer, you must edit the registry directly. Go to the HKLM\Software\Microsoft\Windows NT\CurrentVersion\Print\Printers*printer* key (where *printer* is the name of the printer you want to modify), and set the SpoolDirectory value to the path you want to use.

Command-Line Utilities for Managing Shared Resources

Some users prefer a terse command prompt to a wizard or even an MMC window. If you're in that group, you'll want to use Net.exe for managing resource sharing.

In the following sections, we describe only the most common Net commands (and their most common parameters) for managing network connections. This isn't an exhaustive reference, however. You can get more information from online help or by typing **net help *command***, replacing *command* with the word that follows *net* in the examples. For instance, to get more information about the Net Use command, type **net help use**. This provides more help than typing **net use /?**, which shows only the command syntax.

Net Share

The Net Share command lets you view, create, modify, or delete shared resources on your computer.

Viewing Share Information

Typing **net share** with no parameters causes the command to display a list of the shared resources on your computer, as shown in the following sample:

```
C:\>net share

Share name        Resource                                    Remark
_____

IPC$                                                          Remote IPC
D$                D:\                                          Default share
C$                C:\                                          Default share
print$            D:\WINDOWS\System32\spool\drivers
                                                              Printer Drivers
ADMIN$            D:\WINDOWS                                   Remote Admin
HyperSnap         C:\HyperSnap
SharedDocs        D:\DOCUMENTS AND SETTINGS\ALL USERS\DOCUMENTS

LJ4000            LPT1:              Spooled             HP LaserJet 4000 Series PS
The command completed successfully.
```

If you follow Net Share with the name of a local shared resource, it displays information about that share. For example, the command **net share shareddocs** displays the following:

```
C:\>net share shareddocs
Share name       SharedDocs
Path             D:\DOCUMENTS AND SETTINGS\ALL USERS\DOCUMENTS
Remark
Maximum users    No limit
Users            JAN                CARL
Caching          Manual caching of documents
The command completed successfully.
```

Adding or Modifying a Share

You can share the folder C:\Spreadsheets, for use by an unlimited number of users, and add the comment "Budgets" with the following command:

```
C:\>net share Spreadsheets=C:\spreadsheets /unlimited /remark:"Budgets"
Spreadsheets was shared successfully.
```

Setting a share name "equal" to a folder creates a share. To modify an existing share, you use only the share name (and no folder), as in the following command, which changes the remark on the Spreadsheets share to "Year 2005 Budgets":

```
C:\>net share Spreadsheets /remark:"Year 2005 Budgets"
The command completed successfully.
```

Several parameters can be used with the Net Share command, as shown in Table 30-4.

Table 30-4. **Useful Parameters for the Net Share Command**

Parameter	Description
/Users:*number*	Sets the maximum number of concurrent users
/Unlimited	Lets the maximum number of users connect to the share at one time
/Remark:*"text"*	Adds or changes a comment that appears in Details view in Windows Explorer
/Cache:manual, /Cache:documents, /Cache:programs, or /Cache:no	Sets the document and program caching option for offline files; for details, see "Setting Caching Options on the Server," page 789

Deleting a User Share

To remove a share, simply use the /Delete switch with the Net Share *sharename* command:

```
C:\>net share spreadsheets /delete
spreadsheets was deleted successfully.
```

Net Use

The Net Use command connects your computer to shared resources on other computers. It can also disconnect, or display, all the resources to which you are connected.

Viewing Connections

Type **net use** with no parameters to display the resources to which you are currently connected:

```
C:\>net use
New connections will be remembered.


Status       Local      Remote                      Network


OK           G:         \\everglades\programs        Microsoft Windows Network
OK           K:         \\everglades\document        Microsoft Windows Network
OK           P:         \\everglades\company         Microsoft Windows Network
OK           LPT2       \\badlands\lj4000            Microsoft Windows Network
                        \\www.msnusers.com\xxxxx@msn.com
                                                     Web Client Network
The command completed successfully.
```

Adding a Mapped Network Drive

You can create drive mappings with a command like this:

```
C:\>net use e: \\badlands\spreadsheets
The command completed successfully.
```

This maps the network share Spreadsheets on the computer named Badlands to the local drive letter E. If you want to use the next available drive letter, use an asterisk (*) instead of the drive letter and colon. You can add any of the parameters shown in Table 30-5.

Table 30-5. Useful Parameters for the Net Use Command

Parameter	Description
password	Enter your password following the share name if a password is required.
/User:*domain**username*	To connect with a user name that is different from the one you are currently logged on with, you can use the /User parameter. The domain name is necessary only if you are not in the same domain as the resource you're connecting to. You can also enter the domain and user name in the format of an e-mail address (for example, *user@domain*).
/Delete	Disconnects the connection. You need only specify the drive letter and /Delete to disconnect.
/Persistent:yes or /Persistent:no	The yes option causes connections to persist so that they are reconnected the next time you log on.

Disconnecting a Mapped Drive

To disconnect a mapped drive, simply use the /Delete switch with the Net Use command:

```
C:\>net use e: /delete
e: was deleted successfully.
```

Net Session

The Net Session command lets you view or disconnect connections between your computer and clients that are accessing it.

Viewing Session Information

Type **net session** with no parameters to display the current connections to your computer:

```
C:\>net session

Computer          User name      Client Type          Opens Idle time

_____
\\127.0.0.1                      Windows 2002 2600    1 01:20:24
\\GLACIER         CARL           Windows NT 1381      0 00:00:07
The command completed successfully.
```

Disconnecting a Session

Following Net Session \\computername, append /Delete to disconnect a session. If you don't include \\computername, all active sessions are disconnected.

Net File

The Net File command lets you view or close the open shared files on your computer. Typing **net file** with nothing following it causes Net File to list all the open files, including a file ID, the user name of the person who has the file open, and the number of locks each has:

```
C:\>net file

ID        Path                              User name     # Locks

_____
24        E:\Catalog                        JAN           0
32        C:\spreadsheets\Q1 Budget.xls     CARL          3
The command completed successfully.
```

You can close a file by following Net File with the ID of the file and /Close:

```
C:\>net file 24 /close
The command completed successfully.
```

Net Statistics

The Net Statistics command displays the statistics log for the local Workstation or Server service. Type **net statistics workstation** to view the Workstation statistics. Type **net statistics server** to view the Server statistics.

The Workstation statistics log looks like this:

```
C:\>net statistics workstation
Workstation Statistics for \\SEQUOIA


Statistics since 7/26/2004 4:06 PM


  Bytes received                                 232765115
  Server Message Blocks (SMBs) received             394263
  Bytes transmitted                               65653800
  Server Message Blocks (SMBs) transmitted          393773
  Read operations                                   187879
  Write operations                                    1258
  Raw reads denied                                       0
  Raw writes denied                                      0

  Network errors                                         0
  Connections made                                      20
  Reconnections made                                    24
  Server disconnects                                     7

  Sessions started                                     102
  Hung sessions                                          0
  Failed sessions                                        0
  Failed operations                                      0
  Use count                                            126
  Failed use count                                       2

The command completed successfully.
```

Chapter 31

Remote Access Options

If you're like many twenty-first century knowledge workers, you have a computer at your office and another one at home. How many times have you arrived home, planning to catch up on some work, only to find that you don't have the files you need? Or worse, that you don't have the programs you need installed on your home computer? Microsoft Windows XP offers several features that enable you to retrieve the items you need without hopping in the car and driving back to the office.

At Home with Windows XP

Remote access is most useful in a business setting, so it should come as no surprise that Windows XP Professional is more capable than Windows XP Home Edition when it comes to staying in touch with the office. Remote Desktop is not available in Windows XP Home Edition. If you want to set up your computer to *allow* access using Remote Desktop, you must be running Windows XP Professional. However, you can use Remote Desktop Connection under Windows XP Home Edition to *connect* to a computer running Windows XP Professional. (In fact, you can run the Remote Desktop Connection software under earlier Windows versions, too.)

Don't confuse Remote Desktop with the Remote Assistance capability of the Windows XP Help And Support Center, either. Remote Assistance allows a friend or help desk professional to take over a remote computer's screen temporarily to diagnose or repair a persistent problem; that feature—which is covered in "Connecting to Another PC with Remote Assistance," page 92—works equally well with Windows XP Professional and Home Edition.

The capability to create secure virtual private networks (VPNs) between computers is identical in both Windows XP editions. You can set up either Windows XP Professional or Home Edition to function as a VPN server. Likewise, the wizard that lets you connect to a remote VPN server is the same in both editions.

The most exciting of these features is Remote Desktop, which lets you operate your office computer from home. This goes way beyond being able to download a few forgotten files. You're able to see exactly what is displayed on the other computer's display and, more importantly, operate that computer as if you were sitting right in front of it. You have access to all of the other computer's files, applications, and network resources.

With Remote Desktop, you can work from home using the full capabilities of your office computer. If you need to wait at home for a repair person (do they ever come within the scheduled time?!), you can continue to work just as productively as if you were at your office. If you're stuck working over the weekend, at least you can do it from the comfort of home!

Remote Desktop can work in the other direction too: If, after working all night to finish up a project at home, you forget to bring documents to work, you can connect to your home computer from your office network. Again, using Remote Desktop, you have complete control to view and operate the computer from afar.

Remote Desktop can be useful within the confines of a single network as well. For example, you can use it to solve a problem on another computer without trudging over to the other computer, whether it's in the next cubicle or upstairs in the bedroom. You can manage it from your own desktop.

Windows XP can also serve as the connection point for a single virtual private network (VPN) connection. With a VPN, you use the Internet to connect a computer to your network. In effect, this makes your home computer merely another computer on your office network. You have full access to network resources, just as if your computer were physically connected to the local area network (LAN).

Both Remote Desktop and VPN connections are encrypted, so your information is secure, even if you're making a connection over the public Internet.

The basic difference between Remote Desktop and a VPN is that with Remote Desktop, your computer takes control of a remote computer, whereas with a VPN connection, your computer becomes another node on the network. With Remote Desktop, applications run on the remote computer (your computer is effectively used as a dumb terminal); with a VPN, applications run on your computer. Both can be incredibly valuable, and in this chapter we explain how to set them up and use them.

Setting Up a Remote Desktop Connection to Another Computer

Remote Desktop allows you to work on your Windows XP Professional computer from any other computer. It's based on the Terminal Services technology that first appeared in server versions of Windows NT and Windows 2000.

> **Note** Remote Desktop is not available in Windows XP Home Edition. However, you can use Remote Desktop Connection on a computer running Home Edition to connect to a computer running Windows XP Professional.
>
> If you want to connect to a remote computer that's running Windows XP Home Edition, you're not completely out of luck. Two other programs—while not as flexible and powerful as Remote Desktop—might serve your needs, at least for an occasional connection. The first is Remote Assistance; for more information, see "Connecting to Another PC with Remote Assistance," page 92. The other program is NetMeeting; for more information, see "Other Communications Tools Included with Windows XP," page 1202. In addition, you can use a third-party program called VNC (the name is short for Virtual Network Computing) to set up remote access to any computer running a 32-bit version of Windows. You'll find more details about the program on the RealVNC Web site, at *http://www.realvnc.com*.

What You Need to Use Remote Desktop

The requirements for using Remote Desktop are pretty simple: You need two computers that are connected via a local area network, the Internet, or a dial-up connection.

> **Note** The computer that you want to control—the one at the remote location—is called the *remote computer*. The computer you want to use to control the remote computer is called the *client computer*.

These are the requirements for the two computers:

- **Remote computer** You need a computer running Windows XP Professional. (Windows XP Home Edition doesn't include the required components for hosting Remote Desktop sessions.) This computer must have a connection to a local area network or to the Internet, or it must have a modem that's configured to answer incoming calls automatically. If you're going to connect to this computer over the Internet, its Internet connection must have a known, public IP address. (For ways around this last requirement, see "Finding Your Remote Computer on the Internet," page 1047.)

● **Client computer**   You need a computer running nearly any version of Windows: Windows XP (all versions), Windows 2000 (all versions), Windows Me, Windows 98, Windows 95, Windows NT, or Windows for Workgroups. You must install client software (included on the Windows XP Professional CD-ROM) on the client computer. This computer must have access to the remote computer via a network connection, a virtual private network, or a dial-up connection.

Setting Up the Remote Computer

Before you can connect to a remote computer, you must enable Remote Desktop on the remote computer. To set up a computer to accept Remote Desktop connections, follow these steps:

1 Log on as a member of the Administrators group.

2 Open the System Properties dialog box (press the Windows logo key+Break or, in Control Panel, open Performance And Maintenance, System) and then click the Remote tab.

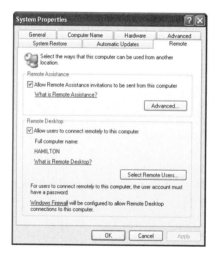

3 Under the Remote tab, select Allow Users To Connect Remotely To This Computer.

At this point, any of the following user accounts (as long as the account has a logon password) can be used to connect remotely to the computer:

- The account currently logged on
- All members of the local Administrators group
- All members of the local Remote Desktop Users group

> **Note** In the interest of security, only accounts that require a password to log on can be used to make a remote connection.

4 If you want to change which users can connect remotely, click Select Remote Users. The Remote Desktop Users dialog box appears.

■ To add a user to the Remote Desktop Users group, click Add. Then type the user's name in the Select Users dialog box that appears (or click Advanced, Find Now to select names from a list). You can type the name of any local user account or, if your computer is in a domain, any domain user account. You can add multiple users by separating each user name with a semicolon.

■ To delete a user from the Remote Desktop Users group, select the user's name in the Remote Desktop Users dialog box and click Remove.

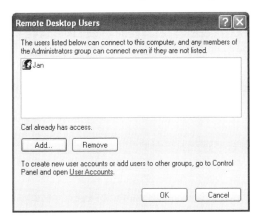

If you're going to connect from another computer on your local area network, that's all you need to do to set up the remote computer. If Windows Firewall is turned on, an exception for Remote Desktop is created automatically when Remote Desktop is enabled.

If you're planning to connect to the remote computer via a dial-up connection, you must install a modem, configure it to answer automatically, and then set up an incoming connection.

> For information about installing a modem, see "Setting Up a New Device," page 135. For information about setting up an incoming connection, see "Configuring a Remote Access Server for Dial-Up Access," page 1068.

If you're going to connect over the Internet, you must take the following additional steps:

● If the Internet connection is protected by a firewall—and it should be—you must open the port used by Remote Desktop, port 3389. If you use Windows Firewall, included with Windows XP Service Pack 2, Windows automatically opens the necessary port when you enable Remote Desktop. Confirming that is simple:

   1 In Control Panel, open Windows Firewall.

   2 Click the Exceptions tab and verify that Remote Desktop is selected.

Your computer is now configured to allow incoming Remote Desktop requests. If you want to restrict which IP addresses are allowed to connect, take these additional steps:

   1 With Remote Desktop selected on the Exceptions tab in Windows Firewall, click Edit.

   2 In the Edit A Service dialog box, click Change Scope.

   3 In the Change Scope dialog box, select Custom List and specify the IP address of the computers you want to allow.

If you use a hardware firewall (or different software firewall), you need to configure it to allow incoming access to TCP port number 3389.

Note You *can* use a different port for Remote Desktop connections. Although there's seldom reason to do so, changing to a different port can provide increased security because you don't expose a listening port where malevolent hackers expect to find Remote Desktop. For details about changing the port, see Microsoft Knowledge Base article 306759, "How to change the listening port for Remote Desktop."

● If the remote computer is on a network *and* it's not connected directly to the Internet, you must create a virtual private network (VPN). To do that, set up the computer, or the router that is connected to the Internet, so that it allows incoming VPN connections. (For details, see "Allowing Remote Access via a Virtual Private Network," page 1065.) This is the typical setup for an office network that you want to connect to from your home.

Note If your router doesn't have VPN capability, configure it for port forwarding. Set up a rule that forwards port 3389 requests to the internal IP address of the remote computer. See your router's instruction manual for how to do this or contact your ISP to perform the configuration.

Finding Your Remote Computer on the Internet

To connect through the Internet, the remote computer (or the computer it uses to connect to the Internet, if it's part of a local area network) must have a known public IP address. Otherwise, how are you going to address this computer from elsewhere on the Internet? The best method is to have a fixed (static) IP address for your Internet connection. But your ISP might not offer static addresses for the type of Internet access account you have. Dial-up accounts, in particular, are likely to use dynamic addressing, where your computer is assigned a different IP address each time you connect to the ISP. Many "always-on" connections, such as cable or DSL, also use dynamic addressing. (Some broadband ISPs use dynamic addressing, but as long as you maintain a connection your address *almost* never changes.)

If the Internet connection to the remote computer doesn't have a fixed IP address, you have a couple of options:

- You (or someone else with physical access to the remote computer) can type **ipconfig** at a command prompt to learn the network adapter's current IP address. (If the computer has more than one network adapter, be sure that you find the one that's connected to the Internet. If you can't identify it by its description, take a look at the IP address: It's *not* the one in the 10.*x.x.x*, 169.254.*x.x*, 172.16.*x.x*–172.31.*x.x*, or 192.168.*x.x* ranges. Those addresses are reserved for private networks; if you see one of those addresses you know the adapter is not connected to the public Internet.)

- You can use a dynamic DNS service, such as those offered by Dynamic Network Services (*http://www.dyndns.org*), TZO (*http://www.tzo.com*), and DHS International (*http://www.dhs.org*). (A Web search for "dynamic DNS service" will turn up many more options.) Such services typically rely on software installed on your remote computer that monitors the computer's IP address. Whenever the IP address changes, the resident software notifies the service provider's dynamic domain name servers. Each domain name server updates its table that correlates your domain name with an IP address—allowing you (or others) to always find your computer by using your registered domain name instead of a numeric IP address, even when the numeric address changes.

Inside Out

Connecting to a computer on a private network via the Internet

To connect to a remote computer that's not directly connected to the Internet, you must first establish a VPN connection to the network. Then you can start Remote Desktop Connection and connect to the desktop of any remote network computer on which Remote Desktop is enabled. You can specify the computer by its name or private IP address. (You can't connect to the computer directly over the Internet because it doesn't have a public IP address.)

However, if you can't use a VPN for some reason, there is another way to get to the desktop of a remote network computer: Set up Remote Desktop on a computer with an Internet connection as well as on the computer that you want to connect to. Use Remote Desktop Connection to connect to the computer with the Internet connection. Then, using the remote desktop, connect to the remote desktop of the other network computer you want to use. (In other words, you'll have a remote desktop within a remote desktop.) It's a bit cumbersome and confusing, but it works! And this approach might be slightly faster because it doesn't require the overhead of VPN encryption and tunneling.

Setting Up the Client Computer

If the client computer—the one that you want to use to connect to the desktop of a remote computer—is running Windows XP, you don't need to install any additional software. Remote Desktop Connection, the client software, is installed by default in both Windows XP Professional and Windows XP Home Edition.

If you use Windows 95, Windows 98, Windows Me, Windows NT 4, or Windows 2000 on the client computer, you must install Remote Desktop Connection, which is included on the Windows XP CD. The easiest way to install it is to insert the CD and, on the menu that appears, click Perform Additional Tasks, Set Up Remote Desktop Connection. (If the menu doesn't appear, open the CD in Windows Explorer. Double-click the Setup.exe icon in the CD's root folder to display the menu. Alternatively, you can start the Remote Desktop Connection setup program directly by double-clicking Msrdpcli.exe in the \Support\Tools folder.)

Note Msrdpcli.exe has been updated since Windows XP was first released. If you have an original Windows XP CD instead of one that has the latest service pack integrated (or if you're not sure), you should download the latest version of the client installation program from Microsoft, at *http://www.microsoft.com/windowsxp/pro/downloads/rdclientdl.asp*.

Inside Out

Taking the Remote Desktop Connection client software with you

Because of its importance, you might not want to carry your original Windows XP CD with you—particularly if it's in its original sleeve or if you've written the CD key on the CD itself. This makes an inviting target for a thief who happens to see it on your car seat. The only file you need from the CD is Msrdpcli.exe in the \Support\Tools folder, so you might want to copy it to a CD-R disc, Zip disk, or USB flash drive. (This file is over 3 MB in size, so it won't fit on an ordinary floppy disk.)

However, if the computer on which you want to install Remote Desktop Connection has Microsoft Installer support, you can get everything you need on a single floppy disk. Microsoft Installer support is built into Windows 2000 and Windows Me, and you have it on other Windows-based computers if you've installed Microsoft Office 2000 or Microsoft Internet Explorer version 5 or later.

Open Msrdpcli.exe in a program that opens .zip archives, such as WinZip. (Msrdpcli.exe is actually a self-extracting .zip archive.) Extract the file named Msrdpcli.msi and copy it to a floppy disk; it's smaller than 800 KB. (The other files in Msrdpcli.exe merely install Microsoft Installer, so they're unnecessary if you already have it.)

Finally, you can keep the disk at home and download the Remote Desktop Connection software to the computer where you're planning to use it. If the computer has a good enough connection to allow remote access, you'll have no trouble with the 3.4-MB download. You'll find the file on the Microsoft site, at *http://www.microsoft.com/windowsxp/pro/downloads/rdclientdl.asp*.

Configuring a Web Server for Use with Remote Desktop Web Connection

In some cases (for example, if you use a public Internet terminal while traveling), it's not feasible to install the Remote Desktop client software. That's okay; with the right setup, you can access your remote computer over the Internet using only Internet Explorer 4 or later.

Note You must still configure the remote computer—which might not be the same computer as the Web server—to allow remote connections. For details, see "Setting Up the Remote Computer," page 1044.

To make this work, the remote computer must be on a network that has a computer configured as a Web server using Internet Information Services (IIS). (For details on installing and configuring IIS, see Chapter 32, "Hosting a Web or FTP Site.") If you didn't install it as part of the initial IIS setup, you must install the Remote Desktop Web Connection component, which you do as follows:

1   In Control Panel, open Add Or Remove Programs.

2   Click Add/Remove Windows Components.

3   Select Internet Information Services (IIS) and click Details.

4   Select World Wide Web Service and click Details.

5   Select Remote Desktop Web Connection, making sure that its check box is selected.

6   Click OK and Next, as needed, to finish the Windows Components Wizard.

After the Remote Desktop Web Connection component is installed, you must also set the appropriate permissions. To do that, follow these steps:

1   In Control Panel, open Administrative Tools, Internet Information Services.

2   Under the name of your computer in the tree pane, navigate to Web Sites\Default Web Sites\Tsweb.

3   Right-click Tsweb and choose Properties. Then click the Directory Security tab, shown in Figure 31-1.

4   Under Anonymous Access And Authentication Control, click Edit to display the Authentication Methods dialog box shown in Figure 31-2.

5   Select Anonymous Access and then click OK in each dialog box.

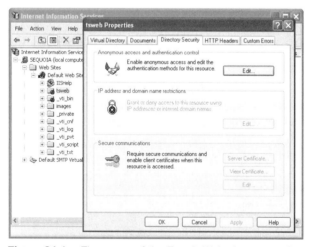

Figure 31-1.   The name of the Tsweb Web site comes from Terminal Services, the feature now known as Remote Desktop.

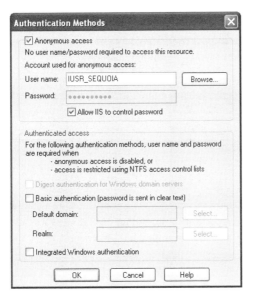

Figure 31-2. At the IIS level, you want to allow anonymous access. Remote Desktop takes care of authentication.

Using Remote Desktop Connection

After you've set up the remote computer to accept remote desktop connections and installed Remote Desktop Connection on the client computer, the rest is easy.

Connecting to a Remote Desktop

To use Remote Desktop Connection, the client computer must be connected to the remote computer. If they're on the same local area network (that is, you want to view the desktop of another computer on your network), that's already done. Similarly, if the remote computer has a public IP address (and the client computer is also connected to the Internet), they're connected. But if you plan to use a dial-up connection or if you plan to connect to a computer that doesn't have a direct Internet connection, you must first connect the computers using a dial-up connection or a VPN connection.

Then start Remote Desktop Connection. Click Start and choose All Programs, Accessories, Communications, Remote Desktop Connection. A dialog box like the one shown in Figure 31-3, on the next page, appears. In the Computer box, type the name of the remote computer or its IP address. Then click Connect.

> **Note** After a successful connection to a remote desktop, the name of the remote computer is added to the list in the Computer box. Thereafter, you can simply select it from the list (if it isn't already selected) instead of typing the name each time.

Figure 31-3. You can specify the remote computer by name or IP address.

Troubleshooting

Your firewall blocks outbound access.

If you have a firewall that blocks unknown outbound Internet traffic (such as ZoneAlarm), it prevents your initial attempt to connect to your remote desktop. Configure the firewall to enable Mstsc.exe (the file name of the Remote Desktop Connection program) to make outbound TCP connections on port 3389.

Unless you've changed the default settings, your screen goes black except for a small title bar at the top of the screen. In a moment, a logon dialog box appears, as shown in Figure 31-4. Enter the user name and password of an account that is a member of the Remote Desktop Users group on the remote computer.

If the account is already logged on to the remote computer—or if no one is logged on to the remote computer—then the remote computer's display appears on your computer, either in a window or a full-screen display.

If someone else is already logged on to the computer (that is, a user account other than the one with which you're making the remote connection), Windows lets you know that you'll be forcing that person to log off. The message you see—and the effect it has—depends on whether Fast User Switching is enabled on the remote computer.

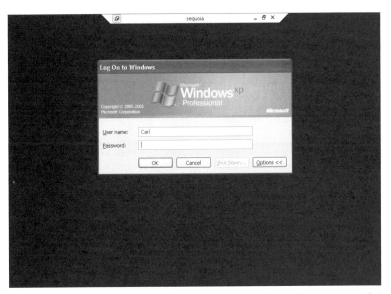

Figure 31-4. By default, Remote Desktop Connection takes over your full screen, regardless of the screen resolution of the remote computer.

● **Fast User Switching enabled** You'll see a message similar to the one shown in Figure 31-5. If you choose Yes, a message is displayed on the remote computer, as shown in Figure 31-6, but if that user doesn't respond within a few seconds, he or she is unceremoniously bumped off. (While it sounds drastic, this also allows you to connect to a desktop that someone has left logged on but is no longer using. Just as in local Fast User Switching, the other user's session remains logged on, but inaccessible.)

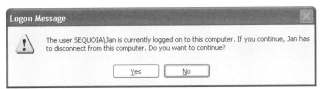

Figure 31-5. You'll know right away if someone else is logged on, which gives you the opportunity to cancel your Remote Desktop Connection session.

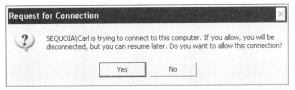

Figure 31-6. If you attempt to connect while someone else is using the remote computer, they'll see this message, which allows them to reject your intrusion.

● **Fast User Switching disabled**   You'll see a more strongly worded message, as shown in Figure 31-7. If you choose Yes, the person at the remote computer is logged off without warning—and without an opportunity to save any open documents.

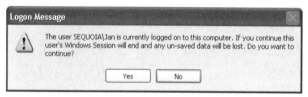

Figure 31-7.   If you connect to a remote computer on which Fast User Switching is disabled, the person currently using the computer will be logged off without warning.

Caution   It's important to note that only one user at a time can control the desktop of a computer running Windows XP Professional. If someone logs on locally to the remote computer, the remote session is immediately disconnected without warning to the users at either end of the connection. (The good news is that no data is lost when the remote user is disconnected. It works the same as when you switch users with Fast User Switching; the first session remains logged on and all applications continue running, but the new session has control of the desktop.) Particularly with the Welcome screen and Fast User Switching enabled, it's all too easy for this to happen. Someone seeing the Welcome screen on a computer with nobody around might naturally assume that the computer is not being used and is available for his or her use.

Therefore, if you use Remote Desktop and other people have physical access to your remote computer while you're connected remotely, you should disable the Welcome screen. At the very least, consider disabling Fast User Switching. Although it doesn't prevent another user from knocking you off, the user who tries to log on locally to the remote computer at least gets a message that explains who is connected remotely and warns that logging on will disconnect the remote user and cause the loss of unsaved data.

Whether you disable the Welcome screen and Fast User Switching or not, logging on locally with the same account that's currently connected remotely disconnects the remote user without warning. This is a good reason to create a separate user account for each person in your office or home (and for each person to log on with his or her account only); it's not likely that one person will be in two places at once!

While you use the remote computer, the remote computer's monitor (if turned on) does not display what you see on the client computer. If you could actually see the remote computer's screen, you'd notice that as soon as someone logs on remotely, the remote computer displays the Welcome screen. If the Welcome screen has been disabled, the remote computer displays the Unlock Computer dialog box. In either case, a person who has physical access to the remote computer can't see what you're doing (other than the fact that you have a certain number of programs running) at the client computer.

> For information about disabling the Welcome screen and Fast User Switching, see "Controlling How Users Log On," page 239. For information about locking and unlocking a computer, see "Logging Off or Locking Your Computer," page 248.

Connecting from a Web Browser

If you set up a Web server on your network, you can connect to a remote desktop without using the Remote Desktop Connection client program; instead, the remote desktop appears in a Web browser window. For details about setting up the Web server for this purpose, see "Configuring a Web Server for Use with Remote Desktop Web Connection," page 1049.

To connect to the remote desktop, you'll need a TCP/IP connection to the network or the Internet, and you must be running Internet Explorer 4 or later. Remote Desktop Web Connection installs an ActiveX control on the client computer. To make the connection, simply type the URL for the Remote Desktop Web Connection home directory in Internet Explorer's Address bar. By default, the URL is *http://server/tsweb/*, where *server* is the name or IP address of the server. On an intranet (or if you've already made a VPN connection to your network), simply use the computer name. If you're connecting over the Internet, the server must have a registered domain name or a known IP address. Internet Explorer then displays a page like the one shown in Figure 31-8.

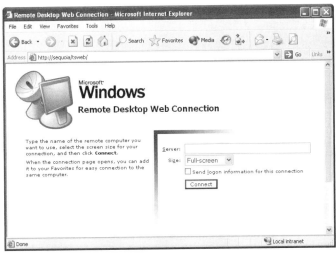

Figure 31-8. Your initial view of the remote computer looks like this.

In the Server box, type the name of the remote computer you want to view; it doesn't have to be the same computer as the Web server. In the Size box, select a screen size. (If you select Full Screen, Internet Explorer uses the screen resolution of the client computer; otherwise, the remote desktop appears in a resizable window.) Then click Connect. The first time you connect from a client computer, Windows displays a security warning about an ActiveX control that you must download. After you click Yes to accept the download, the remote desktop logon dialog box appears—just as it does when you use the Remote Desktop Connection program. After you provide your user name and password, the desktop appears in your Internet Explorer window, as shown in Figure 31-9, and you can interact with it exactly as if you were at the remote computer.

> **Tip** Bookmark the remote desktop
>
> After you get to the remote desktop, save it as a favorite in Internet Explorer. (Open the Favorites menu and choose Add To Favorites.) That way, you can bypass the Remote Desktop Web Connection screen next time. But this method has other advantages: The server name, screen size, and user name (if you select Send Logon Information For This Connection and specify a user name before clicking Connect) are encapsulated in the stored URL—so you needn't enter this information again.

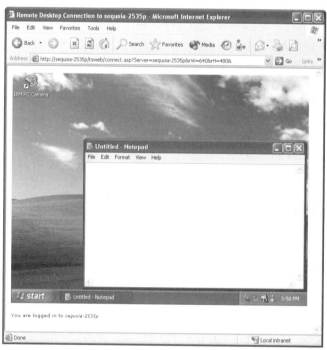

Figure 31-9. Your remote desktop in an Internet Explorer window is fully functional.

Working with Different Screen Resolutions

Whether you connect to a remote computer using Remote Desktop Connection or Remote Desktop Web Connection, by default, the remote computer takes over your entire screen. It uses the resolution of the client computer, regardless of the resolution set on the remote computer. At the top of the screen, a small title bar appears, as shown in Figure 31-4 on page 1053. This title bar lets you switch between your own desktop and the remote desktop. Table 31-1 explains each button on the title bar.

Table 31-1. Remote Desktop Connection Full-Screen Title Bar

Button	Description
📌	The Pushpin button locks the title bar in place. If you click the push-pin, the title bar disappears completely, retracting into the top of the screen. To make the title bar reappear, move the mouse pointer to the top edge of the screen. To keep the title bar visible, click the pushpin again.
–	The Minimize button reduces the remote desktop to a taskbar button on your own desktop.
▣	The Restore button displays the remote desktop in a resizable window on your own desktop. To return to full-screen view, click the window's Maximize button.
✕	The Close button disconnects the remote computer (but does not log you off the remote computer) and closes Remote Desktop Connection. You can pick up where you left off by reopening Remote Desktop Connection and reconnecting or by logging on locally at the remote computer.

Tip   Hide the title bar

If you seldom use the Remote Desktop Connection title bar and it gets in your way, you can hide it by clicking the Pushpin button. (To make it visible again, "bump" the top of the screen with the mouse pointer.) If you rarely use the title bar, you can prevent it from showing up at all. Before you connect, click the Options button in the Remote Desktop Connection dialog box. Click the Display tab, and then clear the Display The Connection Bar When In Full Screen Mode check box.

You might prefer to not use your full screen for the remote desktop. You set this—along with a number of other options—before you connect to the remote computer. After you start Remote Desktop Connection, click the Options button to expand the dialog box. Then click the Display tab, which is shown in Figure 31-10. You can set the screen resolution to any size, from 640×480 up to the current resolution of the client computer (not the remote computer), or you can set it to full screen by moving the slider all the way to the right.

Figure 31-10. Screen resolution is determined by the client computer.

Note Changes you make to settings that appear when you click Options become the default settings for new Remote Desktop Connection sessions. These settings are saved in a hidden file called %UserProfile%\My Documents\Default.rdp.

Troubleshooting

Colors are washed out.

The screen resolution of a Remote Desktop Connection session is determined entirely by the client computer. The number of colors, however, is set to the lowest value set on either computer. At the client computer, you specify the number of colors on the Display tab. On the remote computer, the number of colors is set by Group Policy. If this value is lower than the client setting, it prevails. The Terminal Services and Remote Desktop server in Windows Server 2003 defaults to 8-bit color (256 colors). To increase the number of colors that the remote computer delivers, on the remote computer, open Group Policy (Gpedit.msc). Navigate to Computer Configuration\Administrative Templates\ Windows Components\Terminal Services, and double-click the Limit Maximum Color Depth policy. Select Enabled and then specify the maximum color depth you want to allow for remote connections.

Accessing Local Resources

While you use Remote Desktop Connection, it's immediately apparent that you have control of the remote computer. You see its desktop, Start menu, and so on. That's terrific if the remote computer has everything you need. But you'll often want to use local resources and information from the client computer as well as from the remote computer. In addition, you might want to move information between the two computers. With Remote Desktop Connection, you can do so easily with the following features:

- **Clipboard**   When you copy or cut text or graphics on either the remote computer or the local computer, it's saved on the Clipboard. It's then available for pasting in documents on either computer. Similarly, you can cut or copy files or folders from a Windows Explorer window on either computer and paste them into a folder on the other computer.

  If you want to disable this capability as a security measure, you must use Group Policy on the remote computer. At a command prompt, type **gpedit.msc** to open Group Policy and navigate to Computer Configuration\Administrative Templates\Windows Components\ Terminal Services\Client/Server Data Redirection. Enable the Do Not Allow Clipboard Redirection policy.

- **Disk drives**   You can access your own drives through My Computer on the remote desktop. As shown in Figure 31-11, each drive on the client computer appears on the remote desktop in the My Computer's Other group. You can navigate to any folder or file on your computer, and then use any of the usual methods to copy, move, rename, open, delete, and so on.

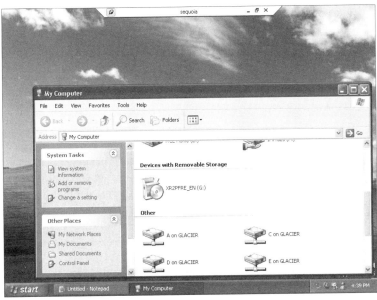

Figure 31-11.   Drives on the client computer (Glacier, in this figure) appear in My Computer on the remote computer (Sequoia).

- **Printers**   Your local printers appear in the remote computer's Printers And Faxes folder. Their entries have "(from *clientcomputername*)" appended to each printer name. To print to a local printer, you simply select its name in a Print dialog box.

> **Note** For Clipboard and disk drives features to work, Disk Drives must be selected on the Local Resources tab before you connect. To use the printers feature, Printers must be selected.

Troubleshooting

Sounds don't play.

Remote Desktop Connection uses User Datagram Protocol (UDP) for transmitting audio data. If sounds don't play at all, it might be because a firewall is blocking this UDP traffic. Check your firewall logs and, if the firewall is blocking the traffic, create a rule that permits it to pass.

If a firewall isn't blocking sounds, the problem might be that the UDP packets are being dropped. Audio data is considered to be relatively unimportant, which is why it uses UDP, a protocol that, by design, permits data to be lost. If you're pushing the bandwidth limits of your connection, audio data disappears in favor of accurate transfer of screen images and other data. You can make more room in the pipe by lowering the number of colors (to 256 colors, for example).

Inside Out

Control Remote Desktop settings with Group Policy

You can force the setting of most items on the Local Resources, Display, Programs, and Experience tabs by using Group Policy. Dozens of other settings are also available, including a number of security-related options and the ability to automatically disconnect remote desktop sessions after a period of inactivity. To make these settings, open Group Policy (Gpedit.msc) and navigate to Computer Configuration\AdministrativeTemplates\Windows Components\Terminal Services and its subfolders. In the details pane, click the Extended tab, and then select a policy to see its description. For more information about Group Policy, see Appendix F, "Group Policy."

If you're connecting to another computer on your local area network, you might not need your local drives and printers to appear on the remote desktop. The drives and printers you need might already be available on the remote computer; allowing Remote Desktop Connection to add an entry for each one merely clutters your windows with a lot of duplicated drive and printer icons. And if you're connecting over a slow modem connection, you might not want to show them, because using those shortcuts merely provides a slow round-trip path to your local resources. To prevent their appearance, before you make the connection, click Options in the Remote Desktop Connection dialog box. Then click the Local Resources tab, shown in Figure 31-12.

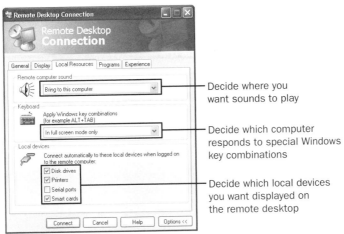

Decide where you want sounds to play

Decide which computer responds to special Windows key combinations

Decide which local devices you want displayed on the remote desktop

Figure 31-12. You control which of the client computer resources are available in the remote desktop window.

On the Local Resources tab, you also specify which computer should play the sounds generated by the remote computer. On a fast connection, you'll probably want them to play on the client computer (select Bring To This Computer). On a slow connection, you're better off selecting Do Not Play. The Leave At Remote Computer option, apparently, is to scare the wits out of anyone who happens to be sitting by the remote-controlled computer!

Using the Keyboard with Remote Desktop Connection

When the Remote Desktop Connection window is active, almost every key you press is passed to the remote computer. Certain key combinations, however, can be processed by the client computer, depending on the setting you make in the Keyboard section of the Local Resources tab of the Remote Desktop Connection dialog box (shown in Figure 31-12). You can specify that the key combinations shown in the first column of Table 31-2 are sent to the remote computer all of the time, only when the remote desktop is displayed in full-screen mode, or never.

Table 31-2. Special Keys in Remote Desktop Connection

Key Combination for Client Computer	Equivalent Key Combination for Remote Desktop Session	Description
Alt+Tab	Alt+Page Up	Switches between programs
Alt+Shift+Tab	Alt+Page Down	Switches between programs in reverse order
Alt+Esc	Alt+Insert	Cycles through programs in the order they were started
N/A	Ctrl+Alt+Break	Switches the remote desktop between a window and full screen
Ctrl+Alt+Delete	Ctrl+Alt+End	Displays the Windows Security dialog box (if the remote computer is joined to a domain) or Task Manager (if the remote computer is not joined to a domain)
Ctrl+Esc	Alt+Home	Displays the Start menu
N/A	Alt+Del	Displays the Control menu of the active window
Shift+Print Screen	Ctrl+Alt+Plus (on numeric keypad)	Captures a bitmap image of the remote desktop and places it on the Clipboard
Alt+Print Screen	Ctrl+Alt+Minus (on numeric keypad)	Captures a bitmap image of the active window and places it on the Clipboard

If you select On The Local Computer, key combinations from the first column of Table 31-2 are always applied to the client computer. To get the equivalent function on the remote computer, press the key combination shown in the second column. The same is true if you select In Full Screen Mode Only and the remote session is displayed in a window.

If you select On The Remote Computer, key combinations from the first column are applied to the remote computer. Key combinations in the second column are ignored (unless they have some function in the active application on the remote desktop). The same is true if you select In Full Screen Mode Only and the remote session is displayed in full-screen mode. One exception is the Ctrl+Alt+Delete combination, which is always applied to the client computer. Regardless of your Local Resources tab setting, you must press Ctrl+Alt+End to obtain the same result on the remote computer. As an alternative, in the remote session open the Start menu and choose Windows Security.

Configuring Performance Options

When you first use Remote Desktop Connection, you might notice that the remote desktop doesn't display a background. Disabling the background is one of several settings you can make that affect the speed of your remote session. How you set these options depends in large measure on the speed of the connection between the two computers. If you're using a dial-up connection, you should disable as many features as possible to reduce the amount of information that must be transmitted across the wire. On the other hand, if you're connecting to another desktop on your local area network, you might as well enable all features to enjoy the full experience of working at the remote computer.

The performance-related options are on the Experience tab of the Remote Desktop Connection dialog box, shown in Figure 31-13. To quickly select an appropriate set of options, select the speed of your connection from the list box.

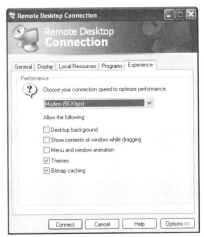

Figure 31-13. Remote Desktop Connection has a default collection of settings for each connection speed.

Use those settings or select your own options. The last two options on the Experience tab are not as comprehensible as the others:

- **Themes** Clearing the Themes check box disables the Windows XP visual styles, causing everything to display using the Windows Classic visual style—the one used in earlier versions of Windows. (For information about visual styles, see "Changing Colors, Fonts, and Visual Effects," page 481.)

- **Bitmap Caching** Unlike the other options on the Experience tab, you get the fastest performance if you *select* (not clear) Bitmap Caching. Bitmap caching can speed up your connection by storing frequently used images on a local drive.

Saving a Remote Desktop Configuration

Changes you make in the expanded Remote Desktop Connection dialog box are automatically saved in %UserProfile%\My Documents\Default.rdp, and they're automatically used the next time you open Remote Desktop Connection. But you might want to have several different Remote Desktop Connection configurations for connections to different computers. If you have a portable computer, you might want different settings for use with different connections to the same computer (for example, dial-up versus LAN).

To save a configuration, simply make all your settings, click the General tab (see Figure 31-14), and click Save As. By default, Remote Desktop Connection offers to save your configuration file in %UserProfile%\My Documents.

Figure 31-14. Options for saving or opening saved connection settings are on the General tab.

To reuse a stored configuration at a later time, start Remote Desktop Connection, click Options, click Open, and then double-click the stored file. More simply, double-click the stored file in Windows Explorer. For the quickest access to a frequently used remote desktop configuration, drag a shortcut to your Start menu or the Quick Launch toolbar.

Disconnecting a Remote Session

When you're through with a Remote Desktop Connection session, you can either disconnect or log off.

If you disconnect, your programs continue to run on the remote computer. It's effectively like pressing the Windows logo key+L with Fast User Switching enabled: The Welcome screen is visible, and the remote computer is available for another user. If you log on later—either locally or through a remote connection—you can pick up right where you left off. To disconnect, in the remote session, open the Start menu and choose Disconnect, which appears in place of the Turn Off Computer (or Shut Down, on domain-based computers) command. A simpler alternative is to click the Close button on the title bar of the remote session. Either way, a confirmation dialog box awaits your answer before Remote Desktop Connection pulls the plug.

Logging off closes all your programs before disconnecting. To log off, in the remote session, open the Start menu and choose Log Off.

You can also turn off or restart the remote computer. To perform either task, in the remote session, press Ctrl+Alt+End or open the Start menu and choose Windows Security. If the remote computer is joined to a domain, the Windows Security dialog box appears; click Shut Down to turn off or restart the computer. If the remote computer is not a domain member, Windows Task Manager appears. Its Shut Down menu offers Turn Off, Restart, and Log Off commands.

Allowing Remote Access via a Virtual Private Network

A *virtual private network* (*VPN*) is a means of connecting to a private network (such as your office network) via a public network, such as the Internet. It combines the virtues of a dial-up connection to a dial-up server (the ability to use all of your network resources and protocols just as if you were connected directly to the network) with the ease and flexibility of an Internet connection. By using an Internet connection, you can travel worldwide and still, in most places, connect to your office with a local call to the nearest Internet access phone number. And if you have a high-speed Internet connection (such as cable or DSL) at your computer (and at your office), you can communicate with your office at full Internet speed, which is much faster than any dial-up connection using an analog modem. *Tunneling* provides a secure, cost-effective way to connect two computers (or two networks) that are each connected to the Internet. Instead of paying the phone company to use its cables and set up special protocols at each end, you leverage the existing Internet infrastructure and its transmission protocols. Tunneling protocols dig underneath the protocol of the intervening network to create the illusion of a direct path between the two separated networks.

This path is created by encrypting each IP packet or frame (depending on the protocol) and wrapping it inside another packet or frame with new header information for traveling through the intervening network. That is, when a network frame (if we're talking about a frame-based protocol) created on one of the computers is destined for a computer on the other side of the tunnel, the entire frame is encrypted and a new header that routes the encrypted frame through the intervening network is attached. When the new frame gets to the other side, the new header is stripped off, and the original frame is decrypted and routed forward just as though it had never left the original local network. When you put all of these pieces together, you end up with a virtual private network. Tunneling protocols are the core of VPNs.

Three tunneling protocols are in wide use today:

- **Point-to-Point Tunneling Protocol (PPTP)**   PPTP allows IP, IPX, and NetBEUI frames to be encrypted and then wrapped in an IP header to be sent across an intervening network.

- **Layer 2 Tunneling Protocol (L2TP)**   L2TP allows IP, IPX, and NetBEUI frames to be encrypted and then sent over any IP, X.25, Frame Relay, or ATM intervening network.

- **IP Security (IPSec) Tunnel Mode**   IPSec Tunnel Mode allows IP packets to be encrypted and then encapsulated in an IP header to be sent across an intervening network.

Windows XP uses PPTP or L2TP for tunnel connections. Only Windows Server 2003 or Windows 2000 Server can act as a VPN server using L2TP. Windows XP can, however, connect to a VPN server using L2TP. Windows XP uses IPSec to enhance the security of all network interactions.

Configuring a VPN Server

A number of third-party VPN solutions are available, and they're often appropriate for allowing VPN access to a corporate network. For a standalone computer or a small network, where you need only a single incoming connection at any time, Windows XP has everything you need built in.

You can make your computer a remote access server so that others can connect to it via a VPN and then access shared folders on your local drives. If your computer is connected to a local area network, incoming VPN connections can also browse the network and access shared resources elsewhere on the network.

> **Note**   To create or modify incoming connections, you must be logged on as a member of the Administrators group.

To enable others to connect to your computer, follow these steps:

1 In Control Panel, open Network Connections.
2 Under Network Tasks, click Create A New Connection. The New Connection Wizard appears.

> **Note**   If you have not configured a modem and a dialing location, the Location Information dialog box appears. This dialog box asks for the name of your country and your area code (or city code). If your computer doesn't have a modem or you don't plan to ever use the computer to dial a phone number, you might be tempted to simply close this dialog box without providing the requested information. Because of a bug in Windows, however, you might not be able to complete the other steps unless you enter an area code and click OK.

3 On the New Connection Wizard's first page, click Next.

4 On the Network Connection Type page, select Set Up An Advanced Connection, and click Next.

5 On the Advanced Connection Options page, select Accept Incoming Connections, and click Next.

6 If a Devices For Incoming Connections page appears, simply click Next. (These options are for setting up an incoming dial-up connection, direct cable connection, or infrared connection.) This page appears only if your computer has an installed modem, serial port, parallel port, or IrDA port.

7 On the Incoming Virtual Private Network (VPN) Connection page, select Allow Virtual Private Connections, and click Next.

To receive VPN connections over the Internet, your computer's IP address (more precisely, the IP address of your connection to the Internet, if your computer has multiple network adapters) must be known on the Internet. This IP address is assigned to you by your Internet service provider. (For ways to work with dynamic addresses, see "Finding Your Remote Computer on the Internet," page 1047.)

8 On the User Permissions page, select the check box next to the name of each user you want to allow to make an incoming connection.

Windows lists all of the local user accounts on your computer. As shown below, you can add (or delete) user accounts from this page, which can save you a visit to the User Accounts program.

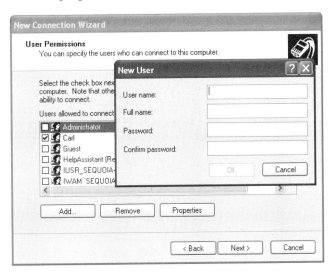

When you're finished with the User Permissions page, click Next.

9   On the Networking Software page, select the check box next to the name of each network component you want to use for an incoming connection.

For an incoming connection to work, the calling computer and your computer have to "speak" the same network protocol. Click Install to add a new networking component. For more information about installing network components, see "Installing and Configuring Protocols," page 968.

When you're finished with the Networking Software page, click Next, and then click Finish.

Configuring a Remote Access Server for Dial-Up Access

If your computer—the one you want to use as a VPN server—doesn't have a full-time Internet connection and a static IP address, you might consider using a dial-up connection instead. You'll need a modem that's configured to answer automatically.

Follow the same steps just described in "Configuring a VPN Server," but replace steps 6 through 8 with these steps:

6   On the Devices For Incoming Connections page, select the modem you want to use.

7   On the Incoming Virtual Private Network (VPN) Configuration page, select Do Not Allow Virtual Private Connections.

8   On the User Permissions page, select the check box next to the name of each user you want to allow to make an incoming connection.

You might want to set callback options, which can be used as an additional security measure for dial-up connections as well as to determine who pays for the phone call. To set callback options for a particular user, select the user name, click Properties, and then click the Callback tab. If you select an option other than Do Not Allow Callback, when your computer receives a call, it authenticates the user, disconnects the call, and then dials the user's modem. Use the following guidelines to make your selection:

●   Select Do Not Allow Callback if you want the remote user to make a connection with a single call to your computer.

●   Select Allow The Caller To Set The Callback Number if you want the caller to be able to specify a phone number for a return call.

●   Select Always Use The Following Callback Number and specify a phone number if you want your computer to call the user at a particular number. This reduces the likelihood that an intruder who has come upon a valid user name and password can access your system.

> **Tip** Require encryption
>
> By default, the VPN connection does not require that users encrypt all transmitted data and passwords. You can improve security by requiring encryption. In the Network Connections folder, right-click the Incoming Connections icon and choose Properties. Click the Users tab and select the Require All Users To Secure Their Passwords And Data check box. Before a user can connect, he or she should open Network Connections on the client computer and open the properties dialog box for the VPN connection. On the Security tab, Require Data Encryption (Disconnect If None) must be selected.

Configuring Firewalls and Other Network Settings for VPN Access

With a simple network configuration and Windows XP running at each end of the connection, your VPN should be ready to go without any further ado. If you're unsuccessful at making a connection to the VPN server or you're unable to browse network resources, a few additional configuration steps are required.

Troubleshooting

You can't connect to the VPN from another computer.

After you set up a VPN connection on another computer, you might not be able to connect. This can occur if a firewall at either end of the connection blocks VPN traffic.

At the server, when you use the New Connection Wizard to create an incoming VPN connection, the wizard automatically configures the built-in Windows Firewall appropriately. You can confirm that by visiting Control Panel, opening Windows Firewall, clicking the Advanced tab, and, in the Network Connection Settings box, clicking Settings. You should see entries for Incoming Connection VPN (L2TP), Incoming Connection VPN (PPTP), and IP Security (IKE); they should all be selected.

If you use a different firewall—software or hardware—you'll need to configure it similarly. For PPTP connections (the type most commonly used with a Windows XP–based VPN), you must open port 1723 for TCP communication. (L2TP connections, which use port 1701, require a machine certificate for authentication and are available only when the VPN server is on a network with Windows Server 2003 or Windows 2000 Server. L2TP, therefore, is a topic that's beyond the scope of this book.) IPSec uses a UDP connection on port 500.

If the firewall on your client computer filters outbound traffic as well as incoming connections, you'll need to open port 1723 on that computer as well.

If you're certain that firewalls at each end are not blocking traffic, yet you still can't connect, the problem might be in between. Some ISPs block VPN traffic or allow it only with certain types of accounts. Check with your ISP for information about its policies.

Troubleshooting

You can't browse the remote network.

If you're able to connect with the VPN server but you can't see any of the other computers on the network, you might need to change some network settings. In particular, you need to be sure that the incoming VPN connection has an IP address in the same subnet as the rest of your local area network.

On the server, open the Network Connections folder, right-click the Incoming Connections icon, and choose Properties. In the Incoming Connections Properties dialog box, click the Networking tab, select Internet Protocol (TCP/IP), and click Properties to display the following dialog box.

Select if you want incoming connections to see other computers on your network

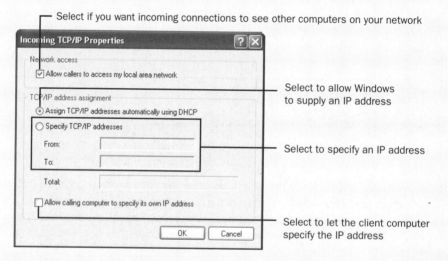

Select to allow Windows to supply an IP address

Select to specify an IP address

Select to let the client computer specify the IP address

On the client, open the Network Connections folder, right-click the icon for the VPN connection, and choose Properties. In the properties dialog box, click the Networking tab, select Internet Protocol (TCP/IP), and click Properties. Check this dialog box against the server's Incoming TCP/IP Properties dialog box. If the server is set up to assign an address, select Obtain An IP Address Automatically. If the server is configured to let the client supply its own IP address, select Use The Following IP Address, and specify an address in the same subnet as the VPN server.

Connecting to a Virtual Private Network

To connect to your Windows XP VPN server, you don't need to run Windows XP; you can connect with any version of Windows.

Troubleshooting

Other Internet services stop working when you make a VPN connection.

When you make a VPN connection, you might find that you can no longer browse the Internet using Internet Explorer, hold conversations using Windows Messenger, or use other applications that access the Internet. This occurs when the VPN connection is configured to use the default gateway on the remote network for Internet access. When you make a VPN connection, Windows adds to the IP routing table a new default route that uses the connection to the VPN server. That new route is assigned the lowest metric, which means that it's used in place of your original default route—and therefore prevents access to some locations. Although this is a useful feature when you connect to some corporate networks, it's generally of little use when you're connecting to a single computer or a small workgroup.

To fix the problem, follow these steps:

1. In Control Panel, open Network Connections, right-click the VPN connection, and choose Properties.
2. Click the Networking tab, select Internet Protocol (TCP/IP), and click Properties.
3. In the Internet Protocol (TCP/IP) Properties dialog box, click Advanced.
4. On the General tab of the Advanced TCP/IP Settings dialog box, clear the Use Default Gateway On Remote Network check box.

You should then be able to use other Internet applications while your VPN connection is active.

To set up a VPN connection on a computer running Windows XP, follow these steps. (The steps are quite similar for users of other Windows versions.)

1. In Control Panel, open Network Connections.
2. Under Network Tasks, click Create A New Connection. The New Connection Wizard appears.
3. On the New Connection Wizard's first page, click Next.
4. On the Network Connection Type page, select Connect To The Network At My Workplace, and click Next.
5. On the Network Connection page, select Virtual Private Network Connection, and click Next.

> **Note** If you want to make a dial-up connection to a remote access server, select Dial-Up Connection instead. The rest of the wizard is straightforward.

6 On the Connection Name page, type a descriptive name for the connection, and click Next.

7 If you need to dial to connect to the Internet, select Automatically Dial This Initial Connection and select your dial-up Internet connection from the list. If you have a full-time connection, select Do Not Dial The Initial Connection, and click Next.

8 On the VPN Server Selection page, type the host name (for example, mycompany.com) or the IP address (for example, 123.45.67.89) of the computer you want to connect to, click Next, and then click Finish.

To connect to a VPN, open the VPN connection in your Network Connections folder. If you don't already have a connection to the Internet open, Windows offers to connect to the Internet. Once that connection is made, the VPN server asks for your user name and password. Enter them correctly, click Connect, and the network resources should be available to you in the same way they are when you connect directly to the network.

> **Tip**   Share your VPN connection
> You can share a VPN connection in the same way that you share an Internet connection. For more information, see "Sharing an Internet Connection," page 978.

Chapter 32

Hosting a Web or FTP Site

Microsoft Windows XP Professional includes Internet Information Services (IIS) 5.1, software that allows you to host Web and File Transfer Protocol (FTP) sites. IIS provides a Web server, an FTP server, and a Simple Mail Transfer Protocol (SMTP) virtual server. You might already be familiar with IIS—IIS 5.0 is included with Windows 2000 Professional, and a scaled-down version of IIS, Personal Web Server (PWS), is included with Windows 98. IIS is not included with Windows XP Home Edition, nor can it be installed separately.

What You Can and Can't Do with IIS in Windows XP Professional

The version of IIS included with Windows XP Professional is not as versatile or as powerful as those included with server editions of Windows. Its principal limitations are that it lets you create only one Web site and one FTP site, and it allows a maximum of 10 simultaneous TCP connections. (Practically speaking, because some Web pages might require multiple connections, this can mean that no more than seven users can access your Web or FTP site at any one time.) To use IIS with more than 10 simultaneous connections or to create multiple Web or FTP sites, you need one of the server editions of Microsoft Windows.

The connection limit precludes using Windows XP Professional as a platform for hosting an e-commerce site or any other kind of site that's intended to reach the public at large. But IIS on Windows XP Professional can still be very useful within an organization.

At Home with Windows XP

Windows XP Home Edition does not include IIS. If you upgrade to Windows XP Home Edition from a version of Windows on which PWS was previously installed, the software will no longer work. As a result, the information in this chapter applies only to users of Windows XP Professional.

First, if you're a Web developer, IIS provides a server that you can use for developing and testing your work before you move it to a larger server. Second, small and medium-sized organizations or workgroups can use IIS on Windows XP Professional to host an *intranet*, a private network based on Internet technology. If your workgroup needs an FTP site to use as a repository for shared files, IIS on Windows XP Professional should meet your needs more than adequately (although, as we explain later in this chapter, WebDAV is a more robust and secure way to share files). Finally, if what you intend to create is a public Web site that will be used primarily by extended family members or a small club or school, the 10-connection limit might not present a serious obstacle.

Installing Internet Information Services

IIS is not installed by default unless you installed Windows XP Professional as an upgrade and Personal Web Server or IIS 5.0 was installed on your previous operating system. To install IIS from scratch, follow these steps:

1 In Control Panel, open Add Or Remove Programs.

2 Click Add/Remove Windows Components.

3 In the Windows Components Wizard, select Internet Information Services (IIS), as shown in Figure 32-1, and click Details. A list of optional subcomponents appears.

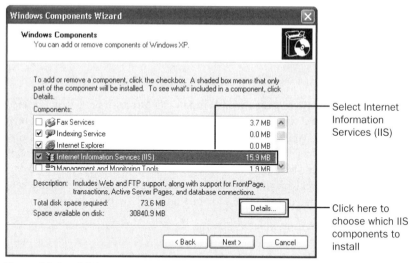

Figure 32-1.   IIS is not installed by default. Use the Windows Components Wizard to install it.

Chapter 32

4   Select the check boxes next to the subcomponents you want to install, and clear those for subcomponents you don't want to install. (See the following section for a discussion of what each of these components is used for.) Click OK to complete the installation.

The following optional subcomponents are available:

- **Common Files**   This selection installs a core group of files required by other components of IIS. If you attempt to clear this check box you'll be warned that doing so will disable most of the other IIS components.

- **Documentation**   The Documentation option, selected by default, puts 9 MB of help files in the folder %SystemRoot%\Help\Iishelp. You'll need this documentation to master IIS, but if you administer several IIS-hosted Web sites from a single workstation, you might not want to install the documentation on each system.

- **File Transfer Protocol (FTP) Service**   If you're planning to set up an FTP site, be sure to select this check box.

- **FrontPage 2000 Server Extensions**   Installed by default, the Microsoft FrontPage Server Extensions are a set of server-side programs that enable you to include forms, hit counters, and full-text search capability on your Web site. The extensions also make it easier for you to keep your site up to date, by letting you publish revisions directly from FrontPage. If you choose to install this feature, Microsoft recommends that you update to the FrontPage 2002 Server Extensions, which are available online at *http://msdn.microsoft.com/library/en-us/dnservext/html/fpse02win.asp*. (Be sure to download and install any security updates referred to in association with these server extensions.)

> **Note**   FrontPage is Microsoft's Web authoring tool. FrontPage 2000 and FrontPage 2002 are available individually and with selected versions of Microsoft Office 2000 and Office XP, respectively. The most recent version, FrontPage 2003, is still a member of the Office family but is available only as a standalone package. For more information about FrontPage and the FrontPage 2000/2002 Server Extensions, see *http://www.microsoft.com/frontpage*. If you have a copy of FrontPage 2002, you can install a specialized version of the FrontPage 2002 extensions called SharePoint Team Services. These extensions add a variety of special features to your Web site, including threaded discussions and the ability for Office users to directly open, edit, and save files in document libraries that can also be accessed through Internet Explorer. A more recent version of SharePoint called Windows SharePoint Services is available only with Windows Server 2003 and cannot be installed on Windows XP Professional. For more information, see *http://www.microsoft.com/sharepoint*.

● **Internet Information Services Snap-In**   The IIS snap-in gives you the ability to administer IIS via Microsoft Management Console (MMC). If you choose not to install it, you will need to use scripts to manage your server.

● **SMTP Service**   SMTP provides you with the means to set up a mail system that can be used on an internal network or over the Internet. Check with your ISP before installing this software. For security reasons, many Internet service providers prohibit the use of SMTP servers other than their own; Internet connections that allow SMTP traffic represent a potential security risk from spammers who relay junk mail through the server, effectively hiding its true origin. Configuring and securing an SMTP server is a complex job that is beyond the scope of this book. If you choose to install the SMTP service, you can find more information by opening %SystemRoot%\Mail.chm.

● **World Wide Web Service**   The World Wide Web Service allows your IIS-hosted site to serve pages over the Internet. This service isn't optional; not installing it effectively disables IIS. However, it has optional sub-components. Click Details to see the subcomponents and select the ones you want to install.

> **Note**   By default, Windows Firewall blocks access from external computers to port 80, which effectively disables IIS. Before you can allow others to access your Web server, you must either disable Windows Firewall or configure an exception that allows incoming traffic to reach port 80. For more details on how to accomplish this task, see "Allowing Connections Through the Firewall," Chapter 7, page 199.

Using the Internet Information Services Snap-In

IIS 5.1 provides an MMC snap-in that you can use for administering all details concerning your Web and FTP sites. Figure 32-2 shows the snap-in as it appears immediately following the installation of IIS. The IIS snap-in can be opened at any time from the Administrative Tools folder (in the Performance And Maintenance category) of Control Panel.

Like other MMC snap-ins, the IIS snap-in presents two panes. On the left is the console tree, on the right the details pane. (For more information about using and customizing MMC, see Appendix C, "Using and Customizing Microsoft Management Console.") Sites and directories (folders) appear in the console tree. Subdirectories and files contained within the currently selected console-tree item appear in the details pane.

The console tree represents the directory structure of your Web and FTP sites, in much the same manner as the folder tree in Windows Explorer depicts the structure of your ordinary disk storage. At the highest level of the outline is the name of the computer whose IIS installation you're administering. By default, the console displays the local computer. To connect to a remote computer, select a computer name in the console tree and then choose Action, Connect. (You must have the necessary permissions, of course.)

Under the computer name entry in the console tree are Web Sites, FTP Sites, and Default SMTP Virtual Server. The Web Sites and FTP Sites entries are superfluous in Windows XP, because you are allowed to create only one of each site type.

IIS initially assigns default names to your Web and FTP sites (Default Web Site and Default FTP Site), and these names appear at the next branch level. You can rename the sites by right-clicking their entries and choosing Rename from the shortcut menu. By default, your Web site and FTP site are located at %SystemDrive%\Inetpub\Wwwroot and %SystemDrive%\Inetpub\Ftproot, respectively. (On a default installation of Windows XP, these folders are located in the root of drive C.)

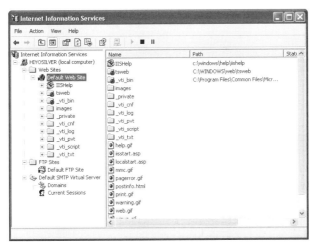

Figure 32-2. The IIS snap-in for the MMC lets you administer every detail of your site.

At the level below your site names appear the names of folders. In IIS documentation, folders are called *directories*, following the MS-DOS and UNIX traditions. Directories are of two types: ordinary and virtual. An *ordinary directory* is just like a folder in Windows Explorer. For example, the Images directory in Default Web Site, an ordinary directory, corresponds to the folder C:\Inetpub\Wwwroot\Images on a typical Windows XP installation.

A *virtual directory* is a pointer to a folder located elsewhere—on your local hard disk or another computer. The details pane of the IIS snap-in displays path information for virtual directories. In Figure 32-2, for example, you can see that IISHelp is a virtual directory whose real location is C:\Windows\Help\Iishelp.

> For information about how and why to create virtual directories, see "Creating Virtual Directories," page 1087.

To take an action affecting any component of this structure, the simplest approach is usually to right-click the component and choose a command from the shortcut menu. For example, you can view the properties dialog box and modify properties for your Web site by right-clicking Default Web Site and choosing Properties from the shortcut menu. Figure 32-3 below shows the Documents tab of the Default Web Site Properties dialog box.

Figure 32-3. The Documents tab of the Web Site Properties dialog box displays the names of possible home pages and the order in which IIS will search for them.

Accessing Your Web and FTP Sites

As you develop your sites, you can browse your work locally by pointing your browser to *http://localhost* (to view your Web site) or *ftp://localhost* (to access your FTP site). If you set up your Web site to require an encrypted connection, use *https* instead of *http*.

The home directories of your sites are mapped to your domain name or computer name. So to reach your Web sites from another computer on your local area network, you can type **http://computername**, replacing *computername* with the network name of the computer on which you're running IIS. To reach your sites from outside your local area network, users type either ***http://domainname***, where *domainname* is a fully qualified domain name that points to your computer, or ***http://IP_address***. (To access your FTP site, replace the *http://* protocol with *ftp://*.)

Until you have created a default Web page, a trip to *http://localhost* generates the display shown in Figure 32-4, as well as the IIS documentation in a second browser window, shown in Figure 32-5. Users who browse your site from somewhere other than your own computer see an "under construction" page. As Figure 32-3 shows, your Web site is set initially to use the following as default home pages: Default.htm, Default.asp, Index.htm, and Iisstart.asp. When you address the root of the Web site without specifying a document, IIS displays the first of those four documents that it finds. When you first install IIS, the only one of those four pages that exists is Iisstart.asp, the script that displays the welcome page and documentation locally and the under construction page for remote browsers. When you begin creating your own site, your home page will take priority over Iisstart.asp, so these greetings will no longer appear.

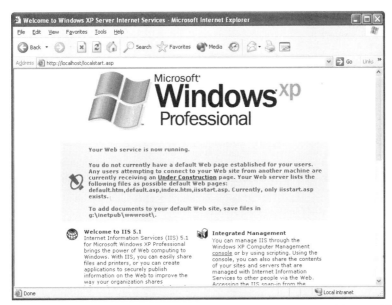

Figure 32-4. The first time you access your site locally, you might see this welcome page and (in a second window) the IIS documentation. Users browsing remotely will see an "under construction" page.

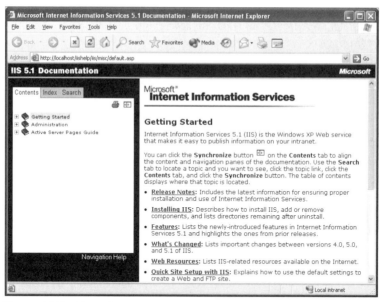

Figure 32-5. You might see this IIS documentation window in addition to the welcome page the first time you access your site locally.

Using the IIS Documentation

The documentation for IIS appears if you direct your browser to *http://localhost* without having created a home page for your Web site. You can get to the documentation at any other time by pointing your browser to *http://localhost/iishelp*. If you're working in the IIS snap-in and want to look up something quickly in the IIS help files, you might find it simpler to open the help files within the snap-in. In either the console tree or the details pane, right-click IISHelp under Default Web Site (or the name of your site if you've created one), and then choose Browse from the shortcut menu. The help files will appear in the console's details pane. To return the console to its more conventional purposes, click on another part of the console tree, or right-click IISHelp again and choose View, Detail from the shortcut menu.

To search the IIS documentation, you must be running the Indexing Service. If the Indexing service is not running on your system, follow these steps:

1 Choose Start, Run, and then type **services.msc**. (There are other ways to get to the Services console, but this is often the simplest.)

2 In the details pane of the Services console, double-click Indexing Service.

3 On the General tab of the Indexing Service Properties dialog box, click Start. To ensure that the Indexing Service will run each time you run Windows XP, select Automatic in the Startup Type list.

Configuring Site Properties

To inspect and configure properties that affect your entire Web or FTP site, right-click either Default Web Site or Default FTP site in the console tree. Then choose Properties from the shortcut menu. Figure 32-6 shows the Home Directory tab of the Default Web Site Properties dialog box.

Specifying a Home Directory

Your Web site and FTP site each must have a home directory. The home directory is the starting point for everything offered by your site. It contains a home page document—typically named Index.htm or Default.htm—that contains links to other pages served by your site. As noted earlier, the default locations for your Web and FTP sites' home directories are %SystemDrive%\Inetpub\Wwwroot and %SystemDrive%\Inetpub\Ftproot, respectively. To change the location of your site to somewhere else on your local hard disk, supply the appropriate path in the Local Path box on the Home Directory tab of the Web site's or FTP site's Properties dialog box. To change the location to another computer on your network, choose A Share Located On Another Computer. The box labeled Local Path then changes to Network Directory and the Browse button changes to a Connect As button. You can supply the appropriate server and directory information in the Network Directory box and click the Connect As button to supply your logon credentials for the network share.

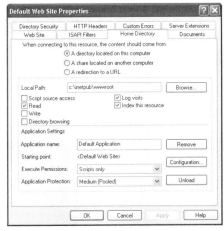

Figure 32-6. On the Home Directory tab of a site's properties dialog box, you can specify the location of the home directory, enable logging and indexing, and configure IIS permissions for the site.

Tip For maximum control over access to your Web and FTP content, it's best to place that content on NTFS drives. If you use FrontPage 2002 Server Extensions, your site must be located on an NTFS drive.

You can also redirect your entire Web site to a different URL. If you move your site, this is a way of leaving a forwarding address for users who don't have the new URL. When you choose A Redirection To A URL, you specify the new URL and select any or all of the following options:

- **The Exact URL Entered Above**   This option redirects all requests for any page in the specified site or virtual directory to the location you specify, such as *http://newsite/ default.htm*.
- **A Directory Below This One**   This option redirects requests for your current home directory to one of its child directories.
- **A Permanent Redirection For This Resource**   This option causes IIS to send a 301 Permanent Redirect message to requesting browsers. Some browsers can use this information to update their bookmarks or favorites lists with the new URL.

Redirection to another URL is not an available option for your FTP site.

Specifying a Default Web Site Document

To specify the document that your Web site serves in response to a URL that references the root of the site but doesn't specify a document name, go to the Documents tab of the Web site's properties dialog box, shown in Figure 32-3 on page 1078. Be sure that Enable Default Document is selected. The list of default documents can contain more than one document. IIS searches for documents using the order in which they're listed and serves the first one it finds. To add a document to the list, click Add. To remove one, select it and click Remove. Use the arrow buttons to change the order of the listed documents.

Note that if you clear Enable Default Document, a browser that references the home directory without a document name will receive an Error 403 "You are not authorized to view this page" message.

To append an HTML-formatted footer to every document served by your site, select Enable Document Footer and specify an HTML file. Be aware that appending an HTML footer can impact the performance of your site.

Setting Connection Limits and Timeout Parameters

IIS running on Windows XP Professional allows a total of 10 simultaneous connections, counting both the connections to your Web site and those to your FTP site. You can't increase this number. On the FTP site, you can decrease the maximum, however. You might consider doing this if you run both a Web site and an FTP site and you want to reserve some of your connections for users of your Web site. You could also set this value to 0 as a way of temporarily excluding users from the FTP site.

To change the connection limit for your FTP site, right-click Default FTP Site in the console tree in the IIS snap-in, choose Properties from the shortcut menu, and then click the FTP Site tab. Enter a number from 0 through 10 in the Limited To box.

Both your Web site and your FTP site are set by default to maintain an inactive connection for 900 seconds (15 minutes). After this period of time has elapsed, the TCP connection is closed, freeing that connection for another user. If your sites frequently use the maximum number of connections, you might consider lowering this timeout value. That way, you'll reduce the chance that someone will be locked out of your site while another user is holding a connection open without interacting with the site. Lowering the timeout threshold unnecessarily can negatively impact users' experience with your sites, however, by forcing their browsers to re-establish connections after short periods of inactivity.

Understanding Property Inheritance

You can set properties at three levels: site, directory (or virtual directory), and file. These levels form a hierarchy, with site at the highest position and file at the lowest. Properties set at higher levels are ordinarily passed on to (inherited by) lower levels. A property change at the site level, for example, is passed on to every directory and virtual directory in the site.

If, however, you have explicitly made a property change at the directory or file level, a property change at a higher level is not necessarily passed on to the lower level. Instead, IIS presents an Inheritance Overrides dialog box like the one shown here that allows you to choose which levels should retain their current settings and which should inherit the higher-level change.

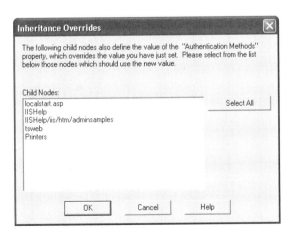

To change the connection timeout value for either your Web site or your FTP site, right-click the site in the console tree, choose Properties from the shortcut menu, and go to the Web Site or FTP Site tab. Then enter a new value in the Connection Timeout box.

Enabling and Configuring Activity Logs

IIS can maintain plain-text log files of all activities on both your Web site and your FTP site. You can read these files in Notepad or another text editor to get an idea of what's going on at your sites. Analyzing activity logs can help you determine who's visiting your sites and what features are most and least used. Figure 32-7 shows an example of an FTP log.

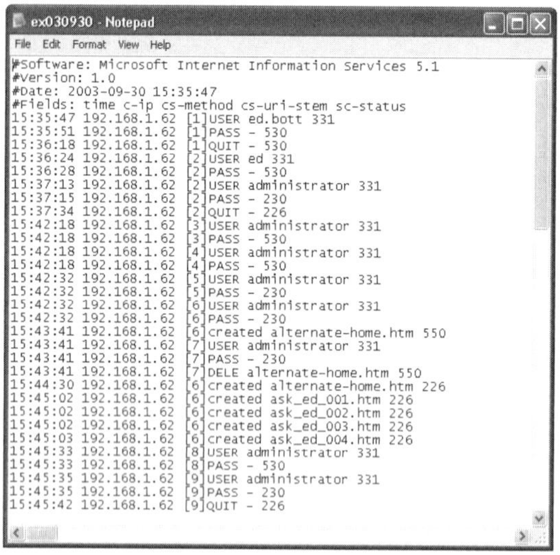


```
#Software: Microsoft Internet Information Services 5.1
#Version: 1.0
#Date: 2003-09-30 15:35:47
#Fields: time c-ip cs-method cs-uri-stem sc-status
15:35:47 192.168.1.62 [1]USER ed.bott 331
15:35:51 192.168.1.62 [1]PASS - 530
15:36:18 192.168.1.62 [1]QUIT - 530
15:36:24 192.168.1.62 [2]USER ed 331
15:36:28 192.168.1.62 [2]PASS - 530
15:37:13 192.168.1.62 [2]USER administrator 331
15:37:15 192.168.1.62 [2]PASS - 230
15:37:34 192.168.1.62 [2]QUIT - 226
15:42:18 192.168.1.62 [3]USER administrator 331
15:42:18 192.168.1.62 [3]PASS - 530
15:42:18 192.168.1.62 [4]USER administrator 331
15:42:18 192.168.1.62 [4]PASS - 530
15:42:32 192.168.1.62 [5]USER administrator 331
15:42:32 192.168.1.62 [5]PASS - 230
15:42:32 192.168.1.62 [6]USER administrator 331
15:42:32 192.168.1.62 [6]PASS - 230
15:43:41 192.168.1.62 [6]created alternate-home.htm 550
15:43:41 192.168.1.62 [7]USER administrator 331
15:43:41 192.168.1.62 [7]PASS - 230
15:43:41 192.168.1.62 [7]DELE alternate-home.htm 550
15:44:30 192.168.1.62 [6]created alternate-home.htm 226
15:45:02 192.168.1.62 [6]created ask_ed_001.htm 226
15:45:02 192.168.1.62 [6]created ask_ed_002.htm 226
15:45:02 192.168.1.62 [6]created ask_ed_003.htm 226
15:45:03 192.168.1.62 [6]created ask_ed_004.htm 226
15:45:33 192.168.1.62 [8]USER administrator 331
15:45:33 192.168.1.62 [8]PASS - 530
15:45:35 192.168.1.62 [9]USER administrator 331
15:45:35 192.168.1.62 [9]PASS - 230
15:45:42 192.168.1.62 [9]QUIT - 226
```

Figure 32-7. IIS can keep plain-text logs of activities at your Web and FTP sites, allowing you to track who is visiting the sites and what features are most popular.

> **Note** It's important to distinguish IIS's activity logs from both the event logs that Windows XP maintains and the auditing of file and folder access. For information about event logs, see Chapter 38, "Monitoring System Activities with Event Viewer." For information about auditing, see Chapter 13, "Auditing Security."

By default, logging is enabled for both Web and FTP sites, and IIS creates daily logs using the W3C Extended format—a space-delimited text format developed by the World Wide Web Consortium (W3C). (You can read the details of the W3C specification at *http://www.w3.org/TR/WD-logfile.html.*) To change these parameters, right-click Default Web Site or Default

FTP Site, choose Properties from the shortcut menu, and then click the Web Site or FTP Site tab. If you don't have a lot of free disk space and you don't care about activity logging, clear the Enable Logging check box. To use a different logging format, choose from the Active Log Format list.

The following formats are available for Web site logging:

- W3C Extended Log File Format
- Microsoft IIS Log File Format
- NCSA Common Log File Format

The NCSA format is not available for FTP sites, and the ODBC logging format, available on IIS running on server editions of Windows, is not available in Windows XP Professional. All three available formats generate space-delimited text files. The W3C format is the most versatile of the three, because it allows you to specify which kinds of information you want to track. Its one possible inconvenience is that it records times in Greenwich Mean Time. The other two formats use local (server) time.

To specify additional options relating to activity logging, select a log format on the Web Site or FTP Site tab and then click the Properties button next to it. The corresponding logging properties dialog box will appear. Figure 32-8 shows the Extended Logging Properties dialog box for the W3C Extended format.

Figure 32-8. You can change the rollover frequency or maximum size of your log files, and if you're using the W3C Extended format, you can specify which fields to include in the log.

By default, IIS creates a new log file beginning at midnight each day (select the Use Local Time For File Naming And Rollover option if you want these logs to remain in sync with your local time) and allows the file to grow without size limit. Files are stored in %SystemRoot%\ System32\LogFiles\W3SVC1 (for Web sites) and %SystemRoot%\System32\LogFiles\ MSFTPSVC1 (for FTP sites). IIS uses a file-naming pattern based on the current (local) date. You can use the option buttons to change the logging frequency (or to create a single log file of limited or unlimited size) and the Log File Directory box to store the files in a different location.

To specify which fields you want to include in a W3C Extended Format log, click the Extended Properties tab. Then select the Extended Properties check box and the check boxes for fields that you want to include.

Configuring Content Ratings

The Platform for Internet Content Selection (PICS) specification defines metalabels that are associated with content on Web pages. The standard was originally devised to describe potentially objectionable content, so that parents and teachers could control Internet access by children. The standard has since been extended to define actions that can be taken on the basis of content labels.

The version of IIS included with Windows XP includes a content rating interface that is based on an obsolete system originally devised by the Recreational Software Advisory Council. That organization no longer exists; its successor, the Internet Content Rating Association (ICRA), provides a similar capability that is compatible with the PICS standard. On its Web site (*http://www.icra.org/faq/server*), ICRA provides detailed instructions for labeling content on a Web site.

When Internet Explorer's Content Advisor feature is enabled, access to all "unrated" sites is blocked by default. Thus, for a simple Web site hosted on Windows XP Professional, the most likely reason to apply content rating labels is to identify a site that has *no* objectionable material.

To apply a single content rating that indicates all pages on your Web site are free of objectionable content, follow these steps:

1 Right-click Default Web Site and choose Properties from the shortcut menu.
2 On the HTTP Headers tab of the Default Web Site Properties dialog box, click Add. (Do not click Edit Ratings.)
3 In the Custom Header Name field of the Add/Edit Custom HTTP Header dialog box, enter **pics-label**.
4 In the Custom Header Value box, enter the following text: (**pics-1.1 "http:// www.icra.org/ratingsv02.html" l r (cz 1 lz 1 nz 1 oz 1 vz 1)**).
5 Click OK to save your changes.

After you've added this custom header, all pages from your site will be sent with the appropriate header information. Because the header indicates that all content is safe, all browsers should be able to accept your content, even if the Content Advisor feature is enabled or another PICS-compatible filtering system is in use.

Creating Virtual Directories

As stated earlier, a virtual directory is an alias for a conventional directory located elsewhere on the computer that hosts your Web or FTP site or on another network computer. Creating content in a virtual directory has certain advantages over creating it in an ordinary directory:

- Virtual directories enhance security by hiding the actual location of your content from users.

- Virtual directories simplify access to your content. Even if all your content is created on the same computer, the likelihood is that some of it will be deeply nested in your hard disk's folder structure. In such cases, the alias for your virtual directory will probably have a shorter path than the directory's actual location.

- Virtual directories are easier to relocate. If you reorganize your hard disk, you don't have to change the URL for the relocated content. All you have to do is change the alias so that it points to the content's new location.

- Virtual directories facilitate the distribution of effort. With virtual directories, you can delegate the creation of portions of your Web content to various employees or groups, and that content doesn't need to reside on a single computer.

To create a virtual directory, you can do either of the following:

- Right-click an existing folder in Windows Explorer and choose either Sharing And Security or Properties (it doesn't matter which—they both take you to the same place) from the shortcut menu. On the Web Sharing tab, shown in Figure 32-9, make sure Default Web Site (or the name of your site, if you've customized it) is selected in the Share On box. Then select Share This Folder.

- In the Internet Information Services console, right-click the parent directory of the new virtual directory (to create a top-level directory, right-click Default Web Site). Choose New, Virtual Directory from the shortcut menu. Then follow the steps presented by the Virtual Directory Creation Wizard.

The first method works only for local folders. The second can be used with remote as well as local folders. To specify a remote folder, you must enter a Universal Naming Convention (UNC) path, which takes the form *server**share*, in the Virtual Directory Creation Wizard. (You can't specify a local drive letter that you have mapped to a remote folder.) After you enter the UNC path, the wizard will prompt you for the credentials you use to log on to the remote computer.

Chapter 32

Figure 32-9. You can turn an existing folder into a virtual Web directory by selecting Share This Folder on the Web Sharing tab of its Properties dialog box.

As the last step in the creation of a virtual directory (by either method), you will be asked to specify access permissions and application permissions for the new directory. For information about making these decisions, see "Setting IIS Permissions," page 1092.

Controlling Access to Your Sites

IIS and Windows XP together provide three mechanisms by which you can control access to the directories and files served by your Web and FTP sites:

- Authentication
- IIS permissions
- NTFS permissions

Authentication is the process by which Windows and IIS determine who's trying to access a resource on your site and whether that person is authorized to do so. *Permissions* are rules that determine what an authenticated user is allowed to do with a resource. IIS permissions apply uniformly to all users. *NTFS permissions*, in contrast, allow you to make different rules for different user accounts or groups of user accounts. Of course, NTFS permissions can be applied only to directories and files stored on NTFS drives.

> **Note** Because NTFS permissions are a feature of the NTFS file system, rather than of IIS, they are discussed elsewhere in this book. For information about setting NTFS permissions, see "Controlling Access with NTFS Permissions," page 282.

> **Note** An additional authentication feature—the ability to grant or deny access to your site based on the IP address or domain name of the visitor—is available only in the server editions of Windows.

Authentication options and IIS permissions can be applied to any level of your site—to the site itself, to a particular directory, or to a particular file. You might, for example, allow anonymous access to most of your site (making it available to the general public, without qualification) but use another form of authentication in conjunction with NTFS permissions to restrict access to private areas.

Understanding Authentication Methods

For Web sites, IIS allows you to choose anonymous access and/or three forms of authentication:

- Basic authentication
- Advanced digest authentication
- Integrated Windows authentication

Of these, basic authentication is the least secure and integrated Windows authentication is the most secure. In the remainder of this section, we explain how to configure each of these authentication options.

> **Note** Client certificates can be used in place of user names and passwords in any of the authentication methods. For more information, see "Authenticating Users with Client Certificates," page 1099.

You can use authentication methods in combination with one another and in combination with anonymous access. If anonymous access is enabled, IIS uses it whenever possible—that is, it logs the client on anonymously unless the client is trying to access a resource that is protected by NTFS permissions (in which case it attempts to establish an authenticated connection). If anonymous access is not enabled and you have selected more than one authentication method, IIS uses the most secure method it can. For example, it uses integrated Windows authentication in preference to basic or advanced digest authentication, if the client computer and the computer running IIS meet the requirements for integrated Windows authentication.

The options for FTP sites are fewer than those for Web sites. FTP sites can be set up either for anonymous access or to use basic authentication. Because the methods available to FTP sites provide less security than those available to Web sites, Microsoft recommends that, if possible, you use Web Distributing Authoring and Versioning (WebDAV) as a method of sharing files over the Internet, rather than FTP. For information about WebDAV, see "Sharing Files with WebDAV," page 1099.

Anonymous Access

Using anonymous access means that your site or resource is available to any client; the client is not required to provide a name or password. IIS "impersonates" anonymous visitors to your site, using a special account called IUSR_*computername* that was created when you installed IIS.

The IUSR_*computername* account has the following characteristics:

- It is a member of the Guests group.
- A user cannot change the password.
- The password never expires.

When someone attempts to reach a directory or file at your site anonymously, IIS checks to see whether NTFS permissions restrict IUSR_*computername*'s access to that resource. If they do not, an anonymous connection is established. If they do, and you have configured the resource to allow other forms of authentication, IIS tries to use those other methods, beginning with the most secure method. If authentication is achieved, a connection is established. Otherwise, the user receives an "HTTP 403 access denied" error message.

You should use anonymous access in circumstances where the need for security is low and for resources that you want to make available to the general public.

Basic Authentication

When IIS uses basic authentication, the client's browser presents the user with a logon dialog box. The user must enter an account name and password that can be validated by the computer hosting your site (or its domain controller) to establish a connection. If the credentials are not valid, IIS gives the user two more tries before returning an "access denied" error message.

The advantage of basic authentication is that it is part of the HTTP 1 standard and therefore can be used by any browser running on any operating system. The disadvantage is that logon credentials are transmitted using Base64 encoding (sometimes called *uuencoding*) and can be intercepted and decoded.

> **Note** Creating a secure connection eliminates the principal problem of basic authentication—the fact that logon credentials are transmitted without effective encryption. The drawback to using a secure connection is that it slows performance. For more information, see "Using SSL to Secure Basic Authentication," page 1098.

Advanced Digest Authentication

The advanced digest authentication method eliminates the principal defect of basic authentication—that client credentials are sent across the network in a form that can be intercepted and decoded. With advanced digest authentication, IIS transmits a realm name to the client browser. The client browser prompts the user for logon credentials, and then creates an MD5 *hash* (a form of encryption) from the realm name and the user's logon credentials. This hash is transmitted back to IIS, which submits the hash to your domain controller for verification.

The requirements for advanced digest authentication are as follows:

- The client browser must be Internet Explorer 5 or later.
- The user and the computer running IIS must be members of, or be trusted by, the same domain.
- The user must have a valid Windows user account stored in Active Directory on the domain controller.
- The domain controller must be running Windows Server 2003.

The computer running IIS must be running Windows XP. Advanced digest authentication represents a security improvement over digest authentication, a form of authentication that was introduced with Windows 2000. If your domain controller is running Windows 2000 Server, rather than Windows Server 2003, IIS uses digest authentication instead of advanced digest authentication. The only difference between the two is that in digest authentication the user's password is stored in clear text on the server; in advanced digest authentication, the password is stored as an MD5 hash. In either case, the transmission of credentials across the network is hashed.

Integrated Windows Authentication

Using integrated Windows authentication, IIS can authenticate a user without requiring the transmission of logon credentials across the network. The authentication takes place by means of a cryptographic exchange between the client and IIS that involves hashing. Because logon credentials are not transmitted, this form of authentication is more secure than digest or advanced digest authentication. It has the following limitations, however:

- The client must be running Internet Explorer 2 or later.
- This form of authentication does not work over HTTP proxy connections.

Chapter 32

Specifying Authentication Methods

You can allow anonymous access and/or specify authentication methods at the site level, at the directory level (which includes files and subdirectories), and at the file level. For information about how settings at one level affect other levels, see "Understanding Property Inheritance," page 1083.

To specify settings, follow these steps:

1   Right-click the appropriate item in the console tree or details pane of the Internet Information Services console and choose Properties from the shortcut menu.

2   Click the Directory Security or File Security tab (File Security, if you've right-clicked a file; otherwise, Directory Security) in the item's Properties dialog box.

3   In the Anonymous Access And Authentication Control section, click Edit.

4   Fill out the Authentication Methods dialog box, shown below in Figure 32-10.

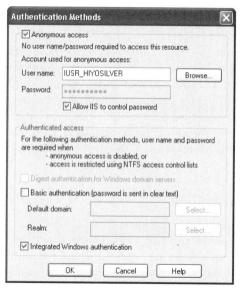

Figure 32-10.   You can use authentication methods in combination with one another.

Setting IIS Permissions

IIS permissions control what users can do after they have accessed a resource on your Web or FTP site. Unlike NTFS permissions, IIS permissions are applied uniformly to all clients. If the IIS permissions for a directory differ from the NTFS permissions, the more restrictive permissions are applied.

IIS permissions can be applied to files, directories, virtual directories, or entire sites. For information about how settings at one level affect settings at other levels, see "Understanding Property Inheritance," page 1083.

To apply IIS permissions, follow these steps:

1   Right-click the appropriate item in the console tree or details pane and choose Properties from the shortcut menu.

2   In the item's properties dialog box, click the Home Directory, Virtual Directory, or File tab (the tab name you see matches the selection type you made in the console tree).

Figure 32-11 shows the Home Directory tab of the Default Web Site Properties dialog box. In the figure, the highlighted controls are the ones concerned with IIS permissions.

Figure 32-11. Use the controls highlighted here to set IIS permissions.

3   To configure IIS permissions, set or clear the following check boxes:

■   Read (set by default). Allows users to view directory or file content and properties.

■   Write. Allows users to change directory or file content and properties.

■   Script Source Access. Allows users to access source files. If Read is also selected, users can read script source code. If Write is also selected, users can modify source code. If neither Read nor Write is selected, Script Source Access is unavailable.

■   Directory Browsing. Allows users to view file directories.

The following options are available in the Execute Permissions list:

■   None. Disables scripts (such as ASP applications) and executables.

■   Scripts Only. Enables scripts (such as ASP applications) but disables executables.

■   Scripts And Executables. Enables both scripts and executables.

Chapter 32

Tightening Security with the IIS Lockdown Wizard

Adding any server software to a computer poses security risks, and IIS is no exception. By inviting other computers to connect to yours, you expose yourself to a wide assortment of potential problems, ranging from viruses and worms that are targeted at IIS (such as the infamous Nimda and Code Red worms), to exploits that allow outside attackers to break into your server and launch attacks against the rest of your network or the Internet at large.

How do you make sure you've installed the proper IIS updates and configured your server settings properly? We recommend using a freely available tool called the Internet Information Services Lockdown Wizard (sometimes referred to as the IIS Lockdown tool). This officially sanctioned wizard steers you through the sometimes tricky process of determining which IIS features you need, disabling the features you don't need, and eliminating common security holes. You can read about the wizard and download the most current version of the tool at *http://www.microsoft.com/technet/security/tools/locktool.mspx*.

Before using the IIS Lockdown Wizard, visit Windows Update and install all current security patches for Windows XP and IIS. After completing this task, download the wizard, and then run it by following these steps:

1   Open Windows Explorer, browse to the folder where you saved the downloaded file, and double-click the executable file, Iislockd.exe.

2   Click Next on the introduction and license agreement pages. The Select Server Template page appears.

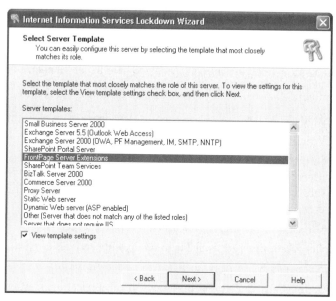

3   Select the template that most closely matches how you use IIS. (To see detailed settings in remaining pages of the wizard, click View Template Settings.) Click Next to continue.

4   Review each page of the wizard. Be certain to select Install URLScan Filter On The Server. (This feature protects the Web server from attacks that use deliberately malformed URLs to try to crash the server and leave the computer in a state where it might execute arbitrary code of the attacker's choosing.) Click Next to display the Ready To Apply Settings page.

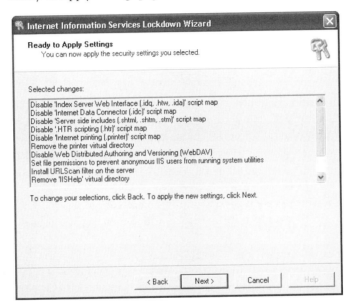

5   Review the proposed changes to be certain they're appropriate. If everything looks right, click Next. The wizard applies new, tighter security settings; disables unneeded and potentially vulnerable services; removes sample files and scripts; and so on.

6   After the changes are made, the wizard displays a summary of its actions. Click the View Report button to see a short log file. Click Next, and then click Finish to close the wizard.

Caution   After completing its work, the IIS Lockdown Wizard saves a concise report of its actions in %SystemRoot%\System32\Inetsrv\Oblt-rep.log. You'll find a more detailed log file in the same folder, saved as Oblt-log.log. Even if the wizard ran with no problems, do not delete these log files! You'll need them later if you need to rerun the wizard for any reason.

Chapter 32

If you have problems accessing IIS after running the wizard, you can undo the changes the wizard made. Just run the wizard again. You can reverse all its modifications and then lock down IIS with a different set of options. For troubleshooting purposes, try selecting or clearing specific options to see which option is the source of the problem you are experiencing.

Enabling a Secure (Encrypted) Connection

IIS can use Secure Sockets Layer (SSL) to create an encrypted connection between your Web site and its clients. SSL employs public-key encryption, at either 40-bit or 128-bit strength. When users log onto your Web site over a secure connection, they do so using a URL that begins with *https* instead of *http*.

Enabling SSL entails the use of *certificates*, digital documents that allow servers and clients to authenticate each other. Certificates come in three flavors:

- **Server certificates** are used to identify servers to Web browsers and to supply the public key for SSL encryption. Whenever a user connects to a resource on your server using the HTTPS protocol (as opposed to HTTP), the server first identifies itself with its server certificate. After the browser accepts the certificate, an encrypted SSL connection is established using the server's private key at the server and public key at the browser.

- **Client certificates** are used to identify Web browsers to servers. A secure site can require browsers to identify themselves with a client certificate as part of the authentication step.

- **Certification Authority (CA) certificates** provide the trust value for server and client certificates. Internet Explorer keeps a list of known and trusted CAs. When a user browses to a secure Web page, the Web server's server certificate is sent to the browser. The browser checks the CA that issued the server certificate. If the CA is on the list of trusted CAs, the certificate is accepted automatically. If the CA is not on the list, a dialog box is displayed, giving the user the option of accepting or rejecting the certificate.

To enable a secure connection to your Web site, directory, virtual directory, or file, follow these steps:

1 Right-click the appropriate object in the console tree or details pane and choose Properties from the shortcut menu.

2 Click the Directory Security or File Security tab in the object's Properties dialog box.

3 In the Secure Communications section of the dialog box, click Edit. (If the Edit button is not available, you need to obtain and install a server certificate. See "Obtaining a

Chapter 32

Server Certificate" below.) The Secure Communications dialog box appears, as shown in Figure 32-12 below.

4 Select Require Secure Channel (SSL) at the top of the Secure Communications dialog box.

Figure 32-12. To establish an encrypted connection, use these options after installing a server certificate.

Note If you don't require SSL, users can still try to create an SSL connection to your site by using *https* instead of *http*. If your server has a server certificate installed, a secure connection is created, even though you have not required it. If your server does not have a server certificate installed, the user receives a "This page cannot be displayed" error message.

Obtaining a Server Certificate

The process for obtaining a server certificate involves creating a certificate request (in the form of a request file), submitting the request to a CA, obtaining the approved certificate, and installing the certificate on your computer. The Web Server Certificate Wizard handles most of this process.

The Web Server Certificate Wizard generates a request for a server certificate and installs the certificate after it has been granted. If you are connected to a domain server running Enterprise Certificate Services, the wizard submits your request online. The wizard also detects out-of-date or about-to-expire certificates.

To start the Web Server Certificate Wizard, follow these steps:

1 Right-click Default Web Site (or the name of your site, if you've customized this setting) and choose Properties from the shortcut menu.

2 Click the Directory Security tab in the properties dialog box.

3 Click Server Certificate under Secure Communications and complete the wizard.

Using SSL to Secure Basic Authentication

You can set up a Web site to use basic authentication and require an SSL communication link. If you do so, an SSL link is made before authentication is performed. The user name and password are therefore transmitted in an encrypted form. All user interaction with the Web site will use SSL, however, and hence will run more slowly.

You can also configure a Web site for basic authentication without requiring an SSL link, and users can request SSL themselves if they want to protect their logon credentials. The user can do this by addressing your site with *https* instead of *http*. If you have a server certificate installed, an encrypted logon occurs, and all pages on your site will use the secure link. However, if the link was created by user request, the user can manually change a URL from *https* to *http* after authentication takes place, and the remainder of his or her interaction with your site will be unencrypted and will not incur the SSL performance overhead.

Authenticating Users with Client Certificates

Client certificates can be used in place of user names and passwords in any of the authentication schemes requiring them. You accomplish this by mapping client certificates to Windows user accounts. If certificate mapping is used, when the client's certificate is received by the server, it is checked against the mapping and, if a corresponding user account exists, the user is logged on using that account.

Two ways of mapping certificates are available: one to one and many to one. In *one-to-one mapping*, each user's certificate is mapped to an account. The server must have an exact copy of each user's certificate to create the mappings.

In *many-to-one mapping*, client certificates are mapped by rules that relate a set of certificate parameters to a user account. In this scenario, copies of the certificates are not needed. However, this means that many-to-one mapping is not as secure as one-to-one mapping.

Follow these steps to enable certificate mapping:

1. Choose Accept Client Certificates in the Client Certificates section of the Secure Communications dialog box, shown in Figure 32-12.

2. Select Enable Client Certificate Mapping and then click Edit.

3. In the ensuing dialog box, choose how you want to map the certificates:

    ▪ To create a one-to-one mapping, click the 1-To-1 tab and then click Add. Select a certificate to use and the user account to which it should be mapped.

    ▪ To create a many-to-one mapping, click the Many-To-1 tab, click Add, and follow the wizard to select certificate fields to use in the mapping rules.

Sharing Files with WebDAV

Web Distributed Authoring and Versioning (WebDAV) is an extension of the HTTP 1.1 protocol that allows users running Windows 2000 and later (and Internet Explorer 5 or later) to read and write files on a virtual directory managed by IIS. Because a WebDAV directory, unlike an FTP site, can employ all of the authentication methods supported by IIS, Microsoft recommends the use of WebDAV in preference to FTP for sharing files among users of Windows 2000 and later.

Chapter 32

Setting Up a WebDAV Directory

To set up a directory for sharing via WebDAV, simply create a virtual directory in your Web site. You can do this in either of two ways:

- Right-click the directory in Windows Explorer, choose Sharing And Security from the shortcut menu, select the Web Sharing tab, and then choose Share This Folder.
- Right-click Default Web Site in the IIS snap-in, choose New, Virtual Directory from the shortcut menu, and then follow the steps of the Virtual Directory Creation Wizard.

As the last step in either process, you need to assign IIS permissions for the shared directory. Figure 32-13 shows the dialog box you'll see if you start in Windows Explorer. (A similar dialog box appears if you begin with the IIS snap-in.)

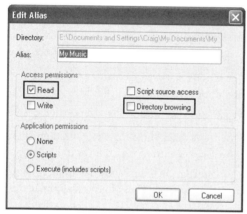

Figure 32-13. Read permission is enabled by default in a WebDAV directory. To provide usability comparable to that of an FTP site, select Directory Browsing as well.

Read permission is enabled by default. To provide functionality comparable to what an FTP site would offer, be sure to select Directory Browsing. If you want users to be able to modify existing files in the directory or create new ones, select Write as well. If you enable Write permission, however, you should choose None in the Application Permissions box. Otherwise, users will be able to upload and execute potentially damaging scripts or executables.

Using a WebDAV Directory

Assuming you have enabled read, write, and directory browsing permissions, users with appropriate credentials (or any user, if you enable anonymous access) can work with your WebDAV directory as they would with their own local file system. They can use the Add

Network Place Wizard to create a shortcut to the directory in My Network Places and then display the shared folder in Windows Explorer. If they use Office 2000 or later, they can create, publish, edit, and save documents in the WebDAV directory, exactly as they would with a local folder. And, if they open the directory in Internet Explorer, the directory looks and behaves just like an FTP site, as shown in Figure 32-14.

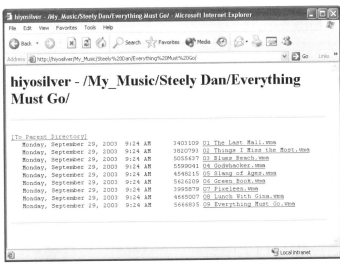

Figure 32-14. A WebDAV directory opened in Internet Explorer 5 or later looks and acts like an FTP site.

Setting Up IIS for Internet Printing

IIS supports the Internet Printing Protocol (IPP). Whenever you share a printer and you are running IIS, the shared printer becomes available over the Internet. Users to whom you've given permission can view and manage printers in a Web browser in much the same way that they can using the Printers And Faxes folder for local and network printers. In an Internet Explorer window, open *http://*hostname/*printers* for a list of shared printers on *hostname*. *Hostname* can be a computer name (for an intranet), a domain name, or an IP address. Three shared printers are shown on the next page.

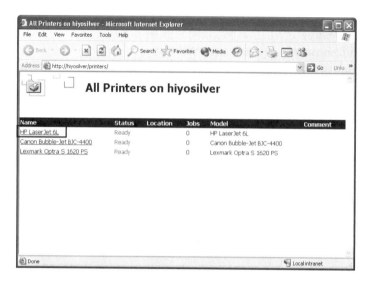

You can select one of the printers to open a page showing its status, queuing, and control options, as shown here.

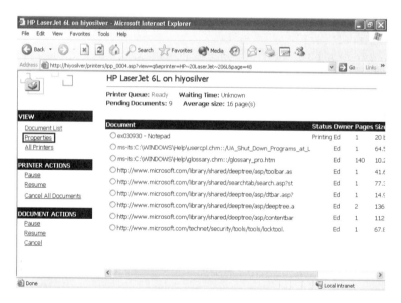

You can then click the Properties link in the left pane under View to generate a page of information about the selected printer, including the estimated wait time and information about the printer's capabilities.

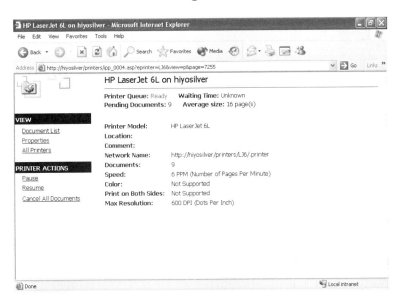

To use a printer shared via IPP, follow these steps:

1 Choose Start, Printers And Faxes.

2 In the Printers And Faxes folder, click Add A Printer under Printer Tasks.

3 When the Add Printer Wizard opens, click Next.

4 On the Local Or Network Printer page, select the second option, A Network Printer, Or A Printer Attached To Another Computer, and then click Next. The Specify A Printer page appears.

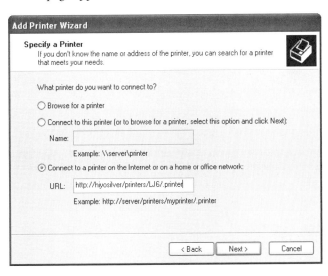

5 Select Connect To A Printer On The Internet Or On A Home Or Office Network.

6 Specify a URL of the form *http://*hostname/*printers*/printername/*.printer*, where *host-name* is the network name of the computer running IIS (you can enter a domain name, a computer name, or an IP address) and *printername* is the name under which the printer is shared. For example, for the printer shared as LJ6 on the computer named Hiyosilver, you would type **http://Hiyosilver/printers/LJ6/.printer**. Click Next and then complete the wizard.

You might be prompted to select drivers for the printer on your local machine, or to insert a disk containing such drivers, as part of the installation process.

After the printer is installed, use the IPP printer exactly as you would any other local or networked printer.

Chapter 33

Working with Windows Domains

A standalone computer is a rare sight these days; most personal computers are connected to one or more other computers as part of a network. Computers on a network can be part of a workgroup or a domain.

In a *workgroup*, the security database (including, most significantly, the list of user accounts and the privileges granted to each one) for each computer resides on that computer. When you log on to a computer in a workgroup, Microsoft Windows checks its local security database to see if you've provided a user name and password that matches one in the database. Similarly, when network users attempt to connect to your computer, Windows again consults the local security database. A workgroup is sometimes called a *peer-to-peer network*.

By contrast, a *domain* consists of computers that share a security database stored on one or more domain controllers running a member of the Windows Server 2003, Windows 2000 Server, or Windows NT Server families. When you log on using a domain account, Windows authenticates your credentials against the security database on a domain controller.

At Home with Windows XP

By design, Windows domains are intended for use on business networks. Only the most fanatical of computer hobbyists would consider installing a domain controller on a small home network. Thus, you shouldn't be surprised to learn that access to most domain features requires Windows XP Professional.

Computers running Windows XP Home Edition cannot join a domain. If you're running Home Edition, however, you *can* access shared domain resources, such as folders and printers. For details, see "Accessing Domain Resources from a Computer Running Windows XP Home Edition," page 1122.

When you have more than a handful of computers in a network, they become much easier to manage when configured as a domain. For example, instead of re-creating a database of user accounts on each computer, you create each account only once. A domain environment also offers much greater power and flexibility. For example, you can easily set up roaming user profiles, which allow users to log on at any network computer and see the same personalized desktop, menus, applications, and documents. A domain using Active Directory, a feature of Windows 2000 Server and Windows Server 2003 (but not Windows NT Server), also offers a fully searchable directory service that allows network users to easily find shared resources, contacts, users, and other directory objects. In addition, these server families offer IntelliMirror, a collection of technologies that offer centralized

- User data management
- Software installation and maintenance
- User settings management

In this chapter we make no attempt to explain how to configure a domain or use its management capabilities. Those are features of the server acting as the domain controller, and they're well documented in the numerous books about server versions of Windows. Rather, our intent here is to explain how to use your computer running Windows XP in a domain environment, focusing on how this is different from using Windows XP in a workgroup.

Domains vs. Workgroups

In addition to the location and use of the all-important security database, you'll notice a number of differences—some trivial and some that can have a significant effect on the way you use Windows—when your computer is joined to a domain. Many of these changes are designed to make Windows XP work the same way that Windows 2000 Professional works in a domain environment, which eases the training and support burden on administrators. A domain-based computer running Windows XP Professional differs from a workgroup-based computer in the ways described in the following sections.

Logon and Logoff

Many differences appear from the moment you turn on your computer. The logon and logoff screens and procedures on a domain-based computer encompass the following changes:

- **Logon screen** The Welcome screen is unavailable in a domain environment. Instead, you use the "classic" logon, which prompts you to press Ctrl+Alt+Delete and then enter your user name (if it isn't already entered from your last session) and password. For more information about using the classic logon, see "Logging On to a Domain," page 1123.

- **Automatic logon**   In a workgroup environment, you can easily set up your computer to log on automatically so that you don't need to enter your password. (Ironically, you use the domain version of User Accounts to achieve this. For details, see "Bypassing the Logon Screen," page 244.) In a domain environment, you must delve into the registry to set up automatic logon. For details, see "Logging On Automatically," page 1124.

- **Logon scripts**   In a domain environment, a domain administrator can set up scripts that run automatically each time you log on to your computer. These scripts, which are typically stored and administered on the domain controller, can be used to provide software updates, new virus definitions, and other information to your computer; set up network connections; start programs; and perform other tasks. A computer that's not joined to a domain can't run domain logon scripts. Although you can create local logon scripts for workgroup computers, they're generally less powerful and, of course, they're not centrally managed for all computers on the network.

- **Forgotten passwords**   Password hints aren't available with the classic logon that's used in a domain environment. Nor can you create or use a Password Reset Disk, which allows you to set a new password if you can't remember your current one. A domain administrator can change the password for your domain account. Any user who is a member of the local Administrators group can change the password for any local account. For details about using these features in a workgroup, see "Recovering from a Lost Password," page 266.

- **Fast User Switching**   Fast User Switching, a fantastic feature that allows a user to log on without requiring the current user to first log off, is not available on domain-based computers. Application compatibility and other technical issues prevent its use. For information about Fast User Switching, see "Configuring Fast User Switching," page 246.

- **Workstation locking**   On a computer that's joined to a domain, pressing the Windows logo key+L locks a workstation so that only the currently logged-on user or an administrator can unlock it. (In a workgroup, Windows logo key+L invokes Fast User Switching.) For details about locking, see "Logging Off or Locking Your Computer," page 248.

- **Logoff and Shutdown screens**   Instead of the big, colorful buttons that appear when you choose to log off or shut down a workgroup computer, a computer joined to a domain displays dialog boxes similar to those in Windows 2000, as shown in Figures 33-1 and 33-2. They serve the same function and they're no harder or easier to use; they are simply intended to ease the transition to Windows XP for corporate users.

Figure 33-1.   Domain users see this utilitarian Log Off Windows dialog box.

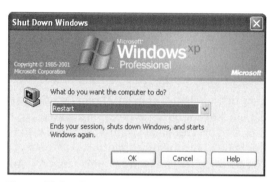

Figure 33-2. To shut down a domain-based computer, you select from a list and click OK. Windows displays your previous selection as the default option.

File Sharing and Security

The methods for sharing files with other users of your computer and with other users on your network are significantly different on a domain-based computer:

- **Simple File Sharing** Although the option to enable Simple File Sharing remains in the Folder Options dialog box (and indeed, it's selected by default), Simple File Sharing is not available in a domain environment.

  Without Simple File Sharing, the Security tab appears in the properties dialog box for all printers and for all folders and files on NTFS drives. When you're logged on as a member of the local Administrators or Power Users group, the Sharing tab, with which you set network access permissions, appears in the properties dialog box for all folders.

  Most importantly, without Simple File Sharing, network users are authenticated as themselves. To access local resources, their account must be granted appropriate permissions, either directly or through their membership in a group.

> For more information about Simple File Sharing, see "Simple File Sharing vs. Windows 2000–Style Sharing," page 230, and "Simple File Sharing vs. Advanced Permissions," page 275. For information about how sharing options can affect sharing over a network, see Chapter 30, "Managing Shared Folders and Printers."

- **Shared Documents** On computers in a workgroup environment, the local Shared Documents folder, %AllUsersProfile%\Documents, occupies a prominent place in My Computer. Particularly when Simple File Sharing is enabled, it is the default and easiest location for storing folders and files that you want to share with other users on your computer or on your network.

When your computer is joined to a domain, however, you're likely to forget that Shared Documents exists. My Computer no longer includes a Files Stored On This Computer group. If your computer was in a workgroup and you ran the Network Setup Wizard before you joined a domain, the folder continues to be shared as Shared Documents. If you have not run the Network Setup Wizard, the folder is not set up as a network share by default. Either way, by default, only local users and groups have permissions to access the folders and files within Shared Documents. If you want to grant permissions to domain users, you should add the appropriate domain groups to the folder's access control list (ACL). For information about modifying the ACL, see "Controlling Access with NTFS Permissions," page 282.

- **Windows Firewall** On a domain-based computer, Windows Firewall supports two profiles. One profile (the domain profile) is used when the computer is connected to the domain and the other (the standard profile) is used when the computer is not connected—a common scenario for mobile computers in a corporate environment. Windows Firewall maintains a separate list of exceptions and settings for each profile. It switches profiles automatically when you connect or disconnect the computer from the domain network. (If you connect the computer to a different network, such as a home network, it uses its standard profile.)

> For more information about Windows Firewall, see "Blocking Intruders with Windows Firewall," page 194.

Networking

Not surprisingly, configuring a network and finding network resources in a domain environment rely on centralized servers.

- **Network Setup Wizard** The Network Setup Wizard, which is designed to help you set up a home or small office network, does not run on a computer that's joined to a domain. (For information about the Network Setup Wizard, see "Using the Network Setup Wizard," page 960.) To perform comparable tasks in a domain environment, you (or a network administrator) must first configure your network connection so that your computer is on the domain's subnet; the remaining tasks are taken care of when you join a domain. (For details, see "Joining a Domain," page 1115.)

- **Network Tasks** When you open My Network Places, the links that appear in the task pane vary depending on whether your computer is part of a workgroup, a Windows NT domain, or an Active Directory domain, as shown in Figure 33-3. In addition, your options for browsing and searching the network vary. For details, see "Finding Files, Printers, and Users," page 1125.

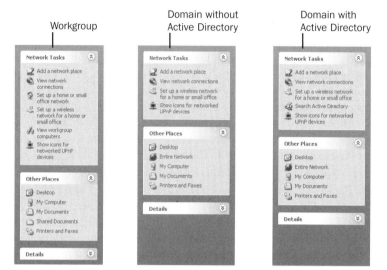

Figure 33-3. Note that Shared Documents appears in Other Places only in a workgroup. You can browse computers in a domain by clicking Entire Network.

Security Center

Security Center, a feature that was introduced with Service Pack 2 for Windows XP, is turned off by default on computers that are joined to a domain. With Security Center turned off, no icon appears in the notification area and, more importantly, Security Center doesn't monitor your computer's essential security settings (firewall, automatic updates, and antivirus) as it does on a workgroup computer. In this state, you can still open Security Center from Control Panel, but all you get is an assemblage of links to other Control Panel programs and related information, as shown in Figure 33-4. The status section—which monitors and advises you of the current state of your firewall, Automatic Updates, and antivirus programs—is absent. Security Center is neutered by default in a domain-based computer because the domain administrator typically has more powerful security tools available and will want to centrally administer security settings.

You can enable Security Center for a domain-based computer and use it just as if you're working on a computer that is *not* joined to a domain. To do that, follow these steps:

1 At a command prompt, type **gpedit.msc** to open Group Policy.
2 In Group Policy, open Computer Configuration\Administrative Templates\Windows Components\Security Center.
3 Double-click the Turn On Security Center (Domain PCs Only) policy.
4 Select Enabled and click OK.
5 Restart your computer.

Figure 33-4. On a domain-based computer, Security Center is reduced to a collection of links. Compare this figure with Figure 7-3 on page 191, which shows Security Center on a workgroup computer.

> **Note** These steps explain how to use the local Group Policy object to enable Security Center for all users on a computer. This policy is also available in Windows Server 2003. Therefore, if your domain controller runs Windows Server 2003 (not Windows 2000 Server), you can use domain-based policy to make this setting. For more information on settings policies, see Appendix F, "Group Policy."

> For more information about Security Center, see "Monitoring Windows XP Security," page 190.

Computer and User Management

Because domain user accounts are managed at the domain level, the account-management tools that you see on a workstation have a different appearance and functionality than those on a workgroup computer.

- **User Accounts** When you open User Accounts in Control Panel, you get a different version depending on whether your computer is joined to a domain or not. The two versions have similar capabilities; the difference is more style than substance. The workgroup version follows the newer style of Windows XP, complete with graphics and links to wizard-like dialog boxes. For information about the workgroup version of User Accounts, see "Working with User Accounts," page 232.

  The domain version uses a traditional dialog box that's nearly identical to its Windows 2000 predecessor. For information about this version, see "Advanced Account Setup Options," page 252.

● **Group Policy**   A computer in a workgroup or in a non–Active Directory domain can use the local Group Policy object to make a large number of settings and impose a number of restrictions—but these settings and restrictions apply to only a single computer, and they apply to all users on that computer. In a domain with Active Directory, many more Group Policy settings are available. More importantly, they're centrally managed and they can be selectively applied to computers, users, groups, domains, and other divisions. This is a huge topic that's covered in great depth in the resource kits for the Windows 2000 Server and Windows Server 2003 families. You can learn about local Group Policy—and get a hint of the power available in domain-based policy—by reviewing Appendix F, "Group Policy."

Miscellaneous User Interface Elements

Some of the other differences between domain-based and workgroup-based computers including the following.

● **Ctrl+Alt+Delete**   In a domain environment, pressing Ctrl+Alt+Delete after you're logged on displays the Windows Security dialog box (shown in Figure 33-5), a time-honored path to options for locking, logging off, shutting down, and other tasks. In a workgroup that's configured to use the Welcome screen for logons, pressing Ctrl+Alt+Delete opens Windows Task Manager. (In fact, this behavior is linked to the Welcome screen, not domain membership per se.)

Figure 33-5.   Many longtime Windows NT and Windows 2000 users are in the habit of pressing Ctrl+Alt+Delete and then Enter to lock their workstation.

● **Time synchronization**   The appearance of an Internet Time tab in Control Panel's Date And Time Properties dialog box depends on domain membership. In a workgroup environment (or in a Windows NT–based domain), you use this tab to synchronize your computer's clock with an Internet time server. This feature is unavailable on computers joined to a domain using Windows 2000 Server or Windows Server 2003.

In fact, this is not merely a user interface change, nor is it a feature that's missing from domain-based computers. It's actually related to the authentication method used by domain controllers. Windows 2000 Server and Windows Server 2003 use Kerberos V5 authentication. One part of Kerberos V5 authentication relies on close synchronization between times on the client workstations and on the server; if transmitted data between them is tagged with a time that's not identical, it's deemed to be invalid. For this reason, a computer that's joined to a domain that uses Windows 2000 Server or Windows Server 2003 as its domain controller always synchronizes its internal clock to the domain controller—not to an external time source. The domain controller should be configured to get its time from an accurate time source.

Like local logons and workgroup logons, Windows NT Server uses the Windows NT challenge/response (also known as NTLM challenge/response) authentication protocol instead of Kerberos V5 authentication. Clients in a Windows NT domain can be configured to retrieve the time from the domain controller or another Windows time server via NetBIOS (synchronizing all computers in a domain is still a good idea, but not essential), or they can be configured to independently contact an Internet time server.

> **Note** **Setting your computer's clock**
> If your computer is in a Windows NT domain, you can synchronize your clock with the domain controller by including this line in a batch program that runs at startup (either as a logon script or by inclusion in your Start menu's Startup group):
>
> ```
> net time /domain /set /y
> ```
>
> If your computer is not in a domain, synchronize your clock using Date And Time Properties. In Control Panel, open Date And Time (or simply double-click the clock in the notification area). Click the Internet Time tab, select the Automatically Synchronize With An Internet Time Server check box, and then click Update Now. (If you prefer a command-line utility, use W32tm /Resync. The Net Time command does *not* work with SNTP, the Internet time protocol.)
>
> If your computer is in an Active Directory domain, you shouldn't set the clock directly; let Windows synchronize automatically with the domain controller.
>
> For more information about synchronizing with an Internet time server, click the Time Synchronization link on the Internet Time tab in Date And Time Properties.

- **Start menu** A couple of trivial changes differentiate the Start menu in a domain environment. No picture appears by the user's full name at the top of the menu, and the command to quit appears as Turn Off Computer on a workgroup computer and Shut Down in a domain. Why? Simply to more closely resemble the Windows 2000 interface that's familiar to many domain users.

Inside Out

Use domain resources *and* retain access to workgroup-only features

As a domain user, you might want to use features that are available only in a workgroup setting. (Fast User Switching is the feature that many domain users miss the most.) Depending on how your domain is configured, which domain-dependent features you need, and whether you need to share your own computer's resources with other domain users, you might decide that you're better off *not* joining a domain. In such a case, you can still have access to shared files and printers. Here's how:

1 If your computer is already joined to a domain, join a workgroup (doing so removes your domain membership), as explained in "Leaving a Domain," page 1122.

2 Log on using your local account.

3 Set the name of your workgroup to be the same as the domain name. (This isn't essential, but it makes browsing the network easier.)

4 In Control Panel, open User Accounts, click your account name, and then click Manage My Network Passwords under Related Tasks in the left pane.

5 In the Stored User Names And Passwords dialog box, click Add.

6 In the Logon Information Properties dialog box, type ***domainname**** (where *domainname* is the name of your domain) in the Server box. In the User Name and Password boxes, enter the credentials for your domain account, not your local account.

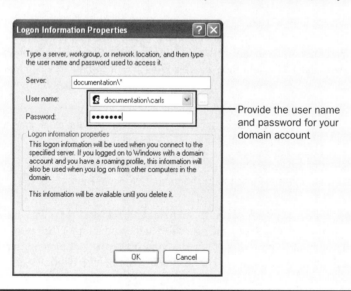

Provide the user name and password for your domain account

Adding a credential this way (instead of providing your user name and password each time you try to view the resources of a different domain computer) gives you immediate access to all domain file and printer resources for which your domain account has permissions. You have effectively linked your domain account to your local account. Be aware that your domain logon script won't run and that several other domain-only features (such as Group Policy) won't be effective; also, the domain administrator might prevent you from logging on this way. In addition, some privileges (such as the ability to use the domain's proxy server) might be limited to members of the Domain Users group or some other global group. Your local account can't be included in a global group.

Entering Domain Credentials

When you enter your user name, Windows needs to know which security database to look in to find the name. In some dialog boxes (such as the Log On To Windows dialog box), you enter your user name in one box and select the name of the domain or computer in another box. Other dialog boxes, however, provide only a User Name box. Windows assumes that you're entering the name of an account on the resource you're trying to access, so in most cases you don't need to enter the name of a domain or computer. In some cases, however, you must provide the name of the computer or domain as well as your user name; you enter both pieces of information in the User Name box. If the security database is on a computer running Windows NT, use the form *domainname\username* (for example, **documentation\ carls** or, for a local account on a computer named Sequoia, **sequoia\carls**). If the security database is on a computer running Windows 2000, Windows XP, or Windows Server 2003, you can use that form or the newer *username@domainname* form (for example, **carls@documentation.swdocs.com** or **carls@sequoia**).

Joining a Domain

To join a domain, your computer must have a computer account set up on the domain controller. You can do this before, during, or after you install Windows XP Professional on your computer:

- Before you set up Windows XP, an administrator can create the computer account on the domain controller. In Windows 2000 Server or Windows Server 2003, you use the Active Directory Users And Computers console to add a computer account; in Windows NT Server, you use Server Manager.

- During installation, the Setup program asks whether you want to join a workgroup or domain. If you elect to join a domain, you can create a computer account (if you haven't already set one up), provided that you can furnish the name and password of a domain administrative account that has authority to add domain computer accounts (typically, an account that's a member of the Domain Admins group). You can provide this information whether you run Setup in an interactive or unattended fashion.

● After installation, you can join a domain from the Computer Name tab of the System Properties dialog box. (Details of this method are provided below.) Again, if you haven't already set up a computer account on the domain controller, you can set one up from here—as long as you provide the name and password of a domain administrator account. To join a domain after you've set up Windows, follow these steps:

1 Log on as a member of the local Administrators group.

2 In Control Panel, open System (in the Performance And Maintenance category). Alternatively, right-click My Computer and choose Properties.

3 In the System Properties dialog box, click the Computer Name tab.

Tip **Skip the Network Identification Wizard**

The Computer Name tab has two buttons that perform essentially the same task. Clicking the Network ID button starts the Network Identification Wizard, which, over the course of a half dozen pages or more, helps you to join a domain. The Change button achieves the same result with a single dialog box, as described in this section.

However, the Network Identification Wizard does offer one advantage: It helps you add a single domain user account to a local user group. For more information about this task, see "Adding Domain Accounts to Your Local Account Database," page 1119.

4   Click Change to open the Computer Name Changes dialog box, shown below.

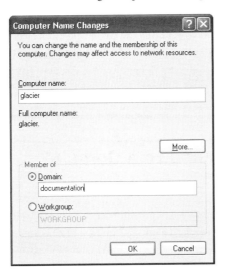

5   Select Domain, type the name of your domain, and then click OK. Another Computer Name Changes dialog box appears.

6   Type the user name and password of an account that has permission to join your computer to the domain. By default, members of the global Domain Admins group have this permission.

7   Restart your computer when prompted.

Chapter 33

Tip   Use resources on another domain

Your computer can be joined to only one domain. But if you routinely use resources from another domain, you can add credentials for other domains that allow access to those domains' resources. In Control Panel, open User Accounts. Click the Advanced tab and then click Manage Passwords. Click Add and then specify the name of the other domain's computer that has the shared resources (in the form *domainname\computername*), along with your user name and password for the other domain.

Is Your Computer Joined to a Domain?

Unless you're aware of some of the subtle visual and operational differences between domains and workgroups described earlier in this chapter, your computer's domain membership status might not be immediately obvious. The most reliable way to determine this at a glance is to open System Properties and click the Computer Name tab. Below Full Computer Name appears either the word *Workgroup* or *Domain*, along with the name of the workgroup or domain.

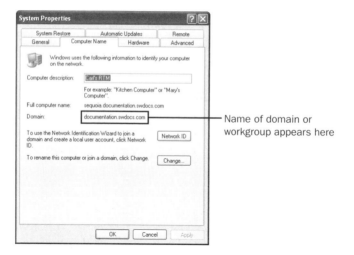

Name of domain or workgroup appears here

You can glean some other interesting information about your domain status by using the Whoami command-line utility, which you can find on the Windows XP CD-ROM in the \Support\Tools\Support.cab file. (You can install all the support tools utilities by running \Support\Tools\Setup.exe.) Open a command prompt window and type **whoami** to find out the user name of the currently logged-on user; the user name is preceded by the domain name if you're logged on using a domain account or the computer name if you're using a local account. Type **whoami /groups** to see a list of all the local and global security groups to which your account belongs.

Adding Domain Accounts to Your Local Account Database

When you join a domain using the procedure described in the previous section, Windows adds two global security groups to your local account database.

- The domain's Domain Admins group is added to your local Administrators group.
- The domain's Domain Users group is added to your local Users group.

You can confirm these additions by opening Local Users And Groups (type **lusrmgr.msc** at a command prompt) and examining the properties of the Administrators group and the Users group, as shown in Figure 33-6.

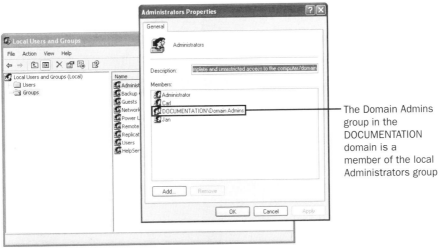

The Domain Admins group in the DOCUMENTATION domain is a member of the local Administrators group

Figure 33-6.   Adding domain accounts gives domain users access to local resources.

Placing these groups in your local account database gives their members the same privileges on your computer as local members of the group. For example, any member of the Domain Admins group can log on to your computer locally and have all the rights and permissions accorded to local administrative accounts.

> **Note**   Don't worry: Membership in a local group doesn't automatically allow access to your files over a network connection. Only folders that you choose to share are available on the network. And permissions that you apply to the shared folders restrict who can access the folders and what they can do with their contents. For more information about sharing on a network, see Chapter 30, "Managing Shared Folders and Printers."

By default, your domain account is a member of the Domain Users group. Therefore, when you log on to your computer using your domain account, you'll have all the privileges of a member of the local Users group. (In other words, you won't have very many privileges; you'll be a limited user.) You might want to add your domain account to a more high-powered group. You can do this in either of two ways:

- At the domain controller, add your account to a global group that has the privileges you need. For example, adding your account to the Domain Admins group gives you instant membership in the local Administrators group—not only of your computer, but of all computers in the domain. Depending on the size of your domain and your role in the organization, this may be entirely inappropriate, of course. But a domain administrator might choose to add your account to another group that has privileges that fall somewhere in between those of Domain Users and Domain Admins.

- At your computer, you can add your domain account (or another global group of which you're a member) to your local account database.

To exercise the second option—adding a domain account to your local account database— you can use either User Accounts or Local Users And Groups. User Accounts is the better tool for adding individual user accounts; Local Users And Groups lets you add groups more easily.

To add a user account, follow these steps:

1 In Control Panel, open User Accounts.

2 On the Users tab, click Add.

3 In the Add New User dialog box, type the user name and domain name of the account you want to add (or click Browse, Advanced, Find Now to select from a list of domain user accounts), and then click Next.

4 In the next dialog box, select the local group with the access level you want and then click Finish.

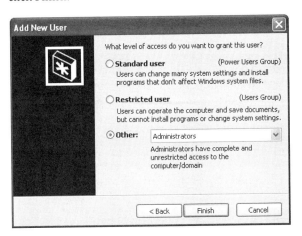

To add a global user account or global group to your local account database, follow these steps:

1 At a command prompt, type **lusrmgr.msc** to open Local Users And Groups.

2 Open the Groups folder, and then double-click the name of the group to which you want to add a user or group.

3 Click Add, Advanced. The Select Users dialog box appears.

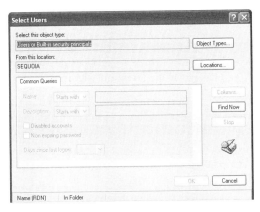

4 Be sure the domain name appears in From This Location. If it does not, click Locations and select the domain name.

5 Click Find Now to display a list of users and groups.

6 Select the users or groups you want to add (hold down the Ctrl key as you click to select multiple names), and then click OK.

For more information about using Local Users And Groups, see "Using the Local Users And Groups Snap-In," page 255.

Leaving a Domain

The procedure for leaving a domain and joining a workgroup is similar to the procedure for joining a domain, described earlier in this chapter. To join a workgroup, follow these steps:

1 Log on as a member of the local Administrators group.

2 Open System Properties and click Computer Name, Change.

3 Select Workgroup and then type the workgroup name. A workgroup name can contain up to 15 characters. It cannot be the same as the name of any computer in the workgroup, and it cannot contain any of the following characters:

    ; : " < > * + = \ | ? ,

4 If you're leaving an Active Directory domain, in the dialog box that appears, enter the user name and password of a domain account that has permission to remove the computer from the domain.

Accessing Domain Resources from a Computer Running Windows XP Home Edition

A computer running Windows XP Home Edition cannot be joined to a domain. Moreover, you can't manually add entries to the list in the Stored User Names And Passwords dialog box using Home Edition. However, Home Edition users who have a domain user account *can* access shared folders and printers in a domain. If your Home Edition computer is connected to the domain, either through a local area connection or a virtual private network (VPN) connection, you can use either of the following techniques to access domain resources:

● In Windows Explorer's Address bar, type the network path to the resource you want to use, in the form *servername**sharename*. For example, to open the Document share on a server named Everglades, type **\\everglades\document**. In a few moments, a dialog box requests your user name and password. Enter the credentials for your domain account, not the local account you use to log on to your own computer. The folders in the share then appear in Windows Explorer.

● Open My Network Places and click View Workgroup Computers. If your workgroup name is the same as the domain name, other computers in the domain become visible. (If your workgroup name is not the same as the domain name, click Microsoft Windows Network under Other Places. Then double-click the domain name to see its computers.) Double-click a computer icon, and the request for user name and password appears. Enter your domain credentials, and the computer's shared resources appear.

Credentials you enter using these methods persist throughout your session, but are discarded when you log off. Therefore, typing an address or browsing to a network resource works fine for ad hoc connections. But if you regularly connect to the same resources, there's a better way that lets you avoid the (sometimes lengthy) wait for the password request dialog box and the requirement to enter your network credentials repeatedly: Set up a batch program that makes your network connections, and run the batch program each time you log on (or each time you connect to the network). To set up such a batch program, follow these steps:

1 Start Notepad.

2 For each network resource you want to connect with, type a Net Use command on a separate line. Use the format **net use *servername**sharename password* /user:*username*,** where *servername* is the name of the computer, *sharename* is the name of a shared folder, *password* is the password for your domain account, and *username* is the user name for your domain account. For example, to connect to the Document share on the computer named Everglades using Carl's domain account, you'd enter

```
net use \\everglades\document WdYw2Gt /user:carls
```

> **Caution**   Your network password is stored as plain text in the batch program. If you don't want to expose your password in this way, replace it with an asterisk (*). Then Windows prompts you to enter the password when you run the batch program.

3 Save the file, giving it a name with either a .cmd or .bat extension. You might place it on the desktop or in your Startup folder.

Logging On to a Domain

When your computer is joined to a domain, you ordinarily log on using your domain account. Doing so loads the portions of your profile stored on network servers, applies domain-based Group Policy objects, and lets you use any resources throughout the domain for which your account has requisite permissions.

Alternatively, you can log on using a local account. But if you have a desktop computer that's permanently attached to the network, there's seldom any reason to do so. Even most local administrative tasks are just as easily handled—either locally or remotely—by a domain account that's a member of the local Administrators group. If you have a portable computer, you might want to use a local account when your computer is not connected to the network. It's not necessary to do that, however, because Windows uses a locally cached version of your profile if the domain controller is unavailable. Using separate accounts for local and network logons can make it more complicated to manage permissions on your locally stored documents.

To log on to a domain, wait for the Welcome To Windows dialog box to appear and press Ctrl+Alt+Delete. Doing so displays the Log On To Windows dialog box, shown in Figure 33-7. Type the user name and password for your domain account, and be sure that your domain name is selected in the Log On To box. (To log on using a local user account, type the user name and password, and select the computer name in the Log On To box.)

Figure 33-7. If the Log On To box doesn't appear, click the Options button.

Logging On Automatically

If your computer is in a secure location where only you (and others you trust) have physical access to it, you might want to set it up so that you don't need to press Ctrl+Alt+Delete and then enter your user name and password each time you start the computer. By making some changes in the registry, you can set up your computer to log on automatically.

> **Caution** With automatic logon, anyone with physical access can start your computer and log on using your credentials. The logged-on individual then has access to all of your files (including encrypted files), network resources, and even Web sites for which you've cached your password. There's another risk to this scheme: Your password is stored in plain text in the registry. Authenticated users on the network who have remote access to your registry can view your password.

With those risks in mind, if you're confident that automatic logon doesn't pose a security risk for you, follow these steps to set it up:

1 Log on as a member of the Administrators group.
2 Type **regedit** at a command prompt to open Registry Editor.

Chapter 33

3 Open the HKLM\Software\Microsoft\Windows NT\CurrentVersion\Winlogon key.

4 Change the setting of the AutoAdminLogon value to 1.

5 Open the DefaultDomainName value and type the name of your domain.

6 Open the DefaultUserName value and type the user name of the account you want logged on automatically.

7 If the DefaultPassword value doesn't exist, create a new string value of that name.

8 Open the DefaultPassword value and type the password for the user account you specified in step 6.

After you complete these steps, the account you specified logs on automatically each time you turn on the computer.

If you decide you no longer want to log on automatically, an easy method is available that doesn't require venturing into the registry again:

1 In Control Panel, open User Accounts.

2 On the Users tab, select Users Must Enter A User Name And Password To Use This Computer.

Selecting this check box makes two essential changes in the registry: It changes the AutoAdminLogon value back to 0 and it deletes the DefaultPassword value altogether. (The other registry changes you made to enable automatic logon are quite harmless and can safely remain in place.) For more information about classic logon, see "Controlling How Users Log On," page 239.

Finding Files, Printers, and Users

In general, you can browse a domain to find its shared resources in much the same way you browse a workgroup. Start by opening My Network Places. In a workgroup environment, the View Workgroup Computers link under Network Tasks displays all of the computers in your workgroup. In a domain environment, there isn't a corresponding link. (See Figure 33-3 on page 1110.) To browse the computers in your domain, click Entire Network (under Other Places) and then double-click Microsoft Windows Network. This displays an icon for each domain and workgroup in your network; double-click a domain name to see its computers. Figure 33-8 shows a small network. (Three domains in a network this size is unusual, but we use this approach to separate test systems from our production network.)

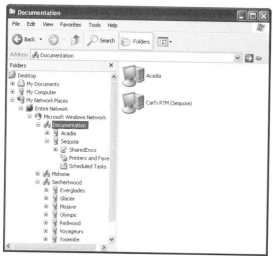

Figure 33-8. The Folders Explorer bar illustrates the network hierarchy.

If your domain controller uses Active Directory, a service included with Windows 2000 Server and Windows Server 2003, there's a better way. Instead of browsing for network objects (such as applications, files, printers, and users), you can search Active Directory. Predefined searches help you locate users, contacts, and groups; computers; printers; shared folders; and organizational units. To start a search, click the Search Active Directory link under Network Tasks in My Network Places. Select the type of object you're searching for and then enter your criteria. The search application window, shown in Figure 33-9, is well organized and easy to figure out.

After you enter your criteria, click Find Now. The window enlarges, and the results of your search appear in a list at the bottom of the window.

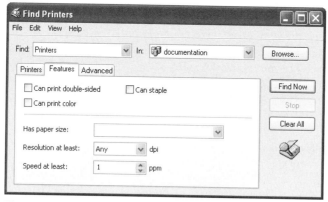

Figure 33-9. In a large organization, you can use this Active Directory search page to locate a printer that has certain features you need.

Part 7

Using E-mail, Fax, and Messaging

Chapter 34

Using and Customizing Outlook Express

Why Outlook Express? You probably use at least one suite of office applications, which means you probably already have a program to send and retrieve your e-mail. So why would you want to use Microsoft Outlook Express—especially considering that its name suggests it's just a lightweight, scaled-down, miniature version of Microsoft Outlook (the scheduling, contact management, and e-mail client component of Microsoft Office)?

At Home with Windows XP

Outlook Express 6 is absolutely identical in Windows XP Home Edition and Professional. All the information in this chapter applies to users of both editions of Windows XP.

Names can be deceiving. Outlook Express might not have quite the power of Outlook, but it would be a mistake to consider it lightweight. If you've dismissed Outlook Express because you're already happily sending and receiving e-mail with another product, here are some reasons to reconsider your decision:

- **Identities** Outlook Express's identities feature allows multiple users to send and receive mail, each using separate accounts and storing their messages and address books in private sets of folders. This feature was originally intended for use with earlier versions of Windows, in which a family shares a single copy of Outlook Express running on a single computer. In Microsoft Windows XP, this feature is much less compelling, because each user can have a separate account with a private copy of Outlook Express. With the help of Fast User Switching, any user on a shared computer can easily and quickly access his or her own mail. Outlook Express identities are still useful for individuals who want to create multiple e-mail "personalities" that share a common address book. For some suggestions on how you can benefit from using Outlook Express identities, see "Managing Identities," page 1143. For more information about sharing contacts, see "Managing Contacts," page 1145.

- **Newsgroups**   Outlook Express is both an e-mail client and a capable newsgroup client. If you take advantage of the Internet's vast array of public and proprietary newsgroups, you might want to employ the same application for accessing both your mail account and your newsgroups. That way you can integrate e-mail and newsgroup messages into a common topic-oriented folder structure. For more details on setting up and using newsgroup accounts, see "Using Newsgroups," page 1169.

- **Hotmail**   You can use Microsoft's free Hotmail service (using either a hotmail.com or msn.com address) with any Internet connection. You don't need an e-mail client to access Hotmail accounts—any Web browser will do. However, with Outlook Express, you can use Hotmail more effectively: You can access your Hotmail accounts from the same place you access your industry-standard SMTP/POP3 e-mail accounts. Outlook Express gracefully deals with both account types, setting up a separate folder tree for each Hotmail account. Outlook Express also enables you to work with Hotmail messages offline. You can use it to read and answer mail when you're away from your Internet connection. Then, when you reconnect, Outlook Express synchronizes your offline work with the Hotmail server, sending your replies and alerting you to new messages that have arrived.

Reality Check

Outlook Express doesn't inspire a passionate response from Windows users. Based on our anecdotal surveys, Windows power users typically prefer other, more powerful e-mail programs, including Outlook and a variety of non-Microsoft alternatives. Most collections of Windows tips and tricks give short shrift to Outlook Express. On the Internet, a small handful of Outlook Express experts provide generally accurate collections of tips, troubleshooting advice, and links to third-party add-ins and utilities. The best online repository of Outlook Express information we've found is Inside Outlook Express (*http://insideoe.tomsterdam.com),* maintained by Microsoft MVP Tom Koch. Microsoft's public Outlook Express newsgroup (part of the Internet Explorer 6.0 group at *http://communities.microsoft.com/newsgroups/default.asp?icp=InternetExplorer)* also offers accurate answers and tips.

In general, the criticisms, complaints, and comments we read about Outlook Express fall into two basic categories: security and spam blocking.

Security Concerns

Because Outlook Express is the default e-mail client in every recent version of Windows, it's a natural target for writers of worms, viruses, Trojan horses, and other hostile software. Many recent attacks have attempted to exploit known security vulnerabilities in the HTML-rendering engine Outlook Express shares with Internet Explorer. So far, every known security hole has been blocked by a patch made available via Windows Update before exploits made it into the wild, and antivirus software developers typically respond to new strains within hours. In Windows XP, security-conscious Outlook Express users can take advantage of the effective (albeit extreme) option to completely disable HTML-rendering capabilities and read new mail in plain text. For more information on this feature, see "Setting Security Options," page 1142.

An additional Outlook Express security feature, introduced in Windows XP Service Pack 1, blocks virtually all attachments in e-mail messages. Unfortunately, this feature (which we describe in detail in "Blocking Dangerous Attachments," later in this chapter) is too sweeping to be of any practical benefit. Because it prevents users from opening or saving even benign attachments (such as pictures and PDF files), it's more likely to frustrate users than to reassure them. Tweaking the list of blocked file types takes skills that are beyond those of most ordinary users, and so they take the path of least resistance: completely disabling attachment blocking.

Spam Blocking

In recent years, the volume of unsolicited commercial e-mail—*spam*—has increased to staggering levels, to the point where it threatens to overwhelm legitimate messages. Outlook Express includes two features that can be pressed into service to block spam, but neither one is particularly effective. Adding an e-mail address or an entire domain to the Blocked Senders list instructs Outlook Express to automatically delete any incoming messages from that sender. Unfortunately, this technique is completely ineffective against the overwhelming majority of modern spam. Message rules, which filter incoming e-mail based on its content, offer slightly more promising options, but require a disproportionate amount of effort to be effective. For more information on both options, see "Blocking Obnoxious Mail," page 1164.

Getting Started with Outlook Express

Getting started with Outlook Express involves a few relatively painless steps: setting up your accounts, tailoring the program's visual presentation so that the information you need is at hand but your screen isn't overwhelmed with details you don't require, and making a few decisions in the Options dialog box.

Setting Up Accounts

The Internet Accounts dialog box (choose Tools, Accounts) is where you set up, review, edit, and delete accounts. Accounts are organized into three categories: Mail, News, and Directory Service. Each category gets a tab in the dialog box. For your convenience, the dialog box lists your accounts of all three types on an All tab (see Figure 34-1).

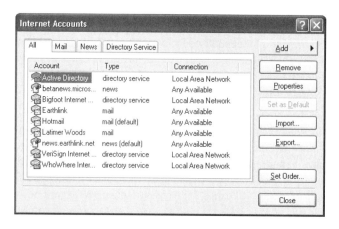

Figure 34-1. The All tab of the Internet Accounts dialog box provides a consolidated list of your mail, news, and directory service accounts.

Mail and news accounts are presumably self-explanatory: They allow you to send and receive e-mail and newsgroup messages. Directory service accounts are different—and might better be described as connections than as accounts. A *directory service* is a repository of information about people and businesses. When you don't know someone's e-mail address, you can try to find it by connecting to a directory service and performing a search. You can also configure things so that Outlook Express checks incomplete e-mail addresses in your outbound messages against one or more directory services. For more information about directory services, see "Creating a Directory Service Account," page 1134.

Creating a Mail Account

If you start Outlook Express without already having established a mail account, the Internet Connection Wizard appears to guide you through the steps necessary to create your first account. If you need to create an additional account, or if you canceled out of the wizard when you first got to it and are ready now to create your first account, choose Tools, Accounts. In the Internet Accounts dialog box, click Add, Mail. You'll be greeted by the Your Name page of the Internet Connection Wizard. The wizard already knows your name, of course, but this first page gives you the chance to change the way your name is presented to recipients of your e-mail messages. For example, if your name is Prasanna Samarawickrama, but you'd rather your recipients see your messages as coming from Prasanna (without the last name), you can make the necessary changes here. When you complete the first page of the wizard, click Next to move to the second page.

Tip **Keep it simple**

It might be tempting to add some flourish to your name on the Your Name page of the Internet Connection Wizard—your academic or professional credentials, for example. But remember that what you put here is likely to be added to the address books of your personal and business contacts. If you want to identify yourself elaborately, do so in a signature (choose Tools, Options, and then click the Signatures tab), rather than on the Your Name page. You can change the signature over time and use personalized signatures for different audiences.

The wizard's second page is called Internet E-Mail Address. Here you specify the address that will be added to your recipients' address books if they exercise an Add Sender to Address Book command in their e-mail software. By default, this is also the address that your recipients will use if they click Reply to answer your e-mail. If you want replies to go to a different address, you'll need to edit the properties for your account after you've finished with the wizard. (See the Inside Out sidebar "Finish Setting Up New Accounts," page 1136, for more details.)

On the wizard's E-Mail Server Names page, you'll need to supply server addresses for your inbound and outbound mail. If you're not sure what to enter on this screen, contact your Internet Service Provider (ISP) or network administrator. Outlook Express supports three server protocols for inbound mail: POP3, IMAP, and HTTP. If your inbound server uses POP3 or IMAP, you'll need to specify a separate server address for outbound mail. (The outbound server uses the SMTP protocol.) If your inbound mail uses HTTP (as Hotmail does, for example), you'll only need to specify one server address. The outbound server edit box will be grayed out in that case, and a new box will appear in which you can specify your HTTP mail provider. If you choose Hotmail, the remaining server field will be conveniently filled in for you. (In fact, if you entered a hotmail.com address on the wizard's previous page, all options on this page should already be filled in correctly.) If you enter an msn.com address, Outlook Express may automatically fill in values for you; if the POP3 option is selected when you attempt to set up an MSN account, you need to choose Other and fill in that box yourself, entering the server name *http://oe.msn.msnmail.hotmail.com/cgi-bin/ hmdata*. Click Next to move on.

Note As of this writing, only Hotmail and MSN support HTTP mail via Outlook Express. Although many other companies offer Web-based mail services, none of them can be configured to work with Outlook Express.

On the Internet Mail Logon page of the wizard, supply your logon information—the name of your account, as given to you by your ISP or other service provider, and your password. A Remember Password option on this screen will be selected by default. If you're concerned

Chapter 34

that someone else might try to use your computer to access your e-mail account, clear this check box. You'll then be prompted for the password the first time you send or retrieve mail in an Outlook Express session.

After you've supplied the logon information, click Next, then Finish. You're ready to use the new account.

> **Tip**   Export a copy of your account information
> If you don't ever want to be bothered to recreate an e-mail account, choose Tools, Accounts, select the account name, and then click Export. Outlook Express will save your account settings (including your password) in encrypted format in an .iaf file. If you ever need to re-establish the account—on this computer or another—you can import that .iaf file into Outlook Express. Because the saved settings include your password, you should be concerned about security—store the file offline, using a suitably private backup medium, such as a floppy disk locked in a filing cabinet.

Creating a News Account

Creating a newsgroup account is just like creating a mail account, except that you provide the address of an NNTP server instead of mail servers. Choose Tools, Accounts; click Add, News; and then follow the wizard. On the first two pages, provide your display name (the name that other newsgroup users will see when you post messages) and your return e-mail address. On the third page, supply the server details. If your news server does not require you to log on (many do not), leave the My News Server Requires Me To Log On option unselected. Most Internet service providers maintain an NNTP server for use by their subscribers. If you're setting up access to a private news server or if you subscribe to a commercial news server—that is, a news server that does require a logon—select this option, and then supply logon details on the ensuing page.

Creating a Directory Service Account

By default, Outlook Express provides access to your Active Directory and several public Lightweight Directory Access Protocol (LDAP) servers. (Active Directory is a service that provides information about objects available on a domain-based network. In standalone or workgroup settings, Outlook Express ignores the Active Directory account.) With these directory "accounts" established, you can look for people or businesses on the Internet (or in your Active Directory) by pressing Ctrl+E (or by clicking the Find button on the toolbar and then choosing People from the Find menu). As Figure 34-2 shows, the Find People dialog box

Using and Customizing Outlook Express

includes a drop-down list of available directory services (as well as your own address book). If you have the server and logon information, you can make additional LDAP servers available by choosing Tools, Accounts, and then clicking Add, Directory Service.

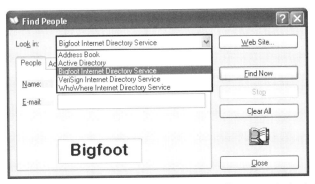

Figure 34-2. The Find People dialog box allows you to look for a contact in any of your established directory service accounts.

When you create e-mail messages, Outlook Express checks your addressees against your address book. If you type an addressee's name on the To line, for example, Outlook Express retrieves the addressee's e-mail address from the address book. If you type part of a name and Outlook Express can't figure out who you're trying to address, it presents a list of possible matches. By default, the program does not check addressees against entries in LDAP servers. However, you can add this form of lookup as follows:

1 Choose Tools, Accounts.

2 On the Directory Service tab (or All tab) of the Internet Accounts dialog box, select the name of a directory service, and then click Properties.

3 On the General tab of the directory service's Properties dialog box, select Check Names Against This Server When Sending Mail.

Editing Account Information

After you've used the Internet Connection Wizard to create an account, you can use the account's Properties dialog box to modify any of the information you gave the wizard. To open an account's Properties dialog box, choose Tools, Accounts. Select the name of the account and then click Properties.

Chapter 34

Inside Out

Finish setting up new accounts

You have no choice but to use the Internet Connection Wizard to set up a new mail account initially. However, if you're a sophisticated mail user, you should visit the properties dialog box for each mail account after completing initial setup. Several options found there are particularly useful, including the following:

- **Mail Account (General tab)** Use this option to change the name displayed in the Accounts dialog box. By default, the account name is the same as the mail server for SMTP/POP3 accounts; Hotmail accounts use the word *Hotmail* and a number to identify multiple accounts. Change this if you've created several versions of the same account with different properties for different uses, or if you have multiple Hotmail/MSN accounts.

- **Reply Address (General tab)** Enter an e-mail address here if you want to specify a return address other than the address from which you sent the original message. The address you enter will appear in the To line when your recipient uses the Reply option in his or her e-mail client. Use this option, for instance, if you send messages from a Hotmail account while traveling because your regular SMTP server is unavailable but you want replies to be sent to the POP3 account you normally use for personal e-mail.

- **My Server Requires Authentication (Servers tab)** Select this option if you are connecting to an SMTP server that requires an extra authentication step as an antispam measure—many servers require that you log on to the POP3 server first (using your user name and password) before being allowed to send messages.

- **Leave A Copy Of Messages On Server (Advanced tab)** This option comes in handy if you're checking your work e-mail from a computer at home (or vice-versa) but you want to maintain a complete archive of messages on the other computer. You can check for new messages at home; when you return to the office, your mail program will download those messages into your Inbox.

Customizing the Look of Outlook Express

Figure 34-3 shows all of Outlook Express's optional visual elements. Unless you're using a large monitor at high resolution, you probably don't want all these elements crowding your display. Everything in Outlook Express's presentation is optional, except for the title bar, the menu bar, and the message list. To tell the program what you want to see, choose View, Layout, and then select or clear check boxes in the Window Layout Properties dialog box.

Outlook bar

Views bar   Folders list   Folder bar   Toolbar

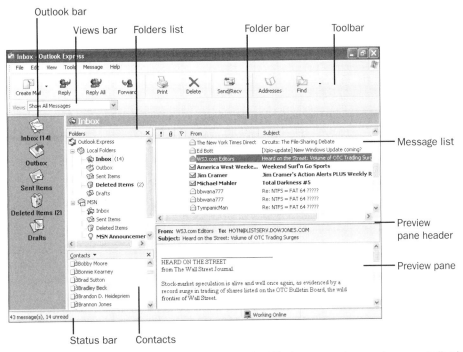

Message list

Preview
pane header

Preview pane

Status bar   Contacts

Figure 34-3. Everything in this display except the title bar, menu bar, and message list is optional

Previewing Messages

The preview pane displays the contents of the currently selected message. When you're scanning mail or newsgroup messages, you can save yourself a lot of time by scanning the first few lines of each message in the preview pane, rather than opening each message and reading it in its own window. However, using the preview pane also exposes you to the dark side of e-mail, because it allows potentially hostile scripts to run without any action on your part. It also downloads any HTML content, including potentially offensive images and "Web bugs" that can confirm to mail senders that you received their message and at least previewed it.

If you choose to display the preview pane, you can position it either below the message list or alongside it. You can also choose whether or not to include the preview pane header. As you can see in Figure 34-3, the header doesn't provide any information that can't also be displayed in the column headings of the message list, so if you're short on visual space, you can economize by eliminating the preview pane header.

Chapter 34

Caution A number of viruses and worms in recent years have taken advantage of vulner-abilities in the HTML-rendering capabilities of Outlook Express to automatically install hostile code. If you're diligent about applying security patches and keeping your antivirus software updated, you're generally safe from these types of attacks. However, you run a small but significant risk of infection on those rare occasions when a new virus or worm appears that exploits a previously unknown vulnerability, or one for which a patch has not been released. If your approach to computer security is extra-cautious, bordering on paranoid, you should disable the preview pane so that you can scan incoming messages and delete suspicious content before it has a chance to do any damage.

Navigating Folders

Outlook Express uses folders to organize messages. When you first run Outlook Express, the program creates one set of folders, called Local Folders, that are used for any POP3 e-mail accounts you configure. It also provides Outbox and Drafts folders that are shared by all your accounts. In addition to the Local Folders tree, Outlook Express creates a separate set of folders for each HTTP and IMAP account you use, as well as a set of folders for each of your news accounts. Figure 34-3, for example, shows two branches of folders in the Outlook Express tree (folder list)—Local Folders and MSN. Scrolling the folders list would reveal additional branches of folders for news accounts. All of these folder branches are subsumed under a heading called Outlook Express.

Figure 34-3 shows the three visual elements that you can use to navigate your folders—the folders list, the folder bar, and the Outlook bar. Of these, the Outlook bar is the least useful because it provides access to only a few folders (initially the top-level folders in the Local Folder tree; you can add other folders by right-clicking them and choosing Add To Outlook Bar). You can right-click any empty space in the Outlook bar and choose the Small Icons option to make room for more such icons, but unless you're lavishly fixed for screen real estate, you might as well pass on the option to display the Outlook bar. (The Outlook bar originated with Microsoft Outlook, which puts it to better use by including selections that take advantage of its unique personal information management capabilities, such as Contacts, Tasks, Notes, Journal, and Calendar. In a revealing design decision, presumably based on feedback from usability testing, the Outlook bar was removed from Outlook 2003.)

The folders list provides familiar controls for navigating folders and subfolders. Like the Folders bar in Windows Explorer, it comes with a convenient Close button, so you can easily bump it out of the way if you occasionally need a wider perspective on your message list and preview pane. (To redisplay it, choose View, Layout, and then select Folder List.)

The folder bar isn't that useful if you're displaying the folders list. With the folders list absent, however, it turns into a handy drop-down list. Click its heading and your entire folder structure unfolds, allowing easy navigation. Thus, if you opt to show the folder bar but not the folders list, you get a broad view of your messages without sacrificing mobility.

For an even more economical layout, you can hide the Outlook bar, the folders list, *and* the folder bar. When you want to move to a different folder, press Ctrl+Y. The Go To Folder dialog box appears, as shown in Figure 34-4, allowing you to navigate to any folder.

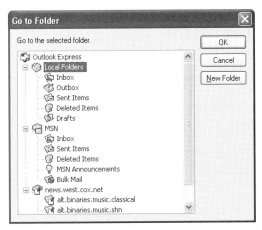

Figure 34-4. If you prefer not to display the folders list alongside your messages, you can navigate by pressing Ctrl+Y to summon this dialog box.

Displaying Contacts

If you choose to display contacts, Outlook Express presents a list of everyone in your address book alongside your message list and preview pane. Having the contacts list visible can sometimes simplify message addressing. Double-click a person's name in the list, and Outlook Express opens a New Message window, with the message already addressed to that person. On the other hand, the contact list typically crowds out the folders list, so many users prefer not to display it. If you forego the contacts list, you can always find your contacts by opening your address book (press Ctrl+Shift+B; click the Addresses button on the toolbar; or choose Tools, Address Book).

Tip   Use your contact list to send instant messages

If you use Windows Messenger and Outlook Express, your Windows Messenger contacts appear at the top of Outlook Express's contacts pane. A green icon appears next to any contacts who are currently online. If a contact is online, you can initiate an instant message conversation with that person by double-clicking his or her name in the contacts pane. For more information about Windows Messenger, see "Introducing Windows Messenger," page 1204.

Chapter 34

Setting Basic Options

The Options dialog box (choose Tools, Options) offers a great many choices, some of which you should make right away, others of which you can defer or ignore.

Checking for Mail at Regular Intervals

By default, Outlook Express checks every 30 minutes to see whether you have new mail. You can change that interval (or disable automatic checking) on the General tab of the Options dialog box. Whether or not you fetch mail on a schedule, you can send and receive at any time by pressing Ctrl+M. This keyboard shortcut checks all your e-mail accounts, unless you have disabled automatic e-mail checking for a particular account (choose Tools, Accounts, select the account you want to check manually, click the Properties button, and clear the Include This Account When Receiving Mail Or Synchronizing option on the General tab). To check a particular account only, choose Tools, Send And Receive (or click the down arrow at the right of the Send/Recv button on the toolbar), and then select the account you want to check.

Outlook Express also ordinarily looks for mail at startup (that is, when you launch Outlook Express) and plays a sound to announce the arrival of a message. You can disable these defaults by clearing check boxes on the General tab of the Options dialog box. If you want sound notification but prefer a different tune, choose Sounds And Audio Devices from Control Panel (in Category view it's located in Sounds, Speech, And Audio Devices). Select the Sounds tab and then change the sound associated with the New Mail Notification event.

Minimizing Connect Time with Dial-Up Accounts

If you use a dial-up connection for e-mail, you should check a few configuration settings to make sure Outlook Express behaves the way you want it to. On the General tab of the Options dialog box, you'll find a setting labeled If My Computer Is Not Connected At This Time. This determines what Outlook Express should do if you're checking for mail at scheduled intervals and you're offline during a scheduled time.

On the assumption that you might not always be connected to a phone line (you might be using a portable computer, for example), Outlook Express's default setting is Do Not Connect. If you're hooked up to the phone line most of the time, you might want to change to Connect Only When Not Working Offline. When you take your portable computer on the road and don't have a dial-up connection at your disposal, choose Work Offline from Outlook Express's File menu to let the program know when it would be pointless to dial.

Whether your computer is stationary or mobile, if you use the same telephone line for voice and data, if your ISP bills you by the hour, or if you incur tolls for your e-mail calls, go to the Connection tab of the Options dialog box, and select Hang Up After Sending And Receiving.

Using and Customizing Outlook Express

Controlling the Format of Outbound Messages

Most e-mail client programs nowadays can read HTML. Many newsgroup clients cannot. Therefore, Outlook Express formats outbound mail by default in HTML, leaving news posts in plain text. You can change these defaults on the Send tab of the Options dialog box.

If most of your correspondents have e-mail programs that can read HTML but some do not, you can set up Outlook Express so that it allows you to compose new messages in HTML by default but offers to convert messages to plain text when sending to recipients whose Address Book entries are tagged for text only. To ensure that a particular person receives only plain-text mail from you, open that person's record in Address Book by double-clicking the entry or by right-clicking it and choosing Properties. On the Name tab, select Send E-mail Using Plain Text Only and save the contact record. Whenever you send a message, Outlook Express checks the list of recipients; if you're about to send an HTML-formatted message to a contact whose record is designated as plain text only, you'll see a dialog box that allows you to send the message in HTML, convert it to plain text, or cancel the Send operation and return to the message editing window. Be aware that if you send HTML to a recipient whose program cannot handle HTML, you'll have a disgruntled correspondent to answer to.

> For more information about using Address Book, see "Managing Contacts," page 1145.

> **Tip**   Turn off HTML while composing a message
> If you forget to suppress HTML formatting in a recipient's address book entry, you can still turn it off while composing a message. In the New Message window, choose Format, Plain Text.

Making Outlook Express the Default Mail and News Handler

Near the bottom of the General tab of the Options dialog box, you'll find options for making Outlook Express the default mail handler and the default news handler. The default handlers are the programs that an Internet browser (such as Internet Explorer) turns to when you choose the browser's Mail or News command. For example, if you click the Mail button on the Internet Explorer toolbar, and then choose New Message, Internet Explorer launches Outlook Express's New Message window—if Outlook Express is the default mail handler. The default mail handler is also the program that springs to life if you click a mailto link on a Web page or other document.

If you do not make Outlook Express the default handler for either mail or news, but no other mail or news client is installed on your system, Windows will treat Outlook Express as the default anyway (although it might not update the Options dialog box to say so). If you do make Outlook Express the default handler and decide subsequently to use a different mail or news handler, use *that* program's menus and dialog boxes to make it the default. Outlook Express itself does not have an "undefault" command.

Chapter 34

> **Tip** **Create an Outlook Express shortcut**
>
> If your computer is running Windows XP Service Pack 1 or later and has been customized to hide access to one or more Windows programs, you may not be able to select Outlook Express as your default e-mail program. In fact, you may not be able to find a program icon of any sort for Outlook Express. In this configuration, you can still run Outlook Express by opening the Run dialog box and entering the command **msimn.exe**. You can also manually create a shortcut to Outlook Express using %programfiles%\Outlook Express\msimn.exe as the target.
>
> For more details about the option to hide Outlook Express and other integrated Windows programs, see "Selecting a Web Browser and Other Middleware Components," page 64.

Setting Security Options

Before you begin using Outlook Express, you should click Tools, Options, and then select the Security tab in the Options dialog box to review your security settings. Make sure that the following options are selected:

- Restricted Sites Zone (More Secure)
- Warn Me When Other Applications Try To Send Mail As Me

Both are selected by default, but it's a good idea to check anyway.

Outlook Express shares the settings for the two most restrictive security zones available in Internet Explorer—the Internet zone and the Restricted Sites zone. By setting Outlook Express to follow the security restrictions observed in the Restricted Sites zone, you get the maximum protection that you have set for this zone in Internet Explorer. This setting goes a long way toward warding off potential viruses and Trojan horses. If something does make it past your defenses, the Warn Me option will provide protection against those viruses that replicate themselves by trying to hijack Outlook Express and its mail-sending capabilities.

It's worth noting that ActiveX controls and scripts are always disabled in Outlook Express, even if you've enabled them in the corresponding security zone for Internet Explorer. Also, the Warn Me capability is useless against modern viruses and worms that incorporate their own SMTP server to send infected messages without getting involved with Outlook Express.

> **Note** If you're concerned about e-mail security, we recommend our other book, *Microsoft Windows Security Inside Out* (Microsoft Press, 2002), which covers the topic in much greater detail than we can here, with a special emphasis on Outlook Express and Outlook.

In Windows XP Service Pack 1, Microsoft introduced an important new security feature in Outlook Express: the Read All Messages in Plain Text option. HTML-formatted e-mail and newsgroup messages can pose a host of problems. Pornographic spam messages, for instance, can display shocking images in your Inbox. Spam senders can confirm that your e-mail address is valid by embedding coded images in HTML-formatted messages and then checking the server logs to see which ones were downloaded in an e-mail client. You can short-circuit both types of threats by configuring Outlook Express to read all messages in plain text only. To enable this feature, choose Tools, Options, click the Read tab, and select the Read All Messages In Plain Text option. When you choose this option, you can read the text portions of any messages sent as multipart MIME messages; the HTML portions will appear as an attachment that can be viewed in Internet Explorer.

> **Note** Beginning with Windows XP Service Pack 1, Microsoft introduced yet another security feature to Outlook Express—the capability to block potentially dangerous attachments. For a full discussion of the workings (and serious limitations) of this feature, see "Blocking Dangerous Attachments," page 1166.

Managing Identities

As we mentioned earlier in this chapter, the developers of Outlook Express originally devised the identities feature as a way for multiple users of the same computer to share a single copy of Outlook Express while still maintaining separate accounts, messages, and address books. With Windows XP, this feature is hardly necessary; it's much more practical for each person to have a separate user account, logging on with Fast User Switching to check their e-mail without disturbing another person's work.

But you might find it handy to switch between multiple *identities*, even if you're the only user of your computer. Having two or more identities is especially useful if you have multiple e-mail accounts and you want to maintain strict separation between them. For instance, you might create one identity for work, where you send and receive mail using your company's SMTP and POP3 servers. In another identity, you would send and receive personal messages from the account at your home ISP, along with two or three Hotmail accounts you use for shopping online. And you might use yet another identity for browsing newsgroups; by carefully configuring the settings in your news account, you can ensure that your "real" e-mail addresses for home and work are never published on a public newsgroup where they can be picked up by spammers.

Each identity is completely separate, with its own set of mail and news accounts, its own folders and message-handling rules, and a private address book. (However, a Shared Contacts folder in the Windows Address Book lets you create address book records that are visible to every identity.) When you switch between identities, Outlook Express actually shuts down and restarts, loading the new settings.

To start working with multiple identities, choose File, Identities, Manage Identities. As Figure 34-5 shows, Outlook Express initially uses a single identity, called Main Identity. You might want to replace this moniker with a real name—your own, perhaps, or a phrase that describes the purpose of the identity—Ed's Work Mail, Ed's Personal Mail, or

Newsgroups Only, for instance. To change the name of the default identity, select Main Identity in the Manage Identities dialog box and click Properties. In the Identity Properties dialog box, in addition to renaming the identity, you can assign a password to it, so that only those who know the password can open the identity in Outlook Express, or delete the identity if it's already open.

Figure 34-5. Outlook Express is initially set up with a single identity, called Main Identity. Use this dialog box to add others and rename Main Identity.

An identity password might discourage casual browsing of your mail, but it won't thwart even a modestly talented intruder. To make your e-mail inaccessible to others, password-protect your Windows XP user account, and make your store folder (the folder in which Outlook Express stores your messages) private. Be aware that your Address Book contacts can be seen by others, even if you do password-protect your user account. (For information about the Outlook Express store folder, see "Relocating Your Message Store to Simplify Backup," page 1173. For information about making folders private, see "Keeping Your Own Files Private," page 280.)

To create a new identity, in the Manage Identities dialog box, choose New, type a name, and type a password if you want one. That's all there is to it.

On opening, Outlook Express always returns to the identity that was in use when the program was closed—regardless of how the Manage Identities dialog box is filled out. To switch identities, choose File, Switch Identity. The first time you switch to a newly created identity, the Internet Connection Wizard prompts you to create a new account. If you want to use the same account settings in more than one identity, you'll need to recreate the account in each one.

> **Tip** Consolidate identities
>
> Change your mind about using identities? You can use Outlook Express's Import command to import messages from one identity into another. Click File, Import, Messages, Microsoft Outlook Express 6, and then specify the identity you want to import from. After you have consolidated all your messages into the main identity's folders, you can delete the identities you no longer need.

Managing Contacts

Outlook Express is tightly integrated with Address Book, a separate application designed to be shared by programs that use contact information—e-mail programs, fax clients, teleconferencing software, and the like. You can run Windows Address Book from Outlook Express by simply clicking the Addresses button on the toolbar. You can close it by pressing Esc. (If the toolbar isn't visible, click Tools, Address Book.) You can also run Address Book from the Start menu; look for it under Accessories, or choose the Run command and type **wab**.

Figure 34-6 below shows Address Book. As you can see, the program presents four columns of information, beginning with name and e-mail address. You can change the order in which the four columns appear by dragging them to the left or right. You can change the sort order by clicking on the column head by which you want to sort.

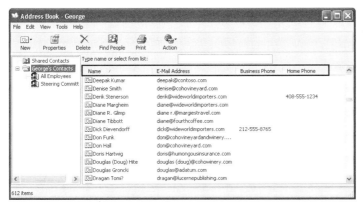

Figure 34-6. Address Book's four-column display is sorted by default by Name, with names presented in first-last order.

Names appear in Address Book, by default, in first name-last name order. You can override this when you create a new contact (click the arrow beside the Display box and choose from the list), but it's not advisable to do so. When you use Outlook Express facilities for adding contact names directly from e-mail messages (for example, the names of people you reply to via e-mail), those names almost always arrive in first-last order. If some of your contacts are listed last-first and others first-last, you wind up with a jumbled address book.

You'll also notice that Address Book doesn't know or care about the formatting of telephone numbers. If you want consistency, you have to enforce it upon yourself.

Organizing Contacts in Folders

The address book shown in Figure 34-6 includes two panes. The left pane contains a Shared Contacts folder for contacts shared between all identities using Outlook Express and a folder containing the current identity's contacts. The current identity's contacts are normally visible only to the current identity.

If your system does not display a left pane, choose View, Folders And Groups.

The entries in the left pane—Shared Contacts and George's Contacts in Figure 34-6—are folders. To organize your contacts more effectively, you can add folders of your own to any existing folder. To add a folder, right-click its parent and choose New, New Folder.

To move a contact from one folder to another, select the contact's name in the right pane and then drag it to the appropriate folder in the left pane. To make a personal contact visible to other identities, for example, drag it from the right pane and drop it on the Shared Contacts heading in the left pane.

Chapter 34

Sharing Contacts with Microsoft Outlook

Earlier versions of Address Book gave you the option of using your Outlook Contacts folder in Outlook Express. If you accepted this option, Address Book became a front end to Outlook, visible in Outlook Express and any other applications that used Address Book. Contacts added via Outlook thus became accessible to Outlook Express, and contacts added to Address Book by means of Outlook Express options (such as Outlook Express's option to add the names of people you reply to via e-mail) became usable in Outlook.

This integration with Outlook is still available in Address Book 6 (the version shipped with Windows XP), but only via an undocumented registry edit. To share contact information between Outlook and Address Book, open Registry Editor and go to HKCU\Software\Microsoft\WAB\WAB4. Add the DWORD value UseOutlook to this key (if it isn't already present), and set it to 1. To return to the unintegrated state, return to this registry value and either delete it or set it to 0.

The tradeoff for integration between Outlook and Address Book is that it precludes using identities in Address Book. If you are using Outlook integration and you display the Folders And Groups pane in Address Book, you see the subfolders of your Outlook Contacts folder instead of your shared contacts and personal contacts. (You can still use multiple identities in Outlook Express—this limitation affects only the display of information in Address Book.)

> **Tip** View other identities' contacts
>
> Address Book normally shows only the current identity's contacts and shared contacts. This is a convenience feature, not a security feature. You can see the contacts of all the identities defined in Outlook Express by starting Address Book from a command line—type the command string **wab/a**. (If Address Book doesn't immediately display identity names in a left pane, choose View, Folders And Groups.) If you don't want other users to see your contacts, don't use identities.

> **Note** You cannot copy a contact by holding down Ctrl as you drag. Duplicate entries in Address Book create inefficiency, so the application doesn't encourage copying. (You can copy a contact, however, by right-clicking it, choosing Copy, moving to the destination, right-clicking again, and then choosing Paste.)

Adding Individual Contacts and Distribution Lists

To directly add someone to your address book, right-click the folder you want the contact to appear in, and choose New, New Contact. (Alternatively, select the folder and then choose File, New Contact.) A seven-tabbed dialog box appears, in which you can enter as much or as little information as you need.

You can also add groups to your address book. When you send mail to a group, Outlook Express parses the group name into its individual member names and sends your message to everyone in the group. To create a group, follow these steps:

1 Right-click the appropriate parent folder in Address Book and choose New, New Group. The properties dialog box for the new group opens, as shown in Figure 34-7 on the next page.

2 Enter a group name (the name that you will choose when you address your outgoing mail).

3 Add names to the group. You can populate the group with contacts several ways:

   ■ To add contacts that are already in your address book, click Select Members.

   ■ To add a new contact to the group and also an individual entry to the address book, click New Contact.

   ■ To add a new contact to the group but not create a separate individual entry for that contact, fill out the Name and E-Mail boxes, and then click Add.

4 Optionally, enter additional information about the group itself on the Group Details tab of the properties dialog box.

Click to add contacts from
your address book

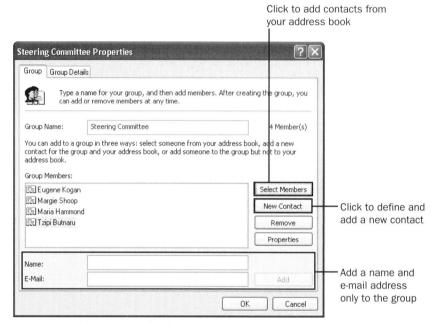

Click to define and
add a new contact

Add a name and
e-mail address
only to the group

Figure 34-7. To create a distribution list, assign a group name and then add contacts (from your address book or new contacts) to the group.

Adding Contacts Who Have Multiple E-Mail Addresses

You can enter multiple e-mail addresses on the Name tab of a contact's address book record. When you do this, Address Book requires that you designate one of the addresses as the default. When addressing a message to a contact with multiple e-mail addresses, if you specify the contact's name (as opposed to e-mail address) on the To line, Outlook Express looks up the name in your address book and uses the default mail address. In other words, you don't get to choose the address at the time you send the message. If you want control over which address is used, you need to specify the e-mail address, not the name, on theTo line.

An alternative—and better—approach is to create separate address book entries for each of your contact's multiple e-mail addresses. You don't need to use different names when you do this (but you can if you want to). If John Doe has six e-mail addresses and you create six John Doe records in Address Book, when you create a message with John Doe on the To line, Outlook Express will present a dialog box asking you to choose an address.

Adding Contacts from E-Mail Messages

By default, when you reply to an e-mail message, Outlook Express adds the name of the person you reply to (and of everyone else who received that message, if you clicked Reply All) to your address book. In everyday situations, this can be a useful service. Junk senders don't land in your address book, because you don't reply to their spam, but contacts you find worth responding to are added. If you frequently reply to "one off" messages from strangers, however, this setting can clutter up your address book with irrelevant names. To turn off this default behavior, choose Tools, Options, go to the Send tab, and clear Automatically Put People I Reply To In My Address Book.

You can also add senders to your address book without replying to their mail. In the message list, you can right-click a message and choose Add Sender To Address Book. Alternatively, you can open the message in its own window (double-click the message in the message list) and then, in the message window, choose Tools, Add To Address Book, Sender. There's a subtle but important difference between these two approaches. If you add the sender to your address book from the message list, the new contact is added forthwith. If you add the sender to your address book from the message window, you get to see and edit the new contact record before committing it to the address book. This technique gives you an opportunity to add more information about the entry or change the display name while it's fresh in your mind.

Troubleshooting

Your address book is full of duplicates.

Over time, your address book will almost certainly accumulate some duplicate entries. The most common reason for duplication is that the people you correspond with send their messages from different systems with differing account identification. For example, suppose a friend buys a new computer and sets up an e-mail account (in Outlook Express or another e-mail client), uses the same e-mail address as before, but presents his name in a slightly different way (with a middle initial, perhaps). When you respond to mail sent from that new setup, Outlook Express adds a new entry to your address book. Fortunately, although the clutter in your address book might bother you, it has no adverse effect on Outlook Express.

You will also undoubtedly accumulate address book entries that you simply don't recognize. For example, you join a mailing list and receive a confirmation message from the list administrator that requires you to reply. Typically, when you reply, a new address book entry is added that consists only of an e-mail address. When you look at that entry later, you have no idea whose address it is or why the entry is there.

Again, the only negative consequence is clutter. If it bothers you, you can either turn off the automatic creation of address book entries from messages you send in reply (choose Tools, Options, go to the Send tab, and then clear Automatically Put People I Reply To In My Address Book), or you can periodically cruise through your address book, using your Delete key to clear out the clutter.

From within the message window, you can also add other folks to your address book. If you receive a message that has gone to other addressees as well, you can add them all at once by choosing Tools, Add To Address Book, Everyone On To List. (Note that this method doesn't catch recipients on the Cc line.) Or you can add any particular addressee by right-clicking that person's name—in any part of the address portion of the message—and choosing Add To Address Book.

Tip Unmask mysterious senders

Occasionally, you might receive a message from someone identified only by an inscrutable e-mail address. You can look up the address in your address book by right-clicking the address and choosing Find from the shortcut menu. If you don't find the sender's identity that way, try clicking the address and pressing Ctrl+C to copy it. Then press Ctrl+E to open the Find People dialog box. Choose an LDAP server from the Look In list, click to position the insertion point in the E-Mail box, and press Ctrl+V to paste the address you copied. Then click Find Now to search for information over the Internet.

Exchanging Electronic Business Cards (vCards)

Address Book supports the vCard format, which allows you to exchange electronic business cards with other users via e-mail. To send your business card to another user, first create an address book record for yourself. Then select your record in Address Book, and choose File, Export, Business Card (vCard). This creates a file with the extension .vcf. Now create a message and attach this .vcf file. For information about attaching files to e-mail messages, see "Adding Attachments," page 1157.

Tip Keep your vCard up to date

If you created your electronic business card file a while ago and you're not sure the information is up to date, you can create one that is current each time you send it. Compose your e-mail message, open Address Book from the message's Tools menu, and then drag your name (or that of the business card you want to send) from Address Book into the body of the message and drop it there. A new .vcf file is instantly attached to the message. You can add as many of these business cards as you like before sending your message. But note that this shortcut won't update the .vcf file on your hard disk.

You can have Outlook Express include your business card in all outgoing mail or news messages. To do this, first create your card, as described in the previous paragraph. Then choose Tools, Options, and go to the Compose tab. In the Business Cards section of the dialog box, select Mail, News, or both Mail and News, and then select the contact name from the list.

To store an associate's electronic business card, double-click the attached .vcf file. The vCard appears as an address book record. Then click Add To Address Book.

> **Note** If double-clicking a .vcf file does not display the vCard in Address Book, then your .vcf files are probably associated with some other application (such as Outlook). You can fix this by choosing Tools, Folder Options in Windows Explorer. Go to the File Types tab, select VCF in the Extensions column of the Registered File Types list, click Change, and then select Address Book.

Importing and Exporting Contacts

Address Book can import contacts from other Address Book files, as well as from comma-separated values (.csv) files and a few other formats. It can also write (export) your contact data in Address Book (.wab) or .csv formats, or as a Microsoft Exchange Personal Address Book.

Importing Address Book Data

To import data from another Address Book (.wab) file, choose File, Import, Address Book in Outlook Express or File, Import, Address Book (WAB) in Address Book. Address Book imports all records in the selected file. If an imported name has the same name as a record in the current file, Address Book tries to merge the data without creating a duplicate record. But if conflicts exist between imported data and existing data—say, for example, that an existing record has one business phone number and an imported record of the same name has another—Address Book does not import the conflicting record. Folder assignments in the imported data are ignored, but group assignments are preserved.

Importing Data from Other Programs

To import information from another contact manager, choose File, Import, Other Address Book in either Outlook Express or Address Book. Choose a file format from the list and then click Import.

If you specify a .csv file for import, Address Book will ask you to map the import file's fields (columns) to Address Book fields. If the .csv file doesn't include field headings (not an unlikely circumstance), you will have to use data in the first record of the .csv file as your guide for creating this mapping. Blank fields in the first record can make this difficult. To get around this problem, either make sure that the first record is completely filled out before exporting to .csv from the source program (your other contact manager), or import the .csv file into a spreadsheet program and add field headings there. Then resave the file in .csv format and import it into Address Book.

If the .csv file that you're importing includes records whose names match records already in your address book, the import routine will ask whether you want to replace the existing record. If you answer no, the program will not import that entry.

Exporting the Address Book to a .wab File

To export your address book as an address book (.wab) file, choose File, Export, Address Book (WAB) in Address Book. Note that when you write Address Book data to an existing .wab file, the exported data replaces the existing data. It is not merged with the existing file. Thus, exporting to a .wab file is a good way to back up your contact list but not a method of merging your data with someone else's.

Exporting the Address Book to a .csv File

To export your address book as a .csv file, open Address Book and choose File, Export, Other Address Book. In the dialog box that appears, select Text File (Comma Separated Values), and then click Export. A wizard will prompt you for a file name, and a list of Address Book fields will appear. Select the fields you want to export and then click Finish.

> **Tip**   **Try importing first**
>
> Exporting to a .csv file is an excellent way of getting your contact data into a spreadsheet or database program. (It's also the simplest, most effective way we know to back up and restore the contents of your address book.) If you're trying to merge Address Book data with information in another contact management program, however, you should check first to see whether the other program can import .wab files directly. That way you can avoid potential mismatches of Address Book fields with fields in the other contact management program.

Printing Your Address Book

You can turn your address book into a handy printed phone or address list for easy access to contact information when you're away from your computer. To print, click the Print button on the Address Book toolbar. To print particular records only, select the ones you want (hold down Ctrl while selecting nonadjacent records), and then click Print.

The Print Style section of the Print dialog box offers three options:

- **Memo**   This option prints all the information you've stored for the selected contacts.
- **Business Card**   This option prints full name, job title, company name, business address, all phone numbers, and all e-mail addresses.
- **Phone List**   This option prints full name and all phone numbers. The printed list includes alphabetical separators.

Backing Up Your Address Book

As we noted earlier, the easiest way to back up your address book is to export it to a text file. To restore the backed-up addresses, open Address Book and choose File, Import, Other

Address Book; choose Text File (Comma Separated Values) from the list of available formats; and browse to the previously exported file.

You can also back up the file in which your address book data resides. Doing so involves a few more steps than a simple export and offers no compelling advantage over that method. You'll find this data in a .wab file nested many folders deep on your local hard disk.To discover its location, choose Help, About Address Book. To get to the folder containing this file (so that you can copy it), do the following:

1 Select its path in the About dialog box (select everything but the file name itself), and press Ctrl+C to copy it.

2 Choose Run from the Start menu and then press Ctrl+V to insert the path into the Open text box.

3 Click OK and the folder will be displayed in Windows Explorer.

Address Book backs up your data as you work in a file with the extension .wa~. The backup file is stored in the same folder as its companion .wab file. If your .wab file becomes corrupt, your .wa~ file might still be good. To find out, rename the .wa~ file to give it the expected .wab extension.

The location of your .wab and .wa~ files is recorded in the registry key HKCU\Software\Microsoft\WAB\WAB4\Wab File Name. If for any reason you need to move the file, be sure to update this registry key. Otherwise, Address Book will simply create a new file in the default location.

Sending Mail

Sending e-mail is straightforward: Address the message, compose the message, attach files as needed, set a priority level if needed, request a receipt if desired, and click Send. To send on "plain paper," start by clicking the Create Mail button on Outlook Express's toolbar. To send a message on "stationery," click the arrow next to the Create Mail button and then select your stationery from the menu. Outlook Express responds with a New Message window.

For more information about stationery, see "Using Stationery," page 1156.

Addressing the Message

If you use multiple e-mail accounts, the first thing to do when you open the New Message window is make sure the program is sending from the account you want to use. If you don't see the right address on the From line, click the arrow to open the list and then choose a different address. (If you have configured only one e-mail account the From line does not appear by default.)

Chapter 34

On the To line, you can enter either a contact's name (if the name is in your address book) or a contact's e-mail address. By default, Outlook Express will complete the address for you as soon as you have typed enough characters to make your intention unambiguous. To change this setting, choose Tools, Options, open the Send tab, and select or clear Automatically Complete E-Mail Addresses When Composing.

Note Create a shortcut for your pen pal
If you regularly send e-mail to the same person, you might want to create a desktop short-cut for that person. Double-clicking the shortcut will then take you to a New Message window with the envelope already addressed. To create such a shortcut, choose New, Shortcut on your desktop. In the Command Line box, type mailto: followed immediately (with no space) by the recipient's name or e-mail address.

To send a message to multiple recipients, type a comma or semicolon after each recipient's name or address. If you send to a group that you have defined in Address Book, be aware that your recipients will see the name (or address) of each member of the group, not the group name. To send to multiple recipients without making each recipient's name or address visible to all the others, use the Bcc (blind courtesy copy) line. If you leave the To line blank, the To field in the recipient's e-mail program says "Undisclosed-Recipient" and all other addressees on the Bcc line are invisible.

Tip Display the Bcc line
The New Message window in Outlook Express doesn't ordinarily display a Bcc line, and it can be difficult to find. To display the Bcc line, choose View, All Headers in the New Message window. The All Headers setting is persistent, though. After you have displayed the Bcc line in a new message, it appears in all subsequent new messages—until you turn it off again.

Composing the Message

Adding text to a new message is as easy as typing. In a plain text message, no formatting is available. If you use HTML formatting, however, the New Message window displays a formatting toolbar full of rich formatting options. You can choose fonts and point sizes, create bulleted lists, indent paragraphs, and do practically anything else that you might do in a word processor program. The toolbar even includes a style list (see Figure 34-8) that can simplify your formatting tasks.

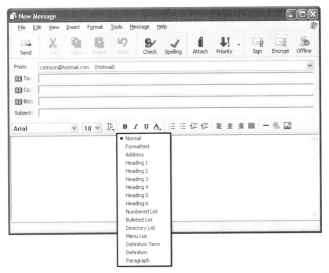

Figure 34-8. HTML support in Outlook Express allows you to do almost anything in an e-mail message that you might do in a word processor—including using defined styles.

Choosing a Font

Outlook Express uses Arial as the default font for all your messages. That means that everyone who uses Outlook Express and accepts the default uses the same font. If you prefer something distinctive, choose Options from the Outlook Express Tools menu. In the Options dialog box, on the Compose tab, click Font Settings and then choose a font. (You can do this separately for mail and news.) It's best to pick a font that most Windows users have. If you select Haettenschweiler Bold (or some other obscure font), recipients who haven't installed your off-the-beaten-track font will see whatever Windows decides to substitute. You can also set the default style, size, and color of the font.

Working Directly with HTML Code

If you're an HTML expert, you can do even more in the way of formatting than the Formatting toolbar allows. You can add animations, scripts, and anything else that you might put on a Web page. To work directly in HTML code, choose View, Source Edit in the New Message window. The tabs that appear along the bottom of the window allow you to switch views while composing your message. The Edit tab provides the same WYSIWYG view as you see when Source Edit view is turned off. The Source tab view shows HTML code along with your text, and the Preview tab attempts to show all elements of your HTML code in action, even some that might not fully display in the Edit window. However, you can't edit in Preview mode.

The Source Edit setting is persistent. If you turn it on, it stays on in subsequent messages until you turn it off again.

Using Stationery

Want a colorful background for your e-mail? Choose from one of the many stationery selections offered by Outlook Express. If you don't find one to your liking on the numbered list that appears when you click the arrow next to the Create Mail button, choose Select Stationery from that menu. You'll find a larger assortment in the Select Stationery dialog box that appears. You can click Edit to modify an existing stationery choice or click Create New to have the Stationery Setup Wizard help you design your own. A word of caution: Recipients using text-only e-mail clients may see your background as an attached image file. Before settling on a stationery, make certain that your message will be readable in a plain-text format.

Inserting Hyperlinks

To insert a hyperlink into an e-mail message, choose Insert, Hyperlink in the New Message window. The most common use for a hyperlink is to point the recipient of your e-mail message to a Web site of interest. But, as Figure 34-9 shows, you can insert many other kinds of links as well.

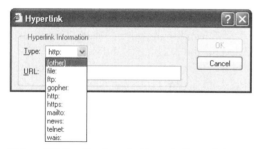

Figure 34-9. By choosing Insert, Hyperlink, you can add links of any sort to your messages.

Inserting Your Signature

A *signature* is a block of text or graphics that you add to a message. Your signature would normally contain your name and e-mail address and any other information (a favorite quotation, perhaps) that you want to include. To create a signature in Outlook Express, choose Tools, Options, click the Signatures tab, and then click New. In the Edit Signature section of the dialog box, shown in Figure 34-10, type the text of your signature. Alternatively, select the File option and use the Browse button to find a text or HTML file. You can create as many signatures as you want in this manner.

Figure 34-10. Specify the text or file you want to appear at the end of your messages.

To add your signature automatically to every message, select Add Signatures To All Outgoing Messages. If you have more than one signature, click the Set As Default button to mark the one you want used automatically.

To add your signature to some but not all messages, leave the Add Signatures To All Outgoing Messages check box clear. Then when you want to use a signature, click Insert, Signature in the New Message window. If you have more than one signature on file, a Signature submenu will appear, from which you can choose the one you want.

Adding Attachments

An attachment is a file that's sent with an e-mail message. To add an attachment, click the Attach button on the New Message window's Standard Buttons toolbar, and then specify the file you want to attach. (Alternatively, you can simply drag a file from Windows Explorer into the New Message window.) The size of the attached file appears in parentheses in the Attach box, following the file name; avoid sending oversize attachments unless you're certain that your outgoing mail server and the recipient's incoming server can handle them properly.

Setting a Priority Level

Messages are sent at normal priority by default. To flag an outgoing message as high or low priority, choose Message, Set Priority in the New Message window. Then select from the submenu that appears. How the high-priority or low-priority message appears to your recipient depends on the e-mail client program he or she is using, of course. If you view such a message in Outlook Express or Microsoft Outlook, the message list shows a red exclamation point (high priority) or a downward-pointing blue arrow (low priority) in the message list, with a corresponding text banner in the message window.

Requesting a Receipt

By choosing Tools, Request Read Receipt in the New Message window, you can ask your recipient to send confirmation that he or she has received your message. (To send a receipt request with every message, choose Tools, Options in Outlook Express. Click the Receipts tab and select Request A Read Receipt For All Sent Messages.) Receipt requests are anything but foolproof. Depending on the e-mail client program your recipient is using, and how that program is configured, your recipient might see something comparable to the following.

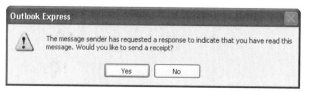

If your recipient doesn't want to acknowledge receipt, there's not much you can do about it.

Tip You don't have to send a receipt

It can be annoying to see a receipt request pop up when you select a message header. If you find such requests intrusive, choose Tools, Options. On the Receipts tab, choose Never Send A Receipt. Alternatively, if you want to send receipts but don't want to be bothered with the request, select Always Send A Read Receipt. Outlook Express will then send receipts to anyone who requests them—without asking permission or telling you that a receipt was requested.

Reading and Organizing Mail

When Outlook Express retrieves your mail, it puts each new message in the Inbox folder, unless you have set up a rule to move it to some other folder. Unread messages appear in the message list in boldface type, accompanied by a closed envelope icon. After you read a message, its entry changes to normal type with an open envelope icon. Messages you have replied to or forwarded are also marked with distinctive icons in the message list. To read a message in a separate window, double-click it in the message list.

Viewing and Saving Attachments

Messages with attachments are identified in the message list by a paper clip icon. In the message window, the name of the attachment appears on an Attach line in the header area, above the message text. To open an attachment, double-click it on the Attach line. To save the attachment instead of opening it, right-click it and choose Save As—or drag it onto your desktop or into Windows Explorer. Of course, e-mail attachments can carry viruses, which is why anyone who uses Windows and receives e-mail should install effective antivirus software and keep it up to date. In addition, you can take a number of precautions to reduce the likelihood that a dangerous virus will sneak onto your computer by way of an e-mail attachment. For details, see "Blocking Dangerous Attachments," page 1166.

Watching, Ignoring, and Flagging Messages

Figure 34-11 shows the Outlook Express message list with all four of its optional iconic columns displayed. By glancing at these columns, you can see that one message in the list (with the paper clip) includes an attachment, one (with the "no" icon—the red circle with a slash through it) is marked to be ignored, another (with the spectacles) is marked to be watched, four have been flagged for attention, two are marked with an exclamation point to indicate they are high priority, and two others show a blue arrow indicating low priority. The remaining messages in the priority column (the second column from the left in Figure 34-11) have no icon, which means that they were sent at normal priority.

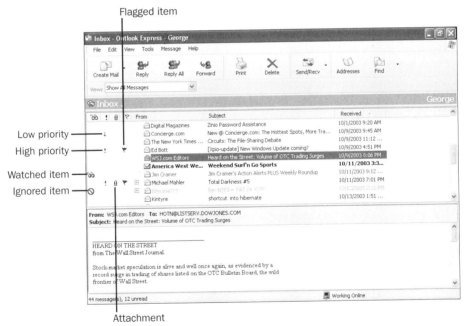

Figure 34-11. Outlook Express uses distinctive icons to identify watched and ignored messages.

If you don't see all of these iconic columns, you can make them visible by choosing View, Columns. In the Columns dialog box, select the check boxes for the columns you want to see, clear those for the columns you don't want to see, and use the Move Up and Move Down buttons to change the order in which columns appear. To return to the default column arrangement, click Reset.

You can mark a message with a watch or ignore icon by clicking in the Watch/Ignore column in the message list. Your first click there inserts a watch icon; a second click changes that to an ignore icon, and a third click clears the column. When a message is marked to be watched, Outlook Express displays the message entry in a contrasting color (red, by default; to change that, go to the Read tab of the Options dialog box). When you mark a message to be ignored, Outlook Express displays the entry in gray.

Tip   Create custom views of hot (or not-so-hot) topics

The watch/ignore icons are most useful in newsgroups, but they can also come in handy in e-mail folders. For instance, if you subscribe to several mailing lists that generate hundreds of messages, you can mark some conversation threads to be watched and others to be ignored. Then, to cut down the clutter, you can create custom views to show only watched messages or to hide ignored messages. To change the display of messages, choose View, Current View, Customize Current View, and then fill in the blanks as explained in the next section.

To flag a message (that is, to display a red flag in the Flag column), choose Message, Flag Message. (You can do this either in Outlook Express or in the Message window.) The flag means whatever you want it to mean; it's just a way of calling particular messages to your attention. If you always want to flag messages from a particular sender (your spouse, for example), you can set up a rule to do that. For more information about rules, see "Using Rules to Organize Messages," on the facing page.

Using Views to Hide Particular Kinds of Messages

Outlook Express comes with three standard message views:

- Show All Messages
- Hide Read Messages
- Hide Read Or Ignored Messages

The default view is Show All Messages, and this view is applied by default to all folders. To apply a different view to a particular folder, choose View, Current View, and then select one of the views listed in the upper portion of the submenu. Or if you have the Views bar displayed in Outlook Express, you can click the Views bar arrow and then choose the view.

Using and Customizing Outlook Express

To apply a view to all of your folders, follow these steps:

1 From the View menu, choose Current View, Define Views.

2 In the Define Views dialog box, select the view you want, and then click Apply View.

3 In the Apply View dialog box, choose All Of My Folders.

By creating your own custom views, you can also arrange to have particular categories of messages hidden or displayed, in all folders or in particular folders. To create a custom view, choose View, Current View, Define Views. In the Define Views dialog box, choose New. Working from top to bottom in the New View Dialog box, shown in Figure 34-12, build your view: Select one or more check boxes to define conditions (1); click each blue link and fill out the dialog box to define conditions further (2); and finally, supply a name for the new view (3).

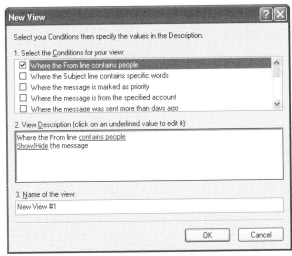

Figure 34-12.   You can use the New View dialog box to specify which kinds of messages should be hidden or displayed.

Using Rules to Organize Messages

Outlook Express allows you to create message rules to manage mail and newsgroup posts. You can use rules to store messages with a particular characteristic—a particular sender or subject line, for example—in a different folder, or to automatically send a reply, forward the message, or discard it without downloading it from your mail server. Rules can be a real time-saver if you receive a lot of routine (or junk) mail, if you subscribe to multiple high-traffic mailing lists, if you want to forward your mail to a different address when you're not able to receive it, or if you want to reply to all incoming messages with an out-of-the-office message while you're away. Rules are similar to custom views, except that you can do much more with rules. (Note also that rules apply only to Internet mail accounts. IMAP and HTTP accounts do not recognize client-side rules you create in Outlook Express.)

> **Tip** Use rules to highlight friends and family
>
> If you decide to use message rules as a spam-fighting technique, don't fall into the trap of trying to build a library of rules that can identify incoming spam based on its contents. That's a losing battle. Instead, use rules as a positive filtering mechanism, identifying messages from friends, family, associates, and trusted businesses. Then assume that anything that isn't captured by these filters is probably unwanted and send it to a Junk Mail folder. Although you're likely to get some false positives initially, you can fine-tune your message-handling rules to allow those exceptions.

Creating a New Rule

To create a new rule, choose Tools, Message Rules, and then choose either Mail or News. This section describes the creation of a mail rule, but the procedure is the same for news rules. Figure 34-13 shows the New Mail Rule dialog box.

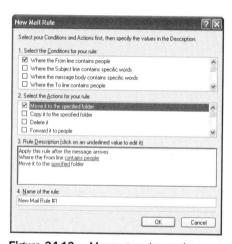

Figure 34-13. Message rules make your computer sort the mail for you.

Follow these general steps to create a new rule:

1 At number 1 of the dialog box, Select The Conditions For Your Rule, select one or more check boxes.

   These check boxes define the conditions under which your rule is to be carried out.

2 At number 2, Select The Actions For Your Rule, select one or more check boxes.

   These check boxes define the actions that you want Outlook Express to perform.

3 After you have selected the conditions and actions, click each blue link that appears at number 3 of the dialog box, Rule Description.

These links that appear and the dialog boxes they open help you to further define conditions and actions.

4 Finally, at number 4, change the default name for your new rule to a more descriptive one, and click OK.

Sending an Automatic Reply

You might receive certain types of mail to which you would like to send an automatic reply. To create such a rule you choose the action Reply With Message, but you must first create and save the reply message you want to have sent:

1 Create a message without an addressee.

2 In the New Message window, choose Save As and specify a file name and path.

3 Create a new rule, specifying the conditions that will trigger the rule and specifying Reply With Message as the action that will be carried out.

   This places a blue link in the Rule Description section (number 3) of the New Mail Rule dialog box.

4 Click the link and specify the file name of the reply message you saved.

Using Negative Criteria

You can create a rule based on a negative criterion—for example, all messages that do *not* come from a particular sender (or a group of senders). To do this, first set up the rule using a positive criterion (all messages that *do* come from a particular sender). After you have finished specifying your criterion, you will see an Options button (if you chose messages from a particular sender as your criterion, the Options button will appear on the Select People dialog box). Click this button to open the Rule Condition Options dialog box, shown in Figure 34-14. In this dialog box, select the Message Does Not Contain The People Below option.

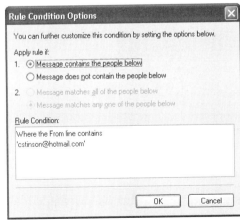

Figure 34-14. Message rules can use negative as well as positive criteria.

Using Multiple Criteria

In rules that involve people, content, or accounts, you can specify multiple criteria. For example, if you wanted messages that contained either "make money" or "work from home" (phrases commonly found in spam) to be deleted from the mail server, you could select Where The Message Body Contains Specific Words in the first section of the New Mail Rule dialog box, click the Contains Specific Words link, type **make money** and click Add, and then type **work from home** and click Add. The rule would then take effect if mail arrived in your Inbox that contained either phrase. (In other words, the phrases would be linked by the logical operator *or*.)

To make the rule affect only those messages containing *both* phrases, first set up the criterion in the normal way. Then click the Options button in the Type Specific Words dialog box to open the Rule Condition Options dialog box. Then select the Message Matches All Of The Words Below option.

Creating a Rule from a Selected Message

As a handy timesaver, Outlook Express allows you to create a rule based on the sender of a current message. If you receive a message from someone and you know immediately that you want all mail from that person to be handled by a rule, select the message in the message list and choose Message, Create Rule From Message. The New Mail Rule dialog box will appear, already set up to apply the new rule to messages from the selected sender.

Blocking Obnoxious Mail

No one is immune from spam. By most estimates, unwanted mail now makes up the lion's share of e-mail traffic on the Internet, and spammers are engaged in (and mostly winning) a cat-and-mouse game to get past filters and into your Inbox.

Outlook Express's Blocked Senders list offers one way to ward off certain types of junk mail. When you get a message from someone you never want to hear from again, select the message in the message list and click Message, Block Sender. You'll see a dialog box similar to this one.

If you make a mistake or change your mind about a blocked sender, you can restore him or her to your good graces. Choose Tools, Message Rules, Blocked Senders List. Select the sender you want to restore, and then click Remove. Alternatively, you can keep the entry in your list but clear either or both of the check boxes for blocking mail and news messages. This way, you can be selective in the kinds of blocking you apply, and you can quickly reapply blocking if it becomes appropriate again.

Tip **Don't rely on the Blocked Senders list to kill spam**
You might be tempted to use the Blocked Senders list to block junk mail (aka spam). For the most part, this strategy is doomed to failure, because the worst forms of spam come from "throwaway" e-mail addresses that are used only once, or from accounts where the sender's address is forged. Adding this sort of address to your Blocked Senders list has no practical effect because you're not likely to ever receive a message from that sender again. The Blocked Senders list is most effective in blocking unscrupulous junk mailers who persist in sending unwanted e-mail messages using addresses from the same domain. Most such firms claim to be using "opt-in" lists and include language that implies that you signed up for their annoying missives. To block all future messages from these pests, open the Blocked Senders dialog box and enter only the domain name. This step indiscriminately eliminates all mail from an entire domain, so use it with care! (And for many more suggestions on how to fight back against spam, see Chapter 11, "Blocking Spam," in *Microsoft Windows Security Inside Out*.)

Searching for Messages

The Edit, Find command in Outlook Express can help you locate a lost, buried, or forgotten e-mail message in either the current folder or all folders. If you like keyboard shortcuts, press Shift+F3 to search the current folder, Ctrl+Shift+F (*not* Ctrl+Shift+F3) to search all folders, or F3 to repeat your last search. As Figure 34-15 shows, you can search each component of the message header as well as message text, and you can specify other qualifiers as well—the date the message was received, whether the message was flagged, and whether the message included one or more attachments. Messages meeting any criterion appear at the bottom of the dialog box. You can use the Find dialog box's Message menu to read, reply to, or forward found messages. Unfortunately, Outlook Express does not allow you to save the criteria for a search so that you can reuse it.

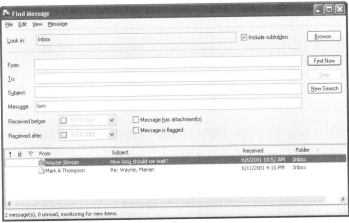

Figure 34-15. The Find Message dialog box locates messages that match specified conditions.

> **Note** Find a message the moment it arrives
> If you leave the Find Message dialog box open, the system continues to monitor incoming messages, adding appropriate ones to the list of found messages. This can be handy if you receive a large volume of mail and need to watch for messages covering particular topics.

Saving Messages Outside Outlook Express

You can save any message as a separate file by selecting the message and choosing File, Save As. The saved file will have the extension .eml and will be associated with Outlook Express (unless you install another e-mail client that claims that extension or you change the association yourself). Because .eml files are simple text files, you can also open them with any text editor, including Notepad; if the message contains HTML formatting, the text editor will display the source code. From your desktop or Windows Explorer, you can reread the message at any time by double-clicking it—whether or not Outlook Express is running. You can also use this technique to back up and restore one or more messages. Save the messages in a folder in Windows Explorer; to restore the messages, drag them into the Outlook Express window and drop them on a folder icon.

> **Tip** Save important messages
> It's not smart to entrust critical information exclusively to Outlook Express's message store. If your message store becomes corrupted for any reason, or if you purge old messages periodically (something you *should* do), you could inadvertently lose or destroy some vital bit of correspondence. To protect yourself, save a copy of anything you must not lose.

Blocking Dangerous Attachments

As most computer users know from (sometimes painful) experience, the most common mode of delivery for viruses and worms is in the form of e-mail attachments. The writers of hostile software use a variety of psychological techniques to induce you to run an infected attachment, such as forging e-mail headers to make it appear as though the message came from a friend or trusted business contact and making the attachment appear to be a fun and innocuous game, screen saver, or photo attachment. How can you protect yourself from the very real risks of infection?

For starters, install antivirus software, keep it up to date, and make sure that it's running at all times. A good antivirus program will detect infected e-mail attachments when they arrive; even if the antivirus program doesn't integrate with your e-mail software, it should intercept a hostile attachment if you try to save or open the file. Train all users of your computer in the proper handling of file attachments. *Never* open an unexpected e-mail attachment, even if it appears to come from a trustworthy source. When in doubt, pick up the phone or send an e-mail message to the sender and ask them what's in the attachment they sent. If you can't reach the sender and you still have doubts, delete the file.

Using and Customizing Outlook Express

For maximum security, you can use the attachment-blocking capabilities in Outlook Express 6. This feature prevents you from opening or saving certain types of file attachments that are potentially dangerous. After installing Windows XP Service Pack 1 or later, in fact, attachment blocking is automatically enabled, with no warning to the user and no obvious indication of how to disable it. Unfortunately, the list of files that Outlook Express considers hazardous is so sweeping that you may find this feature more frustrating than helpful. The list starts with executable files (those with the extensions .exe, .bat, .pif, and so on), which represent the bulk of potentially hostile attachments; but it also blocks a much longer list of normally useful files, including compressed file archives (.zip), Adobe Portable Document Files (.pdf), and Office documents (.doc, .xls, and so on). If you intend to use this feature and still exchange attachments via e-mail, be prepared to do a significant amount of tweaking to the default settings first.

To enable or disable attachment blocking, choose Tools, Options. On the Security tab, select or clear Do Not Allow Attachments To Be Saved Or Opened That Could Potentially Be A Virus. With this option selected, Outlook Express examines all attachments and displays a warning banner when it finds one or more attachments on its prohibited list, as shown in Figure 34-16.

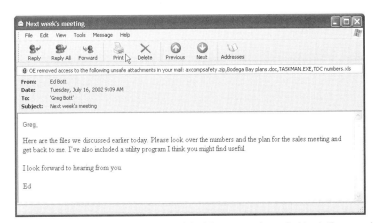

Figure 34-16. With attachment blocking turned on, Outlook Express blocks access to even these harmless .zip files and Microsoft Office documents.

To relax some of the restrictions so that Outlook Express allows certain types of attachments to pass through its filters, you need to make the following adjustments:

1 Open Windows Explorer and choose Tools, Folder Options.

2 Click the File Types tab, and then scroll through the Registered File Types list until you find the extension for the file type you want to change. Select that entry in the list.

3 Click the Advanced button.

4 In the Edit File Type dialog box, clear the Confirm Open After Download check box.

5 Click OK to close the Edit File Type dialog box, and then click Close in the Folder Options dialog box.

Repeat steps 1–4 for any other file types that you want to designate as safe. (Note that this option is not available for executable file types. Also, be aware that changing this setting for any file type will affect the way it's handled in Internet Explorer as well.)

Troubleshooting

You received an e-mail message containing an attachment you know is safe, but Outlook Express won't let you open or save it.

Unlike the similar feature in Outlook 2000 and 2002, you can easily work around attachment blocking in Outlook Express. To temporarily restore access to a blocked attachment, choose Tools, Options, click the Security tab, and clear the Do Not Allow Attachments To Be Saved Or Opened That Could Potentially Be A Virus check box. Close the dialog box to return to the message, where you'll find that the attachment is now available for you to work with. Afterward, be certain to turn the safety feature back on.

Using Hotmail and Other Server-Based Systems

Hotmail accounts and other e-mail accounts that use HTTP or IMAP differ from POP3 accounts in that messages are kept on the account provider's server and can be accessed from any computer via the Internet. When you set up such an account in Outlook Express, the account provider creates a folder structure for you. These folders reside on the server and are mirrored on your own system. Depending on the account provider, you might or might not have the opportunity to pick and choose which of the service's folders you want to use (in Hotmail, you do not have this choice, although you can add your own custom folders to those provided by the service). Your HTTP or IMAP folders appear in a part of the folder tree separate from the Local Folders section used by your POP3 accounts.

When you send and receive mail using a server-based system (a process called *synchronization*), you have the option of downloading all messages, new messages only, message headers only, or nothing. To specify your synchronization preferences, select the root folder in the appropriate part of your folder tree. For example, with a Hotmail account, you would select the folder called Hotmail. As Figure 34-17 shows, you can then specify synchronization settings individually for each of the folders maintained by the server.

To change a synchronization setting for a folder, select the folder and click Settings. If you get a lot of mail, only some of which you need, and you're on a slow dial-up connection, you might want to set your Inbox to download headers only. To download the message body for an item of interest, you can double-click its header. Unless you enjoy reading unsolicited commercial messages, you'll probably want to set Hotmail's Bulk Mail folder to download nothing—that is, not to synchronize. If you don't need local copies of your sent messages, you can also opt not to synchronize the Sent Items folder.

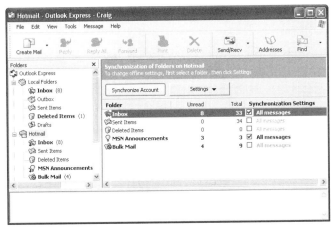

Figure 34-17. Select a folder and click Settings to specify that you want all messages in that folder to be synchronized with your local copy.

Using Newsgroups

Newsgroups function much like server-based mail systems. Messages reside on a server. You create a local mirror of the server (or a portion thereof!) and synchronize it periodically by downloading headers, new messages, or all messages. One major difference is that, rather than giving you a simple folder structure (such as the one that Hotmail downloads for you), the news server typically hosts thousands of newsgroups. You choose the ones you care about by *subscribing* to them, and these subscribed newsgroups become subfolders in the news section of your Outlook Express folder tree. Another difference is that newsgroup messages (often called *posts*) are visible to everyone who has access to the news server. Your account is not private.

The first time you select a news server in your folder tree, Outlook Express offers to download a list of newsgroups available from the server. When the downloading is complete (be patient), you will see the Newsgroup Subscriptions dialog box, which will look similar to Figure 34-18. Icons for each of your newsgroup accounts will appear in the left pane, and the All tab will display an alphabetical list of your server's many offerings. You can filter the list by typing some text on the Display Newsgroups Which Contain line.

By default, Outlook Express downloads newsgroup names but not descriptions of the groups' content. If you need the descriptions as well, go to the Properties dialog box of your newsgroup account (click Tools, Accounts, select the account, and click Properties). On the Advanced tab, select Use Newsgroup Descriptions. Then return to the Newsgroup Subscriptions dialog box and click Reset List (be *really* patient this time).

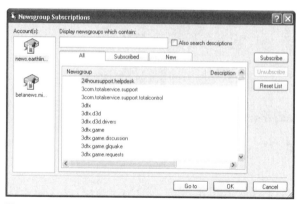

Figure 34-18. The list of your server's newsgroups is likely to be enormous. Use the Display Newsgroups Which Contain box to zero in on groups of interest.

After you have found a group you're interested in, select its name on the All tab and click Subscribe. You can subscribe to as many groups as you want. Outlook will create a subfolder for each group. If you lose interest in a group, choose its entry in the folders list and click the Unsubscribe button.

Marking Headers Offline for Later Download

The newsgroups you're interested in might well hold thousands of posts each. If you're using a dial-up connection, you probably don't want to download all of those messages. Instead, you can set Outlook Express to download the headers only. Then, while offline, you can scan the headers, marking the ones you care about for subsequent downloading. When you reconnect, you can download the full contents of the marked messages.

Setting Synchronization Options

To set your newsgroups for header download, or to choose a different synchronization option, select the news server in your folders list. You'll see a display similar to the one shown in Figure 34-17, except that your subscribed newsgroups will be listed instead of a set of Hotmail folders. Select a newsgroup in the right pane, click Settings, and choose a synchronization option. As with server-based e-mail, your choices are All Messages, New Messages Only, Headers Only, and Don't Synchronize.

Selecting Headers While Offline

While you're offline, you can mark headers for subsequent full download. Select a newsgroup in the left pane and a header in your message list, and then choose Tools, Mark For Offline. From the submenu, you can then choose Download Message Later, Download Conversation Later, or Download All Messages Later. Typically, you'll want to choose Download Conversation Later. Then, when you reconnect and synchronize, Outlook Express will download the marked message and all responses that use the same subject.

> **Tip** **Save time by using the Mark For Offline column**
>
> If the Mark For Offline column appears in your message list (it does, by default, when you're working with newsgroups), you can click in that column beside a header to mark that message for subsequent downloading. The Mark For Offline column is headed by a downward-pointing arrow. When you click in the column next to a message you want to download, an arrow appears beside the marked message. If you mark a message that has a plus sign beside it (indicating that there are responses to the message), Outlook Express will download the message and all responses when you synchronize. To remove a mark after you have clicked in the Mark For Offline column, click again.

Using Rules to Mark Newsgroup Posts for Download

Message rules work similarly with newsgroup items as with e-mail messages. (For more information about rules, see "Using Rules to Organize Messages," page 1161.) One of the actions you can choose that is unique to newsgroup rules, however, is Mark It For Download. While you're offline, if you find a topic of interest in a newsgroup, but you see that there are numerous, widely scattered messages on that topic, you can create a rule that looks for a keyword in the header and marks all headers with that keyword for download. Apply the rule, and you've saved yourself the time and bother of seeking all those messages manually.

Downloading New Messages Only

If you're managing to stay current with the posts in a newsgroup, you can take advantage of the New Messages Only synchronization setting. When you connect, Outlook Express will download only those messages that you haven't already read.

What if this is your strategy, but occasionally you fall behind? For that situation, the program provides the Catch Up command. Right-click a newsgroup and choose Catch Up, and when you connect to the server, Outlook Express will consider all of its messages as read. Then you can start fresh, downloading new messages as they arrive.

 Inside Out

Delete unwanted messages for good

In Windows XP Service Pack 1 and later, Microsoft has fixed a long-standing bug in the Outlook Express news-reading capability. Want to get rid of a message you downloaded from a newsgroup? Press the Delete key. In previous versions, this key did nothing. With the proper updates installed, it permanently zaps the unwanted message from your local folders and ensures that you don't download it again.

Chapter 34

Saving Messages Before They're Deleted from the Server

Because Outlook Express mirrors the newsgroup server when you synchronize, when messages are deleted from the server (as they eventually must be, to make room for new posts), they are also removed from Outlook Express. To preserve important messages, copy them into one of your local folders, or save them as disk files. To save a message, choose File, Save As. Outlook Express gives the file the extension .nws. You can reopen a saved message by double-clicking it in Windows Explorer.

Maintaining Outlook Express

If you use Outlook Express regularly for a period of months or years, you will undoubtedly accumulate a large store of messages. Eventually, the size of your message store will begin to slow the program down. To keep it performing nimbly, you need to clean out your folders periodically.

When you delete messages, Outlook Express moves them to the Deleted Items folder. This folder functions like the Windows Recycle Bin. It holds deleted items, just in case you want to see them again. To delete items permanently, you need to take the separate step of deleting them from the Deleted Items folder. Outlook Express does this for you automatically when you quit—provided you have told it to do so. To set up this behavior, choose Tools, Options. On the Maintenance tab, select Empty Messages From The 'Deleted Items' Folder On Exit.

Simply deleting messages will not significantly reduce the size of your message store, however. When you delete a message, Outlook Express marks the item as deleted but does not remove it from the disk file in which the folder is stored. Thus, over time, you can accumulate a significant amount of wasted disk space. Under these circumstances, Outlook Express's performance will suffer, even though the apparent contents of your folders is relatively small.

To reclaim the wasted disk space, you have to take a second step, called compacting. You can set Outlook Express to do this for you automatically when the wasted space reaches some specified percentage of your overall message store. To do this, choose Tools, Options. On the Maintenance tab, shown in Figure 34-19, select Compact Messages In The Background. Then specify a value in the box next to Percent Wasted Space.

If you prefer to compact on demand, rather than having the program do it for you, click Clean Up Now on the Maintenance tab of the Options dialog box. To compact all of your folders, specify Outlook Express in the Local File(s) For list in the Local File Clean Up dialog box. To compact a particular folder, click Browse and then select the folder.

Using and Customizing Outlook Express

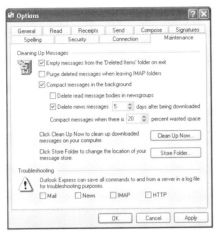

Figure 34-19. Select Compact Messages In The Background to avoid bloat in your message store.

Relocating Your Message Store to Simplify Backup

By default, Outlook Express creates the message store in a deeply nested, hidden folder. (The precise location is %UserProfile%\Local Settings\Application Data\Identities\{*identity_number*}\ Microsoft\Outlook Express, where *identity_number* is a unique 32-character alphanumeric ID.) To locate yours, choose Tools, Options. On the Maintenance tab, click Store Folder. You'll see something like the following.

You can back up from a folder this deeply nested, but you'll find it easier to do so if you move the message store to a more accessible location. (We recommend that you keep the message folders in your profile, but choose a location that's easier to find in your folder hierarchy.)

To move your message store to a place where your backup routine can more easily find it, follow these steps:

1 Create the folder you want to use—for example, you could create a folder called My Messages in your My Documents folder.

2 Choose Tools, Options.

3 On the Maintenance tab, click Store Folder.

Chapter 34

4 In the Store Location dialog box, click Change to open the Browse for Folder dialog box.

5 Select the new store folder you created and click OK.

Close Outlook Express. The program will move your messages the next time you start the program.

> **Note** Each identity uses its own message store. If you use identities and want to move your store folders to locations where they can be easily found, create new repository folders for each identity, and then repeat the change procedure for each.

> **Caution** If you look in your message store folder, you'll find a file named Folders.dbx and an additional .dbx file for each of your Outlook Express folders. The Folders.dbx file contains the structural information about your Outlook Express identity, and each remaining .dbx files contains an index of messages stored in a corresponding Outlook Express folder. If you delete the Folders.dbx file, Outlook Express will create a new folder structure the next time you start the program, creating a top-level folder for each .dbx file it finds, without regard to any subfolders you may have created previously. Don't try to reorganize your folder tree by manipulating other .dbx files directly, however. If you rename or delete a file other than Folders.dbx, you'll just confuse—and possibly disable—Outlook Express. Because the location of your message store is recorded in the registry (the Store Root value is in HKCU\Identities\{*GUID*}\Software\Microsoft\Outlook Express\5.0), you're also asking for trouble if you try to move the store folder in Windows Explorer. Let Outlook Express do it for you.

Archiving Old Messages

Outlook Express does not include a command for archiving old messages. But you can accomplish the task by following these steps:

1 Create a new folder with a suitable name—such as Messages 2004. If you want to keep received and sent messages separate, create one folder for each.

2 Open the Find dialog box. Use the Outlook Express Find command (choose Edit, Find, Message, or press Ctrl+Shift+F).

3 In the Find Message dialog box, use the Received Before control to locate the messages you want to archive.

4 When the messages have been found, drag them into your archival folder(s).

5 Close Outlook Express.

6 Open your message store in Windows Explorer. Look for a .dbx file with the name of your archival folder.

Using and Customizing Outlook Express

7 Copy the folder to a location outside the message store. Repeat for your second archival folder if you archived sent and received messages separately.

8 Reopen Outlook Express and delete the archival folder(s).

If you need to reopen the archived messages at a later date, recreate empty folder(s) in Outlook Express with the same name as the archival folders. Close Outlook Express, copy the archival folders back into your message store (overwriting the empty archival .dbx file(s) in the message store), and then reopen Outlook Express.

Moving Your Outlook Express Files to a New Computer

If your new computer is networked with your old one, it's not too hard to move your entire Outlook Express setup to the new rig. You can use the Files And Settings Transfer Wizard, as described in "Moving Windows Settings and Files," page 45. This option has the advantage of moving all your messages, account settings, and rules in one graceful procedure. However, it is possible to perform this task manually.

First, on the old machine, back up each of your accounts and your address book. To back up an account, choose Tools, Accounts, select the account name, and click Export. To back up your address book, open Address Book and choose File, Export, Address Book (WAB). Now determine the location of your message store by choosing Tools, Options, clicking the Maintenance tab, and clicking Store Folder. You might want to write this path down or copy it to the Clipboard (by pressing Ctrl+C) so that you can find the folder more easily in Windows Explorer.

On the new machine, import your accounts and address book. To import an account, choose Tools, Accounts, and click Import. To import your address book, open Address Book and choose File, Import, Address Book (WAB). Next, choose Tools, Options. On the Maintenance tab of the Options dialog box, click Store Folder to discover the location of your new store folder.

To complete the move, close Outlook Express and copy all files from your old store folder to your new one. When you reopen Outlook Express, everything should be there.

> **Tip** Avoid the hassle of backing up
>
> If the procedures for manually backing up Outlook Express seem needlessly complex, then consider using one of several excellent third-party utilities specifically designed for backing up and exporting your messages and e-mail settings. We recommend the free OEBackup program, available at *http://www.oehelp.com/OEBackup/Default.aspx*. In addition to backing up messages, account settings, and address book contents, it also picks up the Blocked Senders list, message rules, and signatures. For a price, you can choose a more polished utility, including Outlook Express Backup Wizard (*http://www.outlook-express-backup.com*) or ABF Outlook Express Backup (*http://www.abf-soft.com/outlook-express-backup.shtml*).

Chapter 34

Sending and Receiving Faxes

Microsoft Windows XP includes a fax component (referred to as Fax Services, or Fax for short) that lets you send, receive, and manage faxes using your computer's fax modem. With Fax installed, you can transmit documents directly from the applications that create them (your word processor, for example), send a scanned image, or address a fax recipient directly from a supported e-mail client (Microsoft Outlook, for example). You can use one of the four cover page templates that come with Fax, or you can use the program's cover page editor to design your own template. Fax is one of the hidden gems of Windows XP. If you've worked with earlier Windows fax components (Personal Fax for Windows in Windows 2000 or At Work Fax in Windows 95/98), you'll probably find the user interface of the current version an improvement. Management tasks that used to be dispersed between various interface elements, for example, are now consolidated into a single console, and the integration between Fax and Outlook (and with the rest of Microsoft Office) is smoother than before. Office users, for example, will appreciate the fact that Fax now uses the Office Address Book or Contacts folder, instead of requiring you to maintain a separate list of fax recipients in Windows Address Book.

At Home with Windows XP

All of the features for sending, receiving, and managing faxes, as well as those for designing and managing fax cover pages, are available in both editions of Windows XP. Because Windows XP Home Edition always uses Simple File Sharing, Home Edition users might notice one minor difference between Fax on their systems and Fax on a Windows XP Professional system that is not using Simple File Sharing. With Simple File Sharing in effect, the Fax Security tab in the Fax Properties dialog box is not normally visible. Home Edition users can make that tab visible and work with fax security settings, however, simply by holding down the Ctrl key when opening the properties dialog box. (For more information about fax security settings, see "Managing Security," page 1199. For information about Simple File Sharing, see "Simple File Sharing vs. Windows 2000–Style Sharing," page 230, and "Simple File Sharing vs. Advanced Permissions," page 275.)

Installing Fax

If you perform a clean setup of Windows XP, Fax is not installed, even if your computer has a supported fax device. You need to install the fax component as a separate step. (If you upgrade to Windows XP from a Windows 2000 or Windows 95/98 system that has an earlier Windows fax component installed, Windows XP installs the Windows XP fax component *and* preserves your earlier configuration. For more information, see "Upgrading an Earlier Windows Fax Component," page 1179.)

To install Fax, log on to an account in the Administrators group, open Add Or Remove Programs in Control Panel, and then click Add/Remove Windows Components in the left pane. In the Windows Components Wizard (shown in Figure 35-1), select Fax Services. Then click Next and be prepared to insert your Windows XP CD if requested.

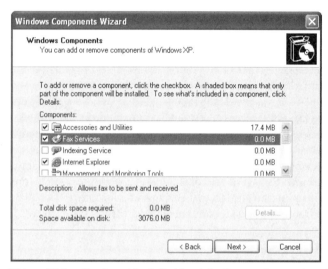

Figure 35-1. Fax is not installed by default on a clean setup. Use Add Or Remove Programs in Control Panel to install it.

Installing Fax adds the following items to your Start menu (choose All Programs, Accessories, Communications, Fax):

- Fax Console
- Fax Cover Page Editor
- Send A Fax

Sending and Receiving Faxes

The first of these, Fax Console, is the principal tool for configuring and managing fax activities in Windows XP. Note that it is not an MMC console; the MMC-hosted Fax Management Console of Windows 2000 has been eliminated in Windows XP.

Installing Fax also adds the Fax service to the list of services that appears in the Services MMC console (Services.msc) and, provided you have a supported fax device installed on the local computer, creates a new printer named Fax. The Fax printer appears alongside other local and remote printers in your Printers And Faxes folder, as well as in your applications' Print dialog boxes. In general, faxing a document in Windows XP is as simple as directing output to the Fax printer.

Upgrading an Earlier Windows Fax Component

If you have been using At Work Fax in Windows 95/98 or Personal Fax for Windows in Windows 2000, your old software will no longer work in Windows XP. When you upgrade, the Windows XP Setup program installs Fax and preserves as much as possible of your earlier fax configuration and archives. In the case of the Windows 2000 upgrade, Fax will retain your device configuration, sender information, and cover pages. The first time you open Fax Console, you'll be given the opportunity to import your Windows 2000 fax archives. If you decline, you can import them later by clicking File, Import, Sent Faxes or File, Import, Received Faxes in Fax Console. In the case of the Windows 95/98 upgrade, your device configuration, sender information, and cover pages will be preserved, but you will not be able to import your Windows 95/98 archives into Fax Console. Your existing faxes will be preserved as TIFF files, however, and you will be able to review them in Windows Explorer or any application that reads TIFF files.

Configuring Fax

To configure Fax—that is, to specify your sender information, answering parameters, and other details governing the behavior of the fax application—log on to an administrator account. Then run Fax Console. The first time you do this, the Fax Configuration Wizard appears. The wizard guides you through most of the essential configuration steps, as described in the following paragraphs. When you've completed the wizard's questionnaire, you'll want to open the Fax Properties dialog box to take care of a few additional configuration details.

(If the Fax Configuration Wizard does not appear when you run Fax Console, you—or someone else—have already been through the wizard process. You can always return to the wizard by clicking Tools, Configure Fax from Fax Console.)

Chapter 35

Sharing Fax Among Users at the Same Computer

If you share a fax device with other users of your computer, keep the following details in mind:

- Each user can supply his or her own personal data for use on cover pages. Fax Cover Page Editor comes with four generic cover page templates that are available to all users. Users can create personally customized versions of these templates or design new templates from scratch. But regardless of whether you transmit with a generic cover page template or one that you have tailored in some way, the resulting cover page will incorporate your own information, not that of another user at your computer. (For more about Fax Cover Page Editor, see "Creating Personal Cover Pages," page 1196.)

- Each user has access to his or her own address book for specifying addressee fax numbers.

- Each user can set his or her own default "printing" characteristics. For example, one user can set Fax to transmit in portrait orientation at letter size, and another can opt for landscape orientation at Quarto, and Fax will maintain these per-user settings. (For details, see "Choosing Paper Size, Image Quality, and Orientation," page 1184.)

- Users can express individual preferences about how they are to be notified of fax events—whether an icon should appear in the notification area, whether Fax Console should appear when a fax is being sent or received, and whether fax events should be announced with certain sounds. (For details, see "Setting Tracking Preferences," page 1185.)

- All configuration details besides those mentioned above are maintained in common for all users. Under default security settings, these common configuration details are accessible only to administrative accounts. (For more information, see "Managing Security," page 1199.)

- All users share a common set of archival folders in Windows Explorer for sent and received faxes.

Providing Information About Yourself

The information solicited by the Fax Configuration Wizard's Sender Information page, shown in Figure 35-2, is used by Fax Cover Page Editor to generate appropriately filled-out cover pages. Include as many or as few details as you want to appear on your cover pages. Note that theTools, Sender Information command in Fax Console returns you to a slightly reorganized version of this dialog box, in case you want to make changes without going through the whole wizard process again.

Selecting a Fax Device and Configuring Send and Receive Settings

By default, Fax is set up to allow you to send but not to receive. You can adjust these settings on the wizard's Select Device For Sending Or Receiving Faxes page, shown in Figure 35-3. In the Please Select The Fax Device list, choose the device you want to enable (if it isn't already selected). Note that if your system has multiple local fax devices, you can switch between them on this screen. Fax can support only one local device at a time, however.

If you select Enable Receive, Fax defaults to answering automatically on the second ring. You can adjust that ring parameter or opt to answer manually. If you choose Manual Answer, you'll need to use a menu command or command button to make your modem pick up the phone.

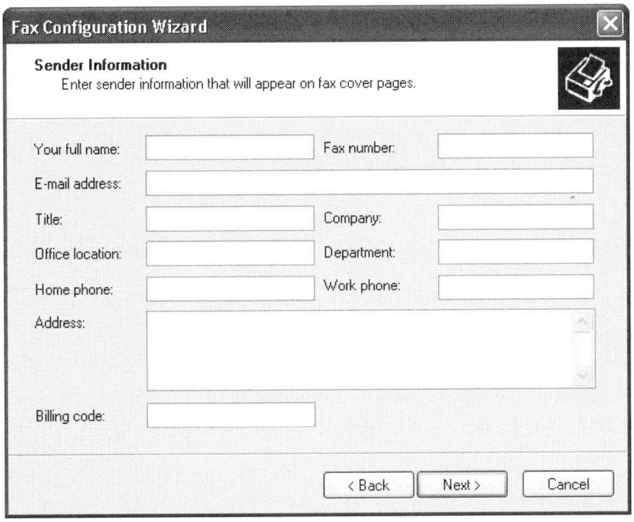

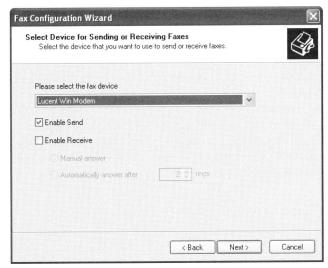

Figure 35-2. The fields on the wizard's Sender Information page supply data to Fax Cover Page Editor.

Figure 35-3. Fax can support one local device at a time; if you have more than one, select the device you want to use on this page of the wizard.

Specifying Your Transmitting Station Identifier (TSID)

If you have selected Enable Send on the Select Device For Sending Or Receiving Faxes page, the wizard asks next for your transmitting station identifier (TSID). The TSID is a string of up to 20 characters that tells your fax recipients where your faxes are coming from. (If your fax modem and telephone service support caller ID, your outbound transmissions might also identify you. Of course, for caller ID to work, your recipient must also have phone service and a fax device that support caller ID.) When you send a fax, the receiving device prints your TSID at the top of each page (unless it has been set up not to do so). It is customary, but not essential, to put your fax number in the TSID.

If you have more than one local fax device, you can set a separate TSID string for each device. For details, see "Making Other Device-Specific Settings," page 1185.

Specifying Your Called Subscriber Identification (CSID)

Provided you have selected Enable Receive on the Select Device For Sending Or Receiving Faxes page, the wizard next prompts for your Called Subscriber Identification (CSID). Like the TSID, the CSID is a string of up to 20 characters. The CSID provides information to senders about the person they have reached. When someone sends you a fax, the fax application on your system sends back your CSID. It's customary, but not required, to put your fax number in the CSID.

Like the TSID, described in the preceding section, the CSID string can be device specific. The Fax Configuration Wizard assigns a common CSID to all local devices. If you have more than one device and want to individualize their CSIDs, see "Making Other Device-Specific Settings," page 1185.

Routing Received Faxes to a Printer or Folder

If you have enabled your fax modem to receive, the Fax Configuration Wizard's Routing Options page, shown in Figure 35-4, gives you the options of sending all incoming faxes to a printer and saving an extra copy of each received fax in a file folder. By default, received faxes are stored as TIFF files in a folder specified on the Archives tab of the Fax Properties dialog box. (To get to this dialog box, choose Tools, Fax Printer Configuration in Fax Console, and then click the Archives tab.) By default, the archive folder is %AllUsersProfile%\Application Data\Microsoft\Windows NT\MSFax\Inbox. The wizard's Routing Options page gives you a way to create a duplicate set of files for faxes you receive.

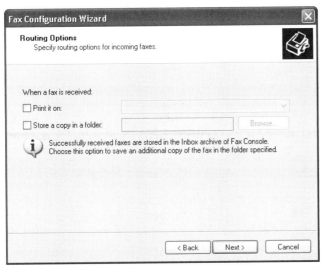

Figure 35-4. The wizard's Routing Options page gives you the opportunity to copy incoming faxes to a printer and folder.

Tip   Keep track of your received faxes
The default archive location for received faxes is in the lower depths of your file system, five levels below the All Users profile. You're likely to miss this remote folder when setting up backup routines. To ensure that you don't lose important faxes, consider using the Routing Options page to create copies in a folder that you can more easily incorporate into a backup routine, such as My Documents\Faxes. (Alternatively, you can change the default archive location, using the procedures outlined in "Specifying the Locations of Fax Console's Inbox and Sent Items Folders," page 1186.)

 # Troubleshooting

Your faxes can't be routed to an Outlook Inbox.

Unfortunately, the option to route incoming faxes to an Outlook Inbox, available in the Windows 2000 fax software, has been eliminated in Windows XP. For more information and a suggested workaround, see Microsoft Knowledge Base article 311794, "The Windows XP–Based Fax Service Does Not Transfer Incoming Faxes Your Inbox in Outlook 2000 or Outlook 2002." There's also no longer an option to have the fax service notify you by e-mail if a fax arrives.

Choosing Paper Size, Image Quality, and Orientation

By default, the fax driver is set to deliver output at letter size, 200 × 200 dpi, and portrait orientation. You can change any of these details by visiting the General tab of the Fax Properties dialog box. To get to the Fax Properties dialog box, choose Tools, Fax Printer Configuration in Fax Console; or open Printers And Faxes in Control Panel, right-click Fax, and choose Properties from the shortcut menu. Then click the Printing Preferences button to open the Fax Printing Preferences dialog box. Paper size, image quality, and orientation are per-user settings, and nonadministrative users can make changes on the Fax Preferences tab.

Setting Retry Characteristics and Discount Hours

The retry parameter, which tells Fax how often and how frequently to keep trying to send a fax if the first attempt fails, is a device-specific setting. If you have multiple fax devices, you can assign different retry values to each. Because the setting is device specific, it's a little harder to find than some of the other Fax configuration options.

The default retry values are three attempts at 10-minute intervals. If you prefer more retries or a shorter interval, open the Fax Properties dialog box. Click the Devices tab, select the device you want to configure, and then click Properties to open the properties dialog box for the selected device (as shown in Figure 35-5). You can express your retry preferences on the Send tab of this dialog box.

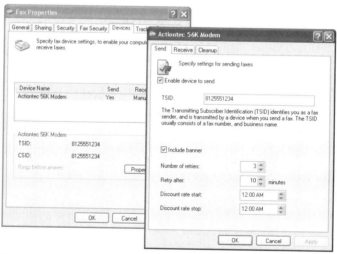

Figure 35-5. Open the Fax Properties dialog box to set retry characteristics and discount hours for a local fax device.

If your telephone service costs less at particular hours of the day, or if you simply prefer sending faxes at off-peak hours (because they're more likely to get through without encountering busy signals, for example), you can indicate those "discount hours" on the Send tab of the device-specific properties dialog box (shown in Figure 35-5). When you send a fax, you'll have the opportunity to schedule it to begin during the discount period.

Making Other Device-Specific Settings

Fax uses a common device driver for all local fax devices. If you have more than one local device, you can make several device-specific settings, in addition to the retry parameters and discount hours described in the previous section. To make any of these settings, choose Tools, Fax Printer Configuration in Fax Console; click the Devices tab; select a device; and click Properties. The following device-specific settings are available:

- TSID (on the Send tab)
- CSID, answer mode, and routing of received faxes (on the Receive tab)
- Scheduled removal of failed faxes from Fax Console's Outbox folder (on the Cleanup tab)

Setting Tracking Preferences

By default, Fax provides both sound and visual feedback on its activities. When sending or receiving, for example, Fax normally displays Fax Monitor, shown in Figure 35-6. Fax Monitor can help you recognize and correct an error condition, such as the absence of a dial tone, or let you know how many pages of your outbound fax have been sent successfully, in case the transmission is interrupted.

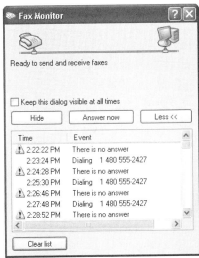

Figure 35-6. Fax Monitor, displayed by default while Fax is sending or receiving, gives feedback about success and failure.

Chapter 35

Additionally, Fax's tracking defaults include an icon in the notification area that appears while a document is coming or going (and stays visible, marked with a red *X*, if an outbound fax fails) and various sound events—a ringing tone when someone dials your fax number, for example, and a "ta-da" to signal a successful send. All these settings can be configured—on a per-user basis—on the Tracking tab of the Fax Properties dialog box. (Click Configure Sound Settings on the Tracking tab to turn sound notification on or off for particular sound events.)

You'll notice that Fax Monitor includes an Answer Now button. If you have your fax device set up to answer manually (for example, if you use the line for both voice and fax), clicking this button is an easy way to get your modem to pick up the phone. It's not the only way, however. If you want to answer manually, but don't like having Fax Monitor pop up when the phone rings, you can use the File, Receive A Fax Now command in Fax Console instead.

If you decide to keep the sound events active but don't care for the sounds that Windows has chosen, open Sounds And Audio Devices in Control Panel and go to the Program Events list on the Sounds tab. You'll find the four fax events—Fax Error, Fax Line Rings, Fax Sent, and New Fax—not under a Fax heading, where you would probably expect to see them, but under the Windows Explorer heading.

Specifying the Locations of Fax Console's Inbox and Sent Items Folders

The Archives tab in the Fax Properties dialog box, shown in Figure 35-7, lets you override the default storage locations for received and sent faxes. As mentioned earlier, these default locations, subfolders of %AllUsersProfile%\Application Data\Microsoft\Windows NT\MSFax, seem almost calculated to discourage browsing and easy backup.

Figure 35-7. You can choose to archive faxes in any folders you like, including ones easier to find than the default locations shown here.

You don't have to rely on Windows Explorer for browsing, of course; you can do it from within Fax Console instead. But backup is another matter. If you want to include your fax archives in a regular backup routine, consider moving them to a more accessible location. If multiple users share a computer configured for Fax services, be sure to select a location that is available to all users, such as a subfolder in the Shared Documents folder.

Faxing a Document or Cover Page

To fax a document, simply print it—using Fax (or whatever you have renamed your fax device) as the "printer." You can do this from your word processor or spreadsheet program, from the Photo Printing Wizard (if, for example, you want to fax a scanned image), or from any other application. When output is directed to the fax device, the Send Fax Wizard appears. The wizard begins by asking for the names and fax numbers of your recipients, as shown in Figure 35-8.

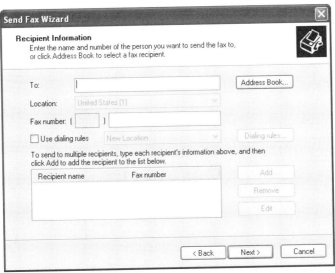

Figure 35-8. You can specify as many recipients as you like on the Send Fax Wizard's Recipient Information page. Click Address Book to fetch addressees and distribution groups from your Windows Address Book or Office Address Book.

Tip Sending multiple pictures via Fax

You can use the Photo Printing Wizard to transmit multiple images as successive pages of a multipage fax. In Windows Explorer, open the folder containing the images you want to send. Then click Print Pictures in the task pane, select each image you want to transmit in the Photo Printing Wizard, and select your fax device as the printer to use.

Chapter 35

On the Recipient Information page, you can specify as many recipients as you like, either by entering names and telephone numbers directly (clicking Add after each entry) or by clicking Address Book and selecting addressees from your Windows Address Book or Office Address Book (if Office is installed, Fax automatically uses the Office Address Book or Contacts folder). Addressees fetched from an address book can either be individuals or distribution groups. If you select a distribution group, the Send Fax Wizard parses the group into individual address-ees and displays each name and fax number in the list of recipient names at the bottom of the dialog box. If you select an address book entry that does not include a fax number, the Send Fax Wizard warns you that it has rejected the entry when you try to complete the send.

If you're entering names directly on the Recipient Information page, you will usually find it easiest to select the Use Dialing Rules check box. Then when you enter an area code in the first box adjacent to Fax Number, Windows will supply the appropriate dialing prefixes, according to whatever rules you have set up in Control Panel, Phone And Modem Options. (If you have not yet set up dialing rules or if you need to edit your dialing rules, click the Dial-ing Rules button on the Recipient Information page.)

Once you have finished addressing your fax, click Next to proceed to the wizard's next page, Preparing The Cover Page (shown in Figure 35-9). If you want to send a cover page, enable the Select A Cover Page Template With The Following Information option and choose from the list of available templates in the Cover Page Template list. Then fill in the Subject Line and Note boxes. You can also click Sender Information to check or edit the data that Cover Page Editor will feed to your selected template. (This information is drawn from the information you supplied during setup, as described in "Providing Information About Yourself," page 1180. For more about cover pages, see "Creating Personal Cover Pages," page 1196.)

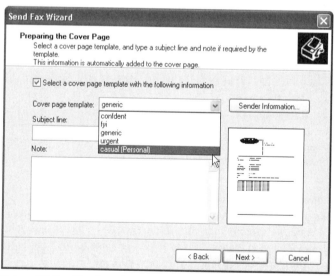

Figure 35-9. The list of available cover page templates includes the four that Fax Cover Page Editor supplies by default, any templates that the Windows XP Setup program has car-ried over from an earlier fax component, and any personal templates you have created.

Finally, click Next to schedule your fax (as shown in Figure 35-10). You can send it immediately, during discount hours, or at a specific time during the next 24 hours.

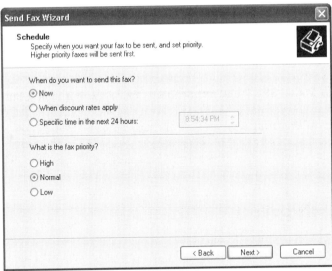

Figure 35-10.   You can send a fax now, during discount hours, or at a specific time of day.

The bottom of the wizard's Schedule page gives you three priority options. When you have multiple jobs in an outbound fax queue, jobs of a given priority and of a given time status (Now, for example, or When Discount Rates Apply) are sent in the order they were created. If you're going to create a queue of documents to be sent later in the day, you can ensure that particular items are transmitted ahead of the others by assigning them High priority. You can change the priority of faxes that have been queued for later sending or delete one or more queued faxes; see "Managing the Outbox Queue," page 1192, for details.

Troubleshooting

Fax won't send via a remote fax device.

If you read the section entitled "Using Remote Fax Resources" in the Help file for Fax Console (in Fax Console, choose Help, Help Topics, and find the topic on the Contents tab), you might easily conclude that Fax can use both local fax devices and fax devices shared by other computers in your workgroup. That, unfortunately, is not the case. The only remote fax resources that Fax can use are those provided by a supported fax server product, such as Microsoft Small Business Server or Windows Server 2003. The Fax Properties dialog box does include a Sharing tab, but for now the sole purpose of that tab is to let you know that you can't share a local fax device.

On the wizard's final page, you can review your settings. You can also click the Preview Fax button to look over the document and cover page that Fax is preparing to send, make sure that the cover page includes the appropriate information, and so on. If anything's amiss, you can back out, fix, and resend.

Faxing a Cover Page Only

To send only a cover page, with or without a note, choose File, Send A Fax, in Fax Console; or choose Send A Fax from the All Programs menu (Accessories, Communications, Fax). The process is the same as for sending a document, except that the option to skip the cover page is unavailable. On the Preparing A Cover Page portion of the wizard, fill in the Subject Line box and use the Note box to create the text of your message. (You can leave the Subject Line or the Note box blank, but not both. You must fill in at least one of these fields when the only page you're faxing is the cover page.)

Faxing from Microsoft Outlook

You can create messages in Outlook (and other supported e-mail programs) and transmit them as faxes from your Outlook Outbox. To do this, you must first install the Fax Mail Transport. In Outlook 2002 or Outlook 2003, follow these steps:

1 Choose Tools, E-Mail Accounts.
2 Select Add A New E-Mail Account, and click Next.
3 Select Additional Server Types, and click Next.
4 Select Fax Mail Transport, and click Next.
5 Close and then reopen Outlook.

To include cover pages with the faxes you transmit from Outlook, perform these steps:

1 Choose Tools, E-Mail Accounts.
2 Select View Or Change Existing E-Mail Accounts, and click Next.
3 Select Fax Mail Transport, and click Change.
4 In the Fax Mail Transport dialog box (shown in Figure 35-11), select Include A Cover Page With Faxes, select the cover page template you want to use as a default (you'll still be able to use other cover page templates for particular messages), and then click OK.

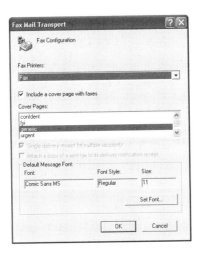

Figure 35-11. You can configure Outlook to use a particular cover page template by default, but you can't change the font used by your Outlook faxes.

Addressing Faxes in Outlook

Once you have installed Fax Mail Transport in Outlook, you can address messages to fax recipients by selecting their names from your Office Address Book or Contacts folder. Outlook will recognize fax numbers and route your messages to Fax. If you include both e-mail addressees and fax addressees, Outlook will process the e-mail first, and then deliver the fax addressees to Fax.

As an alternative to selecting names from an address book, you can enter fax addressees directly on the To: line, using either of the following formats:

- [Fax:*name@faxnumber*]
- [Fax:*faxnumber*]

For example, any of the following would be acceptable:

- [Fax:Ed Bott@+1 (480) 555-0101]
- [Fax:+1 (480) 555-0101]
- [Fax:Ed@555-0101]
- [Fax:555-0101]

Note that the square brackets are essential. If you include the name of your addressee and you're using a cover page template, Fax will feed the name to the template.

Chapter 35

Overriding the Cover Page Default in Outlook

To use a nondefault cover page template in an Outlook fax message, choose Tools, Microsoft Fax Service Attributes in Outlook's Message window. This command is not available when you are using Microsoft Word as your e-mail editor.

Managing the Outbox Queue

Outbound faxes pending delivery are held by Fax Console in a queue, essentially like a printer queue. You can inspect the queue by clicking Outbox in Fax Console's folder tree, and you can print, view, save, and e-mail items in the queue by choosing commands from the File menu. Once jobs have arrived in the Outbox, you can't rearrange the sequence in which they'll be sent. But you can pause an item to let the item following it be transmitted first, and then resume the paused item when you're ready to send it.

If Fax fails to complete a transmission—for example, because it tried to send a fax using the allotted number of retries and received a busy signal on each try—the item remains in the Outbox, its icon marked with a red X. To try again, right-click the item and choose Restart.

> **Tip** Clean out failed faxes
> If you find your Outbox awash in failed items, you can have Fax Console clean out such items periodically. Choose Tools, Fax Printer Configuration. Click the Devices tab, select your fax device, and click Properties. On the Cleanup tab of the device's Properties dialog box, select Automatically Delete Failed Faxes After and specify an interval in days.

If Fax fails to send a job but has not used up the allotted retries, it displays Retrying in the Outbox's Status column (as shown in Figure 35-12) and moves on to another job in the queue. The Scheduled Time column then displays the time of the first job's next scheduled retry. (If these columns do not appear in your Outbox, choose View, Add/Remove Columns.) If you change your retry parameters while jobs are pending retry, Fax maintains the current retry schedule but applies your changes to subsequent retries.

Figure 35-12. The Outbox's Status, Scheduled Time, and Extended Status columns let you know when Fax will retry an unsuccessful send and why the send failed on its last try.

Chapter 35

Caution If you decide to cancel a job while Fax is in the process of sending it, don't delete the item from the Outbox. Instead, click Disconnect in Fax Monitor. (ChooseTools, Fax Monitor in Fax Console, if you don't see Fax Monitor.) While Fax Console will attempt to abort the transmission if you delete an outgoing fax from the Outbox, in some configurations this action may fail.

Archiving Sent Faxes

When Fax has successfully sent a job, it moves it from the Outbox to the Sent Items folder, where you can manipulate it in all the usual ways (double-click it to view it, for example, or choose Save As to create a copy). Fax does not include an archival procedure per se. The Sent Items folder *is* the archive for sent faxes; you can change its location by choosing Tools, Fax Printer Configuration and then clicking the Archives tab. But you can't remove items from the Sent Items folder automatically on the basis of their age or export a selection of items. The best way to preserve selected items while clearing out the Sent Items folder is to work with those items in Windows Explorer. As Figure 35-13 shows, you can use Windows Explorer to open %AllUsersProfile%\Application Data\Microsoft\Windows NT\MSFax\SentItems (or whatever folder you have chosen to use for sent items). You can then use Windows Explorer's Filmstrip and Thumbnails views to examine faxes you've sent. Unfortunately, you'll have to cope with Fax's thoroughly inscrutable file-naming convention, which appends a dollar sign and a 12-digit alphanumeric code to the 36-digit security ID (SID) of the currently logged-on account. The result is a file name that is guaranteed to be both unique and indecipherable.

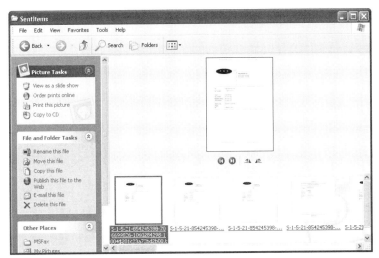

Figure 35-13. All users at a computer share common fax archival folders in Windows Explorer. File names, based on security identifiers, are long and potentially confusing.

Chapter 35

Receiving Faxes

If you have set up Fax to answer automatically, all you have to do to receive a fax is make sure your modem's cable is plugged into a phone jack and that the Fax service is running. Fax does the rest, notifying you of a message's arrival in the manner you have selected (see "Setting Tracking Preferences," page 1185). Once a fax has been successfully received, an entry for it appears in Fax Console's Inbox folder and, if requested, a copy appears at your printer or in your routing folder (see "Routing Received Faxes to a Printer or Folder," page 1182).

If you've set up your system to answer manually, you can have Fax pick up the phone by clicking Answer Now in Fax Monitor (choose Tools, Fax Monitor in Fax Console if you don't see Fax Monitor), by choosing Fax Console's File, Receive A Fax Now command, or by clicking the icon that appears in your notification area when your telephone rings. You'll probably want to have a distinctive sound assigned to the Fax Line Rings sound event, so that you don't miss any calls (see "Setting Tracking Preferences," page 1185).

Tip Give incoming faxes a distinctive ring

How do you share a phone line so that you can use it for voice calls and fax calls without having to manually intercept each fax? Ask your phone service provider if they offer a service called "distinctive ring." With this service (which goes by other names as well), you pay a small extra charge to have a second phone number assigned to your existing phone line. When a caller connects to this number, your phone rings with a distinctive sound that's different from the one associated with regular voice calls. If your modem also supports this capability (not all modems do so, unfortunately), you can add the proper initialization string to the modem's properties (AT-SDR=2 in the case of our old but reliable Supra Faxmodem) and "train" the modem to answer only calls that are identified by the distinctive ring. Give your contacts the new number as your dedicated fax line.

Reading Received Faxes

Faxes arrive in the Inbox folder as TIFF files. (Faxes of more than one page use the multipage TIFF format.) When you double-click an item in any folder in the Fax Console, Windows displays it, using whatever application is currently associated with the .tif file extension. If you have installed Microsoft Office, the application associated with TIFF files is probably Microsoft Office Document Imaging (as shown in Figure 35-14). This TIFF viewer has the virtue of providing page thumbnails for multipage documents and also includes optical character recognition (OCR) capability. Figure 35-15 shows an OCR rendition of the first page of the fax shown in Figure 35-14. It's not perfect by any means, but it's a leg up if you need to edit the text you receive.

Sending and Receiving Faxes

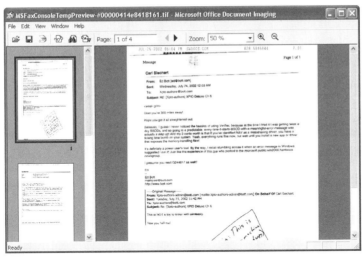

Figure 35-14. Double-click a fax in Fax Console's Inbox folder to display it in your system's default TIFF viewer.

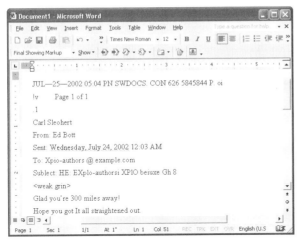

Figure 35-15. The OCR capability in Microsoft Office Document Imaging produced this approximation of the text displayed in Figure 35-14.

If you don't have Office, your system probably uses Windows Picture And Fax Viewer to display your faxes. This application doesn't provide thumbnails. But you can move between pages of a multipage document by clicking the Next Page and Previous Page buttons along the bottom of the window (shown in Figure 35-16 on the next page), or by pressing the Page Up and Page Down keys.

Figure 35-16. Use the Next Page and Previous Page buttons to move between pages in Windows Picture and Fax Viewer.

Archiving Received Faxes

Received faxes accumulate in your Inbox forever, unless you move them manually. Fax Console does not include a date-based archival procedure, nor does it allow you to create additional folders or subfolders. You can delete or save (that is, copy) items individually from the Inbox. Or you can work with them in Windows Explorer, by opening %AllUsersProfile%\ Application Data\Microsoft\Windows NT\MSFax\Inbox (or whatever other folder you've chosen to use for your received items).

Creating Personal Cover Pages

Using Fax Cover Page Editor, you can customize any of the four cover page templates supplied with Fax. You can also create new templates from scratch. The resulting personal cover pages become available to your own user account only.

Although the Fax folder in your Start menu includes a command to launch Fax Cover Page Editor, the simplest way to start building a personal cover page is to choose Tools, Personal Cover Pages in Fax Console. The dialog box that appears lists any personal cover pages you have already created. If you want to work with a blank slate and create your own template from scratch, click New. To edit an existing cover page, select it and click Open. To customize one of the four common cover pages, click Copy, and select the one you want. The selected item then appears in the Personal Cover Pages dialog box, where you can rename it if you want or simply open it and begin customizing. Figure 35-17 shows Fax Cover Page Editor with the common cover page Confdent.cov, unmodified.

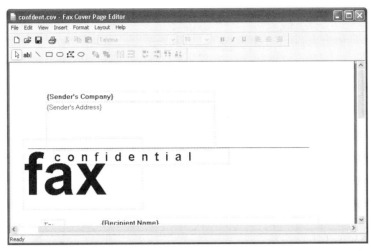

Figure 35-17. You can use Fax Cover Page Editor to modify supplied cover page templates or create your own.

Selecting, Sizing, and Moving Objects

Every element on a cover page that's bounded by a dotted line in Fax Cover Page Editor is a distinct object. To size or move an object, begin by clicking it. Black handles appear around the selected object's perimeter. To change an object's size, drag one of the handles. To move an object, position the mouse along the perimeter, but not on a handle. A four-headed arrow appears beside the normal mouse pointer. Drag the object to its new location. If you change your mind, press Ctrl+Z or choose Edit, Undo.

To move two or more objects at once, hold down Ctrl and click each object. The objects become temporarily grouped and will move together.

Aligning Objects

You can use the View, Grid Lines command to display light-blue grid lines in the editor. These might help you in positioning objects. However, it's usually easier to align objects by choosing Layout, Align Objects. Options on the Align Objects submenu let you line up objects flush left or flush right. You can also top align and bottom align objects or center objects horizontally or vertically.

Spacing Objects Evenly

To ensure that three or more objects have equal vertical or horizontal space between them, first hold down Ctrl and click the objects. Then choose Layout, Space Evenly, Across or Layout, Space Evenly, Down.

Centering Objects on the Page

To center one or more objects on the page, vertically or horizontally, first hold down Ctrl and click the objects. Then choose Layout, Center On Page, Width or Layout, Center On Page, Height.

Changing the Z-Order of Stacked Objects

If two or more objects lie atop one another, the order in which they're stacked is called the *z-order*. To change the z-order of an object relative to others, select the object and choose Layout, Bring To Front or Layout, Send To Back.

Adding Fixed Text

Fixed text is text that doesn't change (as distinguished from fields, which are replaced by information about the sender, recipient, or content of a fax).To add fixed text, follow these steps:

1 Click the Text tool button on the Drawing toolbar. (If the Drawing toolbar isn't visible, choose View, Drawing Toolbar.)

2 Click one corner of the place where you want the object to go. Then drag to the diagonally opposite corner. A perimeter rectangle with black handles appears as you drag.

3 Type your text within the object perimeter. Use the Format, Font and Format, Align Text options (or their toolbar equivalents) to get the text looking the way you want it.

Note that new objects don't affect the placement of existing objects. If you want to insert a line of text between two lines, you must first drag objects out of the way to make room for the incoming text.

Inserting Fields, Images, and Graphics

Objects that begin and end with braces—such as {Sender's Company} and {Sender's Address} in Figure 35-17—are fields. When your fax is sent, these fields will be replaced by the appropriate data. To add fields to a cover page, use the Insert menu. The available fields appear in three submenus: Recipient, Sender, and Message.

To place an image on a cover page, first open or create that image in another application (such as Microsoft Paint). Copy the image to the Clipboard, and then paste it onto your cover page. The pasted image will appear in the upper left corner; you can use the mouse to drag it into place. To insert lines and shapes, use the Line, Rectangle, Rounded Rectangle, Polygon, and Ellipse tools on the Drawing toolbar. To use any of these other than the Polygon tool, click the tool, click the cover page approximately where you want to start drawing the object,

Chapter 35

and drag to the size you want. You can move and resize the objects after you first place them on the page. To use the Polygon tool, click each vertex of the polygon. When you have finished, double-click to close the polygon.

Holding down Shift while you drag constrains the Line, Rectangle, Rounded Rectangle, and Ellipse tools. Shift-dragging with the Line tool creates a horizontal, vertical, or 45-degree diagonal line. Shift-dragging with the Rectangle and Rounded Rectangle tools creates a square and a rounded square, whereas Shift-dragging with the Ellipse tool creates a circle.

Previewing and Saving

The File, Print Preview command gives you a look at your work, more or less the way it will appear in a fax viewer (with fields, instead of data). The Save command puts a copy of the template in %UserProfile%\My Documents\Fax\Personal Cover Pages, the default location for personal cover pages. To save the cover page elsewhere, use File, Save As.

Managing Security

Under default permissions for a fax device, administrative accounts have complete control over all local fax resources and can view and edit security settings. Nonadministrative users can view and manage (copy, print, delete) faxes that they have sent but not those sent by other users. Nonadministrative accounts can view all successfully received faxes (including faxes received by other user accounts) but cannot manage any received faxes. Nonadministrative users cannot see entries in Fax Console's Incoming folder—the folder that Fax Console uses while a fax reception is in progress.

To view or edit fax security settings, open the Fax Properties dialog box. You can do this by choosing Tools, Fax Printer Configuration in Fax Console or by opening Printers And Faxes in Control Panel, right-clicking Fax, and choosing Properties from the shortcut menu.

The Fax Properties dialog box includes two security tabs, labeled Security and Fax Security. The Security tab offers options that are common to all printers. To work with permissions that deal specifically with fax queues and documents, use the Fax Security tab. Neither the Security tab nor the Fax Security tab is normally visible on a computer that is using Simple File Sharing (this includes all computers running Windows XP Home Edition). To make the Fax Security tab appear if you don't see it, close the Fax Properties dialog box and reopen it while holding down Ctrl. The Security tab is visible only on systems that are not using Simple File Sharing.

The basic permissions available for a fax device are listed in Table 35-1 on the next page. In addition to these basic permissions, a much more granular set of permissions is available. To change any of these settings, click Advanced on the Fax Security tab of the Fax Properties dialog box. Then select the name of a user or security group, and click Edit. These steps display the dialog box shown in Figure 35-18 on the next page.

Table 35-1. Basic Fax Permissions and Privileges

Permission	Privileges
Fax	Fax a document; view all faxes in the Inbox
Manage Fax Configuration	Configure the fax device
Manage Fax Documents	Print and manage all faxes, including those owned by other users

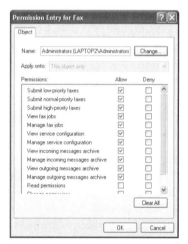

Figure 35-18. If the basic fax permissions don't entirely meet your needs, you can micromanage permissions with the help of these advanced settings.

Chapter 36

Communicating Over the Internet

The ubiquity of Internet connections—many of them at broadband speeds and always on—provides an ideal medium for instant, interactive communications. E-mail is terrific for communications where you don't need an immediate response. Telephone communications are, of course, essential in business and personal intercourse. Instant messaging with a program like Microsoft Windows Messenger provides a third communications method that offers a number of advantages:

- It's interactive. You can exchange questions and answers in real time instead of sending e-mail messages back and forth over a period of hours, days, or weeks.

- It's not as intrusive as telephone communications. If you choose, you can continue working in other programs or on other activities while you carry out an instant messaging session.

- It's more private. Users can control the display of their availability on other users' screens. You can block specific people from seeing your availability and from sending you messages. As with caller ID, you can see who is trying to reach you before you answer. Strangers can't join your conversation, as they can in an Internet chat session.

- It's versatile. As with e-mail, you can send and receive text and files. You can also make audio connections, as you would with a telephone. In addition, you can send and receive video, you can work collaboratively with a whiteboard or a program, and you can take control of another user's computer with that person's permission.

At Home with Windows XP

All of Windows Messenger's features are available in Windows XP Home Edition as well as Windows XP Professional. The optional Group Policy setting that prevents Windows Messenger from running is not available in Home Edition. But if you're a Home Edition user and don't want Windows Messenger to run, you can keep it from appearing by making a small registry modification. For details, see "Disabling Windows Messenger in Windows XP Home Edition," page 1209.

Other Communications Tools Included with Windows XP

Windows Messenger provides a seamless, integrated way for users to participate in text chat, voice and video communication, and data collaboration. As such, it provides the functionality of other programs that were included in earlier versions of Windows. In addition to the messaging capabilities inherited from MSN Messenger, Windows Messenger incorporates audio and videoconference capabilities of Microsoft NetMeeting and Phone Dialer.

Although they don't appear on the Start menu, NetMeeting and Phone Dialer are included in Windows XP. (Note that the version of Phone Dialer included with Windows XP is the sophisticated conferencing application introduced with Windows 2000, not the rudimentary eight-number speed dial program of the same name that was included with Windows 95 and Windows 98.) You might want to use these tools, separately from Windows Messenger, in certain situations:

- If you want to view a directory of and connect with other users whom you don't know, but who may share common interests, use NetMeeting or Phone Dialer. With both programs, you can connect to an Internet location server (ILS), which lists lots of other people who are out there waiting for your call.

- If you've already stored NetMeeting conferencing information (that is, names of conferencing servers and the addresses of users) as entries in your Microsoft Outlook Express address book, use NetMeeting. You can continue working with those contacts as you always have. (On the other hand, you might want to suggest that your contacts switch to Windows Messenger so that you can both enjoy its advantages.)

- If you want to use a sophisticated speed-dial system for making voice calls over standard telephone lines, use Phone Dialer.

- If you want to hold a voice conference or videoconference with more than two people simultaneously, use Phone Dialer.

- If you want to use Whiteboard or application sharing with more than two people simultaneously, use NetMeeting.

- If you want to hold a voice or video conversation, share applications, or use Whiteboard with a user who doesn't have Windows Messenger, use NetMeeting.

NetMeeting

To start NetMeeting, open the Start menu, choose Run, and type **conf**. If you use NetMeeting regularly, you'll want to create a shortcut to its executable, %ProgramFiles%\Netmeeting\ Conf.exe. The first time you run NetMeeting, a wizard asks you to provide your name and e-mail address so that you can be found in a directory. (Even if you choose not to list your name in a directory, an ILS server needs this information to know when you're online and how to route NetMeeting calls to your computer.) After completing the wizard, the main NetMeeting window opens, as shown in Figure 36-1.

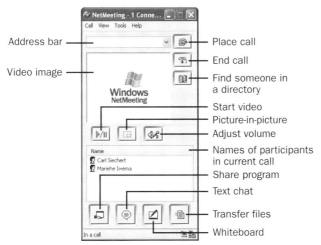

Figure 36-1. The main NetMeeting window provides the tools to make, accept, and control your calls, along with a list of people in the current conversation and a video window.

To learn more about NetMeeting, open its Help menu and choose Help Topics. The Help menu includes several links to online information but, because Windows Messenger has largely supplanted NetMeeting, some of these links no longer work. The mother lode of NetMeeting information, the NetMeeting Resource Kit, is available for download at *http://www.microsoft.com/windows/netmeeting/corp/reskit/*.

Phone Dialer

To start PHone Dialer, open the Run dialog box and type *dialer*. If you want to create a shortcut, you'll find Dialer.exe in the %ProgramFiles%\Windows NT folder. With Phone Dialer, you can mkae videoconference calls to other users on the Internet or on your local area network, as shown in Figure 36-2.

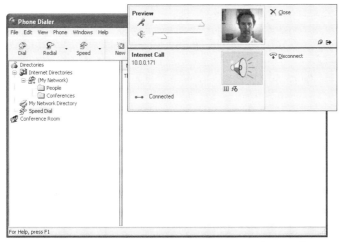

Figure 36-2. Using Phone Dialer, you can make video calls over network connections as well as voice calls over the network or telephone lines.

Introducing Windows Messenger

Windows Messenger is the latest version of a program originally known as MSN Messenger. (MSN Messenger is a separate product, similar in many ways to Windows Messenger. For details, see "Windows Messenger vs. MSN Messenger: What's the Difference?" page 1215.) With Windows Messenger, you can set up a list of contacts and then check it to see which of your contacts is online at any time. Windows Messenger lets you engage in a conference with one or many users across the Internet or a local area network. If your computer has a sound card, a microphone, and speakers, you can talk to another person in something approximating real time. If you have a video camera connected to your computer, you can exchange video images. With or without audio and video equipment, you can "chat" with others, exchange drawings and diagrams by means of a virtual whiteboard, send and receive files, and even work together in a shared program. You can also use Windows Messenger to initiate a Remote Assistance session, in which one user can view and control the computer of another user from a remote location.

For information about using Windows Messenger for Remote Assistance, see "Connecting to Another PC with Remote Assistance," page 92.

Windows Messenger can also serve as an alert service. With Microsoft Alerts, a free service, you can receive alerts about events on your calendar, changes in selected stock prices, current news (from MSNBC), and other events you choose. Third-party enhancements to Windows Messenger offer additional functionality. Windows Messenger provides a platform that developers can use to create other services and features.

Note Windows Messenger can be updated through dynamic update during setup (the Windows XP Setup program can check the Internet for updates), by Windows Update, or in response to messages displayed by Windows Messenger.

Note Don't confuse Windows Messenger with the Messenger service, a system service that you can control with the Services console (Services.msc). Despite the similar names, the two have nothing to do with each other. The Messenger service can be used for broadcasting a text message to one or more computers on your network. Applications can use this service for such things as notifying you that a print job is complete or that the system is running on battery backup power. You don't need to run the Messenger service to use Windows Messenger—in fact, in Windows XP Service Pack 2, the Messenger service is disabled by default.

What You Need to Use Windows Messenger

The basic requirement to run Windows Messenger is simple:You need a working Internet connection and a .NET Passport. (This is true even if you plan to use Windows Messenger only to converse with others on your local area network, because your list of contacts is available only when you're connected to the Internet.) If you want to make voice calls or video calls, you'll need some additional hardware:

- To be able to hear others speak, add a sound card and speakers or a headset.
- To add your own voice to the fray, connect a microphone to the sound card.
- To send your picture to others, add a Web camera.

> **Note** For voice calls or video calls, you'll obviously get better quality with greater bandwidth. Cable or DSL connections are ideal, but you can actually get decent results with a dial-up connection. At a bare minimum, you'll need a 28,800 bps modem that's connected at 28,800 bps.

If your computer is protected from the Internet by a router other than the built-in Internet Connection Sharing, the router must support UPnP if you want to use Messenger features other than instant text messaging and file transfers. For more information about router and firewall configuration, see "Punching Through a Firewall," page 1206.

A .NET Passport provides the connection to the server where your contacts are stored. Because your contacts are stored on a central server, they're available to you no matter where you are when you sign in using your Passport. If you haven't already obtained a .NET Passport and linked it to your user account, you can do so through the User Accounts option in Control Panel. But an easier way is to simply double-click the Windows Messenger icon in the notification area.

Unless your account is already linked to a .NET Passport, this action opens the .NET Passport Wizard. The wizard helps you obtain a .NET Passport if you don't have one and then links it to your user account so that you can sign in automatically whenever you log on to your computer.

> For more information about .NET Passports, see "Setting Up a .NET Passport," page 269.

Chapter 36

Note When Microsoft started its Passport service, you had to have an e-mail address at hotmail.com, msn.com, or passport.com to get a Passport. You can still use one of those addresses if you have one (or you can use the wizard to set up a Microsoft Hotmail account), but you can now link a Passport to *any* e-mail address.

Punching Through a Firewall

If your computer connects directly to the Internet, or connects through a UPnP-compliant router, and if you're using Windows Firewall, you're in great shape for using all of the features of Windows Messenger. This combination deals perfectly with the dynamic port assignments required by Windows Messenger.

Troubleshooting

Windows Messenger stops working when you make a VPN connection.

You might encounter problems using Windows Messenger while you're also using a virtual private network (VPN) connection. If you have a conversation open and then connect to a VPN server, your conversation might stop. You'll receive no indication that the call has been interrupted (other than the fact that the person you're talking with no longer responds to your messages). Similarly, the person at the other end has no indication that you're no longer in the conversation.

The reason for this is that the default configuration of a VPN connection attempts to use the default gateway on the remote network (that is, the default gateway for the VPN server) for Internet connections while the VPN connection is active. This setup is useful in situations where you're connecting to a corporate network and then using *its* ISP to connect to the Internet. If you have your own connection to the Internet, there's usually no reason to use such a setup.

To fix the problem, follow these steps:

1 In Control Panel open Network Connections.

2 Right-click the VPN connection and choose Properties.

3 Click the Networking tab, select Internet Protocol (TCP/IP) and click Properties.

4 In the Internet Protocol (TCP/IP) Properties dialog box, click Advanced.

5 On the General tab of the Advanced TCP/IP Settings dialog box, clear the Use Default Gateway On Remote Network check box.

Thereafter, you should be able to use Windows Messenger (and any other applications that access the Internet, such as Microsoft Internet Explorer) while your VPN connection is active.

Communicating Over the Internet

On the other hand, if you use a router that was purchased before late 2001 and you have not recently upgraded its firmware, your router probably does not support UPnP, and therefore won't allow you to make voice and video connections over the Internet. In addition, you might need to open some ports to enable certain other features. If you have such a setup, check with the manufacturer of your router. Many manufacturers have promised firmware upgrades that enable UPnP, as well as incorporating UPnP support in their new products.

One of the key jobs of a router is network address translation (NAT), which converts the internal LAN address of a computer into a public IP address. NAT effectively shields your network computers from the Internet. But it also makes it difficult to connect computers on separate private networks in a peer-to-peer fashion. UPnP is a new industry standard that makes it possible for computers to detect devices on a network and work with one another. When it comes to traversing NAT devices, UPnP enables applications such as Windows Messenger to navigate the gateway. You can find more information about UPnP at Microsoft TechNet, *http://www.microsoft.com/technet/prodtechnol/winxppro/evaluate/upnpxp.mspx*, and at the UPnP Forum site, *http://www.upnp.org*.

If you're using a firewall other than Windows Firewall, you might need to open the following ports:

- **Instant messaging**   Windows Messenger uses a TCP connection to port 1863 if possible. If that's not available, Messenger connects using the same connection the Web browser uses. If that's the only available connection method, you'll be limited to using Windows Messenger for instant messaging. If you're using a proxy server, open the Tools menu in Windows Messenger and choose Options. Click the Connection tab and provide the requested information, which depends on the type of proxy server you have.

- **File transfer**   Windows Messenger allows up to 10 simultaneous file transfers, each on a separate port, using TCP connections to ports 6891 through 6900.

- **Whiteboard and application sharing**   Like NetMeeting, Windows Messenger uses TCP connections to port 1503 for Whiteboard and application sharing.

- **Voice and video**   These services use dynamically assigned ports. More importantly, they require UPnP support to get to an IP address on the internal network.

Setting Startup Options

By default, Windows Messenger starts each time you log on and its icon appears in the notification area. You can prevent this from happening by double-clicking the icon to open the main Windows Messenger window. (You don't need to sign in.) Click Tools, Options, and click the Preferences tab. Under General, clear the Run This Program When Windows Starts check box. Doing so removes the MSMSGS value from HKCU\Software\Microsoft\Windows\CurrentVersion\Run.

Chapter 36

> **Note** If you don't have a Passport associated with your user account, you can't open Windows Messenger to make this change until you complete the .NET Passport Wizard. However, there is a way around this roadblock without editing the registry directly. Open Outlook Express and choose Tools, Windows Messenger, Options. You can then make the change described above as well as the three that follow.

Note, however, that the icon also appears whenever you start Outlook Express. You can prevent that from happening by making the following additional settings:

- On the Preferences tab of Messenger's Options dialog box, clear the Allow This Program To Run In The Background check box.
- In Outlook Express, click Tools, Options. On the General tab, clear Automatically Log On To Windows Messenger.
- Don't display the Contacts pane in Outlook Express. To prevent it from appearing, choose View, Layout, and clear the Contacts check box.

Before you go to great lengths to exterminate Windows Messenger, be aware that when only its icon appears, Messenger uses an insignificant amount of memory. And if you don't like seeing the icon, set it to be hidden all of the time. For details, see "Removing Unneeded Icons from the Notification Area," page 494.

If you're really intent on preventing Windows Messenger from starting up—ever—you can uninstall it. The easiest way is to enter the following at a command prompt:

```
rundll32 advpack.dll,LaunchINFSection %systemroot%\inf\msmsgs.inf,BLC.Remove
```

(This command string is case-sensitive.) Be aware, however, that removing Windows Messenger can affect other components; if you don't like it, you're best off leaving it in place and ignoring it.

> **Note** If you remove Windows Messenger, starting Outlook Express with the Contacts pane displayed takes an inordinately long time (because Outlook Express tries in vain to launch Windows Messenger). You can retain the Contacts pane but eliminate this delay by adding a registry value. In the HKLM\Software\Microsoft\Outlook Express key, create a new DWORD value named Hide Messenger, and then set its data to 2.

If you have previously set Passport to sign in automatically on your computer and you want to change that so that when you connect to the Internet you don't automatically sign in, follow these steps:

1 In Control Panel, open User Accounts.
2 Click your account name (if you're an administrator) and then click Manage My Network Passwords under Related Tasks in the task pane.
3 Select the Passport.Net* (Passport) entry and click Remove.

Thereafter, when you log on and connect to the Internet, you remain signed off until you explicitly sign in. If you select Sign Me In Automatically in the .NET Messenger Service sign-in dialog box, you'll again sign in automatically each time you connect to the Internet.

Using Group Policy to Disable Windows Messenger

Windows XP Professional users can prevent Windows Messenger from running as follows:

1 At a command prompt, type **gpedit.msc**.
2 Navigate to Local Computer Policy\Computer Configuration\Administrative Templates\ Windows Components\Windows Messenger.
3 Enable the Do Not Allow Windows Messenger To Be Run policy.

These steps prevent Windows Messenger from running, regardless of whether you try to start it directly or another application (such as Outlook Express) attempts to run it. (Note that the other policy setting, Do Not Automatically Start Windows Messenger Initially, is ineffective.) However, if you enable Windows Messenger to run at startup by selecting Run This Program When Windows Starts in Windows Messenger's Options dialog box, Windows Messenger runs at startup, policy notwithstanding.

Disabling Windows Messenger in Windows XP Home Edition

If you're running Windows XP Home Edition, you don't have access to the Group Policy console, but you can disable Windows Messenger by modifying the registry. Proceed as follows:

1 Open HKLM\Software\Policies\Microsoft, and create a new subkey named Messenger.
2 In the Messenger key, create a new subkey named Client.
3 In the Client subkey, create a new DWORD value named PreventRun.
4 Set the data value for PreventRun to 1.

Starting Windows Messenger

If Windows Messenger is set to run at startup, you can open it by double-clicking its notification area icon. Otherwise, you can start Windows Messenger by choosing it from the All Programs menu. When you're not signed in to Passport, the icon looks like the one shown here on the left. If you are signed in, it looks like the one on the right.

Either way, Windows Messenger opens. If you have not signed in, the program prompts you to do so. Otherwise, the appearance of the window is comparable to that shown in Figure 36-3.

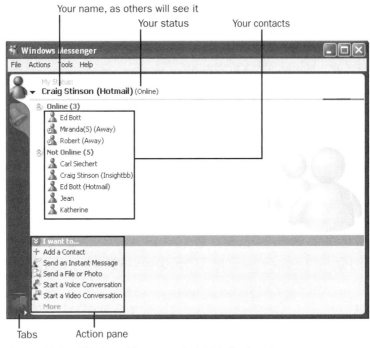

Figure 36-3. Windows Messenger's initial display shows your current status, the name and status of each contact, an action pane, and more.

The name and status that appear at the top of the window, under My Status, is what your contacts see. You can change the name (from your e-mail address to your first name, for example) on the Personal tab of the Options dialog box (choose Tools, Options). To change your status (from Online to Be Right Back, for example), choose your name.

Below your own name appear the names of your contacts, along with their current status. By default, Windows Messenger sorts the contacts according to whether they're offline or online, counting everyone who has signed into their Passport accounts as online, even though some of those contacts might be busy, out to lunch, or tied up in some other manner. As an alternative to this arrangement, you can create your own ad-hoc groupings and sort contacts by the groups you create. In Figure 36-4, for example, we've created two new groups called Work and Play. (To create a group, click Tools, Manage Groups, Add A Group. Then, while the default group name (New Group) is selected, type the name you want to use.)

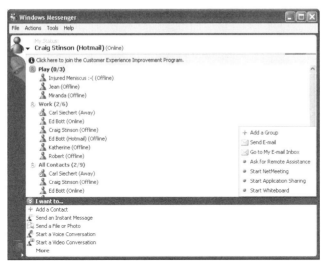

Figure 36-4. Windows Messenger lets you create your own categories of contacts and sort by category.

To sort contacts by groups instead of by online/offline status, choose Tools, Sort Contacts By, Groups. To move a contact from one group to another, right-click it (not in the All Contacts section but in its current group) and choose Move Contact To.

Along the left edge of the window, you might see a panel of tabs. These provide quick access to related services, such as Microsoft Alerts. To configure the tab display, click Tools, Show Tabs. An action pane appears near the bottom of the window, under the heading I Want To. If you click the More link, an expanded set of actions appears as shown in Figure 36-4. If you have a lot of contacts, you might want to collapse the action pane by clicking the chevron beside the I Want To heading. (All the actions are accessible via the Actions and Tools menus, in any case.)

Tip   Double-click to sign in

If you sign out of Windows Messenger (or if you're disconnected due to a network problem), you can sign in again by clicking (or right-clicking) the notification area icon and choosing Sign In from the shortcut menu. But when you do that, you have to re-enter your password. You can bypass the password request by simply double-clicking the notification area icon. That action opens Windows Messenger, which has a link you can click to sign in—without re-entering your password.

Chapter 36

Placing or Receiving a Call

Windows Messenger offers three types of calls: instant message (text), voice, and video. You can send an instant message in any of the following ways:

- Double-click the name of an online contact.
- Click Send An Instant Message in the action pane, or choose Actions, Send An Instant Message. Then select the name of an online contact in the Send An Instant Message dialog box. To send a message to someone who's not on your contacts list, click the Other tab, and then enter the e-mail address of the person you want to reach.
- Click or right-click the notification area icon and choose Send An Instant Message.

> **Tip** Send an instant message from Outlook Express
>
> You don't have to open Windows Messenger to send an instant message; you can initiate a conversation from Outlook Express. Display the Contacts pane (choose View, Layout and select Contacts); your online contacts appear at the top of the list. Double-click an online contact to send an instant message.

A conversation window opens on your computer, similar to the one shown in Figure 36-5. Type your message in the box at the bottom of the window and then click Send.

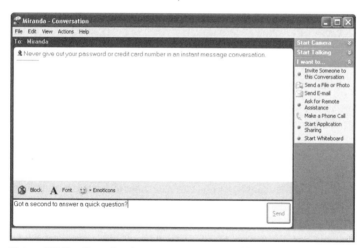

Figure 36-5. Type the text you want to send in the box at the bottom of the conversation window.

When you send your message, an alert window appears on the recipient's screen, as shown in Figure 36-6, and a sound plays. In addition, a brightly colored flashing button appears on the recipient's taskbar. (For all this to happen, of course, the recipient must have Windows Messenger running and must be signed in to Passport.) The text of the alert message is actually a link; the recipient can click the text to open a conversation window on his or her screen. The alert window, however, remains on-screen for only a few seconds. If the recipient misses that opportunity, clicking the taskbar button opens the conversation window. (The flashing, thankfully, stops after a few more seconds, but the bright color remains until the recipient opens—or closes without restoring—the conversation window.)

Tip Customize your alerts

Windows Messenger can display an alert window whenever one of your contacts comes online and when you receive an instant message. In addition, it can play a sound upon each of these events. If you want to limit the number of intrusions or change the sounds that play, open the Tools menu and choose Options. Click the Preferences tab and then make your settings in the Alerts section. As an alternative to disabling sound alerts altogether, you might want to consider assigning quieter tones to Windows Messenger events—by visiting the Sounds And Audio Devices section of Control Panel. Near the bottom of the Program Events list on the Sounds tab of the Sounds And Audio Devices Properties dialog box, you'll find a group of events under the heading Windows Messenger. Configure to taste.

Figure 36-6. The text of an alert window is a clickable link.

Until the recipient opens the conversation window and begins typing a response, you'll have no idea whether the person is at his or her computer. But when the person at the other end of the conversation begins typing, a message in the status bar alerts you to that fact, even before you receive a response.

Chapter 36

> **Tip** Receive other types of alerts
>
> Microsoft Alerts is a service that can send reminders of appointments, due dates, birthdays, and so on; alerts of changes in the price of stocks you're interested in; and more. You can set these alerts to arrive as instant messages when you're running Windows Messenger. (You can also set them up to be delivered to your e-mail address or pager, and you can choose different delivery options depending on your Windows Messenger status.) To learn more and to start setting reminders, visit *http://alerts.microsoft.com*.

Working with Your List of Contacts

It's easiest to initiate a conversation with someone in your contact list. First off, you can see at a glance who among your contacts is online and who is not, as shown in Figure 36-7. Secondly, you can start a conversation by double-clicking the name of an online contact or choosing the name from a menu; no typing is needed.

> **Tip** Contact someone who's not online
>
> To reach a contact who is not online—or who does not respond to an instant message— right-click the contact name and choose Send Mail.

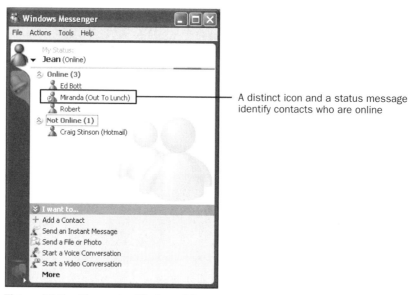

A distinct icon and a status message identify contacts who are online

Figure 36-7. The main Windows Messenger window shows which contacts are online— including those who are online but possibly unavailable.

Windows Messenger vs. MSN Messenger: What's the Difference?

Windows Messenger is included with all versions of Windows XP and is installed by default. As an alternative to, or in addition to, Windows Messenger, you can use MSN Messenger for text, audio, and video messaging. MSN Messenger is not included with Windows XP, but if you use MSN you probably already have it, and if you don't have it, you can download it free from *http://messenger.msn.com*. With both programs on board, you can use whichever you prefer. If you have more than one Passport account, you can log on to both messaging tools at the same time. (You can't be logged onto the same Passport account on both programs at once, however.)

The most obvious difference between MSN Messenger and Windows Messenger is that the former is a consumer-oriented product with—as you might expect—lots of connections to MSN itself. Tabs along the side panel in MSN Messenger provide quick access to MSN Shopping, MSN Games, MSN Money, MSNBC, and more. An ever-changing (but also ever-present) advertising panel appears at the bottom of MSN Messenger's main window.

Other differences are less visible but equally important. Both products support communication via .NET Messenger Service, but Windows Messenger also allows users to communicate via Sessions Initiation Protocol (SIP) servers and Microsoft Exchange Server. If you work in an environment where SIP servers are available or use an Exchange Server–based e-mail system, you might find messaging with colleagues (particularly where audio or video is involved) quicker and more trouble-free using those options instead of .NET Messenger Service. (To use SIP or Exchange accounts, choose Tools, Options in Windows Messenger, click the Accounts tab, and select either My Contacts Include Users Of A SIP Communications Service or My Contacts Include Users of Exchange Instant Messaging—or both.)

On the other hand, if you want to play Mozaki Blocks, Cubis, Hexic, Bejeweled, or a variety of other games with online contacts, MSN Messenger is for you. MSN Messenger also includes a Make A Phone Call command that has been dropped from versions 4.7 and later of Windows Messenger. If you have an account with an Internet telephony service, you can use this command to connect by phone with contacts who don't happen to be online.

Our take: It's good to have both programs on hand, but for simple text messaging we favor the ad-free Windows Messenger. For more details about the two messaging programs, see Knowledge Base article 330117, "Running Both Windows Messenger and MSN Messenger 5.0 in Windows XP" (*http://support.microsoft.com/?kbid=330117*).

To add someone to your contact list, click the Add A Contact link or choose Tools, Add A Contact. The Add A Contact Wizard appears, asking you to decide whether you want to type the contact's e-mail address or search for the contact. Select the default option, By E-Mail Address Or Sign-In Name.

Chapter 36

The search option, which lets you specify a name and location, is not likely to be fruitful. It can search your Outlook Express address book or the Hotmail member directory. However, it doesn't search the Outlook Express address book thoroughly; it checks only contacts that you have added manually, not the addresses that are added automatically when you reply to a message. The Hotmail member directory has its own limitations: It includes only a subset of Hotmail members. (For privacy reasons, many Hotmail members choose not to list their names or provide fake information.) You must enter an exact match for the directory entry; partial names won't produce hits. If you feel compelled to try anyway, leave the Country/ Region box set to (Any). With a country selected, the directory search sometimes fails to produce any results.

After you enter an e-mail name (or find the match you were looking for in a name search), Windows checks the .NET Passport servers to see whether the person has a Passport. If he or she does not, the wizard can send an e-mail message on your behalf that explains how to get a Passport and set up Messenger. If your new contact already has a Passport, a dialog box, shown in Figure 36-8, appears on your contact's computer that alerts him or her to the fact that you've added this person to your contact list. (If Messenger isn't running on the contact's computer at that time, the message appears when the contact next signs in.) Note that this dialog box is an offer that your contact is allowed to refuse! If your contact does not want to be contacted, he or she can select the Block The Person From Seeing When You Are Online And Contacting You option button.

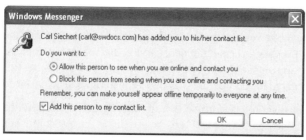

Figure 36-8. Windows Messenger advises your new contact about your action, and offers the contact an opportunity to rebuff your advance—or to reciprocate by adding you to his or her contact list.

Tip Add contacts from Outlook Express

If you've saved e-mail contacts in Outlook Express (or in Address Book), you can quickly convert them to online contacts that appear in your Windows Messenger contact list. In Outlook Express, display the Contacts pane. (Choose View, Layout, and select Contacts.) Right-click a contact and choose Set As Online Contact. (Note that this option isn't available in the Address Book window; you must use the Contacts pane in Outlook Express.) Windows then checks to see if a .NET Passport is associated with the e-mail address of the contact you selected and reports its findings, just as the Add A Contact Wizard does.

To delete a contact you no longer want, right-click it and choose Delete Contact.

Preserving Your Online Privacy

With the increasing numbers of reports of identity theft, stalkers, cons, scams, viruses, worms, and other nasty possibilities, people are understandably wary about exposing personal information on the Internet. Windows Messenger and the supporting .NET Passport technology have a number of features that allow you to protect your privacy. To begin with, unlike Internet relay chat (IRC) programs, Windows Messenger conversations are limited to your friends and associates or, at the very least, to people who have your e-mail address and your permission to converse. You can learn about .NET Passport privacy policies, including descriptions of which personal information is available to others, by visiting the Microsoft .NET Passport site at *http://www.passport.com/consumer/privacypolicy.asp*.

Protecting Your Identity

You determine what name others see if you're listed in their contact list or if you're in a conversation. You can choose to use only your first name or a totally anonymous handle of your invention. To specify the name that others see, open the Tools menu and choose Options. On the Personal tab, shown in Figure 36-9, type the name that you want displayed.

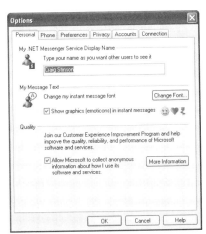

Figure 36-9. You can choose how you want to be identified to your contacts.

Protecting Your E-mail Address

The e-mail address that's linked to your Passport appears in the conversation window while you're in a call. If you don't want that address known publicly, use another. Free e-mail addresses are available from Hotmail and a number of other online services. Changing the address associated with your existing Passport doesn't always work; you're better off obtaining a new Passport that's associated with the new address you want to use.

Note When you create a Passport, you can provide a phony e-mail address; Passport has no way of confirming your address during the sign-up process. However, it's not a good idea to do that. When you first sign in with your new Passport, Windows Messenger asks you to confirm your e-mail address. Passport does this by sending a message to the address you provided, to which you must respond. The message that Passport sends informs the recipient that someone has set up a password with that e-mail address. (This is done to prevent people from posing as someone else by using an address such as *president@white-house.gov*, for example.) Until you respond appropriately, Windows Messenger asks you to confirm your address at each logon. And although you can use Messenger to contact others without confirming your address, the text "(E-Mail Address Not Verified)" appears next to each occurrence of your name in a conversation window, alerting your correspondents to the fact that they might not be talking with the person they think they are.

Protecting Your Phone Numbers

You can choose to make your phone numbers available to people who have you listed in their contact list. To make your phone numbers available, click the Phone tab in the Options dialog box. You can specify up to three phone numbers (identified as home, work, and mobile). If you supply one or more phone numbers, a contact can right-click your name in his or her own contact list and choose Make A Phone Call. This action allows your contact to reach you via an Internet-to-phone service. Naturally, you should publish your phone numbers only if you're willing to be called by anyone who has you in his or her contact list.

Tip Use multiple Passports

The settings you make in Windows Messenger—display name, phone numbers, and so on—are the same for everyone who reaches you through a particular Passport. You can't, for example, display one name for some contacts and a different name for others, or selectively hide your phone numbers or online status. To work around this limitation, create a different Passport for each of your "identities"—one for personal friends, one for business associates, and one for people you meet through an online special interest group, for example.

To switch between identities, you must sign out (choose File, Sign Out, or click the notification area icon and choose Sign Out) and then sign back in; you can be signed in using only one Passport at a time. You can bend this rule by creating multiple user accounts as well—each with its own Passport. Use Fast User Switching to switch between them; they can all remain signed in simultaneously, although you can still only work with one Passport at a time.

Blocking Other Users

You can prevent other users from contacting you or from viewing your online status. When you block a user, if you're in that user's contact list your status is always shown as Not Online. If the blocked user tries to send a message (by entering your e-mail address), it's immediately returned to the sender. You never receive any indication that the blocked user is trying to contact you. You can block a user in any of several ways:

- When you receive notification that the user has added you to his or her contact list (as shown in Figure 36-8), select the Block option.
- If the user is in your contact list, right-click the name and choose Block.
- If you are in a conversation with someone you want to block, click the Block button. (If you're conversing with more than one person, select the name of the person you want to block from the list that appears.) When you do this, it appears to the blocked user that you've gone offline. Conversation windows remain open on both computers.
- Choose Tools, Options, and click the Privacy tab, shown in Figure 36-10. The lists show everyone in your contact list as well as any others you've blocked. Select a name and click Block or Allow to move the name between My Allow List and My Block List.

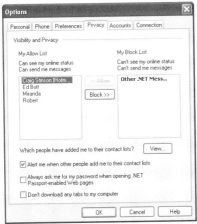

Figure 36-10. Blocking users prevents them from seeing whether you're online and sending you messages.

Finding Out Who's Watching You

People who have you on their contact list can see when you're online. If you're in the habit of setting your status (letting people know when you're available and when you're not), they can track your whereabouts by knowing when you're on the phone, when you're at lunch, and so on. You can find out who's able to keep tabs on you by choosing Tools, Options, Privacy to display the dialog box shown in Figure 36-10. Then click View to see the names of all users who have added you to their contact list.

Chapter 36

Timesaving Tips for Sending and Receiving Instant Text Messages

These tips and shortcuts will help to make your instant messaging sessions more productive:

- **Use the notification area icon.**   Instead of opening the Windows Messenger window when you want to start a conversation, click the notification area icon. On the shortcut menu that appears, choose Send An Instant Message to display a menu of all of your contacts who are currently online.

- **Right-size the conversation window.**   If you're not going to send and receive video, hide the sidebar (the pane on the right side of the conversation window that has the Start Camera link at the top). To do that, in the conversation window choose View, Show Sidebar. Then adjust the window size so that the text is easy to read and the conversation easy to follow.

- **Use a distinctive font.**   By using a font that's different in style and color from that used by your correspondents, it's easier to follow a conversation in the conversation window; it gives you a unique "voice." The same font appears on your screen and on the other person's screen; if he or she doesn't have the font you specify, Windows substitutes the closest available font. To change fonts while a conversation window is open, click Change Font (in the sidebar) or choose Edit, Change Font. You can set your preference in the main Windows Messenger window by choosing Tools, Options, Personal, Change Font.

- **Send hyperlinks.**   If you're discussing information that's on the Web, type or paste a URL link to the information as ordinary text. The recipient can click the link to jump immediately to the Web site.

- **Use a keyboard macro program.**   If you often type the same text—whether it's your standard witty comeback or some boilerplate text that you send as part of a help desk troubleshooting process—obtain and use a keyboard macro program. Such programs (one example is American Systems' EZ Macros—*http://www.americansys.com*) look for user-defined abbreviations as you type, expanding them to their full length when it encounters them. Some keyboard macro programs even have an option that simulates typing, so that your conversation partner won't know your secret.

- **Use emoticons.**   Even though they're considered banal by some language purists, in casual conversation emoticons can express a lot with only two or three keystrokes. The three dozen available icons include a happy face, a smooch-ready pair of lips, a thumbs-up gesture, and more. The most commonly used emoticons are available in the gallery that appears when you click Emoticons at the bottom of the conversation window. To see a larger list of available icons, along with the keystrokes necessary to produce each one, click the ellipsis box in the lower right corner of the Emoticon gallery. Note: If you type a keyboard shortcut for an emoticon, and the desired item doesn't appear, choose View, Enable Emoticons in the conversation window.

Hiding Your Online Status

Assuming that you're willing to let everyone who has added you to his or her contact list see what you're up to, you can set your status by right-clicking your name in the Windows Messenger window and selecting a description. If the Windows Messenger window isn't open, you can set your status by clicking the Windows Messenger icon in the notification area and choosing My Status. By setting your status to Appear Offline, your name appears in the Not Online list of others' contact lists. You can continue to see the status of your contacts and continue using Windows Messenger—but other users can't tell that you're online.

Tip Hide your online status selectively

Setting your status to Appear Offline makes you appear offline to everyone who has your name in his or her contact list. If you want to hide out from only a few individuals but remain visible to others, block certain users. The easiest way to do that is to include them in your contact list. You can then right-click their name and choose Block to go undercover. When you're ready to resurface, right-click again and choose Unblock.

Adding Other Participants to a Conversation

You can have a text chat (but not a voice call or video call) with up to five people including yourself. You initiate this type of chat by opening a conversation window, as described earlier in this chapter. (For details, see "Placing or Receiving a Call," page 1212.) You then add participants—one at a time—by clicking Invite Someone To This Conversation in the sidebar or choosing Actions, Invite Someone To This Conversation.

Note that you can add participants at any time during the conversation. However, if you want all participants to be included in the conversation from the beginning, open a conversation window and invite all participants before you send your first message.

Any participant in a conversation can add others to the fray. The To box at the top of the conversation window (just below the menu bar) shows the display names and e-mail addresses of all participants other than yourself.

Saving an Online Session as a File

Windows Messenger does not have a built-in logging feature that automatically records your every word. You can, however, save the content of the conversation window at any time. Simply choose File, Save. Doing so saves the entire transcript in a plain text file with a .txt extension.

Although this method is convenient, a plain text file loses the fonts, colors, and indentation that can enhance readability. A better alternative is to select the text you want to preserve (or choose Edit, Select All to select the entire transcript), copy the text, and then paste it into an application (such as Microsoft Word or WordPad) that can accept formatted text. That way,

Chapter 36

it looks just the way it does in the conversation window. Copying and pasting has the added benefit of allowing you to include only the parts of the conversation you want to preserve.

Note Whether you save the transcript as a plain text file or copy it to the Clipboard, you lose all emoticons and other icons, such as the ones that appear before system-generated messages.

Making Audio Connections

In the past, voice conversations over the Internet were often of such poor quality that the capability was of little value. With Windows Messenger, the quality has improved to the point where you're likely to consider it a viable alternative to telephone conversations in most cases. Windows Messenger achieves this level of quality by introducing three significant technological improvements:

- The voice delay has been reduced to as little as 70 milliseconds. A delay of that length (or only slightly greater) is hardly noticeable. You'll sometimes encounter greater delays on phone calls that are carried by satellite.

- Windows Messenger selects appropriate voice codecs (coders and decoders) based on network conditions. For communications on a local area network or a broadband connection that provides great bandwidth and minimal delay, Messenger uses codecs that provide telephone-like quality. If network throughput decreases or delay increases beyond a certain point, Windows automatically switches to a lower bit rate. When network conditions improve, Windows automatically steps up to a higher quality.

- Windows Messenger supports acoustic echo cancellation, allowing you to use an ordinary microphone and speakers. (Without acoustic echo cancellation, excessive echo can necessitate the use of a headset.) Note that acoustic echo cancellation might not work on some systems. For more information, see Microsoft Knowledge Base article 295952, "The Acoustic Echo Cancellation Technology May Not Work with Various Sound Cards" (*http://support.microsoft.com/?kbid=295952*).

Before you make your first audio connection, you should run the Audio And Video Tuning Wizard. It helps you to select a camera, microphone, and speakers (if your computer has more than one of any of these components), and to set speaker and microphone volume. To run the wizard, in the Windows Messenger window, choose Tools, Audio Tuning Wizard. Rerun the wizard whenever you install a new camera, microphone, speakers, or headset.

To make an audio connection, you can start with an existing conversation window—one in which you're exchanging instant text messages. Simply click Start Talking in the sidebar. (If the sidebar isn't visible, choose Actions, Start Talking.) Or you can initiate a new conversation as a voice call. In the main Windows Messenger window, choose Actions, Start A Voice Conversation.

Either way, the speaker and microphone controls appear, and you'll see a message like the one shown in Figure 36-11.

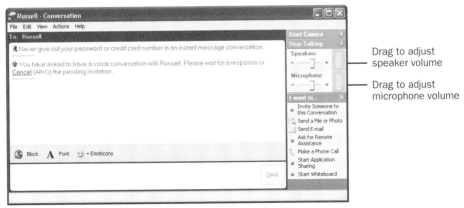

Figure 36-11. The person at the other end must agree before you can have a voice conversation.

The recipient sees a similar message and has the choice of accepting or declining your invitation by clicking a link or pressing a shortcut key. When he or she does so, a message notifies both of you about the action. The conversation window remains open regardless of the recipient's response to your invitation. You can continue to send and receive instant messages in the conversation window while you carry out the voice conversation.

To end the voice conversation, either close the conversation window (to break off the connection entirely) or click the Stop Talking link in the sidebar (to end the voice conversation only).

Using Your Webcam to Make Video Calls

If your computer has a video camera attached, you can send video as well as audio. Depending on the speed of your connection, the motion may be jerky and you'll get some digital artifacts—but the quality can be surprisingly good. And even if the person at the other end of the conversation doesn't have a camera, you can send your picture.

Before you make your first video connection, you should run the Audio And Video Tuning Wizard. (In the Windows Messenger window, choose Tools, Audio Tuning Wizard.) The wizard shows an image from your camera, which you can review to be sure that the camera is positioned properly and that the colors look good. If the colors require adjustment, you'll need to use the software that came with your camera to change the settings.

The procedure for participating in a video conversation is almost identical to that for holding a voice conversation. Start by opening a conversation window, using any of the techniques described earlier in this chapter. Then click the Start Camera link in the sidebar. (If the sidebar isn't visible, choose Actions, Start Camera.) This link opens the video window as well as

Chapter 36

the speaker and microphone controls (because a video call always includes voice messaging also) and sends an invitation to the other person, who can accept or decline your offer. If he or she accepts, the cameras start rolling and soon you'll see the other person's picture on your screen, as shown in Figure 36-12.

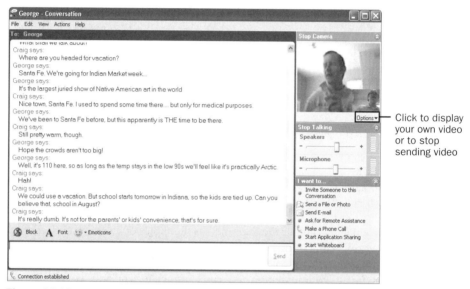

Click to display your own video or to stop sending video

Figure 36-12. Be sure that you look your best before you begin sending video!

To see what your own video looks like, click the Options button (right below the video image) and choose Show My Video As Picture-In-Picture. This displays your outgoing picture in a small box in the corner of the video image. To see a full-size image of your own video, you must run the Audio And Video Tuning Wizard—but you can't do that while you're in a video call.

There are several ways to stop sending video—and each way has a slightly different effect:

- If you want to stop sending video but keep the voice and instant message conversations alive, click Options and choose Stop Sending Video. You continue to receive video from the other party. To turn your camera back on, choose the same command again.

- If you want to stop the video and voice conversations but keep the conversation window open for instant messages, click Stop Camera or Stop Talking; both links shut down video and voice.

- If you want to break the connection completely, close the conversation window.

Sending and Receiving Files

Windows Messenger provides a convenient method of sending a file to another Passport user. Using Messenger to send files provides some advantages over sending files as e-mail attachments:

- Many e-mail client programs, including Outlook, make it impossible to send or receive files of certain types. This is a surefire way to prevent the spread of some viruses and worms, but it becomes a hassle when you and your correspondent *know* that you're working with a safe file and would like a handy way to exchange it. Windows Messenger provides the handy way.

> **Caution** Windows Messenger doesn't put up roadblocks to files the way Outlook does—but be aware of the extra risk and responsibility this incurs. With Messenger, you *can* send or receive a virus-infected file. It's up to you to know the identity of the file sender and, more important, to scan each file you receive with a virus-scanning program. (Even trustworthy and knowledgeable sources can inadvertently send you an infected file.)

- When you send a file as an e-mail attachment, the sender and the recipient each end up with two copies of the file—one that's saved in a folder and one that's saved with the e-mail message. (By default, most e-mail programs save a copy of each message you send.) The extra copy can be a problem, particularly if your messages are stored on a mail server (such as Hotmail or the one at your ISP) that limits the amount of disk space you can use for stored messages. Windows Messenger copies a file directly from a folder on one computer to a folder on the other computer, without leaving extra copies lying about.
- Some mail servers limit the size of attachments. Windows Messenger imposes no such limit.

> **Note** You can't send a file if your conversation includes more than one other person.

> **Note** Before you send or receive files, you must be sure that your firewall or proxy server is configured properly. Windows Messenger uses TCP connections to ports 6891 through 6900. Each port is used for transferring a single file; by opening all 10 ports you can transfer up to 10 files concurrently. If you're using Windows Firewall as your firewall, it's already configured to allow file tranfers.

Chapter 36

To send a file, follow these steps:

1 If you haven't yet started a conversation, right-click the name of the contact you want to send to and choose Send A File Or Photo. If you already have a conversation window open, click Send A File Or Photo (in the sidebar) or choose File, Send A File Or Photo.

A standard File Open dialog box appears.

2 Navigate to the folder that contains the file you want to send, select the file, and click Open.

Messenger displays an estimate of the file transfer time and, on the recipient's computer, an invitation to accept the file.

3 The recipient must click the Accept link.

File transfer commences immediately; its progress is displayed in the status bar. Either the sender or the recipient can cancel the transfer at any time by clicking the Cancel link in the status bar. When the transfer is complete, Messenger displays a notification of completion and a link to the file, as shown in Figure 36-13. The recipient can click the link to open the file with its associated program.

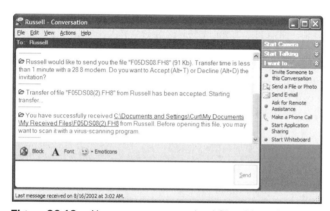

Figure 36-13. You can open a received file with a single click—but you should scan an executable program for viruses before running it.

By default, all files you receive are stored in %UserProfile%\My Documents\My Received Files. You can open that folder to work with your received files by choosing File, Open Received Files in any Windows Messenger window. If you want to change the location for received files, in the main Windows Messenger window, choose Tools, Options. Click the Preference tab and then click Browse to navigate to the folder you want to use.

Communicating Over the Internet

 Troubleshooting

Advanced features in Windows Messenger don't work.

If you experience problems with file transfer, audio connections, video connections, or online meetings while using Windows Messenger, try the following steps:

- Make sure your router (if you use a router) supports UPnP and that its firmware is up to date.
- Make sure that any firewall features of your router are not blocking ports required by Windows Messenger.
- Be sure that you're using version 5 or later. (Choose Help, About Windows Messenger, to determine which version you're currently using. You can download version 5 from the Microsoft Download Center from *http://www.microsoft.com/windows/messenger*.) Version 5 solved problems that some users experienced when connecting to the .NET Messenger service in earlier versions.
- If you're using Windows Firewall, delete and re-create the exception for Windows Messenger. Open Windows Firewall (in Control Panel, Security Center), click the Exceptions tab, select Windows Messenger, and click Delete. The next time you run Messenger, a Security Alert dialog box informs you that Windows Firewall is blocking Windows Messenger, select Unblock This Program and clik OK. If you *still* have problems with Windows Messenger and Windows Firewall, reset the firewall to its default state. (In Windows Firewall, click the Advanced tab and then click Restore Defaults.)
- If all else fails, try using MSN Messenger. Some users have reported success with MSN Messenger with tasks at which Windows Messenger failed.

Using Windows Messenger for Online Meetings

Windows Messenger inherits two collaboration features that were previously available only in NetMeeting: Whiteboard and application sharing.

Whiteboard is an electronic equivalent of the whiteboard in a conference room. With it, you can enter text and draw shapes as well as create freehand drawings. It also includes a feature that's more akin to a conference-room easel than a whiteboard: the ability to create multiple pages of drawings.

With application sharing, users in a meeting can view and control a program that's running on one participant's computer. With this capability, you can work together on a document or presentation, for example.

Note To display help for NetMeeting, the application responsible for the whiteboard and application-sharing features in Windows Messenger, type **hh conf.chm** at a command prompt.

Chapter 36

Using Whiteboard

Whiteboard, shown in Figure 36-14, is a drawing program that functions superficially like Microsoft Paint, except that it's designed for sharing drawings, diagrams, screen shots, and other images with another Passport user. Anything you create in the Whiteboard window is visible to both parties in the conversation, and either participant can modify the Whiteboard contents at any time.

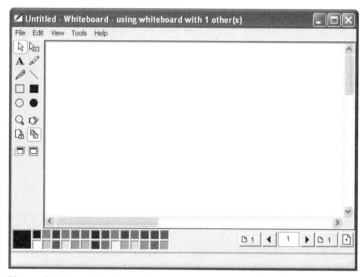

Figure 36-14. Whiteboard is a drawing program that lets you share images with another user in a Windows Messenger conversation.

To run Whiteboard, use any of these methods:

- If you haven't yet started a conversation, right-click the name of the contact you want to work with and choose Start Whiteboard.

- If you already have a conversation window open, click the Start Whiteboard link in the sidebar, or choose Actions, Start Whiteboard.

- If the Sharing Session window, shown in Figure 36-15, is already open, click the Whiteboard button.

Figure 36-15. Sharing Session manages shared applications as well as Whiteboard.

A small Sharing Session window appears. A moment later, after the invitation is accepted and the two machines negotiate a connection, the Whiteboard window appears.

> **Note** Closing the Sharing Session window also closes Whiteboard and stops sharing applications.

Like Paint, Whiteboard includes editing and line-width tools displayed to the left of the drawing window, and a color palette displayed below. You can enlarge the available drawing space by hiding the toolbar. (Choose Tool Bar from the View menu.) With the toolbar removed, you can use commands on the Tools menu to switch between editing tools and use the Tools menu's Line Width command to change line width. Table 36-1 provides an overview of the available tools.

Table 36-1. Whiteboard Tools

Tool	Description
Tools for Creating, Selecting, and Editing	
	Selector Use the Selector tool when you want to move, cut, copy, or recolor part of a drawing. Click the Selector tool, and then click anywhere on the object you want to manipulate. To select more than one object, drag a rectangle over the group of objects you want to manipulate.
	Eraser The Eraser tool works exactly like the Selector tool except that it deletes what you select. Click an object once, and the object is gone. Although Whiteboard has no Undo command, its Edit menu does have an Undelete command. After you have deleted something, the Undelete command stays active until you use it, even if you subsequently add new objects to your drawing. However, only the last deletion can be restored.
	Text To add text, click the Text tool and then click once where you want the text to go. Whiteboard displays a small rectangle for your text and expands the rectangle as you type. Words do not wrap; to begin a new line, press Enter. To change the font, click the Font Options button that appears when you select the Text tool; to change the text's color, click a color in the palette. Note that font and color changes always affect everything in the text rectangle.
	Highlighter The Highlighter tool works just like the Pen tool (described next), except that, if you choose an appropriate color, it creates transparent lines. Thus, for example, you can use yellow highlighting to emphasize particular words in a text object without obliterating the highlighted text. Highlighting works best with light colors.
	Pen The Pen tool lets you add freehand elements to your drawing. Click the tool, click the line width and color you desire, click a starting point in the drawing window, and hold down the mouse button while you move the mouse.

Chapter 36

Table 36-1. Whiteboard Tools

Tool	Description
	Line The Line tool creates straight lines in the current width and color. Note that Whiteboard's Line tool, unlike Paint's, doesn't constrain lines to particular angles when you hold down the Shift key. If you want perfect diagonals, horizontals, or verticals, you can do your work in Paint and then paste it into Whiteboard.
	Unfilled Rectangle The Unfilled Rectangle tool creates a rectangle in the current line width and color. Note that Whiteboard lacks Paint's ability to constrain rectangles into squares. If a perfect square is what you need, it's best to create it in Paint and paste it into Whiteboard.
	Filled Rectangle The Filled Rectangle tool creates a solid rectangle in the current color. Note that Whiteboard has no counterpart to Paint's Fill With Color tool. If you want a rectangle filled with one color and outlined with another, use Paint and paste into Whiteboard.
	Unfilled Ellipse The Unfilled Ellipse tool creates an ellipse in the current line width and color. If you need a perfect circle, use Paint and paste.
	Filled Ellipse The Filled Ellipse tool creates a solid ellipse in the current color.
	Select Area The Select Area tool lets you paste a selected portion of any window into your drawing, making it easy to show the state of some program or document to your conference mate. When you click the tool, Whiteboard displays a message telling you to select an area on the screen. Then it gets out of the way and lets you drag the area you want to paste. The area you select is pasted into the upper left corner of the whiteboard. Drag it to place it where you want it.
	Select Window The Select Window tool works just like the Select Area tool except that it lets you paste an entire window into your drawing. When you click the tool, Whiteboard displays a message saying that the next window you click will be pasted into your drawing. Then it gets out of the way and lets you click the window you want to paste. Note that with some programs, you get only the client area of the window you click. If you click in a Microsoft Word window, for example, the visible part of whatever Word document you're working in, along with Word's ruler (if displayed) and toolbar, is pasted into your drawing. You don't get the Word menu bar or title bar. Note also that if the window you click is displaying two or more document windows, only the active document window is pasted. To capture the entire window, click its title bar instead of clicking in the client area. After you paste your window, the window becomes a selected object. You can drag it to reposition it.

Table 36-1. **Whiteboard Tools**

Tool	Description
	Insert New Page Whiteboard lets you create multi-page documents. To insert a new page after the current page, click the Insert New Page button. To move between pages, click the controls next to the Insert New Page button— or press Ctrl+Page Up or Ctrl+Page Down.
Tools for Controlling the View	
	Zoom Clicking the Zoom tool enlarges your drawing. Clicking again returns it to normal size. If you're not displaying the toolbar, you can choose Zoom from the View menu.
	Remote Pointer Clicking the Remote Pointer tool displays a hand with an outstretched index finger. You can move the hand to draw attention to a particular part of your drawing. Click the tool a second time to make the hand disappear. Each Whiteboard participant has his or her own remote pointer that others can see but not move.
	Lock Contents Click the Lock Contents tool to prevent others from making changes to the contents of the whiteboard. When the whiteboard is locked, click the Unlock Contents tool (it's the same button) so other users can make changes to the whiteboard.
	Synchronize You can use the Synchronize tool to view a Whiteboard page privately. (Ordinarily, when someone switches to a different page, everyone's whiteboard changes so that everyone in the meeting is, well, on the same page.) Click Unsynchronize and move to a different page, and only your whiteboard changes. When you click Synchronize, everyone's whiteboard switches to the page you're viewing.

Whiteboard is object-oriented, rather than pixel-oriented (like Paint). When you create one object on top of another, they remain distinct objects. You can change the z (stacking) order of selected objects that lie atop one another by choosing Send To Back or Bring To Front from the Edit menu.

Collaborating on a Document over the Network

You can share any number of programs running on your computer with another person. Your program appears in a window on the other person's computer, and either person can control the shared program.You can use this ability, for example, to collaborate on a document or alternate moves in a game. Meanwhile, you can continue your conversation—via instant messages, voice, and or video—in the conversation window.

Chapter 36

To begin sharing programs, use any of these methods:

- If you haven't yet started a conversation, right-click the name of the contact you want to work with and choose Start Application Sharing.

- If you already have a conversation window open, click the Start Application Sharing link in the sidebar, or choose Actions, Start Application Sharing.

- If the Sharing Session window, shown in Figure 36-15 on page 1228, is already open, click the App Sharing button.

After the invitation is accepted and a connection is established, any of these actions displays a Sharing window similar to the one shown in Figure 36-16.

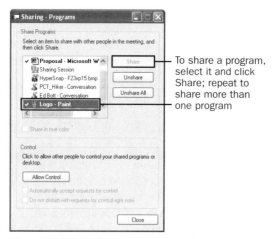

To share a program, select it and click Share; repeat to share more than one program

Figure 36-16. When you agree to share programs, a menu of available programs appears.

To share a program, select it and click Share. The window for the shared application immediately opens in a window on the other person's computer, as shown in Figure 36-17. If you choose to share your desktop, the other user sees your entire desktop; you can't select individual applications to be shared. Similarly, if you share one or more applications, Desktop becomes unavailable for sharing in the list.

Tip Share your desktop

If you want to share your desktop, Windows Messenger can provide an ad hoc alternative to Remote Desktop. That feature offers a number of capabilities that are not available by sharing your desktop as an application with Windows Messenger. But it also requires some additional setup and preparation. For details, see "Setting Up a Remote Desktop Connection to Another Computer," page 1043.

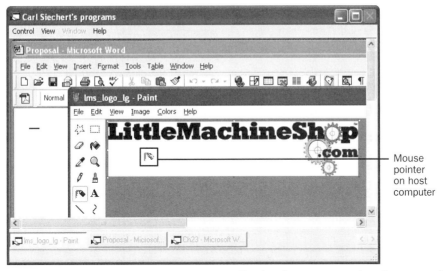

Mouse
pointer
on host
computer

Figure 36-17. As soon as you share an application, it appears on the other person's screen.

The windows for the programs you share appear on the other computer exactly as they appear on your own. The other user sees your mouse pointer, insertion point, selection, and so on just as you do. If the window for a shared application is partly or completely covered by a window that is not shared, the covered portion is obscured on the other user's screen by a background pattern.

Note When you share an application, all instances of that application are shared. For example, if you have several Word documents open, sharing any one of them causes all of them to become shared. Furthermore, any additional documents you open are also shared.

To enable the other user to control shared applications running on your computer, return to the Sharing window (shown in Figure 36-16) and click Allow Control. Once you've allowed control, the other user requests control by opening the Control menu and choosing Request Control. If you consent to the request by clicking Accept in the dialog box that appears, the other user takes over control of your mouse pointer, and his or her keystrokes are passed to the active application. The other user can relinquish control at any time by choosing Control, Release Control. You can retake control yourself by clicking a mouse button or pressing any key. If you press Esc while the other user has control, you not only take control, but you also immediately prevent the other user from taking control again. (This is equivalent to opening the Sharing window and clicking Prevent Control.)

Chapter 36

Inside Out

Share applications with more than one person

You might want to share Whiteboard or another application with more than one other user. Although Windows Messenger allows up to five people in an instant messaging conversation, Whiteboard and application sharing are limited to two people. If you have a two-way conversation going with Whiteboard open, for example, and you then invite another person to start Whiteboard, Sharing Session asks if you want to drop the first sharing session so that you can open another. Or, if you have a three-way conversation going and you then invite one of the other users to start Whiteboard, Windows Messenger breaks out that request into a separate two-way conversation window.

To get around the two-person limit, use NetMeeting, as follows:

1 While you're signed in to Passport (but not using Whiteboard or application sharing), open the Run dialog box and type **conf** to start NetMeeting.

2 Click the Find Someone In A Directory button. In the Find Someone window that opens, be sure that Microsoft Internet Directory is shown in the address bar. Your online contacts should appear in the window.

3 Click the name of each contact you want to invite. Note that the other users don't need to have NetMeeting running. If they're running Windows Messenger, they'll receive your invitation in Messenger, which starts NetMeeting for them.

4 Click the Share Program, Whiteboard, or Transfer Files button to open a window that lets you collaborate with all others in the call.

Note When you receive a request to take control, the name might not be the same as the Windows Messenger display name of the other user. That's because this feature is actually borrowed from NetMeeting, and the name is picked up from the Options dialog box in NetMeeting.

The other options in the Sharing window deserve a little explanation:

- **Automatically accept requests for control** When selected, the other user gains control immediately upon choosing Control, Request Control. Your permission is not required.

- **Do not disturb with requests for control right now** If the other user requests control while this check box is selected, he or she immediately sees a message that says you're busy right now. You get no indication that the other user is trying to gain control.

System Maintenance and Recovery

Chapter 37

Performing Routine Maintenance

Your personal computer is a curious combination of digital data and temperamental machinery. To keep your system running smoothly, it pays to perform some regular maintenance tasks. In particular, it's wise to do the following on a regular basis:

- Check your disks for file system and media errors.
- Defragment your hard disks to optimize file access.
- Make sure that you always have enough space on your hard disk by getting rid of files you no longer need and compressing files if necessary.
- Perform regular backups of data and system files.

Checking Disks for Errors

Errors in disk media and in the file system can cause a wide range of Windows problems, ranging from an inability to open or save files to blue-screen errors and widespread data corruption. Microsoft Windows XP is capable of recovering automatically from many disk errors, especially on drives formatted with NTFS.

At Home with Windows XP

With one glaring exception, the tools and techniques described in this chapter work identically in Windows XP Home Edition and Windows XP Professional. That exception is the Backup Utility program. In Home Edition, it's not installed by default, although in this chapter we explain how to install it. There's another Backup Utility gotcha for Home Edition users, however, and this one has no workaround: The Automatic System Recovery feature works only in Windows XP Professional.

To perform a thorough inspection for errors, you can manually run the Windows XP Check Disk utility, Chkdsk.exe. Two versions of this utility are available—a graphical version that performs basic disk-checking functions, and a command-line version that provides a much more extensive set of customization options.

To check for errors on a local disk, follow these steps:

1   Open My Computer, right-click the icon belonging to the drive you want to check, and then choose Properties from the shortcut menu.

2   On the Tools tab, click the Check Now button.

3   In the Check Disk dialog box, shown here, select from the following options.

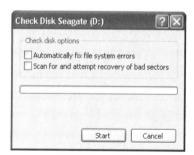

- **Automatically Fix File System Errors**   Select this option if you want Windows to automatically repair any file system errors. If this option is not selected, Check Disk reports any errors it finds but does not change them. This option is the equivalent of running the Chkdsk command with the /F switch, as described later in this section.

■ **Scan For And Attempt Recovery Of Bad Sectors**   Select this option to perform an exhaustive check of the entire disk, locate bad sectors, and recover readable information stored in defective locations. Note that selecting this option automatically repairs file system errors as well, even if the previous option is cleared. This option is the equivalent of running the Chkdsk command with the /R switch.

If you simply want to see a report of file system errors without making any changes to disk structures, leave both boxes unchecked.

4 Click Start to begin the disk-checking process. The green progress bar provides feedback as the error-checking tool goes through several phases.

If you select the Automatically Fix File System Errors option on a drive that currently has open files, Windows is unable to run the utility immediately. In that case, you see the message shown here.

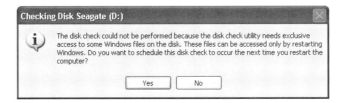

Click Yes to schedule the disk check to run the next time you start your computer. The disk check occurs during the character-mode startup phase of Windows; during this period your computer is not available for you to perform any other tasks. When your computer starts, Windows notifies you that it's about to perform a scheduled disk check; by default, you have 10 seconds to cancel the operation and boot normally instead.

After Check Disk completes its operation, it reports its results. If the disk check turns up no errors, you see a Disk Check Complete dialog box. If Check Disk uncovers any errors, it writes a message to the Event log and displays a dialog box listing the errors it found and the repairs it made.

Caution   Although Check Disk is a useful tool and sometimes a lifesaver, it can cause you headaches if used without some planning. Once started, the Check Disk operation cannot be stopped except by pressing your computer's power switch. On very large drives (60 GB and larger), the full disk check can takes hours or even days to complete.

Longtime users of Windows 95, Windows 98, or Windows Me are probably accustomed to seeing the ScanDisk program run automatically after a power failure or other unexpected shutdown. Windows XP, however, behaves differently. Check Disk runs automatically after an abnormal shutdown only if a specific bit in the registry is set, indicating that the file system is "dirty"—that is, that it has data that it did not properly read or write when it was shut down. If the file system wasn't doing anything when the system shut down, the dirty bit will not be set. Because NTFS volumes keep a journal of all disk activities, they are able to recover and remain clean even if you shut down in the middle of a disk write. Check Disk is most likely to run automatically at startup only on FAT32 volumes, after an unexpected shutdown.

Inside Out

Cancel checks with Chkntfs

Two additional and well-hidden Windows commands are crucial to the operation of the Check Disk utility. The first of these, Autochk.exe, runs automatically any time you specify that you want to schedule a disk check to run at startup. The second, Chkntfs, is especially useful if you change your mind and decide you want to cancel a scheduled check. At a command prompt, type **chkntfs /x** *d*: (where *d* is replaced by a drive letter) to exclude the drive specified. Chkntfs has another nifty trick: It can tell you whether a disk is dirty. At a command prompt, simply type **chkntfs** *d*:. For more details about these commands, see Knowledge Base article 218461, "Description of Enhanced Chkdsk, Autochk, and Chkntfs Tools in Windows 2000" (*http://support.microsoft.com/?kbid=218461*).

The command-line version of Check Disk gives you considerably more options. It also allows you to schedule disk-checking operations using the Scheduled Tasks folder (as described in "Scheduling Tasks to Run Automatically," page 592). To run this command in its simplest form, log on using an account in the Administrators group, open a Command Prompt window (by typing **cmd** in the Run box, for instance), and then type **chkdsk** at the prompt. This command runs Chkdsk in read-only mode, displaying the status of the current drive but not making any changes. If you add a drive letter after the command (**chkdsk d:**, for instance), the report applies to that drive.

You can use any combination of the following switches at the end of the command line to modify its operation:

- **/F** Instructs Chkdsk to fix any errors it detects. This is the most commonly used switch. The disk must be locked. If Chkdsk cannot lock the drive (as is always the case with the system drive), it offers either to check the drive the next time you restart the computer or to dismount the volume you want to check before proceeding. Dismounting is a drastic step; it invalidates all current file handles on the affected volume and can result in loss of data. You should decline the offer. When you do, Chkdsk will make you a second offer—to check the disk the next time you restart your system. You should accept this option.

- /V   On FAT32 volumes, /V displays verbose output, listing the name of every file in every directory as the disk check proceeds. On NTFS volumes, this switch displays cleanup messages (if any).
- /R   Identifies bad sectors and recovers information from those sectors if possible. The disk must be locked. Be aware that this is a time-consuming and uninterruptible process.

The following switches are valid only on NTFS volumes:

- /I   Performs a simpler check of index entries (stage 2 in the Chkdsk process), reducing the amount of time required.
- /C   Skips the checking of cycles within the folder structure, reducing the amount of time required.
- /X   Forces the volume to dismount, if necessary, and invalidates all open file handles. This option is intended for server administrators. Because of the potential for data loss, it should be avoided in normal use with Windows XP Professional or Home Edition.
- /L[:*size*]   Changes the size of the file that logs NTFS transactions. If you omit the *size* parameter, this switch displays the current size. This option is intended for server administrators. Because of the potential for data loss, it also should be avoided in normal use with Windows XP Professional or Home Edition.

Troubleshooting

When you run Chkdsk at the Recovery Console, some options are not available.

The Chkdsk command used when you boot to the Recovery Console is not the same as the one used within a full Windows session. Only two switches are available for this version:

- **/P**   Performs an exhaustive check of the current disk
- **/R**   Repairs damage on the current disk

If your system is able to boot to Windows either normally or in Safe Mode and you suspect that you have disk errors, you should use the full Chkdsk command. For more details, see "Making Repairs from the Recovery Console," page 1295.

Defragmenting Disks for Better Performance

On a relatively new system with a speedy processor and plenty of physical memory, hard disk performance is the single biggest bottleneck in everyday operation. Even on a zippy hard disk, it takes time to load large data files into memory so you can work with them. The problem is especially noticeable with databases, video clips, and CD images, which can easily consume hundreds of megabytes.

Chapter 37

On a freshly formatted disk, files load fairly quickly, but over time, performance can degrade because of disk fragmentation. To understand how fragmentation works, it helps to understand the basic structure of a hard disk. The process of formatting a disk divides it into *sectors*, each of which contains space for 512 bytes of data. The file system combines groups of sectors into *clusters*, which are the smallest units of space available for holding a single file or part of a file.

For more details about how to choose a size and format for disk partitions, see "Working with Partitions, Volumes, and Disks," page 753.

On a 10-GB NTFS drive, the cluster size is 4 KB. On a FAT32 drive of the same size, clusters are 8 KB. Thus, when you save a 20-MB movie clip on a drive that size, Windows divides the file into approximately 2,560 pieces (NTFS) or 1,280 pieces (FAT32).

When you save this file for the first time on a freshly formatted hard disk, Windows writes it in contiguous clusters. Because all the clusters that hold individual pieces of the file are physically adjacent to one another, the mechanical components of the hard disk can work very efficiently, scooping up data in one smooth operation. As a bonus, the Windows disk cache is able to anticipate the need for data and fetch nearby clusters that are likely to contain other parts of the file, which can then be retrieved from the fast cache rather than from the relatively slow disk.

Unfortunately, hard disks don't stay neatly organized for long. When you add data to an existing file, the file system has to allocate more clusters for storage, typically in a different physical location on the disk. As you delete files, you create gaps in the once-tidy arrangement of contiguously stored files. As you save new files, especially large ones, the file system uses all these bits of free space, scattering the new files over the hard disk in many noncontiguous pieces. The resulting inefficiency in storage is called *fragmentation*; each time you open or save a file on a badly fragmented disk, disk performance suffers, sometimes dramatically, because the disk heads have to spend extra time moving from cluster to cluster before they can begin reading or writing data.

Using Disk Defragmenter

The Disk Defragmenter utility improves performance by physically rearranging files so that they're stored in contiguous clusters. In addition to consolidating files and folders, the utility also consolidates free space, making it less likely that new files will be fragmented when you save them. Windows XP includes a graphical utility that works as a snap-in with Microsoft Management Console. A command-line version of this utility (new in Windows XP) allows you to schedule defragmentation so that it occurs automatically, at regular intervals. For details about setting up a defragmentation schedule, see "Scheduling Tasks to Run Automatically," page 592.

Note   Get a more powerful defragmenter
Like many Windows utilities, Disk Defragmenter offers a basic set of features that are sufficient for average users. If you want more bells and whistles, you'll need to pay extra for a
third-party alternative. Your easiest choice is Executive Software's Diskeeper utility (*http://
www.diskeeper.com*), which is a full-featured version of the exact same utility bundled with
Windows XP. The full version allows you to schedule continuous defragmentation in the background and also allows you to perform boot-time defragmentation of the page file, which the
built-in Windows utility doesn't touch. Defrag Manager (*http://www.winternals.com/es/
solutions/DefragManager.asp*) is targeted toward network administrators, and it allows you
to defragment hard disks on computers throughout your network. Symantec's Norton
System Works package (*http://www.symantec.com/sabu/sysworks/basic*) also includes
a capable disk defragmenter, as does Raxco's PerfectDisk (*http://www.raxco.com*).
Before installing any disk utility, be sure to verify that the version you've purchased is compatible with Windows XP.

To open the graphical Disk Defragmenter console, use any of the following techniques:

- From the All Programs menu, choose Accessories, System Tools, Disk Defragmenter.
- From the My Computer window, right-click any drive icon and choose Properties from
  the shortcut menu. Then click the Tools tab and click Defragment Now.

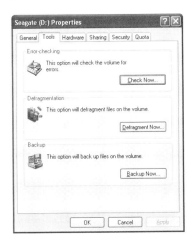

- Run Dfrg.msc from a command prompt.
- Right-click the My Computer icon on the Start menu and choose Manage from the
  shortcut menu. In the Computer Management console, open the Storage option in the
  console pane and select Disk Defragmenter.

In Disk Defragmenter's upper pane, select the disk you want to operate on. To find out how seriously fragmented the disk is currently, click Analyze. As Figure 37-1 shows, Disk Defragmenter presents a graphical fragmentation display and makes a recommendation about whether your disk needs to be defragmented. For more details about the condition of your disk, click View Report. Disk Defragmenter responds with statistics about the overall level of fragmentation and lists the most highly fragmented files, as shown in Figure 37-2.

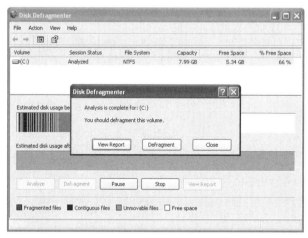

Figure 37-1. If the level of fragmentation exceeds a preset threshold, Disk Defragmenter recommends defragmentation.

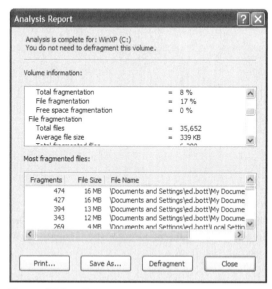

Figure 37-2. This report format lets you see overall fragmentation percentages and identify files that are most widely scattered.

To begin the defragmentation process, click the Defragment button. (You must be logged on as a member of the Administrators group to perform most defragmenting tasks.) While Disk Defragmenter is running, you see a graphical display that indicates the progress of the operation; use the Pause or Stop button at any time to halt the process.

Inside Out

Dedicate a partition for CD burning

The best way to avoid disk fragmentation is to start with a completely clean slate. If you routinely work with CD images, for instance, consider creating a separate partition that's big enough to temporarily hold the files you're working with. A 2-GB partition, for instance, is big enough to hold a CD image and all temporary files associated with it. Keep that drive empty except when you plan to create a CD, at which time you can copy files to it for burning. Using this strategy, you can be certain that fragmentation won't have a deleterious impact on your CD-burning performance.

Running Disk Defragmenter Using a Command Line

Disk defragmentation can be a time-consuming process, so you might not want to spend the time on a drive that is only slightly fragmented. On the other hand, any disk defragmenter will do a more thorough job—and finish its work more quickly—on a disk that is only slightly fragmented. (On a highly fragmented disk or a disk that's nearly full, it's probable that some large or highly fragmented files will remain fragmented even after the process has finished.) Therefore, you might want to adopt the strategy of running Disk Defragmenter routinely during hours when your computer is otherwise idle. The best way to do this is by creating a batch file that uses a command line to run Disk Defragmenter and then creating a scheduled task to run the batch file. (For information about creating scheduled tasks, see "Scheduling Tasks to Run Automatically," page 592. For information about creating batch files, see "Automating Command Sequences with Batch Programs," page 606.)

The command-line version of the Defrag utility uses the exact same program code as the graphical version. To use this command, type **defrag** *d*: at any command prompt, where *d* is the drive letter or mount point of an existing volume. (For an explanation of mount points, see "Assigning and Changing Drive Letters or Drive Paths," page 765.) You can use the following switches with the Defrag command:

- **/A** Analyzes the selected drive or volume and displays a summary of the analysis report.
- **/V** Displays complete (verbose) reports. When used in combination with /A, this switch displays only the analysis report. When used alone, it displays both the analysis and defragmentation reports.
- **/F** Forces defragmentation of the volume even if the amount of free space is low.

Troubleshooting

The Disk Defragmenter utility does not fully defragment the drive.

A volume must have at least 15 percent free space before Disk Defragmenter can completely defragment the volume. If you have less free space available, the operation will run, but only partial defragmentation will result. Check the value at the right of the drive entry in the Defragmenter console to confirm current free space values for the selected drive. If necessary, delete or move files to make extra room.

You cannot defragment a volume that Windows has marked as possibly containing errors. To troubleshoot this possibility, enter **chkdsk** *d:* **/f** at any command prompt, substituting the letter of the drive in question. Chkdsk will report and repair any file-system errors it finds.

Disk Defragmenter does not defragment files in the Recycle Bin. Empty the Recycle Bin before defragmenting.

Additionally, Disk Defragmenter does not defragment the following files: Bootsect.dos, Safeboot.fs, Safeboot.csv, Safeboot.rsv, Hiberfil.sys, and Memory.dmp. In addition, the Windows page file is never defragmented. (See the text following this sidebar to learn how to work around this issue.)

With some large files, it takes several passes to fully defragment the files in question. If the View Report option shows one of these stubborn files, try moving it to another drive before running a full defragmentation pass. After defragmentation is complete, move the file back to its original location. You should be able to copy the file to the newly optimized drive without any problems.

Disk Defragmenter will pass over any files that are currently in use. For best results, shut down all running programs before running the utility. For even better results, log off and log back on (using an account in the Administrators group) before continuing.

The command-line Disk Defragmenter does not provide any progress indicator except for a blinking cursor. To interrupt the defragmentation process, click in the command window and press Ctrl+C.

Using Disk Defragmenter's Analysis Report, you can determine whether your page file is fragmented. (For an explanation of how the page file works, see "Making the Most of Virtual Memory," page 415.) Although page file fragmentation is normally not a serious issue, a severely fragmented page file can reduce your system's performance. Disk Defragmenter cannot consolidate your page file, because Windows holds it open while you work. However, if you have more than one volume available (even if the second volume is on the same physical hard disk as your system drive), you can work around the problem as follows:

1 Open Control Panel and double-click the System icon.

2 On the Advanced tab of the System Properties dialog box, click the Settings button under Performance.

3 On the Advanced tab of the Performance Options dialog box, click Change under Virtual Memory.

4 From the list of available drives, choose a volume other than the one that holds your current page file. This drive will hold your temporary page file.

5 Choose the Custom Size option, enter settings in the Initial Size and Maximum Size boxes to match your current page file, and click Set.

6 Select the drive that contains the fragmented page file, set the Initial Size and Maximum Size boxes to 0, and then click Set.

7 Reboot to allow your system to stop using the old page file and begin using the new one.

8 Defragment the drive that previously held your page file. This consolidates the free space on that volume so that your new page file will be stored in contiguous space.

9 Repeat steps 1 through 6, this time creating a page file on the original disk and eliminating the temporary page file you created. Then reboot to allow the new, defragmented page file to take over.

Managing Disk Space

In the digital era, Parkinson's Law has an inescapable corollary: Data expands to fill the space allotted to it. Gargantuan hard disks encourage consumption, and digital media files (not to mention Windows itself) supply plenty of bits to be consumed. It's surprisingly easy to run low on disk space, and the consequences can be deleterious to your system. If you run low on storage, Windows might not have enough room to expand its page file, or it might be unable to create temporary files. In addition, essential features such as Indexing Service and System Restore may stop working properly. At that point, you start seeing ominous error messages and (possibly) degraded performance.

To pare down on disk space consumption, you can do any or all of the following:

- Clear out temporary files that you no longer need.
- Uninstall programs you don't need.
- Uninstall Windows components you don't need.
- Delete documents you don't need.
- On NTFS volumes, use real-time file compression.

> **Tip** **Stop "low disk space" messages**
>
> When you're running low on disk space, Windows displays a warning message in the notification area at the right of the taskbar. Clicking the balloon opens the Disk Cleanup utility and allows you to clean out unwanted files. If you'd prefer not to see these messages, you can disable them globally by adding a value in the registry. (Unfortunately, this option cannot be applied to individual drives.) Open Registry Editor and select the following key:
>
> HKCU\Software\Microsoft\Windows\CurrentVersion\Policies\Explorer\
>
> Choose Edit, New, DWORD Value, and name the new value NoLowDiskSpaceChecks. Set the data value to 1. Close Registry Editor to apply the change. Windows will no longer display these warnings.

Cleaning Up with Disk Cleanup

The simplest way to make room on any drive is with the help of the Disk Cleanup utility, Cleanmgr.exe. If you click a "low disk space" warning, this tool opens automatically. You can start it manually at any time by choosing the Disk Cleanup shortcut (from the All Programs menu, choose Accessories, System Tools). If you use this option, Windows prompts you to select a local drive letter. To begin working directly with a local drive, right-click the drive icon in the My Computer window, choose Properties from the shortcut menu, and then click Disk Cleanup on the General tab of the properties dialog box. Figure 37-3 shows a system with nearly a gigabyte of space that can be recovered easily.

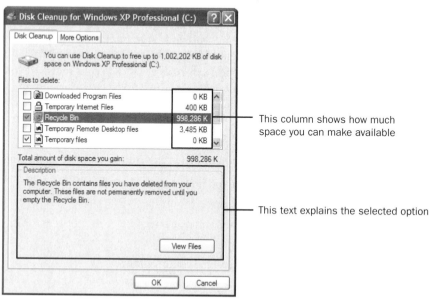

Figure 37-3.   Select or clear options from this list to make additional disk space available on the selected drive.

Most of the Disk Cleanup options are fairly self-explanatory and merely consolidate functions already scattered throughout the Windows interface. For instance, you can empty the Recycle Bin, clear out the Temporary Internet Files folder, and delete files left behind by Indexing Service. (Avoid cleaning out the Downloaded Program Files folder, which contains generally useful ActiveX and Java add-ins.) When you simply use these default settings, the Disk Cleanup utility is strictly an interactive tool. Each time you run the utility, you must select options you want to run and then click the OK button to actually perform the cleanup.

Caution   Disk Cleanup includes one confusing option that can leave an inordinate amount of wasted space on your hard disk if you don't understand how it works. When you run Disk Cleanup, one of the available options offers to delete Temporary Files; the accompanying Help text explains that these are unneeded files in the Temp folder. Unfortunately, this option may display a value of 0, even if your Temp folder contains tens or even hundreds of megabytes of useless files. The reason? Although the Help text doesn't explain it clearly, this value lists only files in your Temp folder that are more than one week old. If you want to completely clean out this folder, you'll need to do so manually. Close all running programs and type **%temp%** in the Run dialog box; from the resulting Windows Explorer window, delete everything you find. You may discover that some files are not available for deletion until you reboot.

The overwhelming majority of Windows users never realize that Disk Cleanup offers three cool switches that are documented only here and in Knowledge Base article 315246, "How to Automate the Disk Cleanup Tool in Windows XP."

To automate the cleanup process, use the following switches:

- **/D** *driveletter*   Runs Disk Cleanup using the drive letter you specify in place of *driveletter* (for example, **type cleanmgr /d c:**, to apply the utility to drive C).

- **/Sageset:***n*   Opens a dialog box that lets you select Disk Cleanup options, creates a registry key that corresponds to the number you entered, and then saves your settings in that key. Enter a number from 0 through 65535 in place of *n*.

- **/Sagerun:***n*   Retrieves the saved settings for the number you enter in place of *n* and then runs Disk Cleanup without requiring any interaction on your part.

To use these switches, follow these steps:

1 Open a Command Prompt window and type the command **cleanmgr /sageset:200**. (This number is completely arbitrary; you can choose any other number from 0 through 65535 if you prefer.)

2 In the Disk Cleanup Settings dialog box, shown in Figure 37-4, choose the options you want to apply whenever you use these settings. For this example, select the Temporary Setup Files, Debug Dump Files, Old Chkdsk Files, and Setup Log Files options.

3 Click OK to save your changes in the registry.

4 Create a shortcut that uses the command **cleanmgr /sagerun:200**. Save the shortcut in the Windows folder using a descriptive name—Weekly Cleanup, for instance.

5 Open Control Panel's Scheduled Tasks folder and start the Add ScheduledTask Wizard. When prompted to select the program you want Windows to run, click Browse and select the shortcut you just created. Follow the wizard's remaining prompts to schedule the command to run at regular intervals.

6 Repeat steps 1–5 for other Disk Cleanup options you want to automate.

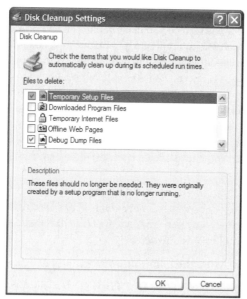

Figure 37-4. When you use the /Sageset switch, you can work with an expanded set of options that are not available interactively.

Tip Expedite Disk Cleanup by skipping file compression

Disk Cleanup normally begins by checking to see how much space it could recover by compressing old files on your hard disk. This analysis phase can keep your computer busy—and keep you waiting an annoyingly long time. If you're not inclined to compress old files at this time anyway, you can streamline the cleanup process by preventing Disk Cleanup from performing its analysis. One way to do this is to use the /Sageset switch to specify a cleanup routine *sans* compression. Alternatively, with a registry edit, you can simply remove Compress Old Files from Disk Cleanup's list of options. Run Registry Editor, navigate to HKLM\Software\ Microsoft\Windows\CurrentVersion\Explorer\VolumeCaches\Compress old files. Delete the data from the default value of this key, close Registry Editor, and Disk Cleanup will no longer concern itself with the compression of old files. To return the utility to its default behavior, retrace your steps to the same registry key and reenter as the key's default value the GUID that you earlier removed: {B50F5260-0C21-11D2-AB56-00A0C9082678}.

Tip Make the most of Disk Cleanup shortcuts

Disk Cleanup shortcuts can be tremendously useful for routine maintenance. For instance, you might want to create one batch file that automatically empties the Temporary Internet Files folder every time you log on to your computer and another that automatically compresses old files every week or two. If you create a shortcut that empties the Recycle Bin, it's best not to add it to the Scheduled Tasks folder, where it can inadvertently toss files you later discover you wanted to recover; instead, save this shortcut and run it as needed.

The More Options tab in the Disk Cleanup dialog box provides three more Clean Up buttons.

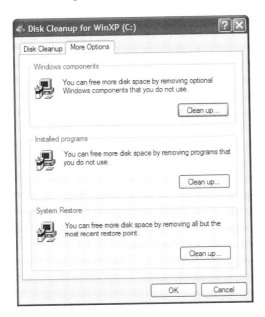

The top two buttons (in the Windows Components and Installed Programs sections) take you to the Add Or Remove Programs dialog box, where you can remove Windows components and programs. (For details, see "Adding and Removing Windows Components," page 60, and "Uninstalling Programs," page 124.) The third button, under System Restore, lets you remove all but the most recent System Restore checkpoint. This option can recover a dramatic amount of space, but you should choose it only if you're certain you won't need to roll back your configuration to one of the saved versions you're about to delete.

As an alternative to deleting all but the most recent restore point, you might want to consider reducing the amount of space that System Restore is allowed to use. By default, System Restore creates restore points until it has devoted 12 percent of your disk space to this purpose—at which point it begins removing old restore points to make room for new ones. (On disks smaller than 4 GB, the default allocation is 400 MB.) If you're frequently running short of disk space, consider allocating a smaller percentage to System Restore. To configure System Restore, right-click My Computer, choose Properties, and click the System Restore tab of the System Properties dialog box. Select the disk you want to configure (if you have more than one), and adjust the Disk Space To Use slider. For more information about System Restore, see "Undoing Configuration Mistakes with System Restore," page 1288.

Using NTFS File Compression

One of the many advantages of choosing the NTFS file system over FAT32 is that it offers on-the-fly compression. Don't confuse this capability with the clunky and unreliable DriveSpace compression schemes found in Windows 98 and Windows ME. The NTFS version is slick and essentially seamless. All you have to do is set an attribute for an NTFS file (or an entire folder), and Windows XP compresses it, decompressing it automatically when you open it.

To compress an NTFS file or folder, right-click its icon in Windows Explorer, choose Properties from the shortcut menu, and click the Advanced button. In the Advanced Attributes dialog box, shown in Figure 37-5, select Compress Contents To Save Disk Space.

Tip   Use compression sparingly

A little compression goes a long way. In general, NTFS compression is most effective when used on files that are not already compressed. Bitmap images, Microsoft Word documents, and database files are highly compressible. Because music files (in MP3 and WMA format) and JPEG and GIF images are already compressed, NTFS compression provides little benefit and incurs a noticeable performance hit. By all means, avoid compressing the folders that contain Windows system files and log files that the operating system uses regularly. The negative effect on performance is especially severe here.

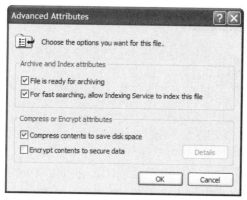

Figure 37-5.   You can compress a single file, a folder full of files, or an entire drive—but only on a drive formatted with NTFS.

To compress an entire volume at once, right-click the drive in Windows Explorer and follow the same procedure. You'll be asked to confirm that you really want to do this for every file in the volume. When you say yes, the system begins compressing files, one at a time. The process can take hours to complete; fortunately, it only needs to be done once. You can continue working while Windows is busy compressing files. If the system needs to compress an open file, you'll be notified with a dialog box. At that point, you can close the file in question and click Retry, or click Ignore or Ignore All.

Troubleshooting

When you select the encryption option, the compression button in the Advanced Attributes dialog box is cleared.

For security and performance reasons, encryption and compression are mutually exclusive attributes for files stored on an NTFS volume. If the file is compressed, it can't be encrypted, and vice versa. For more information about file encryption, see Chapter 11, "Encrypting Confidential Information." If you need to combine compression with security, consider using password-protected Zip files, which offer good (but not great) encryption along with efficient compression capabilities. Use the third-party WinZip program (*http://www.winzip.com*) or the Compressed Folders feature in Windows XP (as described in "Using Zipped Folders," page 706).

When you compress a folder, that attribute affects files that you move or copy later, according to the following rules:

- If you create a new file in a compressed folder, the new file is compressed.
- If you copy a file into a compressed folder, the file is compressed.
- If you move a file from a different NTFS volume into a compressed folder, the file is compressed.
- If you move a file into a compressed folder on the same NTFS volume, the file retains whatever compression setting it had originally and is not automatically compressed.
- If you move a compressed file into an uncompressed folder on the same NTFS volume, the file retains the compressed attribute. However, if you move a compressed file to an uncompressed folder on a different NTFS partition, the file loses the compression attribute.

> **Tip** **Highlight compressed files**
>
> If you use on-the-fly compression, take advantage of an option in Windows Explorer that displays compressed files and folders in an alternate color. That way, you can see at a glance which files and folders are compressed. To verify that this feature is enabled, open Windows Explorer and choose Tools, Folder Options. On the View tab, make sure that Show Encrypted Or Compressed NTFS Files In Color is selected. By default, the names and other details of compressed files appear in blue within Windows Explorer.

Smart Backup Strategies

Hard disks are amazing yet fragile mechanical devices. Packed with ultra-miniature electronics that zoom along at thousands of revolutions per minute, it's no wonder that they fail more often than any other component in the average computer. When a disk crashes, it's usually impossible to recover your data without spending a small fortune at a data recovery service.

And even if your hardware never lets you down, human error can wreak havoc with data. You can press the wrong key and inadvertently delete a group of files you meant to move. If you're not paying attention, you might absentmindedly click the wrong button in a dialog box, saving a new file using the same name as an old one, wiping out an irreplaceable document in the process.

In any of those circumstances, you're almost certainly going to lose some data. When a hard disk crashes, for instance, all files you've created or saved since your last backup are gone for good. But you can avoid the worst data losses if you get into the habit of backing up regularly.

Using the Windows XP Backup Program

Windows XP includes an enhanced version of the powerful Backup Utility (Ntbackup.exe) originally included with Windows 2000. This utility is installed by default on Windows XP Professional. Using this utility, you can back up all or part of the data on your computer's local drives and on shared network folders.

Although Backup Utility was originally designed for use on networks equipped with tape drives, the overwhelming majority of Windows users will choose the much simpler option of saving backup sets to a file, either on a second local drive, on a shared network folder, or on a high-capacity removable storage medium such as an external USB drive.

> **Note** If you're running Windows XP Home Edition, you won't find Backup Utility on the Start menu or even in Add Or Remove Programs. It *is* included, though; you just need to know where to look. To install Backup Utility, you need your Windows XP Home Edition CD. Use Windows Explorer to open the Valueadd\Msft\Ntbackup folder, and then double-click Ntbackup.msi.
>
> If your computer came with only a "system recovery" CD instead of a full Windows CD, finding Ntbackup.msi is not as easy. Look on the CD that was furnished and on any additional hard disk partitions set up on your computer. Some manufacturers provide the Windows files more or less intact, whereas others embed them in compressed disk image files. (Compaq systems with Windows XP Home Edition pre-installed, for example, have Windows files stored within Drive Image files on drive D.) Also, if you happen to have the disk imaging program that was used to create the disk image files, you can use it extract the Windows files you need.

To start Backup Utility, run Ntbackup.exe from a command prompt, or choose the Backup shortcut from All Programs, Accessories, System Tools. The default view is a straightforward wizard that walks you through the backup process quickly and efficiently. Make sure you've logged on using an account in the Administrators group and then follow these steps:

1. After clicking past the Backup Or Restore Wizard's Welcome page, choose the Back Up File And Settings option and click Next.

2. The What To Back Up page, shown in Figure 37-6, presents the following four options.

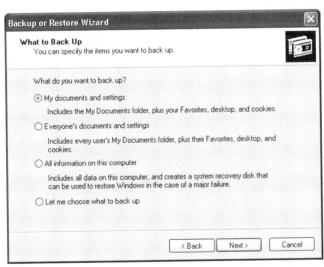

Figure 37-6. The complete backup option (All Information On This Computer) can consume a frightful amount of disk space; for most Windows users, the top two options are adequate.

- **My Documents And Settings**   The explanatory text here is confusing; if you choose this option, you effectively back up your entire user profile, including the My Documents folder, the Application Data folder, and the contents of your desktop. This backup does not include any data stored outside your profile. (If you've moved the My Documents folder to a different location than its default, this option will not work properly. You must select the correct location manually, using the fourth option in this list.)

- **Everyone's Documents And Settings**   This option backs up all user data stored in individual profiles—in other words, the entire contents of the Documents And Settings folder.

- **All Information On This Computer**   This option backs up all data on all local drives and creates an Automated System Recovery disk (see the following section for a description of this option).

- **Let Me Choose What To Back Up**   Choosing this option lets you pick individual files, folders, and drives to back up.

3   Choose the fourth option and click Next to proceed to the Items To Back Up page shown next. (You won't see this page if you select one of the other options.)

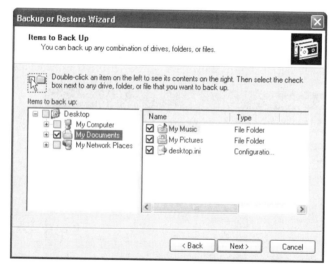

4   Select the check box next to each item you want to back up. Click Next to open the Backup Type, Destination, And Name page.

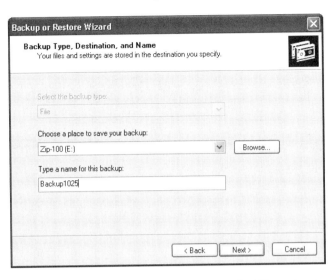

5 Choose the backup type. On most systems, the File option is selected by default and no other options are available. If your system includes a tape drive that is compatible with Backup Utility, you can select it from the Select The Backup Type list. If you select a file as the destination (as most people will), select a local or network drive from the Choose A Place To Save Your Backup list and enter a name for the file. Click Next to continue.

6 On the Completing The Backup Or Restore Wizard page, click Finish to begin the backup immediately, or click the Advanced button to choose additional options.

Tip **Back up to a CD or DVD**

Windows XP Backup Utility does not support backing up directly to CD or DVD recorders. However, if you plan your backups carefully, you can accomplish the same goal in a two-step process. Back up to a file first, and then copy that backup file to a recordable CD or DVD. If you need to restore data from your backup set, you can do so directly from the CD or DVD. For this procedure to work, you must ensure that you have enough free disk space to hold your backup files; you also have to plan your backups so that the resulting backup files will fit onto the target media. If you're backing up to CDs, for example, this might entail reorganizing your backup sets into multiple groups, with each one under 650 MB in size.

Most of the Advanced options are self-explanatory. The most confusing option is the choice of five backup types:

● A *normal backup* backs up all selected files and clears their archive attributes (so that subsequent differential or incremental backups copy only those files that have changed since their normal backup).

● An *incremental backup* copies selected files that have changed since the most recent normal or incremental backup and clears these files' archive attributes. If you perform a normal (full) backup every Monday, you can perform an incremental backup on Tuesday through Friday. As part of each incremental backup, Backup Utility will pick up only those files that have been changed since the last backup, which should take significantly less time than a full backup. In case of data loss, you would restore the normal backup and each succeeding incremental backup.

● A *differential backup* copies selected files that have changed since the most recent normal or incremental backup but does not clear the files' archive attributes. Subsequent differential backups continue to copy all files that have changed since the most recent normal or incremental backup. If you perform a full backup on Monday and a differential backup on each succeeding day of the week, you could restore your data by using the full backup and the most recent differential backup.

● A *copy backup* copies all selected files but does not clear archive attributes. A copy backup is useful as a way of archiving particular files without affecting your overall backup routine.

● A *daily backup* copies all selected files that have changed on the current day, without clearing the files' archive attributes. This procedure represents a way of backing up a particular day's work without affecting the overall backup routine and is best used as part of a scheduled task that runs late at night, after you've quit work for the day.

It's relatively easy to schedule backups so that they occur effortlessly and automatically. When you complete the Backup Or Restore wizard, click the Advanced button and then click Next until you reach the When To Back Up page, where you're given the opportunity to schedule the job you just saved. Choose the Later option and enter a descriptive name for the combination of settings you just created and the schedule you're about to specify—My Documents Weekly Backup, for instance. Then click the Set Schedule button and choose the frequency, start time, and other settings for the scheduled backup, as shown below.

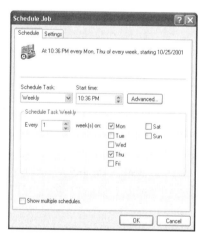

After setting the schedule, you'll need to enter and confirm the user name and password of an administrator account, and then click Finish to close the wizard. To review the backup task you've created, open Scheduled Tasks in Control Panel.

Note Backup Utility, like most backup programs, uses each file's archive attribute to determine whether to include the file in a backup. The *archive attribute* is a single bit in the file's directory entry. When a file is created or modified, its archive attribute is turned on. When a file is backed up using a normal or an incremental backup, the archive attribute is cleared. You can view (and set, if you like) the archive attribute for a file by right-clicking the file in Windows Explorer and choosing Properties. On the General tab, click the Advanced button; the first check box in the Advanced Attributes dialog box represents the archive attribute. (On a FAT-formatted drive, the Archive check box appears on the General tab.)

Troubleshooting

Backup Utility stops during a backup.

The version of Backup Utility initially shipped with Windows XP would stop during a scheduled backup if one or more files or folders scheduled to be backed up had been moved or deleted prior to the backup. This bug was resolved by a hotfix in September 2003. If you have kept current, via Windows Update, with patches and service packs for Windows XP, your version of Backup Utility is probably already corrected. If not, you can read Knowledge Base article 828402, "Backup (NTBackup.exe) Stops During the Backup Process and Event 8017 Is Logged," for information on how to obtain the hotfix.

Although we all hope we never have to deal with data loss, the law of averages says that sooner or later you'll have a disk crash. When that happens, reach for your backup disks and begin the restore process.

To restore data from a backup, start Backup Utility in Wizard Mode and choose the Restore Files And Settings option. Follow the prompts to restore individual files or an entire backup set. At the conclusion of the wizard, click the Advanced button and choose one of the following three options from the Where To Restore page:

- **Original Location** As the name implies, this option puts the files back in the same location as they were when you backed them up. This is the correct choice if you're restoring an entire backup set to a freshly formatted drive; if you're restoring a backup set to a drive that contains data, be careful that you don't inadvertently overwrite newer files with older ones from the backup. To avoid that potentially disastrous outcome, on the subsequent How To Restore page, select Replace Existing Files If They Are Older Than The Backup Files.

- **Alternate Location** Use this option to specify that you want to restore the specified files to a different location than where they were originally stored. After you finish restoring files, you can manually compare old and new files.
- **Single Folder** Use this option when you're restoring just a few files from a backup set and you want them to be easy to find.

Creating an Automatic System Recovery Backup

The Backup program included with Windows XP Professional offers a new feature called Automated System Recovery (ASR). Don't be misled by the name: The procedure isn't fully automated, and it won't necessarily recover your entire system. In fact, the procedure requires a substantial amount of advance preparation, and its stated purpose is to restore your system partition in the event of a catastrophic failure. After you learn what ASR can and can't do, you can decide how you want to use this backup option or whether you want to rely on another solution.

> **Caution** The Automated System Recovery feature is not available on systems running Windows XP Home Edition. Confusingly, Backup Utility allows you to create an ASR backup; however, because the option to restore this backup is not available, you're unable to use it properly.

Most people find out the hard way that Automated System Recovery works only if you prepare a complete backup in advance. Creating an ASR backup set saves the complete contents of your system drive to the backup media you select, such as a second physical disk, a network folder, or a tape drive. In addition, ASR saves information about your current arrangement of disk partitions, system files, and detected hardware on a floppy disk. The combination can quickly and effectively restore your system configuration; however, it does not back up or restore data on drives other than the system volume. For that task, use Backup Utility in Wizard Mode and choose the option to back up everything on the computer.

Inside Out

Make sure you have some free space

At the time it begins saving a backup set, Backup Utility creates a "volume snapshot" using free disk space on any available NTFS drive. If you have sufficient space, you can continue to use the computer while a backup is in progress, and you don't need to close any open files. If your system is short on free space, however, Backup Utility can't create the snapshot, and you may find that open files are not properly backed up.

Chapter 37

If you have a large amount of data on drives other than the system drive and you have an effective strategy to back up those files, you might decide to use the ASR Preparation Wizard to back up only the system drive. In that case, follow these steps:

1 Start Backup Utility (Ntbackup.exe) in Advanced Mode. (If the utility starts in Wizard Mode, click the Advanced Mode link to switch views.)

2 On the Backup Utility Welcome page shown next, click the Automated System Recovery Wizard button.

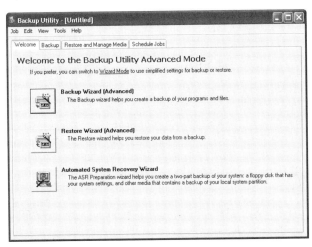

3 Click past the Welcome page to display the Backup Destination page, shown in Figure 37-7, and then choose where you want the backup file to be created.

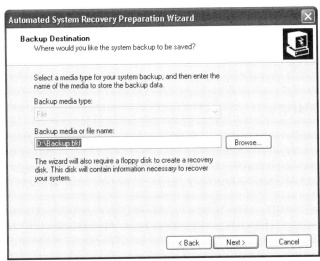

Figure 37-7. If a compatible tape drive is available, you can select it from the Backup Media Type list. Otherwise, select a local folder or network drive as the destination.

Make sure the destination you select has at least enough room to hold all data on the system drive, minus the page file and hibernation file. Click Next to continue.

4 On the final page of the wizard, click the Finish button to begin backing up files from the system drive.

5 When prompted, insert a floppy disk to store the system recovery information.

Save the backup media and the recovery disk in a safe place. In the event of a catastrophic failure of your system partition, you can boot using the Windows XP CD, press F2 to run Automated System Recovery when prompted by Windows Setup, and then follow the prompts to restore your system.

Backing Up with Partition Imaging

One of the limitations of the Windows XP Backup Utility—in addition to its inability to use recordable CDs and DVDs as target media—is the fact that it can't copy system files that are in use while it runs. Backup Utility uses *shadow copying* to work around this problem. It creates a copy of all files that are open when a backup process begins, and then it copies these "shadows" to the backup media. However, to give yourself an extra measure of security, you might want to consider adding a third-party partition-imaging product to your backup toolkit.

File-oriented backup tools, such as Backup Utility, copy files individually. Imaging tools create bit-by-bit copies of entire partitions. By booting into their own versions of DOS and working outside Windows, they are able to make exact copies of your entire system state, including your registry hives and all other system files. Because an imaging product replicates an entire partition, it requires a spare partition as the target medium. This approach typically incorporates data compression, however, so the target partition does not need to be as large as the one on which your data resides.

Some leading imaging products are Drive Image (Symantec Corporation, *http://www.powerquest.com/driveimage*) and Symantec Ghost (Symantec, *http://www.symantec.com/sabu/ghost*).

Other Backup Options

As an ideal backup strategy, we recommend that you use an imaging product for a periodic total backup and rely on Backup Utility (or a third-party file-oriented backup program) for more frequent interim backups. You can effectively use any combination of the following options as well, depending on your data, your hardware, and your personal preferences:

- **Files And Settings Transfer Wizard** Although this utility was designed to move data and settings from an old machine to a new one, it makes a surprisingly effective backup tool as well. Follow the instructions outlined in "Saving Files and Settings to a Folder or Drive," page 49.

- **Compressed folders and other Zip utilities**   If you have a relatively modest amount of personal data, you might find it easier to zip files using the built-in compressed folders feature or a third-party utility such as WinZip. You can then copy the resulting archive file to a safe location or to removable media.

- **Simple copies**   If you have plenty of disk space, you can open two copies of Windows Explorer and drag a folder from one location to another—to make a copy on a network drive, for instance. This option doesn't allow you to easily keep track of changed files, but it's uncomplicated.

- **Third-party file-syncing utilities**   Programs like FileWare's FileSync (*http://www.fileware.com*) allow you to set up mirror images of important data folders, typically on a network drive or an Internet-based server. The software keeps your local copy in sync with the network-based copy, replacing changed files and removing deleted files. If you inadvertently erase a local copy, or if a disk crash wipes out your local disk, you can recover your data from the network.

Chapter 38

Monitoring System Activities with Event Viewer

In Microsoft Windows XP, an *event* is any occurrence that is potentially noteworthy—to you, to other users, to the operating system, or to an application. Events are recorded by the Event Log service, and their history is preserved in three log files: Security (Secevent.evt), Application (Appevent.evt), and System (Sysevent.evt). Event Viewer, a Microsoft Management Console snap-in supplied with Windows XP, allows you to review and archive these three event logs.

Why would you want to do this? The most likely reasons are to troubleshoot problems that have occurred, to keep an eye on your system in order to forestall problems, and to watch out for security breaches. If a device has failed, a disk has filled close to capacity, a program has crashed repeatedly, or some other critical difficulty has arisen, the information recorded in the event logs can help you—or a technical support specialist—figure out what's wrong and what corrective steps are required. Watching the event logs can also help you spot serious problems before they occur. If trouble is brewing but hasn't yet erupted, keeping an eye on the event logs may tip you off before it's too late. For example, if a network adapter is failing intermittently or a network cable is improperly connected, you might begin to see items in the event log showing frequent disconnections from and reconnections to the network. Finally, you can use one of the event logs (the Security log) to track such things as unsuccessful logon attempts or attempts by users to read files for which they lack access privileges. Such occurrences might alert you to actual or potential security problems in your organization.

At Home with Windows XP

Event Viewer works exactly the same way in both versions of Windows XP. In Windows XP Home Edition, only certain predefined events are recorded in the Security log, but that topic is covered in Chapter 13, "Auditing Security."

Types of Events

Security events are recorded in the Security log, Secevent.evt. Monitoring these events is called *auditing* and is the subject of Chapter 13, "Auditing Security." In the remainder of this chapter, we focus on the other two event logs, the Application log (Appevent.evt) and the System log (Sysevent.evt). The Application and System logs record application events and system events, respectively.

Application events are generated by applications, including programs that you install, programs that come with Windows XP, and operating system services. For example, events relating to Microsoft Office, the backup program that comes with Windows XP, and the Windows XP Fax service are all recorded in the Application log.

System events are generated by Windows XP itself and by installed components, such as device drivers. If a driver fails to load when you start a Windows XP session, for example, that event is recorded in the System log.

(If you're curious about what elements of your system generate events and where those events are recorded, use Registry Editor to open the following registry key: HKLM\System\Current-ControlSet\Services\Eventlog. Then inspect the subkeys Application, Security, and System. Each entity capable of generating an event has a subkey under one of those three keys.)

> For details about using Registry Editor, see Chapter 41, "Editing the Registry."

The System and Application logs recognize three types of events, each identified by a unique icon.

⊗	**Errors** These are events that represent possible loss of data or functionality. Examples of errors include events related to a malfunctioning network adapter and loss of functionality caused by a device or service that doesn't load at startup.
⚠	**Warnings** These events represent less significant or less immediate problems than error events. Examples of warning events include a nearly full disk, a timeout by the network redirector, and data errors on a backup tape.
ⓘ	**Information** These are other events that Windows XP logs. Examples of information events include someone using a printer connected to your computer and a successful dial-up connection to your ISP.

Keeping Track of Computer Events

To start Event Viewer, do one of the following:

- In Control Panel, click Performance And Maintenance, Administrative Tools, Event Viewer.

- At a command prompt, type **eventvwr.msc**.

You can also run Event Viewer by right-clicking My Computer and choosing Manage. The Computer Management console that appears includes the Event Viewer snap-in, along with a number of other administrative tools.

Figure 38-1 shows an example of what you might see when you open Event Viewer. The console tree displays the names of the three event logs, allowing you to move from one log to another. The details pane presents a columnar view of the current log.

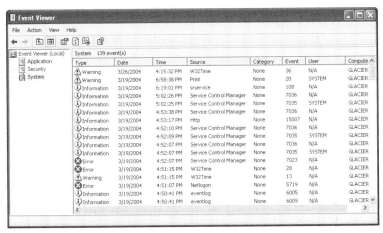

Figure 38-1. Event Viewer's details pane shows the important particulars of each event in the log selected in the console tree.

Figure 38-1 shows all eight of Event Viewer's columns. You can use the Add/Remove Columns command on the View menu to hide columns you don't need or to change the order in which columns appear. By default, events are sorted chronologically, with the most recent located at the top of the list. You can change the sort order by clicking column headings.

Note that, while the details pane includes some useful information, it doesn't provide many details about why events occurred or what they portend. You can get more of that information by inspecting the details for individual events (see "Examining Event Details," page 1269.) Here is a column-by-column rundown of what the details pane does display:

- **Type** Events in the System and Application logs are of three types: Information, Warning, and Error. The icon at the left side of the Type column helps you spot the event types in which you're interested.

- **Date and Time** The Event Log service records the date and time each event occurred in Greenwich mean time, and Event Viewer translates those time values into dates and times appropriate for your own time zone.

- **Source** The Source column reports the application or system component that generated an event.

- **Category** Some event sources use categories to distinguish different types of events they may report. Many sources do not. As you can see, none of the sources shown in Figure 38-1 uses categories.

- **Event** All events are identified by a numerical value. This number is associated with a text description that appears when you view an event's properties. There's no system-wide code in use here—each event source's designer simply decides what numbers to use and records those numbers in a file—and there's no requirement that each event source use a unique set of numbers. After spending some time in your event logs, however, you might begin to recognize particular events by their arbitrary numbers. For example, events 6006 and 6009, generated by the Event Log service itself (listed as eventlog in the Source column), occur respectively when the Event Log service is stopped and started. Because the Event Log service is ordinarily never stopped while your computer is running, these events represent system shutdown and restart.

- **User** The User column records the user account associated with each event. Not all events are associated with a particular user account. Many events, particularly system events, are not generated by a particular user. These events show up as N/A.

- **Computer** The Computer column records the computer on which the event occurred.

Daylight Saving Time, Remote Computers, and Changes to the System Clock

When you move from standard time into daylight saving time or vice versa, Event Viewer changes the displayed Time (and possibly Date) values for events that have already occurred. For example, if an event occurred at 6 P.M. in standard time, after you move into daylight saving time that event will appear as if it had occurred at 7 P.M. That's because Event Viewer applies a single offset from Greenwich mean time to all events in its logs and decrements that offset by one hour when you change from standard into daylight saving time.

If you monitor events on remote computers in other time zones, be aware that Event Viewer always displays those events' dates and times in your (local) time zone. It records occurrences in Greenwich mean time but applies your time zone's Greenwich mean time offset for display purposes. Thus, for example, an event occurring at noon in New York will be reported in Los Angeles as having occurred at 9 A.M.

If you change the clock on your system, the times reported in event logs do not change, because your offset from Greenwich mean time has not changed. If you change your time zone, however, Event Viewer applies the new offset and changes the times displayed for all events in the log.

Examining Event Details

To learn more about an event than Event Viewer's details pane tells you, you need to display individual information for the event. Select the event you're interested in and do one of the following:

- Double-click the event.
- Press Enter.
- Choose Properties from Event Viewer's Action menu.

Figure 38-2 on the next page shows the Event Properties dialog box for an event in the System log.

The summary information in the top third of the Event Properties dialog box is identical to the information that appears in Event Viewer's columnar details pane. The description in the middle third of the window is the plain-language description of what has occurred. For localization purposes, this information is kept separate from the log (.evt) file. Each event type is mapped to descriptive text that lives elsewhere, in whatever file the application's or component's designer chose to use. (The event message file is recorded in the EventMessageFile registry value in HKLM\System\CurrentControlSet\Services\Eventlog*logname**eventsource*, where *logname* is the name of the log—System, for example—and *eventsource* is the name of the application or component that generates the event in question.)

Some events generate binary data that can be useful to programmers or support technicians who are familiar with the product that generated the event. If binary data is available, it appears in the bottom third of the Event Properties dialog box.

If you want to view details for other events, you can do so without returning to the details pane: Click the arrow buttons in the upper right corner of the properties dialog box to move to the previous or next event in the list.

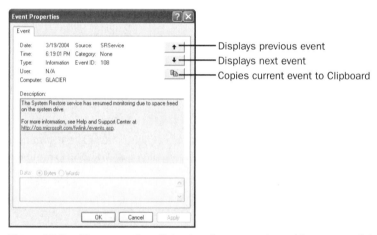

Figure 38-2. The properties dialog box for an event provides a textual description and binary data that are not shown in the main Event Viewer window.

Directly below the Next Event button, near the upper right corner of the window, is a handy Copy button, as shown in Figure 38-2. Clicking here sends the entire contents of the Event Properties dialog box to the Clipboard, allowing you, for example, to paste the information into an e-mail message and send it to a support technician. (You can also copy some or all of the text in the dialog box by selecting it and pressing Ctrl+C. Use this technique to selectively copy field data from the top of the dialog box as well as information in the Description and Data boxes.)

> **Tip** Find better descriptions on the Web
>
> The Description field in some events is a model of clarity and completeness. Others, however, leave much to be desired. You can usually find more information on the Web by searching for "event id" followed by the Event ID number. One particular site deserves mention: EventID.Net (*http://eventid.net*). Here you can search for information by event ID and source; results typically include a clear description, links to relevant knowledge base articles, and comments and suggestions from knowledgeable users.

Searching for an Event

The Find command on Event Viewer's View menu allows you to locate particular items in the current log. The Find dialog box, shown in Figure 38-3, includes a Description box in which you can specify all or a portion of an event's descriptive text. To locate the most recent event that involved any kind of failure, for example, you would select the first event in the log (assuming you've kept the default chronological sort order), choose Find, type **fail** in the Description field, and click Find Next.

Figure 38-3. You can use this dialog box to find a particular event.

Filtering the Log Display

As you can see from a cursory look at your System log, events can pile up quickly, obscuring those of a particular type (such as print jobs) or those that occurred at a particular date and time. To filter a log so that Event Viewer displays only the items you currently care about, right-click the log's name in the console tree and choose Properties. Then fill out the Filter tab of the log's properties dialog box (it looks much like the Find dialog box shown in Figure 38-3), and click OK. To restore the unfiltered list, return to this dialog box and click Restore Defaults.

With the help of the New Log View command on the Action menu, you can quickly switch between filtered and unfiltered views of a log—or between one filtered view and a different filtered view. Simply select the log in which you're interested, right-click, and then choose New Log View. Event Viewer adds the new view to the console tree. Select the new view and filter to taste. Now you can move between views by navigating the console tree.

Working with Log Files

In general, you don't need to do anything with the log (.evt) files. But you might want to limit their size, archive their content, or clear them—tasks that are explained in the following sections.

Setting Log File Size and Longevity

Log files don't continue to pile up new events forever. If they did, they would eventually consume an unmanageable amount of disk space. By default, each log file has a maximum size of 512 KB. You can adjust that downward or upward in 64-KB increments.

> **Caution** Although Event Viewer lets you specify a size for each log as large as 4 GB, don't attempt it. The total combined size of the three event logs should not exceed 300 MB. (Fortunately, there's seldom a reason to make them anywhere near that big.) That's because Event Viewer uses memory-mapped files, which means that all three log files are loaded into system memory. Other services also vie for the same pool of system memory, and are constrained by a 1-GB limit on the amount of this type of memory used by any one process. If the system is unable to allocate memory for system-mapped files, you'll undoubtedly experience significant performance degradation and encounter errors such as lost events.

Also by default, events in each log file have a minimum longevity of seven days. That means that if a file reaches its maximum size, new events overwrite the oldest ones—but only if the oldest ones are at least seven days old. That too is an adjustable parameter.

To change either a log file's maximum size or its events' minimum longevity, select the log in question in the console tree. Then choose Properties from the Action menu. Figure 38-4 shows a log file's properties dialog box. (You must have administrative privileges to use this dialog box; otherwise, all the controls appear dimmed.)

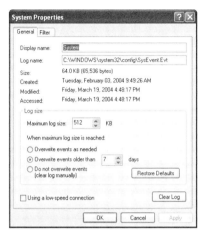

Figure 38-4. The properties dialog box allows you to control the size and lifespan of your event logs.

If the Event Log service is unable to add new events to a log, either because you have told it never to overwrite or because it has reached capacity before the oldest events have reached their minimum age, you'll receive a warning message. Then you can remedy the situation, either by simply clearing the log or by archiving and then clearing it.

Archiving and Clearing Log Files

To archive a log, select it in the console tree, and choose Save Log File As from the Action menu. In the dialog box that appears, be sure to choose the default file type, Event Log (*.evt). The resulting file includes all events (ignoring the current filter, if any) and all the recorded information (including the binary details).

To clear a log, either click the Clear Log button in the log's properties dialog box (see Figure 38-4) or select the log in the console tree and choose Clear All Events from the Action menu. You must have administrative privileges to clear a log.

Displaying an Archived Log File

After you have saved a log file in the .evt format, you can redisplay its contents at any time by using the Open Log File command on the Action menu. You need to tell the system what kind of log file—Application, Security, or System—you're reopening when you specify the file's name.

A reopened archive appears as a new entry in the console tree. You can view it, filter it, and search it, just as you would any other log file. You can also delete it—something you can't do to the default Application, Security, and System logs.

Chapter 38

Troubleshooting

An error message says you don't have enough disk space to record events.

If you run out of space on the disk where your log files reside, the Event Log service will be unable to record new events and you will receive an error message to that effect. If you cannot create free space on the full disk, you can work around the problem by changing the default location of the log files. Doing so requires three modifications to your registry, as follows:

1 Run Registry Editor.

2 Navigate to the key HKLM\System\CurrentControlSet\Services\Eventlog\Application.

3 Double-click the File value.

4 Change the File value's data to specify a path to a disk that isn't full. For example, if the current data is located in %SystemRoot%\System32\Config\Appevent.evt and you have room to put the Appevent.evt file in E:\SomeFolder, change the File value's data to E:\SomeFolder\Appevent.evt.

   The folder you specify must exist, or the change won't take effect.

5 Repeat these steps to change the location specified by the File value in HKLM\System\CurrentControlSet\Services\Eventlog\Security and HKLM\System\CurrentControlSet\Services\Eventlog\System.

6 Close Registry Editor.

7 Restart your computer.

For additional information about modifying the registry, see Chapter 41, "Editing the Registry."

Exporting Log File Information

Saving a log in its native (.evt) format creates a complete replica of the log, but you can view that replica only in Event Viewer (or a third-party application capable of reading native event logs). However, Event Viewer can export log data to tab- or comma-delimited text files, and you can easily import these into database, spreadsheet, or even word processing programs. When you save a log in one of these formats, you get everything in the log except the binary data associated with certain events.

To save an entire log file in a text format, select the log in the console tree, choose Save Log File As from the Action menu, and then select either Text (Tab Delimited) or CSV (Comma

Delimited) from the Save As Type list. The Save Log File As command always exports all of the current log, regardless of how the log might be filtered for display purposes.

If you want to generate a text report showing only particular kinds of events, first filter the log to display those events, and then use the Action menu's Export List command. Like the Save Log File As command, Export List provides tab- and comma-delimited options. It also offers the option to save in Unicode—something that could prove handy if your local language includes non-Latin characters. Do not, however, select the Save Only Selected Rows check box in the Export List dialog box unless you want a report that includes only column headers and a single event.

Backing Up Log Files

Because the Event Log service is ordinarily running at all times, the three log files—Appevent.evt, Secevent.evt, and Sysevent.evt—are generally open at all times. *Do not try to back up these log files using Windows Explorer or the command line!* Windows Explorer and the Copy command will copy your open log files without complaint, but if you copy them back to your %SystemRoot%\System32\Config folder (the default log file location), Event Viewer will find them corrupted and will be unable to display their contents.

Fortunately, Windows XP Backup Utility (Ntbackup.exe) can back up and restore log files without corrupting them in the process. You can use Backup Utility to schedule regular back-ups of your log files. For information about Backup Utility, see "Using the Windows XP Backup Program," page 1254.

 Troubleshooting

Your log files are corrupt.

If Event Viewer reports on startup that one or more of your log files is corrupt, you can rem-edy the situation as follows:

1 Disable the Event Log service. (For information about disabling a service, see "Start-ing and Stopping Services," page 1380.)

2 Restart Windows XP.

3 Delete the corrupt log(s)—Appevent.evt, Secevent.evt, and/or Sysevent.evt—from %SystemRoot%\System32\Config (or wherever they may be). Your existing event data will be lost, but a new log file will be created when the service is restarted, and that log will start to accumulate new events.

4 Reenable the Event Log service, and start the service.

5 If the Event Log service doesn't restart successfully, then restart Windows XP.

Note that you cannot delete or rename the log files while the Event Log service is running.

Chapter 38

Using Third-Party Tools to Monitor Events

Several third-party tools are available to help you monitor events. While some of these tools are directed at helping monitor events across a large enterprise, others provide features useful on small networks and individual computers.

These products provide the capability to perform one or more of the following actions:

- Monitor multiple computers from one workstation
- Organize information and print reports
- Schedule monitoring activities
- Monitor other types of logs in addition to event logs, such as Web server logs
- Send reports or notifications via e-mail
- Provide real-time monitoring and notification of events
- Enable Web-based remote viewing of events

Examples of programs that provide some or all of these capabilities include:

- WDumpEvt (*http://www.eventlog.com*)
- InTrust (*http://www.aelita.com/products/intrust/*)
- EventReporter (*http://www.eventreporter.com*)
- ELM Log Manager (*http://www.tntsoftware.com/products/elm*)

> **Tip** View only errors in the logs
>
> The Help And Support Center offers an alternative view of the system logs. This view merges the content from all three logs, but it shows only the errors (not warnings or information events)—which are typically the most significant events. To see this view of events, click Start, Help And Support Center. From the Help And Support Center home page, click Use Tools To View Your Computer Information And Diagnose Problems, Advanced System Information, View The Error Log.

> **Note** A terrific tool for tracking down the cause of some sporadic, unexplained crashes is Driver Verifier Manager, which checks each device driver to verify that it conforms to Windows standards. (Faulty drivers are responsible for many computer crashes.) For information about Driver Verifier Manager, see the Troubleshooting tip on page 154. You can find further details online at *http://www.microsoft.com/whdc/devtools/tools/verifier.mspx*.

The topics in this chapter all deal with operating system crashes—problems that cause the entire system to become unusable or, at the very least, unstable. Fortunately, such crashes are rare. A more likely occurrence in Windows is an application crash, in which a particular application locks up. Before reviewing techniques for coping with operating system crashes, we'll survey the messages that Windows displays in response to application crashes and your options for reporting such crashes to Microsoft.

Using and Configuring Windows Error Reporting

If you've ever had to resort to terminating an unresponsive (hung) application with Windows Task Manager, or if you've ever had an application roll over and die without apparent provocation on your part, you've probably seen a request, similar to the one shown in Figure 39-1, that you send information to Microsoft. This entreaty comes from Windows Error Reporting, a fault-response component built into Windows XP and enabled by default. Windows Error Reporting, which replaces the Dr. Watson module that was a staple of earlier Windows versions (the doctor has retired but still consults on request; see "What Happened to Dr. Watson?," page 1284), serves two purposes. First, it provides information to Microsoft that might help the company improve its product line. (Microsoft engineers really do use this information for solving problems and for making improvements, both to Windows and to Microsoft applications, such as Microsoft Office. In fact, a large number of the fixes in Windows XP Service Pack 1 and Service Pack 2 are the result of submitted error reports. In addition, this information is available to other software publishers, so that they can make necessary fixes to their programs.) Second, in some cases, submission of crash data can enable Microsoft to provide Web links to a software update that will prevent subsequent occurrences of the same crash, or to information (usually in the form of a Knowledge Base article) about steps that you can take to avoid the problem in the future.

Windows never transmits this information without your permission. If you consent, the information transmitted by Windows Error Reporting in response to an application crash includes a snapshot (a "mini-dump") of the memory allocated to the faulting application. If that application has open data files, that memory snapshot *could* conceivably include sensitive information stored in those files. The information is transmitted over a secure (https) Internet connection and stored in a secure database with controlled access, however, and Microsoft asserts that it will not intentionally use anything transmitted by Windows Error Reporting to identify users. You can read the company's data collection policy statement on the Microsoft Online Crash Analysis Web site at *http://oca.microsoft.com/en/dcp20.asp*.

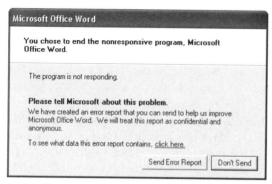

Figure 39-1. Windows Error Reporting, in response to an application crash, gives you the opportunity to send data about the crash over a secure Internet connection to Microsoft.

Windows Error Reporting data, moreover, is not available to support engineers. If you follow up a crash report with a call to Microsoft's Product Support Services, the person you talk to will not have access to the data you sent. If the crash is repeatable, the support technician might ask you to generate and upload a Dr. Watson log, which will include details that might enable the technician to solve your problem. (For information about how to do this, see "What Happened to Dr. Watson?," page 1284.)

To learn more about what Windows Error Reporting will send if you grant permission, you can click the Click Here link shown in Figure 39-1. You will then see something comparable to Figure 39-2. The Error Signature information at the top of this display includes the name and version number of the faulting application (in the case of an application crash), as well as the name of the module (the section of code) where the problem occurred. The first paragraph of the Reporting Details section provides a little more description of the type of information that Windows Error Reporting proposes to send. (The remainder of the Reporting Details section is a brief policy statement. Clicking the second Click Here link at the bottom of this dialog box takes you to the full policy statement mentioned on the previous page.)

If you're still undecided about whether to transmit or not, it's a good idea to click the first Click Here link in the dialog box shown in Figure 39-2. The technical information that will appear (Figure 39-3 shows this detail for our example application crash) might include the names of files that you can inspect yourself before making your decision.

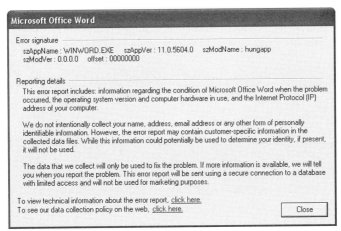

Figure 39-2. Clicking Click Here in the dialog box shown in Figure 39-1 takes you to this brief description of the information that Windows Error Reporting proposes to send.

After Windows Error Reporting transmits your crash data (if you permit it do so), you might see a link to additional information about the occurrence—and possibly to a Web site where you can download a possible remedy. Figure 39-4, for example, shows the screen that appeared following transmission of the data described in Figure 39-3.

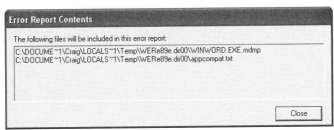

Figure 39-3. The Error Report Contents dialog box provides additional information about the data files Windows Error Reporting proposes to transmit (which you might be able to inspect before sending).

Whether or not you choose to send error data, application crashes are memorialized in the Application event log. The event record provides the brief description that was shown in Figure 39-2. If you elect to share your news with Microsoft, the Application log records that fact in a separate record, which includes a fault bucket number (see Figure 39-5) that might assist a support technician in researching your problem. (For information about reading event logs, see Chapter 38, "Monitoring System Activities with Event Viewer.")

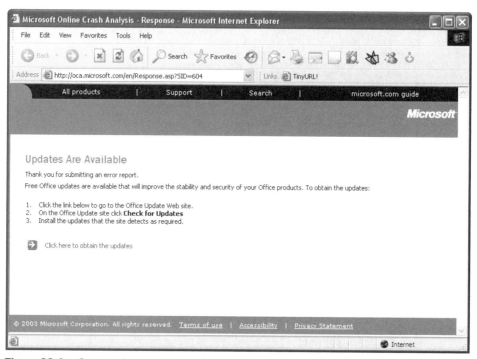

Figure 39-4. One good reason to send error data is that you might be provided with a link to a download that can keep the untoward event from recurring.

Figure 39-5. If you allow Windows Error Reporting to send crash data to Microsoft, the resulting entry in the Application event log includes a fault bucket number that may help support technicians diagnose your problem.

Windows Error Reporting and System Crashes

Figures 39-1 through 39-5 illustrate screens that you might see in the aftermath of an application crash. Windows shuts down the faulting application in such a case, but is otherwise unperturbed. In the case of a kernel-mode, or system, crash, you'll either see a Blue Screen of Death (BSOD) or your system will reset. In either case, the next time a member of the Administrators group logs on, that person will see a screen similar to Figure 39-1 that announces, "The system has recovered from a serious error." The administrator will be invited to notify Microsoft, and the data collection policy that might affect the administrator's decision will be exactly the same as that applying to an application crash. The inducements to consent are higher, however, because a workaround or software update that prevents similar shutdowns in the future might be available. Even if no such fix is available, it might be worth your while to visit Microsoft's Online Crash Analysis site (*http://oca.microsoft.com*). Microsoft analyzes all system error reports (prioritizing them on the basis of number of occurrences), and lets you track the status of your misfortune for 180 days after the event. (You'll need a Microsoft Passport to track your problem's status.)

Configuring Windows Error Reporting

Windows Error Reporting asks permission to notify Microsoft with each error event. No blanket opt-in is available. You can opt out in a general way, however. To disable Windows Error Reporting for all crashes or specific types of crashes, right-click My Computer, choose Properties, click the Advanced tab, and then click Error Reporting. You will see the dialog box shown in Figure 39-6.

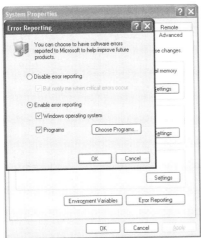

Figure 39-6. Using this dialog box, you can opt out of error reporting, globally, or for specific types of crashes.

To opt out of all error reporting, select Disable Error Reporting. (Unless the system in question is completely unmonitored, you should probably leave the But Notify Me When Critical Errors Occur check box selected.) If you do not disable error reporting globally, you can disable it separately for either kernel-mode crashes (Windows Operating System) or application crashes (Programs). And if you click Choose Programs, a second dialog box appears, in which you can enable error reporting for specific applications or for all programs except those that you enumerate. (If you are developing a program yourself, for example, and you expect an occasional crash from that program, you might want to exempt it from Windows Error Reporting.)

What Happened to Dr. Watson?

In previous versions of Windows, a diagnostic tool with the colorful name of Dr. Watson for Windows was enabled by default. Dr. Watson, shown in Figure 39-7, generated various kinds of crash dump files in the event of application errors. The doctor plays this role no longer, at least by default. He is still present in Windows XP, however (%SystemRoot%\System32\Drwtsn32.exe), and he does go back on duty if you disable Windows Error Reporting. If you experience a repeatable application error and you call Microsoft Support Services for help, the technician you talk to might ask that you disable Windows Error Reporting (see the previous section), reenact the crash, collect a Dr.Watson log, and upload the log to Microsoft.

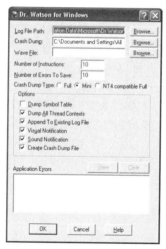

Figure 39-7. You can still use Dr. Watson to generate a detailed crash log.

Using Advanced Startup Options

When you experience problems at startup, you can choose from a similar set of options on two separate menus. From Windows XP Professional and Home Edition, you can access the Advanced Options menu, shown here, by pressing F8 at the menu that prompts you to choose an operating system. (If Windows starts without displaying a startup menu, press F8 after your system finishes displaying startup messages from the BIOS but before the Windows logo appears.)

```
Windows Advanced Options Menu
Please select an option:

    Safe Mode
    Safe Mode with Networking
    Safe Mode with Command Prompt

    Enable Boot Logging
    Enable VGA Mode
    Last Known Good Configuration (your most recent settings that worked)
    Directory Services Restore Mode (Windows domain controllers only)
    Debugging Mode

    Start Windows Normally
    Reboot
    Return to OS Choices Menu

Use the up and down arrow keys to move the highlight to your choice.
```

If Windows hangs at startup, use the power switch or the reset button to restart your system. You should see the Startup Recovery menu, shown here, which offers many of the same troubleshooting options as the Advanced Options menu.

```
We apologize for the inconvenience, but Windows did not start successfully.  A
recent hardware or software change might have caused this.

If your computer stopped responding, restarted unexpectedly, or was
automatically shut down to protect your files and folders, choose Last Known
Good Configuration to revert to the most recent settings that worked.

If a previous startup attempt was interrupted due to a power failure or because
the Power or Reset button was pressed, or if you aren't sure what caused the
problem, choose Start Windows Normally.

    Safe Mode
    Safe Mode with Networking
    Safe Mode with Command Prompt

    Last Known Good Configuration (your most recent settings that worked)

    Start Windows Normally

Use the up and down arrow keys to move the highlight to your choice.
Seconds until Windows starts: 20
```

Using Safe Mode

As in previous Windows versions, Windows XP gives you the option to start your system in Safe Mode if you're unable to reliably start in normal mode. In Safe Mode, Windows uses only those services and drivers that are absolutely required to start your system. The operating system starts with a minimal set of drivers and services, using a generic video driver at a resolution of 640×480, with support for your keyboard, mouse, monitor, local storage, and default system services. In Safe Mode, Windows does not install support for audio devices and nonessential peripherals, including most devices connected via USB ports. (USB keyboards and mice may be used in Safe Mode only if your system BIOS includes the option to recognize and enable these devices.) In Safe Mode, Windows ignores all startup programs as well, whether they're specified in a startup group on the All Programs menu or in the registry.

> **Note** Unlike previous Windows versions, the base video driver in Windows XP will display 24-bit color in Safe Mode; the 640 x 480 resolution, however, cannot be adjusted.

In Safe Mode, you can access most essential configuration tools, including Device Manager, System Restore, Registry Editor, and Backup Utility. Virtually all Help And Support Center features are available in Safe Mode as well, with the noteworthy exception of the Group Policy features in Advanced System Information. You can use these tools to disable the system services, device drivers, or startup applications that are preventing your computer from starting.

If Windows appears to work properly in Safe Mode, you can safely assume that there's no problem with the basic services. Use Device Manager, Driver Verifier Manager, and Event Viewer to try to figure out where the trouble lies. If you suspect that a newly installed device or program is the cause of the problem, you can remove the offending software while you're running in Safe Mode. Use Device Manager to uninstall or roll back a hardware driver; try the Add Or Remove Programs option in Control Panel to remove a program. Then try restarting the system normally to see whether that resolved the problem.

> For more details about working with device drivers, see "Managing Installed Drivers," page 152. For advice on the right way to remove a Windows program, see "Uninstalling Programs," page 124.

If you need access to network connections, choose the Safe Mode With Networking option, which loads the base set of Safe Mode files and adds drivers and services required to start Windows networking. Note that this option will do you no good on a portable computer with a PC Card (PCMCIA) network adapter, because PC Card peripherals are disabled in Safe Mode.

The third Safe Mode option, Safe Mode With Command Prompt, loads the same stripped-down set of services as in Safe Mode, but uses the Windows XP command interpreter (Cmd.exe) as a shell instead of the graphical Windows Explorer (Explorer.exe). This option is recommended only for diehard command-line aficionados.

Tip   **Put Safe Mode on the menu**

If you routinely test hardware, software, and drivers that require you to switch into Safe Mode, you don't have to go through the hassle of pressing F8 at precisely the right time and choosing from the startup menu. Instead, add one or more Safe Mode options to the list of available operating systems that Windows displays at startup.

To install this option, follow these steps:

1. Right-click My Computer on the Start menu and choose Properties.

2. On the Advanced tab, click the Settings button in the Startup And Recovery section.

3. In the Startup And Recovery dialog box, click the Edit button to open Boot.ini in Notepad.

4. Under [Operating Systems], select the entire line that contains the settings for your default operating system choice and copy it to the bottom of the list.

5. Append the following set of switches to the end of the newly copied line:

   `/safeboot:minimal /sos /bootlog`

   (Replace *minimal* with *network* if you want the shortcut to start Windows in Safe Mode with networking.)

6. Change the description in quotation marks to "Windows XP Safe Mode" and then save the file.

Restoring the Last Known Good Configuration

Every time you successfully start Windows in normal mode, the operating system makes a record of all currently installed drivers and the contents of the registry key HKLM\SYSTEM\CurrentControlSet. This record comes in handy if you install a driver or make a hardware configuration change that causes your system to hang at startup. When Windows displays the Startup Recovery menu, you can choose the Last Known Good Configuration option. This menu choice restores the previous, working registry key, effectively removing the changes that are causing the problem.

In general, System Restore is a more reliable alternative than the Last Known Good Configuration menu choice, because it restores all Windows system files and the entire registry rather than just a single key. (For more information, see "Undoing Configuration Mistakes with System Restore," page 1288.)

Chapter 39

Caution If you suspect that a driver change is causing system problems and you don't have a recent System Restore point to return to, don't log on in normal mode. As soon as you log on in normal mode, Windows resets the Last Known Good Configuration information, effectively removing your safety net. If you suspect problems, start Windows in Safe Mode and perform basic troubleshooting first. Logging on in Safe Mode does not update the Last Known Good Configuration information, so you can safely roll back to the Last Known Good Configuration if Safe Mode troubleshooting is unsuccessful.

Other Startup Options

Four additional choices on the Advanced Options menu are of use in specialized circumstances:

- **Enable Boot Logging** When you select this option, Windows starts up normally and creates a log file that lists the names and status of all drivers loaded into memory. To view the contents of this file, look for Ntbtlog.txt in the %SystemRoot% folder. If your system is hanging because of a faulty driver, the last entry in this log file may identify the culprit.

- **Enable VGA Mode** This option starts the computer in standard VGA mode using the current video driver (not the plain-vanilla Vga.sys driver used in Safe Mode). Use this option to recover from video problems that are caused not by a faulty driver but by incorrect settings, such as an improper resolution or refresh rate.

- **Directory Services Restore Mode** Although this option appears on the Advanced Options menu for Windows XP Professional, it is only used with domain controllers running Windows 2000 Server or Windows Server 2003. Ignore it.

- **Debugging Mode** This choice starts Windows XP in kernel debug mode. To take advantage of this capability, you must connect the system to another computer using a serial connection on COM2. The other computer must run a compatible debugger to perform troubleshooting and system analysis.

Undoing Configuration Mistakes with System Restore

System Restore is a Windows XP service that runs in the background, building a log of changes to system files and taking periodic snapshots of the system state, including information about user accounts, hardware and software settings, and files required for startup. At regular intervals (once per day, by default), and whenever particular kinds of changes to your system occur (such as the installation or removal of applications or drivers), System Restore creates a *restore point*. These enable you to return your system to a prior condition in the event of a destabilizing change. In addition to the restore points that System Restore generates automatically, you can create and name your own restore points at any time.

Restore point data is stored in hidden archives for safekeeping and limited in size to a set percentage (12 percent, by default) of the drive on which Windows is installed. (On drives smaller than 4 GB, the default maximum size is 400 MB.) Individual restore points are maintained for a particular length of time (the default is 90 days). When a restore point reaches its age threshold, the system automatically deletes it. If the disk-space threshold is reached, the system deletes the oldest restore point to make room for a new one.

All of these parameters—the frequency with which the system creates periodic restore points, the length of time restore points are kept, and the maximum amount of drive space devoted to restore-point data—are user configurable. (See "Configuring System Restore Options," page 67, for details.)

If you encounter a problem that causes Windows to become unstable, you can start the System Restore Wizard in normal or Safe Mode and roll back your system files and registry to those saved from a previous date—when, presumably, your system worked properly. System Restore can't perform miracles, but it can be a lifesaver in the following situations:

- **You install a program that conflicts with other software or drivers on your system.** If uninstalling the program doesn't cure the problem, you can restore your system configuration to a point before you installed the program.

- **You install one or more updated drivers that cause performance or stability problems.** Rather than using the Driver Rollback feature from Device Manager, use System Restore to restore all previously installed drivers.

- **Your system develops performance or stability problems for no apparent reason.** This scenario is especially likely if you share a computer with other family members or coworkers who casually install untested, incompatible software and drivers. If you know the system was working properly on a certain date, you can use a restore point from that date or earlier and be reasonably confident that your system will return to proper operation.

Caution You cannot count on System Restore to protect you from viruses, worms, Trojan horses, and other malware. In fact, if your system contracts a virus, files stored in restore points created after that point might be infected also, and you run the risk of restoring the virus along with your system files. To be safe, use a reliable antivirus program, keep it up to date, and don't open e-mail attachments unless you're certain they're safe.

Chapter 39

What System Restore Does and Does Not Monitor

A list of file types that System Restore monitors appears in the file %SystemRoot%\System32\ Restore\Filelist.xml. (You can also view a list of monitored file extensions on the MSDN Library site at *http://msdn.microsoft.com/library/default.asp?url=/library/en-us/sr/sr/ monitored_file_extensions.asp*.) In addition to listing the file types that are monitored, Filelist.xml also enumerates specific files and folders that System Restore ignores. Separate exclusion lists are maintained in the values of two registry keys: HKLM\System\ ControlSet001\Control\BackupRestore\FilesNotToBackup and HKLM\System\ControlSet001\ Control\BackupRestore\KeysNotToRestore.

The short version of all this detail is this: System Restore monitors system files and registry keys (archiving this information before any changes are made and encapsulating the change data in periodic restore points), and it ignores all user data. System Restore does *not* monitor the following files and folders:

- Any files of any type stored in the following personal data folders: My Documents, Favorites, Cookies, Recycle Bin, Temporary Internet Files, History, and Temp
- Image and graphics files, including bitmap and JPEG files, and files that use extensions commonly associated with data files, such as .doc, .xls, .mdb, and .pdf
- The page file (virtual memory) or hibernation file
- E-mail files managed by Microsoft Outlook or Outlook Express

System Restore also refrains from restoring Windows logon passwords and hints. In other words, if you have changed passwords during the lifespan of your restore points, you can't inadvertently roll your system back to a point where your current password will be invalid.

When System Restore Creates Restore Points

Windows creates an initial restore point when you install or upgrade to Windows XP. You can create a restore point manually at any time. In addition, Windows XP creates restore points automatically whenever you take any of the following actions:

- **You install an unsigned device driver.** When you attempt to install an unsigned hardware driver, Windows displays a warning message. If you choose to continue, the system creates a restore point before completing the installation. If the driver causes problems, you can use the System Restore Wizard to completely remove the driver.

For more details about driver signing, see "A Crash Course in Device Drivers," page 129.

- **You install an application using an installer that's compatible with System Restore.** Applications that use Windows Installer (including Office) and InstallShield Professional version 6.1 or later fall into this category.

- **You install a Windows update or patch.** Windows creates a restore point automatically whenever you download and install an update using Windows Update or the Automatic Updates feature.

- **You restore a prior configuration using System Restore.** Each time you perform a restore operation, System Restore saves your current configuration, allowing you to undo the restore if necessary.

- **You restore data from a backup set created with the Backup Utility.** Each time you use Backup Utility to restore files (in Advanced or Wizard mode), System Restore creates a restore point. If restoring the backed-up files causes problems with Windows system files, you can quickly restore a working configuration.

> **Caution** Don't rely on System Restore to protect you from data loss or backup mistakes. Restoring a backed-up configuration can undo damage only to your Windows system files; a restore point does not protect data files. If you inadvertently delete working data files or overwrite them with out-of-date backup copies, you will not be able to recover your data files unless you have a recent backup set.

Finally, System Restore creates restore points at regular intervals, regardless of user activity. By default, System Restore creates a restore point every 24 hours if you leave your computer on. If you shut down your computer, the System Restore service creates a new restore point when you restart, if the most recent restore point was more than 24 hours ago. These periodic restore points are created while the system is idle, but the process is quick and does not require an extensive stretch of idle time.

Using System Restore

To create a restore point or to return your system to an earlier state, open the Start menu and choose to All Programs, Accessories, System Tools, System Restore. (Alternatively, you can start System Restore by clicking Undo Changes To Your Computer With System Restore in the Help And Support Center. Or you can simply click Start, Run, and type **%systemroot%\ system32\restore\rstrui.exe**. On the Welcome To System Restore screen, shown on the next page, choose Create A Restore Point or Restore My Computer To An Earlier Time. (A third option, Undo My Last Restoration, will also be available if you have just completed a reversion to one of your restore points.)

Chapter 39

Choose the top option to restore
a previous system configuration

System Restore

Welcome to System Restore   ⑦ Help

You can use System Restore to undo harmful changes to
your computer and restore its settings and performance.
System Restore returns your computer to an earlier time
(called a restore point) without causing you to lose recent
work, such as saved documents, e-mail, or history and
favorites lists.

Any changes that System Restore makes to your computer
are completely reversible.

Your computer automatically creates restore points (called
system checkpoints), but you can also use System Restore
to create your own restore points. This is useful if you are
about to make a major change to your system, such as
installing a new program or changing your registry.

System Restore Settings

To begin, select the task that you want to perform:

⦿ Restore my computer to an earlier time

◯ Create a restore point

◯ Undo my last restoration

To continue, select an option, and then click Next.   Next >   Cancel

The Undo option appears only after
you've performed a restore operation

Inside Out

Make System Restore better with NTFS

Are you looking for a good reason to convert the drive that contains your Windows files from
FAT32 to NTFS? System Restore takes full advantage of the NTFS file system in two ways.
First, your backed-up files are protected from accidental deletion by NTFS permissions. The
restore files are saved in the hidden System Volume Information folder, where only the System account is authorized to access them. On FAT32 volumes, by contrast, any user can
undermine the effectiveness of System Restore by accidentally or deliberately deleting
restore points. Second, the System Restore service uses NTFS compression to minimize
the amount of space each restore point takes. This on-the-fly compression takes place in
the background, when your system is idle, so it has no deleterious effect on performance.

If you're creating a restore point, you'll have an opportunity to supply a descriptive name. Don't worry about the date and time; System Restore will add that for you.

To restore the system to a previous configuration, you must be logged on as a member of the Administrators group. Shut down all running programs and make sure that no other users are logged onto the machine (either in inactive local sessions or across the network) before proceeding. When you choose Restore My Computer To An Earlier Time and click Next, you'll see a screen similar to the following.

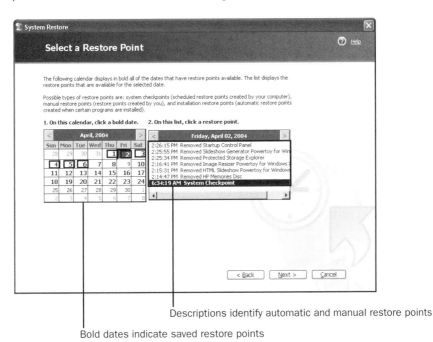

Descriptions identify automatic and manual restore points

Bold dates indicate saved restore points

On the calendar, select the date you want to restore to. Then, if multiple restore points for that date are available, select the one you want to use. (Note that the periodic restore points that are created automatically are identified as System Checkpoint.) After you make your selection and click Next, a Confirm Restore Point Selection screen appears. When you give the go-ahead, System Restore copies files and settings from the selected restore point. It then restarts your system automatically. If the results are not what you expected, run System Restore again and then select the Undo My Last Restoration option.

Chapter 39

System Restore Dos and Don'ts

You don't have to be a science fiction fan to appreciate the potential for problems with time travel. In the case of System Restore, sending your system back in time may change more than you bargained for:

- If you create a new user account and then use System Restore to roll back your system configuration to a point before the new account was created, that user will no longer be able to log on, and you will receive no warning. (The good news is that System Restore does not wipe out data files, so if the new user created any data files, they'll still be intact.)

- If you change your computer or workgroup name or domain membership and then perform a restore operation that takes you back to a time before the change was effective, Windows warns you that you may lose access to some network resources. After the restore operation, you might need to change the name of the computer or workgroup.

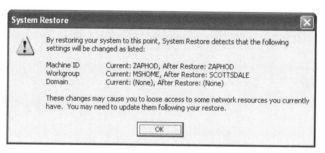

- System Restore does not uninstall programs, although it does remove executable files and DLLs. To avoid having "orphaned" program shortcuts and files, make a note of any programs that you installed after the date of the restore point you're about to roll back to. If you don't want the program anymore, uninstall it (using Add Or Remove Programs in Control Panel) before running the restore operation. If you want to continue using the program, reinstall it after the restore is complete.

- Any changes made to your system configuration using Recovery Console are not monitored by System Restore. This can produce unintended consequences if you make major changes to system files and then roll back your system configuration with System Restore.

- Although you can restore your system to a previous configuration from Safe Mode, you cannot create a new restore point in Safe Mode. As a result, you cannot undo a restore operation that you perform in Safe Mode. If possible, you should always start Windows in normal mode to perform a restore operation.

- If you upgrade from Windows Me to Windows XP or from Windows XP Home Edition to Windows XP Professional, all your existing restore points will be wiped out.

- When you install a service pack, you can save or reset restore points. If you choose the reset option, all existing restore points are lost and System Restore uses the new configuration as the baseline for future restore points.

- You cannot shut down System Restore temporarily. If you use Control Panel to stop System Restore from monitoring one or more drives, Windows deletes all saved restore points on the selected drives. If you then reenable System Restore monitoring, the deleted restore points are not recreated.

> For more details about changing the way System Restore works, see "Configuring System Restore Options," page 67.

Inside Out

Run System Restore with a script

You can use a Windows Management Instrumentation (WMI) script to operate System Restore, either locally or remotely. Such a script can be used to create restore points, list restore points, return a system to a restore point, or view the status of a restore operation. For examples of how to do these things, see "System Restore Scripting Samples" on the Microsoft site at *http://www.microsoft.com/windowsxp/pro/techinfo/productdoc/scriptsamples.asp*.

Making Repairs from the Recovery Console

What do you do if you can't start Windows in normal or Safe Mode? Don't give up hope. You may be able to get back to work by using the Recovery Console, a stripped-down command-line environment that provides a limited set of tools you can use to diagnose and repair problems. The Recovery Console is not for the faint of heart. But if you're experienced with working outside a graphical environment, it can be tremendously useful.

The chief advantage of the Recovery Console over Safe Mode is that it works even when your Windows system files are corrupted. Using the Recovery Console, you can perform any of the following tasks:

- Use, copy, rename, or replace Windows system files and folders
- Enable or disable services or devices (these changes take effect the next time you start Windows)
- Repair the file system boot sector or the Master Boot Record (MBR)
- Rebuild or repair the Windows boot menu
- Create and format drives

To start the Recovery Console from the Windows CD, follow these steps:

1 Insert the Windows CD and restart your computer. Follow your computer's prompts to start from the CD. (You may need to adjust settings in the computer's BIOS to enable the option to start from a CD.)

2 Follow the setup prompts to load the basic Windows startup files. At the Welcome To Setup screen, press R to start the Recovery Console.

3 If you have multiple options on the Windows startup menu, enter the number of the Windows installation you want to access from the Recovery Console.

Caution If you have only a single Windows installation to choose from, you might be tempted to just press Enter at this point. Don't do it. You must type the number of the Windows installation to start the Recovery Console. If you press Enter, Windows restarts. Also, resist the temptation to select the entry for another Windows version from this menu. Although the Recovery Console automatically detects Windows 2000 and Windows NT installations on multiboot systems, logging on to one of these operating systems is not recommended, because you risk damaging the earlier operating system's core files if you perform any repairs. To repair installations of Windows 2000, use the Recovery Console from that operating system version. To repair a Windows NT installation, use the Windows NT Emergency Repair Disk.

4 When prompted, type the Administrator password. If you're using the Recovery Console on a system running Windows XP Home Edition, this password is blank by default, so just press Enter.

5 At the command prompt, enter Recovery Console commands directly.

6 To quit the Recovery Console and restart the computer, use the Exit command.

Tip Add the Recovery Console to the startup menu
With a modest amount of advance preparation, you can add the Recovery Console to the Windows XP boot menu. In this configuration, the Recovery Console files are stored on the same drive that holds your Windows system files, and you don't need to hassle with BIOS options or boot CDs to recover from serious problems. You'll find step-by-step instructions for configuring this option in "Adding the Recovery Console," page 76.

Recovery Console Restrictions

Although the Recovery Console prompt looks identical to the command prompt that you're familiar with from MS-DOS or the Windows XP command interpreter (Cmd.exe), it's not the same. After logging on to the Recovery Console, your actions are severely limited. You may access files only in the following locations:

- The root directory of any volume.
- The %SystemRoot% folder and subfolders of the selected Windows XP installation. On a typical clean setup or an upgrade from Windows 98 or Windows Me, this is usually C:\Windows.
- The Recovery Console Cmdcons folder and any subfolders (if you installed the Recovery Console as a startup option).
- Files and folders on removable disks, including floppy disks, CDs, and Zip disks.

Note In addition to these security-based restrictions, technical limitations impose additional restrictions on Windows XP Professional systems that use dynamic disks. If your system is configured with one or more dynamic disks, see Knowledge Base article 227364, "Dynamic Volumes Are Not Displayed Accurately in Text-Mode Setup or Recovery Console."

Chapter 39

If the Recovery Console did allow unlimited access to files and folders on your hard disk, it would pose a serious security hole, especially on systems running Windows XP Home Edition, where the Administrator password is blank. To prevent unauthorized access, the Recovery Console imposes the following limits on your actions when you log on:

- If you try to access folders other than those described in the previous list, you will receive an "access denied" message. Specifically, you cannot read from or write to the following folders: Program Files, Documents And Settings, and disks or folders containing other Windows installations. These restrictions apply on NTFS and FAT32 volumes alike.
- Write access to removable disks is disabled. This prevents you from copying files to floppy disks and other removable media. If you try to copy a file to a removable disk, you receive an "access denied" message.
- You cannot change the local Administrator account password from the Recovery Console. In fact, if you use Windows XP Home Edition, you have to jump through several hoops to even add a password to the local Administrator account, as explained in "Securing the Administrator Account," page 251.
- No text editing tools are available in the Recovery Console.

Using Recovery Console Commands

After you've logged on to Recovery Console, you can type **help** to see a list of all available commands. Type **help** *commandname* or use the /? switch after a command name to learn its syntax. Although many of Recovery Console's commands are similar to those used in the Windows XP command interpreter (Cmd.exe) and its MS-DOS predecessor (Command.com), the Recovery Console versions of each command typically offer fewer options (switches). Also, unless you tweak the Recovery Console environment as outlined in "Customizing the Recovery Console" on page 1300, these commands do not accept wildcard specifications. Table 39-1 summarizes the commands available from the Recovery Console prompt.

Table 39-1. Recovery Console Commands

Command	Effect
Attrib	Sets or clears attributes (Read Only, Hidden, System) for a single file or folder
Batch	Executes commands from a text file
Bootcfg	Automatically scans all local disks for Windows installations and configures and repairs entries in the operating system menu (Boot.ini)
Cd or Chdir	Changes folders
Chkdsk	Checks and, if necessary, repairs or recovers a drive; marks bad sectors and recovers readable information; requires that the Autochk.exe command be located in the %SystemRoot%\System32 folder or on the Windows CD
Cls	Clears the screen
Copy	Copies a file
Del or Delete	Deletes a single file
Dir	Displays folder contents and attributes for all files in the specified folder, including hidden and system files
Disable	Disables a service or driver
Diskpart	Manages the partitions on basic disk volumes; note that this command is not the same as the one available at a normal command prompt and should never be used with dynamic disks
Enable	Enables a service or driver
Exit	Closes the Recovery Console and restarts the computer

Chapter 39

Table 39-1. **Recovery Console Commands**

Command	Effect
Expand	Extracts a file from a compressed (.cab) file on a local disk or removable media such as the Windows CD
Fixboot	Writes a new partition boot sector onto the partition you specify
Fixmbr	Repairs the Master Boot Record of the specified disk, usually the system partition
Format	Formats a primary partition, volume, or logical drive using the file system you specify
Help	Displays a list of all available commands
Listsvc	Lists all available services and drivers and their current start types
Logon	Lists all detected installations of Windows XP, Windows 2000, and Windows NT and allows you to choose which installation you want to log on to; if you type an incorrect password three times, the system restarts
Map	Lists drive letters, file system types, partition sizes, and mappings to physical devices; intended for use with basic disks only and may return inaccurate information when used with dynamic disks
Md or Mkdir	Creates a new folder or subfolder in the specified location
More	Displays a text file, pausing at each screenful; use Enter and the spacebar to scroll through a file one line at a time and one screen at a time, respectively
Rd or Rmdir	Removes a folder
Ren or Rename	Renames a file
Set	Displays or modifies Recovery Console environment variables (for details on the usage of this command, see "Customizing the Recovery Console," next page)
Systemroot	Sets the current folder to the %SystemRoot% folder of the current Windows installation
Type	Displays a text file

Chapter 39

1299

Customizing the Recovery Console

With a little advance preparation, you can overcome at least some of the Recovery Console limitations listed here when running Windows XP Professional (this technique will not work with Home Edition). Doing so requires that you use the Set command to change system variables in the Recovery Console environment. By default, the Set command is disabled. To enable it, you must change system settings using Group Policy. After logging on as an administrator, follow these steps:

1 From any command prompt, type **gpedit.msc** to open the Group Policy editor.

2 In the console tree, select Local Computer Policy\Computer Configuration\Windows Settings\Security Settings\Local Policies\Security Options.

3 In the list of policies on the right, double-click the entry for Recovery Console: Allow Floppy Copy And Access To All Drives And All Folders.

4 Select the Enabled option and then click OK.

After enabling this policy, you can start the Recovery Console, log on with the local Administrator password, and use any of the following commands to expand your capabilities. Note that the space around each equal sign is required. (To see the current settings for all four parameters, type **set** and press Enter.)

- **Set allowwildcards = true**   Allows you to use the * and ? wildcards with Recovery Console commands

- **Set allowallpaths = true**   Permits you to use the Cd command to list files and sub-folders in all folders on all local disks

- **Set allowremovablemedia = true**   Allows you to copy files from local drives to removable media

- **Set nocopyprompt = true**   Eliminates the warning message that appears when you copy one or more files that overwrite existing files using Recovery Console commands

Repairing Damaged Boot Files

The most common cause of problems with boot files is the improper use of third-party disk utilities or failed attempts to create a multiboot system. If the setup program for another operating system is incompatible with Windows XP, it might overwrite or damage essential startup files. The following are repair techniques available from the Recovery Console for common problems:

- **The Boot.ini file is corrupt or missing.**   From the Recovery Console, type **bootcfg /scan** to list all available Windows installations on all available disks. Use **bootcfg /rebuild** to automatically replace the existing Boot.ini file; use **bootcfg/add** to append a Windows installation to Boot.ini without changing existing entries.

- **Critical system files are damaged or missing.** You can restore Ntldr, Ntoskrnl.exe, Ntdetect.com, and driver files from the Recovery Console. If the file exists on the Windows CD, use the Copy command and enter the source and destination; Windows expands compressed files automatically. If the file is stored within a .cab file, such as Driver.cab, use the Expand command.

- **Another operating system replaced the Windows XP boot sector code.** Start Recovery Console from the Windows CD and use the Fixboot command to rewrite the boot sector code. Restart your computer.

Enabling and Disabling Services and Drivers

Because services operate at a privileged level alongside crucial operating system components, it's possible for a poorly written third-party service to crash your system. Likewise, buggy hardware drivers can interfere with startup, in some cases so severely that you encounter STOP errors even when attempting to start in Safe Mode. If you suspect that a hardware driver or a service such as an antivirus scanner or a remote-control utility is causing your problems and you can't start Windows even in Safe Mode, use these three Recovery Console commands to identify the offending service and enable or disable it:

- **Listsvc** Enter this command to display a complete list of all services and drivers on your system, along with their current status and any optional comments. This list is long and not exactly packed with helpful information. You might need to scroll through many screens and look carefully to identify the driver or service in question. It may help if you have documentation from the developer of the suspect driver or service that lists the names of specific driver and service files.

- **Disable** Enter this command followed by the name of the service or driver you want to stop and press Enter. The Disable command sets the start type of the service to SERVICE_DISABLED. Before doing so, it displays the current start type value of the service: SERVICE_BOOT_START, SERVICE_SYSTEM_START, SERVICE_AUTO_START, or SERVICE_DEMAND_START. Make a note of this value so that you can reenable the device or service properly if necessary.

- **Enable** If after troubleshooting you determine that the device you disabled is not causing your problem, use this command, followed by the service or device name and the start type value you noted when you disabled the service or device.

Repairing and Reinstalling Windows

When all attempts to repair your system fail, you may be able to repair your Windows XP installation using the Windows Setup program. As a last resort, you can reinstall Windows over an existing installation and hope that the new installation will recover enough of your old settings to allow you to retrieve your data files.

Chapter 39

1301

The repair option is quick and painless and typically does not adversely affect user settings. To exercise this option, start from the Windows CD as if you were going to do a clean install. It's easy to become confused during this process, because the word *repair* appears in two different places when you start your computer using the Windows CD. At the Welcome To Setup screen, do not choose the option to repair your installation using the Recovery Console. Instead, press Enter, which starts the Windows Setup program. After you accept the license agreement, Windows searches your system for existing Windows installations. When you reach the screen that lists your current Windows installation, select it from the list and press R to start the repair process. The remainder of this procedure requires the same steps as if you were performing a clean installation; when Setup finishes, your system files should be refreshed and your existing data and settings should be accessible again.

Caution Before you reinstall Windows over an existing installation, be sure to read Knowledge Base article 315341, "How to Perform an In-Place Upgrade (Reinstallation) of Windows XP." Also, be aware that if your computer came with Windows XP pre-installed and if you reinstall from the hardware vendor's CD, you are very likely to restore your system to exactly the state it was in when you received it. That's what hardware vendors' "recovery" CDs are typically designed to do. Instead of repairing your system with the vendor's recovery disc, consider using a fresh (and up-to-date) retail copy of Windows XP. For more details about reinstalling Windows on preinstalled systems, see Knowledge Base article 312369, "You May Lose Data or Program Settings After Reinstalling, Repairing, or Upgrading Windows XP."

In cases of severe disk damage or registry corruption, a repair installation will not be effective; the only alternative is to reformat the disk and install a clean copy of Windows.

Chapter 40

Troubleshooting Windows Errors

If Windows has ever suddenly and unexpectedly shut down, you've probably experienced that sinking feeling in the pit of your stomach. When Microsoft Windows XP encounters a serious problem that makes it impossible for the operating system to continue running, it shuts down immediately and displays an ominous text message whose technical details begin with the word *STOP* in capital letters. Because a STOP error typically appears in white letters on a blue background, this type of message is often referred to as a blue-screen error or the Blue Screen of Death (BSOD). Fortunately, this type of error is rare in Windows XP, but it can occur at any time, especially when you install new hardware or software. When a STOP error appears, it means that there is a serious problem that demands your immediate attention.

Windows XP includes a variety of information sources and debugging tools that you can use to identify the cause of STOP errors. Many of the tools are intended for use by developers with professional debugging tools. These topics are covered in more detail in *Microsoft Windows XP Professional Resource Kit, Second Edition* (Microsoft Press, 2003). If you know where to look, however, you can learn a lot from these error messages, and in many cases you can recover completely by using standard troubleshooting techniques.

At Home with Windows XP

All of the advice in this chapter applies equally to Windows XP Home Edition and Professional. If you use the Recovery Console to repair Windows XP Home Edition, note that the built-in Administrator account has a blank password. When you're prompted for a password, just press Enter to continue.

Decoding STOP Errors

STOP errors may look cryptic, but they often contain detailed information about the underlying cause of the problem that can enable you to diagnose and repair the condition that's causing your system to fail. STOP errors may appear under any of the following circumstances:

- **During Windows Setup**   This type of STOP error is almost always caused by a faulty device driver, a piece of hardware that is in the process of failing, or an incompatible system BIOS. You may see a STOP error during Windows Setup if you attempt a clean install on a system that uses a high-speed disk controller whose drivers are not included with the Windows XP CD. To avoid encountering this STOP error, which occurs when Windows is suddenly unable to access the disk containing temporary Setup files, you must press F6 when prompted at the beginning of Setup and provide the correct drivers.

- **At startup**   If you see a STOP message during startup on a system where Windows XP previously ran properly, the cause of the error is usually an incompatible service or device driver. If you recently installed a new software application or a new device, that is the most likely culprit.

- **While Windows is running**   This kind of STOP error can be caused by drivers, services, or defective hardware and can be difficult to diagnose. The text of the STOP error usually provides important clues.

This chapter includes a list of common STOP errors, with suggestions on how to respond to each one.

Troubleshooting

Your computer hangs on startup.

What should you do if your computer powers up properly but Windows hangs during startup? Find the Windows CD, use it to start your computer, and start the Recovery Console. To identify the driver or system file that may be responsible for the problem, modify Boot.ini. Add the /Noguiboot and /Sos switches, as explained in "Modifying Boot.ini," page 74. After restarting your computer, you'll see a listing for each driver and service as it loads. The last one in the list is the most likely culprit. You can then use Recovery Console's stripped-down command-line environment to disable a rogue service or replace a corrupted file. You'll find detailed instructions for working with Recovery Console in "Making Repairs from the Recovery Console," page 1295.

How to Read a STOP Error

The exact text of a STOP error varies, according to what caused the error. But the format is predictable, as the example in Figure 40-1 shows.

You can gather important information from the following message details:

- **Symbolic error name**   This is the message that the error returned to the operating system. It corresponds to the STOP error number that appears at the bottom of the screen. In this example, the symbolic error name is DRIVER_IRQL_NOT_LESS_OR_EQUAL.

- **Troubleshooting recommendations**   This generic text applies to all STOP errors of the specified type. Depending on the error number, you may be told to check available disk space, uninstall a piece of hardware, or remove or update recently installed drivers or software.

- **Error number and parameters**   Developers call this section *bugcheck information*. The text following the word *STOP* includes the error number (in hexadecimal notation, as indicated by the 0x at the beginning of the code) and up to four parameters that are specific to the error type.

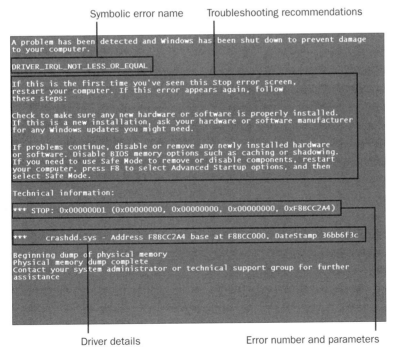

Figure 40-1.   Decoding the information in a STOP error can help you find the underlying problem and fix it.

In this example, the error code is 0x000000D1 (or just D1), which indicates a driver that tried to use an improper memory address. The parameters, in order, identify the memory address the driver tried to access; the interrupt request level, which Windows uses to determine the order in which to respond to hardware and software requests; whether the driver tried to read from or write to memory (the 0 means this was a read operation); and the memory address from which the illegal request originated.

● **Driver information** In some (but not all) STOP errors, this line lists the name of the driver associated with the error. If a file name appears here, check to see if the driver is digitally signed. If necessary, you can use Recovery Console or start Windows in Safe Mode to remove or roll back the driver.

> For more details about recovering from startup problems manually, see "Using Recovery Console Commands," page 1298. For information about removing, disabling, and rolling back drivers, see "Managing Installed Drivers," page 152.

Inside Out

The accused may not be guilty

Don't automatically assume that a file listed in the driver information section of a STOP error is corrupt or needs replacing. In some cases, such a reference means that another service or driver created a system instability that caused the listed program to crash when it performed a perfectly legal operation. For instance, in a STOP 1E error message, you might see a reference to a system file called Win32k.sys, the Multi-User Win32 Driver. In that case, the actual cause of the crash may be a "remote control" program. Start Windows in Safe Mode and try to disable the program, or use Recovery Console to remove the service.

If the system restarts immediately after a STOP error, you may not have time to note the details of the message. However, with rare exceptions, the operating system is able to capture these details in the event log. To see the gory details, follow these steps:

1 After your system restarts, open Control Panel's Administrative Tools folder and then open Event Viewer.

2 From the console pane on the left, click the System log.

3 To filter the event log so that it shows error events only, choose View, Filter; click the Filter tab; and clear all the Event Types check boxes except Error.

4 Scroll through the list of entries until you find one whose Date and Time fields reflect the date and time your computer crashed. The Source field for this error will probably be Save Dump or System Error.

5 Double-click that entry to open the event record that lists the STOP error information, as shown on the facing page.

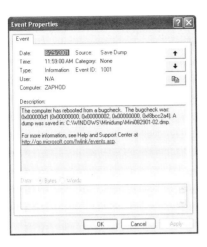

Note that the symbolic error name does not appear. However, you can use this log entry to identify the numeric error code and parameters for the error.

General Advice for Dealing with STOP Errors

If you experience a STOP error, don't panic. Instead, run through the following trouble-shooting checklist to isolate the problem and find a resolution:

- **Look for a driver name in the error details.** If the error message identifies a specific file name and you can trace that file to a driver for a specific hardware device, you may be able to solve the problem by disabling, removing, or rolling back that driver to an earlier version. The most likely offenders are network interface cards, video adapters, and disk controllers. For more details about managing driver files using Device Manager, see "Managing Installed Drivers," page 152.

- **Don't rule out hardware problems.** In many cases, software is the victim and not the cause of blue-screen errors. Damaged hard disks, defective physical RAM, and over-heated CPU chips are three common hardware failures that can result in STOP errors. If the errors seem to happen at random and the message details vary each time, there is a very good chance that you are experiencing hardware problems.

- **Ask yourself, "What's new?"** Be suspicious of newly installed hardware devices and software programs. If you added a new device recently, remove it temporarily and see whether the problem goes away. Take an especially close look at software in the categories that install services or file-system filter drivers—these hook into the core operating system files that manage the file system to perform tasks such as scanning for viruses. This category includes backup programs, multimedia applications, antivirus software, and CD-burning utilities. You may need to permanently uninstall or update the program to resolve the problem.

Chapter 40

1307

- **Search the Knowledge Base.**   Make a note of the error code and all parameters. Search the Knowledge Base using both the full and short formats. For instance, if you're experiencing a KMODE_EXCEPTION_NOT_HANDLED error, use 0x0E and 0x0000000E as your search keywords.

- **Check your system BIOS carefully.**   Is an update available from the manufacturer of the system or motherboard? STOP errors are especially common in connection with Advanced Configuration and Peripheral Interface (ACPI) machines, where flaws in the BIOS may trip up the operating system. Also, check the BIOS documentation carefully—resetting all BIOS options to their default settings can sometimes resolve an issue caused by over-tweaking.

- **Are you low on system resources?**   STOP errors are sometimes the result of a critical shortage of RAM or disk space. If you can start in Safe Mode, check the amount of physical RAM installed and look at the system and boot drives to see how much free disk space is available. You may be able to free space by running the Disk Cleanup utility, as described in "Managing Disk Space," page 1247.

- **Is a crucial system file damaged?**   To reinstall a driver, restart your computer and press F8 when prompted to start Windows in Safe Mode. To repair a damaged system file that prevents you from starting even in Safe Mode, boot from the Windows XP CD and use Recovery Console. From Recovery Console's special-purpose command prompt, the Copy command automatically expands compressed files on the fly when you copy from the CD to a local drive.

Tip   Try an alternate driver

Experienced support engineers recommend that you use the hardware driver that was made specifically for your device. However, if an unsigned, device-specific driver causes STOP errors, you might have success by using a more recent driver for a product in the same family, even if the model name is not identical. This strategy is most likely to work with printers; it is least likely to be successful with video adapters and network interface cards.

How to Troubleshoot Specific STOP Errors

The general troubleshooting steps outlined in the previous section apply to all STOP errors. Details provided by specific STOP errors, however, can help you narrow down the cause of the error and get to a solution quickly. This section lists the most common STOP error codes, with suggested troubleshooting actions and external resources for additional information.

STOP 0x0000000A or IRQL_NOT_LESS_OR_EQUAL

A kernel-mode process or driver attempted to access a memory location without authorization. This STOP error is typically caused by faulty or incompatible hardware or software. The name of the offending device driver often appears in the STOP error and can provide an important clue to solving the problem.

If the error message points to a specific device or category of devices, try removing or replacing devices in that category. If this STOP error appears during Setup, suspect an incompatible driver, system service, virus scanner, or backup program.

STOP 0x0000001E or KMODE_EXCEPTION_NOT_HANDLED

The Windows XP kernel detected an illegal or unknown processor instruction, often the result of invalid memory and access violations caused by faulty drivers or hardware devices. The error message often identifies the offending driver or device. If the error occurred immediately after installing a driver or service, try disabling or removing the new addition.

STOP 0x00000024 or NTFS_FILE_SYSTEM

A problem occurred within the NTFS file-system driver. A similar STOP error, 0x23, exists for FAT32 drives. The most likely cause is a hardware failure in a disk or disk controller. Check all physical connections to all hard disks in the system and run the Check Disk utility (Chkdsk.exe) using the instructions outlined in "Checking Disks for Errors," page 1237.

STOP 0x0000002E or DATA_BUS_ERROR

Failed or defective physical memory (including memory used in video adapters) is the most common cause of this STOP error. The error may also be the result of a corrupted hard disk or a damaged motherboard.

STOP 0x0000003F or NO_MORE_SYSTEM_PTES

Your system ran out of page table entries (PTEs). The cause of this relatively uncommon error may be an out-of-control backup program or a buggy device driver. Knowledge Base article 256004, "How to Troubleshoot 'STOP 0x0000003F' and 'STOP 0x000000D8' Error Messages in Windows 2000," (*http://support.microsoft.com/?kbid=256004*), describes modifications to the Windows registry that may resolve the problem.

STOP 0x00000050 or PAGE_FAULT_IN_NONPAGED_AREA

A hardware driver or system service requested data that was not in memory, causing an exception error. The cause may be defective physical memory or incompatible software, especially remote control and antivirus programs. If the error occurs immediately after installing a device driver or application, try to use Safe Mode to remove the driver or uninstall the program.

Chapter 40

STOP 0x00000077 or KERNEL_STACK_INPAGE_ERROR

The system attempted to read kernel data from virtual memory (the page file) and failed to find the data at the specified memory address. This STOP error can be caused by a variety of problems, including defective memory, a malfunctioning hard disk, an improperly configured disk controller or cable, corrupted data, or a virus infection.

STOP 0x00000079 or MISMATCHED_HAL

No, this message has nothing to do with Hal, the paranoid computer in the classic film *2001: A Space Odyssey*. Instead, this message identifies a mismatch between the Windows XP hardware abstraction layer (HAL) and the Windows XP system files. This error most often occurs on ACPI machines, when ACPI BIOS settings are changed unexpectedly. To disable or reenable ACPI features, reinstall Windows XP after making changes in the BIOS. For more details, read Knowledge Base article 237556, "How to Troubleshoot Windows 2000 Hardware Abstraction Layer Issues" (*http://support.microsoft.com/?kbid=237556*).

STOP 0x0000007A or KERNEL_DATA_INPAGE_ERROR

This STOP error has the same underlying cause as 0x77 errors: A page of kernel data was not found in virtual memory (the page file). This might be due to incompatible disk or controller drivers or hardware problems, such as an improperly terminated SCSI device, bad blocks on the hard disk, or a conflict with the BIOS or other firmware on a disk controller. Run the Windows XP Check Disk utility as detailed in "Checking Disks for Errors," page 1237. If the disk manufacturer has a more comprehensive disk utility, use it to do a thorough check of each physical hard disk on the system.

STOP 0x0000007B or INACCESSIBLE_BOOT_DEVICE

Windows XP was unable to locate the system partition or boot volume during the startup process. This problem may occur after repartitioning disks, adding new disks, or upgrading a disk controller and its drivers. In that case, entries in the Boot.ini file no longer point to the correct partitions. If the error occurs after upgrading the disk controller, verify that the new hardware is configured properly. Then start your system with the Windows XP CD, log on to the Recovery Console, and use the Bootcfg command to scan for available Windows installations and repair the Boot.ini file automatically.

STOP 0x0000007F or UNEXPECTED_KERNEL_MODE_TRAP

Hardware failure is the most common cause of this error. You are most likely to see this STOP error if you have defective memory chips, mismatched memory modules, a malfunctioning CPU, or a failure in your fan or power supply that causes overheating. The error is especially

Chapter 40

likely to occur on systems where the CPU has been tweaked to run past its rated speed, a process known as "overclocking." The first parameter immediately after this STOP error number identifies the specific cause of the error, as explained in Knowledge Base article 137539, "General Causes of STOP 0x0000007F Errors."

STOP 0x0000009F or DRIVER_POWER_STATE_FAILURE

A driver is currently in an inconsistent or invalid power state after shutting down, suspending to Standby or Hibernate mode, or resuming from either of those modes. This error is not limited to hardware drivers. It can also be caused by file-system filter drivers, such as those installed by antivirus programs, backup utilities, and remote control programs. The name of the offending driver file often appears in the STOP error. As a troubleshooting technique, try uninstalling unsigned hardware drivers or the software that uses the named driver. Knowledge Base article 266169, "How to Troubleshoot Problems with Standby Mode, Hibernate Mode, and Shutting Down Your Computer in Windows 2000," (*http://support.microsoft.com/ ?kbid=266169*), provides additional suggestions for resolving this type of error.

STOP 0x000000C2 or BAD_POOL_CALLER

A kernel-mode process or driver attempted to perform an illegal memory allocation. The problem can often be traced to a bug in a driver or software. It is also occasionally caused by a failure in a hardware device. You can find detailed debugging instructions for this error in Knowledge Base article 265879, "How to Debug 'Stop 0xC2' or 'Stop 0x000000C2' Error Messages."

STOP 0x000000D1 or DRIVER_IRQL_NOT_LESS_OR_EQUAL

This is one of the most common STOP errors (see Figure 40-1). The error typically occurs when a driver tries to access an improper memory address. Check for unsigned drivers, and be especially suspicious of recently installed or updated antivirus programs, disk utilities, and backup programs, which may install a faulty file-system filter driver.

STOP 0x000000D8 or DRIVER_USED_EXCESSIVE_PTES

If a poorly written driver causes your computer to request large amounts of kernel memory, you may run out of page table entries (PTEs) and see this error message. The underlying cause of the error and troubleshooting suggestions are identical to those found in the STOP 0x3F message.

STOP 0x000000EA or THREAD_STUCK_IN_DEVICE_DRIVER

You may see this error message after you install a new video adapter or an updated (and poorly written) video driver that causes the system to pause indefinitely while waiting for the video hardware. To resolve the problem, replace the video adapter or use a different video driver.

Chapter 40

STOP 0x000000ED or UNMOUNTABLE_BOOT_VOLUME

Windows XP was unable to gain access to the volume containing boot files. If you see this STOP message while attempting to upgrade a system to Windows XP, verify that you have compatible drivers for the disk controller and check the drive cabling to make sure it is configured properly. If you're using ATA-66 or ATA-100 drivers, make sure you have an 80-connector cable, not a standard 40-connector IDE cable. See the troubleshooting suggestions for STOP 0x7B errors as well. In some cases, this error will spontaneously correct itself after you restart your system.

STOP 0x000000F2 or HARDWARE_INTERRUPT_STORM

This hardware-related STOP error can be extremely frustrating to experience and even more vexing to troubleshoot. The Windows XP kernel detects an *interrupt storm* when a device fails to release an interrupt request (IRQ). This failure is usually caused by a poorly written device driver or a bug in firmware. To isolate the problem, try to determine which device is associated with the file name listed in the driver information section of the STOP message. Then use Device Manager or the System Information tool to identify other devices using the same IRQ, as described in "Viewing and Changing Resource Assignments," page 149. Remove all the devices identified as using that IRQ and add them back, one at a time, until the problem recurs.

STOP 0xC000021A or STATUS_SYSTEM_PROCESS_TERMINATED

This message indicates a serious security problem with Windows XP—a user-mode subsystem, such as Winlogon or the Client Server Runtime Subsystem (Csrss.exe), is compromised. The most common cause of this problem is a third-party program, and the solution is usually to remove that program. This error can also occur if a backup set has been partially restored, causing a mismatch in system files, or if system permissions have been incorrectly modified so that the System account no longer has permission to access system files and folders.

STOP 0xC0000221 or STATUS_IMAGE_CHECKSUM_MISMATCH

File or disk corruption problems (including a damaged page file) and faulty hardware are the most common causes of this type of STOP error. The message usually includes the name of the damaged file at the end of the symbolic error name or on a line by itself; you might be able to restore the file from the Windows XP CD using Recovery Console. Restoring the Last Known Good Configuration might also help to resolve this problem.

Customizing How Windows Handles STOP Errors

When Windows encounters a serious error that forces it to stop running, it takes the following actions:

1 The system displays a STOP message.

2 Based on the preferences defined for the current Windows installation, the system writes debugging information to the page file. When the computer restarts, this information is saved as a *crash dump file*, which can be used to debug the specific cause of an error.

3 Again based on the current preferences, the system either pauses with the STOP message on the screen or restarts when the crash dump information has been saved.

You can customize two crucial aspects of this process by defining the size of the crash dump files and specifying whether you want Windows to restart automatically after a STOP message appears. By default, Windows XP automatically restarts after a STOP message. That's the preferred strategy in response to a random, isolated STOP error. But if you're experiencing chronic STOP errors, you may have more troubleshooting success by reconfiguring Windows to halt at the STOP message and wait for you to manually restart the system. To make this change, follow these steps:

1 Open the System Properties dialog box from Control Panel. (As a shortcut, click the Start button, right-click My Computer, and choose Properties.)

2 Click the Advanced tab and then click the Settings button under the Startup And Recovery heading.

3 In the Startup And Recovery dialog box, clear the Automatically Restart check box.

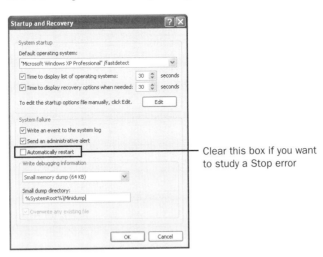

Clear this box if you want to study a Stop error

4 Click OK to make the change effective.

Chapter 40

From the same dialog box, you can also define the settings for crash dump files. By default, Windows XP saves the smallest possible amount of information in a 64 KB file. After recovering from a STOP error, the system displays the dialog box shown below. If you choose the Send Error Report option, the Small Memory Dump file is automatically sent to Microsoft.

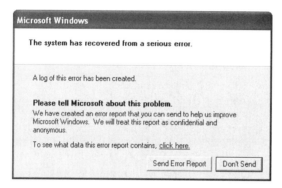

Tip Clean up mini-dump files

If you have a rash of STOP errors, mini-dump files can consume hard disk space unnecessarily. To clean the debris manually, open the %SystemRoot%\MiniDump folder and delete any files you find there. To automatically remove these files, use the Cleanup Manager options described in "Cleaning Up with Disk Cleanup," page 1248.

In most cases, the information in a Small Memory Dump file is not sufficient to thoroughly debug an error. In the case of persistent STOP errors, a Microsoft support technician may ask you to create a more thorough crash dump file. To do so, open the Startup And Recovery dialog box using the steps outlined above, and change the selection in the Write Debugging Information list to one of the following options:

- **Kernel Memory Dump**   This option includes memory allocated to kernel-mode drivers and programs, which are most likely to cause STOP errors. Because it does not include unallocated memory or memory allocated to user-mode programs, it will usually be smaller in size than the amount of RAM on your system. The exact size varies, but in general you can expect the file to be approximately one-third the size of installed physical RAM. The crash files are stored in %SystemRoot% using the file name Memory.dmp.

- **Complete Memory Dump**   This option saves the entire contents of physical memory; as a result, it will be equal in size to your installed RAM. This can cause problems on systems with large amounts of RAM installed. On a system with 1,024 MB of RAM installed, a crash dump file will use up 1 GB of disk space! The crash files are stored in %SystemRoot% using the file name Memory.dmp.

Caution Change memory dump options only when requested to do so by a support engineer and change the options back to their default settings after troubleshooting is complete.

When It's Time to Ask for Outside Help . . .

The Online Crash Analysis feature, which is new in Windows XP, allows the operating system to automatically send debugging information to Microsoft Product Support Services after a serious error occurs. This action takes place only with your permission. You can send the information anonymously or you can use your Microsoft Passport to send an acknowledged upload. In the latter case, a support technician may contact you to request more details. With luck, the technician can suggest a course of action that allows you to recover from the error.

You can upload crash reports manually, using the Online Crash Analysis Web site. After uploading a crash report, you can check the status of your issue by returning to the site.

For more details, visit *http://oca.microsoft.com*.

Chapter 40

Editing the Registry

If you've ever read anything about the registry, you've seen the warnings: Do not try this at home—really. Making changes to the registry directly, as opposed to letting your software do it for you, is hazardous. An errant edit can bring your system down. That's why Microsoft Windows is set up so that you normally don't have to get involved with the registry. When you change some detail about your system's configuration using Control Panel, Control Panel writes the necessary updates to the registry for you, and you needn't be concerned with how it happens. When you install a new piece of hardware or a new program, a myriad of registry modifications take place; again, you don't need to know the details.

But because the designers of Windows couldn't provide a user interface for every conceivable customization you might want to make, sometimes working directly with the registry is the only way to get a job done. And sometimes, even when it's not the only way, it might be the fastest way. So Microsoft Windows XP provides you with a registry editor that you should know how to use—safely. This chapter tells you how.

At Home with Windows XP

The basic structure of the registry is identical in Windows XP Home Edition and Professional. To view and edit data in either edition of Windows XP, use the Registry Editor utility, which works exactly the same way in Home Edition as in Professional, including the ability of administrators to set permissions on individual subkeys. The only material in this chapter that does not apply to Home Edition users is the information about using Group Policy to prevent unwanted modifications to the registry, because Group Policy is not included in Home Edition.

Understanding the Structure of the Registry

Before you begin browsing or editing the registry, it's good to know a bit about how this database is built. Figure 41-1 shows a portion of a system's registry, as seen through Registry Editor, the registry editor supplied with Windows XP. As shown in the figure, the registry consists of the following five *root keys*: HKey_Classes_Root, HKey_Current_User, HKey_Local_Machine, HKey_Users, and HKey_Current_Config. For simplicity's sake and typographical convenience, this book, like many others, abbreviates the root key names as HKCR, HKCU, HKLM, HKU, and HKCC, respectively.

Root keys, sometimes called *predefined keys*, contain subkeys. Registry Editor displays this structure as an outline. In Figure 41-1, for example, HKCU has been opened to show the top-level subkeys: AppEvents, Console, Control Panel, Environment, Identities, Keyboard Layout, Network, Printers, Remote, SessionInformation, Software, Unicode Program Groups, Volatile Environment, and Windows 3.1 Migration Status. A root key and its subkeys can be described as a path, like this: HKCU\Console. Root keys and their subkeys appear in Registry Editor's left pane.

R.I.P. Regedt32

Windows 2000 included two registry editors: Regedit.exe and Regedt32.exe. The functionality of Regedt32 has been incorporated into Registry Editor 5.1, the version shipped with Windows XP, and Regedt32 doesn't exist anymore. Typing **regedt32** at a Windows XP command prompt runs a 4-KB stub whose only function is to execute Regedit.exe.

In Windows 2000, Regedt32 suffered from a nonintuitive interface, but it could do a few things that the slicker-looking Regedit could not. The most important advantage of Regedt32 was that it enabled you to modify the permissions settings associated with registry keys—something that Regedit could not do. But overall, Regedit was the more versatile editor, with a Windows Explorer–style display and the ability to search for keys and values. In Windows XP, instead of using Regedit for most registry work and Regedt32 for the occasional task that Regedit can't handle, you can manage everything with a single editor. (To set permissions for a key in Regedit 5.1, right-click the key, and then choose Permissions from the shortcut menu.)

The only significant feature of Regedt32 that has not been incorporated into Registry Editor 5.1 is read-only mode. If you're accustomed to browsing the registry in Regedt32's read-only mode and don't feel comfortable without that feature, be sure to set a restore point before you begin browsing. If anything goes awry, you can use System Restore to return to the restore point.

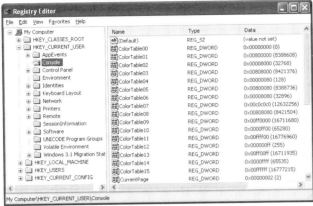

Figure 41-1.   The registry consists of five root keys, each of which contains many subkeys.

> **Note**   The registry is the work of many hands, and capitalization and word spacing are not always consistent. With readability as our goal, we have made our own capitalization decisions for this book, and our treatment of names frequently differs from what you see in Registry Editor. No matter. Capitalization is irrelevant. Spelling and spacing must be correct, however.

Subkeys, which we call *keys* for short, can contain subkeys of their own. Whether they do or not, they always contain at least one *value*. In Registry Editor, that value is known as the *default value*. Many keys have additional values. The names, data types, and data associated with values appear in Registry Editor's right pane. As Figure 41-1 shows, the HKCU\Console key has many values—ColorTable00, ColorTable01, and so on.

The default value for many keys—including HKCU\Console—is not defined. You can therefore think of an empty default value as a placeholder—a slot that could hold data but currently does not.

All values other than the default always include the following three components: name, data type, and data. As Figure 41-1 shows, the ColorTable00 value of HKCU\Console is of data type REG_DWORD. The data associated with this value (on the system used for this figure) is 0x00000000. (The prefix *0x* denotes a hexadecimal value. Registry Editor displays the decimal equivalent of hexadecimal values in parentheses after the value.)

A key with all its subkeys and values is commonly called a *hive*. The registry is stored on disk as several separate hive files. The appropriate hive files are read into memory when the operating system starts (or when a new user logs on) and assembled into the registry. You can see

Chapter 41

1319

where the hives of your system physically live by examining the values associated with HKLM\System\CurrentControlSet\Control\HiveList. Figure 41-2 shows the HiveList key for one of the systems used for this book.

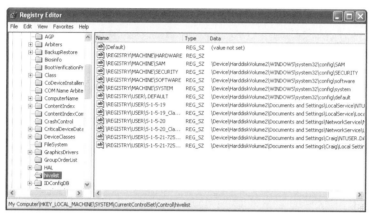

Figure 41-2. You can find the names and locations of the files that make up your registry in HKLM\System\CurrentControlSet\Control\HiveList.

Notice that one hive, \Registry\Machine\Hardware, has no associated disk file. This hive, which records your hardware configuration, is completely volatile; that is, Windows XP creates it fresh each time you turn your system on. Notice also the path specifications for the remaining hive files. Windows assigns drive letters after assembling the registry, so these paths do not specify drive letters.

If you explore the folders containing your hive files, you'll find hidden files with the extensions .log and .alt associated with each hive. The .log files are transaction files that record changes made to the associated hive. The .alt files are copies of the hive files. If a hive file is corrupted, Windows reconstitutes the registry using the associated .alt file.

Registry Data Types

The registry uses the following data types:

- **REG_SZ**   The *SZ* stands for zero-terminated string. This is a variable-length string that can contain Unicode as well as ANSI characters. When you enter or edit a REG_SZ value, Registry Editor terminates the value with a 00 byte for you. A quick scan of the registry reveals that REG_SZ is one of the most common data types and that it's often used for numeric as well as textual data. (See, for example, the values of HKCU\Control Panel\Desktop.) The default values of most keys, where defined, are of type REG_SZ.

- **REG_MULTI_SZ**   This data type contains a group of zero-terminated strings assigned to a single value.

- **REG_EXPAND_SZ**   This data type is a zero-terminated string containing an environment variable, such as %SystemRoot%. If you need to create a key containing a variable name, use this data type, not REG_SZ.

- **REG_BINARY**   As its name suggests, the REG_BINARY type contains binary data—0s and 1s.

- **REG_DWORD**   This data type is a "double word"—that is, a 32-bit numeric value. Although it can hold any integer from 0 to 2^{32}, the registry often uses it for simple Boolean values (0 or 1) because the registry lacks a Boolean data type.

- **REG_QWORD**   This data type is a "quadruple word" (64 bits) and is supported only by Windows XP 64-Bit Edition.

- **REG_LINK**   The REG_LINK data type is a pointer to another section of the registry. For example, the HKCU root key consists of REG_LINKs to a specific user's data stored under HKU. When a user logs on, HKCU is mapped to point to the appropriate user-specific information in HKU. The REG_LINK type allows programs that need information about the current user's preferences or history to get that information from a single source, HKCU, without having to know who's logged on. You can't create REG_LINK values through Registry Editor. It can be done only through the registry application programming interfaces (APIs).

- **REG_NONE**   The rare REG_NONE type is used only in unusual circumstances in which the presence or absence of a value is significant but the value's data is not.

- **REG_FULL_RESOURCE_DESCRIPTOR, REG_RESOURCE_LIST, and REG_RESOURCE_REQUIREMENTS_LIST**   These three data types provide information about the resources used or required by various components of your system.

Environment Variables

As we note in the list of registry data types, the REG_EXPAND_SZ data type is used for environment variables. These strings, which contain information about the environment for the system and for the user who's currently logged on, can save time and keystrokes when used in batch files and shortcuts and at the command line. In addition, some programs use environment variables to determine where to store user data and temporary files. To use an environment variable in a command or a dialog box, surround the variable name with percent signs; this tells Windows to look up the current value for that variable in the registry and use that value in the command or path where you entered it.

Some environment variables can save a significant number of keystrokes. For instance, typing **cd %allusersprofile%** at a command prompt switches to the All Users profile folder, where shared documents and settings are stored. In a default installation, the full path name is nearly twice as long: C:\Documents and Settings\All Users. You can also use environment variables to create shared shortcuts that work differently for each user. A shortcut that points to the %UserProfile%\My Documents folder, for instance, will always open the My Documents folder of the user who's currently logged on.

Windows XP creates a group of default system variables, including several that define the location of Windows system files. Only an administrator can change a system variable. However, any user can add, edit, or remove user variables, which are exclusive to the user who created them and can be used in scripts and batch files.

To view and edit all variables, open the System option in Control Panel, and click the Environment Variables button on the Advanced tab. Click the New button to add a variable name and value, click the Edit button to change an existing variable, or click the Delete button to remove a variable. You can also see a list of all currently defined environment variables by opening a Command Prompt window and entering the **set** command.

Avoiding Registry Mishaps

The two most important things to know about Registry Editor are that it copies your changes immediately into the registry and that it has no Undo command. Registry Editor doesn't wait for you to issue a File, Save command (it has no such command) before making changes permanent. And after you have altered some bit of registry data, the original data is gone forever—unless you remember it and restore it yourself or unless you have some form of backup that you can restore. Registry Editor is therefore a tool to be used sparingly and soberly; it should not be left open when not in use.

Backing Up Before You Edit

One relatively safe way to edit your registry is to back up the section you're interested in before you make any changes to it. If something goes wrong, you can usually use your backup file to restore the registry to the state it was in when you backed up.

Registry Editor's File, Export command lets you save all or portions of your registry in several different formats (see "Understanding Registry Editor's Export Options," on page 1323). The best format to use before editing the registry is the registry hive format. This option saves a binary image of a selected portion of the registry. You won't be able to read the resulting file (choose one of the text-file options if that's what you need to do), but if you need to restore the keys you've worked on, you can be confident that this format will do the job correctly. To export a registry hive, select a key in Registry Editor's left pane, and then choose File, Export. In the Save As Type list of the Export Registry File dialog box, choose Registry Hive Files. The resulting file will include the selected key and all its subkeys and values. Note that although an All option will appear to be available in the Export Range section of the Export Registry File dialog box, you cannot save your entire registry as a hive file.

Understanding Registry Editor's Export Options

Registry Editor can export data in four formats: Registration Files, Win9x/NT4 Registration Files, Text Files, and Registry Hive Files. You choose these options from the Save As Type list in the Export Registry File dialog box.

The Registration Files option creates a .reg file, a text file that can be read and edited in Notepad or another similar program. A .reg file can be *merged* into a Windows XP or Windows 2000 registry. When you merge a .reg file, its keys and values replace the corresponding keys and values in the registry. Using .reg files allows you to edit your registry "off line" and add your changes to the registry without even opening Registry Editor.

The Win9x/NT4 Registration Files option also generates a .reg file, but one in an older format used by earlier versions of Windows. The principal difference between the two formats is that the current format uses Unicode and the older format does not. Use the Win9x/NT4 Registration Files option only if you need to replicate a section of your registry in the registry of an older system.

The Text Files option, like the Registration Files option, creates a file that can be read in Notepad or another text editor. The principal advantage of this format is that it cannot accidentally (or intentionally) be merged into the registry. Thus it's a good way to create a record of your registry's state at a particular time. Its disadvantage, relative to the .reg-file format, is its size. Text files are considerably larger than corresponding .reg files, and they take longer to create.

The Registry Hive Files option, discussed earlier (see "Backing Up Before You Edit," on the previous page) creates a binary image of a selected portion of the registry. It's the format of choice if you want to back up before working in Registry Editor.

If you need to restore the exported hive, select the same key in Registry Editor's left pane, choose File, Import, and specify the file. You'll see a confirmation prompt letting you know that your action will overwrite (replace) the current key and all its subkeys. This is your last chance to make sure you're importing the hive into the right location, so take a moment to make sure you've selected the correct key before you click OK.

Chapter 41

> **Tip** Create hive files using the Console Registry Tool
>
> As an alternative to exporting a hive with Registry Editor's File, Export command, you can use the Save operation of the Console Registry Tool (Reg.exe). This option lets you back up a portion of the registry, as a hive file, without opening Registry Editor. For more information about the Console Registry Tool, see "Editing the Registry from the Command Line," page 1335.

Registry Editor's File menu includes Load Hive and Unload Hive commands, as well as hive file options within the Import and Export commands. Loading a hive, unlike importing one, adds the hive to the registry without replacing anything. You can perform this action only when you select either the HKLM or HKU root key. Loading a hive creates an entirely new subkey directly subordinate to one of these two root keys. The Unload Hive command becomes available only when you select a hive that you have previously loaded.

As an alternative to saving and restoring hive files, you can save and restore .reg files. This approach is fine if you're not going to add new values or subkeys to the section of the registry you're working with. If you do add data, however, importing an unedited .reg file that you saved before adding your new data will not remove the new data. It will return existing data to its former state but won't alter the data you've added.

> For more information about using .reg files, see "Using .Reg Files to Automate Registry Changes," page 1328.

Using System Restore to Save the Registry's State

The System Restore utility takes snapshots of your system's state, at prescribed time intervals or on demand, and allows you to roll your system back to an earlier state (called a *restore point*) if you experience problems. Most of the registry is included in the restore point (the keys that are not included are listed at HKLM\System\ControlSet001\BackupRestore\ KeysNotToRestore). Creating a restore point before you begin working in the registry is an excellent way to protect yourself against mishap.

> For information about using System Restore, see "Undoing Configuration Mistakes with System Restore," page 1288.

Backing Up and Restoring the System State

Backup Utility, the backup program supplied with Windows XP, includes an option to back up your system state. If you exercise this option, the utility creates copies of your registry hives on your backup medium as well as in the folder %SystemRoot%\Repair. Backing up the system state—either with Backup Utility or a comparable third-party program—should be part of your regular maintenance routine. In the event that your registry hive files become corrupt, you can use their backups to rebuild your system.

For details about using Backup Utility, see "Using the Windows XP Backup Program," page 1254.

Browsing and Editing with Registry Editor

Because of the registry's size, looking for a particular key, value, or data item can be daunting. Registry Editor's Find command (choose Edit, Find or press Ctrl+F) works in the forward direction only and does not wrap around when it gets to the end of the registry. If you're not sure where the item you need is located, select the highest level in the left pane (My Computer, if you're searching your own registry) before issuing the command. If you do have an approximate idea where the item you want is located, you can save time by starting at a node closer to (but still above) the target.

Inside Out

Search—and replace—faster with third-party tools

To put the matter kindly, Registry Editor's Find command does not set any speed records (no positive records, at any rate). Nor does it perform the kind of search-and-replace operations that are commonplace in text editors. Given the fact that registry changes take effect immediately, the absence of search-and-replace can be seen as a safety feature. If you don't take the precaution of backing up your registry before editing, you risk the possibility of carelessly replacing all instances of one string with another.

If you take reasonable precautions, however, and if you need to edit your registry more than now and then, you might want to consider using a third-party product to enhance the native capabilities of Registry Editor. "Reasonable precautions" here means backing up and avoiding unprompted search-and-replace. If you're going to replace all instances of one string with another, let the registry tool prompt you before making each replacement.

For blazingly fast search operations, we recommend 4Developers' Registry Crawler (*http://4developers.com/regc/*). Registry Crawler collects all instances of a registry search string in a results window. A single click on any of the results takes you to the exact location of the string in Registry Editor, allowing you to make a careful, manual replacement.

Registry Toolkit by Funduc Software (*http://www.funduc.com*) provides automated (prompted or unprompted) replace, as well as quick searching. Wildcards and regular expressions may be used in search operations, and replacements can be reversed with an Undo command.

Chapter 41

After you have located an item of interest, you can put it on the Favorites list to simplify a return visit. Choose Favorites, Add To Favorites, and supply a friendly name (or accept the default). If you're about to close Registry Editor and know you'll be returning to the same key the next time you open the editor, you can skip the Favorites step, because Registry Editor always remembers your last position and returns to that position in the next session.

> **Tip**   **Use the keyboard**
> Registry Editor includes a number of time-saving keyboard shortcuts. To move to the next subkey that starts with a particular letter, simply type that letter when the focus is in the left pane; in the right pane, use the same trick to jump to the next value that begins with that letter. To open a key (revealing its subkeys), press Right Arrow. To move up one level in the subkey hierarchy, press Left Arrow. To move to the top of the hierarchy (My Computer), press Home. To quickly move between the left and right panes, use the Tab key. In the right pane, press F2 to rename a value, and press Enter to open that value and edit its data. Once you get the hang of using these keyboard shortcuts, you'll find it's usually easier to zip through the subkey hierarchy with a combination of arrow keys and letter keys than it is to open outline controls with the mouse.

Changing Data

You can change the data associated with a value by double-clicking the value in Registry Editor's right pane. Registry Editor pops up an edit window appropriate for the value's data type. So, for example, suppose you have applications that think your name is Preferred Customer (a common mistake on systems that come with Windows XP pre-installed). You can set matters right by using Registry Editor's Find command to locate the data "Preferred Customer." Doing this will eventually take you to HKLM\Software\Microsoft\Windows NT\CurrentVersion. Selecting this key in the left pane and double-clicking the Registered-Owner value in the right pane causes Registry Editor to display an Edit String window (shown in Figure 41-3), in which you can replace the current data with your own name.

Figure 41-3.   When you double-click a data item in Registry Editor's right pane, the editor displays an edit window appropriate for the item's data type.

> **Tip** While you're working in the right pane, Registry Editor doesn't do much to highlight the current subkey in the left pane. The current subkey is differentiated from all the others by an open folder icon and a gray highlight, but it's not always easy to find that open folder icon at a glance. The best way to remind yourself which subkey you're working in is to look at the status bar, which always displays the full path of the current subkey. If you don't see the status bar, choose View, Status Bar.

Adding or Deleting Keys

To add a key, select the new key's parent in Registry Editor's left pane, choose Edit, New, and then choose Key from the submenu. The new key arrives as a generically named outline entry, exactly the way a new folder does in Windows Explorer. Type a new name. To delete a key, select it and then press the Delete key.

Adding or Deleting Values

To add a value, select the parent key and choose Edit, New. Choose the type of value you want to add from the submenu. Table 41-1 shows the value types for each of the five data type names as they appear on the Edit, New submenu. The value you select will appear in the right pane with a generic name. Type over the generic name, press Enter twice, enter your data, and press Enter once more. To delete a value, select it and press Delete.

Table 41-1. Menu Names for Registry Data Types

Menu Name	Registry Data Type
String Value	REG_SZ
Binary Value	REG_BINARY
DWORD Value	REG_DWORD
Multi-String Value	REG_MULTI_SZ
Expandable String Value	REG_EXPAND_SZ

Monitoring Registry Changes

Sometimes it can be useful to monitor the changes that take place in your registry—particularly the changes that occur as the result of installing a new program or device. Windows XP does not provide a registry monitoring tool, unfortunately. Using native Windows tools, the best you can do is employ the venerable Command Prompt program

Chapter 41

Fc.exe to compare registry export files that you create before and after an important registry change. Export a .txt file or .reg file from the branch of the registry that you expect to change (or the entire registry if you're not sure), install the program or driver (or do whatever it is whose registry effects you want to monitor), repeat the export process (using a different file name), and then, at a command prompt, type

```
fc /u before.reg after.reg > regcomp.txt
```

(Substitute the actual names of your snapshot files for *before.reg* and *after.reg*.)

The /U switch, which tells Fc to use Unicode, is necessary because .reg files use Unicode. The > symbol saves Fc's output to a text file, which you can then inspect in Notepad or another text editor.

If that process seems like too much work (it certainly does to us), take a look at Active Registry Monitor, a product by SmartLine Software that is available at *http://www.protect-me.com/arm*. Active Registry Monitor lets you create any number of before-and-after snapshots of your registry and highlights all differences between any two snapshots.

To track registry changes in real time, we recommend Regmon (*http://www.sysinternals.com/ntw2k/source/regmon.shtml*), developed by Mark Russinovich and Bryce Cogswell. Regmon can tell you exactly which processes have read or written to your registry and when each such operation has occurred. Filtering commands let you restrict the program's output to particular sections of the registry or to particular kinds of operations. For example, if you expect a program to be making changes to keys within HKCU\Software, you can limit Registry Monitor's output to writes within that key.

Using .Reg Files to Automate Registry Changes

The .reg files created by Registry Editor's File, Export command are plain text, suitable for reading and editing in Notepad or any similar editor. Therefore, they provide an alternative method for editing your registry. You can export a section of the registry, change it offline, and then merge it back into the registry. Or you can add new keys, values, and data to the registry by creating a .reg file from scratch and merging it. A .reg file is particularly useful if you need to make the same changes to the registry of several different computers. You can make and test your changes on one machine, save the relevant part of the registry as a .reg file, and then transport the file to the other machines that require it.

Figure 41-4 shows a portion of a .reg file. In this case, the file was exported from the HKCU\Software\Microsoft\Windows\CurrentVersion\Explorer\Advanced key, shown in Figure 41-5.

Editing the Registry

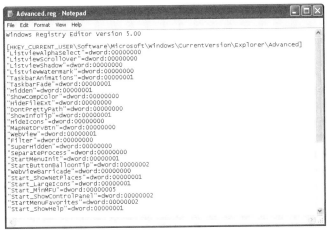

Figure 41-4. A .reg file is a plain-text file suitable for offline editing. This .reg file was exported from the key shown in Figure 41-5.

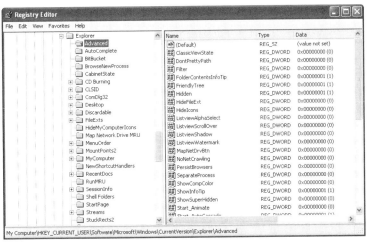

Figure 41-5. This key's name, values, and data are recorded in the .reg file shown in Figure 41-4.

Chapter 41

1329

Identifying the Elements of a .Reg File

As you review the examples shown in the two figures, note the following:

- **Header line**   The file begins with the line *Windows Registry Editor Version 5.00.* When you merge a .reg file into the registry, Registry Editor uses this line to verify that the file contains registry data. Version 5 (the version shipped with Windows XP) generates Unicode text files. If you want to share registry data with a system running Windows NT or Windows 95/98/Me, choose the Win9x/NT4 Registration Files option from the Save As Type field in Registry Editor's Export Registry File dialog box. Otherwise, the Windows 95/98/Me or Windows NT version of Registry Editor will be unable to recognize the file's Unicode characters. (A Windows 2000 registry will be able to read the Unicode file, however.) To create a .reg file that's suitable for import into Windows 95/98/Me or Windows NT 4 from scratch, use the header *REGEDIT4* instead of *Windows Registry Editor Version 5.00.*

- **Key names**   Key names are delimited by brackets and must include the full path from root key to the current subkey. The root key name must not be abbreviated. (Don't use HKCU, for example.) Figure 41-4 shows only one key name, but you can have as many as you please.

- **The default value**   Undefined default values do not appear in .reg files. Defined default values are identified by the special character @. Thus, a key whose default REG_SZ value was defined as MyApp would appear in a .reg file this way:

  `"@"="MyApp"`

- **Value names**   Value names must be enclosed in quotation marks, whether or not they include space characters. Follow the value name with an equal sign. Notice that the value names shown in Figure 41-4 do not appear in the same order as in Figure 41-5. The .reg file displays values in the order they appear in the registry. Registry Editor, however, sorts them for your editing and browsing convenience. If you're creating a .reg file from scratch, the value order is insignificant.

- **Data types**   REG_SZ values don't get a data type identifier or a colon. The data directly follows the equal sign. Other data types are identified as follows:

Data Type	Identifier
REG_DWORD	dword
REG_BINARY	hex
REG_EXPAND_SZ	hex(2)
REG_MULTI_SZ	hex(7)
REG_RESOURCE_LIST	hex(8)
REG_FULL_RESOURCE_DESCRIPTOR	hex(9)
REG_RESOURCE_REQUIREMENTS_LIST	hex(a)
REG_NONE	hex(0)

A colon separates the identifier from the data. Thus, for example, a REG_DWORD value of 00000000 looks like this:

```
"Keyname"=dword:00000000
```

- **REG_SZ values**   Ordinary string values must be enclosed in quotation marks. A backslash character within a string must be written as two backslashes. Thus, for example, the path D:\Lotus\123\Addins is written like this:

```
"D:\\lotus\\123\\addins\\"
```

- **REG_DWORD values**   DWORD values are written as eight hexadecimal digits, without spaces or commas. Do not use the *0x* prefix.

- **All other data types**   All other data types, including REG_EXPAND_SZ and REG_MULTI_SZ, appear as comma-delimited lists of hexadecimal bytes (two hex digits, a comma, two more hex digits, and so on). The following is an example of a REG_MULTI_SZ value:

```
"Addins"=hex(7):64,00,3a,00,5c,00,6c,00,6f,00,74,00,00,75,00,73,00,5c,00,
\31,00,32,00,33,00,5c,00,61,00,64,00,64,00,69,00,6e,00,73,00,5c,00,
\64,00,71,00,61,00,75,00,69,00,2e,00,31,00,32,00,61,00,00,00,00,00,00,00
```

- **Line-continuation characters**   You can use the backslash as a line-continuation character. The REG_MULTI_SZ value shown above, for example, is all one stream of bytes. We've added backslashes and broken the lines for readability, and you can do the same in your .reg files.

- **Line spacing**   You can add blank lines for readability. Registry Editor ignores them.

- **Comments**   To add a comment line to a .reg file, begin the line with a semicolon.

Using a .Reg File to Delete Registry Data

.Reg files are most commonly used to modify existing registry data or add new data. But you can also use them to delete existing values and keys.

To delete an existing value, specify a hyphen character as the value's data. For example, to use a .reg file to remove the value ThumbnailSize from the key HKCU\Software\Microsoft\Windows\CurrentVersion\Explorer, add the following lines to the .reg file:

```
[HKEY_CURRENT_USER\Software\Microsoft\Windows\CurrentVersion\Explorer]
"ThumbnailSize"=-
```

To delete an existing key with all its values and data, insert a hyphen in front of the key name (inside the left bracket). For example, to use a .reg file to remove the key HKCR\.xyz\shell and all its values, add the following to the .reg file:

```
[-HKCR\.xyz\shell]
```

Merging a .Reg File into the Registry

To merge a .reg file into the registry from within Registry Editor, choose File, Import. Registry Editor adds the imported data under the appropriate key names, overwriting existing values where necessary.

The default action for a .reg file is Merge—meaning merge with the registry. Therefore, you can merge a file into the registry by simply double-clicking it in Windows Explorer and answering the confirmation prompt.

Caution Because the default action for a .reg file is to merge it into the registry, if you want to edit the file, *don't* double-click it. Instead, right-click the file and choose Edit from the shortcut menu. (If you accidentally double-click, answer No to the confirmation prompt.)

Working with a Remote Computer's Registry

You can use Registry Editor to connect to the registry of another computer on your network. Choose File, Connect Network Registry, and then fill out the ensuing dialog box with the name of the computer to which you want to connect. The remote computer's name will appear as a top-level entry in Registry Editor's left pane, with its HKLM and HKU keys listed below, as shown in Figure 41-6.

Note To make changes to the remote computer's registry, you must be logged on as an administrator or a member of the Administrators group on both your computer and the remote computer.

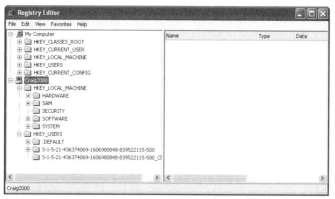

Figure 41-6. With appropriate permissions, you can use Registry Editor to work with a remote computer's registry as well as your own.

Changing Registry Key Permissions

By default, administrators and the System account have full control over all registry keys. The creator/owner of a particular key has full control over that key. (For example, a user typically has full control over all subkeys of HKCU while that user is logged on.) In other registry contexts, a user's default permissions allow read access but nothing more. If you attempt to change a registry key for which you have read access only, Registry Editor presents the appropriate editing dialog box but rejects your edit.

You can prevent changes to an individual registry key and its subkeys (but not to individual values) by editing the permissions for that key. Registry permissions work the same way as permissions assigned to files and folders on an NTFS drive; for each account or group, you can allow full control, allow read access, deny access to the key, or set special permissions. To change permissions for a key, right-click it, and then choose Permissions from the shortcut menu. The Permissions dialog box, shown in Figure 41-7, closely resembles the Security dialog boxes in Windows Explorer when Simple File Sharing is disabled.

Figure 41-7. In most contexts, administrators have full control over data stored in the registry.

Chapter 41

Inside Out

Use the restricted SID to test a suspicious program

Compare the permissions assigned to a registry key with those available to files and folders, and you will notice one significant difference. In the Group Or User Names box for the HKEY_LOCAL_MACHINE, HKEY_CURRENT_USER, and HKEY_USERS keys, you'll find an entry called RESTRICTED. On all these keys (and their subkeys), the Restricted SID is limited to Read permissions.

This security feature, available in both editions of Windows XP, is designed to protect you from programs that you don't fully trust. To take advantage of this protection, launch a program by using the Run As command (right-click the icon for a program or shortcut and choose Run As from the shortcut menu). If you choose to run the program using the credentials of the current user, the Protect My Computer And Data From Unauthorized Program Activity check box will be selected by default.

Leaving this option selected runs the program using your credentials but adds the Restricted token, thereby preventing the program from making any changes to the registry. Thus you can safely run the program and see whether it generates any error messages or displays any unusual behavior. Because programs' normal (and desired) behavior often entails changes to the registry, this is not an option you want to use with programs you do trust. You'll also want to avoid using this option with programs designed to install software; setup programs are almost always designed to make changes to the registry and will invariably fail when given the permissions assigned to the Restricted SID.

On a shared computer running Windows XP Professional, you might decide that certain users should be denied all access to registry editing tools. To enforce the ban, you can use

Group Policy, as described in Appendix F, "Group Policy." From the Group Policy console, open User Configuration\Administrative Templates\System. Double-click the Prevent Access To Registry Editing Tools setting, and change it to Enabled. Unfortunately, this solution cannot be applied easily to a single user: It locks out all users—you included. To lock out a particular user only, follow these steps (carefully!):

1 If the user whose access you want to disable has a limited account, change it to an administrator's account. (You must have administrative rights to perform this change.) Then log on using that user's credentials.

2 In Registry Editor, navigate to HKCU\Software\Microsoft\Windows \CurrentVersion\Policies.

3 Select the System subkey. If this key does not exist, create it.

4 Create a new DWORD value named DisableRegistryTools and set it to 1.

This user will no longer be able to run Registry Editor or merge a .reg file into the registry. To undo the change and re-enable this user to use Registry Editor, follow these steps:

1 Log on using the credentials of the locked-out user and create a shortcut with Regedit.exe as the target.

2 Right-click the shortcut and choose Run As. Supply the credentials of a different account in the Administrators group.

3 Browse to HKLM\Software\Microsoft\Windows NT\CurrentVersion\ProfileList.

4 Select each SID under this key and look at the value ProfileImagePath. At the end of this string is the name of the user. Find the SID that matches the user whose access you're trying to restore.

5 Select the key HKU\[SID]\Software\Microsoft\Windows\CurrentVersion\Policies \System, where [SID] is the SID that you identified in the previous step.

6 Change the value for DisableRegistryTools to 0 and close Registry Editor.

Editing the Registry from the Command Line

The Console Registry Tool for Windows (Reg.exe), installed by default in all versions of Windows XP, enables you to perform registry operations without using Registry Editor. By incorporating Reg.exe commands in batch files or scripts, you can automate registry activities, as well as take conditional actions based on the state of a local or remote registry. For example, you can query a registry value and then edit that value (or take another action) if the data meets some criterion. Virtually the entire feature set of Registry Editor is available in Reg.exe (one exception: the Export operation in Reg.exe exports Unicode .reg files only). And you can do at least one thing in Reg.exe that's impossible to do in Registry Editor: Change the data type of a key's default value. (For an example of how this can be useful, see "Including Environment Variables in Command Strings," page 688.)

For syntax information about the Console Registry Tool, open a Command Prompt window and type **reg /?** (or simply **reg**). As you'll see, the tool's basic syntax is

```
reg operation [parameter list]
```

where *operation* is one of the eleven items listed in Table 41-2, and *parameter list* is one or more items (the name of a subkey or value, for example) pertinent to the specified operation. You can get additional syntax details about an operation by typing **reg *operation* /?**. For example, to learn more about how to use the Query operation, type **reg query /?**.

Table 41-2. Console Registry Tool Operations

Operation	Effect
Add	Adds a key, value, or data item
Compare	Compares one value with another or all values under a particular key with all values under another key
Copy	Copies a value or key from one location in the registry to another
Delete	Deletes a key or value
Export	Exports a key as a Unicode .reg file
Import	Imports a .reg file (to the local registry only)
Load	Loads a hive file to a specified new key
Query	Returns the data associated with a specified value or with all values of a specified key
Restore	Loads a hive file into an existing key, overwriting that key
Save	Creates a hive file
Unload	Unloads a hive file

Some guidelines to note about Reg.exe's syntax:

- Reg.exe requires that you abbreviate the names of root keys. Use HKLM, for example, not HKey_Local_Machine.
- If a key or value name includes spaces, enclose the name within quotation marks.
- If you're incorporating a Reg.exe command in a batch file and that command includes an environment variable, enclose the variable name within double percent signs, not single percent signs. Otherwise, the command interpreter will expand the variable name before passing it to Reg.exe.

All Reg.exe operations issue Errorlevel values that can be tested in batch programs. For all operations except Compare, these values are 0 if the operation is successful and 1 if unsuccessful. Compare returns 0 if the operation is successful and all compared values are identical, 1 if the operation is unsuccessful, or 2 if the operation is successful and there are differences in the compared values. For more information about batch programs, see "Using Batch Commands," page 607.

Appendixes

Appendix A

Windows Versions at a Glance: Professional, Home Edition, and More

Since its introduction in 2001, the Microsoft Windows XP family has doubled in size. Initially, your choices were limited to two alternatives: Windows XP Home Edition and Windows XP Professional. In 2002, Windows XP Tablet PC Edition and Windows XP Media Center Edition joined the lineup, and both of these late editions have been updated significantly in Windows XP Service Pack 2. To understand the differences between the four editions of Microsoft Windows XP, just remember these facts:

- Windows XP Professional contains everything included in Windows XP Home Edition and more.
- Windows XP Tablet PC Edition and Windows XP Media Center Edition contain everything included in Windows XP Professional, along with additional special features that work only with specific hardware devices.
- Both Windows XP Home Edition and Windows XP Professional are sold as retail products, which are packaged in shrink-wrapped boxes with a CD, and in OEM versions, which are available only with a new computer or other hardware and may or may not include a CD.
- Windows XP Tablet PC Edition and Windows XP Media Center Edition are sold only with new computers that meet the specifications for those operating systems.

Throughout this book—in the "At Home with Windows XP" sidebars that appear at the beginning of each chapter and elsewhere—we point out the features that are unavailable in Home Edition. In some cases, we provide a hidden work-around to obtain a Professional feature in Home Edition (for example, editing the registry instead of using Group Policy). But in fact, for computers in a home or small business, the differences between those two editions are few.

The operating system kernel is identical in all editions. The Web browser works the same, as do all the file and folder management tools and techniques in Windows Explorer. Some default settings are different, depending on the edition in use; for instance, the taskbar is locked by default in Windows XP Home Edition but not in Professional. Regardless of which edition you use, you'll find most of the same system management utilities and troubleshooting tools, and there's no difference in multimedia-oriented accessories such as Windows Media Player or Windows Movie Maker.

To discover the true differences between Windows XP Home Edition and Professional, you need to dig a little deeper. As Table A-1 shows, most of the differences are obvious only when you use specialized hardware or try to access advanced security and networking features and capabilities. (Note that all features described in this table are also available in Windows XP Tablet PC Edition and Windows XP Media Center Edition, which are based on Windows XP Professional.)

If you consider yourself a power user, we predict you'll prefer Windows XP Professional (or one of its variants). But that doesn't mean you need to upgrade every machine on your network. All editions of Windows XP coexist happily on a peer-to-peer network and, for that matter, get along well with earlier Windows versions and even with computers running other operating systems. (If your network is set up as a domain using Windows 2000 Server or a member of the Windows Server 2003 family, however, you must use Windows XP Professional to join the domain.)

Table A-1. Key Features Available Only in Windows XP Professional

Feature	Description
Support for multiple processors	Windows XP Professional supports symmetric multiprocessor (SMP) designs that employ up to two CPUs. If you install Windows XP Home Edition on an SMP system, it will not use the second processor.
Support for 64-bit CPUs	Systems built around a 64-bit Intel Itanium, AMD Athlon, or AMD Opteron processor must use a 64-bit version of Windows XP Professional.
Advanced security features	Several sophisticated security capabilities are specific to Windows XP Professional, including support for Encrypting File System and Internet Protocol Security (IPSec), as well as the ability to assign complex access controls to files.
Automated System Recovery	The Backup program in Windows XP Professional includes tools that let you easily rebuild a system from scratch in the event of a catastrophic failure.
Internet Information Services	Windows XP Professional allows you to set up a personal Web server using Internet Information Services (IIS) 5; you must install third-party software to use Windows XP Home Edition as a Web server.

Table A-1. Key Features Available Only in Windows XP Professional

Feature	Description
Remote Desktop Connection	With this feature, you can configure a Windows XP Professional machine to allow remote access, either across a local area network or over the Internet. The client machine can be running any 32-bit or 64-bit version of Windows, including Windows 95/98/Me, Windows 2000, Windows Server 2003, or any version of Windows XP. You cannot make a remote connection to a system running Windows XP Home Edition (although it does include the similar Remote Assistance feature, which allows a remote user to share the desktop for support and training purposes).
Offline files	The offline files feature lets you open and edit network files from a computer running Windows XP Professional, even when that computer isn't connected to the network. When you reconnect, Windows synchronizes your offline files with their network versions.
Domain membership	On a corporate network, Windows XP Professional can join a domain and take advantage of domain-based management features such as group policies and roaming profiles. A system running Windows XP Home Edition can access domain resources such as printers and servers, but it does not exist as an object in the domain.
Dynamic disks	Windows XP Professional allows you to create disk volumes that span multiple hard drives; this capability allows you to increase the storage capacity and performance of drives. Windows XP Home Edition supports only basic volumes, which follow the same basic partitioning rules as disk structures created in Windows 95/98 and Windows Me.
System administration	Windows XP Professional includes a number of management tools and utilities that let you customize your system and lock it down in ways that cannot be done in Home Edition. Foremost of these tools is Group Policy, which includes myriad settings for controlling the way your system is used. Windows XP Professional also includes support for security templates, which let you apply an assortment of security settings to your own computer and to others on your network. Additionally, a handful of Microsoft Management Console snap-ins and command-line utilities are specific to Professional.

Working with the Command Prompt

Microsoft Windows XP allows you to enter commands, run batch programs, and run applications by typing commands at the command prompt. If you're accustomed to performing administrative tasks at the command line, you don't need to change your ways in Windows XP. You can open multiple Command Prompt sessions, each session protected from any failures that might occur in other sessions.

Starting and Ending a Command Prompt Session

To get to the command prompt, do any of the following:

- Choose Start, All Programs, Accessories, Command Prompt.
- Choose Start, Run, and type **cmd**, with or without command-line arguments.
- Double-click the Cmd icon in your %SystemRoot%\System32 folder.
- Double-click any shortcut for Cmd.exe.

You can open as many Command Prompt windows as you like. With each additional window, you start another Command Prompt session. For example, you might want to open two Command Prompt windows to see two directories in side-by-side windows. To open another Command Prompt window, type **start** or **start cmd** at the command prompt. (These commands produce the same result. If you don't type a program name after typing **start**, Windows assumes that you want to start Cmd.exe.)

At Home with Windows XP

The Command Prompt window works identically in Windows XP Home Edition and Windows XP Professional. The only disadvantage for Home Edition users is that the Help And Support Center in Windows XP Professional includes more detailed information about command-line utilities.

> **Tip** **Start a command-line program with AutoRun**
>
> By setting a registry value, you can make a particular application, command, batch file, or script run any time Command Prompt starts. For information about this feature, see "Using AutoRun to Execute Commands When Command Prompt Starts," page 1346.

When the Command Prompt window is active, you can end a Command Prompt session in any of the following ways:

- Type **exit** at the command prompt.
- Click the Close button.
- Click the Control menu icon and choose Close.
- Double-click the Control menu icon.

If you are running a character-based program in the Command Prompt window, you should use the program's normal exit command to quit the program before attempting to close the window and end the Command Prompt session; otherwise, it's possible that you'll lose unsaved data. However, if you are sure that the program doesn't have any unsaved files, you can safely and quickly close it using one of the last three methods in the preceding list. If a program is running, a dialog box appears asking whether or not you really want to terminate the program.

Starting Command Prompt at a Particular Folder

You can add a shortcut menu command to a folder file type that will allow you to right-click any folder in Windows Explorer and start a Command Prompt session focused on that folder.

 The companion CD includes a file named Cmdhere.inf, a setup file that automates the process described below. To add a CMD Prompt Here command to the folder context menu, right-click Cmdhere.inf and choose Install.

The easiest way to add this capability is to use the Cmdhere.inf file on the companion CD or to install the Open Command Window Here PowerToy, available as an unsupported download from Microsoft. (For details about this and other Windows XP PowerToys, visit *http://www.microsoft.com/windowsxp/pro/downloads/powertoys.asp*.) You can also add this functionality manually, by using the following procedure to edit the registry:

1 In Notepad or another plain-text editor, create a file with the following data:

```
Windows Registry Editor Version 5.00
[HKEY_CLASSES_ROOT\Folder\shell\Cmd Here]

@="CMD &Prompt Here"
[HKEY_CLASSES_ROOT\Folder\shell\Cmd Here\command]
@="cmd.exe /k pushd %L"
```

Appendix B

2 Save the file, using the extension .reg. (For example, save the file as Cmdhere.reg.)

3 Double-click the new .reg file, and click Yes at the prompt to add the information to the registry.

Inside Out

Cmd.exe vs. Command.com

Cmd.exe is the Windows XP command processor. Command.com, the 16-bit command processor of MS-DOS days, is still supported, but unless you have a legacy application that requires it, you should use Cmd.exe. You can run external MS-DOS commands, batch files, and other executables with either processor, but Cmd includes a few internal commands not available in Command.com, and some of the internal commands common to both have additional options in Cmd. Only Cmd understands long file names, and most of the command-line syntax, described later in this appendix, is available only with Cmd.

These steps create a new command that appears on the shortcut menu whenever you right-click a folder in Windows Explorer. Choosing this command opens a new Command Prompt session, with the selected folder current.

Starting Command Prompt and Running a Command

The /C and /K command-line arguments allow you to start a Command Prompt session and run a command—an MS-DOS command or a batch file, for example. The difference between the two is that Cmd /C *commandstring* terminates the Command Prompt session as soon as *commandstring* has finished executing, whereas Cmd /K *commandstring* keeps the Command Prompt session open after *commandstring* has finished. Note the following:

- You must include either /C or /K if you want to specify a command string as an argument to Cmd. If you type **cmd** *commandstring*, the command processor simply ignores *commandstring*.

- While *commandstring* is executing, you can't interact with the command processor. To run a command and keep the Command Prompt window interactive, use the Start command. For example, to run Mybatch.bat and continue issuing MS-DOS commands while the batch file is running, type **cmd /k start mybatch.bat**.

- If you include other command-line arguments along with /C or /K, the /C or /K must be the last argument before *commandstring*.

For more information about using Command Prompt's command-line syntax, see "Using Cmd's Command-Line Syntax," page 1349.

Cmd.exe and Other Command Prompts

Cmd.exe, the application whose name is Command Prompt, is only one of several forms of command prompts available in Windows XP. Others include the Run command on the Start menu, the Address toolbar, the Address bar in Windows Explorer, and the Address bar in Microsoft Internet Explorer. In many ways, these command prompts function alike. You can start a Windows-based application from any of them, for example. (If you start from Internet Explorer, you need to include an explicit path specification, or Internet Explorer will try to find a URL that matches your command string.) What's exceptional about Cmd.exe is that it allows you to execute internal MS-DOS commands (that is, commands that are not stored in discrete .exe files).

Using AutoRun to Execute Commands When Command Prompt Starts

Command Prompt's equivalent to the old MS-DOS Autoexec batch mechanism is a feature called AutoRun. By default, Command Prompt executes on startup whatever it finds in the following two registry values:

- The AutoRun value in HKLM\Software\Microsoft\Command Processor
- The AutoRun value in HKCU\Software\Microsoft\Command Processor

The AutoRun value in HKLM affects all user accounts on the current machine. The AutoRun value in HKCU affects only the current user account. If both values are present, both are executed—HKLM before HKCU.

Both AutoRun values are of data type REG_SZ, which means they can contain a single string. (You can enter a multi-string value, but Windows XP ignores all but the first string.) To execute a sequence of separate Command Prompt statements, therefore, you must use command symbols or store the sequence as a batch program, and then use AutoRun to call the batch program.

To specify an AutoRun value, open a registry editor and navigate to the Command Processor key in either HKLM or HKCU. Create a new string value there, and name it AutoRun. Then specify your command string as the data for AutoRun, exactly as you would type it at the command prompt.

To disable AutoRun commands for a particular Command Prompt session, start Command Prompt with /D. For more about Command Prompt's command-line syntax, see "Using Cmd's Command-Line Syntax," page 1349.

Using Commands

In most respects, entering commands or running programs at the Windows XP command prompt is the same as using the command prompt of any other operating system—MS-DOS, OS/2, UNIX. If you've used one command prompt, you've used them all. Every operating system has a command to delete files, another to display lists of files, another to copy files, and so on. The names and details might differ, but it's the same cast of characters.

The commands and features available at the Windows XP command prompt most closely resemble those of MS-DOS 5—with some important enhancements and additions.

Appendix B

> **Tip**   Type /? for help
> You can get help on any Command Prompt command by typing its name followed by /?. For example, to see a list and explanation of the command-line switches for the Dir command, type **dir /?**. Alternatively, type the word **help** followed by the command name—for example, **help dir**. For help with network-related commands, precede your help request with **net**. For example, type **net view /?** or **net help view** for information about the Net View command (with the Net commands, **net help** *command* provides more detailed help than **net** *command* **/?**). You can also type **help** with no arguments to get a list of the internal commands and system utilities provided with Windows XP.

Starting Programs

You can start all kinds of programs at the command prompt—programs for Windows XP, earlier versions of Windows, or MS-DOS—so you don't need to know a program's origin or type to run it. If it's on your disk, simply type its name (and path, if needed) followed by any parameters. It should run with no problem.

If you're starting a character-based program, it runs in the Command Prompt window. When you terminate the application, the command prompt returns. If you start a Windows-based program, it appears in its own window.

In early versions of Windows NT, if you ran a Windows-based program from Command Prompt, the Command Prompt session remained inaccessible until the Windows-based program ended. To continue using Command Prompt after launching a Windows-based program, you had to launch the program with the Start command. That behavior has changed. In Windows XP (and in Windows 2000), the Command Prompt session remains accessible by default. If you prefer the old behavior, launch your program with the Start command, using the /Wait switch:

```
start /wait myprog.exe
```

The /Wait switch is useful only if you need the old behavior for some reason. The Start command has other options that are more useful, however. For instance, for Windows-based programs, you can use /Min or /Max to open a program in a minimized or maximized window. For character-based programs, you can enter (in quotation marks) the title that you want to appear on the program window. Place any parameters or switches that you use with the Start command *before* the name of the program or command you want to start. Anything after the program name is passed to the program as a command-line parameter and is ignored by Start.

For more information about the Start command, type **start /?** at the command prompt.

Using Command Extensions

Command extensions are changes or additions to the following internal commands: Del, Erase, Color, Cd, Chdir, Md, Mkdir, Prompt, Pushd, Popd, Set, Setlocal, Endlocal, If, For, Call, Shift, Goto, Start, Assoc, and Ftype. For example, with command extensions enabled, you can use Cd or Chdir to switch to a folder whose name includes space characters, without enclosing the path specification in quotation marks. For details about a particular command's extensions, type the command name followed by /?. (You can also type **help**, followed by the command name.)

Command extensions are available only in Cmd.exe, not in Command.com, and are enabled by default. Set the DWORD value EnableExtensions in HKLM\Software\Microsoft\Command Processor to 0 to disable them for all user accounts at the current machine. Set EnableExtensions in HKCU\Software\Microsoft\Command Processor to 0 to disable them for the current user account. Start Command Prompt with /E:off or /E:on to disable or enable command extensions for the current session, regardless of the registry settings.

Using File-Name and Folder-Name Completion

Command Prompt offers an invaluable file-name and folder-name completion feature that can save you the trouble of typing long paths or file names. If you start typing a command string and then press Tab (the default *completion character*), Command Prompt proposes the next file or folder name that's consistent with what you've typed so far. For example, to switch to a folder that starts with the letter Q, you can type **cd q** and press the folder-name completion character as many times as necessary until the folder you want appears.

By default, the completion character for both file names and folder names is the Tab key. You can select a different completion character by using Tweak UI (part of the Windows XP PowerToys collection, described in "Customizing Windows XP with Tweak UI," page 501). To make this change manually, modify the registry values of HKCU\Software\Microsoft\Command Processor\CompletionChar and HKCU\Software\Microsoft\Command Processor\PathCompletionChar. These DWORD values specify the file and folder completion characters, respectively, for the current user. (To change the settings for all users, modify the same keys in HKLM.) If you decide to experiment with these registry settings, keep in mind the following: If CompletionChar is defined and PathCompletionChar is either absent or set to the hexadecimal value 0x40, the CompletionChar setting works for both file completion and folder completion. In all cases, the completion characters should be specified as hexadecimal values—for example, 0x9 for Tab, 0x4 for Ctrl+D, 0x6 for Ctrl+F, 0xC for Ctrl+L, and so on.

Settings made via HKLM are added to those made via HKCU. In other words, you can set completion characters for all users via HKLM, and individual users can add their own completion characters via HKCU.

You can also override the registry settings for an individual Command Prompt session by starting the session with Cmd /F:on or Cmd /F:off. Cmd /F:on starts a Command Prompt session with Ctrl+D as the path-completion character and Ctrl+F as the file-completion character, disabling the completion characters set in the registry. Cmd /F:off starts a Command Prompt session with no completion characters, regardless of your registry settings. Cmd /F:on and Cmd /F:off both disable the Tab key as a completion character.

Tip Use wildcards for file-name and folder-name completion

Command Prompt recognizes wildcards in file and path specifications. Typing **cd pro***, for example, might take you to your Program Files folder (depending, of course, on where you are when you type it). Because you can include multiple wildcards in a string, you can even create formulations such as cd pro*\com*\mic* to get to Program Files\Common Files\Microsoft Shared.

Using Cmd's Command-Line Syntax

The complete command-line syntax for Cmd.exe is

```
cmd [/a | /u] [/q] [/d] [/e:on | /e:off] [/f:on | /f:off] [/v:on |
/v:off] [[/s] [/c | /k] commandstring]
```

All arguments are optional.

- **/A|/U**   This argument lets you specify the encoding system used for text that's piped to a file or other device. Use /A for ANSI or /U for Unicode. (The default is ANSI.)

- **/Q**   The /Q argument starts Command Prompt with echo off. (With echo off, you don't need to include an @echo off line to suppress screen output in a batch program. To turn echo back on after starting Command Prompt with /Q, type **echo on** at the command prompt.)

- **/D**   The /D argument disables execution of any AutoRun commands specified in the registry. (For more information, see "Using AutoRun to Execute Commands When Command Prompt Starts," page 1346.)

- **/E:on | /E:off**   The /E argument allows you to override the current registry settings that affect command extensions. (See "Using Command Extensions," page 1348.)

- **/F:on | /F:off**   The /F argument allows you to override the current registry settings regarding file-name and folder-name completion. (See "Using File-Name and Folder-Name Completion," page 1348.)

- **/V:on | /V:off**   The /V argument lets you enable or disable delayed variable expansion. With /V:on, for example, the variable *!var!* is expanded only when executed. The default is /V:off. To turn on delayed variable expansion as a default, add the DWORD value DelayedExpansion to HKLM\Software\Microsoft\Command Processor (for all users at the current machine) or HKCU\Software\Microsoft\Command Processor (for the current user account only), and set DelayedExpansion to 1. (Delayed variable expansion is useful in conditional statements and loop constructs in batch programs. For more information, type **help set** at the command prompt.)

- **/S [/C | /K] commandstring**   The alternative /C and /K arguments allow you to run a command when Command Prompt starts—with /C terminating the session at the command's completion and /K keeping it open. Including /S before /C or /K affects the processing of quotation marks in *commandstring*. For more information, see "Starting Command Prompt and Running a Command," page 1345.

If you do not include /S, *and* there are exactly two quotation marks in *commandstring*, *and* there are no "special" characters (&, <, >, (,), @, ^, or |) in *commandstring*, *and* there are one or more white-space characters (spaces, tabs, or linefeeds, for example) between the two quotation marks, *and commandstring* is the name of an executable file, then Command Prompt preserves the two quotation characters.

If the foregoing conditions are not met and if the first character in *commandstring* is a quotation mark, Command Prompt strips the first and last quotation marks from *commandstring*.

Editing the Command Line

When working at a command prompt, you often enter the same command several times, or enter several similar commands. If you make a mistake when typing a command line, you don't want to retype the whole thing—you just need to fix the part that was wrong. Windows XP includes a feature that recalls previous commands and allows you to edit them on the current command line. Table B-1 lists these editing keys and what they do.

Table B-1. Command-Line Editing Keys

Key	Function
Up Arrow	Recalls the previous command in the command history
Down Arrow	Recalls the next command in the command history
Page Up	Recalls the earliest command used in the session
Page Down	Recalls the most recent command used
Left Arrow	Moves left one character

Table B-1. Command-Line Editing Keys

Key	Function
Right Arrow	Moves right one character
Ctrl+Left Arrow	Moves left one word
Ctrl+Right Arrow	Moves right one word
Home	Moves to the beginning of the line
End	Moves to the end of the line
Esc	Clears the current command
F7	Displays the command history in a scrollable pop-up box
F8	Displays commands that start with characters currently on the command line
Alt+F7	Clears the command history

The command-line recall feature maintains a history of the commands entered during the Command Prompt session. To display this history, press F7. A window appears that shows the commands you have recently entered. Scroll through the history with the arrow keys to select the command you want. Then press Enter to reuse the selected command, or press the Left Arrow key to place the selected text on the command line without executing the command. (This allows you to edit the command before executing it.)

It's not necessary to display the pop-up window to use the command history. You can scroll through the history within the Command Prompt window with the Up Arrow and Down Arrow keys.

The F8 key provides a useful alternative to the Up Arrow key. The Up Arrow key moves you through the command history to the top of the command buffer and then stops. F8 does the same, except that when you get to the top of the buffer, it cycles back to the bottom. Furthermore, F8 displays only commands in the buffer that begin with whatever you typed before you pressed F8. Type **d** at the command prompt (don't press Enter), and then press F8 a few times. You'll cycle through recently entered commands that start with *d*, such as Dir and Del. Now type **e** (after the *d*), and press F8 a few more times. You'll cycle through Del commands along with any others that start with *de*. You can save a lot of keystrokes using F8 if you know the first letters of the command you're looking for.

Using Wildcards

Windows XP, like MS-DOS, recognizes two wildcard characters: ? and *. The question mark represents any single character in a file name. The asterisk matches any number of characters.

In MS-DOS, the asterisk works only at the end of the file name or extension. Windows XP handles the asterisk much more flexibly, allowing multiple asterisks in a command string and allowing you to use the asterisk character wherever you want.

Appendix B

Using Command Symbols

Old-fashioned programs that take all of their input from a command line and then run unaided can be useful in a multitasking system. You can turn them loose to perform complicated processing in the background while you continue to work with other programs in the foreground. Windows XP includes features that make command-line programs easier to run and more powerful. These features also allow you to chain programs together so that later ones use the output of their predecessors as input.

In order to work together better, many command-line programs follow a set of conventions that control their interaction:

- By default, programs take all of their input as lines of text typed at the keyboard. But input in the same format also can be redirected from a file or any device capable of sending lines of text.

- By default, programs send all of their output to the screen as lines of text. But output in the same format also can be redirected to a file or another line-oriented device, such as a printer.

Programs are written to set a number called a return value when they terminate, to indicate the results of the program. When programs are written according to these rules, you can use the symbols in Table B-2 to control a program's input and output, and to connect or chain programs together.

Table B-2. Command Symbols

Symbol	Purpose
<	Redirects input
>	Redirects output
>>	Appends redirected output to existing data
|	Pipes output
&	Separates multiple commands in a command line
&&	Runs the command after && only if the command before && is successful
||	Runs the command after || only if the command before || fails
^	Treats the next symbol as a character
(and)	Groups commands

The Redirection Symbols

As in MS-DOS and UNIX, Command Prompt sessions in Windows XP allow you to override the default source for input (the keyboard) or the default destination for output (the screen).

Redirecting output   To redirect output to a file, type the command followed by a greater than sign (>) and the name of the file. For example, to send the output of the Dir command to a file instead of the screen, type the following:

```
dir /b *.bat > batch.lst
```

This command line creates a file called Batch.lst that contains the names of all the .bat files in the current folder.

Using two greater than signs (>>) redirects output and appends it to an existing file. For example:

```
dir /b *.cmd >> batch.lst
```

This command line appends a list of .cmd files to the previously created file containing .bat files. (If you use >> to append to a file that doesn't exist, Windows XP creates the file.)

Redirecting input   To redirect input from a file, type the command followed by a less than sign (<) and the name of the file. The Sort and More commands are examples of commands that can accept input from a file. The following example uses Sort to filter the file created with the Dir command above.

```
sort < batch.lst
```

The input file, Batch.lst, contains a list of .bat files followed by a list of .cmd files (assuming you have some of each in the current folder). The output to the screen is the same list of files sorted alphabetically by file name.

Redirecting Input and Output

You can redirect both input and output in a command line. For example, to use Batch.lst as input to the Sort command and send its output to a file named Sorted.lst, type the following:

```
sort < batch.lst > sorted.lst
```

Standard output and standard error   Programs can be written to send their output either to the standard output device or to the standard error device. Sometimes programs are written to send different types of output to each device. You can't always tell which is which because, by default, both devices are the screen.

The Windows XP Type command illustrates the difference. When used with wildcards (something you can't do with the Type command in MS-DOS or Windows 95/98/Me), the Type command sends the name of each matching file to the standard error device and sends the contents of the file to the standard output device. Because they both go to the screen, you see a nice display with each file name followed by its contents.

However, if you try to redirect output to a file like this:

```
type *.bat > std.out
```

the file names still appear on your screen because standard error is still directed to the screen. Only the file contents are redirected to Std.out.

Windows XP allows you to qualify the redirection symbol by preceding it with a number. Use 1> (or simply >) for standard output and 2> for standard error. For example:

```
type *.bat 2> err.out
```

This time the file contents go to the screen and the names are redirected to Err.out. You can redirect both to separate files with this command line:

```
type *.bat 2> err.out 1> std.out
```

The Pipe Symbol

The pipe symbol (|) is used to send or *pipe* the output of one program to a second program as the second program's input. Piping is commonly used with the More utility, which displays multiple screens of output one screenful at a time. For example:

```
help dir | more
```

This command line uses the output of Help as the input for More. The More command filters out the first screenful of Help output, sends it to the screen as its own output, and then waits for a keypress before sending more filtered output.

The Command Combination Symbols

Windows XP allows you to enter multiple commands on a single command line. Furthermore, you can make later commands depend on the results of earlier commands. This feature can be particularly useful in batch programs and Doskey macros, but you might also find it convenient at the command prompt.

To simply combine commands without regard to their results, use the & symbol:

```
copy a:file.dat & edit file.dat
```

But what if there is no File.dat on drive A? Then it can't be copied to the current drive, and the Edit command will fail when it can't find the file. Your screen will be littered with error messages. Windows XP provides two command symbols for better control over situations like this:

- The && symbol causes the second command to run only if the first command succeeds.
- The || symbol causes the second command to run only if the first command fails.

Consider this modified version of the earlier example:

```
copy a:file.dat && edit file.dat
```

With this command line, if the Copy command fails, the Edit command is ignored.

Sometimes you want the opposite effect: Execute the second command only if the first fails:

```
copy a:file.dat || copy b:file.dat
```

This command line tries to copy the file from drive A. If that doesn't work, it tries to copy the file from drive B.

The Escape Symbol

Some command symbols are legal characters in file names. This leads to ambiguities. You can resolve such ambiguities by using the caret (^) as an escape to indicate that whatever follows it is a character rather than a command symbol.

Consider the following command line:

```
copy f:\cartoons\Tom&Jerry
```

This copies the file F:\Cartoons\Tom to the current folder, and then executes the Jerry command—probably not what you wanted. You might think that because there is no space before or after the & symbol, the system will know that you are referring to the file name Tom&Jerry. Not true. When a command symbol appears on the command line, whatever follows it is assumed to be a command, space or no space. Use the caret as shown below to indicate that you are referring to a file name.

```
copy f:\cartoons\Tom^&Jerry
```

Alternatively, instead of using the ^ symbol, you can enclose a file specification that includes command symbols (or other troublesome characters, such as spaces) within quotation marks to achieve the same effect. For example:

```
dir "f:\cartoons\Tom&Jerry"
```

Pausing or Canceling Commands

You can pause or cancel a command that you enter at the command prompt as the command is running. (Keep this in mind if you accidentally request a directory of all the files—or worse, enter a command to delete all the files—on a huge network server drive!)

To pause the output of a command, press Ctrl+S or the Pause key. To resume output, press any key.

If you have enabled QuickEdit mode for your Command Prompt window (see "Setting Other Options," page 1362), simply click in the window to pause command output. To resume output, right-click in the window.

To cancel a command, press Ctrl+C or Ctrl+Break. With either key, your command is canceled, and the command prompt returns. Be aware, though, that any action (such as deleting files) that occurs before you cancel the command is done—and cannot be undone.

Simplifying Command Entry with Doskey Macros

The Doskey utility lets you encapsulate command strings as easy-to-enter macros. For example, by typing the following at the command prompt:

```
doskey 50=mode con:lines=50
```

you create a macro named 50 that executes the command string *mode con:lines=50*. To run a macro, you simply enter its name (in this example, 50) at a command prompt. You can create as many macros as you like with Doskey, but your macros are effective only for the current Command Prompt session. To create a reusable set of Doskey macros, save them in a plain-text file, using an editor such as Notepad. Then load them from the command prompt, using Doskey's /Macrofile switch. For example, if your macros are stored in the file C:\MyMacros.txt, typing

```
doskey /macrofile=c:\mymacros.txt
```

makes those macros available for the current Command Prompt session. If you regularly use the same macro file, consider using the AutoRun feature to load your macros. See "Using AutoRun to Execute Commands When Command Prompt Starts," page 1346.

Doskey macros can use replaceable parameters, in much the same way batch files can. (For more information, see "Replaceable Parameters," page 620.) The difference between a Doskey parameter and a batch-file parameter is that the former uses a dollar-sign prefix instead of a percentage symbol. Parameters 1 through 9 thus are identified as $1 through $9. For example, the Doskey macro assignment

```
doskey lines=mode con:lines=$1
```

allows you to switch your display by typing **lines** followed by the number of lines you want.

In Doskey macros, $* represents all the arguments passed, even if there are more than nine.

You can use redirection, piping, and command combination symbols in Doskey macros, but you must insert a caret (^) before each such symbol. For example, the following assignment creates a macro that pipes output through the More filter:

```
doskey mtype=type $* ^| more /e
```

For more information about using Doskey, type **doskey /?** at the command prompt.

Using Environment Variables

Command-prompt operating systems traditionally use environment variables as a means for programs to share information and read global settings. (Windows XP—and applications written for Windows XP—use the registry for the same purpose.) To use an environment variable in a command, program, or address, enclose it between percent signs, like this example: %UserName%.

Viewing Environment Variables

The Set command allows you to examine as well as set environment variables. To examine the current environment variables, open a Command Prompt window and type **set** (without any arguments). Windows XP displays a list of all the current environment variables and their values, as the following example shows:

```
ALLUSERSPROFILE=D:\Documents and Settings\All Users
APPDATA=D:\Documents and Settings\Craig\Application Data
CommonProgramFiles=D:\Program Files\Common Files
COMPUTERNAME=FAFNER
ComSpec=D:\WINNT\system32\cmd.exe
HOMEDRIVE=D:
HOMEPATH=\Documents and Settings\Craig
LOGONSERVER=\\FAFNER
NUMBER_OF_PROCESSORS=1
OS=Windows_NT
Path=D:\WINDOWS\system32;D:\WINDOWS;D:\WINDOWS\System32\Wbem
PATHEXT=.COM;.EXE;.BAT;.CMD;.VBS;.VBE;.JS;.JSE;.WSF;.WSH
PROCESSOR_ARCHITECTURE=x86
PROCESSOR_IDENTIFIER=x86 Family 6 Model 8 Stepping 6, GenuineIntel
PROCESSOR_LEVEL=6
PROCESSOR_REVISION=0806
ProgramFiles=D:\Program Files
PROMPT=$P$G
SESSIONNAME=Console
SystemDrive=D:
SystemRoot=D:\WINDOWS
TEMP=D:\DOCUME~1\Craig\LOCALS~1\Temp
TMP=D:\DOCUME~1\Craig\LOCALS~1\Temp
USERDOMAIN=FAFNER
USERNAME=Craig
USERPROFILE=D:\Documents and Settings\Craig
windir=D:\WINDOWS
```

Modifying Environment Variables

Command Prompt gets its environment variables from three sources:

- Any variables set in your Autoexec.bat file
- System variables, as recorded in HKLM \SYSTEM\CurrentControlSet\Control\Session Manager\Environment
- User variables, as recorded in HKCU\Environment

When you log on, Windows XP scans the Autoexec.bat file in the root folder of your boot drive for environment variables initialized with Set statements. If you don't want Windows XP to scan your Autoexec.bat file for Set statements, open a registry editor and navigate to HKCU\Software\Microsoft\Windows NT\CurrentVersion\Winlogon. Then change the data associated with the ParseAutoexec value from 1 to 0. System and user variables are both stored in the registry, but you don't need to launch a registry editor to change them. Open Control Panel, System instead. Click the Advanced tab, and then the Environment Variables button. To change system variables, you must be logged on as a member of the Administrators group.

Predefined Environment Variables

Many of the environment variables in the preceding example are ones that Windows XP automatically sets with information about your system. You can use these values in batch programs, Doskey macros, and command lines—and if you're a programmer, in the programs you write. The system-defined environment variables include the following:

- **Information about your place in the network**   COMPUTERNAME contains the name of your computer, USERDOMAIN contains the name of the domain you logged on to, and USERNAME contains your logon name.

- **Information about your computer**   PROCESSOR_ARCHITECTURE contains the type of processor (such as "x86"), and PROCESSOR_IDENTIFIER, PROCESSOR_LEVEL, and PROCESSOR_REVISION provide specific information about the processor version.

- **Information about Windows XP**   SystemRoot contains the drive and folder in which Windows XP is installed; SystemDrive contains only the drive letter.

- **Information about your programs**   When you type a program name (to start the program) without typing its path, Windows XP looks first in the current folder. If the program isn't located in the current folder, Windows XP looks in each folder listed in the Path variable.

- **Information about the command prompt**   PROMPT contains codes that define the appearance of the command prompt itself. (For details, type **prompt /?** at the prompt.)

Environment changes made via Control Panel affect your next and subsequent Command Prompt sessions (not the current ones, of course). Changes made via Autoexec.bat are not effective until the next time you log on. In case of conflicting assignments, user variables take precedence over system variables, which take precedence over variables declared in Autoexec.bat. The Path variable, however, is cumulative. That is, changes made in any venue are appended to any changes made in other avenues. (But changes made via Autoexec.bat or HKCU\Environment are not effective until your next logon.)

Within a given Command Prompt session, you can change environment variables by means of Set statements. Such statements affect only the current session and any applications (including additional Command Prompt sessions) spawned from the current session.

> **Note** The Autoexec.nt file has no effect on the Command Prompt environment. Autoexec.nt affects MS-DOS–based applications only. Command Prompt, although it is the MS-DOS command interpreter, is itself a Windows XP–based application.

Customizing Command Prompt Windows

You can customize the appearance of a Command Prompt window in several ways. You can change its size, select a font, and even use eye-pleasing colors. And you can save these settings independently for each shortcut that launches a Command Prompt session, so that you can make appropriate settings for different tasks.

To customize a Command Prompt window, you make settings in a properties dialog box that you can reach in any of three ways:

- Right-click a shortcut that opens a Command Prompt window, and choose Properties from the shortcut menu. Changes you make here affect all future Command Prompt sessions launched from this shortcut.

- Click the Control menu icon in a Command Prompt window, and choose Properties from the Control menu. (If Command Prompt is running in full-screen mode, press Alt+Enter to switch to window display.) Changes you make here affect the current session. When you leave the properties dialog box, you'll be given the option of propagating your changes to the shortcut from which this session was launched. If you accept, all future sessions launched from that shortcut will have the new properties.

- Click the Control menu icon in a Command Prompt window, and choose Defaults from the Control menu. Changes here do not affect the current session. Instead, they affect all future sessions, except those launched from a shortcut whose properties you have modified. They also affect future sessions in character-mode, MS-DOS–based applications that do not have a program-information file (PIF) and do not store their own settings.

Setting the Window Size and Position

To change the screen position where a newly launched Command Prompt window appears, open the window's properties dialog box and click the Layout tab (see Figure B-1).

The dialog box maintains two different sizes—the screen buffer size and the window size. The width for both sizes is specified in columns (characters); the height is specified in rows (text lines).

The screen buffer settings control the size of the "virtual screen," which is the maximum extent of the screen. Standard screen sizes are 80 × 25, 80 × 43, or 80 × 50, but you can set your Command Prompt screen to any size you want. (Some programs that you launch from a Command Prompt session, however, might work correctly only with standard screen sizes. In such cases, Windows XP automatically adjusts the screen buffer size to the closest size that the program understands.)

The window size settings control the size of the Command Prompt window on your screen. In most cases, you'll want it the same size as the screen buffer. But if your screen is crowded, you can reduce the window size. If you do, scroll bars are added so that you can scroll to different parts of the virtual screen. The window size settings cannot be larger than the screen buffer size settings.

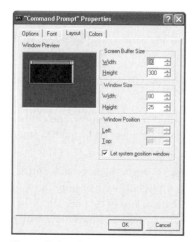

Figure B-1. Settings on the Layout tab control the number of lines and characters per line that a Command Prompt window can display.

Because you size a window by specifying how many rows and columns of characters it should have, the size of those characters also affects the amount of space the window occupies on your display. For information about changing the character size, see "Selecting a Font" on the next page.

Setting the Window Size and Position Visually

Rather than guess at the settings for window size and position, you can use the following procedure:

1. Open a Command Prompt window.
2. Drag the window's borders to adjust its size and drag its title bar to adjust its position.
3. Click the Control menu icon and choose Properties.
4. Click the Layout tab. You'll see the settings that reflect the window's current condition.
5. Click OK to apply these settings.
6. Select Save Properties For Future Windows With Same Title (or Modify Shortcut That Started This Window, if you started the session from a shortcut instead of from the Run command) to retain the settings for future sessions.

Selecting a Font

Unlike most Windows–based applications, applications in a Command Prompt can display only one font at a time. Your choice is relatively limited, as you'll see if you click the Font tab in the Command Prompt window's properties dialog box. Figure B-2 shows the Font tab of the Command Prompt's properties dialog box.

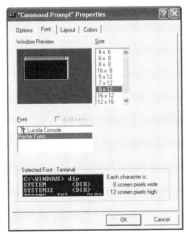

Figure B-2. The small window at the bottom of this dialog box shows an actual-size sample of the selected font; the window at the top shows the relative size and shape of the Command Prompt window if you use the selected font.

You should make a selection in the Font list first because your choice here determines the contents of the Size list. If you select Lucida Console, you'll find point sizes to choose from in the Size list. If you select Raster Fonts, you'll find character widths and height in pixels.

Setting Colors

You can set the color of the text and the background of the Command Prompt window. You can also set the color of the text and the background of pop-up windows that originate from the command prompt, such as the command history.

To set colors, click the Colors tab in the Command Prompt window's properties dialog box, shown in Figure B-3.

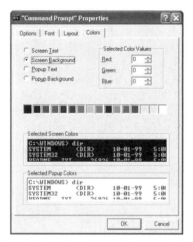

Figure B-3. You can set separate foreground and background colors for the Command Prompt window and pop-up windows, such as the command history window that appears when you press F7.

Setting Other Options

The Options tab in the Command Prompt window's properties dialog box, shown in Figure B-4 on the next page, offers a variety of options that affect how your Command Prompt window operates.

- **Cursor Size**   These options control the size of the blinking cursor in a Command Prompt window.
- **Display Options**   This setting determines whether your Command Prompt session appears in a window or occupies the entire screen.

- **Command History**   These options control the buffer used by Doskey:
  - **Buffer Size**   specifies the number of commands to save in each command history.
  - **Number Of Buffers**   specifies the number of command history buffers to use. (Certain character-based programs other than Cmd.exe use Doskey's command history. Doskey maintains a separate history for each such program that you start.)
  - **Discard Old Duplicates,**   if selected, uses the history buffers more efficiently by not saving duplicate commands.
- **QuickEdit Mode**   This option provides a fast, easy way to copy text from (and paste text into) Command Prompt windows with a mouse. (If you don't select QuickEdit Mode, you can use commands on the Control menu for copying and pasting text.)
- **Insert Mode**   This option (on by default) allows you to insert text at the cursor position. To overstrike characters instead, clear the Insert Mode check box.

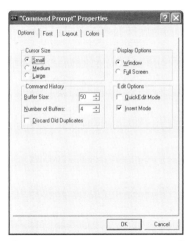

Figure B-4.   You can set cursor size, the size of your command history buffer, and other specifications on the Options tab.

Appendix C

Using and Customizing Microsoft Management Console

Microsoft Management Console (MMC) is an application that hosts administrative tools. By itself, MMC performs no administrative services. Rather, it acts as host for one or more modules called *snap-ins*. The snap-ins do the useful work. MMC simply provides user-interface consistency so that you or the users you support see more or less the same style of application each time you need to carry out some kind of management task. The combination of MMC with one or more snap-ins is called an MMC *console*.

Creating snap-ins requires expertise in ActiveX programming. You don't have to be a programmer, however, to make your own custom MMC consoles. All you need to do is run MMC, start with a blank console, and add one or more of the snap-ins available on your system. (You'll find a list of these in one of MMC's dialog boxes.) Alternatively, you can customize some of the MMC consoles supplied by Microsoft or other vendors simply by adding or removing snap-ins.

At Home with Windows XP

MMC works identically in all versions of Microsoft Windows XP. However, certain MMC snap-ins are not included in Windows XP Home Edition; see Table C-1 on page 1372 for details.

Note MMC snap-ins are not stored as executable files and cannot be opened directly from a command line or from Windows Explorer unless they are first added to a console and saved using the .msc extension. Typically, snap-ins are contained in dynamic link libraries (DLLs), and details about a snap-in must be added to the registry before you can add the snap-in to an MMC console. You can view details about all available snap-ins by opening Registry Editor (Regedit.exe) and browsing to HKLM\Software\Microsoft\MMC\SnapIns.

Why might you want to customize your MMC consoles? Because neither Microsoft nor any other vendor can anticipate your every need and desire. Perhaps you would like to take some of the functionality from two or more existing MMC consoles and combine them into a single console. (You might, for example, want to combine the Fax Service Management console with the Event Viewer console, the latter filtered to show only those events generated by the Fax service.) Or perhaps you would like to simplify some of the existing consoles by removing snap-ins that you seldom use.

You also might find MMC customization worthwhile if you support others in your organization who occasionally need to perform administrative tasks. You can set up consoles that supply only the functionality that your colleagues need, removing or disabling components that might be distracting or confusing. Some of the snap-ins available on your system, for example, are designed to administer remote as well as local computers. If the user you're supporting needs to be able to administer only his or her own machine, you might want to create a custom console for that person that has remote-administration capabilities disabled.

Running MMC Consoles

MMC consoles have, by default, the extension .msc, and .msc files are associated by default with MMC. Thus you can run any MMC console by double-clicking its file name in a Windows Explorer window or by specifying the file name on a command line.

MMC consoles can be run in author mode or in three varieties of user mode. Author mode gives you full access to MMC's menus and options. In user modes, elements of MMC's functionality are removed.

By default, when you run an MMC console, the console runs in the mode it was last saved in. But you can always run any console in any mode you need to.

Running a User-Mode Console in Author Mode

To run a console in author mode, right-click its file in a Windows Explorer window and choose Author from the shortcut menu. Alternatively, you can run a console in author mode using the following command-line syntax:

```
name.msc /a
```

where *name* is the file name of the console file.

Running a Console and Specifying a Target Computer

Many of the consoles supplied by Microsoft are set up to operate on the local computer by default, but—provided that you have the appropriate permissions—they can also be used to manage remote computers. To open such a console and specify a target computer, use this command-line syntax:

```
name.msc /computer=computername
```

Be aware that if you use the /Computer switch with a console that has not been set up to allow remote-computer management, you will not get an error message. Instead, you will simply get the console applied to the default (typically, the local) computer. In the console tree, you can look at the top-level entry for a snap-in to confirm that you're working with the correct target computer.

Some of the consoles supplied with Windows that are designed to work with remote as well as local computers include a menu command for connecting to a different computer. The Computer Management console (Compmgmt.msc), for example, allows you to switch from one computer to another while the console is running. Others, such as Shared Folders (Fsmgmt.msc), can be used with remote computers, but these consoles manage the local computer unless you specify a different target computer on the command line.

Using MMC Consoles

Notwithstanding the fact that MMC is intended to provide user-interface consistency across administrative applications, actual MMC consoles can take on quite a variety of appearances. Compare the Computer Management console (Compmgmt.msc) with the Disk Management console (Diskmgmt.msc), for example.

MMC is designed to be extremely flexible. Snap-ins can add elements to the MMC user interface, and console designers can hide or display UI elements as needs dictate. Nevertheless, *most* of the consoles that come with your operating system look somewhat like Figure C-1 so we can make a few generalizations about their use.

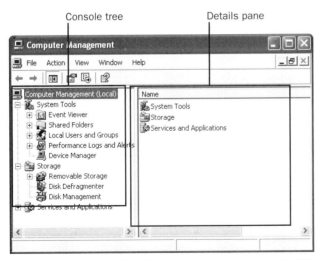

Figure C-1. Most of the MMC consoles that come with Windows XP include a console tree and a details pane.

Appendix C

Console tree and details pane   If the console is divided into panes vertically, the one on the left contains the *console tree* and the one on the right is called the *details pane*. The console tree shows the organization of the console and allows for easy navigation between snap-ins. Outline controls in the console tree function just the way they do in Windows Explorer. The vertical split bar between the console tree and details pane can be dragged to the left or right, like its counterpart in Windows Explorer. The details pane shows information related to the item currently selected in the console tree.

Action and View menus   The Action menu, if present, provides commands specific to the current snap-in. In other words, this is the menu you use to carry out administrative tasks. The View menu, if present, allows you to choose among alternative ways of presenting information. In many MMC consoles, for example, the View menu offers Large Icons, Small Icons, List, and Details commands, just like the View menu in Windows Explorer. The View menu might also include a Customize command. This command presents the Customize View dialog box shown in Figure C-2, which allows you, among other things, to hide or display the console tree.

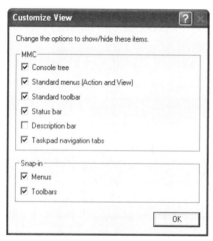

Figure C-2.   You can use the Customize View dialog box to control various elements of the MMC console.

Shortcut menus   Whether or not an Action menu is present, you'll probably find that the easiest way to carry out an administrative task is to right-click the relevant item in the console tree or the details pane and choose an action from the item's shortcut menu. That's because the shortcut menu always includes all the actions available for the selected item. (If you don't immediately find the command you need, look for an All Tasks command; the action you want is probably on the All Tasks submenu.) The shortcut menu also always includes a Help command.

Working with content in the details pane If the details pane provides a tabular presentation, like the one shown in Figure C-1, you can manipulate content using the same techniques you use in Windows Explorer. You can sort by clicking column headings, control column width by dragging the borders between column headings (double-click a border to make a column just wide enough for the widest entry), and rearrange columns by dragging headings.

To hide or display particular columns, look for a Choose Columns command on the View menu. Here you can specify which columns you want to see in the details pane, as well as the order in which you want to see them.

Exporting details pane data to text or .csv files Many MMC consoles include Action-menu commands for saving data in binary formats. In most consoles that produce tabular displays, however, you can also use the Export List command to generate a tab-delimited or comma-delimited text file, suitable for viewing in a word processing, spreadsheet, or database program. If this command is available, you'll find it on the Action menu or any shortcut menu.

Creating Your Own MMC Consoles

Creating your own MMC console or modifying an existing one involves the following steps (not necessarily in this order):

- Running MMC with no snap-in, or opening an existing MMC console in Author mode
- Displaying the console tree if it's not already visible
- Adding folders to the console tree if appropriate for your needs
- Adding or removing snap-ins and, if appropriate, extensions (modules that extend the functionality of snap-ins)
- Adding or removing ActiveX controls and Internet links, if appropriate
- Adding taskpad views (customized pages that appear within the details pane of a snap-in), if appropriate
- Manipulating windows and other display elements to taste
- Adding items to the Favorites menu, if appropriate
- Naming the console and choosing an icon for it
- Choosing Author mode or one of the three User modes
- Further restricting user options, if appropriate
- Using the File menu to save your .msc file

Running MMC with No Snap-In

To run MMC with no snap-in, simply type **mmc** on a command line. An empty, Author-mode MMC console appears, as shown in Figure C-3.

MMC is a multiple-document-interface (MDI) application (the Console Root window is a child window), although most of the consoles supplied with Windows XP do their best to disguise this fact. You can create consoles with multiple child windows, and those windows can be maximized, minimized, restored, resized, moved, cascaded, and tiled.

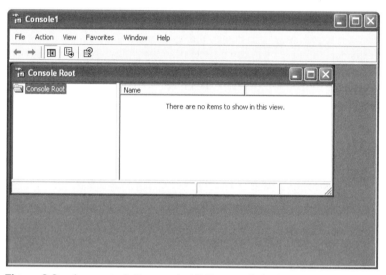

Figure C-3. An empty Author-mode MMC console looks like this.

Displaying the Console Tree

If the console tree is not visible in the application you're creating or modifying, choose Customize View from the View menu. In the Customize View dialog box (see Figure C-2), select the Console Tree check box. You can also use this dialog box to control other elements of the MMC display.

Adding Folders to the Console Tree

If the console you're designing will include several snap-ins, you might want to consider using folders to create logical subdivisions within your console tree. To see how folders can be helpful, check out the Computer Management application (Compmgmt.msc). Computer Management uses three folders—System Tools, Storage, and Services And Applications. These folders allow the user to control the amount of detail shown in the console tree and simplify navigation from one point in the application to another.

Appendix C

To add one or more folders to an MMC application:

1 Choose File, Add/Remove Snap-In (or press Ctrl+M).

2 In the Snap-Ins Added To field of the Add/Remove Snap-In dialog box, choose the parent of the new folder. (In a brand new MMC application, this folder must be Console Root.)

3 Click Add.

4 In the Add Standalone Snap-In dialog box, select Folder and then click Add. Repeat if you want more folders, and then click Close.

5 In the Add/Remove Snap-In dialog box, click OK.

6 In the console tree, right-click the new folder, choose Rename, and supply a meaningful name.

Adding Snap-Ins and Extensions

The contents of a console can consist of a single snap-in, or you can craft a hierarchically organized, completely personalized, everything-but-the-kitchen-sink management tool. Regardless of complexity, the process of building a console requires that you add one snap-in at a time. To add a snap-in to your application:

1 Choose File, Add/Remove Snap-In (or press Ctrl+M).

2 In the Snap-Ins Added To field of the Add/Remove Snap-In dialog box, choose the parent of the new snap-in. This folder can be Console Root or a folder that you've already added.

3 Click Add.

4 In the Add Standalone Snap-In dialog box, select the snap-in you want and then click Add.

    If the selected snap-in supports remote management, you might see a dialog box similar to the one shown in Figure C-4.

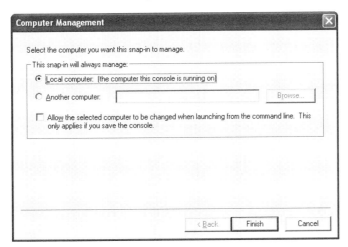

Figure C-4. If your snap-in can manage a remote computer, you will see a dialog box similar to this.

Appendix C

5   Supply the name of the computer you want to manage. Also select the check box if you want the user of your custom console to be able to specify the target computer by means of a command-line switch. (This option is not available for all remote-management snap-ins.) Then click Finish.

Some snap-ins come with optional extensions. You can think of these as snap-ins for snap-ins—modules that provide additional functionality to the selected snap-in.

6   To add an extension to a snap-in, select the snap-in from the Standalone tab of the Add/Remove Snap-In dialog box, and then click the Extensions tab. There you can select the extensions that you want to use. When you have finished adding extensions, click OK.

Table C-1 lists the available snap-ins included with a base installation of Windows XP and Service Pack 2.

Table C-1. Available MMC Snap-Ins

Snap-In Name	Description
ActiveX Control	Select this option to add a previously installed ActiveX control to the current console as if it were a snap-in. The list of available controls includes all installed ActiveX controls, not just those visible within Internet Explorer. Few ActiveX controls are suitable for use in an MMC console, making this option useful mostly to developers.
Certificates	Using this snap-in, you can view currently installed certificates for the current user, a service account, or a computer. Choosing any option except the current user allows you to specify additional details, including the name of a service or a remote computer. A more accessible version of this tool is available from Control Panel, Internet Options; click the Certificates button on the Content tab.
Component Services	This snap-in, also primarily intended for developers, allows you to view and manage settings for programs that use COM+ and DCOM to communicate with the operating system and with each other.
Computer Management	Use the assortment of tools in this snap-in to manage system settings, storage, and services. Most users will access this snap-in through the Administrative Tools folder or by right-clicking the My Computer icon and choosing Manage; either option opens the preconfigured Computer Management console, which contains only this snap-in.
Device Manager	View properties for installed hardware devices and drivers using this snap-in, which is more commonly available from the System option in Control Panel; this snap-in is also available in the Device Manager console (Devmgmt.msc) and as one node in the Computer Management console.

Table C-1. **Available MMC Snap-Ins**

Snap-In Name	Description
Disk Defragmenter	This snap-in, which is also accessible via the Computer Management console, allows you to analyze and defragment any local hard disk volume. When you select a task, this snap-in calls one of two external programs (Dfrgntfs.exe or Dfrgfat.exe) to perform any actions.
Disk Management	Use this snap-in to manage partitions and volumes on local hard disks; it calls Dmadmin.exe, which actually does the work. You can also gain access to the snap-in via its own saved console (Diskmgmt.msc) and as one node in the Computer Management console.
Event Viewer	This is yet another snap-in that you're more likely to access from its standard saved console file (Eventvwr.msc), which is available on the Start menu (All Programs, Administrative Tools, Event Viewer) or from the Computer Management console. For more details on how to view and interpret event logs, see Chapter 38, "Monitoring System Activities with Event Viewer."
Folder	The sole purpose of this snap-in is to help you organize consoles that contain multiple snap-ins. By using folders to arrange complex consoles, you can simplify their use.
Group Policy	This is perhaps the most powerful and most misunderstood of all MMC snap-ins. Although Group Policy is most often used to administer Windows domains, you can also use it to tighten control over a standalone computer running Windows XP, as we explain in Appendix F, "Group Policy." This snap-in is not included with Windows XP Home Edition.
Indexing Service	Use this snap-in to enable, disable, and manage file-system indexes, which improve system performance when searching for files and folders. For more details, see "Using Indexing Service and Query Language," page 724.
IP Security Monitor	If you've enabled Internet Protocol Security (IPSec), you can monitor the status of your secure connections using this snap-in.
IP Security Policy Management	With the help of this snap-in, you can configure IPSec, which enables you to carry on secure communications over standard Internet connections. This feature is complex and confusing, and most people don't require this level of security; if you need in-depth explanations and step-by-step instructions, see Chapter 17, "Securing Ports and Protocols," in our other book, *Microsoft Windows Security Inside Out for Windows XP and Windows 2000* (Microsoft Press, 2003).

Appendix C

1373

Table C-1. Available MMC Snap-Ins

Snap-In Name	Description
Link To Web Address	Technically, this menu choice isn't a snap-in at all; rather, it allows you to add any URL to a console, so that you can view a Web page or access another resource via HTTP instructions. See the text that follows this table for more details.
Local Users And Groups	Manage user and group accounts on a single computer using this snap-in, which provides a range of features not accessible through the simplified User Accounts Control Panel option in Windows XP, as we explain in "Advanced Account Setup Options," page 252. This snap-in produces an error message if you try to access the user account database on a computer running Windows XP Home Edition.
Performance Logs And Alerts	Use this snap-in to set up a battery of performance data counters, trace event logs, and performance alerts. Most users will access this set of tools through the saved Performance console (Perfmon.msc), which also includes the System Monitor snap-in. For more details on this extremely useful tool, see "Advanced System Performance Measurement," page 431.
Removable Storage Management	Expect to safely ignore this snap-in, unless you have a "jukebox" style backup device. Although its name might conjure up images of CD-RW and Zip drives, this snap-in is actually intended for managing libraries of backup tapes, typically used only in very large enterprises.
Resultant Set Of Policy	Use this fairly esoteric snap-in to view policies that have been applied to a particular computer and to predict what their effect will be on a specific user. This snap-in is not included with Windows XP Home Edition.
Security Configuration And Analysis	For anyone interested in advanced security, this snap-in is practically irresistible. It allows you to use security template files to apply consistent security policies to computers and users. For more details, see Chapter 12, "Securing Your Computer with Templates." This snap-in is not included with Windows XP Home Edition.
Security Templates	Use this snap-in to edit security templates used with the Security Configuration And Analysis snap-in. It is not included with Windows XP Home Edition.
Services	Using this snap-in, you can start, stop, and configure services running on a local or remote computer. Most users will access these tools using the Services console (Services.msc) or the Services And Applications node in the Computer Management console.

Table C-1. **Available MMC Snap-Ins**

Snap-In Name	Description
Shared Folders	With the help of this snap-in, you can view and manage shared folders, monitor current sessions, and see which network users have opened files on a local or remote computer. Although this snap-in can be run from Windows XP Home Edition, it does not perform any useful functions; see "Managing Shared Folders," page 1013, for more details.
WMI Control	Windows Management Instrumentation (WMI) is an essential system service that allows remote and local monitoring of hardware and software. In theory, you can control and configure WMI settings using this snap-in; in practice, no user-configurable options are available on a default installation of Windows.

Adding ActiveX Controls and Internet Links

The Add Standalone Snap-In dialog box includes the entries ActiveX Control and Link To Web Address, as well as snap-ins. If you choose ActiveX Control, a new wizard appears, allowing you to choose and configure the control you want to add.

If you choose Link To Web Address, the dialog box that appears lets you specify a hyperlink or browse to an Internet resource. The hyperlink you enter does not have to be a Web URL. It can be another kind of Internet URL (mailto, for example) or a link to a local or network folder. If you do specify a Web link, MMC displays the Web content in the details pane when you select the link in the console tree.

Adding Taskpad Views

A *taskpad* is a customized page that appears within the details pane of a snap-in. With it, you can create icons that encapsulate menu commands, command strings, scripts, URLs, and shortcuts to Favorites items. Navigational tabs at the bottom of a taskpad view make it easy for a user to switch between the taskpad view and a normal view of the same data. You can suppress these tabs (by means of the Customize View dialog box) if you don't want to give your console's users this freedom.

To create a taskpad view, start by selecting an item in the console tree to which you want to apply the view. As you'll see, when you create your taskpad view, you have the option of applying it only to the selected console-tree item or to all items at the same outline level.

Next, right-click the selected console-tree entry and choose New Taskpad View from the shortcut menu. The New Taskpad View wizard appears. The sample table at the right side of the wizard's second page makes the options pretty self-explanatory. The default choices work well in most situations.

Appendix C

The default selections in the wizard's third screen apply the new taskpad view to all comparable console-tree items and make the taskpad the default view for those items. Moving on from this screen, you have the opportunity to assign a name and some descriptive text to the new view.

In the wizard's final screen, select the Start New Task Wizard check box if you want to create one or more task shortcuts. This selection summons a new wizard that walks you through the process of creating your first shortcut. On the final page of this wizard, select Run This Wizard Again if you have additional shortcuts to create.

Manipulating Windows

With the New Window From Here command on the Action menu, you can create a new child window rooted on the current console-tree selection. You might want to use this command to create multiple-window applications—for example, a console consisting of the Indexing Service in one window and a filtered list of Index Service events in a second window. After you've created your windows, you can use Window menu commands to tile or cascade them.

You can also use the New Window From Here command to remove the Console Root item that appears atop your default console tree:

1 Select the first item below Console Root.
2 Choose New Window From Here from the Action menu (or right-click and choose it from the shortcut menu).
3 Close the original window (the one with Console Root).

Controlling Other Visual Elements

The Customize View command on the View menu allows you to hide or display various elements of the MMC visual scene, including taskbars, menus, and the navigational tabs that appear below taskpad views. Note that selections in the Customize View dialog box take effect immediately—you don't need to hit an Apply button or leave the dialog box. Therefore, you can easily try each option and see whether you like it.

Using the Favorites Menu

The Favorites menu allows you to store pointers to places within your console tree. If you create a particularly complex MMC console, you might want to consider using Favorites to simplify navigation. To add a console-tree item to your list of favorites, select that item and then choose Add To Favorites from the Favorites menu.

Appendix C

Naming Your Console

To assign a name to your console, click File, Options. Your entry in the field at the top of the Options dialog box will appear on the title bar of your console, regardless of the file name you apply to its .msc file. If you do not make an entry here, MMC will replace Console1 with the console's eventual file name. Click Change Icon to select an alternate icon for the console. You can select an icon from any DLL or executable file.

Choosing Between MMC's Three User Modes

In the Console Mode field of the Options dialog box (click File, Options), you can choose between MMC's three User modes:

- User Mode—Full Access (In this mode, the top-level menu is present but the Console menu has a single command: Exit.)
- User Mode—Limited Access, Multiple Window
- User Mode—Limited Access, Single Window

In both limited-access modes, the top-level menu disappears, leaving users to work with only the two snap-in menus: Action and View (provided that you haven't suppressed those menus via the Customize View command). In the single-window limited-access mode, the current child (snap-in) window is maximized, and MMC essentially loses its MDI character. If you have two or more child windows open at the time you save an MMC console in single-window mode, a confirmation prompt warns you that the user will see only the current child window.

In multiple-window limited-access mode, MMC retains its MDI character (whether or not you've created multiple child windows), allowing child windows to be minimized, maximized, restored, resized, and repositioned.

Imposing Further Restrictions

If you choose one of the three user modes, the two check boxes at the bottom of the Options dialog box become available. Your choices are as follows:

Do Not Save Changes To This Console   With this check box cleared (its default), MMC saves the state of your application automatically when a user closes it. The user's selection in the console tree, for example, is preserved from one use to the next. If you always want your users to see the same thing each time they run the console, select this check box.

Allow The User To Customize Views   This check box, selected by default, keeps the Customize View command available, allowing your users, for example, to hide or display the console tree. Clear the check box if you want to deny users access to this option.

Appendix C

Saving a Console

The final step in the process of creating an MMC console is, of course, to save the file. Choose File, Save As, enter a file name in the Save As dialog box, and choose a location (the default location is the Administrative Tools folder in the Start Menu\Programs folder for your profile). Click Save. The resulting shortcut is saved as a file of type Microsoft Saved Console, with the .msc extension.

Appendix D

Managing Services

A *service* is a specialized program that performs a function to support other programs. Many services operate at a very low level (by interacting directly with hardware, for example) and need to run even when no user is logged on; for this reason, they are often run by the System account (which has elevated privileges) rather than by ordinary user accounts. Microsoft Windows XP includes services as varied as the Event Log service, which keeps a database of event messages, and the Telnet service, which allows remote users to log on to your computer using a command-line interface.

In this appendix, you'll learn how to view the installed services; start, stop, and configure them; and install or remove them. We'll also take a closer look at some of the services used in Windows XP and show you how to configure them to your advantage.

Using the Services Snap-In

You manage services with the Services snap-in for Microsoft Management Console (MMC), shown in Figure D-1 on the next page. To view this snap-in, type **services.msc** at a command prompt.

The Extended and Standard views in the Services console are functionally equivalent. The Standard view replicates the presentation found in the Windows 2000 version of Services.msc. The Extended view provides descriptive information of the selected service in the space at the left edge of the details pane. This space also sometimes includes links for starting, stopping, or pausing the selected service. Unless you need to constrain the console display to a small area of your screen, you'll probably find the Extended view preferable to the Standard view.

At Home with Windows XP

The procedures for managing services are identical in both versions of Windows XP. Note, however, that not all services included with Windows XP Professional are installed in Windows XP Home Edition.

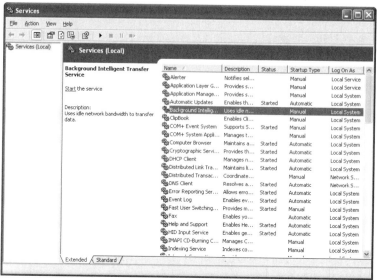

Figure D-1. Use the Services console to start, stop, and configure services.

The Services console offers plenty of information in its clean display. You can sort the contents of any column by clicking the column title, as you can do with other similar lists. To sort in reverse order, click the column title again. In addition, you can:

- Start, stop, pause, resume, or restart the selected service, as described in the following section

- Display the properties dialog box for the selected service, in which you can configure the service and learn more about it

Starting and Stopping Services

Most of the essential services are set to start automatically when your computer starts, and the operating system stops them as part of its shutdown process. But sometimes you might need to manually start or stop a service. For example, you might want to start a seldom-used service on the rare occasion when you need it. (Because running services requires system resources such as memory, running them only when necessary can improve performance.) On the other hand, you might want to stop a service because you're no longer using it. A more common reason, however, for stopping a service is because it isn't working properly. For example, if print jobs get stuck in the print queue, sometimes the best remedy is to stop and then restart the Print Spooler service.

Appendix D

Tip If a service allows pausing, try pausing and then continuing the service as your first step instead of stopping the service. Pausing can solve certain problems without canceling jobs in process or resetting connections.

To change a service's status, select it in the Services console. Then click the appropriate link in the area to the left of the service list (if you're using the Extended view and the link you need appears there). Alternatively, you can use the VCR-style controls in the toolbar, or right-click and choose the corresponding command.

▶	Start, Resume	Starts a service that isn't running, or resumes a service that has been paused.
■	Stop	Stops a running service.
‖	Pause	Pauses a running service. Pausing a service doesn't remove it from memory; it continues to run at a level that varies depending on the service. With some services, pausing allows users to complete jobs or disconnect from resources but does not allow them to create new jobs or connections.
■▶	Restart	Stops a running service and then restarts it.

You can also change a service's status by opening its properties dialog box and then clicking one of the buttons on the General tab. Taking the extra step of opening the properties dialog box to set the status has only one advantage: You can specify start parameters when you start a service using this method. This is a rare requirement.

Not all services allow you to change their status. Some prevent stopping and starting altogether, whereas others permit stopping and starting but not pausing and resuming. Some services allow these permissions to only certain users or groups. For example, most services allow only members of the Power Users and Administrators groups to start or stop them. Which status changes are allowed and who has permission to make them are controlled by each service's discretionary access control list (DACL), which is established when the service is created on a computer.

Appendix D

Configuring Services

To review or modify the way a service starts up or what happens when it doesn't start properly, view its properties dialog box. To do that, simply double-click the service in the Services console. Figure D-2 shows an example.

Figure D-2. You specify a service's startup type on the General tab, where you can also find the actual name of the service above its display name.

Setting Startup Options

On the General tab of the properties dialog box (see Figure D-2), you specify the startup type:

- **Automatic**   The service starts when the computer starts.
- **Manual**   The service doesn't start automatically at startup, but it can be started by a user, a program, or a dependent service.
- **Disabled**   The service can't be started.

You'll find other startup options on the Log On tab of the properties dialog box, as shown in Figure D-3.

> **Note** If you specify a logon account other than the local System account, be sure that account has the requisite rights. Go to the Local Security Policy console (click Start, Run, and type **secpol.msc**), and then go to Security Settings\Local Policies\User Rights Assignment and assign the Log On As A Service right to the account.

Appendix D

Figure D-3. On the Log On tab, you specify which user runs the service, and you can also specify which hardware profiles use the service.

Specifying Recovery Actions

For a variety of reasons—hardware not operating properly or a network connection down, for example—a service that's running smoothly might suddenly stop. Settings on the Recovery tab of the properties dialog box, shown in Figure D-4 on the next page, allow you to specify what should happen if a service fails.

You might want to perform a different action the first time a service fails than on the second or subsequent failures. The Recovery tab enables you to assign a particular response to the first failure, the second failure, and all subsequent failures, from among these options:

- **Take No Action** The service gives up trying. In most cases, the service places a message in the event log. (Use of the event log depends on how the service was programmed by its developers.)
- **Restart The Service** The computer waits for the time specified in the Restart Service After box to elapse and then tries to start the service.
- **Run A File** The computer runs the program that you specify in the Run File box. For example, you could specify a program that attempts to resolve the problem or one that alerts you to the situation.

Figure D-4. Use the Recovery tab to specify what should happen if the service fails.

● **Reboot The Computer** Drastic but effective, this option restarts the computer after the time specified in the Restart Computer Options dialog box elapses. In that dialog box, you can also specify a message to be broadcast (using the Messenger service, if that service is enabled) to other users on your network, warning them of the impending shutdown.

> **Note** Because of potential security risks, the Messenger and Alerter services are disabled by default in Windows XP Service Pack 2. In earlier versions of Windows, these services were set to start automatically.

Troubleshooting

Your service fails and the failure log doesn't record it.

If you set up a service to log on using an account other than the local System account and the service fails, you won't get the dump file or Dr. Watson log that the failed service would otherwise generate. This occurs because the system attempts to access the desktop of the service's logon account and it's unable to do so. To work around this problem, reconfigure the service to use the local System account and select the Allow Service To Interact With Desktop option. (Of course, this workaround doesn't help if the only way to *run* the service is by allowing it to log on with a different account.)

Viewing Dependencies

Many services rely on the functions of another service. If you attempt to start a service that depends on other services, Windows first starts the others. If you stop a service upon which others are dependent, Windows also stops those services. Before you either start or stop a service, therefore, it's helpful to know what other services your action might affect. To obtain that information, go to the Dependencies tab of a service's properties dialog box, shown in Figure D-5.

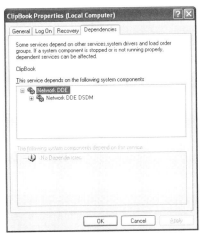

Figure D-5. The Dependencies tab shows which services depend on other services.

Determining a Service's Name

As you view the properties dialog box for different services, you might notice that the service name (shown at the top of the General tab) is often different from the name that appears in the Services console (the display name) and that neither name matches the name of the service's executable file. (In fact, the executable for many services is either Services.exe or Svchost.exe.) The General tab shows all three names.

> **Tip** A detailed description of Svchost.exe appears in Knowledge Base article 314056, "A description of Svchost.exe in Windows XP" (*http://support.microsoft.com/?kbid=314056*).

So how does this affect you? When you work in the Services console, you don't need to know anything other than a service's display name to find it and work with it. But if you use the Net command to start and stop services (as explained in the following section), you might find using the actual service name more convenient; it is often much shorter than the display name. You'll also need the service name if you're ever forced to work with a service's registry entries, which can be found in the HKLM\System\CurrentControlSet\Services*service* sub-key (where *service* is the service name).

And what about the executable name? You might need it if certain users have problems running a service; in such a case, you need to find the executable and check its permissions. Knowing the executable name can also be useful, for example, if you're using Windows Task Manager to determine why your computer seems to be running so slowly. The Processes tab shows only executable names, many of which are inscrutable.

As mentioned earlier, you can find the actual name of each service and its executable name by looking at the General tab of the service's properties dialog box. For your reference, Table D-1 shows the names for all the services that are commonly installed with Windows XP Professional. Note that your system might have other services installed—by Microsoft or by another publisher—or it might not have all of these installed.

Table D-1. Names of Services in Windows XP

Display Name	Service Name	Executable Name
Alerter	Alerter	Svchost.exe
Application Layer Gateway Service	ALG	Alg.exe
Application Management	AppMgmt	Svchost.exe
Automatic Updates	Wuauserv	Svchost.exe
Background Intelligent Transfer Service	BITS	Svchost.exe
ClipBook	ClipSrv	Clipsrv.exe
COM+ Event System	EventSystem	Svchost.exe
COM+ System Application	COMSysApp	Dllhost.exe
Computer Browser	Browser	Svchost.exe
Cryptographic Services	CryptSvc	Svchost.exe
DCOM Server Process Launcher	DcomLaunch	Svchost.exe
DHCP Client	Dhcp	Svchost.exe
Distributed Link Tracking Client	TrkWks	Svchost.exe
Distributed Transaction Coordinator	MSDTC	Msdtc.exe

Table D-1. **Names of Services in Windows XP**

Display Name	Service Name	Executable Name
DNS Client	Dnscache	Svchost.exe
Error Reporting	ERSvc	Svchost.exe
Event Log	Eventlog	Services.exe
Fast User Switching Compatibility	FastUserSwitching Compatibility	Svchost.exe
Fax	Fax	Fxssvc.exe
Help And Support	Helpsvc	Svchost.exe
HTTP SSL	HTTPFilter	Svchost.exe
Human Interface Device Access	HidServ	Svchost.exe
Indexing Service	Cisvc	Cisvc.exe
IPSEC Services	PolicyAgent	Lsass.exe
Logical Disk Manager	Dmserver	Svchost.exe
Logical Disk Manager Administrative Service	Dmadmin	Dmadmin.exe
Messenger	Messenger	Svchost.exe
MS Software Shadow Copy Provider	SwPrv	Dllhost.exe
Net Logon	Netlogon	Lsass.exe
NetMeeting Remote Desktop Sharing	mnmsrvc	Mnmsrvc.exe
Network Connections	Netman	Svchost.exe
Network DDE	NetDDE	Netdde.exe
Network DDE DSDM	NetDDEdsdm	Netdde.exe
Network Location Awareness (NLA)	Nla	Svchost.exe
Network Provisioning Service	xmlprov	Svchost.exe
NT LM Security Support Provider	NtLmSsp	Lsass.exe
Performance Logs And Alerts	SysmonLog	Smlogsvc.exe
Plug And Play	PlugPlay	Services.exe
Portable Media Serial Number	WmdmPmSp	Svchost.exe
Print Spooler	Spooler	Spoolsv.exe
Protected Storage	ProtectedStorage	Lsass.exe

Appendix D

1387

Table D-1. Names of Services in Windows XP

Display Name	Service Name	Executable Name
QoS RSVP	RSVP	Rsvp.exe
Remote Access Auto Connection Manager	RasAuto	Svchost.exe
Remote Access Connection Manager	RasMan	Svchost.exe
Remote Desktop Help Session Manager	RDSessMgr	Sessmgr.exe
Remote Procedure Call (RPC)	RpcSs	Svchost.exe
Remote Procedure Call (RPC) Locator	RpcLocator	Locator.exe
Remote Registry	RemoteRegistry	Svchost.exe
Removable Storage	NtmsSvc	Svchost.exe
Routing And Remote Access	RemoteAccess	Svchost.exe
Secondary Logon	seclogon	Svchost.exe
Security Accounts Manager	SamSs	Lsass.exe
Security Center	wscsvc	Svchost.exe
Server	lanmanserver	Svchost.exe
Shell Hardware Detection	ShellHWDetection	Svchost.exe
Smart Card	SCardSvr	Scardsvr.exe
Smart Card Helper	SCardDrv	Scardsvr.exe
SSDP Discovery Service	SSDPSRV	Svchost.exe
System Event Notification	SENS	Svchost.exe
System Restore Service	srservice	Svchost.exe
Task Scheduler	Schedule	Svchost.exe
TCP/IP NetBIOS Helper	LmHosts	Svchost.exe
Telephony	TapiSrv	Svchost.exe
Telnet	TlntSvr	Tlntsvr.exe
Terminal Services	TermService	Svchost.exe
Themes	Themes	Svchost.exe
Uninterruptible Power Supply	UPS	Ups.exe
Universal Plug And Play Device Host	Upnphost	Svchost.exe

Appendix D

1388

Table D-1. Names of Services in Windows XP

Display Name	Service Name	Executable Name
Upload Manager	Uploadmgr	Svchost.exe
Utility Manager	UtilMan	Utilman.exe
Volume Shadow Copy	VSS	Vssvc.exe
WebClient	WebClient	Svchost.exe
Windows Audio	AudioSrv	Svchost.exe
Windows Firewall/Internet Connection Sharing (ICS)	SharedAccess	Svchost.exe
Windows Image Acquisition (WIA)	Stisvc	Svchost.exe
Windows Installer	MSIServer	Msiexec.exe
Windows Management Instrumentation	Winmgmt	Svchost.exe
Windows Management Instrumentation Driver Extensions	Wmi	Svchost.exe
Windows Time	W32Time	Svchost.exe
Wireless Zero Configuration	WZCSVC	Svchost.exe
WMI Performance Adapter	WmiApSrv	Wmiapsrv.exe
Workstation	lanmanworkstation	Svchost.exe

Note Like file names, the names of services are not case sensitive. In Table D-1, we capitalized the service names exactly as they appear in the registry. Although the capitalization style is sometimes inconsistent, you're likely to see this same capitalization whenever a particular service name is mentioned in documentation.

Appendix D

Recommended Startup Settings for Services

On a typical computer running Windows XP, literally dozens of services are installed by default. What do all of these services do? Do you really need to have each of these running? Table D-2 lists the services you're likely to see on a base installation of Windows XP with Service Pack 2. In each case, we've included a brief description of the service, the account it uses for logon purposes, and our recommendations for setting the startup type (Automatic, Manual, or Disabled).

Table D-2. Service Descriptions and Startup Settings

Service	Log On As	Description	Recommended Startup Type
Alerter	Local Service	Provides an administrative alert (a pop-up message box function) that can be accessed via the Net Send command. Works in conjunction with the Messenger service.	Disabled. Change to Manual and start the service if an application requires the ability to send administrative alerts. (You will need to start the Messenger service as well.)
Application Layer Gateway Service	Local Service	Lets third-party software vendors write plug-ins that enable their protocols to pass through the Windows Firewall and work behind Internet Connection Sharing.	Manual
Application Management	Local System	Provides Assign, Publish, and Remove services for Windows Installer. Also required by the Add New Programs command in the Add Or Remove Programs section of Control Panel.	Manual. The service is stopped until needed by Windows Installer or Add Or Remove Programs, after which it remains running. Do not disable.
Automatic Updates	Local System	Checks for updates and patches at the Windows Update site and downloads or installs them automatically if you have selected those options.	Automatic. (Use Automatic Updates in Control Panel to configure the downloading and installation of updates.)
Background Intelligent Transfer Service	Local System	Allows queuing and background transfer of files (such as Windows updates) between a local computer and an HTTP server, using otherwise idle network bandwidth.	Manual. The service is started when required, then stopped again when transfer is complete.

Table D-2. Service Descriptions and Startup Settings

Service	Log On As	Description	Recommended Startup Type
ClipBook	Local System	Provides support for the Clip-Book Viewer application, which lets users share their Clipboard contents over the network.	Manual on computers that use ClipBook Viewer; Disabled for all others. (With this service disabled, you can still view local Clipboard contents using Clipbrd.exe.)
COM+ Event System, COM+ System Application	Local System	System services that enable communication between applications using the Component Object Model (COM).	Manual
Computer Browser	Local System	Allows a system to act as a "browse master." In a Windows-based workgroup, one computer is always designated the browse master and keeps a list of which computers are present on the network. If the browse master becomes unavailable, the remaining computers on the network elect a new browse master.	Automatic. (If one computer on your network is always on and is very reliable, you can set the Computer Browser to Automatic on that computer and set it to Disabled on the others.)
Cryptographic Services	Local System	Provides verification services for digitally signed files (such as device drivers and ActiveX controls), among other system-level cryptographic functions.	Automatic
DHCP Client	Local System	Acquires network settings (IP addresses and DNS names) from a Dynamic Host Control Protocol (DHCP) server at startup.	Automatic; may be set to Disabled if network settings are configured manually.

Table D-2. Service Descriptions and Startup Settings

Service	Log On As	Description	Recommended Startup Type
Distributed Link Tracking Client	Local System	Maintains links between shortcuts and target files on NTFS volumes within a computer and on computers within a Windows domain. Ensures that shortcuts and OLE links continue to work if a target file is moved or renamed.	Automatic. (Stopping or disabling this service prevents Windows from repairing shortcut links when target files are renamed or moved.)
Distributed Transaction Coordinator	Network Service	Supports Microsoft Transaction Server (MTS); primarily used in applications based on Microsoft SQL Server.	Manual
DNS Client	Network Service	Caches records of DNS lookups to improve performance. Required if using IPSec.	Automatic; may be set to Manual or Disabled if you prefer not to use DNS caching.
Error Reporting	Local System	Allows the operating system and applications to automatically report errors to Microsoft. To disable this feature, open Control Panel, System, and click the Error Reporting button on the Advanced tab; then select Disable Error Reporting.	Manual; Disabled if you have turned off Windows Error Reporting.
Event Log	Local System	Maintains the system event log; this crucial service should never be disabled.	Automatic
Fast User Switching Compatibility	Local System	Supports applications when multiple users are logged on to a single computer using the Fast User Switching feature of Windows XP. (For details, see "Controlling How Users Log On," page 239.)	Manual

Table D-2. **Service Descriptions and Startup Settings**

Service	Log On As	Description	Recommended Startup Type
Fax	Local System	Provides fax capabilities; this is an optional service. (For more details, see Chapter 35, "Sending and Receiving Faxes.")	Manual; Automatic if you want your computer to receive faxes.
Help And Support	Local System	Provides access to Help And Support Center in Windows XP. Most attempts to access Help And Support will cause this service to start.	Automatic
HTTP SSL	Local System	Enables Internet Information Services (IIS) to perform Secure Sockets Layer (SSL) functions.	Automatic on systems that are running IIS; Manual or Disabled on others.
Human Interface Device Access	Local System	Handles the wheels and custom navigation buttons on some mice and keyboards, as well as the volume buttons on USB speakers; a standard 102-key keyboard and PS/2 mouse do not require this service.	Automatic; Disabled if you have no hardware that requires this support.
IMAPI CD-Burning COM Service	Local System	Used by the built-in CD-burning feature in Windows XP.	Manual; may be set to Disabled if you don't have a CD-RW drive.
Indexing Service	Local System	Builds an index of files on your computer to speed up searches. (See "Using Indexing Service and Query Language," page 724, for more details.)	Automatic; set to Disabled if you prefer not to use Indexing Service.
IPSEC Services	Local System	Manages IPSec policy, starts the Internet Security Key Management Protocol (ISAKMP/Oakley), and loads the IP security driver.	Automatic if you use IPSec; otherwise, set to Manual.

Appendix D

Table D-2. **Service Descriptions and Startup Settings**

Service	Log On As	Description	Recommended Startup Type
Logical Disk Manager	Local System	Detects and monitors new hard disk drives and sends information about disk volumes to Logical Disk Manager Administrative Service.	Automatic; do not disable if dynamic disks are present.
Logical Disk Manager Administrative Service	Local System	Supports the Disk Management (Local) snap-in used in the Disk Management (Diskmgmt.msc) and Computer Management (Compmgmt.msc) consoles; this service runs when needed for configuration tasks and then stops.	Manual
Messenger	Local System	Used, along with the Alerter service, by the Net Send command-line utility to send administrative alerts. Not related to Windows Messenger or MSN Messenger.	Disabled
MS Software Shadow Copy Provider	Local System	Allows the Windows Backup utility (and other compatible backup programs) to use the volume shadow copy feature, which takes a "snapshot" of open files so they can be backed up.	Manual
Net Logon	Local System	Used only for authentication of account logon events in Windows domains.	Manual
NetMeeting Remote Desktop Sharing	Local System	Supports the desktop-sharing feature of Microsoft NetMeeting. If you don't use NetMeeting, running this service is a potential security risk.	Manual on computers that use NetMeeting; Disabled on all other computers.

Table D-2. Service Descriptions and Startup Settings

Service	Log On As	Description	Recommended Startup Type
Network Connections	Local System	Manages objects in the Network And Dial-Up Connections folder; unless you disable it, this service starts automatically when it's needed.	Manual
Network DDE, Network DDE DSDM	Local System	These two services support Dynamic Data Exchange (DDE) over networks; very few modern Windows programs use Network DDE.	Disabled; Manual if you're certain a program you use requires Network DDE.
Network Location Awareness (NLA)	Local System	Supports the ability to use multiple network configurations; used primarily on notebook computers and when Windows Firewall or ICS is in use.	Manual
NT LM Security Support Provider	Local System	Provides authentication support for applications and systems that use the NTLM authentication protocol (including systems running Windows NT).	Manual
Performance Logs And Alerts	Network Service	Collects performance data that you can display and analyze using the Performance console (Perfmon.msc). The service also enables you to run a program and send a message when specific performance conditions occur. (Note that the "Send a network message" action in the Performance console requires the Alerter service to be running.)	Manual

Appendix D

Table D-2. Service Descriptions and Startup Settings

Service	Log On As	Description	Recommended Startup Type
Plug And Play	Local System	Detects and configures Plug and Play hardware devices. This service is an essential part of Windows and should never be disabled.	Automatic
Portable Media Serial Number	Local System	Retrieves the serial number of any portable music device connected to a computer running Windows XP; used to manage digital rights when transferring protected media files.	Automatic if you have a portable music player; may be set to Manual or Disabled on all other computers.
Print Spooler	Local System	Manages print jobs on local and network printers. If this service is stopped, applications do not see any printers installed.	Automatic
Protected Storage	Local System	Provides encrypted storage of passwords, private keys, and other sensitive data; Microsoft Internet Explorer and Microsoft Outlook Express are two programs that use this service.	Automatic
QoS RSVP	Local System	Provides a mechanism for an application to gracefully share bandwidth with other applications. (The name stands for Quality of Service Resource Reservation Protocol.) Applications must be QoS-aware for this service to be used; the only common QoS-aware application that ships with Windows is NetMeeting.	Manual

Table D-2. Service Descriptions and Startup Settings

Service	Log On As	Description	Recommended Startup Type
Remote Access Auto Connection Manager	Local System	Automatically dials a connection (a connection to a dial-up ISP, for instance, or a VPN connection) when necessary to connect to a remote network.	Manual; may be set to Disabled if you never use dial-up connections of any kind.
Remote Access Connection Manager	Local System	Creates network connections of all types in the Network And Dial-Up Connections folder; also required by Windows Firewall and ICS.	Manual
Remote Desktop Help Session Manager	Local System	Manages and controls the Remote Assistance feature of Windows XP.	Manual; may be set to Disabled if you have no intention of using Remote Assistance and want to reduce possible security risks.
Remote Procedure Call (RPC)	Network Service	Supports RPC functionality that is used throughout Windows. If this service is turned off, Windows will not start.	Automatic
Remote Procedure Call (RPC) Locator	Network Service	Manages the RPC name service database, enabling RPC clients using the RpcNs family of application programming interfaces (APIs) to locate RPC servers. Almost no applications written in the last decade use these APIs.	Disabled unless you have third-party applications that require it.
Remote Registry	Local Service	Lets a user at a remote computer modify the registry on your computer. This feature is typically used only in large organizations and represents a security risk if not carefully configured.	Automatic if your network uses this feature; Disabled on all other computers.

Appendix D

Table D-2. **Service Descriptions and Startup Settings**

Service	Log On As	Description	Recommended Startup Type
Removable Storage	Local System	Poorly documented service used primarily to manage "jukebox"-style tape backup devices; rarely used on workstations.	Manual; may safely be set to Disabled on computers where no removable storage is available.
Routing And Remote Access	Local System	Provides support for LAN-based routing, specifically incoming dial-up and VPN connections.	Manual if you use any such connections; Disabled on all other computers.
Secondary Logon	Local System	Allows a user to start a program using an alternative user name and password (using Run As); this service can be effectively used by Scheduled Tasks and by administrators.	Automatic
Security Accounts Manager	Local System	Manages security information for all local accounts. This service is essential to the proper operation of Windows and should never be disabled.	Automatic
Security Center	Local System	Monitors security settings (such as the status of Windows Firewall).	Automatic
Server	Local System	Supports network file and printer sharing and provides RPC support.	Automatic
Shell Hardware Detection	Local System	Provides AutoPlay support for removable storage media, flash media, PC cards, and external USB and IEEE 1394 fixed drives.	Automatic
Smart Card, Smart Card Helper	Local Service	Supports smart card authentication hardware; typically used in large, security-conscious organizations.	Manual

Table D-2. **Service Descriptions and Startup Settings**

Service	Log On As	Description	Recommended Startup Type
SSDP Discovery Service	Local Service	The Simple Service Discovery Protocol (SSDP) provides a mechanism for UPnP devices to announce their presence on the network so that other computers can "discover" them. In late 2001, a buffer overflow vulnerability was patched in this service (Microsoft Security Bulletin MS01-059). Windows Firewall depends on UPnP to provide incoming connections to systems behind the firewall. If SSDP is disabled, you can't use Remote Desktop and Remote Assistance to access systems across the Internet.	Manual
System Event Notification	Local System	Tracks system events such as logon, network, screen-saver starts, and power events.	Automatic
System Restore Service	Local System	Creates and manages System Restore checkpoints. For more details about setting up this essential safety net, see "Configuring System Restore Options," page 67.	Automatic; may be set to Disabled if you turn off System Restore completely.
Task Scheduler	Local System	Runs programs in the Scheduled Tasks folder.	Automatic
TCP/IP NetBIOS Helper	Local Service	Provides support for NetBIOS over TCP/IP and NetBIOS name management services; provided for compatibility with Windows 2000.	Automatic

Appendix D

Table D-2. Service Descriptions and Startup Settings

Service	Log On As	Description	Recommended Startup Type
Telephony	Local System	Supports programs that control telephony devices (typically modems) and IP-based voice connections. ICS and Windows Firewall also start this service.	Manual
Telnet	Local System	Allows a remote user to access a computer's resources and run programs from the command line. Most Windows users will never use Telnet and should consider it a potential security risk.	Manual on computers where Telnet access is desired; Disabled on all other computers.
Terminal Services	Local System	Supports a variety of features in Windows XP that allow multiple users to connect to a computer interactively and to display desktops and applications on remote computers. This service is an essential component in Remote Desktop, Remote Assistance, and Fast User Switching.	Manual
Themes	Local System	Provides support for visual effects associated with the look and feel of Windows XP.	Automatic; may be set to Disabled if you have chosen the Windows Classic look (open Control Panel, Display, Themes) and do not intend to use any of the new interface features.

Table D-2. Service Descriptions and Startup Settings

Service	Log On As	Description	Recommended Startup Type
Uninterruptible Power Supply	Local Service	Allows an uninterruptible power supply (UPS) to notify the computer when power has failed and the battery is running low. This service requires that the UPS be connected to the computer using a serial or USB cable, and that the UPS service be configured via Control Panel, Power Options.	Manual
Universal Plug And Play Device Host	Local Service	Allows the operating system to send UPnP announcements on behalf of non-computer peripherals, such as printers and cameras. The peripheral must provide the drivers and software to support UPnP.	Manual; Automatic if you use any UPnP devices.
Upload Manager	Local System	Manages synchronous and asynchronous file transfers between computers on a network.	Automatic
Utility Manager	Local System	Enables a variety of tools, including Microsoft Narrator, designed to make Windows XP more accessible to users with visual impairments; this is an optional service.	Manual

Appendix D

Table D-2. **Service Descriptions and Startup Settings**

Service	Log On As	Description	Recommended Startup Type
Volume Shadow Copy	Local System	Manages the volume shadow copy, a feature of Windows XP that backup programs can use to take a "snapshot" of volumes with open files so that they can perform a complete backup without requiring the user to shut down all running programs.	Manual
WebClient	Local Service	Allows Windows programs to create, access, and modify Internet files using Web Distributing Authoring and Versioning (WebDAV); uncommon in everyday use.	Manual
Windows Audio	Local System	Manages audio devices	Automatic
Windows Firewall/ Internet Connection Sharing (ICS)	Local System	Provides Network Address Translation, address translation, and firewall services on networks.	Automatic
Windows Image Acquisition (WIA)	Local System	Provides image acquisition support for SCSI, IEEE 1394, USB and serial digital still image devices.	Manual
Windows Installer	Local System	Supports installation, repair, and removal of programs that use instructions contained in Windows Installer (.msi) files.	Manual. (Applications that need the service will start it.)
Windows Management Instrumentation	Local System	Provides information about your system configuration to Windows and to third-party applications; if this service is stopped, most Windows-based software will experience problems.	Automatic

Appendix D

Table D-2. **Service Descriptions and Startup Settings**

Service	Log On As	Description	Recommended Startup Type
Windows Management Instrumentation Driver Extensions	Local System	Communicates information between the operating system and any WMI-compatible drivers.	Manual
Windows Time	Local System	Allows you to synchronize the date and time on a computer with a remote server using options you set on the Internet Time tab of Control Panel, Date And Time.	Automatic; may be set to Manual or Disabled if you prefer to set the time manually or use alternate synchronization software.
Wireless Zero Configuration	Local System	Supports automatic configuration of wireless LAN (802.11) adapters.	Automatic if your computer uses a wireless network adapter; may be safely set to Manual or Disabled otherwise.
WMI Performance Adapter	Local System	Implements performance counters as part of Windows Management Instrumentation.	Manual
Workstation	Local System	Makes network connections with remote computers. Many Windows functions depend on this service being available.	Automatic

Appendix D

1403

Managing Services from a Command Prompt

If you want to control services via a batch program—or if you simply prefer working at a command prompt—you can use variants of the Net command. Don't be dissuaded by the name—the Net command manages all services, not only network services. Table D-3 shows the Net commands to use for managing services.

Table D-3. Net Commands for Managing Services

Command	Description
Net Start	Displays a list of running services.
Net Start *service*	Starts the *service* service. For *service*, you can use either the actual service name or its display name. For example, **net start schedule** and **net start "task scheduler"** are equivalent. For a list of services installed by default with Windows XP Professional, see Table D-1 on page 1386. Surround multiword service names with quotation marks.
Net Stop *service*	Stops the *service* service. The service must be started before you can stop it.
Net Pause *service*	Pauses the *service* service. The service must be started before you can pause it. Many services don't permit pausing.
Net Continue *service*	Resumes the *service* service. The service must be paused before you can resume it.

Viewing System Information

Whether it's for troubleshooting purposes or just out of curiosity, you'll occasionally need to find out more about your computer system: what kind of hardware you have, what software is installed, and so on. This appendix provides an overview of the tools included with Microsoft Windows XP for displaying information about your system.

Finding Basic Information About Your Computer

For answers to basic questions about your operating system and computer, there's no better place to start than the General tab of the System Properties dialog box, shown in Figure E-1 on the next page. No matter where you are in Windows or what your preferred input method is, System Properties is only a few clicks or keystrokes away. You can open System Properties in any of the following ways:

- Press the Windows logo key+Break.
- Right-click My Computer and choose Properties. (This works just about any place that My Computer appears, including on the Start menu, on the desktop, in Windows Explorer's task pane, and in a Windows Explorer window.)
- In Control Panel, open System (in the Performance And Maintenance category).
- At a command prompt, type **sysdm.cpl**.

At Home with Windows XP

The command-line utility Systeminfo.exe is not available in Windows XP Home Edition. All the other information tools described in this appendix are available in both editions of Windows XP.

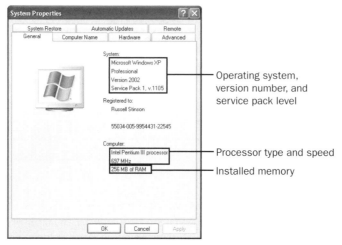

Figure E-1.   System Properties provides essential information.

From System Properties, it's a short hop over to Device Manager, shown in Figure E-2. Device Manager shows detailed information about your installed hardware, including information about drivers. If you already have System Properties open, click the Hardware tab and then click Device Manager. You can open Device Manager directly, without first passing through System Properties, by typing **devmgmt.msc** at a command prompt.

Note   Device Manager shows the devices. For details about how to use this information, see Chapter 5, "Setting Up and Troubleshooting Hardware."

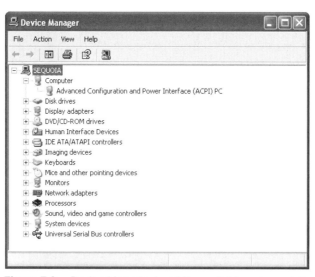

Figure E-2.   Device Manager is a Microsoft Management Console (MMC) snap-in that lists installed devices.

Tip **Use Computer Management**

The Device Manager snap-in is included in the Computer Management console, along with a number of other useful snap-ins. You can open Computer Management in any of the following ways:

- Right-click My Computer and choose Manage.
- In Administrative Tools (if it's not on your Start menu, go to Control Panel's Performance And Maintenance category), open Computer Management.
- At a command prompt, type **compmgmt.msc**.

Finding Information in the Help And Support Center

The most attractive display of system information appears in the Help And Support Center. In addition to presenting copious information in an eye-catching format, the Help And Support Center pages include links to troubleshooters, updates, and help text. Figure E-3 shows an example of Help And Support Center resources.

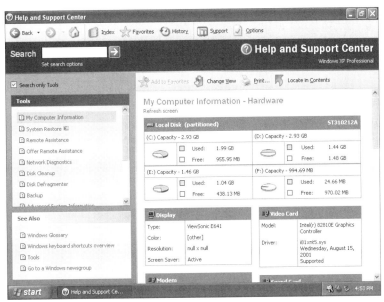

Figure E-3. The Help And Support Center offers a wealth of system information—after you find the right links.

Although the presentation in the Help And Support Center is nice, finding the information you need requires that you pick the right links. Start your journey at the Help And Support Center home page. On the right side, under Pick A Task, click Use Tools To View Your Computer Information And Diagnose Problems. Then, in the list of Tools that appears in the left pane, click My Computer Information. A list of links then appears in the right pane; each leads to a different report about your system.

Digging Deeper with Dedicated System Information Tools

If you want just the straight scoop about your configuration without any visual enhancements, Windows offers two tools with similar names, Systeminfo and System Information.

- **Systeminfo** Systeminfo.exe is a command-line utility that displays information about your Windows version, BIOS, processor, memory, and a few more esoteric items. Figure E-4 shows sample output.

System Up Time shows the elapsed time since your computer was last restarted

Figure E-4. The command-line utility Systeminfo.exe provides an easy way to gather information on all your network computers in a single database.

To run Systeminfo, at a command prompt, type **systeminfo**. In addition to the list format shown in the figure, Systeminfo offers two formats that are useful if you want to work with the information in another program: Table (fixed-width columns) and CSV (comma-separated values). To use one of these formats, include the /Fo switch in the command. You'll also need to redirect the output to a file. For example, to store comma-delimited information in a file named Info.csv, enter the following command:

```
systeminfo /fo csv > info.csv
```

The /S switch allows you to get system information about another computer on your network. (If your user name and password don't match that of an account on the target computer, you'll also need to use the /U and /P switches to provide the user name and password of an authorized account.) When you've gathered information about all the computers on your network, you can import the file you created into a spreadsheet or database program for tracking and analysis. The following command appends information about a computer named Badlands to the original file you created.

```
systeminfo /s badlands /fo csv >> info.csv
```

> **Note**   Systeminfo.exe is not available in Windows XP Home Edition.

- **System Information**   System Information—often called by the name of its executable, Msinfo32.exe—is a techie's paradise. It provides all manner of information about your system's hardware and software in a no-frills window. In addition, it serves as a menu to other diagnostic tools. The following sections discuss System Information in greater detail.

Finding and Decoding Information in System Information

System Information displays a wealth of configuration information in a clear display, as shown in Figure E-5. You can search for specific information, save information, view information about other computers, and even view a list of changes to your system.

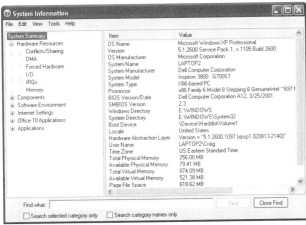

Figure E-5.   System Information is for viewing configuration information only; you can't use it to actually configure settings.

To start System Information, use any of the following methods:

- In the Run dialog box, type **msinfo32**.
- In a Command Prompt window, type **start msinfo32**.
- Click Start and choose All Programs, Accessories, System Tools, System Information.
- From the home page in the Help And Support Center, click Use Tools To View Your Computer Information And Diagnose Problems, Advanced System Information, View Detailed System Information (Msinfo32.exe).
- In the About dialog box of many applications, including Microsoft Office applications (the dialog box you reach by choosing Help, About), click System Info.

You navigate through System Information much as you would through Windows Explorer or an MMC console: You click a category in the left pane to view its contents in the right pane. Table E-1 provides a summary of available information in System Information. Because the tool is *extensible*—which means that other programs can provide information about themselves in a format that can be displayed in System Information—you might see additional categories and additional information on your system.

Table E-1. Information Available in Msinfo32.exe

Category	Description
System Summary	Information similar to that provided by Systeminfo.exe: Windows version, computer name, computer make and model, processor, BIOS version and date, memory summary.
Hardware Resources	Information about shared system resources, such as I/O ports and IRQs; device conflicts; DMA channels in use; devices with manually specified resources instead of system-assigned resources; I/O ports in use; IRQs in use; and memory addresses used by devices.
Components	Information about each installed hardware device, including resources used and device descriptions, drivers, and current status.
Software Environment	Information about drivers, environment variables, open print jobs, mapped network connections, running tasks, loaded system-level DLLs, services, Start menu program groups, programs that run at startup, file associations for OLE objects, and application crashes.
Internet Settings	Information about files used by Microsoft Internet Explorer, your Internet connection, temporary Internet files, certificates, and Internet Explorer security settings.
Applications	Application-specific information that can be added to System Information by your installed programs; Office, for example, lists detailed information about everything from file versions to installed fonts to default page layout settings.

To search for specific information, use the Find What box at the bottom of the System Information window. (If the Find bar is not visible, choose Edit, Hide Find.) The Find feature is basic but effective. A couple of things you should know:

- Whenever you type in the Find What box to start a new search, Find begins its search at the top of the search range (the entire namespace unless you select Search Selected Category Only)—not at the current highlight.

- Selecting Search Category Names Only causes the Find feature to look only in the left pane. When this check box is cleared, all text in both panes is searched.

Exporting System Information

You can preserve your configuration information—always helpful when reconstructing a system—in several ways:

- You can save the information as an .nfo file. You can subsequently open the file (on the same computer or on a different computer with System Information) to view your saved information. To save information in this format, choose File, Save. Saving this way always saves the entire collection of information.

- You can save all or part of the information as a plain text file. To save information as a text file, select the category of interest and choose File, Export. If you want to save all the information as a text file, select System Summary before you save.

- You can print all or part of the information. Select the category of interest, choose File, Print, and be sure that Selection is selected under Page Range. To print everything, select All under Page Range—and be sure to have lots of paper on hand. Depending on your system configuration, the number of installed applications, and so on, your report could top 100 pages.

Regardless of how you save your information, System Information refreshes (updates) the information immediately before processing the command.

Tip   **Save your system information periodically**
Saving system configuration information when your computer is working properly can turn out to be very useful when you have problems. Comparing your computer's current configuration with a known, good baseline configuration can help you spot possible problem areas. You can open multiple instances of System Information, so that you could have the current configuration displayed in one window and a baseline configuration displayed in another.

Viewing System Information History

System Information maintains a one-month history of key parts of your configuration. It updates its history records by taking a daily snapshot, and it also records any differences from the last snapshot that it encounters whenever you run System Information. Armed with this information, you can go back and see what configuration changes occurred shortly before a problem started; this might help to isolate a problem.

You can view configuration changes by choosing View, System History. Select a date in the View Changes Since box and select a category. (Only top-level categories appear in this view.) As shown in Figure E-6 on the next page, the display is rather dense. However, you can use a couple of techniques to focus on information of interest:

- Click a column heading to sort the records by that field.
- Use the Find feature.

Appendix E

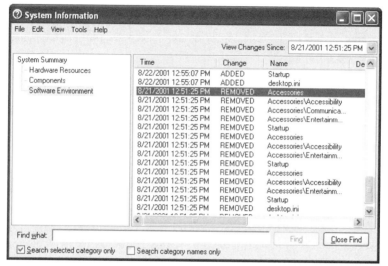

Figure E-6. In this System Information history display, you can see that several folders were removed from the Start menu.

Using System Information to Open Other Diagnostic Tools

The Tools menu in System Information contains commands that open other tools for displaying system information, which can be helpful in diagnosing problems. These tools include:

- **Net Diagnostics** Network Diagnostics displays detailed information about your network connections. In addition to displaying configuration information, it performs a number of tests for network connectivity (such as pinging other computers on your network and your DNS server).

- **DirectX Diagnostic Tool** DirectX Diagnostic Tool displays information about DirectX components, which use hardware acceleration to enhance video and audio performance. In addition, DirectX Diagnostic Tool performs several compatibility tests. You can open DirectX Diagnostic Tool directly by typing **dxdiag** at a command prompt.

> **Tip** Try a third-party utility
>
> In addition to the tools included with Windows XP, you can choose from a wide array of third-party utilities that poke around inside your computer to uncover details about installed hardware and software. Two tools that we recommend are Karen Kenworthy's Computer Profiler (*http://www.karenware.com/powertools/ptprofiler.asp*) and the Belarc Advisor (*http://www.belarc.com/free_download.html*).

Appendix F

Group Policy

Group Policy is a highly touted feature of Active Directory, which is part of Microsoft Windows Server 2003 and Windows 2000 Server. In that environment, Group Policy is indeed an enormously powerful feature that lets administrators configure computers throughout sites, domains, or organizational units. In addition to setting standard desktop configurations and restricting what settings users are allowed to change, administrators can use Group Policy to centrally manage software installation, configuration, updates, and removal; specify scripts to run at startup, shutdown, logon, and logoff; and redirect users' special folders (such as My Documents) to the network. Administrators can customize all these settings for different computers, users, or groups.

But Group Policy can also be a useful tool for managing computers on a small network or even for managing a single computer. Using only the local Group Policy Object on a computer running Windows XP Professional, you can:

- Manage registry-based policy—everything from configuring the desktop to hiding certain drives to preventing the creation of scheduled tasks. These settings—and hundreds more—are stored in the HKLM and HKCU branches of the registry, which you can edit directly. But Group Policy provides two distinct advantages: It's much easier to use than a registry editor, and it periodically updates the registry automatically (thereby keeping your policies in force even if the registry is somehow modified by other means).

- Assign scripts for computer startup, computer shutdown, user logon, and user logoff. (For details, see "Using Scripts That Run at Logon, Logoff, Startup, and Shutdown," page 556.)

- Specify security options.

At Home with Windows XP

In a nutshell: Group Policy is not available in Windows XP Home Edition. Home Edition users can use none of the procedures described in this chapter, nor can they use the various Group Policy settings that are described elsewhere in the book.

In a domain environment, Group Policy enables an administrator to apply policy settings and restrictions to users and computers (and groups of each) in one fell swoop. With a workgroup, you must make similar Group Policy settings on each computer where you want such restrictions imposed.

Starting Group Policy

You make Group Policy settings using the Group Policy snap-in for Microsoft Management Console (MMC), shown in Figure F-1. Windows XP Professional includes an MMC console that shows only this snap-in, but you won't find it on the Start menu. To open the console, go to Start, Run and type **gpedit.msc.** You must be logged on as a member of the Administrators group to use Group Policy.

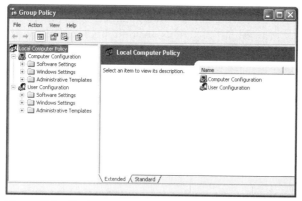

Figure F-1. Typing gpedit.msc at a command prompt opens the Group Policy console.

If your computer is joined to a domain with Active Directory–based policies, and if you have appropriate domain administrative privileges, you can configure Group Policy to display snap-in extensions that let you view and modify domain policies as well as extensions for the local Group Policy object. (For more information, see "How Local Group Policy Settings Interact with Active Directory–Based Group Policy Settings," page 1420.) However, because the focus of this book is Windows XP, in this chapter we explore only the local Group Policy object.

Starting Group Policy for a Remote Computer

With some MMC snap-ins (for example, Computer Management), you can use a menu command to switch from the local computer to another computer on your network. This is not the case with Group Policy, which, once started, directs its attention toward a single computer. You can, however, start Group Policy with its gaze turned toward another computer. To do that, you must have administrative privileges on both your own computer and the other computer. Even without Windows Server 2003 (or Windows 2000 Server) and Active Directory, you can administer all the computers on your network from a single console. (A key difference is that you must set local Group Policy on each computer rather than setting Active Directory–based Group Policy that automatically applies to all computers.) You can use either of two methods to start Group Policy for a remote computer: a command-line parameter or a custom MMC console.

The simplest method is to append the /Gpcomputer parameter, as we did in this example:

```
gpedit.msc /gpcomputer:"redwood"
```

The computer name that follows /Gpcomputer can be either a NetBIOS-style name (such as redwood) or a DNS-style name (for example, redwood.swdocs.local), which is the primary naming form used by Windows Server 2003 and Windows 2000 Server domains. In either case, you must enclose the computer name in quotation marks.

An alternative method for starting Group Policy is to create a custom console that opens another computer's local Group Policy object. The advantage of this approach is that you can create a single console that can open Group Policy for every computer you want to manage. To create a custom console, follow these steps:

1 Go to Start, Run and type **mmc**.

2 Open the File menu and choose Add/Remove Snap-In.

3 On the Standalone tab, click Add.

4 Select Group Policy and click Add.

5 In the Select Group Policy Object dialog box, click Browse.

6 On the Computers tab, select Another Computer, and then type the name of the computer or click Browse, Advanced, Find Now to select it from a list.

7 Click OK and then click Finish.

8 Repeat steps 4 through 7 to add other computers to the console.

9 Click Close and then click OK.

Appendix F

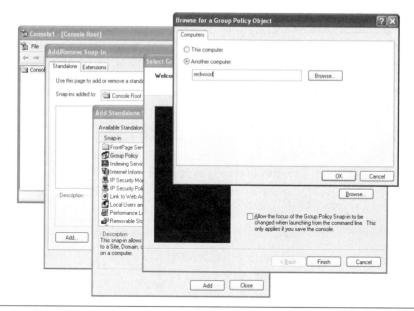

For more information about MMC, see "Creating Your Own MMC Consoles," page 1369.

Customizing the Group Policy Window

The Group Policy console provides some easily overlooked options that you won't find in other MMC snap-ins: You can add or remove administrative templates, and you can restrict the view to show only the policies that have been configured.

Adding or Removing Policy Templates

The Administrative Templates folders (under Computer Configuration and User Configuration) are extensible. The Administrative Templates policies are defined in an .adm file. Windows XP includes several .adm files, of which four are displayed by default, as shown in Table F-1.

You might want to remove the templates that contain policies you never use, or you might want to add a custom template provided with another program. For example, the Office 2003 Editions Resource Kit includes policy templates for managing Microsoft Office; for details, visit *www.microsoft.com/office/ork*.

To add or remove a policy template, right-click Administrative Templates (either folder) and choose Add/Remove Templates. After you make your changes and click Close in the Add/Remove Templates dialog box, both Administrative Templates folders reflect your new selections.

Table F-1 .**Administrative Template Files Included with Windows XP**

File Name	Description
Conf.adm (displayed by default)	Conferencing settings for Microsoft NetMeeting that appear in Administrative Templates\Windows Components\NetMeeting (under Computer Configuration and User Configuration)
Inetcorp.adm	Microsoft Internet Explorer settings for use with Internet Explorer Administration Kit (IEAK), not Group Policy
Inetres.adm (displayed by default)	Internet Explorer settings that appear in Administrative Templates\Windows Components\Internet Explorer (under Computer Configuration and User Configuration)
Inetset.adm	Internet Explorer settings for use with IEAK, not Group Policy
System.adm (displayed by default)	Wide variety of settings for Windows XP, encompassing most of the policies that appear in Group Policy
Wmplayer.adm (displayed by default)	Windows Media Player settings that appear in User Configuration\Administrative Templates\Windows Media Player
Wuau.adm	Windows Update settings that appear in Computer Configuration\Administrative Templates\Windows Components\Windows Update (installed as part of Windows XP Service Pack 1 or later)

Adding a policy template merely copies the .adm file to %SystemRoot%\System32\GroupPolicy\Adm; removing a template deletes the copy in that folder. Adding or removing policy templates does not change the underlying policy settings, if there are any; it only controls whether those policies are displayed in Group Policy.

Displaying Only Policies You Want

With only the standard templates installed, Group Policy offers hundreds of policies that you can set. Many of these policies might be for areas of Windows that you never use; therefore, including them in the Group Policy console only produces clutter. Windows now offers a way to selectively filter the list of displayed Administrative Templates policies to include only the ones that might interest you.

To use this feature, right-click Administrative Templates and choose View, Filtering. In the Filtering dialog box, shown in Figure F-2 on the next page, you can choose to hide items that apply only to certain versions of Windows or Internet Explorer. (This is useful primarily when you're remotely editing policies on another computer, which might not be running Windows XP.) After you configure your local Group Policy as you want it (as described later in this chapter), you can clean up the display by hiding the myriad policies that you aren't interested in: Select Only Show Configured Policy Settings.

Appendix F

1417

As with adding or removing policy templates, filtering the display of policies does not change the underlying policy settings, if there are any; it only controls whether those policies are displayed in Group Policy.

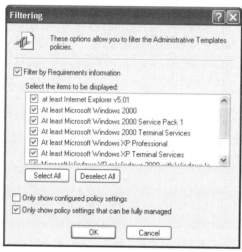

Figure F-2. You can hide policies that you're not interested in.

Unlike the Add/Remove Templates command, filtering applies only to the Administrative Templates folder that you select. If you want to filter the policies in both Computer Configuration and User Configuration, you must repeat the process in each folder.

Understanding the Local Group Policy Object

A *Group Policy object* (often abbreviated as GPO) is simply a collection of Group Policy settings. In a domain based on Windows Server 2003 or Windows 2000 Server, Group Policy objects are stored at the domain level and affect users and computers based on their membership in sites, domains, and organizational units. Each computer running Windows XP has a single *local Group Policy object*. Because it doesn't rely on a server version of Windows, that's the one we focus on here.

The local Group Policy object is stored as a series of files and folders in the hidden %SystemRoot%\System32\GroupPolicy folder. By default, the local Administrators group and the operating system itself have Full Control permissions for this folder and all the objects it contains; Authenticated Users has Read & Execute permissions. The GroupPolicy folder typically contains the following files and folders:

- **Gpt.ini** This file stores information about which extensions (identified by their globally unique identifier, or GUID) contain modified settings and whether the Computer Configuration or User Configuration branch is disabled.

- **Adm** This folder contains the administrative templates (stored as .adm files) that are in use. (See "Adding or Removing Policy Templates," page 1416.)

- **User**   This folder holds a file named Registry.pol, which contains registry settings that apply to users. The User folder includes these subfolders:

  - Microsoft\IEAK contains settings for the items that appear in the \User Configuration\Windows Settings\Internet Explorer Maintenance folder in Group Policy.

  - Scripts includes two folders, Logon and Logoff, which contain the scripts that run when a user logs on or logs off.

- **Machine**   This folder holds another file Registry.pol file; this one contains registry settings that apply to the computer. Within the Machine folder is a Scripts subfolder that holds two folders, Startup and Shutdown; these contain the scripts that run when the computer starts up or shuts down.

> **Note**   Some of these files and folders are created only when you run Group Policy and make some settings.

How Group Policy Works

The majority of the Group Policy settings are in the Administrative Templates extension of the Group Policy snap-in. (The content of the Administrative Templates folders is derived from the .adm files in the Group Policy object.) When you configure a policy in the Administrative Templates folder (that is, you select either Enabled or Disabled and, optionally, set a value), Group Policy stores that information as a custom registry setting in one of the two Registry.pol files. As you'd expect, Group Policy uses the copy of Registry.pol in %SystemRoot%\System32\GroupPolicy\Machine for settings you make in the Computer Configuration\Administrative Templates folder in Group Policy and uses the copy in the User folder for settings you make in User Configuration\Administrative Templates.

Computer-related Group Policy settings—those stored in Machine\Registry.pol—are copied to the appropriate registry keys in the HKLM hive when the operating system initializes and during the periodic refresh. User-related settings (in User\Registry.pol) are copied to the appropriate keys in HKCU when a user logs on and during the periodic refresh.

> **Note**   Group Policy settings—either local or Active Directory–based—take precedence over user settings (that is, settings that you make through Control Panel and other methods available to ordinary users). This is because Group Policy settings are not written to the "normal" registry key for a particular setting; instead, they're written to a value in a "policies" key. For example, if you use the Taskbar And Start Menu Properties dialog box to disable personalized menus, the data in the Intellimenus value in the HKCU\Software\Microsoft\Windows\CurrentVersion\Explorer\Advanced key changes. But if you use Group Policy, the Intellimenus value in the HKCU\Software\Microsoft\Windows\CurrentVersion\Policies\Explorer key changes instead. In cases of conflicts, the value in the Policies key overrules the other.

The *periodic refresh* occurs at intervals that you define as a Group Policy setting. By default, the Registry.pol files are copied to the registry every 90 minutes plus a random offset of 0 to 30 minutes. (The random offset is intended for Active Directory–based policies; on a large network, you wouldn't want all the refresh activity occurring simultaneously. For local Group Policy, the offset serves no useful purpose but is added anyway.) By enabling and modifying the Group Policy Refresh Interval For Computers setting in Computer Configuration\Administrative Templates\System\Group Policy and the Group Policy Refresh Interval For Users setting in User Configuration\Administrative Templates\System\Group Policy, you can change the interval and the random offset. You can set the interval to any value from 0 minutes (in which case settings are refreshed every 7 seconds) through 64,800 minutes (45 days).

To refresh Group Policy settings immediately, type **gpupdate** at a command prompt. To display a list of optional switches for Gpupdate.exe, type **gpupdate /?**.

Note The Gpupdate command replaces the functionality of the Secedit/Refreshpolicy command, which was introduced in Windows 2000.

How Local Group Policy Settings Interact with Active Directory–Based Group Policy Settings

If your computer is joined to a domain, it might be affected by Group Policy settings other than those you set in the local Group Policy object. Group Policy settings are applied in this order:

1 Settings from the local Group Policy object

2 Settings from site Group Policy objects, in administratively specified order

3 Settings from domain Group Policy objects, in administratively specified order

4 Settings from organizational unit Group Policy objects, from largest to smallest organizational unit (parent to child organizational unit), and in administratively specified order at the level of each organizational unit

Policies applied later overwrite previously applied policies, which means that in a case of conflicting settings, the highest-level Active Directory–based policy settings take precedence. The policy settings are cumulative, so all settings contribute to the effective policy. The effective policy is called the *Resultant Set of Policy (RsoP)*.

To see which settings are in effect for a particular user, you can use a command-line tool (Gpresult.exe). To display your RSoP, simply type **gpresult** at a command prompt. Type **gpresult /?** for information about other options.

The Help And Support Center also includes a tool that shows effective Group Policy settings for the current user. To use that tool, open the Help And Support Center. On the home page, click Use Tools To View Your Computer Information And Diagnose Problems on the right, Advanced System Information in the left pane, and View Group Policy Settings Applied in the right pane. Figure F-3 shows an example.

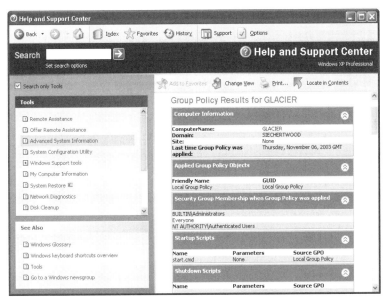

Figure F-3. The Group Policy tool in the Help And Support Center shows which settings are in effect—something that's not readily apparent in a domain environment.

Types of Settings

The Computer Configuration branch of Group Policy includes a variety of computer-related settings, and the User Configuration branch includes a variety of user-related settings. The line between computer settings and user settings is often blurred, however. Because local Group Policy settings apply to all users, your best bet for discovering the policies you need is to examine them all. You'll find a treasure trove of useful settings, including many that can't be made any other way short of hacking the registry. In the Administrative Templates folders, you'll find more than 240 computer settings and more than 440 user settings, which makes this sound like a daunting task—but you'll find that you can quickly scan the policies in each folder and ignore most of them.

To learn more about each policy, simply select it, as shown in Figure F-4 on the next page. If you have selected the Extended tab at the bottom of the window, a description of the selected policy appears in the center pane.

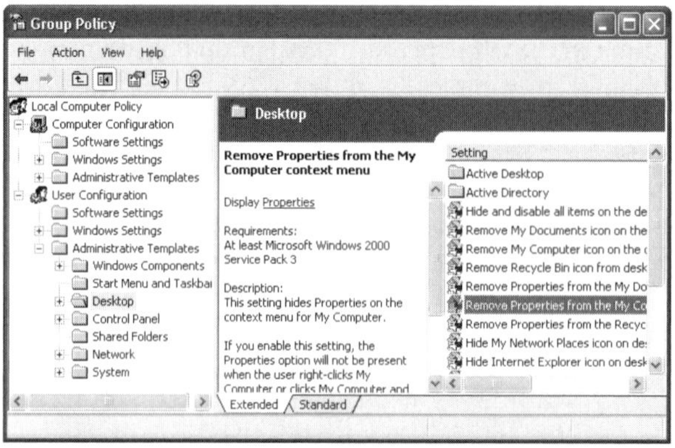

Figure F-4. The Extended tab includes a description of the selected policy.

You can speed up the application of Group Policy settings by disabling those you don't use. To see at a glance which types of policies are in use, right-click Local Computer Policy (at the top of the Group Policy console tree) and choose Properties. In the dialog box that appears, shown in Figure F-5, the Revisions line under Summary shows the number of Computer Configuration and User Configuration settings in use. If either value is 0 (or if you want to disable Group Policy settings for some other reason), select the appropriate check box under Disable.

Figure F-5. You can selectively disable computer-related or user-related Group Policy settings.

Note Some settings appear in both User Configuration and Computer Configuration. In a case of conflicting settings, the Computer Configuration setting always takes precedence.

Making Settings

Each policy in the Administrative Templates folders of Group Policy has one of three settings: Not Configured, Enabled, or Disabled. By default, all policies in the local Group Policy object are initially set to Not Configured. (The policies in the Windows Settings folders do not have a Not Configured option and therefore have other default settings.)

To change a setting, in the Group Policy console, simply double-click the name of the policy you want to change or click the Properties link that appears in the center pane of the Extended tab. The properties dialog box then appears. The dialog box for each policy under Administrative Templates looks much like the one shown in Figure F-6. The Setting tab includes the three options—Not Configured, Enabled, and Disabled—and a large area where you can make policy-specific settings. Controls in the center area appear dimmed and are unavailable unless you select the Enabled option. (Many simple policies leave this area blank because the policy needs no further setting.) The Explain tab provides detailed information about the policy (the same information that appears in the center pane of the Extended tab). The only place you're likely to find more information about each policy is in Group Policy Settings Reference for Windows, a Microsoft Excel spreadsheet that is included on this book's companion CD.

Figure F-6. Properties dialog boxes for all Administrative Templates policies are similar to the one shown here.

Both tabs include Previous Setting and Next Setting buttons, which make it convenient to go through an entire folder without opening and closing the properties dialog box for each policy individually.

Note Pay close attention to the name of each policy, because the settings can be counterintuitive. A number of policies begin with the word *Disable* (for example, Disable Active Desktop in User Configuration\Administrative Templates\Desktop\Active Desktop). For those policies, if you want to *allow* the specified option, you must select the *Disable* setting. (In other words, you must disable the disabling policy.) Conversely, if you want to prohibit the option, you must select Enable.

Making Different Settings for Different Users

Centrally managed Group Policy settings—that is, those that are stored in Active Directory in Windows Server 2003 or Windows 2000 Server—can be applied to individual users, computers, or groups of either. You can have multiple sets of Active Directory–based Group Policy objects, allowing you to create an entirely different collection of settings for different users or computers.

Such is not the case with local Group Policy. Local Group Policy settings apply to all users who log on to the computer. (If the computer is joined to a domain, however, the local settings might be overridden by Active Directory–based settings. For details, see "How Local Group Policy Settings Interact with Active Directory–Based Group Policy Settings," page 1420.) You can't have multiple sets of local Group Policy objects.

Although you can't have customized settings for each of several different groups, you can effectively have two groups of users: those who are affected by local Group Policy settings and those who are not. This duality affects only the User Configuration settings; Computer Configuration settings are applied before anyone logs on.

You can do this because local Group Policy depends on users having Read access to the local Group Policy object, which is stored in the %SystemRoot%\System32\GroupPolicy folder. Policies are not applied to users who do not have Read access; therefore, by denying Read access to administrators or others whom you don't want to restrict, you free those users from control by group policies.To use this method, follow these steps:

1 Make the Group Policy setting changes that you want.

2 In Windows Explorer, right-click the %SystemRoot%\System32\GroupPolicy folder and choose Properties. (GroupPolicy is a hidden folder; if you can't find it in System32, choose Tools, Folder Options, View, Show Hidden Files And Folders.)

3 On the Security tab of the GroupPolicy Properties dialog box, select the Administrators group and select the Deny check box for the Read permission. (If you want to exclude any other users or groups from Group Policy control, add them to the Group Or User Names list and then deny their Read permission.)

> **Note** You must deny the Read permission rather than simply clear the Allow check box. Otherwise, all users will continue to inherit Read permission because of their automatic membership in the Authenticated Users group.

At your next logon using one of the Read-disabled user accounts, you'll find that you're no longer encumbered by Group Policy settings. Without Read permission, however, you'll find that you're also unable to run Group Policy—so you can't view or modify Group Policy settings. To regain that power, you need to revisit the GroupPolicy Properties dialog box and grant yourself Full Control permission.

> **Tip** Create an account for managing Group Policy
> As an alternative to modifying permissions each time you want to work with Group Policy, consider setting up a separate user account for configuring Group Policy. Instead of denying Read permission for the Administrators group (step 3 of the preceding procedure), add your own user account to the Group Or User Names list, and deny Read permission for it. Create a new account—your Group Policy configuration account—and make it a member of the Administrators group. Finally, set up a shortcut to Gpedit.msc. When you want to review or modify Group Policy settings, right-click the shortcut, choose Run As, and enter the name and password of your configuration account.

Keep in mind that, even without the aforementioned security shenanigans, the default security settings effectively produce two groups of users. Although the local Group Policy settings apply to all users (clarification: all users who have Read access to the local Group Policy object), only members of the local Administrators group can view or change these settings.

If customizing the effects of Group Policy settings based on group membership is important to you, you should install Windows Server 2003 or Windows 2000 Server and set up Active Directory. But the methods described in this section can provide an easy compromise solution.

Index to Troubleshooting Topics

Index to Troubleshooting Topics

Index to Troubleshooting Topics

R

S

Index

X

Z

About the Authors

Ed Bott   is a best-selling author and award-winning journalist who has been a part of the personal computer industry since the days when an 8-MHz 80286 was a smokin' machine. Ed's feature stories and columns about Microsoft Windows have appeared regularly in print and on the Web for more than 15 years, and he has written books on nearly every version of Microsoft Windows and Microsoft Office—so many, in fact, that he's lost count of the exact number. Ed is a three-time winner of the Computer Press Award and a two-time recipient of the Jesse H. Neal award from American Business Press. *Microsoft Windows Security Inside Out for Windows XP and Windows 2000*, which he coauthored with Carl Siechert, earned the Award of Merit from the Society for Technical Communication in 2003. After spending three years living in Microsoft's neighborhood in Redmond, Washington, Ed and his wife Judy exchanged the gray and damp of the Northwest for the sunny Southwest and have never been happier.

Carl Siechert   began his writing career at age eight as editor of the *Mesita Road News*, a neighborhood newsletter that reached a peak worldwide circulation of 43 during its eight-year run. Following several years as an estimator and production manager in a commercial printing business, Carl returned to writing with the formation of Siechert & Wood Professional Documentation, a Pasadena, California firm that specializes in writing and producing product documentation for the personal computer industry. Carl is a coauthor of several books published by Microsoft Press, including *Field Guide to MS-DOS 6.2, Microsoft Windows 2000 Professional Expert Companion*, and *Microsoft Windows Security Inside Out*. Carl hiked the Pacific Crest Trail from Mexico to Canada in 1977 and would rather be hiking right now. He and his wife Jan live in southern California.

Craig Stinson,   an industry journalist since 1981, is a contributing editor of *PC Magazine* and was formerly editor of *Softalk for the IBM Personal Computer*. Craig is the author of *Running Microsoft Windows 98* and a coauthor of *Microsoft Excel Inside Out* and *Running Microsoft Windows 2000 Professional*, all published by Microsoft Press. Craig is an amateur musician and has reviewed classical music for various newspapers and trade publications, including *Billboard*, the *Boston Globe*, the *Christian Science Monitor*, and *Musical America*. He lives with his wife and children in Bloomington, Indiana.

The authors have set up a Web site for readers of this book. At the site, you can find updates, corrections, and more useful tips. In addition, you can discuss Windows XP with the authors and with other readers. We hope you'll join us at *http://www.xpinsideout.com*.

Work smarter—*conquer your software from the inside out!*

Microsoft® Windows® XP Inside Out, Second Edition	Microsoft Office System Inside Out— 2003 Edition	Microsoft Office Access 2003 Inside Out	Microsoft Office FrontPage® 2003 Inside Out
ISBN: 0-7356-2044-X	ISBN: 0-7356-1512-8	ISBN: 0-7356-1513-6	ISBN: 0-7356-1510-1
U.S.A. $44.99	U.S.A. $49.99	U.S.A. $49.99	U.S.A. $49.99
Canada $64.99	Canada $72.99	Canada $72.99	Canada $72.99

Hey, you know your way around a desktop. Now dig into the new Microsoft Office products and the Windows XP operating system and *really* put your PC to work! These supremely organized software reference titles pack hundreds of timesaving solutions, troubleshooting tips and tricks, and handy workarounds into a concise, fast-answer format. They're all muscle and no fluff. All this comprehensive information goes deep into the nooks and crannies of each Office application and Windows XP feature. And every INSIDE OUT title includes a CD-ROM packed with bonus content such as tools and utilities, demo programs, sample scripts, batch programs, an eBook containing the book's complete text, and more! Discover the best and fastest ways to perform everyday tasks, and challenge yourself to new levels of software mastery!

Microsoft Press has other INSIDE OUT titles to help you get the job done every day:

Microsoft Office Excel 2003 Programming Inside Out
ISBN: 0-7356-1985-9

Microsoft Office Word 2003 Inside Out
ISBN: 0-7356-1515-2

Microsoft Office Excel 2003 Inside Out
ISBN: 0-7356-1511-X

Microsoft Office Outlook 2003® Inside Out
ISBN: 0-7356-1514-4

Microsoft Office Project 2003 Inside Out
ISBN: 0-7356-1958-1

Microsoft Office Visio® 2003 Inside Out
ISBN: 0-7356-1516-0

Microsoft Windows XP Networking Inside Out
ISBN: 0-7356-1652-3

Microsoft Windows Security Inside Out
for Windows XP and Windows 2000
ISBN: 0-7356-1632-9

To learn more about the full line of Microsoft Press® products, please visit us at:

microsoft.com/mspress/

Microsoft Press products are available worldwide wherever quality computer books are sold. For more information, contact your book or computer retailer, software reseller, or local Microsoft Sales Office, or visit our Web site at **microsoft.com/mspress**. To locate your nearest source for Microsoft Press products, or to order directly, call 1-800-MSPRESS in the United States. (In Canada, call 1-800-268-2222).

In-depth learning solutions *for*
every software user

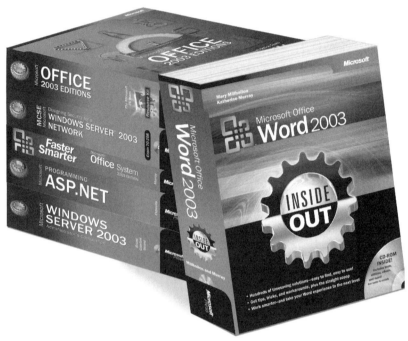

The tools you need to put technology to work.

Microsoft Press produces in-depth learning solutions that empower home and corporate users, IT professionals, and software developers to do more exciting things with Microsoft technology. From beginning PC how-to's to developer reference titles to IT training and technical resources, we offer hundreds of computer books, interactive training software, and online resources, all designed to help build your skills and knowledge—how, when, and where you learn best.

To learn more about the full line of Microsoft Press® products, please visit us at:

microsoft.com/mspress

Microsoft Press products are available worldwide wherever quality computer books are sold. For more information, contact your book or computer retailer, software reseller, or local Microsoft Sales Office, or visit our Web site at **microsoft.com/mspress**. To locate your nearest source for Microsoft Press products, or to order directly, call 1-800-MSPRESS in the United States. (In Canada, call 1-800-268-2222).

Self-paced training that
works as hard as you do!

Microsoft® Windows® XP Step by Step Deluxe, Second Edition ISBN: 0-7356-2113-6 U.S.A. $39.99 Canada $57.99	Microsoft Office Project 2003 Step by Step ISBN: 0-7356-1955-7 U.S.A. $29.99 Canada $43.99	Microsoft Office Excel 2003 Step by Step ISBN: 0-7356-1518-7 U.S.A. $24.99 Canada $35.99	Microsoft Office FrontPage® 2003 Step by Step ISBN: 0-7356-1519-5 U.S.A. $24.99 Canada $35.99

Information-packed STEP BY STEP courses are the most effective way to teach yourself how to complete tasks with the Microsoft Windows operating system and Microsoft Office applications. Numbered steps and scenario-based lessons with practice files on CD-ROM make it easy to find your way while learning tasks and procedures. Work through every lesson or choose your own starting point—with STEP BY STEP'S modular design and straightforward writing style, *you* drive the instruction. And the books are constructed with lay-flat binding so you can follow the text with both hands at the keyboard. Select STEP BY STEP titles also prepare you for the Microsoft Office Specialist credential. It's an excellent way for you or your organization to take a giant step toward workplace productivity.

Microsoft Press has other STEP BY STEP titles to help you get the job done every day:

Home Networking with Microsoft Windows XP Step by Step
ISBN: 0-7356-1435-0

Microsoft Office Word 2003 Step by Step
ISBN: 0-7356-1523-3

Microsoft Office Outlook 2003 Step by Step
ISBN: 0-7356-1521-7

Microsoft Office System Step by Step—2003 Edition
ISBN: 0-7356-1520-9

Microsoft Office PowerPoint 2003 Step by Step
ISBN: 0-7356-1522-5

Microsoft Office Access 2003 Step by Step
ISBN: 0-7356-1517-9

To learn more about the full line of Microsoft Press® products, please visit us at:

microsoft.com/mspress

Microsoft Press products are available worldwide wherever quality computer books are sold. For more information, contact your book or computer retailer, software reseller, or local Microsoft Sales Office, or visit our Web site at **microsoft.com/mspress**. To locate your nearest source for Microsoft Press products, or to order directly, call 1-800-MSPRESS in the U.S.
(in Canada, call 1-800-268-2222).

Learn how to get the job done every day—
faster, smarter, and easier!

Faster Smarter
Microsoft Office
FrontPage® 2003
ISBN: 0-7356-7-
U.S.A. $19.99
Canada $28.99

Faster Smarter
Microsoft® Office
System—2003 Edition
ISBN: 0-7356-1921-2
U.S.A. $19.99
Canada $28.99

Faster Smarter
Microsoft
Windows® XP
ISBN: 0-7356-1857-7
U.S.A. $19.99
Canada $28.99

Faster Smarter
Home Networking
ISBN: 0-7356-1869-0
U.S.A. $19.99
Canada $28.99

Discover how to do exactly what you do with computers and technology—faster, smarter, and easier—with FASTER SMARTER books from Microsoft Press! They're your everyday guides for learning the practicalities of how to make technology work the way you want—fast. Their language is friendly and down-to-earth, with no jargon or silly chatter, and with accurate how-to information that's easy to absorb and apply. These everyday guides—covering topics from Microsoft Windows XP to XML programming—provide clear explanations, easy numbered steps, and visual examples to help you get the job done fast.

Microsoft Press has other FASTER SMARTER titles to help you get the job done every day:

Faster Smarter PCs
ISBN: 0-7356-1855-0

Faster Smarter Web Page Creation
ISBN: 0-7356-1860-7

Faster Smarter Microsoft Windows 98
ISBN: 0-7356-1858-5

Faster Smarter HTML & XML
ISBN: 0-7356-1861-5

Faster Smarter Beginning Programming
ISBN: 0-7356-1780-5

Faster Smarter Internet
ISBN: 0-7356-1859-3

Faster Smarter Digital Video
ISBN: 0-7356-1873-9

Faster Smarter Digital Photography
ISBN: 0-7356-1872-0

To learn more about the full line of Microsoft Press® products, please visit us at:

microsoft.com/mspress

Microsoft Press products are available worldwide wherever quality computer books are sold. For more information, contact your book or computer retailer, software reseller, or local Microsoft Sales Office, or visit our Web site at **microsoft.com/mspress**. To locate your nearest source for Microsoft Press products, or to order directly, call 1-800-MSPRESS in the U.S.
(in Canada, call 1-800-268-2222).

Microsoft® Windows® Server 2003 Enterprise Edition 180-Day Evaluation

The software included in this kit is intended for evaluation and deployment planning purposes only. If you plan to install the software on your primary machine, it is recommended that you back up your existing data prior to installation.

System requirements

To use Microsoft Windows Server 2003 Enterprise Edition, you need:

- Computer with 550 MHz or higher processor clock speed recommended; 133 MHz minimum required; Intel Pentium/Celeron family, or AMD K6/Athlon/Duron family, or compatible processor (Windows Server 2003 Enterprise Edition supports up to eight CPUs on one server)
- 256 MB of RAM or higher recommended; 128 MB minimum required (maximum 32 GB of RAM)
- 1.25 to 2 GB of available hard-disk space*
- CD-ROM or DVD-ROM drive
- Super VGA (800 × 600) or higher-resolution monitor recommended; VGA or hardware that supports console redirection required
- Keyboard and Microsoft Mouse or compatible pointing device, or hardware that supports console redirection

Additional items or services required to use certain Windows Server 2003 Enterprise Edition features:

- For Internet access:
  - Some Internet functionality may require Internet access, a Microsoft Passport account, and payment of a separate fee to a service provider; local and/or long-distance telephone toll charges may apply
  - High-speed modem or broadband Internet connection
- For networking:
  - Network adapter appropriate for the type of local-area, wide-area, wireless, or home network to which you wish to connect, and access to an appropriate network infrastructure; access to third-party networks may require additional charges

Note: To ensure that your applications and hardware are Windows Server 2003–ready, be sure to visit **www.microsoft.com/windowsserver2003**.

* Actual requirements will vary based on your system configuration and the applications and features you choose to install. Additional available hard-disk space may be required if you are installing over a network. For more information, please see **www.microsoft.com/windowsserver2003**.

Uninstall instructions

This time-limited release of Microsoft Windows Server 2003 Enterprise Edition will expire 180 days after installation. If you decide to discontinue the use of this software, you will need to reinstall your original operating system. You may need to reformat your drive.

© 2003 Microsoft Corporation. All rights reserved.

Microsoft and Windows are either registered trademarks or trademarks of Microsoft Corporation in the United States and/or other countries.

0103 Part No. X09-41357

What do you think of this book?
We want to hear from you!

Do you have a few minutes to participate in a brief online survey? Microsoft is interested in hearing your feedback about this publication so that we can continually improve our books and learning resources for you.

To participate in our survey, please visit:

www.microsoft.com/learning/booksurvey

And enter this book's ISBN, 0-7356-2043-1. As a thank-you to survey participants in the United States and Canada, each month we'll randomly select five respondents to win one of five $100 gift certificates from a leading online merchant.* At the conclusion of the survey, you can enter the drawing by providing your e-mail address, which will be used for prize notification *only*.

Thanks in advance for your input. Your opinion counts!

Sincerely,

Microsoft® Learning

Learn More. Go Further.

To see special offers on Microsoft Learning products for developers, IT professionals, and home and office users, visit: *www.microsoft.com/learning/booksurvey*

* No purchase necessary. Void where prohibited. Open only to residents of the 50 United States (includes District of Columbia) and Canada (void in Quebec). Sweepstakes ends 6/30/2005. For official rules, see: *www.microsoft.com/learning/booksurvey*